Schroeder's Collectible TOYS
Antique to Modern Price Guide

OUR #1 BESTSELLING TOY BOOK

2010 TWELFTH EDITION

COLLECTOR BOOKS
A Division of Schroeder Publishing Co., Inc.

Front cover: Robots and Space Toys, Stratoliner 10-3 (Huki), Germany, 8", MIB, $850.00 (photo courtesy Morphy Auctions); Musical Toys, Drum, lithographed tin with Boy Scout scenes, black wooden bands, 8" diameter, 1920s, VG, $200.00 (photo courtesy James D. Julia, Inc.); Breyer, Other Animals, Benji, tan matt/semigloss with shading, 1978 – 1979, $30.00 (photo courtesy Felicia Browell); Pin-Back Buttons, Lone Ranger (The), Lone Ranger and Silver in orange cloud of dust with blue sky, yellow ribbon and boots adornment, 1¼" diameter button, $70.00 (photo courtesy www.serioustoyz.com); Paper-Lithographed Toys, Firehouse and Horse-Drawn Fire Pumper, Bliss, 1895, EX+, $2,500.00 (photo courtesy McMasters Harris Auction Company); Building Blocks and Construction Toys, Halsam American Logs, #815, with senior-size ¾" logs, VG, $40.00 (photo courtesy www.serioustoyz.com). Dolls, Betsy McCall, Ideal, 14", hard plastic body, rooted hair, EX, $200.00 (Photo courtesy McMasters Harris Auction Company); Windups, Frog, Kellerman, lithograph tin, 4½", NM, $1,150.00 (photo courtesy James D. Julia, Inc.); Fisher-Price, #770 Dopey and Doc, 1938, G, $850.00 (photo courtesy Morphy Auctions); Paper Dolls, Pals and Pets, Saalfield #2612, 1952, $35.00 (photo courtesy Mary Young).

Back cover: Smith-Miller, PIE semi, L-Mack, 1950s, 27", VG+, $385.00 (photo courtesy www.serioustoyz.com); Strauss, Long Haulage Truck, VG+, $500.00 (photo courtesy James D. Julia, Inc.); Matchbox, Mack Model AC truck, light blue version, 'Acorn Storage,' 1985, $15.00 to $20.00 (photo courtesy Dana Johnson); Chein, Hercules Series, Ready-Mixed Concrete Truck, 17", VG, $2,750.00 (photo courtesy Morphy Auctions); Marx, Emergency Squad No. 2, pressed steel with plastic ladders, battery-operated, 14", VG, $75.00 (photo courtesy www.serioustoyz.com); Pressed Steel, Trucks and Vans, Ambulance, Sturditoy, 1920s, 25", EX, $15,000.00 (photo courtesy James D. Julia, Inc.); Wyandotte, Stake Truck, pressed steel, 1940s, 15½", VG+, $330.00 (photo courtesy Noel Barrett Antiques & Auctions Ltd.).

Cover design: Beth Summers
Book design: Terri Hunter
Managing Editor: Amy Sullivan
Contributing Editors: Donna Newnum, Loretta Suiters, and Sharon Huxford
Copy Editor: Laurie Swick
Editorial Assistants: Kim Vincent, Beth Ray

Collector Books
P.O. Box 3009
Paducah, Kentucky 42002-3009

www.collectorbooks.com

Copyright © 2010 Schroeder Publishing Co., Inc.

The current values of this book should be used only as a guide. They are not intended to set prices, which vary from one section of the country to another. Auction prices as well as dealer prices vary greatly and are affected by condition as well as demand. Neither the editor nor the publisher assumes responsibility for any losses that might be incurred as a result of consulting this guide.

Searching for a Publisher?

We are always looking for knowledgeable people considered to be experts within their fields. If you feel that there is a real need for a book on your collectible subject and have a large comprehensive collection, contact Collector Books.

Proudly printed and bound in the
United States of America

The big news this year is we've added more color photographs than ever before! Toys themselves are all about color, and we show you just how beautiful some of the vintage lithographed tin toys can be, especially the battery-ops and windups made in Germany, Japan, and the United States from the 1930s through the 1950s and beyond. Many photos are of the spectacular higher-end toys that some of us seldom see. We're keeping up with today's trends and preferences, so you'll note that some categories where there is little interest have been omitted, while information on topics that today's collectors focus on the most have been expanded. With the help of our advisors, toy dealers, and many major auction houses, our goal is to provide our readers with fresh information issue after issue. The few categories that remain unchanged year after year are those that are as complete as we can make them, and the values are checked and rechecked for every new edition to make sure that all of our information is current. We've dropped the dealer codes that were used in past editions, since few if any toy dealers still put out catalogs. (FYI: Many of the country's top dealers are referenced in the Directory of Advisors and Contributors in the back of the book.) We hope you will enjoy this all-new twelfth edition.

How the market has changed since our first edition! It continues to evolve as technological advances give both buyers and sellers more flexibility. Auction houses are now combining live auctions with the internet. Some of the major auction houses have set up their own websites and are utilizing online auction sites such as eBay and Live Auctioneers. This results in high prices for good toys, simply because these auctions have world-wide exposure. (If you opt to do your buying in this venue, it is important to note that depending on which auction site you deal with, from 15% to 25% will be added to the 'hammer' price.)

On the other hand, standard internet auctions such as those on eBay are resulting in such a high volume of sales (many by sellers who have neglected to do even basic research), the market is literally flooded with toys. This is a venue that favors the buyer, and very often the one who exercises patience and diligence will be rewarded by winning a desirable item at a much lower price than usual. But there are still high shipping charges to reckon with, and condition, being relative, is sometimes hard to convey or grasp from a word description, as standards of the buyer compared to the seller often differ.

Shows are rebounding, not only here but abroad as well. 'European toy shows are picking up in both number and quality as evidenced in the twice-annual Paris Toy Show and numerous shows in England and Italy,' to quote our advisor Scott Smiles. Cindy Sabulis (our doll advisor and author of several books on dolls) reports that doll shows are still popular with collectors, 'as some collectors, including those who have previously been burnt by online purchases, prefer to hold a doll in their hands before they buy it, rather than purchase one from online sources.' She goes on to say that 'there are some newer collectors who are just learning that there is such a thing as a doll show. At every show we do we meet new collectors attending for the first time who are discovering the joy of on-the-spot buying after learning of a show from an ad or an online listing.' This observation can apply not only to dolls but to any field. As prices began to sag from their high in the nineties, the number of toy shows declined. Despite the fact that there are fewer toy shows being held in the United States than in the 1980s and 1990s, today's younger collectors are still able to re-discover the thrill a big toy show has to offer. The downside is that very often the dealers who sell directly may have higher prices on their merchandise, and in this transitional timeframe (traditional selling vs. internet) may be more attuned to the past rather than the present. Today more than ever the selling price of any toy in question is simply determined through bartering between buyer and seller.

Tin toy mechanicals in general have started to experience an overall decrease in value, especially for the more common examples. Fluctuations have been small but more constant. The exception would be character toys such as Disney, Popeye, and comic characters, which continue to appreciate in value over time. Another area that continues to show price increases seems to be toys from quality manufacturers, especially Lehmann, Martin, Marx, and Unique Art. Quoting Scott Smiles again, 'More and more collectors...indicate a willingness to purchase toys from these manufacturers because of who made them. Themes that continue to be popular are space, robots, western or cowboy/Indian, clowns and amusement park, or circus tin toys.' Smiles notes that tin toys are 'becoming more of a newspaper item' in publications with sections on antiques that feature articles on special interests with photos and pricing.

It goes without saying that the rare and excellent condition toys continue to fetch the higher prices. Everyone wants to own the best, and many are willing to pay well for the privilege. Because of the volume of merchandise that passes through internet auctions on any given day, condition has become an even weightier worth-assessing factor than ever before. Dealers report that toys in played-with condition are slow to sell as collectors can locate better examples in a relatively short period of time. Unless priced reasonably, 'played-with' toys are passed by more often than not.

Looking ahead, our board of advisors agrees that the soft end of the market will firm up when the abundance of the more contemporary toys eventually diminishes. As new collectors seek the toys of their youth, many will gravitate to older or newer toys, expanding their collections in both directions outside the parameters of their memories. This foible of human nature will assure the future value of collectible toys.

The state of the overall economy at this point in the United States does have an impact on the toy and collectibles market. One of our dolls advisors, Cindy Sabulis, author of *Collector's Guide to Dolls of the 1960s and 1970s* and *Collector's Guide to Tammy, the Ideal Teen*, says that collectibles, including dolls, are luxury items, and like all luxury items, sales drop in a bad economy. 'Prices on dolls have been lower than normal the past couple of years,' Sabulis states. 'This is good news for buyers as bargains abound, but not so good for sellers. The good news for sellers is that even in a struggling economy, sales on mint and rare items still command high prices, although it takes a little longer than it used to to find a buyer willing to pay that high price. The collectibles market is similar to the stock market with highs and lows. When prices are low, it is a good time to buy. When prices are high, it's a good time to sell those items that don't mean as much to you. If you're considering buying items for investment, vintage items often appreciate in value more than reproduction items, although there are exceptions. The better the condition of the vintage items, the easier it will be to sell it when the time comes. Of course as with anything, you should buy what you like, not what you think will appreciate in value, because you will be disappointed if the item ends up dropping lower in value than what you paid for it.'

Our advice: continue to add high quality toys to your collection. There are some real bargains out there right now. Future values are impossible to predict, but if you buy what you like in the best condition you can afford, your collections will continue to appreciate over the long term.

Our suggested values in most cases are prices realized at auction (buyer's premium included; postage if it is charged) and should be regarded simply as a starting point for the transaction.

There are two main factors determining selling price: the attitude of the individual collector (how strongly he desires to own) and the motivation of the dealer (does he need to turn over his merchandise quickly to replenish and freshen his stock, or can he wait for the most opportune time to turn it over for maximum profit). Where you buy affects prices as well. One of our advisors used this simple analogy: while a soda might cost you $2.50 at the ballpark, you can buy the same thing for 39¢ at the corner 7-11. So all we (or anyone) can offer is whatever facts and information we can compile, and ask simply that you arrive at your own evaluations based on the data we've provided, adapted to your personal buying/selling arena.

We hope you enjoy our book and that you'll be able to learn by using it. We don't presume to present it as the last word on toys or their values — there are many specialized books by authors who are able to devote an entire publication to one subject, covering it from 'A' to 'Z,' and when we're aware that such a book exists, we'll recommend it in our narratives.

Concept. Basically, this book is a market report compiled from many sources, meant to be studied and digested by our readers, who can then better arrive at their own conclusion regarding prices. Were you to ask ten active toy dealers for their opinions as to the value of a specific toy, you would no doubt get ten different answers, and who's to say which is correct? Quite simply, there are too many variables to consider. Where you buy is critical. Condition is certainly subjective, prices vary from one area of the country to another, and probably the most important factor is how badly you want to add the item in question to your collection or at what price you're willing to sell. So use this as a guide along with your own observations.

The Directory contains names and addresses of our advisors who you may feel free to contact. If you're looking for an appraisal, some may charge a fee. Be sure to ask. If you would like a reply, be sure to send an SASE with your mailing. There is also a section on 'Clubs, Newsletters, and Other Publications' devoted to specific areas of toy collecting.

Toys are listed by name. Every effort has been made to list a toy by the name as it appears on the toy itself, or on the original box. There have been very few exceptions made, and then only if the collector-given name is more recognizable. For instance, if we listed 'To-Night Amos 'n' Andy in Person' (as the name appears on the box), few would recognize the toy as the Amos 'n' Andy Walkers. But these exceptions are few. Sizes may have been rounded off to the next inch on some of the larger items.

Sources of our suggested values. The values listed in this guide have come from recent major auctions, internet sources, and dealer/advisor collections. Our advisors as well as most collectors have various viewpoints regarding auction results. Some feel they're too high to be used to establish prices while others prefer them to 'asking' prices that can sometimes be speculative. You'll have to make that call yourself. Because the average auction-consigned toy is in especially good condition and many times even retains its original box, it will naturally bring higher prices than the norm. And auctions often offer the harder-to-find, more unusual items. Unless you take these factors into consideration, prices may seem high, when in fact, they may not be at all. Some fear that prices may be driven up by high reserves, but not all galleries have reserves. If an auction item has been listed more than once in the same condition but with different prices, we'll average the price for that item.

Categories that have priority. Obviously there are thousands of toys that would work as well in one category as they would in another, depending on the preference of the collector. For instance, a Mary Poppins game would appeal to a games collector just as readily as it would to someone who bought character-related toys of all kinds. The same would be true of many other types of toys. We tried to make our decisions sensibly and keep our sorts simple. We'll guide you to those specialized categories with cross-references and 'See Alsos.' If all else fails, refer to the index.

Price ranges. Once in awhile, you'll find a listing that gives a price range. These result from our having found varying prices for the same item. We've taken a mid-range — less than the highest, a little over the lowest, if the actual difference in the selling prices was too wide to really be helpful.

Condition — how it affects value, how to judge it. The importance of condition can't be stressed enough! Unless a toy is exceptionally rare, it must be excellent or better to really have much collector value. But here's where the problem comes in: though each step downward on the grading scale drastically decreases a toy's value, as the old saying goes, 'beauty is in the eye of the beholder.' What is acceptable wear and damage to one individual may be regarded by another as entirely too degrading. Criteria used to judge condition even varies from one auction company to the next, so we had to attempt to sort them all out and arrive at some sort of standardization. Auction galleries often describe missing parts, repairs, and paint touch-ups, summing up overall appearance in the condition code. Remember that a toy, even in mint restored condition, still isn't worth as much as one in mint original condition.

These are the conditions codes we have used throughout the book and their definitions as we have applied them:

M – mint. Unplayed with, brand new, flawless.
NM – near mint. Appears brand new except on very close inspection.
EX – excellent. Has minimal wear, very minor chips and rubs, a few light scratches.
VG – very good. Played with, loss of gloss, noticeable problems, several scratches.
G – good. Some rust, considerable wear and paint loss, well used.
F – fair. Obviously played with, noticeable flaws, but still desirable for a collection.
P – poor. Generally unacceptable except for a filler.

Because we do not use a three-level pricing structure as many of you are used to and may prefer, we offer this table to help you arrive at values for toys in conditions other than those that we give you. If you know the value of a toy in excellent condition and would like to find an approximate value for it in near mint condition, for instance, just run your finger down the column under 'EX' until you find the approximate price we've listed (or one that easily factors into it), then over to the column headed 'NM.' We'll just go to $100.00, but other values will be easy to figure by addition or multiplication.

G	VG	EX	NM	M
40/50%	55/65%	70/80%	85/90%	100%
5.00	6.00	7.50	9.00	10.00
7.50	9.00	11.00	12.50	15.00
10.00	12.00	15.00	18.00	20.00
12.00	15.00	18.00	22.00	25.00
14.00	18.00	22.50	26.00	30.00
18.00	25.00	30.00	35.00	40.00
22.50	30.00	37.50	45.00	50.00
27.00	35.00	45.00	52.00	60.00
32.00	42.00	52.00	62.00	70.00
34.00	45.00	55.00	65.00	75.00
35.00	48.00	60.00	70.00	80.00
40.00	55.00	68.00	80.00	90.00
45.00	60.00	75.00	90.00	100.00

Condition and value of original boxes and packaging. When no box or packaging is referred to in the line or in the narrative, assume that the quoted price is for the toy only. Please read the narratives! In some categories (Corgi, for instance), all values are given for items mint and in original boxes. When the box is present, condition codes (for example: 'EXIB' or 'MIB') will be relevant to both toy and box. If a box is less than excellent, the condition of the box alone will be in parenthesis immediately following the condition code for the toy itself. Collector interest in original boxes, cards, and packaging is a recent but growing trend, and today many people will pay very high prices for them, depending on scarcity, desirability, and condition. The more colorful, graphically pleasing boxes are favored, and those with images of well-known characters are especially sought after. Just how valuable is a box? Again, this is very subjective to the individual. We posed the question to several top collectors around the country, and the answers they gave ranged from 25% to 75% above mint-no-box prices, generally speaking.

• • • • • • • • • • • • • • Listing of Standard Abbreviations • • • • • • • • • • • • • •

These abbreviations have been used throughout this book in order to provide you with the most detailed descriptions possible in our limited space. No periods are used after initials or abbreviations. When two dimensions are given, height is noted first. When only one measurement is given, it will be the greater — height if the toy is vertical, length if it is horizontal. (Remember that in the case of duplicate listings representing various conditions, we found that sizes often varied as much as an inch or more.)

att .... attributed to
bkgrd ....background
bl ....blue
blk .... black
b/o .... battery-operated
brn ....brown
BRT ....black rubber tires
c .... copyright
ca ....circa
cb ....cardboard
CI ....cast iron
compo...composition
dbl ....double
dk...dark
ed ....edition
emb..embossed
EX...excellent
EXIB...excellent in box
EXIC ....excellent in container
EXIP...excellent in package
F...fair
fr..frame, framed
ft, ftd...feet, foot, footed
G ....good
GE ....glass eyes
GIB..good in box
gr ....green
H ....height, high
hdl..handle, handled
IB .... in box
illus..illustrated, illustration
inscr...inscribed
Int'l...International
jtd .... jointed
L ....long, length
lg...large
litho..lithographed
lt..light, lightly
M ....mint
MBP ....mint in bubble pack
mc..multicolored
MDW...metal disk wheels
Mfg or mfg..manufacturing
MIB ....mint in box
MIP ....mint in package
MOC...mint on card
MOT ....mint on tree

MSW ....metal spoke wheels
NM..near mint
NOS ....new old stock
NP ....nickel plated
NPDW .... nickel-plated disk wheels
NPP...........................National Periodicals Publications
NPSW .... nickel-plated spoke wheels
NRFB .... never removed from box
NRFC ....never removed from card
NRFP............................ never removed from package
orig .... original
o/w .... otherwise
P .... poor
PE ....painted eyes
pk.. pink
pkg...package
PMDW ....painted metal disk wheels
pnt ....paint, painted
pr ....pair
Prod .... Products, Productions
prof ....professional
PS ....pressed steel
r/c...remote control
rnd .... round
rpl .... replaced
rpnt ....repainted
rpr ....repaired
rstr ....restored
sgn ....signed
sm .... small
sq ....square
sz .... size
turq...turquoise
unmk...unmarked
unpnt... unpainted
VG.. very good
VGIB..very good in box
W .... width
WDE ....Walt Disney Enterprises
WDP ....Walt Disney Productions
wht ....white
WRT ....white rubber tires
WS ....wingspan
WWT ....whitewall tires
w/ .... with
w/up ....windup
yel ....yellow

A. C. Gilbert

The A.C. Gilbert Company, best known for the Erector Set, also marketed various types of scientific activity sets, magic sets, and games. Gilbert started producing the Erector Set in 1913. Over the years, collectors have divided the sets into three basic categories. Type I sets include those from the years 1913 to 1923, Type II from 1924 to 1962, and Type III from 1963 to 1988. Each type underwent a major revamping. Although the A.C. Gilbert Company was sold in 1961 to the Jack Wrather Group, the Gilbert name was used until 1976.

The following listings are from a Leslie Hindman auction and are complete sets unless noted otherwise.

For more information, refer to Clubs, Newsletters, and Other Publications in the back of this guide.

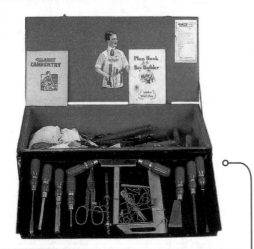

A. C. Gilbert
Big Boy Tool Chest, red metal box, EX, $75.00.
(Photo courtesy www.serioustoyz.com)

A. C. Gilbert
Carpentry Set, #780, 1920s, black wood box, EX+, $1,000.00. (Photo courtesy Leslie Hindman Auctioneers)

A. C. Gilbert
Erector Set, #A, 1931, Locomotive, red wood box, EX, $2,500.00. (Photo courtesy Leslie Hindman Auctioneers)

Air-Kraft Set, #A103, 1919, cb box, VG $1,800.00
Brik-tor Set, cb box, EX.. $650.00
Carpenter's Outfit, #6325, cb box, EX+ $400.00
Chemistry Outfit for Boys, bl cb box, VG $350.00
Chemistry Set, #12065, folding cb box, VG+ $350.00
Coin Tricks, #2010, 1920, cb box, EX........................... $2,500.00
Designer & Toy Maker Set, 1920s, cb box, EX $300.00
Electric Toys & Tricks Set, #3003, cb box, EX................ $500.00
Electrical Set, #3002, 1920s, cb box, EX....................... $500.00
Electrical Set, #3005, 1920s, New Erector..., cb box, EX . $425.00
Erector Set, #A, 1927, cb box, EX+ $1,500.00
Erector Set, #B, 1929, Accessory Set, red wood box, EX. $900.00
Erector Set, #S, 1935, Skyscraper Set, red cb box, VG+ . $1,150.00
Erector Set, #2, 1918, cb box, EX................................ $125.00
Erector Set, #4, 1922, blk wood box, VG+ $350.00
Erector Set, #4, 1924-33, red cb box, VG $175.00
Erector Set, #4½, 1938, red cb box, NM $500.00
Erector Set, #4½, 1941-42, red cb box, EX.................... $300.00
Erector Set, #5, 1923, blk wood box, VG...................... $1,600.00
Erector Set, #6, 1915, wood box, EX............................ $250.00
Erector Set, #6, 1933, gr metal box, EX $400.00
Erector Set, #6, 1950, Whistle Kit, red cb box, EX......... $250.00
Erector Set, #7, 1915, wood box, EX............................ $850.00
Erector Set, #7, 1923, wood box, EX+ $1,500.00
Erector Set, #7, 1928-29, Steam Shovel, wood box, VG+ ..$200.00
Erector Set, #7, 1931, Steam Shovel, red wood box, VG.. $300.00
Erector Set, #7, 1934, red metal box, EX $800.00
Erector Set, #7½, 1926, wood box, EX.......................... $4,500.00
Erector Set, #7½, 1929, White Truck Set, wood box, EX . $450.00
Erector Set, #7½, 1934, bl-gr metal box, VG $575.00

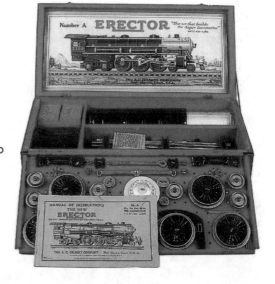

Erector Set, #7½, 1946, bl cb box, EX................................ $300.00

Erector Set, #8, 1915, stained wood box, VG+................ $950.00

Erector Set, #8, 1925, wood box, VG........................... $1,550.00

Erector Set, #8, 1929, Zeppelin (Trail Blazing), red wood box, EX.. $3,000.00

Erector Set, #8½, 1935, Automotive, bl metal box, EX.. $725.00

Erector Set, #10, Junior Erector, yel cb box, EX.............. $275.00

Erector Set, #10, 1922, stained wood box, VG+.............. $950.00

Erector Set, #10½, 1937, bl-gr metal box, EX $2,750.00

Erector Set, #10½, 1951, Amusement Park, red metal box, EX... $250.00

Erector Set, #10½, 1942, Electric Train Set, bl metal box, VG... $1,200.00

Erector Set, #12½, 1949 (early), Walking Giant, red metal box, EX.. $1,150.00

Erector Set, #12½, 1949 (late), Walking Giant, red metal box, VG.. $300.00

Erector Set, #12½, 1956, Walking Robot, red metal box, EX+ .$575.00

Erector Set, #15, Senior Wheels Machinery, cb box, G . $550.00

Erector Set, #44, 1918-19, Master Engineer's Set, wood box, EX... $1,200.00

Erector Set, #77, 1928, Steam Shovel, red wood box, VG...$200.00

Erector Set, #10021, Young Builders, cb tube container, EX...$100.00

Erector Set, #10052, 1958, red metal box, EX $75.00

Erector Set, #10053, 1959, 50th Anniversary, cb box, EX..$75.00

Erector Set, #10072, 1958, Musical Ferris Wheel, red cb box, EX+.. $500.00

Erector Set, #10083, Amusement Park, red metal box, EX+ ..$800.00

Erector Set, #10092, 1958, Walking Robot, red metal box, NM $2,000.00

Kaster Kit Jr Set, #3, 1933, red cb box, EX+ $400.00

Light Experiments, 1920s, blk cb box, EX+ $750.00

Magnetic Fun & Facts Set, #2, cb box, EX+ $200.00

Magnetic Fun & Facts Set, #6507, 1920s, wood box, EX+ ...$2,000.00

Meteor Game, #1053, 1920, cb box, EX $100.00

Microscope Set, #8, cb box, EX....................................... $200.00

Mineralogy Set, #2, 1920s, cb box, EX+ $500.00

Mysto Magic Show Set, #2½, cb box, EX.......................... $200.00

Mysto Magic Show Set, #3, 1938, cb box, EX $350.00

Mysto Magic Show Set, #3A, 1933, cb box, VG $350.00

Mysto Magic Show Set, #5, 1933, red metal box, EX+... $725.00

Mysto Magic Show Set, #5, 1947, cb box, EX+ $500.00

Mysto Magic Show Set, #6, 1952, cb box, EX $850.00

Mysto Magic Show Set, #20, 1950, cb box, EX+ $2,275.00

Mysto Magic Show Set, #25, red fabric-covered hinged box, EX.. $2,500.00

Mysto Magic Show Set, #2001, 1916, EX+ $500.00

Mysto Magic Show Set, #2002, 1917, cb box, VG $100.00

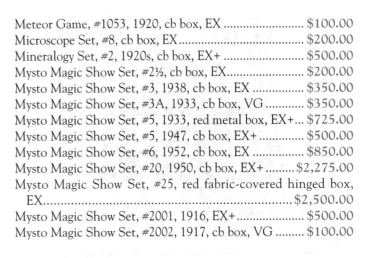

A. C. Gilbert

Erector Set, #10032, 1960, Engineer's Set, cardboard tube container, metal screw lid, VG, $100.00. (Photo courtesy Leslie Hindman Auctioneers)

A. C. Gilbert

Erector Set, #10, 1928, stained wood box with eight drawers, EX+, $10,800.00. (Photo courtesy Leslie Hindman Auctioneers)

A. C. Gilbert

Glass Blowing Set, #2, cardboard box, unused, EX (EX box), $450.00. (Photo courtesy Leslie Hindman Auctioneers)

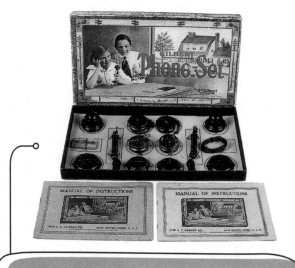

A. C. Gilbert

Phono-Set, #3505, 1918 – 1921, cardboard box, EX+, $1,500.00. (Photo courtesy Leslie Hindman Auctioneers)

A. C. Gilbert

Tele-Set, #3502, 1922, cardboard box, EX, $300.00. (Photo courtesy Leslie Hindman Auctioneers)

Mysto Magic Show Set, #2003, 1920, cb box, EX+	$300.00
Mysto Magic Show Set, #2006, 1923, wood box, EX	$550.00
Mysto Magic Show Set, #2006, 1925, cb box, EX	$400.00
Mysto Magic Show Set, #2007, 1929, red wood box, EX.	$500.00
Nurse's Outfit for Girls, 1918, blk cb box, EX	$1,775.00
Opto Kit, #6, red cb box, EX	$500.00
Pak O' Fun Moovy Sho, cb box, EX	$575.00
Problem Puzzles, #1034, cb box, VG	$75.00
Puzzles Set, #1003, cb box, EX	$75.00
Sixty-Six (66) Stunts w/an Electric Motor, #205, 1922, cb, EX+	$850.00
Soldering Outfit, #7002, 1919, cb box, EX	$450.00
Swinging Aeroplane Set C, 1919, cb box, EX+	$3,000.00
Swinging Clown, #B677, 1920s, cb box, VG	$300.00
Toy Balloon Outfit, #600, cb box, EX	$600.00
Tubular Toy Set, 1937-38, EX	$200.00
Wireless Telegraph Outfit, 1920, cb box, EX	$800.00

A. C. Gilbert

Weather Bureau, #6533, 1920, cardboard box, EX+, $3,000.00. (Photo courtesy Leslie Hindman Auctioneers)

• • • • • • • • • • • • • • • **Action Figures and Accessories** • • • • • • • • • • • • • •

You will find a wide range of asking prices from dealer to dealer, and under the influence of the internet, prices fluctuate greatly. Be critical of condition! Original packaging is extremely important. In fact, when it comes to recent issues, loose, played-with examples are seldom worth more than a few dollars. When no size is given, assume figures are 3¾" or standard size for that line. Listings for 'loose' figures that come with accessories are complete unless noted otherwise.

See also Character, TV, and Movie Collectibles; Dolls and Accessories, Celebrity Dolls; GI Joe; Star Trek; Star Wars.

A-Team, accessory, Combat Headquarters (w/4 figures), Galoob, MIB, $50 to $65.00

A-Team, accessory, Command Chopper & Enforcer Van, MIP, $20 to...$25.00

A-Team, accessory, Corvette (w/Face figure), Galoob, M, $30 to...$35.00

A-Team, accessory, Interceptor Jet Bomber (w/Murdock figure), Galoob, MIP, $50 to...........................$55.00

A-Team, accessory, Off Road Attack Cycle, Galoob, MIP, $20 to $25.00

A-Team, accessory, Patrol Boat (w/Hannibal figure), Galoob, MIB, $25 to $30.00

A-Team, accessory, van w/removable roof, Galoob, M, $25 to $35.00

A-Team, figure, 3¾", Bad Guys, set of 4 (Cobra, Python, Rattler & Viper), Galoob, MOC (all on 1 card), $50 to...........$60.00

A-Team, figure, 3¾", Soldiers of Fortune, set of 4, Galoob, MOC (all on 1 card), $50 to $60.00
A-Team, figure, 6½", Amy Allen, MOC, $45 to $55.00
A-Team, figure, 12", Mr T, nontalking, Galoob, MIB, $30 to..$40.00
A-Team, figure, 12", Mr T, talking, Galoob, MIB, $50 to..$60.00
Action Jackson, accessory, Campmobile, Mego, MIB........$75.00
Action Jackson, accessory, Fire Rescue Pack or Parachute Plunge, Mego, MIB, ea $12 to..$18.00
Action Jackson, accessory, Jungle House, Mego, MIB, ea $175 to...$225.00
Action Jackson, accessory, Scramble Cycle, Mego, MIB ...$45.00
Action Jackson, accessory, Strap-On Helicopter, Mego, MIB, $12 to...$18.00
Action Jackson, accessory, Water Skooter, Mego, NRFB, $12 to...$18.00
Action Jackson, figure, any color hair or beard except blk figure, Mego, MIB, ea $25 to..$30.00
Action Jackson, figure, blk, Mego, MIB, $35 to $40.00
Action Jackson, outfit, any, Mego, MIP, ea $8 to...............$12.00
Adventures of Indiana Jones, see Indiana Jones (Adventures of)
Alien, figure, Alien, 18", Kenner, M, $175 to.................. $200.00
Alien, figure, Alien, 18", Kenner, MIB, $450 to............. $500.00
Aliens, accessory, Evac Fighter or Hovertread, Kenner, MIP, $15 to...$20.00
Aliens, accessory, Power Loader or Stinger XT-37, Kenner, MIP, ea $15 to $20.00
Aliens, figure, Series 1, Apone, Bishop, Bull Alien, Drake, Gorilla Alien or Hicks, Kenner, MOC, ea $8 to $10.00
Aliens, figure, Series 1, Queen Alien, Kenner, MOC, $15 to...$20.00
Aliens, figure, Series 1, Ripley or Scorpion Alien, Kenner, MOC, ea $10 to $15.00
Aliens, figure, Series 2, Flying Queen Alien, Queen Face Hugger or Snake Alien, Kenner, MOC, ea $10 to $15.00
Aliens, figure, Series 3, Arachnid Alien, Clan Leader Predator, King Alien or Swarm Alien, Kenner, MOC, ea $12 to..$18.00
Aliens, figure, Series 3, Atax, Cracked Tusk Predator, Kill Krab or Lava Predator, Kenner, MOC, ea $12 to $18.00
Aliens, figure, Series 3, Mantis Alien, Night Cougar Alien or Night Storm Predator, Kenner, MOC, ea $8 to.............$12.00
Aliens, figure, Series 3, Panther, Rhino, Spiked Tail, Stalker or Wild Boar, Kenner, MOC, ea $8 to $12.00
Aliens, figure set, Series 2, Alien vs Predator, Kenner, MOC, $18 to...$22.00
American West, figure, Buffalo Bill Cody or Cochise, Mego, MIB, ea $65 to..$75.00
American West, figure, Buffalo Bill Cody or Cochise, Mego, MOC, $80 to..$90.00

American West, figure, Davy Crockett, Mego, MIB, $90 to...$100.00
American West, figure, Davy Crockett, Mego, MOC, $125 to.$135.00
American West, figure, Shadow (horse), Mego, MIB, $125 to..$135.00
American West, figure, Sitting Bull, Wild Bill Hickok or Wyatt Earp, Mego, MIB, ea $70 to $80.00
American West, figure, Sitting Bull, Wild Bill Hickok or Wyatt Earp, Mego, MOC, ea $100 to $125.00
American West, playset, Dodge City, Mego, MIB, $150 to... $175.00
ANTZ, figure, any, Playmates, 1998, MOC, ea $3 to $5.00
Archies, figure, any, Marx, 1975, MOC, ea $65 to $75.00
Avengers, figure gift sets, Ant-Man/Giant Man, Hulk, Iron Man, The Wasp, Toy Biz, MOC, ea $18 to $22.00
Avengers, figures, any character from any series, Toy Biz, MOC, $6 to..$10.00
Banana Splits, figure, any, Sutton, 1970s, MIP, ea $120 to..$130.00
Batgirl, see Super Heroes
Batman, see also Captain Action, Comic Action Heroes, Pocket Super Heroes, Super Heroes, or Super Powers
Batman (Animated), accessory, Aero Boat, BATV Vehicle, Batcycle or Bat-Signal Jet, Kenner, 1992-95, MIP, ea $18 to..$22.00
Batman (Animated), accessory, Batcave, Kenner, MIP, $100 to.$130.00
Batman (Animated), accessory, Batmobile, Kenner, MIP, $50 to...$60.00
Batman (Animated), accessory, Crime Stalker, Hoverboat, Ice Hammer or Joker Mobile, Kenner, MIP, ea $15 to $20.00

Action Figures and Accessories
• •
Archie Series, figures, any character, bendable vinyl, Jesco, 6", MOC, each $20.00 to $25.00.
(Photo courtesy Paris & Susan Manos)

Batman (Animated), accessory, Robin's Dragster, Kenner, MIP, $200 to.. $230.00

Batman (Animated), accessory, Street Jet or Turbo Batplane, Kenner, MIP, ea $18 to.................................$26.00

Batman (Animated), figure, Anti-Freeze, Bane, Bruce Wayne, Ground Assault or Infrared Batman, Kenner, MOC, ea $8 to... $12.00

Batman (Animated), figure, Battle Helmet Batman, High-Wire Batman or Poison Ivy, Kenner, MOC, ea $28 to............$35.00

Batman (Animated), figure, Bola Trap Robin or Sky Dive Batman, Kenner, MOC, ea $8 to.................................$12.00

Batman (Animated), figure, Catwoman, Radar Scope Batman or Rapid Attack Batman, Kenner, MOC, ea $22 to...........$26.00

Batman (Animated), figure, Combat Belt Batman, Kenner, MOC, $28 to...$35.00

Batman (Animated), figure, Knight Star Batman, Lightning Strike Batman or Mech-Wing Batman, Kenner, MOC, ea $8 to...$12.00

Batman (Animated), figure, Man-Bat, Kenner, MOC, $12 to...$16.00

Batman (Animated), figure, Penguin, Kenner, MOC, $45 to ..$50.00

Batman (Animated), figure, Riddler, Tornado Batman or Two Face, Kenner, MOC, ea $22 to $26.00

Batman (Animated), figure set, Ninja Batman & Robin, Kenner, MOC, $18 to...$22.00

Batman (Crime Squad), accessory, Attack Jet or Batcycle, Kenner, MOC, $18 to...$22.00

Batman (Crime Squad), figure, any character, Kenner, MOC, ea $8 to..$12.00

Batman (Dark Knight), accessory, Batcycle, Kenner, MIP, ea $18 to..$22.00

Batman (Dark Knight), accessory, Batjet, Kenner, MIP, $40 to $45.00

Batman (Dark Knight), accessory, Batmobile, Kenner, MIP, $85 to $100.00

Batman (Dark Knight), accessory, Batwing, Kenner, MIP, $60 to..$70.00

Batman (Dark Knight), accessory, Bola Bullet, Kenner, MIP, $30 to..$40.00

Batman (Dark Knight), accessory, Joker Cycle, Kenner, MIP, $12 to..$18.00

Batman (Dark Knight), figure, Blast Shield, Claw Climber, Power Wing, Thunder Whip, Kenner, MOC, ea $20 to $30.00

Batman (Dark Knight), figure, Bruce Wayne, Kenner, MOC, $18 to..$22.00

Batman (Dark Knight), figure, Crime Attack or Iron Winch, Kenner, MOC, ea $18 to $22.00

Batman (Dark Knight), figure, Knockout Joker, Kenner, MOC, $45 to..$55.00

Batman (Dark Knight), figure, Night Glider, Kenner, MOC, $30 to..$40.00

Batman (Dark Knight), figure, Sky Escape Joker, Kenner, MOC, $22 to..$28.00

Batman (Movie), accessory, Batcave Master Playset, Toy Biz, MIB, $65 to $75.00

Batman (Movie), accessory, Batmobile (Turbine Sound), Toy Biz, MIB, $25 to $30.00

Batman (Movie), accessory, Joker Cycle (Detachable Launching Sidecar), Toy Biz, MIB, $20 to......................................$25.00

Batman (Movie), figure, Batman (any except sq jaw), Toy Biz, MOC, ea $10 to $15.00

Batman (Movie), figure, Batman (sq jaw), Toy Biz, MOC, $18 to $22.00

Batman (Movie), figure, Bob (Joker's Goon), Toy Biz, MOC, $20 to..$25.00

Batman (Movie), figure, Joker (hair curl), Toy Biz, MOC, $20 to..$25.00

Batman (Movie), figure, Joker (Squirting Orchid), Toy Biz, MOC, $18 to..$22.00

Batman & Robin, accessory, Batgirl's Icestrike Cycle, Kenner, MIP, $15 to..$20.00

Batman & Robin, accessory, Batmobile, Batmobile (Sonic) or Ice Hammer, Kenner, MIP, ea $18 to............................$22.00

Batman & Robin, accessory, Ice Fortress, Kenner, MIP, $8 to...$12.00

Action Figures and Accessories
• •
Batman (Dark Knight), figures, Shadow Wing and Wall Scaler, Kenner, MOC, each $18.00 to $22.00.

Batman & Robin, accessory, Iceglow Bathammer, Kenner, MIP, $25 to..$35.00

Batman & Robin, accessory, Jet Blade, Kenner, MIP, $18 to ...$22.00

Batman & Robin, accessory, Night Sphere, Kenner, MIP, $20 to..$30.00

Batman & Robin, accessory, Wayne Manor Batcave, Kenner, MIP, $45 to..$55.00

Batman & Robin, figure, 5", Bane, Batman (Ambush Attack) or Batman (Battle Board w/Ring), Kenner, ea $6 to...........$10.00

Batman & Robin, figure, 5", Batgirl, Kenner, MIP, $4 to.....$6.00

Batman & Robin, figure, 5", Batgirl w/Icestrike Cycle, Kenner, Deluxe, MIP, $18 to...$22.00

Batman & Robin, figure, 5", Batman, Kenner, Deluxe, MIP, $10 to..$12.00

Batman & Robin, figure, 5", Batman (Aerial Combat), Kenner, Series 1, MIP, $18 to...$22.00

Batman & Robin, figure, 5", Batman (Blast Wing) or Batman (Rooftop Pursuit), Kenner, Deluxe, MIP, ea $8 to..........$10.00

Batman & Robin, figure, 5", Batman (Heat Scan), Batman (Hover Attack) or Batman (Ice Blade), Kenner, MIP, ea $6 to $10.00

Batman & Robin, figure, 5", Batman (Ice Blade & Ring), Kenner, MIB, $6 to $10.00

Batman & Robin, figure, 5", Batman (Laser Cape & Ring), Kenner, MIP, $6 to $10.00

Batman & Robin, figure, 5", Batman (Neon Armor & Ring), or Batman (Rotoblade & Ring), Kenner, MIP, ea $6 to $10.00

Batman & Robin, figure, 5", Batman (Neon Armor) or Batman (Snow Tracker), Kenner, MIP, ea $6 to $10.00

Batman & Robin, figure, 5", Batman (Sky Assault & Ring) or Batman (Thermal Shield & Ring), Kenner, MIP, ea $10 to $12.00

Batman & Robin, figure, 5", Batman (Snow Tracker) or Batman (Wing Blast), Kenner, MIP, ea $6 to..............................$10.00

Batman & Robin, figure, 5", Bruce Wayne (Battle Gear), Kenner, MIP, $6 to $10.00

Batman & Robin, figure, 5", Jungle Venom Poison Ivy, Robin (Iceboard) or Robin (Razor Skate), Kenner, MIP, ea $4 to $6.00

Batman & Robin, figure, 5", Mr Freeze (Ice Terror) or Robin, Kenner, Deluxe, MIP, ea $6 to $10.00

Batman & Robin, figure, 5", Mr Freeze (Iceblast), Kenner, Series 1, MIP, $8 to $12.00

Batman & Robin, figure, 5", Mr Freeze (Jet Wing w/Ring), Kenner, Series 2, MIP, ea $18 to.................................$22.00

Batman & Robin, figure, 5", Mr Freeze (Ultimate Armor w/ Ring), Kenner, MIP, ea $10 to $12.00

Batman & Robin, figure, 5", Robin, Kenner, Deluxe, MIP, $10 to..$12.00

Batman & Robin, figure, 5", Robin (Glacier Battle), Kenner, Deluxe, MIP, $12 to...$15.00

Batman & Robin, figure, 5", Robin (Talon Strike) or Robin (Triple Strike), Kenner, MIP, ea $4 to $6.00

Batman & Robin, figure, 12", Batgirl, Kenner, MIB, $30 to ..$36.00

Batman & Robin, figure, 12", Batman, Kenner, MIB, $20 to ..$28.00

Batman & Robin, figure, 12", Batman & Poison Ivy (set), Kenner, MIP, $35 to..$45.00

Batman & Robin, figure, 12", Ice Battle Batman, Mister Freeze or Robin, Kenner, MIB, ea $20 to...............................$25.00

Action Figures and Accessories
• • • • • • • • • • •
Batman and Robin, figure, 5", Frostbite, Kenner, MOC, $6.00 to $10.00.

Batman & Robin, figure, 12", Ultimate Batman or Ultimate Robin, Kenner, MIB, ea $18 to.....................................$22.00

Batman & Robin, figure set, 5", Batman vs Poison Ivy, Kenner, MIP, $35 to..$45.00

Batman & Robin, figure set, 5", Challengers of the Night, Kenner, MIP, $12 to...$18.00

Batman & Robin, figure set, 5", Cold Night at Gotham, Brain vs Brawn or Guardians of Gotham, Kenner, MIP, ea $8.....$12.00

Batman & Robin (Adventures of), accessory, Night Sphere w/ Batman figure, series 1, Kenner, MIP, $35 to.................$45.00

Batman & Robin (Adventures of), figure, any character from any series, Kenner, MOC, $8 to.....................................$12.00

Batman & Robin (Adventures of), figure set, Rogues Gallery, series 2, Kenner, 1997, MIP, $45 to.............................$50.00

Batman Forever, accessory, Batboat or Batwing, Kenner, MIB, ea $22 to..$28.00

Batman Forever, accessory, Batcave, Batmobile or Triple Action Vehicle Set, Kenner, MIB, ea $35 to.............................$45.00

Batman Forever, accessory, Robin Cycle, Kenner, MIB, $10 to $15.00

Batman Forever, accessory, Wayne Manor, Kenner, MIB, $45 to $55.00

Batman Forever, figure, Attack Wing Batman, Laser Disc Batman or Lightwing Batman, Kenner, MOC, ea $20 to....$28.00

Batman Forever, figure, Batarang Batman or Ice Blade Batman, Kenner, MOC, ea $10 to...$15.00

Batman Forever, figure, Blast Cape Batman, Fireguard Batman, or Hydro Claw Robin, Kenner, MOC, ea $10 to...........$15.00

Batman Forever, figure, Bruce Wayne or The Riddler, Kenner, MOC, ea $40 to $45.00

Batman Forever, figure, Manta Ray Batman, Martial Arts Robin or Neon Armor Batman, Kenner, MOC, ea $12 to........$16.00

Batman Forever, figure, Night Hunter Batman, Power Beacon Batman or Recon Hunter Batman, Kenner, MOC, ea $12 to . $16.00

Batman Forever, figure, Riddler (w/Bazooka) or Triple Strike Robin, Kenner, MOC, ea $10 to $12.00

Batman Forever, figure, Skyboard Robin, Solar Shield Batman or Sonar Sensor Batman, Kenner, MOC, ea $12 to............$16.00

Batman Forever, figure, Street Biker Robin or Street Racer Batman, Kenner, MOC, ea $12 to......................................$16.00

Action Figures and Accessories
• • • • • • • • • •
Batman Forever, figure, Transforming Bruce Wayne, Kenner, MOC, $12.00 to $16.00.

Action Figures and Accessories
• •
Batman Returns, figures, Hydro Charge and Jungle Tracker, Kenner, MOC, each $10.00 to $12.00.

Batman Forever, figure, Talking Riddler, Tide Racer Robin, Kenner, MOC, ea $18 to $22.00

Batman Forever, figure, Transforming Grayson, MOC, ea $12 to $16.00

Batman Forever, figure, Two-Face or Wing Blast Batman, Kenner, MOC, ea $12 to $16.00

Batman Forever, figure set, any, Kenner, MOC, ea $38 to.$42.00

Batman Returns, accessory, All-Terrain Batskiboat, Kenner, MIP, $35 to $45.00

Batman Returns, accessory, Bat Cave Command Center, Kenner, MIB, $55 to $65.00

Batman Returns, accessory, Bat Cycle, Kenner, MIP, $18 to.$22.00

Batman Returns, accessory, Batmissile Batmobile, Kenner, MIB, $65 to $75.00

Batman Returns, accessory, Batmobile, Kenner, MIP, $60 to....$70.00

Batman Returns, accessory, Bruce Wayne Custom Coupe (w/figure), Kenner, MIB, $22 to $28.00

Batman Returns, accessory, Camo Attack Batmobile, Kenner, MIP, $50 to $60.00

Batman Returns, accessory, Robin Jetfoil, Kenner, MIP, $15 to..$20.00

Batman Returns, accessory, Sky Blade, Kenner, 1992, MIP, $30 to...$35.00

Batman Returns, accessory, Sky Drop, Kenner, MIP, $25 to .. $30.00

Batman Returns, figure, Aerostrike Batman, Air Attack Batman or Arctic Batman, Kenner, MOC, ea $10 to $12.00

Batman Returns, figure, Bola Strike Batman, Bruce Wayne or Catwoman, Kenner, MOC, ea $12 to $16.00

Batman Returns, figure, Claw Climber Batman, Crime Attack Batman or Deep Dive Batman, Kenner, MOC, ea $10 to........$12.00

Batman Returns, figure, Firebolt Batman or Rocket Blast Batman, Kenner, MOC, ea $20 to.............................$25.00

Batman Returns, figure, Glider Batman or High Wire Batman, Kenner, MOC, ea $10 to...................................$12.00

Batman Returns, figure, Laser Batman or Night Climber Batman, Kenner, MOC, ea $10 to.............................$12.00

Batman Returns, figure, Penguin Commandos or Robin, Kenner, MOC, ea $12 to $16.00

Batman Returns, figure, Polar Blast Batman, Powerwing Batman or Shadow Wing Batman, Kenner, MOC, ea $10 to......$12.00

Batman Returns, figure, 16", Batman, Kenner, MIB, $60 to .. $65.00

Battlestar Galactica, accessory, Colonial Scarab, Mattel, MIB, $65 to...$70.00

Battlestar Galactica, accessory, Colonial Stellar Probe or Colonial Viper, Mattel, MIB, ea $65 to $75.00

Battlestar Galactica, figure, 3¾", Baltar or Boray, series 2, Mattel, MOC, ea $75 to $80.00

Battlestar Galactica, figure, 3¾", Cylon Commander or Lucifer, series 1, MOC, ea $105 to.............................. $115.00

Battlestar Galactica, figure, 3¾", Daggit, Imperious Leader, series 1, Mattel, MOC, ea $28 to...............................$32.00

Battlestar Galactica, figure, 3¾", series 1, Commander Adama or Cylon Centurian, Mattel, MOC, ea $38 to...................$42.00

Battlestar Galactica, figure, 12", Colonial Warrior or Cylon Centurian, Mattel, MIB, ea $80 to $90.00

Beetlejuice, accessory, any, Kenner, 1989-90, MIP, ea from $8 to $18.00

Beetlejuice, figure, Adam Maitland, Kenner, 1989-90, MOC, $8 to..$12.00

Beetlejuice, figure, Exploding Beetlejuice, Kenner, 1989-90, MOC, $4 to..$6.00

Beetlejuice, figure, Harry the Haunted Hunter or Old Buzzard, Kenner, 1989-90, MOC, ea $8 to $10.00

Beetlejuice, figure, Shipwreck Beetlejuice or Shish Kabob Beetlejuice, Kenner, 1989-90, MOC, ea $8 to..........................$10.00

Beetlejuice, figure, Showtime Beetlejuice or Spinhead Beetlejuice, Kenner, 1989-90, MOC, ea $8 to.........................$10.00

Beetlejuice, figure, Street Rat or Teacher Creature, Kenner, 1989-90, MOC, ea $10 to...$12.00

Beetlejuice, figure, Talking Beetlejuice, Kenner, 1989-90, MIP, $35 to...$40.00

Best of the West, accessory, Buckboard w/Horse & Harness, Marx, MIB, $200 to.. $225.00

Best of the West, accessory, Circle X Ranch, Marx, MIB, $275 to $300.00

Best of the West, accessory, Covered Wagon, Marx, MIB, $200 to $225.00

Best of the West, accessory, Fort Apache Playset, Marx, MIB, $350 to $375.00

Best of the West, accessory, Jeep & Horse Trailer, Marx, MIB, $125 to... $150.00

Best of the West, accessory, Travel Case, Marx, unused, M, $50 to...$75.00

Best of the West, figure, Bill Buck, Marx, 1967, EX (w/some or all accessories), $200 to.............................. $250.00

Best of the West, figure, Bill Buck, Marx, 1967, NMIB (w/some or all accessories), $300 to $350.00

Best of the West, figure, Captain Maddox, bl body, Marx, 1967, EX (w/some or all accessories), $50 to............................$75.00

Best of the West, figure, Captain Maddox, bl body, Marx, 1967, NMIB (w/some or all accessories), $100 to $125.00

Best of the West, figure, Chief Cherokee, Marx, 1965, EX (w/some or all accessories), $50 to $75.00

Best of the West, figure, Chief Cherokee, Marx, 1965, NMIB (w/some or all accessories), $150 to $175.00

Best of the West, figure, Daniel Boone, Marx, 1965, EX (w/some or all accessories), $75 to $100.00

Best of the West, figure, Daniel Boone, Marx, 1965, NMIB (w/some or all accessories), $125 to $175.00

Best of the West, figure, Davy Crockett, Marx, 1965, EX (w/some or all accessories), $75 to $100.00

Best of the West, figure, Davy Crockett, Marx, 1965, NMIB (w/some or all accessories), $200 to $225.00

Best of the West, figure, Fighting Eagle, Marx, 1967, EX (w/some or all accessories), $50 to $100.00

Best of the West, figure, Fighting Eagle, Marx, 1967, NMIB (w/some or all accessories), $175 to $200.00

Best of the West, figure, General Custer, Marx, 1967, EX (w/some or all accessories), $50 to............................$75.00

Best of the West, figure, General Custer, Marx, 1967, NMIB (w/some or all accessories), $100 to $150.00

Best of the West, figure, Geronimo, Marx, 1967, EX (w/some or all accessories), $25 to...$75.00

Best of the West, figure, Geronimo w/Pinto, Marx, 1967-70s, mail-in, NMIB (w/some or all accessories), $125 to.... $150.00

Best of the West, figure, Geronimo w/Storm Cloud, Marx, 1967-70s, NMIB (w/some or all accessories), $75 to $100.00

Best of the West, figure, Jamie West, Marx, 1967, EX (w/some or all accessories), $25 to....................................$50.00

Best of the West, figure, Jamie West, Marx, 1967, NMIB (w/some or all accessories), $75 to $100.00

Best of the West, figure, Jane West, Marx, 1966, EX (w/some or all accessories), $35 to....................................$50.00

Best of the West, figure, Jane West, Marx, 1966, NMIB (w/some or all accessories), $75 to $100.00

Best of the West, figure, Jane West w/Flame, Marx, 1966, NMIB (w/some or all accessories), $85 to....................... $125.00

Best of the West, figure, Janice West, Marx, 1967, EX (w/some or all accessories), $20 to....................................$30.00

Best of the West, figure, Janice West, Marx, 1967, NMIB (w/some or all accessories), $75 to $100.00

Best of the West, figure, Jay West, Marx, 1967, EX (w/some or all accessories), from, $20 to....................................$30.00

Best of the West, figure, Jay West, Marx, 1967, NMIB (w/some or all accessories), $75 to $100.00

Best of the West, figure, Jed Gibson, bl body, Marx, 1967, NMIB (w/some or all accessories), $600 to........................... $800.00

Best of the West, figure, Jed Gibson, blk body, Marx, 1967, M (w/some or all accessories), $300 to $400.00

Best of the West, figure, Johnny West, Marx, 1965, EX (w/some or all accessories), $25 to....................................$50.00

Best of the West, figure, Johnny West, Marx, 1965, NMIB (w/some or all accessories), $100 to $125.00

Best of the West, figure, Johnny West w/Comanche, Marx, 1967, MIB (w/some or all accessories), $125 to..................... $150.00

Best of the West, figure, Johnny West w/Thunderbolt, Marx, 1967, NMIB (w/some or all accessories), $100 to $125.00

Best of the West, figure, Josie West, Marx, 1967, EX (w/some or all accessories), $15 to....................................$30.00

Best of the West, figure, Josie West, Marx, 1967, NMIB (w/some or all accessories), $50 to $75.00

Best of the West, figure, Princess Wildflower, Marx, 1974, EX (w/some or all accessories), $30 to $50.00

Best of the West, figure, Sam Cobra, Marx, 1972, EX (w/some or all accessories), $35 to...$50.00

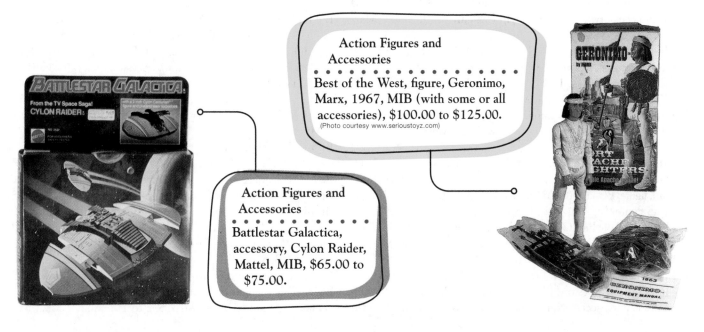

Action Figures and Accessories

Best of the West, figure, Geronimo, Marx, 1967, MIB (with some or all accessories), $100.00 to $125.00.

(Photo courtesy www.serioustoyz.com)

Action Figures and Accessories

Battlestar Galactica, accessory, Cylon Raider, Mattel, MIB, $65.00 to $75.00.

Best of the West, figure, Sam Cobra, Marx, 1972, NMIB (w/some or all accessories), $125 to $150.00

Best of the West, figure, Sam Cobra w/Thunderbolt, Marx, 1975, NMIB (w/some or all accessories), $100 to $150.00

Best of the West, figure, Sheriff Garrett, Marx, 1973, NM (w/some or all accessories), $40 to $60.00

Best of the West, figure, Sheriff Garrett, Marx, 1973, NMIB (w/some or all accessories), $125 to $150.00

Best of the West, figure, Sheriff Garrett w/Horse, Marx, 1973, mail-in figure set, NM (w/mailer), $175 to.................. $200.00

Best of the West, figure, Zeb Zachary, Marx, 1967-69, NM (w/some or all accessories), $125 to $150.00

Best of the West, figure, Zeb Zachary, Marx, 1967-69, NMIB (w/some or all accessories), $200 to $250.00

Best of the West, horse, Comanche, Marx, 1967, NMIB, $65 to $75.00

Best of the West, horse, Flame, Marx, 1966, NM, $35 to..$45.00

Best of the West, horse, Pancho, Marx, 1967, NM, $35 to $45.00

Best of the West, horse, Thunderbolt, blk, Marx, NMIB, rare, $75 to.. $100.00

Big Jim, accessory, Baja Beast, Mattel, MIB, $75 to...........$85.00

Big Jim, accessory, Boat & Buggy Set, Mattel, MIB, $50 to ... $65.00

Big Jim, accessory, Devil River Trip (w/figure & alligator), Mattel, MIB, $45 to $55.00

Big Jim, accessory, Jungle Truck, Mattel, MIB, $45 to.......$55.00

Big Jim, accessory, Motorcross Honda, Mattel, MIB, $45 to $55.00

Big Jim, accessory, Rescue Rig, Mattel, MIB, $75 to....... $100.00

Big Jim, accessory, Safari Hut, Mattel, M, $30 to...............$40.00

Big Jim, accessory, Sky Commander, Mattel, MIB, $65 to..$75.00

Big Jim, accessory, Sport Camper w/Boat, Mattel, MIB, $75 to $100.00

Big Jim, figure, Big Jack, Big Jeff, Big Josh, Dr Alec or Dr Steel, Mattel, MIB, ea $50 to...$60.00

Big Jim, figure, Big Jack (Gold Medal), Mattel, MIB, $70 to $80.00

Big Jim, figure, Big Jim, MIB, $65 to $85.00

Big Jim, figure, Big Jim (Gold Medal), Mattel, MIB, $100 to .$115.00

Big Jim, figure, Big Jim (Gold Medal Olympic Boxing Match), Mattel, MIB, $150 to $175.00

Big Jim's PACK, accessory, Beast, Mattel, MIB, $85 to .. $110.00

Big Jim's PACK, accessory, Blitz Rig, Mattel, MIB, $90 to...$110.00

Big Jim's PACK, accessory, Frogman, Mattel, MIB, $40 to ..$45.00

Big Jim's PACK, accessory, Hard Hat Gunner, Mattel, MIB, $35 to...$45.00

Big Jim's PACK, accessory, Howler, Mattel, MIB, $55 to ..$65.00

Big Jim's PACK, accessory, LazerVette, Mattel, MIP, $80 to .. $90.00

Big Jim's PACK, accessory, Martial Arts, Mattel, MIB, $10 to....$15.00

Big Jim's PACK, accessory, Secret Spy, Mattel, MIB, $55 to.. $65.00

Big Jim's PACK, accessory, Swamp Patrol, Mattel, MIB, $120 to.. $130.00

Big Jim's PACK, accessory, SWAT, Mattel, MIB, $35 to ...$45.00

Big Jim's PACK, figure, Big Jim (Commander), gold pants, Mattel, MIB, $175 to $225.00

Big Jim's PACK, figure, Big Jim (Commander), wht pants, Mattel, MIB, $120 to $130.00

Big Jim's PACK, figure, Big Jim (Double Trouble), Mattel, MIB, $185 to.. $200.00

Big Jim's PACK, figure, Dr Steel, Mattel, MIB, $100 to . $115.00

Big Jim's PACK, figure, Torpedo Fist, Mattel, MIB, $125 to ...$135.00

Big Jim's PACK, figure, Warpath or The Whip, Mattel, MIB, ea $125 to... $135.00

Big Jim's PACK, figure, Zorack the Enemy, Mattel, MIB, $125 to $135.00

Bionic Woman, accessory, Bubblin' Bath 'n Shower, Kenner, MIB, $50 to $75.00

Bionic Woman, accessory, House Playset, Kenner, MIP, $25 to $50.00

Bionic Woman, accessory, Sports Car, Kenner, MIB, $90 to...$110.00

Bionic Woman, figure, Fembot, Kenner, MIB, $200 to .. $225.00

Bionic Woman, figure, Jaime Sommers, Kenner, MIB, $125 to $150.00

Bionic Woman, figure, Jaime Sommers (w/Mission Purse), Kenner, MIB, $160 to... $180.00

Bionic Woman, outfits, any, Kenner, MOC, ea $25 to......$35.00

Black Hole, figure, 3¾", Captain Holland, Dr Alex Durant or Dr Hans Reinhardt, Mego, MIB, $22 to $28.00

Black Hole, figure, 3¾", Harry Booth or Kate McCrae, Mego, MOC, $22 to...$28.00

Black Hole, figure, 3¾", Humanoid, Mego, MOC, $700 to .$750.00

Black Hole, figure, 3¾", Maximillian, Mego, MOC, $70 to.....$80.00

Black Hole, figure, 3¾", Old BOB, Mego, MOC, $175 to ..$200.00

Black Hole, figure, 3¾", Pizer, Mego, MOC, $45 to...........$55.00

Black Hole, figure, 3¾", Sentry Robot, Mego, MOC, $70 to...$80.00

Black Hole, figure, 3¾", STAR, Mego, MOC, $325 to... $350.00

Black Hole, figure, 3¾", VINcent, Mego, MOC, $65 to....$75.00

Black Hole, figure, 12", Captain Holland or Dr Alex Durant, Mego, MIB, ea $70 to...$80.00

Black Hole, figure, 12", Dr Hans Reinhardt, Mego, MIB, $70 to... $80.00

Black Hole, figure, 12", Harry Booth, Mego, MIB, $85 to .$95.00

Black Hole, figure, 12", Kate McCrae, Mego, MIB, $90 to ..$100.00

Blackstar, accessory, Battle Wagon, Galoob, MIB, $70 to .$80.00

Blackstar, accessory, Ice Castle, Galoob, MIB, $125 to... $150.00

Blackstar, accessory, Triton, Galoob, MIB, $100 to $125.00

Blackstar, accessory, Warlock, Galoob, MIB, $125 to..... $150.00

Blackstar, figure, Blackstar, Galoob, MIB, $20 to...............$30.00

Blackstar, figure, Blackstar (w/Laser Light), Galoob, 1983, MOC, $40 to..$45.00

Blackstar, figure, Devil Knight (w/Laser Light), Galoob, 1983, MOC, $45 to..$55.00

Blackstar, figure, Gargo, Galoob, 1983, MOC, $30 to $35.00

Blackstar, figure, Gargo (w/Laser Light), Galoob, 1983, MOC, $40 to..$45.00

Blackstar, figure, Kadray, Galoob, 1983, MOC, $35 to......$40.00

Blackstar, figure, Kadray (w/Laser Light), Galoob, 1983, MOC, $35 to..$40.00

Blackstar, figure, Klone (w/Laser Light), Galoob, 1983, MOC, $45 to..$50.00

Blackstar, figure, Lava Loc (w/Laser Light), Galoob, 1983, $40 to..$45.00

Blackstar, figure, Mara, Galoob, 1983, MOC, $55 to.........$60.00

Blackstar, figure, Meuton, Galoob, 1983, MOC, $35 to $40.00

Blackstar, figure, Neptul (w/Laser Light), Galoob, 1983, MOC, $50 to..$55.00

Blackstar, figure, Overlord, Galoob, 1984, MOC, $20 to ..$25.00

Blackstar, figure, Overlord (w/Laser Light), Galoob, 1984, MOC, $40 to..$45.00

Blackstar, figure, Palace Guard, Galoob, 1984, MOC, $25 to ..$30.00

Blackstar, figure, Palace Guard (w/Laser Light), Galoob, 1984, MOC, $35 to...$40.00

Blackstar, figure, Tongo, Galoob, 1983, MOC, $35 to.......$40.00

Blackstar, figure, Tongo (w/Laser Light), Galoob, 1983, MOC, $35 to..$40.00

Blackstar, figure, Vizar (w/Laser Light), Galoob, 1983, MOC, $35 to..$40.00

Blackstar, figure, White Knight (w/Laser Light), Galoob, 1983, MOC, $40 to...$45.00

Bonanza, accessory, wagon (4-in-1), American Character, M, $45 to..$50.00

Bonanza, accessory, wagon (4-in-1), American Character, MIB, $75 to... $100.00

Bonanza, figure, Ben, Little Joe, Hoss or Outlaw, American Character, M, ea $50 to...$60.00

Bonanza, figure, Ben, Hoss or Outlaw, American Character, MIB, ea $150 to... $175.00

Bonanza, figure w/horse, any, American Character, M, ea $75 to... $85.00

Bonanza, figure w/horse, any, American Character, MIB, ea $175 to... $225.00

Bonanza, horse, any, American Character, M, ea $25 to...$30.00

Bonanza, horse, any, American Character, MIB, ea $65 to....$75.00

Buck Rogers, accessory, Draconian Marauder, Mego, MIB $75 to... $85.00

Buck Rogers, accessory, Land Rover, Mego, NMIB, $40 to...$45.00

Buck Rogers, accessory, Laserscope Fighter, Mego, MIB, $40 to... $45.00

Buck Rogers, accessory, Star Fighter, Mego, MIB, $65 to ..$75.00

Buck Rogers, accessory, Star Fighter Command Center, Mego, MIB, $75 to... $100.00

Buck Rogers, accessory, Star Seeker, Mego, MIP, $65 to....$75.00

Buck Rogers, figure, 3¾", Adrella, Mego, MOC, $15 to....$18.00

Buck Rogers, figure, 3¾", Buck Rogers, Mego, MOC, $60 to ..$65.00

Buck Rogers, figure, 3¾", Dr Huer, Draco or Killer Kane, Mego, MOC, ea $18 to $22.00

Buck Rogers, figure, 3¾", Draconian Guard, Mego, MOC, $18 to...$22.00

Buck Rogers, figure, 3¾", Tiger Man or Wilma Deering, Mego, MOC, $24 to $28.00

Buck Rogers, figure, 3¾", Twiki, Mego, MOC, $35 to $40.00

Buck Rogers, figure, 12", any accept Tiger Man, Mego, MIB, ea $65 to..$75.00

Buck Rogers, figure, 12", Tiger Man, Mego, MIB, $125 to ...$130.00

Bug's Life, figure, any character, Mattel, 1998, MOC, ea $4 to $6.00

Captain Action, accessory, Action Cave, Ideal, MIB, $600 to..$675.00

Captain Action, accessory, Anti-Gravitational Power Pack, Ideal, MIB, $225 to $250.00

Captain Action, accessory, Directional Communicator, Ideal, MIB, $275 to $325.00

Captain Action, accessory, Headquarters, Ideal, MIB, $450 to $550.00

Captain Action, accessory, Inter-Galactic Jet Mortar, Ideal, MIB, $275 to $325.00

Captain Action, accessory, Parachute Pack, Ideal, MIB, $200 to $230.00

Captain Action, accessory, Silver Streak Amphibian Car, Ideal, MIB, $1,000 to $1,200.00

Captain Action, accessory, Silver Streak Garage, Ideal, MIB, $1,800 to.................................... $2,000.00

Captain Action, accessory, Survival Kit, Ideal, MIB, $250 to..$275.00

Captain Action, accessory, Weapons Arsenal, Ideal, MIB, $200 to... $225.00

Captain Action, figure, Action Boy, Ideal, 1967, MIB, $875 to $900.00

Captain Action, figure, Action Boy, Ideal, 1968, MIB, $1,000 to $1,100.00

Captain Action, figure, Action Boy (space suit), Ideal, MIB, $900 to.................................... $1,000.00

Captain Action, figure, Aquaman, Ideal, NM to M, $150 to .$200.00

Captain Action, figure, Captain Action, Ideal, MIB (Lone Ranger box), $525 to..................................... $550.00

Captain Action, figure, Captain Action, Ideal, MIB (parachute offer), $675 to $700.00

Captain Action, figure, Captain Action, Ideal, MIB (photo box), $875 to.................................... $900.00

Captain Action, figure, Captain Action, Ideal, NM (from box w/ parachute offer), $250 to................................. $275.00

Captain Action, figure, Captain Action, Ideal, NM (from Lone Ranger box), $200 to................................... $225.00

Captain Action, figure, Captain Action, Ideal, NM (from photo box), $275 to $300.00

Captain Action, figure, Dr Evil, Ideal, MIB (photo box), $450 to $475.00

Captain Action, figure, Dr Evil, Ideal, NM (from photo box), $250 to $265.00

Captain Action, outfit, Aqualad, Ideal, MIB, $800 to.... $900.00

Captain Action, outfit, Aqualad, Ideal, NM, $275 to $300.00

Captain Action, outfit, Aquaman (no ring), Ideal, EX, $100 to $150.00

Captain Action, outfit, Aquaman (no ring), Ideal, MIB, $600 to $625.00

Captain Action, outfit, Aquaman (w/ring), Ideal, MIB, $900 to $950.00

Captain Action, outfit, Aquaman (w/ring), Ideal, NM to M, $200 to $225.00

Captain Action, outfit, Batman (no ring), Ideal, MIB, $700 to $725.00

Captain Action, outfit, Batman (no ring), Ideal, NM to M, $175 to $225.00

Captain Action, outfit, Batman (w/ring), Ideal, MIB, $1,000 to $1,200.00

Captain Action, outfit, Buck Rogers (w/ring), Ideal, MIB, $2,000 to $2,500.00

Captain Action, outfit, Buck Rogers (w/ring), Ideal, NM to M, $425 to $500.00

Captain Action, outfit, Captain America (no ring), Ideal, MIB, $825 to $875.00

Captain Action, outfit, Captain America (w/ring), Ideal, MIB, $950 to $1,100.00

Captain Action, outfit, Flash Gordon (no ring), Ideal, MIB, $750 to $775.00

Captain Action, outfit, Flash Gordon (no ring), Ideal, NM to M, $175 to $225.00

Captain Action, outfit, Flash Gordon (w/ring), Ideal, 1967, MIB, $750 to $775.00

Captain Action, outfit, Flash Gordon (w/ring), Ideal, 1967, NM to M, $200 to... $250.00

Captain Action, outfit, Green Hornet (w/ring), Ideal, MIB, $6,500 to...$7,000.00

Captain Action, outfit, Green Hornet (w/ring), Ideal, NM to M, $2,000 to...$2,500.00

Captain Action, outfit, Lone Ranger (no ring), Ideal, MIB, $650 to $675.00

Captain Action, outfit, Lone Ranger (no ring), Ideal, NM to M, $175 to $225.00

Captain Action, outfit, Lone Ranger (w/ring), Ideal, MIB, $900 to $950.00

Captain Action, outfit, Phantom (no ring), Ideal, MIB, $725 to $750.00

Captain Action, outfit, Phantom (no ring), Ideal, NM, $175 to $200.00

Captain Action, outfit, Phantom (w/ring), Ideal, MIB, $850 to $875.00

Captain Action, outfit, Robin, Ideal, MIB, $1,000 to..$1,250.00

Captain Action, outfit, Robin, Ideal, NM to M, $300 to. $350.00

Captain Action, outfit, Sgt Fury, Ideal, MIB, $725 to $775.00
Captain Action, outfit, Sgt Fury, Ideal, NM, $175 to $200.00
Captain Action, outfit, Spider-Man, Ideal, MIB, $7,000 to ..$7,500.00
Captain Action, outfit, Spider-Man, Ideal, NM, $550 to . $650.00
Captain Action, outfit, Steve Canyon (no ring), Ideal, MIB,
 $600 to... $650.00
Captain Action, outfit, Steve Canyon (no ring), Ideal, NM to
 M, $200 to.. $250.00
Captain Action, outfit, Steve Canyon (w/ring), Ideal, MIB, $775
 to... $800.00
Captain Action, outfit, Steve Canyon (w/ring), Ideal, NM to M,
 $175 to.. $225.00
Captain Action, outfit, Superboy, Ideal, MIB, $900 to . $1,000.00
Captain Action, outfit, Superboy, Ideal, NM to M, $300 to ...$350.00
Captain Action, outfit, Superman (w/accessories & Krypto the
 dog), Ideal, NM, $200 to... $250.00
Captain Action, outfit, Superman (w/Krypto the dog), Ideal,
 MIB, $650 to $750.00
Captain Action, outfit, Tonto (w/ring), Ideal, MIB, $900 to . $1,000.00
Captain America, see Captain Action and Marvel Super Heroes
Charlie's Angels (Movie), figure, any, Jakks Pacific, MIB, ea $20
 to...$25.00
Charlie's Angels (TV Series), accessory, Adventure Van, Hasbro,
 MIB, $70 to..$80.00
Charlie's Angels (TV Series), figure, any, Hasbro, MOC, ea $75
 to...$85.00
Charlie's Angels (TV Series), figure gift set, Kelly, Kris &
 Sabrina, MIP, $175 to... $200.00
CHiPs, accessory, motorcycle & ramp for 3¾" figures, Mego, MIP,
 $45 to...$55.00
CHiPs, accessory, motorcycle for 3¾" figures, Mego, MIP, $25
 to... $35.00
CHiPs, accessory, motorcycle for 8" figures, Mego, MIP, $75
 to $80.00
CHiPs, figure, 3¾", Jimmy Squeaks or Wheels Willie, Mego,
 MOC, ea $14 to...$16.00
CHiPs, figure, 3¾", Jon or Ponch, Mego, MOC, ea $18 to.$22.00
CHiPs, figure, 3¾", Sarge, Mego, MOC, $28 to.................$30.00
CHiPs, figure, 8", Jon or Ponch, Mego, MOC, ea $35 to...$40.00
CHiPs, figure, 8", Sarge, Mego, MOC, $45 to....................$50.00
Clash of the Titans, figure, Kraken, Mattel, rare, MOC, $300
 to...$325.00
Clash of the Titans, figure, Thallo, Mattel, MOC, $35 to .$40.00
Clash of the Titans, horse, Pegasus, Mattel, MOC, $65 to .$70.00
Clash of the Titans, horse & figure set, Pegasus & Perseus, Mat-
 tel, MIB, $100 to.. $125.00
Comic Action Heroes, accessory, Batcopter, w/Batman figure,
 Mego, MIP, $100 to.. $125.00
Comic Action Heroes, accessory, Batmobile, w/Batman figure,
 Mego, MIP, $145 to.. $155.00
Comic Action Heroes, accessory, Collapsing Tower w/Wonder
 Woman figure & Invisible Plane, Mego, MIP, $200 to . $225.00
Comic Action Heroes, accessory, Exploding Bridge w/Batmobile,
 Mego, MIP, $175 to.. $200.00
Comic Action Heroes, accessory, Fortress of Solitude w/Super-
 man figure, Mego, MIP, $175 to $200.00
Comic Action Heroes, accessory, Spider-Car w/Spider-Man &
 Green Goblin figures, Mego, MIP, $250 to.................. $275.00

Comic Action Heroes, accessory, The Mangler, Mego, MIP, $250
 to $275.00
Comic Action Heroes, figure, Aquaman, Batman, Captain
 America or Joker, Mego, MOC, ea $70 to.....................$75.00
Comic Action Heroes, figure, Aquaman, Batman, Captain
 America or Joker, Mego, NM to M, ea $25 to................$30.00
Comic Action Heroes, figure, Green Goblin, Mego, MOC, $120
 to $130.00
Comic Action Heroes, figure, Green Goblin, Mego, NM to M,
 $25 to...$30.00
Comic Action Heroes, figure, Hulk, Mego, MOC, $50 to.$55.00
Comic Action Heroes, figure, Hulk, Mego, NM to M, $18 to..$22.00
Comic Action Heroes, figure, Penguin, Shazam or Spider-Man,
 Mego, MOC, ea $70 to...$80.00
Comic Action Heroes, figure, Penguin, Shazam or Spider-Man,
 Mego, NM to M, ea $20 to.......................................$25.00
Comic Action Heroes, figure, Robin, Superman or Wonder
 Woman, Mego, MOC, ea $60 to $65.00
Comic Action Heroes, figure, Robin, Superman or Wonder
 Woman, Mego, NM to M, ea $60 to.............................$70.00
Commando (Schwarzenegger), figure, 3¾", any except Matric,
 Diamond Toymakers, MOC, ea $24 to..........................$28.00
Commando (Schwarzenegger), figure, 3¾", any except Matrix,
 Diamond Toymakers, NM to M, ea $8 to......................$12.00
Commando (Schwarzenegger), figure, 3¾", Matrix, Diamond
 Toymakers, MOC, $120 to.. $128.00
Commando (Schwarzenegger), figure, 3¾", Matrix, Diamond
 Toymakers, NM to M, $35 to.......................................$45.00
Commando (Schwarzenegger), figure, 6", any except Matrix,
 Diamond Toymakers, M, ea $24 to $28.00
Commando (Schwarzenegger), figure, 6", any except Matrix,
 NM to M, $28 to...$32.00
Commando (Schwarzenegger), figure, 6", Matrix, Diamond Toy-
 makers, MIP, $65 to...$70.00
Commando (Schwarzenegger), figure, 6", Matrix, Diamond Toy-
 makers, NM to M, $24 to..$28.00
Commando (Schwarzenegger), figure, 18", Matrix, Diamond
 Toumakers, MIB (red box), $265 to........................... $280.00

Commando (Schwarzenegger), figure, 18", Matrix, Diamond Toymakers, MIB (blk box), $165 to $180.00

Commando (Schwarzenegger), figure, 18", Matrix, Diamond Toymakers, NM to M, $65 to $75.00

DC Comics Super Heroes, see also Super Heroes

DC Comics Super Heroes, figure, Aquaman, Batman or Bob the Goon, Toy Biz, MOC, ea $10 to $12.00

DC Comics Super Heroes, figure, Flash, Flash II, Joker or Mr Freeze, Toy Biz, MOC, ea $10 to $12.00

DC Comics Super Heroes, figure, Green Lantern, Hawkman or Two Face, Toy Biz, MOC, ea $18 to $22.00

DC Comics Super Heroes, figure, Riddler, Toy Biz, MOC, $8 to $12.00

DC Comics Super Heroes, figure, Penguin, missile firing (long), Toy Biz, MOC, $15 to $18.00

DC Comics Super Heroes, figure, Penguin, missile firing (short), Toy Biz, MOC, $24 to $28.00

DC Comics Super Heroes, figure, Penguin, umbrella-firing, Toy Biz, MOC, $8 to $10.00

DC Comics Super Heroes, figure, Superman, Toy Biz, MOC, $24 to $28.00

DC Comics Super Heroes, figure, Wonder Woman, Toy Biz, MOC, $15 to $18.00

Defenders of the Earth, figures, Flash Gordon, Garaz, Lothar, Mandrake, Ming or Phantom, Galoob, 1985, MIP, ea $20 to $25.00

Defenders of the Earth, vehicles, Claw Copter, Flash Swordship, Garax Swordship, Galoob, 1985, ea $20 to $30.00

Dick Tracy (TV Cartoon Series), figure, The Blank, Playmates, 1990, M, $35 to $45.00

Dick Tracy (TV Cartoon Series), figure, The Blank, Playmates, 1990, MOC, $65 to $75.00

Dick Tracy (TV Cartoon Series), figures, any except The Blank, Playmates, 1990, M, ea $3 to $5.00

Dick Tracy (TV Cartoon Series), figures, any except The Blank, Playmates, 1990, MOC, ea $6 to $8.00

Dukes of Hazzard, accessory, 3¾", Cadillac w/Boss Hogg or Police Car w/Sheriff Roscoe, Mego, M, ea $30 to $40.00

Dukes of Hazzard, accessory, 3¾", Cadillac w/Boss Hogg or Police Car w/Sheriff Roscoe figure, MIP, ea $65 to $75.00

Dukes of Hazzard, accessory, 3¾", Daisy's Jeep or General Lee w/ Bo & Luke figures, Mego, M, ea $20 to $25.00

Dukes of Hazzard, accessory, 3¾", Daisy's Jeep w/figure or General Lee w/Bo & Luke figures, Mego, MIP, ea $45 to............. $50.00

Dukes of Hazzard, figure, 3¾", Bo or Luke Duke, Mego, MOC, ea $15 to...$18.00

Dukes of Hazzard, figure, 3¾", Boss Hogg or Daisy, Mego, MOC, ea $20 to...$25.00

Dukes of Hazzard, figure, 3¾", Cletus, Cooter, Coy, Rosco, Jesse or Vance, Mego, MOC, ea $25 to...................................$30.00

Dukes of Hazzard, figure, 8", Bo or Luke, Mego, MOC, $25 to..$28.00

Dukes of Hazzard, figure, 8", Boss Hogg, Mego, MOC, $30 to.$35.00

Dukes of Hazzard, figure, 8", Coy (Bo) or Vance (Luke), Mego, MOC, ea $45 to $48.00

Dukes of Hazzard, figure, 8", Daisy, Mego, MOC, $45 to...$48.00

Emergency, accessory, Fire House, LJN, MIP, $200 to $225.00

Emergency, accessory, Rescue Truck, LJN, MIP, $250 to.. $275.00

Emergency, figure, John or Roy, LJN, MOC, ea $75 to......$85.00

Fantastic Four, see also Marvel Super Heroes and Super Heroes (8" Mego)

Fantastic Four, accessory, Fantasticar, Toy Biz, 1995, MIB, $30 to...$35.00

Fantastic Four, accessory, Mr Fantastic Sky Shuttle, Toy Biz, 1995, MIB, $18 to $22.00

Fantastic Four, accessory, The Thing's Sky Cycle, Toy Biz, 1995, MIP, $18 to $22.00

Fantastic Four, figure, 5", any character, Toy Biz, 1995, MIB, ea $8 to...$10.00

Fantastic Four, figure, 10", any character, Toy Biz, 1995, MIB, MIB, $8 to..$10.00

Fantastic Four, figure, 14", electronic, Galactus, Toy Biz, 1995, MIP, $35 to $45.00

Fantastic Four, figure, 14", electronic, Talking Thing, Toy Biz, 1995, MIP, $18 to $22.00

Flash Gordon, figure, Dale Arden, Mego, MOC, $80 to ...$90.00

Flash Gordon, figure, Dr Zarkov, Mego, MOC, $100 to . $115.00

Flash Gordon, figure, Flash Gordon, Mego, MOC, $100 to.. $115.00

Flash Gordon, figure, Ming the Merciless, Mego, MOC, $80 to $90.00

Ghostbusters, accessory, Firehouse Headquarters, Kenner, 1986, MIP, $75 to $100.00

Ghostbusters, figure, Ecto-Glow characters, Kenner, 1991, MIP, ea $20 to $25.00

Happy Days, accessory, Fonz's Garage, Mego, MIB, $150 to ...$175.00

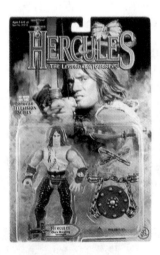

Happy Days, accessory, Fonz's Jalopy or Motorcycle, Mego, MIB, ea $70 to $80.00

Happy Days, figure, any, Mego, MOC, ea $65 to $75.00

Happy Days, figure, Fonzie, Mego, MIB, $75 to $85.00

Hercules (The Legend Continues), accessory, Hercules Tower of Power, Toy Biz, 1995-97, MIP, $8 to $10.00

Hercules (The Legend Continues), Monsters, any, Toy Biz, 1995-97, MOC, ea $8 to $10.00

Hercules (The Legendary Journeys), figure, 10", any character, Toy Biz, 1995-97, MOC, $18 to.....................................$20.00

Hercules (The Legendary Journeys), figure set, 5", Xena & Gabrielle, Toy Biz, 1997, MOC, $30 to $35.00

Hook, accessory, Lost Boy Attack Raft, Mattel, MIP, $18 to . $22.00

Hook, accessory, Lost Boy Strike Tank, Mattel, MIP, $18 to ...$22.00

Hook, figure, Captain Hook (Multi-blade), Mattel, MOC, $8 to $12.00

Hook, figure, Captain Hook (Skull Armor) Deluxe, Mattel, MOC, $24 to..$28.00

Hook, figure, Captain Hook (Swiss Army), Mattel, MOC, $16 to $20.00

Hook, figure, Captain Hook (Tall Terror), Mattel, MOC, $8 to .. $12.00

Hook, figure, Lost Boy Ace, Mattel, MOC, $8 to..............$12.00

Hook, figure, Lost Boy Attack Croc, Deluxe, Mattel, MOC, $16 to...$20.00

Hook, figure, Lost Boy Ruffio, Mattel, MOC, $8 to.........$12.00

Hook, figure, Lost Boy Thud Butt, Mattel, MOC, $16 to..$20.00

Hook, figure, Peter Pan (Air Attack), Mattel, MOC, $8 to.....$12.00

Hook, figure, Peter Pan (Battle Swing), Mattel, MOC, $12 to ..$16.00

Hook, figure, Peter Pan (Food Fighting), Mattel, MOC, $12 to $16.00

Hook, figure, Peter Pan (Learn to Fly), Deluxe, Mattel, MOC, $24 to..$28.00

Hook, figure, Pirate Bill Jukes, Mattel, MOC, $8 to..........$12.00

Hook, figure, Pirate Smee, Mattel, MOC, $10 to $14.00

Incredible Hulk, figure, 6", any character, Toy Biz, 1996-97, MOC, $8 to...$10.00

Incredible Hulk (Outcasts), figure, 5", any character, Marvel/Toy Biz, 1997, MOC, ea $6 to.......................................$8.00

Incredible Hulk (Smash & Crash), figure, 5", any character, Marvel/Toy Biz, 1996-97, MOC, ea $8 to $10.00

Incredible Hulk (Transformations), figure, 6", any character, MOC, ea $8 to..$10.00

Indiana Jones & the Temple of Doom, figure, Giant Thuggee, LJN, MOC, $125 to $150.00

Indiana Jones & the Temple of Doom, figure, Indiana, LJN, MOC, $250 to $275.00

Indiana Jones & the Temple of Doom, figure, Mola Ram, Kenner, MOC, $175 to.. $200.00

Indiana Jones in Raiders of the Lost Ark, accessory, Arabian Horse, Kenner, MIB, $125 to.. $150.00

Indiana Jones in Raiders of the Lost Ark, accessory, Convoy Truck, Kenner, MIB, $100 to... $125.00

Indiana Jones in Raiders of the Lost Ark, accessory, Map Room, Kenner, MIB, $100 to $125.00

Indiana Jones in Raiders of the Lost Ark, accessory, Streets of Cairo, Kenner, MIB, $75 to $100.00

Indiana Jones in Raiders of the Lost Ark, accessory, Well of the Souls Action Playset, MIB (sealed), $125 to.............. $150.00

Action Figures and Accessories
• • • • • • • • • • • • • •
Hook, figure, Peter Pan (Swashbuckling), Mattel, MOC, $8.00 to $12.00. (Photo courtesy www.gasolinealleyantiques.com)

Action Figures and Accessories
• • • • • • • • • • • • • •
Indiana Jones in Raiders of the Lost Ark, figure, 3¾", Indiana Jones, with whip, Kenner, 1982, MOC, $200.00 to $225.00.

Indiana Jones in Raiders of the Lost Ark, figure, Belloq, Kenner, MOC, $55 to $60.00

Indiana Jones in Raiders of the Lost Ark, figure, Belloq (Ceremonial Robe), M (mailing bag), $25 to.............................$30.00

Indiana Jones in Raiders of the Lost Ark, figure, Belloq (Ceremonial Robe), MOC, $725 to... $750.00

Indiana Jones in Raiders of the Lost Ark, figure, Cairo Swordsman, Kenner, MOC, $30 to $35.00

Indiana Jones in Raiders of the Lost Ark, figure, German Mechanic, Kenner, MOC, $55 to $60.00

Indiana Jones in Raiders of the Lost Ark, figure, Indiana, 12", Kenner, MIB, $200 to $225.00

Indiana Jones in Raiders of the Lost Ark, figure, Indiana (German Uniform), Kenner, MOC, $70 to..............................$75.00

Indiana Jones in Raiders of the Lost Ark, figure, Marion Ravenwood, Kenner, MOC, $200 to $225.00

Indiana Jones in Raiders of the Lost Ark, figure, Sallah, Kenner, MOC, $70 to $75.00

Indiana Jones in Raiders of the Lost Ark, figure, Toht, Kenner, MOC, $25 to $30.00

Inspector Gadget, accessory, Gadgetmobile, Tiger Toys, 1992, MIP, $60 to...$65.00

Inspector Gadget, figure, any Inspector, Tiger Toys, 1992, MOC, ea $12 to...$18.00

Inspector Gadget, figure, Dr Claw, Tiger Toys, 1992, MOC, $24 to...$26.00

Inspector Gadget, figure, MAD agent w/Bazooka, Penny & Brian, Tiger Toys, 1992, MOC, ea $18 to.......................$22.00

Inspector Gadget, figure, 11", complete, Galoob, 1983, MIB, $75 to.. $100.00

James Bond, figure, Bond (Pierce Brosnan), 12", Medicom, MIB, $75 to..$85.00

James Bond (Moonraker), figure, Bond, 12", Mego, MIB, $140 to.. $160.00

James Bond (Moonraker), figure, Bond, 12", w/suit & accessories, Mego, MIB, $450 to $475.00

James Bond (Moonraker), figure, Drax or Holly, 12", Mego, MIB, $150 to.. $175.00

James Bond (Moonraker), figure, Jaws, 12", Mego, MIB, $450 to..$475.00

James Bond (Secret Agent 007), accessory, Aston Martin car, w/ ejecting passenger, b/o, bump-&-go action, 12" L, NM, $225 to... $300.00

James Bond (Secret Agent 007), accessory, Dr No's Dragon Tank & Largo's Hydrofoil Yacht, Gilbert, 1965, MOC, $25 to.......$30.00

James Bond (Secret Agent 007), figure, 4", 'M,' Moneypenny or Odd Job, Gilbert, 1965, MIP, $18 to..............................$22.00

James Bond (Secret Agent 007), figure, 4", Domino, Dr Noor Largo, Gilbert, 1965, MIP, $18 to $22.00

James Bond (Secret Agent 007), figure, 4", Goldfinger, Gilbert, 1965, MIP, $24 to $28.00

James Bond (Secret Agent 007), figure, 12", Odd Job, wht judo outfit, Gilbert, 1965, MIB, $300 to............................. $350.00

James Bond (Spy Who Loved Me), figure, Bond (Roger Moore) in ski gear, 12", Hasbro, 1999, MIB $55.00

James Bond (Thunderball), accessory, Disguise Kit #16255, Gilbert, MIB, $325 to... $350.00

Johnny Apollo (Astronaut), figure, Jane Apollo, Marx, MIB, $100 to.. $125.00

Johnny Apollo (Astronaut), figure, Johnny Apollo, Marx, MIB, $150 to.. $175.00

Johnny Apollo (Astronaut), figure, Kennedy Space Center Astronaut, Marx, MIB, $130 to $150.00

Jurassic Park, dinosaur, any, Kenner, 1993, MOC, ea $6 to...$12.00

Jurassic Park, figure, any character, Kenner, 1993, MOC, ea $6 to.. $12.00

Knight Rider, accessory, Knight 2000 Voice Car w/Michael figure, Kenner, MIB, $45 to $50.00

Knight Rider, figure, Michael Knight, Kenner, MOC, $18 to..$20.00

Legend of the Lone Ranger, accessory, Western Town, Gabriel, MIB, $75 to $100.00

Legend of the Lone Ranger, figure, Buffalo Bill Cody, Gabriel, MOC, $24 to...$28.00

Legend of the Lone Ranger, figure, Butch Cavendish, Gabriel, MOC, $24 to...$28.00

Legend of the Lone Ranger, figure, Lone Ranger, Gabriel, MOC, $24 to...$28.00

Legend of the Lone Ranger, figure, Tonto, Gabriel, MOC, $14 to.. $18.00

Legend of the Lone Ranger, figure w/horse, any set, Gabriel, MOC, ea $45 to...$55.00

Legend of the Lone Ranger, horse, Scout, Gabriel, MOC, $18 to.. $22.00

Legend of the Lone Ranger, horse, Silver, Gabriel, MOC, $28 to.. $32.00

Legend of the Lone Ranger, horse, Smoke, Gabriel, MOC, $24 to.. $26.00

Lone Ranger, see also Captain Action

Lone Ranger Rides Again, accessory, Blizzard Adventure, Gabriel, MIB, $25 to...$30.00

Lone Ranger Rides Again, accessory, Carson City Bank Robbery, Gabriel, MIB, $45 to...$50.00

Lone Ranger Rides Again, accessory, Hidden Rattler Adventure, Gabriel, MIB, $25 to...$30.00

Lone Ranger Rides Again, accessory, Landslide Adventure, Gabriel, MIB, $25 to...$30.00

Lone Ranger Rides Again, accessory, Mysterious Prospector, Gabriel, MIB, $70 to...$75.00

Action Figures and Accessories

Lone Ranger Rides Again, accessories, Tribal Tepee and Prairie Wagon, Gabriel, MIB, each $25.00 to $30.00.

Action Figures and Accessories

James Bond (Secret Agent 007), figure, 12", Bond in white shirt and swim trunks, snorkling, Gilbert, 1965, MIB, $325.00 to $350.00.
(Photo courtesy Morphy Auctions on LiveAuctioneers.com)

Lone Ranger Rides Again, accessory, Red River Flood Waters, MIB, $25 to $30.00

Lord of the Rings, creature, Charger of the Ringwraith, Knickerbocker, 1979, MIP, $155 to $165.00

Lord of the Rings, creature, Frodo's Horse, Knickerbocker, 1979, MIP, $155 to $165.00

Lord of the Rings, creature, Ringwraith, Knickerbocker, 1979, MIP, $275 to $300.00

Lord of the Rings, figure, any, Knickerbocker, 1979, MIP, $100 to.. $115.00

Lord of the Rings, figure, any, Toy Vault, 1998-99, MOC, ea $12 to...$18.00

Love Boat, figure, any 4" character, Mego, 1982, MOC, ea $18 to $22.00

Mad Monster Series, accessory, Mad Monster Castle, Mego, 1974, MIB, $550 to $600.00

Mad Monster Series, figure, 8", Dreadful Dracula, Mego, 1974, MIB, $150 to $175.00

Mad Monster Series, figure, 8", Frankenstein, Mego, 1974, MIB, $125 to $150.00

Mad Monster Series, figure, 8", Horrible Mummy, Mego, 1974, MIB, $125 to $150.00

Mad Monster Series, figure, 8", Human Wolfman, Mego, 1974, MIB, $125 to $150.00

Major Matt Mason, accessory, Astro Trac, Mattel, MIB, $100 to.. $125.00

Major Matt Mason, accessory, Fireball Space Cannon, Mattel, MIB, $275 to $300.00

Major Matt Mason, accessory, Gamma Ray Guard, Mattel, MIB, $$75 to... $100.00

Major Matt Mason, accessory, Moon Suit Pak, Mattel, MIB, $75 to $100.00

Major Matt Mason, accessory, Rocket Launch, Mattel, MIB, $70 to...$80.00

Major Matt Mason, accessory, Satellite Locker, Mattel, MIB, $65 to...$75.00

Major Matt Mason, accessory, Space Crawler Action Set (w/figure), Mattel, MIB, $100 to.. $125.00

Major Matt Mason, accessory, Space Probe, Mattel, MIB, $$70 to..$80.00

Major Matt Mason, accessory, Space Station, Mattel, MIB, $300 to $325.00

Major Matt Mason, accessory, Uni-Tred & Space Bubble, Mattel, MIB, $125 to $150.00

Major Matt Mason, figure, Callisto, Mattel, M, $90 to... $100.00

Major Matt Mason, figure, Callisto, Mattel, MOC, $225 to . $250.00

Major Matt Mason, figure, Captain Lazer, Mattel, M, $130 to....$140.00

Major Matt Mason, figure, Captain Lazer, Mattel, MOC, $275 to.. $325.00

Major Matt Mason, figure, Doug Davis (w/helmet), Mattel, M, $115 to.. $125.00

Major Matt Mason, figure, Doug Davis (w/helmet), Mattel, MOC, $275 to... $300.00

Major Matt Mason, figure, Jeff Long, Mattel, M, $170 to ...$180.00

Major Matt Mason, figure, Jeff Long (w/helmet), Mattel, MOC, $500 to... $550.00

Major Matt Mason, figure, Major Matt Mason, Mattel, M, $75 to...$85.00

Major Matt Mason, figure, Major Matt Mason, Mattel, MOC, $175 to $200.00

Major Matt Mason, figure, Scorpio, Mattel, M, $350 to. $375.00

Major Matt Mason, figure, Scorpio, Mattel, MOC, $800 to . $850.00

Major Matt Mason, figure, Sgt Storm, Mattel, MOC, $375 to..$400.00

Man From UNCLE, accessory, Arsenal Set #1 or #2, Gilbert, MIP, $35 to...$45.00

Man From UNCLE, accessory, Jumpsuit Set, Gilbert, MIP, $40 to...$50.00

Man From UNCLE, accessory, Scuba Set, Gilbert, MIP, $50 to $75.00

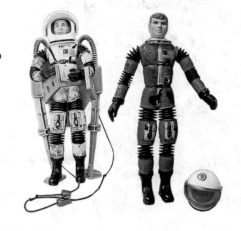

Man From UNCLE, figure, Illya Kuryakin or Napoleon Solo, Gilbert, M, ea $175 to..$200.00

Man From UNCLE, figure, Illya Kuryakin or Napoleon Solo, Gilbert, MIB, ea $325 to.. $375.00

Marvel Comics Super Heroes, see also Incredible Hulk

Marvel Super Heroes, accessory, Training Center, Toy Biz, MIB, $25 to..$35.00

Marvel Super Heroes, figure, Annihilus, Deathlok, Hulk, Human Torch, Mr Fantastic or Thing, Toy Biz, MOC, ea $15 to.... $18.00

Marvel Super Heroes, figure, Daredevil, Toy Biz, MOC, $34 to $38.00

Marvel Super Heroes, figure, Dr Doom or Dr Octopus, Toy Biz, MOC, ea $24 to $28.00

Marvel Super Heroes, figure, Green Goblin (back lever) or Thor (back lever), Toy Biz, MOC, ea $25 to.....................$28.00

Marvel Super Heroes, figure, Green Goblin (no lever) or Thor (no lever), Toy Biz, MOC, ea $24 to $28.00

Marvel Super Heroes, figure, Human Torch (fireball flinging action), Toy Biz, MOC, $15 to $18.00

Marvel Super Heroes, figure, Invisible Woman (catapult), Toy Biz, MOC, $15 to..$18.00

Marvel Super Heroes, figure, Invisible Woman (vanishing), Toy Biz, MOC, $50 to..$55.00

Marvel Super Heroes, figure, Mr Fantastic (5-way stretch), Toy Biz, MOC, $18 to..$20.00

Marvel Super Heroes, figure, Punisher (cap-firing or machine gun sound), Silver Surfer (chrome), Toy Biz, MOC, ea $15 to $18.00

Marvel Super Heroes, figure, Spider-Man (ball joints or web tracer), Toy Biz, MOC, ea $15 to............................$18.00

Marvel Super Heroes, figure, Spider-Man (web climbing or web-shooting), Toy Biz, MOC, ea $30 to $35.00

Marvel Super Heroes, figure, Venom (Living Skin Slime Pores) or Venom (Tongue-Flicking), Toy Biz, MOC, ea $18 to .$22.00

Marvel Super Heroes (Secret Wars), accessory, Doom Copter, Mattel, MOC, $45 to $55.00

Marvel Super Heroes (Secret Wars), accessory, Doom Copter (w/ Dr Doom figure), Mattel, MOC, $75 to $100.00

Marvel Super Heroes (Secret Wars), accessory, Doom Cycle, Mattel, MOC, $18 to..$22.00

Marvel Super Heroes (Secret Wars), accessory, Doom Cycle (w/ Dr Doom figure), Mattel, MOC, $30 to $35.00

Marvel Super Heroes (Secret Wars), accessory, Doom Roller, Mattel, MOC, $18 to..$22.00

Marvel Super Heroes (Secret Wars), accessory, Freedom Fighter, Mattel, MOC, $25 to..$30.00

Marvel Super Heroes (Secret Wars), accessory, Tower of Doom, Mattel, MOC, $40 to..$45.00

Marvel Super Heroes (Secret Wars), accessory, Training Center, Mattel, MOC, $20 to..$25.00

Marvel Super Heroes (Secret Wars), figure, Baron Zemo, Mattel, MOC, $24 to..$28.00

Marvel Super Heroes (Secret Wars), figure, Captain America, Mattel, MOC, $24 to..$28.00

Marvel Super Heroes (Secret Wars), figure, Daredevil, Mattel, MOC, $30 to..$35.00

Marvel Super Heroes (Secret Wars), figure, Dr Doom, Dr Octopus, Kang or Magento, Mattel, MOC, ea $18 to............$22.00

Marvel Super Heroes (Secret Wars), figure, Falcon, Mattel, MOC, $40 to..$45.00

Marvel Super Heroes (Secret Wars), figure, Hobgoblin, Mattel, MOC, $65 to..$70.00

Marvel Super Heroes (Secret Wars), figure, Iron Man, Mattel, MOC, $24 to..$28.00

Marvel Super Heroes (Secret Wars), figure, Spider-Man (blk outfit), Mattel, MOC, $40 to....................................$45.00

Marvel Super Heroes (Secret Wars), figure, Spider-Man (red & bl outfit), Mattel, MOC, $28 to...............................$32.00

Marvel Super Heroes (Secret Wars), figure, Wolverine (blk claws), Mattel, MOC, $110 to.................................... $115.00

Marvel Super Heroes (Secret Wars), figure, Wolverine (silver claws), Mattel, MOC, $38 to..................................$42.00

Marvel Super Heroes (Talking), figure, any, Toy Biz, MIP, ea $20 to..$25.00

M*A*S*H, accessory, 3¾", Ambulance (w/Hawkeye figure), Tri-Star, MIP, $40 to...$45.00

M*A*S*H, accessory, 3¾", Helicopter (w/Hawkeye figure), Tri-Star, MIP, $40 to...$45.00

M*A*S*H, accessory, 3¾", Jeep (w/Hawkeye figure), Tri-Star, MIB, $35 to $40.00

M*A*S*H, accessory, 3¾", Military Base, Tri-Star, MIB, $75 to $100.00

M*A*S*H, figure, 3¾", BJ, Col Potter, Father Mulcahy, Hawkeye, Klinger or Winchester, Tri-Star, MOC, ea $15 to...$20.00

M*A*S*H, figure, 3¾", Hot Lips, Tri-Star, MOC, $20 to.$25.00

M*A*S*H, figure, 3¾", Klinger (in dress), Tri-Star, MOC, $30 to..$35.00

Masters of the Universe, accessory, Battle Cat, Mattel, MIP, $45 to..$55.00

Masters of the Universe, accessory, He-Man & Wind Raider, Mattel, MIP, $80 to $90.00

Masters of the Universe, accessory, Jet Sled, Mattel, MIP, $12 to..$18.00

Masters of the Universe, accessory, Mantisaur, Mattel, MIP, $24 to..$28.00

Masters of the Universe, accessory, Monstroid, Mattel, MIP, $40 to..$45.00

Masters of the Universe, accessory, Night Stalker, Mattel, MOC, $25 to..$35.00

Action Figures and Accessories
• • • • • • • • • • • •
Marvel Super Heroes, figure, Captain America (Shield Launcher), Toy Biz, MOC, $18.00 to $22.00.
(Photo courtesy Morphy Auctions on LiveAuctioneers.com)

Masters of the Universe, accessory, Panthor, MIP, $35 to..$40.00

Masters of the Universe, accessory, Screech, Mattel, MIP, $35 to $45.00

Masters of the Universe, accessory, Stilt Stalker, Mattel, MIP, $18 to $22.00

Masters of the Universe, accessory, Weapons Pak, Mattel, MIP, $12 to $18.00

Masters of the Universe, accessory, Zoar, Mattel, MIP, $28 to ..$32.00

Masters of the Universe, figure, Battle Armor He-Man, Mattel, MOC, $50 to $55.00

Masters of the Universe, figure, Battle Armor Skeletor, Mattel, MOC, ea $35 to $40.00

Masters of the Universe, figure, Beast Man, Mattel, MOC, $85 to $95.00

Masters of the Universe, figure, Blade, Mattel, MOC, $55 to..$60.00

Masters of the Universe, figure, Blast Attack, Mattel, MOC, $45 to $50.00

Masters of the Universe, figure, Buzz-Off, Buzz-Off Hordak or Clawful, MOC, ea $35 to $40.00

Masters of the Universe, figure, Clamp Champ, Mattel, MOC, $60 to $65.00

Masters of the Universe, figure, Dragstor the Evil Horde, Mattel, MOC, $50 to $55.00

Masters of the Universe, figure, Evil-Lyn, Mattel, MOC, $100 to $115.00

Masters of the Universe, figure, Extender, Mattel, MOC, $40 to $45.00

Masters of the Universe, figure, Faker II, Mattel, MOC, $65 to $75.00

Masters of the Universe, figure, Fisto or Grizzlor, Mattel, MOC, ea $35 to $40.00

Masters of the Universe, figure, Grizzlor (blk), Mattel, MOC, $120 to $130.00

Masters of the Universe, figure, Gwilder, Mattel, MOC, $40 to $45.00

Masters of the Universe, figure, He-Man, Mattel, MOC, $200 to.$210.00

Masters of the Universe, figure, He-Man (Thunder Punch), Mattel, MOC, $50 to $55.00

Masters of the Universe, figure, Hordak, Mattel, MOC, $60 to $65.00

Masters of the Universe, figure, Horde Trooper, Mattel, MOC, $130 to $135.00

Masters of the Universe, figure, Jitsu or King Hiss, Mattel, MOC, ea $35 to $40.00

Masters of the Universe, figure, King Randor, Mattel, MOC, $80 to $85.00

Masters of the Universe, figure, Leech, Mattel, MOC, $35 to..$40.00

Masters of the Universe, figure, Man-at-Arms, Mattel, MOC, $105 to $115.00

Masters of the Universe, figure, Man-E-Faces, Mattel, MOC, $60 to $70.00

Masters of the Universe, figure, Mantenna, Mattel, MOC, $35 to $40.00

Masters of the Universe, figure, Mekaneck, Mattel, MOC, $50 to $55.00

Masters of the Universe, figure, Mer-Man, Mattel, MOC, $108 to $115.00

Masters of the Universe, figure, Modulok, Mattel, MOC, $35 to $40.00

Masters of the Universe, figure, Moss Man or Multi-Bot, Mattel, MOC, ea $35 to $40.00

Masters of the Universe, figure, Ninjor, Mattel, MOC, $75 to.$85.00

Masters of the Universe, figure, Orko, Mattel, MOC, $45 to ..$55.00

Masters of the Universe, figure, Rattlor, Mattel, MOC, $35 to ..$40.00

Masters of the Universe, figure, Rio Blast, Mattel, MOC, $45 to $55.00

Masters of the Universe, figure, Roboto, Mattel, MOC, $35 to $40.00

Masters of the Universe, figure, Rokkon, Mattel, MOC, $30 to $35.00

Masters of the Universe, figure, Rotar, Mattel, MOC, $65 to...$75.00

Masters of the Universe, figure, Saurod, Mattel, MOC, $40 to..$50.00

Masters of the Universe, figure, Scare Glow Spector, Mattel, MOC, $120 to $130.00

Masters of the Universe, figure, Skeletor, Mattel, MOC, $175 to $200.00

Masters of the Universe, figure, Snake Face, Mattel, MOC, $65 to $75.00

Masters of the Universe, figure, Snout Spout, Mattel, MOC, $50 to $60.00

Masters of the Universe, figure, Sorceress, Mattel, MOC, $80 to . $90.00
Masters of the Universe, figure, Spikor, Mattel, MOC, $35 to $40.00
Masters of the Universe, figure, Sssqueeze, Mattel, MOC, $60 to .. $70.00
Masters of the Universe, figure, Stratos, Mattel, MOC, $115 to . $125.00
Masters of the Universe, figure, Sy-Klone, Mattel, MOC, $35 to . $45.00
Masters of the Universe, figure, Teela, Mattel, MOC, $110 to.... $120.00
Masters of the Universe, figure, Trapjaw, Mattel, MOC, $65 to.... $75.00
Masters of the Universe, figure, Tri Klops, Mattel, MOC, $55 to . $65.00
Masters of the Universe, figure, Tung Lasher, Mattel, MOC, $40 to.. $50.00
Masters of the Universe, figure, Twistoid, Mattel, MOC, $70 to... $80.00
Masters of the Universe, figure, Two-Bad, Mattel, MOC, $35 to.. $45.00
Masters of the Universe, figure, Webstor, Mattel, MOC, $35 to... $45.00
Masters of the Universe, figure, Whiplash, Mattel, MOC, $30 to... $40.00
Masters of the Universe, figure, Zodac, Mattel, MOC, $125 to .. $135.00
Micronauts, accessory, Astro Station, Mego, MIP, $20 to . $25.00
Micronauts, accessory, Battle Cruiser, Mego, w/figure, MIP, $65 to.. $75.00
Micornauts, accessory, Crater Cruncher, w/figure, Mego, MIP, $50 to.. $55.00
Micronauts, accessory, Galactic Command Center, Mego, MIP, $75 to... $100.00
Micronauts, accessory, Galactic Cruiser, w/figure, Mego, MIP, $50 to.. $55.00
Micronauts, accessory, Giant Acroyear, Mego, MIP, $60 to.. $65.00
Micronauts, accessory, Hornetroid, Mego, MIP, $45 to $50.00
Micronauts, accessory, Hydra, w/figure, Mego, MIP, $50 to . $55.00
Micronauts, accessory, Hydro Copter, Mego, MIB, $30 to.. $40.00
Micronauts, accessory, Mega City, Mego, MIP, $35 to....... $35.00
Micronauts, accessory, Microrail City, Mego, MIP, $40 to. $45.00
Micronauts, accessory, Mobile Exploration Lab, Mego, MIP, $30 to.. $40.00
Micronauts, accessory, Neon Orbiter, Mego, MIP, $20 to.. $25.00
Micronauts, accessory, Photon Sled w/Figure, Mego, 1976, unused & unassembled, MIP, $30 to.............................. $40.00

Micronauts, accessory, Rocket Tubes, Mego, MIP, $45 to.. $55.00
Micronauts, accessory, Star Searcher, Mego, MIP, $35 to.. $45.00
Micronauts, accessory, Stratastation, Mego, MIP, $30 to.... $40.00
Micronauts, accessory, Ultronic Scooter, Mego, MIP, $40 to. $50.00
Micronauts, accessory, Warp Racer, w/figure, Mego, MIP, $40 to.. $50.00
Micronauts, figure, Andromeda, Mego, MIP, $20 to.......... $30.00
Micronauts, figure, Antron, Mego, MIP, $100 to............ $125.00
Micronauts, figure, Baron Karza, Mego, MIP, $25 to.......... $35.00
Micronauts, figure, Biotron, Mego, MIP, $20 to.............. $30.00
Micronauts, figure, Centaurus, Mego, MIP, $200 to........ $225.00
Micronauts, figure, Force Commander, Mego, MIP, $65 to.... $70.00
Micronauts, figure, Galactic Defender or Galactic Warrior, Mego, MOC, ea $35 to $40.00
Micronauts, figure, Giant Acroyear, Mego, MIP, $60 to.... $65.00
Micronauts, figure, Kronos, Mego, MIP, $200 to............ $225.00
Micronauts, figure, Lobros, Mego, MIP, $200 to $225.00
Micronauts, figure, Membros, Mego, MIP, $100 to $125.00
Micronauts, figure, Microtron, Mego, MIP, $70 to............. $75.00
Micronauts, figure, Nemesis Robot, Mego, unused, MIP, $55 to.. $60.00
Micronauts, figure, Oberon, Mego, unassembled, MIP, $45 to.. $50.00
Micronauts, figure, Pharoid w/Time Chamber, Mego, MOC (unpunched), $45 to $50.00
Micronauts, figure, Phobos Robot, Mego, MIP, $70 to $75.00
Micronauts, figure, Repto, Mego, MIP, $100 to $115.00
Micronauts, figure, Time Traveler, Mego, MIP, $45 to....... $50.00
Official World's Greatest Super Heroes, see Super Heroes
One Million BC, accessory, Tribal Lair, Mego, MIB, $175 to . $200.00
One Million BC, accessory, Tribal Lair Gift Set (w/5 figures), MIB, $350 to $375.00
One Million BC, creature, Dimetrodon, Mego, MIB, $200 to.. $225.00
One Million BC, creature, Hairy Rhino, Mego, MIB, $250 to ... $275.00
One Million BC, creature, Tyrannosaur, Mego, MIB, $250 to $275.00

Planet of the Apes, accessory, Action Stallion, r/c, Mego, 1970s, M, $50 to $65.00

Planet of the Apes, accessory, Action Stallion, r/c, Mego, 1970s, MIB, $75 to $110.00

Planet of the Apes, accessory, Battering Ram, Jail, or Dr Zaius Throne, Mego, 1970s, MIB, ea $35 to $45.00

Planet of the Apes, accessory, Catapult & Wagon, Mego, 1970s, MIB, $140 to $150.00

Planet of the Apes, accessory, Forbidden Zone Trap, Fortresor Treehouse (w/5 figures), Mego, 1970s, MIB, ea $175 to..........$225.00

Planet of the Apes, accessory, Village, Mego, 1970s, MIB, $175 to... $225.00

Planet of the Apes, figure, 5", any Bend 'n Flex, MOC, ea $20 to $25.00

Planet of the Apes, figure, 7", any, Hasbro, 1999, MIP, ea $5 to $8.00

Planet of the Apes, figure, 8", Astronaut, any, Mego, 1970s, MIB, $225 to... $250.00

Planet of the Apes, figure, 8", Dr Zaius or Galen or Mego, 1970s, MIB, ea $175 to... $200.00

Planet of the Apes, figure, 8", Dr Zaius or Galen, Mego, 1970s, MOC, ea $75 to $100.00

Planet of the Apes, figure, 8", General Urko, General Ursus or Soldier Ape, Mego, 1970s, MIB, ea $240 to................ $260.00

Planet of the Apes, figure, 8", General Urko, General Ursus or Soldier Ape, Mego, 1970s, MOC, ea $200 to.............. $225.00

Planet of the Apes, figure, 12", any, Hasbro, 1999, MIP, $20 to $30.00

Pocket Super Heroes, accessory, Batcave, Mego, MIB, $275 to...$325.00

Pocket Super Heroes, accessory, Batmachine, Mego, MIB, $100 to... $125.00

Pocket Super Heroes, accessory, Batmobile (w/Batman & Robin), Mego, MIB, $175 to $225.00

Pocket Super Heroes, accessory, Spider-Car (w/Spider-Man & the Hulk), Mego, MIB, $70 to $80.00

Pocket Super Heroes, accessory, Spider-Machine, Mego, MIB, $75 to... $125.00

Pocket Super Heroes, figure, Aquaman, Captain America or Green Goblin, Mego, MOC (wht card), ea $90 to $110.00

Pocket Super Heroes, figure, Batman, Mego, MOC (red card), $65 to.. $75.00

Pocket Super Heroes, figure, Batman, Mego, MOC (wht card), $120 to... $130.00

Pocket Super Heroes, figure, Incredible Hulk, Mego, MOC (red card), $28 to..$32.00

Pocket Super Heroes, figure, Incredible Hulk, Mego, MOC (wht card), $38 to..$42.00

Pocket Super Heroes, figure, Jor-El or Lex Luthor, MOC (red card), $18 to...$22.00

Pocket Super Heroes, figure, Robin, Mego, MOC (red card), $55 to...$65.00

Pocket Super Heroes, figure, Robin, Mego, MOC (wht card), $90 to.. $110.00

Pocket Super Heroes, figure, Spider-Man, Mego, MOC (red card), $45 to...$55.00

Pocket Super Heroes, figure, Spider-Man, Mego, MOC (wht card), $90 to.. $110.00

Action Figures and Accessories
• • • • • • • • • • • • • • • • •
Planet of the Apes, figure, 8", Astronauts, any, Mego, 1970s, MIB, $225.00 to $250.00.
(Photo courtesy Morphy Auctions on LiveAuctioneers.com)

Action Figures and Accessories
• •
Planet of the Apes, figures, 8", Cornelius and Zira, Mego, 1970s, MOC, each $75.00 to $100.00. (Photo courtesy Morphy Auctions on LiveAuctioneers.com)

Pocket Super Heroes, figure, Superman, Mego, MOC (red card), $35 to..$45.00

Pocket Super Heroes, figure, Superman, Mego, MOC (wht card), $70 to..$80.00

Pocket Super Heroes, figure, Wonder Woman, Mego, MOC (wht card), $70 to $80.00

Power Lords, figure, any, MOC, ea $20 to........................$30.00

Rambo, accessory, .50 Caliber Anti-Aircraft Gun or .50 Caliber Machine Gun, Coleco, MIP, ea $10 to $15.00

Rambo, accessory, Defender 6x6 Assault Vehicle, Coleco, MIB, $28 to..$32.00

Rambo, accessory, SAVAGE Strike Cycle, Coleco, MIB, $18 to $22.00

Rambo, accessory, SAVAGE Strike Headquarters, Coleco, MIB, $50 to..$60.00

Rambo, accessory, Skyfire Assault Copter, Coleco, MIB, $28 to. $32.00

Rambo, accessory, Skywolf Assault Jet, Coleco, MIB, $25 to...$30.00

Rambo, accessory, Swamp Dog, Coleco, MIB, $18 to........$22.00

Rambo, accessory, 106 Recoilless Anti-Tank Gun, Coleco, MIP, ea $10 to $15.00

Rambo, figure, Black Dragon, Chief, Colonel Troutman, General Warhawk or Gripper, Coleco, MOC, ea $8 to...............$12.00

Action Figures
and Accessories
• • • • • • • •
Pocket Super Heroes,
figure, General Zod,
Mego, MOC (red card),
$20.00 to $30.00. (Photo
courtesy Wallace M. Chrouch)

Action Figures and Accessories
• •
**Robin Hood Prince of Thieves, accessory, Battle
Wagon, Kenner, NRFB, $25.00 to $35.00.** (Photo
courtesy www.gasolinealleyantiques.com)

Rambo, figure, Dr Hyde, Snakebite, TD Jackson or X-ray, Coleco, MOC, ea $18 to $22.00

Rambo, figure, KAT, Mad Dog, Nomad, Rambo or Rambo w/Fire Power, Coleco, MOC, ea $8 to $15.00

Rambo, figure, Sgt Havoc, Turbo or White Dragon, Coleco, MOC, ea $8 to $15.00

Robin Hood & His Merry Men, figure, Friar Tuck, Mego, MIB, $60 to..$70.00

Robin Hood & His Merry Men, figure, Little John, Mego, MIB, $150 to $160.00

Robin Hood & His Merry Men, figure, Robin Hood, Mego, MIB, $275 to.. $300.00

Robin Hood & His Merry Men, figure, Will Scarlet, Mego, MIB, $250 to... $275.00

Robin Hood Prince of Thieves, accessory, Bola Bomber, Kenner, 1991, MIP, $8 to.....................................$12.00

Robin Hood Prince of Thieves, accessory, Net Launcher, Kenner, 1991, MIP, $10 to...$15.00

Robin Hood Prince of Thieves, accessory, Sherwood Forest Playset, Kenner, 1991, MIP, $55 to..........................$65.00

Robin Hood Prince of Thieves, figure, Azeem, Little John or Sheriff of Nottingham, Kenner, 1991, MOC, ea $12 to.$18.00

Robin Hood Prince of Thieves, figure, Friar Tuck w/Battle Staff, Kenner, 1991, MOC, $15 to $25.00

Robin Hood Prince of Thieves, figure, Robin Hood (either head) w/Cross Bow, Kenner, 1991, MOC, ea $12 to $18.00

Robin Hood Prince of Thieves, figure, Robin Hood w/Long Bow, Kenner, 1991, MOC, $12 to $18.00

Robin Hood Prince of Thieves, figure, The Dark Warrior or Will Scarlet, Kenner, 1991, MOC, $12 to.....................$18.00

Robocop (Ultra Police), accessory, Robo-Command vehicle w/ figure, Kenner, MIB, $25 to.................................$35.00

Robocop (Ultra Police), accessory, Robo-Jailer vehicle, Kenner, MIB, $38 to...$42.00

Robocop (Ultra Police), figure, any, Kenner, 1988-90, MOC, ea, $15 to...$25.00

Robotech, accessory, Armoured Cyclone, Matchbox, MIB, $35 to..$45.00

Robotech, accessory, Bioroid Hover Craft, Matchbox, MIB, $20 to..$30.00

Robotech, accessory, Bioroid Invid Fighter, Dana's Hover Cycle, or Excaliber MkVI, Matchbox, MIB, ea $35 to..............$45.00

Robotech, accessory, Gladiator, Invid Scout Ship, Invid Shock Trooper or Raider X, Matchbox, MIB, ea $35 to...........$45.00

Robotech, accessory, SDF-1 Playset, Matchbox, MIB, $425 to.$475.00

Robotech, accessory, Spartan, Tactical Battle Pod or Veritech Fighter, Matchbox, MIB, ea $35 to........................$45.00

Robotech, accessory, Veritech Hover Tank or Zentraedi Officer's Battle Pod, Matchbox, MIB, ea $30 to $45.00

Robotech, accessory, Zentraedi Powered Armor, Matchbox, MIB, $40 to..$50.00

Robotech, figure, 3¾", Bioroid Terminator, Lisa Hayes or Micronized Zentraedi, Matchbox, MOC, ea $12 to.............$18.00

Robotech, figure, 3¾", Corg, Lunk, Max Sterling, Miriya (red) or Rick Hunter, Matchbox, MOC, ea $20 to...............$25.00

Robotech, figure, 3¾", Dana Sterling or Roy Fokker, Matchbox, MOC, ea $28 to $32.00

Robotech, figure, 3¾", Miriya (blk), Matchbox, MOC, $60 to... $70.00

Robotech, figure, 3¾", Miriya (red), Matchbox, MOC, $18 to... $22.00

Robotech, figure, 3¾", Rand, Robotech Master or Zor Prime, Matchbox, MOC, ea $10 to................................$18.00

Robotech, figure, 3¾", Scott Bernard, MOC, $40 to $45.00

Robotech, figure, 6", any character, Matchbox, MOC, ea $18 to... $22.00

Robotech, figure, 8", Armoured Zentraedi, Matchbox, MIP, $20 to..$25.00

Robotech, figure, 12", Dana Sterling, Lisa Hayes, Lynn Minmei or Rick Hunter, Matchbox, MIB, ea $45 to..................$55.00

Schwarzenegger Commando, see Commando (Schwarzenegger)

She-Ra Princess of Power, accessory, Crystal Castle or Crystal Falls, Mattel, 1984-86, MIP, ea $55 to $65.00

She-Ra Princess of Power, figure, Angella, Bow, Castaspella or Double Trouble, Mattel, 1984-86, MOC, ea $12 to.......$18.00

She-Ra Princess of Power, figure, any creature, Mattel, 1984-86, MIP, ea $35 to...$45.00

She-Ra Princess of Power, figure, Castaspella, She-Ra or Shower Power Catra, Mattel, 1984-86, MOC, ea $35 to $45.00

She-Ra Princess of Power, figure, Catra, Mattel, 1984-86, MOC, $40 to...$50.00

She-Ra Princess of Power, figure, Entrapta, Flutterina, Frosta, Glimmer or Kowl, Mattel, 1984-86, MOC, ea $18 to....$22.00

She-Ra Princess of Power, figure, Loo-Kee, Mermista, Peekablue, Perfuma or Spinerella, Mattel, 1984-86, MOC, ea $18 .$22.00

She-Ra Princess of Power, figure, Netossa, Mattel, 1984-86, MOC, $20 to...$30.00

She-Ra Princess of Power, figure, Starburst She-Ra or Sweet Bee, Mattel, 1984-86, MOC, ea $35 to $45.00

She-Ra Princess of Power, outfit, any, Mattel, 1984-86, MIP, ea $10 to...$15.00

Six Million Dollar Man, accessory, Backpack Radio, Kenner, MIP, $20 to...$30.00

Six Million Dollar Man, accessory, Bionic Cycle, Kenner, MIP, $18 to...$22.00

Six Million Dollar Man, accessory, Bionic Mission Vehicle, Kenner, MIP, $75 to...$85.00

Six Million Dollar Man, accessory, Bionic Transport & Repair Station, Kenner, MIB, $85 to $95.00

Six Million Dollar Man, accessory, Mission Control Center, Kenner, MIB, $100 to $125.00

Six Million Dollar Man, accessory, OSI Headquarters, Kenner, MIB, $75 to...$85.00

Six Million Dollar Man, accessory, Venus Space Probe, Kenner, MIB, $300 to $325.00

Six Million Dollar Man, figure, Bionic Bigfoot, Kenner, MIB, $175 to... $200.00

Six Million Dollar Man, figure, Oscar Goldman, Kenner, MIB, $90 to... $110.00

Six Million Dollar Man, figure, Steve Austin, Kenner, MIB, $100 to... $125.00

Six Million Dollar Man, figure, Steve Austin (Biosonic Arm), Kenner, MIB, $400 to $425.00

Six Million Dollar Man, figure, Steve Austin (w/engine block or girder), Kenner, MIB, $145 to...................................... $155.00

Space: 1999, accessory, Moonbase Alpha, w/figures, Mattel, MIB, $175 to... $200.00

Space: 1999, figure, any except Zython Alien, Mattel, MOC, ea $60 to...$70.00

Space: 1999, figure, Zython Alien, Mattel, MOC, $270 to... $280.00

Spider-Man (New Animated Series), accessory, 5", Daily Bugle Play Set, Toy Biz, 1994-96, MIP, $15 to.........................$25.00

Spider-Man (New Animated Series), figure, 5", any except Rhino or S-M w/Web Cannon, Toy Biz, 1994-96, MOC, ea $10 to...$15.00

Spider-Man (New Animated Series), figure, 5", Rhino, Toy Biz, 1994-96, MOC, $18 to...$22.00

Spider-Man (New Animated Series), figure, 5", Spider-Man (w/ cannon), Toy Biz, 1994-96, MOC, $18 to.....................$22.00

Spider-Man (New Animated Series), figure, 10", any character, Mattel, 1994-96, MIP, ea $25 to $35.00

Spider-Man (New Animated Series), Projectors, any, Toy Biz, 1994-96, MIP, ea $12 to...$18.00

Starsky & Hutch, accessory, car, Mego, MIB, $150 to.... $175.00

Super Heroes, see also DC Comics Super Heroes and Pocket Super Heroes

Super Heroes, accessory, Batcave, Mego, 1974, NMIB, $150 to...$175.00

Super Heroes, accessory, Batman's Wayne Foundation playset, Mego, 1977, rare, NMIB $600.00

Super Heroes, figure, 8", see also Super Heroes (Fantastic Four) and Super Heroes (Fist Fighting)

Super Heroes, figure, 8", Aquaman, Mego, MIB (solid), $750 to $775.00

Super Heroes, figure, 8", Aquaman, Mego, MIB (window box) or MOC, ea $125 to $150.00

Super Heroes, figure, 8", Aquaman, Mego, MOC, $150 to..$175.00

Super Heroes, figure, 8", Batgirl, Mego, MIB or MOC, ea $300 to $325.00

Super Heroes, figure, 8", Batman (pnt cowl), Mego, MIB or MOC, $150 to $175.00

Super Heroes, figure, 8", Batman (removable cowl), Mego, MIB (solid box), $1,000 to... $1,100.00

Super Heroes, figure, 8", Batman (removable cowl), Mego, MIB (window box), $750 to... $850.00

Super Heroes, figure, 8", Batman (removable cowl), Mego, MOC, $300 to $350.00

Super Heroes, figure, 8", Captain America, Mego, MIB, $225 to $250.00

Super Heroes, figure, 8", Captain America, Mego, MOC, $145 to $155.00

Super Heroes, figure, 8", Catwoman, Mego, MIB, $300 to.... $350.00

Super Heroes, figure, 8", Catwoman, Mego, MOC, $1,500 to $1,750.00

Super Heroes, figure, 8", Clark Kent, Mego, MIB, $1,500 to $1,750.00

Super Heroes, figure, 8", Conan, Mego, MIB, $350 to.... $375.00

Super Heroes, figure, 8", Conan, Mego, MOC, $475 to . $500.00

Super Heroes, figure, 8", Dick Grayson, Mego, MIB, $1,500 to $1,750.00

Super Heroes, figure, 8", Falcon, Mego, MIB, $125 to.... $150.00

Super Heroes, figure, 8", Falcon, Mego, MOC, $1,200 to ..$1,600.00

Super Heroes, figure, 8", Green Arrow, Mego, MIB, $400 to.... $450.00

Super Heroes, figure, 8", Green Arrow, Mego, MOC, $1,500 to $1,750.00

Super Heroes, figure, 8", Green Goblin, Mego, MIB, $275 to ...$300.00

Super Heroes, figure, 8", Green Goblin, Mego, MOC, $1,500 to $1,750.00

Super Heroes, figure, 8", Iron Man, Mego, MIB, $100 to.. $125.00

Super Heroes, figure, 8", Iron Man, Mego, MOC, $425 to...$450.00

Super Heroes, figure, 8", Isis, Mego, MIB, $200 to.......... $250.00

Super Heroes, figure, 8", Isis, Mego, MOC, $100 to $125.00

Super Heroes, figure, 8", Joker, Mego, MIB or MOC, $150 to. $175.00

Super Heroes, figure, 8", Lizard, Mego, MIB, $175 to..... $250.00

Super Heroes, figure, 8", Lizard, Mego, MOC, $1,500 to....$1,750.00

Super Heroes, figure, 8", Mr Mxyzptlk (open mouth), Mego, MIB, $70 to $80.00

Super Heroes, figure, 8", Mr Mxyzptlk (open mouth), MOC, $155 to.. $165.00

Super Heroes, figure, 8", Mr Mxyzptlk (smirk), Mego, MIB, $145 to.. $155.00

Super Heroes, figure, 8", Penguin, Mego, MIB, $155 to . $165.00

Super Heroes, figure, 8", Penguin, Mego, MOC, $100 to.. $125.00

Super Heroes, figure, 8", Peter Parker, Mego, MIB, $1,500 to $1,750.00

Super Heroes, figure, 8", Riddler, Mego, MIB, $275 to... $325.00

Super Heroes, figure, 8", Riddler, Mego, MOC, $1,500 to ..$1,750.00

Super Heroes, figure, 8", Robin (pnt mask), Mego, MIB, $145 to.. $155.00

Super Heroes, figure, 8", Robin (pnt mask), Mego, MOC, $90 to...$110.00

Super Heroes, figure, 8", Robin (removable mask), Mego, MIB (window box), $700 to.. $725.00

Super Heroes, figure, 8", Robin (removable mask), Mego, rare, MIB (solid box).. $5,600.00

Super Heroes, figure, 8", Shazam, Mego, MIB, $175 to .. $200.00

Super Heroes, figure, 8", Shazam, Mego, MOC, $140 to . $160.00

Super Heroes, figure, 8", Spider-Man, Mego, MIB, $75 to..$100.00

Super Heroes, figure, 8", Spider-Man, Mego, MOC, $50 to... $60.00

Super Heroes, figure, 8", Supergirl, Mego, MOC, $450 to ..$500.00

Super Heroes, figure, 8", Superman, Mego, MIB (solid box), $725 to.. $775.00

Super Heroes, figure, 8", Superman, Mego, MOC, $125 to ..$150.00

Super Heroes, figure, 8", Tarzan, Mego, MIB, $150 to.... $175.00

Super Heroes, figure, 8", Tarzan, Mego, MOC, $220 to.. $230.00

Super Heroes, figure, 8", Thor, Mego, MIB, $400 to....... $425.00

Super Heroes, figure, 8", Thor, Mego, MOC, $450 to $475.00

Super Heroes, figure, 8", Wonder Woman, Mego, MIB, $350 to $375.00

Super Heroes, figure, 8", Wonder Woman, Mego, MOC, $475 to..$525.00

Super Heroes, figure, 12½", see also Super Heroes (Fly-Away Action)

Super Heroes, figure, 12½", Batman, Magnetic, Mego, MIB, $200 to.. $225.00

Super Heroes, figure, 12½", Batman, Mego, MIB, $125 to...$150.00

Super Heroes, figure, 12½", Captain America, Mego, MIB, $175 to $200.00

Super Heroes, figure, 12½", Incredible Hulk, Mego, MIB, $75 to $100.00

Super Heroes, figure, 12½", Jor-El (Superman's father), Mego, MIB, $100 to $150.00

Action Figures and Accessories
• • • • • • • • • • • • • • • • • • • •
Super Heroes, figure, 8", The Incredible Hulk, Mego, MOC, $50.00 to $60.00. (Photo courtesy Morphy Auctions on LiveAuctioneers.com)

Action Figures and Accessories
• •
Super Heroes, figures, 8", Mego, Supergirl, MIB (window box), $500.00 to $525.00; Superman, MIB (window box), $200.00 to $300.00. (Photo courtesy Morphy Auctions on LiveAuctioneers.com)

Action Figures and Accessories

Super Heroes (Bend 'n Flex), figures, 5", Mego: Catwoman, M, $65.00 to $75.00; Wonder Woman, M, $45.00 to $55.00; Supergirl, M, $65.00 to $75.00; Batgirl, M, $45.00 to $65.00. (Photo courtesy Wallace M. Chrouch)

Super Heroes, figure, 12½", Lex Luthor, Mego, MIB, $100 to .$150.00

Super Heroes, figure, 12½", Spider-Man, Mego, MIB, $100 to $150.00

Super Heroes, figure, 12½", Superman, Mego, MIB, $75 to ..$100.00

Super Heroes, figure, 12½", Superman, Web Shooting, Mego, MIB, $125 to $150.00

Super Heroes (Bend 'n Flex), figure, 5", Aquaman, Mego, MOC, $100 to.. $115.00

Super Heroes (Bend 'n Flex), figure, 5", Batman, Mego, MOC, $75 to.. $100.00

Super Heroes (Bend 'n Flex), figure, 5", Captain America, Mego, MOC, $75 to $100.00

Super Heroes (Bend 'n Flex), figure, 5", Joker, Mego, MOC, $100 to.. $125.00

Super Heroes (Bend 'n Flex), figure, 5", Mr Mxyzptlk, Mego, MOC, $100 to... $125.00

Super Heroes (Bend 'n Flex), figure, 5", Penguin, Mego, MOC, $125 to.. $150.00

Super Heroes (Bend 'n Flex), figure, 5", Riddler, Mego, MOC, $125 to.. $150.00

Super Heroes (Bend 'n Flex), figure, 5", Robin, Mego, MOC, $75 to... $100.00

Super Heroes (Bend 'n Flex), figure, 5", Shazam, Mego, MOC, $100 to... $125.00

Super Heroes (Bend 'n Flex), figure, 5", Spider-Man, Mego, MOC, $100 to... $125.00

Super Heroes (Bend 'n Flex), figure, 5", Superman or Wonder Woman, Mego, MOC, $75 to..................................... $100.00

Super Heroes (Bend 'n Flex), figure, 5", Tarzan, Mego, MOC, $50 to...$75.00

Super Heroes (Fantastic Four), figure, 8", Human Torch, Mego, MIB, $75 to...$85.00

Super Heroes (Fantastic Four), figure, 8", Human Torch, Mego, MOC, $45 to...$55.00

Super Heroes (Fantastic Four), figure, 8", Invisible Girl, Mego, MIB, $140 to $150.00

Super Heroes (Fantastic Four), figure, 8", Invisible Girl, Mego, MOC, $55 to...$65.00

Super Heroes (Fantastic Four), figure, 8", Mr Fantastic, Mego, MIB, $140 to $150.00

Super Heroes (Fantastic Four), figure, 8", Mr Fantastic, Mego, MOC, $55 to...$65.00

Super Heroes (Fantastic Four), figure, 8", Thing, Mego, MIB, $300 to.. $325.00

Super Heroes (Fantastic Four), figure, 8", Thing, Mego, MOC, $55 to...$65.00

Super Heroes (Fist Fighting), figure, 8", Robin, Mego, MIB, $375 to.. $425.00

Super Heroes (Fist Fighting), figure, 8", Joker, Mego, MIB, $550 to.. $575.00

Super Heroes (Fist Fighting), figure, 8", Riddler, Mego, MIB, $550 to $575.00

Super Heroes (Fly Away Action), figure, 12½", Batman, Mego, $120 to.. $130.00

Super Heroes (Fly Away Action), figure, 12½", Batman (Magnetic), Mego, MIB, $200 to $250.00

Super Heroes (Fly Away Action), figure, 12½", Incredible Hulk, Mego, MIB, $100 to... $150.00

Super Heroes (Fly Away Action), figure, 12½", Robin, Mego, MIB, $200 to $250.00

Super Heroes (Fly Away Action), figure, 12½", Robin (Magnetic), Mego, $225 to.. $275.00

Super Heroes (Fly Away Action), figure, 12½", Spider-Man, Mego, $150 to... $175.00

Super Heroes (Fly Away Action), figure, 12½", Superman, Mego, MIB, $130 to $140.00

Superman (Animated), figure, Anti-Kryptonite Superman or Brainiac, Kenner, 1995, MOC, ea $8 to $12.00

Superman (Animated), figure, Capture Claw Superman, Electro Energy Superman, Kenner, 1995, MOC, ea $15 to $20.00

Superman (Animated), figure, Capture Net Superman or City Camp Superman, Kenner, 1995, MOC, ea $8 to $12.00

Superman (Animated), figure, Cyber Crunch Superman or Fortress of Solitude Superman, Kenner, 1995, MOC, ea $18 to.....$22.00

Action Figures and Accessories

Super Heroes (Fist Fighting), figure, 8", Batman, Mego, MIB, $400.00 to $425.00. (Photo courtesy Morphy Auctions on LiveAuctioneers.com)

Action Figures and Accessories
• • • • • • • • • • • • • • • • • • • •
Super Heroes (Fly Away Action), figure, 12½", Captain America, Mego, MIB, $175.00 to $200.00. (Photo courtesy Wallace M. Chrouch)

Action Figures and Accessories
• • • • • • • • • • • • • • • • • • • •
Superman (Man of Steel), figure, Lex Luthor, Kenner, 1995 – 1996, MOC, $18.00 to $22.00.

Superman (Animated), figure, Darkseid or Evil Bizarro, Kenner, 1995, MOC, ea $25 to $30.00

Superman (Animated), figure, Deep Dive Superman or Electro Energy Superman, Kenner, 1995, MOC, ea $8 to $12.00

Superman (Animated), figure, Flying Superman or Fortress of Solitude Superman, Kenner, 1995, MOC, ea $8 to........$12.00

Superman (Animated), figure, Kryptonite Escape Superman, Kenner, 1995, MOC, $15 to $20.00

Superman (Animated), figure, Lex Luthor or Neutron Star Superman, Kenner, 1995, MOC, ea $8 to $12.00

Superman (Animated), figure, Metallo, Kenner, 1995, MOC, $18 to...$22.00

Superman (Animated), figure, Power Swing Superman or Supergirl, Kenner, 1995, MOC, ea $15 to $20.00

Superman (Animated), figure, Quick Change Superman or Strong Arm Superman, Kenner, 1995, MOC, ea $8 to..$12.00

Superman (Animated), figure, Tornado Force Superman or Vision Blast Superman, Kenner, 1995, MOC, ea $15 to.$20.00

Superman (Animated), figure, Ultra Shield Superman or X-Ray Vision Superman, Kenner, 1995, MOC, ea $8 to...........$12.00

Superman (Man of Steel), figure, Blast Hammer Steel (Deluxe), Kenner, 1995-96, MOC, $8 to..$12.00

Superman (Man of Steel), figure, Conduit, Laser Superman, Kenner, 1995-96, MOC, ea $8 to $12.00

Superman (Man of Steel), figure, Power Flight Superman or Solar Suit Superman, Steel, Kenner, 1995-96, MOC, ea $8 to $12.00

Superman (Man of Steel), figure, Street Guardian Superman or Superboy, Kenner, 1995-96, MOC, ea $8 to $12.00

Superman (Man of Steel), figure, Ultra Heat Vision Superman or Ultra Shield Superman, Kenner, 1995-96, MOC, ea $8 to $12.00

Superman (Man of Steel), figure set, Cyber-Link Superman & Cyber-Link Batman, Kenner, 1995, MOC, $18 to $22.00

Superman (Man of Steel), figure set, Hunter-Prey Superman & Doomsday, Kenner, 1995, MOC, $12 to.....................$15.00

Super Monsters, figure, Count Dracula, Frankenstein, The Mummy or Wolfman, Ahi, 1960s, MOC, ea $150 to.. $175.00

Super Naturals, accessory, Ghost Finder, Tonka, 1986, MIB, $25 to...$30.00

Super Naturals, accessory, Lionwings Battle Creature, Tonka, 1986, MIB, $20 to $25.00

Super Naturals, figure, any character, Tonka, MOC, ea $15 to...$20.00

Super Powers, accessory, Batcopter, Kenner, MIB, $100 to ... $125.00

Super Powers, accessory, Batmobile, Kenner, MIB, $100 to.....$125.00

Super Powers, accessory, carrying case, Kenner, M, $30 to .$35.00

Super Powers, accessory, Darkseid Destroyer, Kenner, MIB, $45 to...$55.00

Super Powers, accessory, Delta Probe One, Kenner, MIB, $30 to.. $35.00

Super Powers, accessory, Hall of Justice, Kenner, MIB, $200 to.$225.00

Super Powers, accessory, Kalibak Boulder Bomber, Kenner, MIB, $20 to...$30.00

Super Powers, accessory, Lex-Sor 7, Kenner, MIB, $20 to.$30.00

Super Powers, accessory, Supermobile, Kenner, MIB, $30 to....$40.00

Super Powers, figure, Aquaman, Kenner, MOC, $40 to $50.00

Super Powers, figure, Batman, Kenner, MOC, $90 to..... $100.00

Super Powers, figure, Brainiac, Kenner, MOC, $25 to.......$35.00

Super Powers, figure, Clark Kent, Kenner, MOC (mail-in), $50 to...$60.00

Super Powers, figure, Cyborg, Kenner, MOC, $270 to ... $280.00

Super Powers, figure, Darkseid, Kenner, MOC, $15 to......$20.00

Super Powers, figure, Desaad, Kenner, MOC, $20 to.........$25.00

Super Powers, figure, Dr Fate, Kenner, MOC, $55 to $65.00

Super Powers, figure, Firestorm, Kenner, MOC, $30 to.....$40.00

Super Powers, figure, Golden Pharaoh, Kenner, MOC, $75 to.. $85.00

Super Powers, figure, Green Arrow, Kenner, MOC, $45 to ... $55.00

Super Powers, figure, Green Lantern, Kenner, MOC, $55 to ...$65.00

Super Powers, figure, Hawkman, Kenner, MOC, from, $55 to...$65.00

Super Powers, figure, Joker, Kenner, MOC, $20 to $30.00

Super Powers, figure, Kalibak, Kenner, MOC, $20 to........$30.00

Super Powers, figure, Lex Luthor, Kenner, MOC, $15 to ..$20.00

Super Powers, figure, Mantis, Kenner, MOC, $20 to.........$30.00

Super Powers, figure, Mister Freeze, Kenner, MOC, $60 to ... $70.00

Super Powers, figure, Mister Miracle, Kenner, MOC, $125 to...$135.00

Super Powers, figure, Orion, Kenner, MOC, $30 to $40.00

Super Powers, figure, Parademon, Kenner, MOC, $25 to ..$30.00

Super Powers, figure, Penguin, Kenner, MOC, $45 to.......$55.00

Super Powers, figure, Plastic Man, Kenner, MOC, $100 to... $115.00

Super Powers, figure, Red Tornado, Kenner, MOC, $45 to....$55.00

Super Powers, figure, Samurai, Kenner, MOC, $90 to.... $100.00

Super Powers, figure, Shazam, Kenner, MOC, $65 to........$75.00

Super Powers, figure, Steppenwolf, Kenner, MIP (mail-in), $15 to...$20.00

Super Powers, figure, Steppenwolf, Kenner, MOC, $65 to .$75.00

Super Powers, figure, Superman, Kenner, MOC, $90 to. $100.00

Super Powers, figure, Tyr, Kenner, MOC, $45 to $55.00

Teen Titans, figure, Aqualad, Mego, MOC, $325 to....... $350.00

Teen Titans, figure, Aqualad, Mego, NM, $150 to.......... $175.00

Teen Titans, figure, Kid Flash, Mego, MOC, $425 to $450.00

Teen Titans, figure, Kid Flash, Mego, NM, $150 to $175.00

Teen Titans, figure, Speedy, Mego, MOC, $475 to $500.00

Teen Titans, figure, Speedy, Mego, NM, $275 to $300.00

Teen Titans, figure, Wondergirl, Mego, MOC, $475 to .. $500.00

Teen Titans, figure, Wondergirl, Mego, NM, $175 to $200.00

Teenage Mutant Ninja Turtles, figure, Donatello or Leonardo, Playmates, 1988, 1st series, ea $15 to..............................$20.00

Teenage Mutant Ninja Turtles, figure, Michelangelo or Raphael, Playmates, 1988, 1st series, MOC, ea $15 to..................$20.00

Universal Monsters, figure, 8", Creature From the Black Lagoon, Remco, 1979, MIP, $175 to $225.00

Universal Monsters, figure, 8", Dracula, Remco, 1979, MIP, $75 to.. $125.00

Universal Monsters, figure, 8", Frankenstein, Remco, 1979, MIP, $30 to...$50.00

Universal Monsters, figure, 8", Mummy, Remco, 1979, MIP, $30 to...$50.00

Universal Monsters, figure, 8", Phantom of the Opera, Remco, 1979, MIP, $225 to $275.00

Universal Monsters, figure, 8", Wolfman, Remco, 1979, MIP, $125 to.. $150.00

Waltons, accessory, barn or country store, Mego, MIB, ea $100 to.. $150.00

Waltons, accessory, farm house only, Mego, M, $100 to. $125.00

Waltons, accessory, farm house w/6 figures, Mego, MIB, $400 to.. $425.00

Waltons, accessory, truck, Mego, MIB, $65 to $75.00

Waltons, figure set, John Boy & Mary Ellen, Mom & Pop or Grandma & Grandpa, Mego, MIB, ea set $65 to $75.00

Welcome Back, Kotter, figure, 9", Barbarino, Mattel, 1976, MOC, $65 to $75.00

Welcome Back, Kotter, figure, 9", Epstein, Mr Kotter or Washington, Mattel, 1976, MOC, ea $45 to..........................$55.00

Wizard of Oz, accessory, Emerald City (w/7 8" figures), Mego, MIB, $350 to $375.00

Wizard of Oz, accessory, Munchkin Land, Mego, MIB, $250 to $275.00

Wizard of Oz, accessory, Witch's Castle, Mego, MIB, $475 to . $525.00

Wizard of Oz, accessory, Wizard of Oz & His Emerald City (w/8" Wizard figure only), Mego, MIB, $100 to $125.00

Wizard of Oz, figure, 4", Munchkins, any, Mego, MIB, ea $150 to $160.00

Wizard of Oz, figure, 8", any except the Wicked Witch or the Wizard, MIB, ea $40 to $50.00

Wizard of Oz, figure, 8", Wicked Witch, Mego, MIB, $90 to... $115.00

Wizard of Oz, figure, 8", Wizard, Mego, MIB, $250 to.... $275.00

Wonder Woman (TV Series), figure, Nubia or Queen Hippolyte, Mego, M, ea $100 to $125.00

Wonder Woman (TV Series), figure, Steve Trevor, Mego, NRFB, ... $100.00

Wonder Woman (TV Series), figure, Wonder Woman (w/Diana Prince outfit), Mego, M, $200 to $225.00

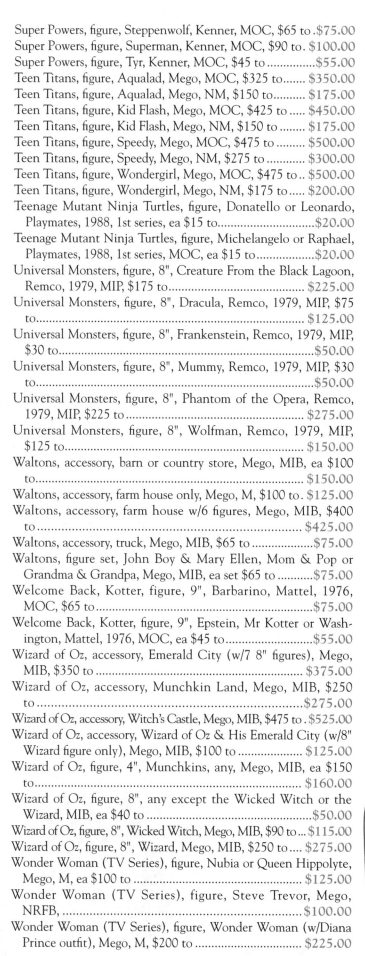

Action Figures and Accessories

Super Powers, figure, Cylcotron, Kenner, MOC, $45.00 to $55.00. (Photo courtesy www. serioustoyz.com)

Action Figures and Accessories

Super Powers, figure, Flash, Kenner, MOC, $20.00 to $25.00. (Photo courtesy www.serioustoyz.com)

Action Figures and Accessories

Super Powers, figure, Martian Manhunter, Kenner, MOC, $40.00 to $50.00. (Photo courtesy www.serioustoyz.com)

Action Figures and Accessories

Super Powers, figure, Wonder Woman, Kenner, MOC, $55.00 to $65.00. (Photo courtesy www.serioustoyz.com)

World's Greatest Super Heroes, or Official World's Greatest Super Heroes, see Super Heroes or Pocket Super Heroes

World's Greatest Super Knights, figure, Black Knight, Mego, MIB, $325 to $375.00

World's Greatest Super Knights, figure, Ivanhoe, Mego, MIB, $225 to $275.00

World's Greatest Super Knights, figure, King Arthur, Mego, MIB, $175 to $225.00

World's Greatest Super Knights, figure, Sir Galahad, Mego, MIB, $275 to $325.00

World's Greatest Super Knights, figure, Sir Lancelot, Mego, MIB, $275 to $325.00

WWF, accessory, Official WWF Monster Ring (Get Ready to Rumble), Jakks, 1996, MIB (sealed), $35 to $45.00

WWF, accessory, Raw is War Monster Ring, Jakks, MIB (sealed), $60 to $70.00

WWF, accessory, Titan Sports Wrestling Stars Sling 'Em Fling 'Em Wrestling Ring, LJN, 1986, EX (P box), $30 to $40.00

WWF, figure, Adam Bomb, Hasbro, 1994, MOC, $15 to .. $20.00

WWF, figure, Akeem, Hasbro, MOC, $35 to $40.00

WWF, figure, All Star Wrestlers Tag Team w/Jimmy Garvin, Precious & Steven Regal, Remco, MOC, $40 to $50.00

WWF, figure, All Star Wrestlers Tag Team w/The Long Riders (Wild Bill Irwin & Scott Hog Irwin), Remco, MOC, $30 to $40.00

WWF, figure, Billy Jack Haynes, LJN, 1985, MOC, $30 to $40.00

WWF, figure, Bret Hart (Superstars #1), Jakks, MOC, $15 to $20.00

WWF, figure, Capt Lou Albano (red lapel), LJN, Series 3, MOC, $25 to $30.00

WWF, figure, Classy Freddie Blassie, LJN, Series 3, MOC, $25 to $30.00

WWF, figure, Crush, Hasbro, 1993, MOC (yel card), $20 to $25.00

WWF, figure, Crush, Hasbro, 1994, MOC (gr card), $45 to .. $50.00

WWF, figure, Diesel (Superstars #3 reissue), Jakks, MOC, $12 to $18.00

WWF, figure, Doink the Clown, Hasbro, 1993, MOC, $8 to .. $10.00

WWF, figure, Dusty Rhodes, Hasbro, MOC, $200 to $225.00

WWF, figure, Greg 'The Hammer' Valentine, Hasbro, 1992, MOC, $15 to $20.00

WWF, figure, Hacksaw Jim Duggan, Hasbro, 1990, MOC, $8 to $10.00

WWF, figure, Hacksaw Jim Duggan, Hasbro, 1993, MOC, $8 to $10.00

WWF, figure, Hacksaw Jim Duggan, Hasbro, 1994, MOC, $8 to $10.00

WWF, figure, Harley Race, LJN, 1985, MOC, $75 to........ $80.00

WWF, figure, Honky Tonk Man, Hasbro, MOC, $20 to.. $25.00

WWF, figure, Hulk Hogan, any except mail-in, Hasbro, MOC, $8 to $12.00

WWF, figure, Hulk Hogan, mail-in, Hasbro, MIP, $45 to.. $55.00

WWF, figure, Hulk Hogan, wht shirt, knee pads & shoes, red shorts, LJN, MOC (bl card), $350 to $375.00

WWF, figure, Hulk Hogan, wht shirt, knee pads & shoes, red trunks, LJN, MOC (blk card), $300 to $325.00

WWF, figure, Hulk Hogan, yel trunks, no shirt, LJN, 1984, MOC (bl card), $75 to $85.00

WWF, figure, Hulk Hogan as Thunderclips, Appleworks, 1985, MOC, $25 to $30.00

WWF, figure, Hulk Hogan vs Big John Studd, 2-pack, LJN, 1985, MOC, $25 to $30.00

WWF, figure, Iron Sheik, LJN, 1985, MOC, $30 to $40.00

WWF, figure, Jake 'The Snake' Roberts, Hasbro, MOC, $8 to... $12.00

WWF, figure, Jesse 'The Body' Ventura, LJN, Series 3, MOC, $20 to $25.00

WWF, figure, Jim 'The Anvil' Neidhart, Hasbro, MOC, $6 to $10.00

WWF, figure, Jimmy 'Superfly' Snuka, Hasbro, 1990, MOC, $10 to $15.00

WWF, figure, Jimmy 'Superfly' Snuka, LJN, 1984, MOC, $80 to $90.00

WWF, figure, Jimmy 'Superfly' Snuka, Rock 'n' Wrestling, LJN, 1985, MOC, $30 to $35.00

WWF, figure, Jimmy Hart (w/no hearts on megaphone), LJN, Series 3, MOC, $25 to $30.00

WWF, figure, King Kong Bundy, LJN, 1985, MOC, $35 to ... $45.00

WWF, figure, Legion of Doom w/Animal & Hawk, Hasbro, 1990, MOC, $15 to $20.00

WWF, figure, Lex Lugar, Hasbro, MOC, $12 to $18.00

WWF, figure, Ludvig Borga, Hasbro, 1994, MOC, $30 to . $35.00

Action Figures and Accessories
• •
Terminator 2, figure, Battle Damage Terminator (or any other character), Kenner, 1992, MOC, each $10.00 to $20.00.

Action Figures and Accessories
• •
Welcome Back, Kotter, figure, 9", Horshack, Mattel, 1976, MOC, $45.00 to $55.00. (Photo courtesy www.whatacharacter.com)

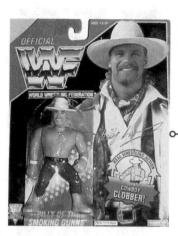

Action Figures and Accessories
• •
WWF, figure, Billy 'Smoking Gunns' Gunn,
Hasbro, 1994, MOC, $15.00 to $20.00.

Action Figures and Accessories
• •
WWF, figures, Big John Studd and Randy
'Macho Man' Savage, LJN, MOC, each
$175.00 to $200.00.

WWF, figure, Luscious Johnny Valiant, LJN, 1985, MOC, $30 to $40.00

WWF, figure, Macho Man, Hasbro, 1990, MOC, $20 to ... $25.00

WWF, figure, Magnificent Maraco, LJN, Series 3, MOC, $25 to $30.00

WWF, figure, Mean Gene Okerlund, LJN, 1985, MOC, $25 to $35.00

WWF, figure, Mr Perfect (w/Perfect Plex), Hasbro, MOC, $20 to $25.00

WWF, figure, New Age Outlaws (2-Tuff #2), Jakks, MOC, $10 to $15.00

WWF, figure, Nikolai Volkoff, LJN, 1985, MOC, $25 to .. $35.00

WWF, figure, Randy Macho Man Savage, w/Macho Masher, Hasbro, MOC, $30 to $35.00

WWF, figure, Ravishing Rick Rude, 'Rude Awakening Headlock' pose, Hasbro, 1990, MOC, $30 to $35.00

WWF, figure, Razor Ramon, Hasbro, MOC (yel or red card), ea $20 to $25.00

WWF, figure, Razor Ramon, Hasbro, 1994, MOC (bl card), $30 to $35.00

WWF, figure, Ricky 'The Dragon' Steamboat, LJN, 1985, MOC, $10 to $15.00

WWF, figure, Rowdy Roddy Piper, Hasbro, MOC, $25 to. $30.00

WWF, figure, Shawn Michaels, Hasbro, 1994, MOC, $10 to ... $15.00

WWF, figure, Sid Justice, Hasbro, MOC, $10 to $15.00

WWF, figure, Tatanka, Hasbro, MOC, $10 to $15.00

WWF, figure, Ted Arcidi, LJN, 1985, MOC, $30 to $40.00

WWF, figure, Ted Dibiase, blk tux w/purple lapels & cummerbun, LJN, 1985, MOC, $50 to $55.00

WWF, figure, Ted Dibiase (Million Dollar Man), in blk tux w/ gold lapels & cummerbun, Hasbro, 1990, MOC, $20 to. $25.00

WWF, figure, Ted Dibiase (Million Dollar Man), in blk wrestling trunks & boots, Hasbro, 1994, MOC, $15 to $20.00

WWF, figure, The Rockers w/Marty Jannetty & Shawn Michaels, Hasbro, 1990, MOC, $20 to $25.00

WWF, figure, The 1-2-3 Kid, Hasbro, 1994, MOC, $35 to .. $40.00

WWF, figure, Typhoon w/Tidal Wave, Hasbro, MOC, $25 to $30.00

WWF, figure, Undertaker (mail-in), Hasbro, MOC, $45 to... $55.00

WWF, figure, Undertaker & Kane (2-Tuff #4), Jakks, MOC, $10 to $15.00

WWF, figure, Undertaker Warrior, w/Graveyard Smash, Hasbro, 1992, MOC, $15 to $20.00

WWF, figure, Undertaker Warrior, w/Warrior Wham, Hasbro, 1992, MOC, $40 to $45.00

WWF, figure, Vince McMann, LJN, Series 5, MOC, $50 to.. $60.00

WWF, figure, Warlord, Hasbro, MOC, $10 to $15.00

WWF, figure, WWF Referee, LJN, 1987, MOC, $35 to $45.00

WWF, figure, Yokozuna, Hasbro, 1994, MOC, $25 to $30.00

Xena Warrior Princess, figure, 6", any character, Toy Biz, 1998, MOC, ea $5 to $10.00

Xena Warrior Princess, figure, 12", any character, Toy Biz, 1998, MOC, ea $18 to $25.00

X-Files, figure, any character except Fireman w/Cryolitter, McFarlane, 1997, MOC, ea $6 to $10.00

X-Files, figure, Fireman w/Cryolitter, McFarlane, 1997, MOC, $12 to $15.00

X-Men/X-Force, figure, Arctic Armor Cable, Avalanche, or Cable Cyborg, Toy Biz, MOC, ea $5 to $10.00

X-Men/X-Force, figure, Black Tom or Bonebraker, Toy Biz, MOC, $10 to $15.00

X-Men/X-Force, figure, Bridge or Brood, Toy Biz, MOC, ea $5 to $10.00

X-Men/X-Force, figure, Cable I, Cable II or Cable III, Toy Biz, MOC, ea $10 to $15.00

X-Men/X-Force, figure, Cable IV, Toy Biz, MOC, $10 to.. $15.00

X-Men/X-Force, figure, Cannonball (pk), Toy Biz, MOC, $10 to $15.00

X-Men/X-Force, figure, Cannonball (purple), Toy Biz, MOC, $5 to $10.00

X-Men/X-Force, figure, Commando, Toy Biz, MOC, $5 to .. $10.00

X-Men/X-Force, figure, Deadpool (1992), Toy Biz, MOC, $12 to $15.00

X-Men/X-Force, figure, Deadpool (1995) or Domino, Toy Biz, MOC, ea $5 to $10.00

X-Men/X-Force, figure, Forearm, Genesis, Gideon or Grizzly, Toy Biz, MOC, ea $5 to $10.00

X-Men/X-Force, figure, Kane I or Kane II, Toy Biz, MOC, ea $5 to $10.00

X-Men/X-Force, figure, Killspree or Killspree II, Toy Biz, MOC, ea $5 to $10.00

X-Men/X-Force, figure, Krule or Kylun, Toy Biz, MOC, ea $5 to $10.00

X-Men/X-Force, figure, Longshot, Mojo, Nimrod, Pyro, Quark, Random, Rictor or Rogue, Toy Biz, MOC, ea $5 to $10.00

X-Men/X-Force, figure, Rogue, Toy Biz, MOC, $24 to $28.00

X-Men/X-Force, figure, Sabretooth I or Sabretooth II, Toy Biz, MOC, ea $5 to $10.00

X-Men/X-Force, figure, Shatterstar I, Shatterstar II or Shatterstar III, Toy Biz, MOC, ea $5 to...$10.00

X-Men/X-Force, figure, Silver Samurai, Slayback, Stryfe or Sunspot, Toy Biz, MOC, ea $5 to..$10.00

X-Men/X-Force, figure, Urban Assault, Warpath I, Warpath II, or X-Treme, Toy Biz, MOC, ea $5 to $10.00

Zorro (Cartoon Series), figure, Captain Ramon or Sgt Gonzoles, Gabriel, MOC, ea $20 to $25.00

Zorro (Cartoon Series), figure, Tempest or Picaro, Gabriel, MOC, ea $50 to $60.00

Zorro (Cartoon Series), figure, Zorro or Amigo, Gabriel, MOC, ea $30 to $35.00

Action Figures and Accessories
• • • • • • • • • • • • • •
X-Men/X-Force, figure, The Blob, Toy Biz, MOC, $10.00 to $15.00.

Activity Sets

Activity sets that were once enjoyed by so many children are finding their way back to some of those same kids, now grown up. The earlier editions in particular carry very respectable price tags when they can be found complete or near complete.

The following listings are for examples that are complete unless noted otherwise.

See also A.C. Gilbert; Character, TV, and Movie Collectibles; Coloring, Activity, and Paint Books; Disney; Playsets; and other specific categories.

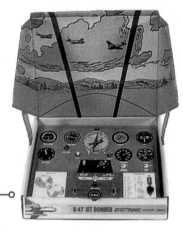

Activity Sets
• • • • • • • • • •
B-47 Jet Bomber Electronic Control Panel, 23x23", NMIB, $175.00.
(Photo courtesy Bertoia Auctions on LiveAuctioneers.com)

Activity Sets
• • • • • • • • • •
Creative Clips, Fisher-Price Arts & Crafts, 1983 – 1984, MOC, $25.00. (Photo courtesy Brad Cassity)

Adam's Magic Set, 1950s, MIB (sealed).......................... $175.00

Barney's Auto Factory Motorized Assembly Line, Remco, 1961, NMIB $175.00

Bill Ding w/Clowns, Strombecker, complete & unused, MIB... $175.00

Casting Race Car Set, Master Caster, 1974, unused, EX+IB...$25.00

Colorforms My House Printer Kit, 1962, EXIB..................$25.00

Colorforms Totem Pole Kit, 1958, NMIB $35.00

Creepy Crawlers, see Thingmaker

Crime Lab, Amsco, 1976, unused, MIB, $40 to $50.00

David Berglas Conjouring Tricks Magic Set, Kay Ltd/London, EXIB, $75 to... $100.00

Design-O-Marx Set, 1960s, scarce, unused, MIB, $40 to...$50.00

Ding-Dong School Finger Paints, Milton Bradley, 1950s, MIB...$25.00

Ding-Dong School Peg-a-Picture, Whitman, 1953, unused, EX+ $25.00

Easy Bake Oven, Kenner, 1960s, NMIB............................$40.00

Etch-A-Sketch, Ohio Art, 1960, 1st issue, unused, MIB, $125 to.. $150.00

Famous Monsters Plaster Casting Kit, Rapco, 1974, complete & unused, MIB, $75 to...................................... $100.00

Fist Faces, Remco, 1966, NMIB, $25 to $30.00

Foto-Fun Printing Set, Fun-Built, 1958, unused, MIB.......$50.00

Hocus-Pocus Magic Set, Adams, 1962, unused, MIB, $65 to $75.00

Hocus-Pocus Magic Set, Adams, 1976, NMIB, $35 to $40.00

Jack Frost Paint Set, Hasbro, 1950s, unused, EXIB............$25.00

Jerry the Magician's Complete Magic Act, 1940s-50s, unused, EX (in photo envelope) $50.00

Joe Thomas' Magic Kit, Cardes Co, 1940, unused, NMIB.$50.00

Johnny Toymaker Car Molding Set, EXIB, $40 to.............$50.00

Thingmaker Mini Dragon Maker Pak, Mattel, 1967, MIB (sealed) $150.00
Tinker Fish, Toy Tinkers, 1927, EXIB $50.00
Tinker Spots, Toy Tinkers, 1930s, EXIB $50.00
Tinkerbeads No 4, Toy Tinkers, 1928, EX (in tin container). $75.00
Trix Stix, Harry Dearly, 1952, MIP $50.00
Vac-U-Form Playset, Mattel, 1962, NMIB $100.00
Voodini Magic Set, Transogram, 1960, NMIB $50.00
Winky Dink Paint Set, Pressman, 1950s, EX $75.00
Wonder Box Magic, Royal, 1954, unused, NMIB $150.00
Wood Doh Modeling Compound, 1959, 'Recommended By Captain Kangaroo' on display box w/3 cans, unused, MIB. ..$40.00
Young Magician's Box of Tricks, Saalfield, 1958, NMIB....$50.00

Junior Doctor Kit, Hansfeld Bros, 1953, NM, $75 to...... $100.00
Kooky Kakes, Mattel, unused, MIB $50.00
Magic Kit of Tricks & Puzzles, Transogram, 1960s, MIB, $65 to $75.00
Magic Set, w/10 tricks, Redhill, 1930s-40s, MIB $50.00
Magic Wand, Porter Chemical, 1928, EXIB $150.00
Magician Magic Set, features Bill Bixby, 1974, NMIB $75.00
Master Magic, Sherms S set, 1930s-40s, EXIB $100.00
Meccano Foundry Kit, 1930s, EXIB (wood box) $400.00
Mighty Men & Monster Makers Set, 1978, EXIB.............. $30.00
Mister Funny Face Clay & Plastic, 1953, EXIB $100.00
Monster Machine, Gabriel, MIB $25.00
Mosaic Paint-by-Number, Transogram, 1960s, NMIB $125.00
Motorized Monster Maker, Topper, 1960s, EXIB $100.00
Mr Magic Art, Adams, 1960s, NMIB $50.00
Mr Potato Head & His Tooty Frooty Friends, Hasbro, 1950, MIB $50.00
Mr Potato Head & Pete the Pepper Set, Hasbro, 1960s, MIB..$30.00
Mr Potato Head In the Parade Set, Hasbro, 1960s, MIB...$35.00
Picture Maker Hot Birds Skyway Scene, Mattel, 1970s, MIB...$75.00
Play Poster Paints, Kenner, 1972, unused, MIB $20.00
Play-Doh Fun Factory, 1960s, rare, MIB $50.00
Playstone Funnies Kasting Kit w/11 Extra Molds, Allied Mfg, 1930s, EX+IB $225.00
Power Mite Work Shop, Ideal, 1969, EXIB..................... $125.00
Power Shop, Mattel, 1960s, NMIB $75.00
Pre-Flight Training Cockpit, Einson, 1942, NMIB............ $50.00
Shaker Maker Pictures, Ideal, MIB.......................... $25.00
Shrunken Head Apple Sculpture, Milton Bradley, 1975, MIB. $75.00
Silly Putty, 1950s, unused, MIP $35.00
Sneaky Pete's Magic Show, Remco #702, 1950s-60s, EXIB ... $85.00
Space Faces, Pressman, 1950s, unused, NMIB $175.00
Space Scientist Drafting Set, 1950s, EXIB.................... $65.00
Starmaster Astronomy Set, Reed, 1950s, EXIB $50.00
Tasket Basket Shape Sorter, Holgate, 1953, NM $35.00
Thingmaker (Triple), Mattel, EXIB $125.00
Thingmaker Featuring Creeple Peeple, Mattel, 1965, MIB. $100.00
Thingmaker Creepy Crawlers, 1st issue, Mattel, 1964, EXIB...$75.00
Thingmaker Creepy Crawlers II, Mattel, 1978, NMIB......$50.00
Thingmaker Fright Factory, Mattel, MIB (sealed) $150.00
Thingmaker Fun Flowers Maker Pak, Mattel, 1966, EXIB .$30.00
Thingmaker Giant Creepy Crawlers Maker Pak #2, Mattel, 1965, EXIB $75.00
Thingmaker Men Set, Mattel, 1965, EXIB $75.00

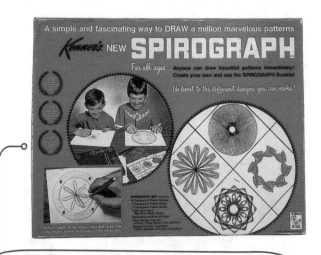

• Advertising •

The assortment of advertising memorabilia geared toward children is vast — plush and cloth dolls, banks, games, puzzles, trucks, radios, watches, and much, much more. And considering the popularity of advertising memorabilia in general, when you add to it the crossover interest from the realm of toys, you have a winning combination! Just remember to check for condition very carefully. Signs of play wear are common. Think twice about investing much money in soiled items like cloth or plush dolls, since stains are often impossible to remove.

For more information we recommend *Cracker Jack Toys* and *Cracker Jack, the Unauthorized Guide to Advertising*, both by Larry White; *Pepsi-Cola Collectibles, Vols. I, II,* and *III*, by Bill Vehling and Michael Hunt; and *Antique & Contemporary Advertising, B.J. Summers' Guide to Coca-Cola,* and *Collectible Soda Pop Memorabilia*, all by B.J. Summers (Collector Books).

Advisor: Larry White, Cracker Jack

See also Buddy L (and other vehicle categories); Character, TV, and Movie Collectibles; Disney; Pin-Back Buttons; Premiums; other specific categories.

A&W Root Beer, bears, bean-stuffed plush, 2 different, 1997-98, M, ea $15 to..$20.00

AC Spark Plugs, figure, AC man w/1 arm extended & other on hip, wht & gr w/AC on chest, gr hat, 6", EXIB........... $150.00

AC Spark Plugs, figure, Sparky the Horse, inflatable vinyl w/ logo, 24x15" L, Ideal, 1960s, EX $100.00

AC Spark Plugs, pull toy, wht horse in wht bathtub on 4 wheels, slush metal, 'Spark Plugs need cleaning too,' 4½", EX ...$45.00

Alka-Seltzer, Speedy figure, vinyl, 5½", 1960s, EX, $250 to.$275.00

Allied Van Lines, doll, gr uniform & hat, 14", Lion Uniform Inc, MIB... $1,200.00

Allied Van Lines, truck, Buddy L, PS, orange & blk tractor w/ van trailer, BRT w/red hubs, 30", prof rstr $750.00

Allied Van Lines, truck, Buddy L, 1941, PS, ride-on, orange & blk, BRT w/red hubs, w/handcart, handle, 29", EX ..$1,800.00

Allied Van Lines, truck, Grimland, metal, orange & blk w/silver trailer top, 7½", NM+IB.. $150.00

Alpo, Dan the Dog w/up figure, walks on his front paws, 3", 1970s, EX+ $12.00

American Stores Co, puzzle, 'Pride of the Plantation,' fr-tray, 15x12", VG $50.00

Arctic Circle Drive-In, Acey figural bank, 6", EX $50.00

Atlas Van-Lines Inc, semi truck, Buddy L, PS, 29", EXIB ...$1,725.00

Aunt Jemima, Breakfast Bear, plush, 13", M....................$175.00

Aunt Jemima, dolls, Aunt Jemima, Diana, Mose & Wade, stuffed printed oilcloth, 9" to 12", 1950s, NM, ea $40 to $50.00

Aunt Jemima, Jr Chef Pancake Set, Argo Industries, 1949, EX... $150.00

Barney's Sandpaper, paper doll set, bear doll w/various outfits, 11x8" uncut sheet, Behr-Manning Co, 1930s, EX+ $25.00

Baskin-Robins, Pinky the Spoon figure, bendable vinyl, 5", 1990, MIP..$10.00

Bazooka Bubble Gum, doll, Bazooka Joe, stuffed print cloth, 19", 1970s, NM, $25 to...$30.00

Betty Crocker, Doll & Bake Set, stuffed print cloth doll w/baking kit, Kenner, 1970s, unused, MIB....................................$25.00

Big Boy, bank, plastic figure wearing red & wht checked overalls, 9", 1970s, NM, $12 to $18.00

Big Boy, comic book, Adventures of Big Boy #1, NM $250.00

Big Boy, comic book, Adventures of Big Boy #2-#5, NM, ea...$50.00

Big Boy, comic book, Adventures of Big Boy #6-#10, NM, ea....$35.00

Big Boy, comic book, Adventures of Big Boy #11-#100, NM, ea... $25.00

Big Boy, comic book, Adventures of Big Boy #101-#250, NM, ea... $10.00

Big Boy, doll, stuffed cloth w/'Big Boy' on wht T-shirt, red & wht overalls, 15", MIP ('Yes, I'm Your Pal' on header).........$25.00

Big Boy, kite, paper w/Big Boy logo, 1960s, M $100.00

Big Boy, kite, paper w/Big Boy logo, 1960s, unused, MIP.. $250.00

Big Boy, nodder figure, 1960s, NM, $20 to......................$25.00

Big Boy, yo-yo, wood w/die-stamp seal, 1960s, M $10.00

Blue Bonnet Margarine, doll, Blue Bonnet Sue, stuffed cloth w/ yel yarn hair, 1980s, NM...$5.00

Borden, baby rattle, Baby Beauregard figure standing in diaper sucking on bottle, hard plastic, 5", 1950s, VG $125.00

Borden, bank, Beauregard, red plastic figure, 5", Irwin, 1950s, EX $65.00

Borden, Elsie's Funbook Cut-Out Toy & Games, 1940s, EX.. $65.00

Borden, Elsie's Good Food Line, punch-out train, cb, 25x27", 1940s, unpunched, M (EX envelope) $150.00

Advertising
A&P Super Markets, Local Delivery Truck, Marx, pressed steel, 19", EX+IB, $600.00.

Advertising
Borden, doll, Elsie the cow, plush with vinyl head, makes 'moo' sound, 12", 1950s, EX, $50.00.

Borden, figure, Elsie, PVC, 3½", M, $10 to $20.00

Borden, figure, Elsie, vinyl, aqua dress w/striped shirt, wht apron, gold felt shoes & bib, 22", EX+ $100.00

Borden, game, Elsie the Cow, Jr Edition, EXIB.............. $125.00

Borden, nightlight, Elsie the Cow head figure, rubber-type compo, 9", NM $175.00

Borden, pull toy, Elsie ('The Cow That Jumped Over the Moon'), wood, 1940s, EX+...$35.00

Borden, push-button puppet, Elsie the Cow, wood, NM.. $150.00

Borden, truck, Keystone #D402, PS, wht w/red Borden's decal, 9", EXIB.. $375.00

Bosco Chocolate, doll, Bosco the Clown, vinyl, EX+........$50.00

Bradford House Restaurants, figure, Bucky Bradford standing on base reading 'It's Yum Yum Time,' vinyl, 9", 1976, EX ...$35.00

Burger Chef, hand puppet, Burger Chef, cloth body & hat w/ vinyl head, 1970s, EX...$10.00

Burger Chef, pillow figure, Burger Chef, stuffed printed cloth, 1970s, EX..$12.00

Burger King, doll, Burger King, stuffed cloth, 16" (1973 or 1977) or 18" (1980), NM, ea...$10.00

Burger King, doll, Magic King, 20", Knickerbocker, 1980, MIB.. $20.00

Burger King, Home of the Whopper Cheeseburger Set, plastic, Multi Toys, 1987, unused, MIB.....................................$15.00

Buster Brown, hobby horse, wood w/pnt advertising as saddle, 28x36", very rare, VG $300.00

Buster Brown, kite, 1940s, NM $40.00

Buster Brown Shoes, airplane, top wing trimotor w/'BB Shoes' decal on top of wing, PS, Steelcraft, 1930, 22" WS, EX...........$2,070.00

Buster Brown Shoes, bank, molded plastic ball shape w/busts of Buster Brown & Tige on top, 1960s, 3½" dia, EX...........$25.00

Buster Brown Shoes, booklet, 'Playing Movies w/Buster Brown,' 1910s-20s, 20 pgs, EX+...$75.00

Buster Brown Shoes, clicker, tin shoe sole form, bl (Blue Ribbon) lettering on yel, VG $20.00

Buster Brown Shoes, paddle ball toy, Froggy the Gremlin graphics on die-cut cb, Ed McConnel, 1940s, EX+ $75.00

Buster Brown Shoes, shoebox w/Treasure Hunt Game on side, 1930s, unused, $50 to...$75.00

Butterfinger Candy Bar, plush, Butterfinger Bear, 15", 1987, M $25.00

Campbell's Soup, book, 'Campbell Kids Have a Party,' Rand McNally/Elf, 1954, EX $12.00

Campbell's Soup, coloring book, 'A Story of Soup,' 1977, EX..$25.00

Campbell's Soup, comic book, 'Captain America & Campbell Kids,' 1980s promo, EX+...$25.00

Campbell's Soup, doll, boy, pirate, 10", Home Shopper, 1995, EX (in soup can box) $80.00

Campbell's Soup, doll, boy & girl, beanbag type in Alphabet Soup outfits, 8", 2001, MIP, ea $12.00

Campbell's Soup, doll, boy & girl, chef outfits, compo w/molded hair, pnt shoes & socks, 12", Horsman, MIB, pr.......... $250.00

Campbell's Soup, doll, boy & girl, farm kids dressed in denim, 7", 2000, MIB, ea...$12.00

Campbell's Soup, doll, boy & girl, Paul Revere & Betsy Ross attire, 10", 1976, M, ea..$50.00

Campbell's Soup, doll, boy & girl, pnt vinyl w/movable heads, 7", Product People, 1970s, NM, pr...................................$50.00

Campbell's Soup, doll, boy & girl, stuffed cloth, 1970s, MIB, pr $75.00

Campbell's Soup, doll, boy or girl, vinyl w/rooted hair, red & wht checked outfits, 1988, special edition, MIP, ea $20.00

Campbell's Soup, doll, chef, 12", M $50.00

Campbell's Soup, doll, girl, cheerleader, vinyl, 1967, 8", EX.. $75.00

Campbell's Soup, doll, girl, rubber & vinyl w/cloth outfit, 8", Ideal, 1955, NM, minimum value $125.00

Campbell's Soup, game, Campbell Kids Shopping Game, Parker Bros, 1955, scarce, NMIB..$65.00

Campbell's Soup, kaleidoscope, replica of soup can, 1981, EX..$40.00

Campbell's Soup, mug, molded plastic Campbell Kid head, 1960s premium, unused, MIB (plain mailer box) $15.00

Campbell's Soup, playset, Campbell Kids Chuck Wagon Set, Amsco Toys, NMIB.. $100.00

Campbell's Soup, semi truck, diecast metal, 'M'm M'm Good!' & Kids perched on crescent moon on trailer, 12½", MIB...$50.00

Campbell's Soup, wristwatch, 4 different, 1980s, MIB, ea.$50.00

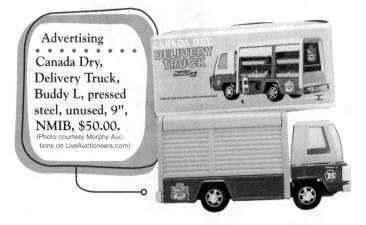

Castile Soap, Paul's Soap Circus ark, paper on wood, hinged roof, 15 prs of animals, 3 figures, 5 singles, 10", EX $150.00

Castoria, Mammy Castoria doll, uncut front/back printed images on oilcloth, 11x14", EX..$85.00

Cheer, doll, Cheer Girl, plastic w/cloth clothes, 10", Procter & Gamble, 1960, NM.....................................$20.00

Cheetos, doll, Chester Cheetah, 18", NM $40.00

Chevron, The Chevron Cars, Freddy 4-Wheeler, unused, MIB $6.00

Chiquita Bananas, doll, stuffed printed cloth, 15", 1975, M .. $20.00

Chuck-E-Cheese, bank, vinyl figure, 7", EX.....................$10.00

Chuck-E-Cheese, doll, plush, 'Show Biz Pizza Time,' 10", 1996, M $10.00

Chuck-E-Cheese, hand puppet, plush, 9", 1992, EX..........$12.00

Coca-Cola, ball & cup, wooden ball on string attached to cup on handle w/Coke advertising, 1960s, NM......................$45.00

Coca-Cola, bang gun, 'G Man'/'It's the Real Thing,' M $20.00

Coca-Cola, bank, can shape w/repeated red & wht diamond design, NM $85.00

Coca-Cola, bank, pig wearing hat, red plastic w/wht 'Drink Coca-Cola'/'Sold Everywhere,' on sides, EX..................$35.00

Coca-Cola, book, 'Freckles & His Friends,' Whitman Better Little Book, 1927 premium, VG+.............................$35.00

Coca-Cola, carousel, metal w/mc Coca-Cola graphics, EX...$50.00

Coca-Cola, cooler & bottle, plastic, 5", 1950s, NM $150.00

Coca-Cola, doll, Buddy Lee dressed as Coca-Cola route driver, 13", 2nd limited edition, 1997-98, M $250.00

Coca-Cola, figure, bear holding Coke bottle, wht plush, 1990s, MIB..$15.00

Coca-Cola, figure, Frozen Coca-Cola mascot, stuffed cloth, 1960s, NM.. $150.00

Coca-Cola, game, Broadsides, Milton Bradley, 1940s-50s, VG+ $150.00

Coca-Cola, game, checkers, metal pegs fit in holes on board w/ wave logo, 1970s, NM+ $75.00

Coca-Cola, game, Double-Six Dominos, brn vinyl case w/Sprite Boy logo, 1970s, EX..$40.00

Coca-Cola, jigsaw puzzle, Teenage Party, NMIB............. $100.00

Coca-Cola, playset, Playtown Luncheonette w/the 'Drink Coca-Cola' logo, Playtown Prod #800, 1940s, unused, NMIB..$275.00

Coca-Cola, truck, Buddy L, plastic, A-frame bed w/screened sides, 2 cases & metal cart, yel, 12", VG...................... $100.00

Coca-Cola, truck, Buddy L, PS, friction, red 'Sign of Good Taste' logo over 2 wht stripes, 8", VG $175.00

Coca-Cola, truck, Buddy L, PS, #5426, yel w/chrome grille, WRT, w/plastic cases & bottles, 15", EX $300.00

Coca-Cola, truck, Les-Paul, Mac cab w/ad header on 2-tiered bed, 22½", NM $400.00

Coca-Cola, truck, Marusan, 1950s, tin, friction, center ad divider, yel w/bl, 4-wheeled, 8", EXIB $1,150.00

Coca-Cola, truck, Marx, plastic, 2-tiered, yel w/red detail, w/ cases, 11", NMIB.. $275.00

Coca-Cola, truck, Marx, PS, #0991, stake truck, yel w/Sprite Boy sign, covered wheels, 20", VG $250.00

Coca-Cola, truck, Marx, PS, stake bed, red & yel, 20½", G+ $275.00

Coca-Cola, truck, Marx, tin, #1088, stake truck, red, yel & bl w/'Take Home Today' sign, 18", EX............................. $500.00

Coca-Cola, truck, Metalcraft, 1930s, PS, A-frame bed, electric lights, orange & yel, 10 bottles, 12", EX+ $1,300.00

Coca-Cola, truck, Metalcraft, 1930s, PS, A-frame bed, simulated lights, orange & yel, 10 bottles, 12", VG $450.00

Coca-Cola, truck, Sanyo, tin, wht, yel & red, BRT, 13", NMIB $375.00

Coca-Cola, truck, Smith-Miller, aluminum Chevy cab w/ open wood sq bed w/metal railed divider, orig wood load, 14", EX $475.00

Coca-Cola, truck, Smith-Miller, aluminum Ford cab w/open wood A-frame bed w/divider, orig wood load, red, 14", VG+ $2,000.00

Coca-Cola, truck, Smith-Miller, 1940s, PS & wood, Ford cabover w/A-frame bed, red, wooden cases, 14", VG+ $2,000.00

Coca-Cola, truck, Smith-Miller, 1950s, PS, GMC cab w/2-tiered bed, red, BRT, cases w/glass bottles, 14", NOS $1,500.00

Coca-Cola, truck, Solido, 1936 Ford pickup, diecast, 1/18 scale, NM $35.00

Coca-Cola, truck, Tipp, 1950s, tin, Volkswagen delivery w/open bay & center ad panel, friction, cases & bottles, 9", EX ..$650.00

Coca-Cola, vehicle, Taiyo, 1950s, tin, Ford Taxi, friction, 9", MIB $400.00

Coca-Cola, vehicle, Taiyo, 1950s, tin, sedan, friction, red & wht, 10½", NMIB $125.00

Coca-Cola, vehicle, Taiyo, 1950s, tin, Volkswagen van bus, EX $225.00

Cocamalt, jigsaw puzzle, 'The Flying Family,' 6½x10", 1932, complete, EX (w/orig envelope) $35.00

Cracker Jack, baseball bat, No 2 wooden child-sz, rare, EX .$50.00

Cracker Jack, charm, boot w/loop on heel, pot metal, 1" L, 1920s, EX $10.00

Cracker Jack, charm, ice skate, pot metal, 1⅛" L, 1920s, EX ... $8.00

Cracker Jack, charm, seahorse, marbleized plastic, 1¹⁵⁄₁₆", 1960s, M $8.00

Cracker Jack, Checkers goat wagon, 1½", EX+ $75.00

Cracker Jack, chenile chicken figure, NM $7.50

Cracker Jack, game, Drawing Made Easy, paper, NM $35.00

Cracker Jack, spinner, 'Keep 'Em Flying,' metal, NM $55.00

Cracker Jack, standup figure, buffalo, plastic, 1⅝" L, 1940s, M .$10.00

Cracker Jack, standup figure, circus elephant w/1 foot on tub, plastic, 1¾", 1950s, M $8.00

Cracker Jack, standup figure, duck, plastic, 2", 1950s, M...$10.00

Cracker Jack, standup figure, Indian chief, plastic, 1", 1950s, M $8.00

Cracker Jack, standup figure, lamb, plastic, 1½", 1950s, M $8.00

Cracker Jack, standup figure, monkey, plastic, 1¾", 1950s, M.. $9.00

Cracker Jack, Toonerville Trolley, litho tin, 2", VG $225.00

Crayola, figure, Crayola Ballerina, plush, 14", Gund, M....$10.00

Crayola, figure, Crayola Bear, plush, 7½", EX $15.00

Cream of Wheat, doll, chef, stuffed cloth, holds printed image of 'Cream of Wheat' bowl, w/apron & hat, 16", 1949, G . $1,000.00

Curél Lotion, doll, Curél Baby, plastic w/jtd arms & legs, 6", 1980, EX $20.00

Curad, bank, The Taped Crusader, plastic, 8", NM $6.00

Curtiss Candies, tandem truck, Buddy L, PS, 2-color cab w/'Baby Ruth' & 'Butterfinger' box trailers, 39", VG............ $1,200.00

Curtiss Candies, van truck, Buddy L, 1949, PS, horizontal 2-color pnt, 'Butterfinger' decal on tall box van, 24", EX $1,200.00

Advertising
Coca-Cola, dispenser, red and white, with four miniature glasses, 1960s, NM, $75.00. (Photo courtesy www.serioustoyz.com)

Advertising
Cracker Jack, Angelus Marshmallow horse-drawn wagon, tin, 2", EX+, $50.00; Angelus Marshmallow truck, tin, 2", EX, $75.00. (Photo courtesy Wm Morford)

Advertising
Cracker Jack, Shadowgraphs, $130.00.
(Photo courtesy Larry White)

Advertising

Curity, Miss Curity doll, dressed in nurse's uniform, 17", NM, with mailing box (Fair box), $100.00. (Photo courtesy Morphy Auctions on LiveAuctioneers.com)

Advertising

Dairy Queen, hand puppet, Curly, white cloth body with pink hands and chest logo, vinyl head, 1950s, NM, $175.00. (Photo courtesy www.gasolinealleyantiques.com)

Advertising

Dairy Queen, doll, Dairy Queen Kid, stuffed cloth, 1974, EX, $20.00.

Advertising

Domino's Pizza, figure, Noid, bendable rubber, 7", 1986, NM, $6.00. (Photo courtesy www.whatachaacter.com)

Dairy Queen, figure, Chips Ahoy Blizzard boy, bendable vinyl, 4¼", M $8.50

Dairy Queen, figure, Marsh Mallo, plush moose, 7", 1980s, EX... $12.00

Dairy Queen, figure, Sweet Nell, plush, 12", 1974, EX......$20.00

Dairy Queen, whistle, plastic ice-cream cone shape, 2", NM.....$5.00

Del Monte, figures, Fluffy Lamb, Lushie Peach or Reddie Tomato figures, plush, 1980s, NM, ea.............................$20.00

Domino's Pizza, figure, Noid, plush, 16", Matchbox Toys, 1987, EX...$12.00

Domino's Pizza, figure, Noid, plush, 19", 1988, MIP..........$20.00

Domino's Pizza, figure, Noid , PVC, boxer, 2¾", 1988, NM+... $5.00

Domino's Pizza, figure, Noid, PVC, sorcerer, 2½", 1980s, MIP...$6.00

Domino's Pizza, game, Noid Ring Toss, Larami, 1989, NRFC ..$10.00

Domino's Pizza, yo-yo, 'Nobody Delivers Faster,' plastic, Humphery, NM+ $5.00

Dots Candy, doll, Dots Candy Baby, beanbag type w/vinyl face & hands, Hasbro, 1970s, MIB $15.00

Douglas Oil Co, figure, Freddy Fast, vinyl, jtd, Dakin, 1976, NM $75.00

Dubble Bubble Bubble Gum, beanie, mc suede w/metal top button, rnd 'Fleers...' logo on front, 1930s, rare, EX+....... $100.00

Dunkin' Donuts, koala bears, plush, 2 different, 4½", EX+, ea...$6.00

Eli's Cheesecake, doll, cloth, holding lg wht cloth fork, 6", EX...$8.00

Energizer Batteries, figure, Energizer Bunny, beanbag type, 7", Creata, 1999, MIP...$15.00

Energizer Batteries, figure, Energizer Bunny, plush, blk & turq rubber flip flops, blk sunglasses, 22", 1990s, MIP............$25.00

Energizer Batteries, flashlight, Energizer Bunny w/movable arms & head, 4", MIP $8.00

Eskimo Pie, doll, stuffed cloth, 15", 1964-74, EX, $15 to ..$20.00

Eveready Batteries, bank, Black Cat, plastic, 1980s, EX+ .$12.00

Fanny Farmer Candies, delivery truck, tin, friction, red & wht, 8", Japan, 1950s, G...$50.00

Fig Newtons, doll, balancing cookie on her head & holding lg cookie in her hand, 4½", Nabisco, 1980s, NM.............$15.00

Firestone, truck, Buddy L, 1953, PS, 'Tire Service,' bl, cream & orange, 24", EX...$1,500.00

Flintstones Vitamins, doll, Fred Flintstone, inflatable vinyl w/ removable plastic clothes, 1970s, M $12.00

Franco-American Spaghetti, hand puppet, King Sauce, cloth body w/vinyl head, 1966, NM...................................... $100.00

Fruit Stripe Gum, figure, Yipes, plush, 15", NM+ $50.00

Funny Face Drink, see also Ramp Walkers category

Funny Face Drink, book, 'How Freckle Face Strawberry Got His Freckles,' Pillsbury, 1965, EX $25.00

Funny Face Drink, masks, die-cut paper images of 6 different characters, Pillsbury, 1960s, unused, M, ea $200 to..... $250.00

Funny Face Drink, pitcher, Goofy Grape, molded plastic, Pillsbury, 10", EX, $65 to $75.00

General Electric, majorette figure, pnt wood bead type, jtd, holds baton, red & wht w/gold trim, 19", EX.......................$450.00

General Mills, Atomic Submarine, plastic, fires torpedoes, 12", made for Cheerios by Ideal, 1958, NM $225.00

General Mills, bank, Twinkles the Elephant, Trix cereal, 1965, MIP $50.00

General Mills, Cocoa Puffs Train, litho tin, w/up, 1959, 12" L, NM $100.00

General Mills, Cocoa Puffs Train Station Tent, 1961, EX...$100.00

General Mills, hand puppet, Champy the Lion, cloth body w/ vinyl head, Wheaties, 1957, EX+ $75.00

General Mills, mask, Count Chocula, plastic, 1970s, NM+ ..$35.00

General Mills, pencil topper, Frankenberry, 1½", NM.......$15.00

General Mills, Wacky Racer, any, 1969, NM, ea $50.00

General Mills, Walky Squawky Talkies, Trix cereal, 1965, MIP..$50.00

Green Giant, bank, Little Sprout figure, compo, plays 'Valley of the Green Giant' song, 8½", EX $50.00

Green Giant, doll, girl, vinyl w/rooted hair, yel & gr dress & hat, corn motif on purse, 17", 1950s, M $40.00

Green Giant, figure, Green Giant w/arms crossed, vinyl, 9", M $100.00

Green Giant, figure, Little Sprout talker, MIP...................$55.00

Green Giant, flashlight, Little Sprout figural handle, gr, M ...$50.00

Green Giant, jump rope, Little Sprout handles, MIP $20.00

Hamburger Helper, figure, Helping Hand, plush, 14", M...$10.00

Hardee's, doll, Gilbert Giddyup, stuffed printed cloth, 1971, EX..$25.00

Harley-Davidson, figure, Harley Hog, 9", M $25.00

Hawaiian Punch, game, Mattel, 1978, NMIB...................$50.00

Hawaiian Punch, doll, Punchy, beanbag type, 10", 1997, MIP...$15.00

Hawaiian Punch, doll, Punchy, plush, 15", 1983, NM........$20.00

Heinz, delivery truck, Metalcraft, PS, wht w/ad decals, electric lights, BRT, 12", EX $325.00

Heinz, delivery truck, Metalcraft, PS, wht w/ad decals, electric lights, BRT, 12", G $150.00

Heinz, doll, Heinz Baby, squeeze vinyl, 9", Hungerford, 1950s, NRFP (poly bag w/header card) $175.00

Heinz, H-57 Rocket Blaster, w/instructions, MIB............$15.00

Heinz, talking alarm clock, plastic, rnd base, 10x6", 1980s, NM $125.00

Hershey's, bank, Hershey Bar, red plastic candy bar vending machine, 6", Felsenthal & Sons, EX+IB....................$75.00

Hershey's, figure, Hershey's Bear in sweater, plush, 7", NM.$8.00

Hobo Joe Restaurants, bank, Hobo Joe figure on rnd base w/ name, NM+ $75.00

Hobo Joe Restaurants, figure, Hobo Joe, vinyl w/cloth outfit, complete w/dog & newspaper, 9", Dakin, NM+ $150.00

Hoover, coloring book, clown w/sweeper on cover, 1960s, partially colored, EX..$25.00

Hush Puppies, plush dog, 10", Presents, 1980s, NM $15.00

Icee, bank, Icee Bear figure, vinyl, 8", 1970s, EX $20.00

IGA, Express HO Scale Electric Train Set, complete, 1997, MIB..$85.00

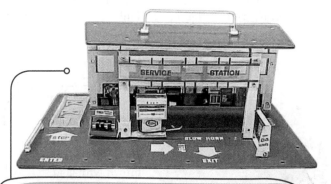

Advertising

Esso, gas station, pressed steel and Masonite, 1960s, 12x17x18", NM, $50.00. (Photo courtesy www.gasolinealleyantiques.com)

Advertising

Funny Face Drink, mugs, various character faces painted on plastic, Pillsbury, 3", M (in mailer box), each $30.00. (Photo courtesy www.gasolinealleyantiques.com)

Advertising

Franco-American Spaghetti, hand puppet, Dragon, cloth body with vinyl head, 1966, NM, $120.00. (Photo courtesy www.gasolinealleyantiques.com)

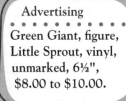

Advertising

Green Giant, figure, Little Sprout, vinyl, unmarked, 6½", $8.00 to $10.00.

Advertising

Hot Point, hand puppet, cloth body with logo on chest, vinyl head, 1950s, EX+, scarce, $250.00. (Photo courtesy www.gasolinealleyantiques.com)

Advertising

Hush Puppies, 26 Secret Password Decoder, 1968 premium, M, $25.00. (Photo courtesy www.gasolinealleyantiques.com)

Jell-O, hand puppet, Mr Wiggle, red vinyl, 1966, M $125.00

Jet Ball Sneakers, Super Space Ring, plastic, 1950s, unassembled, MIP...$75.00

KC Pistons, nodder figure, plastic, NM $200.00

Keebler, bank, Ernie, ceramic, 10", M.............................$50.00

Keebler, doll, Ernie, cloth beanbag type, 5", EX+ $6.00

Keebler, doll, Ernie, vinyl, 7", 1970s, NM.........................$25.00

Keebler, mug, Ernie, plastic figure, 3", NM $10.00

Kellogg's, Battery Powered Electric Train, 1957-59, MIP.. $100.00

Kellogg's, canteen, yel plastic w/Pop! decal, 5½" dia, Rice Krispies, 1973, NM...$12.00

Kellogg's, Color Magic Cards, Rice Krispies, 1930s, complete & unused, EX+ (EX+ envelope) $50.00

Kellogg's, Crater Critters, 8 different, 1968-72, M, ea $35.00

Kellogg's, hand puppets, Snap! Crackle! & Pop!, cloth bodies w/ vinyl heads, Rice Krispies, 1940s, EX, ea......................$75.00

Kellogg's, jigsaw puzzle, 'Keep Going With...,' shows child throwing baseball, 8x6", 1930s, NM $65.00

Kellogg's, Pep Model Warplanes, any in series, unpunched, 1940s, M, ea...$30.00

Kellogg's, Story Book of Games #1, Sambo, Cinderella, Three Little Pigs, etc, 1950s, VG $55.00

Kellogg's, Superman Satellite Launcher, 1956, M.............$40.00

Kentucky Fried Chicken, bank, Colonel Sanders figure w/cane, sm rnd base, 12½", Starling Plastics, 1965, EX+.............$30.00

Kentucky Fried Chicken, coloring book, Favorite Chicken Stores, 1960s, EX...$25.00

Kentucky Fried Chicken, hand puppet, Colonel Sanders, plastic, 1960s, EX...$20.00

Kentucky Fried Chicken, mask, Colonel Sanders, molded plastic, 1960s, NM...$55.00

Kentucky Fried Chicken, nodder, Colonel Sanders, 'Kentucky Fried Chicken' on base, 7½", pnt compo, 1980s, EX......$65.00

Kentucky Fried Chicken, nodder, Colonel Sanders figure holding a bucket of chicken & cane, plastic, 7", NM.................$12.00

Kentucky Fried Chicken, figure, Wacky Wobbler, PVC Colonel Shanders, MIB..$20.00

Knoor Soup, doll set, hard plastic, dressed in costumes from various countries, Best Foods, 1963-64, M............................$15.00

Kool-Aid, bank, mascot pitcher standing on base, hard plastic, mechanical actions, 7", 1970s, NM.............................$50.00

Kool-Aid, figure, Kool-Aid man w/barbells, PVC, 2", EX ...$4.00

Kraft, figures, Cheesasaurus Rex in various sporting poses, PVC, 1990s, M, ea..$10.00

Kraft, pull toy, Kraft TV Theater cameraman seated on rolling camera base, plastic, Velveeta premium, 1950s, EX $100.00

Kraft, wristwatch, Macaroni & Cheese, 1980s, M $10.00

Lee Jeans, doll, Buddy Lee as train engineer in Lee overalls, bl shirt & bl & wht striped hat, 13", EX $150.00

Lee Jeans, doll, girl, stuffed denim w/various yarn hair styles, EX+...$40.00

Lifesavers, bank, cb & metal cylinder w/Lifesavers graphics, 12", 1960s, EX...$20.00

Little Caesar's Pizza, doll, Pizza Pizza man holding slice of pizza, plush, 1990, EX...$5.00

Little Debbie, doll, vinyl w/cloth dress & straw hat, 11", 1980s, NM...$75.00

Log Cabin Syrup, pull toy, Log Cabin Express, NMIB... $900.00

M&M Candy, peanut figure, bendable arms & legs, 7", M, ea $15.00

Advertising

Jewel Tea, delivery truck, pressed steel, brown with gold advertising, 10", 1940s, EX, $35.00. (Photo courtesy Randy Inman Auctions)

MOTHER GOOSE

Advertising

Kellogg's, Mother Goose booklet, Rice Krispies, illustrated by Vernon Grant, 16 pages, 1935, EX, $25.00. (Photo courtesy www.gasolinealleyantiques.com)

M&M Candy, peanut figure, cloth beanbag type, golfer or witch, 6", M, ea $10.00

M&M Candy, plain figure, cloth beanbag type, various colors, M, ea $5.00

M&M Candy, plain figure, plush, 4½", M $5.00

M&M Candy, plain figure, plush, 8", M $8.00

M&M Candy, plain figure, plush, 12", M $10.00

M&M Candy, plain figure, plush, 48" from fingertip to fingertip, NM $75.00

M&M Candy, plain figure dressed as bride, 36", EX $40.00

Maypo Oat Cereal, bank figure, Marky Maypo, plastic, 1960s, EX $100.00

McDonald's, bank, Grimace, ceramic, purple w/pnt features, 9", 1985, NM $20.00

McDonald's, bank, Grimace, compo, 1985, NM................$15.00

McDonald's, bank, Ronald McDonald bust, plastic, Taiwan, 1993, EX $40.00

McDonald's, bop bag, Grimace, inflatable vinyl, name in blk across front, 9", 1978, MIP..$12.00

McDonald's, dish set, plate, bowl & cup w/character scenes, Plastic Manufacturing, 1991, NM+....................................$25.00

McDonald's, doll, Fry Girl, stuffed cloth, 4", 1987, M $5.00

McDonald's, doll, Fry Girl, stuffed cloth, 12", 1987, NM ..$10.00

McDonald's, doll, Fry Guy, stuffed cloth, 12", 1987, NM ..$12.00

McDonald's, doll, Grimace, plush w/plastic eyes, 8", M $10.00

McDonald's, doll, Hamburglar, cloth w/purple stripes, 15", early 1970s, NM $20.00

McDonald's, doll, Hamburglar, cloth w/vinyl head & hat, cloth cape, blk stripes, 11", 1980s, NM+ $20.00

McDonald's, doll, Ronald McDonald, cloth, raised arm, 13", 1987, NM $20.00

McDonald's, doll, Ronald McDonald, cloth w/plastic head, yarn hair, real lace shoes, 15", Dakin, 1991, M......................$15.00

McDonald's, doll, Ronald McDonald, stuffed body w/plastic head, hands & shoes, yarn hair, sm Grimace in pocket, 20", M..$50.00

McDonald's, doll, Ronald McDonald, vinyl w/cloth costume, 7", Remco, 1976, MIB $30.00

McDonald's, game, McDonald's, Milton Bradley, 1975, MIB ..$25.00

McDonald's, game, Playland Funburst, Parker Bros, 1984, MIB $20.00

McDonald's, hand puppet, Ronald or Grimace, cloth bodies w/ vinyl heads, 1993, MIB, ea..$45.00

McDonald's, playset, McDonaldland, Remco, 1976, MIB ..$125.00

McDonald's, puzzle, fr-tray, shows Ronald performing magic tricks in front of audience, Golden #4552A, 1984, NM+ $30.00

Minneapolis Garments, paper doll set, 'Miss Minneapolis,' 4 different seasons, 7x11", 1930s, uncut, EX+, ea..................$25.00

Naugahyde, Nauga Monster, red Naugahyde w/yel felt features, 10", 1960s, EX $125.00

Naugahyde, Nauga Monster, tan Naugahyde w/tan felt features, 10", 1970s, VG $40.00

New Haven Animated Character Watches, die-cut cb stand-up, A Oakley/D Tracy/G Autry images, 12x9", 1950s, no watches, VG $125.00

Old Dutch Cleanser, pull toy, Dutch Cleanser girl w/moving head & arms on base emb 'Old Dutch,' Hubley, 1932, NM. $8,000.00

Oscar Mayer, Weinermobile, plastic, 5x10", later version, EX.$25.00

Advertising

Kraft, delivery truck, Smith-Miller, pressed steel, 1950s, 14", EX, $200.00. (Photo courtesy Randy Inman Auctions)

Advertising

M&M Candy, dispensers, red plain and yellow peanut, large, 1991, M, each, $15.00. (Photo courtesy Bill and Pat Poe)

Advertising

McDonald's, doll, Ronald McDonald, stuffed printed cloth, two different versions, 17", Chase Bag Co., 1970s, EX, each, $20.00. (Photo courtesy Gary Henriques and Audre DuVall)

Advertising

McDonald's, hand puppet, Hamburglar, 1993, MIB, $45.00. (Photo courtesy www.gasolinealleyantiques.com)

Oscar Mayer, Wienermobile, plush, 14x33", EX+ $25.00
Pepsi-Cola, pull toy, bear pushing 5¢ Hot Dog car w/bell & Pepsi-Cola umbrella, wood, 9", Fisher-Price, 1940s, EX $200.00
Pepsi-Cola, truck, Marx, plastic, open bay w/6 cases of bottles, VGIB $175.00
Phillips '66, Power Yacht Set, plastic, b/o, box serves as gas station dock, 18", 1966, unused, MIB $300.00
Planters Peanuts, Mr Peanut Carousel Truck, plastic, 4" L, Acme Plastics, 1950s, NM $300.00
Planters Peanuts, Mr Peanut Jet Racer, plastic, 2x5" L, Elmar Toy Co, 1950s, NMIB $250.00
Planters Peanuts, Mr Peanut Train Set, plastic, 4½" L, Elmar Toy Co, 1950s, EX+ $150.00
Planters Peanuts, Mr Peanut Vendor, plastic, 5x6" L, 1950s, NMIB $400.00
Planters Peanuts, Mr Peanut Walking Man, plastic w/up figure, 8", NMIB $250.00
Plymouth Road Runner, puzzle, fr-tray, bl Plymouth Road Runner & Road Runner cartoon character on wht, 10x14", c 1967, EX $100.00
Pop-Rite Popcorn, doll, stuffed print cloth, 12", VG $15.00
Pure Oil Co, tanker truck, Metalcraft, 1930s, dk bl w/NP grille, electric headlights, skirted wheel wells, 15", G $500.00
RCA, doll, Radiotron Man, pnt wood bead-type w/chest banner, 16", Maxfield Parris design, 1920s, VG $450.00
Reddy Kilowatt, nodder, cowboy outfit, 6½", 1960s, EX+ ... $200.00
Robin Hood Shoes, spinner top, tin w/wooden shaft, 1½" dia, NM+ $50.00
Sambo's Restaurant, tiger, plush w/'Sambo's' lettered diagonally across chest, 7", Dakin, 1970s, EX $25.00
Seven Day Coffee, doll ad, shows 4 different mail-in ready-to-stuff nursery rhyme characters, 9x11", Arbuckle Bros, EX $32.00

Seven-Up, doll, Fresh-Up Freddie, pnt squeeze vinyl, 9", 1959, NM $235.00

Shell, stake truck, Metalcraft, PS, red w/yel stake bed, BRT, 4 oil cans & cart, 12", G+ $200.00

Shell, tank truck, Buddy L, 1938, PS, ride-on w/handle, red & orange, 30", rare, VG+ $5,000.00

Shell, tank truck, Buddy L, PS, yel w/yel & red diagonal pnt on hood, BRT w/red hubs, 20", rstr $450.00

Shell, truck, Buddy L, PS, yel w/red 'Shell' on sides, open curved back, covered wheels, 13", w/3" oil can bank, EX $325.00

Sunshine Biscuits, stake truck, Metalcraft, PS, red & bl, NP grille, 12", VG+ $200.00

Texaco, tanker truck, Buddy L, 1950s, PS, cab w/tank trailer, red w/wht lettering, 24", EX $225.00

Texaco, tanker truck, Buddy L, 1958, PS, red w/'Texaco' lettered on sides of tank, 1-pc, 8-wheeled, EX $75.00

Western Auto, semi truck, Marx, 1960s, PS, red cab w/silver trailer, 'Family Store & Catalog Order Center,' 24", VG $115.00

Wrigley's Gum, truck, Buddy L, 1934, PS, electric lights, gr, BRT w/red hubs, 'Spearmint' ads, 23", EX $5,175.00

Wrigley's Gum, truck, Buddy L, 1938, PS, International cab, 'Railway Express Agency,' gr & yel, 'Spearmint' ads, 25", EX $1,800.00

Advertising
USDA Forest Service, figure, Smokey Bear, Dakin, 1970s, 8", NMT, $30.00. (Photo courtesy www.whatacharacter.com)

Advertising
Sinclair, tank truck, pressed steel, professionally restored, 17", $500.00. (Photo courtesy Randy Inman Auctions)

Advertising
Spaghetti-O's, bowl, ceramic, 8½" diameter, MIB, $25.00. (Photo courtesy www.gasolineantiques.com)

Advertising
USDA Forest Service, doll, Smokey Bear, plush, Knickerbocker, 1972, 6½", MIB, $55.00. (Photo courtesy www.whatacharacter.com)

Advertising
Texaco, tanker ship, battery-operated, plastic, 27", EX+IB (box reads Exclusive Texaco Dealer Offer), $450.00. (Photo courtesy Morphy Auctions on LiveAuctioneers.com)

Advertising
Wrigley's Spearmint Gum, toy semi-truck, Corgi, trailer designed as gum pack, MIB, $75.00. (Photo courtesy Vectis Co. on LiveAuctioneers.com)

• • • • • • • • • • • • • • Advertising Signs, Ads, and Displays • • • • • • • • • • • •

Advertising Signs, Ads, and Displays
• •
Arcade Cast Iron Toys, lithographed tin sign, depicts kids looking at toy display, 12x14", 1931, M, $200.00. (Photo courtesy Arneson Auction Service on LiveAuctioneers.com)

Comic Book Heroes Stickers/Bubble Gum, display box w/36 sealed packs of bubble gum w/stickers, Tops, 1974, EX+IB $200.00

Davy Crockett Badges, display card w/12 diecast badges, orange w/red lettering, 11x10", G+ $100.00

Davy Crockett Iron-on Emblems, display card, complete w/3 rows of 4¾" dia emblems (33 total), 16x12" card, NM $150.00

Dennis the Menace Flashlights, cb display card w/10 of 12 'key chain' flashlights, shows Dennis shining light, NM $500.00

Dinky Toys, counter display sign, 'Your Best Choice...Always Something New!,' black & red on orange, 10x15", G+ .$75.00

Dinky Toys, die-cut cb stand-up sign, illustrated boy shouting & pointing to 'Dinky Toys' lettering, about 8x15", NM.. $215.00

Dinky Toys, window sign, 'No 133 1965 Ford Cortina,' mc graphics on wht paper, unused gummed corners, 6x9½", NM+ $60.00

Advertising Signs, Ads, and Displays
• •
Duncan Jeweled Professional Yo-Yo Tops 69¢, display box with die-cut header, complete with 12 yo-yo tops, NM, $2,250.00. (Photo courtesy Morphy Auctions on LiveAuctioneers.com)

Advertising Signs, Ads, and Displays
• •
Creamsicle (Buck Rogers for), paper sign, 8x20", 1930, EX, $1,100.00. (Photo courtesy Morphy Auctions on LiveAuctioneers.com)

American Flyer Lines, lighted sign, red, wht & bl shield above 'Trains & Accessories Sold Here' in bl on wht, 12x9", NM+ $50.00

Bat Masterson Twirling Canes, die-cut cb display w/image of Gene Barry, complete w/NM 12 canes, EX display box $675.00

Batman's TV Sweepstakes, ad, Procter & Gamble, 1966, 14x11", NM $55.00

Batman Wallets, die-cut cb sign w/lettering over logo, Standard Plastic/Mattel/NPP, 1960s, fits on rack, 6x16", EX $75.00

Best of Walt Disney Comics 1934 to 1952 (A Golden Special), cb display box w/24 reissue books from 1974, EX+ $325.00

Build-A-Set Fast Freight Complete $1.00, die-cut cb display, 25" wide, M (NOS) $100.00

Advertising Signs, Ads, and Displays
• •
Ingersoll Mickey Mouse Watches, 3-D cardboard stand-up, features Mickey serenading Minnie with banjo, 15x11", EX, $800.00.

Erector, magazine ad, 'Boys! Look at all the Spectacular Buzz-With-Action Models..., features Superman, 9x6", 1948, VG $8.50

Funny Frostys Club (Join the/Ask Us!), die-cut cb stand-up display of Sandy (Orphan Annie's dog) w/sign, 30x15", 1930s, VG $550.00

Gabby Hayes Prospector's Hat Only 75¢/Quaker Puffed Wheat Puffed Rice, store sign, 1950s, NM $200.00

Gabby Hayes Western Gun Collection, cb folder display w/ complete set of 6 guns, premiums for Quaker, 1951, 7x12", EX $125.00

Gene Autry World's Greatest Cowboy & Champion World's Wonder Horse, die-cut cb stand-up, 59x31", EX $400.00

Guns by Hubley, blk metal hook rack w/litho tin header sign, no guns, 1950s-60s, 17x23x7", EX $100.00

Howdy Doody Keychain Puzzles, display card w/11 plastic Howdy Doody keychain puzzle figures, 12x8", NM...............$100.00

Ingersoll (The New) Aero Wrist Watch $3.25/Always on Time, cb die-cut sign, features Mickey Mouse & lg watch, 37x50", EX $675.00

Ingersoll Presents Walt Disney Double Feature, paper sign, 12x18", EX..$115.00

Ingersoll Sterling Silver Rings, die-cut cb display w/9 Mickey Mouse & Donald Duck rings, 'Latest Attraction...' VG ..$115.00

Krazy Kat Balloons, cb tri-fold display w/assortment of balloons featuring Krazy Kat, Ashland Rubber, 1950s, 14" T, EX.$50.00

Lionel Commando Assault Train, cb display, tan 'windshield' shape w/battlefield graphics & closeup insets, EX $30.00

Lionel Trains, magazine ad, 'Two Majestic New Diesels featured by Lionel Trains,' text/graphics, blk/wht, 9x6", 1948, VG...$8.00

PEZ, display, molded plastic head image of Peter PEZ the clown holding Pilot PEZ, 2-sided, fits rack, 18", 1960s, EX+. $150.00

Rin-Tin-Tin Cavalry Rifle Pen, full-color newspaper ad from Nabisco Shredded Wheat, 6½x13", 1956, EX $25.00

Roy Rogers Cowboy Flashlights, die-cut cb display w/5 flashlights, EX $800.00

Roy Rogers Straight Shooter Gun Puzzle Key Chains, cb display card w/2 gun key chains, EX $75.00

Sgt Preston's 10 in 1 Trail Kit, full color newspaper ad promoting Quaker cereal premium, 1958, NM+ $25.00

Squirt, paper litho sign, '18" Squirt Doll for $2.95...$5.95 Value!,' 10x21", 1962, M..$50.00

Steiff, peacock store display, 35" L, EX.......................$275.00

Superhero Finger Puppets, display box w/8 ea of 4 characters, Hulk, Thor, Spider-Man, Capt America, Imperial, 1978, EX+ $200.00

Superman Wallets, cb display w/5 vinyl wallets (holds 12), 19x17", Standard Plastic Prod, 1966, M wallets/VG+ display...$350.00

Thundercaps, cb display box w/die-cut header, Magic/Marxie/ Super Sound Caps, Marx, 1950s, 12x4x25" L, VG $50.00

Tom Mix Records 'Now Available'/'Straightshooters...Everyone's Favorite!,' red, wht & bl paper banner, M $200.00

Tootsietoy, w/up Lincoln Zepher & Roamer trailer on cb display, 9x13", NM...$3,250.00

Winchester Roller Skates, magazine ad, 'Strength! Speed!,' boy on skates, w/text, blk & wht, 8x5", 1923, EX..................$8.00

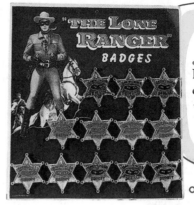

Advertising Signs, Ads, and Displays
Lone Ranger Badges, cardboard display card with badges, 11", NM+, $250.00. (Photo courtesy Morphy Auctions on LiveAuctioneers.com)

Advertising Signs, Ads, and Displays
Matchbox, display case with five cars and boxes, NM, $225.00. (Photo courtesy Morphy Auctions on Live Auctioneers.com)

Advertising Signs, Ads, and Displays
Meccano, working counter display with AC transformer mounted on back, shows man in car, 11x12", 1930s, EX, $550.00.

Advertising Signs, Ads, and Displays
Tasty Food Limited, cardboard sign with free toy train offer, metal engine and three cars, 1920s, VG, $630.00.
(Photo courtesy Morphy Auctions on LiveAuctioneers.com)

• Aeronautical •

Toy manufacturers seemed to take the cautious approach toward testing the waters with aeronautical toys, and it was well into the second decade of the twentieth century before some of the European toy makers took the initiative. The earlier models were bulky and basically inert, but by the 1950s Japanese manufacturers were turning out battery-operated replicas with wonderful details that advanced with whirling motors and flashing lights.

See also Battery-Operated Toys; Cast Iron, Airplanes; Gasoline-Powered Toys; Model Kits; Pull and Push Toys; Robots and Space Toys; Windup, Friction, and Other Mechanical Toys.

AA NC-2100 Airliner (American Airlines), Marx, PS, 4 props, 27½" WS, VG $365.00

AF Lines Air Service Top Wing #555, American Flyer, PS, rubber tires, orange & bl, 19" WS, NM $3,000.00

Air Canada DC-9, Japan, tin, friction, w/'T' tail, 16" WS, EX+ $250.00

Air France Super G Constellation, Jostra, tin, friction, 4 props, 20" WS, VG+ $475.00

Airmail Monocoupo (Top Wing), Girard, w/up, tin, disk wheels, w/pilot, VG $165.00

Airways Express World Tours, tin, 13" WS, VG $150.00

American Airlines DC-7 Flagship Allison, Linemar, tin, friction, 4 props, 18½" WS, VG+ $175.00

American Airlines Electra N305AA, Linemar, tin, b/o, 4 props turn 1 at a time, 20" WS, NMIB $850.00

American Airlines Jet-Powered Electra Flagship (Lockheed L-188), Linemar, 1958, 4 props, flashing lights, 20" WS, EX $150.00

American Airlines Lockheed Electra, Yonezawa, tin/plastic, b/o, 4 props, 15" WS, NMIB $225.00

American Airlines Lockheed Electra II, Nomura, tin/plastic, b/o, 4 props, 16½" WS, EX+ $150.00

American Airlines NC-2100 Flagship, Marx, ca 1950, silver, 4 props, wooden wheels, 28" WS, EX $300.00

American Airlines Twin Engine Passenger Plane, Haji, tin/plastic, b/o, 15" WS, NMIB $125.00

American DC 10, Hong Kong, tin/plastic, friction, 13" WS, EXIB $100.00

American Eagle Navy Fighter, Hubley, diecast metal, folding wings, single prop, 10" WS, NMIB $100.00

Army Scout NX-107 ('Little Jim' Top Wing), Murray Mfg, ca 1929, PS, single prop, 22" WS, VG $475.00

Army Scout Plane, Steelcraft, 1930s, PS, trimotor, 22½" WS, VG $275.00

B-45, Bandai, tin, friction, pilot lithoed on cockpit, advances w/ both props turning, 6" WS, NMIB $175.00

Beechcraft Baron 3400, Masudaya, tin, r/c, twin engine, 2 figures under clear dome, 16" WS, NMIB $150.00

Beechcraft F50ND (Duke), Joustra, tin, friction, 15½" WS, NMIB $125.00

Beechcraft N1607N, Nomura, tin, friction, single engine, 13" WS, NMIB $100.00

Bell Airacuda XFM, Hubley, diecast metal, rear-mount props, 10" WS, VG $600.00

Biplane, early, PS, friction, tapering cylinder fuselage w/flat nose, orange w/gr tail, bull's-eye decals, 14", VG $425.00

Biplane, PS, friction, extra-long fuselage, single prop, MDW, w/ pilot, 15" L, VG $425.00

Biplane, PS, friction, prop on flat-end nose, orange w/bull's-eye insignias on top wing, removable gr tail wing, 14", VG ... $425.00

Bleriot, Germany, 1905, tin, w/up, pilot seated above wings, yel & orange, 5½" L, VG+ $550.00

Aeronautical
• • • • • • • • • • • • • •
Air Mail NX77 Biplane, American National, pressed steel, swastika symbols on top wing, 24" wingspan, EX, $9,775.00. (Photo courtesy Morphy Auctions)

Aeronautical
• • • • • • • • • • • • • •
Army Scout Plane, Steelcraft, 1930s, pressed steel, 'Buster Brown Shoes' decal on top of wing, trimotor, gray and red, 22½" wingspan, EX, $2,070.00. (Photo courtesy Morphy Auctions)

Aeronautical
• • • • • • • • • • • • • •
American Airlines DC-7C Flagship California, Yonezawa, 1950s, tin, four props, flashing lights, moving figures, 24" wingspan, EX+, $790.00. (Photo courtesy www.serioustoyz.com)

Blue Bird B-753 Anphibious Air Plane, Suzuki & Edwards, tin, friction, 13" WS, NMIB $300.00

BOAC Skycruiser, Marx (Hong Kong), tin, r/c, 4 props, 7½" WS, EX+IB $125.00

Boeing 377 Stratocruiser, Wyandotte, 1940s, PS, chrome w/red tail, 4 props, wooden wheels, 13" WS, NM $75.00

Boeing 727, Masudaya, tin/plastic, b/o, 16" WS, EX+IB . $175.00

Bomber, Marx, litho tin, w/up, 4 props, camo pattern, 18" WS, EX $250.00

Bomber TC-1029, Tippco, litho tin top wing, w/up, 14" WS, EX $1,000.00

Bristol Bulldog T360 Top Wing, Suzuki & Edwards, tin, b/o, single prop, 14" WS, NMIB $175.00

Capital Airlines Boeing 377 Strato Clipper, Linemar, tin, r/c, 14" WS, EX+ $125.00

Cessna N0210 Top Wing, tin, friction, single prop, 21" WS, EX $150.00

Cessna Skymaster NI705Z, Cragstan, 1950s, friction, front/rear single props, dbl tail, 11½" WS, NMIB $150.00

Cessna 180 N7570A Top Wing, Yoshida, friction, single engine, lithoed pilot, 12" WS, NMIB $125.00

Cessna 310L N6717X, Nomura, tin & plastic, friction, lithoed windows, 25" WS, NMIB $450.00

China Clipper, Wyandotte, PS, wooden wheels, decal reads 'China Clipper,' wht w/red top wing, 13" WS, EX $225.00

China Clipper, Wyandotte, PS, wooden wheels, decals read 'PAA China Clipper,' 13" WS, NMIB $475.00

Comet DH-106, Masudaya, tin, friction, 9" WS, EXIB .. $150.00

Convair 880 Jetliner, Marusan, 1960, tin, friction, 13" WS, NM $135.00

Curtiss Jenny Trainer HK-47, S&E, tin, friction, 15" WS, EX (Poor box) $100.00

Curtiss Jenny Trainer N-X-388, S&E, tin, friction, 15" WS, NM+IB $175.00

Defense Bomber, Wyandotte, PS, 2 props, 13" WS, EX . $175.00

Dirigible, see also Zeppelin

Dirigible G-FAAW/R 107, Japan, prewar, w/up, red, wht & bl tin, 6½" L, VG $225.00

Douglas Sea Plane, CK/Japan, w/up, litho tin, 3 props, 14" WS, VG+ $3,080.00

Empire Express Top Wing, tin, 18" WS, VG $150.00

F-ANNY Passenger Plane, Joustra, litho tin, w/up, electric light, 4 props, 20½" WS, EX+ $500.00

F-80, Cragstan, tin, friction, 7" WS, NMIB $175.00

Flying Fort B177, wood, collapsible wings, 4 props, 24" WS, VG $100.00

Flying Tiger Line, Nomura, tin/plastic, b/o, 4 props, 14" WS, NMIB $300.00

Folding Wing Jet, Hubley, diecast metal, retractable wheels, EXIB (7x6" box) $165.00

German Fighter Plane, Lehmann, gr w/German swastika on tail, 5½" WS, EXIB $875.00

Giant Flyer Top Wing, Strauss, ca 1925, PS, single engine, 19" WS, VG $285.00

Girard Mechanical Toys Top Wing Monocoupe, Marx/Girard, tin, w/up, pilot in open cockpit, 12" L, EXIB (box reads Wood's) $575.00

GRAF Zeppelin, see Zeppelin (GRAF)

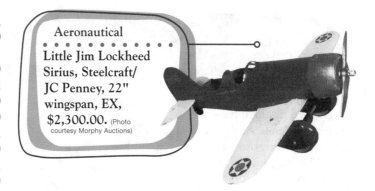

HK 542 Air Liner, Germany/US Zone, tin, w/up, 4 props, 10" WS, EX $125.00

HUKI 10-3 Stratoliner, Huki/Germany, tin, friction, 8", MIB. $950.00

Imperial Airways G-AALB Top Wing Trimotor, Tri-ang, beige w/ red wing, NP props, 24" WS, EX $2,185.00

Japanese Fighter Sea Plane E14-12, Yonezawa, litho tin, wi/up key atop cockpit, w/pontoons, 12" WS, EX+ $600.00

Japanese Zero Fighter, Leadworks Inc, ca 1987, tin, nonpowered, gr camo w/Japanese emblems, 15" WS, MIB $85.00

KLM Royal Dutch Airlines Multi Action Electra Jet, TN, 1960s, 4 props, 16½" WS, NMIB $100.00

Little Jim, see also NX-271 Trimotor Top Wing

Mailplane, Strauss, w/up, tin, 10" WS, EX+ $400.00

Monocoupe, see Army Scout NX-107, NX-271 Trimotor Top Wing

Monocoupe, Wyandotte, gr fuselage w/orange wings, NP wheels & prop, 18" WS, VG $140.00

NASA Space Shuttle Challenger/Flying Jet Plane #905, Taiwan, b/o, tin/plastic, Challenger atop plane, 13" WS, MIB. $175.00

Navy Aqua Plane, Linemar, tin, r/c, single prop, w/pontoons, 13" WS, EX $475.00

Navy Fighter, Hubley Kiddie Toy, diecast metal, folding wings, retractable wheels, 6½" L, EX+IB $200.00

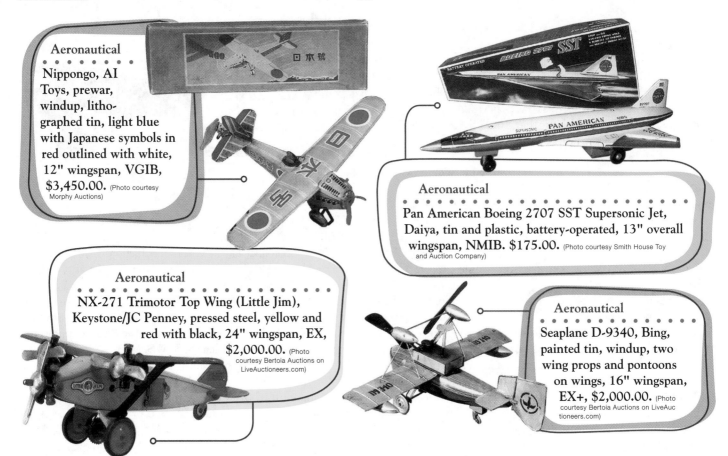

Aeronautical

Nippongo, AI Toys, prewar, windup, lithographed tin, light blue with Japanese symbols in red outlined with white, 12" wingspan, VGIB, $3,450.00. (Photo courtesy Morphy Auctions)

Aeronautical

Pan American Boeing 2707 SST Supersonic Jet, Daiya, tin and plastic, battery-operated, 13" overall wingspan, NMIB. $175.00. (Photo courtesy Smith House Toy and Auction Company)

Aeronautical

NX-271 Trimotor Top Wing (Little Jim), Keystone/JC Penney, pressed steel, yellow and red with black, 24" wingspan, EX, $2,000.00. (Photo courtesy Bertoia Auctions on LiveAuctioneers.com)

Aeronautical

Seaplane D-9340, Bing, painted tin, windup, two wing props and pontoons on wings, 16" wingspan, EX+, $2,000.00. (Photo courtesy Bertoia Auctions on LiveAuctioneers.com)

Navy Fighter (P-47?), Bandai, tin, friction, single engine, dk bl, clear dome cockpit w/pilot, 14" WS, NM+IB $1,250.00

Navy Grumman Cougar F9F-8 Fighter, Sankei, tin, r/c, fold-up wings, 10½" WS, EX $225.00

Navy Grumman Panther F9F-5, Yonezawa, tin, friction, fold-up wings, 6 missiles, 12" WS, NM $400.00

Navy Jet Launching Station, Linemar, tin, friction, jet launches & fires missiles, 9½" L, EX... $1,300.00

Northwest Airlines DC-7, Asahitoy, tin, friction, 4 props, 19" WS, VGIB... $500.00

Northwest Boeing 377 Stratocruiser, Alps, tin, friction, 4 props, 14" WS, NMIB.. $850.00

Northwest DC-7C, Marx, tin/plastic, b/o, 4 props, 14" WS, NM+IB... $175.00

NX-110 Top Wing, Steelcraft, trimotor, gray w/red wing & tail, star decals on wing tips, red props, 22½" WS, VG+.... $700.00

NX-269 Trimotor Top Wing (Keystone Air Mail), Keystone, 1930s, PS, yel & red, 24" WS, VG $900.00

NX-4542 Ford Trimotor Top Wing, Nomura, tin, friction, 15" WS, NM+IB... $550.00

P-35 Bomber, Marx, PS, twin props, 15½" WS, VG....... $100.00

P-35 Fighter, Marx, PS, single prop, 13½" WS, VG $85.00

P-40 Fighter, Hubley, diecast metal, twin NP props, dbl tail, 12½" WS, VG $400.00

P-51 Mustang, HTC, tin, friction, single prop, 10" WS, VG+ ..$100.00

P-51 Yoshiya, tin, friction, single prop, 6½" WS, NMIB. $150.00

Pan American Boeing 377 Strato Clipper, Alps, tin, friction, 14" WS, NMIB $750.00

Pan American Boeing 707 Jet Clipper America, Linemar, 1960s, tin, b/o, 4 light-up engines, 18" WS, VG $100.00

Pan American Boeing 707, Yonezawa, tin, b/o, 18" WS, NM+IB.. $400.00

Pan American Boeing 747, tin & plastic, b/o, 13" WS, NMIB...$125.00

Pan American China Clipper, Wyandotte, PS, 4 props, 13" WS, VG $100.00

Pan American DC-8 Clipper Meteor, Yonezawa, 1950s, tin, b/o, 4 light-up engines, 18" WS, VG+.............................. $100.00

Pan American N774PA, Marx #1678, ca 1952, PS, 27½" WS, unused, MIB $1,090.00

Pan American World Airways N-1401 Strato Clipper, Momoya, friction, 11" WS, EX+IB $200.00

Pan American World Airways Passenger Plane, Marx, PS, 4 props, 28" WS, VG+ $150.00

Piper Cherokee JA3567, Nomura, tin, friction, single engine, red, wht & bl, 13" WS, EXIB.................................... $125.00

Rescue Helicopter (Electric Pylon), Tri-ang, b/o, yel plastic, 7½" L, EX..$50.00

Seaplane (Spirit of Liberty), Liberty, 1929, wood, w/up, 22" L, VG $900.00

Seaplane F260, JEP, 1930s, tin w/compo pilot, w/up, wht flying duck emblem, 19" WS, VG............................... $2,000.00

Sikorsky-Type Plane, Wyandotte, PS, twin props, 9" WS, EX. $115.00

Skycruiser 700 (Four-Motored Transport), Marx, tin, friction, 18" WS, EX $200.00

Skycruiser 700 (Two-Motored Transport), Marx, tin, friction, 18" WS, EXIB... $275.00

Small Gee Bee (Top Wing), Asakusa, tin, w/up, w/Pegasus logo, 6" WS, VG+ $100.00

SNM T9172 Spitfire, Lincoln Int'l, tin, friction, single prop, yel/gr camo, red/wht/bl bull's-eye emblems, 10" WS, NMIB... $200.00

Sonic Jet Plane, Marx, plastic, friction, 10" WS, NM+IB...$200.00

Spirit of St Louis N-X-211 Top Wing, HTC, tin, friction, 12" WS, EXIB................$325.00

Stratocruiser, Wyandotte, PS, 4 NP props, wooden wheels, 13" W, VG................$225.00

Super Main Liner DC-4, Wyandotte, PS, 3-tail model w/4 props, 13" WS, G................$100.00

Tiger X-15 Top Wing, Usagiya, tin, friction, 7½" WS, NM+IB................$100.00

Tip Top Giant Flyer (Top Wing), PS, single prop, 20" WS, EX................$275.00

Top Wing, see also N-X4542 Ford Trimotor Top Wing

Top Wing, see also NX-110 Top Wing; NX-269 Trimotor Top Wing; NX-271 Trimotor Top Wing

Top Wing Monocoupe, Kingsbury, 1930s, PS, w/up, BRT, 18" WS, EX................$175.00

Top Wing Monocoupe, Turner, PS, wht w/red wing, MDW, 20" WS, G................$200.00

Top Wing Monocoupe F255, JEP, litho tin, w/up, striped wing w/ number & 2 bull's-eye emblems, 19" WS, VG............$900.00

Top Wing Monocoupe 574, Distler, w/up, litho tin, yel & blk, 2 disk wheels w/wht tires & red hubs, 5" L, EX................$375.00

Torpedo Bomber, 1950s, PS, single prop, wooden wheels, 13" WS, EX................$140.00

Transport Plane, Wyandotte, PS, 4 props, 13" WS, EX .. $100.00

Transport Plane, Wyandotte, PS/tin, nonpowered, twin props, 13" WS, EX $100.00

Transport Plane (aka Army Airacuda), Wyandotte, 1940s, PS, nonpowered, twin props, 9" WS, EX+ $125.00

TWA Boeing 707, Marx, tin/plastic, b/o, 14" WS, NMIB ...$100.00

TWA Boeing 707, Yonezawa, tin/plastic, b/o, 17" WS, EXIB.. $200.00

Twin-Seat Single Engine, Steelcraft, PS, 17" WS, EX.... $400.00

United Airlines N71025 DC-7, Cragstan, 1950s, tin, friction, 4 props, 8½", EX+ $225.00

United Boeing 737, Nomura, tin/plastic, b/o, 13" WS, NMIB..$125.00

United DC-7 (4-Motor Airplane), Linemar, tin, friction, silver w/red, wht & bl trim, 12½" WS, EX+IB................$275.00

United DC-7C, Yonezawa, tin, b/o, 4 props, wht & gray w/bl & red trim, 23" WS, VG+ $325.00

United DC-8, Yonezawa, tin, friction, 13" WS, EXIB.... $100.00

US Army Bomber, Marx, tin, w/up, army gr w/red, wht & bl star emblems, yel & blk trim on nose, 18" WS, NM $125.00

US Mail Plane NX130, Steelcraft, PS, 22" WS, VG $350.00

USAF BK 252, ET/Japan, litho tin, friction, 4 props, turrets on fuselage, 19" WS, VG $250.00

USAF Boeing B-50 Superfortress, Yonezawa, tin, friction, 4 props, 19" WS, VG+ $575.00

USAF Convair B-36 Bomber, Yonezawa, tin, friction, 26" WS, EX+ $1,500.00

USAF F-9F Fighter Jet, M, tin, friction, 6" WS, NMIB . $125.00

USAF F-47 Thunderbolt, HTC, tin, friction, single prop, 10" WS, NMIB $250.00

USAF Lockheed Hercules Transport Plane, Masudaya, tin, friction, 4 props, EXIB $1,350.00

USAF Lockheed C-5A Galaxy, Nomura, tin/plastic, b/o, 15" WS, NMIB $175.00

USAF X-15 Jet, Masuya, 1959, tin, friction, wht w/blk & red detail, 9½" L, EX $72.00

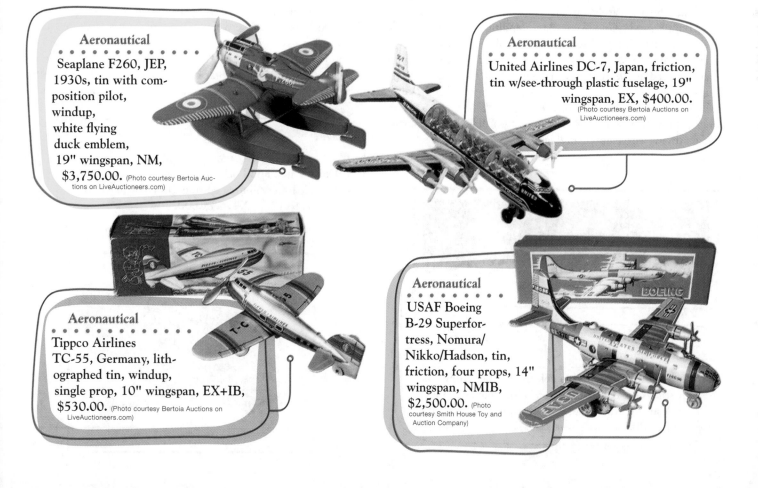

Aeronautical
Seaplane F260, JEP, 1930s, tin with composition pilot, windup, white flying duck emblem, 19" wingspan, NM, $3,750.00. (Photo courtesy Bertoia Auctions on LiveAuctioneers.com)

Aeronautical
United Airlines DC-7, Japan, friction, tin w/see-through plastic fuselage, 19" wingspan, EX, $400.00. (Photo courtesy Bertoia Auctions on LiveAuctioneers.com)

Aeronautical
Tippco Airlines TC-55, Germany, lithographed tin, windup, single prop, 10" wingspan, EX+IB, $530.00. (Photo courtesy Bertoia Auctions on LiveAuctioneers.com)

Aeronautical
USAF Boeing B-29 Superfortress, Nomura/Nikko/Hadson, tin, friction, four props, 14" wingspan, NMIB, $2,500.00. (Photo courtesy Smith House Toy and Auction Company)

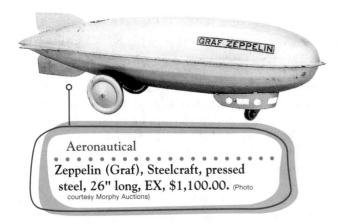

Victory Biplane, Eagle Mfg, 1919, pnt tin, 5x5", EX+ $600.00
Wings Top Wing, tin, w/up, yel w/red detail, 16" WS, VG.$1,200.00
Zeppelin, see also Dirigible
Zeppelin, Steelcraft, PS, wht w/blk eagle decals, BRT w/red hubs, 25" L, some overpnt $1,450.00
Zeppelin (Los Angeles), Strauss, w/up, tin w/celluloid prop, 9½" L, G.. $200.00
Zeppelin (Macon), Steelcraft, PS, electric headlight, wht, 25", VG $1,200.00
Zeppelin R-101, Japan, prewar, w/up, tin w/celluloid props, 11" L, EX.. $850.00

Animation Cels

Some toy enthusiasts enjoy collecting character animation cels to complement their collections. Prior to the 1950s, these works of art were made of a celluloid material, thus the name 'cel.' Along with the original production cels, we have included some of the more recent sericels and limited editions, which are highly collectible in their own right. Although we have only listed animation cels, background sketches, model sheets, storyboards, and preliminary sketches are also sought after by collectors. The following listings are from recent auctions.

Bambi, cel/Courvoisier bkgrd, Bambi's mother looking back at Bambi in forest w/rays of light, Disney, 1942, 5x6", EX+ $1,265.00
Black Cauldron, prod cel/no bkgrd, Tara & the Horned King, Disney, 1985, 11x14", NM $250.00
Bugs Bunny, prod cel/bkgrd, Bugs in tux on stage addressing audience, sgn Friz Freleng/Warner Bros, fr, 10x12", EX $250.00
Bugs Bunny, prod cel/bkgrd, Bugs on knees by lg tree trunk in forest, 10x16", Warner Bros, EX $50.00
Bugs Bunny, prod cel/no bkgrd, Bugs standing w/red book in hand looking back, Warner Bros, 7½x9½" (visible), VG $115.00
Bugs Bunny, prod cel/no bkgrd, half-figure of Bugs leaning w/finger pointed up, Warner Bros, 10½x12½", NM............. $115.00
Bugs Bunny & Yosemite Sam, prod cel/bkgrd, '1001 Rabbit Tales,' interior confrontation scene, fr, 9x12", EX....... $200.00
Bugs Bunny & Yosemite Sam, sericel, from 'High Diving Sam,' Sam diving into empty barrel, ed of 750, vertical, EX. $325.00

Cinderella, prod cel, half-figure of smiling Fairy Godmother looking up against yel bkgrd, Disney, 1950s, EX+ $460.00
Clarabelle Cow & Two of Donald Duck's Nephews, prod cel/no bkgrd, Disney, 1950s, fr, 8x10" (visible), NM.............. $200.00
Crusader Rabbit, pnt cel/no bkgrd, Crusader Rabbit on prancing horse w/bl blanket, Jay Ward, fr, 7x9" (visible), NM .. $575.00
Daffy Duck, prod cel, Daffy seated at lg computer, sgn Chuck Jones, Warner Bros 1994 TV special, fr, 9½x12", EX .. $170.00
Daffy Duck, prod cel/bkgrd, Daffy appearing to be floating among stacks & bags of money & gold, Warner Bros, 10x16", EX .$115.00
Donald Duck, prod cel/no bkgrd, Donald in wide stance looking downward w/mean expression, Disney, 1940s, 11½x8", EX+ $400.00

Elmer Fudd, prod cel, profile view of Elmer high-stepping, sgn Chuck Jones, Warner Bros, 1980, 4x6", EX $115.00

Fantasia, cel setup/Courvoisier bkgrd, Dewdrop Fairy on floating leaf, Disney, 1940s, 5x6", EX $1,955.00

Fantasia, prod cel/Courvoisier bkgrd, Cupid chasing Pegasus against rainbow background, Disney, 1940s, 8x7", NM $1,735.00

Fantasia, prod cel/no bkgrd, Centaurette looking back & holding lg leaf over her head, Disney, 1940s, 8x7", EX $460.00

Fantasia, prod cel/no bkgrd, 2 prs of thistle & orchid Russian dancers, Disney, 1940s, 8x12", VG $315.00

Jiminy Cricket, prod cel/no bkgrd, lg colorful figure w/look of surprise, Disney, 1950s, fr, 8x11" (visible), G $145.00

Lady & the Tramp, prod cel/no bkgrd, Lady in wide stance looking up, Disney, fr, 8x11" (visible), NM $630.00

Little Mermaid, prod cel/no bkgrd, half-figures of Ariel & Prince Eric facing each other, Disney, fr, 9x11" (visible), NM.. $865.00

Little Mermaid, 3-cel setup/print bkgrd, Ariel & Sebastian in throne room, Disney, fr, 10x12½" (visible), NM $4,600.00

Little Mermaid, 5-cel setup/bkgrd, Ariel in water w/Scuttle perched on her leg, w/rocks, Disney, fr, 10x14" (visible), NM $4,600.00

Marvin the Martian, prod cel/no bkgrd, White Monster holding Marvin in his left hand, Warner Bros, 1950s, 10x12", NM $85.00

Mickey Mouse & Pluto, prod cel/no bkgrd, Mickey & Pluto eyeing something, Disney, 1950s, 10⅛x12½", NM $288.00

Mickey Mouse Club, prod cel/bkgrd, Bandleader Mickey on trampoline held by 4 bears, Disney, 1955, fr, 11x14", EX $690.00

Nine to Five, cel setup/pnt bkgrd, features characters in courtyard, 20th Century Fox, fr, 11x15" (visible), NM $300.00

Pink Panther, cel setup, PP & Inspector Clouseau at doorway w/'Editing' above, De Patie-Freleng, 9x11" (visible), NM.. $85.00

Pink Panther, cel/bkgrd, Inspector Clouseau in interior scene scene w/open door, DePatatie-Freleng, 10x14", EX $140.00

Pinocchio, prod cel/Courvoisier bkgrd, Jiminy Cricket meets seahorse in seaweed, Disney, 1940, 10x9", NM $4,025.00

Porky Pig, prod cel, from 'A Connecticut Rabbit in King Arthur's Court,' Porky in castle hall, Warner Bros, 11x15", EX...$85.00

Sheriff Hoot Kloot & Dracula, prod cel/bkgrd, pr in western scene w/mountains, sgn Friz Freleng, 10x13", EX...........$85.00

Simpsons, prod cel/no bkgrd, 'Bart the General,' scruffy looking Bart, Klasky Csupo/Gracie Films, 1990, 11x13", M $175.00

Sleeping Beauty, cel setup/laser bkgrd, Aurora talking to owl in forest, Disney, fr, 12x10" (visible), NM $2,185.00

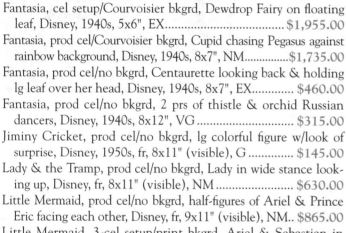

Sleeping Beauty, cel setup/print bkgrd, Flora & Merryweather in peasant garb, Disney, 1959, fr, 8x10" (visible), NM $400.00

Sleeping Beauty, cel/custom print bkgrd, Maleficent as dragon at cliff's edge against yel sky, Disney, 1959, 10x13", EX.. $2,070.00

Sleeping Beauty, prod cel/no bkgrd, Flora changing from red to bl during magic flight, Disney, 1959, 6x9", EX $288.00

Taz & Speedy Gonzales, prod cel, from 'Daffy Duck's Fantaxtic Island,' sgn Friz Freleng, Warner Bros, fr, 9x12", EX ... $230.00

Tom & Jerry, prod cel/no bkgrd, Tom as 1 of the 'Two Musketeers,' MGM, 1952, 11x16", EX $60.00

Who Framed Roger Rabbit?, cell/bkgrd, Jessica (in color) & Eddie Valient (blk & wht), Disney, 10x15", NM $230.00

Woody Woodpecker, prod cel/pnt bkgrd, 'Woodpecker in the Rough,' Walter Lantz, 1952, 11x13", M $115.00

Yellow Submarine, prod cel/no bkgrd, John, inside the submarine, EX... $400.00

Yellow Submarine, prod cels (2)/no bkgrd, Dancing Girls, EX $300.00

Yellow Submarine, prod cel,/no bkgrd, Captain Fred, EX..$400.00
Yellow Submarine, prod cel/no bkgrd, Paul, EX.............$550.00
Yellow Submarine, prod cel/no bkgrd, Ringo, EX $85.00
Yellow Submarine, prod cel/bkgrd, Ringo running from behind piano, bkgrd from 'Hey Bulldog' sequence, EX............$300.00
Yellow Submarine, prod cel/no bkgrd, Blue Meanie, trimmed.$400.00

Animation Cels

Superman, sericel, 'Clark Kent's Secret Secret,' Clark transforms into Superman, one of 350, 1997, framed 23x40", $725.00. (Photo courtesy www.serioustoyz.com)

Animation Cels

Yogi Bear, sericel, 'Do or Diet,' one of 2,500, 1996, framed 19x17", M, $235.00. (Photo courtesy www.serioustoyz.com)

• • • • • • • • • • • • • • • Banks • • • • • • • • • • • • • • •

The impact of condition on the value of a bank cannot be overrated. Cast-iron banks in near-mint condition with very little paint wear and all original parts are seldom found and may bring twice as much (if the bank is especially rare, up to five times as much) as one in average, very good original condition with no restoration and no repairs. Overpainting and replacement parts (even screws) have a very negative effect on value. Mechanicals dominate the market, and some of the hard-to-find banks in outstanding, near-mint condition may exceed $20,000.00! (Here's a few examples: Girl Skipping Rope, Calamity, and Mikado.) Modern mechanical banks are also collectible and include Book of Knowledge and James D. Capron banks, which are reproductions with full inscriptions stating that the piece is a replica of the original. Still banks are widely collected as well, with more than 3,000 varieties having been documented. Beware of unmarked modern reproductions. All of the banks listed are cast iron unless noted otherwise.

The following listings were compiled from various auction sources. Dan Iannotti provided the listings for the modern mechanical banks; he is listed in the Directory.

For more information we recommend *The Dictionary of Still Banks* by Long and Pitman; *The Penny Bank Book* by Moore; *The Bank Book* by Norman; and *Penny Lane* by Davidson. For information on porcelain and ceramic banks we recommend *Collector's Guide to Banks* by Beverly and Jim Mangus and *Ceramic Coin Banks* by Tom and Loretta Stoddard.

See also Advertising; Battery-Operated Toys; Character, TV, and Movie Collectibles; Chein; Disney; other specific categories.

Key:
B of K — Book of Knowledge   JH — John Harper   SH — Shepard Hardware
J&ES — J&E Stevens   K&R — Kyser & Rex

MECHANICAL

Acrobat, J&ES, EX $2,875.00
Artillery Bank, B of K, NM $125.00
Artilley Bank, J&ES, pnt version, rnd trap, EX $725.00
Artillery Bank, SH, Confederate or Union soldier, EX, ea....$875.00
Atlas Bank, VG+ $1,250.00
Bad Accident, J&ES, G $1,000.00
Bad Accident, J&ES, VG+ $2,100.00
Bad Accident (Upside-Down Lettering), J&ES, EX+ .$2,585.00
Bill E Grin, J&ES, EX+ $2,250.00

Bill E Grin, J&ES, VG+ $1,500.00
Bird on Roof, J&ES...$1,950.00
Boy & Bulldog, Judd, VG $650.00
Boy on Trapeze, B of K, NM $150.00
Boy on Trapeze, J Barton & Smith, EX $4,000.00
Boy on Trapeze, J Barton & Smith, NM $6,000.00
Boy on Trapeze, J Barton & Smith, VG $1,700.00
Boy Scout Camp, J&ES, VG $2,750.00
Boy Stealing Watermelon, K&R, EX $6,325.00

Banks, Mechanical
Boy Scout Camp, J & E Stevens, EX, $6,600.00.

Banks, Mechanical
Chief Big Moon, J & E Stevens, EX, $2,575.00. (Photo courtesy James D. Julia, Inc.)

Banks, Mechanical
Bread Winner's Bank, J & E Stevens, EX+, $33,350.00. (Photo courtesy James D. Julia, Inc.)

Banks, Mechanical
Chimpanzee Bank, Kyser & Rex, EX, $3,750.00. (Photo courtesy Morphy Auctions on LiveAuctioneers.com)

Banks, Mechanical
Calamity, J & E Stevens, NM, $29,000.00. (Photo courtesy James D. Julia, Inc.)

Banks, Mechanical
Circus Bank, Shepard Hardware, NM, $100,800.00. (Photo courtesy Morphy Auctions on LiveAuctioneers.com)

Boy Stealing Watermelon, K&R, VG (2nd casting) $500.00
Bull Dog Bank, J&ES, EX...$1,135.00
Bull Dog Bank, J&ES, G..$450.00
Bull Dog Bank, J&ES, VG+ $750.00
Butting Buffalo, B of K, NM $125.00
Butting Buffalo, K&R, EX+...$38,500.00
Butting Goat, Judd, EX...$2,300.00
Cabin Bank, J&ES, G...$250.00
Cabin Bank, J&ES, VG..$625.00
Calamity, J&ES, EX..$12,000.00
Cat & Mouse (Cat Balancing), B of K, NM $150.00
Cat & Mouse (Cat Balancing), J&ES, EX $2,700.00
Cat & Mouse (Cat Balancing), J&ES, NM $8,950.00
Circus Bank, SH, G..$4,000.00
Clown (Black Face), litho tin, EX....................................$485.00
Clown on Globe, James Capron, NM $350.00
Clown on Globe, J&ES, EX+...$4,300.00
Clown on Globe, J&ES, G...$1,300.00
Creedmor, B of K, M...$170.00
Creedmor, J&ES, EX+...$1,500.00

Creedmor, J&ES, VG $450.00
Creedmor, Starkie's, aluminum, VG................................$200.00
Dapper Dan, Marx, litho tin, EX+IB.............................$2,875.00
Darktown Battery, J&ES, EX...$3,800.00
Darktown Battery, J&ES, G..$1,200.00
Dentist, B of K, EX...$125.00
Dentist, J&ES, VG...$4,300.00
Dinah, JH, EX...$850.00
Dinah, JH, VG..$630.00
Dog on Turntable, Judd, EX..$1,800.00
Dog on Turntable, Judd, rare pnt version, NM+ $3,750.00
Dog Tray Bank 1880, K&R, EX......................................$7,000.00
Eagle & Eaglets, B of K, M $175.00
Eagle & Eaglets, J&ES, EX+...$1,400.00
Eagle & Eaglets, J&ES, VG..$750.00
Elephant (Three Stars), unknown mfg, EX....................$500.00
Elephant & Three Clowns, J&ES, VG $900.00
Elephant w/Howdah (Locked), Gurney, later version w/1 tree
    stump, EX+...$1,900.00

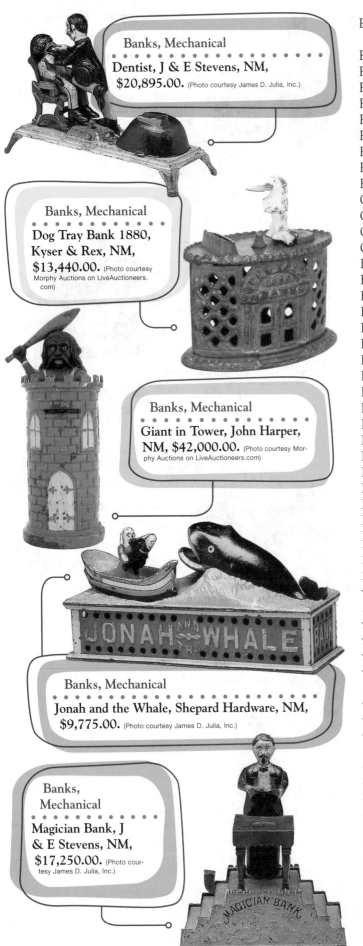

Banks, Mechanical
Dentist, J & E Stevens, NM, $20,895.00. (Photo courtesy James D. Julia, Inc.)

Banks, Mechanical
Dog Tray Bank 1880, Kyser & Rex, NM, $13,440.00. (Photo courtesy Morphy Auctions on LiveAuctioneers. com)

Banks, Mechanical
Giant in Tower, John Harper, NM, $42,000.00. (Photo courtesy Morphy Auctions on LiveAuctioneers.com)

Banks, Mechanical
Jonah and the Whale, Shepard Hardware, NM, $9,775.00. (Photo courtesy James D. Julia, Inc.)

Banks, Mechanical
Magician Bank, J & E Stevens, NM, $17,250.00. (Photo courtesy James D. Julia, Inc.)

Elephant w/Howdah (Man Pops Out), Enterprise, Mfg, VG	$315.00
Elephant w/Howdah (Pull Tail), Hubley, VG	$275.00
Fidelity Trust Savings Bank, Barton Smith, rpnt	$285.00
Football Bank, JH, NM	$11,000.00
Freedman's Bureau, wood, VG	$230.00
Frog Bank (Two Frogs), J&ES, VG	$750.00
Frog on Rock, Kilgore, NM+	$1,300.00
Frog on Rock, Kilgore, VG	$375.00
Frog on Round (Lattice) Base, J&ES, VG	$800.00
Frog on Round Base, J&ES, VG	$500.00
Gem, Judd, G	$650.00
Girl Skipping Rope, J&ES, EX	$18,400.00
Girl Skipping Rope, J&ES, VG	$13,225.00
Globe Savings Bank, Enterprise Mfg, EX	$2,185.00
Hall's Excelsior, J&ES, VG+	$650.00
Hall's Lilliput Bank, J&ES, VG	$460.00
Hen & Chick, J&ES, EX	$2,070.00
Hold the Fort (5 Holes), EX+	$860.00
Home Bank (No Dormers), J&ES, VG	$1,380.00
Hoop-La, JH, G	$600.00
Horse Race (Flanged Base), J&ES, VG+	$6,325.00
Horse Race (Straight Base), J&ES, NM+	$19,550.00
Humpty Dumpty, B of K, M	$125.00
Humpty Dumpty, SH, VG	$300.00
I Always Did 'Spise a Mule, B of K, NM	$145.00
I Always Did 'Spise a Mule (Boy on Bench), J&ES, VG	$900.00
I Always Did 'Spise a Mule (Jockey), J&ES, VG	$850.00
Independence Tower, Enterprise Mfg, VG	$575.00
Indian Shooting Bear, B of K, M	$195.00
Indian Shooting Bear, J&ES, G	$600.00
Indian Shooting Bear, J&ES, NM	$4,885.00
Indian Shooting Bear, J&ES, VG	$1,300.00
Initiating Bank (1st Degree), Novelty Works, NM	$62,100.00
Initiating Bank (2nd Degree), Novelty Works, EX+	$12,650.00
Jolly 'N,' Greece, aluminum, moving eyes, jtd arm, rectangular base, VG	$550.00
Jolly 'N,' J&ES, G	$285.00
Jolly 'N,' JH, top hat, eyes move, EX	$670.00
Jolly 'N,' JH, top hat, eyes move, VG	$400.00
Jolly 'N,' SH, moving eyes, fixed ears, jtd arm, brn face w/red lips & wht teeth, red shirt w/blk tie, VG+	$300.00
Jolly 'N,' Sydenham & Mcoustra/England, G	$285.00
Jolly 'N,' Starkie's, aluminum, VG	$150.00
Jolly 'N,' Starkie's, CI, moving eyes, fixed ears, jtd arm, blk face w/pk lips & wht teeth, blk top hat, red shirt, VG	$400.00
Jolly 'N,' Urlwin/New Zealand, aluminum, gr shirt, EX	$430.00
Jonah & the Whale, B of K, M	$135.00
Jonah & the Whale, SH, EX	$2,130.00
Jumbo (on Wheels), VG+	$200.00
Leap Frog, B of K, NM	$175.00
Leap Frog, SH, G	$875.00
Leap Frog, SH, VG	$1,500.00
Lion & Two Monkeys, James Capron, NM	$450.00
Lion & Two Monkeys, K&R, G	$450.00
Lion & Two Monkeys, K&R, VG	$750.00
Lion Hunter, J&ES, VG	$2,200.00
Little Moe, Chamberlain & Hill, EX+	$600.00

Lost Dog, Judd, EX.. $400.00
Magician Bank, B of K, M $150.00
Magician Bank, B of K, MIB $225.00
Magician Bank, J&ES, VG $4,370.00
Mammy & Child, K&R, EX+................................ $5,750.00
Mammy & Child, K&R, VG $2,200.00
Mason Bank, SH, EX $3,900.00
Mason Bank, SH, EXIB (wooden box) $13,225.00
Monkey & Coconut, J&ES, VG............................ $2,400.00
Monkey Bank, Hubley, EX $675.00
Monkey w/Tray, Germany, tin, EX+ $200.00
Mosque, Judd, EX+ $3,500.00
Mule Entering Barn, J&ES, NM........................... $2,500.00
Multiplying Bank, J&ES, EX $1,800.00
Multiplying Bank, J&ES, G $825.00
Novelty Bank, J&ES, EX $4,125.00
Novelty Bank, J&ES, EX rpnt $975.00
Novelty Bank, J&ES, G $350.00
Organ Bank, B of K, NM $150.00
Organ Bank (Boy & Girl), K&R, EX $1,200.00
Organ Bank (Cat & Dog), K&R, EX $1,200.00
Organ Bank (Medium w/Monkey), K&R, VG $400.00
Organ Bank (Miniature w/Monkey), K&R, EX............ $850.00
Organ Bank (Miniature w/Monkey), K&R, VG............ $450.00
Organ Grinder & Performing Bear, K&R, VG $2,875.00
Owl (Slot in Book), Kilgore, VG $255.00
Owl (Slot in Head), Kilgore, VG $255.00
Owl (Turns Head), B of K, NM $150.00
Owl (Turns Head), J&ES, EX $475.00
Owl (Turns Head), J&ES, G $275.00
Paddy & the Pig, B of K, NM $175.00
Paddy & the Pig, J&ES, EX $4,400.00
Peg-Leg Beggar, Judd, VG................................... $2,000.00
Pelican (Man Thumbs Nose), J&ES, EX $1,250.00
Pig in Highchair, J&ES, VG.................................... $860.00
Popeye Knockout Bank, Straits Mfg, 1930s, litho tin, VG.... $200.00
Presto Bank, K&R, VG+ $250.00
Punch & Judy, B of K, NM $150.00
Punch & Judy (Large Letters), SH, EX $2,500.00
Punch & Judy (Small Letters), SH, EX $2,500.00
Rabbit in Cabbage Patch, Kilgore, EX $650.00
Rabbit Standing (Small), Lockwood, EX $700.00
Reclining Chinaman, J&ES, EX $6,500.00
Rooster, K&R, EX $800.00
Rooster, K&R, G $325.00
Santa at Chimney, SH, EX $1,900.00
Santa at Chimney, SH, G $690.00
Shoot the Chute, J&ES, NM $2,500.00
Signal Cabin, Distler, VG+ $150.00
Speaking Dog, SH, EX+ $1,650.00
Speaking Dog, SH, VG... $750.00
Stump Speaker, SH, EX $850.00
Tammany Bank, B of K, NMIB $200.00
Tammany Bank, J&ES, NM $1,600.00
Tammany Bank, J&ES, VG $500.00
Tank & Cannon, Starkie's, EX $550.00
Teddy & the Bear, B of K, NM $135.00
Teddy & the Bear, J&ES, G.................................. $500.00

Banks, Mechanical
Multiplying Bank, J & E Stevens, NM, $2,800.00. (Photo courtesy Morphy Auctions on LiveAuctioneers.com)

Banks, Mechanical
Organ Bank (Medium with Monkey), Kyser & Rex, NM+, $2,015.00. (Photo courtesy Morphy Auctions on LiveAuctioneers.com)

Banks, Mechanical
Panorama Bank, J & E Stevens, EX, $4,255.00. (Photo courtesy James D. Julia, Inc.)

Banks, Mechanical
Professor Pug Frog's Great Bicycle Feat, J & E Stevens, NM, $51,750.00. (Photo courtesy James D. Julia, Inc.)

Banks, Mechanical
Reclining Chinaman, J & E Stevens, NM, $14,000.00. (Photo courtesy Morphy Auctions on LiveAuctioneers.com)

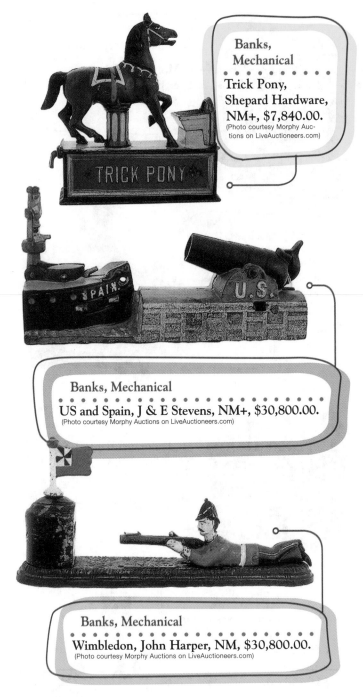

Banks, Mechanical

Trick Pony, Shepard Hardware, NM+, $7,840.00.
(Photo courtesy Morphy Auctions on LiveAuctioneers.com)

Banks, Mechanical

US and Spain, J & E Stevens, NM+, $30,800.00.
(Photo courtesy Morphy Auctions on LiveAuctioneers.com)

Banks, Mechanical

Wimbledon, John Harper, NM, $30,800.00.
(Photo courtesy Morphy Auctions on LiveAuctioneers.com)

Watch Dog Safe, J&ES, EX $925.00
William Tell, B of K, M $200.00
William Tell, J&ES, EX $1,600.00
William Tell, J&ES, G $450.00
World's Fair, J&ES, VG $650.00
World's Fair (Columbus), J&ES, NM $4,600.00
Zoo Bank, K&R, EX $1,840.00

REGISTERING

Beehive Dime Register, H&H, 1891, NP CI, 5½", EX ... $175.00
Captain Marvel Magic Dime Saver, litho tin, 2½" sq, VG+ ...$150.00
Cash Register Savings Bank, US, 1889, CI w/paper litho insert
   under glass face, rnd, 3-footed, 6", NM $1,900.00
Coin Registering Bank, K&R, EX+ $8,050.00
Davy Crockett Frontier Dime Bank, litho tin box, 2½" sq,
   EX $140.00
Home Five-Coin Savings bank (Cash Register), American Can
   Co, 7", VG+ $75.00
Jackie Robinson Daily Dime Register Bank, US, litho tin box,
   2½", EX $450.00
Keep 'Em Flying Dime Register Bank, litho tin, 2½" sq, VG ..$250.00
Keep 'Em Rolling Dime Register Bank, litho tin, 2½" sq,
   VG $250.00
Keep 'Em Sailing Dime Register Bank, litho tin, 2½" sq, VG ..$250.00
Mickey Mouse Dime Register, litho tin, 2½" sq, VG+ $450.00
New York World's Fair Daily Dime Register, RMS Sales Corp,
   litho tin box w/diagonal corners, NMOC $70.00
Penny Register (Pail), K&R, bail handle, 3", EX $175.00
Popeye Daily Dime Register, litho tin box, red & yel, 2½" sq, EX
   (in orig pkg) $150.00
Recording Dime Bank, NP CI, registering window in front, 6½",
   EX $200.00
Spar-Uhr, Germany, litho tin, registering clock on front, 5¾",
   EX+ $175.00
Time Registering Bank, Ives Blakeslee and Williams, PAT 1891,
   metal, VG $300.00

Banks, Registering

Little Orphan Annie, Save A Dime A Day, tin, 3" wide, 1936, VG, $225.00.
(Photo courtesy Bertoia Auctions)

Teddy & the Bear, J&ES, VG $1,000.00
Thrifty Animal Bank, Buddy L, PS, VG $115.00
Toad on Stump, J&ES, VG $630.00
Trick Dog, Hubley, solid base, EX $500.00
Trick Dog, Hubley, solid base, NM $1,075.00
Trick Dog, Hubley, 6-part base, G $175.00
Trick Pony, B of K, NM $185.00
Trick Pony, SH, VG $500.00
Uncle Remus, B of K, M $150.00
Uncle Remus, K&R, VG+ $3,450.00
Uncle Sam, SH, G $800.00
Uncle Sam, SH, VG $1,800.00
Uncle Sam Bust, Ives, Blakeslee & Williams, EX+ $925.00
Uncle Tom (Stars on Lapels), K&R, VG+ $700.00
US & Spain, B of K, M $150.00

STILL

Andy Gump (Seated Reading Newspaper), Arcade, 4½",
   EX $1,380.00
Apple on Leafy Twig, K&R, ca 1882, 3x5", EX $1,725.00
Aunt Jemima, AC Williams, standing w/hand on hip & spoon in
   hand, 6", NM $450.00
Baby in a Cradle, japanned, 4", EX $1,840.00
Bank Building (Eagle Finial), 10x5½", VG $2,875.00

Baseball Player, AC Williams, early version, standing w/bat, 6", EX $1,090.00

Battleship Maine, bl w/gold trim, 7", EX $1,000.00

Bear Begging, AC Williams, upright on haunches w/begging paws, gold, 5½", EX $115.00

Bear Standing (Left Foot Forward), JH, japanned, 6", EX ... $115.00

Bear Stealing Pig, bear standing upright w/pig in his arms, gold pnt, 5½", EX $650.00

Beauty, rearing horse on base, 'Beauty' emb on sides, blk w/gold accents, 5", NM $400.00

Blackpool Tower, Chamberlin & Hill, japanned, 7½", EX+ . $400.00

Boston State House, Smith & Egge, late 1800s, 7", rpnt .. $3,750.00

Boy Eating Watermelon on Haystack, pnt chalkware, 7x6", EX $115.00

Boy Scout, US, 1910, holds 'Boy Scout Camp' flag, 7", EX... $550.00

Boy w/Large Football, Hubley, kneeling w/football over head, gold pnt, 5", EX $1,600.00

Buster Brown & Tige, AC Williams, ca 1910, bl w/red scarf, 5½", G $175.00

Camel w/Trunk on Back Resting, K&R, 1889, 'Bank' emb on sides of trunk, japanned w/gold accents, 2½x5", G $315.00

Cannon, Hubley, ca 1914, gr w/red spokes, 3x7", rpnt.. $1,035.00

Captain Kidd, figure w/shovel standing next to tree trunk on grass base, mc pnt, 5½", EX $100.00

Carpenter Safe, JH, figure standing w/hammer & saw, 4½", EX $3,250.00

Castle w/2 Towers, JH, japanned, 7", VG $750.00

Cat Playing w/Ball, AC Williams, gray w/gold ball, 5¾", VG.. $430.00

Cat Seated, Germany, gray w/bl bow, hinged head for coin retrieval, w/lock, 4", G $375.00

City Bank, Judd, seated teller at front steps, bronze, 5½", EX.. $315.00

Clown Head, Germany, blk face w/sm blk top hat on red head scarf, 4", EX $630.00

Columbia Tower, Grey Iron, japanned, 7", G $575.00

Crown Bank, J&ES, 'Bank' building, wht w/gr & red trim, bl highlights, 3", EX+ $325.00

Cupola Bank, J&ES, ca 1872, 4", EX $250.00

Dolphin (Boy in Boat), gold, 4", EX $375.00

Dolphin (Boy in Boat), rare brass finish, 4", EX+ $575.00

Donkey, AC Williams, saddled, 4½", EX+ $175.00

Doughboy, Grey Iron, ca 1919, khaki uniform, 7", EX ... $200.00

Dreadnought Bank (United We Stand), English, 6¾", EX ..$350.00

Eagle w/Union Shield, 1880, wings down, silver, 4", G.. $400.00

Egg Man, Arcade, caricature of William Howard Taft, gold pnt, 4", VG+ $1,900.00

Eiffel Tower, Syndenham & McOustra, 1908, 8½", EX+ . $1,300.00

Elephant Seated on Box w/Trunk Down, 4", VG $460.00

Elephant w/Howdah (Flat), Harris Toy, ca 1904, walking w/stiff legs, 3½x4½", VG+ $485.00

Flat Iron Building, Kenton, triangular, 6½", EX $300.00

Flat Iron Building, Kenton, triangular, 8½" (scarce sz) ... $750.00

Football Player, AC Williams, gold, 5", EX $460.00

Foxy Grandpa, Hubley, standing w/hands in pockets, 5½", EX $175.00

Gas Stove Bank, Bernstein, ca 1901, orante casting, 5½", EX.$285.00

General Butler, J&ES, 7", EX $1,750.00

Gingerbread House, brn w/mc detail, woman at door, 2 kids outside, 4½x4", EX $5,750.00

Girl Standing on Thimble, Germany, pnt lead, girl in pilgrim-like hat and shawl, 6", EX $550.00

Golliwog, England, ca 1890, 5½", EX $400.00

Hold the Fort, 5" H, EX $900.00

Independence Hall, Enterprise Mfg, gold overall, 11½" L, EX $1,200.00

Indian Family, JH, 1905, bust images of chief, wife & child, copper finish, 4x5", EX $1,100.00

Banks, Still
Black Man Seated on Cotton Bale, 5", EX, $4,825.00. (Photo courtesy Morphy Auctions on LiveAuctioneers.com)

Banks, Still
Fido Seated on Pillow, painted cast iron, 7½" long, NM, $785.00. (Photo courtesy Morphy Auctions on LiveAuctioneers.com)

Banks, Still
Buster Brown/Good Luck, black horse with 5" Buster Brown and Tige horseshoe, M, $300.00. (Photo courtesy Morphy Auctions on LiveAuctioneers.com)

Banks, Still
Football Player, Hubley, 5", VG, $1,780.00. (Photo courtesy James D. Julia, Inc.)

Indian w/Tomahawk, Hubley, 5", EX+ $460.00

Little Red Riding Hood (Safe), JH, 1907, 5", EX $3,750.00

Mailbox, Kenton, gr w/emb 'Letters', 'Lift Up', 'US Mail' & eagle highlighted in gold, no post, 4x3½", EX+ $430.00

Maine (Battleship), Grey Iron, bl w/gold trim, 5x6½", EX..$1,500.00

Maine (Battleship), Grey Iron, japanned, 5" H, EX $375.00

Mammy, see also Aunt Jemima

Mammy w/Hands on Hips, Hubley, red & wht, 5", EX+ . $200.00

Mammy w/Spoon, AC Williams, 6", VG $115.00

Mary & Her Lamb, gr dress w/wht pinafore, red stockings, wht lamb, 4⅜", G.. $255.00

Merry-Go-Round, Grey Iron, semi-mechanical, 4½", VG ..$350.00

Mosque, AC Williams, 'Bank' emb over arched door, yel w/red trim, 4¼", G.. $255.00

Mulligan the Cop, AC Williams, emb advertising on back, 6", EX $900.00

Ohio Mutual Building & Loan Co Building, 11", G....... $345.00

Old South Church (Boston), gold pnt, 9x6x4", VG.... $3,500.00

Oregon (Battleship), J&ES, 5x6", Fair.......................... $285.00

Oriental Camel, US, rocking base, 5x4", EX $600.00

Owl, Vindex, brn w/wht chest, yel & blk eyes, 4¼", EX. $200.00

Palace, Ives, 1885, red w/gold trim, 8" L, NM+ $9,200.00

Pig (I Made Chicago Famous), blk w/gold emb lettering on sides, 4", EX.. $400.00

Policeman, Arcade, w/club & hand on hip, 5¾", VG..... $140.00

Policeman Safe, JH, 1907, figure standing in front of safe w/billy club & hand on hip, 5", EX.................................... $5,500.00

Professor Pug Frog, AC Williams, ca 1905, gold pnt, 3¼", VG.$85.00

Rabbit on Base, wht on gr base emb Bank/1884, 2¾", some rpnt.. $345.00

Red Goose Shoes, Arcade, red goose w/gold trim, 3½", EX+ ..$430.00

Rhino, Arcade, blk, 5", G.. $250.00

Rooster w/Man's Face, Chanticleer, ca 1911, gold w/flesh-tone face, 4½", EX...$10,925.00

Santa Claus w/Tree, Hubley, 6", VG $350.00

Santa Safe, JH, 1907, Santa standing holding bag over shoulder, red w/silver bag, 4", VG $3,750.00

Save & Smile Money Box, England, 4", EX.................... $225.00

Save & Smile Santa, England, blk w/red hat, 7", EX...... $375.00

Save for a Rainy Day (Duck), Hubley, wht duck w/blk umbrella & top hat standing on red tub w/emb lettering, 5½" ... $350.00

Seal on Rock, Arcade, gold, 4½" L, VG......................... $315.00

Sharecropper, see also Give Me a Penny

Sharecropper, AC Williams, 5½", EX $200.00

Silo, Marietta, electroplated, 5½", EX+ $1,500.00

Songbird Perched on Stump, AC Williams, gold w/bronze highlights, 5", EX... $375.00

Squirrel w/Nut, sitting upright, gold, 4", VG $400.00

St Bernard w/Backpack, AC Williams, 8" L, EX+ $115.00

Statue of Liberty, Kenton, silver, 10", EX...................... $690.00

Stop/Save Bank, Dent, 1920s, gray stop sign post w/red & gr lights, 4½", VG... $315.00

Stork Safe, JH, 1907, 'Copyrighted' emb diagonally on front, copper-look finish, 5½", EX+ $1,400.00

Teddy Roosevelt Bust, AC Williams, gold pnt, 5", EX ... $200.00

Three Wise Monkeys, AC Williams, 1917, see, hear & speak no evil, gold w/red trim, 3½", VG $315.00

Tower Bank 1890, K&R, japanned w/red, gold & silver highlights, 7x2½", EX.. $950.00

Water Wheel, NP, tin base, 4½", EX+ $1,300.00

World's Fair Administration Building, US, red, wht & gold, 6", EX $650.00

Yellow Cab, Arcade, blk & orange w/screened rear windows, slot in roof, 7¾", VG.. $750.00

Banks, Still
• • • • • • • • •
Give Me a Penny (Sharecropper), Wing/Hubley, 6", NM, $250.00. (Photo courtesy Morphy Auctions on LiveAuctioneers.com)

Banks, Still
• • • • • • • • •
Mammy with Hands on Hips, Hubley, 5¼", MIB, $335.00. (Photo courtesy Morphy Auctions on LiveAuctioneers.com)

Banks, Still
• • • • • • • • •
Palace, Ives, 1885, cast iron, japanned with gold trim, 8" long, NM, $8,960.00. (Photo courtesy Morphy Auctions on LiveAuctioneers.com)

Banks, Still
• • • • • • • • •
Santa Claus with Tree, Hubley, 6", NM, $1,120.00. (Photo courtesy Morphy Auctions on LiveAuctioneers.com)

Banks, Still
· · · · · · · · · · · · · · · · · · · ·
State Bank, Kenton, 8", NM,
$1,000.00. (Photo courtesy Morphy Auctions on
LiveAuctioneers.com)

Banks, Still
· · · · · · · · · · · · · · · · ·
US Air Mail Mailbox,
Dent, 6½", EX, $630.00.
(Photo courtesy James D. Julia, Inc.)

Barbie® Doll and Friends

Barbie doll has been around for 50 years now, having first been introduced in 1959. Since then her face has changed three times. She's been blond and brunette, her hair has been restyled over and over, and it's varied in length from above her shoulders to the tips of her toes. She's worn high-fashion designer clothing and pedal pushers. She's been everything from an astronaut to a veterinarian, and no matter what her changing lifestyle requires, Mattel (her 'maker') has provided it for her.

Though Barbie doll items from recent years are bought and sold with fervor, those made before 1970 are the most sought after. You'll need to do a lot of studying and comparisons to learn to distinguish one Barbie doll from another, but it will pay off in terms of making wise investments. There are several books available; we recommend them all: *Barbie Doll Fashion, Vol. I, 1959 – 1967, Vol. II, 1968 – 1974,* and *Vol. II, 1975 – 1979,* all by Sarah Sink Eames; *Barbie, The First 30 Years, 1959 through 1989 and Beyond,* by Stefanie Deutsch and Bettina Dorffman; *Collector's Encyclopedia of Barbie Doll Exclusives & More, Collector's Encyclopedia of Barbie Doll Collector's Editions,* and *Barbie Doll Around the World,* all by J. Michael Augustyniak.

As a general rule, a mint-in-box doll is worth around twice as much as a mint doll with no box. A doll that has been played with and shows some use is worth half as much as the mint doll with no box (or even less). Never-removed-from-box examples sell at a premium.

DOLLS

Allan, 1964, straight legs, red-pnt hair, MIB $75.00
Allan, 1965, bendable legs, MIB $200.00
Barbie, 1958-59, #1, blond or brunette, MIB, ea $5,000 to . $5,250.00
Barbie, 1959, #2, blond, MIB, $5,000 to $5,250.00
Barbie, 1959, #2, brunette, MIB, $6,000 to.................. $6,250.00
Barbie, 1960, #3, blond or brunette hair, MIB, ea $925 to .. $1,025.00
Barbie, 1960, #4, blond, MIB, $475 to $525.00
Barbie, 1960, #4, brunette, MIB, $375 to........................ $425.00
Barbie, 1961, #5, blond, MIB, $325 to $350.00
Barbie, 1961, #5, brunette, MIB.................................... $375.00
Barbie, 1962, #5, redhead, MIB, $475 to........................ $500.00
Barbie, 1962, #6, any color hair, MIB, ea $350 to.......... $375.00
Barbie, 2001, blk or wht, NRFB....................................$45.00
Barbie, 2002, blk, NRFB...$35.00
Barbie, 2002, wht, NRFB...$40.00
Barbie, 2003, blk or wht, NRFB, ea...............................$50.00
Barbie, 2003, redhead, NRFB............................,........ $100.00
Barbie, American Beauty Queen, 1991, blk or wht, MIB..$15.00
Barbie, American Girl, 1965, blond or brunette, NRFB, ea..$1,500.00
Barbie, American Girl, 1965, redhead, MIB................ $2,000.00
Barbie, American Girl, 1965, redhead, NRFB............ $2,500.00
Barbie, American Girl, 1966, Color-Magic, MIB $1,800.00
Barbie, American Girl, 1966, side-part, blond, NRFB. $3,000.00
Barbie, Angel Face, 1982, MIB, $25 to $30.00
Barbie, Angel of Hope, 1999, Timeless Sentiments, blk or wht,
    NRFB..$55.00

Barbie, Animal Lovin', 1989, blk or wht, MIB $12.00
Barbie, Anne Klein, 1996, NRFB....................................$55.00
Barbie, Applause Style, 1990, NRFB...............................$20.00
Barbie, Arctic, 1996, Dolls of the World, NRFB $25.00
Barbie, Army Desert Storm, 1993, Stars & Stipes, blk or wht,
    NRFB..$25.00
Barbie, Astronaut, 1985, blk or wht, NRFB......................$25.00
Barbie, Autumn in Paris, 1998, City Season Collection,
    NRFB..$45.00
Barbie, Avon Representative, 1999, wht, blk or Hispanic,
    NRFB $40.00
Barbie, Ballerina Barbie on Tour, 1976, #1, NRFB $75.00
Barbie, Ballet Lessons, 2000, blk or wht, NRFB $15.00
Barbie, Ballroom Beauties, 1997, NRFB $45.00
Barbie, Barbie Celebration, 1987, NRFB..........................$30.00
Barbie, Barbie Sign Language, 1999, blk or wht, NRFB $20.00
Barbie, Bath Magic, 1992, NRFB....................................$15.00
Barbie, Baywatch, 1995, blk or wht, NRFB $20.00
Barbie, Beach Blast, 1989, NRFB....................................$15.00
Barbie, Beautiful Bride, 1978, MIB $60.00
Barbie, Benefit Ball, 1992, NRFB....................................$45.00
Barbie, Bicyclin', 1994, NRFB..$25.00
Barbie, Birthday Party, 1993, NRFB................................$30.00
Barbie, Birthday Wishes, 1999, blk, NRFB $25.00
Barbie, Blossom Beautiful, 1992, NRFB......................... $225.00
Barbie, Brazilian, 1990, Dolls of the World, NRFB...........$25.00
Barbie, Bridesmaid, 1991, NRFB....................................$30.00
Barbie, Bubble-Cut, 1961-62, redhead, MIB.................. $175.00
Barbie, Bubble-Cut, 1962, blond or brunette, MIB $175.00

Barbie Doll and Friends, Dolls
• •
Barbie, Party Pretty Barbie, 1990, MIB, $25.00. (Photo courtesy Margo Rana)

Barbie Doll and Friends, Dolls
• • • • • • • • • • • • • • • • • • • •
Barbie, Southern Beauty Barbie, 1991, Winn Dixie, MIB, $30.00. (Photo courtesy Margo Rana)

Barbie, Bubble-Cut, 1965, side part, any hair color, MIB.. $875.00
Barbie, Busy Talking, 1972, MIB $200.00
Barbie, Butterfly Princess, 1995, any, NRFB $25.00
Barbie, California Dream, 1988, MIB $15.00
Barbie, Calvin Klein, 1996, Bloomingdale's, NRFB $40.00
Barbie, Camp, 1994, NRFB $25.00
Barbie, Career Girl, 1964, MIB $750.00
Barbie, Carnival Cruise Lines, 1997, NRFB $30.00
Barbie, Carolina Fun, 1995, NRFB $20.00
Barbie, Catwoman, 2004, NRFB $20.00
Barbie, Celebration, 1986, NRFB $65.00
Barbie, Celebration Cake, 1999, any, NRFB $20.00
Barbie, Charity Ball, 1998, blk or wht, NRFB $30.00
Barbie, Chataine, 2003, NRFB $425.00
Barbie, Children's Doctor, 2000, NRFB $20.00
Barbie, Chinese, 1993, Dolls of the World, NRFB $20.00
Barbie, Cinderella, 1996, NRFB $25.00
Barbie, Circus Star, 1995, NRFB $70.00
Barbie, City Sophisticate, 1994, NRFB $50.00
Barbie, Color Magic, 1966, blond, MIB (plastic box).. $1,600.00
Barbie, Color Magic, 1966, midnight blk, MIB (plastic box) .. $2,400.00
Barbie, Color Magic, 2004, blond, NRFB $175.00
Barbie, Color Magic, 2004, brunette, NRFB $40.00
Barbie, Color Magic, 2004, redhead, NRFB $200.00
Barbie, Color Me, 1998, NRFB $15.00
Barbie, Cool & Sassy, 1992, NRFB $25.00
Barbie, Cool Times, 1989, NRFB $15.00
Barbie, Country Rose, 1997, NRFB $50.00
Barbie, Cut & Style, 1995, any, NRFB $20.00
Barbie, Dance 'N Twirl, 1994, NRFB $35.00
Barbie, Dance Magic, 1990, NRFB $20.00
Barbie, Day-to-Night, 1985, NRFB $45.00
Barbie, Dazzlin' Date, 1992, NRFB $25.00
Barbie, Detective, 2000, Best Buy, NRFB $20.00
Barbie, Dinner Date, 1998, redhead, NRFB $20.00
Barbie, Disney Fun, 1992, NRFB $35.00
Barbie, Doctor, 1988, NRFB $25.00
Barbie, Dorothy (Wizard of Oz), 1994, Hollywood Legends Series, NRFB $75.00
Barbie, Dramatic New Living, 1970, MIB $200.00
Barbie, Dream Date, 1983, NRFB $30.00
Barbie, Dream Glow, 1986, blk, MIB $25.00

Barbie, Dream Glow, 1986, Hispanic, MIB $45.00
Barbie, Dream Glow, 1986, wht, MIB $35.00
Barbie, Dream Time, 1988, NRFB $25.00
Barbie, Dress 'N Fun, 1994, any, NRFB $15.00
Barbie, Dutch, 1994, Dolls of the World, MIB $25.00
Barbie, Earring Magic, 1993, blk or wht (blond), NRFB ... $15.00
Barbie, Earring Magic, 1993, brunette, NRFB $20.00
Barbie, Easter, 1997, NRFB $15.00
Barbie, Easter Party, 1995, NRFB $20.00
Barbie, Eliza Dolittle (My Fair Lady), 1995, Hollywood Legends, NRFB $75.00
Barbie, Elizabethan, 1994, Great Eras, MIB $50.00
Barbie, Enchanted Evening, 1991, JC Penney, NRFB $50.00
Barbie, Enchanted Princess, 1993, Sears, NRFB $75.00
Barbie, Eskimo, 1982, Dolls of the World, NRFB $45.00
Barbie, Evening Sparkle, 1990, Hill's, NRFB $35.00
Barbie, Fabulous Fur, 1986, NRFB $55.00
Barbie, Fantastica, 1992, MIB $55.00
Barbie, Fantasy Goddess of Asia, 1998, Bob Mackie, NRFB... $150.00
Barbie, Fashion Play, 1983-91, NRFB $20.00
Barbie, Fashion Jeans, 1981, MIB $55.00
Barbie, Fire Fighter, 1995, blk or wht, Toys R Us, NRFB .. $30.00
Barbie, Flight Time, 1990, NRFB $20.00
Barbie, Fountain Mermaid, 1993, blk or wht, NRFB, ea ... $20.00
Barbie, Free Moving, 1974, NRFB $125.00
Barbie, French Lady, 1997, Great Eras Collection, NRFB. $50.00
Barbie, Gap Barbie, 1996, blk or wht, NRFB $65.00
Barbie, Garden Party, 1989, NRFB $20.00
Barbie, Glinda (Wizard of Oz), 2000, NRFB $40.00
Barbie, Goddess of the Sun, 1995, Bob Mackie, NRFB $75.00
Barbie, Gold Medal Skater or Skier, 1975, NRFB $75.00
Barbie, Great Shapes, 1984, blk or wht, NRFB $15.00
Barbie, Great Shapes, 1984, w/Walkman, NRFB $20.00
Barbie, Growin' Pretty Hair, 1971, NRFB $325.00
Barbie, Hispanic, 1980, MIB $60.00
Barbie, Holiday, 1988, NRFB $325.00
Barbie, Holiday, 1989, NRFB $150.00
Barbie, Holiday, 1990, NRFB $75.00
Barbie, Holiday, 1991, NRFB $75.00
Barbie, Holiday, 1992, NRFB $50.00
Barbie, Holiday, 1993, NRFB $50.00
Barbie, Holiday, 1994, NRFB $65.00

Barbie, Holiday, 1995, NRFB $45.00
Barbie, Holiday, 1996, NRFB $35.00
Barbie, Holiday, 1997, NRFB $35.00
Barbie, Holiday, 1998, NRFB $20.00
Barbie, Ice Capades (50th Anniversary), 1990, NRFB......$20.00
Barbie, Inline Skating, 1996, NRFB.....................$20.00
Barbie, Island Fun, 1988, NRFB..........................$15.00
Barbie, Japanese, 1984, Dolls of the World, NRFB...........$40.00
Barbie, Jewel Essence, 1996, Bob Mackie, NRFB $125.00
Barbie, Julia (TV Nurse), 1969, Twist 'N Turn or talking, any
    issue except 2-pc outfit, NRFB $275.00
Barbie, Julia (TV Nurse), 1969, Twist 'N Turn, 2-pc outfit,
    NRFB..$375.00
Barbie, Knitting Pretty, 1964, pk, NRFB.....................$1,265.00
Barbie, Knitting Pretty, 1965, royal bl, NRFB................$635.00
Barbie, Korean, 1988, Dolls of the World, NRFB.............$35.00
Barbie, Lights 'N Lace, 1991, NRFB $15.00
Barbie, Lily, 1997, FAO Schwarz, NRFB $150.00
Barbie, Live Action, 1970, NRFB $175.00
Barbie, Live Action on Stage, 1970, NRFB $275.00
Barbie, Magic Curl, 1982, NRFB..........................$25.00
Barbie, Malibu, 1971, MIB $55.00
Barbie, Malibu (Sunset), 1975, MIB $35.00
Barbie, Malt Shop, 1993, Toys R Us, NRFB $30.00
Barbie, Medieval Lady, 1995, Great Eras Collection, NRFB....$60.00
Barbie, Mexican (International), 1989, Dolls of the World,
    NRFB...$25.00
Barbie, Miss America, 1972, Kellogg Co, NRFB $175.00
Barbie, Moon Goddess, 1996, Bob Mackie, NRFB...........$75.00
Barbie, Moonlight Magic, 1993, Toys R Us, NRFB $60.00
Barbie, Music Lovin', 1985, NRFB.......................$25.00
Barbie, My First Barbie, 1981, NRFB....................$25.00
Barbie, NASCAR 50th Anniversary, 1998, NRFB...........$25.00
Barbie, Native American #1, 1993, Dolls of the World,
    NRFB...$35.00
Barbie, Neptune Fantasy, 1992, Bob Mackie, NRFB $525.00
Barbie, Nifty Fifties, 2000, Great Fashions of the 20th Century,
    NRFB...$50.00
Barbei, Ocean Friends, 1996, NRFB $15.00
Barbie, Opening Night, 1993, Classique Collection, NRFB.. $50.00
Barbie, Oreo Fun, 1997, Toys R Us, NRFB $20.00
Barbie, Paleontologist, 1997, Toys R Us, NRFB $25.00
Barbie, Party in Pink, 1991, Ames, NRFB $20.00
Barbie, Peach Blossom, 1992, NRFB......................$40.00
Barbie, Peach Pretty, 1989, K-Mart, MIB....................$35.00
Barbie, Peaches 'N Cream, 1984, blk or wht, MIB $35.00
Barbie, Pen Friend, 1996, NRFB $20.00
Barbie, Pepsi Spirit, 1989, Toys R Us, NRFB....................$75.00
Barbie, Perfume Pretty, 1988, blk or wht, NRFB $20.00
Barbie, Pet Doctor, 1996, brunette, NRFB...................$25.00
Barbie, Phantom of the Operea, 1998, FAO Schwarz, NRFB .. $90.00
Barbie, Picnic Pretty, 1992, Osco, NRFB...................$30.00
Barbie, Pilgrim, 1995, American Stories Collection, NRFB.. $15.00
Barbie, Pink & Pretty, 1982, MIB $50.00
Barbie, Pink Sensation, 1990, Winn Dixie, NRFB............$25.00
Barbie, Pioneer, 1995 or 1996, American Stories Collection,
    NRFB, ea $15.00
Barbie, Police Officer, 1993, blk or wht, Toys R Us, NRFB....$75.00

Barbie, Polly Pockets, 1994, Hill's, NRFB.........................$25.00
Barbie, Portrait in Blue, 1998, blk or wht, Wal-Mart, NRFB...$20.00
Barbie, Pretty Changes, 1978, NRFB......................$35.00
Barbie, Queen of Hearts, 1994, Bob Mackie, NRFB....... $175.00
Barbie, Queen of Sapphires, 2000, Royal Jewels, NRFB. $115.00
Barbie, Quick Curl, 1972, NRFB..........................$75.00
Barbie, Quick Curl, 1974, Miss America, blond, NRFB....$80.00
Barbie, Quick Curl, 1974, Miss America, brunette, NRFB..$130.00
Barbie, Quick Curl, 1976, Deluxe, NRFB....................$80.00
Barbie, Rappin' Rock, 1992, NRFB.........................$25.00
Barbie, Rendezvous, 1998, NRFB...........................$50.00
Barbie, Rising Star Barbie, 1998, Grand Old Opry, NRFB .$75.00
Barbie, Rocker, 1986, 1st issue, NRFB $25.00
Barbie, Rockettes, 1993, FAO Schwarz, NRFB $100.00
Barbie, Romantic Wedding 2001, 2000, Bridal Collection,
    NRFB...$50.00
Barbie, Russian, 1989, Dolls of the World, NRFB $25.00
Barbie, Safari, 1983, Disney, NRFB.......................$25.00
Barbie, Sapphire Sophisticate, 1997, Toys R Us, NRFB....$30.00
Barbie, Savvy Shopper, 1994, Bloomingdale's, NRFB $40.00
Barbie, School Spirit, 1993, blk or wht, Toys R Us, NRFB...$30.00
Barbie, Scottish, 1981, Dolls of the World, NRFB $75.00
Barbie, Sea Princess, 1996, Service Merchandise, NRFB..$25.00
Barbie, Sentimental Valentine, 1997, Hallmark, NRFB....$25.00
Barbie, Serenade in Satin, 1997, Barbie Couture Collection,
    MIB...$80.00
Barbie, Shampoo Magic, 1996, NRFB......................$15.00
Barbie, Snowboard, 1996, NRFB...........................$20.00
Barbie, Snow Princess, 1994, blond, Enchanted Seasons,
    NRFB $80.00
Barbie, Snow Princess, 1994, brunette, Mattel Festival,
    NRFB... $1,100.00
Barbie, Snow White, 1999, Children's Collector Series, NRFB.. $25.00
Barbie, Something Extra, 1992, Meijer, NRFB.................$25.00
Barbie, Southern Belle, 1994, Great Eras Collection, NRFB...$50.00
Barbie, Sports Star, 1979, NRFB $25.00
Barbie, Spring Parade, 1992, blk or wht, NRFB................$35.00
Barbie, Standard, 1967, any hair color, MIB..................$425.00
Barbie, Starlight Dance, 1996, Classique Collection, NRFB...$30.00
Barbie, Starlight Splendor, 1991, Bob Mackie, NRFB.... $275.00

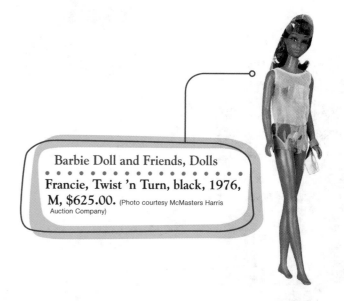

Barbie Doll and Friends, Dolls
• •
**Francie, Twist 'n Turn, black, 1976,
M, $625.00.** (Photo courtesy McMasters Harris
Auction Company)

Barbie, Steppin' Out Barbie 1930s, 1999, Great Fashions of the 20th Century, NRFB $45.00
Barbie, Strawberry Sorbet, 1999, Avon, NRFB $20.00
Barbie, Sugar Plum Fairy, 1997, Classic Ballet Series, NRFB ... $30.00
Barbie, Sun Gold Malibu, 1984-85, any, NRFB $20.00
Barbie, Sun Lovin' Malibu, 1979, NRFB $25.00
Barbie, Sun Valley, 1973, NRFB $125.00
Barbie, Sunsational Malibu, 1981, wht or Hispanic, NRFB ... $30.00
Barbie, Super Hair, 1987, blk or wht, NRFB $20.00
Barbie, Super Size, 1977-79, NRFB $130.00
Barbie, Super Size Bride, 1977-79, NRFB $250.00
Barbie, Swan Lake Ballerina, 1998, blk or wht, Classic Ballet, NRFB $30.00
Barbie, Swedish (International), 2000, Dolls of the World, NRFB $25.00
Barbie, Swirl Ponytail, 1964, blond or brunette, NRFB . $625.00
Barbie, Swirl Ponytail, 1964, platinum, NRFB $1,300.00
Barbie, Swirl Ponytail, 1964, redhead, NRFB $625.00
Barbie, Talking, 1968, side ponytail, blond, brunette or redhead, NRFB $400.00
Barbie, Talking, 1970, blond, brunette or redhead, NRFB ... $475.00
Barbie, Ten Speeder, 1973, NRFB $30.00
Barbie, Thailand, 1998, Dolls of the World, NRFB $25.00
Barbie, That Girl, 2003, Pop Culture Collection, NRFB .. $35.00
Barbie, Twirly Curls, 1982, wht or Hispanic, MIB, ea $25.00
Barbie, Twist 'N Turn, 1967, long straight red hair w/bangs, MIB $575.00

Barbie, Twist 'N Turn, 1969, flipped hairdo, blond or brunette, NRFB $475.00
Barbie, Twist 'N Turn, 1971, any color hair, eyes centered, MIB $575.00
Barbie, Unicef, 1989, NRFB $20.00
Barbie, University Barbie (Indiana), 1998, NRFB $15.00
Barbie, University Barbie (Xavier), 1999, NRFB $15.00
Barbie, Winter Fantasy, 1990, FAO Schwarz, NRFB $75.00
Barbie, Wonder Woman, 2000, Pop Culture Collection, NRFB $45.00
Barbie, Working Woman, 1999, blk or wht, NRFB $25.00
Barbie, Yuletide Romance, 1996, Hallmark, NRFB $25.00
Brad, Talking, 1970, NRFB $225.00
Brad, 1970, darker skin, bendable legs, NRFB $200.00
Cara, Free Moving, 1974, MIB $115.00
Casey, Twist 'N Turn, 1968, blond or brunette, NRFB ... $300.00
Chris, 1967, any hair color, MIB $200.00
Christie, Beauty Secrets, 1980, MIB $50.00
Christie, Fashion Photo, 1978, MIB $60.00
Christie, Golden Dream, 1980, MIB $40.00
Christie, Kissing, 1979, MIB $50.00
Christie, Pink & Pretty, 1982, NRFB $40.00
Christie, Pretty Reflections, 1979, NRFB $75.00
Christie, Sunsational Malibu, 1982, NRFB $55.00
Christie, Superstar, 1977, MIB $80.00
Christie, Talking, 1970, MIB $250.00
Christie, Talking, 1970, NRFB $300.00
Christie, Twist 'N Turn, 1968, redhead, MIB $300.00
Francie, 1966, bendable legs, brunette, MIB $375.00
Francie, Busy, 1971, NRFB $325.00
Francie, Growin' Pretty Hair, 1971, MIB $150.00
Francie, Malibu, 1971, NRFB $50.00
Francie, Twist 'N Turn, 1967, blk or wht (blond or brunette), MIB $1,200.00
Francie, Twist 'N Turn, 1969, blond or brunette, long or short hair, MIB $425.00
Francie, 1966, straight leg, blond or brunette, MIB $325.00
Francie, 30th Anniversary, 1996, NRFB $50.00
Ginger, Growing Up, 1977, MIB $115.00
Jamie, New & Wonderful Walking, 1970, blond hair, MIB $200.00
Kelley, Quick Curl, 1972, NRFB $80.00
Kelley, Yellowstone, 1974, NRFB $300.00
Ken, 1961, flocked hair, blond or brunette, NRFB $150.00
Ken, 1962, pnt hair, blond or brunette, NRFB $100.00
Ken, 1963, pnt hair, ¾" shorter, NRFB $125.00
Ken, 1965, bendable legs, blond or brunette, NRFB $325.00
Ken, Air Force, 1994, Stars 'N Stripes, NRFB $30.00
Ken, Arabian Nights, 1964, NRFB $400.00
Ken, Army, 1993, blk, NRFB $35.00
Ken, Beach Blast, 1989, NRFB $15.00
Ken, California Dream, 1988, NRFB $15.00
Ken, Crystal, 1984, blk, NRFB $20.00
Ken, Dream Date, 1983, NRFB $30.00
Ken, Fashion Jeans, 1982, NRFB $25.00
Ken, Flight Time, 1990, NRFB $25.00
Ken, Fraternity Meeting, 1964, NRFB $375.00
Ken, Free Moving, 1974, MIB $75.00

Barbie Doll and Friends, Dolls
• • • • • • • • • • • • •
Ken, Talking Busy, 1972, MIB, $160.00; NRFB, $200.00. (Photo courtesy Sarah Sink Eames)

Barbie Doll and Friends, Dolls
• • • • • • • • • • • • •
Ken, Dr. Ken, 1964, NRFB, $375.00. (Photo courtesy Stefanie Deutsch)

Ken, Funtime, 1975, NRFB $65.00
Ken, Gold Medal Skier, 1975, NRFB $75.00
Ken, Hawaiian, 1981, NRFB $40.00
Ken, Henry Higgins, 1996, Hollywood Legends Series, NRFB $35.00
Ken, Horse Lovin', 1983, NRFB $30.00
Ken, In-Line Skating, 1996, FAO Schwarz, NRFB $20.00
Ken, Jewel Secrets, 1987, NRFB $20.00
Ken, Live Action on Stage, 1971, NRFB....................$150.00
Ken, Malibu, 1976, NRFB $30.00
Ken, Marine Corps, 1992, Stars 'N Stripes, NRFB $25.00
Ken, Mod Hair, 1974, MIB $175.00
Ken, New Look, 1976, longer or shorter hair, NRFB, ea ...$75.00
Ken, Ocean Friends, 1996, NRFB $15.00
Ken, Rhett Butler, 1994, Hollywood Legends Series, NRFB.. $35.00
Ken, Rocker, 1986, MIB $30.00
Ken, Sport & Shave, 1980, MIB $40.00
Ken, Sun Lovin' Malibu, 1979, NRFB $25.00
Ken, Sunset Malibu, 1971, NRFB $60.00
Ken, Super Sport, 1982, MIB $20.00
Ken, Superstar, 1977, MIB....................................... $100.00
Ken, Talking, 1970, NRFB $115.00
Ken, Walk Lively, 1972, MIB $150.00
Ken, Western, 1982, MIB $20.00
Midge, 1963, straight legs, brunette hair, MIB.............. $130.00
Midge, 1965, bendable legs, any color hair, MIB $450.00
Midge, Cool Times, 1989, NRFB $15.00
Midge, Earring Magic, 1993, NRFB $20.00
Midge, Ski Fun, 1991, MIB $30.00
Midge, 30th Anniversary, 1992, porcelain, MIB...............$60.00
Nikki, Animal Lovin', 1989, NRFB $15.00
PJ, Deluxe Quick Curl, 1976, MIB...........................$55.00
PJ, Fashion Photo, 1978, MIB $75.00
PJ, Free Moving, 1974, MIB $75.00
PJ, Free Moving, 1976, MIB $85.00
PJ, Gold Medal Gymnast, 1975, MIB.........................$80.00
PJ, Live Action, 1971, MIB $225.00
PJ, Malibu, 1978, MIB $55.00
PJ, Malibu (Sun Lovin'), 1979, MIB $50.00
PJ, Malibu (Sunsational), 1982, MIB $30.00
PJ, Malibu (The Sun Set), 1971, blond hair, MIB.............$55.00
PJ, New & Groovy Talking, 1969, orig swimsuit, beads & glasses, NM $150.00
Ricky, 1965, MIB $130.00
Scott, 1979, MIB...$55.00
Skipper, 1964, straight legs, any hair color, MIB............ $130.00
Skipper, 1965, bendable legs, any hair color, MIB $150.00
Skipper, Deluxe Quick Curl, 1975, NRFB $65.00
Skipper, Dramatic New Living, 1970, MIB................... $130.00
Skipper, Growing Up, 1976, MIB............................. $100.00
Skipper, Hollywood Hair, 1993, NRFB $25.00
Skipper, Homecoming Queen, 1989, NRFB $20.00
Skipper, Malibu, 1977, MIB $50.00
Skipper, Malibu (Sunsational), 1982, MIB $40.00
Skipper, Music Lovin', 1985, NRFB.........................$25.00
Skipper, Super Teen, 1980, NRFB.............................$20.00
Skipper, Totally Hair, 1991, NRFB............................$25.00
Skipper, Twist 'N Turn, 1969, any hairstyle or color, MIB....$230.00

Skipper, Western, 1982, NRFB.................................$40.00
Skipper, Workout Teen Fun, 1988, NRFB $25.00
Skooter, 1965, any hair color, straight leg, MIB $130.00
Skooter, 1966, bendable legs, any color hair, MIB $275.00
Stacey, Talking, any hair color, MIB $430.00
Stacey, Twist 'N Turn, 1969, any hair color, NRFB $450.00
Teresa, All American, 1991, MIB $25.00
Teresa, Country Western Star, 1994, NRFB.................$25.00
Teresa, Rappin' Rockin', 1992, NRFB.......................$30.00
Tutti, 1967, any hair color, MIB $175.00
Whitney, Style Magic, 1989, NRFB..........................$15.00

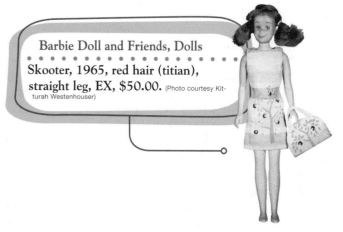

Barbie Doll and Friends, Dolls

Skooter, 1965, red hair (titian), straight leg, EX, $50.00. (Photo courtesy Kiturah Westenhouser)

CASES

Barbie, All That Jazz outfit, 1967, NM..........................$40.00
Barbie, Circus Star, FAO Schwarz, 1995, M $25.00
Barbie, Easter Parade, 1961, EX+ $20.00
Barbie, Goes Travelin', 1965, EX+ $75.00
Barbie, Madison Avenue, blk w/pk hdl, FAO Schwarz, 1992, M $35.00
Barbie & Ken, Barbie in Party Date & Ken in Sat Night Date, blk vinyl, 1963, EX...$50.00
Barbie & Midge, Barbie in Raincoat & Midge in Sorority Meeting, NM $50.00
Barbie & Stacey, Sleep 'N Keep, 1960s, NM $75.00
Francie & Casey, Francie in Groovy Get-Up & Casey in Iced Blue, rare, NM+ $75.00
Ken, gold vinyl w/blk plastic handle, metal clasp, w/hang tag, 1962, NM $35.00

Barbie Doll and Friends, Cases

Barbie, Fashion Queen Barbie, 1963, vinyl with mirror and wig stand, $100.00. (Photo courtesy Connie Craig Kaplan)

Ken, w/3 smaller images of Barbie in casual wear, gr, 1961, NM $35.00

Midge, Movie Date, 1964, NM $35.00

Miss Barbie, blk patent, 1963, NM+ $150.00

Miss Barbie, wht vinyl, w/orig wig, wig stand & mirror, rare, EX.. $75.00

Skipper, School Days, 1964, NM...............................$65.00

Skipper & Scooter, 1965, NM....................................$150.00

Skooter, in Country Picnic outfit chasing butterflies, 1965, rare, NM $125.00

Tutti, Play Case, bl or pk vinyl w/various scenes, EX.........$30.00

CLOTHING AND ACCESSORIES

Barbie, After Five, #934, 1962, NRFP................................$80.00

Barbie, All That Jazz, #1848, 1968, NRFP.................. $150.00

Barbie, All Turned Out, #4822, 1984, NRFP.....................$20.00

Barbie, American Airlines Stewardess, #984, 1961, NRFP... $175.00

Barbie, Baby Doll Pinks, #3403, 1971, NRFP $100.00

Barbie, Backyard Barbecue, #5719, 1983, NRFP $20.00

Barbie, Balleria, #989, 1961, NRFP...........................$175.00

Barbie, Beach Dazzler, #1939, 1981, NRFP.....................$10.00

Barbie, Beach Party, #5541, 1983, NRFP $20.00

Barbie, Best Bow, Pak, 1967, NRFP $175.00

Barbie, Bouncy Flouncy, #1805, 1967, NRFP $300.00

Barbie, Bridal Brocade, #3471, 1971, NRFP $250.00

Barbie, Bride's Dream, #947, 1963, NRFP....................... $225.00

Barbie, Brunch Time, #1628, 1965, NRFP $375.00

Barbie, Camping, #7702, 1973, NRFP $45.00

Barbie, Caribbean Cruise, #1687, 1967, NRFP................ $230.00

Barbie, Change Abouts, Pak, 1968, NRFP $150.00

Barbie, Cheerleader, #876, 1964, NRFP......................... $175.00

Barbie, Cinderella, #872, 1964, NRFP $450.00

Barbie, City Sparklers, #1457, 1970, NRFP $125.00

Barbie, Close-Ups, #1864, 1969, NRFP $125.00

Barbie, Club Meeting, #1672, 1966, NRFP.................. $400.00

Barbie, Cruise Stripes, #918, 1959, NRFP...................... $175.00

Barbie, Debutante Ball, #1666, NRFP.....................$1,500.00

Barbie, Disco Dazzle, #1011, 1979, NRFP.......................$15.00

Barbie, Dream Wraps, #1476, 1969, NRFP $80.00

Barbie, Drizzle Dash, #1808, 1967, NRFP $200.00

Barbie, Drum Majorette, #875, 1964, NRFP................... $225.00

Barbie, Enchanted Evening, #983, 1960, NRFP $325.00

Barbie, Evening Gala, #1660, 1966, NRFP $400.00

Barbie, Evening Outfit, #2221, 1978, NRFP.....................$30.00

Barbie, Eye Popper, #1937, 1981, NRFP $10.00

Barbie, Fab Fur, #1493, 1969-70, complete, very scarce, EX (no pkg)...$350.00

Barbie, Fancy Free, #943, 1963, NRFP.............................$75.00

Barbie, Fashion Luncheon, #1656, NRFP $1,500.00

Barbie, Floral Petticoat, #921, 1959, NRFP.....................$75.00

Barbie, Formal Occasion, #1697, complete, VG to EX (no pkg) $125.00

Barbie, Formal Occasion, #1697, NRFP..........................$525.00

Barbie, Fraternity Dance, #1638, NRFP $600.00

Barbie, Friday Night Date, #979, 1960, NRFP.................$225.00

Barbie, Fringe Benefits, #1701, 1965, NRFP.....................$60.00

Barbie, Fun at the Fair, #1624, NRFP $300.00

Barbie, Fun Fakes, #3412, 1971, NRFP $100.00

Barbie, Fur Sighted, #1796, 1970, NRFP.........................$20.00

Barbie, Galaxy A Go-Go, #2742, 1986, NRFP.................$30.00

Barbie, Garden Party, #0931, 1962, NRFP $175.00

Barbie, Garden Party, #5701 or #5835, 1983, NRFP, ea $10.00

Barbie, Gay Parisienne, #964, complete, VG+ (no pkg) . $425.00

Barbie, Glamour Group, #1510, 1970, NRFP $350.00

Barbie, Glimmer Glamour, #1547, 1968, complete, very scarce, EX (no pkg) $350.00

Barbie, Gold 'N Glamour, #1647, NRFP.....................$1,500.00

Barbie, Graduation, #945, 1963, NRFP $75.00

Barbie, Great Coat, #1459, 1970, NRFP.........................$90.00

Barbie, Happy Go Pink, #1868, 1969, NRFP.................$200.00

Barbie, Have Fun, Pak, 1966, NRFP $325.00

Barbie, Holiday Dance, #1639, 1965, NRFP $550.00

Barbie, Homecoming, #16076, 1996, NRFP.....................$30.00

Barbie, In Blooms, #3424, 1971, NRFB $90.00

Barbie, Indian Print Separates, #7241, 1975, NRFP..........$35.00

Barbie, Invitation to Tea, #1632, 1965, NRFP................$550.00

Barbie, Jumpin' Jeans, Pak, 1964, NRFP.........................$85.00

Barbie, Lady in Blue, #2303, 1978, NRFP.......................$15.00

Barbie, Little Red Riding Hood & the Wolf, #880, 1964, NRFP..$550.00

Barbie, Lunch Date, #1600, NRFP $150.00

Barbie, Madras Mad, #3485, 1972, NRFP $120.00

Barbie Doll and Friends, Clothing and Accessories

Barbie, Barbie-Q Outfit, #962, 1959 – 1962, loose, NM, $75.00; MIP, $170.00. (Photo courtesy Sarah Sink Eames)

Barbie Doll and Friends, Clothing and Accessories

Barbie, Beautiful Bride, #1698, 1967, loose, M, $800.00; MIP, $2,500.00. (Photo courtesy Sarah Sink Eames)

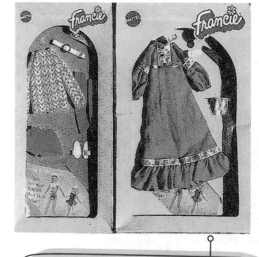

Barbie Doll and
Friends, Clothing
and Accessories
• • • • • • • • • •
Barbie, Get-Ups 'n
Go, #9742, 1977
– 1978, NRFP,
$15.00. (Photo courtesy
Sarah Sink Eames)

Barbie Doll and
Friends, Clothing and
Accessories
• • • • • • • • • • • • • •
Barbie, Knitting Pretty,
#957, 1963, loose, M,
$200.00; MIP, $350.00.
(Photo courtesy Sarah Sink Eames)

Barbie Doll and Friends, Clothing
and Accessories
• • • • • • • • • • • • • •
Francie, Little Kits, #3275, 1972, NRFP,
$125.00; Long View #3282, 1972,
$85.00. (Photo courtesy Stefanie Deutsch)

Barbie, Masquerade, #944, 1963, NRFP $200.00	Barbie, Shimmering Magic, #1664, 1966-67, NRFP.... $1,500.00
Barbie, Midi-Marvelous, #1870, 1969, NRFP $160.00	Barbie, Silken Flame, #977, 1960, NRFP $175.00
Barbie, Movie Groovie, #1866, 1969, NRFP $125.00	Barbie, Silver Serenade, #3419, 1971-72, NRFP $350.00
Barbie, Music Center Matinee, #1663, 1966-67, EX (no pkg) $250.00	Barbie, Ski Party Pink, #5608, 1983, NRFP $10.00
	Barbie, Slip On Wrap 'n Tie, #1910, 1981, NRFP $10.00
Barbie, Nighty-Negligee Set, #965, 1959-64, MIP $140.00	Barbie, Snap Dash, #1824, 1968, NRFP.......................... $140.00
Barbie, Now Knit, #1452, 1970, NRFP $100.00	Barbie, Sophisticated Lady, #993, 1963-64, NRFP $275.00
Barbie, Overall Denim, #3488, 1972, NRFP $110.00	Barbie, Sophisticated Lady, #993, 1963-64, VG (no pkg) .$40.00
Barbie, Pajama Pow, #1806, complete, EX (no pkg)....... $125.00	Barbie, Star of the Snow in Golden Glow, #9741, 1977, NRFP $15.00
Barbie, Party Date, #958, 1963, MIP.............................. $225.00	
Barbie, Patio Party, #1708, 1965, NRFP..........................$50.00	Barbie, Sugar Plum Fairy, #9326, 1976, NRFP...................$40.00
Barbie, Pedal Pushers, Pak, 1968, NRFP $120.00	Barbie, Swingin' Easy, #955, 1963, NRFP $225.00
barbie, Perfect Beginnings, #60, 1970, NRFP $90.00	Barbie, Topsy Twosider, #4826, 1984, NRFP....................$10.00
Barbie, Perfectly Pink, #4805, 1984, NRFP $10.00	Barbie, Trail Blazer, #1846, 1968, NRFP $250.00
Barbie, Plush Pony, #1873, 1969, NRFP $175.00	Barbie, Two-Way Tiger, #3402, 1971, NRFP.................... $110.00
Barbie, Poodle Parade, #1643, NRFP $1,000.00	Barbie, Velvet Touch, #2789, 1979, NRFP $15.00
Barbie, Poodle Parade, #1643, 1965, complete, EX+ (no pkg)... $275.00	Barbie, Walking Pretty Pak, 1971, NRFP........................ $130.00
	Barbie, Wild 'N Wonderful, #1856, 1968-69, NRFB...... $200.00
Barbie, Rain or Shine, #2788, 1979, NRFP $15.00	Barbie, Yellow Go, #1816, 1967, NRFP........................... $800.00
Barbie, Raincoat, #949, 1963, NRFP $100.00	Barbie & Stacey, All the Trimmings Fashion Pak, #0050, 1970, MOC $75.00
Barbie, Rare Pair, #1462, 1970, NRFP $125.00	
Barbie, Reception Line, #1654, 1966, NRFP $550.00	Francie, Checkmates, #1259, 1966, NRFP...................... $150.00
Barbie, Red Flair, #939, 1962, NRFP.............................. $175.00	Francie, Cheerleading Outfit, #7711, 1973, NRFP............$80.00
Barbie, Royal Ball, #2668, 1979, NRFP $15.00	Francie, Dancing Party, #1257, NRFP............................ $275.00
Barbie, Scene-Stealers, #1845, 1968, NRFP $240.00	Francie, First Formal, #1260, 1966, NRFP $200.00
Barbie, Scuba Do's, #1788, 1970, NRFP $65.00	Francie, Furry-Go-Round, #1294, Sears Exclusive, 1967, NRFP..$500.00
Barbie, Sea-Worthy, #1872, 1969, NRFP $225.00	Francie, Hip Knits, #1265, 1966, NRFB $225.00
Barbie, Shape-Ups, #1782, 1970-71, NRFP $200.00	Francie, It's a Date, #1251, 1960s, NRFP $150.00
Barbie, Sharp Shift, #20, 1970, NRFP............................. $110.00	Francie, Merry-Go-Rounders, #1230, MIP...................... $150.00
Barbie, Sheath Sensation, #986, 1961, NRFP................. $150.00	Francie, Peach Plush, #3461, 1971, NRFP $250.00
Barbie, Shimmering Magic, #1664, 1966-67, complete, EX (no pkg) $400.00	Francie, Quick Shift, #1266, 1966, NRFP....................... $200.00
	Francie, Sissy Suits, #1228, 1969, MIB $125.00

Barbie Doll and Friends, Clothing and Accessories
• • • • • • • • • • • • • • • • • • • •
Ken, Fashion Original Business Suit, #7246, 1975, $60.00. (Photo courtesy Stefanie Deutsch)

Barbie Doll and Friends, Clothing and Accessories
• •
Ken, Get-Ups 'n Go, Casual Suit, #9167, 1976, $70.00. (Photo courtesy Sarah Sink Eames)

Barbie Doll and Friends, Clothing and Accessories
• •
Ken and Brad Accessories, #3384, 1972, NRFC, $90.00; #8627, 1973, NRFP, $40.00. (Photo courtesy Stefanie Deutsch)

Francie, Slightly Summery Fashion Pak, 1968, NRFP.......$95.00
Francie, Sugar Sheers, #1229, 1969-70, NRFP $125.00
Francie, Summer Number, #3454, 1971-72 & 1974, MIP ..$175.00
Francie, Totally Terrific, #3280, 1972, MIP..................... $225.00
Francie, Wedding Whirl, #1244, 1970-71 & 1974, complete, M $275.00
Francie & Casey, Cool It! Fashion Pak, 1968, MIP $50.00
Francie & Stacey, Culotte-Wot?, #1214, 1968-69, MIB. $300.00
Francie & Stacey, Tennis Time, #1221, 1969-70, MIP ... $150.00
Fun at McDonald's, #4276, 1983, NRFP...........................$15.00
Jazzie, Mini Dress, #3781 or #3783, 1989, NRFP, ea..........$10.00
Ken, A Go-Go, #1423, 1960s, NRFP.............................. $725.00
Ken, Army & Air Force, #797, 1963, EX (no pkg)............$70.00
Ken, Army & Air Force, #797, 1963, NRFP.................... $250.00
Ken, Beach Beat, #3384, 1972, NRFP..............................$80.00
Ken, Best Man, #1425, 1960s, NRFP $1,500.00
Ken, Big Business #1434, 1970, NRFP.............................$75.00
Ken, Blazer, Pak, 1962, NRFP $25.00
Ken, Breakfast at 7, #1428, 1969, NRFP.........................$70.00
Ken, Campus Corduroys, #1410, 1964, NRFP $75.00
Ken, Casual All-Stars, #1436, 1970, NRFP $50.00
Ken, Casual Suit, #9167, 1976, NFRB.............................$70.00
Ken, Cool 'N Casual, #3379, 1972, NRFP........................$70.00
Ken, Country Clubbin', #1400, 1964, NRFP $100.00
Ken, Date Night, #5651, 1983, NRFP..............................$10.00
Ken, Date w/Barbie, #5824, 1983, NRFP $10.00
Ken, Denims for Fun, #3376, 1972, NRFP.......................$70.00
Ken, Doctor, #7705, 1973, NRFP....................................$80.00
Ken, Double Play, #4886, 1984, NRFP............................$10.00
Ken, Fountain Boy, #1407, 1964, NRFP........................ $250.00
Ken, Fraternity Meeting, #1408, 1964, NRFP $75.00
Ken, Fun on Ice, #791, 1963, NRFP.............................. $125.00
Ken, Goin' Huntin', #1409, 1964, NRFP $125.00
Ken, Going Bowling, #1403, 1964, NRFP $50.00
Ken, Graduation, #795, 1963, NRFP $65.00
Ken, Groom, #9596, 1976, NRFP $15.00
Ken, Gym Shorts & Hooded Jacket, #2795, 1979, NRFP .$60.00
Ken, Here Comes the Groom, #1426, 1960s, NRFP.... $1,500.00
Ken, Hiking Holiday, #1412, 1965, NMIP...................... $225.00
Ken, In Hawaii, #1404, 1960s, NRFP $200.00
Ken, In the Limelight, #2802, 1979, NRFP $20.00
Ken, Jazz Concert, #1420, 1966, NRFP......................... $275.00
Ken, Midnight Blues, #1719, 1972, NRFP..................... $115.00
Ken, Mod Madras, #1828, 1972, NRFP......................... $115.00
Ken, Night Scene, #1496, 1971, NRFP.......................... $100.00
Ken, Olympic Hockey, #7247, 1975, NRFP......................$70.00
Ken, Pepsi Outfit, #7761, 1974, NRFP............................$40.00
Ken, Play Ball, #792, 1963, NRFP................................. $120.00
Ken, Prince (The), #0772, 1964-65, M, no pkg............. $150.00
Ken, Rally Day, #788, 1962, NRFP $90.00
Ken, Roller Skate Date, #1405, 1964, NRFP $130.00
Ken, Running Start, #1404, 1981, NRFP.........................$10.00
Ken, Safari, #7706, 1973, NRFP.....................................$70.00
Ken, Sea Scene, #1449, 1971, NRFP $60.00
Ken, Ship-Shape, #4885, 1984, NRFP $10.00
Ken, Sportsman, Pak, 1964, NRFP..................................$90.00
Ken, Suede Scene, #1439, 1971, NRFP $60.00
Ken, Summer Job, #1422, 1966, NRFP.......................... $450.00

Ken, Tuxedo, #787, 1961, complete, EX (no pkg) $40.00
Ken, United Airlines Pilot Uniform, #7707, 1973, NRFP..$100.00
Ken, Vest Dressed, #2799, 1979, NRFP $15.00
Ken, Victory Dance, #1411, 1964, NRFP $155.00
Ken, Way-Out West, #1720, 1972, NRFP.......................$65.00
Ken, Well Suited, #1407, 1980, NRFP...........................$10.00
Ken, Western Winner, #3378, 1972, NRFP $60.00
Ken, White Is Right Fashion Pak, 1964, NRFP $40.00
Ken & Brad, Sun Fun Fashion Pak, 1971, MIP.................$75.00
Midge, Orange Blossom, #987, 1962, NRFP...................$75.00
Ricky, Let's Explore, #1506, 1965-67, NRFC...................$50.00
Skipper, All Over Felt, #3476, NRFP............................ $150.00
Skipper, All Spruced Up!, #1941, 1967, NRFP $145.00
Skipper, Ballerina, #3471, 1971, NRFP..........................$75.00
Skipper, Beach, #7848, 1974, NRFP $50.00
Skipper, Beach Party, #1409, 1980, NRFP.....................$10.00
Skipper, Bicentennial Fashions, #9165, 1976, NRFP $70.00
Skipper, Budding Beauty, #1731, 1970, NRFP $75.00
Skipper, Check the Suit, Pak, 1971, NRFP......................$45.00
Skipper, Chill Chasers, #1926, 1966, NRFP $75.00
Skipper, Chilly Chums, #1973, 1969, NRFP................... $125.00
Skipper, City Shopping, #2809, 1979, NRFP...................$15.00
Skipper, Cookie Time, #1912, 1965, NRFP $125.00
Skipper, Daisy Crazy, 1970, #1732, M..........................$30.00
Skipper, Dressed in Velvet, #3477, 1971, NRFP............. $125.00
Skipper, Get-Ups 'N Go Flower Girl, #7847, 1974-76, MIP...$100.00
Skipper, Hearts 'N Flowers, #1945, 1967, NRFB $300.00
Skipper, Ice Skatin', #3470, 1971-72, MIP $150.00
Skipper, Jeepers Creepers, #1966, 1969, NRFP.............. $125.00
Skipper, Lacey Charmer & Partytimer, #9746, 1977, NRFP..$15.00
Skipper, Masquerade, #1903, 1964, NRFP $160.00
Skipper, Nifty Knickers, #3291, 1972, NRFP...................$85.00
Skipper, Olympic Skating, #7251, 1975, NRFP.................$70.00
Skipper, Party Pair, #3297, 1972, NRFP.........................$90.00
Skipper, Platter Party, #1914, 1965, NRFP $125.00
Skipper, Popover, #1943, 1967, NRFP $175.00
Skipper, Rain or Shine, #1916, 1965, NRFP....................$95.00
Skipper, Real Sporty, #1961, 1968, NRFP $200.00

Skipper, School's Cool, #1976, 1969-70, MIP................ $200.00
Skipper, Shoe Parade Fashion Pak, 1965, NRFP..............$45.00
Skipper, Skimmy Stripes, #1956, 1968, MIP.................. $200.00
Skipper, Tea Party, #1924, 1966, NRFP $175.00
Skipper & Fluff, Fun Runners, #3372, 1972, MIP.............$50.00
Skipper & Fluff, Some Shoes Fashion Pak, 1971, MIP......$65.00
Skipper & Fluff, Super Snoozers, #3371, 1972, NRFB.......$55.00
Tutti, Birthday Beauties, #3617, 1968, NRFP $160.00
Tutti, Pink PJs, #3616, 1968-69, MIP........................... $150.00
Twiggy, Twiggy Turnouts, #1726, 1968, NRFP $250.00

FURNITURE, ROOMS, HOUSES, AND SHOPS

Action Sewing Center, 1972, MIB.................................$50.00
Barbie & Midge Queen Size Chifferobe (Susy Goose), NM. $100.00
Barbie & Skipper Deluxe Dream House, Sears Exclusive, 1965,
    MIB, minimum value $175.00
Barbie & The Beat Dance Cafe, 1990, MIB $35.00
Barbie & the Rockers Hot Rockin' Stage, 1987, MIB $40.00
Barbie Beauty Boutique, 1976, MIB.............................$40.00
Barbie Cafe Today, 1971, MIB.................................. $400.00
Barbie Cookin' Fun Kitchen, MIB $100.00
Barbie Dream Armoire, 1980, NRFB............................$35.00
Barbie Dream Bed & Nightstand, 1984, pk, MIB.............$25.00
Barbie Dream Glow Vanity, 1986, MIB $20.00
Barbie Dream House Bedroom, 1981, MIB......................$6.00
Barbie Dream Kitch-Dinette, #4095, 1964, MIB $600.00
Barbie Dream Store Makeup Department, 1983, MIB.......$40.00
Barbie Fashion Wraps Boutique, 1989, MIB $35.00
Barbie Lively Livin' Room, MIB $50.00
Barbie Playhouse Pavilion, Europe, MIB.......................$75.00
Barbie's Apartment, 1975, MIB................................. $140.00
Barbie's Room-Fulls Firelight Living Room, 1974, MIB. $100.00
Barbie Unique Boutique, Sears Exclusive, 1971, MIB.... $185.00
Coot Tops Skipper T-Shirt Shop, 1989, complete, MIB....$25.00
Francie House, 1966, complete, M............................. $150.00

Barbie Doll and Friends, Furniture, Rooms, Houses, and Shops
• •
Barbie-Tutti Playhouse, 1966, #3306, with doll, EX, $75.00. (Photo courtesy Connie Craig Kaplan)

Go-Together Chaise Lounge, MIB $75.00
Go-Together Dining Room, Barbie & Skipper, 1965, MIB.... $50.00
Go-Together Lawn Swing & Planter, 1964, complete, MIB... $150.00
Ice Capades Skating Rink, 1989, MIB $70.00
Living Pretty Cooking Center, 1988, MIB.................$25.00
Magical Mansion, 1989, MIB............................. $125.00
Party Garden Playhouse, 1994, MIB $275.00
Pink Sparkles Armoire, 1990, NRFB $25.00
Pink Sparkles Starlight Bed, 1990, MIB................ $300.00
Skipper Dream Room, 1964, MIB $300.00
Skipper's Jeweled Vanity (Susy Goose), Sears Exclusive, 1965, NRFP $100.00
Superstar Barbie Beauty Salon, 1977, MIB $55.00
Surprise House, 1972, MIB............................. $100.00
Susy Goose Canopy Bed, 1962, MIB.................... $150.00
Susy Goose Four Poster Bed Outfit, M $35.00
Susy Goose Mod-A-Go-Go Bedroom, 1966, NRFB.... $2,300.00
Susy Goose Wardrobe, 1962, EX........................$35.00
Tutti Playhouse, 1966, M............................. $100.00
World of Barbie House, 1966, MIB $175.00

GIFT SETS

Ballerina Barbie on Tour, 1976, MIB..................... $175.00
Barbie & Ken Campin' Out, 1983, MIB $75.00
Barbie Dance Club & Tape Player Set, #4217, 1989, MIB.$75.00
Barbie's Olympic Ski Village, MIB.......................$75.00
Barbie's Wedding Party, 1964, MIB.................... $700.00
Barbie Snap 'N Play Deluxe Gift Set, JC Penney Exclusive, 1992, MIB..$40.00
Barbie 35th Anniversary Gift Set, 1994, NRFP............. $150.00
Birthday Fun at McDonald's, 1994, NRFB.................$75.00
Cinderella, 1992, NRFB $125.00
Dance Sensation Barbie, 1985, MIB $35.00
Dramatic New Living Skipper Very Best Velvet, Sears Exclusive, 1970-71, NRFB $1,500.00

Golden Dreams Glamorous Nights, 1980, NRFB $100.00
Halloween Party Barbie & Ken, Target, 1998, NRFB........$65.00
Happy Meal Stacie & Whitney, JC Penney Exclusive, 1994, MIB $30.00
Ken Red, White & Wild, Sears Exclusive, 1970, NRFB.. $525.00
Living Barbie Action Accents, Sears Exclusive, 1970, MIB ...$450.00
Malibu Barbie Beach Party, M (M case)....................$75.00
Malibu Ken Surf''s Up, Sears Exclusive, 1971, MIB $350.00
New 'N Groovy PJ Swingin' in Silver, MIB $770.00
Night Night Sleep Tight Tutti, NRFB........................... $300.00
Pretty Pairs Nan 'N Fran, 1970, NRFB $250.00
Skipper Party Time, 1964, NRFB $500.00
Stacey Nite Lighting, Sears Exclusive, 1969, NRFB.... $2,000.00
Sun Sensation Barbie Spray & Play Fun, Wholesale Clubs, 1992, MIB...$60.00
Superstar Barbie Fashion Change-Abouts, 1978, NRFB.. $100.00
Talking Barbie Golden Groove Set, Sears Exclusive, 1969, MIB $1,500.00
Talking Barbie Perfectly Plaid, Sears Exclusive, 1971, MIB .. $500.00
Tutti & Todd Sundae Treat, 1966, NRFB $500.00
Wedding Party Midge, 1990, NRFB $150.00

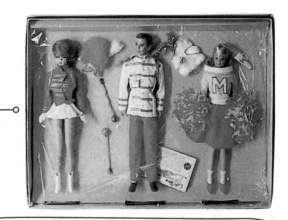

Barbie Doll and Friends, Gift Sets
• •
Barbie, Ken, and Midge on Parade Gift Set, 1964, #1014, NMIB, $925.00. (Photo courtesy James D. Julia, Inc.)

Barbie Doll and Friends, Gift Sets
• • • • • • • • • • •
Twirly Curls Barbie Gift Set, 1983, #4079, MIB, $80.00. (Photo courtesy Paris and Susan Manos)

VEHICLES

Allan's Roadster, 1964, aqua, MIB $500.00
ATC Cycle, Sears Exclusive, 1972, MIB $65.00
Austin Healy, Irwin, 1962, red & wht, very rare, NRFB .. $3,500.00
Barbie & Ken Dune Buggy, Irwin, 1970, pk, MIB........... $250.00
Barbie & the Rockers Hot Rockin' Van, 1987, MIB........$60.00
Barbie's Own Sports Car, NMIB $150.00
Barbie Silver 'Vette, MIB..$30.00
Barbie Travelin' Trailer, MIB.....................................$40.00
Beach Buggy for Skipper, Irwin, 1964, rare, MIB, minimum
    value $500.00
Beach Bus, 1974, MIB $45.00
California Dream Beach Taxi, 1988, MIB......................$35.00
Ken's Classy Corvette, 1976, yel, MIB $75.00
Ken's Dream 'Vette, 1981, dk bl, MIB........................ $100.00
Ken's Hot Rod, Sears Exclusive, 1964, red, MIB........... $900.00
Snowmobile, Montgomery Ward, 1972, MIB $65.00
Sports Plane, Sears Exclusive, 1964, MIB $3,600.00
Star 'Vette, 1977, red, MIB....................................... $100.00
Starlight Motorhome, 1994, MIB................................$45.00
Sunsailer, 1975, NRFB...$55.00
Western Star Traveler Motorhome, 1982, MIB $50.00
1957 Belair Chevy, 1989, 1st edition, aqua, MIB........... $150.00
1957 Belair Chevy, 1990, 2nd edition, pk, MIB.............. $125.00

MISCELLANEOUS

Barbie & the Rockers, purse, vinyl, w/comb & cologne, M ..$15.00
Barbie Dictionary, vinyl w/head image of Bubble-Cut Barbie
    encircled by lettering & stars graphics, 1963, G.............$20.00
Barbie Disco Record Player, 1976, M $75.00
Barbie Ge-Tar, 1965, MIP... $375.00
Barbie Nurse Kit, Pressman, 1962, M....................................$85.00
Barbie Pretty-Up Time Perfume Pretty Bath, 1964, complete,
    M.. $150.00
Barbie Pretty-Up Time, w/brush, comb & mirror, 1960s, MIP ..$125.00
Barbie Shrinky Dinks, 1979, MIB $30.00
Book, Barbie's Fashion Success, Random House, 1962, hard-
    cover, EX $20.00
Carrying Case, cloth w/vinyl trim, Barbie's name & allover
    flower design, grip hdl, zipper, VG $75.00
Coloring Book, Barbie & Ken, 1963, unused, NM $50.00
Coloring Book, Francie, Whitman #1094, 1967, unused, NM...$20.00
Embroidery Set, Barbie & Ken, 1962, complete, rare, NMIB.$150.00
Francie Electric Drawing Table, 1966, M $60.00
Game, Barbie 35th Anniversary, Golden, 1994, MIB........$60.00

Knitting for Barbie, cb canister w/metal ends, complete contents,
    VG $30.00
Ornament, Holiday Barbie, Hallmark, 1993, 1st edition, MIB.$75.00
Paper Dolls, Barbie, Whitman #4601, 1963, uncut, M......$85.00
Paper Dolls, Midge Cut-Outs, Whitman #1962, 1963, uncut,
    NM $150.00
Party Set, 31-pc pk & wht plastic set w/graphics, cups, plates,
    silverware, pots & pans, 1983, MIB (sealed) $35.00
Pencil Case, Barbie, Ken & Midge, 1964, M $100.00
Puzzle, jigsaw, Barbie & Ken, Whitman, 1963, 100 pcs,
    MIB..$40.00
Quick Curl Miss America Beauty Center, Sears Exclusive, 1975,
    MIB..$75.00
Sweet Sixteen Promotional Set, 1974, M $70.00
Tea Set, Barbie 25th Anniversary, 1984, complete, M ... $150.00
Wagon, Camp Barbie, 1995, 34", EX $50.00
Yo-yo, Spectra Star, plastic w/paper sticker, MIP................$5.00

Barbie Doll and Friends, Miscellaneous
Barbie Cut-Outs, Whitman, #1962, 1963, unused M, $85.00. (Photo courtesy Lorraine Mieszala)

Barbie Doll and Friends, Miscellaneous
Wallets, vinyl with graphics, 1962, EX, each $25.00. (Photo courtesy Connie Craig Kaplan)

• • • • • • • • • • • • • • • Battery-Operated Toys • • • • • • • • • • • • • • •

From the standpoint of being visually entertaining, nothing can compare with the battery-operated toy. Most (probably as much as 95%) were made in Japan from the 1940s through the 1960s, though some were distributed by American companies such as Marx, Ideal, and Daisy, who often sold them under their own names. So even if they're marked, it's sometimes almost impossible to identify the manufacturer. Though batteries had been used to power trains and provide simple illumination in earlier toys, the Japanese toys could smoke, walk, talk, drink, play instruments, blow soap bubbles, and do just about anything else humanly possible to dream up and engineer. Generally, the more actions the toy performs, the more collectible it is. Rarity is important as well, but first and foremost to consider is condition. Because of their complex mechanisms, many will no longer work. Children often stopped them in mid-cycle, rubber hoses and bellows aged and cracked, and leaking batteries caused them to corrode, so very few have survived to the present intact and in good enough condition to interest a collector. Although it is sometimes possible to have them repaired, it is probably better to wait on a better example. Original boxes have considerable impact on the value of a battery-op and can sometimes be counted on to add from 30% to 50% (and up), depending on the box's condition, of course, as well as the toy's age and rarity.

Sometimes the name of a toy will appear on the toy itself; on occasion, the name on the box will be different. When this is the case, we have started our descriptive line by the name that appears on the toy first; the box name will follow in parenthesis. Some cross referencing has been used to help identify toys without boxes. For more information we recommend *Collecting Toys* by Richard O'Brien.

Note: The following listings are for toys in working order, and boxes are in excellent condition or better unless noted otherwise.

Advisor: Tom Lastrapes

See also Aeronautical; Boats; Games; Guns; Japanese (and Other) Tin Vehicle Replicas; Marx; Robots and Space Toys; Tin Vehicles.

Battery-Operated Toys
• • • • • • • • • • • • • • • •
Accordion Bear (lighted eyes), Kraemer, EXIB, $800.00. (Photo courtesy Morphy Auctions on LiveAuctioneers.com)

Battery-Operated Toys
• • • • • • • • • • • • •
Astro Dog, Y, 1960s, tin and plastic, remote control, MIB, $100.00. (Photo courtesy www.serioustoyz.com)

ABC Toyland Express, MT, 1950s, 15", NM.....................$50.00
Accordion Bear, Alps, 1950s, 11", EX............................ $325.00
Accordion Player Hobo (w/Monkey), Alps, 1950s, NMIB.$450.00
Acro-Chimp Porter, YM, 1960s, 9", NMIB......................$75.00
Acrobatic Umbrella, lady in cloth outfit holding tin umbrella, 10", GIB... $100.00
Air Control Tower (w/Airplane & Helicopter), Bandai, 1960s, 10½", EXIB... $250.00

All Stars Mr Baseball Jr, K, 1950s, 8", EXIB $825.00
Amphibious Car, plastic, red, cream & wht w/blk stripe, drives & floats, 10½" L, EX+IB.. $100.00
Animal Yacker/Crackers the Talking Plush Parrot, MIB . $175.00
Animated Squirrel, S&E, 1950s, 9", MIB $100.00
Annie Tugboat, Y, 1950s, 12½", NM+ $150.00
Answer Game Machine (Robot), Ichida, 1960s, 15", NMIB .$450.00
Antique Fire Car, TN, 1950s, 10", EXIB..........................$75.00
Antique Gooney Car, Alps, 1960s, 9", EX+......................$75.00
Arthur A-Go-Go, Alps, 1960s, 10", NM+IB.................. $375.00
Arthur A-Go-Go, Alps, 1960s, 10", VG......................... $175.00
Aston Martin Secret Ejector Car, #M101, r/c, 11", EX... $250.00
Auto-Matic (Rock 'N Roll Monkey), see Rock 'N Roll Monkey
B-Z Porter (Baggage Truck), MT, 1950s, 8" L, EXIB....... $125.00
B-Z Rabbit, MT, 1950s, 7" L, EX $100.00
Baby & Carriage Pony Tail Girl, Rosko/S&E, 1950s, 8" H, EXIB...$175.00
Baby Carriage, TN, 1950s, 13", EXIB.............................. $125.00
Baggage Porter, Cragstan, plush dog pulling 2-wheeled stake cart, 12", EXIB... $125.00
Ball Blowing Clown (w/Mystery Action), TN, 1950s, cloth costume, 11", EXIB... $175.00
Ball Playing Bear, 1940s, bear, goose, umbrella & celluloid balls in spiral wire on tin base, 11", EXIB $900.00
Balloon Blowing Monkey (Lighted Eyes), Alps, 1950s, plush w/ cloth overalls, 12", EXIB.. $125.00
Balloon Vendor, Y, 1960s, tin w/cloth outfit, 11", GIB... $125.00
Barber Bear, TN, 1950s, plush, tin base, 10", EXIB $400.00
Barky Puppy, Alps, r/c, plush, 9" H, EXIB.........................$50.00
Barney Bear the Drumming Boy, Alps, 1950s, r/c, 11", NM+IB.$100.00
Bartender, TN, 1960s, wht-haired gent in red jacket standing behind tin bar, 12", EXIB..$80.00
Batman Flying Batplane, Remco 1966, r/c, plastic, performs aerial stunts, 12", EXIB $125.00
Batman Zoomcycle, DC Comics, 1977, unused, MIB........$75.00
Batmobile, Taiwan, tin & plastic, w/Batman & Robin figures, 12", EX+IB $250.00
Batmobile (Mystery Action/Blinking Warning Light/Engine Noise), Ahi, 1970s, blk w/red trim, Batman figure, 12", EX $225.00
Bear Target Game, MT, 1950s, tin, 9", NMIB................. $300.00
Bear the Cashier, MT, 1950s, plush, 8" , EXIB............... $250.00
Bear the Shoe Maker, TN, 1950s, 8½", EX+.................... $200.00
Bear the Shoe Maker, TN, 1950s, 8½", EXIB $300.00
Bear the Xylophone Player, Y, 1950s, r/c, plush & tin, 10", EX .$275.00
Beauty Parlor, Y, 1950s, 9½", EX $400.00

Battery-Operated Toys
· ·
Baby Bertha the Watering Elephant, Mego, 1960s, 9" long, MIB, $475.00. (Photo courtesy Don Hultzman)

Battery-Operated Toys
· · · · · · · · · · · · ·
Batman, Nomura, 1960s, tin and vinyl, 12", NM+IB, $6,780.00. (Photo courtesy Smith House Toy and Auction Company)

Beethoven the Piano Playing Dog, see Pianist (Jolly Pianist)

Big Dipper, Technofix, 1960s, 3 cars on track, 21" L, EX. $150.00

Big John the Chimpee Chief, Alps, 1960s, chimp in Indian headdress seated at drum, 13", EXIB................$50.00

Big Ring Circus (Circus Parade), MT, 1950s, truck, 13", EXIB $200.00

Big Top Champ Circus Clown, Alps, 1960s, 14", NMIB. $100.00

Big Wheel Ice Cream Truck, Taiyo, 1970s, 10", EX...........$75.00

Bimbo the Drumming Clown, Cragstan, 1950s, r/c, 11", EXIB...$225.00

Birdwatcher Bear, MT, plush, seated w/bird on paw, 10", EX ... $450.00

Black Smithy Bear, TN, 1950s, plush bear seated at anvil, 10", EXIB $325.00

Black Tap Dancer, Japan, tin figure in straw hat, plaid jacket & striped pants on round base, 11", EX $150.00

Blacksmith Bear, A-1, 1950s, plush bear standing at anvil & fire pit, 9", EXIB $375.00

Blinky the Clown, Amico Toy, r/c, EXIB........................ $250.00

Blushing Frankenstein, Nomura, tin & vinyl, 13", NMIB ...$175.00

Blushing Gunfighter, Y, 1960s, tin w/cloth shirt, 11", NMIB...$125.00

Blushing Willie, Y, 1960s, wht-haired gent pouring himself a drink, 10", EXIB $75.00

Bobby Drinking Bear, Y, 1950s, r/c, plush, 10", VGIB.... $425.00

Bomber Pilot, Yoshia, tin & plastic, 9" WS, VGIB......... $250.00

Bongo Monkey (w/Bongo Drums & Lited Eyes), Alps, 1960s, plastic hat, 10", EXIB.. $150.00

Bowling Bank, ASC/Daniel Imports, 1960s, 10", unused, MIB $100.00

Brave Eagle (Beating Drum & Raising War-Hoop), TN, 1950s, cloth outfit, 13", MIB.. $125.00

Bruin the Bear & His Ball Playing Act, Cragstan, tin & celluloid, 10", NMIB.. $500.00

Bruno Accordion Bear, Y, 1950s, r/c, 10", EXIB $350.00

Bubble Bear, MT, 1950s, blows bubbles, 9½", EXIB........ $275.00

Bubble Blowing Boy, Y, 1950s, 8", NMIB $225.00

Bubble Blowing Monkey, Alps, 1950s, 11", EXIB........... $125.00

Bubble Blowing Musician, Y, 1950s, 10", NMIB............. $225.00

Bubble Blowing Popeye, Linemar, 1950s, 12", EXIB.... $1,000.00

Bubble Blowing Popeye, Linemar, 1950s, 12", NMIB.. $1,200.00

Bubble Blowing Popeye, Linemar, 1950s, 12", VG $450.00

Bubble Blowing Washing Bear, Y, 1950s, 8", EXIB......... $300.00

Bubble Kangaroo, MT, 1950s, 9", NMIB...................... $300.00

Bubble Lion, MT, 1950s, 7", EXIB $125.00

Bubbling Bull (Wild West Rodeo), Linemar, 1950s, 8", NMIB... $175.00

Bulldozer (Tractor), ISI, 1950s, r/c, tin w/blk rubber treads, driver in open seat, 8½", NMIB.. $125.00

Bumper Automatic Control Bus, Bandai, 15", EXIB $225.00

Bunny the Busy Secretary, MT, plush & tin, 7½", NMIB . $600.00

Bunny the Magician, Alps, 1950s, plush, 14", EXIB....... $325.00

Burger Chef, Y, 1950s, plush & tin, 9", EXIB.................. $175.00

Busy Housekeeper (Bear), Alps, 1950s, pushing sweeper, plush w/ cloth dress, 9", EXIB...................................... $250.00

Busy Housekeeper (Rabbit), Alps, 1950s, pushing sweeper, plush w/cloth dress, 10", EXIB.. $250.00

Busy Secretary, Linemar, 1950s, 7½" H, EXIB $250.00

Cadillac (Musical Open Car), Yoshiya, w/cowboy driver, 9", NMIB $450.00

Calypso Joe, Linemar, 1950s, r/c, 10", EX $300.00

Camera Shooting Bear, see Cine Bear (Camera Shooting Bear)

Cappy the Happy Baggage Porter, Alps, 1960s, 12", MIB...$275.00

Captain Kidd Pirate Ship, Y, 1960s, 13", rare, MIB........ $275.00

Champion Weight Lifter, TM, 1960s, plush monkey w/lg barbell, 10", EXIB $250.00

Chap the Obedient Dog, Rosko, 1960s, MIB...................$75.00

Charlie the Drumming Clown, see Cragstan Melody Band (Charlie the Drumming Clown)

Charlie the Funny Clown, Alps, 1960s, clown in cloth outfit on circus car, 10" L, EXIB.................................. $175.00

Charlie Weaver Bartender, TN, 1960s, NMIB................ $125.00

Chee Chee Chihuahua, Mego, 1960s, 8", EX $25.00

Cheerful Dachshund, Y, 1960s, r/c, plush, 9", EXIB $50.00

Chef Cook, Y, 1960s, 9", EXIB.................................... $175.00

Chimpy the Jolly Drummer, Alps, plush monkey seated at drum w/cymbals, 9", EXIB...$50.00

Chippy the Chipmunk, Alps, 1950s, 12", NMIB............. $100.00

Cindy the Meowing Cat, Tomiyama, 1950s, 12", EX.........$35.00

Circus Fire Engine, MT, 1960s, tin & plastic, 11", EX.... $125.00

Circus Lion, Rock Valley, 1950s, plush, seated on drum, w/whip & carpet, 10", EXIB $375.00

Circus Parade, see Big Ring Circus

Clancy the Great, Ideal, 1960s, MIB............................. $225.00

Climbing Linesman (Clown), TPS, 1950s, clown climbing metal rod atop vehicle, 24" (assembled), EXIB $650.00

Clown & Lion, MT, 1960s, clown spins up & down pole as lion roars, tin base, 13", NMIB.. $325.00

Clown & Magician, Cragstan, #40244, 1950s, cloth costume, VGIB $200.00

Clown on Roller Skates, Japan, r/c, litho tin w/cloth costume, 6½", EX.. $400.00

Clucking Clara, CK, 1950s, NM $50.00

Coffeetime Bear, TN, 1960s, plush & tin, 10", EXIB...... $250.00

College Jalopy, Linemar, 10", NMIB $375.00

Collie, Alps, 1950s, r/c, plush, barks & begs, eyes light up, EXIB $75.00

Comic Choo Choo, Cragstan, 1960s, 10", EX $35.00

Comic Hungry Bug (Volkswagen Beetle), Tora, 1960s, 8", NMIB $80.00

Coney Island Penny Machine, Remco, NMIB................ $125.00

Coney Island Rocket Ride, Alps, 1950s, tin, 13½", NMIB ..$850.00

Cragstan Crapshooter, Y, 1950s, 9½", NMIB $150.00

Cragstan Dog Shuttling Train, Yonezawa, 38" L, NMIB. $125.00

Cragstan Melody Band (Daisy the Jolly Drumming Duck), Alps, 1950s, plush & tin, eyes light up, 9", EXIB.................. $200.00

Cragstan Melody Band (Mambo the Jolly Drumming Elephant), 9", EXIB.. $175.00

Cragstan Playboy, 1960s, 13", EXIB $125.00

Cragstan Remote Driving-Dashboard Control Car (1959 Buick), Nomura, 11½", NMIB... $425.00

Cragstan Roulette Man, Y, 1960s, 9", unused, MIB........ $200.00

Cragstan Telly Bear, S&E, 1950s, plush, tin desk, 9", EXIB.. $275.00

Cragstan Tootin'-Chuggin' Locomotive w/Mystery Action (Santa Fe), tin, 24", EXIB... $125.00

Cragstan Two-Gun Sheriff, r/c, 10", EXIB $125.00

Crowing Rooster, Y, 1950s, plush, wht, yel & orange, 9", EXIB..$75.00

Cycling Daddy, Bandai, 1960s, 10", EXIB $125.00

Cymbal Playin' Monkey, r/c, lt brn plush w/pointed hat, metal cymbals, 12", EXIB...$50.00

Daisy the Jolly Drumming Duck, see Cragstan Melody Band (Daisy the Drumming Duck)

Dalmatian (The Jolly Drumming Dog), Cragstan, plush, 9", EXIB $150.00

Dancing Dan (w/His Mystery Mike), Bell, 1950s, 16", EXIB... $175.00

Dancing Merry Chimp, Kuramochi, 1960s, 11", NM $150.00

Dancing Sam, litho tin, 11", EX.................................... $200.00

Dandy the Happy Drumming Pup, Cragstan, 1950s, 9", EXIB..$125.00

Dandy Turtle, DSK, 1950s, 8", M $150.00

Dashee the Derby Hat Dachshund, Mego, 1970s, r/c, plush w/ plastic hat, MIB...$80.00

Dentist Bear, S&E, 1950s, plush & tin, 10", MIB........... $275.00

Dilly Dalmatian, Cragstan, 1950s, r/c, plush, 8", VGIB.. $100.00

Dip-ie the Whale, SH, 1960s, 13", M $125.00

Disney Acrobat (Donald Duck), Linemar, celluloid figure on wire apparatus, EXIB.. $575.00

Disney Acrobat (Mickey Mouse), Linemar, celluloid figure on wire apparatus, 9", EXIB... $575.00

Disney Acrobat (Pluto), Linemar, 9", VGIB................... $450.00

Disney Piston Race Car, Masudaya, Mickey Driver, 9", NMIB...$100.00

Distant Early Warning Radar Station, see Radar N Scope

Dixie the Dog (Dachshund), Linemar, r/c, 10", EXIB $75.00
Dolly Dressmaker (Seamstress), TN, 1950s, 6", NMIB... $375.00
Donald Duck, Linemar, 1960s, 8", EXIB $300.00
Donald Duck Locomotive, MT, 1970, tin & plastic, 9", M..$125.00
Dozo the Steaming Clown, Rosko, 1960s, 14", VGIB $275.00
Dream Boat (Rock 'N Roll Hot Rod), TN, tin, 7", EX... $175.00
Dream Boat (Rock 'N Roll Hot Rod), TN, tin, 7", NMIB...$400.00
Drinking Captain, S&E, cloth outfit, 12", EXIB............. $125.00
Drinking Dog, Y, plush & tin, NMIB........................... $100.00
Drinking Licking Cat, TN, 1950s, tin & plush, NMIB .. $250.00
Dune Buggy (w/Surf Board), TPS, w/driver, 10", EXIB .. $100.00
El Toro, TN, 1950s, tin, NMIB $200.00
Electronic Periscope-Firing Range, Cragstan, 1950s, VGIB....$150.00
Emergency Service Truck, Nomura, tin, AAA on vehicle &
    driver's back, 9½", NMIB... $575.00
Expert Motor Cyclist, MT, 1950s, tin, 12", EX $375.00
Father Bear, MT, 1950s, plush, in rocking chair reading & drink-
    ing, EXIB $175.00
FBI Godfather Car, Bandai, 1970s, 10", MIB.................. $125.00
Feeding Bird Watcher, Linemar, 1950s, 7", EX+IB......... $450.00
Fido the Xylophone Player, Alps, 1950s, plush, 9", EXIB . $175.00
Fighter F-50 Jet Plane, KO, 'chunky' plastic plane w/pilot under
    clear dome, 9", EXIB $175.00
Fighting Bull, Alps, 1950s, 15", MIB.............................. $100.00
Fire Boat, MT, 1950s, 15", MIB..................................... $350.00
Fire Tricycle, TN, tin, w/driver, 10", EXIB.................... $650.00
Fishing Bear (Lighted Eyes), Alps, 11", EXIB $225.00
Fishing Panda Bear (Lighted Eyes), Alps, 1950s, plush & tin,
    11", EX+IB $275.00
Flexi the Pocket Monkey, Alps, 1960s, 12", MIB $125.00
Flintstone Yacht, Remco, 1960s, 17", NM+.................... $175.00
Flying Circus, Tomiyco, 14" H, EXIB............................ $650.00
Ford Mustang Fastback 2x2, plastic, lt bl, 16", EXIB (box marked
    2x2 Cool & 'Pow!') $150.00
Frankenstein (Mod Monster — Blushing Frankenstein), TN,
    1960s, standing on litho tin base w/name, 13", EX+IB . $175.00
Frankenstein Monster, Nomura/Rosko, cloth outfit, EXIB ..$175.00
Frankenstein Poynter, 1970s, mostly plastic, standing on 'rock'
    base, red & wht suit, belly showing, 13", EXIB $150.00
Frankie the Roller Skating Monkey, Alps, 1950s, r/c, plush w/
    cloth outfit, 12", VGIB... $125.00
Fred Flintstone's Bedrock Band, Alps, 1960s, 10", MIB.. $500.00
Fred Flintstone's Bedrock Band, Alps, 1960s, 10", VGIB.. $300.00
French Cat, Alps, 1950s, 10" L, MIB $75.00
Friendly Joco My Favorite Pet, Alps, 1950s, r/c, dressed monkey,
    10", EXIB.. $125.00
Funland Cup Ride, Kanto, 7" wide, NMIB $250.00
Galloping Horse & Rider, Cragstan, 12", EXIB $225.00
Gino Neapolitan Balloon Blower, Rosko, 1960s, 11", EXIB...$175.00
Godzilla Monster, Marusan, 1970s, 12", NMIB $600.00
Good Time Charlie, MT, 1960s, 13", EXIB...................... $150.00
Gorilla, see also Roaring Gorilla Shooting Gallery or Walking
    Gorilla
Gorilla, TN, 1950s, r/c, wht or brn plush, 10", EXIB...... $300.00
Grand-Pa Panda Bear, MT, 1950s, plush, in rocker, 9", NMIB..$200.00
Grandpa Bear (Smoking & Rocking w/Lighted Pipe), Alps,
    plush, 9", EXIB $225.00
Grasshopper, MT, 1950s, 6", M $350.00

Battery-Operated Toys
• • • • • • • • • • • • • • • • • • • •
Dennis the Menace (Playing Xylophone), TN,
1950s, 8", EXIB, $200.00.

Battery-Operated Toys
• • • • • • • • • • • • • • • • • • • •
Disney Fire Department
No. 6, Aerial Ladder Truck,
friction with battery-operated
Donald climbing ladder, Pluto
driver, Mickey at rear, 18", EX,
$900.00. (Photo courtesy Morphy Auctions on
LiveAuctioneers.com)

Battery-Operated
Toys
• • • • • • • • • • • • • •
Drumming Mickey
Mouse, Linemar, remote
control, lighted eyes,
11", EXIB, $975.00.
(Photo courtesy Don Hultzman)

Green Caterpillar, Daiya, tin & fabric, 10", NMIB......... $200.00
Green Hornet Secret Service Car, ASC, 1960s, 11", EX+.... $700.00
Gypsy Fortune Teller, Ichida, 1950s, 10", EXIB........... $1,250.00
Hamburger Chef, K, 1960s, 8", MIB............................... $250.00
Handy-Hank Mystery Tractor w/Light, TN, 1950s, 11",
    NMIB... $125.00
Happy 'N Sad Magic Face Clown, Y, 1960s, r/c, 11", EXIB .. $200.00
Happy Band Trio, MT, 1970s, 11", NMIB....................... $500.00
Happy Drive Car, see Speed Star 3
Happy Fiddler Clown, Cragstan, 1950s, cloth outfit, 10", MIB...$300.00

Happy Naughty Chimp, Daishin, 1960s, 10", EXIB $50.00

Happy Santa, Alps, 1950s, r/c, plush, walking w/drum, 11", EXIB..$150.00

Happy Singing Bird, MT, 1950s, 3" L, M $75.00

Happy the Clown Puppet Show, Y, 1960s, 10", EXIB..... $275.00

Hasty Chimp, Y, 1960s, 9", MIB..................................$75.00

High Jinks at the Circus, TN, 1950s, 10", NMIB $225.00

Hobo Accordion Player w/Monkey, Alps/Cragstan, 11", NMIB $350.00

Hoop Zing Girl, Linemar, 1950s, 12", MIB.....................$300.00

Hoopy the Fishing Duck, Alps, 1950s, 10", NMIB........ $375.00

Hooty the Happy Owl, Alps, 1960s, 9", EXIB $100.00

Hot Rod #158 (Dream Boat), TN, 1950s, teen driver, 10", NM $275.00

Hovercraft (Brace), TPS, 1950s, r/c, 8", NMIB..............$225.00

Hungry Cat, Linemar, 1960s, cat swipes at fishbowl, 9", EXIB ..$350.00

Hungry Hound Dog, 1950s, 10", NMIB.........................$300.00

Hungry Sheep, MT, 1950s, r/c, plush, 8" H, EXIB.......... $200.00

Hy-Que the Amazing Monkey, TN, 1960s, plush, 17", EXIB.$225.00

I May Look Busy/I'm the Boss (Telephone Bear), see Telephone Bear

Ice Cream Baby Bear, MT, 1950s, 10", rare, NM $325.00

Indian Joe, Alps, 1960s, beats drum between legs, 12", VG...$50.00

Indian Signal Choo-Choo, Kanto Toys, 1960s, 10", EXIB .$50.00

Jig-Saw Magic, Z Co, 1950s, 7x7x9", MIB $100.00

Joco the Drinking Monkey, Linemar, 1950s, plush w/plastic face, in tux & top hat, 10", EXIB...$125.00

Johnny Speed Mobile, Remco, 1960s, 15", MIB.............. $175.00

Jolly Bambino, Alps, 1950s, plush monkey in highchair, 9", MIB..$525.00

Jolly Daddy the Smoking Elephant, Marusan, 1950s, r/c, plush in cloth outfit, 9", VGIB...$150.00

Jolly Peanut Vendor, Cragstan, plush bear, 9", EXIB $325.00

Jolly Pianist, see Pianist (Jolly Pianist)

Journey Pup, S&E, 1950s, 8" L, M..................................$50.00

Jumbo (the Elephant), Alps, 1960s, r/c, plush w/circus blanket & headdress, picks up pole w/truck, 10" H, VGIB...........$175.00

Jumbo the Bubble Blowing Elephant, Y, 1950s, 7", NMIB...$150.00

Jumping Rabbit (Light-up Eyes), Japan, 1950s, 10", NMIB.$100.00

Jungle Jumbo, BN-C Toy, 1950s, hunter on elephant, 10", EXIB...$375.00

Jungle Trio, Linemar, 8", NMIB $750.00

King Zoor, Ideal, 1961, 26" L, very rare, M $500.00

Kissing Couple, Ichido, 1950s, 11", MIB.........................$325.00

Knight in Armor Target Game, 1950s, 12" figure, NMIB. $375.00

Knitting Grandma (Lighted Eyes), TN, 1950s, plush bear, 9", VGIB $125.00

Lady Pup Tending Her Garden, Cragstan, 1950s, cloth outfit, 9", EXIB $250.00

Laughing Clown (Robot), Waco, mc plastic, 14", NMIB. $200.00

Leo the Growling Pet Lion (w/Magic Face-Change Action), Tomiyama, 1970s, 9", MIB $175.00

Light-A-Wheel Lincoln, Rosko, 1950s, bump-&-go action, 11", NM $150.00

Linemar Music Hall, 6", EXIB.......................................$150.00

Lite-O-Wheel Go-Kart, Rosko, 1950s, 11", EXIB $175.00

Little Indian, TN, 1960s, 9", rare, NM..........................$175.00

Little Poochie in Coffee Cup, Alps, 1960s, 9", M..............$75.00

Loop the Loop Clown, TN, 1960s, 12", EXIB...................$75.00

Lucky Cement Mixer, MT, 1960s, 12", M.........................$75.00

Mac the Turtle w/The (Whiskey) Barrel, Y, 1960s, 9", EXIB..$150.00

Magic Action Bulldozer, TN, 1950s, 10", MIB $150.00

Magic Beetle, Linemar, 7", EXIB.....................................$50.00

Magic Man (Clown), Marusan, 1950s, r/c, puffs smoke, 12", EXIB $250.00

Magic Snow Man, MT, 1950s, w/broom, 11", EXIB $150.00

Major Tooty (Drum Major), Alps, tin, 11", NM+IB....... $175.00

Mambo the Jolly Drumming Elephant, see Cragstan Melody Band

Man From UNCLE Headquarters Transmitter, NMIB ... $200.00

Marching Bear, Alps, 1960s, plush, drums/cymbals, 10", EXIB $125.00

Marshal Wild Bill, Y, 1950s, r/c, cloth outfit, 11", VGIB. $150.00

Marvelous Locomotive, 1950s, TN, 10", M $50.00

Marvelous Mike, Saunders, 1950s, 17", EXIB $200.00

McGregor, TN/Rosko import/Japan, 1960s, tin figure seated on trunk holding cane, cloth outfit, 12", MIB................. $175.00

Melody Camping Car, Y, 1970s, 10", NM $150.00

Mew-Mew the Walking Cat, MT, 1950s, r/c, plush, 7", VGIB $75.00

Mexicali Pete the Drum Player, Alps, 1960s, 10", EXIB. $175.00

Mickey Mouse Locomotive, MT, 1960s, 9", NM $100.00

Battery-Operated Toys
• • • • • • • • •
Hungry Baby Bear, Y, 1950s, plush momma and baby, 9", EXIB, $150.00. (Photo courtesy Don Hultzman)

Battery-Operated Toys
• • • • • • • • •
Main Street, Linemar, 1950s, 20", rare, NMIB, $1,200.00. (Photo courtesy Don Hultzman)

Mickey Mouse & Donald Duck Fire Truck, MT, 1960s, 16", EXIB $325.00

Mickey Mouse Drummer, Linemar, r/c, plush w/plastic face, light-up eyes, tin drum, EX $400.00

Mickey Mouse Melody Railroad, Frankonia/Japan, 1967, VGIB... $375.00

Mickey the Magician, Linemar, 1960s, 10", EXIB $2,000.00

Mickey the Magician, Linemar, 1960s, 10", VG $650.00

Mini Poodle w/Bone, TN/Rosko, 1950s, r/c, plush, 11" L, NMIB $75.00

Mischief (Mischievous Monkey), MT, 1950s, 13", EXIB. $250.00

Miss Friday the Typist, TN, 1950s, 8", EXIB $250.00

Monkee Mobile, ASC, 1960s, 12", EX $325.00

Monkee Mobile, ASC, 1960s, 12", EXIB $575.00

Monkey on a Tricycle, Masudaya, plush & tin, 9" H, VG+ .. $150.00

Monkey the Shoe Maker, TN, 1950s, 9", rare, NMIB $500.00

Monorail Set, Haji, 1950s, complete, EXIB $175.00

Mother Bear (Sitting & Knitting in Her Old Rocking Chair), MT, 1950s, plush, 10", EXIB...................................... $125.00

Mother Duck & Baby, see Worried Mother Duck & Baby

Mother Goose, Cragstan, plush, 10", VGIB.....................$75.00

Mr Al-E-Gator (Amazing), Alps, 1950s, 12", unused, MIB.. $200.00

Mr Baseball, see All Stars Mr Baseball Jr

Mr Fox the Magician (w/The Magical Disappearing Rabbit), Y, 1960s, 9", EXIB $550.00

Mr Fox the Magician (w/The Magical Disappearing Rabbit), Y, 1960s, 9", NM $300.00

Mr Magoo Car, Hubley, 1960s, 9", EXIB......................... $275.00

Mr McPooch Taking a Walk & Smoking His Pipe, SAN, 1950s, r/c, EXIB $150.00

Mumbo Jumbo Hawaiian Dancer, Alps, 1960s, 10", MIB...$225.00

Mumbo Jumbo Hawaiian Dancer, Alps, 1960s, 10", VG . $100.00

Musical Comic Jumping Jeep, Alps, 12", M $125.00

Musical Ice Cream Truck, Bandai, 1960s, 11", NM $150.00

Musical Jackal, Linemar, 1950s, 10", very rare, MIB...... $750.00

Musical Jolly Chimp, C-K, 1960s, 10", EXIB....................$80.00

Musical Marching Bear, Alps, 1950s, r/c, 10", NMIB..... $400.00

Musical Melody Mixer, Taiyo, 1970s, 11", M................. $100.00

Mystery Action Tractor, Japan, 1950s, 7", MIB $100.00

Mystery Plane, TN, 1950s, 10", EXIB $250.00

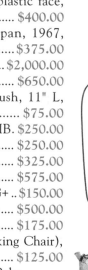

Mystery Police Car, TN, 1960s, 10", NM........................ $150.00

Naughty Dog & Busy Bee, MT, plush, 10", EXIB $65.00

NBC Television/RCA Victor Truck, Linemar, 9", VG+ . $500.00

O-Mar-X (Western Style Music Box), Linemar, 5", NMIB.. $250.00

Ol' McDonald's Farm Truck, Tomy, 1960s, tin w/plastic animals & driver, 10½", NM (G box) $75.00

Ol' Sleepy Head RIP, Y/Toy-A-Joy Spesco import, 1950s, 9", NM..$300.00

Overland Stage Coach, MT, 1950s, 15", EXIB $175.00

Pa Pa Bear, Marusan, r/c, standing smoking pipe, 9", MIB...$100.00

Battery-Operated Toys

Oldtimer Train Set, Cragstan, 1950s, MIB, $200.00.

Battery-Operated Toys

Police Patrol Auto-Tricyle, Japan, 1950s, MIB, $600.00. (Photo courtesy Smith House Toy and Auction Company)

Battery-Operated Toys

Police No. 5 Patrol Car, Japan, 1950s, policeman in white open car with siren on hood, bump and go action, 10" long, NM, $75.00. (Photo courtesy Smith House Toy and Auction Company)

Peppermint Twist Doll, Haji, 1950s, 12", EXIB $250.00

Peppy Puppy w/Bone, Y, 1950s, 7", NMIB $50.00

Perky Pup, Alps, 1960s, r/c, plush, 8½", MIB....................$75.00

Pet Turtle, Alps, 1960s, 8", NMIB.................................. $150.00

Pete the Talking Parrot, TN, 1950s, 18", M.................... $150.00

Peter the Drumming Rabbit (Lighting Eyes), Alps, 1950s, r/c, 12", EXIB.. $175.00

Pianist (Jolly Pianist), Marusan, 1950s, plush dog at tin piano, 8½", NMIB $200.00

Picnic Bunny (It Drinks), Alps, 1950s, plush, 10", NMIB ..$125.00

Picnic Monkey, Alps, 1950s, 10", EXIB $175.00

Picnic Poodle, STS, 1950s, 7" L, NMIB............................$50.00

Pierrot Monkey Cycle, MT, 1950s, 9", EXIB................... $300.00

Piggy Cook, Y, 1950s, 10", EXIB $175.00

Pinky the Juggling Clown, Japan, 1950s, cloth outfit, 19", MIB $275.00

Pinocchio Playing Xylophone, Rosco, 9½", EXIB........... $225.00

Pioneer Covered Wagon, Ichida, 1960s, 15", EXIB........ $125.00

Pipie the Whale, Alps, 1950s, 12", NM $150.00

Pistol Pete, Marusan, 1950s, 10", EXIB......................... $300.00

Playful Puppy w/Caterpillar, MT, 8" H, EXIB $125.00

Playing Monkey, S&E, 10", NMIB.................................. $150.00

Pluto, Ilco/WDP, 1960s or 1970s, r/c, plastic, 5x10", MIB ..$100.00

Pluto, Linemar, 1960s, r/c, plush, 10", EXIB $65.00

Pluto Lantern, Linemar, tin figure w/glass middle, 7", EXIB....$250.00

Popcorn Eating Bear, MT, 1950s, EX $100.00

Popeye, see also Smoking Popeye

Popeye & Olive Oyl Tumbling Buggy, Hong Kong, 1981, 7", NMIB $50.00

Pretty Peggy Parrot, Rosko, plush, 11", NMIB................ $275.00

Professor Owl, Y, 1950s, 8", NMIB................................ $425.00

Quick Draw McGraw Target Car w/Baba Looie, EXIB... $200.00

Rabbits & the Carriage, S&E, 1950s, 9", NMIB............. $150.00

Rambling Ladybug, MT, 1960s, 8" EX..............................$50.00

Red Gulch Bar (Western Bad Man), MT, 1960s, 10", VGIB..$450.00

Rex Doghouse, Tel-E-Toy, 1950s, 5", M $125.00

River Steam Boat (w/Whistle & Smoke), MT, 14", VGIB..$75.00

Roaring Gorilla Shooting Gallery, MT, 1950s, 9", NMIB...$225.00

Robo Tank TR2, TN, 1960s, 6", NM+............................. $175.00

Rock 'N Roll Monkey (Auto-Matic), Alps, 1950s, 12", EXIB ..$250.00

Battery-Operated Toys

Popeye in Rowboat, Linemar, 10", EX, $1,800.00. (Photo courtesy Morphy Auctions on LiveAuctioneers.com)

Battery-Operated Toys
• • • • • • • • • • • • • • • •
Popeye Lantern, Linemar, litho-graphed tin figure with glass middle, 7½", EXIB, $550.00.

Battery-Operated
Toys
• • • • • • • • • • • • • • •
Rembrandt the Monkey Artist, Alps, 1950s, 8", rare, NMIB, $475.00.
(Photo courtesy Don Hultzman)

Rocky, Japan, tin (Fred Flintstone look-alike) 4", NMIB.. $100.00
Roller Skating Clown, see Clown on Roller Skates
Root Beer Stand, K, 1960s, 8x8", NM............................. $200.00
Sam the Shaving Man, Plaything Toy Co, 1960s, 12", EXIB..$200.00
Sammy Wong the Tea Totaler, Rosko/TN, 1950s, 10", EXIB.$250.00
Shark U-Control Race Car, Remco #610, 1961, 10", unused, MIB... $150.00
Shoe Shine Bear (Lighted Pipe), TN, 1950s, 9", EXIB .. $200.00
Shooting Bear, Marusan, 1950s, r/c, plush, 10", EXIB $275.00
Shutter Bug, TN, 1950s, 9", EX...................................... $500.00
Shutter Bug, TN, 1950s, 9", NMIB................................ $875.00
Shuttling Train & Freight Yard, Alps, 1950s, 16", EXIB $100.00
Skating Circus Clown, TPS, 1950s, r/c, 6", NM............. $875.00
Skipping Monkey, TN, 1960s, jumps rope, 10", EXIB.......$65.00
Sleeping Baby Bear, Linemar, 10", VGIB........................ $150.00
Smokey Bill on Old-Fashioned Car, TN, 1960s, 9", MIB . $125.00
Smoking Bunny, Cragstan, r/c, plush, NMIB................. $200.00
Smoking Grandpa (in Rocker), SAN, 1950s, 9", NMIB . $150.00
Smoking Pa Pa Bear, SAN, r/c, 8", EXIB $125.00
Smoky Bear, SAN, 1950s, r/c, EXIB................................ $300.00
Smurf Choo Choo w/Headlight, Durham Industries, 1980s, unused, MIB $40.00
Snake Charmer, Linemar, 1950s, 8", NMIB.................... $575.00
Snappy Puppy, Alps, 1960s, plush, 9", VGIB...................$50.00
Sneezing Bear (Lighted Eyes), Linemar, 1950s, 9", EXIB $200.00
Space Patrol (Snoopy), MT, 1960s, 12", EXIB................ $200.00
Space Traveling Monkey, Yanoman, 1960s, 9", EXIB..... $125.00
Spanking Bear, Linemar, 1950s, 10", EXIB $200.00
Sparky the Seal, TN, 1950s, 7" L, NMIB..........................$75.00
Speed Star 3 (Happy Drive Car), Nomura, litho tin w/vinyl driver, 8", NMIB... $150.00
Squirmy Hermy the Snake, HTC, r/c, 12", NMIB.......... $150.00
Strange Explorer, DSK, 1960s, 8", EXIB $275.00
Strutting My Fair Dancer, Haji, 1950s, 9", EXIB $175.00
Strutting Sam, Japan, litho tin artiuclated blk figure on rnd drum-type base, 11", NMIB $375.00
Super Susie, Linemar, 1950s, 8x6", EXIB....................... $600.00
Suzette the Eating Monkey, Linemar, 1950s, 9", EXIB... $475.00
Suzette the Eating Monkey, Linemar, 1950s, 9", G......... $150.00
Swimming Duck, Bandai, 1950s, 8", rare, NM...................$75.00
Swimming Fish, Koshibe, 1950s, 11", NM...................... $125.00

Battery-Operated Toys
• • • • • • • • • • • • • • • •
Sea Hawk Future Car, Japan, 1964, driver seated under plastic dome, 12", EX, $375.00. (Photo courtesy Bertoia Auctions)

Battery-Operated
Toys
• • • • • • • • • • • • • •
Smoking and Shoe Shin-ing Panda Bear, Alps, 1950s, 10", plush, NMIB, $250.00. (Photo courtesy www.serioustoyz.com)

Battery-
Operated
Toys
• • • • • • • • • • • •
Smoking Popeye, Linemar, 9", EXIB, $1,500.00. (Photo courtesy Morphy Auctions on LiveAuctioneers.com)

Battery-Operated Toys
• • • • • • • • • • • • •
Superman (Army) Tank, Linemar, 8½", EXIB, $1,650.00.
(Photo courtesy Bertoia Auctions)

Battery-Operated Toys
• •
Walking Cat, Linemar, 6", remote control, EXIB, $100.00. (Photo courtesy Don Hultzman)

Switchboard Operator, Linemar, 1950s, 7", EXIB........... $500.00

Talking Batmobile, Palitoy (Hong Kong)/DC Comics, 1977, 10", NM+IB.. $175.00

Tarzan, Marusan, 1966, 13", NMIB (Japanese box)........ $975.00

Taxi Cab, Y, 1970s, rear side door opens, bump-&-go action, blinking lights, turning meter, 9", MIB.....................$75.00

Teddy Balloon Blowing Bear, Alps, 1950s, 11", EXIB..... $125.00

Teddy Bear Swing, TN, 1950s, bear on trapeze, 14", NMIB....$475.00

Teddy Go-Kart, Alps, 1960s, 10", EXIB $150.00

Teddy the Artist, Electro Toy/Y, 1950s, 10", EXIB.......... $425.00

Teddy the Champ Boxer, Y, 1950s, 10", EXIB $175.00

Telephone Bear, Linemar, 1950s, 9", EXIB $250.00

Telephone Rabbit, MT, 1950s, 10", EXIB $275.00

The Great Mickey, see Mickey the Magician

Tin Man Robot (The Wizard of Oz), Remco, 1969, plastic, 21", MIB.. $200.00

Tom & Jerry Choo Choo, MT, 1960s, 11", EX+IB $200.00

Tom & Jerry Hand Car, MT, 1960s, tin, MIB $200.00

Tom Tom Indian, Y, 1960s, 11", NMIB........................... $125.00

Topo Gigio Xylophone Player, TN, 1960s, 11", rare, MIB ..$950.00

Tractor (Robot Driver/Visible Lighted Piston Movement), Linemar, 1950s, 10", MIB.. $425.00

Traveler Bear, K, 1950s, r/c, 8", NMIB............................ $350.00

Traveler Bear, K, 1950s, r/c, 8", VG $100.00

Tri-Cycling Clown, MT, 1960s, 12", EX+IB $300.00

Trik-Trak Cross Country Road Rally, Transogram, 1966, complete, NMIB...$50.00

Trumpet Monkey, Alps, 1950s, 10", EXIB...................... $150.00

Tugboat (w/Realistic Noises & Puffs of Real Smoke), SAN/Cragstan, 1950s, 13", EXIB.. $175.00

Tumbles the Bear, YM, 1960s, 9", NMIB $100.00

Tumbling Bozo the Clown, Sonsco, 1970s, 8", M $75.00

Twirly Whirly Rocket Ride, Alps, 1950s, 13", EXIB....... $500.00

Two-Gun Sheriff, see Cragstan Two-Gun Sheriff

Union Mountain Monorail, TN, 1950s, MIB $225.00

VIP the Busy Boss, S&E, 1950s, 8", EXIB....................... $200.00

V8 Roadster, Daiya, vinyl-headed driver, 11", EX........... $200.00

Waddles Family Car, Y, 1960s, MIB $100.00

Wagon Master, MT, 1960s, 18", NM............................... $150.00

Wal-Boot Hobo, Tomy, 1960s, 20", NM $50.00

Walking Bear w/Xylophone, Linemar, 1950s, 10", EXIB . $350.00

Walking Donkey, Linemar, 1950s, r/c, 9", VGIB............. $150.00

Walking Elephant (Carrying Flying Ball), MT, 1950s, r/c, 9", EXIB $100.00

Walking Gorilla, Linemar, r/c, 7", NMIB....................... $275.00

Walking Horse (Cowboy Rider), Linemar, 1950s, r/c, 7", EXIB $350.00

Wee Little Baby Bear (Reading Bear/Lighted Eyes), Alps, 10", EXIB $375.00

Western Bad Man, see Red Gulch Bar

Western Special Locomotive, MT (Masudaya), 1960s, tin, bump-&-go, realistic whistle, 14", EX+ (P box) $50.00

Western Style Music Box, see O-Mar-X

Whistling Hobo, Waco, 1960s, 13", EXIB $100.00

Windy the Juggling Elephant, TN, 1950s, 10", EX+IB... $100.00

Worried Mother Duck & Baby, TN, 1950s, 7", MIB $150.00

Xylophone Ace, 1950s, 6" L, NM $50.00

Yo-Yo Clown, Alps, 1960s, 10", rare, MIB $275.00

Yo-Yo Monkey, Alps, 1960s, 9", NMIB $225.00

Yo-Yo Monkey, YM, 1960s, 12", NMIB........................... $225.00

Yummy Yum Kitty, Alps, 1950s, 10", rare, EXIB............. $750.00

Battery-Operated Toys
• • • • • • • • • • • • • • •
Wonder Wheel Amusement Ride, ATC, lithographed tin, rare version, 10", VG, $2,300.00.
(Photo courtesy Morphy Auctions on LiveAuctioneers.com)

• • • • • • • • • Bicycles and Tricycles • • • • • • • • •

The most interesting of the vintage bicycles are those made from the 1920s into the 1960s, though a few later models are collectible as well. Some of the '50s models were very futuristic and styled with sweeping Art Deco lines; others had wonderful features such as built-in radios and brake lights, and some were decked out with saddlebags and holsters to appeal to fans of Hoppy, Gene, and other Western heroes. Watch for reproductions.

Condition is everything when evaluating bicycles, and one worth $2,500.00 in excellent or better condition might be worth as little as $50.00 in unrestored, poor condition.

Note: A girl's bicycle will bring from 35% to 50% less than a boy's bicycle of the same model.

Advisor: Richard Trautwein

BICYCLES

AMF Spider-Man Jr Roadster, boy's, 1978, EX $150.00
Colson Bullnose, boy's, 1939, light on front fender, EX, rstr..$1,800.00
Columbia Airrider, boy's, 1940-42, EX, $800 to $1,100.00
Columbia Superb, boy's, 1941, VG, $600 to $900.00
Columbia 3-Speed Playbike, boy's, 1970s-80s, VG...........$75.00
Elgin Deluxe, girls, 1940, G, $350 to $550.00
Elgin Robin, boy's, 1937, G $1,500.00
Elgin Sport Model, girl's, 1940s, G, $350 to.................... $550.00
Evans, boy's, 1960s, middleweight truss frame, G $75.00
Hawthorn Comet, boy's, Montgomery Ward, 1938, EX, $600 to.$800.00
Hawthorn Zep, boy's, 1939, w/dual Silver Ray lights, leather seat,
    Riverside wht-wall tires, VG, $2,500 to $3,000.00

Huffy American Thunderbird, boy's, 1960s, G, $75 to... $100.00
Huffy BMX, boy's, 1970s, VG, $100 to $150.00
JC Higgins, boy's, Winderide Spring Fork, EX $1,200.00
JC Higgins Flow Motion, girl's, 1948, G, $100 to $150.00
Monarch Silver King Model M1, boy's, 1938, EX........... $900.00
Monarch Silver King Wingbar, girl's, 1939, EX $600.00
Moulton Mark III, boy's, 1970, G................................. $200.00
Murray Fire Cat, boy's, 1977, VG................................. $250.00
Raleigh Chopper, boy's, 1970s, EX, $150 to.................. $250.00
Raleigh Space Rider 3-Speed, boy's, 1968, EX............... $150.00
Roadmaster Luxury Liner, girl's, 26", EX, $500 to.......... $700.00
Schwinn AutoCycle, 1936, cross bar speedo, twin Seiss head-
    lamps, front fender 'bomb' ornament, VG................ $3,250.00
Schwinn Bantam, girl's, 1960, G $75.00
Schwinn Fair Lady, 1960s, VG $125.00
Schwinn Green Phantom, boy's, 1951, 26", EX...........$1,100.00
Schwinn Lady's Stanford Model BC308, VG, $100 to ... $200.00
Schwinn Mark IV Jaguar, boy's, 1960s, West Wind tires, VG .$800.00
Schwinn Model B, girl's, spring fork & fender headlight, VG .$250.00
Schwinn Red Phantom, boy's, 1950s, rstr, $1,000 to ... $1,300.00
Schwinn Sting Ray, girl's, 1970s, G.................................$55.00
Sears Free Spirit, boy's, 1960s, EX, $100 to.................... $150.00
Sears Spaceliner, boy's, 1960s, G, $100 to...................... $150.00
Shelby Donald Duck, boy's, NM+ (NOS) $5,500.00
Shelby Donald Duck, girl's, NM+ (NOS).................... $4,000.00
Shelby Traveler, boy's, 1938, G $250.00
Sting-Ray Super Deluxe, Schwinn, 1966, boy's, rstr to like new,
    $800 to.. $950.00
Swiss Army, boy's, 1941, VG, $700 to..........................$1,000.00
Vista Banana 3-Speed, boy's, 1970s, 20", M................... $200.00
Western Flyer Buzz Bike 2+1, boy's, 1960-70, G, $150 to . $200.00

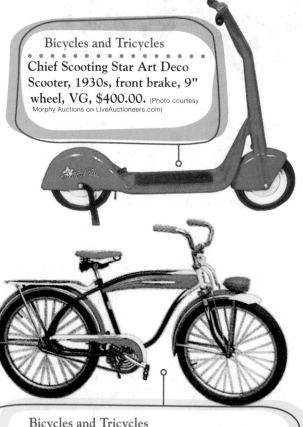

Bicycles and Tricycles
• • • • • • • • • • • • •
Chief Scooting Star Art Deco Scooter, 1930s, front brake, 9" wheel, VG, $400.00. (Photo courtesy Morphy Auctions on LiveAuctioneers.com)

Bicycles and Tricycles
• • • • • • • • • • • • •
Cleveland Deluxe Roadmaster, boy's, prewar, light on front fender, horn on tank, rear carrier, 24", EX, $375.00. (Photo courtesy Copake Auction Inc.)

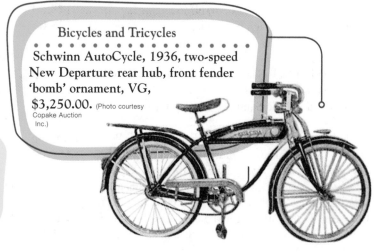

Bicycles and Tricycles
• • • • • • • • • • • • •
Schwinn AutoCycle, 1936, two-speed New Departure rear hub, front fender 'bomb' ornament, VG, $3,250.00. (Photo courtesy Copake Auction Inc.)

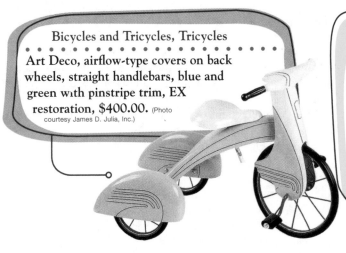

Bicycles and Tricycles, Tricycles

Art Deco, airflow-type covers on back wheels, straight handlebars, blue and green with pinstripe trim, EX restoration, $400.00. (Photo courtesy James D. Julia, Inc.)

Bicycles and Tricycles, Tricycles

Colson Mickey Mouse Tricycle, upper half of Mickey figure decaled on fender with articulated legs reaching pedals, 22", VG, $2,875.00. (Photo courtesy Morphy Auctions on LiveAuctioneers.com)

TRICYCLES

AMF Junior Bike, Junior Toy Corp, perforated wheels, 21", EX..$115.00
AMF Junior Tow-Trike, w/Delta front light, cleated tires, rear boom w/crank & chain pulley, NM $350.00
Art Deco, airflow-type covers on all 3 wheels, hanging bell attached to handlebars, spoke wheels, bright bl, EX rstr $350.00
Colson Fairy, 1920s, chain drive, EX rstr $375.00
Gendron Pioneer, no fenders, 19½", G $375.00
Jaxon, 1950s, w/unusual rear 3 wheels, hard tires, G $350.00
Kiddie Kar Pedal-less Trike, 16", bl, NM........................ $100.00
Mattel V-Room! Trike, w/plastic engine, 35", EX+ $75.00
Murry Airflow Jr, 17½", G $200.00
Steelcraft Streamline, red & wht, 28", M rstr, $500 to ... $800.00
Wooden Model, saddle-type seat, straight handlebars, lg wooden spoke wheels, red w/yel stripe, 42x30", VG $100.00

Bicycles and Tricycles, Tricycles

Pony, 33x9", VG, $180.00. (Photo courtesy James D. Julia, Inc.)

Black Americana

Black subjects were commonly depicted in children's toys as long ago as the late 1870s. Among the most widely collected today are the fine windup toys made both here and in Germany. Early cloth and later composition and vinyl dolls are favorites of many; others enjoy ceramic figurines. Many factors enter into evaluating Black Americana, especially in regard to the handmade dolls and toys, since quality is subjective to individual standards. Because of this, you may find wide ranges in asking prices.

Advisor: Judy Posner

See also Banks; Battery-Operated Toys; Schoenhut; Windup, Friction, and Other Mechanical Toys.

Bank, litho tin cylinder w/blk, yel & red image of minstrel playing banjo, red lid, 4", prewar, NM.................... $175.00
Book, Andy's Exciting Day, England, 1930s, 24 pgs, EX. $125.00
Book, Further Adventures of Wongabilla, Australian, hardcover, 50 pgs, EX.. $300.00
Book, Little Black Sambo, Bannerman, 1949, w/5 mechanical multi-action pgs, 9x18", NM+ $150.00
Book, Little Black Sambo (the Pop-Up), Blue Ribbon, 1934, NM $27.50
Book, Sambo's Family Funbook, 'Fun Games & Puzzles,' featuring JT & the Tiger Kids, restaurant premium, 1978, EX........$30.00
Book, Well Done Noddy!, by Enid Blyton, EX..................$30.00
Clock, bell atop rnd 3-footed chrome case, man in yel jacket & gr tie on face w/blk numbers, 6", EX............................ $850.00
Coloring Book, Little Brown Koko, illus by Dorothy Wadstaff, 1941, 22 pgs, unused, EX.................................... $125.00

Doll, baby, 1920s, blk compo head & hands w/molded features & hair, cloth body, flannel gown, 24", G $335.00
Doll, Dream Baby, AM Germany 341/4-K, pnt hair, glass sleep eyes, closed mouth, 5-pc bent-limb body, orig dress, 15", G.....$400.00
Doll, Dream Baby, Armand Marseille, 1920s, compo body w/brn bisque head, pnt hair, wht gown, 10", EX.................... $275.00
Doll, girl, Gebruder Heubach, 7670-4" on head, bisque, molded eyes, open/close mouth, orig dress, 10", EX $1,200.00
Doll, girl, Simon & Halbig, #0739, wood & compo body w/brn bisque socket head, set eyes, blk wig, cloth dress, EX.. $650.00
Doll, Golliwog, England, prewar, blk stuffed body w/wool hair, googley eyes, bl pants, red tails, ruffled shirt, 19", EX.....$60.00
Doll, Golliwog, England, 1950s, crocheted yarn body w/crocheted bow at neck, lg eyes, red & yel, 7", NM........... $100.00
Doll, Kewpie, standing, nude, compo, jtd shoulders, heart label on chest, 12", VG....................................... $125.00

Doll, lady, ca 1900, blk-pnt oilcloth head & hands, cloth body, caracal wig, gold dress w/wht shawl-like wrap, 24", VG ..$840.00

Doll, Little Red Riding Hood (2-face), Bartenstein, wax-over-maché/compo/wood, blk face/wht face, glass eyes, 18", VG...$1,000.00

Doll, Mammy, ca 1900-10, stuffed blk stockinette, pnt eyes/lips, wht headscarf, neckscarf & apron over dress, 20", EX. $475.00

Doll, Mammy, Norah Wellings, brn velvet w/brn glass eyes, pnt features, blk mohair wig w/print scarf, VG $150.00

Doll, Pretty Pairs (Nan & Fran), bendable arms & legs, in flannel print pajamas w/lace trim, NRFB.................................. $200.00

Doll, stockinette, child, American, early 1900s, stitched features, astrakhan wig, shirt, overalls, hat, 10", EX $500.00

Doll, Topsy-Turvy, late 1900s, stuffed cloth, 4 faces w/embroidered features, cotton dresses w/matching bonnets, 19", EX... $300.00

Figure, Sambo dancing, pnt CI, 2¼", Hubley, 1920s, EX. $150.00

Figure Set, Golliwog musicians, chalkware, 3-pc, 3", Robertson's Marmalade premiums, 3-pc, 3", NM+ $100.00

Game, Chuck Target Game, litho cb, Ottman/USA, 1890s, rare, EXIB $350.00

Game, Chuckler's Game, USA, 1930s, EXIB $100.00

Game, Game of Sambo, ring toss, Parker Bros, 1900s, NM+..$300.00

Game, Jolly Darkie Target Game, McLoughlin Bros, complete, EX+IB $500.00

Game, Little Black Sambo, Cadaco-Ellis, 1940s, complete, EXIB... $100.00

Game, Mr Busby, Milton Bradley, 1905, NMIB.............. $350.00

Game, Muffin & Golly Card Game, 45 cards w/Muffin & friends, England, late 1940s, NMIB.................................. $100.00

Game, Pickaninny Bowling Game, Bavaria/England, 1920s, scarce mini version, EX+IB.. $275.00

Game, Sambo Target, Wyandotte, 1930s, EX $75.00

Game, Zoo Hoo, USA, 1920s, complete, NMIB $125.00

Hand Puppet Set, boy, girl & baby, molded rubber, 3-pc, Child Craft, 1965, EX+ $75.00

Hand Puppet Set, mother, father & grandparents, molded rubber, 4-pc, Child Craft, 1965, EX+..$75.00

Jack-in-the-Box, compo man's head w/pnt features, cloth outfit, paper-on-wood box, 5" (when opened) $125.00

Kobe Toy, acrobat figure, swinging freely over trapeze bar when knob is turned, wood, 5", EX.................................... $375.00

Kobe Toy, figure seated in 3-wheeled cart holds stick in hand, head wobbles, wood, 7", VG.. $225.00

Marionette, Golliwog (Jumpelles), pnt wood w/cloth outfit, 9", Pelham, NMIB $175.00

Marionette, Jambo the Jiver, jtd wood w/cloth outfit, 14", Talent Prod, 1948, VG $225.00

Mechanical Toy, Bojangle Dancer, Clown Toy Co, push the button on tin base & articulated wood dancer performs, NMIB $175.00

Mechanical Toy, Boy Drummer, TT/Japan, w/up celluloid figure, head turns & eyes wobble, 7", EX $350.00

Mechanical Toy, Boy on Velocipede, Stevens & Brown, 1870s, w/up, tin & CI, cloth outfit, 11" L, EX $2,000.00

Mechanical Toy, Boy Riding Donkey Cart, Gunthermann, w/up, litho tin, boy w/whip in 2-wheeled railed cart, 8¼" L, EX. $600.00

Mechanical Toy, boy walker, blk compo head, hands w/lead feet, cloth pants, shirt & neck scarf, 8½", EX.................... $1,375.00

Mechanical Toy, Dancing Man, England, 1930s, flat articulated litho tin figure on rnd base, push tab for action, 8", EX...$550.00

Mechanical Toy, Happy Jack, Krauss/Germany, crank-op litho tin flat figure dances w/hands on hips, top hat, 6", EX $375.00

Mechanical Toy, Harlem Strutter, Socsco, post-war, figure dances under street sign, tin & celluloid, 8½", EXIB $275.00

Mechanical Toy, Hot Mammy, Fisher-Price #810, cloth-dressed doll, w/up, 7", EXIB.. $1,200.00

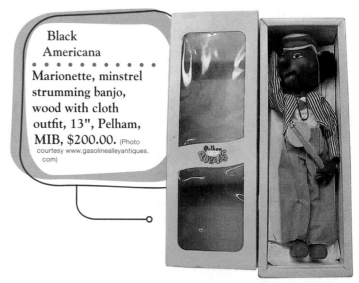

Mechanical Toy, Jazz Saxophone Player, Germany, lever action, flat-sided litho-tin figure, moves arms & legs, 7", EX .. $350.00

Mechanical Toy, Jiggling Jimmy the High Steppin' Tap Dancer, Guiferman, litho tin jtd figure, lever action, 8", EX $125.00

Mechanical Toy, Minstrel Couple, Germany, pnt tin, he w/ cloth coat, she plays instrument & he sways on wheels, 8", VG $7,800.00

Mechanical Toy, musicians (2) seated on beveled base playing banjo & fiddle, w/up, pnt tin, plink-plink sound, 9" L, EX...$1,500.00

Mechanical Toy, Native Dancer, att Gunthermann, w/up, pnt tin, girl w/arms up in gr & yel dress, red trim, 7", VG. $375.00

Mechanical Toy, Native Dancer, rocks back & forth as he plays, 8", Marx USA $125.00

Mechanical Toy, Negro Preacher, Ives, 1880s, w/up, preacher in cloth outfit on wooden podium, 10½", NMIB (wood box) $4,500.00

Mechanical Toy, Pango Pango, native spins & dances as head goes back & forth, 6½", Japan, MIB $150.00

Mechanical Toy, Tap Dancer, Alps, post-war, w/up celluloid figure in cloth outfit dances under street sign, 9", NMIB $250.00

Mechanical Toy, 2 cloth-dressed figures atop wooden box w/pnt tin lid, 8", VG+ $1,750.00

Nodder, boy seated on box holding chalkboard, bisque, 5½", Austria, 1880s, NM $350.00

Nodder, lady w/hand on hip, carved pnt wood, lg head w/ wht eyes, red lips/teeth, thin body, lg feet on sq base, 12", EX $4,000.00

Paper Dolls, Oh Susanna! Musical Pack O' Fun, complete, unused, EX...$50.00

Pull toy, Sambo, Velo, wood, 12" $85.00

Puzzle, Boo Boogey Man, jigsaw, red, wht & bl image of 3 missionaries & 3 natives stranded on island, 4", NMIB.......$50.00

Puzzle, Darktown Fire Brigade, jigsaw, heavy cb, shows stereotypical fire dept scene, Parker Bros, complete, EXIB... $425.00

Puzzle, Golly & 'Noah' loading train (ark) w/animals, jigsaw, litho wood, very scarce, NMIB $100.00

Ramp Walker, Mammy, wood figure in cloth dress & headscarf, 4½", ca 1900, NM $75.00

Roly Poly, clown, papier-maché body, pointed felt hat w/plush brim, wht w/red trim, 7", VG...............................$150.00

Roly Poly, man in suit w/cigar in hand, pnt pressed cb, brn face w/lt tan around eyes, mc clothes, 9½", VG.................$225.00

Sand Pail, litho tin w/'A Present From the Seaside' around rim & beach scene w/2 Golliwogs, 7", England, 1920s, EX.....$200.00

Squeeze Toy, Golliwog figure, pnt rubber, 6", England, 1930s, NM $75.00

Ventriloquist Doll, Sammy, tattered plaid jacket & pants, rpl shirt, 37", EX (poor box)...............................$500.00

• • • • • • • • • • • • • • • • **Boats** • • • • • • • • • • • • • • • •

Though some commercially made boats date as far back as the late 1800s, they were produced on a much larger scale during WWI and the decade that followed and again during the years that spanned WWII. Some were scaled-down models of battleships measuring nearly three feet in length. While a few were actually seaworthy, many were designed with small wheels to be pulled along the floor or out of doors on dry land. Some were steam-powered, while others were windups or even battery-operated. Some of the larger manufacturers were Bing (Germany), Dent (Pennsylvania), Orkin Craft (California), Liberty Playthings (New York), Arnold (West Germany), and Marklin (Germany).

Advisor: Richard Trautwein

See also Battery-Operated Toys; Cast Iron, Boats; Paper-Lithographed Toys; Tootsietoys; Windup, Friction, and Other Mechanical Toys; other specific categories or manufacturers.

Aircraft Carrier, Linemar, 14", litho tin, b/o, w/planes, 1960s, EX+IB $250.00

Aircraft Carrier, Marx, 20", litho tin, b/o, w/2 helicopters, missiles & jets, EXIB.. $360.00

Battleship, Bing, 24", pnt metal, w/up, 2-tone gray, 4 stacks, 8 turrets, 1910-20, G+ $2,875.00

Battleship, Bing, *King Edward*, 29", tin, w/up, gray w/red trim, 3 stacks, 2 masts, 4 lifeboats, rstr $7,500.00

Battleship, Carette, *Nurnberg*, 24", pnt tin, w/up, wht & red, 2 gr masts, rstr $3,850.00

Battleship, Converse, *Oregon*, 17½", litho tin & wood, wht w/red & bl, 1910s, EX+ $850.00

Battleship, Dayton, 10", friction, moveable artillery, wht w/gr 'wavy' bottom, single red stack, 1920s, VG $225.00

Battleship, Dayton, 12", PS, friction, wht, gr, gold & red, w/4 lifeboats, F $125.00

Battleship, Dayton, 18", flywheel, wooden turrets at both ends, orange & wht w/2 red stacks, G $165.00

Battleship, Fleischmann, 10", tin, w/up, gray & blk hull & 2 stacks w/red deck, single mast, 2 gun turrets, G $325.00

Battleship, France (?), *Liberté*, 53", mostly pnt tin w/some wood, gray w/aqua bottom, electric motor, 1920s (?), G $6,000.00

Battleship, Japan, *Yamato*, 8", litho tin, candle-powered, EXIB $60.00

Battleship, Lehmann, *Taku*, 9½", litho tin, w/up, EXIB .. $525.00

Battleship, Marx, *USS Washington*, 14½", litho tin, friction, NM $150.00

Battleship, Orkin, *New York*, 25", PS, w/up, gray w/dk gr hull, VG+ $2,200.00

Battleship, Orkin, *Pennsylvania*, 30", PS, w/up, wooden turrets, 2 fire control towers, EX $2,750.00

Battleship, Orkin, *Wisconsin*, 38", EX $1,550.00

Battleship, Orkin, 30", PS hull w/wooden turrets, 2 masts, 2 stacks, blk & red w/yel stripe, rpnt $700.00

Battleship Fleet, Hess, *Dreadnought*, 8", litho tin, w/up, 1 lg & 2 sm battleships, complete w/tug bars & envelope, EX+ . $650.00

Cabin Cruiser, Boucher, 49", pnt wood, live steam, gr & wht, 2 removable cabin sections, VG $3,575.00

Cabin Cruiser, Fleet Line, *Marlin*, 16", wood, b/o, w/Atwater motor, EXIB, $400 to $500.00

Cabin Cruiser, Japan, *Sea Queen #56*, 10", litho tin, G $100.00

Cabin Cruiser, Linemar, *Vacationer*, 12½", litho tin, w/motor, unused, MIB, $300 to $375.00

Caribbean Luxury Liner, Marx, 14½", litho tin, friction, red wht & bl, NMIB $125.00

Convertible Vessel, Miyazawa, 12", tin, friction, converts from steamship to warship, NMIB $350.00

Cruiser, Arnold, 12", single stack w/2 masts, wht & lt gr hull w/ tan deck, wht cabin, red, wht & bl stack, EX $400.00

Cruiser, Bing, 10", pnt tin, live steam, wht w/gray bottom & rudder, red & gold trim, G $1,800.00

Cruiser, Bing, 28", pnt tin, gray w/blk bottom, 4 stacks, completely railed, some rpnt $3,300.00

Cruiser, Orkin, *USS Marcella*, 18", PS w/NP deck, EX . $2,000.00

Destroyer, Fleischmann, 15", w/up, gray & brn, 2 stacks & masts, 1950s, some rstr $975.00

Destroyer, Ives, 12", pnt tin, gray & blk, 2 stacks & masts, 2 lifeboats, VGIB (#3012 on box) $425.00

Destroyer, *Nomura*, K-55, 8½", litho tin, friction $75.00

Ferryboat, Bing, *Union*, 16", pnt tin, w/up, wht w/wood-tone open ended railed deck, rstr $825.00

Freighter, Fleischmann, *Eggo*, 21", pnt tin, w/up, wht deck w/blk & red hull, some rpnt $825.00

Freighter, Fleischmann, 15", tin, w/up, blk & red hull w/brn deck, wht cabin, blk & red stack, 2 wht masts, EX+ $1,100.00

Freighter, Weeden, 18", pnt tin, steam-powered, single stack, gray, EX, $4,000 to $5,100.00

Gunboat, Bing, 25", pnt tin, w/up, gray w/red trim, 3 stacks, 2 masts, VG $3,850.00

Gunboat, Bing, 27", enameled tin, w/up, 2-tone gr w/4 blk & orange stacks, 6 guns, 2 masts w/crow's nests, EX rstr . $4,700.00

Gunboat, Carette, *Man O' War*, 13", tin, w/up, wht & red hull w/blk pinstripe, lt gr & tan decks, 2 blk stacks, rstr.. $2,250.00

Gunboat, Orobr, 10", pnt tin, wht w/red trim, EX $800.00

Harbour Patrol Boat #117, Japan, 10", litho tin, friction/crank-op, NMIB $75.00

Motorboat, Lang Craft, 11", plastic, b/o, w/outboard motor (in own box), EXIB, $125 to $225.00

Ocean Liner, Arnold, 7", tin, bl & wht, 2 blk stacks w/red stripes, single mast, cabin w/cut-out windows, 1930s, EX $150.00

Ocean Liner, Arnold, 8", tin, inertia drive, blk & red hull, gold deck w/stenciled 'Gettysburg PA,' 2 stacks, EX $375.00

Ocean Liner, Arnold, 14", pnt tin, inertia motor, wht cabin w/ tan deck, bl & red hull, 4 stacks, 2 masts, EX $1,550.00

Boats
• • • • • • • • • • • • • • • • • • • •
Cabin Cruiser, Chein, 15" long, windup, lithographed tin, EXIB, $125.00. (Photo courtesy Smith House Toy and Auction Company)

Boats
• • • • • • • • • • • • • • • • • • • •
Ocean Liner, Bing, Transatlantic, large-scale ship, red and black hull, white cabin, 1920s, 33", $3,000.00 to $4,000.00.

Boats

• • • • • • • • • • • • • • •

Ocean Liner, *George Washington,* **German windup, tin, white/black/red, EX, $4,250.00.** (Photo courtesy Morphy Auctions on LiveAuctioneers.com)

Boats

• • • • • • • • • • • • • • •

Riverboat, Marklin, *Luzern,* **20", tin, windup, cream with red bottom, white cabin and two stacks, two masts, restored, $12,000.00.** (Photo courtesy Morphy Auctions on LiveAuctioneers.com)

Ocean Liner, Bing, *Bremen,* 26", tin, live steam, blk & red hull w/ wht deck, 3 stacks, 2 masts, w/lifeboats, rstr, $4,750 to. $5,900.00

Ocean Liner, Bing, *Savoya,* 25", tin, w/up, red & wht, 2 stacks, 2 masts, EX $11,500.00

Ocean Liner, Bing, Series II of 1912, 32", pnt tin, w/up, red wht & bl w/4 yel stacks, 3 blk masts, EX...........................$8,000.00

Ocean Liner, Bing, 12", pnt tin, w/up, blk & red hull & 3 stacks, wht cabin on yel deck & 2 masts, EX $550.00

Ocean Liner, Bing, 20", tin, w/up, blk & red hull w/wht deck, 3 blk & red stacks, 2 masts, lifeboats, VG $1,900.00

Ocean Liner, Carette, 11", tin, w/up, bl, wht & red hull w/blk pinstripe, wht deck, 3 blk & red stacks, 2 masts, VG.. $650.00

Ocean Liner, Carette, 19", tin, w/up, cream & red hull, wht cabin w/cut-out widows, 2 blk & wht stacks, Am flag, rstr.. $3,250.00

Ocean Liner, Carette, 25", tin, w/up, blk & red hull w/wht pinstripe, wood-tone deck, 4 stacks, 2 masts, 4 lifeboats, EX.. $4,000.00

Ocean Liner, Carette, 27", pnt tin, wht, blk & red bottom w/wht & tan deck, 4 yel & red stacks, 3 crows' nests, VG+. $4,200.00

Ocean Liner, Falk, 16½", tin, w/up, wht & blk hull w/yel deck & 2 masts, 3 red, blk & wht stacks, 4 lifeboats, rstr...... $3,000.00

Ocean Liner, Fleischmann, 7½", tin, w/up, wht cabin w/red deck & hull 2 blk stacks, EX.................................... $275.00

Ocean Liner, Fleischmann, 10", pnt tin, w/up, wht w/bl stripe, brn deck, red accents, 2 stacks, 2 masts, NM+ $500.00

Ocean Liner, Fleischmann, 11½", tin, w/up, wht cabin w/brn deck, blk & red hull, 2 stacks, single mast, EX............ $275.00

Ocean Liner, Fleischmann, 12½", tin, w/up, wht w/bl stripe, red accents, 2 stacks, G $300.00

Ocean Liner, Fleischmann, 13", tin, w/up, blk & red hull w/red & wht deck, 2 stacks & masts, EX $1,100.00

Ocean Liner, Fleischmann, 19", tin, w/up, wht w/med bl stripe & single stack w/key, 2 masts, 1955, EX........................$1,000.00

Ocean Liner, Fleischmann, 20", blk & red hull w/wht deck, 2 stacks (lg key), 2 masts, lifeboats, VG $2,250.00

Ocean Liner, JEP, 14", pnt tin, w/up, wht, blk & red, 3 stacks, 2 masts, some rpnt.. $225.00

Ocean Liner, Liberty, 27", wood w/tin cabins & stacks, w/up, railed sides, VG $2,750.00

Ocean Liner, Marklin, *Augusta Victoria,* ca 1910-20, 29", live steam, wht, blk & red, EX..$16,100.00

Ocean Liner, Unk/Germany, 11", litho tin, w/up, yel & blk w/red deck, twin cabin, 2 stacks, VG.............................. $100.00

Oil Tanker, Fleischmann, 20", tin, w/up, blk & red hull w/wht rails & trim, gr catwalk, 1 stack w/key, 2 lifeboats, G.. $500.00

Oil Tanker, Fleischmann, 20", tin, w/up, blk & red hull w/wht rails & trim, gr catwalk, 1 stack w/key, 2 lifeboats, EX $1,200.00

Patrol Boat, Kasuga, Bing, 20", pnt tin, w/up, wht & red, 2 blk stacks w/red trim, lg turret on bow, rpnt, $1,500 to.. $2,000.00

Patrol Boat, Radiguet, 22", pnt tin, w/up, brn & cream, some rpnt $2,750.00

Phantom Raider, Ideal, 30", changes from freighter to fighting war ship, 1960s, NMIB................................... $150.00

Piggyback Boat, Cragstan/NGS #1406-8, friction, tin w/plastic 'Sea-Land Service' container, NMIB........................... $100.00

Racing Scull, Issmayer, 20½", tin, w/up, 4-man rowing team, VG $4,000.00

Riverboat, Bing, 19½", pnt tin, w/up, wht over red, full canopy, railed deck, w/windows, some rpnt, VG $2,000.00

Riverboat, Carette, 14½", tin, w/up, wht & red hull w/lt bl pinstripe, tan deck, 2 blk stacks w/'smoke' key, rstr $2,750.00

Riverboat, Carette, 16½", tin, w/up, wht, blk & red, red & wht canopy over cabin, rpnt............................... $1,425.00

Riverboat, Carette, 21", tin, w/up, red & wht, canopied, railed bow (w/diners), cabin & stern, rstr $2,200.00

Riverboat, Ernst Plank, *Jupiter,* 17½", pnt tin, wht & red hull w/ yel deck & canopy, VGIB $10,000.00

Riverboat, Fleischmann, 16", tin, w/up, wht & red w/lt bl pinstripe, canoped top w/lg key, rstr $2,500.00

Riverboat, Ives, *Sally,* 10", pnt tin, w/up, wht & red w/red stack & lifeboat, canopied stern, rstr, $300 to $500.00

Rowboat, Arnold, 8", tin, w/up, lt bl & wht w/figure rowing, VGIB $325.00

Rowboat, Arnold, 8", tin, w/up, wht w/bl band, compo oarsman, NM $800.00

Runabout, Liberty, 15", wood & tin, w/up, G, $75 to..... $150.00

Runabout, TMY, 14", pnt wood, w/up, w/windshield & deck setail, American flag, EX, $200 to................................... $275.00

Sailboat, Converse, *Resolute,* 18", PS, fashioned after the America's Cup entries, EX+ $350.00

Sailboat, Gescha, 7½", tin, w/up, red w/red flag atop 2 gray sails w/wht pinstriped, bl trim, EX+ $200.00

Sailboat, Hess, *1045*, 12", litho tin w/litho cb sails, EX... $1,000.00

Sailboat (Racing), Keystone, 17", wood, cloth sails, VGIB.. $125.00

Sea Babe, Fleetline, 13", wood, b/o, NMIB, $125 to $225.00

Sea Hawk, Straits Corp, 18", PS, b/o, working headlight, yel, 1934, NM, $170 to $280.00

Side-Wheeler, Carette, 15", pnt tin, w/up, cream w/red bottom, cream canopy, center stack, rstr $1,000.00

Side-Wheeler, Hess (?), 10", litho tin, flywheel action, 3 stacks, pointed front w/rounded back, VG $400.00

Side-Wheeler, Marklin, *New York*, 19", pnt tin, wht & red w/gold details, NM $7,000.00

Side-Wheeler, Marklin, *Providence*, 26", enameled tin, w/up, red & wht, ca 1905, EX $99,000.00

Speedboat, Boucher, *Polly-Wog*, 23", wood & polished aluminum, live steam/hot air motor, EX+ $7,175.00

Speedboat, German, 29", tin w/wooden deck, G, $600 to .. $850.00

Speedboat, Jacrim Mfg, *Flying Yankee*, #66, 22", wood, w/up motor, 1930s, G $800.00

Speedboat, Japan, 17½", wooden, b/o, wht w/brn deck & dragons on sides, VG+, $350 to $460.00

Speedboat, JEP, *Ruban Bleu*, 20", pnt tin, red w/wht trim, 1930, NMIB, $950 to $1,500.00

Speedboat, *Le Raceret*, 6", bright bl, seated 'captain' figure, EXIB $650.00

Speedboat, Lindstrom, 21", litho tin, w/up outboard motor, red, yel & gr, EX, $500 to $625.00

Speedboat, Lionel, #43, 17", EX $2,300.00

Speedboat, Lionel, #44, tin w/2 compo figures, w/up, EXIB .. $1,400.00

Speedboat, Meccano, *Hornby*, 17½", wood & tin, w/up, VG . $225.00

Speedboat Meccano, *Hornby Racer III*, PS, 17", w/up, yel w/red trim, 1930s, NM, $450 to $550.00

Speedboat, *Miss Canada*, 12", tin, steam-powered, gr & red w/ brass boiler, w/funnel & fuel can, British flag, VG $400.00

SS Moby Dick (Wooden Model Boat), Japan, 15½", b/o, red, wht & bl, NMIB, $400 to $470.00

Steam Launch, Bing, 16½", tin, steam-powered, canopied top, G+ $850.00

Steam Launch, Carette, 18", tin, wht & red w/blk metal filigree-edge canopy, G $1,750.00

Steam Launch, Ernst Plank, 11", tin, steam-powered, wht & red hull, single stack, VG $1,450.00

Steam Launch, Weeden, 15", tin, steam-powered, blk & red hull w/yel deck, VG $475.00

Steam Launch, Weeden, 15", tin, steam-powered, red stack, brass piping, EX+ $750.00

Submarine, Bing, 13", tin, w/up, aqua bl w/copper-color rudder, EX $750.00

Submarine, CK/Japan, 12", tin, hand lever controls prop, wht deck w/gray bottom, gold gun, American flag, EX+IB.. $275.00

Submarine, Fleischmann, *Pennsylvania R-4*, 10", tin, w/up, red & gray, G $100.00

Submarine, Horndlein, 10½", tin, w/up, gray & camo, w/railed observation deck, EX $250.00

Submarine, Jep, *Nautilus 919*, 17", tin, w/up, gray & wht, EXIB $175.00

Submarine, Linemar, *Sea Wolf*, 12½", tin, r/c, NMIB $250.00

Submarine, Remco, *Barracuda Atomic*, 1960s, EXIB $150.00

Submarine, *SSN No 25*, 10", litho tin, crank-op friction, EXIB $200.00

Submarine (Diving), Wolverine, 13", litho tin, w/up, EXIB $175.00

Swamp Boat, Knickerbocker, 13", with pusher type airplane motor, 1950s, NMIB $90.00

Tanker, Fleischmann, 20", tin, w/up, red w/gr stripe, wht deck w/ gr bridge, single stack, 2 masts, EX $2,000.00

Torpedo Boat, Bing, 21", tin, w/up, 2-tone gray w/bl deck, 2 masts, G $875.00

Torpedo Boat, Japan, 17", wood, b/o, bl-gray & red, very detailed, 1950s, EX $500.00

Torpedo Boat, Japan, 32", wood, b/o, bl-gray & red, very detailed, 1950s, EX $700.00

Torpedo Boat, Linemar, PT 107, 11", litho tin, b/o, 1950s, NMIB $175.00

Torpedo Boat, Marusan, P-5701, 11½", tin, friction, gray w/red bottom, wht & blk trim, NMIB $275.00

Tugboat, Carette, 11", tin, w/up, cream, yel, gr & blk, key in single stack atop pilot's cabin, single mast, EX $1,450.00

Tugboat, Hornby, 11", tin, wht & gr w/yel deck & single stack, blk bottom, EX $125.00

Tugboat, Marusan, 12½", litho tin, b/o, NM+IB............. $150.00

Tugboat, Sankei, 9", litho tin, crank-op friction, NM+IB... $100.00

U-Boat, *Nemo*, 15½", tin, w/up, wht w/blk trim, EXIB.... $450.00

Boats

Side-Wheeler, Merklin, *Lorelei*, hand-painted, professionally restored, 13½" long, $6,000.00 to $8,000.00.

Boats

Submarine, Marklin, 31", hand enameled tin with clockwork mechanism, VG to EX, $3,000.00 to $4,000.00.

Warship, Ideal, *Phantom Raider*, 1960s, 30", plastic, EXIB ..$150.00
Yacht, Carette, 18", tin, w/up, yel & red, 1905, EX $1,900.00
Yacht, Tri-Ang, 18", PS, red w/blk trim, 2 cloth sails, NMIB...$175.00
Yacht, Marklin, *Yolanda*, 29", tin, w/up, wht & blk hull w/reddish
    brown deck, tan stack, 2 masts, 4 lifeboats, EX $15,500.00

OUTBOARD MOTORS

Allyn Seafury, 5½", EX+ $250.00
Chester A Pimmer, 7", VG............................... $175.00
K&O, 5", NM $195.00
NBK No 0-4, orange & wht, 4", NOS (in orig box)....... $185.00

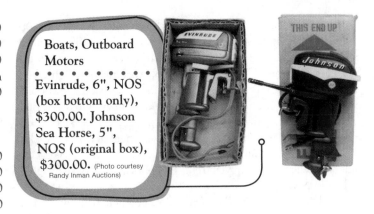

Boats, Outboard Motors. Evinrude, 6", NOS (box bottom only), $300.00. Johnson Sea Horse, 5", NOS (original box), $300.00. (Photo courtesy Randy Inman Auctions)

• • • • • • • • • • • • • • • • • • • Books • • • • • • • • • • • • • • • • • • •

Books have always captured and fired the imagination of children, and today books from every era are being collected. No longer is it just the beautifully illustrated Victorian examples or first editions of books written by well-known children's authors, but more modern books as well.

One of the first classics to achieve unprecedented success was *The Wizard of Oz* by L. Frank Baum — such success, in fact, that far from his original intentions, it became a series. Even after Baum's death, other authors wrote Oz books until the decade of the 1960s, for a total of more than 40 different titles. Other early authors were Beatrix Potter, Kate Greenaway, Palmer Cox (who invented the Brownies), and Johnny Gruelle (creator of Raggedy Ann and Andy). All were accomplished illustrators as well.

Everyone remembers a special series of books they grew up with — the Hardy Boys, Nancy Drew Mysteries, Tarzan, and countless others. And though these are becoming very collectible today, there were many editions of each, and most are very easy to find. Generally the last few in any series will be most difficult to locate, since fewer were printed than the earlier stories which were likely to have been reprinted many times. As is true of any type of book, first editions, or the earliest printings will have more collector value. For more information on series books as well as others, we recommend *Encyclopedia of Collectible Children's Books* by Diane McClure Jones and Rosemary Jones (Collector Books).

Big Little Books came along in 1933, and until edged out by the comic-book format in the mid-1950s, sold in huge volumes. They were printed by Whitman, Saalfield, Goldsmith, Van Wiseman, Lynn, and World Syndicate, and all stuck to the thick hand-sized sagas of adventure. The first hero to be immortalized in this venue was Dick Tracy, but many more were to follow. Some of today's more collectible Big Little Books feature well-known characters like G-Man, Tarzan, Flash Gordon, Little Orphan Annie, Mickey Mouse, and all the Western heroes. For more information we recommend *Big Little Books*, by our advisor, Larry Jacobs.

Little Golden Books were first published in 1942 by Western Publishing Co. Inc. The earliest had spines of blue paper that were later replaced with gold foil. Until the 1970s, the books were numbered from one to 600, while later books had no numerical order. The most valuable are those with dust jackets from the early 1940s or books with paper dolls and activities. The three primary series of books are Regular (1 – 600), Disney (1 – 140), and Activity (1 – 52). Books with the blue or gold paper spine (not foil) often sell at $8.00 to $15.00. Dust jackets alone are worth $20.00 and up in good condition. Paper doll books are generally valued at about $30.00 to $35.00, and stories about TV Western heroes at $12.00 to $18.00. First editions of the 25¢ and 29¢ cover-price books can be identified by a code (either on the title page or the last page); '1/A' indicates a first edition while a 'number/Z' will refer to the twenty-sixth printing. Condition is important but subjective to personal standards. For more information we recommend *Collecting Little Golden Books, Vols. I* and *II*, by Steve Santi. The second volume also includes information on Wonder and Elf books. For further study we recommend *Whitman Juvenile Books* by David and Virginia Brown.

See also Black Americana; Coloring, Activity, and Paint Books; Rock 'n Roll; other specific categories.

BIG LITTLE BOOKS

Alley Oop & Dinny, #763, 1935, G+.....................$15.00
Alley Oop & Dinny in the Jungles of Moo, #1473, 1936, M...$75.00
Andy Panda & the Mad Dog Mystery, #1431, 1947, M.....$40.00
Apple Mary & Dennie Foil the Swindlers, #1130, 1936, VG...$25.00
Betty Boop in Miss Gulliver's Travels, #1158, 1935, M .. $200.00
Betty Boop in Snow White Assisted by Bimbo & Ko-Ko, #1119, 1934, G...$45.00
Billy the Kid, #773, 1935, M $50.00
Blondie & Baby Dumpling, #1415, 1937, M.....................$45.00
Blondie with Baby Dumpling & Daisy, #1429, 1939, M....$35.00

Brenda Star & the Masked Imposter, #1427, 1943, M.......$40.00
Brer Rabbit, #1426, 1947, VG+ $40.00
Buck Rogers & the Planetoid Plot, #1197, 1936, VG+ $45.00
Buck Rogers in the War w/Planet Venus, #1437, 1934, M...$150.00
Buck Rogers 25th Century AD, #742, 1933, G $25.00
Captain Easy Soldier of Fortune, #1128, 1934, M $35.00
Captain Midnight & Sheik Jomak Khan, #1407, 1946, VG....$35.00
Chester Gump Finds the Hidden Treasure, #766, 1934, VG+..$20.00
Cowboy Lingo — Boy's Book of Western Facts, #1457, 1938, M...$50.00

Dan Dunn in Crime Never Pays, #1116, 1934, M $45.00
Danger Trail North, #1177, 1940, M.................................$35.00
Desert Eagle & the Hidden Fortress, #1431, 1941, VG+...$25.00
Dick Tracy & Dick Tracy Jr, #710, 1933, w/ads, G $40.00
Dick Tracy Detective, Adventures of, #W-707, 1933, 1st Big
    Little Book, scarce, G.. $200.00
Dick Tracy from Colorado to Nova Scotia, #749, 1933, VG+ ...$45.00
Dick Tracy in Chains of Crime, #1185, 1936, VG+ $45.00
Ella Cinders & the Mysterious House, #1106, 1934, M.....$85.00
Ellery Queen the Adventures of the Last Man Club, #1406,
    1940, G+ $15.00
Felix the Cat, #1465, 1945, VG+......................................$30.00
Flame Boy & the Indians' Secret, #1464, 1938, VG..........$18.00
Flash Gordon & the Perils of Mongo, #1423, 1940, VG ...$35.00
Flash Gordon & the Tournaments of Mongo, #1171, 1935,
    VG..$45.00
Flash Gordon in the Forest Kingdom Mongo, #1492, 1938,
    G+ $25.00
G-Man & the Gun Runners, #1469, 1940, M $40.00
G-Man & the Radio Bank Robberies, #1434, 1937, M $40.00
Gang Busters Step In, #1433, 1939, VG+...........................$20.00
Gene Autry in Public Cowboy No 1, #1433, 1938, VG+..$25.00
George O'Brien & the Hooded Riders, #1457, 1940, M....$30.00
Ghost Avengers, #1462, 1943, 'See 'em Move Just Flip the
    Pages,' M..$50.00
Green Hornet Returns, #1496, 1941, VG...........................$35.00
Green Hornet Strikes!, #1453, 1940, G $20.00
Hall of Fame of the Air, #1159, 1936, VG+ $18.00
Houdini's Big Little Book of Magic, #715, 1927, VG $35.00
Inspector Wade of Scotland Yard, #1186, 1940, VG+.......$20.00
Jack Swift & His Rockt Ship, #1102, 1934, G....................$8.00
Jackie Cooper in Gangster's Boy, #1402, 1939, VG...........$25.00
Junior Nebb Joins the Circus, #1470, 1939, VG+ $25.00
Laughing Dragon of Oz, #1126, 1934, M $350.00
Little Annie Rooney & the Orphan House, #1117, 1936, VG...$18.00
Little Orphan Annie & Her Dog Sandy, #716, 1933, 1st print-
    ing, M.. $200.00
Little Orphan Annie & the Haunted Mansion, #1482, 1941,
    VG+...$30.00
Lone Ranger & the Black Shirt Highwayman, #1450, 1939,
    VG.. $25.00
Lone Ranger & the Menace of Murder Valley, #1465, 1938,
    VG...$20.00

Lone Ranger & the Secret Killer, #1431, 1937, VG..........$20.00
Mandrake the Magician Mighty Solver of Mysteries, #1454,
    1941, M $55.00
Marge's Little Lulu Alvin & Tubby, #1429, 1947, VG+ $35.00
Men of the Mounted, #755, 1934, VG................................$18.00
Mickey Mouse & Bobo the Elephant, 1935, M................$90.00
Mickey Mouse & the 'Lecto Box, #1413, 1946, VG+ $35.00
Mickey Mouse & the Desert Palace, #1451, 1948, M........$90.00
Mickey Mouse & the Lazy Daisy Mystery, #1433, 1947, VG...$30.00
Mickey Mouse & the Seven Ghosts, #1475, 1940, G+ $28.00
Mickey Mouse Runs His Own Newspaper, #1409, 1937, VG+..$35.00
Mickey Mouse the Detective, #1139, 1934, VG................$35.00
Mickey Mouse the Mail Pilot, #731, 1933, G $45.00
Mutt & Jeff, #1113, 1936, G+...$50.00
Nancy Has Fun, #1487, 1944, M, rare.................................$95.00
Napoleon, Uncle Elby & Little Mary, #1166, 1939, VG...$25.00
Og Son of Fire, #1115, 1936, VG.......................................$18.00
Once Upon a Time, #718, 1933, VG $35.00
Oswald the Lucky Rabbit, #1109, 1934, VG+ $35.00
Our Gang, #1085 or #1315, 1934, VG................................$30.00
Pat Nelson Ace of Pilots, #1445, 1937, VG.......................$18.00
Peggy Brown & the Mystery Basket, #1411, 1941, VG $20.00
Perry Winkle & the Rinkeydinks, #1199, 1937, VG $18.00
Phantom & Desert Justice, #1421, 1941, VG+..................$40.00
Popeye & Olive Oyl, #1458, 1949, VG...............................$25.00
Popeye & the Jeep, #1405, 1937, VG $30.00
Popeye the Sailor Man, #1422, 1947, G+ $18.00
Porky Pig & His Gang, #1404, 1946, VG $30.00
Quiz Book, #1100B, 1938, M..$15.00
Radio Patrol, #1142, 1935, VG..$20.00
Red Barry Undercover Man, #1426, 1939, VG+ $20.00
Red Ryder & Little Beaver on Hoofs of Thunder, #1400, 1939,
    VG..$25.00
Red Ryder & Western Border Guns, #1450, 1942, VG $30.00
Riders of Lone Trails, #1425, 1937, VG+...........................$18.00
Roy Rogers King of the Cowboys, #1476, 1943, VG $18.00
Secret Agent X-9 & the Mad Assassin, #1472, 1938, M...$55.00
Shadow & the Living Death, #1430, 1940, NM............. $250.00
Shirley Temple with Lionel Barrymore in The Little Colonel,
    #1115, 1935, EX $35.00
Skeezix Goes to War, #1414, 1944, VG+............................$25.00
Skippy, #761, 1934, M..$75.00
Skyroads with Hurricane Hawk, #1127, 1936, M $50.00

Smilin' Jack & the Stratosphere Ascent, #1152, 1937, VG+ ..$40.00
Smitty Golden Gloves Tournament, #745, 1934, M..........$50.00
Son of Tarzan, #1477, 1939, VG+.....................................$30.00
Tailspin Tommy & the Lost Transport, #1413, 1940, M....$35.00
Tarzan Escapes, #1182, 1935, VG.....................................$25.00
Tarzan of the Apes, #744, 1933, 1st Tarzan, G.................$25.00
Tarzan the Fearless, #769, 1934, G+................................$15.00
Tarzan's Revenge, #1488, 1938, G+.................................$55.00
Terry & the Pirates, #1156, 1935, VG..............................$35.00
Texas Kid, #1429, 1937, M...$30.00
Three Musketeers, #1131, 1935, VG+...............................$40.00
Tiny Tim in the Big Big World, #1472, 1945, M $65.00
Treasure Island, #720, 1933, VG+....................................$30.00
Uncle Don's Strange Adventure, #1114, 1935, M............$30.00
Union Pacific, #1411, 1939, VG.......................................$35.00
Up Dead Horse Canyon, #1189, 1940, M.........................$25.00
Wash Tubbs & Captain Easy Hunting for Whales, #1455, 1938,
    VG+..$30.00
We Three, #1109, 1935, VG+..$25.00
Windy Wayne & His Flying Wing, #1433, 1942, M..........$30.00
Zane Grey's King of the Royal Mounted Gets His Man, #1452,
    1938, M $40.00
Zip Saunders King of the Speedway, #1465, 1939, VG+ ...$18.00

ELF BOOKS BY RAND MCNALLY

Alice in Wonderland, 1951, VG+......................................$12.00
Animal's Bus Ride, Junior, #8118, VG.............................$6.00
Animal Stories We Can Read, #8031, EX.........................$10.00
Animals at the Seashore, #8125, VG................................$7.50
Big Helpers, #8047, 1953, VG..$7.50
Bremen Town Musicians, Junior, #8066, G+ $5.00
Busy Book, #8402, 1952, VG...$7.50
Busy Bulldozer, #8375, 1952, VG+...................................$8.50
Dennis the Menace, #541, 1956, EX+ $12.00
Early One Morning, Tip-Top, #8656, 1963, VG.................$8.00
Farm Animals, #8735, 1952, EX.......................................$10.00
Farm for Andy, #448, 1951, VG $8.00
Farm Pets, Junior, #8041, VG...$7.50
Fireman Joe, Start Right, #8006, VG................................$8.50
Growing Up, #8397, 1959, VG+..$7.50
House That Jack Built, Junior, #8055, G+ $6.00
How Chicks Are Born, #8153, EX......................................$7.50
Humpty Dumpty & Other Mother Goose Rhymes, Junior, #8001,
    VG $6.00
Jack & Jill & Other Nursery Rhymes, #8395, EX $10.00
Jack Sprat, #8130, VG...$7.50
Jolly Jingle Book, Junior, #8001, VG...............................$6.50
Larry the Canary, #8322, 1959, EX $8.50
Little Boy Blue's Horn, Junior, #8117, EX.......................$8.50
Little Donkey, Junior, #8111, EX+ $10.00
Little Fox, Junior, #8077, 1961, EX $10.00
Little Penguin, Junior, #8057, 1960, EX..........................$10.00
Little Skater, Tip-Top, 1959, EX..$10.00
Mailman Mike, Junior, #8056, VG....................................$8.50
Mother Goose, Tip-Top, #8647, 1971, EX $6.00
Mr Bear's House, #8349, 1953, EX $12.00
Mr Flopears, Start-Right, #8163, EX $10.00

My Bible Book, Tip-Top, #8696, 1946, VG $10.00
My Cowboy Book, Start-Right, #8150, VG........................$6.00
My Truck Book, Junior, #8063, VG...................................$6.50
Night Before Christmas, #8204, 1950s, VG......................$5.00
Noah's Ark, Tip-Top, #8648, 1961, EX $12.00
Noni the Christmas Reindeer, Junior, #8197, 1979, VG $6.50
Number 9 the Little Fire Engine, #444, 1950s, VG+.........$10.00
Outdoor Fun, #479, 1953, EX..$12.00
Pet for Peter, Junior, #8043, EX.......................................$10.00
Pets, #486, 1954, VG+ $10.00
Pocahontas, #575, 1957, G+ $8.50
Pony Express, #8344, 1956, VG $10.00
Runaway Kangaroos, Junior, #8004, VG $6.00
Santa's Runaway Elf, Junior, #8203, VG $5.00
Sergeant Preston & Rex, #569, 1956, VG+ $10.00
Sleeping Beauty, #8050, VG..$6.50
Sleeping Beauty, #8320, 1959, G+ $8.50
Sleeping Beauty, #8683, VG..$6.50
Snow White & the Seven Dwarfs, #8028, 1959, VG $8.00
Squirrel Twins, Tip-Top, #8670, 1972, VG+.....................$10.00
Story of Toby, Junior, #8000, VG $6.50
Surprise!, #8384, 1956, VG...$10.00
Ten Little Monkeys, #8044, VG+ $8.00
Three Billy Goats Gruff, Start-Right, #8136, VG+............$8.00
Three Little Bunnies, #443, 1950, EX+ $18.00
Three Little Puppies, #447, 1953, G+...............................$8.50
Three Wishes, Junior, #8061, 1945, EX............................$8.00
Tim & His Train, #8045, VG+..$8.50
Tom Thumb, Tip-Top, #8684, 1959, EX.............................$10.00
What Can I Do?, #8070, 1961, EX+ $10.00
Wild Animals, #454, 1952, EX+ $10.00
Wonderful Plane Ride, #433, 1949, EX.............................$12.00

LITTLE GOLDEN BOOKS

ABC Rhymes, #543, 1964, A ed, EX $12.00
ABC Rhymes, #543, 1972 ed, VG+....................................$8.50
Aladdin & His Magic Lamp, #371, A ed, 1959, VG $12.00
Ali Baba, #323, 1958, 1st ed, VG+ $12.00
Alice's First Words, #10136-20, 1993, EX $6.00
Animal Daddies & My Daddy, #576, 1968, A ed, VG.........$8.00
Aristocats, #D122, 1970, VG+...$10.00

Books, Little
Golden Books
• • • • • • • •
Littlest Racoon,
Peggy Parrick,
1961, A edition,
NM, $18.00.
(Photo courtesy www.gaso
linealleyantiques.com)

Baby's First Book, #358, 1959, A ed, VG+..........................$20.00
Bambi, #D7, P ed, EX $8.00
Bambi, #101-50, O ed, 1975, VG+ $7.50
Bambi Friends of the Forest, #101-50, N ed, 1975, VG.......$7.50
Bedtime Stories, #002, 10th ed, 1942, EX+ $14.00
Bedtime Stories, #538, J ed, 1940s (?), G+ $7.00
Benji, #111-36, D ed, 1978, EX $10.00
Bettina the Ballerina, #211-69, 1991, A ed, EX+ $12.00
Bobby & His Airplanes, #69, 1949, D ed, VG+.................$12.00
Book of God's Gifts, #112, 1978 ed, VG $8.00
Bozo the Clown, #446, A ed, 1961, EX $16.00
Bugs Bunny & the Health Hog, #10250, B ed, 1986, EX $8.00
Cave Kids, #539, A ed, 1963, VG $16.00
Christmas Carols, #26, H ed, VG.......................................$8.00
Corky, #486, 1962, EX+...$10.00
David & Goliath, #110, 1978 ed, VG $9.00
From Then to Now, #201, 1954, A ed, EX $10.00
Fuzzy Duckling, #557, F ed, 1949, EX...............................$10.00
Gaston & Josephine, #65, 1949, D ed, VG+ $45.00
Golden Egg Book, #304-11, 1962, EX $7.00
Hi Ho! Three in a Row, #188, 1954, A ed, EX $10.00
Howdy Doody & Clarabell, #121, B ed, 1951, EX.............$25.00
Huckleberry Hound Builds a House, #376, C ed, 1959, EX ..$12.00
Huckleberry Hound Safety Signs, #458, A ed, 1961, VG..$10.00
I Don't Want to Go, #208-59, A ed, 1989, EX $8.00
I Think About God, #111, 1978 ed, EX...............................$8.00
Little Cotton Tail, #414, D ed, 1960, EX $9.00
Little Golden Book of Words, #45, D ed, 1948, scarce, EX...$16.00
Little Lulu & Her Magic Tricks, #203, 1954, A ed, w/dust jacket,
    VG $100.00
Lively Little Rabbit, #15, 1943, A ed, EX $25.00
Loopy de Loop Goes West, #417, 1960, EX $15.00
Lucky Puppy, #D89, E ed, 1960, EX+ $11.00
Lucky Puppy, #D89, G ed, 1960, EX $9.00
Mickey Mouse & Goofy The Big Bear Scare, #D138, 1978,
    VG $5.00
Mickey Mouse Picnic, #D15, H ed, 1950, EX $10.00
Mother Goose, #300-10, Y ed, EX.....................................$8.50
Mother Goose Rhymes, #317, A ed, 1958, EX $17.50
Mr Bell's Fixit Shop, #204-42, 1981, E ed, EX+.................$18.00
New Puppy, #370, 1977 ed, EX..$8.00
Night Before Christmas, #20, B ed, 1949, Santa on rooftop put-
    ting toys down chimney, EX...$20.00
Peter Rabbit, #479-1, 1979 ed, EX+ $9.00
Pink Panther in the Haunted House, #110-5, 1980 ed, EX.$8.00
Pinocchio, #D8, T ed, 1948, G+ $9.00
Pinocchio, #104-2, 1979 ed, EX..$9.00
Pocketful of Nonsense, #312-05, 1992, NM+ $7.50
Prayers for Children, #5, M ed, 1942, EX..........................$25.00
Quiz Fun, #5024, A ed, 1959, Giant LGB, EX+ $12.00
Raggedy Ann & Andy & the Rainy Day Circus, #107-2, 1980
    ed, EX $10.00
Santa's Toy Shop, #D16, B ed, 1950, EX...........................$15.00
Scamp, The Adventures of a Little Puppy, #D63, B ed, 1957,
    EX $12.00
Scuffy the Tugboat, #30, D ed, 1946, EX..........................$22.00
Scuffy the Tugboat, #363, C ed, 1955, EX.........................$10.00
Shy Little Kitten, #23, E ed, 1946, EX...............................$25.00

Books, Little Golden Books
• • • • • • • •
The Night Before Christmas, Clement C. Moore, 1949, limited edition, twelfth printing, third cover, NM, $12.00. (Photo courtesy www.gasolinealleyantiques.com)

Shy Little Kitten, #23, I ed, 1946, EX $10.00
Sleeping Beauty, #D61, A ed, 1957, VG+ $10.00
Sleeping Beauty, #104-56, J ed, 1986, EX $7.00
Supercar, #492, 1962, A ed, VG $12.00
Things in My House, #570, A ed, 1968, EX........................$8.00
Through the Picture Frame, #D1, 2nd ed, 1946, VG.........$25.00
Tiger's Adventure, #208, B ed, 1954, VG+ $12.00
Top Cat, #453, A ed, 1962, VG $10.00
Toy Soldiers, #D99, A ed, 1961, VG+ $11.00
Tweety Plays Catch the Puddy Cat, #141, 1978 ed, EX.......$9.00
Twelve Days of Christmas, #526, A ed, 1963, EX..............$12.00
Wild Animals, #499, 1974 ed, EX $10.00
Winnie the Pooh Meets Gopher, #D117, B ed, EX+ $12.00
Woody Woodpecker, #145, B ed, 1952, EX........................$8.00
Words, #45, Y ed, 1948, EX $12.00

POP-UP AND MOVABLE BOOKS

ABC & Number Pop-Up Pictures, Purnell, 1950s, 1st ed,
    EX $18.00
Animal's Merry Christmas, by Kathryn Jackson, 1950, w/pop-up
    tree, EX...$125.00
Buck Rogers Strange Adventures in the Spider Ship, 1935, 3
    pop-ups, VG $115.00
Christmas Treasure Book, Simon & Schuster, 1950, 1 pop-up,
    EX $45.00
Cinderella, A Peepshow Book, Brett Lithographing Co, 1950,
    G $50.00
Dick Tracy — The Capture of Boris Arson, Blue Ribbon Books,
    1935, 3 pop-ups, EX $125.00
Goldilocks & the Three Bears, Blue Ribbon Books, 1934, 3 pop-
    ups, NM...$200.00
Jack & the Beanstalk/Hop O' My Thumb, Bancroft & Co, 1962,
    EX $50.00
Little Orphan Annie & Jumbo the Circus Elephant, Blue Ribbon
    Books, 3 pop-ups, NM+ $250.00
Mickey Mouse Presents Silly Symphonies/Babes in the Woods/
    King Neptune, Dean & Son Ltd, 1st ed, 4 pop-ups, G...$50.00
New Adventures of Tarzan 'Pop-Up,' 3 pop-ups, EX $100.00
Night Before Christmas, illus & animations by Julian Wehr,
    Duenewald, 1949, spiralbound, EX..............................$40.00
Peeps into Fairyland, Philomel Books, 1986 repro of early Ernest
    Nister book, hardcover, EX+..$15.00

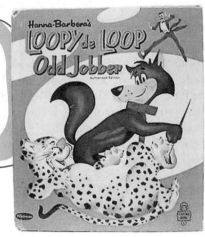

Peter Rabbit the Magician, Strathmore, 1942, spiralbound, VG.. $35.00

Pinocchio, by Marion Merrill, Cima Publishing, 1945, spiralbound, w/dust jacket, VG.............................$32.00

Pop-Goes-The-Joke Book, Hallmark, VG.....................$35.00

Pop-up Minnie Mouse, Blue Ribbon Books, 1933, 3 pop-ups, EX $175.00

Pop-Up Popeye w/the Hag of the Seven Seas, Pleasure Books, 1935, VG...$85.00

Santa's Circus, White Plains Greeting Card Corp, 1952, 3 pop-ups, spiralbound, EX.....................................$40.00

Terry & the Pirates in Shipwrecked, Blue Ribbon/Pleasure Books, 1935, 3 pop-ups, EX...............................$75.00

TELL-A-TALE BY WHITMAN

Animals in Mother Goose, 1970, EX $6.00
Bugs Bunny Keeps a Promise, 1951, VG $6.00
By the Sea, Big Tell-A-Tale, 1966, VG.............................$10.00
Circus Train, 1948, EX+ $18.00
Dodo the Little Wild Duck, 1948, EX+ $15.00
Donald Duck w/Chip 'N' Dale, 1954, EX+ $10.00
Elves & the Shoemaker, 1958, EX.......................................$8.00
Goofy Tiger Hunt, VG...$6.00
Happy, 1964, EX $15.00
Hippity Hop around the Block, 1953, VG $8.00
Hooray for Lassie!, 1964, EX $10.00
House That Jack Built, 1961, VG $6.00
How to Be a Grouch by Oscar the Grouch, 1976, EX $10.00
I Know What a Farm Is, 1969, VG+ $8.00
Lassie & the Deer Mystery, #2442, 1966, EX $15.00
Lassie Finds a Friend, 1960, VG+..$8.00
Little Bear & the Beautiful Kite, 1955, G............................$5.00
Little Henry to the Rescue, 1945, EX+ $15.00
Little Joe's Puppy, 1957, EX $10.00
Little Red Hen, 1953, VG $8.00
Little Red Riding Hood, 1953, EX $7.00
Mother Goose on the Farm, 1975, EX+ $8.00
My Little Book about Our Flag, 1975, EX+ $8.00
My Little Book of Big Machines, 1975, EX+ $8.00
Night Before Christmas, Big Tell-A-Tale, 1965, VG.........$10.00
Nursery Rhymes, 1945, EX+...$10.00

Our America, 1941, VG+..$10.00
Peter's Pencil, 1953, NM+...$12.00
Pinocchio, 1961, VG $7.50
Pony Who Couldn't Say Neigh, 1964, EX $10.00
Prayers for Boys & Girls, 1953, VG+ $6.00
Princess Who Never Laughed, 1961, EX............................$10.00
See-It Goes, 1953, VG..$8.00
Special Pet, 1968, EX..$8.00
Splish, Splash & Splush, 1962, EX....................................$14.00
Surprise in the Barn, VG...$5.00
Tagalong Shadow, 1959, VG $10.00
Three Bears, 1955, VG+..$8.00
Three Little Pigs, 1956, VG $6.00
Tom & Jerry & the Toy Circus, EX $8.00
Tuffy the Tugboat, 1947, EX+...$15.00
Very Best of Friends, 1963, EX $8.00
Walt Disney's Bear Country, 1954, VG $6.00
Walt Disney's Beaver Valley, 1954, EX...............................$8.00
Walt Disney's Lady, 1954, VG $6.00
Water Birds, 1955, VG $5.00
Woody Woodpecker Peck of Trouble Book, 1959, VG........$6.00

WHITMAN

A Little Mother Goose, Tiny Tales, 1959, VG+ $10.00
Annette Sierra Summer, 1960, VG+ $12.00
Buddy Bear's Lost Growl, Tiny Tales, 1959, VG $8.00

Champions All the Way, 1960, EX $8.00
Crusader Rabbit in Bubble Trouble, Top Top Tale, #2468, VG ..$12.00
Donald Duck in the Great Kite Maker, Tiny Tales, 1959, VG ...$10.00
Famous Investigators, 1963, VG+ $10.00
Fun at the Beach, Tiny Tot Tale, 1960, VG+ $10.00
Here's a Bunny, #2210, 1970, washable cloth cover, VG...$12.00
Lion & the Mouse, Top Top Tales, #2483, 1961, EX $12.00
Ludwig von Drake Dog Expert, Top Top Tales, #2482, 1962, VG $10.00
Mother Goose, Top Top Tales, #2478, 1960, EX $10.00
Nurses Who Led the Way, 1961, EX+ $12.00
Pinocchio, Top Top Tales, #2459, 1961, VG $8.00
Playtime, Tiny Tales, 1960, VG..........................$8.50
Plush, Tiny Tales, 1949, VG..............................$8.50
Poppyseed, Top Top Tales, #2475, 1954, EX $15.00
Rain & Shine, Tiny Tales, 1960, EX $10.00
Telling Time, Tiny Tales, 1959, EX $10.00
They Flew to Fame, 1963, EX+ $12.00
Tommy Caboose, Tiny Tales, 1950, VG+ $10.00
Truck That Stopped at Village Small, #2477, 1951, VG $8.00
Tunes for Toddlers, Tiny Tales, 1950, VG+..............$10.00
Twinkles & Sanford's Boat, Top Top Tales, #2477, 1962, EX....$12.00

WONDER BOOKS

Animal's Playground, #825, EX..........................$10.00
Baby Raccoon, #797, 1963, EX $10.00
Baby's Day, #663, EX+ $15.00
Barbie's Adventures, #2048, 1964, VG $8.50
Bingity-Bangity School Bus, #550, 1950, EX $12.00
Brave Fireman & Firehouse Cat, #563, 1951, EX+...........$12.00
Brave Little Duck, #777, 1953, EX......................$10.00
Brave Little Steam Shovel, #555, 1951, EX+ $10.00
Can You Guess? A Romper Room Book, #701R, 1953, EX.$8.00
Casper the Friendly Ghost, #761, 1960, EX..............$10.00
Christ Child Wonder Book, #587, 1953, EX...............$10.00
Copycat Colt, #545, 1951, EX...........................$10.00
Counting Rhymes, #882, VG $8.00
Deputy Dawg's Big Catch, #770, 1961, VG+ $10.00
Dondi, #783, 1961, VG+.................................$12.00
Donkey Who Wanted to Be Wise, #771, c 1961, EX $10.00
Giraffe Who Went to School, #551, c 1951, EX+ $12.00

Hector Crosses the River, #769, c 1961, VG $6.00
Herman & Katnip, #788, 1961, VG.......................$12.00
Hoppy the Curious Kangaroo, #579, 1975, EX $8.00
How Peter Cottontail Got His Name, #668, 1957, VG $8.00
I See the Sky, #746, 1974 edition, VG..................$8.00
It's a Secret, #540, early version, EX $12.00
Johnny Grows Up, #618, 1954, EX.......................$10.00
Joke on Farmer Al Falfa, #736, 1959, EX...............$12.00
Kitten's Secret, #527, 1950, G.........................$6.00
Lassie Come Home, #639, 1956, VG+.....................$8.50
Little Car That Wanted a Garage, #573, 1952, EX...........$10.00
Little Duck Said Quack Quack Quack, #636, 1955, VG...$12.00
Little School House, #710, 1977, VG $8.00
Minute-And-A-Half-Man, #758, 1960, VG $12.00
My First Book of Jokes, #799, 1962, EX $8.00
Peter Rabbit & Reddy Fox, #611, 1954, EX...............$12.00
Pony Engine, #626, 1972 ed, VG+.......................$10.00
Pony Engine, #626, 1983 ed, VG $8.00
Popeye Goes on a Picnic, #697, 1958, G $5.00
Raggedy Ann's Merriest Christmas, #594, 1952, EX.........$18.00
Raggedy Ann's Merriest Christmas, #594, 1952, VG $12.00
Rattle Rattle Train, #655, 1957, EX $8.00
Romper Room Do Dee Book of Manners, #763, 1960, EX..$8.00
Runaway Baby Bird, #748, 1960, EX.....................$8.50
Secret Cat, Easy Reader, 1961, EX $10.00
Surprise Doll, #519, 1949, EX $25.00
Trick on Deputy Dawg, #830, 1964, EX $12.00
Tuggy the Tugboat, #696, 1958, EX.....................$10.00
Water Water Everywhere, #607, c 1953, EX+...............$12.00
What's for Breakfast?, #846, 1974 ed, EX $8.00
Who Goes There?, #779, 1975 ed, c 1961, EX.............$10.00
Wizard of Oz, #543, 1951, EX+.........................$10.00
Wonder Book of Favorite Nursery Tales, #730, 1953, EX..$10.00

MISCELLANEOUS

Adventures of Remi, by Hector Malot, Rand McNally, 1940, G+ $30.00
American Indian Fairy Tales, by WT Larned, Wise-Parslow, 1935, reprint, hardback, VG..........................$12.00
Beautiful Stories of Shakespeare, by E Nesbit, DE Cunningham & Co, 1907, hardback, VG+ $12.00

Belonging Book, Golden Tiny Tale, 1968, EX $15.00

Big Book of Cowboys, Big Treasure Book, by Sidney E Fletcher, 1950, EX...$22.00

Big Susan, by Elizabeth Orton Jones, MacMillan, 1960, hardback, w/dust jacket, VG $30.00

Bobbsey Twins, Saalfield, 1940, hardback, VG..................$10.00

Bobbsey Twins on a Houseboat, by Laura Lee Hope, Grosset & Dunlap, 1915, hardback, VG+......................................$18.00

Bounce the Puppy, A Little Book, John Martin's House, 1948, hardcover, VG...$10.00

Butterflies & Moths, The Golden Library of Knowledge, by Richard A Martin, VG...$8.00

Calico Pup, The Little Color Classics, 1939, EX $32.00

Chocolate War, by Robert Cormier, Pantheon, 1974, hardback, w/dust jacket, EX+ $32.00

Cinderella, by Charles Perrault/Retold by Amy Ehrich, Dial NY, 1985, 1st ed, hardcover, w/dust jacket, VG $10.00

Cowboy Andy, 'I Can Read It All By Myself Beginner's Book,' by Edna Walker Chandler, 1959, hardback, EX $20.00

Danny's Secret, The Little Color Classics, #830, 1940, hardback, EX $15.00

Dobry, by Monica Shannon, Viking Press, 1959, 11th printing, VG+..$12.00

Doctor Dolittle & the Secret Lake, by Hugh Lofting, Lippincott, 1948, 1st ed, hardback, VG...$40.00

Doctor Dolittle in the Moon, by Hugh Lofting, JB Lippincott Co, 1956, hardback, EX $12.00

Doctor Dolittle's Garden, by Hugh Lofting, FA Stokes, 1927, VG+..$25.00

Dorothy of Oz, by Roger S Baum, Morrow, 1989, 1st ed, hardback, w/dust jacket, EX+..$15.00

Down Near the Rabbit Hole, A Little Book, John Martin's House, 1948, hardback, VG...$12.00

East of the Sun & West of the Moon, by Ingri & Edgar Parin d'Aulaire, Viking, 1969 ed, hardback, w/dust jacket, EX...$20.00

Eloise Takes a Bawth, by Kay Thompson, Simon & Schuster, 2002, 1st ed, hardback, EX+ $12.00

Enchanting Fairy Tales, Honey Bear Books, 1989, hardcover, VG $8.00

Famous Fairy Tales, A Sturdibilt Book, 1945, illus by Catherine Barnes, VG $10.00

Fantasy Voyage through Outer Space, by John Hassell, Golden, 1974, EX $20.00

First Book of Horses, by Franklin Watts, 1949, paperback, EX...$6.50

Fixit Man, Treasure Book, #851, 1952, EX.......................$12.00

Flying Kitten, Golden Tiny Tales, 1968, EX+ $15.00

Fun at the Beach, Golden Tiny Tales, 1966, VG $10.00

Good Night Sleep Tight Book, by Mircea Vasiliu, Golden Press, 1973, hardback, w/dust jacket, EX............................. $100.00

Gremlins — To Catch a Gremlin, Western Publising, 1984, EX $8.00

Gulliver's Adventures in Lilliput, by Jonathan Swift, Philomel, 1993, 1st ed, hardback, w/dust jacket, EX.....................$25.00

Hansel & Gretel, Grosset & Dunlap, 1970, hardback, EX .$18.00

Happy Birthday to You!, by Dr Seuss, Random House, 1959, early reprint, VG..$25.00

Happy Prince & Other Stories, by Oscar Wilde, William Morrow/ Books of Wonder, 1991, hardback, w/dust jacket, EX........$18.00

Henny Penny, Read Along With Me/See & Say Reader, Samuel Lowe, 1962, VG $10.00

Here We Go!, by May Windsor, John Martin's House, 1950, EX $12.00

Home for Bunny, Big Golden Book, 1983, VG..................$10.00

Indians & the Old West, by Anne Terry White, Golden Book, Simon & Schuster, 1958, 2nd print, hardback, VG+.......$8.00

Jack & Jill at the Pet Show, A Lolly Pop Book, John Martin's House, 1949, VG+ $12.00

Kathy Martin Courage in Crisis, by Josephine James, 1964, EX...$15.00

Land of Oz a Sequel to the Wizard of Oz, by Frank Baum, Reilly & Lee, 1939, hardback, w/dust jacket, VG+ $42.00

Land of Surprise, McLoughlin Bros, 1938, VG+...............$45.00

Little Auto, by Lois Lenski, Random House, 2001, hardback, w/ dust jacket, EX+ $32.00

Little Chick, A Little Book, John Martin's House, 1948, VG ..$10.00

Little Cottontail, Golden Tiny Tales, by Carl Memling, 1960, VG...$8.00

Little Friends of Mine, A Little Book, John Martin's House, 1948, hardcover, VG...$10.00

Little House in the Big Big Woods, by Laura Ingalls Wilder, Harper & Bros, 1940, VG $35.00

Little Princess, by Frances Hidgson Burnett, Charles Scriber's Sons, 1905, dated 1905, G $125.00

Little Toot, by Hardie Gramatky, Weekly Reader Book Club 1960s ed, c 1939, VG...$12.00

Main Street in Animal Town, Bonnie Book, #4827, 1958, hard-
cover, VG $8.50
Mary Poppins Opens the Door, by PL Travers, Reynal & Hitch-
cock, 1943, hardback, w/dust jacket, EX $32.00
Monkey Shines, by Elinor Andrews, Platt & Munk, 1940,
unstated 1st ed, hardback, VG+ $32.00
Mork & Mindy Story, by Peggy Herz, 1979, paperback, VG .$8.00
My Little Book of Animals, Tiny Book, John Martin's House,
1948, hardcover, VG...$10.00
My Little Book of Nursery Rhymes, A Little Book, John Martin's
House, 1948, hardcover, VG...$10.00
My Little Book of Prayers, A Little Book, John Martin's House,
1948, VG $10.00
My Picture Book, Platt & Munk, 1941, VG+ $42.00
Nutshell Library, by Maurice Sendak, Harper & Row, 1962,
hardback, EX+..$18.00
Old MacDonald Had a Farm, Golden Tiny Tale, 1960, VG .$8.00
On the Farm, A Little Book, John Martin's House, 1948, VG ...$10.00
Pandora, Pied Piper Books, dated 1946, 1st ed, EX............$25.00
Pepper & Salt or Seasoning for Young Folk, by Howard Pyle,
Harper Brothers, 1913, hardback, w/dust jacket, EX......$30.00
Pied Piper of Hamelin, adapted by Sara & Stephen Corrin, 1988,
hardback, w/dust jacket, EX $12.00
Popeye — The Gold Mine Thieves, King Features, c 1935, hard-
back, G $75.00
Rebecca of Sunnybrook Farm, by Kate D Wiggin, Random
House, hardback, w/dust jacket, EX+ $15.00
Rin Tin Tin & the Hidden Treasure, by Charles Spain Verral,
Simon & Schuster Big Golden Book, 1958, EX $12.00
Rip Van Winkle & the Legend of Sleepy Hollow, by Wasington Irving,
Sleepy Hollow Restorations, 1974, 1st printing, EX+..............$12.00
Robin Hood, by Edith Heal, Rand McNally, 1935, hardback, w/
dust jacket, VG+ $32.00
Search for Santa Claus, by Elsa Ruth Nast, Western Printing,
1958, hardback, VG+...$10.00
Sesame Street Pet Show, 1980, hardback, EX......................$8.00
Sleeping Beauty & Other Stories, The Little Color Classics, #96,
1942, hardback, VG $12.00
Snow Queen, by Hans Christian Andersen, Harper & Row,
1985, hardback, EX+ $15.00
Someone's in the Kitchen with Dennis, by Hank Ketcham,
Franklin Watts, 1978, 2nd printing, G+............................$6.00
Storyland, A Sturdi Bilt Book, 1947 reprint, hardback, VG...$8.00
Superman, Random House, 1942, hardback, EX $450.00
Tanglewood Tales, by Nathaniel Hawthorne, Rand McNally,
1913, hardback, VG+...$22.00
Tinderbox, by Hans Christian Andersen, Maxton, 1948, hard-
back, G+...$14.00
Tim McCoy Speedwings, Engel van Wiseman, 1935, VG+..$45.00

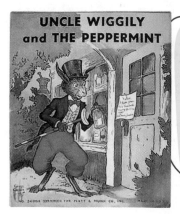

Toby's Adventure, A Little Book, John Martin's House, 1948,
hardback, VG $10.00
Toby Tyler, by James Otis, Saalfield, 1938, hardback, VG.$10.00
Tom Thumb, The Little Color Classics, #893, 1942, VG..$12.00
Tommy's Camping Adventure, Gold Tiny Tale, 1962, EX..$12.00
Tortoise & the Hare, Top Top Tales, #2455, 1963, hardback,
VG+...$10.00
Treasure Book of Favorite Nursery Tales, Treasure Book #856,
1953, hardback, EX $15.00
Tuttle, by Nancy Marohn, John C Winston Co, 1949, hardback,
w/dust jacket, EX..$28.00
Water Babies, by Charles Kingsley, Frederick A Stokes of NY,
1891, hardback, VG $20.00
Wind & the Willows, by Kenneth Graham, Lemon Tree Press,
1982, hardback, w/dust jacket, EX $10.00
Winkle Twinkle Pup, The Little Color Classics, #848, 1941, EX..$15.00
Winnie the Pooh a Tight Squeeze, A Big Golden Book, 1965,
hardback, VG $12.00
Yoo Hoo The Little Elephant, A Little Book, John Martin's
House, 1948, VG+ $10.00

• Breyer • • • • • • • • • • • • • • • • • • •

Breyer collecting seems to be growing in popularity, and though horses dominate the market, the company also made dogs, cats,
farm animals, wildlife figures, dolls, tack, and even accessories such as barns. They've been in continuous production since the 1950s,
all strikingly beautiful and lifelike in both modeling and color. Earlier models were glossy, but since 1968 a matt finish has been used,
though glossy and semiglossy colors are now being reintroduced in special runs. (A special run of Family Arabians was done in the
glossy finish in 1988.)

One of the hardest things for any model collector is to determine the value of his or her collection. The values listed are for models with no significant damage, but may have slight factory overspray or blurred markings (about a 3 on the 4-to-1 scale). A model that has been altered in any way is considered a customized model and has an altogether different set of values than one in the original finish. The models listed herein are completely original. Recently, internet auctions have depressed prices to the point that it's now a buyer's market. For more information, we recommend *Breyer Animal Collector's Guide* by Felicia Browell, Kelly Korber-Weimer, and Kelly Kesicki.

CLASSIC SCALE

American Quarter Horse Foal (#663), Springtime Frolic Gift Set, palomino, wht mane/tail, broken stripe, stockings, 2005..**$8.00**

American Quarter Horse Stallion (#665), Son O' Leo Family, matt chestnut w/shaded lighter points, Wal-Mart, 2007-present...**$9.00**

Andalusian Foal (#3060FO), Spanish Norman Family, matt med gray w/blk points, Toys R Us, 1994................................**$10.00**

Andalusian Mare (#3060MA), Classic Andalusian Family, matt dapple gray w/darker points, socks, 1979-93....................**$10.00**

Andalusian Stallion (#3060ST), Classic Andalusian Family, matt dapple gray, stockings, Sears Wish Book, 1984......**$15.00**

Arabian Foal (#3055FO), matt palomino, bald face, socks/stockings, 1973-82 ....**$13.00**

Arabian Mare (#3055A), Classic Arabian Family, matt alabaster, shaded mane, tail, muzzle, etc, Sears Wish Book, 1984-85. **$17.00**

Arabian Stallion (#3055ST), Classic Arabian Family, sorrel w/flaxen mane & tail, socks, 1971-91................................**$10.00**

Black Beauty (#3040BB), Lath (King of the Wind Set), bay w/blk points, 1990-93 ....**$12.00**

Black Stallion (#3030BS), Shetan (The Black Stallion Returns Set), semigloss blk, natural hooves, 1983-93....................**$11.00**

Bucking Bronco (#190), gray w/darker mane & tail, stockings, 1961-67..**$56.00**

Charging Mesteno (#4812ME), Grulla Charging Mustang & Dun Foal, matt grulla w/darker mane & tail, Wal-Mart, 2003 ..**$10.00**

Cutting Horse (#491), Smart Little Lena, chestnut w/darker mane & tail, hind socks, Limited Ed, 2004 ....**$15.00**

Fighting Mesteno (#4811ME), Azul (Azul & Fausto), matt bl roan w/blk points, gray shading, Wal-Mart, 2001..........**$11.00**

Fighting Sombra (#4811SO), The Challengers Mesteno & Sombra, matt grulla w/blk points, some striping on legs, 1994-97 .... **$14.00**

Ginger (#3040GI), Black Beauty Family, chestnut w/darker mane, tail & hooves, stripe & snip, 1980-93..................**$10.00**

Hobo (#625), The Pony Express, matt buckskin w/blk points, shading, 2001 ....**$24.00**

Hollywood Dun It (#478), Gunner, matt chestnut pinto, apron face, high stockings, 2002 ....**$40.00**

Jet Run (#3035JR), Palomino Warmblood, wht mane & tail, gray-shaded muzzle, hind socks, gray/natural hooves, 1998 ....**$10.00**

Johar (#3030JO), The Black Stallion Returns Set, alabaster w/gray mane, tail & hooves, 1983-93 ....**$11.00**

Keen (#3035KE), Liver Chestnut Appaloosa Sporthorse, darker points, spots in blanket, blaze, socks, 1998....................**$11.00**

Kelso (#601), Black Jet, blk pinto w/wht mane & tail, wht left foreleg, hind stocking, 2 socks, 1995-96 ....**$12.00**

Lipizzan Stallion (#620), alabaster, 1980 ....**$18.00**

Man O' War (#602), Pepe, lt chestnut w/darker mane & tail, stockings, 1991-92..**$13.00**

Merrylegs (#3040ML), Lady Jane Gray (A Pony for Keeps), alabaster w/wht mane & tail, shading, gray hooves, 1990-91.......**$12.00**

Mesteño (#480), Spirit, Kiger Mustang Family, buckskin w/blk points, Wal-Mart, 2002-present......................................**$10.00**

Mesteño's Mother (#4810MO), Paloma (Paloma & Naldo), dapple gray w/wht mane & tail, natural hooves, Wal-Mart, 2002 ....**$10.00**

Morgan Foal (#634), any variation, 2007-present, ea..........**$6.00**

Morgan Mare (#633), Marigold (Breyer Fun Days — Spring), matt shaded chestnut w/lighter mane & tail, 3 socks, 2007......**$11.00**

Morgan Stallion (#632), any variation, 2007-present **$11.00**

Mustang Foal (#065FO), Mustang Family, chestnut pinto, socks, gray hooves, Sears Wish Book, 1985..............................**$10.00**

Mustang Mare (#3065MA), Breyer Mustang Family, bay w/blk points, right hind sock, JC Penney, 1992......................**$15.00**

Mustang Stallion (#3065ST), Three-Piece Family Gift Set, grulla pinto w/darker points on head, hind socks, 1998-99......**$11.00**

Polo Pony, dappled rose gray w/slightly darker points, socks/stockings, 1998-99..**$18.00**

Quarter Horse Stallion, Appaloosa Family, blk appaloosa w/splash spots on rear blanket, Montgomery Ward, 1984..**$18.00**

Rearing Stallion (#180), Little Chaparral (Breyer Show Special), buckskin pinto w/blk & wht mane & tail, pk hooves, 1993..**$22.00**

Rojo (#4812RO), Mateo (Alano & Mateo), smoky blk w/blk points, 1 front/1 back wht sock, Wal-Mart, 2002.............**$9.00**

Breyer, Classic Scale

American Quarter Horse Mare (#682), Bay Mare, matt shaded metallic bay, three socks, natural hooves on feet with white, 2005 – present, $10.00. (Photo courtesy Felicia Browell, Kelly Korber-Weimer, and Kelly Kesicki)

Breyer, Classic Scale
• • • • • • • • • • •
Keen (#686), Warmblood, black and white pinto, semigloss black pinto, star, and stripe, white legs, natural hooves, 2007 – present, **$9.00.** (Photo courtesy Felicia Browell, Kelly Korber-Weimer, and Kelly Kesicki)

Ruffian (#606), dk bay w/blk points, star, left hind sock, 1977-90 .... $14.00

Sagr (#3030SA), The Black Stallion Returns Set, sorrel w/flaxen mane & tail, socks, gray hooves, 1983-93 .... $14.00

Shire A (#627A, turned head), dapple gray, shaded knees, high stockings, 2002-present $10.00

Shire B (#627B, facing forward), Yankee Doodle Dandy, Breyer-Fest Contest Prize, 30 issued, matt bay pinto, bl ribbons, prize for 2007 Stars & Stripes Float Contest $320.00

Silky Sullivan (#603), Spice, bay appaloosa, natural hooves, 1995-96 .... $12.00

Swaps (#604), Prince, matt lt gray w/gray points, socks/stockings, natural hooves, 1993-94 .... $12.00

Terrang (#605), Ambrosia, palomino w/wht mane & tail, blaze, socks/stockings, gray-shaded muzzle knees & hocks, 1997 . $12.00

Wahoo King (#466), Hot Shot — World Barrel Racing Champion, matt buckskin w/blk points, natural hooves, 2007-present $14.00

PADDOCK PALS SCALE

American Saddlebred (#9030), Breyer Parade of Breeds, matt brn pinto, narrow blaze, wht legs, pk hooves, JC Penney, 1988 .... $10.00

American Saddlebred (#9030), Pinto, semigloss bay w/stenciled markings, bicolored mane, wht tail, natural hooves, 2006 .... $6.00

Arabian Stallion (#9001), most variations, 1984-2006, $6 to $10.00

Clydesdale (#9025), Charger, semigloss dapple gray, Hobby Center Toys, 1989 .... $16.00

Clydesdale (#9025), variations other than Charger from Hobby Center Toys (1989), 1984-2006, $6 to............................ $10.00

Morgan Stallion (#9005), Breyer Parade of Breeds, matt dk-shaded bay w/blk points, gray or blk hooves, JC Penney, 1988 .... $9.00

Quarter Horse Stallion (#9015), many variations, 1984-2006, $6 to $8.00

Thoroughbred Stallion (#9010), many variations, 1984-2006, $6 to $10.00

Unicorn (#9020), Montgomery Ward issue, 1985 .... $30.00

Unicorn (#9020), variations other than Montgomery Ward issue (1985), 1984-2006 .... $6.00

STABLEMATE SCALE

American Saddlebred (#5608), Cottontail Express, matt palomino, hind stocking, gray hooves, 2005 .... $6.00

Andalusian (#5606), any variation except Movie Gift (unpnt glow-in-the-dark keychain), 1998-2006, ea $3 to $14.00

Andalusian (Rearing), (#5626), any variation except matt bl roan w/allover wht stars, 2006-present, ea $3 to $4.00

Andalusian (Rearing), (#5626), matt bl roan w/allover wht stars, BreyerFest Special, 2007 .... $14.00

Appaloosa (#5601), any variation, 1998-present, ea $4 to $18.00

Arabian (#5622), any variation except porcelain unicorns, 2006-present, ea $3 to $4.00

Arabian (#5622), Isabel & Chloe, porcelain, metallic silvery wht w/gold horns, grassy base, BreyerFest Special, 2005 ...... $24.00

Arabian Mare (#5011), Butterscotch, matt roan appaloosa, gray-shaded face, mane & tail, 1996 .... $20.00

Arabian Mare (#5011), matt lt red roan w/red points, gray muzzle & ears, wht sock/stockings, 1998 .... $10.00

Arabian Rearing (#5603), any variation except porcelain, 1998-2006, ea $3 to $14.00

Arabian Stallion (#5010), matt alabaster w/lt gray mane & tail, lt gray hooves, 1975-81 .... $18.00

Arabian Stallion (#5010), matt dapple gray w/darker mane & tail, stockings, 1975-76 .... $20.00

Belgian (#5618), any variation except keychain, 2006-07, ea $3 to $4.00

Cantering Foal (#5614), any variation, 2000-present, ea $2 to .. $3.00

Cantering Stock Horse (#5617), Play Mate Palomino, 2007-present $4.00

Cantering Warmblood (#5629), any variation, 2006-present, ea $3 to $4.00

Citation, any variation, 1975-98, ea $6 to $10.00

Clydesdale (#5604), any variation, 1998-2005, ea $4 to ... $14.00

Draft Horse (#5055), matt dapple gray w/darker gray & blk points, socks, gray hooves, 1989-94 .... $10.00

Draft Horse (#5055), matt red sorel w/flaxen mane & tail, right hind sock, Riegseckers, 1985 .... $40.00

Highland Pony (#5628), any American variation, 2006, ea $3 to $4.00

Lying Foal (#5630), any variation except porcelain, 2006-07, ea $2 to $3.00

Morgan Mare (#5038), any variation, 1976-2005, ea $6 to .. $14.00

Morgan Stallion (#5035), matt blk, left hind sock, 1988 .. $12.00

Morgan Stallion (#5035), matt dapple gray w/darker mane & tail, various socks, 1975 .... $24.00

Mustang (#5625), any variation except for BreyerFest or Halloween Special, 2006-07, ea $3 to $4.00

Mustang (#5625), Stripes, matt red roan, BreyerFest Special, 2007 .... $14.00

Native Dancer (#5023), matt gray w/blk points, 1976-94 . $10.00

Paso Fino (#5610), Horses of the World, matt golden palomino w/wht mane & tail, hind socks, w/accessories, TJ Maxx, 2004 .... $8.00

Peruvian Paso (#5619), any variation, 2006-present, ea $3 to ... $4.00

Quarter Horse Mare (#5048), chestnut w/darker mane & tail, stockings, blk hooves, 1976 .... $20.00

Breyer, Stablemate Scale

• • • • • • • • • • • • • • • • • • • •

Morgan Prancing, liver chestnut, 1999, $3.00 to $4.00; red bay with black points and star, J.A.H. Special Edition Stablemates Gift Set, 1998, $5.00 to $9.00. (Photo courtesy Felicia Browell)

Breyer, Stablemate Scale

• • • • • • • • • • • • • • •

Thoroughbred Mare, dark liver chestnut with lighter points, reddish mane and tail, faint low socks, Sears Wishbook, 1998, $3.00 to $8.00. (Photo courtesy Felicia Browell)

Quarter Horse Stallion (#5045), matt buckskin w/blk points, no dorsal stripe, 1976-87 ....$12.00

Quarter Horse Stallion (#5045), matt/semigloss chestnut w/ darker mane & tail, socks/stockings, gray hooves, 1976.$20.00

Saddlebred (#5002), matt blk, gray hooves, 1989-90 ....$12.00

Scrambling Foal (#5613), any variation, 2000-present, $2 to.. $3.00

Scratching Foal (#5616), any variation, 2000-present, ea $3 to . $4.00

Seabiscuit (#5024), matt/semigloss bay w/blk points, some w/ stockings, 1976-90..$14.00

Shetland Pony (#5605), any variation, 1998-2005, ea $3 to.....$14.00

Silky Sullivan (#5022), Saddle Club Stablemates Collection, matt mahogany bay w/blk points, blaze, hind socks, 1996-97..$10.00

Standing Foal (#5631), any variation, 2006-07, ea..............$2.00

Standing Stock Horse (#5621), All American Tribute — Colorado Ranger, matt chestnut appaloosa, BreyerFest Special, 2007 ....$12.00

Standing Stock Horse (#5621), any variation except 2007 BreyerFest Special, 2006-07, ea $3 to $4.00

Swaps (#5021), any variation, 1976-96, ea $6 to...............$13.00

Tennessee Walking Horse (#5624), All American Tribute — Tennessee Walker, matt blk pinto, BreyerFest Special, 2007...$12.00

Thoroughbread Mare (#5026), any variation, 1975-2004, ea $8 to..$14.00

Thoroughbred (#5602), any variation except porcelain, 1998-2006, ea $4 to $12.00

Thoroughbred Lying Foal (#5700LF), any variation except keychains, 1975-2005, ea $5 to $8.00

Thoroughbred Lying Foal (#5700LF), any variation of keychain, 1994-98, ea $14 to...$20.00

Thoroughbred Standing Foal (#5700SF), any variation except keychains, 1975-2005, ea $3 to.......................................$10.00

Thoroughbred Standing Foal (#5700SF), keychains, any variation, 1994-98, ea $21 to $24.00

Trotting Foal (#5615), any variation, 2000-present, ea $2 to.....$3.00

Warmblood (#5607), any variation except porcelain, 1998-present, ea $4 to..$14.00

Warmblood Jumper (#5620), any variation, 2006, ea $3 to..$4.00

TRADITIONAL SCALE

Action Stock Horse Foal (#235), appaloosa, matt gray blanket w/ spatter spots, blk points, blk hooves, 1984-88 ....$14.00

Action Stock Horse Foal (#235), bay pinto, matt w/blk points, socks, gray hooves, 1984-88 ....$13.00

Adios (#50), Adios Famous Standard Bred, matt bay, slightly shaded, blk points, hind socks, chalky version, 1969-80 .$36.00

Adios (#50), Clayton Quarter Horse, matt dapple palomino, wht mane & tail, dk knees & hocks, stockings, 1995-96 ......$24.00

Adios (#50), Standing Quarter Horse Stallion, matt apricot dun w/dk reddish mane, tail & leg joints, socks, 1988-89 .....$31.00

Amber (#488), Black Tie Affair, matt blk blanket appaloosa foal, lacy blanket, high hind stockings, 2004..........................$16.00

American Saddlebred Stallion (#571), Family Saddlebred Trio, shaded gray, wht hind stockings, JC Penney, 2005.........$31.00

Andalusian Stallion (#584), blk, very dk matt bay, shaded, subtle dappling, no markings, 2004-06....................................$28.00

Appaloosa Performance Horse (#99), Foundation, matt bay roan blanket, dappled, right hind sock, 2001-02 ....$26.00

Appaloosa Performance Horse (#99), matt chestnut roan w/dk mane & tail, blanket, spotted, bald face, stockings, 1974-80 ....$26.00

Balking Mule (#207), matt or semigloss liver chestnut/seal brn, may have darker legs, brn or red bridle, 1968-71 ....$81.00

Balking Mule (#207), Molly, glossy gray appaloosa, gray shaded body, dk gray points, blk halter, Collector's Ed, 1999.....$30.00

Belgian (#92), Blackhome Grandeur Lyn, matt shaded lt gray, some speckles, 2003-04 ....$26.00

Belgian (#92), Toby the Vaulting Horse, matt brn or bay pinto, half-&-half tail, 1997 ....$40.00

Big Ben (#483), Stormchaser, matt dapple gray, blk points, 3 socks, star & snip, 2001..$53.00

Black Beauty (#89), Donovan Running Appaloosa Stallion, matt gray, blanket w/chestnut spots, blk points/3 socks, 1995-97 ..$23.00

Black Beauty (#89), matt blk, diamond-shaped star, various stockings, 1979-88..$21.00

Black Stallion (#401), Hyksos the Egyptian Arabian, semigloss Ageless Bronze, dk points, Commemorative Ed, 1991 ...$38.00

Bolya (#490), American Warmblood, matt palomino w/wht mane & tail, odd broad blaze, socks & stockings, 1998-99 ....$24.00

Brighty (#375), Mischief the Holiday Donkey, matt buckskin, gray shaded points, wht muzzle, 2002 ....$27.00

Brown Sunshine (#484), Saddle Mule, matt dk seal bay, blk points, lighter muzzle, no wht, 1998-2000.....................$29.00

Buckshot (#415), Cody, matt dk bay pinto, blk points, 1995...$29.00

Buckshot (#415), Rowdy Yates, matt grulla, darker points & face, 2004-05..$23.00

Cantering Welsh Pony (#104), matt chestnut w/flaxen mane & tail, bald face, stocking, red mane ribbons, 1971-76 ......$36.00

Cantering Welsh Pony (#104), Plain Pixie, matt red roan, cream base color w/red speckles & chestnut shading, 1992-93.$26.00

Cigar (#476), Seabiscuit, matt bay, shaded body, blk points, gray hooves, QVC, 2001..$47.00

Cleveland Bay (#703), Jazz Fusion, glossy dk bay pinto, Just About Horses, 2006.. $248.00

Clydesdale Foal (#84), Quincy, matt chestnut pinto w/ darker mane & tail, socks, rear stockings connect to belly, 1997-98..$19.00

Clydesdale Mare (#83), matt lt bay w/blk mane & tail, shaded face & knees, broad blaze, stockings, gray hooves, 1990-91.......$32.00

Clydesdale Stallion (#80), glossy dapple gray w/darker mane & tail, bald face, stockings, gold hobs, 1962-65..................$94.00

Cody (#471), Cody, matt bay, shaded body, blk points, 1999-2000..$25.00

Donkey (#81), matt gray w/dk mane & tail, pale muzzle, stockings, bay or solid face variations, 1958-74, ea.................$45.00

El Pastor (#61), Desperado, semigloss blk pinto w/patches of wht, broken blaze, high wht stockings, Show Special, 1997 ..$36.00

Family Arabian Foal (#9), Shah, matt bay w/blk mane & tail, narrow blaze, stockings, blk hooves, 1967-74.................$10.00

Family Arabian Mare (#8), Hope, glossy palomino w/wht mane & tail, bald face, stockings, gray hooves, 1961-66..........$16.00

Family Arbian Stallion (#7), Fleck, glossy gray appaloosa w/ splash spots, bald face, wht barrel, blk points, 1963-67..$15.00

Fighting Stallion (#31), Chaparral, matt buckskin pinto w/blk front half of mane, tail & front knees, Limited Ed, 1992 ....$35.00

Fighting Stallion (#31), King, glossy gray appaloosa w/pk & gray shaded muzzle, gray points & hooves, 1961-67...............$92.00

Five Gaiter (#52), Commander, matt sorrel, brn mane/tail, bald face, stockings, red/wht braids, color variation, 1963-86 ...$31.00

Five Gaiter (#52), Commander, matt sorrel, charcoal brn mane & tail, bald face, red & wht braids, color variations, 1963-86 .... $31.00

Foundation Stallion (#64), Azteca, matt dapple gray w/darker mane, tail & points, various socks, hooves, etc, 1980-87..............$24.00

Foundation Stallion (#64), Fugir Cacador Lusitano Stallion, buckskin, shaded muzzle, blk points/stripe, Limited Ed, 1993 ....$27.00

Friesian (#485), Dashing Dan, matt palomino/sorrel w/flaxen mane & tail, lt gray hooves, Sears Wish Book, 1998......$42.00

Fury Prancer (#P45), Lucky Ranger, glossy blk pinto w/rider & accessories, 1956-57 (dates uncertain) $160.00

Galiceno (#100), Freckle Doll, matt bay pinto w/wht patch on left side, blk blaze & points, shaded muzzle, 1994-95.....$22.00

Gem Twist (#495), Commander Riker, matt chestnut w/ slightly darker mane & tail, shaded muzzle, left hind sock, 2004-05..$27.00

Grazing Foal (#151), matt palomino w/wht mane & tail, bald face, stockings, gray hooves, 1964-81 ....$16.00

Grazing Mare (#141), matt bay, bald/blaze face, blk points, front socks, rear stockings, 1961-80...$25.00

Hackney (#496), Arisocrat Champion Hackney, matt bay, blk points, 4 socks, 1995-96...$25.00

Haflinger (#156), Mountain Pony, matt sorrel, gray knees & hocks, 1991-92 ....$22.00

Halla (#63), Halla Famous Jumper, matt bay, sm star, blk points, 1977-85...$24.00

Hanoverian (#58), Gifted, matt bay, w/blaze, blk points, stockings, Limited Ed, 1994..$40.00

Huckleberry Bey (#472), Alaric the Unicorn Stallion, glossy iridescent wht w/bl & lavender shadings, QVC, 2002.......$66.00

Ideal American Quarter Horse (#497), King, matt bay w/ diamond-shaped star, blk points, gray hooves, QVC, 2002 ....$38.00

Breyer, Traditional Scale

Proud Arabian Foal, SS Morning Star, bay pinto with darker points, high white stockings, star, natural hooves, 1997 – 1998, $11.00 to $18.00; Arabian Foal, black with white socks, stockings, and star/stripe, natural hooves, 1999, $10.00 to $13.00. (Photo courtesy Felicia Browell)

Indian Pony (#175), Cheyenne American Mustang, matt roan w/ chestnut shaded head, blk points, left front sock, 1995-96. $38.00

Indian Pony (#175), Ichilay, matt lt gray w/darker points, red speckle roan, various Native American symbols, 1993 ..$34.00

John A Henry (#445), Quiet Foxhunters Set, matt bay w/blk points, low socks, natural hooves, JC Penney, 1992 ....$27.00

Jumping Horse (#300), matt seal brn w/diamond-shaped star, blk points, sepia wall w/gr base, Sears Wish Book, 1982-83.$72.00

Justin Morgan (#65), Tri-Mi Boot Scootin' Boogie, matt blk, broad blaze w/spots, high stockings, natural hooves, 1996-97...$26.00

Khemosabi (#460), Arabian Stallion, matt rose gray, dappling, darker points, socks, striped hooves, 1999-2000.............$24.00

Lady Phase (#40), Paint Mare Grullo, matt gray pinto w/shaded body, stripe, broad blaze, blk points, stockings, 2002 .....$24.00

Lady Phase (#40), Silky Keno, blk pinto w/wht apron face, wht front stockings, all wht hind legs, gray hooves, 2001 .....$28.00

Lady Roxanna (#425), Sahara, matt shaded gray, darker points snipe, right front sock, 'My Favorite Horse' card, 2004-06 ....$20.00

Le Fire (#581), Baby's First Steps Mare & Foal Set, matt palomino w/lighter mane & tail, blaze, socks, QVC, 2002 ...$25.00

Legionario (#68), Medieval Knight, matt gray roan, shaded body, grayish red points, 1993-94 ....$28.00

Llianarth True Briton (#494), Danaway Tango, matt sorrel pinto, wide blaze over chin, tail fades to wht, 2004-06.............$26.00

Lonesome Glory (#572), Afleet Alex, matt red bay, stripe, blk points, low socks on right, Racing Legends Series, 2006.$36.00

Lonesome Glory (#572), Mardi Gras, matt bay semi-leopard appaloosa, dorsal stripe, BreyerFest, 2000.......................$79.00

Lying Down Foal (#245), matt buckskin w/blk mane & tail, shaded muzzle & legs, 1969-73.......................................$23.00

Man O' War (#47), My Prince Thoroughbred, matt med brn chestnut, darker mane/tail, dk brn halter/gold hardware, 1996-97...$25.00

Marabella (#487), Nokomis, glossy bay pinto, shading, blk tail, wht legs, natural hooves, Mid-States Distributing, 2001 ..$39.00

Midnight Sun (#60), Memphis Storm, glossy charcoal w/ wht mane & tail, stockings, pk hooves, red on yel braids, 1995-96 ....$27.00

Midnight Tango (#467), matt blk pinto w/blk & wht mane & tail, right front sock, hind stockings, 2000-01 ....$18.00

Missouri Fox Trotter (#486), Snowflake, matt lt shaded dapple gray w/darker quarters & front legs, wht mane & tail, 1998..$46.00

Misty (#20), matt palomino pinto, dbl eye circles & 'old' Misty pinto pattern, 1972..$86.00

Misty's Twilight (#470), Sundance & Skipper Set, matt bay pinto, apron face, darker points, 3 socks, JC Penney, 1997...........$25.00

Morgan (#48), matt bay, bald face, blk points, varied socks & stockings, 1965-71...$51.00

Morganglanz (#59), Horse Salute Gift Set, matt bay w/blaze, blk points, socks, pk hooves, JC Penney, 1994 ....$26.00

Mustang (#87), American Mustang, matt sorrel w/flaxen mane & tail, darker muzzle, stockings, gray hooves, 1987-89 ..$31.00

Mustang (#87), Diablo, charcoal w/wht mane & tail, bald face, stockings, 1970 ....$110.00

Mustang (#87), Gray Hawk, matt bl roan pinto, Native American markings, QVC, 2002...$42.00

Nokota Horse (#1279), matt gray dun, wht/dk gray shading, speckled, 3 gray hooves/1 natural, Benefit Limited Ed, 2007.......$26.00

Nursing Foal (#3155FO), Pride & Joy, matt lt chestnut, socks, JC Penney, 1996 ....$14.00

Old Timer (#200), matt red roan w/darker mane & tail, dk hooves, bl hat & red band, 1991-93 ....$24.00

Pacer (#46), matt sorrel, flaxen mane & tail, socks, complete w/ accessories & Brenda in racing silks, JC Penney, 1982-83..$74.00

Peruvian Paso Stallion (#576), Magnifico, BreyerFest Special, 2006..$102.00

Phantom Wings (#18), Rough Diamond, matt dk brn pinto w/wht mane & tail, star & narrow stripe, high stockings, 1991-93...$10.00

Phar Lap (#90), Hobo, matt buckskin, blk points, shaded muzzle, natural hooves, 1991-92...$27.00

Pluto (#475), Pluto the Lipizzaner, matt lt gray w/shaded mane, tail, muzzle, knees & hooves, 1991-95 ....$25.00

Pony of the Americas (#155), Pantomine, matt blk appaloosa, hind blanket, star & stripe, socks, 1993-94 ....$20.00

Proud Arabian Foal (#218), matt mahogany bay w/blk & dk gray points & hooves, various socks, 1973-80.......................$16.00

Proud Arabian Mare (#215), matt red sorrel w/lighter flaxen mane, tail & stockings, gray hooves, 1991-92 ....$24.00

Proud Arabian Mare (#215), Sheba, glossy bay w/blk mane & tail, blaze, stockings, old mold, 1956-60 ....$118.00

Proud Arabian Stallion (#215), flocked bay, blk points, blaze, 3 socks, Montgomery Ward, 1984......................................$40.00

Proud Arabian Stallion (#215), matt dapple rose gray, gray muzzle, knees, hocks & hooves, 1989-90 ....$29.00

Quarter Horse Gelding (#97), Tow Bits, matt buckskin, blk points, w/dk brn halter, 1961-80......................................$26.00

Quarter Horse Yearling (#101), Calypso, matt dun w/darker mane & tail, shaded knees, hocks & ankles, stocking, 1995-96...$22.00

Quarter Horse Yearling (#101), matt palomino w/lighter mane & tail, crooked blaze, stockings, gray hooves, 1970-80.......$22.00

Racehorse (#36), Phantom, matt dapple gray, bald face, stockings, blk halter, Just About Horses, 1997......................$31.00

Rejoice (#479), Naranda, matt red bay w/blk points, no wht, Limited Ed, 2002 ....$30.00

Roemer (#465), Flim Flam, matt red bay w/blk points, odd star, snip, 3 socks w/striped hooves, other plain, 2003-04......$30.00

Roy the Belgian (#455), Belgian Brabant, matt gray dun, base gray color w/chestnut shading, darker points, 1991-93 ..$26.00

Rugged Lark (#450), matt red chestnut w/darker mane & tail, hind stocking, gray hooves, JC Penney, 1990.................$26.00

Running Foal (#130), matt buckskin, bald face, blk points, JC Penney, 1983 .... $240.00

Running Foal (#130), matt smoke, bald face, wht points, 1963-70..$26.00

Running Mare (#120), Buckskin Mare, matt alabaster w/lt gray mane, tail & hooves, 1961-72..............................$33.00

Running Mare (#120), Running Horse Family Set, matt bay w/ blk points, Sears Wish Book, 1984 ....$38.00

Running Stallion (#210), matt blk appaloosa, bald face, spotted hind blanket, 1968-81...$25.00

Running Stallion (#210), Xena's Argo, matt palomino w/wht mane & tail, Hollywood Heroe Series, 1999.................$30.00

Saddlebred Weanling (#62), matt palomino/lt chestnut pinto w/wht mane, tail & legs, narrow blaze, Commemorative Ed, 1990 ....$44.00

San Domingo (#67), Comanche Pony, matt palomino w/wht mane & tail, gray shaded muzzle, stockings, 1990-92.....$24.00

San Domingo (#67), Oxydol Rodeo Appaloosa, matt alabaster mottled gray muzzle, pk/natural hooves, 1995-96...........$24.00

Scratching Foal (#168), matt of semigloss red roan w/overdappled roaning & chestnut points, 1970-73 ....$45.00

Sea Star (#16), Chincoteague Foal, matt buckskin w/gray-brn points, star, stripes on forelegs, 1992-93 ....$11.00

Secretariat (#435), Race Horse Set, glossy chestnut, narrow stripe, 3 socks, Sears Wish Book, 1990 ....$38.00

Sham (#410), Best Choice Arabian, matt mahogany bay w/blk points, shaded muzzle, blaze, sock/3 stockings, 1997-98.$23.00

Sham (#410), Prancing Arabian Stallion, matt fleabitten gray, lt points, socks/stockings, pk/natural hooves, 1988-89 ......$23.00

Sherman Morgan (#430), Justin Morgan, glossy shaded bay w/blk points, gray hooves, QVC, 2002 ....$42.00

Shetland Pony (#23), glossy alabaster w/gray mane, tail & hooves, 1960-72 ....$30.00

Shetland Pony (#23), matt sorrel w/flaxen mane & tail, blaze, 3 stockings, 1992-94...$20.00

Silver (#574), Phoenix Rising, matt buckskin pinto w/dk brn points, w/wood base & plaque, QVC, 2002.....................$82.00

Silver (#574), Valentine, glossy mahogany bay w/blk points (no wht), BreyerFest Special, 2001..$70.00

Smart Chic Olena (#595), Tommie Turvey's Joker, semigloss blk pinto w/blk & wht mane & tail, BreyerFest Celebration, 2006.........$54.00

Smoky (#69), Durango, matt dk bronze, Commemorative Ed, 2000..$26.00

Spider Stud (#66), Hightower, matt chestnut, star, right hind sock, 2000-01..$26.00

Spirit (#577), Spirit, Stallion of the Cimarron, matt buckskin w/ blk mane, tail & eyebrows, shaded muzzle/legs, 2002.....$26.00

Stock Foal Horse (#228), Bay Quarter Horse Stock Foal, blk points, hind socks, 1985-87..$13.00

Stock Horse Foal (#228), Gray Quarter Horse Foal, matt shaded gray w/blk points, lighter face, hind socks, 1998 ....$13.00

Stock Horse Mare (#227), American Quarter Horse Mare, matt dapple gray w/blk or dk gray points, socks, 1999-2001 ...$23.00

Stock Horse Mare (#227), Appaloosa Stock Horse Mare (leg up), matt blk appaloosa, stripe or star, socks, 1983-86 ...$21.00

Stock Horse Stallion (#226), Bay Quarter Horse Stock Stallion, matt bay w/blk points, 1981-88..$25.00

Stock Horse Stallion (#226), Shane American Ranch Horse, matt blk roan w/blk points, hind socks, 'R' brand, 1995-96 ....$22.00

Stormy (#19), Buckaroo & Skeeter, matt bay pinto, crescent star, 3 socks, Toys R Us, 1995 ....$11.00

Strapless (#583), Appaloosa Sport Horse, matt blk blanket appaloosa w/lacy blanket, star, high front stockings, 2004-06...$25.00

Stud Spider (#66), Overo Paint, matt chestnut pinto w/darker mane & tail, bald face, stockings, 1979-81 ....$30.00

Sunny Action Foal (#235), matt lt dun, dorsal stripe, lt gray mane & tail, dk gray & brn cannons & ankles, 1994-95 ....$13.00

Susecion (#580), Hall of Fame Arabian Mare, matt gray, shaded face, natural hooves, 2002-05 ....$31.00

Thoroughbred Mare (#3155MA), Pride & Joy, matt lt chestnut, socks, JC Penney, 1996..$24.00

Trakehner (#54), matt bay w/blk points, brand on left thigh, 1979-84 ....$29.00

Western Horse, glossy palomino, stockings, gray hooves, complete w/saddle, bridle, harness, etc, 1950-70....................$26.00

Western Pony, glossy chestnut pinto, chestnut tail w/wht tip, wht mane, bald face, stockings, w/saddle, 1956-67................$34.00

Western Prancing Horse (#110), Cheyenne, matt smoke w/wht mane & tail, bald face, gray hooves & saddle, 1961-76 .$38.00

Wixom (#573), Cedarfarm Wixom, matt blk, slightly dappled, bl tail bow, 2001-03 ....$30.00

Zippo Pine Bar (#466), Impress Me Shannon, matt chestnut appaloosa, extensive semi-leopard markings, Limited Ed, 2005 ....$30.00

OTHER ANIMALS

Alpine Goat (#1512), any variation, 1999-2004, ea $7 to ..$8.00

Australian Shepherd (#1515), matt bl merle w/wht spot on muzzle, wht feet & ruff, 2000-06......................................$6.00

Bear (#306), any variation, 1967-2005, ea $30 to $44.00

Bear Cub (#308), any variation except matt wht (from Bear Family Gift Set), 1967-2005, ea $11 to $28.00

Bear Cub (#308), Bear Family Gift Set, matt wht, reddish eyes, 1992-95..$40.00

Bighorn Ram (#78), matt brn & tan w/lighter head, lower legs & horns, 1997-2005 ....$28.00

Bighorn Ram (#78), matt tan w/wht rump, paler muzzle, ears & eyes, gray hooves, 1969-80...$48.00

Black Angus Bull (#365), blk, 1978-2004...........................$28.00

Black Labrador (#1507), any variation, 1999-2004, ea........$7.00

Boxer (#1), glossy tan, 1958-74..$34.00

Boxer (#1), semigloss woodgrain, wht face stripe w/blk muzzle, 1959-65..$388.00

Brahma Bull (#70), glossy gray, 1958-67 ....$28.00

Buffalo (#76), matt dk brown w/darker shaded head, nape & lower legs, overall darker than other brn models, 1997-99..........$28.00

Breyer, Other Animals
Benji, tan matt/semi-gloss with shading, 1978 – 1979, $30.00.
(Photo courtesy Felicia Browell)

Breyer, Other Animals
Border Collie (#1158), matt black and white, 2000 – 2006, $6.00. (Photo courtesy Felicia Browell, Kelly Korber-Weimer, and Kelly Kesicki)

Calf (#347), Holstein Calf, matt blk & wht pinto, 1972-73 ..$20.00

Charolais Bull (#360), matt alabaster, 1975-95 ....$24.00

Cougar (#822), any variation except BreyerFest Special, 2001-03, ea $8.00

Cougar (#822), Kohana, BreyerFest Special, 2002 ....$32.00

Cow (#341), Brown Swiss, matt cocoa, 1972-73 ....$46.00

Cow (#341), Holstein, matt blk & wht pinto pattern, 1972-73..$28.00

Cutting Calf (#492), any variation, 1997-2004, ea..............$6.00

Elephant (#91), battleship gray, 1958-60 ....$64.00

Elk (#77), any variation, 1968-2005, ea $24 to $30.00

English Fox Hound (#1519), any variation, 2001-05, ea.....$7.00

Great Dane (#1520), any variation, 2001-06, ea $7 to........$8.00

Irish Setter (#1526), any variation, 2004..............................$6.00

Jasper the Market Hog (#355), Hog, matt dk chestnut, Hog Breeders Association, 1980...$80.00

Jasper the Market Hog (#355), wht w/gray spots on back, 1974-2000..$13.00

Kitten (#335), Cleopatra or Leonardo Kitten, orange or gray tabby, 1994-95, ea $23.00

Kitten (#335), Siamese, 1966-71......................................$66.00

Lassie (#2), Jester, matt blk, wht & brn, BreyerFest Special, 2001 ....$46.00

Moose (#79), any variation, 1966-2005, ea $28 to $35.00

Mountain Goat (#312), any variation, 1973-89, ea $32 to...$40.00

Polled Hereford Bull (#74), matt red-brn & wht, 1968-2004 ....$29.00

Poodle (#67), matt silver gray w/red collar, 1968-73 ....$44.00

Pronghorn Antelope, matt brn & wht, 1971-76................$60.00

Pronghorn Antelope (#210), matt chestnut, 1997-2005...$29.00

Red Fox (#820), Fox Hunting Gift Set, glossy red chestnut w/ wht & blk, 2001-03...$6.00

Breyer,
Other Animals
• • • • • • • • • • • • • • •
Miniature Sicil-
ian Donkey (#1522),
traditional scale, matt
gray dun, dorsal stripe
and shoulder bars, pale
muzzle, 2001 – 2006,
$8.00. (Photo courtesy Felicia
Browell, Kelly Korber-Weimer, and Kelly Kesicki)

Breyer, Other Animals
• • • • • • • • • • • • • • •
Texas Longhorn Bull (#75),
Babe, matt wedgwood blue,
white legs, bald face, gray hooves, 1960 special
release for Paul Bunyan Restaurant, $700.00.
(Photo courtesy Felicia Browell, Kelly Korber-Weimer, and Kelly Kesicki)

Rin Tin Tin (#327), any variation, 1958-73, ea.................$46.00
Roping Calf, any variation, 1999-2004, ea from 6 to...........$7.00
Spanish Fighting Bull (#73), matt steel gray w/darker shading,
    wht horns, 1997-2004 ....$36.00
St Bernard (#321 ?), Brandy St Bernard, matt golden brn & wht,
    1995-96...$34.00
Texas Longhorn Bull, matt chestnut pinto, gray horns w/dk tips,
    gray hooves, 1990-95...$26.00
Texas Longhorn Bull (#75), Maverick, matt blk & wht pinto w/
    gray striped horns, 1998 ....$56.00

Walking Black Angus Bull (#72), glossy blk, 1960-62.......$77.00
Walking Hereford Bull (#71), any glossy finish except Buford
    (BreyerFest Special) or woodgrain, 1958-81, ea.............$36.00
Welsh Corgi (#1506), any variation, 1999-2006, ea............$5.00
Whitetail Deer (#301BU), buck, 1965-73 ....$11.00
Whitetail Deer (#302DO), doe, 1965-73.......................$11.00
Whitetail Deer (#303FA), fawn, 1965-73.......................$8.00
Wolf (#821), any variation except 2002 BreyerFest Special Ban-
    dit, 2001-06, ea $7 to $10.00
Wolf (#821), Bandit, BreyerFest Special, 2002..................$32.00

• **Buddy L** •

Buddy L vehicles were produced by Fred Lundahl, founder of Moline Pressed Steel Co. Mr. Lundahl first designed the toys for his young son, Buddy. They were advertised as being 'Guaranteed Indestructible,' and indeed they were sturdy and well built pressed-steel toys. Wartime brought on a shortage of heavy-gauge pressed steel, so wood was used as a substitute to make some of the vehicles. Many were based on actual models and some were hydraulically activated. The ride-ons were capable of supporting an adult's weight.

Condition is everything. Remember that unless the work is done by a professional restorer, overpainting and amateur repairs do nothing to enhance the value of a toy in poor condition.

See also Advertising; Aeronautical; Boats; Catalogs.

AUTOMOBILES

Army Staff Car, 1964, 16", EX+ $125.00
Colt Sportsliner, 1960s, any style, 10", NM, ea $40 to $50.00
Colt Utility Car, 1960s, any style, 10", EX+, ea $30 to $40.00
Country Squire Station Wagon, 1963, wht w/wood-grain, 15½",
    EX $100.00
Country Squire Station Wagon, 1965, red w/wood-grain, 15½", EX+....$85.00
Deluxe Convertible Coupe, 1949, top retracts into rumble seat,
    EX+ $375.00
Flivver Coupe, 1920s, 12", NM................................... $1,200.00
Flivver Coupe, 1920s, 12", VG....................................... $475.00
Flivver Roadster, 1920s, 11", EX................................. $1,200.00
Flivver Roadster, 1920s, 11", NM+ $1,500.00
Junior Buggy Hauler, 1970s, 12", NM+ $40.00
Junior Flower Power Sportster, 1969, 6", NM $40.00
Scarab, 1930s, w/up, 10", NM+................................... $400.00
Scarab, 1941, non-mechanical, 10½", EX $150.00
Suburban Station Wagon, 1960s, any style, 16", NM, ea $100 to..$125.00
VW Buddywagen, 1960s, any style, 11", EX+, ea $35.00

CONSTRUCTION

Cement Mixer on Treads, 1929-31, 16", EX $2,600.00
Cement Mixer on Wheels, 1926-29, 15", EX.................. $750.00
Concrete Mixer, 1926, #280, 18", EX............................. $550.00
Derrick (Big), 1920s, 24" H, EX $625.00
Derrick (Small), 1920s, 22" H, EX $525.00
Hoisting Tower, 1928-31, 29" H, G................................. $650.00
Hoisting Tower, 1928-31, 29" H, VG+ $1,200.00
Mobile Construction Derrick, 1950s, any model, 26", EX+.$175.00
Mobile Power Digger Unit, 1950s, any model, EX+ $130.00
Overhead Crane, 1924, 46", VG $650.00
Pile Driver on Wheels, 1920s, #260, VG $650.00
Road Roller, 18", EX.. $1,500.00
Sand Loader, 1920s, any model, 21", EX+ $200.00
Sand Loader, 1930s, 21", EX+ $250.00
Scoop 'N Load Conveyor, 1950s, any model, 18", EX, ea $50
    to $75.00
Side Conveyor Load 'N Dump, 1950s, any model, 21", EX, ea
    $75 to... $100.00

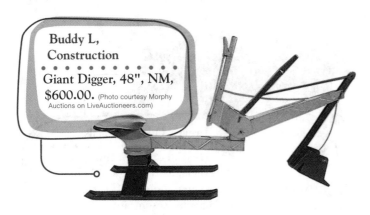

Steam Shovel, 1920s, blk & red, EX+ $550.00
Steam Shovel, 1920s, blk & red, G $200.00
Steam Shovel Truck, 20", VG $300.00
Trencher, rubber treads, 20", EX rstr $1,750.00

FIREFIGHTING

Aerial Ladder & Emergency Truck, 1950s, any model, 22", EX $250.00
Aerial Ladder & Emergency Truck, 1960s, any model, 27", EX .. $150.00
Aerial Ladder Truck, 1920s, open, hydraulic, 39", G $300.00
Aerial Ladder Truck, 1920s, open, hydraulic, 39", NM. $7,500.00
American La France Pumper Truck, 1960s, 25½", EX+ $50.00
Extension Ladder Trailer Fire Truck, 1950s, #5651, 29½", MIB $300.00
Fire & Chemical Truck, 1949, 25", EX+ $150.00
Fire Department Emergency Truck, 1950s, 12½", EX+IB . $200.00
Fire Truck, 1945, enclosed cab, 12", EX+ $150.00
GMC Deluxe Aerial Ladder Truck, 1950s, 28", EX+ $250.00
GMC Hydraulic Aerial Ladder Truck, 1950s, 27", EX+ . $150.00
GMC Pumper Truck, 1950s, w/horn, 15", EX+ $175.00
Hook & Ladder Truck, 1920s, open, 26", EX $1,000.00
Pumper Truck, 1920s, open bench seat, red w/brass detail, MDW, 23", VG $1,800.00
Snorkel Fire Pumper, 1969, any model, 21", NM, ea $75 to ...$150.00

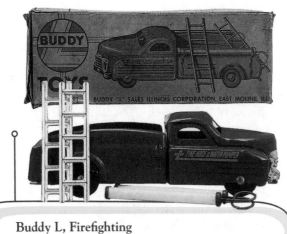

Suburban Pumper, 1960s, red station wagon w/wht plastic bumpers, 15", EX+ $125.00
Water Tower Truck, 1920s, open, 40", NM $4,500.00
Water Tower Truck, 1920s, open, 40", VG $1,500.00

RIDE-ON TOYS

Allied Van Lines, 1941, 29", complete, EX $1,500.00
Automatic Tail-Gate Loader, 1953, 26", complete, VG.. $2,400.00
Baggage Rider, 1940, #819, complete, NM+IB $1,200.00
Curtiss Candies Butterfinger Truck, 1949, 24", complete, EX.. $1,200.00
Dandy Digger, #933, 28", complete, EXIB $150.00
Dump Truck, 1930s International, curved cab, 25", complete, VG $1,000.00
Dump Truck, 1930s International, sq cab w/visor, 20", complete, G+ $500.00
Dump Truck, 1930s International, working headlights, 24", complete, G $550.00
Emergency Towing Truck, 1930s International, 33", no seat or hdl, EX $2,000.00
Fire Aerial Ladder Truck, 1930s International, hydraulic ladder, 42", complete, G+ $2,175.00
Fire Ladder Truck, 1930s International, 42", complete, G... $1,950.00
Fire Truck, 1930s International, electric headlights, 26", no handle, VG $3,150.00
Hydraulic Dump Truck, 1930s International, 26", complete, NM. $2,500.00
Ice Truck, 1930s International, 29", no seat, VG $1,950.00
Junior Excavator, 1940s, 27" L, EX $175.00
Railway Express Agency, 1930s International, 'Wrigley's' gum ad, 25", complete, VG $1,600.00
Sand & Gravel Truck, 1950s, 22", EX $600.00
Shell Fuel Oil, 1938, 30", complete, VG+ $5,000.00
Wrecker, 1934 International, 27", electric lights, complete, VG $1,200.00
Wrecker, 1938 International, 33", complete, VG $1,725.00

TRAINS

Industrial Set, locomotive, flat car, gondola, hopper, lumber car, side-dump, track, 2 switches, 3 stall rnd houses, EX. $1,825.00
Industrial Set, locomotive, tender, rocker dump car, ballast car, flatcar & rack car, orig track, 8" ea, EX $1,000.00
Industrial Set, locomotive & 5 different cars, 24 pcs of curved track, VG+ $500.00

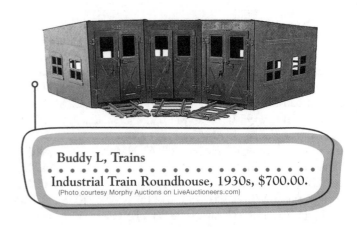

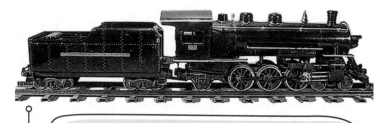

Buddy L, Trains

Outdoor Engine and Trailer, 40", $2,500.00.
(Photo courtesy Morphy Auctions on LiveAuctioneers.com)

Buddy L, Trucks, Buses, and Vans

Army Transport with Tank, 1950s, 26½" overall, EX, $125.00. (Photo courtesy Morphy Auctions on LiveAuctioneers.com)

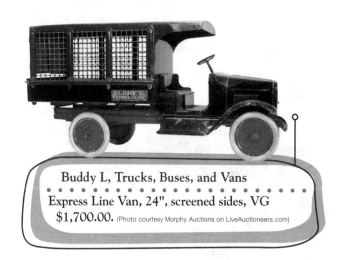

Buddy L, Trucks, Buses, and Vans

Express Line Van, 24", screened sides, VG $1,700.00. (Photo courtesy Morphy Auctions on LiveAuctioneers.com)

Outdoor Ballast Car, 22", EX..................................... $725.00
Outdoor Boxcar, 22", VG+ $450.00
Outdoor Caboose, 19", EX... $950.00
Outdoor Caboose, 19", VG... $575.00
Outdoor Cattle Car, 22", EX.. $850.00
Outdoor Cattle Car, 22", NM $1,000.00
Outdoor Coal Car, 22", EX $625.00
Outdoor Crane on Flatcar, EX................................... $2,075.00
Outdoor Dredger on Flatcar, 30", EX $1,300.00
Outdoor Dump Car, 12", EX......................................$4,025.00
Outdoor Flatcar, 20", EX... $950.00
Outdoor Gondola, 22", VG+ $600.00
Outdoor Hopper, 22", VG $900.00
Outdoor Locomotive & Tender, wood crate only, stamped 'I-NO 1000 Locomotive & Tender,' 50", EX.......................... $600.00
Outdoor Locomotive & Tender, 2 pcs of straight track, 45", G.$700.00
Outdoor Locomotive & Tender, 44" overall, EX.......... $1,800.00
Outdoor Locomotive & Tender 4-6-4, 48" ea, EX $3,450.00
Outdoor Locomotive 4-6-4, 44", G $285.00
Outdoor Pile Driver, 23x22", partial rpnt..................... $800.00
Outdoor Steam Shovel on Flatcar, 23", EX.................. $3,450.00
Outdoor Switch Track, left/right hand switches, orig decals, 82" L, EX.. $625.00
Outdoor Tank Car, yel w/'Shell Co 1721' on sides, 19", EX... $1,150.00
Outdoor Tank Car, 19", VG $800.00
Outdoor Wrecking Crane, 35" L, prof rstr $1,200.00

TRUCKS, BUSES, AND VANS

Air Force Supply Transport Truck, 1950s, bl w/bl cloth canopy, 15", EX.. $125.00
Airway Delivery Truck, 1950s, GMC cab w/box van, gr, 17½", EX.. $250.00
Allied Van Lines Semi, removable van roof, blk & orange, BRT, 6-wheeled, 29", G.. $300.00
Anti-Aircraft Unit w/Electric Searchlight Trailer, 1950s, GMC cab, bl, 24", EX+ $300.00
Army Searchlight Repair-It Truck, 1950s, 15", VG.......... $75.00
Army Supply Corps & Searchlight Repair Truck Set, #5560, complete w/Howitzer gun, 2 ammo boxes & 5 plastic figures, EXIB $500.00
Army Supply Truck, 1956, canvas cover, 14½", NM $75.00
Army Transport, 1940s, gr w/US Army on cloth cover, BRT, 21", G+ $175.00

Atlas Van Lines Semi, gr & wht w/red lettering, silver van top, BRT, logo on doors, 29", NM...................................... $550.00
Auto Transport, 1968, yel cabover, w/3 8" vehicles, 25½", NM $125.00
Baggage Stake Truck, 1930-32, blk cab w/opening doors, yel stake bed, BRT w/red hubs, 26", NM......................$5,320.00
Baggage Truck, 1927, doorless cab, stake sides, chains across back, 26", EX... $1,200.00
Baggage Truck, 1935, blk cab w/non-opening doors, flat or solid sides, 26", EX... $375.00
Big Brute Dumper, 1971, 8", EX+................................... $65.00
Big Brute Mixer Truck, 1971, 7", VG.............................. $25.00
Bus, 1920s, coach w/2 side spares on nose, opening doors, 22 seats, bl-gr, MDW, 29", VG.................................... $3,725.00
Camper Truck, 1960s, WWT, 15", VG $65.00
Camper Truck w/Boat, 1960s, 15", EX+ $75.00
Cement Mixer, 1960s, bl & wht, 7½", NMIB $100.00
Circus Animal Truck, 1960s, yel tractor-trailer, w/8 animals, 10", EX $550.00
City Dray, 1930s, electric lights, 20", EX $450.00
Coal Truck, 1920s, doorless cab, hopper bed, blk & red, NPDW, 24", VG $2,575.00
Coca-Cola Truck, open bay w/ad panel dividing 2 shelves, yel w/ wht-wall BRT, w/8 soda cases & hand cart, 15", EX+ . $615.00
Curtiss Candy Semi, lt bl & wht, drop-down tailgate, 29" rstr $650.00

Buddy L, Trucks, Buses, and Vans
• • • • • • • • • • • • • •
Greyhound Lines, No. 755, 16", EX+IB, $650.00. (Photo courtesy Morphy Auctions on LiveAuctioneers.com)

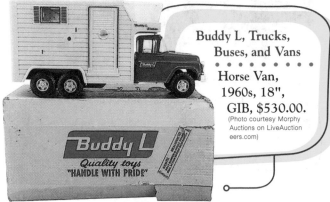

Buddy L, Trucks, Buses, and Vans
• • • • • • • • •
Horse Van, 1960s, 18", GIB, $530.00.
(Photo courtesy Morphy Auctions on LiveAuctioneers.com)

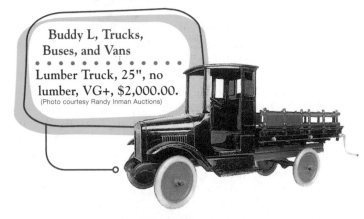

Buddy L, Trucks, Buses, and Vans
• • • • • • • • •
Lumber Truck, 25", no lumber, VG+, $2,000.00.
(Photo courtesy Randy Inman Auctions)

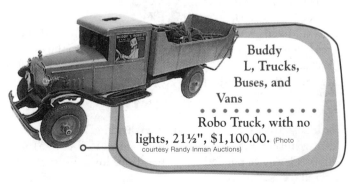

Buddy L, Trucks, Buses, and Vans
• • • • • • • • • •
Robo Truck, with no lights, 21½", $1,100.00. (Photo courtesy Randy Inman Auctions)

Dump Truck, 1920s, electric lights, BRT, 20", VG+ $425.00
Dump Truck, 1920s, open, A-frame dump bed, 24", G... $500.00
Dump Truck, 1920s, open, A-frame dump bed, 24", NM...$2,000.00
Dump Truck, 1920s, open, chain-drive dump bed, MDW, 25", EX $900.00
Dump Truck, 1920s, open, hydraulic dump bed, 24", VG+ ..$1,500.00
Dump Truck, 1930s, electric headlights, blk & red, 20", VG... $575.00
Dump Truck, 1930s, enclosed cab, curved dump bed, BRT, 24", G $200.00
Dump Truck, 1930s, open, hydraulic dump bed, rear dual wheels, 24", EX...$2,500.00
Dump Truck, 1940s, enclosed cab, curved dump bed, blk wooden wheels, 17", VG....................................... $100.00
Dump Truck, 1960s, enclosed cab, side-crank dump bed, BRT, 6-wheeled, 14", VG..$50.00
Electric Emergency Unit, 1950s, yel, 14½", EX $75.00
Emergency Auto Wrecker, 1940s, NP grille, 15", EX $225.00
Emergency Auto Wrecker, 1950s, BRT, 17", VG............ $125.00
Express Line, Tandem Truck, early cab w/2 trailers, electric lights, 3-color, BRT, 40" overall, EX+ $900.00
Express Line Tractor-Trailer, 1930s, box van w/removable roof, electric lights, 23", VG................................... $500.00
Express Line Van, 1920s, screened sides, 24", EX $2,200.00
Express Line Van, 1920s, solid sides, 24", EX.............. $2,200.00
Express Pickup, 1920s, open cab, MSW, blk & red, 24", G... $450.00
Farm Supplies Dump Truck, 1940s, 2-color, 20", EXIB.... $450.00
Fast Freight Semi, 1950s, open U-shaped trailer w/chain across open back, 6-wheeled, 20", NMIB.............................. $650.00
Fast Freight Semi, 1950s, open U-shaped trailer w/chain across open back, 6-wheeled, 20", VG $100.00
Firestone Tire Service Truck, 1940s, 24", VG $600.00
Flivver Contractor's Dump Truck, open seat, MSW, 11", EX ..$2,200.00
Flivver Dump Cart, 1926-30, MSW, 12", VG.............. $1,000.00
Flivver Dump Truck, 1920s, tilting dump bed, MSW, 12", VG...$700.00
Flivver Huckster Truck, 1920s, 12", EX+ $2,400.00
Flivver Pickup Truck, 1920s, 12", G........................... $500.00
Gold Belt Line Bus, 1920s, long-nosed w/side spare, MDW, bl-gr, 30", VG $2,300.00
Hydraulic Dumper, 1920s, open, EX $600.00
Hydraulic Dumper, 1930s, 25", EX $500.00
Hydraulic Dumper, 1950s, 4-wheeled, 'Heavy Hauling,' 21", G.... $75.00
Hydraulic Dumper, 1950s, 10-wheeled, 20", VG $225.00
Hydraulic Dumper, 1960s, turq, BRT, 6-wheeled, 20", VG..$150.00
Ice Truck, 1926-31, VG... $1,950.00
Junior Air Mail Truck, blk & red, 22", VG $2,000.00
Junior Dump Truck, 1930s, blk & red, 24", VG............. $850.00
Machinery Truck, 1950s, 6-wheeled, 23", VG+ $250.00
Merry-Go-Round Truck, 1960s, 14", EX $100.00
Mobile Repair-It Unit Tow Truck, 1950s, complete, 21", EXIB....$400.00
Motor Market Truck, electric lights, BRT, w/grocery product boxes, 20½", VG...$1,000.00
Moving Van, 1920s, roof extends over open seat, blk, 24", G.. $775.00
Moving Van, 1920s, roof extends over open seat, blk, 24", NM $3,500.00
Pickup Truck, 1960s, lt bl, WWT, 12", VG $35.00
Police Squad Truck, 1940s, yel & bl-gr, 21½", EX+ $200.00
Railway Express Semi, 1930s, 'Wrigley's' ad, removable roof, 23", G.. $325.00

Railway Express Van, 1920s, screened sides, 25", EX... $2,000.00

Railway Express Van, 1930s, 'Wrigley's' ad, electric lights, 6-wheeled, 23", EX.. $5,000.00

REA Express Step Van, 1964, gr w/wht trim, WWT, 11½", EX... $115.00

Red Baby Dump Truck, 1920s, 24", EX rstr................. $1,250.00

Red Baby Express Truck, 1920s International, doorless cab, NPSW, 24", EX $1,000.00

Red Baby Pickup, 1920s, doorless cab, 'IHC Sales & Service'/'McCormick-Deering'/'Int'l Harvester' decals, 24", VG+ $4,500.00

Repair-It Unit, divided windshield, wht over red, 6-wheeled, 22", EX $275.00

Repair-It Unit, single windshield, red cab w/wht bed, gr hoist, 6-wheeled, 21", VG+ $100.00

Robotoy Dump Truck, introduced at 1933 Chicago World's Fair, electric lights, red & gr, 21", EX+IB $1,525.00

Rockin' Giraffes Truck, 1960s, WWT, complete w/2 giraffes, 13½", NM $250.00

Sand & Gravel Truck, #3312, 13½", EX+IB $325.00

Sand & Gravel Truck, 1920s, doorless cab, blk w/red undercarriage & hubs, MDW, 26", VG.............................. $500.00

Sand & Gravel Truck, 1930-32, opening doors, headlights, blk w/red undercarriage, BRT w/red emb 'spoke' wheels, 26", EX.. $2,500.00

Sand Loader & Dump Truck, 1950, 25", EX $200.00

Scoop & Dump Truck, 1950s, 4-wheeled, 18", G $75.00

Scoop & Dump Truck, 1950s, 6-wheeled, G...................... $75.00

Scoop & Dump Truck, 1950s, 10-wheeled, 22", G $100.00

Shell Delivery Truck, yel w/red Shell decal on sides of truck bed, w/oil can bank & hand cart, 13", EX+IB.................... $450.00

Stake Truck, 1920s, open seat, 24", VG+...................... $1,650.00

Super Market Truck, #325, w/mini grocery items, 13", VGIB . $300.00

Tank Line Sprinkler Truck, 1920s, 26", G....................... $850.00

Tank Line Sprinkler Truck, 1920s, 26", NM $3,300.00

Tank Line Sprinkler Truck, 1920s, 26", VG................. $1,100.00

Texaco Tanker Truck, red w/wht lettering, 23½", EX $225.00

US Mail 2592 Truck, olive w/cream top, Buy Defense Bonds on sides, 23½", EX... $785.00

Utilities Service Truck, 1950s, GMC, 15", EX.............. $350.00

Van Freight Carriers, #3413, 20", unused, NMIB $400.00

Wrecker, 1920s, open seat, MDW, 26", VG+ $1,450.00

Wrigley's Spearmint Delivery Box Truck, 1960s, 14½", EX... $530.00

Zoo-A-Rama Jeep & Caged Trailer, 1967, 21" overall, NMIB .. $600.00

WOODEN VEHICLES

Army Supply Truck, 1940s, 16", G.....................................$75.00

Army Tank, 11½", VG..$75.00

Buick Station Wagon, electrig headlights, folding rear gate, 18", VG $1,150.00

Fire Aerial Hook & Ladder Truck, 1940s, 33", EX+ $1,750.00

Fire Ladder Truck, 22½", G $75.00

Greyhound Bus, 1940s, bl & wht w/red hubs, 18", VG .. $400.00

Long Distance Moving Van, orange & blk w/yel hubs, 27", EX+ $400.00

Milk Farms Truck, 1940s, wht w/blk top, sliding door, 13", EX.. $400.00

Pontoon Boat, 1940s, w/up motor, 16", NM $2,800.00

Railway Express Truck, #480, sliding side door, rear doors open, 16", VG+ $500.00

Timber Truck, 27", G+.. $250.00

Town & Country 'Woodie' Convertible, working convertible hard top that slides into trunk, 18", EX $500.00

Woody Station Wagon, maroon, WWT, chrome hubs, 19", VG $175.00

Wrecking Truck, 18", G+ $175.00

MISCELLANEOUS

Airplane Hangar & 3 Monocoupes, 20x8", Fair $600.00

Buddy L Savings & Recording Bank, litho tin, lever action, 6½", EX $175.00

Catapult Hangar w/Airplane, 1930s, yel & red monocoupe w/12" WS, gr hangar, VG+ $1,400.00

Fire Station, 1940s, pnt wood, 16x16", EX $500.00

Gas Pump, plastic pump w/magnetic nozzle, 7", EXIB.... $125.00

Tool Box, blk & red wooden box w/metal corners, 11x23", box only, VG+...$50.00

• • • • • • • • • • • • Building Blocks and Construction Toys • • • • • • • • • • • •

Toy building sets were popular with children well before television worked its mesmerizing influence on young minds; in fact, some were made as early as the end of the eighteenth century. Important manufacturers include Milton Bradley, Joel Ellis, Charles M. Crandall, William S. Tower, W.S. Read, Ives Manufacturing Corporation, S.L. Hill, Frank Hornby (Meccano), A.C. Gilbert, The Toy Tinkers, Gebruder Bing, R. Bliss, S.F. Fischer, Carl Brandt Jr., and F. Ad. Richter. (See Anchor Stone Building Sets by Richter in this section.) Whether made of wood, paper, metal, glass, or 'stone,' these toys are highly prized today for their profusion of historical, educational, artistic, and creative features.

Richter's Anchor (Union) Stone Building Blocks were the most popular building toy at the beginning of the twentieth century. As early as 1880, they were patented in both Germany and the USA. Though the company produced more than 600 different sets, only their New Series is commonly found today; these are listed below. Their blocks remained popular until WWI, and Anchor sets were some of the first toys to achieve international 'brand name' acceptance. They were produced both as basic sets and supplement sets (identified by letters A, B, C, or D) which increased a basic set to a higher level. There were dozens of stone block competitors, though none were very successful. During WWI the trade name Anchor was lost to A.C. Gilbert (Connecticut) who produced Anchor blocks for a short time. Richter responded by using the new trade name 'Union' or 'Stone Building Blocks,' sets considered today to be Anchor blocks despite the lack of the Richter's Anchor trademark. The A.C. Gilbert Company also produced the famous Erector sets which were made from about 1913 through the early 1960s.

Note: Values for Richter's blocks are for sets in very good condition; (+) at the end of the line indicates these sets are being reproduced today.

Advisor: George Hardy, Anchor Stone Building Sets by Richter.

American Model Builder Set, EXIB (wood box) $1,020.00
Ges Gesch, Wood Architectural Building Set, Germany, prewar, wooden blocks in various shapes & szs, EXIB (wood box) ..$127.00
Halsam American Logs #815, w/senior-sz ¾" logs, VG $40.00
Ideal Super City Heliport Building Set, 1968, EX (EX vinyl case) $50.00
Ideal Super City Skyscraper Building Set, 1960s, EXIB.....$75.00
JL Wright Lincoln Stones, VG (in 16x12" box) $475.00
Kelmet Steel Engineering Set #1, complete, EXIB $180.00
Kenner Girder & Panel Constructioneer Set #8, EXIB.. $100.00
Kenner Girder & Panel Hydro-Dynamic Double Set #18, VGIB.. $200.00
Kenner Girder & Panel Hydro-Dynamic Single Set #17, VGIB...$175.00
Kenner Girder & Panel International Airport, 1977, EXIB.....$40.00
Kenner Girder & Panel Skyscraper w/Working Elevator Set #72050, NMIB $65.00
Kenner Mold Master Road Builder, 1964, NMIB $125.00
Lionel Construction Set #222, unused, NMIB $100.00

Marklin #2, 1940s, appears unused, VG+IB (cb box)..... $240.00
Marklin Auto-Baukasten, contemporary reissue of the 1930s race car, MIB.. $185.00
Meccano Accessory Outfit #4A, EXIB.............................$90.00
Meccano Aeroplane Constructor #0, EXIB $375.00
Meccano Aeroplane Constructor #1, VGIB $325.00
Meccano Aeroplane Constructor #2, EX+IB................. $450.00
Meccano Roadster Constructor, EXIB $500.00
Meccano Truck & Ship Set, 1930-31, EXIB $1,080.00
Meccano Truck & Ship Set, 1930-36, w/P56 motor, VG+IB .$3,240.00
Meccano Truck Set #110, 1930-31, VGIB..................... $480.00
Metalcraft Spirit of St Louis, 'Builds Over 25 Airplanes,' complete, VGIB $100.00
Metalcraft Spirit of St Louis Airplane Kit, complete, VGIB. $145.00
Modlwood Toys, wooden ready-to-assemble open car, 14½" L, Schoenhut, EXIB $200.00

Building Blocks and Construction Toys
• • • • • • • • • • • • •
Embossing Company Sky-Hy Building Blocks Set #3105, VG+IB, $400.00. (Photo courtesy Noel Barrett Antiques & Auctions Ltd. on LiveAuctioneers.com)

Building Blocks and Construction Toys
• • • • • • • • • • • • •
Kelmet Steel Engineering Set, #10, 1923, complete (wood box), VGIB, $360.00. (Photo courtesy Leslie Hindman Auctioneers)

Pioneer Toys, Daniel Boone Logs, complete w/12-pg booklet, VGIB $175.00

Pyro Design-A-Car...Automobile Designing-Construction Set, 1950s, complete, NMIB $75.00

Questor Big Tinkertoy Construction Set for Little Hands, 1976, EXIB $25.00

Questor Tinkertoy Design Blocks, EXIC............................$30.00

Questor Tinkertoy Giant Engineer, EXIC.........................$25.00

Questor Tinkertoy Junior Architect, EXIC........................$25.00

Questor Tinkertoy Little Designer, EXIC...........................$25.00

Questor Tinkertoy Locomotive & Driver, EXIC................$15.00

Questor Tinkertoy Master Builder, EXIC...........................$25.00

Renwal Busy Mechanic Construction Kit #375-198, EXIB ..$30.00

Schoenhut Aeroplane Builder, unfinished wood, EXIB.. $200.00

Schoenhut Hollywood Home Builder, wood, EXIB........ $200.00

Schoenhut Toy Train to Build, makes 5-pc wooden train set, 11" L, VG+IB.. $300.00

Schuco Elektro Champion Deluxe Set, VGIB............... $325.00

Schuco Montage-Mercedes 190SL Kit, #2097, EX+IB... $165.00

Schuco-Studio Steerable Driving School Car, unused, NMIB.. $200.00

Spalding Big Toy Tinkertoy, 1950s-60s, EXIB....................$50.00

Spalding Curtain Wall Builder No 640, 1959-64, EXIC....$40.00

Spalding Executive Tinkertoy Set, 1966, EXIC.................$35.00

Spalding Junior Tinkertoy Set, 1963, EXIC......................$25.00

Spalding Major Tinkertoy, 1964, EXIC..............................$25.00

Spalding Motorized Tinkertoy, EXIC $60.00

Spalding Teck Tinkertoy, 1963, EXIC................................$25.00

Spalding Tinkertoy Curtain Wall Builder, AD Spalding & Bros #620, 1959, complete, EX (VG+ canister).....................$25.00

Spalding Tinkertoy Panel Builder #600, 1958, EXIC $30.00

Spalding Tinkertoy Panel Builder #800, 1958, EXIC $40.00

Spalding Tinkertoy Wonder Builder, 1953-54, EXIC $30.00

Spalding Tinker Zoo No 717, 1970, EXIC $15.00

Spalding Tinker Zoo No 737, 1962-70, EXIC....................$25.00

Structo Auto-Builder Set #10, unused, EX+IB $1,750.00

Structo Tractor-Builder #11, early 1900s, VGIB............. $600.00

Toy Tinkers Giant Tinker Multi Motion Model Maker Set, VG+IB, $125.00. (Photo courtesy Noel Barrett Antiques & Auctions Ltd. on LiveAuctioneers.com)

ANCHOR STONE BUILDING SETS BY RICHTER

American House & Country Set #206...................... $600.00

American House & Country Set #208...................... $600.00

American House & Country Set #210...................... $700.00

DS Set #E3, w/metal parts & roof stones $80.00

DS Set #3A, w/metal parts & roof stones....................$80.00

DS Set #5, w/metal parts & roof stones..................... $150.00

DS Set #5A, w/metal parts & roof stones................... $150.00

DS Set #7, w/metal parts & roof stones..................... $270.00

DS Set #7A, w/metal parts & roof stones................... $200.00

DS Set #9A, w/metal parts & roof stones................... $250.00

DS Set #11, w/metal parts & roof stones................... $675.00

DS Set #11A, w/metal parts & roof stones................. $300.00

DS Set #13A, w/metal parts & roof stones................. $325.00

DS Set #15, w/metal parts & roof stones.................$1,500.00

DS Set #15A, w/metal parts & roof stones................. $475.00

DS Set #19A, w/metal parts & roof stones................. $475.00

DS Set #21A, w/metal parts & roof stones................. $975.00

DS Set #23A, w/metal parts & roof stones................. $750.00

DS Set #25A, w/metal parts & roof stones.................$1,500.00

DS Set #27, w/metal parts & roof stones.................$6,000.00

DS Set #27B, w/metal parts & roof stones $2,000.00

Fortress Set #402 .... $100.00

Fortress Set #402A $130.00

Fortress Set #404 .... $250.00

Fortress Set #404A $275.00

Fortress Set #406 .... $500.00

Fortress Set #406A $400.00

Fortress Set #408 ....$1,000.00

Fortress Set #408A $800.00

Fortress Set #410 ....$1,800.00

Fortress Set #410A $1,000.00

Fortress Set #412A $1,500.00

Fortress Set #414 ....$5,000.00

German House & Country Set #301 .... $500.00

German House & Country Set #301A $500.00

German House & Country Set #303 ....$1,000.00

German House & Country Set #303A $2,000.00

German House & Country Set #305 ....$3,000.00

GK-AF Great-Castle Set $9,950.00

GK-NF Set #6 (+) $140.00

GK-NF Set #6A (+) $160.00

GK-NF Set #8 .... $300.00

GK-NF Set #8A (+) $180.00

GK-NF Set #10.. $480.00

GK-NF Set #10A (+) $200.00

GK-NF Set #12.. $680.00

GK-NF Set #12A (+) $250.00

GK-NF Set #14A $250.00

GK-NF Set #16..$1,180.00

GK-NF Set #16A $300.00

GK-NF Set #18A $400.00

GK-NF Set #20..$2,000.00

GK-NF Set #20A $500.00

GK-NF Set #22A $500.00

GK-NF Set #24A $600.00

GK-NF Set #26A $1,000.00

GK-NF Set #28 .... $4,000.00	KK-NF Set #13A $300.00
GK-NF Set #28A $1,200.00	KK-NF Set #15A $450.00
GK-NF Set #30A $1,200.00	KK-NF Set #17A $750.00
GK-NF Set #30A $1,200.00	KK-NF Set #19A $2,500.00
GK-NF Set #32B $1,600.00	KK-NF Set #21 .... $4,500.00
GK-NF Set #34 .... $7,000.00	Neue Reihe Set #102 .... $100.00
KK-NF Set #5 .... $110.00	Neue Reihe Set #104 .... $150.00
KK-NF Set #5A $100.00	Neue Reihe Set #106 .... $200.00
KK-NF Set #7 .... $200.00	Neue Reihe Set #108 .... $300.00
KK-NF Set #7A $115.00	Neue Reihe Set #110 .... $600.00
KK-NF Set #9A $120.00	Neue Reihe Set #112 .... $1,000.00
KK-NF Set #11 .... $315.00	Neue Reihe Set #114 .... $1,500.00
KK-NF Set #11A $275.00	Neue Reihe Set #116 .... $2,000.00

• Candy Containers • • • • • • • • • • • • • • • •

As early as 1876, candy manufacturers used figural glass containers to package their candy. They found the idea so successful that they continued to use them until the 1960s. The major producers of these glass containers were Westmoreland, West Bros., Victory Glass, J.H. Millstein, J.C. Crosetti, L.E. Smith, and Jack and T.H. Stough. Some of the most collectible and sought after today are the character-related figures such as Amos 'N Andy, Barney Google, Santa Claus, and Jackie Coogan, to name a few.

There are many reproductions; know your dealer. For a listing of these reproductions, refer to *Schroeder's Antiques Price Guide*.

In the early 1900s, Germany produced candy containers made of composition. Many were of famous advertising and cartoon characters of the time.

For other types of candy containers, see Halloween; Penny Toys; PEZ Dispensers.

Alphonse Emerging From Eggshell w/Feet Showing, pnt compo, 5", Germany, VG.. $175.00

Amos & Andy Car, clear glass w/pnt features, tires & bumper, 4½", EX+ $375.00

Barney Google on Pedestal, glass, 3¾", 1920s, EX.......... $150.00

Battleship on Waves, clear glass w/metal bottom, EX..... $175.00

Bear in Auto, pnt glass, tin cap on radiator, rpnt............ $400.00

Bear on Circus Tub Holding Fan, glass, blow through tube to turn fan, 4¼", TG Stough, ca 1916, VG...................... $175.00

Black Cat for Luck, pnt glass, 4¼", VG+ $1,250.00

Brownie Standing w/Hands on Round Tummy, pnt compo, gr sailor suit, pointed hat, rnd base, 6", Germany, VG.... $150.00

Buddy, litho tin figure leaning on glass candy/coin jar w/pnt screw lid, serves as bank when empty, 4¼", Marx, EX. $300.00

Buster Brown Seated on Tige, pnt compo, 6", Germany, NM.$1,425.00

Butler, compo & cb figure w/wire arms, felt hands, ears, jacket, vest & pants, pnt features, 10", Germany, EX $225.00

Campbell's Kid, pnt compo, bl hat, red coat & yel pants, rnd base, 4½", EX+ $150.00

Charlie Chaplin Standing Next to Barrel, glass w/pnt figure, tin lid, 3¾", EX..$15.00

Easter Rabbit w/Egg-Filled Wheelbarrow, pnt glass, 4", worn pnt $115.00

Felix the Cat, pnt compo roly-poly figure, 5", Germany, EX.. $1,500.00

Foxy Grandpa Seated on Egg, pnt compo, 5", Germany, VG.$150.00

Happy Fat Standing on Drum, 4¾", glass, Borgfeldt, ca 1915, G $100.00

Happy Hooligan Seated Sideways on Chick, pnt compo, 5", Germany, EX $150.00

Happy Hooligan Standing Holding Chicken, compo & wood w/ cloth outfit, 8½", EX... $200.00

Katzenjammer Kid (Fritz) Emerging From Eggshell w/Feet Showing, pnt compo, 5", Germany, EX $125.00

Candy Containers
• • • • • • • • • • • • • • • • •
Donald Duck in Airplane, composition with glittery detail, 9x8", EX, $400.00. (Photo courtesy Morphy Auctions on LiveAuctioneers.com)

Candy Containers
• • • • • • • • • • • • • • • • •
Punch (Punch and Judy), painted composition head with lithographed cardboard tube body, 33", EX, $175.00. (Photo courtesy Noel Barrett Antiques & Auctions Ltd. on LiveAuctioneers.com)

Candy Containers
• • • • • • • • • • • • •
Rabbit Banjo Player with Cup on Round Base, papier-maché, metal glasses, metal coiled neck, ears, and arm, musical, 14", German, $200.00. (Photo courtesy Morphy Auctions on LiveAuctioneers.com)

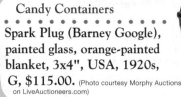

Candy Containers
• • • • • • • • • • • •
Spark Plug (Barney Google), painted glass, orange-painted blanket, 3x4", USA, 1920s, G, $115.00. (Photo courtesy Morphy Auctions on LiveAuctioneers.com)

Liberty Bell, pk glass, bail handle, metal bottom screw lid, EX $850.00
Mama Katzenjammer Standing Holding Switch, pnt compo, w/ eyeglasses, 6", Germany, EX $400.00
Santa Claus Standing by Chimney, glass, 4", LE Smith, 1920s, VG $200.00
Snookums Playing w/Roller Devil's Toy, pnt compo on wood base, Germany, EX $250.00
Uncle Sam Standing on Barrel, glass, 4", ca 1918, EX+ $65.00
Yellow Kid Emerging From Eggshell, pnt compo, 2¾", Germany, EX $300.00

Candy Containers
• • • • • • • • • • • •
Spirit of St. Louis Airplane, glass body with tin topwing and single propeller, metal spoke wheels, Westmoreland, 6½", EX+, $650.00. (Photo courtesy Morphy Auctions)

• Cast Iron •

Realistically modeled and carefully detailed, cast-iron toys enjoyed their heyday from about the turn of the century (some companies began production a little earlier) until about the 1940s when they were gradually edged out by lighter-weight toys that were less costly to produce and to ship. Some cast iron toys were more than 20" in length and very heavy. Many were vehicles faithfully patterned after actual models seen on city streets at the time. Horse-drawn carriages were phased out when motorized vehicles came into use.

Some of the larger manufacturers were Arcade (Illinois), who by the 1920s was recognized as a leader in the industry; Dent (Pennsylvania); Hubley (Pennsylvania); and Kenton (Ohio). In the 1940s, Kenton came out with a few horse-drawn toys which are collectible in their own right but naturally much less valuable than the older ones. In addition to those already noted, there were many minor makers; you will see them mentioned in the listings. For more detailed information on these companies, we recommend *Collecting Toys* by Richard O'Brien (Books Americana).

The following listings have been compiled from major toy auctions with some prices averaged according to condition.

See also Banks; Dollhouse Furniture; Guns; Pull and Push Toys.

AIRPLANES

Air Mail Top Wing, Kenton, 6" WS (more flat-ended wing tips), yel, EX+ $3,000.00
Air Mail Top Wing, Kenton, 6" WS (more rounded wing tips), red, G $475.00
America, Hubley, 17" WS, EX $3,000.00
Bremen, Hubley, 6½" WS, pilot in enclosed cockpit, no raised lettering on wings, EX $825.00
Bremen D1167, Hubley, 10" WS, 2 pilots in open cockpit, NM. $5,100.00
DO-X, Hubley, 3" WS (rare size), red & gray, G $250.00
DO-X, Hubley, 6" WS, M $2,700.00
Fighter Plane, Arcade, 10", royal bl w/yel wings, single prop, EX $475.00
Ford 1417 Top Wing Tri-Motor, Dent, 10" WS, orig casting, EX $3,900.00

Ford 1417 Top Wing Tri-Motor, Dent, 12½" WS, later casting, EX $1,400.00
Friendship, Hubley, 13" WS, NM $3,500.00
Lindy, Hubley, 10" WS, bl w/raised gold lettering (scarce), EX $1,400.00
Lindy, Hubley, 10" WS, gray w/raised red lettering, EX.. $825.00
Lindy, Hubley, 13" WS, gray w/raised red lettering, EX+ . $2,500.00
Lindy, Hubley, 13" WS, gray w/raised red lettering, G.... $975.00
Lindy, North & Judd, 4" WS, red & NP, VG $500.00
Lindy NR211 Sirius, Hubley, 10½", blk & orange, 2 pilots, VG $2,400.00
Los Angeles Zeppelin, Dent, 8", gr, EX $750.00
Los Angeles Zeppelin, Dent, 12", silver w/red trim, VG .. $1,050.00
Los Angeles Zeppelin, Kenton, 11", bl w/gold trim, EX ... $1,400.00

Monocoupe (Side Wings), Arcade, 10" WS, bl & yel, EX+ ...$400.00
Monocoupe (Top Wing), Arcade, 10" WS, blk & orange, EX ...$625.00
Monocoupe (Top Wing), Arcade, 10" WS, blk & orange, NM...$950.00
Monocoupe (Top Wing), Arcade, 10" WS, blk & orange, VG ..$375.00
Sea Gull, Kilgore, 8" WS, VG+.. $625.00
TAT (Trimotor), Kilgore, 11" WS, yel & bl, EX.......... $2,300.00
Travel Air Mystery, Kilgore, 6¾" WS, VG $400.00

Bell Toys

Acrobats (2) on 4-Wheeled Platform, 6", ea balancing bells on
    spinning star, G $925.00
Alligator & Boy on 4-Wheeled Base (Gator Baiter), NN Hill
    Brass Co, 9", some rpnt, VG $1,200.00
Are You a Buffalo?, Gong Bell, 6", EX....................... $12,650.00
Clowns (2) Back-to-Back on Donkey, 9", 4-wheeled base, articu-
    lated action, some rpnt... $1,600.00
Columbia, Gong Bell, 7½", G $1,650.00
Daisy, Gong Bell, 8", 4-wheeled horse sleigh, G+........... $500.00
Ding Dong Bell Pussy's Not in the Well, Gong Bell, 9", EX..$1,500.00
Eagle on Rocker, 5" L, lg bell in mouth, VG.................. $225.00
Elephant w/Bell on Trunk on 4-Wheeled Platform, NN Hill, 7"
    L, articulated trunk, VG.. $450.00

Hello-Hello Monkey, 8½" L, 2-wheeled base w/2 bells, some
    rpnt $750.00
Jack & Jill Rocking, Watrous Mfg, 8", pnt figures back-to-back atop 2
    bells on open band base w/2 lg & 2 sm wheels, EX+.......$1,300.00
Jack & Jill Seesaw, Watrous, Mfg, 7", seesaw attached to center
    bell on open banded 4-wheeled base, EX.................... $950.00
Jockey on Horse, Watrous Mfg, 7", NP CI, jockey on horse on
    bar across 2 bells on 2 MSW, EX+ $1,100.00
Jonah (Whale), NN Hill, 5½", 4-wheeled, EX+ $1,725.00
Lady Driving Pony Cart, Gong Bell, 6", G..................... $200.00
Landing of Columbus, Gong Bell, 7", VG..................... $375.00
Miss Liberty Standing in 4-Wheeled Coach w/Bell, Kyser & Rex,
    8", eagle finial on bell, EX...................................$29,700.00
Monkey on Log w/Coconut, NN Hill, 6", log on 4 wheels w/bell
    at front end, EX $1,000.00
Monkey on Velocipede, J&E Stevens, 8" L, some rpnt.$1,000.00
Rough Riders, Watrous Mfg, 7", 2 riders on horses atop bell on
    banded frame w/4 heart-spoked wheels, EX................ $400.00
Swan Chariot w/Girl Driver, J&E Stevens, 10" L, some rpnt..$900.00
Tramp No 4, Gong Bell, 6" L, VG.............................. $375.00
Whoa Dar Caesar, Ives, 5½", G $500.00

Boats

Battleship Kentucky, J&E Stevens, 10", some rpnt......... $950.00
Battleship Maine, 8½", VG $3,850.00
Battleship New York, Dent, 20", G $450.00
Chris Craft, Kilgore, 11", VG.................................. $2,700.00

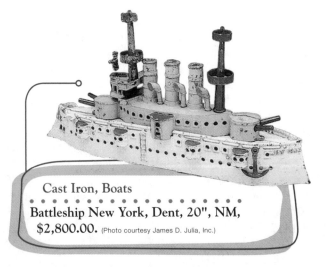

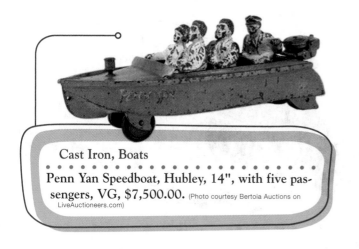

Racing Skull, US Hardware, 14½", 8 oarsmen, EX $2,400.00
Sailboat, Kilgore, 3½", VG+ $1,500.00
Showboat, Arcade, 11", VG $1,725.00
Side-Wheeler Adirondak, Dent, 15", G $550.00
Side-Wheeler City of Chicago, Wilkins, 16", NM $1,100.00
Side-Wheeler City of New York, Wilkins, 15", VG+ .. $1,000.00
Side-Wheeler New Orleans, Wilkins/Harris, 10½", EX.. $975.00
Side-Wheeler Puritan, Wilkins, 11", NM $1,400.00
Side-Wheeler Puritan, Wilkins, 11", VG $500.00
Speedboat Static, Hubley, 10", no driver, G $800.00
Static Motor Boat, Hubley, 9½", w/driver, EX $4,800.00

CHARACTER

Amos 'N' Andy Fresh Air Taxi, Dent, 6", orange, MSW, 2 figures, EX $1,725.00
Andy Gump Car, Arcade, 7", EX $825.00
Buster Brown & Tige Cart, 7", Buster standing in 2-wheeled cart pulled by Tige, VG $350.00
Buster Brown & Tige on 4-Wheeled Base, 7", EX $1,080.00
Chester Gump Horse Cart, Arcade, 7", Chester standing in 2-wheeled basket cart, 1 horse, EX $400.00
Gloomy Gus in Mule Cart, Harris, 7", bed with slant front, 2 MSW, standing figure, G $225.00
Gloomy Gus in Mule Stake Wagon w/Driver, Harris, 13", 2 sm & 2 lg, MSW, G+ $400.00
Happy Hooligan Car, Kenton, 6", open w/smoke stack on rear, MSW, VG $850.00
Happy Hooligan Driving Soap Box Auto, NN Hill, 6", EX.$950.00
Happy Hooligan Goat Cart, Kenton, 8", VG $200.00
Happy Hooligan Mule Cart, Kenton, 6", EX $500.00
Happy Hooligan Nodder in Donkey Cart, Kenton, 6", EX..$300.00
Happy Hooligan Police Patrol, Kenton, 19", 2 horses, Gloomy Gus driver, cop hitting Happy Hooligan, VG $1,600.00
Popeye Patrol Motorcycle, Hubley, 1938, 9", VG $4,025.00
Popeye Spinach Cycle, Hubley, 5½", VG $500.00
Santa Sleigh, Hubley, 15", 1 reindeer, EX $1,600.00
Santa Sleigh, Hubley, 16½", 2 reindeer, VG+ $1,600.00
The Nodders (Foxy Grandpa in Donkey Cart), Kenton, 6x6½", VG $450.00
Uncle Sam in Horse-Drawn Eagle Chariot, Hubley, 10", VG.$1,975.00
Yellow Kid Goat Cart, Kenton, 7½", 2 MSW, standing figure, G $225.00

CIRCUS

Clown in Horse Cart, 7", clown w/lg lollipop seated on 2-wheeled seat pulled by horse, VG $625.00
Clown in Horse-Drawn Chariot, Hubley, 10", lg standing clown figure, 3 horses, VG $575.00
Clown in Pig Cart, Gong Bell, 6", EX $200.00
Elephant Cart, 9", elephant w/circus blanket pulling driver in 2-wheeled shell-shaped seat, VG $625.00
Overland Circus Band Wagon, Kenton, 16", 2 horses, 6 musicians & driver, EX+ $500.00
Overland Circus Band Wagon, Kenton, 16", 2 horses, 6 musicians & driver, later version w/WRT on spoke wheels, EX+. $650.00
Overland Circus Cage Wagon, Kenton, 15", 1 wht bear, 2 horses w/riders, driver, EX+ $275.00
Royal Circus Band Wagon, Hubley, 22½", 4 horses, 6 musicians & driver, EX $2,830.00
Royal Circus Cage Wagon, Hubley, 15", 1 lion, 2 horses, no driver, EX $1,375.00
Royal Circus Cage Wagon, Hubley, 15", 1 wht bear, 2 horses, driver, VG $650.00
Royal Circus Cage Wagon, Hubley, 15", 2 brn bears, 2 horses, driver, EX+ $1,500.00
Royal Circus Cage Wagon, Hubley, 15", 2 elephants, 2 horses, driver, NM $4,500.00
Royal Circus Cage Wagon, Hubley, 15", 2 elephants, 2 horses, driver, VG $925.00
Royal Circus Cage Wagon, Hubley, 15", 2 lions, 2 horses, driver, NM $3,500.00

Cast Iron, Circus
Band Wagon, Hubley, 30", EX+, $20,700.00.
(Photo courtesy James D. Julia, Inc.)

Cast Iron, Circus
Royal Circus Giraffe Wagon, Hubley, 23", large and small giraffes, four horses, EX, $10,450.00.
(Photo courtesy Morphy Auctions on LiveAuctioneers.com)

Royal Circus Cage Wagon, Hubley, 15", 2 lions, 2 horses, driver, VG... $850.00

Royal Circus Cage Wagon, Hubley, 15", 2 rhinos, 2 horses, driver, EX.. $1,800.00

Royal Circus Cage Wagon, Hubley, 15", 2 wht bears, 2 horses, driver, ladder, NM+.............................. $3,500.00

Royal Circus Cage Wagon, Hubley, 15", 2 wht bears, 2 horses, driver, EX.. $1,300.00

Royal Circus Cage Wagon, Hubley, 24", 1 lion, 4 horses, driver, VG... $1,725.00

Royal Circus Calliope Wagon, Hubley, 16", 2 horses, driver, NM... $2,300.00

Royal Circus Calliope Wagon, Hubley, 24", 4 horses, driver, VG $1,725.00

Royal Circus Clown Wagon, Hubley, 16", clown on trapeze, 2 horses, driver, EX................................... $2,000.00

Royal Circus Clown Wagon, Hubley, 16", clown on trapeze, 2 horses, driver, VG.................................... $1,000.00

Royal Circus Giraffe Wagon, Hubley, 16", lg giraffes, 2 horses, driver, EX... $6,325.00

Royal Circus Monkey Wagon, Hubley, 13", monkey on trapeze, 2 horses, driver, EX..................................... $1,950.00

Royal Circus Rhino Wagon (Farmers Head), Hubley, 16", 2 horses, lg head rises & revolves as wagon moves, EX.............. $4,725.00

CONSTRUCTION

Bates 40 Bulldozer, Vindex, 6", new NP driver, VG $3,150.00

Buckeye Ditcher, Kenton, 9", NM $1,200.00

Buckeye Ditcher, Kenton, 12", G................................... $575.00

Caterpillar Tractor, Arcade, 8", steel treads, NP driver, NMIB...$2,500.00

Cement Mixer, 1920s, rubber treads, EX...................... $3,500.00

Cement Mixer, 1940s, #832, VG+ $250.00

Cement Mixer, 1950s, makes motor sound, 10" L, EX+ . $100.00

Cement Truck, 1960s, 8-wheeled, 15", NM+................. $225.00

Construction Crane, 1950s, 20" H, VG......................... $125.00

Construction Derrick, 1950s, VG................................. $175.00

Contractors Dump Wagon, Kenton, 8", high bench seat, 3 dump buckets, NPDW, w/driver, VG+ $600.00

Dandy Digger, 1920s, #33, 28", EX............................... $150.00

Derrick, 1920s, 24", H, VG $500.00

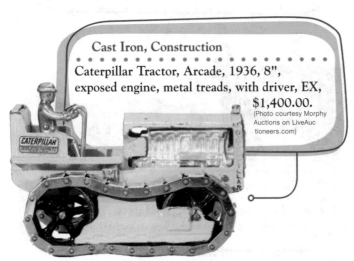

General Digger (Mack), Hubley, 10", swivels, cast driver & worker, EX+... $500.00

General Digger (Mack), Hubley, 10", swivels, cast driver & worker, VG... $375.00

Hoisting Tower, 1920s, #350, 38" H, VG+ $850.00

Huber Road Roller, Hubley, 8", no driver, VG............... $200.00

Huber Road Roller, Hubley, 15", removable standing driver, EX... $1,900.00

Jaeger Cement Mixer, Kenton, 7", MSW, NM $450.00

Jaeger Cement Mixer, Kenton, 7", NPDW, VG............. $150.00

Jaeger Cement Mixer, Kenton, 7", WRT, EX................. $250.00

Jaeger Cement Mixer, Kenton, 9", chain drive, WRT, EX .. $1,375.00

Mobile Power Digger, 1950s, 32", EX+ $175.00

Panama Digger, Hubley, 13", gr Mack cab w/red body, NP shovel, WRT, integral driver & 2 rear figures, EX................. $1,500.00

Pile Driver, 1920s, #260, 23" H, EX+.............................. $900.00

Road Grader, 1970s, yel, 7" L, EX+ $150.00

Sand Loader, 1920s, 18" H, EX+ $200.00

FARM TOYS

See also Horse-Drawn and Other Animals in this section.

Allis-Chalmers Tractor (WC), Arcade, 7", BRT, NP driver, VG... $275.00

Allis-Chalmers Tractor & Dump Trailer, Arcade, 8", WRT, integral driver, EX.. $150.00

Case L Tractor, Vindex, 7", NP driver, VG $1,000.00

Case 3-Bottom Plow, Vindex, 10", EX+ $2,500.00

Cultivision Tractor (A Model), Arcade, 7", BRT, NP driver,
VG $300.00

Farmall Tractor (M Model), Arcade, 7", BRT, NP driver, G...$300.00

Ford Tractor (9N Model), Arcade, 9", BRT, integral driver &
2-bottom plow, VG $850.00

Fordson Tractor, Arcade, 6", metal traction wheels, NP driver,
VG $100.00

Fordson Tractor & Wagon, Skogland & Olson, 14", NP driver,
simulated stake bed, G $1,500.00

Horse-Drawn Mower, Wilkins, 10½", 2-wheeled mower blade w/
high seat, 2 horses, w/driver, VG $1,800.00

Horse-Drawn Plow, Wilkins, 10", 1 horse, 2 MSW, w/driver,
VG $5,175.00

John Deere Combine, Vindex, 13½", figure on platform, EX ..$4,125.00

John Deere Thresher, Vindex, 15", NM $3,500.00

John Deere Tractor (A Model), Arcade, 8", BRT, NP driver &
steering wheels, EXIB.. $1,500.00

John Deere Tractor (D Model), Vindex, 7", VG+ $800.00

John Deere 3-Bottom Plow, Vindex, 9½", EX............. $1,500.00

McCormick-Deering Combine, Arcade, 12", MSW, NM....$650.00

McCormick-Deering Thresher, Arcade, 12", EX+ $800.00

McCormick-Deering Tractor (10-20 Model), Kilgore, 6", rear
metal traction wheels, NP driver, G $400.00

McCormick-Deering Tractor (10-20 Model) w/2-Bottom Plow,
Arcade, 14", VG... $300.00

Oliver Superior Spreader, Arcade, VG........................... $250.00

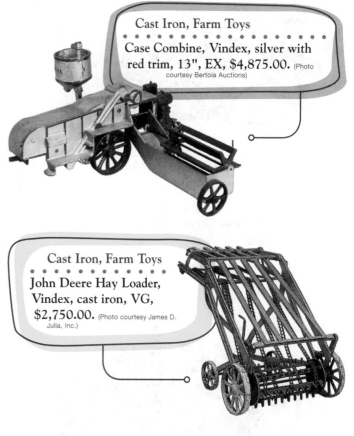

Cast Iron, Farm Toys
Case Combine, Vindex, silver with red trim, 13", EX, $4,875.00. (Photo courtesy Bertoia Auctions)

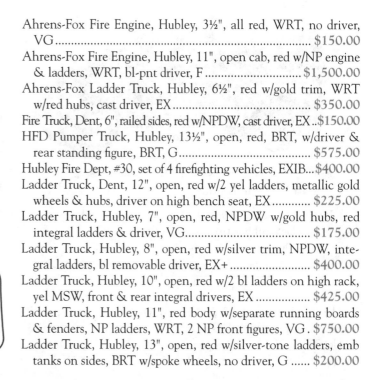

Cast Iron, Farm Toys
John Deere Hay Loader, Vindex, cast iron, VG, $2,750.00. (Photo courtesy James D. Julia, Inc.)

Oliver Tractor & Row Corn Picker, Arcade, 10" overall, BRT,
cast driver, VG $250.00

Oliver 70-Row Crop Tractor, Arcade, 7", BRT, NP driver,
VG... $715.00

FIREFIGHTING

See also Horse-drawn and Other Animals in this section.

Ahrens-Fox Fire Engine, Hubley, 3½", all red, WRT, no driver,
VG... $150.00

Ahrens-Fox Fire Engine, Hubley, 11", open cab, red w/NP engine
& ladders, WRT, bl-pnt driver, F $1,500.00

Ahrens-Fox Ladder Truck, Hubley, 6½", red w/gold trim, WRT
w/red hubs, cast driver, EX $350.00

Fire Truck, Dent, 6", railed sides, red w/NPDW, cast driver, EX ..$150.00

HFD Pumper Truck, Hubley, 13½", open, red, BRT, w/driver &
rear standing figure, BRT, G...................................... $575.00

Hubley Fire Dept, #30, set of 4 firefighting vehicles, EXIB...$400.00

Ladder Truck, Dent, 12", open, red w/2 yel ladders, metallic gold
wheels & hubs, driver on high bench seat, EX $225.00

Ladder Truck, Hubley, 7", open, red, NPDW w/gold hubs, red
integral ladders & driver, VG...................................... $175.00

Ladder Truck, Hubley, 8", open, red w/silver trim, NPDW, integral ladders, bl removable driver, EX+ $400.00

Ladder Truck, Hubley, 10", open, red w/2 bl ladders on high rack,
yel MSW, front & rear integral drivers, EX $425.00

Ladder Truck, Hubley, 11", red body w/separate running boards
& fenders, NP ladders, WRT, 2 NP front figures, VG . $750.00

Ladder Truck, Hubley, 13", open, red w/silver-tone ladders, emb
tanks on sides, BRT w/spoke wheels, no driver, G $200.00

Cast Iron, Farm Toys
Oliver 70-Row Crop Tractor, Arcade, 7", black rubber tires, nickel-plated driver, VG, $715.00.
(Photo courtesy Bertoia Auctions)

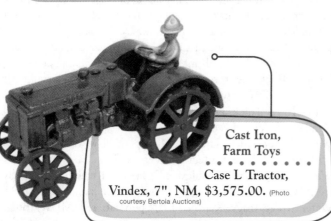

Cast Iron, Farm Toys
Case L Tractor, Vindex, 7", NM, $3,575.00. (Photo courtesy Bertoia Auctions)

Cast Iron, Firefighting
• •
Aherns-Fox Fire Truck, Hubley, 7", open, red, two cast ladders and driver, white rubber tires, M, $2,250.00. (Photo courtesy Morphy Auctions on LiveAuctioneers.com)

Cast Iron, Firefighting
• •
HFD Pumper Truck, Hubley, 13½", NM+, $7,840.00. (Photo courtesy Morphy Auctions on LiveAuctioneers.com)

Cast Iron, Firefighting
• •
Pumper Truck, Arcade, 13", open, red with silver trim, black rubber tires, six cast firemen, EX, $550.00. (Photo courtesy Morphy Auctions on LiveAuctioneers.com)

Ladder Truck, Hubley, 13", open, red w/yel hubs, gold trim, PS ladders, bl-pnt driver, VG+ $450.00

Ladder Truck, Hubley, 15", open frame w/eagles, red, gold trim, yel support, 2 wooden ladders & MSW, integral driver, VG ..$450.00

Ladder Truck, Hubley, 16", open, red w/silver-tone trim, NP ladders & driver, BRT w/NP spokes, EX+ $2,000.00

Ladder Truck, Hubley, 16", open, red w/yel MSW, red wooden ladders, integral front & rear drivers, VG+ $850.00

Ladder Truck, Hubley, 16", open frame, bl w/gold trim, yel wooden ladders, wht-pnt MDW, red hubs, pnt driver, EX+ $550.00

Ladder Truck, Hubley, 20", open, red w/yel hubs, PS ladders, MDW, front & rear drivers, VG+ $1,000.00

Ladder Truck, Hubley, 28", transitional, open 2-wheeled tractor w/driver pulling ladder frame w/driver, wht & red, NM $5,400.00

Ladder Truck, Kenton, 11", open, red w/yel wooden ladders, yel MSW, bl front & rear drivers, EX $1,600.00

Ladder Truck, Kenton, 13", open, red w/yel metal ladders, WRT, bl driver, VG $450.00

Mack Ladder Truck, Arcade, 14", open, red w/yel ladders, WRT w/red hubs, NP driver, VG $500.00

Mack Ladder Truck, Arcade, 18", open, red w/yel ladders, MDW w/red hubs, NP driver, EX $625.00

Patrol Truck, Hubley, 15", bl w/gold rails & trim, bl driver & 6 red firemen seated in back, gray & red MSW, VG+ $325.00

Pumper Car, Hubley, 8½", open, red & silver take-apart body, NP grille, WRT, red hubs, 2 NP figures in front seat, EX .. $150.00

Pumper Truck, Arcade, 13", open later model, red w/silver trim, BRT, gold hubs, 2 firemen in front/2 side/2 rear, EX ... $600.00

Pumper Truck, Arcade, 13", open later model, red w/silver trim, BRT, gold hubs, 2 firemen in front/2 side/2 rear, VG .. $300.00

Pumper Truck, Dent, 10½", open, red w/gold & wht trim, wht-pnt MDW w/yel hubs, driver & rear standing figure, EX...$350.00

Pumper Truck, Hubley, 10", open, red w/gold trim, wht-pnt MDW w/yel hubs, red-pnt cast driver w/bl hat, EX..... $175.00

Pumper Truck, Hubley, 11", open, red w/silver trim, BRT w/spoke wheels, bl-pnt driver, VG... $150.00

Pumper Truck, Hubley, 11", open, red w/yel hubs, brass-colored boiler top, MDW, NP driver, VG+ $350.00

Pumper Truck, Hubley, 11", open, yel w/gold trim, red MSW & integral driver, bell on hood, EX................................... $475.00

Pumper Truck, Hubley, 11", open frame, yel w/blk, red & gold trim, yel & red integral driver, grau & red MDW, G rpnt..........$100.00

Pumper Truck, Hubley, 11", open w/open vents on sides of hood, yel w/red & brass trim, MSW, cast driver, EX.............. $700.00

Pumper Truck, Kenton, 10", open, red w/gold trim, red MSW w/ red spokes, integral driver, EX................................... $450.00

Pumper Truck, Kenton, 10", open, red w/yel hubs, brass boiler top, MDW, integral driver, EX $450.00

Pumper Truck, Kenton, 14", open, red w/silver & gold trim, BRT w/red spoke wheels, bl-pnt driver, VG......................... $175.00

Pumper Truck, Kenton, 14", open, red w/wht boiler, gold trim, wht-pnt MDW w/yel hubs, w/driver, EX $400.00

Water Tower Truck, Dent, 15", open, red w/bl tower, NPDW, red hubs, side lever, EX+ $1,375.00

Water Tower Truck, Hubley, 14", open, bl w/wht tower & red MSW, front & rear integral drivers, VG+ $800.00

Water Tower Truck, Hubley, 22", open, bl w/wht tower & yel MSW, front & rear integral drivers, EX..................... $1,600.00

Water Tower Truck, Kenton, 19", open cab, red, MDW, integral driver, old rpnt... $600.00

HORSE-DRAWN AND OTHER ANIMALS

Adams Express Wagon, Ives, 18", 1 horse, w/driver, VG+ .$1,900.00
Boys Express Co Wagon, Pratt & Letchworth, 17", 2 high-stepping
  horses, low sides, driver on high bench seat, EX $2,000.00
Brake (2-Seat), Hubley, 17", 2 horses, 4 figures, EX.....$7,475.00
Brake (2-Seat), Hubley, 17", 2 horses, 4 figures, VG ...$3,500.00
Brake (3-Seat), Hubley, 20", 2 horses, 6 figures, NM..$9,500.00
Brake (3-Seat), Hubley, 20", 2 horses, 6 figures, VG ...$3,500.00
Brake (4-Seat), Hubley, 28", 4 horse, 8 figures, EX....$10,350.00
Broadway Car Line Trolley, Wilkins, 17", 1 horse, EX.$2,150.00
Broadway Car Line Trolley, Wilkins, 17", 1 horse, VG.$1,900.00
Buckboard, Harris, 13½", 2 horses, w/driver, VG.........$1,500.00
Buckboard, Hubley, 13½" $1,495.00
Bulldog Cart, 7", Egyptian driver, VG............................$750.00
Caisson, Ives, 22", 2 horses w/riders, driver seated on aluminum
  box w/2 MSW, 2-wheeled cannon, EX $2,250.00
Chariot, see also Circus sub-category in this section
Chariot, Hubley, 10", 3 horses, standing figure, VG $475.00
Chief Cart (Fire), Hubley, 11½", 1 horse, w/driver, VG .$150.00
City Delivery Wagon, Harris, 15", 2 horses, w/driver, VG..$1,300.00
Coal & Wood Wagon, Harris, 12", 1 horse, w/driver on high
  bench seat, VG...$400.00
Coal Cart, Ives, 13", 1 mule, tilting body w/slanted sides, blk
  driver, rpnt..$300.00
Coal Cart, Walker, 12", 1 horse, 2 MSW, no driver, VG .$550.00
Coal Wagon, Hubley, 16", 2 horses, w/driver, VG+........$900.00
Consolidated Street RR Streetcar, Wilkins, 14½", 1 horse,
  VG+ $850.00
Contractors Dump Wagon, Arcade, 14", 2 horses, no driver, G..$175.00
Covered Wagon, Kenton, 14", 2 horses, Conestoga-type cover,
  w/driver, VG+ $175.00
Doctor's Buckboard, Hubley, 14", 2 horses, pnt driver, some
  rpnt $300.00
Doctor's Cart, Wilkins, 10", 1 horse, 2 MSW, driver, EX. $500.00
Dog Cart, Pratt & Letchworth, 13", 1 horse, 2 MSW, driver,
  EX+ $2,750.00
Dog-Drawn Cart, Harris, 10½", 2 MSW, driver, VG $475.00
Dray Wagon, Dent, 16", low curved stake bed w/high seat, 1
  horse, w/driver, G $450.00
Dray Wagon, Hubley, 16", 2 horses, stake sides, EX........$300.00
Dray Wagon, Hubley, 23", 2 horses, emb 'Dray' on sides, blk
  driver, EX..$1,600.00
Dray Wagon, Pratt & Letchworth, 11", 1 horse, 2-wheeled,
  standing driver, EX...$275.00
Dray Wagon, Pratt & Letchworth, 14", 1 horse, stake sides,
  driver on high bench seat, EX....................................$650.00
Dray Wagon, Pratt & Letchworth, 17", 2 horses, no sides, driver
  on very high bench seat, VG+....................................$800.00
Dray Wagon, Wilkins, 16½", 2 horses, roof over driver's seat, top
  over bed, EX $850.00
Dray Wagon, Wilkins, 21", 2 horses, w/driver, VG+ $350.00
Dump Cart, Wilkins, 13", 1 horse, w/driver, EX $2,750.00
Express 106 Wagon, Ideal (?), 18", 2 horses, w/driver, VG..$450.00
Farm Wagon, Kenton, 14", box type w/high bench seat, 2 horses,
  blk driver w/'straw' hat, EX+....................................$1,150.00
Fire Chemical Wagon, Wilkins, 19½", 1 cast ladder, 2 horses,
  front/rear firemen, EX...$7,475.00

Cast Iron, Horse-Drawn and Other Animals
• • • • • • • • • • • • • • • • • • • •
Barouche, Pratt and Letchworth, 18", VG,
$3,250.00. (Photo courtesy James D. Julia, Inc.)

Cast Iron, Horse-Drawn and Other Animals
• • • • • • • • • • • • • • • • • • • •
Fire Patrol Wagon, Hubley, 15½", two horses,
with driver and three firemen, NM, $4,200.00.
(Photo courtesy Morphy Auctions on LiveAuctioneers.com)

Cast Iron, Horse-Drawn and Other
Animals
• • • • • • • • • • • • • • • • • • • •
Fire Pumper Wagon, Kenton, 26½", two
horses, with driver, EX, $3,740.00. (Photo cour-
tesy James D. Julia, Inc.)

Fire Chief Cart (623), 10", 1 horse, red w/yel wheels, red-pnt
  driver, EX..$750.00
Fire Chief Wagon (FD), Wilkins, 14", 1 horse, w/driver,
  G+ $1,050.00
Fire Chief Wagon (FD), Wilkins, 14", 1 horse, w/driver, EX..$4,025.00
Fire Hose Reel Cart, Dent, 20", 2 horses, w/driver, VG..$450.00
Fire Hose Reel Cart, Hubley, 12", 1 horse, blk & red, w/driver,
  EX $400.00
Fire Hose Reel Cart, Ives, 17", 2 horses, w/driver, EX..$1,250.00

Fire Hose Reel Cart, Wilkins, 10", 1 horse, red w/2 yel MSW, w/driver, EX.. $650.00

Fire Hose Reel Wagon, Hubley, 20", 2 horses, lg reel on open frame, driver on high bench seat, VG...................... $1,600.00

Fire Ladder Wagon, Carpenter, 24", 2 horses, red w/4 red CI ladders, front & rear drivers, VG $750.00

Fire Ladder Wagon, Dent, 30", 3 horses, wht w/yel wooden ladders, yel MSW, pnt driver, VG.................................... $300.00

Fire Ladder Wagon, Hubley, 21", 2 horses, red w/natural wood ladders, yel MSW, w/driver, G $150.00

Fire Ladder Wagon, Hubley, 27", 2 horses, open frame, 1 yel wooden ladder, G $175.00

Fire Ladder Wagon, Hubley, 33", 2 horses, open frame w/3 ladders on rack, 2 sides ladders, front & rear drivers, NM+ $3,080.00

Fire Ladder Wagon, Ives, 26", 2 horses, front & rear drivers, VG $575.00

Fire Ladder Wagon, Jones & Bixler, 29½", red & yel wooden ladders, 2 horses, front/rear drivers, EX $1,035.00

Fire Ladder Wagon, Pratt & Letchworth, 23½", red wooden ladders, 2 horses, front/rear drivers, EX $2,585.00

Fire Ladder Wagon, Pratt & Letchworth, 29½", yel wooden ladders, 3 horses, front/rear drivers, EX+ $3,735.00

Fire Patrol Wagon, Dent, 16", 3 horses, 5 firemen, EX ... $650.00

Fire Patrol Wagon, Hubley, 13", 3 horses, w/driver & 3 firemen, G.. $325.00

Fire Pumper Wagon, Dent, 21", 3 horses, wht w/gold trim, red MSW, w/driver, EX.. $425.00

Fire Pumper Wagon, Hubley, 10", 2 horses, red w/silver boiler, cast driver, VG $650.00

Fire Pumper Wagon, Hubley, 21", 3 horses, w/driver & rear fireman, VG.. $500.00

Fire Pumper Wagon, Ideal, 22", 3 horses, w/driver & rear fireman, VG...$2,760.00

Fire Pumper Wagon, Ives, 19", 2 horses, no driver, VG.. $675.00

Fire Pumper Wagon, Kenton, 15", 3 horses, w/driver, G.. $315.00

Fire Pumper Wagon, Wilkins, 18", high bench seat, 2 horses, w/driver & rear fireman, G.................................... $1,265.00

Fire Pumper Wagon, Wilkins, 19", lower bench seat, 2 horses, w/driver, G $1,725.00

Fire Water Tower Wagon, Dent, 29", 3 horses, w/driver, prof rstr... $300.00

Fire Water Tower Wagon, Wilkins, 44", 3 horses, w/driver, EX+ $8,500.00

Fire Water Tower Wagon, Wilkins, 44", 3 horses, w/driver, VG... $3,500.00

Gig, Hubley, 11½", 1 horse, 2 MSW, lady driver, G........ $225.00

Gig, Ideal, 9½", 3-sided (slat sides) w/2 spoke wheels, 1 high-stepping horse, w/driver, VG................................... $375.00

Goat Cart, Harris, 13", 2 wht goats, 4 MSW, lady driver, EX. $2,070.00

Hansom Cab, Kenton, 16", 1 horse, w/front driver & lady passenger, EX $200.00

Hansom Cab, Pratt & Letchworth, 11", 1 horse, rear driver, EX+ $1,400.00

Hansom Cab, Pratt & Letchworth, 11", 1 horse, rear driver, G $500.00

Hay Rake, Wilkins, 9", 1 horse, w/driver, G.................. $200.00

Hay Wagon, Hubley, 14", 2 oxen, standing blk driver, EX...$650.00

Horse Cart, Carpenter, 12", horse in galloping motion, 2 standing figures in top hats, VG+ $350.00

Horse Cart, Wilkins, 9½", 1 horse, lady driver, EX $375.00

Ice Wagon, Hubley, 14", 1 horse, w/driver, VG $150.00

Ice Wagon, Hubley, 14", 2 horses, w/driver, NM $600.00

Ice Wagon, Hubley, 14", 2 horses, w/driver, VG $175.00

Landau Coach, Hubley, 15½", 1 horse, w/driver, VG $275.00

Landau Coach, Wilkins, 15", 2 horses, w/2 drivers, VG+ ...$600.00

Log Wagon, Hubley, 15", 2 oxen, blk figure seated sideways on lg log, EX $700.00

Log Wagon, Hubley, 15", 2 oxen, blk figure seated sideways on lg log, VG $550.00

Milk Wagon, Kenton, 13", 1 horse, driver, unused, MIB. $350.00

Milk Wagon, Kenton, 13", 1 horse, driver, VG.............. $100.00

Mower, Wilkins, 10", 2 horses, driver on 2-wheeled seat, w/fold-down mower blade, VG $1,100.00

Mule Cart, J&ES, 9", blk man w/whip, NM $2,875.00

Ox Cart, Carpenter (?), 11", 2-wheeled box cart, yoke of oxen, mk Pat April 24 1883 on bottom of cart, VG.............. $285.00

Ox Cart, 11", blk figure standing in stake cart w/2 MSW, 1 ox, VG $150.00

Patrol Wagon (Fire), Dent, 20", 2 horses, w/driver & 3 firemen, VG $350.00

Patrol Wagon (Police), Dent, 20", 2 horse, w/driver & 4 patrolmen, VG $350.00

Cast Iron, Horse-Drawn and Other Animals
Tally-Ho Coach, Carpenter, 28", G, $31,625.00.
(Photo courtesy James D. Julia, Inc.)

Cast Iron, Horse-Drawn and Other Animals
Street Sweeper, Wilkins, 12½", VG+, $17,250.00.
(Photo courtesy James D. Julia, Inc.)

Phaeton, Hubley, 17", 1 horse, lady driver, EX $1,350.00
Pony Cart, Wilkins, 7½", 1 horse, w/driver, EX+ $750.00
Pony Cart, Wilkins, 9½", 1 horse, w/driver, EX $950.00
Pony Cart, Wilkins, 10½", female driver $920.00
Pony Cart, Wilkins, #140, box only, wooden w/stamped image & lettering, 11" L, EX $675.00
Sand & Gravel Wagon, Kenton, 15", 2 horses, w/driver, G .. $230.00
Sleigh, see also Santa Sleigh in Character sub-category in this section
Sleigh, Dent, 15½", 1 horse, w/driver in top hat, EX ... $1,200.00
Sleigh, Hubley, 14½", ornate swan-like form, 1 horse, lady driver, EX $1,265.00
Stake Wagon, Kenton, 13", 2 horses, no driver, rstr $285.00
Stanhope Gig, Kenton, 10½", 1 horse, w/driver, VG $400.00
Sulky, 8", 2 MSW, 1 horse, w/driver, EX $250.00
Surrey (2-Seat), Pratt & Letchworth, 14½", 1 horse, w/driver in top hat, EX $800.00
Tally-Ho Coach, Carpenter, 28", 4 galloping horses, 7 figures, NM $90,000.00
Tedder, Wilkins, 9", w/driver, very scarce, VG $6,325.00
Tom Mix Circus Wild West Wagon, Arcade, 14", wood wagon, EX $1,870.00
Transfer Wagon, Dent, 17", 2 horses, w/driver, EX $375.00
Victoria Phaeton, Dent, 16", 1 horse, driver on high seat, lady passenger, EX $1,800.00

Motor Vehicles

Note: Description lines for generic vehicles may simply begin with 'Bus,' 'Coupe,' or 'Motorcycle,' for example. But more buses will be listed as 'Coach Bus,' 'Coast to Coast Bus,' 'Greyhound,' 'Interurban,' 'Mack,' or 'Public Service' (and there are other instances); coupes may be listed under 'Ford,' 'Packard,' or some other specific car company; and lines describing motorcycles might also start 'Armored,' 'Excelsior-Henderson,' 'Delivery,' 'Policeman,' 'Harley-Davidson,' and so on. Look under 'Yellow Cab' or 'Checker Cab' and other cab companies for additional 'Taxi Cab' descriptions. We have given any lettering or logo on the vehicle priority when entering descriptions, so with this in mind, you should have a good idea where to look for your particular toy. Body styles (Double-Decker Bus, etc.) have also been given priority.

ACF Bus, Arcade, 11½", MDW, no driver, NM $5,000.00
ACF Bus, Arcade, 11½", WRT, no driver, EX $3,000.00
ACF Bus, Arcade, 11½", WRT, no driver, F $800.00
Ambulance, Arcade, 6", wht w/red cross on door, back lattice windows, EX $400.00
Ambulance, Kenton, 10", MSW, driver, VG $1,100.00
American Oil Co Tank Truck, see Mack American Oil Co Tank Truck
Anchor Truck Co Ford Model T Stake Truck, North & Judd, 9", blk & red, MSW, w/driver, VG $550.00
Arctic Ice Cream Delivery Truck, Kilgore, 8", MDW, no driver, EX $800.00
Arctic Ice Cream Delivery Truck, Kilgore, 8", MDW, no driver, G $300.00
Auto Carrier, Arcade, 24", Ford Model A cab, 4 Model A cars on flatbed trailer, NPSW, VG $1,950.00

Auto Carrier, Hubley, 10", red cab pulling lt bl trailer w/3 lt bl Buick coupes, NPDW, no driver, EX $1,400.00
Auto Carrier, Hubley, 12", w/2 open roadsters, WRT, VG ... $600.00
Auto Express 546 Truck, Kenton, 7", open bench seat, MSW, VG $350.00
Aviation Gas Tank Truck, Kilgore, 12", EX $1,950.00
Bell Telephone Truck, Hubley, 4", WRT, EX $350.00
Bell Telephone Truck, Hubley, 5", WRT, VG $275.00
Bell Telephone Truck, Hubley, 8", NPSW, w/accessories, VG ... $500.00
Bell Telephone Truck, Hubley, 9", NPSW, w/accessories, NM $900.00
Bell Telephone Truck, Hubley, 9", WRT, water tank, w/accessories, EX+ $1,090.00
Bell Telephone Truck, Hubley, 10", MSW, no accessories, G .. $350.00
Bell Telephone Truck, Hubley, 10", WRT, w/accessories, EX.. $800.00
Bell Telephone Truck, Hubley, 10", WRT, w/accessories, NM $1,600.00
Borden's Milk Bottle Truck, Arcade, 6", WRT, G+ $1,100.00
Borden's Milk Truck, Hubley, 6", wht, WRT, pnt grille, VG.. $1,100.00
Breyers Ice Cream Truck, Dent, 8½", orange w/blk top, silver & gold trim, MDW w/red hubs, cast driver, EX $3,500.00
Brinks Express Co (Van) Truck, Arcade, 12", WRT, no driver, extremely rare, EX $34,500.00
Buick Coupe, Arcade, 9", rear spare, WRT w/blk spokes, NP driver, NM $2,500.00
Buick Sedan, Arcade, 9", rear spare, WRT w/blk spokes, NP driver, EX $1,800.00
Bus, Hubley, 8", Deco style short rnd nose, WRT, silver w/red fenders, rear fin & hubs, EX+ $450.00
Bus, Kenton, 10½", orange coach type, wht-pnt MDW w/orange hubs, w/driver, VG $345.00
Bus Line Bus, Dent, 8½", orange w/blk trim, NPDW, no driver, second casting from orig molds, EX $225.00
Bus, Skoglund & Olson, 10½", long nose, open windows, WRT, driver, VG $500.00
Century of Progress, see Greyhound Lines
Champion Gas & Motor Oil Tanker Truck, 8", NPDW, no driver, VG $250.00
Champion Panel Truck, 8", red, WRT w/bl hubs, VG.... $400.00
Champion Police Motorcycle, 7", NPSW, cast driver, NM .. $950.00
Champion Police Motorcycle, 7", WRT, cast driver, EX . $250.00
Champion Police Motorcycle w/sidecar, 6", WRT, w/driver & passenger, VG $350.00
Champion Police Motorcycle w/sidecar, 9", WRT, integral driver & passenger, VG $325.00

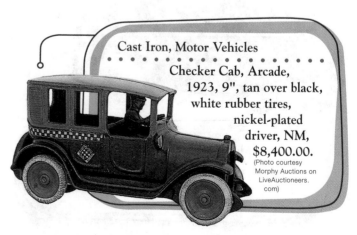

Cast Iron, Motor Vehicles
• • • • • • • • • • • • • • • • •
Checker Cab, Arcade, 1923, 9", tan over black, white rubber tires, nickel-plated driver, NM, $8,400.00.
(Photo courtesy Morphy Auctions on LiveAuctioneers.com)

Checker Cab, Arcade, 8", gr & blk w/blk & wht checked band, wht-pnt MDW w/gr hubs, w/driver, VG $425.00

Checker Cab, Arcade, 9", no visor, deep yel w/blk roof & stripes, WRT & rear spare w/blk hubs, NP driver, NM $2,530.00

Chevy Coupe, Arcade, 8", 1920s model, NPDW, EX $900.00

Chevy Sedan, Arcade, 8", blk w/silver grille & gold headlights, NPDW, EX $2,500.00

Chicago Motor Coach, Arcade, 13", stenciled lettering, no driver or passengers, F $800.00

Chrysler Airflow, Arcade, 4", NP grille, WRT, 'Sundial Shoes' decal, NM $1,350.00

Chrysler Airflow, Hubley, 4½", take-apart body, EX $300.00

Chrysler Airflow, Hubley, 6", take-apart body, NP trim, WRT & rear space, G+ $200.00

Chrysler Airflow, Hubley, 7", take-apart body, EX $650.00

Chrysler Airflow, Hubley, 8", take-apart body, electric lights, WRT, NP trim, VG $425.00

Chrysler Airflow, Hubley, 8", electric lights, WRT, EX . $1,500.00

Coal Truck, see also Mack Coal Truck

Coal Truck, Kenton, 6½", open cab, low slanted back, NPDW, driver, G $500.00

Coast to Coast Bus, Dent, 15", high roof, MDW, no driver, NM $1,300.00

Coast to Coast Bus, Hubley, 7", MDW, integral driver, older rstr $100.00

Coast to Coast Bus, Hubley, 13", NM+ $3,900.00

Coast to Coast Bus, Hubley, 13", VG $1,550.00

Coast to Coast Stake Truck, AC Williams, 7", 6-wheeled, MSW, EX+ $950.00

Contractors Dump Truck, Kenton, 8", open seat, 3 dump compartments, MDW, w/driver, EX................................. $300.00

Coupe, Champion, 7½", red, MSW, no driver, VG $250.00

Coupe, Dent, 6", take-apart body, NP grille, WRT, VG+ ..$1,840.00

Coupe, Freidag, 6", 1924 model, MSW, integral driver, VG+..$275.00

Coupe, Hubley, 9", 1920s model, red w/gold trim, MDW w/bl hubs, NP driver, EX... $1,100.00

Coupe, Kenton, 10", 1928 model w/visor, NP bumper, MSW w/ rear spare, overpnt.. $1,800.00

Coupe, Kilgore, 6", w/visor, NPSW, w/bobbing head driver & passenger, NM $1,100.00

Crash Car, Hubley, 5", WRT, integral driver, EX............ $275.00

Crash Car, Hubley, 6½", NPSW, integral driver, EX+ $400.00

Crash Car, Hubley, 11", 'Indian' decal on tank, BRT w/spokes, removable driver, EX+ $4,250.00

Delivery Truck, Hubley, 10", sq cab w/flat roof, open bed, red w/ yel MSW, driver, EX... $600.00

DeSoto Sedan, Hubley, 4", 1934 model, electric lights, NM . $6,500.00

Dodge Coupe, Arcade, 1926 model, rear spare, some rpnt...$350.00

Double-Decker Bus, see also Chicago Motor Coach

Double-Decker Bus, Arcade, 8", long nose, WRT, no driver or passengers, EX $450.00

Double-Decker Bus, Arcade, 8", snub-nosed, BRT, cast driver, 2 passengers, VG $225.00

Double-Decker Bus, Hubley, 12", gr & red w/gold trim, WRT w/ red hubs, VG $450.00

Double-Decker Bus, Kenton, 8", dk gr w/yel disk wheels, driver & 4 passengers, NM $1,100.00

Double-Decker Bus, Kenton, 10", WRT, no driver or passengers, VG $500.00

Double-Decker Bus, Kenton, 11½", MDW, driver & 7 passengers, EX $650.00

Dump Truck, Kilgore, 8½", bl w/orange dump bed, NPDW, no driver, EX $400.00

Dump Truck, Skoglund & Olsen, 10", flat top cab w/visor, low bed, removable tailgate, MDW, no driver, rpnt........... $400.00

Elgin Street Sweeper, Hubley, 9", pnt driver, NM $6,000.00

Fageol Safety Bus, Arcade, 12", MDW, EX $500.00

Five (5) Ton (Stake) Truck, Hubley, 16", w/driver, G $230.00

Ford Dump Truck, Arcade, 7½", 1929 model, NPSW, EX+ $525.00

Ford Model A Coupe, Arcade, 6½", tin opening rumble seat, yel w/NP grille, WRT w/red hubs, EX $1,000.00

Ford Model A Sedan, Arcade, 7", MSW, no driver, VG+ ..$250.00

Ford Model A Stake Truck, AC Williams, 7", VG+....... $300.00

Ford Model A Tractor & Dump Trailer, Arcade, 13½", gr & red, NPSW, EX... $2,000.00

Ford Model A Wrecker, Arcade, 8", MSW, VG $200.00

Ford Model A Wrecker, Arcade, 11", NPSW, NP driver, EX $500.00

Ford Model A Wrecker, Arcade, 11", NPSW, NP driver, G ...$100.00

Ford Model T Coupe, Arcade, 7", NP driver, EX............ $350.00

Ford Model T Coupe, Arcade, 7", no driver, VG+ $250.00

Ford Model T Sedan, Arcade, 7", 'cloth' top up, no driver, EX..$450.00

Cast Iron, Motor Vehicles
Crash Car, Hubley, 9½", 'Indian' embossed on gas tank, EX, $2,000.00 to $2,500.00. (Photo courtesy Bertoia Auctions)

Cast Iron, Motor Vehicles
Diamond T Gas Truck, Hubley, 7", silver with red detail, white rubber tires, NM+, $880.00.
(Photo courtesy Morphy Auctions on LiveAuctioneers.com)

Ford Model T Stake Truck, Aracde, 7½", NPSW, EX..... $350.00

Ford Sedan, Arcade, 6½", 1934 model, NP grille, WRT, no driver, VG.. $490.00

Ford Sedan w/Trailer, Arcade, 5½" car w/6" trailer, 1937 model, rstr.. $950.00

Freeman's Dairy Truck, Dent, 5½", WRT, w/driver, EX..$1,725.00

Gasoline Tank Truck, AC Williams, 6½", red, WRT w/red wooden hubs, EX... $300.00

Greyhound Bus, Arcade #4400, 9", VGIB $575.00

Greyhound Bus, Arcade, 9", bl & wht w/NP front, WRT, VG.$275.00

Greyhound Lines Bus, Arcade, nickel grill front panel, bl & wht, decals on sides, wht rubber tires, 9" $275.00

Greyhound Lines Century of Progress Chicago 1933 GMC Tandem Bus, Arcade, 7½", WRT, VG................................ $175.00

Greyhound Lines Century of Progress Chicago 1933 GMC Tandem Bus, Arcade, 10½", WRT, G $125.00

Greyhound Lines Century of Progress Chicago 1933 GMC Tandem Bus, Arcade, 11½", EX $125.00

Greyhound Lines Century of Progress Chicago 1933 GMC Tandem Bus, Arcade, 14½", WRT, EX.............................. $400.00

Greyhound Lines Coast to Coast Bus, 7½", BRT, lt bl w/wht stripe & greyhound on sides, EX $300.00

Greyhound Lines GMC Bus, Arcade, 7½", curved top, WRT, NM $725.00

Greyhound Lines GMC Tandem Bus, Arcade, 7", WRT, NM $350.00

Greyhound Lines Great Lakes Exposition 1935 Tandem Bus, Arcade, 11", WRT, G $200.00

Greyhound Lines New York World's Fair Bus, Arcade, 8", EX....$300.00

Greyhound Lines New York World's Fair Bus, Arcade, 11", flat roof, 3 open doors ea side, NP trim, VG...................... $275.00

Greyhound New York World's Fair Tractor Train, Arcade, 7", EX+IB... $425.00

Harley-Davidson Civilian Motorcycle, Hubley, 6", WRT, integral driver, EX... $525.00

Harley-Davidson Civilian Motorcycle w/sidecar, Hubley, 6", MSW, integral, driver, no passenger, NM................. $2,000.00

Harley-Davidson Police Motorcycle, Hubley, 7", WRT, spoke wheels, integral driver w/swivel head, EX.................... $750.00

Harley-Davidson Police Motorcycle, Hubley, 7", WRT, spoke wheels, integral driver w/swivel head, VG.................. $400.00

Harley-Davidson Police Motorcycle, Hubley, 9", BRT w/spoke wheels, driver, VG.................................... $725.00

Harley-Davidson Police Motorcycle w/Sidecar, Hubley, 5", NPSW, integral driver w/removable passenger, NM ... $750.00

Harley-Davidson Police Motorcycle w/Sidecar, Hubley, 9", BRT w/spoke wheels, removable driver & passenger, NM.$1,500.00

Hathaway's Bread Truck, Arcade, 9", WRT, G $575.00

Hill Climber Motorcycle, Hubley, 6½", WRT, civilian driver, G $250.00

Huckster, AC Williams, 7", take-apart body, red & blk, WRT, G $375.00

Ice Truck, see also Mack Ice Truck

Ice Truck, Arcade, 1941, 7", EX................................ $400.00

Ice Truck, Kenton, 7½", open seat w/open railed bed, wht, MDW, red hubs, right-sided driver, EX...................... $300.00

Indian Civilian Motorcycle, Hubley, 9", BRT, removable driver, EX $800.00

Indian Motorcycle, Hubley, 9", BRT, no driver, EX........ $525.00

Indian Police Motorcycle, Globe, 9", 2-cylinder, BRT, spoke wheels, driver, G... $450.00

Indian Police Motorcycle w/Sidecar, Hubley, 9", BRT w/spoke wheels, no driver or passenger, EX............................. $650.00

Indian Police Motorcycle, Hubley, 9", BRT, spoke wheels, removable driver, rare lime gr color, NM......................... $2,500.00

Indian Police Motorcycle, Hubley, 9", BRT, spoke wheels, removable driver, some rpnt.................................... $925.00

Indian Police Motorcycle w/sidecar, Hubley, 8½", red, BRT w/ spoke wheels, w/driver & passenger, VG+.................. $500.00

Indian Police Motorcycle w/Sidecar, Hubley, 9", BRT w/spoke wheels, removable driver & passenger, EX $1,100.00

Indian Traffic Car, see Traffic Car

Indian US Air Mail Motorcycle, Hubley, 9", BRT w/spoke wheels, removable driver, EX.................................... $1,400.00

Interchangeable Set, AC Williams, 4½", #611R, 1 chassis w/4 interchangeable bodies, EXIB.................................... $400.00

International COE Stake Truck, Arcade, 9", yel w/NP grille, no driver, VG... $345.00

International Delivery Van, Arcade, 9½", 1932 model, 2-tone bl w/yel side stripe & hubs, WRT, w/driver, VG+ $475.00

International Dump Truck, Arcade, 11", gr w/red chassis & spokes, WRT w/rear duals, EX $950.00

International Panel Delivery Truck, Arcade, 9", 2-tone bl w/yel stripe & hubs, WRT, NP driver, EX........................ $1,500.00

International Pickup Truck, Arcade, 9", yel, BRT, silver-pnt hubs & grille, EX $400.00

International Red Baby Dump Truck, Arcade, 11", BRT, no driver, VG.. $400.00

International Red Baby Dump Truck, Arcade, 11", NPDW, NP driver, NM.. $1,200.00

International Red Baby Wrecker, Arcade, 11½", WRT, NP driver, EX.............................. $425.00

International Stake Truck, Arcade, 12", gr, cast grille, VG ..$400.00

International Stake Truck, Arcade, 12", gr, NP grille, G . $250.00

J&B Express Stake Truck, Jones & Bixler, 15", open, yel, MSW, no driver, G $350.00

Lammerts Moving Van, Arcade, 13", blk, NPDW, w/driver, EX .$3,500.00

LaSalle Pickup Truck, Dent, 4½", take-apart body, NP grille, WRT, no driver, VG.................................. $485.00

Life Savers Truck, Hubley, 1930, 4", holds roll of Life Savers, bl w/gold highlights, NPDW, no driver, M $2,700.00

Lincoln Touring Car, AC Williams, 9", simulated soft top, NPSW w/rear spare, no driver, VG........................... $575.00

Mack American Oil Co Tank Truck, Dent, 10", open C-style cab, NPDW, w/driver, G $350.00

Mack Coal Truck, Arcade, 10", 'COAL' stenciled on dump bed, BRT, w/driver, G $700.00

Mack Coal Truck, Arcade, 10", 'COAL' stenciled on dump bed, WRT, w/driver, EX+ $1,500.00

Mack Coal Truck, Arcade, 10", 'COAL' stenciled on dump bed, WRT, w/driver, VG $975.00

Cast Iron, Motor Vehicles
• •
International Stake Truck, Arcade, 8", green, cast grille, EX+, $1,455.00. (Photo courtesy Morphy Auctions on LiveAuctioneers.com)

Cast Iron, Motor Vehicles
• •
Packard Sedan, Hubley, 11", metal disk wheels, EX, $10,000.00. (Photo courtesy James D. Julia, Inc.)

Mack Delivery Van, Dent, 7", open C-style cab w/integral driver, emb grid sides, NPDW, EX........................... $150.00

Mack Dump Truck, Arcade, 12", T-bar, low bed, WRT, spoke wheels, G $350.00

Mack Dump Truck, Dent, 14", red w/bl dump bed, yel MSW, w/driver, NM $2,400.00

Mack Dump Truck, Hubley, 8", gray w/red dump bed, WRT w/red hubs, w/driver, VG $285.00

Mack Dump Truck, Hubley, 10½", gr w/red dump bed, WRT w/red hubs, NP driver, VG $400.00

Mack Gasoline Tank Truck, Arcade, 13", gr, CI tank, 'Gasoline' emb on side of tank, MSW, w/driver, VG+ $1,000.00

Mack Gasoline Tank Truck, Arcade, 13", gr, tin tank, 'Gasoline' stenciled on frame, BRT, w/driver, VG $800.00

Mack Gasoline Tank Truck, Arcade, 13", gr, tin tank, 'Gasoline' stenciled on frame, WRT, EX.................................. $1,300.00

Mack Ice Truck, Arcade, 8", ice cube w/tongs, MSW, no driver, VG $315.00

Mack Stake Truck, Arcade, 12", gr, NPSW & driver, EX ..$1,800.00

Mack Stake Truck, Dent, 15", chained sides, red w/yel MSW, no driver, G $285.00

Mack Tank Truck, Arcade, 13", red & blk w/'Pennsylvania Indpendent Co Inc' stenciled in gold, WRT, w/driver, EX.....$2,875.00

Mack Tow Truck, Champion, 8½", open C-style cab, WRT, no driver, G $255.00

Mack Wrecker, Arcade, 10½", MDW, NP driver, VG+ ..$1,265.00

Mack Wrecker, Arcade, 12", MSW, w/driver, G+........... $850.00

Mack Wrecker, Champion, 9", WRT, no driver, rpnt..... $150.00

McNeill's Moving & Storage Van, Arcade, 13", WRT, VG+ $8,625.00

Merchants Delivery Van, Hubley, 6", BRT, spoke wheels, cast driver, VG.. $550.00

Nucar Transport, Hubley, 16", WRT, NP driver, EX....... $350.00

Oil/Gas Tank Truck, Kenton, 10", MSW, w/driver, EX .. $875.00

Packard Sedan, Hubley, 11", MDW, w/driver, NM....$15,000.00

Packard Sedan, Hubley, 11", MDW, w/driver, VG.......$7,500.00

Panel Truck, Arcade, 8", NPDW, side spares, NP driver, EX .$3,575.00

Parcel Express, Dent, 8", NM $9,500.00

Parcel Express, Dent, 8", VG $3,200.00

Parlor Coach Bus, Arcade, 13", WRT w/side spare, driver, EX...$1,050.00

Parmalee Yellow Cab, see Yellow Cab

Patrol Truck, Kenton, 9½", open seat w/open railed bed, bl w/gold trim, WRT w/red hubs, integral driver, EX.......... $750.00

Pickwick Nite Coach, Kenton, 9", VG $825.00

Pickwick Nite Coach, Kenton, 11", EX+.....................$4,200.00

Plymouth Coupe, Arcade, 8½", MDW w/rear spare, cast driver, some old rpnt...................................... $750.00

Police Motorcycle, see also Champion Police Motorcyle, Harley-Davidson Police Motorcycle, or Indian Police Motorcycle

Police Motorcycle, Hubley, 6½", electric headlight, cast driver, VG... $300.00

Police Motorcycle w/sidecar, Hubley, 5", NPSW, cast driver w/removable sidecar & passenger, EX.................. $900.00

Police Motorcycle w/sidecar, Hubley, 8½", BRT w/spoke wheels, removable driver & passenger, pull cord, NMIB $16,800.00

Police Motorcycle w/sidecar, Hubley, 8½", BRT w/spoke wheels, removable driver & passenger, VG $1,800.00

Police Motorcycle w/Two-Wheeled Side Wagon, Kilgore, 6",
 NPSW on cycle, simulated spokes on wagon, integral driver,
 VG.. $500.00
Police Patrol Van, Dent, 9", MDW w/side spare, cast driver,
 VG $1,320.00
Pontiac Roadster, Kilgore, 10", open, cream & bl w/NP detail,
 NPDW, no driver, EX.. $2,750.00
Public Service Bus, Dent, 14", red w/blk top, NPDW, NM... $430.00
Racer, AC Williams, 8", early model, sits high on MSW, w/
 driver, VG... $150.00
Racer, AC Williams, 8½", long nose w/side vents, WRT, 2 inte-
 gral drivers, EX $600.00
Racer, Champion, 8½", long nose, WRT, w/driver, G $230.00
Racer, Hubley, 8½", rear fin, 'flames' shoot out from hood vents,
 silver w/red trim, NPDW, w/driver, VG...................... $600.00
Racer, Hubley, 11", rear fin, 'flames' shoot out from hood vents,
 BRT w/spoke wheels, w/driver, NM...................... $3,500.00
Racer #2, Vindex, 10½", red w/yel hubs, MDW, driver, VG .. $4,200.00
Racer #3, Kenton, 7", boattail, MDW, w/driver, VG+.... $150.00
Racer #5, Hubley, 9½", electric headlights, hood opens to battery
 compartment, NP grille, MDW, driver, EX $3,500.00
Racer #5, Hubley, 9½", hood opens to reveal motor, NP grille,
 BRT, w/driver, VG+ $1,125.00
Red Baby Dump Truck, see International Red Baby Dump Truck
Red Top Cab, Arcade, 5", no driver, VG $800.00
Red Top Cab, Arcade, 8", w/driver, G....................... $600.00
REO Coupe, Arcade, 9", NM+................................$13,000.00
REO Coupe, Arcade, 9", VG................................... $4,000.00
Roadster, Freidag, 6½", bl w/NPDW, 2 drivers, G........... $350.00
Roadster, Hubley, 6", take-apart, open, blk & yel, WRT, red
 wooden hubs, NM...................................... $350.00
Roadster, Hubley, 7", C-type roof over driver's seat w/driver, gray
 w/gold trim, red MSW, NM $2,400.00
Roadster, Kilgore, 8", open, opening rumble seat, NPDW, driver,
 EX $200.00
Roadster, Kilgore, 8", open, opening rumble seat, NPDW, driver,
 NM $400.00
Runabout, Ives, 7½", w/up, bench seat w/center steering bar,
 repro driver, VG $750.00
Runabout, Kenton, 6½", open seat, red w/yel MSW, VG . $200.00
Sedan, Freidag, 8", 1920s model, blk & wht, wht MDW w/blk
 hubs, EX+ $475.00
Sedan, Hubley, 7", lt bl $570.00
Sedan, Kenton, 6½", 1920s model, MDW, no driver, VG...$325.00
Sedan, Vindex, 5½", visor over windshield, MSW, gr pnt includ-
 ing headlights & bumpers, no driver, VG+ $1,100.00
Sedan (Second Generation), Dent, 7½", red w/blk top, silver
 trim, NP rear spare, NPDW, EX+ $400.00
Sprinkler Tank Truck, Kenton, 7", orange, MDW w/red hubs, no
 driver, EX.. $400.00
Standard Brands Delivery Van, Arcade, 9", BRT, NP driver,
 P...$1,725.00
Stutz Roadster, Kilgore, 10½", NP grille, bumpers & windshield,
 NPDW, rear spare, yel w/bl fenders & running boards, VG.$315.00
Stutz Bearcat Open Roadster, Kilgore, 10", NP details, NPDW &
 spoil, EX $3,025.00
Taxi, Arcade, 5", blk & gray, MDW w/bl hubs, VG $450.00
Tank, Arcade, 8", camo colors, rubber treads, G............ $200.00

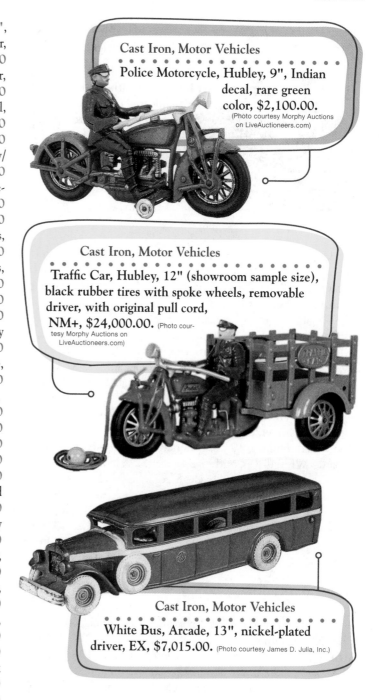

Cast Iron, Motor Vehicles
Police Motorcycle, Hubley, 9", Indian decal, rare green color, $2,100.00. (Photo courtesy Morphy Auctions on LiveAuctioneers.com)

Cast Iron, Motor Vehicles
Traffic Car, Hubley, 12" (showroom sample size), black rubber tires with spoke wheels, removable driver, with original pull cord, NM+, $24,000.00. (Photo courtesy Morphy Auctions on LiveAuctioneers.com)

Cast Iron, Motor Vehicles
White Bus, Arcade, 13", nickel-plated driver, EX, $7,015.00. (Photo courtesy James D. Julia, Inc.)

Touring Car, Kenton, 9", open, hood slants forward, MSW, w/
 driver & lady passenger, VG $500.00
Tractor-Trailer, Arcade, 11", early 4-wheeled tractor, trailer w/2
 sm front wheels & 2 lg rear wheels, red, NPSW, EX... $3,000.00
Traffic Car, Hubley, 9", NPSW, cast driver, EX $1,500.00
Valley View Dairy Truck, Dent, 8", WRT, VG+ $625.00
Vehicle Set, Arcade #3440, 5" to 5½" ea, dump truck, sedan,
 stake truck & wrecker, EXIB................................$1,300.00
White Bus, Arcade, 13", WRT, side spare, no driver, early
 rpnt...$800.00
White Moving Van, Arcade, 13", w/driver, EX........... $4,500.00
White Moving Van, Arcade, 13", w/driver, NM.......... $6,500.00
Woody Station Wagon, Hubley, 6", take apart $460.00
Wrecker, see also Ford Model A Wrecker, Mack Wrecker, Yellow
 Cab Wrecker

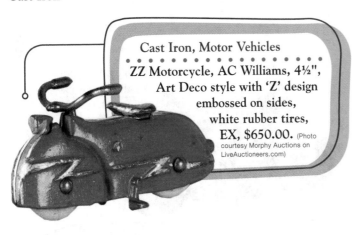

Wrecker, Kenton, 8", open, yel w/blk fenders & red boom &
 hubs, gold trim, MDW, driver, EX $2,750.00

Yellow Baby Dump Truck, Arcade, 11", orange, MDW w/orange
 hubs, NP driver, VG... $500.00

Yellow Cab, Arcade, 5", orange & blk, NPDW w/orange hubs,
 VG... $250.00

Yellow Cab, Arcade, 8", Parmalee, yel w/blk roof, NP grille,
 WRT w/blk hubs, EX $2,150.00

Yellow Cab, Arcade, 8", 1927 GMC, orange & blk, WRT w/
 orange hubs, NP driver, NM $3,500.00

Yellow Cab, Hubley, 1920s, 8", orange, MDW w/orange hubs,
 rear spare, driver, EX $750.00

Yellow Cab, Hubley, 1930s, 8", orange w/blk stripe & running
 boards, WRT, driver, NM.................................... $950.00

Yellow Cab Panel Truck, Arcade, 8", orange & blk w/wht MDW,
 yel hubs, w/driver, NM $7,500.00

Yellow Cab Wrecker, Arcade, 8", blk & orange w/gr boom, WRT,
 spoke wheels, NP driver, VG $315.00

Yellow Coach Double-Decker Bus, Arcade, 13½", WRT, driver,
 EX+.. $950.00

TRAINS AND TROLLEYS

Arcade, locomotive, tender, 2 boxcars, 2 coal trucks & caboose,
 NP, 62" overall, EX+ $375.00

Arcade, locomotive, tender & 2 gondolas, NP, 19½" overall,
 EX $175.00

Arcade, Pennsylvania Wrecker Car, red w/blk boom, NPW,
 13½", rpnt $230.00

Arcade, pile driver, 11", EX................................... $250.00

Arcade, Railplane, 5", EX....................................... $250.00

Arcade, Railplane, 10", G....................................... $85.00

Arcade, Railplane/Pullman, 9", G.......................... $125.00

Arcade, streamliner, 3-pc, 26", VG $375.00

Carpenter, locomotive (Patterned), w/up, 2 sm front MSW w/2
 lg back MSW, 8", VG $400.00

Carpenter, locomotive, tender & 2 flat cars, 19½", F...... $260.00

Dent, locomotive, tender (1085) & 3 coaches, 22½" overall,
 VG+... $250.00

Dent, Toyland's Treasure Chest Train Set, #711, locomotive w/3
 passenger coaches, EXIB $100.00

Grey Iron, locomotive, tender & 3 coaches (300 & 301), NP,
 EX+.. $225.00

Harris, Trolley, 7½", cast conductor figures at either end, M. $250.00

Hubley, Elevated Railway, w/up, locomotive & tender goes
 around trestle track w/4 archways, 30" dia, G+ $9,500.00

Hubley, locomotive, tender (PRR) & 2 coaches (America), 23"
 overall, EX $500.00

Hubley, locomotive (#7 Electric Outline), 2 coaches (1929), 17"
 overall, VG $175.00

Ideal, locomotive (4-4-0/154), tender & 2 coaches, 48" overall,
 worn finish... $350.00

Ives, Circus Train, locomotive, tender, low side rail car & elephant cage car, elephant emb 'Baby,' 30", EX.......... $2,500.00

Ives, Locomotive No 19-11, w/up, blk w/red accents, Pat 1884,
 EX (w/VG orig wooden box) $3,900.00

Ives, locomotive, tender & 2 gondolas (CP/RR), standing figures
 in ea gondola, 23", VG....................................... $500.00

Ives, Trolley, w/up, conductors cast on both end platforms, emb
 'Trolley' on sides, yel, w/guide wire, 7½", overpnt $850.00

Ives, Whist train w/locomotive, tender & 2 coaches w/integral
 passengers in windows, 29", VG $550.00

J&E Stevens, 'Big 6' locomotive w/sm coal tender & 3 coaches,
 42" L, EXIB (wooden box).................................. $850.00

Kenton, locomotive (4-4-0), baggage car (#1200), 2 16" passenger cars (#1201 NYC & Hudson River/Chicago), blk & red,
 VG+... $1,200.00

Kenton, locomotive (600 Camel Back), tender (Erie) & 3 boxcars (yel stock), EX... $1,200.00

Pratt & Letchworth, 4-pc passenger w/#999 engine, Empire
 Express tender, NY Central & Hudson coaches, 16" ea,
 VG $675.00

Pratt & Letchworth, locomotive, w/up, 8", VG.............. $500.00

Welker & Crosby, locomotive, w/up, 2 sm front MSW & 2 lg
 back MSW, 12", EX+ $1,500.00

Welker & Crosby, locomotive, w/up, blk & red, 11", ca 1890,
 EX $1,500.00

Wilkins, locomotive (4-4-0) & tender, 2 coaches, red & blk,
 EX $750.00

MISCELLANEOUS

Amusement Park Ride, Hubley, w/up, 11x9x6" $31,625.00

Arcade Road Construction Set #4329, 7-pc set, EX+IB. $950.00

Arcade Service Station, wht-pnt wood w/gr-stenciled name & 3
 windows, 3 red finials, 6½x12" L, VG......................... $200.00

Arcadia Airport, Arcade, wooden, wht w/red stamping, 12" L,
 NM+... $1,850.00

Bicycle Rider Toy, Ideal, 7½", lg bike w/rider supported by 2 sm
 bikes w/riders on either side, EX $1,200.00

Champion Express Wagon, 8" L, WRT, pull handle, VG ..$55.00

City Bus Terminal, Arcade/FAO Schwarz, 1943, w/2 CI Greyhound buses, NMIB.. $5,000.00

Engine Co No 99 Station, Arcade, wooden, wht w/red trim, 12"
 L, EX+ $875.00

Ferris Wheel, Hubley, CI & PS, w/up, star design w/6 gondolas &
 figures, 17", EX $2,300.00

Ferris Wheel, Hubley, CI & PS, w/up, star design w/6 gondolas &
 figures, 17", G $800.00

Filling Station (Gasoline Motor Oils), Arcade, portico over 2
 pumps, wooden, wht & gr, 12" L, NM+.................... $1,850.00

Fire Dept Alarm Box, free-standing, 4¾", EX+.............. $250.00

Garage, Arcade, wooden, wht & gr, dbl doors open from 1 side, 13" L, EX+ $825.00

Garage, Arcade, wooden, wht & gr, dbl doors open from center, 15" L, EX+ $825.00

Garage, Arcade, wooden, wht & gr, 'Garage' stamped above 5 opening doors, 16" L, NM+ $1,500.00

Gas Pump, Arcade, 'Arcade Gas,' w/crank dial, yel, 6", NM ..$750.00

Marble Game, Kyser & Rex, 4 removable marble shooters & center target cup on ornate sq base, 10x10", VG $1,450.00

Old Dutch Cleanser Pull Toy, Dutch Cleanser girl w/head & arms motion on base emb w/'Old Dutch,' Hubley, 1932, NM $8,000.00

Sign, free-standing lollipop, 'Dont Park Here/Police Department,' 4¾", EX+ $250.00

Sign, free-standing diamond shape, 4¾", NM $300.00

Surfer Girl Pull Toy, Hubley, 7½" L, figure on 3-wheeled base, simulates surfing action when pulled, no cord, G $2,500.00

Traffic Signal, Grey Iron, 9", EX $650.00

Tricyclist, Shimer, 4x3", silver, w/rider, G $200.00

• • • • • • • • • • • • • • • • • •   Catalogs   • • • • • • • • • • • • • • • • • •

In any area of collecting, old catalogs are a wonderful source for information. Toy collectors treasure buyers' catalogs, those from toy fairs, and Christmas 'wish books.' Montgomery Ward issued their first Christmas catalog in 1932, and Sears followed a year later. When they can be found, these 'first editions' in excellent condition are valued at a minimum of $200.00 each. Even later issues may sell for upwards of $75.00, since catalogs from the '50s and '60s contain the toys that are now so collectible.

Action Man, Palitoy, 1980, EX+ $20.00

American Flyer, 1949, G $25.00

Black Beauty Bicycles, 1917, G $50.00

Breyer Animal Creations, 1976, EX $20.00

Buddy L Catalog of Steel Toys for 1935, EX $450.00

Buddy L De Luxe Steel Playthings, 1940, EX $225.00

Capitol Children's Record Albums, 1950s, 14 pgs w/foldouts, EX+ $40.00

Coleco Toys, 1972, EX $10.00

Fisher-Price Toys, 1950, EX $125.00

Galoob, 1973, EX $30.00

Gimbels Christmas, 1953, EX $40.00

Hasbro Romper Room, 1972, EX $50.00

Howdy Doody Merchandise Catalogue, 1955, VG $250.00

Keystone Steam Shovels & Trucks, 1925, 6x4", G $125.00

Kusan Toys, 1968, EX $25.00

Mattel Toys, 1968, NM $40.00

Mego Superstars, 1974, EX $250.00

Mickey Mouse Merchandise, 1936-37, complete, EX $500.00

Ohio Art, 1974, Woody Woodpecker on cover, EX $50.00

Playskool Toys, Learning While Playing, 1950, boy w/pull toy on bl cover, 16 pgs, VG $18.00

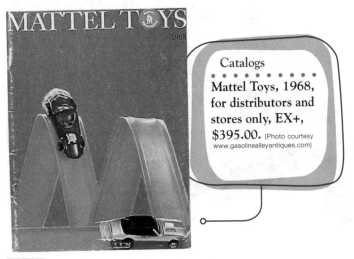

Railroading w/American Flyer, 1946, NM $150.00
Roy Rogers & Dale Evans Catalogue & Merchandise Manual, 1953, 82 pgs, laser copy (not orig) w/spiral binding, M ...$100.00
Schoenhut Perfection Art Dolls, pamphlet, EX................$50.00
Schoenhut's Humpty Dumpty Circus, 1918, VG............ $150.00
Schuco, 1957, 90 pgs, EX.. $325.00
Sears 1960 Christmas Book, 482 pgs, VG $95.00
Sibleys 1956 Christmas Catalog, 84 pgs, EX $25.00
Snow White Merchandising Supplement, 1960s, tie-in campaigns featuring various products & companies, 12 pgs, M...........$50.00
Tinkertoys, 1927, 1931 or 1935, EX, ea..............................$50.00
Tomy Corporation Catalog, 1981, for distibutors & stores, M ..$40.00
Tonka, 1963, NM... $100.00
Ventriloquist Figures by Fred Maher, #1, 1950, 16 pgs, EX.$50.00
Vogue Dolls, 1978, EX $40.00
Walt Disney Character Merchandise 1938-39, complete, EX .$500.00

Character and Promotional Drinking Glasses

Once given away by fast-food chains and gas stations, a few years ago you could find these at garage sales everywhere for a dime or even less. Then, when it became obvious to collectors that these glass giveaways were being replaced by plastic, as is always the case when we realize no more (of anything) will be forthcoming, everyone decided they wanted them. Since many were character-related and part of a series, we felt the need to begin to organize these garage-sale castaways, building sets and completing series. Out of the thousands available, the better ones are those with superheroes, sports stars, old movie stars, Star Trek, and Disney and Walter Lantz cartoon characters. Pass up glasses with worn and faded colors.

There are some terms used in our listings that may be confusing if you're not familiar with this collecting field. 'Brockway' style tumblers are thick and heavy, and they taper at the bottom. 'Federal' is thinner, and top and diameters are equal. Unless another condition or material is indicated in the description, values are for glass tumblers in mint condition.

For more information we recommend *Collectible Drinking Glasses* by Mark E. Chase and Michael J. Kelly and *The Collector's Guide to Cartoon and Promotional Drinking Glasses* by John Hervey. See also PGCA in the Clubs, Newsletters, and Other Publications section in the back of this book.

Character and Promotional Drinking Glasses
Al Capp, 1975, milk glass mug, Dogpatch U.S.A., Daisy and Li'l Abner, $15.00 to $20.00. (Photo courtesy Cathy and Gene Florence)

Al Capp, Shmoos, USF, 1949, Federal, 3 different sizes (3½", 4¾", 5¼"), $10 to $20.00
Al Capp, 1975, flat bottom, Daisy Mae, Li'l Abner, Mammy, Pappy, Sadie, ea $35 to...$50.00
Al Capp, 1975, flat bottom, Joe Btfsplk, $35 to $50.00
Al Capp, 1975, ftd, Daisy Mae, Li'l Abner, Mammy, Pappy, Sadie, ea $35 to $50.00
Al Capp, 1975, ftd, Joe Btfsplk, $40 to $60.00
Animal Crackers, Chicago Tribune/NY News Syndicate, 1978, Eugene, Gnu, Lana, Lyle Dodo, ea $7 to $10.00
Animal Crackers, Chicago Tribune/NY News Syndicate, 1978, Louis, scarce...$25.00
Arby's, see also specific name or series
Arby's, Actor Series, 1979, 6 different, smoke-colored glass w/blk & wht images, silver trim, numbered, ea $3 to..................$5.00
Arby's, Bicentennial Cartoon Characters, 1976, 10 different, 5", ea $8 to $15.00
Arby's, Bicentennial Cartoon Characters, 1976, 10 different, 6", ea $10 to $20.00
Archies, Welch's, 1971 & 1973, many variations in ea series, ea $2 to..$4.00
Baby Huey & Related Characters, see Harvey Cartoon Characters
Batman & Related Characters, see also Super Heroes
Batman Forever, McDonald's, 1995, various emb glass mugs, ea $2 to..$4.00

Character and Promotional Drinking Glasses
· ·
Disneyland, McDonald's series, four different areas of park with Disney character, 1989, each $9.00 to $15.00. (Photo courtesy Gary Henriques and Audre DuVall)

Battlestar Galactica, Universal Studios, 1979, 4 different, ea $7 to..................$10.00

Beatles, Dairy Queen/Canada, group photos & signatures in wht starburst, gold trim, ea $95 to.................... $125.00

Beverly Hillbillies, CBS promotion, 1963, rare, NM...... $200.00

Bozo the Clown, Capitol Records, 1965, Bozo head image around top w/related character at bottom, ea $10 to..................$15.00

Bozo the Clown, Capitol Records, 1965, Bozo on 3 sides only, $8 to..................$10.00

Buffalo Bill, see Western Heroes or Wild West Series

Bugs Bunny & Related Characters, see Warner Bros

Bullwinkle, Rocky & Related Characters, see Warner Bros or PAT Ward

Burger Chef, Friendly Monster Series, 1977, 6 different, ea $15 to..................$25.00

Burger King, see also specific name or series

Burger King, Collector Series, 1979, 5 different Burger King characters featuring Burger Thing, etc, ea $3 to..............$5.00

Burger King, Put a Smile in Your Tummy, features Burger King mascot, $5 to..................$6.00

California Raisins, Applause, 1989, juice, 12-oz, 16-oz, ea $4 to.................. $6.00

California Raisins, Applause, 1989, 32-oz, $6 to $8.00

Captain America, see Super Heroes

Casper the Friendly Ghost & Related Characters, see Arby's Bicentennial Cartoon Characters Series or Harvey Cartoon Characters

Charlie McCarthy & Edgar Bergen, Libbey, 1930s, set of 8, M (EX illus display box) $600.00

Children's Classics, Libbey Glass Co, Alice in Wonderland, Gulliver's Travels, Tom Sawyer, $10 to $15.00

Children's Classics, Libbey Glass Co, Moby Dick, Robin Hood, Three Musketeers, Treasure Island, ea $10 to..................$15.00

Children's Classics, Libbey Glass Co, The Wizard of Oz, $25 to $30.00

Chilly Willy, see Walter Lantz

Chipmunks, Hardee's (no logo on glass), 1985, Alvin, Simon, Theodore, Chipettes, ea $1 to $3.00

Cinderella, Disney/Libbey, 1950s-60s, set of 8 .... $120.00

Daffy Duck, see Warner Bros

Davy Crockett, 1950s, 'Davy Crockett 1786-1836'/'...Indian Fighter/Statesman/Hero of the Alamo,' on horse/canoe, 5", NM $15.00

Dick Tracy, Domino's Pizza, M, $95 to $125.00

Dick Tracy, 1940s, frosted, 8 different characters, 3" or 5", ea $50 to..................$75.00

Dilly Dally, see Howdy Doody

Disney, see also Wonderful World of Disney or specific characters

Disney Characters, 1936, Clarabelle, Donald, F Bunny, Horace, Mickey, Minnie, Pluto, 4¼" or 4¾", ea $30 to................$50.00

Disney's All-Star Parade, 1939, 10 different, ea $25 to......$50.00

Donald Duck, Donald Duck Cola, 1960s-70s, $10 to $15.00

Donald Duck or Daisy, see also Disney or Mickey Mouse (Happy Birthday)

Dynomutt, see Hanna-Barbera

ET, Pepsi/MCA Home Video, 1988, 6 different, ea $15 to .$25.00

ET, Pizza Hut, 1982, ftd, 4 different, $2 to $4.00

Fantasia, see Mickey Mouse (Through the Years)

Flintstones, see Hanna-Barbera

Ghostbusters II, Sunoco/Canada, 1989, 6 different, ea $3 to $5.00

Goonies, Godfather's Pizza/Warner Bros, 1985, 4 different, ea $3 to..................$5.00

Green Arrow or Green Lantern, see Super Heroes

Hanna-Barbera, Pepsi, 1977, Dynomutt, Flintstones, Josie & the Pussycats, Mumbly, Scooby, Yogi & Huck, ea $10 to $20.00

Hanna-Barbera, Welch's, Flintstones, 1962 (6 different), 1963 (2 different), 1964 (6 different), ea $4 to...........................$6.00

Hanna-Barbera, 1960s, jam glasses featuring Cindy Bear, Flintstones, Huck, Quick Draw McGraw, Yogi Bear, rare, ea $60 to $90.00

Happy Days, Dr Pepper, 1977, Fonzie, Joanie, Potsie, Ralph, Richie, ea $6 to $10.00

Happy Days, Dr Pepper/Pizza Hut, 1977, any character, ea $6 to $10.00

Harvey Cartoon Characters, Pepsi, 1970s, action pose, Baby Huey, Hot Stuff, Wendy, ea $8 to $10.00

Harvey Cartoon Characters, see also Arby's Bicentennial Series

Harvey Cartoon Characters, Pepsi, 1970s, static pose, Baby Huey, Casper, Hot Stuff, Wendy, ea $12 to $15.00

Harvey Cartoon Characters, Pepsi, 1970s, static pose, Richie Rich, $15 to...................$20.00

Harvey Cartoon Characters, Pepsi, 1970s, static pose, Sad Sack, scarce, $25 to..................$30.00

He-Man & Related Characters, see Masters of the Universe

Honey, I Shrunk the Kids, McDonald's, 1989, plastic, 3 different, ea $1 to..................$2.00

Hopalong Cassidy, milk glass w/black graphics, Breakfast Milk, Lunch Milk, Dinner Milk, ea $15 to $20.00

Hopalong Cassidy, milk glass w/red & black graphics, 3 different, ea $20 to...................$25.00

Hopalong Cassidy's Western Series, ea $25 to $30.00

Hot Stuff, see Harvey Cartoon Characters or Arby's Bicentennial Cartoon Characters Series

Howard the Duck, see Super Heroes

Howdy Doody, Welch's/Kagran, 1950s, 6 different, emb bottom, ea $10 to..................$15.00

Huckleberry Hound, see Hanna-Barbera

Incredible Hulk, see Super Heroes

Indiana Jones & the Temple of Doom, 7-Up (w/4 different sponsers), 1984, set of 4, $8 to..................$15.00

James Bond 007, 1985, 4 different, ea $10 to.....................$15.00

Joker, see Super Heroes

Jungle Book, Disney/Canada, 1966, 6 different, numbered, 5", ea $30 to..................$65.00

Jungle Book, Disney/Canada, 1966, 6 different, numbered, 6½", ea $20 to..................$40.00

Character and Promotional Drinking Glasses
• •
McDonald's, McDonaldland Collector Series, 1970s, six different, each $2.00 to $3.00. (Photo courtesy Gary Henriques and Audre DuVall)

Character and Promotional Drinking Glasses
• • • • • • • • • • • • •
PAT Ward, Pepsi, late 1970s, static pose, Boris and Natasha, 6", $15.00 to $20.00; Snidley Whiplash, 6", $10.00 to $15.00. (Photo courtesy Mark Chase and Michael Kelly)

Jungle Book, Disney/Pepsi, 1970s, Bagheera or Shere Kahn, unmk, ea $35 to..$60.00

Jungle Book, Disney/Pepsi, 1970s, Mowgli, unmk, $15 to.$20.00

Jungle Book, Disney/Pepsi, 1970s, Rama, unmk, $25 to....$35.00

Laurel & Hardy, see Arby's Actor Series

Leonardo TTV Collector Series, see also Arby's Bicentennial Cartoon Characters

Leonardo TTV Collector Series, Pepsi, Underdog, Go-Go Gophers, Simon Bar Sinister, Sweet Polly, 6", ea $10 to.$15.00

Leonardo TTV Collector Series, Pepsi, Underdog, Simon Bar Sinister, Sweet Polly, 5", ea $6 to......................................$10.00

Little Mermaid, 1991, 3 different sizes, ea $6 to $10.00

Masters of the Universe, Mattel, 1983, He-Man, Man-at-Arms, Skeletor, Teels, ea $5 to..$10.00

Masters of the Universe, Mattel, 1986, Battle Cat/He-Man, Man-at-Arms, Orko, Panthor/Skeletor, ea $3 to..............$5.00

MGM Collector Series, Pepsi, 1975, Tom, Jerry, Barney, Droopy, Spike, Tuffy, ea $5 to...$10.00

MGM Collector Series, Pepsi, 1975, 5", 2 different w/Tom & Jerry against yel background, ea $8 to.............................$12.00

Mickey Mouse, Happy Birthday, Pepsi, 1978, Clarabelle & Horace or Daisy & Donald, ea $5 to $10.00

Mickey Mouse, Happy Birthday, Pepsi, 1978, Donald, Goofy, Mickey, Minnie, Pluto, Uncle Scrooge, ea $5 to..............$7.00

Mickey Mouse, Mickey's Christmas Carol, Coca-Cola, 1982, 3 different, ea $5 to $7.00

Mickey Mouse, Pizza Hut, 1980, milk glass mug, Fantasia, MM Club, Steamboat Willie, Today, ea $2 to $5.00

Mickey Mouse, see also Disney Characters

Mickey Mouse, Through the Years, K-Mart, glass mugs w/4 different images (1928, 1937, 1940, 1955), ea $3 to.............$5.00

Mickey Mouse Club, 4 different w/filmstrip bands top & bottom, ea $10 to..$20.00

Mickey Mouse Club, 6 different characters w/name & club logo on reverse, ea $8 to..$12.00

Mister Magoo, Polomar Jelly, many different variations & styles, ea $25 to..$35.00

Pac-Man, Arby's Collector Series, 1980, rocks glass, $2 to..$4.00

Pac-Man, Bally Midway MFG/AAFES/Libbey, 1980, Shadow (Blinky), Bashful (Inky), Pokey (Clyde), Speedy (Pinky), ea $4 to..$6.00

Pac-Man, Bally Midway Mfg/Libbey, 1982, 6" flare top, 5⅜" flare top or mug, $2 to..$4.00

PAT Ward, see also Arby's Bicentennial Cartoon Characters

PAT Ward, Collector Series, Holly Farms Restaurants, 1975, Boirs, Bullwinkle, Natasha, Rocky, ea $20 to.................$40.00

PAT Ward, Pepsi, late 1970s, action pose, Bullwinkle w/balloons, Dudley in Canoe, Rocky in circus, 5", ea $5 to.............$10.00

PAT Ward, Pepsi, late 1970s, static pose, Boris, Mr Peabody, Natasha, 5", ea $10 to..$15.00

PAT Ward, Pepsi, late 1970s, static pose, Bullwinkle, 5", $15 to.. $20.00

PAT Ward, Pepsi, late 1970s, static pose, Bullwinkle (brn lettering/no Pepsi logo), 6", $15 to..$20.00

PAT Ward, Pepsi, late 1970s, static pose, Bullwinkle (wht or blk lettering), 6", $10 to..$15.00

PAT Ward, Pepsi, late 1970s, static pose, Dudley Do-Right, 5", $10 to..$15.00

PAT Ward, Pepsi, late 1970s, static pose, Dudley Do-Right (blk lettering), 6", $10 to..$15.00

PAT Ward, Pepsi, late 1970s, static pose, Dudley Do-Right (red lettering/no Pepsi logo), 6", $10 to......................................$15.00

PAT Ward, Pepsi, late 1970s, static pose, Rocky, 5", $15 to...$20.00

PAT Ward, Pepsi, late 1970s, static pose, Rocky (brn lettering/no Pepsi logo), 6", $10 to..$15.00

PAT Ward, Pepsi, late 1970s, static pose, Rocky (wht or blk lettering), 6", $10 to..$15.00

PAT Ward, Pepsi, late 1970s, static pose, Snidley Whiplash, 5", $8 to..$10.00

Peanuts Characters, Dolly Madison Bakery, Snoopy for President or Snoopy Sport Series, 4 different ea series, ea $3 to......$5.00

Peanuts Characters, McDonald's, 1983, Camp Snoopy, wht plastic, w/Lucy or Snoopy, ea $5 to..$8.00

Peanuts Characters, milk glass mug, Snoopy for President, 4 different, numbered & dated, ea $5 to................................$8.00

Peanuts Characters, milk glass mug, Snoopy in various poses, $2 to..$4.00

Penguin, see Super Heroes

Pinocchio, Dairy Promo/Libbey, 1938-40, 12 different, ea $15 to..$25.00

Pinocchio, see also Wonderful World of Disney

Pluto, see Disney Characters

Pocahontas, Burger King, 1995, 4 different, MIB, ea...........$3.00

Popeye, Coca-Cola, 1975, Kollect-A-Set, any character, ea $3 to...$5.00

Popeye, Popeye's Famous Fried Chicken, 1978, Sports Scenes, Brutus, Olive Oyl, Swee' Pea, ea $10 to $15.00

Popeye, Popeye's Famous Fried Chicken, 1978, Sports Scenes, Popeye, $7 to...$10.00

Popeye, Popeye's Famous Fried Chicken, 1979, Pals, 4 different, ea $10 to...$15.00

Popeye, Popeye's Famous Fried Chicken/Pepsi, 1982, 10th Anniversary Series, 4 different, ea $7 to $10.00

Quick Draw McGraw, see Hanna-Barbera

Raggedy Ann & Andy, going down slide, skipping rope, stacking blocks, riding in wagon, ea $5 to.............................$10.00

Rescuers, Pepsi, 1977, Brockway tumbler, Bernard, Bianca, Brutus & Nero, Evinrude, Orville, Penny, ea $5 to.............$10.00

Rescuers, Pepsi, 1977, Brockway tumbler, Madame Medusa or Rufus, ea $15 to...$25.00

Richie Rich, see Harvey Cartoon Characters

Riddler, see Super Heroes

Road Runner & Related Characters, see Warner Bros

Robin, see Super Heroes

Rocky & Bullwinkle, see Arby's Bicentennial Cartoon Characters or PAT Ward

Roy Rogers Restaurant, 1883-1983 logo, $3 to $5.00

Sad Sack, see Harvey Cartoon Characters

Scooby Doo, see Hanna-Barbera

Sleeping Beauty, American, late 1950s, 6 different, ea $8 to.....$15.00

Sleeping Beauty, Canadian, late 1950s, 12 different, ea $10 to...$15.00

Smurfs, Hardee's, 1982 (8 different), 1983 (6 different), ea, $1 to...$3.00

Snidley Whiplash, see PAT Ward

Snoopy & Related Characters, see Peanuts Characters

Snow White & the Seven Dwarfs, see also Wonderful World of Disney

Snow White & the Seven Dwarfs, Bosco, 1938, ea $20 to.$30.00

Snow White & the Seven Dwarfs, Libbey, 1930s, verses on back, various colors, 8 different, ea $15 to $25.00

Star Trek, Dr Pepper, 1976, 4 different, ea $15 to..............$20.00

Star Trek, Dr Pepper, 1978, 4 different, ea $25 to..............$30.00

Star Trek II, The Search for Spock, Taco Bell, 1984, 4 different, ea $3 to..$5.00

Star Trek: The Motion Picture, Coca-Cola, 1980, 3 different, ea $10 to..$15.00

Star Wars Trilogy: Empire Strikes Back, Burger King/Coca-Cola, 1980, 4 different, ea $5 to $7.00

Star Wars Trilogy: Return of the Jedi, Burger King/Coca-Cola, 1983, 4 different, ea $3 to $5.00

Star Wars Trilogy: Star Wars, Burger King/Coca-Cola, 1977, 4 different, ea $8 to $10.00

Sunday Funnies, 1976, Brenda Star, Gasoline Alley, Moon Mullins, Orphan Annie, Smilin' Jack, Terry & the Pirates, $5 to $7.00

Sunday Funnies, 1976, Broom Hilda, $90 to...................$125.00

Super Heroes, Marvel, 1978, Federal, flat bottom, Captain America, Hulk, Spider-Man, Thor, ea $40 to.................$75.00

Super Heroes, Marvel, 1978, Federal, flat bottom, Spider-Woman, $100 to..$150.00

Super Heroes, Marvel/7 Eleven, 1977, ftd, Amazing Spider-Man, $25 to..$30.00

Super Heroes, Marvel/7 Eleven, 1977, ftd, Captain America, Fantastic Four, Howard the Duck, Thor, ea $10 to $15.00

Super Heroes, Marvel/7 Eleven, 1977, ftd, Incredible Hulk, $10 to...$15.00

Super Heroes, NPP, 1960s, Batman (Crack Whack Zonk), Robin the Boy Wonder (Clonk Smak Bam), 5", M, ea $25 to.$30.00

Super Heroes, Pepsi Super (Moon) Series/DC Comics or NPP, 1976, Aquaman, Flash, Supergirl, Superman, Wonder Woman, $10 to...$15.00

Super Heroes, Pepsi Super (Moon) Series/DC Comics or NPP, 1976, Batgirl, Batman, Robin, Shazam!, ea $10 to.........$15.00

Super Heroes, Pepsi Super (Moon) Series/DC Comics or NPP, 1976, Green Arrow, $15 to $20.00

Super Heroes, Pepsi Super (Moon) Series/DC Comics or NPP, 1976, Green Lantern, Joker, Penguin, Riddler, ea $15 to.$25.00

Super Heroes, Pepsi/DC Comics, 1978, Brockway, flat bottom, Aquaman, Shazam!, Superman, The Flash, ea $8 to......$10.00

Super Heroes, Pepsi/DC Comics, 1978, Brockway, flat bottom, Batman, Robin, Wonder Woman (red boots), ea $8 to..$15.00

Super Heroes, Pepsi/DC Comics, 1978, Brockway, rnd bottom, Batman, Robin, Shazam!, 5½", ea $15 to $25.00

Super Heroes, Pepsi/DC Comics, 1978, Brockway, rnd bottom, Superman, The Flash, Wonder Woman, ea $15 to $25.00

Superman, M Polanar & Son/NPP, 1964, 6 different, various colors, 4¼" or 5¾", ea $20 to $25.00

Sylvester the Cat or Tweety Bird, see Warner Bros

Tom & Jerry & Related Characters, see MGM Collector Series

Underdog & Related Characters, see Arby's Bicentennial Cartoon Characters or Leonardo TTV Collector Series

Universal Monsters, Universal Studios, 1980, ftd, Creature, Dracula, Frankenstein, Mummy, Mutant, Wolfman, ea $125 to.....$150.00

Walter Lantz, see also Arby's Bicentennial Cartoon Characters

Walter Lantz, Pepsi, 1970s, Chilly Willy or Wally Walrus, ea, $15 to...$20.00

Walter Lantz, Pepsi, 1970s, Cuddles, $30 to $50.00

Walter Lantz, Pepsi, 1970s, Space Mouse, $75 to $150.00

Walter Lantz, Pepsi, 1970s, Woody Woodpecker, $15 to...$20.00

Walter Lantz, Pepsi, 1970s-80s, Anty/Miranda, Chilly/Smelley, Cuddles/Oswald, Wally/Homer, ea $20 to $30.00

Walter Lantz, Pepsi, 1970s-80s, Buzz Buzzard/Space Mouse, $15 to..$20.00

Walter Lantz, Pepsi, 1970s-80s, Woody Woodpecker/Knothead & Splinter, $15 to $20.00

Warner Bros, Acme Cola, 1993, bell shape, Bugs, Sylvester, Tasmanian Devil, Tweety, ea $4 to...$8.00

Warner Bros, Arby's, 1988, Adventures Series, ftd, Bugs, Daffy, Porky, Sylvester & Tweety, ea $25 to.........................$30.00

Warner Bros, Marriott's Great America, 1975, 12-oz, 6 different (Bugs & related characters), ea $20 to.........................$30.00

Warner Bros, Marriott's Great America, 1989, Bugs, Porky, Sylvester, Tasmanian Devil, ea $7 to $10.00

Warner Bros, Pepsi, 1973, Federal 16-oz tumbler, Bugs Bunny, wht lettering, $5 to...$10.00

Warner Bros, Pepsi, 1973, Federal 16-oz tumbler, Cool Cat, blk lettering, $5 to...$10.00

Warner Bros, Pepsi, 1973, Federal 16-oz tumbler, Elmer Fudd, wht lettering, $5 to...$8.00

Warner Bros, Pepsi, 1973, Federal 16-oz tumbler, Henery Hawk or Slow Poke Rodriguez, blk lettering, ea $25 to............$40.00

Warner Bros, Pepsi, 1973, Federal 16-oz tumbler, Speedy Gonzales, blk lettering, $6 to.......................................$10.00

Warner Bros, Pepsi, 1973, wht plastic, 6 different, Bugs, Daffy, Porky, Road Runner, Sylvester, Tweety, ea $3 to..............$5.00

Warner Bros, Pepsi, 1976, interaction, Beaky Buzzard & Cool Cat w/kite or Tasmanian Devil & Porky w/fishing pole, ea $8 to $10.00

Warner Bros, Pepsi, 1976, interaction, Yosemite & Speedy Gonzales panning gold, ea $10 to.............................$15.00

Warner Bros, Pepsi, 1976, interaction, Foghorn Leghorn & Henery Hawk, $10 to $15.00

Warner Bros, Pepsi, 1976, interaction, others, ea $5 to.....$10.00

Warner Bros, Pepsi, 1979, Collector Series, rnd bottom, Bugs, Daffy, Porky, Road Runner, Sylvester, Tweety, ea $7 to $10.00

Warner Bros, Pepsi, 1980, Collector Series, Bugs, Daffy, Porky, Road Runner heads on star, names on band above, ea $6 to..........$10.00

Warner Bros, Six Flags, 1991, clear, Bugs, Daffy, Sylvester, Wile E Coyote, ea $5 to...$10.00

Warner Bros, Six Flags, 1991, clear, Yosemite Sam, $10 to...$15.00

Warner Bros, Welch's, 1974, action poses, 8 different, phrases around top, ea $2 to $4.00

Warner Bros, Welch's, 1976-77, 8 different, names around bottom, ea $5 to $7.00

Warner Bros, Zak Designs, 1991, 4 different tumblers, 4", ea..$5.00

Warner Bros, 1995, Taz's Root Beer/Serious Suds, clear glass mug, $5 to...$7.00

Warner Bros, 1996, 8 different w/ea character against busy bkgrd of repeated characters, names below, ea $4 to $6.00

Warner Bros, 1998, 6 different w/characters against vertically striped background, ea $4 to $6.00

WC Fields, see Arby's Actor Series

Western Heroes, Annie Oakley, Buffalo Bill, Wild Bill Hickok, Wyatt Earp, ea $8 to...$12.00

Western Heroes, Lone Ranger, $10 to..............................$15.00

Western Heroes, Wyatt Earp, fight scene or OK Corral gunfight, name at top, $12 to $22.00

Wild West Series, Coca-Cola, Buffalo Bill, Calamity Jane, ea $10 to $15.00

Wile E Coyote, see Warner Bros

Winnie the Pooh, Sears/WDP, 1970s, 4 different, ea $7 to..$10.00

Wizard of Oz, see also Children's Classics

Wizard of Oz, Coca-Cola/Krystal, 1989, 50th Anniversary Series, 6 different, ea $7 to $10.00

Wizard of Oz, Swift's, 1950s-60s, fluted bottom, Emerald City or Flying Monkeys, ea $8 to $15.00

Wizard of Oz, Swift's, 1950s-60s, fluted bottom, Glinda, $15 to .$25.00

Wizard of Oz, Swift's, 1950s-60s, fluted bottom, Wicked Witch, $35 to..$50.00

Wonder Woman, see Super Heroes

Wonderful World of Disney, Pepsi, 1980s, Alice, Bambi, Lady & the Tramp, Pinocchio, Snow White, 101 Dalmatians, $15 to....$20.00

Woody Woodpecker & Related Characters, see Arby's Bicentennial Cartoon Characters or Walter Lantz

Yogi Bear, see Hanna-Barbera

Yosemite Sam, see Warner Bros

Ziggy, Number Series, 1-8, ea $4 to....................................$8.00

Ziggy, 7-Up Collector Series, 1977, Here's to Good Friends, 4 different, ea $3 to $5.00

• • • • • • • • • • • • • • • **Character Clocks and Watches** • • • • • • • • • • • • • • •

Clocks and watches with dials depicting favorite characters have been manufactured with kids in mind since the 1930s, when Ingersoll made a wristwatch, a pocket watch, and a clock featuring Mickey Mouse. The #1 Mickey wristwatch came in the now-famous orange box commonly known as the 'critter box,' illustrated with a variety of Disney characters. There is also a blue display box from the same time period. The watch itself featured a second hand with three revolving Mickey figures. It was available with either a metal or leather band. Babe Ruth starred on an Exacta Time watch in 1949, and the original box contained not only the watch but a baseball with a facsimile signature.

Collectors treasure the boxes about as highly as they do the watches. Many were well illustrated and colorful, but most were promptly thrown away, so they're hard to find today. Be sure you buy only watches in very good condition. Rust, fading, scratches, or other signs of wear sharply devaluate a clock or a watch. Hundreds have been produced, and if you're going to collect them, you'll need to study *Comic Character Clocks and Watches* by Howard S. Brenner for more information.

Note: Our values are typical of high retail. A watch in exceptional condition, especially an earlier model, may bring even more. Dealers, who will generally pay about half of book when they buy for resale, many times offer discounts on the more pricey items, and package deals involving more than one watch may sometimes be made for as much as a 15% discount.

Advisor: Bill Campbell

See also Advertising.

CLOCKS

Batman Alarm Clock, Bright Ideas, 1989, image of Batman high above city on bl bkgrd, rnd, steel case, 6x5", MIB..........$40.00

Bugs Bunny Alarm Clock, Ingraham, 1940s, Bugs resting w/carrot, 4x4" sq, EX, $150 to $200.00

Bugs Bunny Alarm Clock, Janex, 1970s, molded plastic, Bugs leaning on clock, MIB...$75.00

Charlie McCarthy Alarm Clock, Gilbert, Charlie's head & name on rnd face on base, EX...................................... $775.00

Cinderella Alarm Clock, Bradley/Japan, image of Cinderella leaving slipper on steps, 3" dia, scarce, MIB $125.00

Felix the Cat, Bright Ideas, 1989, MIB $50.00

Garfield Alarm Clock, Sunbeam, 1990s, blk paw print & image of Garfield from the arms up on wht face, 2 bells, 7", MIB....$40.00

Green Hornet Alarm Clock, Official Green Hornet Agent graphics on rnd face, w/up, NM.....................................$75.00

Hopalong Cassidy Alarm Clock, US Time, rnd blk case w/wht name on oblong base, blk & wht Hoppy/Topper, red numbers, NM $300.00

Howdy Doody Alarm Clock, Janex, 'It's Howdy Doody Time,' plastic w/Howdy & Clarabelle figures, 7" L, EXIB....... $150.00

James Bond 007 Wall Clock, 1981, Roger Moore image, NM+ $50.00

Mickey Mouse Alarm Clock, Bayard, 1960s re-issue, Mickey running on wht, arms are clock hands, red metal base, 5", NM+IB $175.00

Mickey Mouse Alarm Clock, Bayard/France, 1930s, EXIB.$1,000.00

Mickey Mouse Alarm Clock, Ingersoll, 1930s, sq metal case w/ Mickey figure on face, electric, 4", EX $425.00

Minnie Mouse Alarm Clock, Bradley, red rnd case w/2 yel bells atop, footed, image & name on face, EXIB.....................$65.00

Peanuts Alarm Clock, Japan, 1988, silver metal case, character faces as numbers, 3½" dia, MIB............................$50.00

Pluto Wall Clock, Allied, plastic figure w/clock attached to his chest, hands shaped as dog bones, 8", EXIB $300.00

Roy Rogers & Trigger Alarm Clock, animated Trigger, Ingraham, desert mountain scene, 4½" sq, EX $275.00

Shmoo Wall Clock, Lux, bl plastic flat figure w/blk features & numbers & hands, working pendulum, 6½", EX+IB.... $400.00

Sleeping Beauty Alarm Clock, Phinney-Walker, 1950s, Sleeping Beauty petting rabbit while surrounded by 3 birds, 5", NM $75.00

Snoopy Alarm Clock, Blessing, 1970s, wht Snoopy w/ears up & appears to be dancing, wht numbers on blk, 5½", EX+ ..$35.00

Snoopy Alarm Clock, Equity, 1970s, Snoopy as tennis player against tan grid-patterned face, ball as second hand, 5", NM $40.00

Superman Wall Clock, New Haven, 1978, b/o, framed w/image of Superman confronting spaceship, NM+ $50.00

Three Little Pigs Alarm Clock, Ingersoll, 1930s, wolf & pigs on red rnd face, 4½", EX.. $450.00

Who's Afraid of the Big Bad Wolf? Alarm Clock, Ingersoll, wolf's head bobs, EX... $825.00

Woody Woodpecker Wall Clock, Model No 535, molded plastic figure of Woody on horse w/clock face, 9", NRFB....... $250.00

POCKET WATCHES

Boy Scouts, Ingersoll, 1937, 'Be Prepared'/'A Scout Is' on yel hands pointing to phrases encircling numbers, 2" dia, EX...........$225.00

Buck Rogers, Ingraham, 1935, Buck & Wilma illus w/copper-colored lightning bolt hands, silver-tone case, EX $500.00

Dan Dare, Ingersoll, 1953, Dan Dare graphics, rnd silver-tone case, EX+ $375.00

Don Winslow in the Navy, New Haven, 1938-39, EX..$1,500.00

Donald Duck, Ingersoll, 1939, full-figure Donald on wht face, chrome case, EXIB (Donald & Mickey on bl box)... $1,100.00

Lone Ranger, w/gun fob, MIB... $800.00

Lone Ranger, w/lapel fob, MIB.. $800.00

Lone Ranger, 1970, rnd chrome case, Lone Ranger & Silver, bl strap, silver chain, NM.. $100.00

Mickey Mouse, Ingersoll, 1930s, w/fob & strap, GIB...... $200.00

Popeye, King Features, ca 1935, Popeye in wide stride on face w/arms as dials, 2nd hand depcits Wimpy chasing burger, EX..$350.00

Popeye, New Haven, 1935, Popeye surrounded by alternating heads & numbers, chrome case, VGIB...................... $625.00

Roy Rogers, Bradley, lg image of Roy w/sm image of Roy & Trigger in background, w/stopwatch feature, EX $600.00

Superman, New Haven, rectangular chrome case, 3-quarter figure, w/stopwatch feature, EX $600.00

Three Little Pigs, Ingersoll, 1930s, wolf & pigs on red face, blk leather strap w/inlayed fob, EXIB $1,725.00

Wizard of Oz, Westclock, 1980s, 4 characters on dial, silver-tone case, unused, MIB $75.00

Woody (Toy Story), Fossil, 1996, limited ed, M (M box & container) $125.00

WRISTWATCHES

Alice in Wonderland, Ingersoll, image of Alice, fabric strap, EXIB (rnd box w/clear plastic teacup), $300 to $350.00

Angelique (Dark Shadows), Abbelare, MIB (coffin box) . $100.00

Annie Oakley, New Haven $175.00

Bambi, US Time, 1948, 1 of 10 in Mickey's 20th Birthday Series, EXIB $175.00

Bambi, US Time, 1948, 1 of 10 in Mickey's 20th Birthday Series, luminescent, MIB $275.00

Barnabas Collins (Dark Shadows), Abbelare, MIB (coffin box) $100.00

Batman, Fossil, 1990, limited ed, complete w/pin, MIB . $175.00

Battlestar Galactica, 1950s, MIB $125.00

Bionic Woman, MX Berger, 1970s, image & lettering on face, vinyl band, NM $75.00

Blondie, Danbros Watch Co/KFS, 1949, rnd chrome case, Blondie, Dagwood & pups on band, NM+IB $950.00

Bongo, US Time, 1948, 1 of 10 in Mickey's 20th Birthday Series, EX $175.00

Buffy & Jody, Sheffield, 1969, image & names on face, visible gears, various bands, M, ea $125.00

Bugs Bunny, Rexall Drug Co/Warner Bros, 1950s, rnd chrome case, animated carrot hands, NM $400.00

Captain Marvel, Fawcett, 1948, rnd chrome case, full figure image, plastic strap, EXIB $750.00

Charlie Brown, Determined, 1970s, baseball scene on yel bkgrd, blk band, EXIB $175.00

Cinderella, Timex, 1950s, full figure on rnd dial, MIB (w/clear plastic slipper) $250.00

Cool Cat, Sheffield, 1960s, full-figure image, VG $50.00

Creature from the Black Lagoon, Fossil, EX $200.00

Daisy Duck, US Time, 1948, 1 of 10 in Mickey's 20th Birthday Series, EXIB $300.00

Dale Evans, Bradley Time #186, 1954, 'Queen of the West Wrist Watch for Girls,' horseshoe portrait, leather band, MIB . $325.00

Davy Crockett, US Time, 1950s, gr plastic case, tooled leather band, unused, MIB (w/powder horn display) $450.00

Dick Tracy, New Haven/Chester Gould, 1951, rnd case, leather band, NM+IB (wht box) $650.00

Dick Tracy, 1935, MIB $600.00

Dizzy Dean, Everbrite-Ingersoll, 1933, scarce, M $1,100.00

Donald Duck, Ingersoll, 1936, leather band w/wht Donalds, EXIB, $2,500 to $3,500.00

Donald Duck, US Time, 1948, 1 of 10 in Mickey's 20th Birthday Series, EX $175.00

Dopey, US Time, 1948, 1 of 10 in Mickey's 20th Birthday Series, EX $175.00

Dracula, Fossil, MIB $175.00

Dr Seuss, Cat in the Hat, 1972, NM $150.00

Evel Knievel, Bradley, 1976, vinyl band, EX $150.00

Flash Gordon, 1950s, MIB $150.00

Flipper, ITF/MGM, glow-in-the-dark image, M.............. $125.00

Frankenstein, Fossil, MIB $175.00

Frankenstein (Universal Monsters), 1995, glow-in-the-dark, MOC $25.00

Gene Autry, New Haven, 1951, Six Shooter, brn leather band, unused, MIB $650.00

Gene Autry, Wilane, 1948, Champion, NMIB............... $400.00

Girl from UNCLE, 1960s, pk face w/blk line drawing & numbers, EX..$65.00

Godzilla, Fossil, w/statuette, MIB.......................... $225.00

Goofy, Helbros/WDP, 1972, runs backwards, animated hands, leather band, MIB $675.00

Hopalong Cassidy, Anniversary, w/watch, neckerchief & steer slide, MIB $150.00

Hopalong Cassidy, Fossil, 100th anniversary ed, EX....... $150.00

Hopalong Cassidy, US Time/William Boyd, 1955, blk plastic dial, decorated band, unused, MIB...................... $525.00

Howdy Doody, Ideal/Kagran, 1950s, rnd dial, plastic band, MIB $650.00

Jiminy Cricket, Ingersoll/US Time, 1948, 1 of 10 in Mickey's 20th Birthday series, VGIB.......................... $400.00

Jiminy Cricket, US Time, 1948, 1 of 10 in Mickey's 20th Birthday Series, luminescent, EX $200.00

Joe Carioca, US Time, 1948, 1 of 10 in Mickey's 20th Birthday Series, EX $175.00

Joe Palooka, New Haven/Ham Fisher, 1948, unused, NMIB..$950.00

Joker, Fossil, 1980s, NMIP.................................$75.00

Josie & the Pussycats, Bradley, 1971, w/3 bands, MIB.... $350.00

Kaptain Kool & the Kongs, 1977, Kaptain Kool on face, M. $100.00

King Kong, Fossil, MIB................................... $175.00

Li'l Abner, New Haven, 1947, animated mule, rare, MIB, $600 to $800.00

Li'l Abner, New Haven, 1947, animated flag, rare, MIB, $600 to...$800.00

Lone Ranger, New Haven, 1939, MIB, $500 to............. $800.00

Man From UNCLE, Bradley, 1960s, MIB (very rare box)...$200.00

Mary Marvel, Marvel/Fawcett, 1948, rnd chrome case, vinyl band, NMIB (oblong cb box) $600.00

Mickey Mouse, Ingersoll, 1930s, oblong chrome case, metal bracelet band, EXIB (box w/Mickey in top hat)....... $1,500.00

Mickey Mouse, Ingersoll, 1930s, oblong gold-tone case, leather band, nonworking o/w EXIB.................................. $1,600.00

Mickey Mouse, Ingersoll, 1930s, rnd chrome case, blk leather band w/2 metal Mickey inlets either side of dial, EXIB............$500.00

Mickey Mouse, Ingersoll, 1930s, rnd chrome case, metal bracelet w/repeated Mickey figures, EX+IB $450.00

Mickey Mouse, Ingersoll, 1930s, rnd gold-tone case, vinyl band, VGIB $150.00

Mickey Mouse, Ingersoll, 1940s, oblong chrome case, leather band, unused, MIB (yel Mickey box)......................... $400.00

Mickey Mouse, Ingersoll, 1940s, rnd chrome case, vinyl band, EXIB (yel Mickey box)... $225.00

Mickey Mouse, Ingersoll, 1950s, rnd chrome case, leather band, GIB $175.00

Mickey Mouse, Ingersoll, 1950s, rnd chrome case, leather band, MIB (plastic Mickey figure) $375.00

Mickey Mouse, US Time, 1940s, oblong case, leather band, VGIB $175.00

Mickey Mouse, US Time, 1948, 1 of 10 in Mickey's 20th Birthday Series, EX $225.00

Minnie Mouse, Timex, 1950s, w/emb celluloid plaque, MIB..$200.00

Orphan Annie, New Haven, oblong case w/image of Annie standing, leather band, NMIB $450.00

Orphan Annie, New Haven, oblong case w/image of Annie standing, leather band, VGIB $175.00

Partridge Family, 1970s, family image on face, NM $175.00

Pinocchio, US Time, 1948, 1 of 10 in Mickey's 20th Birthday Series, luminescent, EX... $175.00

Pluto, US Time, 1948, 1 of 10 in Mickey's 20th Birthday Series, VG $175.00

Popeye, New Haven, 1935, MIB $800.00

Popeye, unknown maker, 1940s, Popeye flanked by heads of Olive Oyl & Wimpy, rnd chrome case, chrome flex band, VG..$75.00

Roy Rogers, Fossil, 1st ed, EX...................................... $150.00

Snow White, EXIB (mirror box) $225.00

Snow White, EX+IB (w/figure) $385.00

Superman, Bradley, MIB..$2,500.00
Superman, Ingraham, bl band w/Superman logo, lightning bolt
   hands, EX, $400 to $600.00
Superman, New Haven, 1938, MIB $1,100.00
Tarzan, Bradley, 1950s, MIB $75.00
Texas Ranger, New Haven, EX.......................................$100.00
Three Little Pigs, Ingersoll, 1934, wolf & pigs on red rnd face,
   metal link band, EX $950.00
Tom Corbett Space Cadett, Ingraham, 1955, rnd chrome case w/
   blk leather band, NMIB (w/cb rocket display) $425.00
Woody Woodpecker, Ingraham, EX $150.00
Wolfman, Fossil, MIB $175.00

• • • • • • • • • Character, TV, and Movie Collectibles • • • • • • • • • •

To the 'baby boomers' who grew up glued to the TV set and addicted to Saturday matinees, the faces they saw on the screen were as familiar to them as family. Just about any character you could name has been promoted through retail merchandising to some extent; depending on the popularity they attain, exposure may continue for weeks, months, even years. It's no wonder, then, that the secondary market abounds with these items or that there is such widespread collector interest. For more information, we recommend *Collector's Guide to TV Toys & Memorabilia, 1960s & 1970s,* by Greg Davis and Bill Morgan; *Howdy Doody* by Jack Koch; *Character Toys and Collectibles, Vols. I* and *II,* and *Cartoon Toys and Collectibles* by David Longest; *The World of Raggedy Ann Collectibles* by Kim Avery; and *Peanuts Collectibles* by Andrea Podley and Derrick Bang.

Note: Although most characters are listed by their own names, some will be found under the title of the group, movie, comic strip, or dominant character they're commonly identified with. The Joker, for instance, will be found in the Batman listings. They are also listed under the cartoon studio name from which they came, such as Hanna-Barbera, Harvey Cartoons, Looney Tunes, etc.

All items are complete unless noted otherwise.

See also Action Figures; Battery-Operated Toys; Books; Chein; Character and Promotional Drinking Glasses; Character Clocks and Watches; Coloring, Activity, and Paint Books: Disney; Dolls; Fisher-Price; Games; Guns; Halloween Costumes; Lunch Boxes; Marx; Model Kits; Movie Posters and Lobby Cards; Paper Dolls; Pin-Back Buttons; Plastic Figures; Puzzles; Play Sets; Ramp Walkers; Records; View-Master; Western; Windup, Friction, and Other Mechanical Toys.

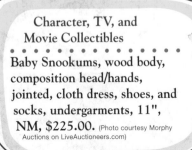

Addams Family, bank, Lurch, ceramic, Korea, 1970s, 8",
   NM+..$200.00
Addams Family, bank, The Thing, b/o, 3½x4½", Poynter Prod,
   1964, NMIB $125.00
Addams Family, doll, Morticia, stuffed cloth, 27", NM $50.00
Addams Family, figure, Morticia, hard plastic w/oversized rubber
   head, 4", 1960s, NM..$100.00
Addams Family, figure, Uncle Fester, vinyl, holding frog in raised
   hand, 5", Remco, 1960s, EX+ $125.00
Addams Family, hand puppets, Gomez, Morticia or Uncle Fester,
   Ideal, 1965, EX, ea..$50.00
Addams Family, Uncle Fester's Mystery Light Bulb, Poynter
   Prod, 1965, EXIB..$125.00
Alf, figure, Stick-Around Alf, plush w/suction cups on hands,
   Coleco, 1988, 8", unused, NRFB $18.00
Alf, figure, stuffed plush, 19", Coleco, 1986, NM+............$25.00
Alf, hand puppet, plush w/'Born to Rock' shirt, Alien Prod,
   NM $20.00
Alf, hand puppet, plush w/'Cookin' w/Alf' apron, 12", Alien
   Prod, 1988, NM...$20.00
Alf, jacks set, ball & 5 jacks, 1980s, MIP...........................$6.00
Alf, mug, ceramic, wht w/decal of Alf admiring self in mirror,
   'You're One of My Favorite Aliens,' Russ Berrie, 1987, M .$8.00
Alvin & the Chipmunks, bubble bath container, any character,
   Colgate-Palmolive, 1960s, M, ea $15.00
Alvin & the Chipmunks, figure, Alvin, plush pull-string talker,
   red sweater w/yel 'A,'19", CBS Toys, 1983, NM+.........$30.00

Alvin & the Chipmunks, figure, Alvin, stuffed cloth, felt-like material, red 'A' on chest, 5", Christy Mfg, 1959, NM...$25.00

Alvin & the Chipmunks, figure, Alvin, stuffed plush, lg yel 'A' on red sweater, red hat, 12", CBS Toys, 1983, NM $15.00

Alvin & the Chipmunks, figure, Simon, stuffed cloth, musical, 13", Knickerbocker, 1963, EX $75.00

Alvin & the Chipmunks, figure, Simon, stuffed plush, gym-shoe feet, wht 'S' on bl shirt, 8", Graphics Int'l, 1987, NM ...$10.00

Alvin & the Chipmunks, figure, Simon, stuffed plush, gym-shoe feet, 13", CBS Toys, 1983, NM+ $15.00

Alvin & the Chipmunks, figure, Simon, vinyl, jtd, bl shorts & wht tanktop, gym shoes, bl glasses, 4", CBS, 1984, NM+ .$5.00

Alvin & the Chipmunks, figure, Theodore, plastic, gr 'T' on wht top, gr shorts & socks, gr & wht shoes, 3", CBS, NM $5.00

Alvin & the Chipmunks, figure, Theodore, stuffed plush, pk 'T' on long gr shirt, 7", Graphics Int'l, 1980s, w/tag, NM+ .$10.00

Alvin & the Chipmunks, figure, Theodore, stuffed plush, talker, red 'T' on long gr shirt, 19", CBS Toys, 1983, NM+ $30.00

Alvin & the Chipmunks, hand puppet, Alvin, full cloth body w/ vinyl head in red hat, Knickerbocker, 1960, EX+ $75.00

Alvin & the Chipmunks, harmonica, red plastic triangular shape w/Alvin decal, Dairy Queen, 1984, NM....................$8.00

Alvin & the Chipmunks, ornament, 3 on sled, emb resin, 4", Adler, MIP...$6.00

Alvin & the Chipmunks, Stuff & Lace Set, Hasbro, 1950s-60s, EX+IB...$75.00

American Tail, Christmas Stockings, Fievel, 3 different, McDonald's premium, 1986, 7", EX+, ea $5.00

American Tail, doll, Fievel, plush w/bl pants & hat, red shirt, 22", Caltoy/Sears, NM $15.00

Amos 'N' Andy, figures, pnt wood bead type w/names on front, 6", EX+, pr..$350.00

Andy Panda, see Walter Lantz

Annie (Movie), wallet, wht vinyl w/name & image of Annie & Sandy, Henry Gordy Int'l, 1981, MIP (sealed)...............$12.00

Archies, any character in car, Burger King, 1991, MIP, ea..$10.00

Archies, figure, Archie, stuffed cloth body w/vinyl head, hands & shoes, cloth outfit, 18½", Presents, 1987, NM...........$30.00

Archies, figure, Reggie, bendable rubber, 6½", Jesco, 1989, NM+ $8.00

Archies, hand puppet, Archie, printed vinyl body w/vinyl head, Ideal, 1973, MIP (header reads 'TV Favorites')...........$125.00

Archies, Jughead Jr Shaver, Ja-Ru, 1986, NRFP.................$10.00

Archies, stencil set, 1980s, MOC.....................................$15.00

Babe, figure, stuffed plush, pk w/felt pouch holding 3 piglets, 12 gr foot pads & 1 red, 13", Equity Toys, 1998, NM.........$12.00

Baby Huey, see Harvey Cartoons

Banana Splits, see Hanna-Barbera

Barney, bank, Barney seated in chair w/mug, blanket & book, vinyl, 7", 1992, MIP...$10.00

Barney, figure, Barney as baseball player catching ball in glove, vinyl, 5", 1990s, NMIP...$10.00

Barney, night-light, plastic figure of Barney in hot-air balloon, 8½", Happiness Express, 1992, MIP.............................$18.00

Barney, ornament, resin figure in Santa hat holding candy cane & gift, 4½", Kurt Adler, 2001, MIP $6.00

Barney Bear, squeeze toy, bare-chested Barney w/arm raised, vinyl, 7", Alan Jay, 1950s, EX $50.00

Barney Google, bank, Spark Plug, pnt CI w/name emb on sides, 7½", EX...$85.00

Barney Google, drum, litho tin w/paper drumsticks, 10" dia, 1920s, VG..$275.00

Barney Google, figure, Spark Plug, wood, felt back blanket, 10½", Schoenhut, EX $250.00

Barney Google, figure set, Barney Google & Spark Plug, stuffed cloth w/glass eyes, cloth dressed, 9" & 12", Knickerbocker, 1930, VG...$1,100.00

Barney Google, figure set, Barney Google & Spark Plug, wood w/ cloth outfits, 7" & 9", Schoenhut, VG $575.00

Barney Google, figure set, Barney Google & Spark Plug, wood w/ cloth outfits, 8" & 9", Schoenhut, EX+ $600.00

Barney Google, hand puppet, Barney, printed cloth body w/ name, vinyl head w/cigar, Gund, 1950s, NM+............$100.00

Barney Google, hand puppet, Snuffy Smith, cloth body w/vinyl head, Gund, 1950s, NM $100.00

Batman, bank, Batman, standing in wide stance, hands on hips on wht stepped base w/red name, ceramic, 7", Lego, 1966, NM...$65.00

Batman, bank, Batman standing on sq base w/hands on hips, name on base compo, 7", NPP/Japan, NM $80.00

Batman, bank, Joker, bust figure w/emb name, plastic, 8", Mego, 1974, EX+...$60.00

Batman, Bat Grenade, shoots caps, Esquire Novelty, unused, M (VG card) $125.00

Batman, Batmobile, plastic, Duncan, 1977, MOC (8x11" card) $50.00

Batman, Batphone Hot-Line, plastic, Marx, 1966, non-working o/w EX $435.00

Batman, bicycle ornament, figure w/cape, 2-tone bl w/yel belt & bl & yel insignia, 8½", 1966, VG....................................$30.00

Batman, bubble bath container, Batman, bl & gray w/yel belt, Kid Care, 1995, unused, M...$10.00

Batman, bubble bath container, Batman or Robin, Colgate-Palmolive, 1960s, NM, ea $30.00

Batman, Climbing Figure, plastic figure, 9", Remco, 1980, MIB $100.00

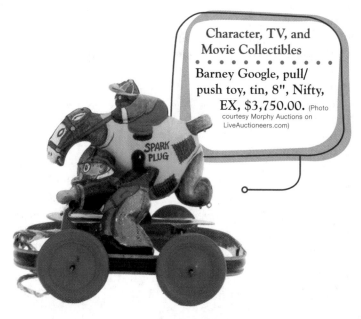

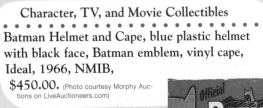

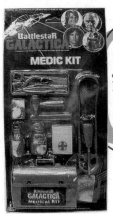

Character, TV, and Movie Collectibles
Batman Helmet and Cape, blue plastic helmet with black face, Batman emblem, vinyl cape, Ideal, 1966, NMIB, $450.00. (Photo courtesy Morphy Auctions on LiveAuctioneers.com)

Character, TV, and Movie Collectibles
Battlestar Galactica Medic Kit, 12-piece set, Lorami, 1978, NRFC, $20.00. (Photo courtesy www.gasolinealleyantiques.com)

Batman, coin set, Transogram, 1966, MIP (sealed) $35.00

Batman, Color Pin-Ups, cb, various images, 11x14", 1966, NMIB, ea $25.00

Batman, Colorforms Adventure Set, 1989, NRFB.............$18.00

Batman, Colorforms Cartoon Kit, 1960s, EXIB.................$50.00

Batman, Colorforms Print Putty, 1966, MIP (sealed) $150.00

Batman, figure, Batman, hard vinyl, jtd, bl shorts, gloves & boots, turq cape, yel belt, 15", Presents, 1988, M $40.00

Batman, figure, Flying Batman, 13", Transogram, 1966, MIP (sealed) $175.00

Batman, figure, Joker, vinyl, jtd arms, cloth jacket & vest, 15", Presents, 1989, EX+ $38.00

Batman, figure, Robin, vinyl, jtd, yel cloth cape, 13", Presents, 1988, NM $35.00

Batman, figure, Super Junior Squeak Toy, Batman or Robin, vinyl, 7", 1978, NM+, ea......................................$20.00

Batman, flashlight, bl plastic box w/red label, 3½", Nasta Industried, 1974, MIB..$75.00

Batman, fork & spoon, name & emb images on hdls, Imperial, 1966, NM $30.00

Batman, gyro spin top w/rip cord, Batman bust at top, 4½", Ahi, 1977, NM $15.00

Batman, hand puppet, Batman, blk cloth body, vinyl head w/flesh-tone face & blk mask, Punching Puppet, 1990, MIP $25.00

Batman, hand puppet, Batman, printed cloth body w/vinyl head, Ideal, 1966, MIP...$75.00

Batman, hand puppet, Batman, vinyl body w/name & molded vinyl head, Ideal, 1966, MIP......................................$150.00

Batman, hand puppet, Robin, vinyl body w/molded vinyl head, Ideal, 1966, NM $75.00

Batman, hand puppet set, Batman & Robin, all vinyl w/lithoed bodies, Ideal, 1966, MIB $1,000.00

Batman, kite, Giant Size, 37", Pressman Toys, 1964, MIP (sealed) $65.00

Batman, lamp, Batman figure next to Batcave on base w/'Batman' logo, shade is Joker's umbrella, 8", Vanity Fair, NM.... $175.00

Batman, mug, wht milk glass w/blk images of Batman on front & back, Westfield, 1966, NM..................................$50.00

Batman, night-light, pnt vinyl figure standing on sq base, cloth cape, 11", EX $75.00

Batman, night-light, 3-quarter figure, 2-tone bl w/yel trim, 3", Cable Electric, 1966, M $40.00

Batman, Oil Painting By Numbers, NPP, 1965, unused, NMIB $140.00

Batman, pencil box, gun shape, 1966, unused, MOC (sealed)..$175.00

Batman, pinball game, Batman & Robin, 22x10", Marx, 1966, NM $100.00

Batman, push-button puppet, Batman, 3", Kohner, 1960s, NM+ $50.00

Batman, scissors, Batman & Robin, Chemtoy, 1973, MOC..$25.00

Batman, Shaker Maker Batman Playset, Ideal, 1974, M (EX sealed box).. $160.00

Batman, Shooting Arcade, 8", Ahi/DC Comics, 1977, unused, NMIB $150.00

Batman, Sip-A-Drink Cup, Batman & Robin, plastic w/built-in straw, NPP, 1966, 5", EX+ $30.00

Batman, Sparkle Paints, Kenner, 1966, EXIB $75.00

Batman, Stardust 'Touch of Velvet Art' by Numbers, Batman & Robin, Hasbro/NPP, 1966, unused, MIP (sealed) $150.00

Batman, Utility Belt, complete w/accessories, Remco, unused, MIB.. $950.00

Batman, wallet, yel vinyl w/mc image & 'Batman' in red, plastic coin holder, magic slate notepad & wood stylus, M $90.00

Batman, Wrist Radios, bl plastic, Remco, 1966, EX, pr....$40.00

Battlestar Galactica, Atomic Yo-Yo, plastic, Larami, 1978, MOC...$35.00

Battlestar Galactica, Colorforms Adventure Set, Deluxe Edition #2359, 1978, MIB....................................$75.00

Battlestar Galactica, ID Set, Larami, 1978, NRFC............$18.00

Battlestar Galactica, Jet Discs, Larami, 1978, NRFC.........$20.00

Battlestar Galactica, wallet, vinyl w/image of space cruiser & name, 1978, NRFC $20.00

Beany & Cecil, bank, Cecil's head, molded plastic, NM...$35.00

Beany & Cecil, Beany-Copter, Mattel, 1961, NMOC $75.00

Beany & Cecil, bubble bath container, Cecil, Purex, 1962, NM.. $20.00

Beany & Cecil, Cecil Disguise Kit, unused, MIB........... $115.00

Beany & Cecil, doll, Beanie, stuffed w/vinyl head, hands & shoes, Bob Clampett, ca 1960, NM $200.00

Beany & Cecil, doll, Beany, plush, Mattel talker, 1961, EXIB.$200.00

Beany & Cecil, hand puppet, Beany, cloth body w/vinyl head, googley eyes, 1950s, EX......................................$75.00

Beany & Cecil, hand puppet, Dishonest John, Mattel talker, 1962, NM $175.00

Beany & Cecil, jack-in-the-box, Mattel, 1961, M.......... $250.00

Beany & Cecil, record player, Vanity Fair, 1961, EX+.... $125.00

Beetle Bailey, doll, Beetle Bailey, printed cloth body w/name, vinyl head, Gund, 1960, NM+..................................... $150.00

Beetle Bailey, doll, General Halftrack, stuffed cloth body, vinyl head, hands & shoes, gr jumpsuit, 15", Toy Works, NM .$20.00

Beetle Bailey, doll, Miss Buxley, stuffed cloth, vinyl head, red cloth dress, red shoes, 15", Sugar Loaf, 1990s, NM+ $20.00

Beetle Bailey, doll, Sgt Snorkel, stuffed body w/vinyl head & hands, flocked shoes, 15", Presents, 1985, EX $30.00

Beetle Bailey, hand puppet, Beetle Bailey, printed cloth body w/ name & vinyl head, Gund, 1960, EX $100.00

Beetle Bailey, stamper set, w/book, crayon & stampers, Ja-Ru, 1980s, complete & unused, MIP.............................$60.00

Ben Casey MD, Paint-by-Number Water Color Set, Transogram #1825, 1962, NRFB (sealed) $175.00

Ben Casey MD, Play Hospital Set, Transogram, 1962, NMIB. $550.00

Ben Casey MD, Sweater Guard, chain w/charms, Bing Crosby Prod, 1962, NRFC...$50.00

Betty Boop, bank, red plastic coin sorter w/Betty Boop graphics, drop a coin & she winks, 8", Mag-Nif, 1986, MIB.........$18.00

Betty Boop, doll, Betty, compo, cloth dress, shoes & socks, 12", Cameo Doll Co, NMIB... $4,250.00

Betty Boop, doll, compo & wood, red-pnt dress, jtd, 12", Cameo Doll Co, EX $1,725.00

Betty Boop, doll, Betty, stuffed cloth, w/guitar, faux red leather boots, zebra pants, 16", Good Stuff, 1999, NM $12.00

Betty Boop, doll, Betty, stuffed cloth, wearing bathing suit w/ chest banner, 13", Ace Novelty, 1989, NM....................$15.00

Betty Boop, doll, Betty, vinyl, jtd, short blk dress, 9½", M Shimmel & Sons, unused, MIP (sealed)..................................$35.00

Betty Boop, doll, Bimbo, wood & compo, jtd, 7", EX..... $325.00

Betty Boop, doll, Ko-Ko the Clown, plush w/rubber head, cloth outfit, 12", Presents, 1987, NM..................................$25.00

Betty Boop, Fancy Rings, set of 9, Ja-Ru, 1990s, unused, MOC $8.00

Betty Boop, mug, ceramic busty head figure w/eyes glancing upward, 4", 1981, NM..$10.00

Betty Boop, nodder, celluloid, operates w/rubber band, 7", EX+IB.. $800.00

Betty Boop, nodder, celluloid operates w/rubber band, 7", VG.. $300.00

Betty Boop, Play Set, includes watch, make-up case, lipstick, eye shadow kit, Ja-Ru, 1994, unused, MOC $8.00

Betty Boop, tea set, wht & bl porc w/various decaled images, 17-pc, Occupied Japan, EXIB..................................... $285.00

Beverly Hillbillies, car w/Jed, Granny, Jethro, Ellie May & Duke (Jed's dog), plastic, crank-op, 23", Ideal, 1960s, NMIB . $875.00

Beverly Hillbillies, doll, Ellie May, complete w/wardrobe, 12", Unique Art, 1964, MIB... $200.00

Beverly Hillbillies, doll, Jane Hathaway, gr skirt & jacket w/yel blouse, 11½", Japan, 1960s, MIB............................... $400.00

Beverly Hills 90210, dolls, any character, 11½", Mattel, 1991, MIB, ea...$50.00

Bevery Hills 90210, frisbee, Wham-O, 1991, NRFP..........$20.00

Bewitched, doll, Samantha, red gown & hat, 11½", Ideal, 1965, M $300.00

Bimbo, figure, stuffed cloth, blk & wht w/name on chest, side-glancing eyes, 12", French Novelty Co, EX.............. $2,500.00

Bionic Woman, bank, vinyl figure in jogging suit running on 'rocky' base, 10", Animals Plus, 1976, EX+ $25.00

Bionic Woman, Paint-By-Number Set, Craftmaster, 1970s, MIB $30.00

Bionic Woman, Pic-A-Show Projector, Kenner, 1979s, MIB..$25.00

Bionic Woman, Play-Doh Action Playset, Kenner, 1970s, MIB $20.00

Bionic Woman, See-A-Show Viewer, Kenner, 1970s, MOC ..$15.00

Bionic Woman, Styling Boutique, Kenner, 1970s, MIB $50.00

Bionic Woman, wallet, bl or pk w/image, Fabergé, 1970s, MIP... $200.00

Blondie, doll, Blondie, molded soft vinyl curly blond hair, red cloth dress, red pnt shoes, 18", Presents, 1985, NM+ $30.00

Blondie, doll, Daisy the Dog, plush, w/orig tag, 1985, EX .$25.00

Blondie, marionette, Dagwood, 14", 1940s, NM+ $200.00

Blondie, paint set, American Crayon, 1940s, EXIB...........$75.00

Blondie, wallet, EX+...$25.00

Blues Brothers, dolls, Elwood & Jake, blk cloth suits, hats & sunglasses, 26", Fun 4 All, 1997, MIB, set......................... $200.00

Blues Brothers, dolls, Elwood & Jake, shiny blk suits, hats & sunglasses, w/accessories, 12", Fun 4 All, 1997, MIB, ea $30.00

Bo-Peep, doll, jtd body w/pnt features, blond mohair wig, pk & wht print dress & hat, w/lamb, 8", Vogue, EX $550.00

Bob Hope, hand puppet, cloth body w/vinyl head, Zany, 1940s, NM $125.00

Character, TV, and Movie Collectibles
Boob McNutt, marionette, Schoenhut, 1920s, 10½", $550.00. (Photo courtesy Morphy Auctions on LiveAuctioneers.com)

Character, TV, and Movie Collectibles
Bozo the Clown, Changeable Blocks, Gaston Manufacturing, 1950s, EXIB, $45.00. (Photo courtesy www.serioustoyz.com)

Bonzo, dexterity game, tin & cb, 4" dia, Germany, EX... $100.00

Bonzo, figure, compo, standing upright, jtd arms & head, lg bl eyes, blk segmented tail, 13", 1920s, G........................ $775.00

Bonzo, figure, stuffed velvet, stitched features, jtd, 22", Chad Valley, 1920s, EX $1,000.00

Bonzo, figure, stuffed velvet, stitched features, orig suede collar, name on foot, jtd, 12", 1920s, VG $550.00

Bonzo, pull toy, Bonzo on scooter, litho tin, pushes & pulls on lever as scooter is pulled, 7" L, Chein, NM $625.00

Boob McNutt, doll, oilcloth w/printed features, cloth outfit, 34", Averill, 1920s, EX $100.00

Boob McNutt, doll, wood w/cloth outfit, 9", Schoenhut, EX ..$475.00

Bozo the Clown, bank, bust figure w/big smile, vinyl, 5", 1987, NM $20.00

Bozo the Clown, Bozo's Pocket Watch, plastic, 2", MIP....$12.00

Bozo the Clown, bubble bath container, Colgate-Palmolive, 1960s, NM..$45.00

Bozo the Clown, Button Ball Game, yel plastic Bozo figure w/ball on string, 3½", MIP...$12.00

Bozo the Clown, Circus Train, plastic, 3-pc w/Bozo in engine, Butchy & Belinda figures, Multiple Toymakers, 1970, MIB.$35.00

Bozo the Clown, Decal Decorator Kit, Meyerscord/Capitol Records, 1950s, EX+ $50.00

Bozo the Clown, doll, stuffed cloth, fuzzy hair, plastic eyes, 7½", Ace Novelty, 1989, NM+ $15.00

Bozo the Clown, doll, stuffed cloth w/soft molded vinyl head, 12", 1972, NM...$25.00

Bozo the Clown, doll, stuffed cloth w/vinyl face, pull-string talker, 21", Mattel, 1962, EX.....................................$35.00

Bozo the Clown, doll, vinyl, jtd, 7½", Dakin, 1974, NM...$28.00

Bozo the Clown, gumball machine, plastic Bozo figure hugging gum globe on base while waving, 10", Leaf Inc, 1994, MIB $28.00

Bozo the Clown, hand puppet, cloth body, vinyl head w/open-mouth smile, Knickerbocker, 1962, EX+ $55.00

Bozo the Clown, puzzle blocks, paper-litho-on-wood, Bozo's portrait changes expressions, 7x7x1", Capitol, 1950s, EX+.$50.00

Bozo the Clown, record player, Transogram, EX $50.00

Bozo the Clown, squeeze toy, Bozo w/hands son hips & looking up, turq w/red, wht & bl trim, 8", Holland Hall, 1964, EX......$50.00

Brady Bunch, banjo, 15", Larami, 1973, MIP....................$50.00

Brady Bunch, Brain Twisters, Larami, 1973, MOC............$25.00

Brady Bunch, Fishin' Fun Set, Larami, 1973, MOC $25.00

Brady Bunch, Fishing Puzzle & Game, Larami, 1973, MOC...$45.00

Brady Bunch, gum cards, complete set of 88 w/images on TV screen, 1969, rare set, EX to NM $600.00

Bringing Up Father, see Maggie & Jiggs

Broom-Hilda, bubble bath container, Lander, 1977, EX....$20.00

Broom-Hilda, doll, stuffed cloth w/yarn hair, 14", Wallace Berrie, 1983, w/orig hang tag, NM+ $30.00

Broom-Hilda, Spurt Stick, vinyl window stock-on reads 'Next Time Bring Your Wife,' 14", Meyercord, 1975, unused, MIP $10.00

Buck Rogers, Buck Rogers & Twiki Communication Set, HG Toys, 1970s, unused, MIB (sealed)................................$30.00

Buck Rogers, Chemical Laboratory, Gropper Mfg, complete, EXIB $1,150.00

Buck Rogers, Crayon Ship box, die-cut cb, American Pencil Co #019, 1930s, EX..$75.00

Buck Rogers, map of the solar system, 18x25", 1933, VG...$200.00

Buck Rogers, pencil box, 5x8½", American Lead Pencil Co, 1936, EX...$75.00

Buck Rogers, ring, flashes from Buck Rogers to Captain America, chrome band, 1960s, NM...$20.00

Buck Rogers, Strato-Kite, Aero-Kite, 1940s, unused & complete w/instructions, EXIP...$50.00

Buck Rogers, Twiki Robot Signal Flasher, b/o figure, 9½", MIB (worn box).. $125.00

Buffy the Vampire Slayer (TV Show), dolls, any character, Diamond Select, 1999, MIB, ea.....................................$30.00

Bugs Bunny, see Looney Tunes

Bullwinkle, see Rocky & Friends

Buster Brown, see also Advertising or Premium categories

Buster Brown, figure, Froggy the Gremlin, soft squeeze rubber, 10", Rempel, 1948, VG+...$65.00

Buster Brown, Magic Hat, blk plastic top hat w/wht Buster figure, Buster pops up, 3", Commonwealth Plastics, 1950s, M..$65.00

Buttercup & Spare-Ribs, doll set, stuffed cloth with printed features, 18½" Buttercup & 12" Spare-Ribs, EX.............. $900.00

Buttercup & Spare-Ribs, pull toy, figures on 4-wheeled platform, tin, 4", Nifty/Chein, VG $650.00

Captain America, Flashmite, Jane X, 1970s, MOC..........$75.00

Captain America, hand puppet, Ideal, 1960s, NM $50.00

Captain America, hand puppet, printed vinyl body w/molded vinyl head, Imperial, 1978, MIP $55.00

Captain America, figure, Mechanical Marvel Super-Heroes, plastic, 5½" Marx, 1968, MIB $225.00

Captain America, Official Utility Belt, Remco, 1979, complete, NRFB..$75.00

Captain America, Skooter, friction drive, Marx, 1968, NRFC $1,000.00

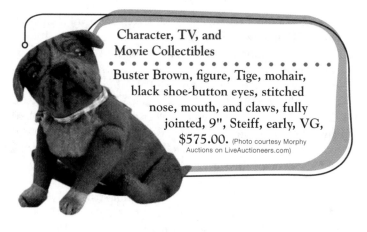

Captain Kangaroo, doll, Captain Kangaroo, Mattel, 1960s, MIB $150.00

Captain Kangaroo, doll, Mr Green Jeans, stuffed cloth w/yel yarn hair, gr outfit w/red & wht plaid shirt, 13", 1960s, M.....$30.00

Captain Kangaroo, hand puppet, cloth body w/vinyl head, Rushton, 1950s, NM+ $75.00

Captain Kangaroo, mug, plastic figural head w/googley eyes, 4", 1950s premium, EX $15.00

Captain Kangaroo, squeeze toy, Captain standing w/hands in pockets, pnt vinyl, 8", 1950s, MIB.......................$50.00

Captain Kangaroo, table cover, character birthday graphics, 54x96", CA Reed, 1950s, unopened, NM+ $50.00

Captain Kangaroo, TV Eras-O-Board Set, Hasbro, 1950s, EXIB $50.00

Captain Marvel, Buzz Bomb (airplane), paper, Fawcett, 1950s, complete & unused, MIP $125.00

Captain Marvel, Flying Captain Marvel punch-out toy, 10x7", Reed & Associates, 1944, unused, MIP (envelope) $45.00

Captain Marvel, Illustrated Soap, 1940s, complete & unused, MIB $650.00

Captain Marvel, key chain, Fawcett, 1940s, EX+ $50.00

Captain Marvel, Magic Flute, cb w/plastic mouthpiece, w/logo & illus on sides, 4½" L, Fawcett, 1940s, EX+ $50.00

Captain Marvel, Magic Lightning Box, Fawcett, 1940s, EX+ ..$75.00

Captain Midnight Playset, EX $200.00

Captain Midnight, playsuit, US Flight Commander, army gr shirt & pants w/Aviator Ace badge, Collegeville, EX $175.00

Captain Video, Space Ship Set, plastic, DuMont/USA, 1950s, rare, MIB $225.00

Car 54 Where Are You?, hand puppet, Patrolman Francis Muldoon, cloth body w/vinyl head, 1961, NM $175.00

Carrot Top, hand puppet, cloth body w/vinyl head, googley eyes, Zaney, 1940s, EX $125.00

Casey Jones, Engineer Doll, 12", EXIB..........................$350.00

Casper the Friendly Ghost, see Harvey Cartoons

Cat in the Hat, see Dr Seuss

Charlie Brown, see Peanuts

Charlie Chaplin, whistle, litho tin figure, 1½", EX.........$175.00

Charlie McCarthy, doll, Eddie Bergen's Charlie McCarthy, compo head w/moving mouth, blk tux, 19", Effanbee, VGIB $450.00

Charlie McCarthy, doll, molded compo w/movable mouth, 12", EX $175.00

Chicken Little, figure, plush w/felt trim, 6", Dakin, EX+ ..$95.00

CHiPs, Colorforms Playset, 1980s, unused, MIB $50.00

CHiPs, Police Set, California Higway Patrol, HG Toys, 1970s, NRFC $55.00

CHiPs, wallet, Imperial, 1981, MOC $25.00

Combat, gum cards, full set of 66 cards w/blk & wht images, 1963, NM $125.00

Crash Dummies, figure, stuffed cloth, plastic eyes, 14", Ace Novelty, 1992, NM+ $12.00

Creature from the Black Lagoon, see Universal Monsters

Curious George, doll, plush beanbag type, 7", Gund, M....$10.00

Curious George, doll, plush, name on red shirt & hat, 10", Toy Network, 1990s, M $10.00

Curious George, doll, plush, wht sweater & red hat, 15", Eden Toys, 1980s, M $20.00

Curious George, jack-in-the-box, litho metal, Schylling, 1995, EX $25.00

Daffy Duck, see Looney Tunes

Daisy Mae, see Li'l Abner

Dan Dare, 'Anatasia,' Jet Plane, press-out, unused, NM....$50.00

Dennis the Menace, doll, Dennis, stuffed cloth & vinyl, cloth outfit, 9", Presents, 1987, w/hang tag, NM+ $30.00

Dennis the Menace, doll, Dennis, stuffed cloth & vinyl, cloth outfit, 13", Mighty Star, MIB $35.00

Dennis the Menace, doll, Dennis, stuffed cloth w/printed features & hair, cloth outfit, 8", Determined, 1976, NM+..$15.00

Dennis the Menace, doll, Dennis, stuffed cloth, stitched nose & mouth, plastic eyes, cloth outfit, 11", Nanco, 1992, NM .$8.00

Dennis the Menace, doll, Dennis, vinyl, walking pose, 9", Hall Syndicate, NM $40.00

Dennis the Menace, doll, Margaret, stuffed cloth & vinyl, synthetic hair, cloth outfit, 10", Presents, 1987, NM...........$30.00

Dennis the Menace, hand puppet, Alice (mother), cloth body w/ vinyl head (open or closed mouth), EX+.......................$60.00

Dennis the Menace, hand puppet, Dennis, plain cloth body w/ vinyl head, 1959, EX $60.00

Dennis the Menace, hand puppet, Dennis, striped body w/vinyl head (lg or sm), Dennis Play Prod, NM.......................$50.00

Dennis the Menace, hand puppet, Henry (father), printed cloth w/vinyl head, w/eyeglasses, EX+ $60.00

Dennis the Menace, hand puppet, Margaret, cloth body w/vinyl head, Hall Syndicate, 1959, NM $100.00

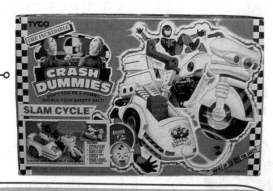

Dennis the Menace, Mischief Kit, Hassenfeld Bros (Hasbro), 1950s, unused, NMIB... $250.00

Dennis the Menace, paint set, Pressman, 1954, complete & unused, MIB $125.00

Dennis the Menace, Stuff 'n Lace Doll, Standard Toycraft, MIP $40.00

Dennis the Menace, whistle, locomotive w/mouthpiece, plastic, 5", Fortune, MIP (w/Dennis the Menace header card) ..$15.00

Deputy Dawg, bubble bath container, Colgate-Palmolive, 1960s, NM $25.00

Deputy Dawg, doll, cloth w/vinyl head, 14", Ideal, 1960s, NM ..$50.00

Dick Dastardly, Flying Propeller, Larami, 1973, MOC $35.00

Dick Tracy, badge, Inspector General/Dick Tracy/Secret Service Patrol, brass, 2½", 1938, scarce, EX+ $250.00

Dick Tracy, bank, Sparkle Plenty in highchair, ceramic, 'Sparkle Plenty Savings Bank'/'Dick Tracy God Father,' 13", EX ...$100.00

Dick Tracy, bubble bath container, Dick Tracy, Colgate-Palmolive, 1965, NM $25.00

Dick Tracy, Candid Camera, complete w/film & plastic carrying case, Seymour Sales, 1950s, NMIB $75.00

Dick Tracy, coloring set, w/pencils & pictures to color, Hasbro, 1967, complete & unused, MIP $100.00

Dick Tracy, doll, Sparkle Plenty, compo w/yel yarn hair, 13", Ideal, NMIB... $350.00

Dick Tracy, fingerprint set, w/microscope, magnifying glass, badge & ink pad, Pressman, 1930s, EXIB $200.00

Dick Tracy, hand puppet, Dick Tracy, printed cloth body (blk suit & tie), w/vinyl head in blk vinyl hat, Ideal, 1961, EX ...$85.00

Dick Tracy, hand puppet, Joe Jitsu, printed cloth w/vinyl head, 1960s, EX+ $30.00

Dick Tracy, handcuffs, metal, John Henry, 1940s, EX+ $30.00

Dick Tracy, Islander Ukette, features Sparkle Plenty, Styron, 1950s, EX+ $75.00

Dick Tracy, magnifying glass, plastic w/attached vinyl case, Larmi, 1970s, unused, MOC $18.00

Dick Tracy, soap figure, Sparkle Plenty, display box simulates bed, 4½" figure, Castile, EXIB................................$50.00

Dick Tracy, Sparkle Paints, Kenner, 1963, complete & unused, NMIB $75.00

Dick Tracy, Sunny Dell Acres playset (Home of Sparkle Plenty), DeLuxe Game Corp, EX $400.00

Dick Tracy, Talking Phone, b/o, 10 different phrases, Marx, 1960s, EX+ $50.00

Dick Tracy, Wrist Radio, receiver on leather band, Da-Myco Prod, 1940s, EXIB $300.00

Dick Tracy, Wrist Radios, Remco, 1950s, EXIB............. $100.00

Doctor Dolittle, Animal Fist Faces, EXIB........................$40.00

Doctor Dolittle, bank, Doctor Dolittle figure standing w/sitting monkey & dog at his side, NM $50.00

Doctor Dolittle, Colorforms Cartoon Kit, 1967, NMIB $30.00

Doctor Dolittle, doll, Doctor Dolittle, pull-string talker, 23", Mattel, 1967, NMIB................................... $100.00

Doctor Dolittle, doll, Doctor Dolittle, talker, Mattel, 1960s, 24", MIB.. $150.00

Doctor Dolittle, doll, Pushmi-Pullyu, talker, Mattel, 1960s, NM $100.00

Doctor Dolittle, hand puppet, Doctor Dolittle, talker, Mattel, 1967, NM $50.00

Doctor Dolittle, Stitch-a-Story, Hasbro, NMIP $25.00

Donkey Kong, figure, stuffed plush w/vinyl face, hands & feet, barrel applique on chest, Etone Int'l, 1982, NM $15.00

Dr Kildare, doll, plastic, 11½", 1960s, rare, MIB............. $450.00

Dr Seuss, bookends, Cat in the Hat, emb red plastic figures, 14" H, M, pr $25.00

Dr Seuss, figure, Cat in the Hat, stuffed plush, 24", Eden, 1979, NM $50.00

Dr Seuss, figure, Cat in the Hat, stuffed plush, 28", Coleco, 1983, NM+...$50.00

Dr Seuss, figure, Grinch, stuffed plush, gr w/red collar, yel plastic eyes, 30", Macy's, 1997, EX+................................$35.00

Dr Seuss, figure, Horton the Elephant, Mattel talker, 1970s, EX+ $75.00

Dr Seuss, figure, Horton the Elephant, plush, Coleco, 1980s, NM+...$75.00

Dr Seuss, figure, Thidwick the Moose, plush, Coleco, 1980s, EX+ $25.00

Dr Seuss, figure, Yertle the Turtle, plush, Coleco, 1980s, EX+...$25.00

Character, TV, and Movie Collectibles

Dr. Seuss, figure, Cat in the Hat, stuffed plush, 25", Douglas Co., 1976, NM, $50.00.
(Photo courtesy www.whatacharacter.com)

Character, TV, and Movie Collectibles

Dukes of Hazzard, Acrylic Paint Set, 'Chase Scene,' Craft Master, 1980, unused, MIB (sealed), scarce, $75.00. (Photo courtesy www.gasolinealley antiques.com)

Dr Seuss, hand puppet, Cat in the Hat, Mattel talker, 1970, EX+ $75.00

Dr Seuss, push-button puppet, Cat in the Hat, Little Kids Inc, 2003, MIP $10.00

Dracula, see Universal Monsters

Dragnet, Crime Lab, Transogram, 1955, incomplete, G+IB .. $50.00

Droopy Dog, hand puppet, cloth & plush body w/molded vinyl head, 12", Turner Ent/MGM, 1989, EX+ $12.00

Droopy Dog, hand puppet, cloth body w/vinyl head, Zaney, 1950s, NM $75.00

Dudley Do-Right, see Rocky & Friends

Dukes of Hazzard, Etch-A-Sketch Action Pak, 6 different reusable screens, Ohio Art, 1980s, NMIP $10.00

Dynasty (TV Series), dolls, Alexis Colby or Krystal Carrington, 19", World Doll, 1985, MIB, ea $175.00

Emergency, fire hat & oxygen mask set, NM $50.00

Emmett Kelly, hand puppet, Willie the Clown character, blk & wht checked body w/vinyl head, Baby Barry, 1950, NM+ $100.00

Emmett Kelly Jr, ventriloquist doll, Horsman, 1978, MIB. $50.00

ET, book, 'Fly Away With ET'/'A Shape Vinyl Book,' 6", Simon & Schuster, 1983, MIP... $12.00

ET, bubble bath container, half figure of ET in bathrobe, Avon, 1984, unused, NMIB $25.00

ET, charm bracelet, enameled metal, Aviva, 1982, MOC (Elliott & ET graphics) $6.00

ET, figure, PVC, w/flower pot, The Original Collectibles, LJN, 1982, M (G card) $10.00

ET, Finger Light, vinyl finger shape, b/o, glows when pressed, 5", Knickerbocker, 1982, MOC............................... $10.00

Family Affair, doll set, Buffy & Mrs Beasley, 10½", Mattel, 1960s, 10½", NRFB $150.00

Family Affair, make-up & hairstyling set, Buffy, Amsco, 1970s, EX $50.00

Fantastic Four, flicker ring, silver-tone plastic w/mc flicker image, vending machine item, 1966, M $65.00

Fat Albert, doll, Little Bill, stuffed cloth & vinyl, 'Hey Hey Hey I'm a Cosby Kid', 22", Remco, 1985, MIB $75.00

Fat Albert, hand puppet, Fat Albert, printed vinyl body w/ molded vinyl head, Ideal, 1973, NM+ $150.00

Fat Albert, hand puppet, Weird Harold, all vinyl, Ideal, 1973, MIP (header card reads 'TV Favorites') $200.00

Felix the Cat, bubble bath container, color variations, Colgate-Palmolive, 1960s, NM.. $25.00

Felix the Cat, figure, compo, jtd arms, name in gold high on chest, gold neck bow, 13", c Pat Sullivan, 1924, EX.. $2,500.00

Felix the Cat, figure, squeeze action w/cloth body, compo head & wooden hands & feet, squeeze legs & arms move, 8", EX $1,450.00

Felix the Cat, figure, stuffed blk body, Yes/No head movement when tail is moved, 10", EX $1,100.00

Felix the Cat, figure, stuffed cloth, cowboy attire w/chaps, vest, hat, gun & holster, 24", Gund (?), 1930s, EX.......... $1,200.00

Felix the Cat, figure, stuffed orange cloth w/papier-maché face, 24", 1930s, EX $1,550.00

Felix the Cat, figure, stuffed plush, blk w/wht face, shoe-button eyes, jtd, 9½", Steiff, 1920s.......................... $5,600.00

Felix the Cat, figure, stuffed plush, toothy grin, lg eyes, 23", Chad Valley (?), 1920s, VG.............................. $1,100.00

Character, TV, and Movie Collectibles
• • • • • • • • • • •
Fat Albert, doll, Remco, 1985, MIB, $90.00. (Photo courtesy www.whatacharacter.com)

Felix the Cat, figure, stuffed plush, 'You're My CATnip' on red satin shirt, 16½", Applause, 1989, w/hang tag, NM $12.00

Felix the Cat, figure, stuffed velvet w/extra long arms, legs & tail, red neck ribbon, 29", 1920s, EX $450.00

Felix the Cat, figure, vinyl, standing w/legs together & arms down at sides, 6", Eastern Moulded Prod, 1962, NM+ ... $50.00

Felix the Cat, figure, wooden, blk & wht bead type w/name on chest, 8", Schoenhut, EX (G box marked 'Felix the Movie Cat')... $550.00

Felix the Cat, figure, wooden, flat-sided w/screwed-on jtd arms & legs, 7", ca 1930, EX $775.00

Felix the Cat, hand puppet, plush body & head w/felt ears, EX... $600.00

Felix the Cat, magic slate, red w/'Felix the Cat Slate' in outline lettering, mc image on header, Lowe #3068, 1950s, EX. $50.00

Felix the Cat, pull toy, 'Felix the Movie Cat,' Felix & 2 mice on on 4-wheeled platform, tin, 8" Nifty/Chein, EXIB... $2,500.00

Felix the Cat, push toy, blk pnt wood w/blk & wht features, jtd arms & legs, VG $250.00

Felix the Cat, sparkler, tin head w/'Copyright by Pat Sullivan'/'Felix' lithoed on tie, Chein/Borgfeldt, EXIB.............. $1,200.00

Felix the Cat, tableware, 20-pc wht china w/Felix decals, red trim, Crown Pottery, EX.................................... $400.00

Felix the Cat, tea set, 14-pc tan lustre w/cups, saucers, plates, creamer & teapot, no sugar bowl, 1940s, EX $400.00

Felix the Cat, Walking Felix, papier-maché figure w/segmented wood tail, 5" figure w/20" walking ramp, EXIB........... $800.00

'Felix the Movie Cat,' Felix & 2 mice on 4-wheeled platform, tin, 8", Nifty/Chein, 1930s, EX............................. $1,600.00

Fievel, see American Tail

Flash Gordon, figure, wood compo, standing on base w/name, 5", rare, NM $275.00

Flash Gordon, hand puppet, cloth body w/vinyl head, KFS, 1950s, EX... $75.00

Flash Gordon, Space Compass, figural compass on yel & bl band w/buckle closure, 1950s, MOC $40.00

Flash Gordon, Space Outfit, w/vest, cummerbund, sleeve cuffs, spats, hat & belt, EX+IB $175.00

Flash Gordon, Strat-O-Wagon, PS wooden wheels & hdl, 6" (w/o hdl), Wyandotte, 1940s, EX $100.00

Flash Gordon, wrist compass, plastic, FG Inc, 1950s, EX .. $65.00

Flintstones, bank, Barney figure standing on 'rock' base, vinyl, 6", 1994, M $12.00

Flintstones, bank, Fred figure hugging gold club, vinyl, 8", NM .$75.00

Flintstones, bank, Wilma holding Pebbles on grassy base incised 'Wilma,' 11", 1970s, NM+ $40.00

Flintstones, bubble bath container, any character, Purex, NM $25.00

Flintstones, Dino, plush w/vinyl head, gr pants w/blk shirt, yel hands & feet, 10", Gund, 1960s, EX $75.00

Flintstones, Doodle Dialer, Winthrop Toy, 1960s, EX+ $50.00

Flintstones, figure, Baby Puss (saber tooth tiger), sitting upright, yel vinyl w/blk spots, gr belt, 10", 1960, rare, NM $150.00

Flintstones, figure, Bamm-Bamm, squeeze vinyl, standing holding club down in front, 6", Sanitoy, 1979, EX+ $18.00

Flintstones, figure, Bamm-Bamm, stuffed cloth, felt hair, hat & outfit, 8", Knickerbocker, 1970s, NMIB $50.00

Flintstones, figure, Bamm-Bamm, vinyl, cloth outfit, jtd, 7", Dakin, 1970s, w/orig hang tag, unused, M.....................$25.00

Flintstones, figure, Bamm-Bamm, vinyl, standing, no club, jtd arms, swivel head, 6", Kenner, 1970s, M $15.00

Flintstones, figure, Bamm-Bamm, vinyl, standing w/club on gray 'rock' base, 5½", 1994, NM $8.00

Flintstones, figure, Barney, stuffed cloth & vinyl, gr-pnt hair, brn fuzzy outfit w/2 patches, 12", Knickerbocker, EX............$75.00

Flintstones, figure, Barney, vinyl, felt outfit, 7" or 8", Dakin, 1970s, NM, ea $45.00

Flintstones, figure, Barney Rubble, vinyl, cloth outfit, jtd head & arms, 7", Dakin, 1970s, orig hang tag, unused, M...........$25.00

Flintstones, figure, Betty, plastic, standing w/arms behind head in gr dress, 3", Imperial, 1976, NM $10.00

Flintstones, figure, Betty, vinyl, standing w/1 arm in front, yel hair, bl dress, open-mouth smile, 12", 1960s, VG...........$50.00

Flintstones, figure, Dino, vinyl, swivel head, jtd arms, 6", Knixies/Knickerbocker, 1962, EX $55.00

Flintstones, figure, Fred, stuffed cloth w/vinyl head, bl fuzzy suit w/yel collar, red tie, 11", Knickerbocker, NM.............. $125.00

Flintstones, figure, Hoppy, vinyl, jtd, Dakin, scarce, MIP ('The Flintstones' header card) $150.00

Flintstones, figure, Pebbles, squeeze vinyl, 6", Sanitoy, 1979, NM $25.00

Flintstones, figure, Pebbles, stuffed cloth, cloth outfit, brn felt hair, printed features, 7", Knickerbocker, 1970s, EX $15.00

Flintstones, figure, Pebbles, vinyl w/cloth outfit, 4½", Knickerbocker, 1970s, EX $10.00

Flintstones, figure, Wilma, squeeze vinyl, seated talking on phone, 5½", Lanco, NM...$40.00

Flintstones, figure, Wilma, stuffed cloth w/orange plush hair, wht dress & necklace, 17", Toy Works, 2000, w/tag, NM $10.00

Flintstones, hand puppet, Barney Rubble, stuffed cloth w/furry outfit, vinyl head, Knickerbocker, 1960s, NM................$50.00

Flintstones, hand puppet, Pebbles, printed cloth body w/name & vinyl head, Ideal, 1966, NM $75.00

Flintstones, iron-on transfer, pictures of Fred, Wilma & Pebbles on pk circle outlined in yel, 7½x6", dated 1976, M........$18.00

Flintstones, Magnet Stickers, pkg of 3 featuring lg Barney, smaller Fred & Bamm-Bamm, c 1979, NRFP $20.00

Flintstones, marionette, Barney, stuffed cloth w/furry outfit, 12", Knickerbocker, 1962, NM...$35.00

Flintstones, mug, any character, molded plastic head, 3", F&F Mold Co, 1970s, NM, ea $12.00

Flintstones, night-light, Barney figure, plastic, 4", Leviton, 1975, MOC $15.00

Flintstones, push-button puppet, any character, Kohner, 1960s, NM, ea...$50.00

Flip the Frog, figure, celluloid, movable arms, 6½", Japan, EX .$100.00

Flip the Frog, stuffed velvet, 6", Dean's Rag Book Co, EX ..$400.00

Flipper, figure, plush, gray & wht w/lt bl sailor's vest & wht sailors hat, 17", Knickerbocker, 1976, NM $35.00

Flying Nun, doll, 4½", Hasbro, 1967, rare, MIB.............. $175.00

Flying Nun, doll, 12", Hasbro, rare, MIB $350.00

Foxy Grandpa, figure, wood w/cloth outfit, 9", Schoenhut, VG+ $2,000.00

Froggy the Gremlin, see Buster Brown

Full House (TV Series), doll, Jesse, vinyl w/cloth outfit, red guitar, 12", Tiger Toys, 1993, MIB $50.00

Full House (TV Series), doll set, Danny's Family, 3" to 7", Tiger Toys, 1993, MIB $50.00

Full House (TV Series), doll set, Jesse's Family, from 3" to 7", MIB...$50.00

G-Men, Fingerprint Set, New York Toy & Game Co, complete, EXIB $300.00

G-Men, pencil box, blk & wht on red, about 5x8½", 1930s, EX...$85.00

Gabby, see Gulliver's Travels

Garfield, bank, figure as hobo w/tooth missing & holding hat w/ slot, vinyl, 8", NM..$20.00

Garfield, bank, figure sitting upright w/eyes half closed, vinyl, 6", Kat's Meow, 1980s, NM+ $15.00

Garfield, comb & brush set, orange plastic figural brush w/blk detail, orange comb w/blk printed detail, Avon, MIP $12.00

Garfield, figure, Arlene, stuffed, pk w/red felt lips, lg plastic eyes, 7", Dakin, 1974, NM...$10.00

Garfield, figure, Odie, stuffed plush, 10½", Dakin, 1983, NM...$12.00

Garfield, figure, PVC, 'Eat Your Heart Out!' on red shirt, 1½", Enesco, 1980s, NMIB...$15.00

Garfield, figure, stuffed plush, 'User Friendly,' 9", Dakin, 1980s, NM+...$12.00

Garfield, gumball machine, 'But It Will Cost You!' or 'Never Trust a Smiling Cat,' Superior Toy, 1970s-80s, NM, ea..$35.00

Garfield, night-light, plastic blk-outlined image of Garfield resting on blk-outlined cloud, 2x3", Prestigeline, MOC......$10.00

Gasoline Alley, pull toy, Skeezix being pulled by Pal, die-cut pressed wood, pnt detail, 6½", Trixie Toy, 1930s, G.......$65.00

Get Smart (TV Series), doll, Agent 99, red dress w/gold belt, 11½", Japan, 1967, rare, MIB....................................... $400.00

Ghostbusters, gumball machine, vinyl ghost in red 'No' symbol atop bl plastic dispenser, 7", Superior Toy, 1986, NM....$12.00

Ghostbusters, Streamer Kite, features the 'No Ghost' symbol & Slimer, Spectra Star, 1989, unused, MIP $12.00

Ghostbusters (The Real Ghosbusters Cartoon Series), Pinball Game, plastic, Ja-Ru, 1986, unused, MOC......................$10.00

Gilligan's Island, doll, Mary Ann in 2-pc swimsuit, 11½", Japan, 1965, rare, MIB $400.00

Gilligan's Island, Gilligan's Floating Island, Playskool, 1977, MIB $150.00

Gomer Pyle (TV Show), gum cards, complete set of 66 blk & wht images, 1960s, all M $75.00

Good Times (TV Series), doll, JJ, stuffed cloth w/molded head, red suit, 15", Shindana, 1975, rare, MIB $150.00

Good Times (TV Series), doll, JJ, talker, stuffed cloth w/'Dyn-O-Mite' label on chest, 21", Shindana, MIB $125.00

Good Times (TV Show), gum cards, complete set of 55, Topps, 1975, EX to NM (w/sealed wax pack) $50.00

Green Hornet, figure, bendable, 6", Lakeside Toys, 1966, MOC..$175.00

Green Hornet, flicker ring, silver base, 1966, EX...............$10.00

Green Hornet, hand puppet, Greenway Prod, 1960s, NM...$250.00

Green Hornet, Humming Bee, swing it around & it makes realistic buzzing noise, 5½", 1966 premium, NM $50.00

Green Hornet, kite, Magic Invisible Kit, plastic, Roalex, 1966, NMIB (sealed).. $400.00

Green Hornet, playing cards, 'Official...52 Card Deck w/40 Official Action Photos,' 1966, unused, MIB...................... $100.00

Green Hornet, Print Putty, Colorforms, 1966, MOC (sealed)..$75.00

Green Hornet, spoon, name & image on enamel oval inlayed on ornate handle, 4½", 1966, M..$25.00

Green Hornet, Stardust 'Touch of Velvet Art By Numbers,' Hasbro, unused, MIB (sealed) $125.00

Green Hornet, wallet, gr vinyl w/name, image & lg insect, Standard Plastic Prod, 1966, NM.................................... $140.00

Gremlins, Colorforms Play Set, 1984, unused, MIB $35.00

Gremlins, doll, Gizmo, plush, 12", Hasbro Softies, 1980s, scarce, NM $25.00

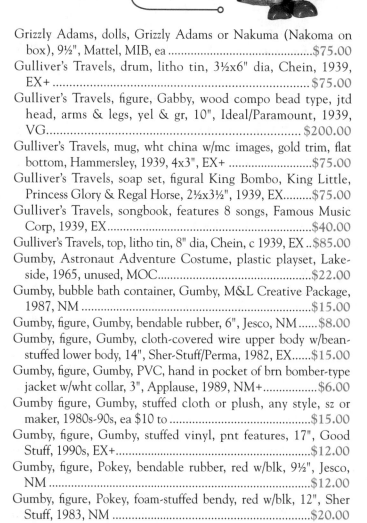

Grizzly Adams, dolls, Grizzly Adams or Nakuma (Nakoma on box), 9½", Mattel, MIB, ea $75.00

Gulliver's Travels, drum, litho tin, 3½x6" dia, Chein, 1939, EX+ $75.00

Gulliver's Travels, figure, Gabby, wood compo bead type, jtd head, arms & legs, yel & gr, 10", Ideal/Paramount, 1939, VG.. $200.00

Gulliver's Travels, mug, wht china w/mc images, gold trim, flat bottom, Hammersley, 1939, 4x3", EX+ $75.00

Gulliver's Travels, soap set, figural King Bombo, King Little, Princess Glory & Regal Horse, 2½x3½", 1939, EX.........$75.00

Gulliver's Travels, songbook, features 8 songs, Famous Music Corp, 1939, EX..$40.00

Gulliver's Travels, top, litho tin, 8" dia, Chein, c 1939, EX ..$85.00

Gumby, Astronaut Adventure Costume, plastic playset, Lakeside, 1965, unused, MOC..$22.00

Gumby, bubble bath container, Gumby, M&L Creative Package, 1987, NM $15.00

Gumby, figure, Gumby, bendable rubber, 6", Jesco, NM......$8.00

Gumby, figure, Gumby, cloth-covered wire upper body w/bean-stuffed lower body, 14", Sher-Stuff/Perma, 1982, EX......$15.00

Gumby, figure, Gumby, PVC, hand in pocket of brn bomber-type jacket w/wht collar, 3", Applause, 1989, NM+.................$6.00

Gumby figure, Gumby, stuffed cloth or plush, any style, sz or maker, 1980s-90s, ea $10 to $15.00

Gumby, figure, Gumby, stuffed vinyl, pnt features, 17", Good Stuff, 1990s, EX+...$12.00

Gumby, figure, Pokey, bendable rubber, red w/blk, 9½", Jesco, NM...$12.00

Gumby, figure, Pokey, foam-stuffed bendy, red w/blk, 12", Sher Stuff, 1983, NM $20.00

Gumby, figure, Prickle, rubber, yel jtd dinosaur, 1980s, NM. $6.00
Gumby, figures w/up, Gumby or Pokey, vinyl, 4", Lakeside, 1966, EX, ea $40.00
Hair Bear, see Hanna-Barbera
Hanna-Barbera, see also Flintstones, Jetsons or Scooby Doo
Hanna-Barbera, Amazing Chan Cork Gun Set w/Target Set, Larami, 1973, unused, MIP $24.00
Hanna-Barbera, bank, Baba Looey, vinyl, orange w/gr sombrero & blk neckerchief, 9", Roclar, 1976, NM $18.00
Hanna-Barbera, bank, Huckleberry Hound sitting upright w/arms crossed, lt bl & pk bowtie, 5", 1980s, NM $20.00
Hanna-Barbera, bank, Huckleberry Hound standing, red w/blk hat, ears & nose, Knickerbocker, 1960s, NM+ $25.00
Hanna-Barbera, bank, Yogi Bear standing w/1 hand on tie, other arm at side, 10", Knickerbocker, 1960s, EX $30.00
Hanna-Barbera, bop bag, Pixie/Dixie reversible images on inflatable vinyl, 8", Kestral, M $50.00
Hanna-Barbera, bubble bath container, any character except Moroco Mole, Purex, 1960s, NM, ea $20 to $25.00
Hanna-Barbera, bubble bath container, Morocco Mole, Purex, 1966, rare, NM+ $65.00
Hanna-Barbera, camera, Yogi Bear, blk plastic w/wht image of Yogi on side, 3x3½", Hong Kong, NM+IB $35.00
Hanna-Barbera, Cartoon Kit, colorforms Huckleberry Hound, 1962, EXIB $150.00
Hanna-Barbera, Cartoonist Stamp Set, features many different characters, 1960s, EXIB $100.00
Hanna-Barbera, chalkboard, Huckleberry Hound, Pressman Toy Co, 1960s, M $50.00
Hanna-Barbera, club membership kit, Banana Splits, 1968, NM (w/mailer) $100.00

Hanna-Barbera, doll, Augie Doggie, plush w/vinyl face, 10", Knickerbocker, 1959, EX+ $40.00
Hanna-Barbera, doll, Baba Looey, stuffed plush & vinyl, lt gr w/ orange vinyl sombrero, 16", Knickerbocker, 1959, EX ...$50.00
Hanna-Barbera, doll, Cindy Bear, stuffed felt, printed features, cloth skirt, 8", Knickerbocker, 1973, NRFB $50.00
Hanna-Barbera, doll, Cindy Bear, stuffed plush w/vinyl face, 16", Knickerbocker, scarce, NM $250.00
Hanna-Barbera, doll, Hair Bear, stuffed plush w/felt vest, belt & neck scarf, furry mop of hair, 8", Sutton & Sons, NM ...$40.00
Hanna-Barbera, figure, Augie Doggie, squeeze rubber, jtd, pale yel w/lt bl collar, 8", Bucky, 1970s, NM+ $75.00
Hanna-Barbera, figure, Dixie, plush w/felt eyes & tie, Knickerbocker, 1959, 13", NM $50.00
Hanna-Barbera, figure, Fleegle (Banana Splits), rubber, pk w/red hat & bowtie, 5", 1968, NM $50.00
Hanna-Barbera, figure, Huckleberry Hound, inflatable vinyl, unused, MIP (pkg reads 'The Flintstones Inflatables')....$25.00
Hanna-Barbera, figure, Huckleberry Hound, squeeze vinyl, policeman, 10", Dell, NM $50.00
Hanna-Barbera, figure, Huckleberry Hound, squeeze vinyl, standing w/blk cane & top hat in hand, 6", Dell, NRFP $50.00
Hanna-Barbera, figure, Huckleberry Hound, squeeze vinyl, w/ice cream cone, airbrushed details, 7", Elizabeth, MIP.........$75.00
Hanna-Barbera, figure, Huckleberry Hound, stuffed plush w/rubber face, red & wht, 18", Knickerbocker, 1959, NM $35.00
Hanna-Barbera, figure, Huckleberry Hound, vinyl, red w/bl top hat & tie, jtd arms, 6", Knickerbocker Knixies, NM $40.00
Hanna-Barbera, figure, Magilla Gorilla, plush w/vinyl head, 19", Ideal, 1960s, NM $100.00
Hanna-Barbera, figure, Magilla Gorilla, squeeze rubber, brn w/red shorts & wht tie blk cane, 6½", Bucky, 1974, NM $65.00
Hanna-Barbera, figure, Magilla Gorilla, stuffed felt w/vinyl head, 7½", Ideal, 1960s, NM $55.00
Hanna-Barbera, figure, Magilla Gorilla, stuffed plush, 8½", Nanco, 1990, NM+ $10.00
Hanna-Barbera, figure, Magilla Gorilla, stuffed ribbed cloth w/pk shorts, 7½", Playtime Toys, 1979, NM+ $20.00
Hanna-Barbera, figure, Mr Jinks, soft rubber, standing w/hands on hips, 8½", Bucky, NM $75.00
Hanna-Barbera, figure, Mr Jinks, stuffed plush w/vinyl face, blk & wht, pk bowtie/buttons, 13", Knickerbocker, 1959, VG...$50.00
Hanna-Barbera, figure, Mushmouse, stuffed felt w/vinyl head, red felt vest, 9", Ideal, 1960s, EX $75.00
Hanna-Barbera, figure, Pixie, vinyl, jtd head & arms, 6", Knickerbocker Knixies, 1962, NM $40.00
Hanna-Barbera, figure, Pixie or Dixie, plush, 12", Knickerbocker, 1960s, NM+ $50.00
Hanna-Barbera, figure, Quick Draw McGraw, stuffed plush, felt hands, feet, hat & gun holster, 13", Nanco, 1989, NM..$15.00
Hanna-Barbera, figure, Quick Draw McGraw, stuffed plush, felt hands, hat & gun holster, 16", Presents, 1985, NM+ $20.00
Hanna-Barbera, figure, Snagglepuss, squeeze vinyl, jtd, standing w/feet together, dk pk w/blk trim, 9", Bucky, EX $75.00
Hanna-Barbera, figure, Snagglepuss, vinyl, pk, 7½", Dakin, 1971, MIP (clear plastic bag w/name & hdl)....................$65.00
Hanna-Barbera, figure, Top Cat, inflatable vinyl, unused, NRFP (pkg reads 'The Flintstone Inflatables') $25.00

Hanna-Barbera, figure, Top Cat, vinyl, seated upright w/legs spread, 1 hand on tummy & waving w/the other, 6", Bucky, NM $35.00

Hanna-Barbera, figure, Wally Gator, stuffed cloth, standing upright, gr w/purple hat, 7", Playtime, 1979, NM $25.00

Hanna-Barbera, figure, Yellow Dog (Banana Splits), plastic w/ vinyl head, jtd arms, 7", Dakin, 1970, EX....................$50.00

Hanna-Barbera, figure, Yogi Bear, jtd head & arms, 8", Dakin, 1970s, VG...$20.00

Hanna-Barbera, figure, Yogi Bear, plastic roly-poly, chimes, 7", Sanitoy, 1979, NM $20.00

Hanna-Barbera, figure, Yogi Bear, squeeze vinyl, seated on log & tugging on tie, 6", Dell, 1960s, EX................................$35.00

Hanna-Barbera, figure, Yogi Bear, stuffed felt, brn w/gr hat & tie, wht collar, 7½", Knickerbocker, 1973, NRFB................$45.00

Hanna-Barbera, figure, Yogi Bear, stuffed pillow type w/printed image, 17", 1977, NM+ $15.00

Hanna-Barbera, figure, Yogi Bear, stuffed plush w/vinyl face, gr felt hat & tie, 18½", Knickerbocker, 1959, EX+.............$50.00

Hanna-Barbera, figure, Yogi Bear, vinyl, jtd arms & head, 6", Knickerbocker Knixies, 1962, EX $35.00

Hanna-Barbera, flashlight, Huckleberry Hound, plastic w/molded face, 7", Laurie Import Ltd, 1976, unused, MIP..............$15.00

Hanna-Barbera, Flickers, Huckleberry Hound, Sonwell, 1960s, unused, NMIB $50.00

Hanna-Barbera, guitar, Snorky Elephant (Banana Splits), 10", 1970s, EX..$25.00

Hanna-Barbera, hand puppet, Droop-A-Long Coyote, cloth body w/vinyl head, Ideal, 1960s, NM $75.00

Hanna-Barbera, hand puppet, Magilla Gorilla, printed cloth body w/name, vinyl head, Ideal, 1960s, NM $75.00

Hanna-Barbera, hand puppet, Mr Jinks, plush body w/vinyl head, Knickerbocker, 1959, NM.....................................$75.00

Hanna-Barbera, hand puppet, Pixie & Dixie, plush bodies w/ vinyl heads, Knickerbocker, 1958, EX+, ea $50.00

Hanna-Barbera, hand puppet, Tweety Bird, cloth body w/vinyl head, Marriott's Great America, 1970, EX+...................$15.00

Hanna-Barbera, hand puppet, Yogi Bear, brn cloth body, vinyl head w/bl hat, NM $75.00

Hanna-Barbera, iron-on transfer, Yogi standing against bl circle outlined in yel & w/name, Holoubek Studios, 1976, M.$18.00

Hanna-Barbera, Kite Fun Book, Top Cat, PG&E premium, 1963, Reddy Kilowatt on back cover, NM................................$35.00

Hanna-Barbera, Kut-Up Kit, Banana Splits, Larami, 1970s, MOC (sealed) $25.00

Hanna-Barbera, Modelcast 'N Color Kit, features Huckleberry Hound & Flintstones, Standard Toycraft, 1960, unused, MIB $100.00

Hanna-Barbera, Modelcast 'N Color Kit, Quick Draw McGraw, Standard Toycraft, 1960, complete, EXIB $50.00

Hanna-Barbera, mug, Fleegle (Banana Splits), plastic head shape, yel w/red tongue & bow tie, 3¼", 1960s, M.........$25.00

Hanna-Barbera, mug, Hair Bear, plastic, bl w/image, 4", 1970s, NM $10.00

Hanna-Barbera, night-light, Yogi Bear Lite/projects Yogi on Ceiling, plastic, 4", Hoyle Prod, 1980s, MIB.......................$25.00

Hanna-Barbera, Pile On Game, Whitman, 1962, complete w/ container, EX+ $20.00

Hanna-Barbera, Play-Doh Playset, Yogi Bear, Kenner, 1980, unused, NRFB $35.00

Hanna-Barbera, Play Fun Set, Atom Ant, Whitman, 1966, NMIB $50.00

Hanna-Barbera, punch-out playset, Atom Ant, Whitman, 1960s, unused, EXIB $75.00

Hanna-Barbera, push-button puppet, any character, Kohner, 1960s, NM+, ea $50 to...$75.00

Hanna-Barbera, puzzle block w/sections of character images to match up, 3", Arby's premium, 1996, NM+ $5.00

Hanna-Barbera, squeeze toy, Pixie & Dixie on wedge of cheese, 'Pixie and Dixie' on cheese, 5½", Dell, 1960s, EX+ $40.00

Hanna-Barbera, Stamp Set, 'Yogi Bear & Huckleberry Hound & Fred Flintstone 25 Piece...,' 1975, unused, MOC..........$15.00

Hanna-Barbera, sticker, Huckleberry Hound, puffy vinyl figure standing w/arms at sides, 7", 1977, MIP........................$10.00

Hanna-Barbera, tambourine, Banana Splits, plastic & cb, 1970s, MIP..$35.00

Hanna-Barbera, wall hook, Yogi & Ranger Smith, plastic, self-adhesive, Tiger Home Prod, 1978, unused, MOC............$8.00

Hanna-Barbera, Wrist Glo Slate, Yo Yogi!, Ja-Ru, 1991, unused, MOC $8.00

Hanna-Barbera, yo-yo, Yogi Bear, molded plastic head w/big smile, 3", Creative Creations, MOC.............................$22.00

Hansel & Gretel, marionette, Hansel or Gretel, Pelham, NMIB, ea $100.00

Hansel & Gretel, marionette, Hansel, nonworking mouth, 14", Hazelle #813, NMIB.. $125.00

Hansel & Gretel, marionette, Hansel, working mouth, 14", Hazelle, NM+... $115.00

Hansel & Gretel, marionette, Witch, working mouth, 14", Pelham, NM+IB... $135.00

Happy Hooligan, doll, wood w/cloth outfit, 8½", Schoenhut, EX+IB.. $2,500.00

Hardy Boys, Sing-A-Long Phonograph, Vanity Fair, electric or b/o, EX...$75.00

Harold Lloyd, whistle, litho tin figure, 2½", EX.............. $200.00

Harvey Cartoons, bubble bath container, Casper the Friendly Ghost, Colgate-Palmolive, 1960s, NM+ $25.00

Harvey Cartoons, doll, Casper the Friendly Ghost, cloth, 15", 1960s, EX+...$50.00

Harvey Cartoons, doll, Casper the Friendly Ghost, talker, terrycloth w/plastic head, 15", Mattel, 1960s, EX+ $100.00

Harvey Cartoons, figure, Wendy, stuffed plush w/vinyl head, 10", Gund Gundikins, 1950s, EX $50.00

Harvey Cartoons, hand puppet, Baby Huey, cloth body w/vinyl head, Gund, 1950s, NM+................................$75.00

Harvey Cartoons, hand puppet, Casper the Friendly Ghost, cloth w/plastic head, 8", 1960s, NM+ $50.00

Harvey Cartoons, hand puppet, Casper the Friendly Ghost, plush, Dakin, 1995, NM...................................$32.00

Harvey Cartoons, hand puppet, Spooky, cloth body w/red trim, vinyl head w/blk hat, Gund, 1950s, NM+ $100.00

Harvey Cartoons, jack-in-the-box, litho tin w/Casper pop-up, EX+..$50.00

Harvey Cartoons, pull toy, Casper playing xylophone, wood, 9" L, 1960s, EX+ $300.00

Harvey Cartoons, push-button puppet, Casper the Friendly Ghost, Kohner, 1950s, EX+ $60.00

Harvey Cartoons, squeeze toy, Casper figure w/'Casper the Friendly Ghost' on chest, 7", Sutton, 1972, NM...........$25.00

Heathcliff, bagatelle games, Heathcliff's Sports Board, 2-pc set w/ basketball & tennis, Smithport, 1983, unused, MOC.....$15.00

Heathcliff, figure, stuffed plush & cloth, printed cowboy outfit w/ hat & red velvet vest, 12", Knickerbocker, 1981, EX+ ..$12.00

Heathcliff, friction toy, plastic, Heathcliff as football player, 8", Talbot Toys, 1982, NRFP...$12.00

Heckle & Jeckle, bank, pnt wood figure, hang tag reads 'Famous Terry Toon Bank,' 8", VG+.. $150.00

Heckle & Jeckle, hand puppet, blk plush bodies w/yel hands & feet, Rusthon Creations, 1950s, ea..............................$75.00

Henry, doll, pnt compo, workable mouth, red/blk striped cap, red jacket, yel pants, blk shoes, 12", EX............................. $125.00

Henry, doll, rubber w/cloth outfit, 9½", Perfekta, 1940s, NM $100.00

Herman & Katnip, figure, Katnip, stuffed plush w/vinyl head, 10", Gund Gundikins, 1950s, EX+ $50.00

Herman & Katnip, hand puppet, Katnip, cloth body w/vinyl head, Gund, 1950s, NM+ $75.00

Hi & Lois, doll, Hi, stuffed cloth w/vinyl head & hands, cloth outfit, brn flocked shoes, 16", Presents, 1985, NM+.......$30.00

Homey Clown, see In Living Color

Honeymooners, doll, Ed Norton (Art Carney), porcelain w/cloth outfit, 16", Effanbee, 1986, NM $125.00

Honeymooners, doll, Ralph Cramden (Jackie Gleason), porcelain w/cloth bus driver's outfit, 16", Effanbee, 1986, NM...... $125.00

Howdy Doody, bank, Clarabell, flocked plastic figure standing on base waving, 9", Straco, 1970s, NM..............................$35.00

Howdy Doody, bank, Howdy in wide stance on base w/name on label, flocked plastic, 9", Straco, 1976, EX+...................$35.00

Howdy Doody, bank, Howdy seated on barrel, ceramic, 6½", Lefton, NM...$75.00

Howdy Doody, bank, Mr Bluster Savings Bank, flocked plastic figure, 9", 1970s, EX+ $35.00

Howdy Doody, bath mitt, terry cloth w/printed image & name, 8", 1950s-60s, EX..$15.00

Howdy Doody, bubble pipe, plastic Clarabell figure, 4½" L, Lido Toy, unused, NMOC...$75.00

Howdy Doody, costume, Howdy Doody, Official Pl-A-Time Costume, shirt, pants & canvas mask, NMIB.................... $100.00

Howdy Doody, doll, Howdy Doody, compo w/pnt hair, glass eyes, cloth outfit, 23", Effanbee, 1950s, EXIB $325.00

Howdy Doody, doll, Howdy Doody, stuffed, compo head/hands, red/ wht checked shirt w/bl neckerchief, red pants, 19", G...... $250.00

Howdy Doody, doll, Howdy Doody, wood bead type w/compo head, cloth neckerchief, 13", Noma/Cameo, NM+IB. $575.00

Howdy Doody, doll, Princess Summerfall-Winterspring, brn Indian outfit, blk pigtails, 7½", Beehler Arts, NM+IB . $100.00

Howdy Doody, Doodle Slate, Stickless Corp, EX $50.00

Howdy Doody, figure, Howdy Doody, chalkware, standing on base w/name, hands at sides, 7", EX................................$20.00

Howdy Doody, figure set, 5 different characters, pnt hard plastic w/movable mouths, 4" ea, 1950s, EX to EX+ $125.00

Howdy Doody, finger puppet, Howdy Doody, full-hand type, foam rubber & cb, 10½x5", Bendy Toys, 1987, NM.......$20.00

Howdy Doody, hand puppet, Buffalo Bob, cloth w/vinyl head, mouth open w/top teeth showing, red felt hands, NM. $100.00

Howdy Doody, hand puppet, Clarabell, cloth body w/felt hands, vinyl head, googley-eyes, EX+ $75.00

Howdy Doody, hand puppet, Howdy Doody, full figure w/eyes & mouth operated from back, 13", Pride Prod, unused, MIB ..$125.00

Howdy Doody, hand puppet, Howdy Doody, plaid cloth body w/ red neckerchief, vinyl head, googley eyes, 1950s, NM . $100.00

Howdy Doody, hand puppet, Princess Summerfall-Winterspring, cloth body, vinyl head, googley eyes, 1950s, NM $75.00

Character, TV, and Movie Collectibles
• • • • • • • • • • • • • • • •
Howdy Dowdy, marionette, Peter Puppet Playthings, 1952, 15", NMIB, $225.00. (Photo courtesy www.seri oustoyz.com)

Howdy Doody, lamp, plastic Howdy figure seated on base, circus-themed lamp shade, 13½" overall, EX $500.00

Howdy Doody, lamp, vinyl head form w/bl neckerchief, 9½" H, Leadworks Inc, 1988, NM..$22.00

Howdy Doody, marionette, Clarabell, wood & compo w/cloth outfit, 15", Peter Puppet Playthings, 1952, NMIB....... $150.00

Howdy Doody, marionette, Clarabell, 15", Pride Prod, EXIB.$100.00

Howdy Doody, marionette, Flub-A-Dub, wood & compo w/cloth outfit, Peter Puppet Playthings, 1950s, EX+ $150.00

Howdy Doody, marionette, Heidy Doody, 14", Pride Prod, NM+IB... $275.00

Howdy Doody, marionette, Howdy Doody, 15", Peter Puppet Playthings, 1952, EXIB $125.00

Howdy Doody, marionette, Howdy Doody as 'Small Fry,' 13", NM+IB... $150.00

Howdy Doody, marionette, Mr Bluster, wood & compo w/cloth outfit, Peter Puppet Playthings, 1950s, EX $200.00

Howdy Doody, marionette, Mr Bluster, 13", Barsbury Puppet, NMIB $180.00

Howdy Doody, marionette, Princess Summerfall-Winterspring, wood & compo w/cloth outfit, Peter Puppet Playthings, 1950s, NMIB $125.00

Howdy Doody, Night Lamp, Magic Twinkle Doll, wood & plastic, 6½", Ahmco Prod, NMIB $175.00

Howdy Doody, night-light, Clarabell head figure, 2", Leco, NMIB $175.00

Howdy Doody, One Man Band, complete w/4 plastic instructions, Trophy Prod, EXIB $150.00

Howdy Doody, pencil w/pencil topper, Howdy's head, pencil emb w/name, 1950s, unused, NM..$50.00

Howdy Doody, plate, ceramic, Howdy the cowboy w/lasso & name on wht, 8½" dia, Smith-Taylor, 1950s, EX+ $50.00

Howdy Doody, Puppettes Set, 4 compo characters, cb box transitions to stage, Molded Latex Prod Inc, VGIB $100.00

Howdy Doody, push-button puppet, any character, Kohner, 1950s, NMIB, ea, $125 to $175.00

Howdy Doody, ring, Clarabell's horn on brass ring w/emb images of Howdy & Clarabell, horn works, EX $150.00

Howdy Doody, ring, flasher, Howdy appears to turn head, 1950s cereal premium, NM+..$50.00

Howdy Doody, sand bucket, plastic w/molded image on bottom, label on front, swing handle, 5½", Ideal, scarce, EX.......$75.00

Howdy Doody, squeeze toy, Clarabell figure, 7", Peter Puppet Playthings, MIB... $150.00

Howdy Doody, squeeze toy, Howdy in airplane w/smiling face, yel rubber, 4½x5½", EX.. $175.00

Howdy Doody, straw holder, molded plastic head clips on side of glass, complete w/straws, Old Colony Paper Prod, NMIB.$75.00

Howdy Doody, Sun-Ray Camera Outfit, complete, Silver Rich Corp, NMIB $125.00

Howdy Doody, ventriloquist doll, Howdy Doody, stuffed body w/vinyl head & hands, 11", Goldberger, 1970s, NMIB......$65.00

HR Pufnstuf, hand puppet, Dr Binkley, Remco, 1970, NM+..$100.00

HR Pufnstuf, hand puppet, Jimmy, printed vinyl body w/molded vinyl head, Remco, 1970, NM $150.00

HR Pufnstuf, hand puppet, Orson, cloth body w/vinyl head, Remco, 1970, NM $150.00

Huckleberry Hound, see Hanna-Barbera

Character, TV, and Movie Collectibles
. . . .
Howdy Doody Wonder Walker, Wall, $85.00.
(Photo courtesy Smith House Toy and Auction Company)

Character, TV, and Movie Collectibles
. . . .
I Love Lucy, doll, Lucy, stuffed cloth with molded plastic face, 28", 1950s, VG, $75.00. (Photo courtesy Morphy Auctions)

Hulk Hogan, hand puppet, red velvety cloth body w/mechanical blk vinyl boxing gloves, vinyl head w/headband, 1980s, NM+ $25.00

Hunchback of Notre Dame, figure, Glow-in-the-Dark Movie Monsters, plastic, 5½", Uncle Milton, 1990, MOC $12.00

I Dream of Jeannie, doll, posable vinyl w/rooted hair, cloth outfit, 6", Remco, 1966, NMIB..$60.00

Ignatz Mouse, see Krazy Kat

In Living Color, figure, Homey D Clown, stuffed clown w/satin-type costume, 24", Acme, 1992, NM+ $25.00

Incredible Hulk, bank, Hulk breaking through wall, vinyl, 10", Renzi, 1977, EX+...$25.00

Incredible Hulk, figure, bendable rubber, 6", Just Toys, 1989, EX+..$8.00

Incredible Hulk, figure, rubber, 5½", 1970s, EX+...............$20.00

Incredible Hulk, figure, vinyl, jtd arms, 14", Toy Biz, 1991, EX ..$25.00

Incredible Hulk, hand puppet, vinyl body w/gr molded vinyl head, blk-pnt hair, Imperial, 1978, EX $35.00

Incredible Hulk, Magic Motion Yo-Yo, Vari-Vue images on sides, Duncan, 1978, MIP...$28.00

Inspector Gadget, squeeze toy, vinyl, figure in trench coat, 6½", Jugasa, 1983, MIP..$50.00

Inspector Gadget, toy telephone, half-figure atop red & bl phone, 10", HG Toys, 1980s, NM $30.00

Iron Man, flicker ring, silver-tone plastic w/mc flicker image, vending machine item, 1966, NM...............................$35.00

J Fred Muggs (Today Show), hand puppet, printed cloth body w/vinyl head, Imperial, 1954, NM.....................................$85.00

James Bond (Secret Agent), playset, Action Toy Set 5, Bond, Moneypenny & Bond's boss 'M,' Gilbert, unused, NRFB..........$55.00

Jerry Mahoney, hand puppet, printed vinyl body w/molded vinyl head, 1966, NM+ $125.00

Jerry Mahoney, ventriloquist doll, 25", Juro Novelty, 1950s, EX+ $150.00

Jetsons, bagatelle game, The Jetsons Space Ball, Marx, VGIB $150.00

Jetsons, fast-food toy, Astro in space car & any other character in space vehicle, Wendy's, 1989, M, ea.................... $6.00

Jetsons, figure, Astro, PVC, begging w/bone in mouth, 2¼", Applause, 1993, M $5.00

Jetsons, figure, Astro, stuffed plush, beige w/gr collar, felt tongue, plastic eyes, 10½", Nanco, 1989, M $10.00

Jetsons, figure, Astro, stuffed plush, gray w/gr collar, plastic eyes, 8", Applause, 1980s-90s, M........................ $10.00

Jetsons, figure, Elroy, stuffed cloth, printed features, fuzzy yel hair & beanie, 12", Dakin, 1986, EX+ $12.00

Jetsons, figure, Elroy, stuffed cloth & vinyl, 5½", Applause, 1990, NM+... $15.00

Jetsons, figure, Judy, vinyl, 2-tone pk cloth outfit, 10", Applause, 1990, NM+.................................. $15.00

Jetsons, figure, Rosie the Robot, 9", Applause, 1990s, NM.. $15.00

Jetsons, hand puppet, any character, cloth body w/vinyl head, Knickerbocker, 1963, NM+, ea...................... $75.00

Jetsons, night-light, Orbity, Elroy & Astro sleeping in bed, bisque, 6" L, Giftique, 1980s, M..................... $35.00

Jetsons, ornament/clock, Astro Multi-Function Countdown Clock, vinyl, digital, 3¾", Radio Shack, 1999, MIB....... $18.00

Jetsons, Star Scope, plastic, Ja-Ru, 1990, MOC (sealed)...$10.00

Joe Palooka, bop bag, inflatable vinyl w/boxer image, Ideal, 1952, 44", NM................................... $65.00

Katnip, see Herman & Katnip

Katzenjammer Kids, doll set, family of 4, cloth/printed features/cloth outfits, 16" to 20", Knickerbocker, 1925-30, EX+............ $5,500.00

Kewpie, tea set, 10-pc wht china set w/Kewpie decals & airbrushed daisy accents, Germany, early 1900s, EX $300.00

Kilo the Boxing Kangaroo, doll, blk & wht stuffed printed cloth w/pk rayon shorts, 16", EX $350.00

King Kong, bank, figure walking over building w/his name emb on front, vinyl, Relic Art Ltd, NM.......................... $150.00

King Kong, pennant, felt w/mc image of King Kong atop the World Trade Center, 'New York City' down side, 25", 1970s, NM..$75.00

Koko the Klown (Out of the Inkwell), hand puppet, cloth body w/vinyl head, Gund, 1962, NM+.................................. $200.00

Krazy Kat, figure, Ignatz Mouse, wood, w/bendable limbs, blk & wht face, Cameo Doll Co/Borgfeldt, ca 1930, VGIB .. $500.00

Krazy Kat, figure, Ignatz Mouse, wood bead type w/bug eyes, blk w/wht hands, feet, nose & chest, 5½", EX+................. $250.00

Krazy Kat, figure, Krazy Kat, hard-stuffed purple cloth w/wht face, gold neck bow, 18", Averill Mfg, 1930s, VG....... $950.00

Krazy Kat, figure, Krazy Kat, wood bead type, blk, wht & yel w/ toothy grin, 7½", Chein, EX $775.00

Krazy Kat, pull toy, Krazy Kat chasing Ignatz Mouse on 4-wheeled platform, EXIB $3,000.00

Krazy Kat, pull toy, Krazy Kat Express (train engine), wood, 12", Int'l Feature Service, 1932, EX $675.00

Krazy Kat, tea set, 16-pc set w/tray, teapot, creamer, sugar, 4 ea cups, saucers & plates, Chein, EX............................... $125.00

Lamb Chop, bubble bath container, Lamb Chop holding duck, Kid Care, unused, w/tag, M................................ $8.00

Lamb Chop, hand puppet, stocking body w/vinyl head, Tarcher Prod, 1960, NM................................. $50.00

Laurel & Hardy, bank, either character, vinyl, 14", Play Pal Plastics, 1970s, NM, ea................................. $45.00

Laurel & Hardy, figure, either character, bendable rubber, 6", Lakeside, 1967, EX+, ea............................. $25.00

Laurel & Hardy, figure, either character, bendable vinyl w/cloth outfit, 8½", Knickerbocker, NM+, ea.................. $40.00

Laurel & Hardy, figure, either character, squeeze vinyl, 5½", Dakin, 1970s, EX, ea.............................. $30.00

Laurel & Hardy, figure, either character, stuffed body w/vinyl head & hands, 12", Goldberger, 1986, NRFB, ea........... $35.00

Laurel & Hardy, figure, either character, vinyl w/cloth clothing, 8", Dakin, 1970s, w/hang tags, MIP, ea................. $50.00

Laurel & Hardy, hand puppet, either character, cloth body w/ vinyl head, Knickerbocker, 1965, NM.................. $65.00

Laurel & Hardy, roly poly figure, Oliver Hardy, vinyl, red, wht & blk, chimes, 11", 1970s, EX............................ $30.00

Laverne & Shirley, doll set, Laverne & Shirley, 11½", Mego, 1977, NMIB $75.00

Laverne & Shirley, Paint-by-Numbers, acrylic paint set, Hasbro, 1981, unused, MIP (sealed)..$20.00

Li'l Abner, bank, 'Can O' Coins, company name on lid, 5", 1953, premum item, unused, M $125.00

Li'l Abner, bank, Papy Yokum standing atop base w/'Dogpatch USA' label on front, compo, 7", Al Capp Ent, 1970s, NM.............$55.00

Li'l Abner, bank, Shmoo figure, molded plastic, various colors, 7", WI Gould, 1940s, w/hang tag, EX $55.00

Li'l Abner, doll, Li'l Abner, vinyl w/cloth outfit, 14", Baby Barry Toys, 1950s, NM...................................... $100.00

Li'l Abner, doll, Mammy or Pappy Yokum, vinyl w/cloth outfit, 14", Baby Barry Toys, 1950s, NM, ea........................... $100.00

Li'l Abner, hand puppet, any character, Ideal, 1960s, NM+, ea...$75.00

Li'l Abner, w/up toy canoe, pnt plastic, w/Abner & Lonesome Polecat, w/up jug activates rowing, 12", 1940s, EX $100.00

Little Audrey, carrying case, 'Around the World With...'/graphics on wht vinyl hat-box shape w/handle, 1960s, EX $55.00

Little Audrey, doll, compo, blk synthetic hair in pigtails, cloth dress, felt hat, shoes & socks, 14", 1950s, EX $275.00

Little Audrey, hand puppet, cloth body w/vinyl head, Gund, 1950s, NM..$75.00

Little Iodine, hand puppet, cloth body w/vinyl head, Gund, 1950s, MIP $100.00

Little King, walking spool toy, pnt wood figure, 4", Jaymar, 1939, VG+IB..$50.00

Little Lulu, bank, Little Lulu standing beside blk fire hydrant, vinyl, 7½", Play Pal, 1970s, EX $25.00

Little Lulu, bank, Little Lulu standing next to baby carriage, 10", Play Pal, 1973, NM+..$55.00

Little Lulu, Cooking Set, plastic, Larami, 1974, MOC (sealed) $15.00

Little Lulu, doll, inflatable vinyl, red dress w/name on breast pocket, 14", Sanitoy, 1973, M..$30.00

Little Lulu, doll, stuffed cloth, red cloth dress w/wht collar & lace trim, 6½", Gund, 1972, MIB....................................$75.00

Little Lulu, squeeze toy, Little Lulu in red dress w/wht purse waving, 6", Romogosa Int'l, 1984, MIP.................................$30.00

Little Orphan Annie, bubble bath container, figural, Lander, 1977, NM $15.00

Little Orphan Annie, costume, cloth dress w/'Leapin' Lizards! It's Little Orphan Annie' on chest, linen mask, 1930s, EX $100.00

Little Orphan Annie, figure set, Annie & Sandy, compo w/pnt features, cloth dress, 12" & 7", EXIB $450.00

Little Orphan Annie, Jack Set, Arcade, 1935, NRFP..... $175.00

Little Red Riding Hood, fork & spoon set, engraved w/name & wolf dressed as grandma in bed, EXIB (box w/bed scene) .$85.00

Little Red Riding Hood, hand puppet, Big Bad Wolf, brn cloth cody w/tie & collar, vinyl head, MPI Toys, 1960, NM . $125.00

Little Red Riding Hood, hand puppet, Grandma, cloth body w/ vinyl head, MPI Toys, 1960, NM...................................$75.00

Little Red Riding Hood, hand puppet, Little Red Riding Hood, cloth body w/vinyl head, MPI Toys, 1960, NM..............$75.00

Little Red Riding Hood, hand puppet, Little Red Riding Hood/ Big Bad Wolf, dbl-sided vinyl head w/cloth body, NM ..$75.00

Little Red Riding Hood, marionette, Big Bad Wolf, nonmovable mouth, 15", Hazelle, NM $150.00

Little Red Riding Hood, marionette, Little Red Riding Hood, red & wht checked outfit, 15", Hazelle, EX+ $100.00

Looney Tunes, Bake A Craft Stained Glass Kit, Foghorn Leghorn, Road Champos, 1991, MOC (sealed)...................$12.00

Looney Tunes, bank, Bugs Bunny in basket of carrots labeled 'What's Up Doc,' 14", Vinyl Prod Corp, 1972, NM $35.00

Looney Tunes, bank, Cool Cat, image on yel on sq metal box, 4x4x1", Warner Bros, EX+....................................$22.00

Looney Tunes, bank, Daffy Duck hugging money bag emb w/dollar sign, ceramic, 6", Good Co, 1989, NM+...................$40.00

Looney Tunes, bank, Porky Pig declaring 'That's All Folks!' on red Looney Tunes logo, ceramic, 8", Good Co, 1989, NM....... $50.00

Looney Tunes, bank, Porky Pig standing w/arms behind back, bisque, 5", 1940s, VG...$75.00

Looney Tunes, bank, Porky Pig standing w/head turned looking up & arms behind back, ceramic, 10", 1990s, NM+.......$15.00

Looney Tunes, bank, Porky standing w/1 arm bent up & 1 arm down, legs togetehr, 6½", Dakin, NM............................$20.00

Looney Tunes, bank, Road Runner & Wile E Coyote figures emb on side of mountain, vinyl, 5", WB stores, 1990s, NM ..$25.00

Looney Tunes, bank, Road Runner running on grassy base, pnt compo, 8", Holiday Fair, 1970s, NM..............................$50.00

Character, TV, and Movie Collectibles

Little Lulu, doll, stuffed cloth with plastic head, yarn hair, 13", Knickerbocker/Saturday Evening Post subscription premium, 1930s, M, $800.00. (Photo courtesy Morphy Auctions)

Character, TV, and Movie Collectibles

Little Orphan Annie, doll set, Annie and Sandy, leather with printed details, 16" Annie, EX, pair, $175.00. (Photo courtesy Morphy Auctions)

Looney Tunes, bank, Road Runner standing on dirt mound, plastic, 12", Dakin, NM..$50.00

Looney Tunes, bank, Speedy Gonzales standing on cheese wedge, vinyl w/cloth outfit, 9½", Dakin, MIP $75.00

Looney Tunes, bank, Tasmanian Devil as 'mean' football player, vinyl, 6½", HEI, 1994, M $15.00

Looney Tunes, bank, Tasmanian Devil standing w/hands clasped in front, closed-mouth smile, vinyl, 5", Dakin, NM+ $75.00

Looney Tunes, bank, Tweety Bird, vinyl, standing on birdcage w/ coin slot, 10", Dakin, 1971, EX.....................................$20.00

Looney Tunes, bank, Tweety Bird, vinyl figure, 6", Dakin, 1976, VG $18.00

Looney Tunes, bank, Tweety Bird atop birdhouse marked Tweety, compo, 9", Holiday Fair, 1971, NM+............................$35.00

Looney Tunes, bank, Tweety Bird perched atop bird cage, vinyl, 10½", Dakin, 1971, NM+...$35.00

Looney Tunes, bank, Yosemite Sam w/'wooden' treasure chest, ceramic, 6", Applause, 1988, M $40.00

Looney Tunes, bookends, big Bugs pushing little Bugs on a cart on hot pk base, 7", Holiday Fair, M, pr $50.00

Looney Tunes, bubble bath container, any character, Colgate-Palmolive, 1960s, NM, ea $20 to....................................$25.00

Looney Tunes, bubble bath container, any character, Kid Care, 1992, NM+, ea $8.00

Looney Tunes, Cartoon-O-Graph Sketch Board, Moss Mfg, 1940s-50s, EXIB $75.00

Looney Tunes, figure, any character, PVC, Arby's, 1988-89, MIP, ea $6.00

Looney Tunes, figure, Bugs Bunny, flocked plastic, gray & wht, 6", Lucky Bell, 1988, NRFC...................................$10.00

Looney Tunes, figure, Bugs Bunny, plastic (hollow), gray & wht w/pk mouth, 5½", Dakin, 1960s-70s (?), NM $12.00

Looney Tunes, figure, Bugs Bunny, stuffed, canvas face, standing holding carrot, 22", M&H Novelty, VG.......................$50.00

Looney Tunes, figure, Bugs Bunny, stuffed cloth, as 'Uncle Sam,' 11", Dakin, 1976, NM...$25.00

Looney Tunes, figure, Bugs Bunny, stuffed cloth, dressed as Mexican w/sombrero & serape, Dakin, 11½", EX...................$15.00

Looney Tunes, figure, Bugs Bunny, stuffed cloth, lying down w/ carrot, 8" L, Dakin (Fun Farm bag), 1978, NM..............$25.00

Looney Tunes, figure, Bugs Bunny, vinyl, 'Happy Birthday,' 12", Dakin Goofy Gram, 1971, NM....................................$38.00

Looney Tunes, figure, Bugs Bunny, vinyl, as 'Uncle Sam,' jtd, 9", Dakin, 1975, MIP..$50.00

Looney Tunes, figure, Bugs Bunny, vinyl, holding carrot, jtd, 11", Dakin, 1971, MIP..$40.00

Looney Tunes, figure, Bugs Bunny, vinyl, standing w/legs apart, hand on hip w/carrot, solid orange, 6", Dakin, 1976, NM.$20.00

Looney Tunes, figure, Bugs Bunny figure w/snap-on superhero costume, 3½", McDonald's, 1991, NM $4.00

Looney Tunes, figure, Cool Cat, vinyl, jtd head & arms, Dakin, 1969, EX...$25.00

Looney Tunes, figure, Daffy Duck, bisque, on flowery grassy base w/1 hand on head & 1 to mouth, 6", Price, 1979, M $28.00

Looney Tunes, figure, Daffy Duck, PVC, as baseball player standing on base, 3", Applause, 1990, MIB ('Official' box)....$10.00

Looney Tunes, figure, Daffy Duck, stuffed cloth pillow type w/ printed image & name, 16", 1970s, NM $15.00

Looney Tunes, figure, Daffy Duck, stuffed plush w/vinyl collar, 15", Mighty Star, 1971, NM......................................$10.00

Looney Tunes, figure, Daffy Duck, vinyl, jtd, as part of barbershop quartet, 9", Applause, NM+ $15.00

Looney Tunes, figure, Daffy Duck, vinyl, standing w/legs together & feet spread, hand on hip, 9", Dakin, 1960s-70s, NM .$20.00

Looney Tunes, figure, Elmer Fudd, vinyl, cloth jacket/pants/shirt/ tie/gloves, plastic hat/shoes, 8½", Dakin, 1970, NM+....$25.00

Looney Tunes, figure, Foghorn Leghorn, vinyl, jtd, 8½", Dakin, 1970s, M...$50.00

Looney Tunes, figure, Henery Hawk, stuffed plush, stuffed felt feet & beak, lg plastic eyes, 18", 1990s, NM+ $15.00

Looney Tunes, figure, Marvin Martian, vinyl, jtd, 8", 1990s, w/ hang tag, NM+ $15.00

Looney Tunes, figure, Merlin the Magic Mouse, vinyl, cloth outfit, 8", Dakin, 1970s, w/orig hang tag, EX $25.00

Looney Tunes, figure, Merlin the Magic Mouse, vinyl, 'I'll Drink That!' on rnd base, 7", Goofy Gram/Dakin, 1970s, EX..$25.00

Looney Tunes, figure, Pepe Le Pew, stuffed vinyl, 8", Ace Novelty, 1997, NM...$8.00

Looney Tunes, figure, Pepe Le Pew, vinyl, jtd, 9", Dakin, 1970s, EX $15.00

Looney Tunes, figure, Pepe Le Pew, vinyl, on base marked 'You're A Real Stinker,' 9", Goofy Gram/Dakin, 1971, MIP......$75.00

Looney Tunes, figure, Petunia Pig, squeeze vinyl, standing w/ hands on hips, 4", Spain, 1990s, NM................$12.00

Looney Tunes, figure, Porky Pig, squeeze rubber, standing w/head cocked & arms behind back, 7", Sun Rubber, 1940s, NM..$50.00

Looney Tunes, figure, Porky Pig, squeeze vinyl, standing w/arms down & palms forward, blk jacket, 5", Dakin, 1960s, NM.............$20.00

Looney Tunes, figure, Porky Pig, squeeze vinyl, waving pose, turq jacket, orange bow tie, Reliance, 1978, NM+ $15.00

Looney Tunes, figure, Porky Pig, stuffed felt, lt violet jacket & yel collar, 16", Warner Bros, VG $175.00

Looney Tunes, figure, Porky Pig, stuffed plush, felt hat, felt features, seated w/legs apart, 8", Dakin, 1975, EX+ $15.00

Looney Tunes, figure, Porky Pig, vinyl, blk cloth cape, wht bowtie, 8", Dakin, 1969, NRFP (Looney Tunes bag) $35.00

Looney Tunes, figure, Porky Pig, vinyl, cloth jacket & bowtie, sm vinyl hat, 7½", Dakin, 1970s, NM+................................$22.00

Looney Tunes, figure, Road Runner, PVC, 4½", Dakin, 1970s, EX $10.00

Looney Tunes, figure, Road Runner, vinyl, standing w/legs together, 9", Dakin, 1968, EX $15.00

Looney Tunes, figure, Road Runner, vinyl, standing w/legs together, 9", Dakin, 1968, NM $25.00

Looney Tunes, figure, Second Banana, vinyl, gray mouse w/yel-pnt turtleneck sweater, 6", Dakin, 1970, EX.................$25.00

Looney Tunes, figure, Tasmanian Devil, bendable foam rubber, 7½", Bendy Toys, 1988, MIP.............................$25.00

Looney Tunes, figure, Tasmanian Devil, bendable vinyl, legs apart, arms up & mouth wide open, 6", Tyco, 1990, NM+ $6.00

Looney Tunes, figure, Tasmanian Devil, PVC, holding heart, 3", Tyco, 1994, MOC (card reads 'Heart Throbs Figurines) .$10.00

Looney Tunes, figure, Tasmanian Devil, rubber arms over head & bent at elbows, tan & gray, 5", 1980, NM $10.00

Looney Tunes, figure, Tweety Bird, flocked plastic, dressed as sheriff, 3", Lucky Bell, 1989, NM+ $8.00

Looney Tunes, figure, Tweety Bird, squeeze vinyl, standing w/ hands on tummy, 5", Dakin, 1970s, NM.......................$20.00

Looney Tunes, figure, Tweety Bird, squeeze vinyl, standing wearing bl neck scarf & diaper, 6", Oak Rubber, 1940s, VG .$25.00

Looney Tunes, figure, Tweety Bird, stuffed cloth, lt yel w/orange beak, seated, 18", Mighty Star, 1971, EX.......................$12.00

Character, TV, and Movie Collectibles
. . . .
Looney Tunes, Music Maker, Bugs Bunny, lithographed tin, Mattel, 1963, 8x6", VG, $35.00.
(Photo courtesy www.whatacharacter.com)

Looney Tunes, figure, Tweety Bird, vinyl, swivel head & feet, 6", Dakin, 1969, NM $25.00

Looney Tunes, figure, Wile E Coyote, plastic, standing w/legs apart, 5", Dakin, 1970s, EX.............................$12.00

Looney Tunes, figure, Wile E Coyote, rubber, 3", Arby's, 1988, M $6.00

Looney Tunes, figure, Yosemite Sam, PVC, standing w/legs apart & guns raised, 2¼", Applause, 1989, NM+ $5.00

Looney Tunes, figure, Yosemite Sam, vinyl, cloth outfit, red fuzzy beard, blk plastic hat, 7½", Dakin, 1968, NM $20.00

Looney Tunes, finger puppet, any character, Starbuck's premium, 2004, M, ea..$4.00

Looney Tunes, finger puppet, any character, vinyl, Dakin, 1970, MIP, ea...$20.00

Looney Tunes, Flash Lite, Bugs Bunny figure, plastic, gray & wht, 5", 1940s, unsued, MIB $25.00

Looney Tunes, game, Dominoes, red plastic w/2 inset pics of LT characters on ea pc, Whitman, 1977, EXIB (Bugs on box) $15.00

Looney Tunes, gumball machine, Bugs Bunny, clear plastic head w/ wht teeth & gray ears, colored base, 10", Tarrson, EX+.....$25.00

Looney Tunes, gumball machine, Bugs Bunny w/arms & legs crossed & carrot next to gum globe, Processed Plastic Co, 1988, EX..$15.00

Looney Tunes, Gumball Pocket Pack Dispenser, any character, Processed Plastic Co, 1989, MOC, ea.....................$10.00

Looney Tunes, hand puppet, any character, vinyl body & head, detergent premium, 1969, NM, ea $20 to......................$25.00

Looney Tunes, hand puppet, Bugs Bunny, cloth body w/vinyl head, googley-eyed, Zany, 1950s, EX+ $65.00

Looney Tunes, ice machine, Marvin Martian, plastic, 12", Saltan, 1990s, NM+ $20.00

Looney Tunes, Looney Toonavision, makes different faces, litho cb w/control knobs, 1950s, VG......................$25.00

Looney Tunes, mug, any character head, 4", Promotional Partners, 1992, M, ea $6.00

Looney Tunes, mug, any character, ceramic, Applause, 1989-1990s, M, ea $10 to $12.00

Looney Tunes, pencil holder/sharpener, Bugs Bunny figure standing eating carrot, compo, 6", Holiday Fair, 1970, NM ...$18.00

Character, TV, and Movie Collectibles
. . . .
Looney Tunes, figure, Wile E. Coyote, Dakin Goofy Gram, 1971, 9½", NM+, $45.00. (Photo courtesy www.whatacharacter.com)

Looney Tunes, pencil topper, Marvin Martian on spacecraft, PVC, 2½", NM+...$5.00

Looney Tunes, pull toy, Porky Pig & Petunia on horses w/4 wheels & bell, paper-litho-on-wood, Brice Novelty #920, 8", EX $100.00

Looney Tunes, pull toy, Tweety Bird twirling figure atop wagon, 9½", Brice Novelty, 1950s, NM $125.00

Looney Tunes, push-button puppet, any character, Kohner, 1960s, EX, ea..$30.00

Looney Tunes, snow dome, Bugs Bunny, 'A 24K Friend' on base, Bug's head & carrot in hand in plastic dome, 3", 1989, NM...........$10.00

Looney Tunes, snow dome, Pepe Le Pew in clear plastic dome on red base marked 'Pour L'Amour,' 3", 1989, NM $15.00

Looney Tunes, snow dome, Wile E Coyote in clear dome, 'Feel Better!' on orange base, 3", Acme, 1989, NM+ $15.00

Looney Tunes, Speedy Gonzales Turbine Tops, Larami, 1973, MOC $30.00

Looney Tunes, squeeze toy, Bugs Bunny, vinyl, waving, glancing eyes, orange gloves, 7", Dakin, 1970s, NM+ $18.00

Looney Tunes, squeeze toy, Daffy Duck as cowboy seated on gray rock, vinyl, Vo-Toys, 1994, NM+ $8.00

Looney Tunes, Stained Glass Kit, features Bugs Bunny, Road Runner, Chamos, 1991, unused, MOC.......................$10.00

Looney Tunes, stationery set, Fancy House Club, unused, MIP.. $6.00

Looney Tunes, wall plaque, Tasmanian Devil figure scowling, mc plastic popcorn-type material, 1973, M $12.00

Lucky Ducky, hand puppet, checked cloth body w/vinyl head, Zany, 1950s, NM $50.00

Maggie & Jiggs, doll, stuffed cloth, cloth outfit, printed features, w/ cigar, 18", Lars of Italy, 1920s, EX ('Bringing Up Father') . $400.00

Maggie & Jiggs, doll set, wood w/cloth outfits, 7" & 9", Schoen-hut, NRFB ('Bringing Up Father')............................$2,750.00

Maggie & Jiggs, doll set, wood w/cloth outfits, w/few accessories, 9" & 13", VGIB ('Bringing Up Father') $350.00

Magilla Gorilla, see Hanna-Barbera

Man From UNCLE, finger puppets, set of 6, unused, NMIB..$325.00

Man From UNCLE, magic slate, Watkins-Strathmore, 1960s, unused, NM...$75.00

Man From UNCLE, Secret Print Putty, USA, 1965, complete & unused, MOC... $100.00

Man From UNCLE, Shooting Arcade, tin & plastic, Marx, 1960s, NMIB $200.00

Man From UNCLE, Target Game, plastic & cb, Ideal, MIB ..$200.00

Marvin the Martian, see Looney Tunes

Mary Hartline, Super Circus Puppet, punch-out cb pcs, Snickers Candy, 1950s, unpunched, M $125.00

Max & Moritz, figures, wood w/cloth outfits, 8", Schoenhut/William Busch, ca 1915, F, pr....................................... $400.00

Merlin the Magic Mouse, see Looney Tunes

Mighty Mouse, bubble bath container, Colgate-Palmolive, 1960s, NM+..$25.00

Mighty Mouse, figure, Mighty Mouse, vinyl, Dakin, 1978, MIP ('Fun Farm')... $125.00

Mighty Mouse, figure, Pearl Pureheart, stuffed cloth w/red cloth jacket, yel hair, 15", A&A Plush Inc, 1990s, NM+........$12.00

Mighty Mouse, figure, vinyl, Dakin, 1978, MIP (Fun Farm)...$125.00

Mighty Mouse, flashlight, figural, 3½", 1970s, MIP $100.00

Mighty Mouse, Merry-Pack, complete collection of 20 games & tops, die-cut litho cb, CBS TV Ent, 1956, unused, EX+ .$75.00

Mister Magoo, bubble bath container, Colgate-Palmolive, 1960s, EX $15.00

Mister Magoo, figure, stuffed cloth w/vinyl head, all yel w/shiny hat, shirt & feet, 13", Cuddle Wit, NM+ $18.00

Mister Magoo, figure, stuffed cloth w/vinyl head & hat, felt outfit w/3 plastic buttons, 16", Ideal, 1960s, NM $100.00

Mr Ed, hand puppet, plush body, vinyl head w/yarn mane, talker, Mattel, 1962, NM $75.00

Mr Rogers' Neighborhood, hand puppet, King, full cloth body w/ weighted base, vinyl head, Ideal, 1976, NM...................$50.00

Mr Rogers' Neighborhood, hand puppet, X the Owl, full cloth body w/weighted base, vinyl head, Ideal, 1976, NM $50.00

Munsters, doll, any character, stuffed cloth w/vinyl head, cloth outfits, about 9", Presents/Hamilton Gifts, NM+, ea $35.00

Munsters, doll, any character, stuffed cloth w/vinyl head, cloth outfit, about 14", Toy Works, unused, MIP, ea................$20.00

Munsters, doll, any character, vinyl w/cloth outfit, 8½" Eddie, Ideal, 1965, NM+, ea $100.00

Munsters, figure, Herman Munster, plastic w/rooted hair, 6", Kayro-Vue, 1964, NM...$45.00

Munsters, hand puppet, any character, printed cloth body w/ vinyl head, Ideal, 1964, EX, ea..$50.00

Muppet Babies, hand puppet, Animal, plush w/plastic eyes, Dakin, 1988, NM $10.00

Muppets, see also Sesame Street

Muppets, bank, Kermit the Frog seated on grassy base w/pk flowers, hand to cheek, 9", Applause, NM+.........................$15.00

Muppets, bubble bath container, any character, Calgon, 1996, M, ea...$8.00

Muppets, figure, Gonzo, Dress-up Muppet Doll, Fisher-Price #858, 1982-83, EX...$15.00

Muppets, figure, Gonzo, stuffed plush w/cloth outfit, plastic eyes, blk/wht plaid pants, chili-pepper tie, 14", Nanco, M $10.00

Muppets, figure, Gonzo, vinyl, seated, yel bird on red outfit, 5", Hasbro, 1984, NM..$8.00

Muppets, figure, Kermit the Frog, Dress-Up Muppet Doll, Fisher-Price #857, EX...$10.00

Muppets, figure, Kermit the Frog, stuffed plush, felt collar, 19", Hasbro, 1985, NM+ $20.00

Muppets, figure, Miss Piggy, stuffed cloth, vinyl head w/synthetic hair, purple gown, 14", Fisher-Price, 1980s, NMIB $25.00

Muppets, figure, Red (Fraggle Rock), plush w/stuffed arms & legs, red shirt, yarn hair, 16", Tommy, 1983, NM $25.00

Muppets, figure, Scooter, stuffed cloth, 17", 1978, EX $20.00

Muppets, hand puppet, Fozzie Bear, plush, Fisher-Price, 1978, NM+ $15.00

Muppets, hand puppet, Miss Piggy, mouth moves, Fisher-Price #855, 1979-80, NM..$10.00

Muppets, hand puppet, Rowlf, brn plush, Fisher-Price #852, 1977, EXIB $35.00

Muppets, hand puppet, Scooter, plush, Fisher-Price #853, 1978-81, NM $10.00

Muppets, kaleidoscope, cb & metal w/lithoed Muppet characters, 9" L, Hallmark, 1981, EX+..$30.00

Muppets, mirror, Deco style ceramic frame w/Miss Piggy figure admiring self in lower left corner, 9", Sigma, 1980s, M ..$75.00

Muppets, Muppet Show Players #846, 1979-83, MIB........$30.00

Muppets, necklace, resin Kermit the Frog as hiker w/backpack, w/lt gr cord & bead, 3½" figure, Just Toys, NM+ $8.00

Muppets, Party Puzzlers, features Kermit the Forg, hallmark, 1981, unused, MOC..$10.00

Muppets, Stick Puppet, any character, Fisher-Price, 1970s-80s, NM, ea...$10.00

Mutt & Jeff, doll set, compo w/cloth outfits, 7", Swiss made, VG $315.00

Mutt & Jeff, drum, litho tin, 13" dia, Converse, EX $300.00

My Favorite Martian, beanie, pk felt, wire antennae w/bells, Benay Albee, 1960s, unused, EX............................$75.00

My Favorite Martian, Martian Magic Tricks Set, Gilbert, 1964, complete & unused, MIB............................ $175.00

My Three Sons, doll set, Robbie's Triplets, Remco, 1969, MIB.$350.00

Nancy, figure, Nancy, stuffed cloth, 6½", Knickerbocker, 1973, MIB (box reads 'Extra! U*Color*It Comic Strip...')......$40.00

Nancy, figure, Nancy or Sluggo, squeeze rubber, 10", Dreamland Creations, 1955, NM, ea..................................$75.00

Nancy, figure, Nancy or Sluggo, stuffed cloth, 6½", Knickerbocker, 1970s, MIB (box reads 'Miniature Rag Doll'), ea..............$40.00

Nanny & the Professor, Colorforms Cartoon Kit, 1971, MIB...$40.00

Natasha Fatale, see Rocky & Friends

New Zoo Revue, hand puppet, Henrietta Hippo, yel cloth body w/vinyl head, lg open mouth, 1970s, NM+ $75.00

New Zoo Revue, mobile, musical, 1975, MIB...................$25.00

Nightmare on Elm Street, doll, Freddy Krueger, talker, removable hat & clothing, Matchbox, 1989, MIB..........................$50.00

Nightmare on Elm Street, figure, Freddy Krueger, Squish 'em, squish & squash him & he pops back up, 4½" (kneeling), MOC $15.00

Nightmare on Elm Street, figure, Freddy Krueger, vinyl w/suction cups, 5½", MOC $15.00

Nightmare on Elm Street, Freddy's Glove, 1984, MOC....$25.00

Nightmare on Elm Street, yo-yo, Freddy Krueger, Spectra Star, 1988, unused, MOC $20.00

Odie, see Garfield

Oswald the Rabbit, crib toy, celluloid & wood bead figure, 7", Irwin, ca 1928, NM+.. $125.00

Oswald the Rabbit, figure, squeeze rubber, 7½", Sun Rubber, 1940s, VG..$50.00

Oswald the Rabbit, figure, stuffed plush w/name on chest banner, orange jacket, laced shoes, 17", Irwin, 1930s, EX........ $450.00

Our Miss Brooks, hand puppet, cloth body w/vinyl head, Zany, 1950s, NM.. $150.00

Out of the Inkwell, see Koko the Klown

Pac-Man, bank, plastic, marked 'Tomy Pac-Man' on front of base, 4½", 1980s, NM+ $15.00

Pac-Man, figure, stuffed plush, yel w/red open mouth, 17", 1980s, NM $15.00

Pac-Man, hand puppet, plush, Commonwealth Toy & Novelty, 1980s, EX...$10.00

Paddington Bear, bank, Paddington seated, flocked plastic w/ cloth coat & hat, 6", Eden Toys, 1980s, EX+ $20.00

Paddington Bear, figure, stuffed cloth, lt bl cloth shirt w/name, blk printed features & ears, 13", Eden Toys, 1970s, NM .$20.00

Partridge Family, bulletin board, 1970s, 18x24", NM..... $100.00

Peanuts, bank, Peppermint Patty in ball cap standing & leaning on baseball bat, compo, 7", Determined, 1972, NM+....$65.00

Peanuts, bank, Snoopy as 'Joe Cool,' on gr base, pnt compo, 6", 1970s, NM+...$35.00

Peanuts, bank, Snoopy Bank, globe w/flags of different countries & various Snoopy images, metal, 5", Ohio Art, 1970s, NM..$40.00

Peanuts, bank, Snoopy in 'Racer,' pnt compo, 4x5", 1970s, EX $50.00

Peanuts, bank, Snoopy in stocking cap & scarf standing holding pr of skis, vinyl, 6", Danara, 1970s, NM $22.00

Peanuts, bank, Snoopy in 'The Express Truck,' pnt compo, 4", 1970s, NM+...$55.00

Peanuts, bank, Snoopy lying on back atop baseball, pnt compo, 5", 1970s, NM $35.00

Peanuts, bank, Snoopy seated upright, clear glass, 6", Anchor Hocking, 1980s, M...$22.00

Peanuts, bank, Woodstock standing, signed Schulz, 6", 1970s, NM+ $30.00

Peanuts, bicycle horn, plastic w/squeeze vinyl Snoopy head, 7", Hollywood Accessories, 1980s, MIP...........................$18.00

Peanuts, bubble bath container, Lucy, Avon, 1970, MIB ..$15.00

Peanuts, bulletin board, cork, Snoopy sniffing 'love' note & 'Notes' lettered at bottom, 18x12", Butterfly Originals, 1980s, MIP..$18.00

Peanuts, bulletin board, cork w/images of Peanuts Gang amidst a musical staff, Schroeder playing piano, 18x13", NM+ ...$12.00

Peanuts, comb & brush set, Charlie Brown figural brush w/6" plastic comb, Avon, 1971, NM+IB..................................$25.00

Peanuts, Cool Writer/Roly Poly Pen Holder, image of 'Joe Cool' on sides, plastic, 3", Butterfly Originals, 1980s, MIB......$15.00

Peanuts, figure, Charlie Brown, bendable vinyl, arms stretched out w/ball glove, 6", 1960s, NM+ $20.00

Peanuts, figure, Charlie Brown, plastic w/cloth pants & shirt, jtd, 7", 1960s, NM $35.00

Peanuts, figure, Charlie Brown, squeeze vinyl, w/bowl of dog food, 5½", Con Agra, 1990s, NM+ $8.00

Peanuts, figure, Charlie Brown, squeeze vinyl, 9", Hungerford, 1950s, EX+ $75.00

Peanuts, figure, Charlie Brown, stuffed cloth w/blk-printed face, orange cloth shirt, Rag Doll, Ideal, 1960s-70s, MIP.......$35.00

Peanuts, figure, Charlie Brown, stuffed terrycloth pillow type w/ printed image, 8½", Determined, 1970s, unused, MIP ...$35.00

Peanuts, figure, Charlie Brown, vinyl, red shirt w/blk zigzag design, blk shorts & shoes, 9", Hungerford, 1950s, MIP $100.00

Peanuts, figure, Linus, bendable vinyl, arms straight out, 5½", 1960s, NM..................................$25.00

Peanuts, figure, Linus, squeeze vinyl, standing w/1 hand up by face & other on tummy, 7", Hungerford, 1950s, EX+ $45.00

Peanuts, figure, Linus, squeeze vinyl, standing w/1 hand up by face & other on tummy, 9", Hungerford, 1950s, EX.......$65.00

Peanuts, figure, Linus, stuffed cloth, printed features, cloth shorts, 8", Rag Doll, Ideal, 1960s, MIP (sealed) $40.00

Peanuts, figure, Linus, stuffed cloth, printed pillow type, 9", Determined, 1970s, MIP (sealed) $35.00

Peanuts, figure, Linus, stuffed cloth body w/vinyl head, sucking thumb, w/blanket, 9", Determined, 1980s, EX $25.00

Peanuts, figure, Lucy, bendable rubber, pk dress, 5", 1969, NM..................................$25.00

Peanuts, figure, Lucy, squeeze vinyl, yel dress, 8", Hungerford, 1950s, NM..................................$65.00

Peanuts, figure, Lucy, stuffed cloth, 'Director of Everything' printed on red shirt, 10", Determined, M $18.00

Peanuts, figure, Lucy, stuffed cloth w/blk printed features & hair, red dress w/bl trim, 7½", Ideal, NRFP..................................$40.00

Peanuts, figure, Lucy, stuffed print cloth, lg wht 'P' on red gym suit, red gym shoes, 6¼", Determined, EX+..................................$10.00

Peanuts, figure, Lucy, vinyl, yel dress, 9", Hungerford, 1950s, EX+..................................$75.00

Peanuts, figure, Peppermint Patty, foam-stuffed printed terry-cloth, 8½", Determined, 1970s, MIP (sealed)..................................$35.00

Peanuts, figure, Peppermint Patty, stuffed cloth, cloth outfit, printed features, Rag Doll, Ideal, 7", MIP..................................$40.00

Peanuts, figure, Peppermint Patty, stuffed cloth, printed outfit & features, 6", Determined, NM..................................$12.00

Peanuts, figure, Sally, squeeze vinyl, standing w/hands to mouth, 5½", Con Agra, 1990s, NM+ $8.00

Peanuts, figure, Schroeder, squeeze vinyl, seated as if playing piano, red-pnt outfit, 8", Hungerford, 1950s, EX.........$125.00

Peanuts, figure, Schroeder, vinyl, orange woven 'Beethoven' sweater, blk cloth trousers, 7½", Pocket Dolls, 1970s, NM..............$35.00

Peanuts, figure, Snoopy, foam-stuffed printed cloth, as train engineer, 8", Determined, 1970s, MIP..................................$30.00

Peanuts, figure, Snoopy, squeeze vinyl, as 'Flying Ace' in airplane, side emb 'Snoopy,' 4x6" L, Danara, 1970s, NM..............$25.00

Peanuts, figure, Snoopy, squeeze vinyl, as sheriff, 6", Danara, 1970s, EX+ $12.00

Peanuts, figure, Snoopy, squeeze vinyl, asleep on tummy w/rump in air, head stretched out, 7½", Con Agra, 1990s, NM $8.00

Peanuts, figure, Snoopy, squeeze vinyl, sitting upright holding yel flower, 4", Danara, 1970s, EX+ $12.00

Peanuts, figure, Snoopy, stuffed cloth w/jeans & name on red shirt, 8", Rag Doll, Ideal, MIP (sealed)..................................$40.00

Peanuts, figure, Snoopy, stuffed plush, cloth sheriff's outfit, 12", Determined, NM..................................$15.00

Peanuts, figure, Snoopy, vinyl, jtd, as astronaut, 9", Determined, 1969, G..................................$100.00

Peanuts, figure, Snoopy, vinyl, jtd, cloth outfit w/'S' on red top, wearing roller skates, 10", Determined, 1980s, EX+.......$28.00

Peanuts, figure, Woodstock, resin, standing w/eyes closed, 4", NM..................................$10.00

Peanuts, figure, Woodstock, stuffed body w/vinyl head & feet, cloth outfit w/name on top, 7", Applause, NM+..............$15.00

Peanuts, figure, Woodstock, stuffed felt w/yarn hair, Determined, 1970s, EX..................................$12.00

Peanuts, friction toy, Woodstock on ice cream scooter, plastic, 6", Aviva, 1970s, EX..................................$22.00

Peanuts, friction toy (Motorized Toy), Woodstock seated atop bird's nest, plastic, 3½", Aviva, 1970s, NRFP..................................$35.00

Peanuts, Friction Wheelie, plastic, Snoopy seated on 3-wheeled scooter, 6", MIP..................................$35.00

Peanuts, gyroscope, Charlie Brown sitting atop globe, 8½", Aviva, 1970s, MIB (box reads 'Snoopy Gyroscope') ... $400.00

Peanuts, Jumbo Coloring Pencils, Empire, unused, MOC...$6.00

Peanuts, kaleidoscope, cb w/allover images of Snoopy laughing, 9", NM..................................$30.00

Peanuts, magic slate, Top Dog, various images of Snoopy, Child Art Prod, 1970s, unused, M (sealed) $15.00

Peanuts, marionette, Charlie Brown, vinyl, jtd, 8", Pelham, 1980s, NRFB..................................$75.00

Peanuts, megaphone, litho tin w/images of Snoopy w/megaphone, Lucy & Charlie Brown, 6", Chein, 1970, EX $25.00

Peanuts, night-light, plastic bulb w/image of Charlie Brown flying kite, 4", 1980s, NM..................................$10.00

Peanuts, push-button puppet, Charlie Brown, Ideal, 1960s, NM+ $35.00

Peanuts, push-button puppet, Snoopy as Joe Cool, Ideal, 1970, NM+..................................$75.00

Peanuts, push-button puppet, Woodstock Flying Trapeze Toy, Aviva, NM...$25.00

Peanuts, Skediddler, Lucy, 4½", Mattel, 1969, MIB........ $125.00

Peanuts, Snoopy Auto Refreshers, stuffed cloth Snoopy figure outline in blk, red collar, 3", Determined, MIP..............$12.00

Peanuts, Snoopy Fun Flashlight, plastic Snoopy figure as Flying Ace, squeeze to light, 4", Garrity, 1980s, MOC $15.00

Peanuts, Snoopy Mini Walker, plastic w/up figure, 3", Aviva, 1970s, MOC...$10.00

Peanuts, Snoopy Photo Ornaments (Paint-by-Number), Craft House, unused, MOC...$15.00

Peanuts, Snoopy's Pound-a-Ball, 17x13", Child Guidance, 1978, EX+IB...$50.00

Peanuts, Snoopy Scissors, plastic, Mattel #7410, 1970s, NM+ .$50.00

Peanuts, soap dish, Charlie Brown figure w/ball glove as soap dish, plastic, wall-mount, Avon, 1970s, NM+IB...........$25.00

Peanuts, tea set, litho tin, Frieda & Schroeder portraits on plates, gang on tray, 7-pc, Chein, spoons missing, EXIB $100.00

Peanuts, top, Peanuts Top, litho tin, musical, 10" dia, Chein, EXIB $75.00

Pebbles, see Flintstones

Pepe Le Pew, see Looney Tunes

Phantom, figure, wood compo, standing w/arms folded on base w/ name, 5", KFS, 1944, EX.. $500.00

Pink Panther, bank, bright pk & red PP golfer figure emb on yel container, plastic, 9x4x2½", 1970s, NM+..............$50.00

Pink Panther, Chatter Chum, Mattel, 1976, NM..............$50.00

Pink Panther, figure, bendable vinyl, skinny, 10", Amscan, 1970s, NM $18.00

Pink Panther, figure, stuffed pk plush in blk satin jacket, plastic eyes, 16", Mighty Star, 1987, NM...................................$25.00

Pink Panther, figure, vinyl, jtd, legs apart, 2-tone tan, 8", Dakin, EX...$25.00

Pink Panther, figure, vinyl, jtd arms only, legs together, 2-tone pk, 8", Dakin, 1971, NM...$28.00

Pink Panther, gumball machine, transparent pk plastic head on yel base, 8", Tarrson Co, 1970s, NM.................................$30.00

Pink Panther, marionette, compo w/cloth outfit, 12", JJK Assoc, 1960s-70s, MIP ('Want-Um Marionettes' on header)....$75.00

Pink Panther, mug, ceramic head form, pk w/dk pk nose, yel eyes, 4½", Royal Orleans, 1980s, NM+ $50.00

Pink Panther, push-button puppet, atop cylindrical candy container, misspelling on label, Taiwan, 1970s, unused, M..$60.00

Pink Panther, windup swimming figure, plastic, Polly Gaz Int'l, 1979, MOC (sealed) $30.00

Pinky & the Brain, figures, vinyl, 3", Dakin, 1990s, NM+, pr..$35.00

Planet of the Apes, bank, Galen figure standing, vinyl, 11", Play Pal Plastics, 1974, NM $35.00

Planet of the Apes, hand puppet, any character, plush, Commonwealth, 1960s, MIP, ea.. $150.00

Pogo, mug, plastic, Albert Alligator decal, angled handle open at bottom, 1970s, NM $10.00

Pogo, figure, Albert Alligator, vinyl, jtd arms, 5½", detergent giveaway, 1969, NM+ $15.00

Pogo, figure, Churchy La Femme, vinyl, jtd arms, swivel head, 5", detergent give-away, 1969, NM $18.00

Pogo, figure, Porky Pine, vinyl, swivel head, standing holding stick, 5", 1969, NM $12.00

Pogo, mug, Churchy La Femme decal on wht plastic, cylindrical w/angled hdl open at bottom, 4", 1970s, NM................$10.00

Popeye, bank, Popeye holding spinach can, vinyl, jtd arms, 6½", EX..$25.00

Popeye, bath toy, vinyl, Popeye leaning forward on boat (soap dish), 5x6" L, Stahlwood, 1950s, VG $40.00

Popeye, bubble bath container, Brutus, Colgate-Palmolive, 1960s, EX..$25.00

Popeye, bubble bath container, Popeye, Colgate-Palmolive, 1960s, NM..$30.00

Popeye, Christmas Tree Set (Lights), set of 6 w/characters on ea Mazda lamp, Reliance, 1930s, NMIB.......................... $175.00

Popeye, Colorforms, Popeye the Weatherman, 1959, NMIB...$45.00

Popeye, dexterity game, Popeye the Juggler, tin w/glass top, 3½x5", Bar-Zim Toys, 1929, NM $100.00

Popeye, figure, Brutus, stuffed body w/vinyl head & hands, flocked hair & beard, w/blk eye, 22", Presents, 1985, NM+...........$25.00

Popeye, figure, Brutus, stuffed body w/vinyl head & hands, toothy grin, synthetic hair & beard, 13", Presents, 1985, NM+ .$20.00

Popeye, figure, compo, jtd limbs, stands w/fists clinched & pipe in mouth, Cameo/KFS, 1935, rstr $575.00

Popeye, figure, Jeep, compo, jtd limbs, yel w/lg red nose, 12", KFS, 1935, VG $575.00

Popeye, figure, Olive Oyl, plush body w/vinyl head, red & wht, 9", Gund Gundikins, 1950s, NM $50.00

Popeye, figure, Olive Oyl, stuffed cloth w/vinyl head, hands & shoes, cloth outfit, 12", Presents, 1985, w/tag, NM........$20.00

Popeye, figure, Olive Oyl, stuffed printed foam, Olive holding flower bouquet, about 6", Crib Mates, 1979, MIP $20.00

Popeye, figure, Olive Oyl, vinyl (hollow), swivel head & waist, arms & legs, 9", Multiple Toys, 1960s, NM $55.00

Popeye, figure, Popeye, foam-stuffed print cloth, 6", Crib Mates, 1979, NRFP ('Stuffed Foam Toy' on header) $20.00

Popeye, figure, Popeye, pnt wood/compo bead-type w/pipe in mouth, 13½", King Features, 1935, VG.......................$300.00

Popeye, figure, Popeye, rubber-&-cloth-over-tin w/up figure that grows taller while eating spinach, 11", 1950s, NM......$200.00

Popeye, figure, Popeye, squeeze vinyl, 4½", Playmakers, 1984, NRFP ('Vinyl Squeaker' on header card) $18.00

Popeye, figure, Popeye, squeeze vinyl, 9", Crib Mates, 1979, EX .$25.00

Popeye, figure, Popeye, stuffed cloth, w/spinach can, 7", Dean's Rag, 1930s, G $150.00

Popeye, figure, Popeye, stuffed cloth w/vinyl head & arms, cloth shirt, 7", Uneeda, 1979, MIB.................................$35.00

Popeye, figure, Popeye, stuffed felt w/cloth outfit, printed face w/ plastic eyes, wooden pipe, can under arm, 11", EX...... $150.00

Popeye, figure, Popeye, stuffed plush, vinyl head, lt gr & wht, 9½", Gund Gundikins, 1950s, EX+.................................$50.00

Popeye, figure, Popeye, stuffed plush, vinyl head winking & pipe in mouth, roly-poly body, chimes, 10", Gund, 1950s, EX $50.00

Popeye, figure, Popeye, vinyl, cloth outfit, jtd head & arms, holding spinach can, 8½", Dakin, 1970s, NM+.................$25.00

Popeye, figure, Popeye, vinyl, jtd, 13½", Cameo, 1950s, EX....$125.00

Popeye, figure, Popeye, wood, pnt bead type w/pipe in mouth, 15", Ideal, EX..$450.00

Popeye, figure, Popeye, wood & compo, jtd, 8", Chein, EX+..$275.00

Popeye, figure, Swee' Pea 'Comic Strip Doll,' stuffed cloth, red sleepware, wht hat w/red ribbon, 10", Columbia Toy, EX $55.00

Popeye, figure, Swee' Pea, foam-stuffed body w/vinyl head & hands, 9½", Uneeda, MIB.....................................$40.00

Popeye, figure, Wimpy, stuffed cloth body w/vinyl head & hands, flocked shoes, cloth outfit, 12", Presents, 1985, M $25.00

Popeye, figure, wood & compo, jtd, 12", Ideal, G+.........$150.00

Popeye, game, Ring Toss, 1980, NRFC.............................$12.00

Popeye, hand puppet, Olive Oyl, cloth body w/vinyl head, Guns, 1950s, EX...$50.00

Popeye, Hip-Pop Ball, solid rubber, 2", Ja-Ru, 1981, NRFP ...$10.00

Popeye, jack-in-the-box, Popeye in the Music Box, Mattel, 1961, VG...$75.00

Popeye, jack-in-the-box, Popeye Spinach Can, 7½", Mattel, 7½", EX+ $275.00

Popeye, lamp, diecast metal boat w/'water' base & flag, Popeye figure in 'smokestack' light bulb, 7", G $200.00

Popeye, lamp, pot metal figure w/arm around post, orig shade w/ Popeye images, 16", Idealite, 1930s, EX lamp/G shade.. $300.00

Popeye, magic slate, lg head of Popeye on header, Lowe, 1963, G...$10.00

Popeye, marionette, Popeye, cloth body w/vinyl head, plastic hands, cloth outfit, 12", Gund, 1950s, NM $75.00

Popeye, marionette, Popeye, compo w/cloth outfit, 12", NRFP ('Want-Up Marionettes' on header card) $75.00

Popeye, Metal Tapping Set, Carlton Dank #333, 1950s, complete, NMIB... $110.00

Popeye, nodder, celluloid, stands w/fists clinched & pipe in mouth, 8", Japan, ca 1935, VGIB $450.00

Popeye, Official Pipe, wood, b/o, Micro-Lite Prod, 1958, MOC...$90.00

Popeye, Paddle Ball, wooden paddle w/rubber ball attached, 9½", M Shimmel Sons Inc, NRFP...$15.00

Popeye, Pin Ball Game, plastic bagatelle, shows Popeye punching Brutus, 7½x4½", M Shimmel & Sons, MOC $12.00

Popeye, playset, Thimble Theatre Mystery Playhouse, complete, Harding Prod, ca 1959, EXIB................................ $975.00

Popeye, Pocket Puzzles, 4 dexterity puzzles on 1 card, Ja-Ru, 1989, NRFC $12.00

Popeye, Popeye Menu Pinball Game, KFS, dated 1935, 23x14", EX $285.00

Popeye, Popeye Music Box (jack-in-the-box), litho tin, Mattel, 11", NM... $650.00

Popeye, pull toy, Popeye & Olive Oyl Stretchy Hand Car, Linemar, litho tin, 6½" L, EX+IB $2,000.00

Popeye, pull toy, Popeye & Olive Oyl w/'Slinky' bodies work handcar on 4-wheeled platform, 8", Linemar, VG $500.00

Popeye, pull toy, Popeye Band Wagon, paper-litho-on-wood, 8½" H, EX $125.00

Popeye, pull toy, Popeye w/spinach can on wheeled surfboard (?), paper-litho-on-wood, articulated arms, 12" H, EX $100.00

Popeye, push-button puppet, any character, Kohner, 1960s, NM, ea $50 to $75.00

Popeye, slide-tile puzzle, blk & wht plastic, 4 character images, Roalex, unused, MOC..$50.00

Popeye, squeeze toy, Olive Oyl's head on squeeze hdl, vinyl, 5", Crib Mates, 1979, NRFP..$18.00

Popeye, squeeze toy, Popeye's head on squeeze hdl, vinyl, 6", Crib Mates, 1979, NRFP $18.00

Popeye, stamp set, Popeye Comics Department, StamperKraft #4007, complete, used, EX $75.00

Popeye, Super Magnet, plastic horseshoe shape, 9½", Laurie Import Limited, 1976, NRFP $15.00

Popeye, Telephone w/Bell, plastic w/Popeye image in center of rotary dial, Larami, 1970s, NRFC..................................$15.00

Popeye, wallet, blk vinyl w/wht 'SS Popeye' life preserver & Vari-Vue image on front, Bernard Cohn Co, 1950s, M..$20.00

Popeye, Whistling Flashlight, Bantamlite, 1950s, MOC. $100.00

Popeye, Wood Slate (chalkboard), Ja-Ru, 1983, NRFC....$12.00

Porky Pig, see Looney Tunes

Power Rangers, bubble bath container, any character, Kid Care, 1994, M $6.00

Punch & Judy, hand puppet, cloth body w/vinyl head, Peter Puppet Playthings, 1949, MIB, ea $75.00

Raggedy Ann & Andy, Animal Friends, Larami, 1977, unused, MOC $12.00

Character, TV, and Movie Collectibles
Popeye, pull toy, SS Popeye, 15½", EX+, $225.00. (Photo courtesy Bertoia Auctions)

Raggedy Ann & Andy, baby rattle, plastic lollipop type w/Andy image on wht, 6", Stahlwood Toy, 1980s, MIP..............$20.00

Raggedy Ann & Andy, bank, Andy in 'Spirit of '76' outfit, vinyl & cloth, 9", Royalty, 1974, NM.................$35.00

Raggedy Ann & Andy, bank, Andy sitting w/arms at sides, red shirt w/wht collar, vinyl, Imco, 1970s, NM $25.00

Raggedy Ann & Andy, bank, Andy standing w/ice cream cone behind back on grassy base, compo, 7", Boudoir Pets, 1969, NM $20.00

Raggedy Ann & Andy, bank, Ann & Andy seated leaning on each other, pnt compo, 6", Determined, 1971, EX+ $25.00

Raggedy Ann & Andy, bank, Ann seated, bl dress w/wht pinafore, ruffled collar/cuffs, blk shoes, 7", Play Pal, 1970s, EX $20.00

Raggedy Ann & Andy, bank, Ann standing w/arms at sides, ceramic, 8", Lefton, 1970s, NM $25.00

Raggedy Ann & Andy, bubble bath container, Ann, Lander, 1960s, NM.................$25.00

Raggedy Ann & Andy, figure, Ann or Andy, inflatable vinyl, 15", Ideal, NM, ea $15.00

Raggedy Ann & Andy, hand puppet, red/wht/bl cloth body, stuffed head, yarn hair, plastic eyes, Knickerbocker, 1960s, NM.................$50.00

Raggedy Ann & Andy, ornament, Andy figure w/arms at sides & legs spread, pnt ceramic, 4", Duncan, 1970s, NM+........$10.00

Raggedy Ann & Andy, pencil sharpener, 6", Janes, 1974, NM ..$25.00

Raggedy Ann & Andy, rag doll, Andy, 5", plaid shirt, lt bl pants, sailor's hat, Knickerbocker, 1976, MIB............$25.00

Raggedy Ann & Andy, rag doll, Andy, 13", red & wht checked shirt, bl pants, wht sailor's hat, Knickerbocker, 1979, MIB............$75.00

Raggedy Ann & Andy, rag doll, Ann, 5", printed wht collar & apron straps outlined in blk, Knickerbocker, 1976, MIB.$25.00

Raggedy Ann & Andy, rag doll, Ann, 12", floral dress w/wht pinafore, Knickerbocker, 1979, NM+IB.................$75.00

Raggedy Ann & Andy, squeeze toy, Ann seated w/hands on tummy in patched outfit, vinyl, 5", EX+.................$15.00

Raggedy Ann & Andy, squeeze toy, Ann standing in pk dress w/ wht apron & collar, 6", Regent Baby Prod, 1970s, MIP .$22.00

Raggedy Ann & Andy, toothbrush, Andy, b/o, Janex, 1973, unused, MIB $45.00

Raggedy Ann & Andy, wall decor, Ann figure standing holding coffeepot, cb, 14", Doll Toy Co, 1972, EX+ $10.00

Rainbow Brite, bubble bath container, Hallmark, 1995, NM .. $8.00

Ren & Stempy, figure, Ren, bendable stuffed cloth w/rubber face, bloodshot eyes, toothy frown, 12", Mattel, 1992, NM+.$15.00

Ren & Stempy, figure, Ren, stuffed plush, fleshy pk, 17", Dakin, 1992, NM $15.00

Ren & Stempy, figure, Talking Ren Hoek, stuffed cloth w/vinyl head, 10", Mattel, 1992, unused, MIP $25.00

Ren & Stempy, Spitballs figure, soft rubber, Ren holding throat as if choking, eyes bulging, rubber, 5", Dakin, 1992, NM $12.00

Richie Rich, figure, Gloria Gad, PVC, 2½", Dimensions, 1981, MOC (sealed) $100.00

Ricochet Rabbit, hand puppet, printed cloth body as sheriff & name across bottom, vinyl head, Ideal, 1960s, NM..... $100.00

Road Runner, see Looney Tunes

Robocop, bubble bath container, Cosway, 1990, NM........$10.00

Rocky & Friends, bank, Bullwinkle standing against tree trunk waving, brn vinyl, 12", Play Pal Plastics, 1973, EX+......$65.00

Rocky & Friends, bank, Bullwinkle standing w/arms down & 'B' on gr sweater, JM Co/Hong Kong, 1977, 10½", NM+. $100.00

Rocky & Friends, bank, Bullwinkle standing w/hands on hips on base, 10", Imco, 1977, EX+.................$50.00

Rocky & Friends, bank, rnd clock shape w/Bullwinkle on face w/arms as clock hands, plastic, 9x6", Larami Corp, 1969, MIP.........$75.00

Rocky & Friends, bank, 'Rocky & His Friends Bank' w/Rocky, Mr Peabody & Bullwinkle holding signs, ceramic, 5x7", 1960s $175.00

Rocky & Friends, bank, Rocky, Bullwinkle, Sherman & Mr Peabody in band, figural ceramic, 5", PAT Ward, c 1960, EX..........$400.00

Rocky & Friends, bop bag, Snidley Whiplash, inflatable vinyl, marked PAT Ward, 1982, M $25.00

Rocky & Friends, bubble bath container, any character, Colgate-Palmolive, 1960s, NM, ea $30.00

Rocky & Friends, Bullwinkle's Double Boomerangs, Larami #3804, 1969, MIP.................$30.00

Rocky & Friends, Bullwinkle's Electric Quiz Game, Larami, 1971, unused, MIP $20.00

Rocky & Friends, figure, Bullwinkle, bendable rubber, 'B' on gr sweater, 7", Jesco, 1991, MOC.................$12.00

Rocky & Friends, figure, Bullwinkle, stuffed plush, 'B' on lt bl tank top, 12", Mighty Star, 1991, EX.................$10.00

Rocky & Friends, figure, Bullwinkle, stuffed plush, 'B' on orange shirt, 16½", Wallace Berry, 1982, NM+.................$25.00

Rocky & Friends, figure, Bullwinkle, stuffed plush, 'B' on red sweater, felt antlers, 12", Dakin, 1978, w/tag, M $45.00

Rocky & Friends, figure, Dudley Do-Right, bendable vinyl, Wham-O, 1972, EX $20.00

Rocky & Friends, figure, Natasha, bendable rubber, purple knee-length dress, Jesco, 1991, MOC.................$10.00

Rocky & Friends, figure, Natasha, bendable rubber, purple knee-length dress, Wham-O, 1972, VG $15.00

Rocky & Friends, figure, Rocky, bendable rubber, 5", Jesco, 1991, MOC $10.00

Rocky & Friends, figure, Rocky, stuffed plush, 12", Wallace Berrie, 1982, NM+.................$20.00

Rocky & Friends, figure, Rocky, stuffed plush w/vinyl head, 9½", 1966, rare, VG $150.00

Rocky & Friends, figure, Rocky, vinyl, jtd, 6½", Dakin, 1970s, MIB ('Cartoon Theater' box) $75.00

Rocky & Friends, figure, Sherman, bendable rubber, 4", Wham-O, 1972, NM $20.00

Rocky & Friends, figure, Snidley Whiplash, bendable rubber, blk & wht w/yel eyes, 5", Wham-O, 1970s, MOC $25.00

Character, TV, and Movie Collectibles
• • • • • • • • • • • • •
Raggedy Ann and Andy, doll, Ann, 31", stenciled heart on chest, original clothing, 1950s, $115.00.
(Photo courtesy James D. Julia, Inc.)

Rocky & Friends, figure set, Bullwinkle & Rocky, plastic, jtd, 5" & 1½", Exclusive Toy Prod, 1998, unused, MIB.............$15.00

Rocky & Friends, pencil case, vinyl w/images of Rocky & Bullwinkle on trapeze bars, zippered, 4x8", 1962, scarce, NM+ $75.00

Rocky & Friends, wallet, Bullwinkle & Rocky, brn vinyl w/wht rope stitching, Larami, MOC.........................$25.00

Rootie Kazootie, handkerchief, cloth w/Gala Poochie Pup in clubhouse, 9x9", RK Inc, 1950s, EX $25.00

Rugrats, bubble bath container, Tommy Kid Care, 1997, NM..$6.00

Rugrats, figure, Phil, vinyl w/cloth outfit, 4½", Mattel, 1998, NRFP...$10.00

Rugrats, hand puppet, Tommy, cloth body w/vinyl head & hands, Mattel, 1998, M..$8.00

Rugrats (Movie), figure, Angelica, vinyl w/yarn hair & cloth outfit, 6", Mattel, 1998, NRFB.............................$10.00

Scooby Doo, bank, Scooby, vinyl, seated upright, 6", 1980, EX $18.00

Scooby Doo, figure, Scooby, hard-stuffed ribbed cloth, 8", Dakin, 1979, NM $15.00

Scooby Doo, figure, Scooby, stuffed plush, felt tongue, seated, 8", Sutton, 1970, NM $25.00

Scooby Doo, figure, Scooby, stuffed plush, standing on all 4s, 7½", Sutton, 1970, NM $30.00

Scooby Doo, figure, Shaggy, bendable rubber, 5½", Equity Marketing, 1999, NM...$5.00

Scooby Doo, night-light, Scooby, Scrappy & Ghost, bisque, 7", 1980s, NM...$25.00

Sesame Street, see also Muppets

Sesame Street, bank, Big Bird hugging lg egg while seated on nest w/'Sesame Street' sign, compo, 6", Gorham, 1978, NM+...$20.00

Sesame Street, bank, Bert figure, vinyl, 13", New York vinyl, 1971, EX+...$25.00

Sesame Street, bank, Cookie Monster standing holding Cookie jar, vinyl, 9½", Illco, 1980s, NM+.........................$15.00

Sesame Street, bath toy, bubble-blowing Elmo figure holding onto blanket, vinyl, 7", Kid Dimension, 1993, NM $10.00

Sesame Street, bath toy, Cookie Monster eating cookie on innertube, vinyl, 4", Playskool, NM $6.00

Sesame Street, Bert Stacking Toy, figural, 10½", Child Guidance, 1975, NMIB $25.00

Sesame Street, bookends, plastic-framed photo images of characters, 7½", WPC Inc, 1980, NM, pr $20.00

Sesame Street, bubble bath container, Elmo, Kid Care, 1997, NM $6.00

Sesame Street, cake topper, Bert figure waving on oval base, plastic, 2½", Wilton, 1980s, M.........................$5.00

Sesame Street, figure, any character, PVC, 4", Jack-in-the-Box premium, MIP, ea $5.00

Sesame Street, figure, Bert, stuffed cloth, 8", Applause, 1980s-90s, NM+...$8.00

Sesame Street, figure, Bert, stuffed cloth, 10", Rag Doll #2601, Knickerbocker, 1975, MIB.........................$35.00

Sesame Street, figure, Bert, stuffed cloth, 18", Applause, 1980s, NM+...$18.00

Sesame Street, figure, Big Bird, PVC, playing guitar, 3½", Tara, 1985, MOC $10.00

Character, TV, and Movie Collectibles
• • • • • • • • • • • • •
Scooby Doo, figure, Scrappy, vinyl, 6½", Dakin, 1982, NM+, $75.00. (Photo courtesy www.whatacharacter.com)

Sesame Street, figure, Big Bird, stuffed plush, stuffed striped cloth legs, bl felt shirt w/name, 10", Hasbro, NM+ $10.00

Sesame Street, figure, Big Bird, stuffed plush, 11" or 13" (fireman's hat), Knickerbocker, 1970s-80s, NM+, ea............$15.00

Sesame Street, figure, Big Bird, stuffed plush, 12", Applause, 1993, NM $10.00

Sesame Street, figure, Big Bird, vinyl, jtd arms, swivel head & torso, 5", Tara Toy, 1985, NM+.........................$6.00

Sesame Street, figure, Cookie Monster, plastic (hollow), standing & waving, bright bl, CBS Inc, 1985, NM+ $10.00

Sesame Street, figure, Cookie Monster, stuffed plush, 'Cookies Make Me Happy' on apron, 12", Applause, NM $10.00

Sesame Street, figure, Cookie Monster, stuffed plush, lg plastic eyes, mouth wide open, 15", Applause, 1980s-90s, EX+ .$10.00

Sesame Street, figure, Cookie Monster, stuffed plush, plastic eyes, 9", musical, sings 'Sing,' Knickerbocker, EX+ $18.00

Sesame Street, figure, Cookie Monster, stuffed plush, plastic eyes, 10", Knickerbocker, 1970s-80s, NM $12.00

Sesame Street, figure, Cookie Monster, stuffed plush, 5", Applause, 1980s, NM+ $8.00

Sesame Street, figure, Count, beanbag plush, gr cape, 8", Tyco Preschool, 1997, NM+.........................$12.00

Sesame Street, figure, Elmo, beanbag plush, plastic eyes, 9", Tyco, 1997, NM+...$8.00

Sesame Street, figure, Ernie, stuffed cloth, felt type w/flat felt hands, blk fuzzy hair, 6", Applause, NM+.........................$8.00

Sesame Street, figure, Ernie, stuffed cloth, orange parachute type, bl shirt w/yel dots, fuzzy blk hair, 12", Tyco, M...............$10.00

Sesame Street, figure, Ernie, stuffed cloth, pillow type w/printed image of Ernie waving, 17", NM+ $15.00

Sesame Street, figure, Ernie, stuffed cloth, vinyl head/hands, striped sweater, print sneakers, 12", Applause, 1980s, NM $15.00

Sesame Street, figure, Grover, stuffed plush, bl w/lg pk nose, plastic eyes, 7", Applause, 1995, M.........................$10.00

Sesame Street, figure, Grover, stuffed plush, bl w/lg pk nose, plastic eyes, 17", Nanco, 2000, NM+.........................$12.00

Sesame Street, figure, Grover, stuffed plush, bl w/lg pk nose, plastic eyes, 30", Nanco, 2003, M $20.00

Sesame Street, figure, Guy Smiley, stuffed cloth, felt-likle w/blk fuzzy hair, 9", Tyco Preschool, 1997, M.........................$10.00

Sesame Street, figure, Honker, beanbag plush, 9", Tyco Preschool, 1997, NM+ $8.00

Sesame Street, figure, Oscar the Grouch, beanbag plush w/plastic eyes, 10", Knickerbocker, EX+ $12.00

Sesame Street, finger puppet, any character, vinyl, Applause, Dakin or Tara Toys, NM, ea $5 to................................$8.00

Sesame Street, friction toy, any character, plastic, 4x6", Illco, 1980s-90s, NM, ea $8 to...$10.00

Sesame Street, globe, w/removable base, 15" H, Rand McNally, 1985, NM $25.00

Sesame Street, hand puppet, Bert, stuffed cloth from head to feet, plastic eyes, Applause, EX...$10.00

Sesame Street, hand puppet, Big Bird, plush w/felt hands & beal, yarn topknot, plastic eyes, Child Guidance, 1980, NM .$15.00

Sesame Street, hand puppet, Cookie Monster, bright bl furry plush w/lg plastic eyeballs, Child Horizon, 1970s, NM ..$20.00

Sesame Street, hand puppet, Oscar the Grouch, shaggy plush, Topper, 1970s, EX+ $20.00

Sesame Street, jack-in-the-box, Big Bird pops up w/guitar, plastic, 10", Playskool, 1986, NM+ $25.00

Sesame Street, lamp, Bert & Ernie w/instruments in wheeled washtub on rnd wooden base, graphical shade, 16", 1970s, NM $35.00

Sesame Street, Party Blowouts, features Big Bird, pkg of 8, Party Maker Beach Prod, 1990, unused, MIP $8.00

Sesame Street, pull toy, Cookie Monster on tricycle, Hasbro, 1982, M...$20.00

Sesame Street, push-button puppet, Ernie standing on base w/ Sesame Street label, 8", Tara Toy Co, EX+....................$20.00

Sesame Street, radio, w/up musical, plastic, shows emb Big Bird on front, 6", Illco, 1980s, NM+ $12.00

Sesame Street, squeeze toy, any character, Playskool, 1980s, NM, ea $8.00

Sesame Street, squeeze toy, Cookie Monster sitting holding cookie jar, vinyl, 4", Child Guidance, 1978, NM..........$12.00

Sesame Street, stuffed plush, Cookie Monster, lg plastic eyes, 8", Nadel & Sons, 1980s, NM+ $12.00

Sesame Street, TV set w/Big Bird figure, musical, plastic, 9x11", Illco, 1980s, EX+ $15.00

Sesame Street, windup toy, Big Bird on tricycle w/name on plaque, plastic, 7", Illco, 1980s, NM $12.00

Shazam, flowerpot, ceramic, wht w/Shazam in flight, 'Super Plants,' 3", 1970s, M...$15.00

Shmoo, see Li'l Abner

Simpsons, bank, any character, vinyl, Street Kids, 1990, NM+ $10.00

Simpsons, doll, any character, stuffed cloth w/vinyl head, cloth outfit, 12", Burger King, 1990, MIP, ea $10.00

Simpsons, doll, any character, vinyl, 4" to 6", Jesco, 1990s, NM+, ea $6 to $8.00

Simpsons, doll, Bart, stuffed cloth, plastic bug eyes, printed nose & mouth, cloth outfit, 18", Dan Dee, 1990, NM $15.00

Simpsons, doll, Bart, stuffed cloth, vinyl head & hands, knit top, bl felt pants & shoes, 5", Dan Dee, 1990, M $8.00

Simpsons, doll, Bart, stuffed cloth w/print face, bl cloth outfit & shoes, 11", Dan Dee, 1990, MOC........................$12.00

Simpsons, doll, Bart, stuffed plush w/vinyl head, cloth outfit, 24", Acme, 1990, NM $20.00

Simpsons, doll, Bart, vinyl, bl cloth shirt & shorts, bl shoes, holding slingshot, 9", Presents, 1990, M...................$15.00

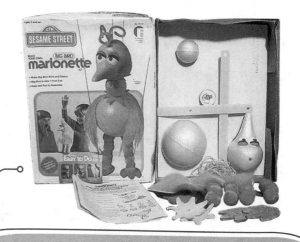

Simpsons, doll, Cooties Man!, stuffed body w/vinyl head, arms & legs, 12", Dan Dee, 1990, NM $15.00

Simpsons, doll, Homer, Talking & Dancing, dressed as Santa, b/o, Gemmy Industries, 2004, MIB................................$20.00

Simpsons, doll, Lisa, stuffed cloth, printed features & necklace, red felt dress & shoes, 11", Dan Dee, 1990, M $12.00

Simpsons, doll, Maggie, stuffed cloth w/vinyl head & hands, bl night gown, 7½", Burger King, 1990, NM+....................$10.00

Simpsons, eight ball, turn ball to reveal answers to questions, image of Bart, 1990s, NM+ $10.00

Simpsons, gumball machine, plastic globe w/Lisa decal, front reads 'The Simpsons,' 6", Rinco, 2000, NM+.................$12.00

Simpsons, soap figure, Bart, 5", Corich, 1990, unused, MIB (box reads 'Wash It, Dude!')..$10.00

Skeezix, see Gasoline Alley

Skippy, figure, pnt bisque, standing on rnd base w/name, 5½", Percy L Crosby, 1930s, VG+ $50.00

Sluggo, see Nancy

Smokey Bear, see Advertising category under USDA Forest Service

Smurfs, bank, Smurf figure standing w/legs together holding wht heart in hand, plastic, bl & wht, 11", Renzi, 1980s, EX.$12.00

Smurfs, Chatter-Chum, any character, plastic, 7", Mattel, 1980s, EX $20.00

Smurfs, figure, Baby Smurf on tummy, stuffed plush in pk pj's, 6½", Applause, 1980s, NM...$10.00

Smurfs, figure, Brainy Smurf, bisque, standing holding book, 4", Wallace Berrie, 1982, M..$20.00

Smurfs, figure, Gargamel, stuffed cloth, 15", M.................$15.00

Smurfs, figure, Greedy Smurf, bisque, in chef's hat & carrying lg birthday cake, 4", Wallace Berrie, 1980s, M...................$20.00

Smurfs, figure, Hefty Smurf, bisque, using mallet to pound Smurf Village sign into ground, Wallace Berrie, 1980, NM+ ...$20.00

Smurfs, figure, Papa Smurf, stuffed red & bl plush w/wht shaggy beard, seated pose, 8", Wallace Berrie, 1980s, NM........$10.00

Smurfs, figure, Papa Smurf, vinyl, jtd, 3¼", Irwin, 1996, MOC (sealed) $10.00

Smurfs, figure, Smurf kneeling & looking up holding candle w/ red flame, squeeze vinyl, 5", Danara, 1984, NM+...........$12.00

Smurfs, figure, Smurf standing w/eyes closed, smiling & hand to chin, squeeze vinyl, bl & wht, 5", Haco, 1980s, NM......$12.00

Smurfs, push-button button, any character, Kohner, 1980s, NM, ea $20 to...$25.00

Smurfs, top, litho tin w/rubber suction cup on bottom, Ohio Art, 1980s, 10x9" dia, EX+...$25.00

Smurfs, toy telephone, Smurf atop desk phone w/rotary dial, plastic, 10" H, HG Toys, 1980s, VG+............................$28.00

Snoopy, see Peanuts

Snuffy Smith, see Barney Google

Soupy Sales, hand puppet, yel cloth body w/red trim ('Soupy Sez Let's Do the Mouse'), vinyl head, Gund, 1965, NM+ . $225.00

South Park, figure, Cartman, stuffed plush, 9", Fun 4 All Corp, 1998, NM $10.00

South Park, figure, Cartman, vinyl, 6", Fun 4 All Corp, 1998, NM+...$10.00

South Park, figure, Kenny McCormick, stuffed plush, head hidden in orange parka, 7", Fun 4 All, 1998, NM+.............$12.00

Space Patrol, space helmet, plastic, Beemak Plastics, 1952, NMIB.$525.00

Spark Plug, see Barney Google

Speedy Gonzales, see Looney Tunes

Spider-Man, bank, bust figure w/arms crossed & blk spider logo on chest, plastic, Street Kids, 1991, NRFP $15.00

Spider-Man, Crazy Foam, unused, 1970s, MIP...................$50.00

Spider-Man, figure, vinyl, jtd arms, 13", Presents/Hamilton Gifts, 1990, M (w/hang tag)...$40.00

Spider-Man, gumball machine, 'Official Big Buckle Secret Gumball Dispenser,' Superior Toy, 1985, MOC (sealed)........$35.00

Spider-Man, hand puppet, plastic body w/vinyl head, 1970s, NM+...$40.00

Spider-Man, Jiggler, rubber figure, Ben Cooper/Hong Kong, 1960s, 6½", NM...$15.00

Spider-Man, Kazoo, plastic head shape, Straco, MOC $50.00

Spider-Man, Magic Motion Yo-Yo, Vari-Vue images on sides, Duncan, 1978, MIP...$20.00

Spider-Man, Webmaker, Chemtoy, 1970s, MIP.................$75.00

Steve Canyon, Jet Helmet, Ideal, 1959, NMIB $75.00

Superman, bank, plastic bust figure, w/orig 'Super Savers' sticker, 8", Mego, 1974, NM+ $30.00

Superman, bubble bath container, Avon, 1978, unused, MIB..$25.00

Superman, bubble bath container, Colgate-Palmolive, 1965, NM..$25.00

Superman, doll, compo w/jtd limbs, w/cloth shirt, shorts & snap-on cape, 15", Imperial Crown Toy Co, 1947, EX $475.00

Superman, figure, wood compo, standing w/hands on hips on base, promo for DC Comics, 5½", Syroco, 1942, EX .$1,375.00

Superman, flicker rings, gold-tone plastic w/various scenes, 1966, EX to NM, ea $125 to $150.00

Superman, hand puppet, printed cloth body w/vinyl head, Ideal, 1965, MIP...$65.00

Superman, Kiddie Paddlers, Super-Swim, 1940s, NMIB.. $150.00

Superman, Krypto-Raygun, flashes picture stories on the wall, plastic, b/o, complete, VGIB...$750.00

Superman, Kryptonite Rock, Pro Arts, 1977, MIB............$75.00

Superman, Movie Style Viewer, complete w/2 films, Acme Plastics, 1955, MIP $200.00

Superman, Movie Viewer, Chemtoy/NPP, 1965, unused, MOC..$25.00

Superman, Muscle Building Set, Peter Puppet Playthings #1001, 1954, complete, EXIB $225.00

Superman, push-button puppet, Kohner, 1960s, M $125.00

Superman, record player, suitcase style w/allover graphics including inside lid, 12x10", 1978, EX....................................$150.00

Superman, wallet, yel vinyl w/snap closure, Standard Plastics (Mattel), 1966, unused, M $85.00

Super Mario Bros, bank, Mario standing w/arms at sides, vinyl, 5½", Applause, 1989, EX...$12.00

Super Mario Bros, figure, Mario, stuffed cloth & vinyl, 12", Applause, 1989, NM+...$20.00

Sylvester the Cat, figure, vinyl, jtd head & arms, 8½", Dakin, 1968, EX...$40.00

Tarzan, clicker, Tarzan & gorilla, litho tin, upper bodies move when clicker is operated, 3", KKK, scarce, EX............. $200.00

Tasmanian Devil, see Looney Tunes

Teddy Roosevelt, figure, wood w/cloth 'safari' outfit, 9½", Schoenhut, VG+.. $550.00

Teenage Mutant Ninja Turtles, bubble bath container, any container, any character, Kid Care, 1990, M.........................$8.00

Teenage Mutant Ninja Turtles, Safety Target Set, Henry Gordy Int'l, 1990s, NRFP...$10.00

Teenage Mutant Ninja Turtles, snow domes, any character w/ Christmas motif, 4", Int'l Silver Co, 1990, NM+, ea $10.00

Tennessee Tuxedo, bubble bath container, w/ice-cream cone, Colgate-Palmolive, 1960s, NM......................$20.00

Thor (Super Hero), hand puppet, printed vinyl body w/molded vinyl head, Imperial Toy, 1978, NM..............................$20.00

Thor (Super Hero), Mechanical Super Heroes figure, plastic, 5½", Marx, 1968, MIB.......................... $225.00

Three Stooges, doll, any, stuffed cloth in blk & wht striped prisoner's suit, 15", Play-by-Play, 1999, NM+ $15.00

Three Stooges, doll, any, stuffed cloth in mismatched plaid outfits, 16", Play-by-Play, 1999, M, ea...............................$15.00

Three Stooges, doll, any, stuffed cloth in skeleton's outfit, 16", Good Stuff, 2002, NM+ $10.00

Three Stooges, hand puppet, any character, printed cloth body w/name, molded vinyl head, 1950s, EX+, ea $125 to.. $150.00

Tom & Jerry, bank, Jerry popping out of cheese wedge, ceramic, 4x5½" L, Gorham, 1981, M $40.00

Tom & Jerry, bank, tin container w/Tom chasing Jerry carrying piggy bank, 'T&J Savings Bank,' 5", Presents, 1989, NM .$12.00

Tom & Jerry, bank, Tom resting atop hamburger, ceramic, 5", Gorham, 1980s, M $50.00

Tom & Jerry, bank, Tom seated w/legs crossed holding sleeping Jerry, ceramic, 6", Gorham, 1980s, M $50.00

Tom & Jerry, bath toy, Jerry in duck intertube on seashell, hole in duck's mouth squirts water, 3", Turner, 1993, NM+.....$5.00

Tom & Jerry, Fight the Friction Mouse, plastic mouse, 3", Larami, 1970s, MOC..................................$12.00

Tom & Jerry, figure, Jerry, plastic, standing showing muscles on gr kidney-shaped base, Marx, 1973, EX+............................$25.00

Tom & Jerry, figure, Tom, bendable rubber, 6", 1979, EX+..$8.00

Tom & Jerry, figure, Tom, plastic, standing w/hands on hips, lt bl & wht w/peachy ears, yel eyes, 6", Marx, 1973, EX+ $25.00

Tom & Jerry, figure, Tom w/2 sm mice in fishing creel, stuffed cloth, vinyl wading boodts, 18", Italian, 1960s, EX..... $725.00

Tom & Jerry, figure set, bendable rubber, Amscan Inc, 1967, MOC...$25.00

Tom & Jerry, figure set, plastic, 6" lt bl Tom & 5" brn Jerry, Marx, 1973, MIB.................................$65.00

Tom & Jerry, hand puppet, Tom, plush body w/vinyl head, 1989, NM.................................$15.00

Tom & Jerry, hand puppet, Tom or Jerry, cloth body w/vinyl head, Zany, 1950s, EX, ea.................................$75.00

Tom & Jerry, kaleidoscope, litho metal, Green Monk, 1970s, NM+.................................$25.00

Tom & Jerry, pull toy, all-in-one Tom & Jerry figure standing on 4-wheeled bl & pk plastic platform, 7", Combex, NM...$50.00

Tom & Jerry, soap figures, Tom or Jerry, unused, MIB (box reads 'Fine Quality Soap'), ea.................................$20.00

Tom & Jerry, squeeze toy, Tom, yel & wht, standing rigidly w/fists clinched at sides, 1970, NM+ $25.00

Tom & Jerry, squeeze toy, Tom leaning back w/legs crossed in life preserver, rubber, 4" L, Lanco, 1990s, M.........................$12.00

Tom & Jerry, Water Gun, Marx, 1973, NMIB..................$50.00

Tom Corbett Space Cadet, costume, w/shirt, pants & belt, Yankiboy, 1950s, NM+IB $225.00

Toonerville Folks (Trolley), figure set, Mickey McGuire/Powerful Katrinka/Skipper/trolley, bisque, Borgfeldt, 1931, NMIB.$225.00

Top Cat, see Hanna-Barbera

Tweety Bird, see Looney Tunes

Umbriago (Jimmy Durante's Friend), printed oilcloth body w/ compo head, American Merchandise, 1945, NM........ $100.00

Uncle Sam, doll, bisque head w/bl glass eyes, wood & compo body w/patriotic cloth outfit, 14", Dressel, VG $630.00

Underdog, bank, standing w/arms at sides, vinyl, 8", Play Pals, 1970s, NM.................................$40.00

Underdog, bank, standing w/elbows out, plastic, JM Co/Hong Kong, 10", NM.................................$40.00

Underdog, bank, standing w/hands on hips, vinyl, 11", Play Pals, 1973, NM+.................................$50.00

Underdog, playset, 'It's a boat — it's a plane — it's a car!, it's Underdog!,' Playskool, 1974, NM+IB $100.00

Universal Monsters, bubble bath container, any monster character, Colgate-Palmolive, NM, ea $50.00

Universal Monsters, bubble bath container, Creature From the Black Lagoon, 10", Colgate-Palmolive, M.....................$90.00

Universal Monsters, bubble bath container, Frankenstein figure, 10", Colgate-Palmolive, EX $60.00

Universal Monsters, bubble bath container, Mummy figure, 10", Colgate-Palmolive, 1960s, EX.................................$60.00

Universal Monsters, bubble bath container, Wolfman, 10", Colgate-Palmolive, NM $65.00

Universal Monsters, Famous Monsters Plaster Casting Kit, Creature From the Black Lagoon, Rapco, 1974, unused, MIB.........$150.00

Universal Monsters, figure, any of 6 'Glow-in-the-Dark Movie Monsters,' about 5", Uncle Milton Industries, 1990, MOC, ea.................................$12.00

Universal Monsters, figure, Dracula, bendable rubber, 6", JusToys, 1991, MOC $10.00

Character, TV, and Movie Collectibles
Teenie Weenie, doll set, oil cloth, 3" – 5¾", 1920s, rare, VG – EX, $150.00. (Photo courtesy Smith House Toy and Auction Company)

Character, TV, and Movie Collectibles
Tom Corbett Space Cadet, doll, composition with cloth outfit, sleep eyes, 7½", EX, $75.00.
(Photo courtesy Smith House Toy and Auction Company)

Universal Monsters, figure, Dracula, stuffed w/printed features, satin cape, cb coffin, Commonwealth Toy Novelty, EX+.$40.00

Universal Monsters, figure, Mummy, vinyl, jtd, 7½", Imperial, MOC (card reads 'Universal Classic Movie Monster') ..$20.00

Universal Monsters, Horoscope Movie Viewer, Multiple Produtcs, 1964, NMIB $1,950.00

Universal Monsters, Magnetic Disguise Set, Wolfman, Imperial, 1987, unused, MOC..................................$10.00

Walter Lantz, bank, Andy Panda figure, plastic, 7", 1970s, NM+ $40.00

Walter Lantz, bank, Andy Panda figure, pnt compo, Crown Toy/ Walter Lantz Prod, 1939, 5", EX..................$75.00

Walter Lantz, bank, Woody Woodpecker popping out of tree trunk, ceramic, 7", Applause, 1980s, MIB $40.00

Walter Lantz, bank, Woody Woodpecker standing w/head turned, hand on hip & pointing up, plastic, 10", Imco, 1977, NM+ $40.00

Walter Lantz, Bubb-A-Loons, Imperial Toy, 1970s, NRFP .$15.00

Walter Lantz, bubble bath container, Woody Woodpecker, Colgate-Palmolive, 1960s, NM..................................$20.00

Walter Lantz, Chilly Willy on skis, vinyl w/cloth cap & scarf, 8½", Royalty Industries, 1970s, NM $35.00

Walter Lantz, figure, Andy Panda, plush beanbag-style body w/tan plastic shoes, California Stuffed Toys, 1982, 10", EX........$25.00

Walter Lantz, figure, any character, plush & vinyl, California Stuffed Toys, 1980s, NM, ea $20 to $25.00

Walter Lantz, figure, Wally Walrus, ceramic, full-length standing pose, 5½", 1950s, NM..................................$90.00

Walter Lantz, figure, Woody Woodpecker, stuffed plush, 13½", Ace Novelty, 1985, NM..................................$12.00

Walter Lantz, figure, Woody Woodpecker, stuffed plush, 19", Ace Novelty, 1989, w/tag, NM..................................$18.00

Walter Lantz, hand puppet, Woody Woodpecker, bl & wht printed cloth body w/name & vinyl head, 1950s, EX.....$75.00

Walter Lantz, hand puppet, Woody Woodpecker, talker, Mattel, 1962, EX+..................................$40.00

Walter Lantz, Magic Draw, featuring Woody Woodpecker, Ja-Ru, 1992, NRFC..................................$8.00

Walter Lantz, Motor Friend friction toy featuring Woody Woodpecker, plastic, 5", Nasta, 1975, EX $18.00

Walter Lantz, mug, Chilly Willy head, molded ceramic, 5 & Dime Inc, 1970s, 4½", NM..................................$20.00

Walter Lantz, w/up hopping Woody Woodpecker w/plush body & vinyl head, plastic hands & feet, 9", Illco, 1980s, NM $30.00

WC Fields, bank, standing, vinyl, 7½", Play Pal, 1970s, EX .$20.00

Welcome Back, Kotter, gum card set, complete set of 53, Topps, 1956, NM to M $45.00

Welcome Back, Kotter, portable record player, Teletone, 1996, NM $60.00

Wendy the Good Little Witch, see Harvey Cartoons

Wizard of Oz, hand puppet, any character, thin vinyl body w/ molded vinyl head, detergent premium, 1960s, EX, ea ..$18.00

Wonder Woman, doll, vinyl, jtd arms, standing w/legs together, golden whip, 15", Presents, 1988, NM+ $50.00

Woodstock, see Peanuts

Woodsy Owl, see Advertising category under USDA Forest Service

Yogi Bear, see Hanna-Barbera

Ziggy, figure, stuffed cloth, 'I Love A Smile' on shirt w/name & 'smiling' heart, 8", Knickerbocker, 1978, NM+..............$12.00

Ziggy, snow dome, 'Your're #1' on base, plastic oval, 1980s, NM. $10.00

Zippy the Monkey, marionette, 13", Peter Puppet Playthings, NM $325.00

Character, TV, and Movie Collectibles

Walter Lantz, bank, Space Mouse, vinyl, standing with hand on stomach, 7", Imco, 1977, NM, $50.00. (Photo courtesy www.whatacharacter.com)

Character, TV, and Movie Collectibles

Wizard of Oz, doll, Cowardly Lion, 50th anniversary edition, 11½", Multi Toys, 1988, MIB, $30.00. (Photo courtesy www.whatacharacter.com)

• **Chein** •

Although the company was founded shortly after the turn of the century, this New Jersey-based manufacturer is probably best known for the toys it made during the '30s and '40s. Wind-up merry-go-rounds and ferris wheels as well as many other carnival-type rides were made of beautifully lithographed tin even into the '50s, some in several variations. The company also made banks, a few of which were mechanical and some that were character-related. Mechanical, sea-worthy cabin cruisers, space guns, sand toys, and some Disney toys were made by this giant company. They continued in production until 1979.

Advisor: Scott Smiles

See also Banks; Character, TV, and Movie Collectibles; Disney; Sand Toys and Pails.

WINDUPS

Aero-Swing, 12", VG.....................................$300.00
Alligator w/Native Rider, 15" L, EX...................$150.00
Alligator w/Native Rider, 15" L, NM+IB..............$250.00
Aquaplane, 1930s version, 7" WS, EX.................$275.00
Aquaplane, 1950s version, 7½" WS, EX+.............$150.00
Army Cannon Truck, Mack 'C'-style cab, 8", EX $150.00
Army Sergeant, 1930s, 5½", EX+ $100.00
Barnacle Bill Floor Puncher, 7", EX $400.00
Barnacle Bill in Barrel, 7", EX $250.00
Barnacle Bill Walker, 6", NM+........................$375.00
Barnacle Bill Walker, 6", VG...........................$175.00
Big Top Tent, 1961, 10", EXIB $225.00
Broadway Trolley, 8", EX $150.00
Cabin Cruiser, 15", MIB $250.00
Cabin Cruiser, 15", VG................................$125.00
Cathedral Organ, #130, crank-op, 9½", NMIB.............$150.00
Chipper Chipmunk, 19½" L, EXIB $100.00
Clown Balancing Parasol on Nose, 1920s, 8", EX..........$250.00
Clown Floor Puncher, 8", EX $650.00
Clown Floor Puncher, 8", NM.........................$800.00
Clown in Barrel, 7", VG+ $350.00
Clown Walking on Hands, #158, 5", EX $150.00
Dan-Dee Dump Truck, 8½", VG+ $275.00
Dan-Dee Oil Truck, 8½", EX+ $425.00
Dan-Dee Roadster, 9", EXIB $900.00
Dan-Dee Skid Truck, 9", EX...........................$700.00
Doughboy, 6", EX+ $200.00
Drum Major, #111, 9", EXIB...........................$775.00
Drummer, #109, 9", EX+IB............................$150.00
Duck, in bellhop's hat & jacket, 1930s, 4", EX+...........$125.00
Easter Bunny Delivery Cart, VG+.....................$200.00
Easter Truck, 8½", EX+ $400.00
Fancy Groceries/Centre Market Delivery Van, 6", EX ...$300.00
Ferris Wheel, #172, 17", G.............................$275.00
Ferris Wheel, #172, 17", NMIB........................$425.00
Fish (Mechanical), #55, 1940s, 11" L, NM $125.00
Greyhound Coast-to-Coast Bus, disk wheels, 9", VG.....$225.00
Happy Hooligan, 6", EX $200.00
Indian Chief Walker, 5", EX............................$200.00
Junior Bus, #219, 9", EX+ $300.00
Junior Bus, #219, 9", VG $175.00
Junior Truck, 8½", EX $150.00
Limousine, 6", EX $300.00
Log Truck, 8½", VG+ $150.00
Marine Sergeant, 1960s, 5", EX........................$200.00
Mickey Mouse Sparkler, die-cut tin head w/name on bowtie, 6", EX.$225.00
Mono-Wing Plane, 6½", 1920s, gr or orange version, EX . $225.00
Navy Frog Man, 12", NMOC...........................$150.00
Noisemaker, 4 musical frogs lithoed on side, 3", EX $50.00
Pan American Sea Plane, 11" WS, EX..................$425.00
Peggy Jane Motor Boat, 14½", NM+IB $150.00
Pelican, #222, 5", NM $125.00
Penguin in Tuxedo, 1940, 4", EX+ $100.00
Playland Merry-Go-Round, #385, 10", EX..............$325.00
Playland Merry-Go-Round, 1950s, #385, 10", NMIB.....$475.00
Playland Whip, #340, 20" L, NMIB.....................$900.00

Chein, Windups
Aero-Swing, 12", NM (VG box), $700.00. (Photo courtesy James D. Julia, Inc.)

Chein, Windups
Krazy Kat Sparkler, 1932, 6", EX, $500.00. (Photo courtesy Morphy Auctions on LiveAuctioneers.com)

Chein, Windups
Popeye Drummer, #252, 7", NM+IB, very rare, $6,500.00. (Photo courtesy Morphy Auctions on LiveAuctioneers.com)

Popeye Carrying Parrot Cages, 8½", VG $325.00
Popeye Drummer, #252, 7", EX $3,000.00
Popeye Drummer, #252, 7", VG $2,000.00
Popeye Floor Puncher, 7" H, EX.............................$1,300.00
Popeye Floor Puncher, 7" H, G+............................$675.00
Popeye Heavy Hitter, 12", EX.................................$3,575.00
Popeye Heavy Hitter, 12", NMIB.............................$10,000.00
Popeye in Barrel, 7", EX..$325.00
Popeye in Barrel, 7", EXIB.....................................$525.00
Popeye Over the Head Puncher, 10", VG....................$3,150.00
Popeye Sparkler, #251, 1930s, figural head, NM+IB....$4,750.00
Popeye Sparkler, head image lithoed on rnd yel bkgrd, 5", EX ..$325.00
Popeye Walker, 6", EX+...$500.00
Rabbit, standing upright w/hands in pockets, 1938, 5", NM..$75.00
Racer #5, boattail w/spare tire, yel & orange, w/driver, 9", VG....$300.00
Ride-A-Rocket (Rocket Ride), #400, 19", EXIB $825.00
Ride-A-Rocket (Rocket Ride), #400, 19", VG $325.00
Roller Coaster, 1930s version, 19" L, EX+ $150.00
Roller Coaster, 1930s version, 19" L, NMIB..................$350.00
Roller Coaster, 1950s version, 19" L, NMIB..................$250.00

Santa Walker, 5½", EX $300.00
Turtle w/Native Rider, 8" L, EX............................ $225.00
Wimpy in Barrel, 8", EX $1,100.00
Yellow Taxi (Main 6531), 8", EX $300.00
Yellow Taxi (Main 7570), 6", VG+....................... $150.00

HERCULES SERIES

Chein, Hercules Series
Mack Crane Truck, #1100, 30", VG+, $1,150.00. (Photo courtesy Morphy Auctions on LiveAuctioneers.com)

Army Truck, cloth cover, 19", EX $600.00
Coal Truck, 20", EX $800.00
Coupe, 18", NM..$1,900.00
Dairy Products Truck, 19½", EX $1,000.00
Dump Truck, open seat, 17½", VG+ $350.00
Fire Hook & Ladder Truck, open seat, 18", EX............$1,200.00
Fire Pumper Truck, open seat, 18", VG $550.00
Ice Truck, 20", EX..$1,200.00
Local & Long Distance Moving & Storage Truck, 8", EX ..$450.00
Motor Express Truck, 16", NM....................................... $875.00
Oil Tank Truck, Mack 'C'-style cab, 19", EX $2,250.00

Oil Tank Truck, open seat, 10", rpnt $425.00
Racer #8, 20", EX+ $3,000.00
Railway Express Agency Truck, 20", G+ $425.00
Ready-Mixed Concrete Truck, Mack 'C'-style cab, 18", EX....$725.00
Roadster, w/rumble seat & luggage rack, 18", EX+IB ..$1,500.00
Royal Blue Line Bus, 18", EX $1,200.00
Royal Blue Line Bus, 18", G $475.00
Royal Blue Line Bus, 18", VG $850.00
Stake Truck, Mack 'C'-style cab, 18½", VG $525.00
Tow Truck, open seat, 18", VG....................................... $350.00

MISCELLANEOUS

Bank, Church, #29, 1950s, VG $50.00
Bank, clown head, mechanical, 1949, 5", EX................. $125.00
Bank, elephant sitting upright on drum, mechanical, 1950s, 5", NM $150.00
Bank, monkey tips hat when coin is inserted, 1950s, 5", M .. $200.00
Bank, Uncle Sam Bank, red, wht & bl litho tin top hat, 3", VG+ $75.00
Bank, Uncle Wiggily, 5", EX $175.00
Horse-Drawn Cart, #174, 12", SC, New York City, VG+, MB, $125 to.. $225.00
Magic Tulip Top, 9½", M (VG box) $75.00
Roly Poly (Clown), 6½", VG.. $100.00
Roly Poly (Monkey), bank, 6½", EX $150.00
Roly Poly (Monkey), 6½", VG+....................................... $125.00
Roly Poly (Rabbit), 6½", EX.. $150.00
Top, Three Little Pigs, 9" dia, VG....................................$75.00
Train, 3-pc, loco/tender #80, Harrison Pullman & Saratoga Pullman, 8½" L, VG $150.00
Yellow Taxi, nonpowered, 1926 on license plate, 7½", EX+ . $250.00

• • • • • • • • • • • • • • • ‹ Circus Toys › • • • • • • • • • • • • • • •

If you ever had the opportunity to go to one of the giant circuses as a child, no doubt you still have very vivid recollections of the huge elephants, the daring trapeze artists, the clowns and their trick dogs, and the booming voice of the ringmaster. What a thrill it was! The circus toys presented here evoke that excitement of the 'Big Top.' All are auction listings.

See also Battery-Operated Toys; Cast Iron; Chein; Marx; Windup, Friction, and Other Mechanical Toys.

American National Circus, Brown, Taggard & Chase, die-cut litho-on-cb animals & performers, EXIB.................... $100.00
Big Top Toy Circus, Britains style w/17" horse-drawn cage wagon, tight rope apparatus, etc, EX........................... $250.00
Bradley's Interchangable Combination Circus, Milton Bradley, ca 1883, complete, EX+IB $175.00

Britain's Mammoth Circus #1539, 21-pc set w/red wooden ring & tub, NMIB...$1,800.00
Britain's Three-Ring Circus, 19 pnt-lead figures, w/accessories, EX $250.00
Cirque International Clowns (2), France, w/up activation for performing on props, 10" H, EX+, pr $475.00

Circus Toys
Marx Super Circus, complete, EXIB, $100.00. (Photo courtesy Bertoia Auctions on LiveAuctioneers.com)

Circus Toys
- -
Three Ring Circus, with Britains figures, includes 19 painted lead figures, two tubs, and three wooden rings, most marked 'England,' 8", EX, $100.00 to $150.00. (Photo courtesy Noel Barrett Antiques & Auctions Ltd.)

Crandall Acrobats, 3 clowns (take-apart) on base, paper on wood, incomplete set, G (10x6" box)...................... $200.00
Crandall Happy Family Circus Cage, 9 flat-sided animals, etc, paper-on-wood, 17" L, VG+ $1,400.00
French Cirque International, 2-cloth-dressed clowns (1 w/internal w/up), 2 wooden donkeys, etc, VG+ $375.00
German Circus Set, pnt compo figures w/wooden accessories, EX (EX 12x12" box) $350.00
Hagenbeck's Menagerie Wagon, elephant-drawn, pnt wood/compo, 22" L wagon, VG+ $1,200.00

Reed Gigantic Circus & Mammoth Hippodome, lithoed wood, crank-op, complete, VG+IB $700.00
Reed Polar Bear Cage Wagon, paper litho on wood, 2 horses, driver, bear & keeper, 26" L, EX $5,500.00
Reeve-Mitchell Pull-A-Part Circus, pnt wood, complete, VG to EX $875.00
Revell Circus World's Greatest Toy Show, plastic jtd animals complete w/circus accessories, 1950, EXIB.................... $90.00
Spears Royal Circus, England, die-cut litho circus personnel w/ wooden props, complete, EXIB................................. $125.00

• Clickers • • • • • • • • • • • • • • • • • •

Previously called 'tin crickets' (and a few of them were even shaped like actual crickets), clickers were produced by German makers and became popular in the late 1800s and early 1900s. They are small metal toys with attached steel springs that click when pressed. The first clickers were made of tin, but more modern versions of the toys are made of plastic. Clickers were commonly used by businesses as advertising premiums.

Interestingly, one of the original intended uses of clickers was for soliders, particularly airborne troops, during the invasion of Normandy in World War II. They used their clickers to signal friendly or unfriendly soldiers. One soldier would click once, and if a click-click twice was heard in return, it meant the other nearby soldier was an ally.

The following listings are auction prices.

Baseball Players, KKK, pitcher throws ball to batter, 3", EX.. $300.00
Black Woman Scrubbing Boy's Back, Gely, 3", EX $700.00
Boxers, Japan, blk boxer & wht boxer move back & forth, NM $85.00
Boxers, unmk, blk boxer & wht boxer move back & forth, 4", VG $75.00
Cat & Dog, Germany, dog gets after cat on brick column, 3", NM $125.00
Cat & Mouse, Germany, cat makes facial expressions & wags tail as he holds mouse by the tail, 5", NM $125.00
Circus Elephant, Gely, plays the cymbal as it moves its head & tail, 2½", EX $135.00
Clown Banjo Player, Germany, eyes & body move as he plays banjo, 5", VG $140.00
Cowboy Kneeling & Shooting, Japan, 3", EX................... $50.00
Cowboy on Rearing Horse, Japan, 4", EX+....................... $50.00
Donkey Eats Grass, Gely, head & tail move, 3", EX $135.00
Egghead Playing Drum, Japan, head moves back & forth, 3½", EX $30.00
Man w/Rolling Pin & Fat Lady, Gely, man uses rolling pin on kneeling fat lady's backside, 3½", VG+....................... $450.00
Me & My Buddy Pistol, Wyandotte, PS, cowboy's arm moves & gun makes 'firing' noise, 8" L, EX.................................$50.00
Military Machine Gunner Prone, Japan, arm moves, 3½", EX ...$50.00

Clickers
- - - - - - - - - - - - - - - -
Blacksmith and Helper, Germany, 4", VG+, $450.00. (Photo courtesy Smith House Toy and Auction Company)

Clickers
- - - - - - - - - - - - - - - -
Clown and Golliwog, Germany, 3½", EX, $275.00. (Photo courtesy Smith House Toy and Auction Company)

Penguin Playing Cello, Japan, 4", EX...................................$50.00
Pig, Frog, Cat or Monkey Playing Cello, Japan, 2¼", EX+,
   ea...$50.00

Stork, Gely, tips hat & opens beak to reveal baby, 3", EX...$225.00
Tarzan & Gorilla Fighting, KKK, 3", EX.......................... $200.00
Tarzan & Native Fighting, KKK, 3", NM........................ $200.00

• • • • • • • • • • • • • Coloring, Activity, and Paint Books • • • • • • • • • •

Coloring, activity, and paint books from the early twentieth century are scarce indeed and when found can be expensive if they are tied into another collectibles field such as Black Americana or advertising; but the ones most in demand are those that represent familiar movie and TV stars of the 1950s and 1960s. Condition plays a very important part in assessing worth, and though hard to find, unused examples are the ones that bring top dollar — in fact, as much as 50% to 75% more than one even partially used.

ABC Country A Paint Book, Whitman, 1938, unused, VG+..$22.00
Alice in Wonderland Coloring Book, Whitman #1045-31, 1976,
   NM $20.00
Amazing Spider-Man Coloring Book, Whitman #1396, 1979,
   'The Monstera Gigantica Plot' (A Plantscaper Caper), unused,
   EX $50.00
Amazing Spider-Man in Seeing Double Coloring Book, Whit-
   man #1639-4, 1976, unused, NM $20.00
Amazing Spider-Man, The Oyster Mystery Coloring Book,
   Whitman #1051, 1976, unused, EX.......................$20.00
Annie Oakley Roundup Coloring Book w/Lofty & Tagg, Whit-
   man, 1955, unused, EX+ $20.00
Baba Looey Coloring Book, Watkins-Strathmore #1853, 1960,
   unused, EX...$32.00
Baloo the Bear From The Jungle Book Coloring Book, Watkins-
   Strathmore #1872-2, 1967, unused, EX.................$25.00
Banana Splits Coloring Book, Whitman #1062, 1969, unused,
   EX $50.00
Barbie, Ken & Midge Coloring Book, Whitman #1640-59, 1963,
   unused, EX...$55.00
Barney Bear Coloring Book, Whitman, 1953, unused, EX+..$25.00
Batman Coloring Book, Whitman #1002, 1967, unused, NM...$15.00
Batman Meets Blockbuster Coloring Book, Whitman #1032,
   1966, unused, NM..$15.00
Batman Vroom! Screech! Coloring Book, Watkins-Strathmore
   #1833-4, 1966, unused, NM..................................$20.00
Batman Zap Crunch Coloring Book, Watkins-Strathmore, 1966,
   unused, NM+...$30.00
Beatles Official Coloring Book, Saalfield, 1964, group on yel
   cover, unused, NM $85.00
Benji Activity Book, Golden, 1983, unused, EX $15.00
Big Daddy Roth Rat Fink Coloring Book, 1992, unused, EX...$45.00
Big-Big Magic Coloring Book, Whitman #2902, 1955, spiral-bound
   w/box of crayons inserted in cover, some use, VG $18.00

Blackbeard's Ghost Coloring Book, Whitman, 1968, unused,
   NM $18.00
Bob Clampett's Beany Coloring Book, Whitman, some use,
   EX...$15.00
Boys & Girls Coloring Book, Whitman #1244, 1960, unused,
   NM $15.00
Brady Bunch Coloring Book, Whitman #1004, 1974, unused,
   EX $18.00
Brady Bunch Coloring Book, Whitman #1657, 1974, unused,
   NM $25.00
Bridal Coloring Book, Whitman #1123, 1959, unused, NM+..$22.00
Buck Rogers Paint Book, 1935, some use, G+ $35.00
Buffy & Jody Coloring Book, Whitman #1640-59, 1969, unused,
   EX $32.00
Bugs Bunny Porky Pig Paint Book, Whitman, 1946, unused,
   EX $35.00
Captain America Coloring Book, Whitman #1181, 1966,
   unused, EX..$25.00

Coloring,
Activity, and
Paint Books
. . . .
Flash Gordon and
His Adventures in
Space, #9545, M
(used), $75.00.

Coloring,
Activity, and
Paint Books
. . . .
Howdy Doody Fun
Book, Whitman
#2187, 1950s,
some use, VG,
$20.00. (Photo courtesy
www.gasolinealleyantiques.
com)

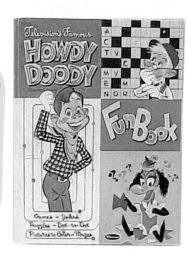

Captain Kangaroo Coloring Book, Watkins-Strathmore #1847, 1957, unused, EX.................................$18.00

Captain Kangaroo Dot to Dot, Whitman #1420, 1959, unused, NM..$20.00

Charmin' Chatty Paper Doll Activity Book, Golden, 1964, unused, VG...$20.00

Children's Modern Drawing & Paint Book, Whitman #W-684, 1927, unused, EX.............................$25.00

Chitty Chitty Bang Bang Coloring Book, Whitman #1654, 1968, unused, NM..............................$20.00

Circus Boy Coloring Book, Whitman, 1957, unused, EX..$15.00

Color Book/288 Pages to Paint & Color, Whitman, 1934, unused, VG+...$55.00

Color Fun, Whitman, 1949, kids waving at train, unused, EX....$25.00

Color Lessons for Little Folks by Milt Youngren, Whitman, 1935, unused, EX...........................$35.00

Connect the Lines (Leo & Lonnie the Lions), 1953, unused, VG+..$16.00

Crayon Fun Coloring Book, Saalfield, 1953, some use, VG+ .. $8.50

Crusader Rabbit Coloring Book, Whitman, 1959, striped Pluto cowering behind CR in armor w/sword & shield, unused, EX...................................$30.00

Dastardly & Muttley Coloring Book, Whitman #1023, 1970, unused, NM+...............................$25.00

Dennis the Menace Coloring Book, Whitman #1135, 1961, unused, EX+.................................$25.00

Ding Dong School Miss Francis Says Let's Color, Whitman, 1954, unused, EX+..........................$15.00

Dinosaurs Color Book, Whitman, 1974, unused, NM+.....$15.00

Disneyland Coloring Book, Whitman #2975-A, 1961, unused, EX.......................................$30.00

Doggie Daddy Coloring Book, Watkins-Strathmore #1883-5, unused, EX.......................................$28.00

Donald Duck Coloring Book, Whitman #2946, 1957, unused, EX.......................................$25.00

Easy Dot to Dot Pictures, Saalfield, 1953, cover features rabbit in sailboat, some use, VG+...........................$8.50

Ed 'Big Daddy' Roth Monster Coloring Book, 1960s, unused, NM+......................................$175.00

Fantasia Paint Book, Whitman, 1940, some use, VG........$32.00

Five in One Paintless Paint/Tracing/Trail of the Dots..., Whitman, 1940, unused, EX.........................$18.00

Flintstones Coloring Book, Whitman #1636, 1961, unused, EX..$30.00

Fluffy Dogs A Big Color/Activity Book, Golden, 1986, unused, NM.......................................$20.00

Fun Activities Till Christmas/192 Pages, Whitman, 1968, unused, EX+.....................................$25.00

Gentle Ben Coloring Book, Whitman #1642, 1968, unused, EX+..$20.00

Giant Whopper Coloring Book, Whitman, 1959, unused, NM..$15.00

Gingham's on the Farm Coloring Book, Whitman #1000-32, 1979, unused, NM+..........................$15.00

Goofy Coloring Book, Whitman #1009, 1972, unused, EX..$18.00

Groovie Goolies Coloring Book, Whitman #1096, unused, M $55.00

Gumby & Gumby's Pal Pokey Coloring Book, Whitman, 1968, unused, NM......................$25.00

Gummi Bears Coloring Fun, Simon & Schuster, 1985, unused, M $80.00

Happy Birthday Paint Book, Whitman, 1939, unused, EX+..$18.00

Howdy Doody Puppet Show Book, Whitman, 1950s, punch-out puppets, unused, EX+........................$100.00

HR Pufnstuf, see also Six Flags Fun Book

HR Pufnstuf Coloring Book, Whitman #1093, unused, M.$80.00

Huey, Dewey & Louie Coloring Book, Whitman, 1961, unused, EX..$15.00

Incredible Hulk At the Circus Coloring Book, Whitman #1040, 1977, unused, NM............................$25.00

Indians Punchout Standups & Coloring, Lowe, 1963, unused, EX..$22.00

Inspector Willoughby Coloring Book, Whitman #1221, 1961, unused, NM+...................................$20.00

It's Fun to Play w/ABC for Very Young Children, Whitman, 1930s-40s (?), unused, EX $18.00

Jem Deluxe Color/Acivity Book, Golden, 1986, unused, M..$50.00

Jingle Bells Novelty Cutouts & Coloring/Paint Book, Whitman, 1950, unused, M..............................$15.00

Jolly Santa Coloring Book, Whitman, 1965, unused, EX..$25.00

Lassie Coloring Book, Watkins-Strathmore, 1956, Timmy, Mom & Lassie on cover, unused, EX.....................$25.00

Lennon Sisters Coloring Book, Watkins-Strathmore #1833, 1958, unused, EX....................................$15.00

Let's Draw, Saalfield, 1953, features wht lamb on blk cover, unused, VG+ $10.00

Liddle Kiddles Coloring Book, Watkins-Strathmore, 1967, unused, EX...$35.00

Little Injuns to Color, Whitman #67510, unused, NM $20.00

Little Kids of Americana Craft Book, Taplinger, 1975, VG..$8.00

Little Lulu Coloring Book, Whitman #1663, 1974, unused, NM+ $20.00

Little Zebra & His Pals Pictures to Color, Saalfield, 1953, some use, VG+ $12.00

Lone Ranger (Adventures of) Coloring Book, Whitman #1653-34, 1975, unused, NM $15.00

Lone Ranger Hi-Yo Silver! Paint Book, Whitman #621, 1938, some use, VG..$35.00

Lord of the Rings Color & Activity Book, Whitman #1254, 1979, unused, EX+ $18.00

Magilla Gorilla Coloring Book, Whitman, 1967, MG playing violin, unused, NM $28.00

Masters of the Universe Adventures of Snake Mountain Coloring Book, Golden #1142-27, 1985, unused, NM............$20.00

Masters of the Universe Giant Color/Acivity Book, Golden #3114, 1985, unused, NM+.....................................$15.00

Mickey Mouse & Pluto Coloring Book, Watkins-Strathmore #1850-5, 1963, unused, EX $18.00

Mickey Mouse Club Dot to Dot, Whitman #1414, 1957, unused, VG $22.00

Mickey Mouse in Surprise for Everyone Coloring Book, Whitman #1664, 1978, unused, NM+ $22.00

Mickey Mouse Paint Book, 1960s repro of a 1930s version (Whitman #627), unused, EX.............................$15.00

Mommy & Me Coloring Book, Whitman, 1954, mother & daughter in matching bl dresses, unused, NM $32.00

Mother Goose Coloring Book, #3411, 1936, 15x10½", unused, G...$15.00

Multiplication Rock Color & Activity Book, Whitman, 1973, unused, NM $30.00

Munsters Coloring Book, Whitman, 1966, shows Herman & Grandpa trying to skateboard, unused, NM.................$200.00

My Little Buckaroo Coloring Book, Whitman, 1949, unused, EX+ $20.00

My Little Pony at the Dream Castle Coloring Book, Happy House, unused, NM.......................................$60.00

Night Before Christmas Coloring Book, Whitman #1125, 1954, unused, EX..$50.00

Old Yeller Coloring Book, Whitman #1199, 1957, unused, EX...$32.00

One Hundred & One Dalmatians Coloring Book (for everyone who loves dogs), Whitman, 1960, unused, EX $30.00

Pebbles & Bamm-Bamm (Teenage) Coloring Book, 1971, some use, EX...$35.00

People & Places Around the World, Whitman #1114, 1959, unused, EX...$15.00

PJ New 'N Groovy Coloring Book, Whitman #1654, 1971, unused, NM $22.00

Pluto Coloring Book, Whitman, 1953, artist Pluto painting himself a bowl of bones w/Mickey looking on, unused, EX ..$30.00

Princess of Power Who's Who Book (A Big Coloring Book), Golden #1152-1, 1985, unused, NM $22.00

Quickdraw McGraw Coloring Book, Whitman, QD startled by Hoss-Face Harry bursting through 'Wanted' poster, some use, VG+..$22.00

Rainbow Brite 'Dome Sweet Dome' Big Coloring Book, Golden #1149-29, 1984, unused, NM.................................$15.00

Restless Gun A Book to Color, Saalfield, 1950s, some use, VG .$20.00

Ricochet Rabbit (128 Pages to Color), Whitman, 1964, unused, EX...$50.00

Rin Tin Tin Coloring Book, Whitman #2958, 1959, some use, VG...$22.00

Rocket Jets Space in Action to Color, Merrill #1595, 1958, unused, EX..$50.00

Roy Rogers Paint Book, Whitman, 1948, some use, VG...$15.00

Santa Claus Coloring Book, Whitman, 1949, Santa admiring tree w/3 lg colorful bulbs, unused, EX............................$18.00

Santa Claus Paint Book, Whitman, 1949, unused, EX......$45.00

Santa's Busy Book/Dot to Dot/Things to Do/Things to Make..., Whitman, 1955, unused, EX..................................$22.00

Santa's Favorite Coloring Book, Watkins-Strathmore #1887, 1965, unused, NM..$20.00

Shirley Temple Coloring Box, Saalfield, 1935, complete w/orig crayons, some use, EX..................................$55.00

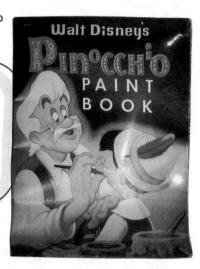

Coloring, Activity, and Paint Books
• • • • • • • • •
Walt Disney's Pinno-chio Paint Book, Whit-man, 1939, $100.00 to $150.00. (Photo courtesy David Longest)

Coloring, Activity, and Paint Books
• • • • • • • • • • • • • •
Walt Disney's Snow White and the Seven Dwarfs Paint Book, 1938, large, $200.00 to $300.00. (Photo courtesy David Longest)

Simple Objects to Color, Bonnie Book #4143, 1950, w/o crayons o/w VG $10.00

Six Flags Fun Book (HR Pufnstuf Characters), 1973, unused, NM+ $400.00

Snagglepuss & Yakky Doodle Coloring Book, Whitman, 1962, unused, NM+...$20.00

Snow White & the Seven Dwarfs Coloring Book, Watkins-Strathmore, 1950s, unused, EX+.....................................$20.00

Snow White & the Seven Dwarfs Coloring Book, Whitman #1024, 1952, unused, EX.................................$30.00

Snow White & the Seven Dwarfs Coloring Book, Whitman #1638, 1974, unused, EX.................................$15.00

Space Ghost Coloring Book, Whitman, 1967, some use, VG+ $18.00

Spike & Tyke Coloring Book, Whitman #2946, 1957, unused, NM+...$20.00

Sugarfoot Coloring Book, Saalfield, 1959, some use, VG..$28.00

Sunshine Fun Family, Whitman #1654-31, unused, EX...$15.00

Super Friends Coloring Book, Whitman #1000, 1975, unused, NM $20.00

Superman Battle 'Bainiac's Biggest Plot'/Giant Comics to Color, Whitman, 1976, unused, EX...$15.00

Superman Coloring Book, Whitman #1005, 1966, unused, NM+ $22.00

Sword & the Stone Coloring Book, Whitman #1637, 1963, unused, NM..$20.00

Tales of the Wizard of Oz Coloring Book, Whitman, 1962, unused, EX..$35.00

Tarzan Coloring Book, Whitman, 1966, Ron Ely cover, unused, EX..$28.00

Things to Make & Do for Christmas, Treasure Books #867, 1950s, unused, VG..$10.00

To Market We Will Go Paint Book, Whitman, 1939, unused, VG+..$25.00

Tom & Jerry Coloring Book, Whitman #2946, 1952, unused, EX+..$25.00

Tom Corbett Space Cadet Coloring Book, Saalfield, 1950s, some use, VG..$25.00

Trace & Color, Whitman #1168-15, 1951, unused, EX+ ..$15.00

Uncle Scrooge Coloring Book, Watkins-Strathmore #1851-6, 1966, unused, EX+ $30.00

Walt Disney's Fairy Tales & Other Favorites Coloring Book, Whitman #1645, unused, EX+..$18.00

Walt Disney's Mickey & His Friends Dot to Dot, Whitman #1260-34, 1979, unused, EX $15.00

Walt Disney World Coloring Book, Whitman #1078, 1971, unused, NM..$20.00

Waltons Coloring Book, Whitman #1028, 1975, unused, NM..$20.00

Whirly Birds Coloring Book, Whitman #1151, 1959, unused, NM $20.00

Winner Coloring Book, Whitman, 1951, unused, EX $18.00

Wonder Woman Faces 'The Menace of the Mole Men' A Book to Color, Whitman, 1965, unused, EX $45.00

Yippee Cowboy Coloring Book, Whitman, 1950, unused, EX .$30.00

Yogi Bear Coloring Book, Whitman #1655, 1961, unused, EX..$30.00

Zorro Trace & Color, Whitman #1414, 1958, unused, EX+ $28.00

• • • • • • • • • • • • • • • • • Comic Books • • • • • • • • • • • •

For more than a half a century, kids of America raced to the bookstand as soon as the new comics came in for the month and for 10¢ an issue kept up on the adventures of their favorite super heroes, cowboys, space explorers, and cartoon characters. By far, most were eventually discarded — after they were traded one friend to another, stacked on closet shelves, and finally confiscated by Mom. Discount the survivors that were torn or otherwise damaged over the years and those about the mundane, and of those remaining, some could be quite valuable. In fact, first editions of high-grade comic books, or those showcasing the first appearance of a major character, often bring $500.00 and more. Rarity, age, and quality of the artwork are prime factors in determining value, and condition is critical. If you want to seriously collect comic books, you'll need to refer to a good comic book price guide such as *The Official Overstreet Comic Book Price Guide*.

Action Comics, DC Comics #96, 1946, NM $3,200.00
Addams Family, Gold Key #3, NM.................................. $150.00
Adventure Comics, DC Comics #43, October 1939, VG+ ..$1,300.00
All Star Comics The Justice Society of America Initiates Johnny Thunder!, DC #6, 1941, VG $700.00
All-American Comics, DC Comics #75, 1946, NM.... $3,000.00
Amazing Fantasy, Marvel, #15, Spider-Man's 1st appearance, VG $3,000.00
Amazing Fantasy, Marvel Comics, #15, Spider-Man, EX+ ..$11,000.00
Amazing Spider-Man, Marvel, #3, 1960s, EX+ $3,200.00
Amazing Spider-Man, Marvel, #16, 1964, NM............ $1,800.00

Amazing Spider-Man, Marvel #100, 1971, NM+ $1,650.00
Amazing Spider-Man, Marvel #129, 1974, NM........... $1,100.00
Amazing Spider-Man, Marvel #252, 1984, NM+ $350.00
Archie's Rival Reggie, Archie #1, 1949, EX+ $975.00
Atom, DC Comics #27, 1966, NM+ $450.00
Atom & Hawkman, DC Comics #39, NM+ $400.00
Atom Ant, Gold Key #1, 1966, NM $1,500.00
Baby Huey & Papa, Harvey #23, 1966, NM $250.00
Bamm-Bamm & Pebbles, Gold Key #1, 1964, NM......... $175.00
Batman, DC Comics #16, VG+ $1,100.00
Batman, DC Comics #47, VG+ $2,400.00
Batman, DC Comics #49, NM $1,600.00
Batman, DC Comics #55, NM $2,375.00
Batman, DC Comics #62, NM $3,200.00
Batman, DC Comics #63, NM $2,100.00
Batman, DC Comics #65, NM $2,300.00
Batman, DC Comics #66, NM $2,000.00
Batman, DC Comics #67, NM $1,600.00
Batman, DC Comics #69, NM $2,800.00
Best of Bugs Bunny, Gold Key #2, 1968, NM................. $125.00
Bonanza, Gold Key #8, 1964, NM................................. $275.00
Boris Karloff Tales of Mystery, Gold Key #4, 1963, NM . $125.00
Boy Commandos, DC Comics #9, 1944, NM $2,100.00
Brave & the Bold, DC Comics #29, EX $550.00
Brave & the Bold, DC Comics #71, NM+ $475.00
Bugs Bunny & Porky Pig, Gold Key #1, 1965, NM $150.00
Bugs Bunny's Vacation Funnies, Dell #3, 1953, NM...... $375.00
Bullwinkle & Rocky, Charlton #1, 1970, NM $250.00
Captain America, Marvel #21, December 1942, EX.... $1,120.00
Captain America Comics, Timely/Marvel, #1, G $3,000.00
Captain America's Weird Tales, Marvel Comics, #74, VG+..$3,500.00
Captain Marvel Adventures, Fawcett #11, 1942, NM+..$5,200.00
Casper's Ghostland, Harvey #61, 1971, NM+ $275.00
Casper the Friendly Ghost, Harvy #8, 1953, EX+ $450.00
Cheyenne, Dell #13, 1959, NM+ $150.00
Colt .45, Dell #6, 1960, NM+ $275.00
Comic Cavalcade, DC Comics #1, Winter 1942, VG . $1,350.00
Daffy Duck, Whitman #101, 1976, NM.......................... $75.00
Daredevil, Marvel #1, EX $2,000.00
Dark Shadows, Gold Key #4, 1970, NM $400.00
Dear Nancy Parker, Gold Key #1, 1963, NM................. $125.00
Deputy Dawg, Gold Key #1, 1965, NM.......................... $450.00
Deputy Dawg Presents Dinky Duck & Hashimoto-San, Gold Key #1, EX+... $150.00
Detective Comics, DC Comics #48, 1941, 1st Batmobile, VG...$375.00
Detective Comics, DC Comics #82, 'Extra Added Attraction Boy Commandos,' NM.. $1,900.00
Detective Comics, DC Comics #93, VG.......................... $800.00
Detective Comics, DC Comics #107, 1946, EX+ $975.00
Detective Comics, DC Comics #225, VG+ $3,000.00
Dick Tracy, Harvey #73, 1954, EX+ $125.00
Dirty Dozen, Dell #1, 1967, NM+ $650.00
Family Affair, Gold Key #1, 1970, NM $225.00
Fantastic Four, Marvel #1, VG+................................... $1,150.00

Comic Books
• • • • • • • •
Air Fighters, Hillman Publications, #1, November 1941, NM, $1,150.00.
(Photo courtesy Morphy Auctions on LiveAuctioneers.com)

Comic Books
Astro Boy, Gold Key #1, 1965, NM, $1,200.00.

Comic Books
• • • • • • • •
Conan the Barbarian, Marvel #1, October 1970, NM, $625.00.

Fantastic Four, Marvel #43, 1965, VG+............................$50.00
Fantastic Four, Marvel #48, NM....................$1,400.00
Fantastic Four, Marvel #100, '100th Anniversary Issue,' NM+.$1,950.00
Fantastic Voyage, Gold Key #2, 1969, NM+....................$375.00
Fat Albert With the Cosby Kids, Gold Key #21, NM........$40.00
Flash, DC Comics #175, 1967, NM $850.00
Flash Gordon, Gold Key #1, 1965, NM $175.00
Flintstones, Gold Key #10, 1963, NM..............................$225.00
Flintstones & Pebbles, Gold Key #50, 1969, NM $250.00
Flintstones on the Rocks, Dell #1, 1961, NM..................$925.00
Fly (Adventures of), Archie #24, 1963, NM....................$175.00
Frankenstein Jr & the Impossibles, Gold Key #1, 1967, NM+ ..$350.00
Friendly Ghost Casper, Harvey #21, 1960, NM+ $325.00
Funky Phantom, Gold Key #1, 1972, NM.......................$225.00
George of the Jungle With Tom Slick & Super Chicken, Gold
    Key #2, 1969, NM+...$300.00
Ghost Rider, Magazine Enterprizes #1, EX....................$600.00
Ghost Rider, Marvel #5, August 1972, NM $650.00
Giant-Size Superheroes Spider-Man, Marvel #1, 1974, NM+ ..$425.00
Girl From UNCLE, Gold Key #5, 1967, NM...................$250.00
Green Lantern, DC Comics #53, 1967, NM+ $550.00
Green Lantern, DC Comics #151, 1982, NM...................$50.00
Hair Bear Bunch, Gold Key #3, NM+.............................$75.00
Happy Days, Gold Key #1, 1979, NM+........................$275.00
Have No Fear...Underdog Is Here!, Gold Key #22, 1976, NM+ ..$275.00
Hector Heathcote, Gold Key #1, 1964, NM+.................$325.00
Hot Stuff, Harvey #58, 1968, NM+ $450.00
Hot Stuff, Harvey #96, 1970, NM....................................$150.00
Huey, Dewey & Louie Junior Woodchucks, Gold Key #2, 1967,
    NM $130.00
Human Torch, Timely Comics #4 (#3), Spring 1941, G+ ..$550.00
I Love Lucy Comics, Dell #11, 1956, NM......................$575.00
I Love Lucy Comics, Dell #28, 1960, NM+ $600.00
I Spy, Gold Key #2, 1966, NM+.....................................$375.00
Incredible Hulk, Marvel #1, VG $1,200.00
Incredible Hulk, Marvel #5, VG+..................................$575.00
Incredible Hulk, Marvel #181, NM...........................$1,350.00
Iron Man (The Invincible), Marvel #2, NM+ $600.00
Jerry Lewis (Adventures of), DC Comics #91, NM+......$275.00
Jetsons, Gold Key #8, 1964, NM $375.00
Jetsons, Gold Key #22, 1965, NM+................................$300.00
Jimmy Olsen, see Superman's Pal Jimmy Olsen
Jonny Quest, Gold Key #1, 1964, EX+...........................$750.00
Journey Into Mystery With Thor, Marvel #112, January 1945,
    NM $600.00
Justice League of America, DC Comics, #2, 1961, EX....$175.00
Justice League of America, DC Comics #5, 1961, VG+ $55.00
Justice League of America, DC Comics #38, 1965, NM....$75.00
Justice League of America, DC Comics #58, 1967, NM. $550.00
King Leonardo & His Short Subjects, Gold Key #2, 1962,
    NM+ $275.00
King Leonardo & His Short Subjects, Gold Key #4, 1963,
    NM..$225.00
Lassie, Dell #44, 1959, NM $200.00
Lassie, Dell #53, 1961, NM $275.00
Lawman, Dell #5, 1960, NM+...$800.00
Leading Comics, DC Comics #1, 5 Favorite Features! (Green
    Arrow), EX...$2,650.00

Comic Books

Dr. Kildare, Dell #9, April – June 1965, NM, $525.00.

Comic Books

Green Hornet, Gold Key #3, August 1967, NM+, $650.00.

Comic Books

Green Lantern, Featuring Menace of the Giant Puppet, DC Comics #1, July – August 1960, EX+, $1,150.00.

Comic Books

Have No Fear...Underdog Is Here!, Gold Key #1, 1975, NM+, $575.00.

Comic Books
• • • • • • •
Hawkman, DC Comics #5, January 1965, NM+, $75.00 to $125.00.

Comic Books
• • • • • • •
Superboy, DC Comics #2, May/June 1949, EX+, $1,150.00. (Photo courtesy Morphy Auctions on LiveAuctioneers.com)

Little Dot, Harvey #83, 1962, NM+ $400.00
Lone Ranger, Dell #3, 1948, NM $900.00
Lone Ranger, Dell #62, 1953, NM+ $325.00
Lone Ranger, Dell #112, 1957, NM $1,175.00
Lone Ranger, Dell #126, 1959, NM $375.00
Lone Ranger, Dell #136, 1960, NM+ $575.00
Lone Ranger's Western Treasury, Dell #1, 1953, NM+ .. $1,950.00
Looney Tunes Comics Merry Melodies, Dell #76, 1948, NM+ .. $1,200.00
Lucy Show, Gold Key #2, 1963, NM $225.00
Mad (Tales Calculated to Drive You), DC Comics #1, 1952, G $575.00
Magilla Gorilla, Gold Key #6, 1965, NM $125.00
Magnus Robot Fighter, Gold Key #14, 1966, NM+ $300.00
Magnus Robot Fighter, Gold Key #16, 1966, NM+ $575.00
Man From UNCLE, Gold Key #3, 1965, NM+ $375.00
Man From UNCLE, Gold Key #6, 1966, NM $200.00
Man From UNCLE, Gold Key #13, 1967, NM+ $225.00
Marvel Comics Mystery, #13, VG $2,000.00
Master Comics, #21, December, 'Captain Marvel in Bulletman,' EX $1,575.00
Mickey Mouse, Gold Key #90, 1963, NM $115.00
Mickey Mouse, Gold Key #116, 1968, NM+ $175.00
Mighty Hercules, Gold Key #1, 1963, EX+ $225.00
Mighty Sampson, Gold Key #2, 1965, NM+ $425.00
Mighty Sampson, Gold Key #16, 1968, NM+ $300.00
Mission Impossible, Dell #1, 1967, NM+ $975.00
More Fun Comics, DC Comics #69, 1941, EX $2,450.00
Munsters, Gold Key #12, 1967, NM+ $425.00
Mutt & Jeff, DC Comics #26, 1947, NM $375.00
Nurse Linda Lark, Dell #5, 1962, NM $175.00
Our Gang With Tom & Jerry, Dell #47, 1948, NM+ $450.00
Outer Space, Charlton #21, 1959, NM $475.00

Peanuts, Dell #7, 1961, NM+ $375.00
Petticoat Junction, Dell #2, 1965, NM $225.00
Phantom, Gold Key #1, 1962, EX+ $225.00
Phantom, Gold Key #11, 1965, NM $275.00
Police Comics, Quality #1, August, G+ $600.00
Popeye, Gold Key #71, 1964, NM+ $150.00
Raggedy Ann & Andy, Dell #1, 1946, VG+ $225.00
Rangers of Freedom, Fiction House #4, 1942, NM $1,275.00
Rawhide, Dell Four Color #1028, 1959, NM+ $1,800.00
Rex Allen, Dell #21, 1956, NM $325.00
Richie Rich, Harvey Comics #1, November 1960, VG+ . $600.00
Rifleman, Gold Key #12, 1962, NM+ $375.00
Ripley's Believe It or Not! True Ghost Stories, Gold Key #1, 1965, NM $175.00
Rocky & His Fiendish Friends, Gold Key #3, 1963, NM. $750.00
Roy Rogers Comics, Dell #1, 1948, NM $2,750.00
Roy Rogers Comics, Dell #30, 1950, NM $575.00
Roy Rogers Comics, Dell #137, 1959, NM $250.00
Scooby Doo, Gold Key #5, 1971, NM+ $575.00
Sensation Comics, DC Comics, #1, DC Comics, Wonder Woman!, VG+ $9,000.00
Seventy Seven (77) Sunset Strip, Gold Key #2, NM $250.00
Sgt Fury & His Howling Commandos, Marvel #13, 1964, 'Starring Captain America & Bucky!,' NM $2,450.00
Shield-Wizard, MJL Magazines #1, EX $1,100.00
Showcase Presents Green Lantern, DC Comics, #22, EX+ .. $3,500.00
Showcase Presents Superman's Girlfriend Lois Lane in Mrs Superman!, DC #9, 1957, G $450.00
Snagglepuss, Gold Key #1, 1962, NM+ $475.00

Comic Books
• • • • • • •
Superman Annual (Giant), DC Comics #1, 1960, NM, $12,000.00.

Comic Books
• • • • • • •
That Darn Cat (Walt Disney's), Gold Key #1, 1966, NM, $320.00.

Space Ghost, Gold Key #1, 1967, NM $1,350.00
Spooky, Harvey #36, 1959, NM+ $550.00
Star Bangled Comics, DC Comics #17, 1943, NM+ ... $8,950.00
Star Trek, Gold Key #45, 1977, NM+ $275.00
Startling Comics, Better Publications #31, 1945, NM.. $2,850.00
Strange Suspense Stories Presents Captain Atom, Charlton #75, 1965, NM+ $1,275.00
Super TV Heroes, Gold Key #3, 1968, NM+ $625.00
Superman, DC Comics #3, 1940, EX $9,500.00
Superman, DC Comics #25, 1943, EX+ $2,100.00
Superman's Pal Jimmy Olsen, DC Comics #109, NM+.. $225.00
Suspense Comics, #3, VG+ $5,200.00
Tales of Suspense, Marvel #39, Iron Man!, EX $4,500.00
Tales of the Unexpected, DC Comics #41, 1959, NM.. $1,750.00
Tales to Astonish, Marvel #27, 1962, VG..................... $625.00
Tarzan, Aurora #1, 1974, NM+ $200.00
Tarzan, Dell #76, 1956, NM+ $300.00
Three Stooges, Dell #1170, 1961, NM+ $1,250.00
Time Tunnel, Gold Key #1, 1967, NM $300.00
Tom & Jerry, Dell #61, 1949, NM $325.00
Tom & Jerry Comics, Wilson #61, 1949, EX+ $175.00
Tom & Jerry Fun House, Gold Key #213, 1962, NM+ ... $275.00
Tom & Jerry Winter Carnival, Dell Giant #2, 1953, NM...$675.00
Top Cat, Gold Key #24, 1968, NM+ $125.00
Top-Notch Comics, MLJ #7, 1940, EX+ $2,650.00
Turok Son of Stone, Dell Four Color #596, EX $350.00
Turok Son of Stone, Gold Key #53, 1966, NM+ $225.00
Twilight Zone (The), Gold Key #17, 1966, NM+.......... $225.00
Uncle Scrooge & Donald Duck, Gold Key Giant #1, 1965, NM.. $325.00
Voyage to the Bottom of the Sea, Gold Key #6, NM+ ... $225.00
Walt Disney Comics & Stories, Dell #1, October 1940, G. $1,200.00
Walt Disney Comics & Stories, Whitman #489, 1981, NM+. $450.00
Walt Disney Comics & Stories, Whitman #502, 1983, NM+. $300.00
Walt Disney's Comics & Stories, Gold Key #309, 1966, NM+ $275.00
Wendy the Good Little Witch, Harvey #53, 1969, NM+...$300.00
Wham Comics, Centaur Publications #1, 1940, VG+ ... $350.00
Whiz Comics, Fawcett #3, G.. $1,000.00
Whiz Comics, Fawcett #4, VG $625.00
Whiz Comics, Fawcett #11, 1940, EX+........................ $2,150.00
Whiz Comics, Fawcett #100, 1948, NM+ $1,400.00
Wild Western, Atlas Comics, September 1948, #3, NM . $750.00
Wild Wild West, Gold Key #1, 1966, EX+ $315.00
Wonder Woman, DC Comics #1, Summer issue, VG . $2,300.00
Wonder Woman, DC Comics #130, 1962, NM............. $725.00
Wonder Woman, DC Comics #135, 1962, NM............. $800.00
Woody Woodpecker Adventure Comics, Gold Key #75, 1963, NM $125.00
Woody Woodpecker's Back to School, Dell #2, 1953, NM..$475.00
World's Finest Comics, DC Comics #5, 1942, EX+ $2,175.00
Wow Comics, Fawcett #1, 'Featuring Mr Scarlett!,' VG . $650.00
Yosemite Sam & Bugs Bunny, Gold Key #35, 1976, NM ..$50.00
Yosemite Sam & Bugs Bunny, Whitman #80, 1983, NM ..$75.00
Young Allies, Timely #16, 1945, NM $4,150.00
Zorro, Gold Key #1, 1967, EX+ $125.00
Zorro, Gold Key #6, 1967, NM+ $200.00
3-D Dolly, Harvey #1, NM $1,500.00

Comic Books
Three Stooges in Orbit, Gold Key #1, 1962, NM+, $700.00.

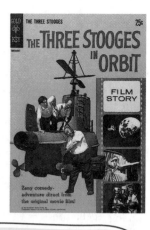

Comic Books
Uncle Scrooge (Walt Disney's) in 'Only a Poor Old Man,' Dell #386, 1952, NM $3,450.00. (Photo courtesy Morphy Auctions on LiveAuctioneers.com)

Comic Books
Voyage to the Bottom of the Sea, Gold Key #8, 1967, NM, $225.00.

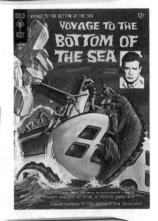

Comic Books
World's Finest Comics, DC Comics #28, May/June 1947, NM, $3,000.00.

Comic Books
Young Allies, Timely #4, 1942, NM, $14,250.00.

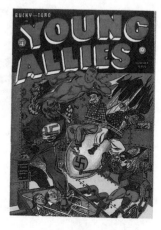

Corgi

The Corgi legacy is a rich one, beginning in 1934 with parent company Mettoy of Swansea, South Wales. In 1956, Mettoy merged with Playcraft Ltd. to form Mettoy Playcraft Ltd. and changed the brand name from Mettoy to Corgi, in of honor of Queen Elizabeth's beloved Welsh Corgis, which she could regularly be seen taking for walks around Buckingham palace.

In 1993, Mattel bought the Corgi brand and attempted, for a short time, to maintain the tradition of producing Corgi quality collectible toys. Shortly afterward, employees of the Welsh manufacturing center purchased back the Corgi Collectibles line from Mattel. In July 1999, the brand was purchased again, this time by Zindart, an American-owned company based in Hong Kong, where the Corgi Classics line is now produced.

Some of the most highly prized Corgi toys in today's collectors' market are the character-related vehicles. The assortment includes the cars of secret agent James Bond, including several variations of his Aston-Martin, his lotus Esprit complete with underwater maneuvering fins, and other 007 vehicles. Batman's Batmobile and Batboat, and The Man From U.N.C.L.E.'s THRUSH-Buster are among the favorites as well.

Values represent models in new condition in their original package unless noted otherwise.

Adams Bros Drag-Star, #165, $40 to $50.00
Adams Bros Probe 16, #384, $35 to $45.00
Air France Concorde, #651-A, $70 to $80.00
Air France Concorde, #651-B, $30 to $40.00
Allis Chalmers Fork Lift, #409, $40 to..........................$50.00
AMC Pacer, #291, $45 to $45.00
AMC Pacer Secours, #484, $60 to $75.00
Aston Martin DB4 Saloon, #218, $125 to $135.00
Austin A-40, #216, 2-tone bl, $80 to $100.00
Austin A-60, #236, right-hand drive, $100 to...............$125.00
Austin A-60, #255, left-hand drive, $125 to.................$150.00
Austin Cambridge, #201, $100 to $125.00
Austin Cambridge, #201, w/motor, $150 to..................$175.00
Austin Healey, #300, red or cream, $140 to..................$150.00
Austin Mini Countryman, #485, $150 to $170.00
Austin Mini Metro, #275, $40 to....................................$50.00
Austin Mini Van, #450, $90 to..$110.00

Austin Taxi, #418, w/Whizzwheels, $45 to $60.00
Austin 7, #225, red, yel interior, $125 to $150.00
Austin 7, #225, yel, red interior, $300 to $325.00
Aveling-Barford Diesel Road Roller, #279, $30 to.............$50.00
Batcopter, #925, $80 to...$95.00
Batman's Bat Bike, #268, $120 to $130.00
Batmobile, #267, 1966 or 1967-72, ea $500 to $550.00
Batmobile, #267, 1973, $400 to.......................................$425.00
Batmobile, #267, 1980-81, $190 to $210.00
Beast Carrier, #58, $50 to $65.00
Beatles Yellow Submarine, #803, 1st issue, $850 to $950.00
Bedford AA Road Service, #408, $140 to $150.00
Bedford AFS Tender, #405, gr w/blk ladder, divided windshield,
    $200 to.. $235.00
Bedford Ambulance, #412, divided windshield, $125 to . $150.00
Bedford Ambulance, #412, single windshield, $125 to... $150.00
Bedford Corgi Toys Van, #422, yel w/bl roof, $200 to..... $250.00
Bedford Daily Express Van, #403, divided windshield, $125
    to $150.00
Bedford Dormobile, #404, cream, maroon or turq, divided windshield, ea $125 to.. $145.00
Bedford Dormobile, #404, friction motor, $175 to.......... $200.00
Bedford Evening Standard Van, #421, $125 to.............. $150.00
Bedford Fire Dept Van, #405, friction motor, $180 to $200.00
Bedford KLG Plugs, #403, friction motor, divided windshield,
    $250 to... $275.00
Bedford Military Ambulance, #414, $100 to.................. $125.00
Bedford Tipper, #494, red & silver, $60 to $70.00
Bell Helicopter, #920, $35 to...$45.00
Bentley Continental, #224, $100 to................................ $115.00
Bentley Mulliner, #274, $80 to.. $100.00
Bertone Runabout, #386, $40 to $50.00

Corgi
American LaFrance Ladder Truck, #97387, white, $50.00 to $65.00. (Photo courtesy Dana Johnson)

Corgi
Aston Martin, competition model, #309, 1962, $125.00 to $135.00.

Corgi
Bentley R Type (1954), #815, $20.00 to $30.00. (Photo courtesy Dana Johnson)

Bertone Shake Buggy, #392, $40 to $50.00
Bluebird Record Car, #153, $125 to $150.00
BMW M1 Racer, #308, $30 to.................................$40.00
BOAC Concorde, #650, 1st issue, $70 to $85.00
BOAC Concorde, #650, 2nd issue, $30 to $40.00
Breakdown Truck, #703, $35 to $45.00
British Chieftain Tank, #903, $60 to..........................$75.00
BRM Racer, #152, $140 to $160.00
Buck Rogers' Starfighter, #647, $80 to $95.00
Cadillac Superior Ambulance, #437, $125 to $150.00
Capt Marvel's Porsche, #262, $55 to $65.00
Chevrolet Astro 1, #347, $80 to...............................$90.00
Chevrolet Caprice Cab, #327, $45 to $55.00
Chevrolet Caprice Classic, #325, $55 to........................$65.00
Chevrolet Caprice Racer, #341, $55 to $60.00
Chevrolet Corvair, #229, $75 to...............................$85.00
Chevrolet Corvette, #310, $150 to $175.00
Chevrolet Corvette Stingray, #300, $150 to $175.00
Chevrolet Corvette Stingray, #337, $90 to $100.00
Chevrolet Fire Chief, #439, $100 to $125.00
Chevrolet Impala, #220, $130 to............................ $140.00
Chevrolet Impala, #248, $120 to............................ $130.00
Chevrolet Impala Taxi, #221, $125 to $150.00
Chevrolet Kennel Service, #486, $125 to $150.00
Chevrolet Police Car, #326, $45 to............................$65.00
Chevrolet SS 350 Camaro, #338, $70 to........................$95.00
Chevrolet Superior Ambulance, #405, $65 to $75.00
Chipperfield's Circus Giraffe Transporter, #503, $150 to . $175.00
Chipperfield's Circus Mobile Booking Office, #426, $300 to ... $350.00
Chipperfield's Circus Poodle Pickup, #511, $525 to $575.00
Chipperfield's Land-Rover Circus Parade, #487, $165 to. $185.00
Chitty Chitty Bang Bang, #266, orig, $350 to $400.00
Chitty Chitty Bang Bang, #266, replica, $125 to........... $150.00
Chrysler Ghia, #241, $65 to $80.00
Chrysler Imperial, #246, metallic bl, $155 to.................. $170.00
Chrysler Imperial, #246, red, $100 to........................ $125.00
Citroen DS19, #210, $125 to $150.00
Citroen DS19 Monte Carlo, #323, $180 to $190.00
Citroen Dyane, #287, $25 to $35.00
Citroen Le Dandy, #259, metallic bl, $165 to................. $180.00
Citroen Le Dandy, #259, metallic maroon, $120 to........ $130.00
Citroen Safari, #436, $95 to $120.00
Citroen Ski Safari, #475, $150 to $175.00
Citroen SM, #284, $50 to....................................$65.00
Citroen Tour de France, #510, $125 to $150.00
Citroen 2 CV, #346, $25 to $35.00
Coca-Cola Van, #437, $55 to $70.00
Commer Ambulance, #463, $90 to $110.00
Commer Lorry, #452, $125 to................................ $150.00
Commer Military Ambulance, #354, $110 to................. $135.00
Commer Military Police, #355, $110 to....................... $135.00
Commer Milk Float, Co-Op, #466, $150 to.................. $175.00
Commer Pickup Truck, #465, $65 to..........................$85.00
Commer Platform Lorry, #454, $150 to...................... $175.00
Commer Police Van, #464, $150 to.......................... $175.00
Commer US Army Field Kitchen, #359, $150 to $175.00
Commer Van, #462, Co-Op, $150 to......................... $175.00
Commer Van, #462, Hammonds, $175 to...................... $200.00

Corgi
Buick Riviera, #245, 1964, $80.00 to $90.00.

Corgi
Charlie Chaplin's Production, 'A Woman of Paris,' yellow and red, #858, $25.00 to $35.00. (Photo courtesy Dana Johnson)

Corgi
Charlie's Angels Custom Van, #434, 1978, MIB, $60.00 to $75.00. (Photo courtesy www.gasolinealleyantiques.com)

Corgi
Chevrolet Sedan (1939), Memphis Fire Department, 2003, $10.00 to $15.00. (Photo courtesy Dana Johnson)

Commer Wall's Ice Cream Van, #453, see Wall's Ice Cream Van
Conveyor on Jeep, #64, $90 to $120.00
DAF City Car, #283, $30 to $55.00
Daily Planet Helicopter, #929, $55 to $65.00
Datsun 240Z, East African Safari, #394, $30 to.................$40.00
Datsun 240Z, US Rally, #396, $30 to.........................$40.00

David Brown Tractor, #55, $40 to $50.00

Detomaso Mangusta, #203, $40 to $55.00

Dick Dastardly's Racer, #809, $175 to $200.00

Disneyland Bus, #470, $45 to $65.00

Dolphin Cabin Cruiser, #104, $90 to $100.00

Dougal's Car, #807, $180 to $200.00

DRAX Helicopter, #930, $170 to $180.00

Dropside Trailer, #100, $25 to $40.00

Elf-Tyrrell Project 34, #161, $45 to $60.00

ERF Cement Tipper, #460, $40 to $55.00

ERF Dropside Lorry, #456, $115 to $140.00

ERF Earth Dumper, #458, $80 to $90.00

ERF Moorhouses Jams Van, #459, $325 to............$350.00

ERF Platform Lorry, #457, $125 to $140.00

Ferrari Berlinetta Le Mans, #314, $55 to............$70.00

Ferrari Daytona 365 GTB4, #323, $50 to............$60.00

Ferrari Formula I, #154, $45 to $60.00

Ferrari 206 Dino Sport, #344, $55 to $65.00

Fiat X1/9, #306, $30 to $40.00

Fiat 1800, #217, $85 to $95.00

Fiat 600 Jolly, #240, $125 to $150.00

Ford Capri, #311, orange, $140 to $150.00

Ford Capri S, #312, $30 to...................................$40.00

Ford Cobra Mustang, #370, $25 to $40.00

Ford Consul, #200, dual colors, $175 to $200.00

Ford Consul, #200, solid colors, $150 to $175.00

Ford Consul, #200, w/motor, $175 to $200.00

Ford Consul Classic, #234, $85 to $100.00

Ford Consul Cortina Estate, #491, $85 to............ $100.00

Ford Consul Cortina Super Estate Car, #444, w/golfer & caddy, $150 to $175.00

Ford Cortina, #313, bronze or bl, $90 to $120.00

Ford Cortina, #313, yel, $275 to $325.00

Ford Cortina GXL Police, #402, $40 to $50.00

Ford Escort, #334, $20 to $30.00

Ford GT 70, #316, $40 to $50.00

Ford Milk Float, #405, $30 to $45.00

Ford Mustang Competition, #325, $75 to............. $100.00

Ford Mustang Organ Grinder Dragster, #166, $35 to $50.00

Ford Mustang Rally, #329, $50 to $70.00

Ford Sierra 2.3 Ghia, #299, $20 to $30.00

Ford Thames Caravan, #420, $125 to $150.00

Ford Thunderbird, #214, $120 to $140.00

Ford Thunderbird, #214, w/motor, $240 to.................... $260.00

Ford Thunderbird, #801, $30 to $40.00

Ford Thunderbird Sport, #215, $115 to $130.00

Ford Tipper Trailer, #62, $25 to $35.00

Ford Zephyr Estate Car, #424, $80 to $95.00

Ford Zephyr Politei, #419, $450 to $475.00

Ford 5000 Super Major Tractor, #67, $70 to $80.00

Ford 5000 Tractor & Scoop, #74, $165 to $175.00

Ford 5000 Tractor & Trencher, #72, $175 to $185.00

Fordson Disc Harrow, #71, $25 to $40.00

Fordson Half-Track Tractor, #54, $200 to $225.00

Fordson Power Major Tractor, #55, $100 to $115.00

Fordson Power Major Tractor, #60, $100 to $125.00

Forward Control Jeep FC-150, #409, $45 to $60.00

Forward Control Jeep Tower Wagon, #478, $100 to....... $125.00

German Rocket Launcher, #907, $80 to $95.00

Ghia Fiat 600 Jolly, #240, $175 to...................... $185.00

Ghia L64 Chrysler V8, #241, $70 to $80.00

Ghia Mangusta De Tomaso, #271, $65 to $80.00

Green Hornet's Black Beauty, #268, $525 to $575.00

Hardy Boy's Rolls Royce Silver Ghost w/Figures, #805, $175 to $200.00

Heinkel Trojan, #233, $75 to $90.00

Hillman Hunter Rally, #302, kangaroo, $130 to.............. $150.00

Hillman Husky, #206, metallic bl & silver, $120 to........ $130.00

Hillman Husky, #206, w/friction motor, $150 to $175.00

Hillman Imp Monte Carlo, #328, $125 to $135.00

Holiday Minibus, #508, $115 to $140.00

Honda Driving School, #273, $20 to $30.00

Honda Prelude, #345, $15 to $25.00

Incredible Hulk Mazda Pickup, #264, $65 to......................$80.00

Iso Grifo 7 Litre, #301, $25 to $35.00

Jaguar E Type, #307, $125 to $150.00

Jaguar E Type, #312, $135 to $145.00

Jaguar Fire Chief, #213, $200 to $225.00

Jaguar Fire Chief, #213, w/suspension, $200 to............ $225.00

Jaguar MK10, #238, any color, $100 to $125.00

Jaguar Police Car, #429, $40 to $55.00

Jaguar XJS, #319, $25 to $40.00

Jaguar XJ12C, #286, $45 to $60.00

Jaguar XK120 Rally, #804, w/spats, $65 to $75.00

Jaguar 2.4 Saloon, #208, $100 to $125.00

Jaguar 2.4 Saloon, #208M, w/friction motor, $150 to..... $175.00

Jaguar 4.2 Litre E Type, #335, $115 to $125.00

Corgi
Fiat 2100, #232, 1961, $75.00 to $90.00.

Corgi
Ford Mustang Fastback 2-2, #348, pop art mustang stock car, 1968, $75.00 to $125.00.

Corgi
• • • • • • • • •
James Bond's Mercedes Saloon, from 'Octo-pussy,' 2003, $12.00 to $16.00. (Photo courtesy Dana Johnson)

Corgi
Lotus Elan, #319, red or blue, $75.00 to $100.00.

Corgi
• • • • • • • • •
Land Rover Breakdown, #417S, 4", NMIB, $75.00 to $100.00. (Photo courtesy www.serioustoyz.com)

Corgi
• • • • • • • • • • • • • • •
Man from U.N.C.L.E with Gun Firing Thrush-Buster, #497, 1966 – 1968, $275.00 to $300.00.

Jaguar 4.2 Litre E Type, #374, $80 to	$100.00
James Bond's Aston Martin, #270, w/tire slashers, $275 to	$325.00
James Bond's Aston Martin, #271, $85 to	$95.00
James Bond's Aston Martin DB5, #261, $300 to	$350.00
James Bond's Citroen 2CV, #272, $65 to	$75.00
James Bond's Ford Mustang, #391, $275 to	$300.00
James Bond's Lotus Esprit, #269, $100 to	$125.00
James Bond's Moon Buggy, #811, $500 to	$530.00
James Bond's Space Shuttle, #649, $85 to	$100.00
James Bond's Toyota 2000 GT, #336, $350 to	$375.00
Japan Air Line Concorde, #651, $450 to	$500.00
Jeep, #419, $25 to	$35.00
Jet Police Helicopter, #931, $55 to	$65.00
John Wolfe's Dragster, #170, $45 to	$60.00
Karrier Bantam Dairy Van, #435, $125 to	$150.00
Karrier Bantam Lucozade Van, #411, $175 to	$200.00
Karrier Bantam Mobile Family Butchers Shop, #413, w/ or w/o suspension, $175 to	$200.00
Karrier Bantam Mobile Grocers, #407, $175 to	$200.00
Karrier Bantam Mr Softee Van, #428, $275 to	$300.00
Karrier Bantam Snack Bar, #471, $250 to	$300.00
Karrier Bantam 2-Ton, #455, bl, $115 to	$140.00
Karrier Bantam 2-Ton, #455, red, $300 to	$350.00
Kojak's Buick, #290, $100 to	$115.00
Lamborghini P400 GT Miura, #342, $90 to	$110.00
Lancia Fulvia Sport, #332, red or bl, $80 to	$100.00
Land Rover Breakdown, #477, w/Whizzwheels, $75 to	$85.00
Land Rover RAC, #416A, $170 to	$180.00
Land Rover RAC Radio Rescue, #416, $200 to	$250.00
Land Rover w/Rice's Pony Trailer & Pony, #GS2, $200 to	$225.00
Land Rover Vote for Corgi, #472, complete w/2 figures, $200 to	$250.00
Land Rover Vote for Corgi, #472, no figures, $150 to	$175.00

Land Rover Weapons Carrier, #357, $145 to	$195.00
Land Rover w/Canopy, #438, $75 to	$100.00
Land Rover 109 WB Pickup, #406, $90 to	$110.00
Land Rover 109 WB Pickup, #406S, spring suspension, $175 to	$200.00
Lincoln Continental, #262, bl, $150 to	$175.00
Livestock Transporter, #484, $70 to	$85.00
London Transport Routemaster, #468, various ad logos, $65 to	$75.00
Lotus Elan, #318, $100 to	$120.00
Lotus Elan, #319, $80 to	$90.00
Lotus Elite, #301, $25 to	$40.00
Lotus Elite, #382, $30 to	$40.00
Lotus John Player, #154, $40 to	$55.00
Lotus Texaco Special, #154, $40 to	$55.00
Lotus XI, #151, regular, $90 to	$110.00
Lotus-Climax F1 Racer, #155, $60 to	$75.00
Lunar Bug, #806, $80 to	$100.00
Magic Roundabout Carousel, #852, $775 to	$825.00
Magic Roundabout Playground, #853, $900 to	$1,100.00
Magic Roundabout Train, #851, $350 to	$375.00
Magnum PI's Ferrari, #298, $50 to	$65.00
Marcos Mantis, #312, $40 to	$60.00

Marcos Volvo 1800 GT, #324, $70 to $95.00
Marcos 3 Litre, #377, $50 to......................................$60.00
Massey-Ferguson Tractor & Fork, #57, $145 to $155.00
Massey-Ferguson Tractor Shovel, #53, $125 to.............$135.00
Massey-Ferguson 165 Tractor, #66, $75 to $95.00
Massey-Ferguson 50B Tractor, #50, $60 to.......................$75.00
Massey-Ferguson 65 Tractor, #50, $100 to $125.00
Massey-Ferguson 65 Tractor w/Shovel, #53, $130 to $150.00
Mazda Camper, #415, $45 to.......................................$60.00
Mazda Maintenence Truck, #413, $50 to.........................$65.00
Mazda Open Truck, #495, $30 to $45.00
Mazda Pickup, #440, $30 to..$45.00
Mazda Pickup, #493, $30 to..$40.00
McLaren Texaco-Marlboro, #191, $60 to........................$75.00
Mercedes Benz C111, #388, $50 to $65.00
Mercedes Benz Unimog, #406, $40 to $50.00
Mercedes Benz 220SE, #230, $90 to $110.00
Mercedes Benz 240 Rally, #291, $20 to..........................$30.00
Mercedes Benz 300SL, #303, $135 to..........................$145.00
Mercedes Benz 300SL, #304, $145 to..........................$155.00
Mercedes Benz 350SL, #393, $50 to............................$65.00
Mercedes Benz 600 Pullman, #247, $75 to......................$90.00
Mercedes Police Car, #412, 'Police' or 'Polizei' decals, $25 to..$35.00
Mercedes 240D Taxi, #411, cream or blk, $60 to.............$75.00
Mercedes 240D Taxi, #411, orange w/blk roof, $45 to.......$60.00
MGA Sports Car, #302, $140 to $155.00
MGB GT, #327, $100 to $125.00
MGC GT, #378, $150 to $175.00
Mini BMC 1000, #200, $45 to $60.00
Mini Cooper Monte Carlo, #317, $175 to $225.00
Mini Cooper Rally, #227, $250 to $275.00
Mini Cooper Rally, #282, $90 to $110.00

Mini Magnifique, #334, $70 to......................................$95.00
Mini Marcos GT850, #341, $60 to.................................$80.00
Mini Metro, #275, colors other than gold, $25 to............$40.00
Mini Metro, #275, gold, $65 to $80.00
Mister Softee's Ice Cream Van, #428, $225 to $250.00
Mobile Camera Van, #479, $150 to $175.00
Monkeemobile, #277, $375 to $425.00
Monte Carlo (1967 Mini Cooper), #339, w/roof rack, $275 to...$325.00
Monte Carlo (1967 Sunbeam IMP), #340, $125 to........$150.00
Monte Carlo BMC Mini Cooper S, #308, $100 to $125.00
Monte Carlo Mini Cooper, #321, 1965, $275 to $325.00
Monte Carlo Mini Cooper, #321, 1966, w/autographs, $575 to....$625.00
Morris Cowley, #202, $125 to $150.00
Morris Cowley, #202, w/friction motor, $150 to $175.00
Morris Mini-Cooper, #249, wicker, $120 to..................$135.00
Morris Mini-Minor, #204, bl, $225 to $250.00
Morris Mini-Minor, #226, $100 to $125.00
Morris Pick-Up, #065, $75 to $100.00
Mr McHenry's Trike, #859, $150 to $175.00
Noddy's Car, #801, blk-face Noddy, $550 to $575.00
Noddy's Car, #801, other than blk-face Noddy, $325 to.$350.00
Noddy's Car, #804, Noddy only, $150 to......................$175.00
NSU Sports Prinz, #316, $75 to $95.00
Oldsmobile County Sheriff's Car, #237, $95 to $120.00
Oldsmobile HQ Staff Car, #358, $125 to $150.00
Oldsmobile Super 88, #235, $80 to $100.00
Oldsmobile Toronado, #264, $100 to $125.00
Oldsmobile Toronado, #276, $75 to $90.00
Opel Senator, #332, Doctor's car, $25 to $30.00
Penguin Mobile, #259, $60 to $75.00
Peugeot 505, #373, $20 to...$30.00
Pinder's Circus Booking Office, #426, $50 to.................$75.00
Platform Trailer, #101, $40 to....................................$50.00
Plymouth US Mail, #443, $125 to..............................$150.00
Police Range Rover, Belgian, #483, $80 to $100.00
Police Vigilant Range Rover, Police, #461, $40 to $55.00
Pontiac Firebird, #343, $100 to $125.00
Pony Trailer, #102, $25 to...$40.00
Pop Art Morris Mini-Mostest, #349, $2,500 to............$3,000.00
Pop Art Mustang Stock Car, #348, $125 to $150.00
Popeye's Paddle Wagon, #802, $525 to $550.00
Porsche Carrera 6, #330, $80 to $90.00

Corgi

MGC GT, competition model, #345, 1969, $275.00 to $325.00.

Corgi

National Motor Museum, #858, red and white, $25.00 to $35.00. (Photo courtesy Dana Johnson)

Corgi

Plymouth Sports Suburban Station Wagon, #219, $90.00 to $110.00.

Porsche Carrera 6, #371, $55 to $65.00
Porsche Polizei, #509, $55 to $65.00
Porsche Ritjks Politie, #509, $150 to $175.00
Porsche 917, #385, $35 to...$50.00
Porsche 924, #303, $20 to $30.00
Porsche 924, #321, $45 to...$55.00
Porsche 924 Police, #430, $30 to $45.00
Professionals Ford Capri, #342, $140 to $160.00
Quad Gun Tank, Trailer & Field Gun, #909, $55 to $70.00
Radar Scanner, #353, $65 to...$80.00
Radio Rescue Rover, #416, $165 to $185.00
RAF Land-Rover, #351, $95 to $120.00
RAF Vanguard Staff Car, #352, $95 to $120.00
Rago Rascal Roller 400, #459, $25 to..............................$50.00
Rambler Marlin Sports Fastback, #263, $75 to $100.00
Range Rover Ambulance, #482, $45 to $55.00
Reliant Bond Bug 700 ES, #389, $45 to $65.00
Renault Alpine, #294, $35 to $45.00
Renault Floride, #222, $90 to $100.00
Renault Turbo, #381, $25 to...$40.00
Renault 11 GTL, #384, $35 to $45.00
Renault 16TS, #202, $45 to $55.00
Renegade Jeep, #448, $25 to...$40.00
Riley Pathfinder, #205, $100 to $125.00
Riley Pathfinder, #205, w/motor, $150 to $175.00
Riley Pathfinder Police Car, #209, $130 to $140.00
Riot Police Wagon, #422, $30 to....................................$40.00
Roger Clark's Ford Capri, #303, gold wheels w/red hubs, $225
   to...$275.00
Roger Clark's Ford Capri, #303, w/Whizwheels, $75 to.. $100.00
Rolls Royce Silver Shadow, #273, $90 to....................... $100.00
Rolls Royce Silver Shadow, #280, silver, $80 to $100.00
Rough Rider Van, #423, $45 to.......................................$60.00
Rover Monte Carlo, #322, $150 to $190.00
Rover Triplex, #340, $25 to..$40.00
Rover 2000, #252, $80 to $95.00
Rover 2000 TC, #275, $70 to..$80.00
Rover 2000 TC, #281, $55 to $65.00
Rover 3500, #338, $20 to $30.00
Rover 3500 Police Car, #339, $30 to.............................$45.00
Rover 90, #204, $140 to $150.00
Rover 90, #204, w/friction motor, $200 to $225.00
Saint's Jaguar XJS, #320, $80 to $90.00
Saint's Volvo, #201, $175 to $200.00
Saint's Volvo P1800, #258, $150 to............................... $200.00
Santa Pod Commuter Dragster, #161, $45 to....................$60.00
Santa Pod Dragster, #163, $40 to $55.00
Sikorsky Helicopter, #922, $35 to $45.00
Sikorsky Helicopter, #923, Military, $35 to.....................$45.00
Silver Jubilee Bus, #471, $45 to......................................$60.00
Smith's-Karrier Joe's Diner Mobile Canteen, #471, $150 to ...$175.00
Smith's-Karrier Potato Frittes Mobile Canteen, #471, $300 to ...$350.00
Space Shuttle (Moonraker), #649, $45 to.........................$60.00
Spider Van, #436, $50 to $70.00
Spiderbuggy, #261, $100 to $125.00
Spidercopter, #928, $80 to...$90.00
Standard Vanguard, #207, $120 to $130.00
Standard Vanguard, #207, w/friction motor, $150 to...... $175.00

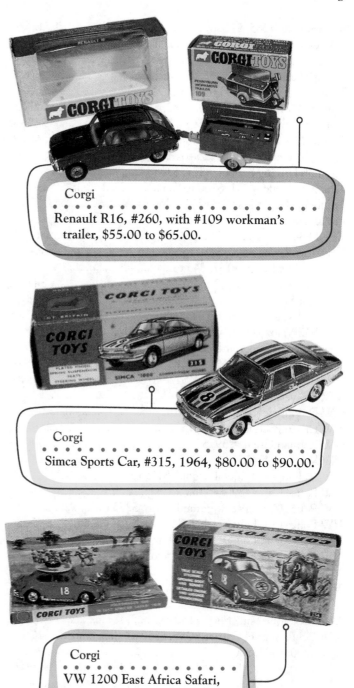

Corgi
• •
Renault R16, #260, with #109 workman's
trailer, $55.00 to $65.00.

Corgi
• •
Simca Sports Car, #315, 1964, $80.00 to $90.00.

Corgi
• •
VW 1200 East Africa Safari,
#256, $225.00 to $250.00.

Starfighter Jet Dragster, #169, $45 to $60.00
Starsky & Hutch Ford Torino, #292, $100 to $125.00
STP Patrick Eagle Racer, #159, $45 to..............................$55.00
Stromberg Helicopter, #926, $120 to $130.00
Studebaker Golden Hawk, #211, no suspension, $125 to ...$150.00
Studebaker Golden Hawk, #211, w/friction motor, $150
   to $175.00
Studebaker Golden Hawk, #211, w/suspension, $150 to . $175.00
Stunt Bike, #681, $250 to...$275.00
Sunbeam Imp Police, #506, $80 to..................................$90.00
Superbike, #266, $75 to $90.00
Superman Van, #435, $50 to $75.00

Supermobile, #265, $70 to..$80.00
Surtees TS9, #150, $40 to...$50.00
SU100 Tank Destroyer, #905, $60 to $75.00
Talbot Matra Rancho, #457, $20 to..................................$30.00
Team Surtees, #153, $45 to..$60.00
Thunderbird Guided Missile, #350, $100 to $125.00
Touring Caravan, #490, $30 to...$45.00
Toyota 2000 GT, #375, $50 to...$60.00
Triumph Acclaim, #276, $25 to...$35.00
Triumph Driving School, #277, $30 to $45.00
Triumph Herald, #231, $100 to $115.00
Triumph TR2 Sports Car, #301, $150 to $175.00
Trojan Heinkel, #233, $80 to $100.00
Tyrell P34 Racer, #162, $50 to...$60.00
US Army Rover, #500, $450 to $500.00
USA Racing Buggy, #167, $45 to.......................................$55.00
Vantastic Van, #432, $30 to..$45.00
Vanwall, #150, $145 to $155.00
Vauxhall Velox, #203, $135 to $145.00
Vauxhall Velox, #203, w/friction motor, $165 to........... $175.00
Vegas Ford Thunderbird, #348, $85 to........................... $105.00
Volvo P-1800, #228, $115 to $125.00
VW Breakdown Truck, #490, $120 to $130.00
VW Delivery Van, #433, $100 to $125.00
VW Driving School, #400, $55 to.......................................$65.00
VW Driving School, #401, $75 to.......................................$85.00
VW Karman Ghia, #239, $75 to $90.00
VW Kombi, #434, $100 to $125.00
VW Pickup, #431, metallic gold, $115 to $135.00
VW Police Car, #489, $45 to...$60.00
VW Police Car, #492, w/gr mudguards, $275 to $325.00
VW Police Car, Politie, #492, $250 to $300.00
VW Police Car, Polizei, #73, $150 to $175.00
VW Police Car, Polizei, #492, $85 to $100.00
VW Polo, #289, $50 to...$60.00
VW Polo, #302, $25 to...$35.00
VW Polo Turbo, #309, $25 to $40.00
VW Toblerone Van, #441, $150 to $175.00
VW US Personnel Carrier, #356, $250 to $275.00
VW 1200, #383, $80 to $90.00
VW 1200, #383, ADAC, $140 to $160.00
VW 1200, #401, $60 to $75.00
VW 1200, Swiss PTT, #383, $125 to............................... $150.00
VW 1200 Rally, #384, $45 to $55.00
Wall's Ice Cream (Commer) Van, #443, $325 to............ $375.00
Wild Honey Dragster, #164, $60 to...................................$70.00
Woolworth Silver Jubilee Bus, #471, $50 to $65.00

CLASSIC SCALE

Bentley (1927), #9001, $70 to.. $80.00
Bentley (1927), #9002, $85 to..$95.00
Daimler 38 (1910), #9021, $60 to $70.00
Ford Model T, #9013, any variation, $60 to.....................$70.00
Renault 12/16 (1910), #9031, $75 to $85.00
Renault 12/16 (1910), #9032, $75 to $85.00
Rolls-Royce Silver Ghost, #9041, $50 to $60.00
World of Wooster (Bentley), #9004, $100 to.................. $125.00

CORGITRONICS

Chevrolet Fire Chief, #1008, $50 to $60.00
Corgitronics Beep Beep Bus, #1004, $50 to.....................$60.00
Corgitronics Firestreak, #1001, $85 to $100.00
Corgitronics Roadtrain, #1002, $65 to............................$75.00
Firestreak, #1011, $40 to $50.00
Ford Torino, #1003, $50 to $60.00
Land Rover & Compressor, #1007, $60 to $70.00
Maestro MG1600, #10029, $50 to $60.00
Police Land Rover, #1005, $50 to $60.00
Roadshow, Radio, #1006, $60 to $70.00

GIFT SETS

Agricultural Set, #5, $425 to $450.00
Avengers John Steed's Vintage Bently & Emma Peel's Lotus
    Elan, #40, 1966, $750 to $775.00
Batboat & Trailer, #107, w/Batman & Robin figures, $200
    to $225.00
Batman Set, #40, $750 to $775.00
Batmobile & Batboat, #3, w/'Bat'-hubs, $600 to............ $625.00
Batmobile & Batboat, #3, w/whizzwheels, $300 to $350.00
Car Transporter Set, #1, $875 to $925.00
Car Transporter Set, #20, $875 to $925.00
Centurion Tank & Transporter, #10, $125 to $150.00
Chipperfield's Circus Crane Truck & Cage, #12, $375 to $400.00
Chopper Squad, #35, $75 to $100.00
Club Racing Set (Juniors), #3020, $175 to $225.00
Combine Harvester Set, #8, $375 to $400.00
Constructor Set, #24, $200 to $225.00
Corporal Missile & Launcher, #9, $850 to $875.00
Country Farm Set, #4, $70 to $80.00
Country Farm Set, #5, w/no hay, $70 to..........................$80.00
Daktari Set, #7, $225 to.. $250.00
Ecurie Ecosse Set, #16, $525 to $600.00
Emergency Set, #18, $90 to $110.00

Corgi
**Riviera Gift Set, Buick Riviera and Boat, #31,
with boat, trailer, and water skier, $250.00 to
$300.00.**

ERF Dropside Lorry & Platform Trailer w/Milk Churns, #21, $350 to.. $375.00

ERF Truck & Trailer, #11, $200 to $225.00

Ferrari Racing Set, #29, $75 to.....................................$90.00

Fiat & Boat, #37, $60 to...$75.00

Ford Sierra & Caravan, #1, $40 to................................$50.00

Ford Tractor & Beast Trailer, #1, $175 to...................... $200.00

Fordson Tractor & Plough, #13, $140 to $150.00

Fordson Tractor & Plough, #18, $175 to $200.00

Giant Daktari Set, #14, $475 to $525.00

Glider Set, #12, $70 to..$80.00

Golden Guinea Set, #20, $275 to.................................. $325.00

Grand Prix Set, #12, $425 to.. $500.00

Jaguar & Powerboat, #38, $70 to..................................$85.00

James Bond Set, #22, $550 to.. $575.00

Jean Richards' Circus Set, #48, $250 to $275.00

Jeep & Motorcycle Trailer, #10, $30 to..........................$50.00

Land Rover & Horsebox, #15, $125 to $175.00

Land Rover & Pony Trailer, #2, $175 to $200.00

Land Rover w/Ferrari Racing Car on Trailer, #17, $400 to.... $475.00

Lions of Longleat, #8, $175 to...................................... $225.00

London Passenger Transport Set, #35, w/policeman, $575 to.. $650.00

Lotus Racing Set, #32, $90 to....................................... $100.00

Machinery Carrier w/Priestman, #27, $225 to $275.00

Matra Rancho & Racer, #26, $70 to..............................$85.00

Mazda Pickup & Dinghy, #28, w/trailer, $60 to $75.00

Military Set, #17, $80 to...$95.00

Oldsmobile Toronado w/Glastren Sportsman Speedboat & Trailer, #36, $250 to $300.00

Peugeot Tour De France, #13, $80 to $100.00

Pinder's Circus Rover & Trailer, #30, $125 to................. $150.00

Pony Club Set, #47, $45 to..$60.00

Racing Car Set, #5, $275 to.. $325.00

RAF Land-Rover & Missile, #3, $225 to $275.00

RAF Land-Rover & Missile, #4, $475 to $550.00

Rallye Monte Carlo Set, #38, $925 to............................ $975.00

Rambler Marlin, #10, w/2 kayaks, trailer & figure, $225 to... $250.00

Renault Tour de France, #13, w/film unit & bicyclist, $250 to ..$275.00

Rocket Age Set, #6, $900 to.....................................$1,250.00

Royal Canadian Mounted Police, #45, $80 to $95.00

Silo & Conveyor, #322, $60 to.......................................$75.00

Silver Jubilee State Landau, #41, $45 to $60.00

Silvertone Set, #15, $1,750 to....................................$2,000.00

Spider-Man Set, #23, $350 to.. $375.00

Super Karts, #26, $25 to..$40.00

Tarzan Set, #36, $250 to... $275.00

Tower Wagon, #14, $125 to.. $175.00

Tractor & Trailer, #7, $125 to....................................... $150.00

Tractor & Trailer, #29, $125 to..................................... $150.00

Tractor & Trailer, #32, $175 to..................................... $200.00

Tractor w/Shovel & Trailer, #9, $150 to......................... $175.00

Unimog Dumper, #2, $150 to.. $175.00

Volkswagen Breakdown Truck w/Trailer & Corgi Styled Cooper Maserati, #25, $175 to $225.00

VW Transporter & Cooper Maseratti, #06, $175 to $200.00

VW Transporter & Cooper Masaratti, #25, $150 to $175.00

Working Converyer on Trailer w/Ford 5000 Super Major Tractor & Driver, #47, $225 to................................... $250.00

HUSKIES

Huskies were marketed exclusively through the Woolworth stores from 1965 to 1969. In 1970, Corgi Juniors were introduced. Both lines were sold in blister packs. Listed below are some of the character-related examples.

Bat Boat, #1003A, Husky on base, $125 to..................... $150.00

Bat Boat, #1003B, Junior on base, $80 to.........................$95.00

Batmobile, #1002A, Husky on base, $200 to $225.00

Batmobile, #1402, Husky Extra, 1st issue w/gray wheels, MOC $200.00

Chitty-Chitty Bang-Bang, #1006A, Husky on base, $200 to.... $225.00

Chitty-Chitty Bang-Bang, #1006B, Junior on base, $175 to...$200.00

Crime Busters Gift Set, #3008, scarce, $825 to............. $900.00

Ironside Police Van, #1007, $125 to............................. $150.00

James Bond Aston Martin, #1001B, Junior on base, $150 to... $200.00

James Bond Bobsleigh, #1011, $300 to $325.00

James Bond's Aston Martin, #1001A, Husky on base, $200 to ...$250.00

Jerry's Banger, #1014, $70 to...$85.00

Monkeemobile, #1004A, Husky on base, $200 to $225.00

Monkeemobile, #1004B, Junior on base, $175 to $200.00

Popeye Paddle Wagon, #1008, $200 to $225.00

Spectre Bobsleigh, #1012, $300 to $325.00

Tom's Go-Kart, #1013, $70 to...$85.00

UNCLE Car, #1005A, Husky on base, $175 to $200.00

UNCLE Car, #1005B, Junior on base, $1,500 to $1,750.00

MAJOR PACKS

Airport Crash Truck, #1103, $100 to $125.00

Airport Emergency Tender, #1118, $80 to $95.00

Bedford Milk Tanker, #1129, $275 to............................ $325.00

Bedford Mobilgas Tanker, #1110, $250 to $300.00

Bedford TK Car Transporter, #1105, $175 to................. $200.00

Bedford US Army Fuel Tanker, #1134, $350 to.............. $375.00

Berliet Container Truck, #1107, $70 to $85.00

Berliet Racehorse Transporter, #1105, $70 to $85.00

Berliet Wrecker, #1144, $75 to......................................$90.00

Bloodhound Guided Missile, #1115, $170 to.................. $180.00

Bloodhound Guided Missile Platform, #1116, $80 to........$90.00

Bloodhound Guided Missile Trolley, #1117, $90 to........ $110.00

Bloodhound Guided Missile w/Launching Ramp, #1108, MIB, $275 to.. $300.00

Bloodhound Guided Missile w/Trolley, #1109, MIB, $290 to.. $310.00

Carrimore Car Transporter, #1101, $250 to $300.00

Carrimore Low Loader, #1100, yel cab, $225 to............. $250.00

Carrimore Low Loader, #1132, $250 to......................... $300.00

Carrimore Machinery Carrier, #1131, $150 to............... $175.00

Chipperfield's Circus Animal Cage, #1123, $150 to....... $175.00

Chipperfield's Circus Crane, #1121, $225 to................. $275.00

Chipperfield's Circus Horse Transporter, #1130, $275 to. $325.00

Corporal Erector & Missile, #1113, $575 to $625.00

Corporal Missile Launching Platform, #1124, $90 to..... $110.00

Corporal Missile on Launching Ramp, #1112, $175 to .. $200.00

Decca Airfield Radar, #1106, $340 to $360.00

Dolphinarium, #1164, $150 to $175.00

Ecurie Ecosse Transporter, #1126, $225 to.................... $275.00

Euclid Bulldozer, #1102, $175 to $200.00
Euclid Crawler Tractor, #1103, $200 to...................... $225.00
Euclid TC-12 Bulldozer, #1107, $225 to $250.00
Ferrymasters Truck, #1147, see Scammell Ferrymasters Truck
Ford Aral Tanker, #1161, $45 to $55.00
Ford Car Transporter, #1159, $55 to $65.00
Ford Car Transporter, #1170, $50 to $60.00
Ford Esso Tanker, #1157, $55 to $65.00
Ford Express Tilt Cab 'H' Series Semi, #1137, $200 to... $225.00
Ford Transit Wrecker, #1140, $55 to $65.00
HDL Hovercraft SR-N1, #1119, $100 to $125.00
Heavy Equipment Transporter, #1135, $450 to............... $500.00
Holmes Wrecker, #1142, $135 to $180.00
Hydrolic Crane, #1101, $60 to $75.00
Hyster Sealink, #1113, $80 to $90.00
International Truck, #1118, gr, $175 to $200.00
Machinery Carrier, #1104, $150 to $175.00

Mack Esso Tanker, #1152, $90 to $100.00
Massey-Ferguson Combine Harvester, #1111, metal blades &
    tynes, $175 to $200.00
Massey-Ferguson Combine Harvester, #1111, plastic blades &
    tynes, $150 to $175.00
Mercedes Truck, #1129, $25 to................................$35.00
Mercedes Unimog Dumper, #1145, $55 to..................$65.00
Mercedes Unimog Snowplough, #1150, $70 to $85.00
Michelin Container Truck, #1108, $45 to $60.00
Michelin Truck, #1109, $60 to................................$75.00
Priestman Cub Luffing Shovel, #1128, $90 to $110.00
Scammell Carrimore Tri-Deck Car Transporter, #1146, $125 to..$135.00
Scammell Co-op Truck, #1151, $300 to..................... $325.00
Scammell Ferrymasters Truck, #1147, $125 to............... $150.00
Simon Snorkel Fire Engine, #1127, $120 to $130.00
Skyscraper Tower Crane, #1155, $70 to.........................$80.00
US Army Troop Transporter, #1133, $175 to................. $200.00

• Diecast •

Diecast replicas of cars, trucks, planes, trains, etc., represent a huge corner of today's collector market, and their manufacturers see to it that there is no shortage. Back in the 1920s, Tootsietoy had the market virtually by themselves, but one by one, other companies had a go at it, some with more success than others. Among them were the American companies of Barclay, Hubley, and Manoil, all of which are much better known for other types of toys. After the war, Metal Masters, Smith-Miller, and Doepke Ohlsson-Rice (among others) tried the market with varying degrees of success. Some companies were phased out over the years, while many more entered the market with fervor. Today it's those fondly remembered models from the 1950s and 1960s that many collectors yearn to own. Solido produced well-modeled, detailed little cars; some had dome lights that actually came on when the doors were opened. Politoy's were cleanly molded with good detailing and finishes. Mebetoys, an Italian company that has been bought out by Mattel, produced several; and some of the finest come from Brooklyn.

In 1968, the Topper Toy Company introduced its line of low-friction, high-speed Johnny Lightning cars to be in direct competition with Mattel's Hot Wheels. To gain attention, Topper sponsored Al Unser's winning race car, the 'Johnny Lightning,' in the 1970 Indianapolis 500. Despite the popularity of their cars, the Topper Toy Company went out of business in 1971. Today the Johnny Lightnings are highly sought after, and a new company, Playing Mantis, is reproducing many of the original designs as well as several models that never made it into regular production.

If you're interested in Majorette toys, we recommend *Collecting Majorette Toys* by Dana Johnson. Dana is also the author of *Collector's Guide to Diecast Toys & Scale Models*; *Toy Car Collector's Guide*; and *Matchbox Toys, 1947 to 2007*.

Values are for examples in mint condition and in the original packaging unless noted otherwise.

See also Corgi; Dinky; Farm Toys; Hot Wheels; Matchbox; Tekno; Tootsietoys.

Diecast
Ahi, Army Truck, 1950s, M, $25.00. (Photo courtesy
www.gasolinealleyantiques.com)

Ahi, Buick, $20 to $25.00
Ahi, Darracq (1904) $15.00
Ahi, Dodge Military Ambulance..$15.00
Ahi, Dodge Military Lumber Truck....................................$15.00
Ahi, Dodge Military Searchlight Truck...............................$12.00
Ahi, Ford Model T (1915), $15 to $20.00
Ahi, Mercedes-Benz 220SE $16.00
Ahi, Midget Racer, $20 to $25.00
Ahi, Rambler (1903) $12.00
Ahi, Renault Floride $16.00
Ahi, Rolls-Royce Silver Wraith, $25 to $30.00
Ahi, Simca Aronde P60 ....$16.00
Ahi, Tank Carrier, 1950s, M...$25.00
Ahi, Volvo PV 544 .... $160.00
Amazing Car Model #600, Ny-Lint, 1946, w/up, tin, NMIB..$150.00
Anker, Alfa Romeo 1300, $20 to $25.00
Anker, Audi 100 ....$18.00
Anker, Renault Rodeo Jeep...$18.00

Asahi Model Pet, Datsun Bluebird UHT $50.00
Asahi Model Pet, Nissan Silvia Coupe $75.00
Asahi Model Pet, Subary 360 ....$135.00
Aurora Cigar Box, Buick Riviera.....................................$35.00
Aurora Cigar Box, Ferrari Berlinetta...............................$35.00
Aurora Cigar Box, Ford J Car, yel, $30 to $40.00
Aurora Cigar Box, Mercury Cougar $35.00
Auto Pilen, Ferrari 512 ....$60.00
Auto Pilen, Mercedes Taxi, $40 to $50.00
Bandai, Hato Bus, bl & wht $20.00
Bandai, Tank Lorry JAL $6.00
Bandii, Mazda RX7 25i $5.00
Bandii, Porsche 903, silver...$16.00
Bandii, Porsche 928, bl, $16 to $20.00
Bang, Ford Mk II Le Mans, bl or blk, ea $25 to $35.00
Barclay, Ambulance, #50, 5" $50.00
Barclay, Army Truck w/Gun, #151 ....$35.00
Barclay, Austin Coupe, 2" $30.00
Barclay, Federal Truck (1937) $25.00
Barclay, Renault Tank, #47 ....$40.00
Barclay, Searchlight Truck, $145 to................................$160.00
Barclay, Streamline Car, #302, 3⅛" $35.00
Barlux, Ferarri B2..$12.00
Barlux, Fiat Ambulance, $25 to $35.00
Barlux, Road Roller $20.00
Barlux, Tyrell-Ford $10.00
BBR, Ferrari 250 GTE (1959), $150 to $180.00
BBR, Ferrari 275 GRB (1965) $175.00
BBR, Ferrari 308 GTB Coupe, red, $165 to $185.00
Bburago, Bugatti Atlantic (1936), Bijoux series $25.00
Bburago, Dodge Viper GTS, metallic bl w/wht racing stripes, $7
   to...$10.00
Bburago, Fiat Tipo, $12 to $15.00
Bburago, Jaguar SS 100, 1937.......................................$30.00
Bburago, Lancia Stratos, 4000 series $12.00
Bburago, Porsche 911S $20.00
Bburago Dump Truck, 1500 series, M, $30 to $35.00
Benbros, AEC Box Van $30.00
Benbros, Armored Car (3¾") & Field Gun (4") $45.00
Benbros, Army Land Rover $25.00
Benbros, Caterpillar Bulldozer, 4½" $55.00
Benbros, Lorry w/Searchlight $50.00
Benbros, Rolls-Royce (1906), $15 to $20.00
Best Toys of Kansas, Pontiac Sedan, #100 ....$45.00
Best Toys of Kansas, Racer #76, 4", $30 to $35.00
Best Toys of Kansas, Sedan, #87 ....$30.00
Best-Box of Holland, Ford Model T Coupe, $24 to $27.00
Best-Box of Holland, Saloon, #501 DAF 1400 ....$27.00
Box Model, Ferrari 250 IM Street, red, #8434 ....$20.00
Britains, Triumph Thunderbird Motorcycle, #9690, 1950s...$75.00
Brooklins, Rover 90 P4 Lansdowne (1957), $45 to $65.00
Brooklins (British Issues), Buick Roadmaster Coupe (1949), $65
   to...$150.00
Brooklins (British Issues), Chevrolet El Camino (1959), $60 to.$75.00
Brooklins (Canadian Issues), Chrysler Newport 4-Door (1940),
   $175 to...$225.00
Brooklins (Canadian Issues), Ford Victoria 2-Door (1930), $100
   to...$250.00

Diecast
• • • • • • •
Brooklins,
Dodge 500
Convertible
(1954), 1990 –
1994, M, $115.00. (Photo
courtesy www.gasolinealleyantiques.com)

Diecast
• • • • • • • •
Diapet, Sunny
Coupe 1200
GL, #212, $24.00.
(Photo courtesy Dana Johnson)

Brooklins (Canadian Issues), Packard (1932) $225.00
Brooklins (Robeddie Models), Saab 99 (1969), $60 to......$85.00
Brumm, any model, ea $18 to $24.00
Brumm, Limited Editions, any model, ea $35 to.............$45.00
Buby, VW Buggy $5.00
Buccaneer, any model, ea $20 to $25.00
Budgie, Birmingham-London Motorway Express Coach, #296,
   NMIB, $75 to $125.00
Budgie, Coast to Coast Refrigeration Truck, #202, 1959, 6",
   EX. $92.00
Budgie, Coast to Coast Refrigeration Truck, #202,1959, 6",
   NMIB, $100 to $125.00
Budgie, Daimler Ambulance, #258, NM+IB, $125 to $175.00
Budgie, Dump Truck $24.00
Budgie, Hansom Cab, #100, 1970s, 4½"..........................$45.00
Budgie, Horse Box, #294, 1960s, 4½"..............................$75.00
Budgie, Lewin Sweepmaster, #300, NM+IB, $175 to $225.00
Budgie, Leyland Cement Mixer, #310, EX+IB, $125 to . $175.00
Budgie, London Taxi Cab, #101, 1970s, 4¼" $50.00
Budgie, Pitt Alligator Low Loader, 1960s, 6½", NMIB... $105.00
Budgie, Plateglass Transporter, #304, 1960s, 4¼", NMIB ..$83.00
Budgie, REA Express Parcel Delivery Truck, #57, 1960s, M..$10.00
Budgie, Refuse Truck, #274, EXIB, $75 to $100.00
Budgie, Rolls-Royce Silver Cloud, #102, $30 to $40.00
Budgie, Routemaster Double-Decker Bus, #236, 1970s, Uniflow
   decals, 4¼" $50.00
Budgie, Rover Squad Car..$15.00
Budgie, Seddon AA Traffic Control Unit, #218, EX+IB, $100
   to... $125.00
Budgie, Tower Glass Co Plateglass Transporter, #304, G+IB, $75
   to... $100.00
CD, Lelage Limousine $100.00
CD, MG Record Car.. $100.00
Chad Valley, Ambulance...$35.00
Chad Valley, Commer Fire Engine, $160 to...................$180.00
Chad Valley, Commer Flat Truck $175.00
Chad Valley, Guy Ice Cream Truck.................................$250.00
Chad Valley, Post Office Van...$35.00

Charbens, Alfa Romeo Racer $120.00

Charbens, Standard 6HP (1903), Old Crock series $18.00

Chrono, Porsche 550 RS (1953), silver, $25 to $39.00

CIJ, Renault Floride, #3/58, 1960.....................................$55.00

Con-Cor, Ferrari Testarossa $8.00

Conquest, Buick Super Hard Top (1955), 3-tone $225.00

Conrad, Haulpak/Wabco Quarry Truck, #272, NMIB, $100 to..$125.00

Conrad, Magirus 4-Axle Dump Truck, #3274 ....$39.00

Conrad, Volkswagen Polo C $10.00

Conrad, Volvo Old Timer Fire Engine (1928) $59.00

Conrad, Volvo Titan L395 Flatbed Truck $48.00

Dalia, Vesper Scooter, gr..$75.00

Dalia-Solido, Jaguar D Le Mans, bl, gr or red.................. $100.00

Dalia-Solido, Porsche F2, silver & red $125.00

Dalia-Tekno, Monza GT Coupe $60.00

Danbury Mint, Ferrari 250 Testa Rossa, red, $110 to...... $135.00

Danbury Mint, Pierce Arrow (1933), silver, $115 to...... $125.00

Diapet, Corvette, #G76, $65 to..$80.00

Diapet, Datsun 280Z Police Car, #P53 ....$18.00

Diapet, Nissan Cedric Ultima Station Taxi, #P29 ....$39.00

Diapet, P68 Lincoln Continental, custom gold finish w/Oriental style rear cover extending over roof, EX+IB, $125 to . $150.00

Dodge Coronet Custom Taxi, #F18, 1970s, M...................$11.00

Doepke, Unit Mobile Crane, 11½", $300 to $400.00

Doepke, Victory 37 Bus (1972) $25.00

Dubuque, Greyhound Bus, 9½" $400.00

Dugu, Benz Victoria (1893), 1964.....................................$40.00

Dugu, Fiat 500A Coupe (1936), 1966.................................$60.00

Dugu, OM Dump Truck, Sispla series.................................$95.00

Durham Classics, Ford Pickup (1953), bl.......................... $120.00

Durham Classics, Lincoln Zephyr Coupe (1938)............ $100.00

Eagle's Race/Eagle Collectibles, Ford Hot Rod (1940), any color, $30 to...$35.00

Efsi, Commer Ambulance, $12 to $16.00

Eligor, Chrysler New Yorker Convertible (1958)...............$25.00

Eligor, Ford Police Sedan (1932), $30 to $35.00

Eligor, Ford Roadster Fire Chief (1932) $25.00

Enchanted, Buick Riveria (1949)..................................... $115.00

Enchanted, Chevy Nomad (1957), $75 to $100.00

Enchanted, Kaiser Manhattan (1953), $75 to $100.00

Enchanted, Packard Victoria (1937)...................................$85.00

Enchantment Land Coach Builders, Chevy Nomad Wagon (1957) $125.00

Enchantment Land Coach Builders, Packard Victoria (1937) ...$95.00

Ertl, American Classics Set, #1741, 1978, 6-pc $45.00

Ertl, Buick (1912), red & blk, 1:43 scale, 1985, $20 to $25.00

Ertl, Chevy Cameo Pickup (1955) $8.00

Ertl, Corvette Coupe (1963), dk bl, 1:18 scale, $30 to $35.00

Ertl, Dodge Ram Truck (1995), blk or red.........................$25.00

Ertl, Dukes of Hazzard, 4-pc set, 1:64 scale, 1991, MIB (sealed) ..$125.00

Ertl, Hawkeye Flatbed (1931), True Value $24.00

Ertl, John Deere 690C Excavator $15.00

Ertl, Plymouth Hemi Roadrunner (1969), yel....................$30.00

France Jouets, Ambulance (GMC Truck), 300 series, 1959... $80.00

France Jouets, Dump Truck (Berlier Straidair), 700 series, 1967 ...$80.00

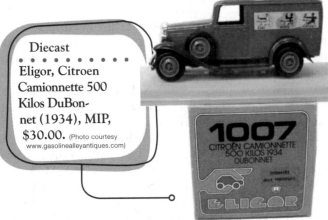

Diecast

Eligor, Citroen Camionnette 500 Kilos DuBonnet (1934), MIP, $30.00. (Photo courtesy www.gasolinealleyantiques.com)

Diecast

Hubley, Auto Transport #492, holds four plastic sedans, conventional cab model, red overall with silver grille and fenders, original box, M, $250.00.

Diecast

Franklin Mint, Bonnie and Clyde's 1932 Ford V8, 1987, MIP, $110.00. (Photo courtesy www.gasolinealleyantiques.com)

Diecast

Hubley, Dump Truck, diecast cab and dump trailer, green and red with silver highlights, dump body spring activated for unloading, 14 rubber tires, 16¼", MIB, $415.00.

France Jouets, Police Jeep, 1965, $60 to............................$75.00
Franklin Mint, Chevy Corvette (1953) $95.00
Franklin Mint, Ford Model T (1913), 1:16 scale, $120 to ..$140.00
Franklin Mint, Ford Mustang (1964), 1:43 scale, $65 to...$75.00
Franklin Mint, Ford Thunderbird (1962), $55 to.............$65.00
Fun Ho!, Land Rover, 1966-78, 1¾", $40 to.....................$60.00
Gama, Ford Taunus 17M, #901, 1959, $45 to....................$55.00
Gama, Mercedes-Benz 300CE, $20 to...............................$30.00
Gama, Opel Rekord, 1978..$35.00
Goldvarg, Chevrolet Bel-Air 4-Door Sedan (1954) $89.00
Goldvarg, Ford Deluxe Sedan (1946), $85 to $100.00
Goodee, GMC Pickup Truck (1953), 3".............................$18.00
Goodee, GMC Pickup Truck (1953), 6".............................$25.00
Goodee, Lincoln Capri Hardtop (1953), 3", $16 to..........$20.00
Goodee, Moving Van...$15.00
Guiloy, Harley-Davidson Custom Sport Motorcycle.........$18.00
Guiloy, Indian Chief Motorcycle (1948), $35 to $45.00
Guisval, Chevy Camero (1979), $16 to $20.00
Guisval, Lincoln 4-Door Sedan (1928)............................$15.00
Guisval, Porsche 959, $16 to $20.00
Hartoy, Wrigley's Mack Box Truck..................................$25.00
Hubley, Aherns-Fox Closed Cab Fire Engine, 1948, EX....$25.00
Hubley, Army Air Combat Squadron Hangar, 5-pc set, folding
    wings, unused, NMIB..$460.00
Hubley, Auto Transport #492, w/3 plastic cars, 14", EX (G+
    box)...$150.00
Hubley, Cement Mixing Truck, red cab w/NP drum on gr bed,
    BRT, 10", NMIB...................................... $440.00
Hubley, Chrysler Airflow, 5", $80 to...............................$95.00
Hubley, Log Truck, 1960s, w/logs, 10", G, $35 to $45.00
Hubley, Poultry Truck, w/accessories, 10", $265 to.........$300.00
Hubley, School Bus, 9½", EX...$70.00
Hubley, Sedan, 1940s, BRT, 7", NM $92.00
Hubley, Tinytoy Kit, LeTourneau-Westinghouse Tournapull
    Scraper, #616K-130, die-cast & plastic (sealed)............$55.00
Hubley, Tractor, orange w/blk rubber tires, 7", $150 to... $175.00
Hubley Kiddie Toy, Convertible, bl, 7", EXIB.................$165.00
Hubley Kiddie Toy, Custom Sports Car, yel, 13", rare $850.00
Hubley Kiddie Toy, De Luxe Sports Car........................$250.00
Hubley Kiddie Toy, Dump Truck, #510, $240 to.............$265.00
Hubley Kiddie Toy, Sedan, #452, 7", $30 to....................$45.00
Hubley Kiddie Toy, Tandem Roto Helicopter, yel, 9", NM...$25.00
Hubley Kiddie Toy, Texaco Tanker Truck, all-in-one w/slanted
    back, 1940s, 5", EX+...$65.00
Hubley Mighty-Metal, Tow Truck, $120 to...................... $135.00
Husky, Aston Martin, DB6, 1960s, NM............................$25.00
Husky, Citroen Safari Ambulance, 1960s $35.00
Husky, Commer Wall Thro' Van, 1960s.............................$45.00
Husky, Ford Camper, 1960s $55.00
Husky, Forward Control Land Rover, removable canopy,
    MIP..$46.00
Husky, Man From UNCLE Gull Wing Car w/2 figures, 1968,
    3" $60.00
Husky, Sunbeam Alpine, 1960s, NM+..............................$40.00
Joal, Adams Probe 16, $35 to $45.00
Joal, Alfa Romeo Giulia 55 ....$25.00
Joal, Chrysler 150, $35 to $45.00
Joal, Ferrari 512S $40.00

Diecast

Hubley, Race Car #22, EX, $40.00.
(Photo courtesy Homestead Auctions on LiveAuctioneers.com)

Diecast

Hubley, Taxi Cabs, Kiddie-Toy, set of three, EXIB, $600.00. (Photo courtesy Morphy Auctions on LiveAuctioneers.com)

Diecast

Johnny Lightning, Shelby Mustang GT 350H (1966), MIP, $225.00. (Photo courtesy www.gasolinealleyantiques.com)

Joal, Ford Fiesta...$25.00
Joal, Jaguar E-Type Roadster..$30.00
Johnny Lightning, Bug Bomb, M, $25 to $35.00
Johnny Lightning, Chevy Impala 91958, MIP..................$25.00
Johnny Lightning, Custom El Camino, 1969.............. $1,250.00
Johnny Lightning, Custom El Camino (1994), M..............$8.00
Johnny Lightning, Custom Eldorado, open doors, M $100.00
Johnny Lightning, Custom GTO, 1969, M.......................$250.00
Johnny Lightning, Custom XKE, doors open, 1969, M .. $125.00
Johnny Lightning, Jet Powered Screamer, 1970, M...........$35.00
Johnny Lightning, Jumpin' Jag, 1970, MIP......................$35.00
Johnny Lightning, Jumpin' Jag, 1970, M, $20 to $25.00
Johnny Lightning, Sand Stormer, 1970, M........................$30.00
Johnny Lightning, Vulture...$70.00
Jouef, Honda Acura NSX, gray..$25.00
JRD, Unic Van Hafa, 1959 ....$195.00
Junkers JU-87B Stuka, #721, NMIP...................................$50.00
Kansas Toy & Novelty, Army Truck, #74, 2¼", $50 to......$65.00
Kansas Toy & Novelty, Bearcat Racer, #26, 4" $90.00
Kansas Toy & Novelty, Convertible Coupe, #35, 2¼".......$50.00

Diecast
• • • • • • •
Lledo, Gold
Lotus Europa,
$9.00 to $12.00. (Photo courtesy Dana Johnson)

Diecast
• • • • • • •
Lone Star, Fiat
2300S Coupe,
MIP, $28.00.
(Photo courtesy www.gaso
linealleyantiques.com)

Diecast
• • • • • • •
Majorette,
Ford Mus-
tang (1965),
MIP (Leg-
ends), $16.00. (Photo
courtesy www.gasolinealleyantiques.com)

Diecast
• • • • • • • • • • • •
Majorette, 3045 Lincoln Super Stretch
Limo, version 2, silver with black landau
roof, $12.00. (Photo courtesy Dana Johnson)

Kansas Toy & Novelty, Midget Racer w/Driver, 3" $40.00
Kemlows, Armored Car $55.00
Kenner Fast 111's, any model, ea $4 to $6.00
Kenner Winner's Circle, Drag Racing models, 1:64 scale, ea $4
    to...$5.00
Kiddie Car Classics, Ford Mustang (1964), 7" $55.00
Kiddie Car Classics, Garton Delivery Cycle (1950), 6¾" ..$45.00
Kirk, Chevrolet Monza GT, $65 to $75.00
Kirk, Chevy Monza Spider $60.00

Kyosho, MGB Mk-1 (1966), gr, red or wht, ea $50 to $65.00
Lansing-Slik Toys, Fastback Sedan, #9600, 7" $40.00
Lansing-Slik-Toys, Roadster, #9701, 3½", $35 to $45.00
Lansing-Slik Toys, Tanker Truck, #9705, 4" $30.00
Leslie-Henry, Cargo Comet Freight Train Set, complete,
    NMIB $125.00
Lledo, Delivery Van, 1983, $15 to.....................................$20.00
Lledo, Ford Model T Tanker, 1983, $15 to $20.00
Lledo, Greyhound Scenicruiser, $18 to $20.00
Lledo, Long Distance Coach, 1985 ....$10.00
Lledo, Volkswagen Cabriolet, red......................................$25.00
Londontoy, Chevy Master DeLuxe Coupe (1941), 6" $32.00
Londontoy, City Bus, 4", $30 to $35.00
Londontoy, Dump Truck, lg, $110 to.............................. $125.00
Londontoy, Ford Pickup (1941), 4" $25.00
Londontoy, Ford Pickup (1941), 6", $35 to $45.00
Lone Star, Chevy Corvette, coral......................................$65.00
Lone Star, Chevy Corvette, wht..$90.00
Lone Star, Dodge Dart Phoenix, metallic bl, $80 to....... $100.00
Lone Star, Ford Mustang Fastback, Flyers #39, $25 to.......$40.00
Lone Star, Roadmaster Impy Cars, Corvette Gran Turismo
    Coupe, #11, 1960s...$37.00
Lone Star, Roadmaster Impy Cars, Fiat 2300S Coupe, #21,
    1960s, MIP $30.00
Lone Star, Roadmaster Impy Cars, Volvo 1800S, #19, 1960s,
    MIP...$30.00
Maisto, Bugatti EB110 (1992), bl or red, M.....................$30.00
Maistro, Ferrari F50 Coupe, yel or red, ea $25 to..............$35.00
Maistro, Jaguar XK8, $10 to $15.00
Majorette, Bernard Circus Truck $18.00
Majorette, Citreon DS..$29.00
Majorette, Citreon Maserati SM, $12 to $15.00
Majorette, Toyota Truck & Trailer, $12 to $15.00
Majorette, VW Golf, red, $5 to...$6.00
Majorette Sonic Flashers, Ambulance, $8 to $12.00
Mandarin, Honda 9 Coupe, $6 to $8.00
Manoil, Bus, 1945-55, $35 to $50.00
Manoil, Fire Engine, 1945-55...$95.00
Manoil, Roadster, 1935-41, $85 to $100.00
Master Caster, Yellow Cab (1947), 7" $225.00
Mebetoys, BMW 320 Rally, 1980, $27 to..........................$35.00
Mebetoys, BMW 2000 CS, #A17, 1960s $40.00
Mebetoys, Lotus JPS, 1973, $65 to $90.00
Mebetoys, Maserati Mistral Coupe, #A-10, 1960s.............$40.00
Mebetoys, Pontiac Firebird (1983), $28 to $35.00
Mebetoys, Porsche 912 Rally, 1974 ....$30.00
Mebetoys, Willys Fire Jeep (1974), $35 to $40.00
Mercury, Alfa Romeo, 1951..$40.00
Mercury, Cadillac 62 Sedan (1949), $140 to $175.00
Mercury, Fiat 131 Fire Chief, 1971 ....$25.00
Mercury, Fiat 131 Wagon & Trailer (1977), $35 to $45.00
Mercury, Jack's Demon Dragster, 1969 ....$29.00
Mercury, Sigma Grand Prix (1969) $35.00
Mercury, Stagecoach, $80 to...$95.00
Midgetoy, American LeFrance Fire Pumper, 1957 ....$19.00
Midgetoy, Jeep, 1960s, red, $8 to.....................................$12.00
Milton, Ford Model T, $27 to...$30.00
Milton, Jaguar 3.8 Saloon..$49.00

Mira, Chevy Pickup (1953) $25.00
Mira, Ford Thunderbird (1956), $30 to $40.00
Mira, Renault Espace Ambulance $19.00
Morestone, Daimler Ambulance $120.00
Morestone, Mercedes Benz Racer $40.00
Navy Fighter-Bomber Squadron, Hubley, #53, 1950s, set of 5, all
    w/folding wings, EX+IB.......................... $920.00
Nicky Toys, Daimler Jaguar 3.4 ....$29.00
Nostalgic, Chevy Corvette (1982) $79.00
Nostalgic, Ford Van (1936), maroon, $55 to $70.00
Nostalgic, LaSalle Roadster (1934) $65.00
NZG, CAT 627 Scraper....................................$59.00
NZG, Kramer Tremo Utility Truck $25.00
NZG, Scania City Bus CN112, $45 to................$55.00
Playart, Jeep, $6 to $12.00
Playart, Man From UNCLE car, 2¾", 1960s, NM........... $109.00
Politoys, Alfa Romeo Giulia GT 1300 Junior, #80, 1960s, MIP....$45.00
Quiralu, Simca Marly Ambulance, 1957....................$129.00
Racing Champions, any, ea $6 to $12.00
Ralstoy, Chevy Step Van (1982) $24.00
Ralstoy, Moving Van, any trade name, ea $39.00
Ralstoy, Safety-Kleen Van, M, $30 to $45.00
Renwal, Pontiac Convertible, $125 to............... $140.00
Rio, any, ea $25 to $35.00
Road Champs, Ford Woodie (1949), $16 to $18.00
Road Champs, Greyhound Eagle Coach $5.00
Sabra/Cragstan, Chevelle Ambulance, #8101, 1960s........$25.00
Sabra/Cragstan, Chevelle Station Wagon, #8100, 1960s ..$15.00
Sabra/Cragstan, Plymouth Barracuda, #8114, 1960s..........$25.00
Sabra/Cragstan, Pontiac GTO, #8107, 1960s $50.00
Sabra/Gamada Koor, Chevrolet Police Car, #8115, 1960s..$20.00
Sabra/Gamda Koor, Toronado, #8109, 1960s $10.00
Sakkura, Toyota Land Cruiser, $24 to $27.00
Schabak, Audi 80 Sedan (1992), $20 to $25.00
Schabak, Ford Transit Van (1986), 1987, $32 to.......$36.00
Schabak, VW Jetta, 1984 ....$20.00
Schuco, Audi 80 LS, 1972, $30 to".................$35.00
Schuco, Krupp Cement Mixer, 3⅝", $55 to $70.00
Schuco, MGA Coupe, 1958, 2", $55 to $75.00
Schuco, Volkswagen Polo, 1975........................$25.00
Scottoys, Fiat 600 Saloon, $30 to $35.00
Siku, Ford Tanus 15M (1967), #V2778, 1968, M $32.00
Siku, Ford 12M, 1963, $36 to........................$40.00
Siku, Jeep w/Trailer, 1964-72...........................$39.00
Siku, Mercedes 300 SL (1963), #V221, 1963 ....$60.00
Siku, Opel Rekford C, #V271, 1968, NM.............$10.00
Siku, Police Bat Transporter, 1989 ....$25.00
Siku, Pontiac GTO (The Judge), 1972-74 ....$49.00
Siku, Volkswagen Vanagon Bus (1973-74) $25.00
Solido, Alpine F3 (1965), 1996 reissue $24.00
Solido, Chrysler Windsor (1946), 1960s, $30 to.......$40.00
Solido, Ford Mustang (1965), 1994....................$24.00
Solido, Ford Tanker (1936), 1994 ....$30.00
Solido, Jaguar XJ 12 (1978), $12 to..................$16.00
Solido, Mack R 600 Fire Engine, $30 to $35.00
Solido, Opel GT, #171, 1960s, MIP $60.00
Solido, Porsche 924, #1324, 1970s, NMIP............$10.00
Solido, Volkswagen Golf, 1981-82, $20 to............$36.00

Spot-On, Aston-Martin D83, $225 to $250.00
Spot-On, Austin 1800 .... $120.00
Spot-On, Ford Consul Classic $165.00
Spot-On, Jaguar Mk 10, $180 to $210.00
Sunnyside, BMW 728 Sedan, $6 to..................$8.00
Tip Top Toy, Coupe, 3½" $39.00
Tip Top Toy, Stake Truck, 5", $55 to................$65.00
Tomica, Cadillac Ambulance, #F-2....................$12.00
Tomica, Datsun Silva Coupe $20.00

Diecast
Schuco, Mercedes Bus, 1950s – 1960s, M, $95.00.
(Photo courtesy www.gasolinealley antiques.com)

Diecast
Siku, Porsche 901, hood opens, jeweled headlights, M, $60.00. (Photo courtesy www.gasolinealleyantiques.com)

Diecast
Siku, Renault R5 Le Car, 1970s – 1980s, MIP, $21.00. (Photo courtesy www.gasolinealleyantiques.com)

Diecast
Solido, DeLage D8/120, M, $22.00.
(Photo courtesy www.gasolinealleyantiques.com)

Tomica, Datsun 200SX, #235-6, $6 to $8.00
Tomica, Ford Texaco Oil Delivery Truck, #F62, 1970s, M ..$5.00
Tomica, Lotus Elite, #F47, $6 to..$8.00
Tomica, Morgan Plus 8, #F26, 1977, NM.............................$5.00
Tomica, Nissan Gloria Van (1967), #F47, 1970s, M..........$11.00
Tomica, Porsche 950 Turbo, #F1, 1979, M..........................$11.00
Tomica, Volkswagen Microbus, #166-F29, $18 to...............$24.00
Tomica Dandy, Nissan Skyline $18.00
Top Gear, Falcon XC Covra, $32 to.......................................$39.00
Tri-Ang, Bentley Touring Car (1938), $120 to...............$150.00
Tri-Ang, Rolls-Royce Sedanca, 1937 ....$150.00
Tri-Ang (Spot-On), Austin A40, EX+IB, $225 to $275.00

Tri-Ang (Spot-On), Jaguar XKSS, EX+IB, $200 to........$250.00
Tri-Ang (Spot-On), MGA (open), NM+IB, $300 to.....$350.00
Tri-Ang (Spot-On), Sunbeam Alpine, NM, $100 to......$150.00
Tri-Ang, Town Coupe (1935), $120 to...........................$150.00
Vitesse, any except Vitesse Victoria, ea.............................$35.00
Vitesse Victoria, any, ea $22 to...$40.00
Western Models, Buick Riviera (1972) $175.00
Yat Ming, Ford Thunderbird (1955), $25 to $35.00
Ziss, Chevrolet Phaeton (1916), 1969, $24 to $32.00
Ziss, Ford Ranch Car (1909), 1966 ....$40.00
Ziss, Opel Commodore Coupe (1971), $36 to $48.00

· **Dinky** ·

Dinky diecasts were made by Meccano (Britain) as early as 1933, but high on the list of many of today's collectors are those from the decades of the 1950s and 1960s. They made commercial vehicles, firefighting equipment, farm toys, and heavy equipment, as well as classic cars that were the epitome of high style, such as the #157 Jaguar XK120, produced from the mid-1950s through the early 1960s. Some Dinkys were made in France; since 1979 no toys have been produced in Great Britain. Values are for examples mint and in the original packaging unless noted otherwise.

AA Motorcycle Patrol, #270, $80 to...............................$100.00
AC Acceca, #167, all cream, $275 to $325.00
AC Acceca, #167, dual colors, $200 to $240.00
AEC Articulated Lorry, #914, $200 to...........................$225.00
AEC Articulated Transporter & Helicopter, #618, $140 to..$150.00
AEC Hoyner Transporter, #974, $125 to $135.00
AEC Tanker, #991, Shell Chemicals, $225 to $235.00
Airport Fire Rescue Tender, #263, $75 to $100.00
Airport Fire Tender, #276, w/flashing light, $125 to.......$150.00
Alfa Romeo Giulia, #514, $175 to $200.00

Alfa Romeo Scarabo, #217, $120 to...............................$140.00
Alfa Romeo 33, #210, $190 to..$220.00
Ambulance, #30F, $265 to..$285.00
ANWB Motorcycle Patrol, #272, $325 to $375.00
Armoured Car, #670, $85 to..$115.00
Armoured Command Vehicle, #677, $120 to $130.00
Armstrong Siddeley, #36A, $215 to $230.00
Armstrong Withworth 'Whitley' Bomber, #62T, $225 to .$250.00
Army Covered Wagon, #623, $140 to..............................$160.00
Army Field Kitchen Cuisine Roulante, #823, $125 to ...$150.00
Army Jeep, #669, $75 to $100.00
Army Personnel, #603, box of 12, $115 to.....................$140.00
Army Water Tranker, #643, $115 to $125.00
Army 1-Ton Cargo Truck, #641, $75 to $85.00
Army 10-Ton Truck, #622, $65 to...................................$75.00
Aston-Martin DB35, #104, $175 to $185.00
Aston-Martin DB5, #110, $130 to $140.00
Atlantean City Bus, #291, $125 to.................................$150.00
Atlantean City Bus, #295, Yellow Pages, $90 to...........$120.00
Atlas COPCO Compressor Lorry, #436, $145 to............$170.00
Austin Atlantic, #106, bl or blk, $195 to.......................$240.00
Austin Atlantic, #106, pk, $385 to.................................$435.00
Austin A105, #176, cream or gray, $150 to....................$175.00
Austin A105, #176, cream w/bl roof, or gray w/red roof, $240 to..$260.00

Austin A105, #176, gray, $170 to	$220.00
Austin Champ, #674, olive drab, $70 to	$90.00
Austin Covered Truck, #30SM/625, $265 to	$285.00
Austin Healey 100, #109, $130 to	$150.00
Austin Healey, #546, $225 to	$250.00
Austin Healey Sprite, #112, $110 to	$135.00
Austin Paramoke, #601, $40 to	$60.00
Austin Somerset, #161, dual colors, $500 to	$525.00
Austin Somerset, #161, solid colors, $100 to	$125.00
Austin Taxi, #254, yel, $200 to	$225.00
Austin 1800 Taxi, #282, $90 to	$110.00
Aveling-Barford Dumper, #924, $175 to	$200.00
Beach Buggy, #227, $35 to	$45.00
Bedford Articulated Lorry, #521, $175 to	$200.00
Bedford Articulated Lorry, #921, $325 to	$350.00
Bedford Fire Engine, #956, $180 to	$200.00
Bedford Forward Control Lorry, #420, $200 to	$225.00
Bedford Refuse Wagon, #987, $225 to	$250.00
Bedford TK Box Van, #450, Castrol, $270 to	$295.00
Bedford TK Tipper, #435, gray or yel cab, $170 to	$210.00
Bedford TK Tipper, #435, silver & bl, $250 to	$275.00
Bedford Van, #260, Royal Mail, $125 to	$150.00
Bedford Van, #410, MJ Hire, Marley or Collectors' Gazette, $160 to	$195.00
Bedford Van, #410, Royal Mail, $35 to	$45.00
Bedford Van, #480, Kodak, $180 to	$200.00
Bedford Van, #482, Dinky Toys, $400 to	$450.00
Beechcraft C-55 Baron, #715, $170 to	$195.00
Bell Police Helicopter, #732, M*A*S*H, $100 to	$125.00
Berliet Fire Pumper, #32E, $185 to	$215.00
Berliet Military Wrecker, #F826, $225 to	$250.00
Berliet Missile Launcher, #620, $165 to	$185.00
Berliet Wrecker, #589, $175 to	$200.00
Big Bedford Lorry, #522, bl & yel, $350 to	$375.00
Big Bedford Lorry, #522, maroon & fawn, $200 to	$225.00
Big Ben Lorry, #408, bl & yel, or bl & orange, $350 to	$375.00
Big Ben Lorry, #408, maroon & fawn, $300 to	$325.00
Blaw-Knox Bulldozer, #561, $120 to	$130.00
Blaw-Knox Heavy Tractor, #563, $100 to	$125.00
Blaw-Knox Heavy Tractor, #963, $175 to	$200.00
BMW 1500, #534, $200 to	$225.00

BOAC Coach, #283, $100 to	$125.00
Brink's Armoured Car, #275, no bullion, $110 to	$140.00
Brink's Armoured Car, #275, w/gold bullion, $175 to	$225.00
Brink's Armoured Car, #275, w/Mexican bullion, $950 to	$1,250.00
Bristol 450, #163, $150 to	$175.00
BRM Racer, #243, $145 to	$165.00
Buick Roadmaster, #545, $190 to	$210.00
Cadillac El Dorado, #131, $140 to	$150.00
Cadillac (1962), #147, $140 to	$160.00
Chevrolet Corvair, #552, $225 to	$250.00
Chevrolet El Camino Pickup, #449, $135 to	$145.00
Chrysler Airflow, #32/30A, $425 to	$450.00
Chrysler Royal Saloon, #39E, $290 to	$310.00
Chrysler Saratoga, #550, $180 to	$200.00
Chrysler Simca 1308/GT, #11542, $115 to	$130.00
Citroen Ambulance, #556, $275 to	$300.00
Citroen DS-19, #522, $130 to	$140.00
Citroen Fire Van, #562, $245 to	$265.00
Citroen ID-19, #539, $225 to	$250.00
Citroen Milk Truck, #F586, $550 to	$625.00
Citroen Police Van, #556, $205 to	$230.00
Citroen 2-CV, #535, $145 to	$155.00
Coles Mobile Crane, #571, $75 to	$100.00
Coles Mobile Crane, #971, $115 to	$125.00
Coles 20-Ton Lorry, #972, mounted crane, yel & blk, $75 to	$85.00
Commando Jeep, #612, $95 to	$120.00
Commer Breakdown Lorry, #430, all colors other than tan & gr, $950 to	$1,300.00
Commer Breakdown Lorry, #430, tan & gr, $195 to	$225.00
Connaught Racer, #236, $170 to	$195.00
Continental Touring Coach, #953, $375 to	$410.00
Conveyancer Fork Lift Truck, #404, $50 to	$75.00
Convoy Army Truck, #687, $125 to	$150.00
Convoy Dumper, #382, $120 to	$145.00
Convoy Farm Truck, #381, $25 to	$35.00
Convoy Fire Rescue Truck, #384, $35 to	$45.00
Convoy Skip Truck, #380, $120 to	$145.00
Cooper-Bristol Racer, #233, $165 to	$185.00
Corvette Stingray, #221, $55 to	$65.00
Cosmic Zygon Patroller, #363, for Marks & Spencer, $230 to	$255.00
Coventry-Climax Fork Lift, #401, orange, $115 to	$140.00
Coventry-Climax Fork Lift, #401, red, $475 to	$550.00
Covered Truck, #584, $225 to	$250.00
Customized Corvette Stingray, #206, $130 to	$160.00

Customized Land Rover, #202, $55 to	$65.00
Customized Range Rover, #203, $35 to	$45.00
Daimler Ambulance, #254, $115 to	$125.00
David Brown Tractor, #305, $175 to	$225.00
Delahaye Fire Truck, #32D, $350 to	$400.00
DeSoto Diplomat, #545, gr, $190 to	$210.00
DeSoto Diplomat, #F545, orange, $155 to	$165.00
DeSoto Fireflite Sedan, #192, $165 to	$185.00
DeSoto USA Police Car, #258, $135 to	$165.00
Dinky Goods Train Set, #784, $150 to	$175.00
Dodge Royal Sedan, #191, $155 to	$165.00
Dodge Tipper, #414, all colors other than royal bl, $170 to	$195.00
Dodge Tipper, #414, royal bl, $190 to	$215.00
Dump Truck, #569, $225 to	$250.00
Dump Truck, #580, $250 to	$275.00
Dumper, #585, $250 to	$275.00
Dumper Truck, #382, $15 to	$25.00
Dunlop Double-Decker Bus, #290, $175 to	$225.00
Duple Luxury Coach, #296, $70 to	$90.00
Eagle Freighter, #359, $75 to	$125.00
Eaton Yale Tractor Shovel, #973, $75 to	$100.00
Electric Dairy Van, #490, Express Dairy, $200 to	$225.00
Electric Dairy Van, #491, NCB or Job Dairies, $200 to	$225.00
Elevator Loader, #564, $150 to	$175.00
Elevator Loader, #964, $175 to	$200.00
Emergency Rescue Paramedic Truck, #267, $75 to	$100.00
ERF Fire Tender, #266, $90 to	$110.00
Estafette Pickup, #563, $195 to	$220.00
Estate Car, #27D/344, $100 to	$125.00
Euclid Rear Dump Truck, #965, $125 to	$145.00
Farm Tractor, #22E, $430 to	$460.00
Farm Tractor & Trailer Set, #399, $250 to	$275.00
Ferrari, #204, $75 to	$85.00
Ferrari P5, #220, $85 to	$90.00
Ferrari 250 GT, #515, $140 to	$150.00
Ferrari 312/B2, #226, $85 to	$90.00
Fiat 1800 Familiate, #548, $150 to	$175.00
Fiat 2300 Pathe News Camera Car, #281, $175 to	$225.00
Fiat 2300 Station Wagon, #172, $140 to	$150.00
Fiat 850, #509, $175 to	$200.00

Field Marshall Tractor, #27N/301, $165 to	$185.00
Fire Engine, #555, w/extension ladder, $130 to	$150.00
Foden Army Truck, #668, $50 to	$70.00
Foden Diesel 8-Wheel, #501, $425 to	$450.00
Foden Dump Truck, #959, $300 to	$325.00
Foden Flat Truck, #503, 1st cab, $425 to	$475.00
Foden Flat Truck, #503, 2nd cab, $250 to	$300.00
Foden Mobilgas Tanker, #941, $725 to	$775.00
Foden Regent Tanker, #942, $525 to	$575.00
Foden Tipper, #432, $100 to	$125.00
Foden 8-Wheel Truck, #901, $450 to	$475.00
Ford Berth Caravan, #188, $135 to	$175.00
Ford Capri, #143, $85 to	$100.00
Ford Capri, #165, $125 to	$135.00
Ford Corsair, #169, $100 to	$125.00
Ford Cortina, #139, $140 to	$150.00
Ford Cortina MKII, #159, $125 to	$175.00
Ford D 800 Snow Plow, Tipper, #439, opening doors, $75 to	$100.00
Ford Escort, #168, $115 to	$125.00
Ford Fairlane, #148, gr, $200 to	$210.00
Ford Fairlane, #149, $120 to	$130.00
Ford Fordor, #170, dual colors, $275 to	$325.00
Ford Fordor, #170, solid colors, $180 to	$230.00
Ford Fordor US Army Staff Car, #170m, $340 to	$365.00
Ford GT Racing Car, #215, $60 to	$70.00
Ford Model T, #475, $165 to	$175.00
Ford Model T w/Santa Claus, #485, $140 to	$160.00
Ford Mustang, #161, $150 to	$175.00
Ford Panda Police Car, #270, $55 to	$65.00
Ford Police Car, #551, $145 to	$165.00
Ford Taunus, #551, Polizei, $145 to	$155.00
Ford Taunus, #559, $145 to	$155.00
Ford Thunderbird, #555, $225 to	$250.00
Ford Transit, #407, $115 to	$140.00
Ford Transit Ambulance, #274, $45 to	$55.00
Ford Transit Fire, #271, Falck, $160 to	$190.00
Ford Transit Fire, #286, $50 to	$75.00
Ford Transit Police Accident Unit, #269, $50 to	$75.00
Ford Transit Van, #416, 1,000,000 Transits, $210 to	$240.00
Ford Transit Van, #416 or #417, ea $115 to	$140.00
Ford Vedette Taxi, #24XT, $140 to	$160.00
Ford Zephyr, #162, $140 to	$160.00
Ford Zodiac MKIV, #164, bronze, $175 to	$225.00
Ford Zodiac MKIV, #164, silver, $150 to	$185.00
Ford Zodiac Police Car, #255, $100 to	$130.00
Ford 40-RV, #132, $130 to	$155.00
Fork Lift, #597, $200 to	$225.00
Gabriel's Model T Ford, #109, $90 to	$110.00
Glouster Javelin, #735, $65 to	$75.00
Goods Yard Crane, #752, $75 to	$100.00
Goods Yard Crane, #973, $200 to	$225.00
Guy Flat Truck, #513, $475 to	$525.00
Guy Flat Truck, #912, $475 to	$500.00
Guy Flat Truck w/Tailboard, #433, $225 to	$275.00
Guy Flat Truck w/Tailboard, #913, $625 to	$650.00
Guy Van, #914, Lyon's, $1,550 to	$1,650.00
Guy Warrior Flat Truck, #432, $450 to	$525.00

Dinky
Foden 14-Ton Tanker, #942, Regent, $500.00 to $525.00. (Photo courtesy Morphy Auctions)

Guy Warrior Snow Plow, #958, $290 to........................ $310.00
Guy Warrior Van, #920, Heinz, $3,000 to.................... $3,250.00
Guy 4-Ton Lorry, #911, $475 to................................. $500.00
Halesowen Harvest Tractor, #27B/320, $65 to...................$85.00
Hawker Executive Jet, #723, $70 to.............................$80.00
Hawker Harrier, #722, $80 to.................................. $100.00
Hawker Hunter, #736, $75 to...................................$85.00
Hawker Hurricane, #718, $125 to............................. $150.00
Hesketh Racing Car, #222, $70 to.............................$80.00
Hesketh Racing Car, #222, Olympus Camera, $135 to .. $160.00
Hillman Imp, #138, $145 to................................... $155.00
Hillman Minx, #175, $135 to.................................. $155.00
Hindle-Smart Electric Lorry, #421, $150 to $175.00
Holden Special Sedan, #196, $100 to......................... $125.00
Honest John Missile Erector, #655, $175 to.................. $200.00
Horse Box, #981, $125 to..................................... $150.00
Howitzer & Tractor, #695, $200 to............................ $225.00
Hudson Commodore Sedan, #171, cream & bl, $375 to . $425.00
Hudson Hornet Sedan, #174, $150 to......................... $175.00
Humber Hawk, #165, $140 to.................................. $160.00
Humber Hawk Police Car, #256, $150 to....................... $175.00
International Road Signs, #771, set of 12, $135 to......... $150.00
Jaguar E-Type, #120, $135 to................................. $145.00
Jaguar Mark 10, #142, $220 to............................... $230.00
Jaguar Motorway Police Car, #269, $125 to $150.00
Jaguar Type-D Racer, #238, $180 to.......................... $200.00
Jaguar XJS Coupe, #219, $100 to............................. $125.00
Jaguar XK120 Coupe, #157, $260 to $280.00
Johnson Dumper, #430, $55 to.................................$65.00
Johnson Road Sweeper, #449, $65 to $75.00
Klingon Battle Cruiser, #357, $80 to...........................$90.00
Ladder Truck, #568, $200 to.................................. $225.00
Lady Penelope's Fab 1, #100, luminous pk, $360 to........ $385.00
Lady Penelope's Fab 1, #100, pk, $240 to..................... $260.00
Lamborghini Marzal, #189, $55 to $65.00
Land Rover Bomb Disposal Unit, #604, $70 to $90.00
Land Rover Breakdown Crane, Falck, #442, $145 to $270.00
Land Rover Pickup, #344, $125 to $150.00
Lawn Mower, #386, $65 to.....................................$75.00
Leopard Anti-Aircraft Tank, #696, $175 to.................. $200.00
Leopard Recovery Tank, #699, $90 to.......................... $110.00
Leopard Tank, #692, $100 to.................................. $125.00
Leyland Cement Truck, #933, $300 to........................ $325.00
Leyland Cement Wagon, #533, $225 to........................ $300.00
Leyland Comet Cement Lorry, #419, $350 to................. $375.00
Leyland Comet Lorry, #417, $275 to $300.00
Leyland Comet Lorry, #531, all colors other than bl or brn, $275
   to... $300.00
Leyland Comet Lorry, #531, bl or brn, $650 to.............. $700.00
Leyland Comet Lorry, #531, orange & bl, $275 to......... $300.00
Leyland Comet Lorry, #931, all colors other than bl & brn, $275
   to... $300.00
Leyland Comet Lorry, #931, bl & brn, $525 to.............. $550.00
Leyland Comet Wagon w/Tailboard, #932, $275 to....... $300.00
Leyland Dump Truck, #925, $250 to $275.00
Leyland Forward Control Lorry, #420, $175 to.............. $200.00
Leyland Octopus Flat Truck, #935, $1,500 to $1,700.00
Leyland Octopus Tanker, Esso, #943, $500 to.................. $550.00

Dinky
• •
Guy Van, #514, Slumberland, $625.00 to $650.00.
(Photo courtesy Morphy Auctions)

Dinky
• •
Guy Van, #918, Ever Ready, $400.00 to
$450.00. (Photo courtesy Lloyd Ralston Toys)

Dinky
• •
Guy 4-Ton Lorry, #511, two-tone blue, $350.00
to $400.00. (Photo courtesy Morphy Auctions)

Leyland Octopus Wagon, #934, all colors other than bl & brn,
   $650 to.. $700.00
Leyland 384 Tractor, #308, $125 to............................. $150.00
Lincoln Continental, #170, $200 to............................ $225.00

Lincoln Premiere, #532, $275 to $300.00
Lockheed Shooting Star Fighter, #733, $35 to............$45.00
Lorry-Mounted Concrete Mixer, #960, $120 to............. $130.00
Lotus Europa, #218, $120 to $140.00
Lotus Formula 1 Racer, #225, $35 to.........................$45.00
Lotus Racer, #241, $55 to $65.00
Loudspeaker Van, #492, $180 to $200.00
Lunar Roving Vehicle, #355, $180 to...................... $215.00
Marrel Multi-Bucket Unit, #966, $175 to...................... $200.00
Maserati Sport 2000, #22, $200 to $225.00
Maserati Racer, #231, $175 to $225.00
Massey-Harris Tractor w/Driver, #300, $220 to $230.00
Matra 630, #200, $130 to $170.00
Medium Artillery Tractor, #689, $90 to $115.00
Mercedes Benz C111, #224, $45 to $55.00
Mercedes Benz Truck, #940, $175 to $200.00
Mercedes Benz Truck & Trailer, #917, $375 to $400.00
Mercedes Benz 190 SL, #526, $190 to $210.00
Mercedes Benz 220 SE, #186, $165 to $175.00
Mercedes Benz 250 SE, #160, $60 to $70.00
Mercedes Benz 600, #128, 1978, $40 to $50.00
Mercury Cougar, #174, $140 to $150.00
Merryweather Fire Engine, #250, $135 to $150.00
Merryweather Fire Engine, #255, $75 to $100.00
Mersey Tunnel Police Van, #255, $130 to.................. $140.00
Messerschmitt, #726, desert camouflage, $95 to $120.00
Messerschmitt, #726, gray & gr, $190 to $215.00
MG Midget, #102, $200 to $225.00
MG Midget, #108, $190 to $210.00
MG Midget, #129, $725 to $775.00
MGB, #113, $125 to $135.00
Michigan Tractor Dozer, #976, $75 to.......................$85.00
Mighty Antar Low Loader w/Propeller, #986, $500 to ... $525.00
Military Ambulance, #626, $65 to $85.00
Mini Clubman, #178, $120 to $145.00
Mini Klingon Cruiser, #802, $120 to...................... $160.00
Mini USS Enterprise, #801, $120 to $160.00
Missile Erector Vehicle w/Corporal Missile & Launching, Plat-
    form, #666, $250 to $275.00
MKI Corvette (boat), #671, $125 to $150.00
Mobile Anti-aircraft Gun, #690, $170 to...................... $195.00
Mobilgas Tanker, #440, $170 to $195.00
Morris Mini Minor, #183, $130 to......................... $160.00
Morris Mini Traveller, #197, dk gr & brn, $400 to $450.00
Morris Mini Traveller, #197, lime gr, $250 to $325.00

Morris Oxford, #159, dual colors, $275 to............... $325.00
Morris Oxford, #159, solid colors, $200 to..................... $225.00
Morris 1100, #140, $130 to............................... $155.00
Moto-Cart, #27G, $65 to...................................$85.00
Motor Patrol Boat, #675, $150 to $175.00
Muir-Hill Dumper, #962, $55 to............................$65.00
Muir-Hill Loader, #437, $55 to............................$65.00
Muir-Hill Loader & Trencher, #967, $55 to................$65.00
NASA Space Shuttle, #364, w/booster, $225 to............ $250.00
NASA Space Shuttle, #366, no booster, $200 to $220.00
Nash Rambler, #173, $135 to $145.00
Observation Coach, #29F/280, $115 to $130.00
Opel Commodore, #179, $150 to.......................... $175.00
Opel Kadett, #540, $150 to............................... $175.00
Opel Kapitan, #177, $130 to.............................. $150.00
Packard Clipper Sedan, #180, $175 to $200.00
Packard Convertible, #132, $155 to $165.00
Packard Super 8 Tourer, #39a, $150 to $175.00
Panhard Armoured Tank, #815, $245 to $270.00
Paramedic Truck, #267, $140 to $165.00
Parsley's Car, #477, $140 to $150.00
Petrol Tanker, #441, Castrol, $195 to.................... $220.00
Petrol Tanker, #442, Esso, $170 to $195.00
Petrol Tanker, #443, National Benzole, $170 to $195.00
Peugeot 203, #24, $190 to $210.00
Peugeot 403, #521, $130 to $140.00
Peugeot 404-U, #553, $190 to $210.00
Peugeot Van, #570, $200 to $225.00
Phantom II, #725, $95 to $120.00
Pink Panther, #354, $230 to $250.00
Plymouth Belvedere, #24D, $125 to $175.00
Plymouth Estate Car, #27F, $125 to $150.00
Plymouth Fury, #115, $80 to..............................$90.00
Plymouth Fury, #137, $115 to............................ $125.00
Plymouth Plaza, #178, bl w/wht roof, $250 to............ $275.00
Plymouth Plaza, #178, pk, gr or 2-tone bl, $145 to......... $155.00
Plymouth Police Racer, #244, $45 to $65.00
Plymouth Stock Car, #201, $40 to $50.00
Plymouth Taxi, #265, $130 to $150.00
Plymouth Taxi, #266, $140 to $160.00
Police Accident Unit, #287, $55 to $65.00
Police Land Rover, #277, $55 to $65.00
Police Mini Clubman, #255, $55 to $65.00
Police Range Rover, #254, $55 to $65.00
Pontiac Parisienne, #173, $75 to......................... $100.00
Porsche 356A Coupe, #182, cream, red or bl, $125 to ... $150.00
Prisoner Mini Moke, #106, $375 to........................ $425.00
Pullmore Car Transporter, #583, $150 to $175.00
Purdey's Triumph TR7, #112, $75 to...................... $100.00
RAC Patrol Mini Van, #273, $175 to $225.00
Racehorse Transporter, #979, $625 to $675.00
RAF Avro Vulcan Bomber, #749, $3,450 to $3,750.00
Rambler Station Wagon, #193, $130 to $150.00
Range Rover, #192, $50 to $75.00
Range Rover Ambulance, #268, $45 to $55.00
Range Rover Fire Chief, #195, $55 to......................$65.00
RCMP Patrol Car, #264, Cadillac or Fairlane, ea $150 to....$175.00
Renault Dauphine, #524, $100 to $130.00

Dinky
• • • • • • • • •
P1B Lightning, #737, NM, $50.00. (Photo courtesy www.serioustoyz.com)

Renault Floride, #543, $150 to $175.00
Renault Mail Car, #561, $175 to $200.00
Renault R8, #517, $125 to.. $150.00
Renault R16, #166, $100 to $125.00
Renault 16-TX, #538, $125 to $150.00
Renault 4L, #518, $100 to $125.00
Richier Road Roller, #F380, $140 to $160.00
Riley, #158, $125 to $150.00
Road Grader, #963, $65 to..$75.00
Rolls-Royce Phantom V, #198, $75 to $100.00
Rolls-Royce Silver Shadow, #158, $150 to $175.00
Routemaster Bus, #289, Esso, purple, $775 to $850.00
Routemaster Bus, #289, Esso, red, $150 to $175.00
Routemaster Bus, #289, Festival of London Stores, $225 to....$250.00
Routemaster Bus, #289, Madame Tussaud's, $175 to $200.00
Routemaster Bus, #289, Silver Jubilee, $125 to $150.00
Rover 3500 Sedan, #180, $50 to $75.00
Rover 75, #156, dual colors, $150 to $200.00
Rover 75, #156, solid colors, $100 to $125.00
Saab 96, #156, $100 to $125.00
Salev Crane, #F595, $165 to $185.00
Scorpion Tank, #690, $175 to $200.00
Service Station, #785, $385 to $420.00
Shell-BP Fuel Tanker, #944, $325 to $350.00
Shell-BP Fuel Tanker, #944, red wheels, $675 to........... $725.00
Silver Jubilee Bus, #297, $65 to $75.00
Simca Tipper Dump Truck, #33, $175 to $185.00
Simca Chambord, #24K, $140 to $160.00
Simca 100, #519, $150 to $175.00
Simca 1500, #523, $125 to $150.00
Singer Gazelle, #168, $175 to $225.00
Singer Vogue, #145, $90 to $110.00
Single-Decker Bus, #283, $120 to $145.00
Spitfire, #700, $225 to $250.00
Spitfire MKII, #741, $130 to... $140.00
Spitfire MKII RAF Jubilee, #700, $165 to...................... $190.00
SRN-6 Hovercraft, #290, $135 to $160.00
Standard Lamp, #755, single arm, $25 to $40.00
Standard Lamp, #756, dbl arm, $25 to $40.00
Standard Vanguard-Spats, #153, $100 to $125.00
Studebaker Golden Hawk, #169, $175 to $200.00
Studebaker Land Cruiser, #172, dual colors, $275 to...... $300.00
Studebaker Land Cruiser, #172, solid colors, $175 to $200.00
Sunbeam Alpine, #107, $170 to...................................... $180.00
Sunbeam Rapier, #166, $145 to....................................... $155.00
Superior Cadillac Ambulance, #288, $90 to $110.00
Superior Criterion Ambulance, #263, $120 to $130.00
Superior Criterion Ambulance, #277, $140 to $160.00
Tank Transporter, #660, $165 to..................................... $185.00
Tank Transporter & Tank, #698, $275 to........................ $300.00
Telephone Service Van, #261, $150 to............................ $200.00
Terex Dump Truck, #965, $275 to $300.00

Thames Flat Truck, #422, bright gr, $225 to $250.00
Thames Flat Truck, #422, dk gr or red, $170 to $195.00
Thunderbird II & IV, #101, $350 to................................ $375.00
Tractor-Trailer, McLean, #948, $400 to $425.00
Trailer, #428, lg, $115 to $140.00
Trailer, #429, $115 to $140.00
Trailer, #551, $75 to...$90.00
Trident Star Fighter, #362, $50 to $75.00
Triumph Herald, #189, $125 to $150.00
Triumph Spitfire, #114, $135 to $160.00
Triumph TR2, #105, $190 to $210.00
Triumph TR2, #111, $275 to $300.00
Triumph 1800 Saloon, #151, $175 to $225.00
Triumph 2000, #135, $90 to $115.00
Trojan Van, #451, Dunlop, $175 to $200.00
Trojan Van, #452, Chivers, $200 to $225.00
Trojan Van #455, Brooke Bond Tea, $175 to $200.00
Turntable Fire Escape, #956, Bedford, $200 to................$225.00
Turntable Fire Escape, #956, Berliet, $250 to $275.00
Twin-Engine Fighter, #731, $30 to $40.00
UNIC Boilot Car Transporter, #894, $400 to $425.00
UNIC Pipe-Line Transporter, #893, $450 to $475.00
Universal Jeep, #405, $115 to...$125.00
US Air Force F-4 Phantom II, #727, $825 to.....................$850.00
US Army Staff Car, #139a, $345 to $375.00
US Army T-42A, #712, $120 to $145.00
US Jeep & 105mm Howitzer, #615, $90 to $115.00
USA Police Car, #251, Pontiac, $130 to............................$150.00
USS Enterprise, #358, $140 to $150.00
USS Enterprise, #371, sm version, $130 to $140.00
Vanguard, #40E, $140 to $160.00
Vanwall Racer, #239, $120 to $140.00
Vauxhall Cresta, #164, $150 to $175.00
Vauxhall Victor, #141, $100 to $125.00
Vauxhall Victor Ambulance, #278, $140 to $160.00
Vauxhall Victor 101, #151, $90 to $110.00
Vauxhall Viva, #136, $100 to $125.00
Vega Major Luxury Coach, #952, $200 to.........................$240.00
Vega Major Luxury Coach, #954, no lights, $175 to $200.00
Vega Major Luxury Coach, #961, $350 to.........................$375.00
Vickers Viscount Airliner, BEA, #708, $180 to $200.00
Viking Airliner, #705, $65 to $75.00
Volvo Police Car, #243, $50 to $75.00
Volvo 1800S, #116, $115 to $125.00
Volvo 265 Estate Car, #122, $40 to $50.00
VW Porsche 914, #208, $70 to $90.00
VW 1300 Sedan, #129, $70 to $80.00
VW 1600 TL, #163, $120 to $130.00
Wayne School Bus, #949, $400 to.....................................$425.00
Westland Sikorsky Helicopter, #716, $120 to $130.00
Zero-Sen, #739, $100 to $125.00
Zygon Marauder, #368, $55 to $65.00

• **Disney** •

Through the magic of the silver screen, Walt Disney's characters have come to life, and it is virtually impossible to imagine a child growing up without the influence of his genius. As each classic film was introduced, toy manufacturers scurried to fill department store shelves with the dolls, games, battery-operated toys, and windups that carried the likeness of every member of its cast. This being the case, along with the heavy marketing by Disney of its merchandise and movies, suggests that people will always collect Disney. Demand will likely shift to reflect the changing eras, as collectors usually tend to seek out items associated with their childhood. This is where you will see prices move upward as demand increases due to the child now becoming an adult.

Vintage Disney will always remain a strong force, as the merchandise manufactured prior to 1950 was produced strictly for user enjoyment and not intended as collectibles. Many of these toys were abandoned by children after use along with the box. For this reason items in excellent or mint condition show the greatest demand. By having the box the value could possibly double.

The internet also has produced a change in value by making the supply increase dramatically and thereby lowering the value. Before the internet, a person would have to spend many hours or weeks in search of a particular collectible by spending much time at flea markets, antique shows, searching the classifieds. Today with a couple of clicks and by doing a search he would find not one but many to choose. Thus, condition and rarity are number one when it comes to evaluation.

For more information we recommend *Collector's Toy Yearbook, 100 Years of Great Toys,* and *Collecting Disneyana* by David Longest (both published by Collector Books); *Stern's Guide to Disney Collectibles* by Michael Stern (there are three in the series); *The Collector's Encyclopedia of Disneyana* by Michael Stern and David Longest; *Disneyana* by Cecil Munsey; *Disneyana* by Robert Heide and John Gilman; *Walt Disney's Mickey Mouse Memorabilia* by Hillier and Shine; *Tomart's Disneyana Update Magazine; Elmer's Price Guide to Toys* by Elmer Duellman; and *Official Price Guide to Disney Collectibles* by Ted Hake.

Advisor: Joel J. Cohen

See also Battery-Operated Toys; Books; Character and Promotional Drinking Glasses; Character Clocks and Watches; Coloring, Activity, and Paint Books; Comic Books; Fisher-Price; Games; Housewares; Lunch Boxes; Marx; Movie Posters and Lobby Cards; Pin-Back Buttons; Plastic Figures; Puzzles; Ramp Walkers; Records; View-Master and Tru-Vue; Western; Windup, Friction, and Other Mechanical Toys.

Disney
• • • • • • • • • •
Bank, Dopey, composition metal base, 7½", WDE, 1939, VG, $60.00. (Photo courtesy www.serioustoyz.com)

Disney
• •
Celluloid Toy, Mickey Mouse and Donald Duck in rowboat, 6" long, EX, $400.00. (Photo courtesy Morphy Auctions on LiveAuctioneers.com)

Bank, Ariel seated on mound of purple coral w/pk snail in her lap, vinyl, 7", NM+ $10.00

Bank, Donald Duck resting on elbows on suitcase emb 'To Walt Disney World,' silver-plated metal, 6", Leonard, EX+....$35.00

Bank, Dumbo seated upright w/trunk curled & looking upward, soft rubber, 7", Walter Jamieson Inc, 1950s-60s, NM.....$28.00

Bank, Jiminy Cricket standing holding closed umbrella at side of head, pnt compo, 6", Crown Mfg, 1940s, F $75.00

Bank, Ludwig Von Drake, hands clasped together as in deep thought, mc plastic, 10", 1961, VG $35.00

Bank, Mickey Mouse standing next to trunk, pnt compo, lock trap on base, 6", Crown Toy Co, 1938, EX $225.00

Bank, Mickey Mouse standing w/hands on hips, pnt aluminum, red shorts, yel hands & feet, 8", France, 1930s, EX $625.00

Bank, Pinocchio bust w/eyes looking up, lg bowtie, 10", Play Pal, 1970s, NM..$28.00

Bank, Three Little Pigs Bank, tin building w/lithoed image of Wolf trying to blow it down, 3", Chein, 1930s, EX $110.00

Bank, 2nd National Duck Bank, litho tin building w/Donald as teller & Mickey & Minnie customers, 6½", EX...........$150.00

Birthday Party Kit, Donald Duck on box, Rendoll Paper Co, 1940s, some use, incomplete o/w VGIB.........................$55.00

Bookrack, die-cut wood, Mickey Mouse & Minnie on ends holding up table top, shelf underneath, 25", VG................$600.00

Bookrack, die-cut wood w/Mickey Mouse & Minnie standing on pnt chairs holding up rod, shelf in between, 42", rare, EX......$1,035.00

Bookshelf, die-cut wood, Clarabelle the cow figures on ends supporting 5 shelves, 52", rare, EX................................$1,500.00

Bubble Bath Container, any character, Colgate-Palmolive, 1960s, NM, ea..$15.00

Bubble Bath Container, any Three Little Pigs character, Tubby Times, 1960s, rare, M $25.00

Bubble Buster, Mickey Mouse, complete w/Bubblets, EXIB.. $300.00

Calendar, 12-pg w/Disney color illustrations & brief stories, for Morrell Meats, 1942, Ketterlinus Litho Mfg, 20x8", EX+........$325.00

Camera, Mick-A-Matic, Child Guidance #880, 1960s, NMIB..$75.00

Candleholders, Mickey Mouse Birthday, set of 5, Cypress Novelty/WDE, 1930s, unopened, NMIB $75.00

Celluloid Toy, see also Figure or Figure Set

Celluloid Toy, Donald Duck figure standing on roly-poly base, 7", Japan, 1930s, EX $450.00

Celluloid Toy, Donald Duck in sleigh pulled by Pluto, 4" L, NM $250.00

Celluloid Toy, Donald Duck roly-poly figure w/coiled neck, bottom bill & closed eyes move, EX $700.00

Celluloid Toy, Mickey Mouse (5) marching over 4½" L curved bridge, NM $175.00

Celluloid Toy, Mickey Mouse (5 1" figures) 'walking' across 6½" platform on carved wood base, Japan, VG...................$125.00

Celluloid Toy, Mickey Mouse & Donald Duck integral figures dancing, 3½", Japan, prewar, EX $400.00

Chalkboard, Mickey Mouse, wood frame w/fold-out legs, top header w/Mickey graphics, 37x17", Falcon Toys, EX+ . $175.00

Charm Bracelet, Snow White & the Seven Dwarfs, 8 pnt metal figures on chain, 1930s, NMOC $115.00

Color-By-Number Oil Set, Disneyland, Hasbro #2195, 1950s, unused, NMIB $65.00

Colorforms, Aristocats, 1960s, MIB $25.00

Colorforms Cartoon Kit, 101 Dalmatians, 1961, NMIB....$15.00

Colorforms Sew-Ons, 'Mickey & Minnie in lots of swell new clothes,' 6 unused cards, 1970s, EXIB...............................$30.00

Comb & Brush Set, Mickey Mouse, blk colorful figural decal of Mickey on 4" brush, 6" comb, H Hughes Co, MIB $65.00

Disneyland Blocks Set, 15 colorful wooden blocks ea featuring 3 different characters, unused, MIB $75.00

Drum, litho tin, Mickey, Minnie & Pluto on yel w/bl & top & bottom, 6½" dia, Ohio Art, EX $100.00

Drum, litho tin, Mickey in top hat leading parade of characters w/instruments on grass, 6½" dia, Ohio Art, VG.............$75.00

Drum, Mickey Mouse parade graphics on cb w/tin top & bottom, 6" H, Happy Hak #601, England, EX........................... $150.00

Drum, Snow White & the Seven Dwarfs, litho tin, w/drumsticks, 11" dia, Chein, EX $125.00

Figure, Baloo (Jungle Book), stuffed rusty brn cloth w/beige felt chest, 2 bottom teeth, 6½", 1960s, NM.........................$30.00

Figure, Bashful (Snow White), stuffed felt w/wht furry beard, eyes looking up, 7", 1960s-70s, NM..............................$25.00

Figure, Bashful (Snow White), stuffed w/molded plastic face, furry beard, cloth outfit, 14", Knickerbocker, 1930s, EX $175.00

Figure, Beast (Beauty & the Beast), vinyl w/furry mane & tail, plush outfit, 15", Dakin, NRFB.......................................$35.00

Figure, Big Bad Wolf, blk fur w/colorful felt features, hat & pants, 18", Lars/Italy, EX+ $700.00

Figure, Chip 'N Dale, rubber, bendable, 4½", Just Toys, 1980s, NM, ea...$10.00

Figure, Cinderella, plush & vinyl, pk & wht, Gund, EX+ .$50.00

Figure, Daisy Duck, bisque, playing croquet, 4", WDP, 1970s, M..$28.00

Figure, Danny (lamb from 'So Dear to My Heart'), plush, blk w/ bl ribbon & button on chest, 1947, VG $175.00

Figure, Dewey, see also Huey, Louie & Dewey

Figure, Dewey (Donald's nephew), plush & vinyl, 'D' on bl sweater, 8", Applause, NM...$10.00

Figure, Dewey (Donald's nephew), vinyl, jtd, Dakin, 1970s, NM... $22.00

Disney
Figure, Bambi, vinyl, jointed legs, 8", Dakin, 1970s, EX+, $25.00. (Photo courtesy www. whatacharacter.com)

Disney
Figure, Captain Hook, vinyl, seated on green base, cloth jacket, hat, and scarf, AD Sutton, 1960s, MIB (Small World Figures), $75.00. (Photo courtesy www. whatacharacter.com)

Disney
Figure, Donald Duck, composition, in parade attire with cape and black fuzzy hat, 9", Knickerbocker/Cossack, 1935, NM, $1,065.00. (Photo courtesy Morphy Auctions on LiveAuctioneers.com)

Figure, Donald Duck, bisque, long-billed, standing w/head turned, hands at sides, 4½", Borgfeldt, VG+ $100.00

Figure, Donald Duck, bisque, long-billed, standing w/head turned, hands on hips, 1¾", WDE, 1930s, EX $65.00

Figure, Donald Duck, bisque, long-billed, standing w/head turned, jtd limbs, bl jacket & hat, 6", WDE, VG $125.00

Figure, Donald Duck, bisque, standing w/paintbrush in hand, head turned, 4", Japan #S1489, EX.............................. $300.00

Figure, Donald Duck, bisque, strutting w/chest out & head upturned, 3½", WDE, 1940s, EX+ $65.00

Figure, Donald Duck, bisque, tangled in garden hose, 3", WDP, 1970s, NM+...$20.00

Figure, Donald Duck, stuffed, Bavarian/Swiss outfit, 20", Lenci, 1950s, EX.. $150.00

Figure, Donald Duck, stuffed, Boy Scout outfit, 30", Lenci, 1950s, NM.. $550.00

Figure, Donald Duck, stuffed, drum major outfit, 16", Knickerbocker, 1930s, VG.. $500.00

Figure, Donald Duck, stuffed, long billed, sailor suit w/red tie, 18½", Knickerbocker, w/tag, VG $500.00

Figure, Donald Duck, stuffed, plush & felt, 9", Character Novelty, EX $200.00

Figure, Donald Duck, stuffed, plush w/vinyl face, open mouth, 9", Gund, 1950s, EX+ $50.00

Figure, Donald Duck, stuffed, velveteen/corduroy/felt, 4 wht plastic buttons on chest, 12", Character Novelty, 1940s, EX......$250.00

Figure, Donald Duck, stuffed, wht velvet w/silk-type beak & feet, bl sailor jacket, stern expression, 15", Krueger, EX...... $900.00

Figure, Donald Duck, vinyl, cloth jacket & hat, 8", Dakin, 1970s, w/orig hang tag, unused, M $25.00

Figure, Donald Duck, wood, pnt bead type w/ball-shaped hands, 3", Fun-E-Flex, 1930s, EX $375.00

Figure, Donald Duck, wood, pnt bead type w/fingered hands, 5", Fun-E-Flex, 1930s, EX+ $700.00

Figure, Dumbo, inflatable vinyl, sitting upright, 18", WDP, 1970s, MIP..$25.00

Figure, Dumbo, vinyl, cloth neck band, yel plastic hat, 7" L, Dakin, 1970s, orig hang tag, EX.........................$22.00

Figure, Dumbo, vinyl, felt eyes, googly eyes, 8½", Knickerbocker, 1941, EX $150.00

Figure, Eeyore, Gund, 1960s, 5", stuffed corduroy w/blk felt features, NM+ $35.00

Figure, Elmer the Elephant, celluloid, standing upright w/movable head/trunk/arms, emb/pnt outfit, 5", Japan, 1930s, EX.. $225.00

Figure, Ferdinand the Bull, chalkware, sitting upright, lg head, 8½", EX...$50.00

Figure, Ferdinand the Bull, compo, jtd legs, flower in mouth, 9" L, Ideal, VG.. $100.00

Figure, Ferdinand the Bull, compo, jtd legs, flower in mouth, 9" L, Ideal, VGIB.. $200.00

Figure, Flip the Frog, compo, jtd arms, Ub Iwerks, 1930s, EX.$600.00

Figure, Flower the Skunk (Bambi), plush, sitting upright, plastic eyes, red neck ribbon, 8", Knickerbocker, 1970, NM $15.00

Figure, Goofy, stuffed, orange shirt & pk vest, gr hat, 17", Mattel, EX $100.00

Figure, Goofy, stuffed, plush w/cloth overalls & shirt, 14", Schuco, 1950s, EX.. $250.00

Figure, Goofy, stuffed plush/felt, bl body w/orange turtleneck shirt, yel feet, 20", G $100.00

Figure, Goofy, vinyl, cloth outfit, vinyl hat & boots, 8", Dakin, 1970s, VG...$20.00

Figure, Grumpy (Snow White), stuffed, wht furry beard, felt features, vinyl belt, 7", 1960s-70s, EX+ $25.00

Figure, Gus (Cinderella), stuffed plush w/felt top & gr felt shoes, 15", Gund, NM+ $200.00

Figure, Huey, Dewey & Louie, vinyl, jtd limbs, 5", Dakin, 1970s, M, ea...$25.00

Figure, Jack Skellington & Zero, 9", Hasbro, 1993, MIB...$45.00

Figure, Jiminy Cricket, wood, pnt bead-type w/felt-brimmed hat & umbrella, 8½", Ideal, 1939, EX+............................ $550.00

Figure, Joe Carioca, stuffed, cloth eyes, stitched mouth, cloth outfit, hat & umbrella, 16", VG.................... $400.00

Figure, Lady (Lady & the Tramp), stuffed, sitting upright, corduroy-type cloth w/felt ears, 7", WDP, NM $75.00

Figure, Mary Poppins, plastic, synthetic hair, yel cloth dress, 12", Gund/WDP, 1960s, NM...............................$75.00

Figure, Mary Poppins, vinyl, jtd, purple dress, blk folded umbrella, 7", Multiple Toys/WDP, 1967, NM+IB $75.00

Figure, Mickey Mouse, bisque, standing next to Pluto, 5½", Borgfeldt, 1930s, EX+ $300.00

Figure, Mickey Mouse, celluloid, wht, blk & red, 8", VG ...$400.00

Figure, Mickey Mouse, compo, cowboy outfit w/double holster & guns, 10", Knickerbocker, EX $750.00

Figure, Mickey Mouse, compo, parade outfit w/cape & blk furry hat, 9", Knickerbocker/Cossack, 1930s, EX.............. $1,200.00

Figure, Mickey Mouse, stuffed, cloth w/plastic shoes, 12", Knickerbocker/Charlotte Clark, 1935, EX $750.00

Figure, Mickey Mouse, stuffed, cowboy outfit w/double holster & guns, red plastic shoes, 10", Knickerbocker, EX $900.00

Figure, Mickey Mouse, stuffed felt, English Guard, blk, red & gold outfit w/red compo shoes, 13", VG+ $850.00

Figure, Mickey Mouse, stuffed felt, printed toothy grin, red shorts, yel feet, 8½", Dean Rag/Borgfeldt, EX.............. $350.00

Figure, Mickey Mouse, stuffed felt, red shorts w/wht buttons, gold hands, orange plastic shoes, 11", Knickerbocker, EX .. $575.00

Figure, Mickey Mouse, stuffed felt, stuffed hands & feet, red shorts, 4½", Steiff, NOS... $700.00

Figure, Mickey Mouse, stuffed velvet, red shorts w/wht buttons, gold face & hands (up to elbows), orange shoes, 16", VG.. $575.00

Figure, Mickey Mouse, stuffed velvet, tan shorts w/wht buttons, gold hands, orange shoes, 9", Steiff, EX.................. $1,150.00

Disney

Figure, Jiminy Cricket, felt, 15", Lars/Italy, EX, $1,800.00. (Photo courtesy Morphy Auctions on LiveAuctioneers.com)

Disney

Figure, Jiminy Cricket, wood/composition, light green body with black felt hat and jacket, orange vest, 10", Knickerbocker, 1940, VG+, $650.00. (Photo courtesy Randy Inman Auctions)

Figure, Mickey Mouse, vinyl, cloth shorts & shirt, jtd, sm, Dakin, EX $22.00

Figure, Mickey Mouse, wood/compo bead-type, fingered hands, 7", Fun-E-Flex, 1930s, EX $500.00

Figure, Mickey Mouse, wood/compo bead type, lollipop hands, 7", Fun-E-Flex, 1930s, EX+ $675.00

Figure, Mickey Mouse, wood/compo bead-type, pancake hands, 5", Fun-E-Flex, 1930s, VG $300.00

Figure, Mickey Mouse, wood/compo bead-type, pancake hands, 7½", Cameo, VG rpnt $315.00

Figure, Mickey Mouse, wood/compo bead-type, pancake hands, 9½", Cameo, VG $400.00

Figure, Minnie Mouse, celluloid, movable head & arms, 5½", Borgfeldt, 1930s, EX $275.00

Figure, Minnie Mouse, stuffed felt, cloth skirt, hat w/flower on long stem, 6", Steiff, no tags, VG.............................. $1,100.00

Figure, Minnie Mouse, stuffed felt, cloth skirt & bloomers, jtd arms, 14", Nifty, VG $350.00

Figure, Minnie Mouse, stuffed felt, plush face, jtd limbs, wht skirt w/blk hem band, wht gloves, orange shoes, 10", EX. $1,400.00

Figure, Minnie Mouse, stuffed felt, toothy grin, blk shoe-button eyes, bl & wht cloth skirt, 8", Dean Rag/Borgfeldt, EX . $450.00

Figure, Minnie Mouse, vinyl, jtd, cloth dress, 8", Dakin, 1970s, NM+ $25.00

Figure, Minnie Mouse, wood bead-type body w/fingered hands, 7", Fun-E-Flex, VG $175.00

Figure, Peter Pan, plastic, jtd, sleep eyes, cloth outfit & hat, 9", Dutchess, 1950s, NM $125.00

Figure, Pinocchio, compo, cloth outfit & hat, 13", Ideal, EX ..$265.00

Figure, Pinocchio, compo, cloth outfit & hat, 20", Ideal, 1940s, EX+ $450.00

Figure, Pinocchio, stuffed plush roly-poly body w/vinyl face, cloth feet, 8", Gund, EX..$35.00

Figure, Pinocchio, stuffed plush w/vinyl face, lime gr & wht, 12", Gund, 1950s, EX+ $50.00

Figure, Pinocchio, vinyl, cloth outfit, plastic hat, jtd, 8", Dakin, w/orig hang tags, unused, M....................................$25.00

Figure, Pinocchio, wood bead-type body w/name on tummy, felt bowtie, 8", Ideal, 1930s-40s, EX+ $200.00

Figure, Pluto, stuffed plush, blonde fur w/blk ears, nose, tail & collar, 12", VG $100.00

Figure, Pluto, vinyl, jtd, 8x9" L, Dakin, 1970s, EX $20.00

Figure, Rabbit (Winnie the Pooh), stuffed ribbed cloth w/felt chest, 6½", Gund, 1960s, NM......................................$35.00

Figure, Shere Khan (Jungle Book), stuffed, 4x6", Gund, 1966, EX $30.00

Figure, Snow White, compo, pnt features, molded hair, cloth dress, 15", Knickerbocker, G $225.00

Figure, Snow White, compo, sleep eyes, swivel neck, synthetic hair, cloth gown, 15", Knickerbocker, VG.................... $335.00

Figure, Tigger, stuffed ribbed cloth w/felt features & stripes, long whiskers, 6" L, Sears, 1960s, NM+........................$35.00

Figure, Tinkerbell, plastic w/synthetic hair, gr velvet dress & gold wings, jtd, 8", Duchess, 1950s, EX+ $65.00

Figure, Tramp (Lady & the Tramp), stuffed plush 2-color roly-poly body w/vinyl face, musical chimes, 9", Gund, EX $40.00

Figure, Winnie the Pooh, stuffed plush w/red cloth top, standing waving, 6½", Gund, 1966, NM+....................................$35.00

Figure Set, Mickey & Minnie, bisque, he w/cane, she w/closed umbrella over arm, 4", Borgfeldt, 1930s, NMIB $250.00

Figure Set, Mickey & Minnie, bisque, Mickey & 2 Minnies playing musical instruments, 3½" ea, Borgfeldt, 1930s, EXIB........$300.00

Figure Set, Mickey & Minnie, bisque, yel shorts/skirt, red buttons/dots, red shoes, 2½", Borgfeldt, NMIB............... $375.00

Figure Set, Mickey & Minnie, celluloid, 6½", VG.......... $450.00

Figure Set, Mickey & Minnie, celluloid, string-jtd, Mickey in red shorts & Minnie in yel top hat, 5", EX+..................... $400.00

Figure Set, Mickey & Minnie, stuffed velvet, blk, red, orange & gold, 6", Steiff, EX, pr..$1,075.00

Figure Set, Mickey Mouse & Minnie, stuffed velvet, red, orange & gold, 11", Steiff, EX, pr $2,200.00

Figure Set, Mickey & Minnie, wood bead-type, Mickey & 2 Minnies, 5", Nifty, EXIB (1 shared box)..................... $925.00

Figure Set, Mickey Mouse, bisque, Baseball Stars, 3-pc, 3¼", Borgfeldt, 1930s, NMIB $650.00

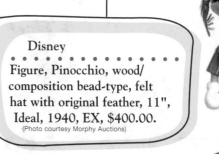

Disney
• • • • • • • • •
Figure Set, Mickey and Minnie, stuffed cloth, Mickey with tag, 18", Knickerbocker, EX, pair, $3,400.00. (Photo courtesy Morphy Auctions on LiveAuctioneers.com)

Disney
• • • • • • • • •
Figure Set, Pinocchio, six figures, bisque, Borgfeldt, EXIB, $400.00. (Photo courtesy Morphy Auctions on LiveAuctioneers.com)

Disney
• • • • • • • • •
Figure Set, Three Little Pigs, stuffed, jointed, 15", EX, $100.00. (Photo courtesy Morphy Auctions on LiveAuctioneers.com)

Disney
• • • • • • • • •
Fun-E-Flex Toy, Mickey Mouse, George Borgfeldt and Co., 7", with box, EX, $2,000.00.
(Photo courtesy Randy Inman Auctions)

Figure Set, Mickey Mouse, bisque, musician, 4-pc, 3½", Japan, EXIB $115.00

Figure Set, Mickey Mouse, Minnie & Pluto, bisque, Mickey & Pluto together, Minnie w/hands on hips, 5½", Japan, VG..........$350.00

Figure Set, Mickey Mouse, Minnie & Pluto, bisque, Mickey w/cane, Minnie w/closed umbrella & Pluto seated, 3", 4", EXIB...$200.00

Figure Set, Seven Dwarfs, stuffed cloth & vinyl, felt eyes, pnt mouths/cheeks, fur beards, 9", Gund, 1967, NM, ea $30.00

Figure Set, Snow White & the Seven Dwarfs, bisque, 2½" dwarfs & 3½" Snow White, Borgfeldt, 1938, EXIB $425.00

Figure Set, Snow White & the Seven Dwarfs, bisque, 13" Snow White, Borgfeldt, 1938, EXIB $400.00

Figure Set, Snow White & the Seven Dwarfs, celluloid, 6" ea, marked 'Foreign,' VGIB $600.00

Figure Set, Snow White & the Seven Dwarfs, compo, cloth outfits, 18" Snow White, Ideal, EXIB (individual boxes) $2,400.00

Figure Set, Snow White & the Seven Dwarfs, stuffed cloth/velvet, pnt features, wht yarn beards, 19" Snow White/14" dwarfs, VG+ $1,000.00

Figure Set, Snow White & the Seven Dwarfs, stuffed felt w/velvet outfits, 16" Snow White/10" dwarfs, Chad Valley, 1930s, NM $1,200.00

Figure Set, Snow White & the Seven Dwarfs, vinyl, 20" Snow White in purple & yel cloth dress, 7" all vinyl dwarfs, VGIB........ $175.00

Figure Set, Three Little Pigs, bisque, musicians, 3½", Borgfeldt, 1930s, NM+IB... $250.00

Figure Set, Three Little Pigs, rubber, Seiberling Rubber Co, 1934, VGIB $825.00

Figure Set, Three Little Pigs & the Big Bad Wolf, bisque, pig musicians & wolf watching, 3½", Borgfeldt, EX to NM $125.00

Flashlight, Minnie chasing Mickey around tree shown on hdl, EX $150.00

Fun-E-Flex, see also Figure, Mickey Mouse

Fun-E-Flex Toy, Mickey & Minnie on sled pulled by Pluto, wood, 10", EX... $750.00

Fun-E-Flex Toy, Pluto in doghouse, wood, EX $550.00

Game, Dopey's Bean Bag Game, Parker Bros, 1938, complete, VGIB.. $75.00

Game, Mickey Mouse Bagatelle, wood w/lg pnt image of Mickey, Chad Valley, 1930s, NMIB $400.00

Game, Mickey Mouse Bagatelle, 24", Marks Bros version, 1930s, VG... $250.00

Game, Mickey Mouse Party Game/Pin the Tail on Mickey, Marks Bros, 1930s, complete, EXIB.............................$50.00

Game, Mickey Mouse Portable Table Tennis, Commonwealth Toy & Novelty, 1930s, EXIB................................... $1,000.00

Game, Mickey Mouse Soldier Set, 8 cb Mickey target figures, w/cork gun, VGIB $275.00

Game, Mickey Mouse Target Game, bull's-eye target w/lg image of Mickey, complete w/toy gun, VGIB........................ $150.00

Game, Pin the Tail on Mickey, Marks Bros, 1935, complete, VGIB..$65.00

Game, Walt Disney's Own Game, Red Riding Hood, Parker Bros, 1930s, EXIB.. $225.00

Hair Bows, Ferdinand the Bull, rayon w/gold metal center, Stark Prod/WDP, 1938, EXOC...$50.00

Hand Puppet, Cinderella, full plush body w/vinyl head & slippers, Gund, 1950s, NM+..$75.00

Hand Puppet, Donald Duck, bl & wht checked cloth body w/red neck bow, vinyl head, Gund, 1950s, NM $50.00

Hand Puppet, Dopey, cloth body w/vinyl head, Gund, 1950s, NM $50.00

Hand Puppet, Dumbo, printed cloth body w/name on chest, gray vinyl head w/red hat, Gund, 1960s, NM $50.00

Hand Puppet, Ferdinand the Bull, cloth body w/compo head, 1938, NM $125.00

Hand Puppet, Goofy, cloth body w/red neck bow, vinyl head w/ red hat, open mouth, Gund, 1950s, NM $35.00

Hand Puppet, Jiminy Cricket, cloth body w/vinyl head, Gund, 1960s, NM $35.00

Hand Puppet, Mickey Mouse, print cloth body w/name across bottom, vinyl head, Korea, 1970s, EX+ $35.00

Hand Puppet, Peter Pan, cloth body w/vinyl head, Gund 1950s, EX $35.00

Hand Puppet, Robin Hood, brn & gr cloth body w/wht collar, vinyl head w/gr felt hat, MPI Toys, 1960s, NM+......... $125.00

Hand Puppet, Sleeping Beauty, cloth body w/vinyl head, eyes closed, Gund, 1950s, NM...$65.00

Hand Puppet, Tinkerbell, cloth body w/vinyl head, Gund, 1950s, NM $35.00

Hand Puppet, Wendy (Peter Pan), cloth body w/vinyl head, Gund, 1950s, NM...$50.00

Jack-in-the-Box, Donald Duck, compo head w/cloth body, wood box w/push-button action, Spear, 1940s, NM $200.00

Jack-in-the-Box, Winnie the Pooh, litho tin, Carnival, 1960s, EX $65.00

Jewelry, pendant, Tinkerbell figure applied to silver-tone metal ring, 1960s, EX $15.00

Kaleidoscope, cb & plastic w/litho images of Disney characters, 7" L, Straco, EX+ $20.00

Lamp, Dopey, ceramic figure, airbrushed details, printed scene on shade, 12", NM.. $150.00

Lamp, Mickey Mouse, ceramic figure in serape & sombrero playing mandolin, Mickey figure in lightbulb, 12", 1940s, VG $300.00

Lamp, Mickey Mouse, figural ceramic base w/Mickey as student on lamp shade, red, yel, bl & beige, 12", EX............... $325.00

Lamp, Mickey Mouse & Minnie, metal ball base w/Mickey pushing Minnie in wheelbarrow on paper shade, EX.......... $400.00

Lamp, Snow White, pnt plaster figure, printed scene on shade, 13½", LaMode/WDE, EX+.. $350.00

Lamp, Snow White & the Seven Dwarfs, dwarfs on base look up next to lamp w/Snow White in forest scene on shade, 12", EX $115.00

Lamp, Snow White & the Seven Dwarfs, figural ceramic dwarf base w/scene of Snow White baking pie on paper shade, 12", EX $400.00

Lantern, Donald Duck figure, plastic head, w/tin & plastic lantern body, tin arms & feet, b/o, 9", Linemar, VGIB..... $400.00

Light Set, Pinocchio Mazda Disneylights, 12-light strand w/character images on lamps, EXIB...$150.00

Magic Slate, Winnie the Pooh, Western Publishing, 1965, unused, NM+..$50.00

Marionette, Alice in Wonderland, working mouth, Hazell, 14", NM $125.00

Marionette, Cinderella, pnt features, synthetic hair, in evening gown, Pelham, 1960s, NMIB $100.00

Disney
Game, Mickey Mouse Circus Game, Marks Brothers, NMIB, $450.00. (Photo courtesy Morphy Auctions on LiveAuctioneers.com)

Disney
Game, Mickey Mouse Spin-N-Win, Northwestern Prod., 1940s, tin, EXIB, $40.00. (Photo courtesy www.serioustoyz.com)

Disney
Hand Puppet, Mickey Mouse, velvet, pie eyes, Steiff, G+, $200.00. (Photo courtesy Morphy Auctions on LiveAuctioneers.com)

Disney
Marionette, Mad Hatter, cloth outfit, Peter Puppet Playthings, EX, $100.00. (Photo courtesy www.gasolinealleyantiques.com)

Disney
• • • • • • • • • • • • • • •
Marionette, Wendy (Peter Pan), talker, composition head and arms, cloth outfit, Peter Puppet Playthings, NM, $125.00.

Disney
• • • • • • • • • • • • • •
Mechanical Toy, Climbing Mickey Mouse, cardboard figure climbs when string is pulled, 9", Dolly Toy Co., 1935, VGIB, $275.00. (Photo courtesy Morphy Auctions on LiveAuctioneers.com)

Disney
• • • • • • • • • • • • • •
Mickey Mouse Bus Lines, with Walt Disney Stars, Gong Bell, #125, pressed wood with tin, with box, 20", EXIB, $650.00. (Photo courtesy Morphy Auctions on LiveAuctioneers.com)

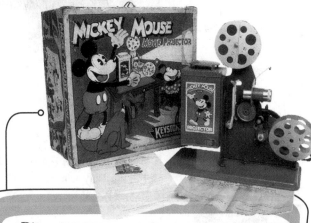

Disney
• • • • • • • • • • • • • • •
Mickey Mouse Movie Projector, with two reels, Keystone, 1934 – 1935, EXIB, $1,000.00.

Marionette, Donald Duck, wood w/cloth jacket, open bill, 9", Pelham, 1976, MIB $95.00

Marionette, Dopey, working mouth, Peter Puppet Playthings, EX+..$125.00

Marionette, Goofy, compo w/cloth outfit, 10", Pelham, 1979, MIB..$95.00

Marionette, Jiminy Cricket, 9½", Pelham, EX+IB..........$125.00

Marionette, Mickey Mouse, compo w/cloth outfit, 1940s, EX.$100.00

Marionette, Minnie Mouse, compo w/cloth outfit, 1940s, EX+ $150.00

Marionette, Peter Pan, ball-shaped head w/pnt features, dk hair, gr felt outfit, wht shoes, 11", Pelham, 1980s, MIB.......$100.00

Marionette Set, Mickey Mouse & Minnie, 12", Peter Puppet Playthings, 1950s, ea EXIB..................................... $225.00

Mechanical Toy, Goofy on tricycle, plastic, friction, 5", Gabriel, 1977, NM $20.00

Mechanical Toy, Happy Birthday Carousel, litho tin, 8" H, Ross Prod, NM+IB $150.00

Mechanical Toy, Mickey Mouse Scooter-Jockey, w/up plastic figure on 3-wheeled scooter, 6", Mavco, EXIB $150.00

Mechanical Toy, Pluto Twirly Tail Toy, w/up plastic figure w/wire tail, 5½", EXIB..$100.00

Mickey Mouse Club Crayons & Stencils, Transogram, 1950s, complete & unused, MIB (sealed) $50.00

Mickey Mouse Explorers Outfit, complete & unused, NMIB.$250.00

Mickey's & Minnie's Merry Moments Stencil Outfit, Spear's, 1930s, complete, EXIB.................................... $150.00

Mini Winders, Donald Duck, plastic w/up, 3", Durham/WDP, 1970s, MOC...$12.00

Mystery Art Set, Mickey Mouse, Dixon/WDE, unused, MIB.$400.00

Nodder, Sleepy (Snow White & the Seven Dwarfs), celluloid figure on rnd tin base, 6", Japan, VG $350.00

Paint Box, Snow White, litho tin, 4x9" L, WD/MM Ltd, 1930s, unused, EX...$50.00

Pencil Case, Peter Pan, cb snap front, sliding drawer, shows Peter looking in trunk full of pencils, 5x9", 1950s, EX............$25.00

Pencil Holder, Dopey figure standing on 'Disneyland' base, ceramic, 4", EX+ $45.00

Pencil Holder, Mickey Mouse w/hole in foot holds pencil, blk & wht pnt compo, w/orig mechanical pencil, 1930s, 7", VG+ $100.00

Pencil Set, Mickey Mouse, cb box w/snap closure, shows Mickey & friends, schoolhouse, 9" L, Japan, 1930s, EX+ $250.00

Pencil Sharpener, Donald Duck, celluloid figure w/hands on hips, 3", EX+ $150.00

Phonograph, Snow White & the Seven Dwarfs PortoFonic, litho tin, 14" dia, VG...$175.00

Pillow Cover, Mickey w/flower, blk, gray & yel on wht cloth, 17x15", Vogue Needlecraft, 1930s, EX $50.00

Pillow Cover, printed cloth w/Mickey & Minnie under Umbrella in the rain, 16" sq, Vogue Needlecraft, ca 1931, EX+ $75.00

Playing Cards, Bambi, Russell Mfg, Vol 4, 1946, NM (in sleeve box) $30.00

Playing Cards, Mickey Mouse, 1930s, 2½x2" cards, NMIB...$40.00

Playing Cards, Three Little Pigs Silly Symphonies, WDE, 1930s, complete deck of 52, NMIB...$65.00

Playset, Mickey Mouse Explorers Outfit, hat, ammo belt & holster w/cap gun, binoculars, pin-back button, LM Eddy, NM+IB $125.00

Pull Toy, Donald Duck Ice Cream Wagon, paper litho on wood, 9", Marx, EXIB.................$200.00

Pull Toy, Donald Duck on 4 wheels, plastic, 4", US Plastics, 1950s, MIP (header reads 'Toy Time...25¢')..................$45.00

Pull Toy, Mickey Mouse & Minnie Mouse on seesaw on 4-wheeled platform, pnt wood bead-type figures, PS base, 10" L, EX.................$2,000.00

Pull Toy, Mickey Mouse Circus, wood Mickey/Minnie figures perform trapeze on 4-wheeled base, 11", Borgfeldt, 1930s, VG.................$1,725.00

Pull Toy, Mickey Mouse in 'Express' cart pulled by Horace Horsecollar, wood cart w/pnt bead-type wood figures, EX.............$4,000.00

Pull Toy, Mickey Mouse pulling 2-wheeled bell, 13" L, N Hill Brass Co, 1936, EX.................$375.00

Pull Toy, Snow White on 2 lg wheels pulled by Doc & Dopey, paper-litho-on-wood figures, metal wheels, 14" L, EXIB .$325.00

Push Puppet, Bambi, Kohner, 1960s, M.................$65.00

Push Puppet, Donald Duck, Gabriel, 1977, NM+.............$35.00

Push Puppet, Donald Duck, Kohner, 1960s, M.................$50.00

Push Puppet, Donald Duck, Kohner, 1960s, Mini Puppet, Kohner, 1960s, M.................$50.00

Push Puppet, Donald Duck, Kohner, 1960s, Tricky Trapeze, NM+.................$25.00

Push Puppet, Donald Duck, Kohner, 1970s, Maxi Puppet, NM.$20.00

Push Puppet, Mickey Mouse, Kohner, 1960s, M.................$50.00

Ride-On Toy, Bambi, natural wood Bambi figure on colorful rocker base, 29", Gong Bell Toy Co, 1956, EX.................$50.00

Ride-On Toy, Mickey Mouse figure on all fours, red & blk w/ yel rockers & seat on Mickey's back, 34", Mengel Co, 1935, VG.................$225.00

Rocker Toy, Mickey Mouse die-cut figure on hands/knees attached to wooden rockers w/seat atop back & hand grips, 35", NM.................$500.00

Rubber Toy, Mickey Mouse Airmail Plane, 6" L, Sun Rubber, EX+.................$75.00

Scrapbook, Disneyland, 'For Pictures & Clippings,' 8½x11", WDP, 1950s, unused, EX+.................$50.00

Shoo-Fly Rocker, die-cut wood Donald Duck figures either side of seat, labeled 'Walt Disney's Donald Duck,' 32" L, EX......$725.00

Shoo-Fly Rocker, die-cut wood Mickey figure on 2 wood rockers w/ metal supports, seat on MM's back, Mengel, 35" L, VG....$285.00

Shoo-Fly Rocker, die-cut wood Mickeys either side of seat w/ curled metal supports, 32" L, WDP, 1940s, G.............$175.00

Shoo-Fly Rocker, Mickey Mouse floating on back in stream pnt on plywood, 35x16", c WDE, G.................$115.00

Shovel, litho tin w/wooden handle, laughing Minnie watches as Mickey hits Donald Duck w/snowball, 27", Ohio Art, EX..$285.00

Sled, Flexible Flyer No 80, 1935, natural wood w/Mickey's name & colorful Mickey & Minnie decal, metal runners, 32".......$250.00

Slinky Figure, Pluto, litho tin head & rear w/Slinky center body on wheels, 8", VG.................$200.00

Snap-Eeze Figures, 12 different on 1 card, Marx, MIB....$100.00

Soap, Mickey Mouse Toilet Soap, 3 unused bars, 2 Mickey's & 1 Clarabelle the Cow, Pictorial Prod, 1930s, MIB.............$65.00

Soap Dish, Ariel (Little Mermaid) holding wht scalloped seashell, vinyl, 6½", Avon, 1991, MIB.................$6.00

Soap Set, Aristocats, 3 character figures, 2½", Avon, 1970s, unused, MIB.................$25.00

Disney

Piano, Mickey Mouse, wood, articulated Mickey and Minnie figures dance when piano is played, 9x10x5", Marks Brothers, VG, $900.00. (Photo courtesy Morphy Auctions)

Disney

Push Puppet, Jiminy Cricket, mini-puppet, Kohner, 1960s, NM, $45.00. (Photo courtesy www.gasolinealleyantiques.com)

Soap Set, Snow White & the Seven Dwarfs, 7 bars ea w/ incised dwarf image & name, Kerk Guild/WDE 1938, unused, NM+IB.................$135.00

Spinikin, Mickey Mouse, plastic, 4", Kohner, 1960s, NM.................$400.00

Squeeze Toy, Donald Duck holding binoculars, 10½", Dell, 1960s, NM.................$50.00

Squeeze Toy, Donald Duck standing w/mouth open, side-glance eyes, 10½", Sun Rubber, 1950s, EX+.................$50.00

Squeeze Toy, Dumbo, 3x4", Kohner Squeez-Mees, 1960s-70s, MIP.................$40.00

Squeeze Toy, Huey, Dewey & Louie in a 'wooden' washtub, 5x6", Sun Rubber, 1950s, VG.................$35.00

Squeeze Toy, Peter Pan, 10", Sun Rubber, 1950s, EX.........$50.00

Tableware, Snow White & the Seven Dwarfs dish set, wht ceramic w/decals, gr trim, 19-pc w/gravy boat, tureen, etc, Japan, 1930s, EX.................$650.00

Tea Set, Donald Duck, wht china w/decals, red trim, 4 cups & saucers, teapot, sugar bowl & creamer, Occupied Japan, EXIB.................$200.00

Tea Set, Donald Duck (Children's Tea Set), litho tin, red & bl w/graphics, pot, tray, 2 cups & saucers, Ohio Art, NMIB.................$275.00

Tea Set, Mickey Mouse & Minnie/Helpmates, litho tin, 6-pc, Ohio Art, VG.................$135.00

Tea Set, Mickey Mouse & Minnie/Helpmates, litho tin, 10-pc, Ohio Art, EXIB.................$800.00

Tea Set, Mickey Mouse & Minnie, wht porc w/decaled blk, wht & red images, tan lustre trim, 17-pc, Japan, EXIB.......$100.00

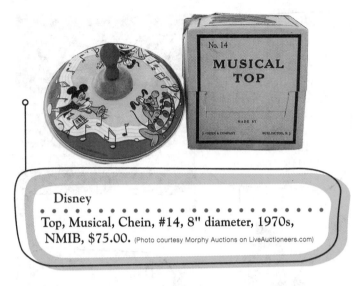

Disney
• •
Top, Musical, Chein, #14, 8" diameter, 1970s, NMIB, $75.00. (Photo courtesy Morphy Auctions on LiveAuctioneers.com)

Tea Set, child's, Snow White, Japan, ca 1937, litho ceramic tea set w/3 cups, saucers, & plates, teapot, gravy boat, sugar & creamer & cake serving plate, featuring Doc, Dopey, Sneezy, & Snow White, EX $325.00

Tea Set, Walt Disney characters, wht china w/gold trim, 15-pc, Beswick, NMIB $400.00

Tea Set, Walt Disney characters, wht china w/various decaled character scenes, 23-pc, Marx, EXIB $325.00

Tea Set, Who's Afraid of the Big Bad Wolf/Three Little Pigs, litho tin, scenes w/gr trim, 13-pc, Ohio Art, EX $400.00

Telephone, Mickey Mouse on candlestick-type phone, NN Hill Brass Co, 1930s, 9", EX $225.00

Toothbrush Holder, Donald Duck figures (2) arm-in-arm, bisque, 4½", early, EX $325.00

Toothbrush Holder, Mickey washing Pluto's face, bisque, 4½", EX $200.00

Top, Disney characters on parade, litho tin, Fretz Bueschel/WDE, 9" dia, EX $375.00

Toy Chest, Mickey Mouse, cb litho w/metal closure & corner support strips, bl, orange, yel & wht graphics, 12x28", VG .. $200.00

Tray, Lady & the Tramp, litho tin w/illustrated 'spaghetti' scene, 13x17", EX $50.00

Tricky Trike, Mickey Mouse, Gabriel, 1977, NRFC $30.00

Wacky Heads (Puppet), Roger Rabbit, foam rubber head, fingers manipulate facial expressions, Applause, 1987, unused, MIP . $10.00

Weather Forecaster, plastic house labeled Mickey Mouse Weather House, 6", post WWII, EXIB $100.00

Whistle, Mickey Mouse, litho tin figure waving, 2½", EX... $135.00

Whistle, Snow White & the Seven Dwarfs, Japan, litho tin w/ images of all, 2½", VG $75.00

• • • • • • • • • • • • • • **Dollhouse Furniture** • • • • • • • • • • • • • • •

Back in the 1940s and 1950s, little girls often spent hour after hour with their dollhouses, keeping house for their imaginary families, cooking on tiny stoves (that sometimes came with scaled-to-fit pots and pans), serving meals in lovely dining rooms, making beds, and rearranging furniture, most of which was plastic, much of which was made by Renwal, Ideal, Marx, Irwin, and Plasco. Jaydon made plastic furniture as well but sadly never marked it. Tootsietoy produced metal items, many in boxed sets.

Of all of these manufacturers, Renwal and Ideal are considered the most collectible. Renwal's furniture was usually detailed; some pieces had moving parts. Many were made in more than one color, often brightened with decals. Besides the furniture, they made accessory items as well as 'dollhouse' dolls of the whole family. Ideal's Petite Princess line was packaged in sets with wonderful detail, accessorized down to the perfume bottles on the top of the vanity. Ideal furniture and parts are numbered, always with an 'I' prefix. Most Renwal pieces are also numbered.

Advisor: Judith Mosholder

Acme/Thomas, carriage, any color combo, ea $6.00

Acme/Thomas, doll, baby, sucking thumb, hard plastic, pk, Thomas, 1¼" $3.00

Acme/Thomas, doll, baby, w/diaper, Thomas, 1⅛" to 2", any $2 to $4.00

Acme/Thomas, doll, Dutch girl, flesh-colored, Thomas, 2⅜" $5.00

Acme/Thomas, doll, girl, hard plastic, yel dress, Thomas, 3½" . $20.00

Acme/Thomas, doll, little brother, w/raised hand, Thomas.. $3.00

Acme/Thomas, hammock, bl w/red supports $20.00

Acme/Thomas, rocker, yel w/gr or yel w/red, ea.................. $4.00

Acme/Thomas, seesaw, bl w/yel horseheads.......................... $6.00

Acme/Thomas, stroller, any color combo.............................. $6.00

Acme/Thomas, swing, single, red w/gr seat & yel 'ropes'... $15.00

Acme/Thomas, Tommy horse, gr w/wht seat $12.00

Allied/Pyro, bed, red w/wht spread..................................... $10.00

Allied/Pyro, chair, dining, pk, red or wht, ea $3.00

Allied/Pyro, chair, kitchen, gray, pk or red, unmk, ea.......... $3.00

Allied/Pyro, cupboard, corner, aqua $8.00

Allied/Pyro, hutch, aqua or red $4.00

Allied/Pyro, night stand, yel... $4.00

Allied/Pyro, piano, blk (unmk), or lt bl (Allied), ea $5.00

Allied/Pyro, radio, floor; yel... $5.00

Allied/Pyro, sofa, aqua or lt bl, unmk................................. $5.00

Allied/Pyro, sofa, yel, unmk... $8.00

Allied/Pyro, stove, wht, unmk.. $4.00

Allied/Pyro, table, kitchen, wht $4.00

Allied/Pyro, tub, lt bl.. $4.00

Allied/Pyro, vanity, aqua, bl or pk, ea $4.00

Arcade, bath set (tub, sink, toilet), pnt CI, wht, VG pnt.. $55.00

Arcade, bathtub, pnt CI, ivory $125.00

Arcade, breakfast nook set (Curtis), 3-pc (table & 2 benches), pnt CI, wht, G $100.00

Arcade, chair, bedroom, pnt CI, dk gr, VG pnt $95.00

Arcade, cupboard (Boone), pnt CI, wht, VG $90.00

Arcade, dresser, arched mirror, 4-drawer, 4-footed, gr, G . $220.00

Arcade, icebox (Leonard), pnt CI, wht, VG $185.00

Fisher-Price, barbecue grill & patio lounge chair, #272, 1983-84, MOC $4.50

Fisher-Price, chair, kitchen, wht & yel.................................$2.00
Fisher-Price, chair, kitchen, wht w/marbleized seat $1.00
Fisher-Price, chair dining, brn w/tan seat............................$2.00
Fisher-Price, cradle, wht $5.00
Fisher-Price, doll family, 1983-85, any, MOC, ea $3.00
Fisher-Price, dresser w/mirror, wht $5.00
Fisher-Price, refrigerator, wht w/yel..................................$5.00
Fisher-Price, sink, kitchen, yel, wht & orange $5.00
Fisher-Price, stove w/hood, yel...$5.00
Fisher-Price, table, kitchen, wht w/red marbleized top $3.00
Fisher-Price, toilet/vanity, bright gr w/wht trim.................$10.00
Ideal, bench, lawn, bl $18.00
Ideal, bird bath, marbleized ivory $18.00
Ideal, buffet, dk brn or dk marbleized brn, ea....................$10.00
Ideal, buffet, red..$15.00
Ideal, chair, dining room, brn w/bl seat, dk marbleized maroon w/
    bl or yel seat, ea..$10.00
Ideal, chair, kitchen, ivory w/various seat colors, ea $5.00
Ideal, chair, sq back, bl swirl, bright gr swirl or med gr swirl, all
    w/brn bases, ea..$15.00
Ideal, chaise lounge, wht $18.00
Ideal, china closet, dk brn swirl or dk marbleized maroon, ea ..$15.00
Ideal, china closet, red..$20.00
Ideal, clothes washer, front load, wht...............................$22.00
Ideal, dishwasher, w/lettering $20.00
Ideal, doll, baby, pnt diaper...$10.00
Ideal, hamper, bl $6.00
Ideal, hamper, ivory $4.00
Ideal, highboy, ivory w/bl..$18.00
Ideal, highchair, collapsible, bl or pk, ea $25.00
Ideal, iron, electric, wht w/blk...$18.00
Ideal, piano w/bench, caramel swirl $35.00
Ideal, playpen, bl w/pk bottom or pk w/bl bottom, ea........$25.00
Ideal, potty chair, pk, complete $15.00
Ideal, radiator..$25.00
Ideal, radio, floor, brn or dk marbleized maroon.................$10.00
Ideal, refrigerator, Deluxe, wht w/blk, opening door, cb back-
    ing $30.00
Ideal, refrigerator, ivory w/blk...$15.00
Ideal, secretary, dk marbelized maroon, complete..............$40.00
Ideal, sewing machine, dk marbleized brn or dk marbleized
    maroon, ea..$20.00

Ideal, shopping cart, bl w/wht baskets, wht w/red or bl baskets,
    ea...$40.00
Ideal, sink, bathroom, bl w/yel or ivory w/blk, ea................$8.00
Ideal, sink, kitchen, ivory w/blk.......................................$15.00
Ideal, sofa, med bl, med gr, med gr swirl or orange-red swirl, all
    w/brn bases, ea..$22.00
Ideal, stool, vanity, ivory w/bl seat....................................$6.00
Ideal, stove, ivory w/blk..$15.00
Ideal, table, coffee, brn or dk marbleized maroon $10.00
Ideal, table, end/nightstand, brn or dk marbleized maroon, ea..$6.00
Ideal, table, kitchen, ivory w/blk..$6.00
Ideal, table, picnic, gr...$20.00
Ideal, table, umbrella, yel w/red umbrella & red pole $25.00
Ideal, television, dog picture, yel detail.............................$45.00
Ideal, toilet, bl w/yel hdl..$10.00
Ideal, toilet, ivory w/blk hdl..$20.00
Ideal, tub, corner, bl w/yel $18.00
Ideal, tub, ivory w/blk..$10.00
Ideal, vacuum cleaner, no bag, bl w/red or yel or gr w/red-yel,
    ea...$20.00
Ideal, vanity w/mirror, dk marbelized maroon, mirror wear...$12.00
Ideal, vanity w/mirror, ivory w/bl, mirror good $18.00
Ideal Petite Princess, bed, #4416-4, bl or pk, complete, w/orig
    box...$30.00
Ideal Petite Princess, books & bookends, Heirloom #4428-9,
    ea...$5.00
Ideal Petite Princess, boudoir chaise lounge, #4408-1, pk,
    MIB...$25.00
Ideal Petite Princess, buffet, Royal #4419-8, complete........$4.00
Ideal Petite Princess, cabinet, Treasure Trove #4418-0......$10.00
Ideal Petite Princess, cabinet, Treasure Trove #4418-09, in orig
    box...$12.00
Ideal Petite Princess, cabinet, Treasure Trove #4479-2, in orig
    box...$12.00
Ideal Petite Princess, candelabra, Fantasia #4438-8, in orig
    box...$22.00
Ideal Petite Princess, candelabra, Royal #4439-6, in orig box ...$15.00
Ideal Petite Princess, chair, dining, Host #4413-1, w/orig box ..$17.00
Ideal Petite Princess, chair, drum, Salon #4411-5, gold or gr, w/
    orig box, ea...$17.00
Ideal Petite Princess, chair, guest dining, #4414-9, in orig box..$17.00
Ideal Petite Princess, chair, host dining, #4474-3, in orig box..$17.00
Ideal Petite Princess, chair, hostess dining, #4415-6............$8.00

Ideal Petite Princess, chair, wing, Salon #4410-7, w/orig box......$15.00

Ideal Petite Princess, chair & ottoman, occasional, #4412-3, lt brn, w/orig box $22.00

Ideal Petite Princess, chest, Palace #4420-6.....................$5.00

Ideal Petite Princess, chest, Palace #4420-6, in orig box ...$17.00

Ideal Petite Princess, clock, grandfather, #4423-0, w/folding screen, in orig box $20.00

Ideal Petite Princess, doll family, father, mother, girl, boy, #9170-5, MIB..$75.00

Ideal Petite Princess, dressing table, #4417-2, complete....$20.00

Ideal Petite Princess, hearthplace, Regency #4422-2, complete..$4.00

Ideal Petite Princess, hearthplace, Regency, #4422-2, complete, in orig box $18.00

Ideal Petite Princess, lamp, table, Heirloom #4428-9 ....$5.00

Ideal Petite Princess, piano & bench, grand, Royal #4425-5.....$25.00

Ideal Petite Princess, piano & bench, grand, Royal #4425-5, in orig box...$30.00

Ideal Petite Princess, planter, Salon #4440-4.....................$15.00

Ideal Petite Princess, planter, Salon #9710-5, in orig box .$18.00

Ideal Petite Princess, sofa, #4407-3, beige/gold, in orig box ...$25.00

Ideal Petite Princess, table, coffee, Salon #4433-9, w/assorted accessories, in orig box $25.00

Ideal Petite Princess, table, dining room, #4421-4.............$15.00

Ideal Petite Princess, table, lyre, #4426-3..........................$5.00

Ideal Petite Princess, table, occasional, #4437-0..................$5.00

Ideal Petite Princess, table, Palace #4431-3 ....$5.00

Ideal Petite Princess, table set, #4426-3, complete $15.00

Ideal Petite Princess, table set, Heirloom, #4428-99, complete in orig box...$27.00

Ideal Petite Princess, table set, occasional, #4437-0, complete, in orig box...$27.00

Ideal Petite Princess, table set, Palace #4431-3, complete.$20.00

Ideal Petite Princess, table set, pedestal, #4427-1, complete, in orig box...$18.00

Ideal Petite Princess, table set, Salon #4433-9, complete, in orig box...$27.00

Ideal Petite Princess, table set, tier, #4429-7, complete, in orig box...$18.00

Ideal Petite Princess, tea cart, rolling, #4424-8, complete, in orig box...$20.00

Ideal Petite Princess, telephone, Fantasy #4432-1 ....$8.00

Ideal Petite Princess, telephone set, Fantasy #4432-1, complete, in orig box $20.00

Ideal Princess, Buddha, #4437-0, metal.............................$15.00

Ideal Princess, clock, grandfather, #4423-0 ....$10.00

Ideal Young Decorator, bathtub, corner, bl w/yel..............$35.00

Ideal Young Decorator, carpet sweeper, 2 rollers, red w/bl hdl...$30.00

Ideal Young Decorator, chair, kitchen, wht.......................$10.00

Ideal Young Decorator, china coset, dk marbleized maroon...$25.00

Ideal Young Decorator, night stand, dk marbleized maroon...$15.00

Ideal Young Decorator, playpen, pk.................................$45.00

Ideal Young Decorator, sofa, right corner section, rose $12.00

Ideal Young Decorator, sofa, sm middle section, rose.........$12.00

Ideal Young Decorator, stove, wht....................................$55.00

Ideal Young Decurator, table, coffee, dk marbelized maroon..$18.00

Ideal Young Decorator, table, kitchen, wht.......................$10.00

Ideal Young Decorator, television, complete.....................$45.00

Ideal Young Decorator, television, no cb backing..............$25.00

Irwin, broom, any color, ea $5.00

Irwin, clothes basket, bright yel, 3" across.........................$4.00

Irwin, dustpan, any color $4.00

Irwin, hoe, orange $3.00

Irwin, pail, dk bl or gr $4.00

Irwin, shovel, gr or orange, ea $3.00

Irwin, spade, bright yel...$3.00

Irwin, watering can, orange $10.00

Irwin Interior Decorator, bathtub, lt gr $5.00

Irwin Interior Decorator, plate, orange..............................$3.00

Irwin Interior Decorator, refrigerator, under-the-counter, yel...$3.00

Irwin Interior Decorator, refrigerator, yel $5.00

Irwin Interior Decorator, toilet, lt gr $5.00

Irwin Interior Decorator, toilet, yel w/chrome $5.00

Jaydon, bed w/spread, bl spread $15.00

Jaydon, chair, bedroom, bl or pk, ea $6.00

Jaydon, chair, living room, ivory w/brn base $8.00

Jaydon, chest w/2 opening drawers, reddish brn................$5.00

Jaydon, cupboard, corner, red $5.00

Jaydon, hamper, red $5.00

Jaydon, lamp, table, ivory w/red shade or red shade, ea $15.00

Jaydon, nightstand, pk $4.00

Jaydon, piano, reddish brn swirl $12.00

Jaydon, piano bench, reddish brn swirl $3.00

Jaydon, refrigerator, ivory w/blk......................................$15.00

Jaydon, sink, bathroom, ivory..$10.00

Jaydon, sink, kitchen, ivory w/blk $15.00

Jaydon, table, dining, reddish brn swirl $5.00

Jaydon, toilet, ivory w/red lid $10.00

Kilgore, lawnmower, reel-type, 3¾" L, EX+ $525.00

Kilgore, Sally Ann Bathroom Set, w/tub, sink, toilet, stool, laundry basket & bisque baby, VG+IB..........................$715.00

Kilgore, Sally Ann Household (Laundry) Set, CI, NOS . $715.00

Kilgore, Sally Ann Playground Set, 5-pc set, CI w/NP wheels, NOS $1,045.00

Lundby, bathroom set w/tub, sink & toilet, gr tile $30.00

Lundby, bed, bl & wht, no pillows.....................................$10.00

Lundby, chair, dining, wht w/gold-striped fabric seat...........$5.00

Lundby, chair, kitchen, red & wht checked seat..................$4.00

Lundby, chair, wht & gold striped fabric $8.00

Dollhouse Furniture
• • • • • • • • • • • • • • •
Kilgore, Sally Ann Dining Room Set, with table and four chairs, sideboard, and cabinet, painted cast iron, EX+IB, $1,045.00. (Photo courtesy Randy Inman Auctions)

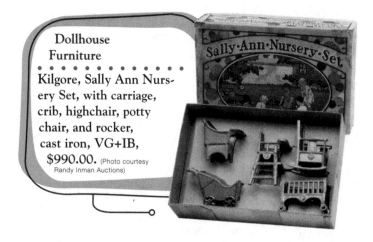

Dollhouse Furniture

Kilgore, Sally Ann Nursery Set, with carriage, crib, highchair, potty chair, and rocker, cast iron, VG+IB, **$990.00.** (Photo courtesy Randy Inman Auctions)

Lundby, dishwasher, red-patterned back splash $8.00
Lundby, fireplace $15.00
Lundby, fireplace, corner, w/logs, wht $15.00
Lundby, garden table & 2 chairs, wood w/metal $20.00
Lundby, light, hanging, red w/gold trim $8.00
Lundby, living room set, Royal, MIP $40.00
Lundby, mirror, wht w/gold trim $5.00
Lundby, night table, 2 drawers, wht $5.00
Lundby, refrigerator, opening door, wht w/blk base $8.00
Lundby, sink, red-patterned backsplash $8.00
Lundby, sofa, wht w/gold striped fabric $10.00
Lundby, stove, red-patterned backsplash $8.00
Lundby, table, dining, wht top $8.00
Lundby, table, kitchen, red $6.00
Lundby, table, living room, walnut $12.00
Marklin, bed, brass w/spindle headboard & footboard, wire springs, cloth bedding, 8¼", VG $330.00
Marklin, bedroom set, 3-pc ormolu w/bed, free-standing full-length mirror, chair, red silk bedding & chair upholstery $935.00
Marklin, fireplace, pnt & copper-plated tin, cherub decor, w/ accessories, 5½", VG+ $350.00
Marklin, settee, 2 chairs & 2 flowerpots, ormolu w/rose satin upholstery, wht ceramic planters w/ormolu flowers, VG $650.00
Marx, hard plastic, ½" scale, any pc except barbecue, curved sofa, jukebox or milk bar, any color, ea $3 to $5.00
Marx, hard plastic, ½" scale, curved sofa or milk bar, bright yel or red, ea $15 to $18.00
Marx, hard plastic, ½" scale, jukebox, bright yel or red, ea .$20.00
Marx, hard plastic, ¾" scale, any pc except iron, swimming pool or upright sweeper, ea $3 to................................$6.00
Marx, hard plastic, ¾" scale, iron, wht $8.00
Marx, hard plastic, ¾" scale, swimming pool (red), upright sweeper (wht), ea $10.00
Marx, soft plastic, ¾" scale, any pc except floor lamp, ea $3 to ... $4.00
Marx, soft plastic, ¾" scale, floor lamp, bright yel or lt yel, ea ..$6.00
Marx Little Hostess, chair, bedroom occasional, ivory w/hot pk seat $8.00
Marx Little Hostess, chair, dining, brn w/red seats, armless, set of 6, boxed $25.00
Marx Little Hostess, chair, occasional, yel $8.00
Marx Little Hostess, chair, occasional, yel, boxed $10.00
Marx Little Hostess, chair, rocking, reddish brn $12.00
Marx Little Hostess, chair, wingback, red, boxed..............$10.00

Marx Little Hostess, chaise, ivory w/bright pk $12.00
Marx Little Hostess, chest, block front, ivory $8.00
Marx Little Hostess, chest, block front, rust or ivory, ea....$12.00
Marx Little Hostess, clock, grandfather, red..................$18.00
Marx Little Hostess, dresser, dbl, ivory......................$8.00
Marx Little Hostess, fireplace, ivory $20.00
Marx Little Hostess, lowboy, red $12.00
Marx Little Hostess, mirror, gilded, boxed $6.00
Marx Little Hostess, mirror, wall $5.00
Marx Little Hostess, refrigerator, avocado....................$25.00
Marx Little Hostess, screen, folding, blk, boxed $10.00
Marx Little Hostess, sideboard, brn...........................$12.00
Marx Little Hostess, sofa, turq................................$8.00
Marx Little Hostess, sofa, turq, boxed $15.00
Marx Little Hostess, table, gate-leg, lt brn, boxed $8.00
Marx Little Hostess, table, gate-leg, rust $15.00
Marx Little Hostess, table, tilt-top, blk $12.00
Marx Little Hostess, table coffee, rnd, brn $8.00
Mattel Littles, armoire $8.00
Mattel Littles, doll, Belinda, w/4 chairs & pop-up room setting $25.00
Mattel Littles, doll, Hedy, w/sofa & pop-up room setting..$22.00
Mattel Littles, doll set, Littles Family (Mr & Mrs & baby)...$22.00
Mattel Littles, table, drop-leaf, w/4 plates & cups $15.00
Mattle Littles, sofa $5.00
Plasco, bathroom set, complete, in orig box w/insert & floor plan $50.00
Plasco, bathtub, any color, ea $4.00
Plasco, bed, brn headboard, yel spread $3.00
Plasco, bedspread, any color, ea..............................$2.00
Plasco, buffet, any color, ea.................................$4.00
Plasco, chair, dining, tan w/paper seat cover.................$4.00
Plasco, chair, dining (w/ or w/o arms), brn or marbelized brn, ea $3.00
Plasco, chair, kitchen, any color, ea.........................$2.00
Plasco, chair, living room, no-base style, dk brn or yel, ea...$3.00
Plasco, chair, living room, w/base, bright gr, lt gr or mauve, ea .$15.00
Plasco, chair, patio, bl w/ivory legs.........................$3.00
Plasco, clock, grandfather, lt brn swirl or dk brn, cb face, ea..$15.00
Plasco, highboy, tan $8.00
Plasco, kitchen counter, no-base style, pk....................$3.00

Dollhouse Furniture

Marx, Series 2000 Breezeway Weathervane, unused, MIB (sealed), $350.00. (Photo courtesy Morphy Auctions on LiveAuctioneers.com)

Plasco, nightstand, brn, med marbleized brn or tan, ea $3.00
Plasco, refrigerator, no-base style, pk or wht, ea.................$3.00
Plasco, refrigerator, wht w/bl base................................$5.00
Plasco, sink, kitchen, no-base style, lt gr w/rose trim, pk or wht, ea $3.00
Plasco, sofa, no-base style, any color, ea..............................$3.00
Plasco, stove, no-base style, pk...$3.00
Plasco, stove, wht w/bl base..$5.00
Plasco, table, coffee, brn, med marbelized brn or tan, ea $3.00
Plasco, table, coffee, tan w/leather top................................$5.00
Plasco, table, dining room side, tan w/yel.........................$4.00
Plasco, table, kitchen, pk..$5.00
Plasco, table, patio (sm), bl w/ivory legs $4.00
Plasco, table, umbrella, bl w/ivory, complete $15.00
Plasco, toilet, turq w/wht...$8.00
Plasco, vanity, w/ or w/o mirror, any color, ea $5.00
Plasco, vanity bench, any color, ea.....................................$5.00
Pyro, see Allied Pyro
Reliable, bathtub, ivory w/bl trim......................................$15.00
Reliable, chair, dining, rust..$5.00
Reliable, chair, kitchen, ivory w/bl seat $5.00
Reliable, chair, living room, bl w/rust base or red w/rust base, ea $15.00
Reliable, doll, baby, hard plastic, any, ea...........................$10.00
Reliable, highboy, rust $8.00
Reliable, piano bench, brn..$4.00
Reliable, piano bench, rust..$25.00
Reliable, radio, floor, rust...$15.00
Reliable, refrigerator, ivory w/bl trim $5.00
Reliable, stove, ivory w/bl trim...$5.00
Reliable, table, dining, rust...$20.00
Reliable, table, kitchen, ivory...$12.00
Reliable, toilet, ivory w/bl seat $5.00
Renwal, baby bath, any color w/decal $15.00
Renwal, bathroom tub/sink/toilet, med bl & turq w/blk....$35.00
Renwal, bed, brn w/ivory spread...$8.00
Renwal, bench, piano/vanity, brn or lt gr, ea $2.00
Renwal, buffet, brn $6.00
Renwal, carriage, doll insert, pk w/pk wheels.....................$30.00

Renwal, chair, barrel, bl w/red base $8.00
Renwal, chair, barrel, med bl w/metallic red base $9.00
Renwal, chair, club, bl w/brn base, pk w/red or metallic red base, ea $8.00
Renwal, chair, club, dk bl w/brn base $15.00
Renwal, chair, folding, gold w/red seat.................................$15.00
Renwal, chair, kitchen, brn w/ivory seats.............................$2.00
Renwal, chair, kitchen, ivory w/blk......................................$5.00
Renwal, chair, kitchen, ivory w/brn or red, red w/yel, ea.....$3.00
Renwal, chair, kitchen, lt gr w/blk seats, ea $5.00
Renwal, chair, teacher's, red $15.00
Renwal, china closet, brn, reddish brn or med maroon swirl, ea $5.00
Renwal, china closet, brn (stenciled) or ivory, ea $15.00
Renwal, china closet, reddish brn, stenciled $8.00
Renwal, clock, kitchen, ivory or red, ea.............................$20.00
Renwal, clock, mantel, ivory or red, ea $10.00
Renwal, cradle, doll insert, lt bl, no decals........................$20.00
Renwal, cradle, doll insert, pk, w/decals............................$25.00
Renwal, desk, student's, any color, ea.................................$12.00
Renwal, desk, teacher's, bl or red, ea..................................$25.00
Renwal, doll, baby (chubby), pnt diaper $45.00
Renwal, doll, baby, flesh or pk, pnt diaper, ea $8.00
Renwal, doll, baby, plain...$8.00
Renwal, doll, baby, pnt suit...$10.00
Renwal, doll, brother, plastic rivets, all yel.........................$20.00
Renwal, doll, father, metal rivets, dk brn suit $25.00
Renwal, doll, mother, metal rivets, rose dress $25.00
Renwal, doll, rubber nursery, ea..$4.00
Renwal, doll, sister, metal rivets, yel dress...........................$25.00
Renwal, dustpan, red or yel, ea $10.00
Renwal, garbage can, red w/yel, no decal $5.00
Renwal, garbage can, yel w/red, w/decal..............................$8.00
Renwal, hamper, nonopening lid, ivory $2.00
Renwal, hamper, opening lid, lt gr $10.00
Renwal, hamper, opening lid, pk $5.00
Renwal, highboy, nonopening drawers, brn $6.00
Renwal, highboy, nonopening drawers, pk...........................$12.00
Renwal, highboy, opening drawers, brn................................$8.00

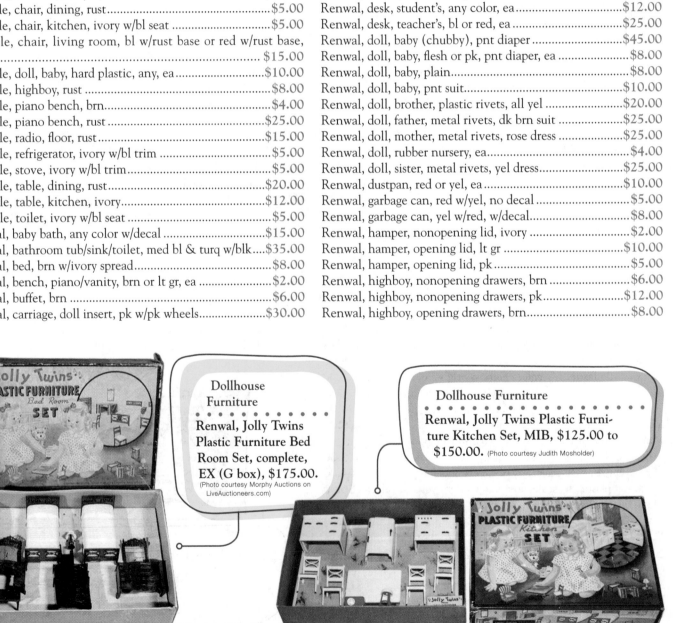

Dollhouse Furniture

Renwal, Jolly Twins Plastic Furniture Bed Room Set, complete, EX (G box), $175.00. (Photo courtesy Morphy Auctions on LiveAuctioneers.com)

Dollhouse Furniture

Renwal, Jolly Twins Plastic Furniture Kitchen Set, MIB, $125.00 to $150.00. (Photo courtesy Judith Mosholder)

Renwal, highchair, pk w/decal................................$25.00
Renwal, ironing board, bl or pk, ea $7.00
Renwal, ironing board & iron, pk w/bl & pk iron, ea........$22.00
Renwal, kiddie car, red w/bl & yel........................$25.00
Renwal, lamp, floor, metallic red w/ivory shade.................$20.00
Renwal, lamp, floor, pk w/ivory shade $50.00
Renwal, lamp, table, brn w/ivory shade........................$6.00
Renwal, lamp, table, caramel w/ivory shade or metallic red w/
  ivory shade, ea $12.00
Renwal, lamp, table, red or metallic red, ea $10.00
Renwal, lamp, table, red w/ivory shade or yel w/ivory shade,
  ea $10.00
Renwal, nursery crib, any color & name, ea.....................$10.00
Renwal, piano, marbleized brn $35.00
Renwal, playground slide, any color, ea......................$22.00
Renwal, playpen, bl w/pk bottom or pk w/bl bottom, ea ...$15.00
Renwal, radio, floor, brn $8.00
Renwal, radio, table, brn.................................$10.00
Renwal, radio, table, red or metallic red, ea $15.00
Renwal, radio/phonograph, brn or red, ea.......................$20.00
Renwal, rocking chair, yel w/red.............................$8.00
Renwal, scale, ivory or red..............................$10.00
Renwal, seesaw, yel w/bl & red or bl w/yel & red, ea.........$25.00
Renwal, server, nonopening door, brn.......................$6.00
Renwal, server, opening door, brn..........................$8.00
Renwal, server, opening door, brn or reddish brn, stenciled...$12.00
Renwal, server, opening drawer, red $15.00
Renwal, sewing machine, any color combo, ea.................$30.00
Renwal, sewing maching, tabletop, red w/bl base $85.00
Renwal, sink, bathroom, dk turq w/blk $8.00
Renwal, sink, bathroom, ivory w/blk, pk w/bl or lt bl, ea $5.00
Renwal, sink, kitchen, ivory w/blk $12.00
Renwal, sink, kitchen, opening door, ivory w/red.............$18.00
Renwal, smoking stand, ivory w/red or red w/ivory, ea $12.00
Renwal, sofa, bright pk w/metallic red base $18.00
Renwal, stool, ivory w/red seat or red w/ivory seat, ea.......$10.00
Renwal, stove, ivory w/blk...............................$12.00
Renwal, stove, opening door, ivory w/red....................$18.00
Renwal, stove, wht w/blk...............................$15.00
Renwal, table, cocktail, brn.............................$6.00
Renwal, table, cocktail, reddish brn $8.00
Renwal, table, dining, orange..........................$15.00
Renwal, table, end/nightstand, brn, lt brn, reddish brn or dk
  maroon, ea $2.00
Renwal, table, end/nightstand, caramel swirl or lt bl, ea $3.00
Renwal, table, end/nightstand, pk or matt pk, ea $4.00
Renwal, table, folding, gold $20.00
Renwal, table, kitchen, brn or yel $8.00
Renwal, table, kitchen, ivory or very deep ivory, ea $5.00
Renwal, table & chairs set, folding, red & gold $120.00
Renwal, telephone, yel w/red.............................$22.00
Renwal, toilet, ivory w/blk or pk w/bl hdl, ea $10.00
Renwal, toydee, bl, w/duck stencil $12.00
Renwal, toydee, bl or matt bl, pk or matt pk, ea $4.00
Renwal, toydee, pk, w/3 Bears decal......................$12.00
Renwal, tub, bathroom, ivory w/blk or pk w/bl, ea $7.00
Renwal, tub, bathroom, med bl & turq w/blk $12.00
Renwal, vacuum cleaner, red w/yel, no decal..................$12.00

Renwal, vacuum cleaner, yel w/red, w/decal $25.00
Renwal, vanity, simplified style w/stenciled mirror, brn.....$12.00
Renwal, washing machine, bl w/pk or pk w/bl, bear decals, ea....$30.00
Sounds Like Home, bed w/night clothes...................$12.00
Sounds Like Home, breakfront..........................$6.00
Sounds Like Home, chair $2.00
Sounds Like Home, dresser w/mirror.....................$6.00
Sounds Like Home, dresser w/music box.................$12.00
Sounds Like Home, hair dryer, bl $5.00
Sounds Like Home, kitchen table $5.00
Sounds Like Home, night table w/electric alarm clock $8.00
Sounds Like Home, shower curtain rod $2.00
Sounds Like Home, sink, electronic.....................$12.00
Sounds Like Home, stove, electronic $12.00
Sounds Like Home, tissue box.........................$5.00
Strombecker, ¾" scale, bathtub, bl or ivory, ea $10.00
Strombecker, ¾" scale, bed, pk, 1940s $8.00
Strombecker, ¾" scale, chair, bedroom/dining, unfinished,
  1930s $6.00
Strombecker, ¾" scale, chair, living room, aqua, dk bl or red,
  1940s-50s, ea $10.00
Strombecker, ¾" scale, clock, grandfather, bl w/blk trim or dk
  peach w/blk trim, ea $15.00
Strombecker, ¾" scale, lamp, floor, unfinished...............$10.00
Strombecker, ¾" scale, nightstand, lt gr or pk, ea $6.00
Strombecker, ¾" scale, scale, dk bl or gr...................$15.00
Strombecker, ¾" scale, sink, aqua or ivory $8.00
Strombecker, ¾" scale, sofa, gr flocking, 1940s $18.00
Strombecker, ¾" scale, stove, ivory, 1940s $8.00
Strombecker, ¾" scale, stove, lt gr, 1940s $15.00
Strombecker, ¾" scale, stove, wht or wht w/blk, 1940s-50s, ea .$18.00
Strombecker, ¾" scale, stove, wht w/ivory trim, 1961 ....$15.00
Strombecker, ¾" scale, table & chairs set, dining, wood finish....$15.00
Strombecker, ¾" scale, television, paper screen, 1961 ....$20.00
Strombecker, 1" scale, living room set, 8-pc w/sofa, chair, foot
  stool, end & library tables, radio, clock & bench........ $135.00
Strombecker, 1" scale, sink, bathroom, gr w/gold swirl $20.00
Strombecker, 1" scale, sofa, gr flocking....................$25.00
Strombecker, 1" scale, stove, ivory w/blk trim $20.00
Strombecker, 1" scale, table, dining, walnut $20.00

Dollhouse Furniture
• • • • • • • •
Strombecker, 1" scale, living room set, wooden, 10 pieces, NMIB, $130.00. (Photo courtesy Lloyd Ralston Gallery on LiveAuctioneers.com)

Tomy-Smaller Homes, armoire, no hangers $10.00
Tomy-Smaller Homes, armoire, w/hangers.......................$15.00
Tomy-Smaller Homes, bathtub...$15.00
Tomy-Smaller Homes, bed, canopy.....................................$15.00
Tomy-Smaller Homes, cabinet, bathroom, w/dbl sink bowls ...$20.00
Tomy-Smaller Homes, cabinet w/television, high $55.00
Tomy-Smaller Homes, cat $10.00
Tomy-Smaller Homes, chair, kitchen...................................$3.00
Tomy-Smaller Homes, checkerboard....................................$5.00
Tomy-Smaller Homes, diary $10.00
Tomy-Smaller Homes, dolls, father, sister or brother, ea......$8.00
Tomy-Smaller Homes, lamp, table $15.00
Tomy-Smaller Homes, mirror, standing................................$15.00
Tomy-Smaller Homes, nightstand $8.00
Tomy-Smaller Homes, oven unit w/microwave & cherry pie ..$55.00
Tomy-Smaller Homes, place mat, yel & orange...................$5.00
Tomy-Smaller Homes, plant, tall...$8.00
Tomy-Smaller Homes, planter, bathroom, no towels.........$10.00
Tomy-Smaller Homes, refrigerator $15.00
Tomy-Smaller Homes, rocker $10.00
Tomy-Smaller Homes, rug, throw...$8.00
Tomy-Smaller Homes, scale...$15.00
Tomy-Smaller Homes, sink/dishwasher, no racks.................$8.00
Tomy-Smaller Homes, sink/dishwasher w/2 racks.............$15.00
Tomy-Smaller Homes, sofa, 2-pc...$12.00
Tomy-Smaller Homes, sofa, 3-pc...$15.00
Tomy-Smaller Homes, speakers $3.00
Tomy-Smaller Homes, stereo cabinet..................................$15.00
Tomy-Smaller Homes, stove w/hood unit $15.00
Tomy-Smaller Homes, table, end $8.00
Tomy-Smaller Homes, table, kitchen....................................$8.00
Tomy-Smaller Homes, television...$50.00
Tomy-Smaller Homes, toilet..$10.00
Tomy-Smaller Homes, towel $5.00
Tomy-Smaller Homes, vanity $15.00
Tomy-Smaller Homes, vanity stool $6.00
Tootsietoy, bed w/headboard, footboard & slats, bl or pk, ea....$20.00
Tootsietoy, buffet, opening drawer, cocoa brn...................$22.00
Tootsietoy, cabinet, medicine, ivory.....................................$25.00
Tootsietoy, chair, bedroom, bl or pk, ea.............................$7.00
Tootsietoy, chair, club, bl..$8.00

Tootsietoy, chair, kitchen, ivory $7.00
Tootsietoy, chair, simple back, no arms $7.00
Tootsietoy, chair, simple back, w/arms, dk brn $8.00
Tootsietoy, chair, tufted look, dk red $20.00
Tootsietoy, chair, XX back, w/ or w/o arms, ea.................$7.00
Tootsietoy, cupboard, non-opening doors, ivory $20.00
Tootsietoy, icebox or stove, non-opening doors, ivory, ea .$20.00
Tootsietoy, lamp, table, bl..$45.00
Tootsietoy, living room set, 5-pc w/2 chairs, floor lamp, footstool
   & side table $65.00
Tootsietoy, nightstand, pk...$10.00
Tootsietoy, piano bench, yel w/tan seat..............................$15.00
Tootsietoy, rocker, bedroom, bl...$12.00
Tootsietoy, rocker, wicker style w/cushion, gold or ivory ...$20.00
Tootsietoy, server, non-opening door, dk brn $22.00
Tootsietoy, table, long, gr crackle $22.00
Tootsietoy, table, rectangular, dk brn $22.00
Tootsietoy, tea cart, dk brn $22.00
Tootsietoy, vanity, blk...$18.00
Tootsietoy (Midget), bed, pk $18.00
Tootsietoy (Midget), dresser, pk $10.00
Tootsietoy (Midget), piano, ivory...$25.00
Tootsietoy (Midget), sofa, 2-pc, right side, red...................$6.00
Tootsietoy (Midget), vanity, pk $10.00
Tynietoy, Astor piano & stool, wood, 3⅜", G $275.00
Tynietoy, bedroom set, bed w/orig mattress & bolster, mirrored
   dresser, rocker, sewing table & side chair, wht wood, G ..$350.00
Tynietoy, bedroom set, canopied bed, 3-drawer dresser &
   Sheraton side chair, orig bed linens, 7½" bed, G......... $500.00
Tynietoy, bedroom set, 6-pc w/bed, nightstand, dresser, highchair,
   straight-back chair & rug, yel, VG.............................. $275.00
Tynietoy, bedroom set, 6-pc w/4-poster bed, dresser, 2 straight-
   back chairs, cradle, rug, natural wood/cloth, VG $465.00
Tynietoy, dining room set, 9-pc w/rnd table, 4 Chippendale chairs,
   sideboard, grandfather clock, mirror, wood, VG $300.00
Tynietoy, grand piano & bench, wood, w/working music box, G .$450.00
Tynietoy, kitchen set, 6-pc w/table, 1 chair, sink, CI stove, cupboard w/backless top shelves, gr-pnt wood, G+ $220.00
Tynietoy, parlor set, 4-pc w/settee, wingback chair & 2 side
   chairs, yel w/floral cloth upholstery, 5", G $550.00
Tynietoy, parlor set, 9-pc w/Astro piano & stool, wingback chair, 2
   shieldback chairs, banjo clock & Empire mirror, VG $660.00

Dollhouse Furniture
• • • • • • • • • • • • • •
Tootsietoy, dining room set, 10 pieces, NMIB, $225.00.
(Photo courtesy Lloyd Ralston Gallery on LiveAuctioneers.com)

Dollhouse Furniture
• •
Tynietoy, bedroom set, Sheraton highboy chest, dresser with mirror, canopy bed with original bedspread and canopy, EX, $1,200.00. (Photo courtesy Noel Barrett Antiques & Auctions Ltd. on LiveAuctioneers.com)

Dollhouses

Dollhouses were first made commercially in America in the late 1700s. A century later, Bliss and Schoenhut were making wonderful dollhouses that, even yet, occasionally turn up on the market, and many were being imported from Germany. During the 1940s and 1950s, American toymakers made a variety of cottages, which are also collectible.

Key: PLW — paper lithograph on wood   PW — painted wood

Bliss, 1½-story, PLW, steps lead to porch w/6 ornate columns, 1 chimney, 3 papered rooms, 23x19x11", VG+ $2,050.00

Bliss, 2-story, 2 rooms, PLW, cut-out & lithoed arched windows, red roof w/bl pnt porch roof, 13x9x6½", VG $600.00

Bliss, 2-story, 2 rooms, PLW w/bl clapboards & yel shingles, sm balcony on full-length front porch roof, 16x11", EX... $800.00

Bliss, 2-story w/attic windows, 4 rooms, PLW, 2nd story balcony, curtained windows, center door, 23x20x11", VG $500.00

Bliss, 2½-story Victorian w/upper side deck, upper & lower railed porches, 2 roof chimneys, front gable, 23x19", VG.. $1,750.00

Christian Hacker, 2-story mansion, w/3 attic dormers on mansard roof, corner molding, working doorbell, 30x28", VG .. $3,100.00

Christian Hacker, 2-story suburban villa, English, 4 rooms, bay window, arched doorway, 31x28", VG $1,800.00

Christian Hacker, 2-story villa w/bow-front facade, opens on ea side to reveal 4 rooms, separate front stairs, 28x18", G $2,750.00

Christain Hacker, 2½-story gambrel, 2 rooms & attic room, 2-sided covered porch, red roof, 22x20x14", G $2,000.00

Converse, 1-story cottage, 1-room, stenciled wood exterior, front porch w/2 turned columns, hinged side, 12x14", VG+. $325.00

Gottschalk, 1-story cottage, 1 room w/access to attic, 3-paneled window on attic dormer, 2-sided porch, 14x14x9", VG ..$300.00

Gottschalk, 2-story mansion/attic, 2 chimneys, upper/lower porches/attic balcony, front opens to rooms, 37x31x20", VG...$8,050.00

Gottschalk, 2-story stable, 2 stalls, PLW, brick/wood facade, bl roof, window opens to loft, 2 compo horses, 12x12", VG $500.00

Gottschalk, 2-story, 2-rooms, front brick facade w/gray sides, gr roof w/2 gray chimneys, lithoed windows, 17x7", F+ .. $500.00

Gottschalk, 2-story, 2 rooms, PLW, 'brick' w/bl roof, cut-out windows, front porch meets extended front, 16x7x10", VG .$850.00

Gottschalk, 2-story, 2-rooms, PLW w/wht-pnt balcony, 2 chimneys, 14½x6½", VG+ $425.00

Gottschalk, 2-story Victorian, 2-room, front bay window, cut-out windows, 'brick' facade, bl roof, 15x10x7½", VG $750.00

Gottschalk, 2-story, 4 rooms, w/porch & balcony, front cut-out windows w/glass, pnt exterior/interior, 22x20x11", F+. $400.00

Gottschalk, 2-story w/attic room, 4 rooms w/2 hallways & 1 flight of stairs, gambrel attic dormer w/balcony, 32x28", G... $3,500.00

Gottschalk, 3-story 6 rooms, working elevator, wood, upper balcony, 2 chimneys, 23x18x13½", G............................. $3,500.00

Reed, 2-story Gutter Roof, PLW, porch w/turned columns, upper full-length balcony, 18x10x9", EX $1,500.00

Schoenhut, bungalow, 3-room, sides open to 2 downstairs rooms, roof opens to attic, wht w/gr roof & shutters, 14x18", G.$125.00

Schoenhut, cottage w/faux gray brick exterior, red roof, wht trim, electrified, 8-pc wood furniture set, 20x13x17", VG... $325.00

Schoenhut, Railroad Station, gray brick facade w/red pressed cb shingle roof, 10½x17", G... $100.00

Dollhouses
Bliss, fire station, No. 2, paper lithograph on wood, with steeple, portico over double doors, 13", G+, $1,430.00. (Photo courtesy Noel Barrett Antiques & Auctions Ltd.)

Dollhouses
Bliss, two-rooms, paper lithograph on wood, R. Bliss on front door, original Eisenglass windows with paper lace curtains, original papered rooms, blue paper shingled roof, soft metal bed, VG, $600.00. (Photo courtesy Noel Barrett Antiques & Auctions Ltd.)

Dollhouses
Bliss, two-story, two-rooms, paper lithograph on wood, front porch, balcony with turned post, yellow brick chimney, original wallpaper, interior includes small scale Waltershausen sofa and chair, wooden chest, rocker, soft metal table and chair, 19", VG, $715.00. (Photo courtesy Noel Barrett Antiques & Auctions Ltd.)

Schoenhut, 2-story Colonial, 4 rooms & attic, cut-out windows w/cloth curtains, red roof, 17x12x15", F.....................$150.00

Schoenhut, 2-story PA colonial style, 4 rooms, 17x17x12", EX.....................................$425.00

Tynietoy, 2-story Nantucket or Saltbox style, 4 rooms, wood, 25x29x25", G $600.00

Tynietoy, 2½-story New England Townhouse, w/2-story side-rooms, electric lights, furnished, 29x48x17", VG+ ..$5,500.00

Unknown, 2-story barn, w/roof & opening door, cut-out window, open stable area w/2 animals, w/saw & rake, 12x15", VG.$225.00

Unknown, 2-story 'gutter' house, 2-room, PLW, front attic dormer & lg-grooved gutter, 11x5½x8", G+ $325.00

SHOPS AND SINGLE ROOMS

Barn, Bliss, PLW & heavy cb, take-apart style w/copula & farm scenes, many stand-up figures, 7 animals, 19x18", EX. $500.00

Bedroom, Marjorie Wentworth, American colonial style w/canopy bed, w/X-acto House of Miniature pcs, 1 doll, 13x22", VG $250.00

Butcher Shop, France, 2 cut-out arched windows at the sides of the front, many accessories, 10x20x10", G.................$800.00

Confectionary Shop, French, 3 front openings w/carved top pediments w/paper labels, many accessories, 20x29x7", EX...$5,500.00

General Store, Germany, PW, ornate back shelving w/clock front, 15 accessories, 8½x17½x11", G $425.00

Kitchen, France, 1900-10, bl & wht, w/tin stove & many accessories, 19x27x8", VG+ $1,100.00

Kitchen, PLW, metal stove w/wooden table & 2 chairs, wooden side table, doll, many accessories, 12x12x18", EX.......$275.00

Kitchen, 1870s, tin, 3-sided, built-in tin chimney & hood, lg tin cabinet w/glass doors, many accessories, 12x22x9", VG.$2,750.00

Parlor, Germany, box folds out to form parlor, w/chairs, hutch, sofa, etc, paper litho scene on front of box, 8x14", VG...........$375.00

Stable, Christian Hacker, PW, 3 stalls, feed room & trainer's area, gabled roof, opening gates, wire bail holder, 27x42x22", VG+.....................................$2,500.00

Stable, England, 1910s, 2 stalls w/hay bins & wooden bench, 12x21", VG $175.00

Store, Gottschalk, back wall w/12 wooden drawers & porcelain labels, many accessories, 13x23x10", VG+...............$1,500.00

Store, Gottschalk, carved clock on back wall w/elaborate pediment & shelf, 20 back drawers, w/accessories, 16x29x14", G+.....................................$3,000.00

• • • • • • • • • • • • • • • • • • Dolls • • • • • • • • • • • • • • • • • • •

Remnants of dolls have been found in the artifacts of most primitive digs. Some are just sticks or stuffed leather or animal skins. Dolls teach our young nurturing and caring. Motherly instincts stay with us — and aren't we lucky as doll collectors that we can keep 'mothering' even after the young have 'left the nest.' Baby dolls come in all sizes and mediums: vinyl, plastic, rubber, porcelain, cloth, etc.

Obviously the entire field of dolls cannot be covered in a price guide such as this. Here we touch upon some of the dolls from the 1950s and 1960s, since a lot of collector interest is centered on these baby boomer dolls.

For in-depth information on dolls of all types, we recommend these lovely doll books: *Doll Values, Antique to Modern*, by Linda Edward; *Madame Alexander Collector's Dolls Price Guide* and *Collector's Encyclopedia of Madame Alexander Dolls, 1948 – 1965*, by Linda Crowsey; *Horsman Dolls: The Vinyl Era*, by Don Jensen; *The Complete Guide to Shirley Temple Dolls* by Tonya Bervaldi-Camaratta; *Collector's Encyclopedia of American Composition Dolls, 1900 – 1950*, Vols. I and II, by Ursula R. Mertz; *Collector's Guide to Dolls of the 1960s and 1970s, Vol. II*, by Cindy Sabulis; *American Character Dolls* by Judith Izen; *Collector's Encyclopedia of Vogue Dolls* by Judith Izen & Carol Stover; *Encyclopedia of Nancy Ann Storybook Dolls* by Elaine Pardee; *Collectible African American Dolls* by Yvonne H. Ellis; and *Celluloid Dolls, Toys & Playthings* by Julie Pelletier Robinson.

See also Action Figures; Barbie Doll and Friends; Character, TV, and Movie Collectibles; Disney; GI Joe; and other specific categories.

Advisors: Linda Edward, author of *Doll Values, Antique to Modern*; Marcia Fanta, www.fantastiquedollsandcollectibles.com (Baby Dolls)

MADAME ALEXANDER

Beatrice Alexander and her sister Rose began making doll clothes and cloth dolls in 1912. But in 1928 she took out the trademark Madame Alexander which she used for her new company. The Madame Alexander Doll Company, which still exists today, is responsible for some of the finest dolls produced in the USA during the 1950s and 1960s. For more information we recommend *Madame Alexander Collector's Dolls Price Guide* and *Collector's Encyclopedia of Madame Alexander Dolls, 1948 – 1965*, both by Linda Crowsey, and *Doll Values, Antique to Modern*, by Linda Edward.

Alice in Wonderland, 1930s, felt mask face w/pnt features, blond yarn hair, orig dress & shoes, 16", rare, G+ $250.00

Alice in Wonderland, 1950s, hard plastic, sleep eyes, blond wig, jtd, orig dress & shoes, 15", VG+IB.....................$150.00

Dolls, Madame Alexander
• • • • • • • • • • •
Davy Crockett, 1950s, #446, 8", hard plastic, EX, $125.00.
(Photo courtesy McMasters Harris Auction Co.)

Dolls, Madame Alexander
• • • • • • • • • • • • • • •
Little Shaver, Madame Alexander, 1963, 11", MIB, $225.00. (Photo courtesy Marcia Fanta)

Dolls, Madame Alexander
• • • • • • • • • • • • • • •
Wendy (Peter Pan), 1950s, #1506, hard plastic, wig, original dress, 14", EX, $1,350.00. (Photo courtesy McMasters Harris Auction Co.)

Alice in Wonderland, 1996, vinyl, sleep eyes, wig, jtd, 15", EX.$200.00

Annabelle, in sweater & skirt w/dbl rickrack border, complete w/ comb & curlers in box, EX $350.00

Cinderella, 1960s, #1235, hard plastic, sleep eyes, blond synthetic wig, jtd, orig outfit, VGIB.................................. $150.00

Cinderella, 1960s, #1235, hard plastic, sleep eyes, wig, jtd, orig bl satin gown, w/tag, 12", NM+IB $600.00

David Copperfield, 1930s, felt mask face w/pnt features, blond mohair wig, blk & wht outfit & hat, 16", EX $400.00

Davy Crockett, 1950s, #446, hard plastic, sleep eyes, red caracul wig, orig outfit & hat, 8", NMIB.................................. $350.00

Little Men (Lissy), 1960s, hard plastic, wig, orig outfit, EX $550.00

Little Men (Nat), 1950s, hard plastic, orig outfit w/gold felt jacket, 14", rare, EX.. $2,100.00

Little Men (Stuffy), 1950s, hard plastic, sleep eyes, wig, orig outfit w/bl felt jacket & hat, 14", rare, EX $2,450.00

Little Men (Tommy Bangs), 1950s, hard plastic, wig, orig outfit, 14", NM.. $875.00

Little Women (Amy), 1959-60, hard plastic, sleep eyes, wig, bent-knee walker, orig outfit, 8", EXIB...................... $425.00

Little Women (Beth), 1949, hard plastic, wig, orig outfit, w/cloverleaf tag, EX+ $625.00

Little Women (Jo), 1950s, hard plastic, wig, orig outfit, tagged, 14", EX+ $375.00

Little Women (Marme), 1950s, hard plastic, wig, orig outfit, tagged, 14", EX $275.00

Little Women (Meg), 1950s, hard plastic, wig, orig outfit, tagged, 14", VG+ $275.00

Oliver Twist, 1930s, felt mask face w/pnt features, blond mohair wig, complete orig outfit, 16", rare, VG $275.00

Peter Pan, 1950s, #1505, hard plastic, wig, orig outfit, 15", EXIB...$1,800.00

Pocahontas, 1967, bent-knee nonwalker, sleep eyes, w/papoose in carrier, brn suede costume, head feather, 8", EX+IB..... $225.00

Prince Charming, 1950s, hard plastic, sleep eyes, caracul wig, orig outfit w/brocade jacket & hat, 18", NMIB $550.00

Prince Charming, 1950s, hard plastic, strung, sleep eyes, caracul wig, orig outfit w/brocade jacket & hat, 14", EXIB $500.00

Scarlett O'Hara, 1940s, compo, sleep eyes, wig, orig lime gr organdy dress w/hat & leatherette shoes, 14", EX $900.00

Snow White, 1939-42, compo, sleep eyes, blk mohair wig, orig outfit w/cape, 16", EX.. $525.00

Snow White, 1950s, hard plastic, strung, sleep eyes, blk wig, orig outfit w/gold lamé waistcoat, 18", EX $650.00

Snow White, 1970s, hard plastic, non-walker, jtd, orig outfit w/ cape, 8", EX $50.00

Sound of Music Set, 1970s, Maria, Louisa, Brigitta, Liesl, Gretl, Friedrich & Marta, plastic, all orig, 8"-12", EX $325.00

Tiny Tim, 1938, mask face w/pnt features, blond wig, blk & wht checked pants & hat, blk jacket w/wht collar, 16", EX.. $300.00

AMERICAN CHARACTER

For more information we recommend *American Character Dolls* by Judith Izen, and *Doll Values, Antique to Modern,* by Linda Edward.

Dolls, American Character
• • • • • • • • • • • • • • •
Little Love Infant, 1942, 20", $350.00. (Photo courtesy Ruth Cayton/Linda Edward)

Little Miss Echo, b/o, 30", EX, $125 to $150.00
Little Miss Echo, b/o, 30", MIB, $225 to...................... $275.00
Tiny Tears, 1950s, 12", VG.. $125.00
Tiny Tears, 1960s, 17", complete, MIB, $125 to $225.00
Tiny Tears (Lifesize), 1963, 21", MIB, $150 to............... $275.00
Tiny Tears (Teenie Weenie), 1964, 8½", orig outfit, EX, $25 to .$30.00
Tiny Tears (Teeny), 1960s, 12", EX, $65 to..................... $100.00

TRESSY

American Character's Tressy doll was produced in this country from 1963 to 1967. The unique feature of this 11½" fashion doll was that her hair 'grew' by pushing a button on her stomach. Tressy also had a little (9") sister named Cricket. Numerous fashions and accessories were produced for these two dolls. Never-removed-from-box Tressy and Cricket items are rare, so unless indicated, values listed are for loose, mint items. A never-removed-from-box item's worth is at least double its loose value.

Advisor: Cindy Sabulis

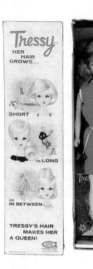

Dolls, American
Character, Tressy
• • • • • • • • • • • •
Doll, Tressy, in original
box, $75.00 to $100.00.
(Photo courtesy Cindy Sabulis)

There were two different materials used for tiny Betsy's hair. The first was a soft mohair sewn into fine mesh. Later the rubber skullcap was rooted with saran which was more suitable for washing and combing.

Betsy McCall had an extensive wardrobe with nearly 100 outfits, each of which could be purchased separately. They were made from wonderful fabrics such as velvet, taffeta, felt, and even real mink. Each ensemble came with the appropriate footwear and was priced under $3.00. Since none of Betsy's clothing was tagged, it is often difficult to identify other than by its square snap closures (although these were used by other companies as well).

Betsy McCall is a highly collectible doll today but is still fairly easy to find at doll shows. Prices remain reasonable for this beautiful clothes horse and her many accessories. Be aware that new versions of this doll are being made today. For more information we recommend *Doll Values, Antique to Modern*, by Linda Edward.

Apartment	$350.00
Beauty Salon	$250.00
Case, Cricket, M	$30.00
Case, Tressy	$30.00
Doll, Pre-Teen Tressy	$30.00
Doll, Tressy & Her Hi-Fashion Cosmetics, MIB	$145.00
Doll, Tressy in Miss America Character Outfit, NM	$65.00
Doll, Tressy in orig dress	$35.00
Doll, Tressy w/Magic Make-Up Face, M	$25.00
Doll Clothes Pattern	$10.00
Gift Pak w/Doll Clothing, NRFB, minimum value	$100.00
Hair Accessory Pak, NRFB	$20.00
Hair Dryer	$25.00
Hair or Cosmetic Accessory Kits, ea minimum value	$50.00
Millinery	$200.00
Outfits, MOC, ea	$40.00
Outfits, NRFB, ea minimum value	$65.00

Case, Betsy McCall's Pretty Pac, rnd vinyl hatbox style w/strap, graphics on front, NM+	$95.00
Doll, American Character, 8", hard plastic, rooted hair, 1957, EX	$350.00
Doll, American Character, 14", vinyl, jtd shoulders & hips, rooted hair, w/trunk & outfits, G	$400.00
Doll, American Character, 14", vinyl w/swivel waist or 1-pc torso, rooted hair, 1958, EX, ea	$500.00
Doll, American Character, 19" or 20", vinyl, rooted hair, 1-pc torso, 1959, EX, ea	$500.00
Doll, American Character, 22", vinyl w/jtd limbs & waist, 5 different colors of rooted hair, 1961, EX, ea	$225.00
Doll, American Character, 29", vinyl w/jtd limbs & waist, 5 different colors of rooted hair, 1961, EX, ea	$300.00
Doll, American Character, 36", Linda McCall (Betsy's cousin), vinyl w/Betsy face, rooted hair, 1959, EX	$350.00

ARRANBEE

Debu 'Teen, 1938 on, compo, slim body, 14", orig clothing, EX	$425.00
Drink 'N Babe, unused, M (in case)	$775.00
Lil Imp, 1960, vinyl, red hair & freckles, 10", EX	$90.00
Littlest Angel, 1956, hard plastic, bent-knee walker, wearing orig clothing, NM	$200.00
Nancy, 1930s, similar to Effanbee Patsy, all compo w/molded hair, wearing orig dress, pnt eyes, EX	$275.00
Nanette, 1949-59, 25", MIB	$550.00
Taffy, 1956, similar to Madame Alexander Cissy, high-heel fashion doll, wearing formal clothing, EX	$165.00

BETSY McCALL

The tiny 8" Betsy McCall doll was manufactured by the American Character Doll Co. from 1957 through 1963. She was made from high-quality hard plastic with a bisque-like finish and hand-painted features. Betsy came in four hair colors — tosca, red, blond, and brunette. She had blue sleep eyes, molded lashes, a winsome smile, and a fully jointed body with bendable knees. On her back there is an identification circle which reads McCall Corp. The basic doll wore a sheer chemise, white taffeta panties, nylon socks, and Maryjane-style shoes and could be purchased for $2.25.

Dolls, Betsy McCall
Doll, Uneeda Doll Co., 1964, 11½",
rigid vinyl body, rooted hair, wore mod
outfits, $125.00 to $225.00. (Photo courtesy
McMasters Harris Auction Co./Linda Edward)

Dolls, Betsy McCall
• • • • • • • • • • • •
Doll, Ideal, 14", hard plastic
body, rooted hair, EX, $200.00.
(Photo courtesy McMasters Harris Auction Co.)

Doll, American Character, 36", vinyl w/Patti Play Pal style body, rooted hair, 1959, EX $325.00

Doll, American Character, 39", Sandy McCall (Betsy's brother), vinyl w/molded hair, red blazer & navy shorts, 1959, EX .$350.00

Doll, Amsco, 8", plastic, complete w/Pretty Pac accessories & booklet, G.. $325.00

Doll, Horsman, 12½", rigid body w/vinyl head, w/extra hair & accessories, 1974, EX..$50.00

Doll, Horsman, 29", rigid plastic teen body w/vinyl head, rooted hair w/side part, orig clothing marked BMc, 1974, MIB..$275.00

Outfit, rain coat, hat umbrella & vinyl boots, blk & wht check w/red trim, red boots, NM+ $75.00

BRIDE

All listings are from current auctions.

Bride, American Character, Sweet Sue, hard plastic, sleep eyes, wig, walker, orig complete outfit, 17", unused, NM (G box).......$125.00

Bride, Madame Alexander, Cissette, 1960s, hard plastic, jtd, blond wig, orig lace-trimmed gown, veil w/floral crown, 10", EX.. $300.00

Bride, Madame Alexander, Cissette, 1960s, hard plastic, jtd, dk brn wig, orig tulle-over-satin gown, 10½", EX $375.00

Bride, Madame Alexander, Godey, 1950s, hard plastic, sleep eyes, blond floss wig, orig satin gown & lacy veil, 14", EX ... $3,700.00

Bride, Madame Alexander, Leslie, black version, 1966-71, orig lacy gown, EXIB (incorrect box) $150.00

Bride, Madame Alexander, Margaret, hard plastic, sleep eyes, blond wig, orig complete satin outfit, 14", unused, NM.$550.0

Bride, Madame Alexander, Mary Rose, 1950s, plastic, sleep eyes, floss wig, orig outfit, 17", EX $525.00

Bride, Madame Alexander, Yolanda, hard plastic w/vinyl head, red wig, orig tiered lacy gown, 1965, EXIB.................... $375.00

Bride & Groom, Madame Alexander, 1950s, bride straight-leg nonwalker & Quiz-Kin groom straight-leg walker, 8", VG, ea.. $225.00

Bridesmaid, Madame Alexander, 1940s, compo, strung, sleep eyes, wig, orig pik gown w/floral hat & muff, 14", EX. $250.00

Groom, Madame Alexander, 1948-49, Godey, hard plastic, wig w/ mutton chops, sleep eyes, orig tux outfit, 14", rare, EX. $3,600.00

CELEBRITY

Celebrity dolls have been widely collected for many years. Except for the rarer examples, most of these dolls are still fairly easy to find, and the majority are priced under $100.00.

Condition is a very important worth-assessing factor, and if the doll is still in the original box, so much the better! Should the box be unopened (NRFB), the value is further enhanced. Using mint as a standard, add 50% for the same doll mint in the box and 75% if it has never been taken out. On the other hand, dolls in only good or poorer condition drop at a rapid pace.

The dolls listed here are not character-related. For celebrity/character dolls see Action Figures; Character, TV, and Movie Collectibles; Rock 'N Roll. For more information we recommend *Doll Values, Antique to Modern*, by Linda Edward.

Abbot & Costello, vinyl in cloth baseball uniforms, w/cassette of the comedy 'Who's on First?,' MIB, set........................ $250.00

Alan Jackson (Country Music Stars), Exclusive Premiere, 1998, 9", MIB...$30.00

Andrew Jackson, Effanbee, 1990, military uniform, 16", MIB.$125.00

Andy Gibb, Ideal, 1979, 7½", MIB...$85.00

Ashley & Mary Kate Olsen, Mattel, 1st issue, Dance & Horse-back Riding sets, 9½", MIB, ea.....................................$30.00

Audrey Hepburn (Breakfast at Tiffany's), Mattel, 1998, 11½", MIB..$50.00

Betty Grable, International Doll Co, 1940s, blond Dynel hair, w/ tag, 19", NM, minimum value $400.00

Beverly Johnson (Real Model Collection), Matchbox, 1989, 11½", MIB $50.00

Brooke Shields, LJN, 1982, pk & gray casual outfit, 11½", MIB $55.00

Brooke Shields, LJN, 1982, Prom Party, 11½", rare, MIB. $150.00

Brooke Shields, LJN, 1982, suntan doll, 11½", MIB..........$65.00

Captain & Tenille, Mego, 1977, 12½", MIB, ea $125.00

Charlie Chaplin (Little Tramp), Milton Bradley/Bubbles Inc, 1972, 19", MIB... $100.00

Cher, Mego, 1976, Growing Hair, 12½", MIB $150.00

Cher, Mego, 1976, pk evening gown, 12½", MIB $125.00

Cher, Mego, 1981, swimsuit, 12", MIB.............................$50.00

Cheryl Ladd, Mattel, 1978, 11½", MIB.............................$85.00

Dolls, Bride
. . . .
Bride, Tiny Kitty, Robert Tonner Doll Co., wedding hat box set, $85.00. (Photo courtesy Elaine Holda/Linda Edward)

Dolls, Celebrity
. . . .
Dolly Parton, Eegee, 1978, 11½", $20.00. (Photo courtesy Talona Griffin/Linda Edward)

Cheryl Tiegs (Real Model Collection), Matchbox, 1989, 11½", MIB..$50.00

Christie Brinkley (Real Model Collection), Matchbox, 1989, 11½", MIB..$50.00

Christy Lane, long red velvet skirt & wht blouse, 1965-70s, 14", M...$25.00

Danny Kaye (White Christmas), Exclusive Premiere, 1998, dressed as Santa, 9", MIB.....................................$45.00

Deanna Durbin, Ideal, compo w/cloth outfit, decal eyes, 21", VG..$530.00

Debbie Boone, Mattel, 1978, 11½", MIB......................$100.00

Deidre Hall (Days of Our Lives), Mattel, 1999, 11½", MIB.....$35.00

Dennis Rodman (Basketball Player), Street Players, 1990s, 12", MIB...$30.00

Diana Ross, Mego, 1977, 12½", MIB........................... $150.00

Diana Ross (of the Supremes), Ideal, 1969, 19", rare, MIB..$600.00

Dick Clark, Juro, 1958, 26½", MIB $450.00

Dionne Quints, Madame Alexander, compo, molded hair, in diapers & bibs, 18" L pnt wood swing w/cloth canopy, VG..........$990.00

Dionne Quints, Madame Alexander, compo, molded hair, sunsuits & bonnets, 7" dolls w/18" swing w/cloth canopy, EX+ . $1,760.00

Dionne Quints, Madame Alexander, compo, molded hair, various colors of dresses & bonnets, 7½", G $275.00

Dionne Quints, Madame Alexander, compo, wigged, orig wool snowsuits, homemade bench, 14", VG $3,850.00

Dolly Parton, Goldberger, 1978, red & silver outfit, 11½", MIB..$100.00

Dolly Parton, Goldberger, 1990s, blk outfit w/silver boots, 12", MIB...$75.00

Donnie & Marie Osmond, Mattel, 1976, 12", MIB, ea $85.00

Dorothy Hamill (Olympic Ice Skater), Ideal, 1977, 11½", MIB $100.00

Dorothy Lamour, Film Star Creations, 1940s-50s, stuffed print cloth w/mohair wig, bathing suit, w/tag, 14", NM....... $135.00

Ekaterina (Katia) Gordeeva (Olympic Ice Skater), Playmates, 1998, 11½", MIB $25.00

Eleanor Roosevelt, Effanbee, 1985, brn dress, 14½", MIB...$125.00

Elizabeth Taylor (Butterfield 8), Tri-Star, 1982, 11½", MIB..$150.00

Elizabeth Taylor (National Velvet), Madame Alexander, 1990, 12", MIB..$100.00

Elvis Presley, Eugene, 1984, issued in 6 different outfits, 12", MIB..$75.00

Elvis Presley, Hasbro, 1993, Jailhouse Rock, Teen Idol or '68 Special, numbered edition, 12", MIB, ea $50.00

Elvis Presley, World Doll, 1984, Burning Love, 21", MIB $125.00

Fanny Brice, compo w/molded hair, cloth outfit, 13", VG ...$140.00

Farrah Fawcett-Majors, see also Charlie's Angels in Character, TV, and Movie Collectibles category

Farrah Fawcett-Majors, Mego, 1977, wht jumpsuit, 12½", MIB..$125.00

Farrah Fawcett-Majors, Mego, 1981, swimsuit, 12", MIB..$50.00

Flip Wilson/Geraldine, Shindana, 1970, stuffed reversible talker, 15", MIB..$85.00

Florence Griffith-Joyner, LJN, 1989, 11½", MIB $65.00

George Burns, Effanbee, 1996, blk tuxedo holding cigar, 17", MIB.. $150.00

George Burns, Exclusive Premiere, 1997, w/accessories, 9", MIB..$25.00

Ginger Rogers, World Doll, 1976, limited edition, MIB. $100.00

Gorbachev, Dreamworks, 1990, 11", MIB.......................$50.00

Grace Kelly (Swan or Mogambo), Tri-Star, 1982, 11½", MIB, ea...$100.00

Groucho Marx, Julius Henry/Effanbee, 1982, 18", MIB . $150.00

Harold Lloyd, 1920s, lithoed stuffed cloth of star standing w/ hands in pockets, 12", EX+... $100.00

Harry Truman, Effanbee, 1988, suit & har, red bow tie, 16", MIB.. $125.00

Humphery Bogart (Casablanca), Effanbee, 1989, 16", MIB.. $150.00

Humphery Bogart & Ingrid Bergman (Casablanca), Exclusive Premiere, 1998, 9", MIB, ea $30.00

Jacklyn Smith, Mego, 1977, 12½", MIB......................... $200.00

Jacklyn Smith, see also Charlie's Angels in Character, TV, and Movie Collectibles category

James Cagney, Effanbee, 1987, pinstripe suit & hat, 16", MIB ..$125.00

James Dean, Dakin, 1985, vinyl w/cloth outfit, pnt hair, jtd, 18", MIB..$35.00

James Dean, DSI, 1994, sweater & pants, 12", MIB $55.00

Jerry Springer, Street Players, 1998, 12", MIB....................$50.00

John Travolta (On Stage...Super Star), Chemtoy, 1977, 12", MIB.. $100.00

Dolls, Celebrity

Marlo Thomas (That Girl), Madame Alexander, 1967, vinyl, Polly face, 17", rare, $800.00. (Photo courtesy McMasters Harris Auction Co./Linda Edward)

Dolls, Celebrity

Sonny Bono, Mego Corp., 12", MIB, $70.00. (Photo courtesy The Museum Doll Shop/Linda Edward)

John Wayne (Great Legends), Effanbee, 1981, Symbol of the West (cowboy outfit), 17", MIB................................... $150.00

John Wayne (Great Legends), Effanbee, 1982, Guardian of the West (cavalry uniform), 18", MIB $150.00

Kate Jackson, Mattel, 1978, 11½", MIB..............................$85.00

Katerina Witt (Olympic Ice Skater), Playmates, 1998, 11½", MIB..$25.00

KISS, Mego, 1978, any from group, 12½", MIB, ea $350.00

Kristi Yamaguchi, Playmates, 1998, 11½", MIB.................$25.00

Laurel & Hardy, Goldberger, 1986, bluejean overalls, 12", MIB $55.00

Laurel & Hardy, Hamilton Gifts, 1991, cloth suits, 16", MIB, ea...$65.00

Laurel & Hardy, 1981, cloth bodies w/porcelain heads, cloth suits, 18" & 21", MIB, ea.....................................$75.00

Leann Rimes (Country Music Stars), Exclusive Premiere, 1998, 9", MIB $30.00

Leslie Uggams, Madame Alexander, 1966, lt pk dress, 17", MIB $350.00

Liberace, Effanbee, 1986, glittery blk & silver outfit w/cape, 16½", MIB $250.00

Louis 'Satchmo' Armstrong, Effanbee, 1984, bl & blk tuxedo, 15½", MIB $250.00

Lucille Ball, Effanbee, 1985, in blk tails & top hat, 15", MIB ..$175.00

Lucille Ball (Hollywood Walk of Fame Collection), CAL-HASCO Inc, 1992, 20", MIB $350.00

Lyndon Johnson, Remco, 1964, plastic, 6", MIB $40.00

Mae West, Hamilton Gifts, 1991, 17", M $50.00

Mae West (Great Legends), Effanbee, 1982, 18", MIB... $125.00

Mandy Moore, Play Along, 2000, 11½", MIB.....................$20.00

Margaret O'Brien, Madame Alexander, 18", EX............ $675.00

Marie Osmond (Modeling Doll), Mattel, 1976, 30", MIB..$150.00

Marilyn Monroe, DSI, 1993, blk gown & wht fur stole, 11½", MIB...$50.00

Marilyn Monroe, Tri-Star, 1982, pk gown & gloves, 16½", MIB $100.00

Marilyn Monroe, Tri-Star, 1982, 2nd issue (different face mold), 11½", MIB $150.00

Mary Martin, Madame Alexander, ca 1949, hard plastic, short curly wig, orig outfit, 14", EX $1,250.00

Marylin Monroe, Tri-Star, 1982, 1st issue (same face mold as 16½" doll), 11½", MIB..................................$75.00

Michael Jackson, LJN, 1984, bl & gold outfit holding microphone, 12", MIB...$75.00

Muhammad Ali, Hasbro, 1997, 12", MIB $45.00

Muhammad Ali, Mego, 1976, 9", MOC $150.00

Nicole Boebeck (Olympic Ice Skater), Playmates 1998, 11½", MIB..$25.00

Patty Duke, Horsman, 1965, 12", rare, MIB.................. $450.00

Penny Marshall or Cindy Williams, see Character, TV & Movie category under Laverne & Shirley

Prince Charles, Goldberg, 1983, dress uniform, 12", MIB...$100.00

Prince William, Goldberg, 1982, christening gown, 18", MIB ..$150.00

Prince William, House of Misbet, 1982, as baby, 18", MIB..$200.00

Princess Diana, Danbury Mint, 1988, pk satin gown, 14", MIB $125.00

Princess Diana, Effanbee (Fan Club), 1982, wedding dress, 16½", MIB.. $225.00

Princess Diana, Goldberg, 1983, wht gown w/wht boa, 11½", MIB.. $100.00

Princess Diana, Way Out Toys, 1990s, Royal Diana, pk dress, 11½", MIB $20.00

Princess Margaret, Dean's Rag Book Co, 1920s, papier-maché over cloth, mohair wig, cloth coat & hat, 14", unused, M.......$350.00

Queen Elizabeth, Effanbee, 1980s, wht satin gown, 14", MIB... $75.00

Queen Elizabeth, Effanbee, 1989, red & wht satin gown, 14", MIB.. $125.00

Randy Travis (Country Music), Exclusive Premiere, 1998, 9", MIB..$30.00

Red Foxx, Shindana, 1976, 2-sided stuffed print cloth talker, 16", MIB... $150.00

Robert Crippen (Astronaut), Kenner, 1997, 12", MIB......$45.00

Ronald Reagan, Dots Okay, 1982, stuffed printed cloth (Reaganomics), 10", MIB $25.00

Rosemary Clooney (White Christmas), Exclusive Premiere, 1998, red gown, 8", MIB $45.00

Rosie O'Donnell, Mattel, 1999, red outfit, 11½", MIB......$30.00

Rosie O'Donnell, Tyco, 1997, The Rosie Doll, stuffed cloth w/ outfit, 14", MIB...$40.00

Selena, Arm Enterprise, 1996, red jumpsuit, 11½", MIB...$85.00

Shari Lewis, Direct International, 1994, rag doll holding Lambchop, 14", MIB...$30.00

Shari Lewis, Madame Alexander, 1959, yel sweater w/gr skirt & hat, 21", MIB... $450.00

Soupy Sales, 1960s, yel sweater & red tie, 11½", MIB $250.00

Vanna White, HSC, 1990, gold dress & purple jumpsuit, 11½", MIB..$55.00

WC Fields, Effanbee, 1980, blk coat, checked pants & gray top hat, 15½", MIB $125.00

WC Fields, Knickerbocker, 1972, stuffed print cloth talker, 16", MIB..$75.00

Willie Nelson, Catena International Inc, 1989, stuffed cloth w/ yarn hair & bandana, 16", M.............................$65.00

Winston Churchill, Madame Alexander, hard plastic, blk tuxedo & hat, 18", VG.. $375.00

DELUXE READING/TOPPER

For more information we recommend *Doll Values, Antique to Modern*, by Linda Edward.

DAWN

Dawn and her friends were made by Deluxe Topper in the 1970s. They're becoming highly collectible, especially when mint in the box. Dawn was a 6" fashion doll who had friends named Angie, Jessica, Glori, and Dale. There were also more elaborate sets such as Model Agencies, Majorettes, and Flower Fantasies. They were issued in boxes already dressed in clothes of the highest style, or you could buy additional outfits, many complete with matching shoes and accessories.

Advisor: Dawn Diaz

Accessory, Dawn's Apartment, complete $50.00
Doll, Dancing Angie, NRFB $50.00
Doll, Dancing Dale, NRFB..$65.00
Doll, Dancing Dawn, NRFB..$50.00
Doll, Dancing Gary, NRFB..$50.00
Doll, Dancing Glori, NRFB..$50.00
Doll, Dancing Jessica, NRFB...$50.00
Doll, Dancing Ron, NRFB...$50.00
Doll, Dancing Van, NRFB..$80.00
Doll, Daphne Model Agency, gr & silver dress NRFB.... $100.00
Doll, Dawn Majorette, NRFB..$80.00
Doll, Denise Model Agency, NRFB $100.00
Doll, Dinah Model Agency, NRFB $100.00

Doll, Gary, NRFB..$40.00
Doll, Jessica, NRFB...$35.00
Doll, Kip Majorette, NRFB $65.00
Doll, Longlocks, NRFB..$35.00
Doll, Maureen Model Agency, red & gold dress, NRFB. $100.00
Doll, Ron, NRFB $40.00
Outfit, Bell Bottom Flounce, #0717, NRFB $20.00
Outfit, Green Slink, #0716, NRFB......................................$20.00
Outfit, Sheer Delight, #8110, NRFB $20.00

OTHER DELUXE READING/TOPPER DOLLS

Lil' Miss Fashion, 1960, 20", MIB $75.00
Suzy Cute, 1964, w/plastic crib, 7", MIB......................... $175.00
Tickles, 1963, talker, MIB...$75.00

EFFANBEE

For more information we recommend *Doll Values, Antique to Modern*, by Linda Edward.

Butterball, 1969, all-vinyl, molded hair, sleep eyes, 12", MIB ... $50.00
Button Nose, 1968-71, vinyl head, cloth body, 18", $25 to...$35.00
Dy-Dee, 1934 on, hard rubber head, sleep eyes, jtd soft rubber body, drink & wet doll, molded hair, 11", NM $225.00
Dy-Dee, 1934 on, hard rubber head, sleep eyes, jtd soft rubber body, drink & wet doll, molded hair, 15", EX.............. $375.00
Fluffy, 1954 on, all-vinyl, molded or rooted hair, 8", MIB .$35.00

Fluffy, 1954 on, all-vinyl, molded or rooted hair, 8", black version, EX $45.00
Fluffy, 1954 on, all-vinyl, molded or rooted hair, 11", EX..$40.00
Lil Sweetie, 1967, nurser w/no lashes or brows, 16", EX....$45.00
Monique, 1978, 16", MIB...$65.00
Most Happy Family, 1958, vinyl, 21" mother, 10" brother & sister, 8" baby, boxed set, MIB $200.00
Patsy, 1928 on, all compo, pnt or sleep eyes, molded hair or wigged, marked Effanbee//Patsy//Pat Pend//Doll, wearing orig clothing, EX $625.00
Tiny Tubber, 1976, 11", all orig, MIB..............................$55.00

FISHER-PRICE

Though this company is more famous for their ruggedly durable, lithographed wooden toys, they made dolls as well. Many of the earlier dolls (circa mid-1970s) had stuffed cloth bodies and vinyl heads, hands, and feet. Some had battery-operated voice boxes. For company history, see the Fisher-Price category. For more information, we recommend *Fisher-Price Toys* by Brad Cassity and *Doll Values, Antique to Modern*, by Linda Edward.

See Also Advertising; Character, TV, and Movie Collectibles; Disney.

Doll, Audrey, #203, 1974-76, MIB...................................$50.00
Doll, Baby Ann, #204, 1974-76, MIB $80.00
Doll, Baby Soft Sounds, #213, MIB..................................$65.00
Doll, Billie, #242, 1979-80, EX...$10.00
Doll, Elizabeth, #205, 1974-75, EX $25.00
Doll, Honey, #208, 1977-80, EX..$20.00

Dolls, Fisher-Price
Doll, Joey, #206, 1975 – 1976, M, $40.00.
(Photo courtesy Brad Cassity)

Dolls, Fisher-Price
Doll, My Friend Mandy, #210, complete with straw hat, pink party dress, stretchy tights, white slip-on shoes, nightgown, and booklet, 1977 – 1978, EX, $25.00. (Photo courtesy Brad Cassity)

Doll, Jenny, #201, 1974-76, MIB.......................................$55.00
Doll, Mandy, #4009, 1985, Happy Birthday, EX $50.00
Doll, Mary, #200, 1974-77, MIB.......................................$60.00
Doll, Mikey, #240, 1979-80, EXIB....................................$45.00
Doll, Muffy, #241, 1979-80, EX $100.00
Doll, My Baby Sleep, #207, 1979-80, EX $25.00
Doll, My Friend Becky, #218, 1982-84, EX.......................$20.00
Doll, My Friend Christie, #8120, 1990, EX, $40 to $75.00
Doll, My Friend Jenny, MIB.. $100.00
Doll, My Friend Jenny, 1978, with doll trunk, outfits & hangers, EX $65.00
Doll, My Friend Mandy, #216, 1984 only, EX...................$35.00
Doll, My Friend Mikey, #205, 1982-84, EX.......................$30.00
Doll, My Friend Nickey, #206, 1985, MIB........................$75.00
Doll, Natalie, #202, 1974-76, MIB....................................$65.00
Doll, Rattle Rag Doll, #419, 1977, EX...............................$30.00
Outfit, Aerobics, #4110, 1985, EX $10.00
Outfit, Let's Go Camping, #222, 1978-79, EX $10.00
Outfit, Miss Piggy's Sailor Outfit, #891, 1981-82, EX $12.00
Outfit, Party Dress Outfit & Pattern, #221, 1978-79, EX ..$10.00
Outfit, Rainy Day Slicker, #219, 1978-80, EX $10.00
Outfit, Springtime Tennis, #220, 1978-82, EX..................$10.00
Outfit, Sunshine Party Dress, #237, 1984, EX.................$10.00
Outfit, Valentine Party Dress, #238, 1984-85, EX.............$10.00

GERBER BABIES

The first Gerber Baby dolls were manufactured in 1936. These dolls were made of cloth and produced by an unknown manufacturer. Since that time, six different companies working with leading artists, craftsmen, and designers have attempted to capture the charm of the winsome baby in Dorothy Hope Smith's charcoal drawing of her friend's baby, Ann Turner (Cook). This drawing became known as the Gerber Baby and was adopted as the trademark of the Gerber Products Company, located in Fremont, Michigan. For further information see *Gerber Baby Dolls and Advertising Collectibles* by Joan S. Grubaugh and *Doll Values, Antique to Modern*, by Linda Edward.

Amsco, 10", pk & wht rosebud sleeper, blk, vinyl, 1972-73, NM, $60 to.. $100.00
Amsco, 10", pk & wht rosebud sleeper, vinyl, 1972-73, NM, $45 to .$55.00
Amsco, 14", baby & feeding set, vinyl, 1972-73, complete, NMIB $85.00
Arrow Rubber & Plastic Corp, 14", bib & diaper, 1965-67 Gerber premium, MIB, $45 to..$60.00
Atlanta Novelty, 12", Baby Drink & Wet, blk, complete w/trunk & accessories, 1979-81, M $100.00
Atlanta Novelty, 12", Bathtub Baby, 1985, MIB, $70 to ...$85.00
Atlanta Novelty, 12", porcelain, #D527, wht satin gown & bonnet, w/pillow & basket, 1982 limited ed, EX+................$50.00
Atlanta Novelty, 12", rag doll, pk or bl, EX $20.00
Atlanta Novelty, 17", Baby Drink & Wet, complete w/trunk & accessories, 1979-81, M, $75 to $85.00
Atlanta Novelty, 17", googly eyes, wht or blk dolls, orig outfit, 1979, unused, MIB, $45 to...$55.00
Atlanta Novelty, 17", 50th Anniversary, stuffed cloth & vinyl w/ eyelet skirt & bib, 1978, NRFB..................................$75.00

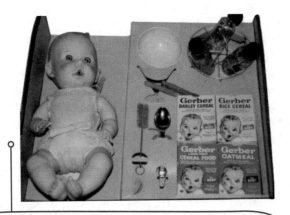

Lucky Ltd, 6", Birthday Party Twins, 1989, NRFB.............$40.00
Lucky Ltd, 16", christening gown, 1989, EX.....................$40.00
Sun Rubber, 11", nude, 1956, EX..................................$50.00
Sun Rubber, 13", mouth open for bottle, in dress, matching panties & bonnet, 1955, NM...$175.00
Sun Rubber, 18", nude, EX..$75.00
Toy Biz, Baby Care Set, 1996, MIB................................$25.00
Toy Biz, Food & Playtime Baby, 1995, MIB, $25 to...........$35.00
Toy Biz, Potty Time Baby, 1994-95, NRFB.....................$25.00

Hasbro

For more information, we recommend *Doll Values, Antique to Modern*, by Linda Edward.

Dolly Darlings

Dolly Darlings (DD in the listings below) are approximately 4" tall and have molded or rooted hair. The molded-hair dolls were sold in themed hatboxes with small accessories to match. The rooted-hair dolls were sold separately and came with a small brush and comb. There were four plastic playrooms that featured the rooted-hair dolls. Hasbro also produced the Flower Darling (FD in the listings below) series which were 2" dolls in flower corsages. The Dolly Darlings and Flower Darlings were available in the mid-to-late 1960s.
   Advisor: Dawn Diaz

DD, Beth at the Supermarket, NRFB...............................$40.00
DD, Cathy Goes to a Party, M (EX case).........................$25.00
DD, Daisy Darling, complete, EX..................................$15.00
DD, Flying Nun, MIB, $50 to..$75.00
DD, Go-Team-Go, dolly only, EX..................................$15.00
DD, Hipster, doll only, EX, $15 to.................................$20.00
DD, Honey, NRFB..$50.00
DD, John & His Pets, M (in case)...................................$30.00
DD, Lemon Drop, doll only, EX, $15 to...........................$20.00
DD, Powder Puff, doll only, EX, $15 to...........................$20.00

DD, School Days, doll only, EX, $15 to...........................$20.00
DD, Shary Takes a Vacation, doll only, EX.......................$10.00
DD, Slick Set, doll only, EX..$20.00
DD, Slumber Party, doll only, EX...................................$20.00
DD, Sunny Day, doll only, $15 to...................................$20.00
DD, Susie Goes to School, M (EX case)............................$25.00
DD, Sweetheart, doll only EX, $15 to..............................$20.00
DD, Tea Time, NRFB...$50.00
DD, Teeny Bikini, doll only, EX, $15 to...........................$20.00
FD, dolls, complete, M, ea $15 to..................................$25.00
FD, dolls, MIP, ea..$50.00
FD, dolls w/o flower pins, ea $7 to.................................$12.00

Jem

The glamorous life of Jem mesmerized little girls who watched her Saturday morning cartoons, and she was a natural as a fashion doll. Hasbro saw the potential in 1985 when they introduced the Jem line of 12" dolls representing her, the rock stars from Jem's musical group, the Holograms, and other members of the cast, including the only boy, Rio, Jem's road manager and Jerrica's boyfriend. The dolls were posable, jointed at the waist, head, and wrists, so that they could be positioned at will with their musical instruments and other accessory items. Their clothing, makeup, and hairdos were wonderfully exotic, and their faces were beautifully modeled. The Jem line was discontinued in 1987 after being on the market for only two years.

Accessory, Video Madness, NRFB..................................$75.00
Clock, rnd neon wall mount w/Jem in center, bl neon & background, 11" dia, unused, M...$55.00
Color, Activity and Paint Books, any, unused, M, ea $20 to..$30.00
Compact, oblong w/Jem image on lid, 3½x4½", M............$12.00
Doll, Aja, NRFB..$245.00
Doll, Banee, NRFB..$35.00
Doll, Clash, NRFB...$65.00
Doll, Flash 'n Sizzle Jem/Jerrica, NRFB..........................$85.00
Doll, Glitter 'n Gold Jem/Jerrica, NRFB..........................$75.00
Doll, Glitter 'n Gold Rio, NRFB.....................................$40.00
Doll, Jetta, MIB...$100.00
Doll, Jetta, NRFB..$110.00
Doll, Kimber, complete, M...$48.00
Doll, Kimber, MIB..$70.00
Doll, Pizzazz, complete, M...$45.00

Doll, Pizzazz, 1st issue, MIB $85.00
Doll, Raya, NRFB $190.00
Doll, Rock 'N Curl, MIB $45.00
Doll, Rock 'n Curl Jem, NRFB $40.00
Doll, Roxy, MIB $100.00
Doll, Shana, NRFB $100.00
Doll, Stormer, NRFB $100.00
Doll, Synergy, NRFB.. $150.00
Eraser Set, Jem (star-shaped), Pizzazz (triangular), MOC ..$90.00
Magic Slate, unused, M $20.00
Outfit, Glitter 'n Gold Midnight Magic, NRFP.........$20.00
Outfit, Glitter 'n Gold Purple Haze, NRFP.....................$35.00
Outfit, How You Play the Game, MIP.........................$135.00
Outfit, Let's Rock This Town, NRFP.........................$70.00
Outfit, Like a Dream, NRFP $70.00
Outfit, Rock 'n Roses, NRFP $70.00
Outfit, Rock Country, NRFP $45.00
Outfit, Set Your Sails, MIP $100.00
Outfit, Sophisticated Lady, NRFP $50.00
Outfit, Splashes of Sound, NRFP $35.00
Outfit, You Can't Catch Me, complete, MIP $100.00

HOLLY HOBBIE

Sometime around 1970 a young homemaker and mother, Holly Hobbie, approached the American Greeting Company with some charming country-styled drawings of children. Her concepts were well received by the company, and since that time over 400 Holly Hobbie items have been produced, nearly all marked HH, H. Hobbie, or Holly Hobbie.

See also Clubs, Newsletters, and Other Publications.

Bubble Bath Container, several figural variations, Benjamin
    Ansehl, 1980s, NM $10.00
Doll, Country Fun Holly Hobbie, 16", 1989, NRFB..........$20.00
Doll, Grandma Holly, 14", MIB $20.00
Doll, Grandma Holly, 24", MIB $25.00
Doll, Holly Hobbie, Amy or Carrie Dream Along, 12", MIB,
    ea.. $15.00
Doll, Holly Hobbie, Bicentennial, 12", MIB.....................$25.00
Doll, Holly Hobbie, Day 'N Night, 14", MIB....................$15.00
Doll, Holly Hobbie, Heather, Amy or Carrie, 6", MIB, ea ..$5.00
Doll, Holly Hobbie, Heather, Amy or Carrie, 9", MIB, ea..$10.00

Doll, Holly Hobbie, Heather, Amy or Carrie, 16", MIB, ea..$20.00
Doll, Holly Hobbie, Heather, Amy or Carrie, 27", MIB, ea..$25.00
Doll, Holly Hobbie, Heather, Amy or Carrie, 33", MIB, ea..$35.00
Doll, Holly Hobbie, scented, clear ornament around neck, 18",
    1988, NRFB...$30.00
Doll, Holly Hobbie, 25th Anniversary, 26", 1994, MIB $55.00
Doll, Holly Hobbie Dream Along, Amy or Carrie, 9", MIB,
    ea..$10.00
Doll, Holly Hobbie Talker, 4 sayings, 16", MIB.............$25.00
Doll, Little Girl Holly, 15", 1980, MIB $20.00
Doll, Robby, 9", MIB $15.00
Doll, Robby, 16", MIB $20.00
Dollhouse, M.. $200.00
Sand Pail, 6", Chein, 1974, EX $25.00
Sewing Machine, b/o, 5x9", Durham, 1975, EX $25.00

HORSMAN

The E.I Horsman Company of New York City existed from 1878 into the 1980s. It was founded by Edward Imeson Horsman as a company that imported, assembled, wholesaled, and distributed various dolls and doll lines.

For more information, we recommend *Horsman Dolls: The Vinyl Era, 1950 to Present,* by Don Jensen.

Baby First Tooth, 1966, vinyl head, limbs, cloth body, open/
    closed mouth w/tongue & 1 tooth, molded tears on cheeks,
    rooted blond hair, pnt bl eyes, 16", EX $40.00
Baby Sofskin, 1972 on, vinyl, 12", EX..............................$25.00
Ballerina, 1957, vinyl, 1-pc body & legs, jtd elbows, 18", EX...$50.00
Bye-Lo Baby, 1972, reissue, molded vinyl head, limbs, cloth body,
    wht nylon organdy bonnet dress, 14", EX.....................$25.00
Bye-Lo Baby, 1980-90s, reissue, molded vinyl head, limbs, bloth
    body, wht nylon organdy bonnet drss, 14", EX $15.00
Campbell's Kids, 1930-40s, all-compo, 13", NM............ $275.00
Drinkee Walker, 1988, NM $50.00
Gold Medal Doll, 1953, vinyl head, soft vinyl foam stuffed body,
    molded hair, 26", NM...................................... $175.00
Jeanie Horsman, 1937, compo head & limbs, molded hair, sleep
    eyes, 14", EX $225.00

Dolls, Holly Hobbie

Trinket box, heart-shaped porcelain, 'Happiness is having someone to care for,' 2x3", WWA, 1973, NM+, $15.00. (Photo courtesy www.whatacharacter.com)

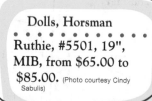

Dolls, Horsman

Ruthie, #5501, 19", MIB, from $65.00 to $85.00. (Photo courtesy Cindy Sabulis)

Lil' David & Lil' Ruth, 1970s, all vinyl, anatomically correct babies, 12", EX, ea $20.00
Poor Pitiful Pearl, 1963, from cartoon by William Steig, 11", EX $100.00
Poor Pitiful Pearl, 1963, from cartoon by William Steig, 17", NM..$175.00
Tessie Talk, 1974, ventriloquist doll, 16", EX..................$40.00

IDEAL

The Ideal Novelty and Toy Company was in business from 1906 through the 1980s, and was based out of Brooklyn, New York. The company produced its own composition dolls in the early years. Later dolls were rubber, hard plastic, vinyl, and cloth.

For more information we recommend *Collector's Guide to Ideal Dolls* by Judith Izen.

CRISSY AND HER FAMILY

Ideal's 18" Crissy doll with growing hair was very popular with little girls of the early 1970s. She was introduced in 1969 and continued to be sold throughout the 1970s, enjoying a relatively long market life for a doll. During the 1970s, many different versions of Crissy were made. Numerous friends followed her success, all with the growing hair feature like Crissy's. The other Ideal 'grow hair' dolls in the line included Velvet, Cinnamon, Tressy, Dina, Mia, Kerry, Brandi, and Cricket. Crissy is the easiest member in the line to find, followed by her cousin Velvet. The other members are not as common, but, like Crissy and Velvet, loose examples of these dolls frequently make their appearance at doll shows, flea markets, and even garage sales. Only those examples that are in excellent or better condition and wearing their original outfits and shoes should command book value. Black versions of the dolls command much higher prices than the white versions.

Advisor: Cindy Sabulis, author of *Dolls of the 1960s and 1970s*

Baby Crissy, black, 1973-76, pk dress, EX $80.00
Baby Crissy, 1973-76, pk dress, EX $65.00
Baby Crissy, 1973-77, re-dressed, $35 to $45.00

Baby Crissy, 1976-76, pk dress, MIB................................$125.00
Brandi, black, 1972-73, orange swimsuit, EX.................$125.00
Cinnamon, Curly Ribbons, black, 1974, EX.....................$75.00
Cinnamon, Curly Ribbons, 1974, EX.................................$45.00
Cinnamon, Hairdoodler, black, 1973, EX..........................$75.00
Cinnamon, Hairdoodler, 1973, EX.....................................$40.00
Crissy, Country Fashion, 1982-83, EX................................$20.00
Crissy, Country Fashion, 1982-83, MIB.............................$45.00
Crissy, Look Around, 1972, EX $40.00
Crissy, Magic Hair, 1977, EX...$30.00
Crissy, Magic Hair, 1977, MIB, $65 to $80.00
Crissy, Magic Hair, 1977, NRFB..$90.00
Crissy, Movin' Groovin', black, 1971, EX.........................$100.00
Crissy, Movin' Groovin', 1971, EX.....................................$40.00
Crissy, Swirla Curla, black, 1973, EX...............................$100.00
Crissy, Swirla Curla, 1973, EX...$35.00
Crissy, Twirly Beads, 1974, MIB..$65.00
Crissy Magic Hair, black, 1977, EX..................................$100.00
Dina, 1972-73, purple playsuit, EX....................................$50.00
Kerry, 1971, gr romper, EX...$55.00
Mia, 1971, turq romper, EX..$50.00
Tara, black, 1976, yel gingham outfit, MIB.....................$200.00
Velvet, Beauty Braider, 1973, EX $35.00
Velvet, Look Around, 1972, EX $35.00
Velvet, Movin' Groovin', 1971, EX.....................................$35.00
Velvet, reissue, 1982, EX $30.00
Velvet, Swirly Daisies, 1974, EX..$35.00
Velvet, Swirly Daisies, 1974, MIB......................................$65.00
Velvet, 1st issue, purple dress, 1970, EX............................$35.00
Velvet Look Around, black, 1972, EX..............................$100.00

FLATSYS

Flatsy dolls were produced from 1968 until 1970 in 2", 5", and 8" sizes. There was only one boy in the 5" line; all were dressed in '70s fashions, and not only clothing but accessory items such as bicycles were made.

In 1994 Justoys reissued Mini Flatsys. They were sold alone or with accessories such as bikes, rollerblades, and jet skis.

Advisor: Dawn Diaz

Ali Fashion Flatsy, NRFP, $45 to.......................................$50.00
Bonnie Flatsy, sailing, NRFP $55.00

Dolls, Ideal, Crissy and Her Family
• • • • • • •
Crissy, Beautiful, grow-hair, orange lace dress, 1969, 18", EX, $40.00.
(Photo courtesy The Museum Doll Shop/Linda Edward)

Dolls, Ideal, Flatsys
• • • • • • •
Grandma Baker, Flatysville series, Catalog #0159-4, complete, M, $25.00 to $30.00.
(Photo courtesy Judith Izen)

Candy, Happy Birthday, complete, EX $25.00
Casey Flatsy, MIB...$55.00
Cory Flatsy, print mini-dress, NRFP, $45 to $50.00
Dale Fashion Flatsy, hot pk maxi NRFP, $45 to $50.00
Dewie Flatsy, NRFP $60.00
Dewie Flatsy Locket, NRFP, $20 to $30.00
Filly Flatsy, complete, EX...$25.00
Gwen Fashion Flatsy, NRFP, $45 to $50.00
Judy Flatsy, NRFP, $55 to...$75.00
Kookie Flatsy, Flatsyville series, complete, M, $25 to........$30.00
Munch Time Flatsy, Mini Flatsy Collection, NRFP, $50 to...$75.00
Slumber Party Flatsy, Mini Flatsy Collection, NRFP, $50 to..$75.00
Spinderella Flatsy, complete, M, $35 to $40.00
Summer Mini Flatsy Collection, NRFP $65.00
Susie Flatsy complete, EX...$25.00

TAMMY

In 1962, the Ideal Novelty and Toy Company introduced their teenage Tammy doll. Slightly pudgy and not quite as sophisticated-looking as some of the teen fashion dolls on the market at the time, Tammy's innocent charm captivated consumers. Her extensive wardrobe and numerous accessories added to her popularity with children. Tammy had a car, a house, and her own catamaran. In addition, a large number of companies obtained licenses to issue products using the 'Tammy' name. Everything from paper dolls to nurse's kits were made with Tammy's image on them. Her success was not confined to the United States; she was also successful in Canada, Japan, and several other European countries.

Interest in Tammy remains high according to Cindy Sabulis, co-author of *Tammy, the Ideal Teen*. Values for quality mint-in-box items remain strong. Loose, played-with dolls are still readily available and can be found for decent prices.

Advisor: Cindy Sabulis

Accessory Pak, baseball bat, catcher's mask, mitt & ball, unknown #, NRFP..$35.00
Accessory Pak, electric skillet & frying pan w/lids, unknown #, NRFP $50.00
Accessory Pak, luggage case, airline ticket & camera, #9183-), NRFP $25.00
Accessory Pak, Misty Hair Color Kit, #9828-5, MIB.........$75.00
Accessory Pak, pizza, princess phone, Tammy's telephone directory, wht scandals, #9184-80, NRFP......................$25.00
Accessory Pak, plate of crackers, juice, glasses, sandals & newspaper, #9179-3, NRFP......................................$30.00
Accessory Pak, poodle on leash, red vinyl purse & wht sneakers, #9186-80, NRFP...$30.00
Accessory Pak, tennis racket, score book & sneakers, #9188-8, NRFP $20.00
Case, Dodi, gr bkgrd, EX..$30.00
Case, Misty, Dutch door-type, blk, EX $30.00
Case, Misty, pk & wht, EX..$25.00
Case, Misty & Tammy, dbl telephone, gr or pk, ea $25.00
Case, Misty & Tammy, hatbox style, EX $30.00
Case, Pepper, front snap closure, red or coral, EX.............$15.00
Case, Pepper, hatbox style, turq, EX..................................$40.00

Case, Pepper, yel or gr, EX..$20.00
Case, Pepper & Dodi, front opening, bl, EX $30.00
Case, Pepper & Patti, Montgomery Ward Exclusive, red, EX..$50.00
Case, Tammy, suitcase type w/doll compartment, closet & accessory compartment, red w/clear see-through front, EX $50.00
Case, Tammy & Her Friends, pk or gr, EX $30.00
Case, Tammy Beau & Arrow, hatbox style, bl or red, EX ..$40.00
Case, Tammy Evening in Paris, bl, blk or red, EX..............$20.00
Case, Tammy Model Miss, dbl trunk, red or blk, EX.........$25.00
Case, Tammy Model Miss, hatbox style, bl or blk, EX.......$30.00
Case, Tammy Model Miss, red or blk, EX...........................$25.00
Case, Tammy Traveller, red or gr, EX $45.00
Coloring Book, Tammy & Thumbilina, Whitman, 1963, unused, EX $32.00
Doll, Bud, MIB, minimum value $600.00
Doll, Dodi, MIB..$75.00
Doll, Glamour Misty the Miss Clairol Doll, MIB $150.00
Doll, Grown Up Tammy, blk, MIB...............................$400.00
Doll, Grown Up Tammy, MIB...$85.00
Doll, Misty, blk, MIB, minimum value..........................$600.00
Doll, Misty, MIB $100.00
Doll, Patti, MIB $200.00
Doll, Pepper, MIB $65.00
Doll, Pepper (Canadian version), MIB..............................$75.00
Doll, Pepper (carrot-colored hair), MIB............................$75.00
Doll, Pepper (trimmer body & smaller face), MIB.............$75.00
Doll, Pos 'N Dodi, M (decorated box) $100.00
Doll, Pos 'N Dodi, M (plain box).....................................$75.00
Doll, Pos 'N Misty & Her Telephone Booth, MIB..........$125.00
Doll, Pos 'N Pepper, MIB..$75.00
Doll, Pos 'N Pete, MIB...$125.00
Doll, Pos 'N Salty, MIB...$125.00
Doll, Pos 'N Tammy & Her Telephone Booth, MIB.......$100.00
Doll, Pos 'N Ted, MIB...$100.00
Doll, Tammy, MIB $100.00
Doll, Tammy's Dad, MIB $65.00
Doll, Tammy's Mom, MIB $85.00
Doll, Ted, MIB $50.00

Dolls, Ideal, Tammy
• • • • • • • • • • • • • • • • • • •
Doll, Pos 'N Misty, Opening Night outfit. Doll, $25.00 to $45.00; outfit, mint and complete, $65.00 to $80.00. (Photo courtesy Cindy Sabulis)

Dolls, Ideal, Tammy
Doll, Pos 'N Pepper, Flower Girl outfit. Doll, $20.00 to $25.00; outfit, mint and complete, $35.00 to $50.00. (Photo courtesy Cindy Sabulis)

Dolls, Ideal, Tammy
Doll, Tammy, top braid, sold as 'switchables,' straight-legged. Doll, $25.00 to $40.00; outfit, $30.00 to $45.00. (Photo courtesy Cindy Sabulis)

Outfit, Dad & Ted, pajamas & slippers, #9456-5, MIB......$20.00
Outfit, Dad & Ted, sports car, coat & cap, #9467-2, NRFP.$20.00
Outfit, Dad & Ted, sweater, shorts & socks, #9476-3, MIP...$25.00
Outfit, Day & Ted, blazer & slacks, #9477-1, NRFP..........$20.00
Outfit, Pepper, After School, #9318-7, complete, M.........$30.00
Outfit, Pepper, Anchors Away, #9316-1, complete, M $35.00
Outfit, Pepper, Flower Girl, #9332-8, complete, M............$50.00
Outfit, Pepper, Happy Holiday, #9317-9, complete, M......$40.00
Outfit, Pepper, Miss Gadabout, #9331-0, MIP $50.00
Outfit, Pepper & Dodi, Light & Lacy, #9305-4, MIP.........$45.00
Outfit, Pepper & Dodi, Sun 'N Surf, #9321-1, MIP...........$75.00
Outfit, Tammy, Beach Party, #9056-3 or #99-6-9, complete, M..$45.00
Outfit, Tammy, Career Girl, #9945-7, complete, M...........$75.00
Outfit, Tammy, Cutie Coed, #9132-2 or #9932-5, complete, M $45.00
Outfit, Tammy, Jet Set, #9155-3 or #9943-2, MIP $100.00
Outfit, Tammy, Knit Knack, #9094-4 or #9917-6, complete, M ...$25.00
Outfit, Tammy, Opening Night, #9954-9, MIP............... $100.00
Outfit, Tammy, Private Secretary, #9939-0, MIP $150.00
Outfit, Tammy's Mom, Evening in Paris, #9421-9, complete, M $40.00
Outfit, Tammy's Mom, Lazy Days, #9418-5, MIP...............$50.00
Pak Clothing, afternoon dress & shoes, #9345-2, NRFP...$45.00
Pak Clothing, nightgown, sandals & 3-pc fruit set, #9242-9, NRFP..$30.00
Pak Clothing, pedal pushers, orange juice, newspaper & hanger, #9224-7, NRFP...$30.00
Pak Clothing, sheath dress, blk belt, shoes & hanger, #9243-7, NRFP..$45.00
Pak Clothing, short-sleeved blouse, red glasses & hanger, #9231-2, NRFP..$20.00

Pak Clothing, skirt, belt, handkerchief, date book & hanger, #9220-5, MIP $30.00
Pak Clothing, skirt & hanger, #9221-3, NRFP $25.00
Pak Clothing, sleeveless blouse, necklace & hanger, #9222-1, NRFP..$25.00
Pak Clothing, sweater, scarf & hanger, #9244-5, NRFP $25.00
Pepper's Jukebox, M...$65.00
Pepper's Pony, MIB... $250.00
Pepper's Treehouse, MIB... $125.00
Tammy & Ted Catamaran, MIB.. $200.00
Tammy Bubble Bath Set, NRFB..$75.00
Tammy Dress-Up Kit, Colorforms, 1964, complete, MIB..$30.00
Tammy Hair Dryer, sq or rnd case, NM...........................$50.00
Tammy's Bed, Dresser & Chair, MIB.................................$65.00
Tammy's Car, MIB $75.00
Tammy's Ideal House, M, minimum value $100.00
Tammy's Jukebox $50.00
Tammy's Magic Mirror Fashion Show, NRFB $50.00

OTHER IDEAL DOLLS

Baby Cuddles, 1930-40, 22", re-dressed, EX.................... $150.00
Baby Giggles, 1967, 15", MIB... $125.00
Baby Snoozie, 1965, 14", w/up knob, EX, $50 to $75.00
Belly Button Baby, 1971, 9½", several variations, MIB, ea .$85.00
Bonnie Braids, 1951-53, Dick Tracy comic strip character, vinyl head, jtd arms, 1-pc body, open mouth, 1 tooth, pnt yel hair, 2 yel saran pigtails, pnt bl eyes, 11½", EX...................... $230.00
Dennis the Menace, 1976, all-cloth, printed doll, comic strip character by Hank Ketcham, blond hair, freckles, wearing overalls, striped shirt, 14", EX...$20.00
Flintstones, Baby Pebbles, 1963-64, all-vinyl toddler, jtd body, outfit w/leopard print, 14", NM $140.00
Harriet Hubbard Ayer, 1953, cosmetic doll, vinyl stuffed head, hard plastic body, wigged or rooted hair, came w/8-pc HH Ayer cosmetic kit, 14", EX $100.00
Harriet Hubbard Ayer, 1953, cosmetic doll, vinyl stuffed head, hard plastic body, wigged or rooted hair, came w/8-pc HH Ayer cosmetic kit, 16", EX $125.00
Johnny Playpal, 1949, 24", NM...................................... $425.00
Kissy, 1960s, 22", MIB, $100 to $125.00
Kissy (Tiny), 1960s, 16", EX, $25 to.................................$65.00
Little Lost Baby, 1968, 22", MIB $125.00
Miss Ideal the Photographer's Model, complete w/Playwave Kit, NMIB, $250 to $300.00
Patti Playful, 1960s, nurse, 36", M.................................. $350.00
Patti Playful, 1970, 16", EX, $45 to $65.00
Patti Prays, 1957, NM...$55.00
Patty PlayPal, 1981, reissue, MIB, $200 to...................... $250.00
Peanuts Gang, 1976-78, all-cloth, stuffed printed dolls from Peanuts cartoon strip by Charles Schulz, Charlie Brown, Lucy, Linus, Peppermint Patty & Snoopy, 14", EX, ea.............$35.00
Penny Playpal, 1959, 32", re-dressed, $300 to................. $350.00
Pos'n Glamour Misty, 1965, 11½", M...............................$45.00
Pretty Curls, 1981-82, Ex..$25.00
Princess Mary, 1950s, 19", M... $175.00
Revlon Doll, EXIB... $300.00
Rub-A-Dub Dolly in Tugboat Shower, 1974-78, 17", MIB..$100.00

Dolls, Ideal, Other
Plassie, Ideal, 1942, 16", $145.00. (Photo courtesy McMasters Harris Auction Co./Linda Edward)

Saucy Walker, 16", EXIB $225.00
Saucy Walker, 22", EX $225.00
Talkytot, 1950s, stuffed body, vinyl face, hand-crank, 25", MIB $195.00
Tearie Dearie Twins, 1963, 9", EX $40.00
Thumbelina, 1960s, 18", NMIB, $150 to $225.00
Thumbelina (Newborn), 1960s, 9½", NM $95.00
Thumbelina (Tiny), 1960s, 14", MIB $185.00
Thumbelina (Tiny), 1960s, 21", NM, $100 to $150.00
Thumbelina (Toddler), 1960s, complete w/walker, NMIB...$125.00
Toni, 1949 on, hard plastic, jtd body, nylon wig, sleep eyes, came w/permanent wave playset, 14", EX $325.00

Toni, 1949 on, hard plastic, jtd body, nylon wig, sleep eyes, came w/permanent wave playset, 16", EX $400.00
Toni, 1949 on, hard plastic, jtd body, nylon wig, sleep eyes, came w/permanent wave playset, 21", EX $450.00
Upsy Dazy, 1973, 15", EX $40.00

KENNER

Kenner Products was a toy company founded in 1947 by three brothers, Albert, Phillip, and Joseph L. Steiner, in Cincinnati, Ohio. It was purchased by Tonka Toys in 1987 and then by Hasbro in 1991, run as a separate division by both. Hasbro closed the Cincinnati offices of Kenner in 2000, and Kenner's product lines were merged into Hasbro's. For more information we recommend *Doll Values, Antique to Modern*, by Linda Edward.

STRAWBERRY SHORTCAKE

Berry Cycle, 1983, MIB $38.00
Big Berry Trolley, 1982, EX..$40.00
Birthday Candle, figural number w/Strawberry Shortcake figure, various numbers, American Greetings, 3½", unused, MOC.......$12.00
Candle, Raspberry Cream, figural, 4½", unused, M............$10.00
Doll, Almond Tea, 6", MIB $30.00
Doll, Angel Cake & Souffle, 6", NRFB.............................$40.00
Doll, Apple Dumpling, 12", cloth w/yarn hair, EX+.........$25.00
Doll, Apple Dumpling & Tea Time Turtle, 6", MIB $75.00
Doll, Apricot, 15", NM...$35.00
Doll, Baby Needs a Name, 15", NM................................$35.00
Doll, Berry Baby Orange Blossom, 6", MIB......................$35.00
Doll, Butter Cookie, 6", MIB...$25.00
Doll, Cafe Olé, 6", MIB $45.00
Doll, Cherry Cuddler, 6", NRFB.....................................$45.00
Doll, Huckleberry Pie, flat hands, 6", MIB.......................$45.00
Doll, Lemon Meringue, 6", MIB......................................$45.00
Doll, Lemon Meringue, 15", cloth w/yarn hair, EX............$25.00
Doll, Lime Chiffon, 6", MIB...$45.00
Doll, Mint Tulip, 6", MIB..$50.00
Doll, Orange Blossom & Marmalade, MIB $45.00
Doll, Peach Blush & Melonie Belle, 6", MIB $115.00
Doll, Purple Pieman w/Berry Bird, posable, MIB..............$35.00
Doll, Strawberry Shortcake & Custard, 6", NRFB.......... $150.00
Doll, Strawberry Shortcake & Strawberrykin, 6", NRFB. $300.00

Dolls, Ideal, Other
Tiny Bamm-Bamm, 1964, all vinyl, jtd body, rooted blond saran hair, painted blue side-glancing eyes, leopard skin suit, cap, club, 12", NM, $125.00. (Photo courtesy Marcia Fanta)

Dolls, Ideal, Other
Tiny Pebbles, 1964 – 1966, hard vinyl body, came with plastic log cradle in 1965, 12", EX, $125.00. (Photo courtesy Marcia Fanta)

Dolls, Kenner, Strawberry Shortcake
Clock, 6", Bradley/ American Greetings, 1981, NM, $35.00. (Photo courtesy www.whatacharacter.com)

Dolls, Kenner, Strawberry Shortcake

Doll, Orange Blossom, Welcome to the World of Strawberry Shortcake, doll, comb, and thank you card/envelope included, MIB, $65.00. (Photo courtesy Sharing My Dolls and Stuff/Linda Edward)

Dolls, Kenner, Strawberry Shortcake

Musical Toy, Strawberry, Kenner, 1984, M, $18.00. (Photo courtesy www.whatacharacter.com)

Dolls, Kenner, Strawberry Shortcake

Strawberryland Miniatures, Sour Grapes with Dregs, scented like grapes, Kenner, MOC, $15.00 to $20.00.

Dolls, Kenner, Strawberry Shortcake

Strawberryland Miniatures, Strawberry Shortcake on a Skateboard, PVC, 2¼", MOC, $15.00. (Photo courtesy www.whatacharacter.com)

Dolls, Kenner, Strawberry Shortcake

Toothbrush Holder, plastic, 5½x7", American Greetings, 1981, $25.00. (Photo courtesy www.whatacharacter.com)

Dollhouse, no accessories, M $200.00
Figure, Almond Tea w/Marza Panda, PVC, 1", MOC $15.00
Figure, Butter Cookie w/Jelly Bear, PVC, 1", MOC $15.00
Figure, Cherry Cuddler w/Goosberry, Strawberryland Miniature, MIP, $15 to $20.00
Figure, Lemon Meringue w/Frappo, PVC, 1", MOC $15.00
Figure, Lime Chiffon w/balloons, PVC, 1", MOC $15.00
Figure, Merry Berry Worm, MIB $35.00
Figure, Mint Tulip w/March Mallard, PVC, MOC $15.00
Figure, Raspberry Tart w/bowl of cherries, MOC $15.00
Figurine, Strawberry Shortcake, ceramic, 5", EX $8.00
Ice Skates, EX $35.00
Lamp, 5½" Strawberry Shortcake on rnd base, pleated shade, American Greetings, 1981, M $35.00
Motorized Bicycle, NM $100.00
Ornament, Custard in Christmas stocking w/candy cane, compo, 4", American Greetings, 1981, NM+ $15.00
Ornament, Raspberry Cream, pnt compo, 3¼", American Greetings, NM+ $15.00
Pillow Doll, Huckleberry Pie, 9", EX $100.00
Roller Skates, EX $35.00
Shoelaces, print on wht American Greetings, 1981, MIP (pkg reads One Two...Tie My Shoe) $10.00
Sleeping Bag, EX $25.00
Storybook Playcase, M $35.00
Stroller, Coleco, M $85.00
Telephone, Strawberry Shortcake figure, b/o, EX $85.00
Tray Table, tin, w/fold-down legs, Friends & Fun Go Together, 13x18x7", American Greetings, 1981, NM+ $15.00
Vase, wht porc, bulbous, Love Grows in Sweet Hearts, gold trim, 4", WWA, 1980, M $25.00

OTHER KENNER DOLLS

Baby Yawnie, 1974, vinyl head, cloth body, 15", EX $15.00
Blythe, 1972, pull string to change color of eyes, 'mod' clothes, 11½", NM $1,200.00
Gabbigale, 1972, 18", MIB $85.00
Nancy Nonsense, 1968, talker, 17", MIB $115.00
Talking Baby Alive, 1992, MIB $125.00

MATTEL

Mattel, Inc. was founded in 1959 by Ruth and Elliott Handler. Probably most noted for producing the ever-popular Barbie® doll, it is one of the most successful toy companies in history, and is still in operation. For more information we recommend *Doll Values, Antique to Modern*, by Linda Edward.

CHATTY CATHY

Chatty Cathy was introduced in the 1960s and came as either a blond or brunette. For five years, she sold very well. Much of her success can be attributed to the fact that Chatty Cathy talked. By pulling the string on her back, she could respond with many different phrases. During her five years of fame, Mattel added to the line with Chatty Baby, Tiny Chatty Baby and Tiny Chatty Brother (the twins), Charmin' Chatty, and finally

Singin' Chatty, Charmin' Chatty had 16 interchangable records. Her voice box was acitvated in the same manner as the above-mentioned dolls, by means of a pull string located at the base of her neck. The line was brought back in 1969, smaller and with a restyled face, but it was not well received.

Note: Prices given are for working dolls. Deduct half if doll is mute.

For more information we recommend *Chatty Cathy Dolls* and *Talking Toys of the 20th Century*, both by Kathy and Don Lewis.

Dolls, Mattel, Chatty Cathy
• • • • • • • • • • • • • • •
Doll, Chatty Cathy, 1960 – 1963, 20", $275.00. (Photo courtesy The Museum Doll Shop/Linda Edward)

Carrying Case, Chatty Baby, bl or pk, NM, ea...................$50.00
Carrying Case, Tiny Chatty Baby, bl or pk, NM, ea..........$40.00
Doll, Charmin' Chatty, EX, $75 to.................................. $150.00
Doll, Chatty Baby, EX, $65 to.....................................$90.00
Doll, Chatty Cathy, any style except for unmarked 1st doll, EX, $75 to.. $150.00
Doll, Chatty Cathy, 1970 reissue, MIB, $35 to.................$50.00
Doll, Chatty Patty, 1980s, MIB.....................................$75.00
Doll, Singin' Chatty, blond hair or brunette, M, $40 to....$75.00
Doll, Tiny Chatty Baby, blk, EX....................................$150.00
Doll, Tiny Chatty Baby, brother, EX, $45 to.....................$65.00
Doll, Tiny Chatty Baby, EX, $35 to.................................$50.00
Outfit, Charmin' Chatty, Let's Go Shopping, MIP............$75.00
Outfit, Charmin' Chatty, Let's Play Together, MIP...........$75.00
Outfit, Chatty Baby, Sleeper Set, MIP $50.00
Outfit, Chatty Cathy, Pink Peppermint Stick, MIP........ $125.00
Outfit, Chatty Cathy, Playtime, MIP $125.00
Outfit, Tiny Chatty Baby, Pink Frill, MIP...................... $100.00
Outfit, Tiny Chatty Baby Bye-Bye, MIP............................$75.00

LIDDLE KIDDLES

From 1966 to 1971, Mattel produced Liddle Kiddle dolls and accessories, typical of the 'little kid next door.' They were made in sizes ranging from a tiny ¾" up to 4". They were all posable and had rooted hair that could be restyled. Eventually there were Animiddles and Zoolery Jewelry Kiddles, which were of course animals, and two other series that represented storybook and nursery-rhyme characters. There was a set of extraterrestrials, and lastly in 1979, Sweet Treets dolls were added to the assortment.

In the mid-1970s Mattel reissued Lucky Locket Kiddles. The dolls had names identical to the earlier lockets but were not of the same high quality.

In 1994 and 1995 Tyco reissued Liddle Kiddles in Strapon, Clip-on, Lovely Locket, Pretty Perfume, and Baby Bottle collections.

Loose dolls, if complete and with all their original accessories, are worth about 50% less than the same mint in the box. Dressed, loose dolls with no accessories are worth 75% less. For more information, refer to *Liddle Kiddles* by Paris Langford.

Advisor: Dawn Diaz

Alice in Wonderliddle, complete, NM............................ $175.00
Animiddle Kiddles, MIP, ea...$75.00
Aqua Funny Bunny, #3532, MIP, $40 to $50.00
Babe Biddle, #3505, complete, M.....................................$50.00
Baby Din-Din, #3820, complete, M $35.00
Baby Rockaway, #3819, MIP $100.00
Beach Buggy, #5003, complete, NM................................$25.00
Beat-A-Diddle, #3510, MIP $500.00
Blue Funny Bunny, #3532, MIP, $40 to..........................$50.00
Calamity Jiddle, #3506, complete w/high saddle horse, M .$50.00
Chitty Chitty Bang Bang Kiddles, #3597, MIP................. $150.00
Chocolottie's House, #2501, MIP....................................$25.00
Cinderriddles Palace, #5068, plastic window version, M...$25.00
Cookin' Kiddles, #3846, complete, M $150.00
Dainty Deer, #3637, complete, M $20.00
Florence Niddle, #3507, complete, M $50.00
Flower Charm Bracelet, #3747, MIP................................$50.00
Flower Pin Kiddle, #3741, MIP.......................................$50.00
Flower Ring Kiddle, #3744, MIP.....................................$50.00
Frosty Mint Kone, #3653, complete, M $35.00
Greta Grape, Kola Kiddle, #3728, complete, M, $35 to $40.00
Greta Griddle, #3508, complete, M $50.00
Heart Charm Bracelet Kiddle, #3747, MIP.......................$50.00
Heart Pin Kiddle, #3741, MIP..$50.00
Heart Ring Kiddle, #3744, MIP......................................$50.00
Henrietta Horseless Carriage, #3641, complete, M, $35 to...$40.00
Hot Dog Stand, #5002, complete, M $25.00
Howard Biff Biddle, #3502, complete, M.........................$75.00
Howard Biff Biddle, #3502, MIP $300.00
Jewelry Kiddles, Treasure Box, #3735, red, M.................$25.00
Jewelry Kiddles, Treasure Box, #5166, gr, rare, M $75.00

Dolls, Mattel, Liddle Kiddles
• • • • • • • • • • • • • • • • • • • •
Heather Hiddlehorse, Skediddle Kiddles series, #3673, 1969 – 1970, M, $85.00. (Photo courtesy Paris Langford)

Kampy Kiddle, #3753, complete, M $85.00

Kiddle & Kars Antique Fair Set, #3806, MIP $300.00

Kiddle Komedy Theatre, #3592, EX....................$35.00

Kiddle Kolognes, #3704, Honeysuckle, MIP...................$75.00

Kiddle Kolognes, #3705 Sweet Pea, M....................$45.00

Kiddles Kolognes, #3710 Gardinia, MIP..................$75.00

Kiddles Kolognes, #3713 Violet, MIP.....................$75.00

Kiddles Sweet Shop, MIP $300.00

King & Queen of Hearts, #3784, MIP....................$150.00

Kleo Kola, Kola Kiddle, #3729, complete, M, $35 to $40.00

Kola Kiddles Three-Pak, #3734, MIP.....................$200.00

Kosmic Kiddles, M, ea $150.00

Lady Crimson, #A3840, MIP...........................$75.00

Lady Lavender, #A3840, MIP...........................$75.00

Laffy Lemon, Kola Kiddle, #3732, MIP....................$75.00

Larky Locket, #3539, complete, EX....................$25.00

Lenore Limousine, #3743, complete, M, $35 to.............$40.00

Liddel Kiddles Kabin #3591, complete, EX................$25.00

Liddel Kiddles 3-Story House, complete, M...............$35.00

Liddle Biddle Peep, #3544, complete, M $150.00

Liddle Diddle, #3503, complete, M $50.00

Liddle Kiddles Kastle, #3522, complete, M................$55.00

Liddle Kiddles Klub, #3301, M $20.00

Liddle Kiddles Kolony, #3571, M $25.00

Liddle Kiddles Kottage, #3534, complete, EX.............$25.00

Liddle Kiddles Open House, #5167, MIP................$40.00

Liddle Kiddles Pop-Up Boutique, #5170, complete, M......$30.00

Liddle Kiddles Pop-Up Playhouse, #3574, complete, M $30.00

Liddle Kiddles Talking Townhouse, #5154, MIB $50.00

Liddle Lion Zoolery, #3661, complete, M $75.00

Liddle Red Riding Hiddle, #3546, complete, M $150.00

Lilac Locket, #3540, MIP $75.00

Limey Lou Spoonfuls, #2817, MIP $25.00

Lois Locket, #3541, complete, M $75.00

Lola Locket, #3536, MIP $75.00

Lolli-Grape, #3656, complete, M $40.00

Lolli-Lemon, #3657, MIP $75.00

Lolli-Mint, #3658, MIP $75.00

Lorelei Locket, #3717, MIP $75.00

Lorelei Locket, #3717, 1976 version, MIP $25.00

Lottie Locket, #3679, complete, M $25.00

Lou Locket, #3537, MIP $75.00

Luana Locket, #3680, complete, M $35.00

Luana Locket, #3680, Gold Rush version, MIP $85.00

Lucky Lion, #3635, complete, M $20.00

Lucky Locket Jewel Case, #3542, M $100.00

Lucky Locket Magic Paper Dolls, Whitman, 1968, EXIB..$30.00

Luscious Lime, Kola Kiddle, #3733, complete, M, $35 to....$40.00

Luscious Lime, Kola Kiddle, #3733, glitter version, complete, M..$50.00

Luvvy Duvvy Kiddle, #3596, MIP $50.00

Millie Middle, #3509, complete, M....................$85.00

Miss Mouse, #3638, MIP $50.00

Nappytime Baby, #3818, complete, M $40.00

Nurse 'N Totsy Outfit, #LK7, MIP.....................$25.00

Olivia Orange Kola Kiddle, #3730, MIP.................$75.00

Pink Funny Bunny, #3552, MIP, $40 to $50.00

Poisies 'N Pink Skediddle Outfit, #3585, MIP $25.00

Rah Rah Skediddle, #3788, complete, M...................$80.00

Rapunzel & the Prince, #3783, MIP $150.00

Robin Hood & Maid Marion, #3785, MIP $150.00

Rolly Twiddle, #3519, complete, M................. $175.00

Romeo & Juliet, #3782, MIP $150.00

Santa Kiddle, #3595, MIP $40.00

Shirley Skediddle, #3766, MIP.........................$60.00

Shirley Strawberry, Kola Kiddle, #3727, complete, M, $35 to .$40.00

Sizzly Friddle, #3513, complete, M....................$50.00

Sizzly Friddle, MIP $300.00

Sleep 'N Totsy Outfit, #LK5, MIP....................$25.00

Sleeping Biddle, #3527, complete, M, $150 to $175.00

Sleeping Biddle, #3527, MOC $300.00

Slipsy Sliddle, #3754, complete, M $65.00

Snap-Happy Bedroom, #5172, complete, M $15.00

Snap-Happy Living Room, #5173, NMIP...................$20.00

Snap-Happy Patio Furniture, #5171, MIP, $20 to.............$25.00

Snoopy Skediddleer & His Sopwith Camel, M.............. $150.00

Suki Skediddle, #3767, complete, M....................$25.00

Surfy Skediddle, #3517, complete, M....................$75.00

Swingy Skiddle, #3789, MIP $200.00

Teeter Time Baby, #3817, complete, M....................$35.00

Teresa Touring Car, #3644, complete, M, $35 to $40.00

Tessie Tractor, #3671, complete, NM....................$85.00

Tiny Tiger, #3636, MIP $50.00

Tracy Trikediddle, #3769, complete, M...................$40.00

Trikey Triddle, #3515, complete, M $50.00

Vanilla Lilly, #2819, MIP...........................$25.00

Windy Fiddle, #3514, complete, M $85.00

World of the Kiddles Beauty Bazaar, #3586, NRFB $300.00

Dolls, Mattel, Liddle Kiddles

Liz Locket, Lucky Locket Kiddle series, #3538, 1967, 2", MOC, $75.00. (Photo courtesy McMasters Harris Auction Co./Linda Edward)

Dolls, Mattel, Liddle Kiddles

Peter Paniddle, #3547, Storybook Kiddles series, MIB, $300.00. (Photo courtesy Paris Langford)

ROCK FLOWERS

Rock Flowers were introduced in the early 1970s as Mattel's answer to Topper's Dawn Dolls. Rock Flowers are 6½" tall and have wire articulated bodies that came with mod sunglasses attached to their heads. There were four girls and one boy in the series with 18 groovy outfits that could be purchased separately. Each doll came with its own 45 rpm record, and the clothing packages were shaped like a 45 rpm record.

Advisor: Dawn Diaz

Dolls, Mattel, Rock Flowers

Doll, Heather, 1970, loose, $15.00. (Photo courtesy The Museum Doll Shop/Linda Edward)

Case, Rock Flowers, #4991 (single doll), vinyl, NM..........$10.00
Case, Rock Flowers on Stage, #4993 (3 dolls), vinyl, NM..$15.00
Doll, Doug, #1177, NRFB, $40 to $50.00
Doll, Heather, NRFB, $40 to...$50.00
Doll, Iris, NRFB, $50 to..$60.00
Doll, Lilac, #1167, NRFB, $40 to.......................................$50.00
Doll, Rosemary, #1168, NRFB, $50 to $60.00
Gift Set, In Concert, Heather, Lilac & Rosemary, NRFB ...$150.00
Outfit, Flares 'N Lace, #4057, NRFP..................................$15.00
Outfit, Frontier Gingham, #4069, NRFP $15.00
Outfit, Jeans in Fringe, NRFP...$15.00
Outfit, Long in Fringe, #4050, NRFP.................................$15.00
Outfit, Overall Green, #4067, NRFP..................................$15.00
Outfit, Tie Dye Maxi, #4053, NRFP...................................$15.00
Outfit, Topped Lace, #4058, NRFP $15.00

UPSY DOWNSYS

The Upsy Downsy dolls were made during the late 1960s. They were small, 2½" to 3½", made of vinyl and plastic. Some of the group were 'Upsys' that walked on their feet, while others were 'Downsys' that walked or rode fantasy animals while upside-down.

Advisor: Dawn Diaz

Foozie Woozie $25.00
Funny Feeder, Gooey Chooey only, EX..............................$25.00
Furry Hurry Wiz-z-zer...$25.00
Hairy Hurry Downsy Wiz-z-er, complete, EX $100.00

OTHER MATTEL DOLLS

Baby Beans, 1970s, several variations, NM, ea $30 to $45.00
Baby Cheerful Tearful, 1966, 6½", MIB $55.00
Baby Cheryl, 1965, talker, MIB..$225.00
Baby Drowsy, 1969, talker, 15", MIB, $175 to..............$225.00
Baby First Step, 1964, b/o, 18", M, $40 to.......................$65.00
Baby First Step, 1967, b/o, 18", longer hair than 1st issue, M, $35 to..$65.00
Baby First Step, 1967, talker, MIB $175.00
Baby Flip-Flop, JC Penney, 1970, talker, MIB.................$125.00
Baby Fun, 1968, 7", complete, EX $55.00
Baby Go Bye-Bye & Her Bumpety Buggy, 1968, 10½", MIB..$225.00
Baby Love Light, 1971, NMIB $55.00
Baby Pat-A-Burp, 1963, 17", EX.......................................$65.00
Baby Secret, 1966, talker, 18", EX.....................................$65.00
Baby See 'N Say, 1964, talker, MIB, $175 to....................$225.00
Baby Sing-A-Long, 1969, talker, 16½", MIB $150.00
Baby Small Talk, 1968, talker, 10", MIB $100.00
Baby Teenietalk, 1966, talker, 17", EX..............................$75.00
Baby Tender Love (Brother), NRFB $125.00
Baby Whisper, 1968, talker, 17½", MIB $150.00
Casper the Friendly Ghost, 1964, pull-string talker, 16", EX...$100.00
Cheerful-Tearful, 1965, 13", orig outfit, NM.....................$65.00
Cheerleader, 1970, talker, several variations, MIB, ea.......$75.00

Dolls, Mattel, Upsy Downsys

Upsys: Baby So-High and her Airo-Zoomer, Flossy Glossy and her Elewetter Fire-Truck, Tickle Pinkle and her Bugabout and mushroom gas pump, and Pudgy Fudgy and her Piggybus. Each $20.00 to $30.00. (Photo courtesy Karen Hickey/Cindy Sabulis)

Dolls, Mattel, Upsy Downsys

Downsys: Miss Information (missing glasses) and her Booth Moose, Pocus Hocus and his Dragon Wagon, Mother What Now and her Go-Getter, and Downy Dilly and her Footmobile. Each $20.00 to $30.00. (Photo courtesy Karen Hickey/Cindy Sabulis)

Cynthia, talker, M..$85.00
Dancerella, 1972, 18", b/o, complete, M, $35 to................$65.00
Dancerina, 1968, 24", b/o, MIB, $225 to $275.00
Drowsy, 1966, talker, MIB $165.00
Gramma & Grandpa, 1968, talkers, MIB, ea $95.00
Hi Dottie, 1972, talker, w/phone, blk, NM.......................$75.00
Little Sister Look 'N Say, Sears, talker, 18", M $150.00
Magic Baby Tender Love, 1978, 14", MIB $125.00
Matty the Talking Boy, 1961, MIB..............................$145.00
Mork & Mindy, 1979, 9", MIB, ea.................................$30.00
Randi Reader, 1968,m talker, 20", MIB $175.00
Sister Belle, 1961, talker, MIB $145.00
Sister Small Talk, 1968, talker, EX $55.00
Small Talk Cinderella, MIB, $100 to $125.00
Somersalty, 1970, talker, MIB....................................$200.00
Swingy, 1968, mechanical dancing doll, 18", EX...........$100.00
Taters, M $125.00
Teachy Keen, Sears, 1966, talker, 16", MIB $175.00
Teachy Keen, Sears, 1966, talker, 16", NM.....................$95.00
Teachy Talk, 1970, talker, MIB $145.00
Tearful Tender Love, 1971, 16", VG+.............................$50.00
Timey Tell, talker, MIB..$110.00
Tippee Toes, 1968-70, mechanical, rides accessory horse, tricycle,
knit sweater, pants, 17", EX $85.00

REMCO

Remco Industries, Inc. of Harrision, New Jersey, was a toy company founded in the 1940s that was best known for toys marketed and sold in the late 1950s and 1960s. The name Remco comes from the two words 'Remote Control.' Remco was one of the first companies to market with television ads.

For more information we recommend *Doll Values, Antique to Modern*, by Linda Edward.

HEIDI AND FRIENDS

Heidi was probably one of Remco's most popular dolls. She was extremely popular from about 1967 into the early 1970s. Heidi was a little blond doll standing about 5½" tall who came with a plastic case. Heidi had a Japanese friend named Jan. Both Heidi and Jan featured magic buttons on their stomachs that made them wave. They were all-vinyl with rooted hair, painted side-glancing eyes, and open/closed mouths.

Heidi, 5½", EX $40.00
Herby, 4½", EX $25.00
Hildy, 4½", EX...$30.00
Jan, Oriental, 5½", MIB..$50.00
Pip, 5½", EX...$35.00
Winking Heidi, 1968, 5½", $20 to $30.00

LITTLECHAP FAMILY

In 1964, Remco Industries created a family of four fashion dolls that represented a typical American family. The Littlechaps family consisted of the father, Dr. John Littlechap, his wife, Lisa, and their two children, Judy and Libby. Their clothing and fash-

ion accessories were made in Japan and are of the finest quality. Because these dolls are not as pretty as other fashion dolls of the era, and their size and placement of arms and legs made them awkward to dress, children had little interest in them at the time. This lack of interest during the 1960s has created shortages of them for collectors of today. Mint and complete outfits or outfits never-removed-from box are especially desirable to Littlechap collectors. Values listed for loose clothing are for ensembles complete with all their small accessoires. If only the main pieces of the outfit are available, then the value could go down significantly.

Dolls, Remco, Littlechap Family Doll, Libby, 10½", $50.00. (Photo courtesy The Museum Doll Shop/Linda Edward)

Carrying Case, EX...$40.00
Doll, Doctor John, MIB...$65.00
Doll, Judy, MIB...$75.00
Doll, Lisa, MIB..$65.00
Family Room, Bedroom or Doctor John's Office, EX, ea. $125.00
Outfit, Doctor John, complete, EX, $15 to.........................$30.00
Outfit, Doctor John, NRFB, $40 to $50.00
Outfit, Judy, complete, EX, $25 to $40.00
Outfit, Judy, NRFB, $35 to $75.00
Outfit, Libby, complete, EX, $20 to $35.00
Outfit, Libby, NRFB, $35 to $50.00
Outfit, Lisa, complete, EX, $20 to $35.00
Outfit, Lisa, NRFB, $35 to...$75.00

OTHER REMCO DOLLS

Baby Crawl-Along, 1967, 20", all orig, EX, $25 to $35.00
Baby Glad 'N Sad, 1967, vinyl & hard plastic, rooted blond hair,
pnt eyes, 14", EX $12.00
Jumpsy, 1970, vinyl & hard plastic, jumps rope, rooted hair, pnt
eyes, molded-on shoes & socks, 14", EX.........................$30.00
Polly Puff, 1970, vinyl, came w/inflatable furniture, 12", MIB ..$45.00
Sweet April, 1971, vinyl, 5½", EX...................................$40.00
Tippy Tumbles, 1968, vinyl, rooted red hair, stationary eyes, does
somersaults, batteries in pocketbook, 16", EX $65.00

SCHOENHUT

Schoenhut dolls are from the late nineteenth century to the early twentieth century. First came the all-wood dolls, then came the dolls with cloth bodies, and later the composition dolls. Their hair was carved or molded and painted or wigged. They had intaglio or sleep eyes, open or closed mouths. For more information we recommend *Doll Values, Antique to Modern*, by Linda Edward.

The following listings are from current auctions.

Baby Boy, 11½", pnt hair & eyes, orig bl & wht sailor-type suit w/ hat, bare feet, VG $225.00

Baby Boy, 12", wig, pnt eyes, closed mouth, re-dressed, EX..$200.00

Boy Walker, 17", wig, intaglio eyes, closed mouth, re-dressed, EX $350.00

Character Boy, 14", wig, intaglio eyes, pouty mouth, re-dressed, G $355.00

Character Boy, 16", #309, wig, intaglio eyes, similing mouth w/2 teeth, orig outfit, VG $3,025.00

Character Boy, 19", wig, intaglio eyes, re-dressed, G $385.00

Character Girl, 14", #313, wig, intaglio eyes, re-dressed, G .$450.00

Character Girl, 16", #16/306, wig, intaglio eyes, closed mouth, orig outfit, EX $4,125.00

Character Girl, 16", #303, wig, intaglio eyes, smiling mouth w/6 teeth, orig outfit, VG.................................. $2,200.00

Girl, 14", wig, intaglio eyes, slightly open mouth, orig outfit, VG $700.00

Girl, 16", carved pnt hair, intaglio eyes, period dress w/blk leather shoes, EX $1,100.00

Girl, 16", wig, intaglio eyes, re-dressed, VG..................... $600.00

Girl, 19" $900.00

Girl Walker, 16", wig, intaglio eyes, closed mouth, orig outfit, VG $300.00

Miss Dolly, 16", #316, wig, pnt eyes, 4 bottom teeth, night clothes & slippers, VG+ $300.00

Miss Dolly, 19½", wood, wig, pnt features, 4 upper teeth, orig outfit, VG $250.00

Nature Baby, 12½", pnt hair, spring-jtd, re-dressed, G.... $110.00

Toddler Boy, 11", wig, pnt eyes, orig outfit w/hat, shoes & socks, VG, A $300.00

Toddler Boy, 11½", pnt hair, spring jtd, orig outfit, G..... $200.00

Toddler Girl, 16", wig, intaglio eyes, re-dressed, VG $400.00

SHIRLEY TEMPLE (1957 – 1963)

In 1957, the Ideal Toy Corporation reintroduced the Shirley Temple doll to a whole new generation of young fans who arose from watching her early movies on television along with a TV show called *The Shirley Temple Storybook*. Shirley herself played a big part in the production of these new dolls, which were made of vinyl with rooted hair and sleep eyes.

Note: The outfits on the dolls listed are original and complete with undergarments, shoes and socks, purses, and hang tags unless noted otherwise.

For more information we recommend *The Complete Guide to Shirley Temple Dolls and Collectibles* by Tonya Bervaldi-Camaratta and *Doll Values, Antique to Modern*, by Linda Edward.

Doll, 12", dress, nylon (various colors), wht lacy trim, wht panties, #9717, 1960, MIB $90.00

Doll, 12", dress, straw hat, wht socks & blk sandals (rare), blk signature purse, 1958, MIB (gold star box)................. $350.00

Doll, 12", Heidi outfit w/gr felt headband, 1959, NM..... $175.00

Doll, 12", ice skating outfit, red shirt & tights w/blk skirt, matching stocking hat, wht shoes, #9561, 1959, NM $300.00

Doll, 12", party dress, yel nylon w/wht lacy trim, straw hat, shoes w/snap closures, 1959, MIB........................... $250.00

Doll, 12", playsuit (1-pc) w/lacy trim, 1961-62, MIB...... $225.00

Doll, 12", Scottie dog applique on red felt skirt, wht blouse, 1960, NM $200.00

Doll, 12", slip (pk satin), pk hair bow, 1958, MIB $200.00

Doll, 12", Wee Willie Winkie outfit, (rare red version), 1959, M (G box)... $250.00

Doll, 13", dress, red w/2 wht Scottie dog appliques, pin-back button at waist, VG $375.00

Doll, 13", dress, wht chiffon type w/bl banded trim & bl dots on under layer, matching hat, early, G............................. $150.00

Doll, 13", dress, wht w/red polka dots & ribbons, pin-back button at waist, EXIB... $2,125.00

Doll, 13", dress, yel w/floral print, wht collar & lace on short puffy sleeves, w/'The World's Darling' pin, early, VG . $450.00

Doll, 15", dress, bl w/wht nylon matador sleeves trimmed in red, 1963, NM $300.00

Doll, 15", dress, lt bl w/wht lace & blk velvet trim, 1959-60, NMIB $275.00

Doll, 15", dress, red w/wht & bl rickrack, red straw hat, 1961, NM $200.00

Doll, 15", dress, yel w/wht lace trim, bl ribbon & flower accents, 1959-60, NM $250.00

Doll, 15", Jr Prom dress, bl & wht checks w/lace & floral trim, 1961, MIB.. $325.00

Doll, 15", jumper, red w/wht blouse, red hair bow, 1962, MIB... $350.00

Doll, 15", Little Red Riding Hood outfit, 1961, NM $300.00

Doll, 16", 1973, Stand Up & Cheer $75.00

Doll, 17", Captain January, bl sailor dress w/red, wht & blk hat, 1960, MIB $325.00

Doll, 17", dress, bl nylon w/bl & wht trim, 1959-60, MIB ..$325.00

Doll, 17", dress, red & wht flocking, 1958, NM $250.00

Doll, 17", pinafore, wht nylon w/blk ribbon trim over pk dress, 1959-60, MIB $325.00

Doll, 17", Stand Up & Cheer, wht nylon dress w/red polka-dots, red trim, 1960, NM $225.00

Doll, 19", dress, taffeta w/bright floral design, 1960, NM. $250.00

Doll, 19", dress, wht nylon w/bl flower design, wht ribbon waist tie, #9532, 1959-60, NM $225.00

Doll, 19", Wee Willie Winkie, red plaid dress w/bl short-sleeved jacket w/3 wht buttons, 1959, NM $350.00

Doll, 36", dress, bl nylon w/lace-trimmed collar, 2 lg pk roses on bodice, 1959, NM $1,200.00

Doll, 36", Heidi dress (scarce) in wht w/gr vest & patterned trim around hemline, straw hat, 1960, NM $2,000.00

Outfit, 12", coat, #9535, brn wool w/dk brn collar, hat & muff, rare, 1958, M $90.00

Outfit, 12", dress, #9509, yel sleeveless V-neck w/bl embroidered floral trim, blk signature purse, 1958, M $60.00

Outfit, 12", dress, #9757, sleeveless w/pear-&-leaf design on wht, red V-neck collar & skirt hem, purse, 1961, M $45.00

Outfit, 12", pajama set, #9501, striped pants w/stripe & lace trim, red or bl, 1958, NM $40.00

Outfit, 12", pajama set, #9541, red & wht 2-pc w/matching stocking cap, 1959, MIB $75.00

Outfit, 12", playsuit, #9527, red 1-pc short-legged romper top w/ red & wht striped skirt, w/signature purse, 1958, M $50.00

Outfit, 12", raincoat, #9510, attached hood, matching belt, clear purse, various patterns, 1959, M $60.00

Outfit, 12", sailor dress, #9543, bl w/red-trimmed wht collar & hat, 1959, M $45.00

Outfit, 17", Rebecca of Sunnybrook Farm, bl denim jumper w/ red & wht checked pockets & blouse, checked headband, 1960, M...$65.00

Shirley Temple's Treasure Board (Magic Slate), Saalfield #8806, 1959, unused, M $25.00

VOGUE DOLL COMPANY

This popular doll company was founded in the 1930s by Jennie Graves in Medford, Massachusetts. Mrs. Graves began her business by dressing German dolls but is probably best known for the little dolls to become known as Ginny, which she introduced in 1948. The Vogue Doll Company is still in existence today and offers many re-creations of the dolls from the 1950s. For more information we recommend *Collector's Encyclopedia of Vogue Dolls* by Judith Izen and Carol Stover, and *Doll Values, Antique to Modern*, by Linda Edward.

Bent Knee Walker, 8", hard plastic, sleep eyes, jtd knees, walker mechanism in body, marked Vogue on head, on torso GINNY // VOGUE DOLLS // INC. // PAT NO. 2687594 // MADE IN U.S.A, 1957-62, MIB $225.00

Ginny, 8", all-vinyl, sleep eyes, straight-leg non-walker, rooted hair, marked Ginny on head, on torso Ginny // VOGUE DOLLS, Inc. 1965-72, NM $40.00

Ginny, 8", all-vinyl, sleep eyes, straight-leg non-walker, rooted hair, marked Ginny on head, on torso Ginny // VOGUE DOLLS©1972 // MADE IN HONG KONG // 3, 1972-77, NM.. $25.00

Ginny, 8", all-vinyl, sleep eyes, slender straight-leg non-walker, rooted hair, marked Ginny on head, on torso Ginny // VOGUE DOLLS©1972 // MADE IN HONG KONG // 3, 1977-82, MIB...$25.00

Jan, 10½", vinyl head, 6-pc hard vinyl body, straight-leg, swivel waist, rooted hair, marked VOGUE, 1958-64, NM..... $125.00

Jeff, 11", vinyl head, 5-pc hard vinyl body, straight-leg, molded pnt hair, marked VOGUE DOLLS, 1958-60 MIB $140.00

Jill, 10½", hard plastic, bent-knee walker, high heeled feet, marked JILL // VOGUE DOLLS // MADE IN U.S.A. © 1957-65, NM $175.00

Molded Lash Walker Ginny, 8", hard plastic, sleep eyes, walker mechanism in body, marked on torso GINNY // VOGUE DOLLS // INC. // PAT NO. 2687594 // MADE IN U.S.A, 1955-57, NM $200.00

Painted Eye Ginny, 8", hard plastic, marked Vogue on head, Vogue Doll on body, 1948-49, VG............................. $325.00

Painted Lash Walker Ginny, 8", hard plastic, sleep eyes, walker mechanism in body, marked on torso GINNY // VOGUE DOLLS // INC. // PAT PEND. // MADE IN U.S.A, 1954, NM.. $250.00

Strung Ginny, 8", hard plastic, sleep eyes, strung joints, marked Vogue on head, Vogue Doll on body, 1950-53, NM $400.00

Strung Ginny, 8", hard plastic, sleep eyes, strung joints, marked Vogue on head, Vogue Doll on body, poodle cut wig, wearing Margie outfit 1950-53, MIB $560.00

Vinyl Walker, 8", vinyl head, hard plastic body, sleep eyes, walker mechanism in body, marked GINNY on head, on torso GINNY // VOGUE DOLLS // INC. // PAT NO. 2687594 // MADE IN U.S.A, 1957-65, NM $40.00

• **Farm Toys** •

It's entirely probable that more toy tractors have been sold than real ones. They've been made to represent all makes and models, of plastic, cast iron, diecast metal, and even wood. They've been made in at least 1/16th scale, 1/32nd, 1/43rd, and 1/64th. If you buy a 1/16th-scale replica, that small piece of equipment would have to be 16 times larger to equal the size of the real item. Limited editions (meaning that a specific number will be made and no more) and commemorative editions (made for special events) are usually very popular with collectors. Many models on the market today are being made by the Ertl company.

See also Cast Iron, Farm Toys; Diecast.

Advisor: John Rammacher

Allis-Chalmers Tractor D-21 w/Duals, #13078, 1/16 scale, MIB $39.00

Allis-Chalmers Tractor Hi-Crop D-19, #13403, 1/64 scale, MIB $39.00

Allis-Chalmers Tractor WD-45, #13080, 1/16 scale, MIB.$23.50

Allis-Chalmers Tractor WD-45 Precision #7, #13101, 1/16 scale, MIB $118.00

Allis-Chalmers Tractor 7060, w/cab, #13185, 1/16 scale, MIB $35.00

Case IH Combine 2388, #14176, 1/64 scale, MIB $11.00

Case IH Cotton Express Picker, #4300, 1/64 scale, MIB ...$11.00

Case IH Planter 12-Row 900, #656, 1/64 scale, MIB...........$4.50

Case IH Round Baler, #274, 1/64 scale, MIB $3.25

Case IH Tillage Plow, #14172, 1/64 scale, MIB $32.50

Case IH Tractor Maxxum MX120, #4487, 1997 Farm Show, 1/16 scale, MIB...$45.00

Case IH Tractor MX135, #1458, 1/64 scale, MIB $5.00

Case IH Tractor MX270, #14134, 1/64 scale, MIB $5.00

Case IH Tractor STX Tracked, #14046, 1/64 scale, MIB.....$8.00

Case IH Tractor 6670 Row Crop, #229, 1/64 scale, MIB.....$3.00

Case IH Tractor 9260 w/4-Wheel Drive, #231, 1/64 scale, 1993 Farm Show, MIB...$9.00

Case Skid Steer Loader 90XT, #4216, 1/64 scale, MIB......$25.00

Case Tractor STX3754 w/4-Wheel Drive, #14005, 1/16 scale, MIB...$70.00

Case Tractor 930 Precision #12, #4284, 1/16 scale, MIB $107.00

Case Tractor 1930 Western SP Precision #15, #14130, 1/16 scale, MIB..$116.00

Caterpillar Flotation Liquid Fertilizer Spreader, #2324, 1/64 scale, MIB...$4.75

Deutz Allis Tractor 7085, #1260, 1/64 scale, 1990 Farm Show, MIB...$11.00

Deutz Allis Tractor 9150 Orlando Show, #1280, 1/16 scale, MIB $200.00

Farmall Crawler 340, #4734, 1/16 scale, MIB $25.00

Farmall Tractor B, #14113, 1/16 scale, MIB......................$23.50

Farmall Tractor F-20 on Rubber, Precision, #299CO, 1/16 scale, VG...$80.00

Farmall Tractor F-20 on Steel, Precision, #638CO, 1/16 scale, VG...$75.00

Farmall Tractor H, #4441, 1/16 scale, MIB $25.00

Farmall Tractor Super M, #14270, 1/16 scale, MIB $22.00

Farmall Tractor 400 Precision, #14007, 1/16 scale, MIB..$110.00

Farmall Tractor 560 w/Mount Picker & Wagon, #14073, 1/64 scale, MIB...$10.50

Ford Tractor F, #872, 1/16 scale, Collector's Ed, MIB $45.00

Ford Tractor 8N, #843, 1/16 scale, MIB $20.00

Ford Tractor 621, #13529, 1/16 scale, MIB $22.00

Ford Tractor 640, #3054, 1/16 scale, MIB $22.00

Ford Tractor 640 Precision 8, #13574, 1/16 scale, MIB .. $112.00

Ford Tractor 641 w/Precision Series Loader, #383, 1/16 scale, MIB...$135.00

Ford Tractor 4000, #3024, 1/64 scale, MIB $3.00

Ford Tractor 5000 Precision, #13503, 1/16 scale, MIB ... $117.00

Ford Tractor 5640 w/Loader, #334, 1/64 scale, MIB.............$5.00

Ford Tractor 7740 Row Crop, #973, 1/16 scale, Collector's Ed, MIB...$50.00

Farm Toys
Allis-Chalmers Tractor AC D-19, 1/16 scale, F, $50.00. (Photo courtesy John Rammacher)

Farm Toys
Deutz 1936 Bauemschiepper, 1/16 scale, $27.00. (Photo courtesy John Rammacher)

Farm Toys
Farmall Tractor 418, diecast metal, 1/16 scale, MIB (box damaged), $25.00.

Farm Toys
Farmall Tractor 544 with loader, 1/16 scale, VG, $90.00. (Photo courtesy John Rammacher)

Farm Toys
Oliver Farm Set, Slik Toy, NM (worn box), $285.00. (Photo courtesy Morphy Auctions on LiveAuctioneers.com)

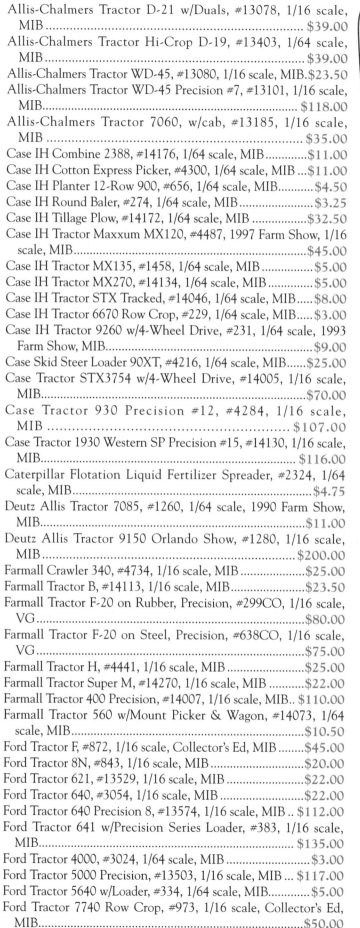

Ford Tractor 7740 w/Loader, #387, 1/64 scale, MIB............$5.00

Ford Tractor 8340 w/Duals, #388, 1/64 scale, MIB $3.50

Ford Tractor 8340 w/4 Wheel Drive, #877, 1/16 scale, Collector's Ed, MIB $50.00

Fordson Tractor, #13573, 1/16 scale, MIB......................$27.00

Heston Skid Steer Loader SL-30, #2267, 1/64 scale, MIB.$42.50

IH Combine 815, #4354, 1/64 scale, MIB.........................$10.50

IH Tractor 460 Precision #11, #4355, 1/16 scale, MIB ... $110.00

IH Tractor 756 w/Cab, #14124, 1/16 scale, MIB.............$35.00

IH Tractor 756 WF, #2308, 1/16 scale, MIB.....................$31.00

IH Tractor 856 WF, 1/16 scale, M $260.00

IH Tractor 1456 Diesel w/Cab, #2311, 1/16 scale, MIB.....$31.00

IH Tractor 1466 Precision, #14204, 1/16 scale, MIB $125.00

John Deere Combine 95, #5819, 1/64 scale, MIB.............$10.00

John Deere Cotton Picker 9986, #15440, 1/64 scale, MIB.$10.50

John Deere Crawler 40, #5072, 1/16 scale, MIB $27.00

John Deere Field Cultivator 2200, #15081, 1/64 scale, MIB... $8.00

John Deere Forage Blower Model 150, #5728, 1/64 scale, MIB $4.00

John Deere Forage Harvester, #566, 1/64 scale, MIB...........$3.00

John Deere Mower Conditioner, #5657, 1/64 scale, MIB....$3.00

John Deere Skid Steer Loader, Ertl, #569, 1/16 scale, MIB..$18.50

John Deere Sprayer, #5752, 1/64 scale, MIB........................$9.00

John Deere Sprayer, #15180, MIB.......................................$8.00

John Deere Tractor D, #5179, 1/16 scale, MIB $26.00

John Deere Tractor G, #5104, 1/16 scale, MIB $20.00

John Deere Tractor 70, #5611, 1/16 scale, MIB $21.00

John Deere Tractor 630 w/Corn Picker & Wagon, #15086, 1/16 scale, MIB..$10.50

John Deere Tractor 4010, #5716, 1/16 scale, MIB $25.00

John Deere Tractor 4040, #5133, 1/16 scale, MIB $30.00

John Deere Tractor 4520, w/duals, 1/16 scale, MIB $42.00

John Deere Tractor 8200, #5064, 1/64 scale, MIB $3.50

John Deere Utility Tractor w/Loader, #517, 1/16 scale, MIB..$22.00

John Deere Wing Disk, #5615, 1/64 scale, MIB...................$3.25

Massey-Ferguson Tractor 1155, #13170, 1/16 scale, MIB ..$43.00

Massey-Ferguson Tractor 3070 w/Front-Wheel Drive, #1107, 1/64 scale, MIB...$3.50

Massey-Ferguson Tractor 3070 w/Loader, #1109, 1/64 scale, MIB $5.00

Massey-Ferguson Tractor 3140 w/Front-Wheel Drive, #1107, 1/64 scale, MIB...$3.50

Massey-Ferguson Tractor 8280 w/Duals, #1352, 1/64 scale, MIB $5.85

New Holland Box Spreader, #308, 1/64 scale, MIB............$3.00

New Holland Combine CR960, #1395, 1/64 scale, MIB...$11.00

New Holland Hay Rake, #369, 1/64 scale, MIB...................$2.65

New Holland Skid Loader LS170, #13562, 1/64 scale, MIB.$4.00

New Holland Tractor TG-255, #13617, 1/64 scale, MIB.....$5.00

New Holland Tractor TM-150 w/4-Wheel Drive, #13560, 1/16 scale, MIB..$40.00

New Holland Tractor 7840 w/Loader, #13588, 1/16 scale, MIB $48.00

New Holland Tractor 8560, #3032, 1/43 scale, MIB..........$11.00

New Holland Wing Disk, #3049, 1/64 scale, MIB $4.00

Oliver Crawler HG, #13079, 1/16 scale, MIB....................$22.00

Oliver Tractor 88 w/Mounted Picker & Wagon, #13051, 1/64 scale, MIB..$10.50

Oliver Tractor 1655 w/Cab, #13186, 1/16 scale, MIB........$35.00

• ‹ **Fisher-Price** › •

Fisher-Price toys are becoming one of the hottest new trends in the collector's marketplace today. In 1930 Herman Fisher, backed by Irving Price, Elbert Hubbard, and Helen Schelle, formed one of the most successful toy companies ever to exist. Located in East Aurora, New York, the company has seen many changes since then, the most notable being the changes in ownership. From 1930 to 1968, it was owned by the individuals mentioned previously and a few stockholders. In 1969 it became an aquisition of Quaker Oats, and in June of 1991 it became independently owned. In November of 1993, one of the biggest sell-outs in the toy industry took place: Fisher-Price became a subdivision of Mattel.

There are a few things to keep in mind when collecting Fisher-Price toys. You should count on a little edge wear as well as some wear and fading to the paint. Pull toys found in mint condition are truly rare and command a much higher value, especially if you find one with its original box. This also applies to playsets, but to command higher prices, they must also be complete, with no chew/teeth marks or plastic fading. Another very important rule to remember is there are no standard colors for pieces that came with a playset. Fisher-Price often substituted a piece of a different color when they ran short. Please note that the dates on the toys indicate their copyright date and not the date they were manufactured.

The company put much time and thought into designing their toys. They took care to operate by their 5-point creed: to make toys with (1) intrinsic play value, (2) ingenuity, (3) strong construction, (4) good value for the money, and (5) action. Some of the most sought-after pull-toys are those bearing the Walt Disney logo. For more information, we recommend *Fisher-Price, A Historical Rarity Value Guide*, by John J. Murray and Bruce R. Fox; and *Fisher-Price Toys* by Brad Cassity.

Additional information may be obtained through the Fisher-Price Collectors' Club, which publishes a newsletter three times a year; their address may be found in the Directory under Clubs, Newsletters, and Other Publications.

Note: With the ever-increasing influence of the internet it is becoming harder and harder to establish book value. A toy can sell for 100% more than the book value or 75% less on the internet. The prices we have listed here are for toys in excellent condition unless noted otherwise.

See also Building Blocks and Construction Toys; Catalogs; Character, TV, and Movie Collectibles; Dollhouse Furniture; Dollhouses; Dolls; Optical Toys; other specific categories.

#5 Bunny Cart, 1948-49 ....$80.00
#6 Ducky Cart, 1948-49 ....$50.00
#7 Doggy Racer, 1942-43 .... $150.00
#7 Looky Fire Truck, 1950-53 & Easter 1954................. $130.00
#8 Bouncy Racer, 1960-62..$45.00
#12 Bunny Truck, 1941-42 ....$65.00
#14 Ducky Daddles, 1941 ....$40.00
#20 Animal Cutouts, 1942-46, duck, elephant, pony or Scottie
   dog, ea..$50.00
#28 Bunny Egg Cart, 1950...$75.00
#50 Bunny Chick Tandem Cart, 1953-54, no number on toy ..$50.00
#51 Ducky Cart, 1950..$50.00
#52 Rabbit Cart, 1950 ....$30.00
#100 Dr Doodle, 1931 .... $550.00
#100 Dr Doodle, 1995, Fisher-Price limited edition of 5,000, 1st
   in series $50.00
#100 Musical Sweeper, 1950-52, plays Whistle While You
   Work $60.00
#101 Granny Doodle & Family, 1931-32 .... $600.00
#102 Drummer Bear, 1931 .... $500.00
#102 Drummer Bear, 1932-33, fatter & taller version $500.00
#103 Barky Puppy, 1931-33 .... $300.00
#104 Lookee Monk, 1931 .... $500.00
#105 Bunny Scoot Toy, 1931, very rare.......................$1,500.00
#109 Lucky Monk, 1932-33 .... $325.00
#110 Chubby Chief, 1932-33 .... $500.00
#111 Play Family Merry-Go-Round, 1972-77, plays Skater's
   Waltz, w/4 figures..$30.00
#112 Picture Disk Camera, 1968-71, w/5 picture disks.......$20.00
#114 Sesame Street Music Box TV, 1984-87, plays People in
   Your Neighborhood...$1.00
#120 Cackling Hen, 1958-66, wht......................................$35.00
#120 Gabby Goose, 1936-37 & Easter 1938 .... $350.00
#121 Happy Hopper, 1969-76..$10.00
#123 Cackling Hen, 1966-68, red litho.............................$35.00
#123 Roller Chime, 1953-60 & Easter 1961 ....$30.00
#124 Roller Chime, 1961-62 & Easter 1963 ....$25.00
#125 Music Box Iron, 1966, aqua w/yel hdl $40.00
#125 Music Box Iron, 1966-69, wht w/red hdl..................$30.00
#125 Uncle Timmy Turtle, 1956-58 ....$50.00
#130 Wobbles, 1964-67, dog wobbles when pulled............$35.00
#131 Toy Wagon, 1951-54.. $225.00
#135 Play Family Animal Circus, 1974-76, complete........$60.00
#136 Play Family Lacing Shoe, 1965-69, complete $60.00
#138 Jack-in-the-Box Puppet, 1970-73.............................$20.00
#139 Tuggy Turtle, 1959-60 & Easter 1961 ....$75.00
#140 Katy Kackler, 1954-56 & Easter 1957 ....$75.00
#141 Snap-Quack, 1947-49 .... $200.00
#142 Three Men in a Tub, 1970-73, w/bell.......................$10.00
#142 Three Men in a Tub, 1974-75, w/flag $5.00
#145 Humpty Dump Truck, 1963-64 & Easter 1965 ....$35.00
#145 Husky Dump Truck, 1961-62 & Easter 1963............$30.00
#145 Musical Elephant, 1948-50 .... $175.00
#146 Pull-A-Long Lacing Shoe, 1970-73, w/6 figures........$50.00
#148 Ducky Daddles, 1942 .... $200.00
#148 Jack & Jill TV Radio, 1959 & Easter 1960, wood & plas-
   tic $30.00
#149 Dog Cart Donald, 1936-37 .... $575.00

Fisher-Price
#156 Circus Wagon, 1942, NM, $500.00. (Photo courtesy Morphy Auctions on LiveAuctioneers.com)

#150 Barky Buddy, 1934-35 .... $475.00
#150 Pop-Up-Pal Chime Phone, 1968-78.........................$15.00
#150 Teddy Tooter, 1940-41 .... $225.00
#150 Timmy Turtle, 1953-55 & Easter 1956, gr shell $75.00
#151 Goldilocks & the Three Bears Playhouse, 1967-71 ..$40.00
#151 Happy Hippo, 1962-63 .... $100.00
#152 Road Roller, 1934-35 .... $525.00
#154 Frisky Frog, 1971-83, squeeze plastic bulb & frog jumps...$10.00
#155 Moo-oo Cow, 1958-61 & Easter 1962 .... $130.00
#155 Skipper Sam, 1934 .... $850.00
#156 Baa-Baa Black Sheep TV-Radio, 1966-67, wood & plas-
   tic $50.00
#156 Jiffy Dump Truck, 1971-73, squeeze bulb & dump bed
   moves..$15.00
#158 Katie Kangaroo, 1976-77, squeeze bulb & she hops..$15.00
#158 Little Boy Blue TV-Radio, 1967, wood & plastic......$50.00
#159 Ten Little Indians TV-Radio, 1961-65 & Easter 1966, wood
   & plastic $20.00
#160 Donald & Donna Duck, 1937 .... $700.00
#161 Creative Block Wagon, 1961-64, 18 building blocks & 6
   wooden dowels fit into pull-along wagon $60.00
#161 Looky Chug-Chug, 1949-52 .... $175.00
#161 Old Woman Who Lived in a Shoe TV-Radio, 1968-70,
   wood & plastic w/see-through window on back $30.00
#164 Mother Goose, 1964-66..$30.00
#166 Bucky Burro, 1955-57 .... $200.00

Fisher-Price
#175 Gold Star Stagecoach, 1954, M (VG box), $250.00. (Photo courtesy Morphy Auctions on LiveAuctioneers.com)

#166 Farmer in the Dell TV-Radio, 1963-66 .... $30.00
#166 Piggy Bank, 1981-82, pk plastic $10.00
#166 Tumbling Tom, 1939, VG $200.00
#168 Snorky Fire Engine, 1960 & Easter 1961, gr litho . $175.00
#170 American Airlines Flagship, 1941, VG $650.00
#170 Change-A-Tune Carousel, 1981-83, music box w/crank hdl, 3 molded records & 3 figures $20.00
#171 Toy Wagon, 1942-47 .... $250.00
#175 Kicking Donkey, 1937-38 .... $425.00
#175 Winnie the Pooh TV-Radio, 1971-73, Sears only $35.00
#177 Donald Duck Xylophone, 1946-52, 2nd version w/'Donald Duck' on hat $325.00
#177 Oscar the Grouch, 1977-84 .... $10.00
#178 What's in My Pocket Cloth Book, 1972-74, boy's version.. $20.00
#179 What's in My Pocket Cloth Book, 1972-74, girl's version $20.00
#180 Snoopy Sniffer, 1938-55 .... $125.00
#183 Play Family Fun Jet, 1970, 1st version $20.00
#185 Donald Duck Xylophone, 1938, mk WDE $500.00
#189 Looky Chug-Chug, 1958-60 .... $100.00
#190 Gabby Duck, 1939-40 & Easter 1941 .... $350.00
#190 Molly Moo-Moo, 1956 & Easter 1957 .... $75.00
#191 Golden Gulch Express, 1961 & Easter 1962 .... $100.00
#192 Playland Express, 1962 & Easter 1963 .... $100.00
#192 School Bus, 1965 .... $50.00
#195 Peek-A-Boo Screen Music Box, 1965-68, plays Mary Had a Little Lamb $25.00
#195 Teddy Bear Parade, 1938 .... $750.00
#198 Band Wagon, 1940-41 .... $300.00
#201 Woodsy-Wee Circus, 1931-32, complete $500.00
#205 Walt Disney's Parade, WDE, 1936-41 .... $250.00
#205 Woodsy-Wee Zoo, 1931-32 .... $750.00
#207 Walt Disney's Carnival, 1936-38, Mickey, Donald, Pluto or Elmer, complete, ea $300.00
#207 Woodsy-Wee Pets, 1931, complete w/goat, donkey, cow, pig & cart $650.00
#208 Donald Duck, 1936-38 .... $175.00
#209 Woodsy-Wee Dog Show, 1932, complete w/5 dogs . $500.00
#210 Pluto the Pup, 1936-38 .... $150.00
#211 Elmer Elephant, 1936-38 .... $175.00
#215 Fisher-Price Choo-Choo, 1955-57, engine w/3 cars.. $75.00
#225 Wheel Horse, 1935 & Easter 1936 .... $500.00
#234 Nifty Station Wagon, 1960-62 & Easter 1963, removable roof $250.00

#237 Riding Horse, 1936 .... $425.00
#250 Big Performing Circus, 1932-38 .... $475.00
#301 Bunny Basket Cart, 1957-59 .... $35.00
#302 Chick Basket Cart, 1957-59 .... $40.00
#302 Husky Dump Truck, 1978-84 .... $15.00
#303 Adventure People Emergency Rescue Truck, 1975-78.. $15.00
#303 Bunny Push Cart, 1957 .... $50.00
#304 Adventure People Wild Safari Set, 1975-78 .... $50.00
#304 Running Bunny Cart, 1957 .... $50.00
#305 Walking Duck Cart, 1957-64 .... $40.00
#306 Bizzy Bunny Cart, 1957-59 .... $40.00
#307 Adventure People Wilderness Patrol, 1975-79 .... $30.00
#307 Bouncing Bunny Cart, 1961-63 & Easter 1964 .... $35.00
#309 Adventure People TV Action Team, 1977-78 .... $50.00
#310 Adventure People Sea Explorer, 1975-80 .... $20.00
#310 Mickey Mouse Puddle Jumper, 1953-55 & Easter 1956 . $115.00
#311 Husky Bulldozer, 1978-79 .... $15.00
#312 Adventure People Northwoods Trail Blazer, 1977-82 .. $20.00
#312 Running Bunny Cart, 1960-64 .... $40.00
#313 Husky Roller Grader, 1978-80 .... $15.00
#314 Husky Boom Crane, 1978-82 .... $25.00
#314 Queen Buzzy Bee, 1956-58 .... $25.00
#315 Husky Cement Mixer, 1978-82 .... $15.00
#316 Husky Tow Truck, 1978-80 .... $15.00
#317 Husky Construction Crew, 1978-80 .... $20.00
#318 Adventure People Daredevil Sports Van, 1978-82 ... $25.00
#319 Husky Hook & Ladder Truck, 1979-85 .... $20.00
#320 Husky Race Car Rig, 1979-82 .... $20.00
#322 Adventure People Dune Buster, 1979-82 .... $10.00
#325 Adventure People Alpha Probe, 1980-84 .... $20.00
#325 Buzzy Bee, 1950-56, 1st version, yel & blk litho, wooden wheels & antenna tips $25.00
#326 Adventure People Alpha Star, 1983-84 .... $20.00
#327 Husky Load Master Dump, 1984 .... $20.00
#328 Husky Highway Dump Truck, 1980-84 .... $20.00
#329 Husky Dozer Loader, 1980-84 .... $15.00
#331 Husky Farm Set, 1981-83 .... $20.00
#332 Husky Police Patrol, 1981-84 .... $15.00
#333 Butch the Pup, 1951-53 & Easter 1954 .... $55.00
#334 Adventure People Sea Shark, 1981-84 .... $20.00
#336 Husky Fire Pumper, 1983-84 .... $15.00
#337 Husky Rescue Rig, 1982-83 .... $20.00
#338 Husky Power Tow Truck, 1982-84 .... $20.00
#339 Husky Power & Light Service Rig, 1983-84 .... $30.00

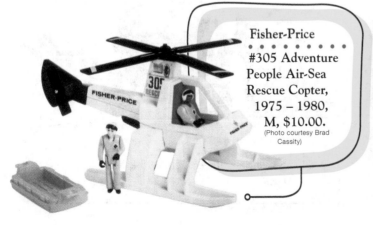

Fisher-Price
#305 Adventure People Air-Sea Rescue Copter, 1975 – 1980, M, $10.00.
(Photo courtesy Brad Cassity)

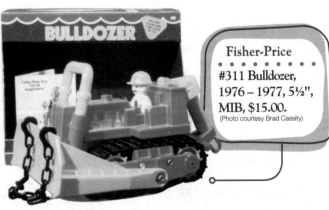

Fisher-Price
#311 Bulldozer, 1976 – 1977, 5½", MIB, $15.00.
(Photo courtesy Brad Cassity)

#344 Copter Rig, 1981-84 ....$10.00
#345 Boat Rig, 1981-84 ....$10.00
#345 Penelope the Performing Penguin, 1935, w/up $800.00
#350 Adventure People Rescue Team, 1976-79.................$15.00
#350 Go 'N Back Mule, 1931-33, w/up.........................$425.00
#351 Adventure People Mountain Climbers, 1976-79......$15.00
#352 Adventure People Construction Workers, 1976-79..$15.00
#353 Adventure People Scuba Divers, 1976-81.................$15.00
#354 Adventure People Daredevil Skydiver, 1977-81.......$10.00
#355 Adventure People White Water Kayak, 1977-80 .....$10.00
#355 Go 'N Back Bruno, 1931 ....$425.00
#356 Adventure People Cycle Racing Team, 1977-81 ......$10.00
#358 Adventure People Deep Sea Diver, 1980-84.............$10.00
#360 Adventure People Alpha Recon, 1982-84 ....$10.00
#360 Go 'N Back Jumbo, 1931-34, w/up $425.00
#365 Puppy Back-up, 1932-36, w/up $800.00
#367 Adventure People Turbo Hawk, 1982-83 ....$10.00
#368 Adventure People Alpha Interceptor, 1982-83.........$10.00
#369 Adventure People Ground Shaker, 1982-83 ....$10.00
#375 Adventure People Sky Surfer, 1978.....................$25.00
#375 Bruno Back-Up, 1932 ....$800.00
#377 Adventure People Astro Knight, 1979-80 ....$15.00
#400 Tailspin Tabby, 1931-38 ....$200.00
#401 Push Bunny Cart, 1942 ....$200.00
#404 Bunny Egg Cart, 1949 ....$50.00
#405 Lofty Lizzy Pop-Up Kritter, 1931-33 ....$200.00
#407 Chick Cart, 1950-53 ....$50.00
#407 Dizzy Dino Pop-Up Kritter, 1931-32 ....$225.00
#410 Stoopy Stork Pop-Up Kritter, 1931-32 ....$225.00
#415 Lop-Ear Looie Pop-Up Kritter, 1934 ....$225.00
#415 Super Jet, 1952 & Easter 1953 ....$200.00
#420 Sunny Fish, 1955 ....$125.00
#422 Jumbo Jitterbug Pop-Up Kritter, 1940.................$75.00
#425 Donald Duck Pop-Up, 1938 & Easter 1939 .... $350.00
#430 Buddy Bronk, VG $2,300.00
#433 Dizzy Donkey Pop-Up Kritter, 1939 ....$100.00
#434 Ferdinand the Bull, 1939 ....$950.00
#440 Goofy Gertie Pop-Up Kritter, 1935 ....$225.00
#440 Pluto Pop-Up, 1936, mk WDP $75.00
#444 Fuzzy Fido, 1941-42 ....$225.00
#444 Puffy Engine, 1951-54 ....$50.00
#444 Queen Buzzy Bee, 1959, red litho.....................$30.00
#445 Hot Dog Wagon, 1940-41...............................$200.00
#445 Nosey Pup, 1956-58 & Easter 1959 ....$30.00
#447 Woofy Wagger, 1947-48.................................$50.00
#450 Donald Duck Choo-Choo, 1941 ....$325.00
#450 Donald Duck Choo-Choo, 1942-45 & Easter 1949 . $100.00
#450 Kiltie Dog, 1936......................................$350.00
#454 Donald Duck Drummer, 1949-50 ....$275.00
#455 Tailspin Tabby Pop-Up Kritter, 1939-42 ....$225.00
#456 Bunny & Container, 1939-40..........................$225.00
#460 Dapper Donald Duck, 1936-37.........................$200.00
#460 Suzie Seal, 1961-63 & Easter 1964.....................$20.00
#461 Duck Cart, 1938-39 ....$225.00
#462 Busy Bunny, 1937......................................$200.00
#465 Donald Duck Choo-Choo, 1942, VG $550.00
#465 Teddy Choo-Choo, 1937 ....$225.00
#466 Busy Bunny Cart, 1941-44..............................$75.00

#469 Donald Duck Cart, 1940........................... $225.00
#469 Rooster Cart, 1938-40 .... $100.00
#470 Tricky Tommy, 1936 .... $350.00
#472 Jingle Giraffe, 1956 .... $175.00
#472 Peter Bunny Cart, 1939-40....................... $125.00
#473 Merry Mutt, 1949-54 & Easter 1955 ....$75.00
#474 Bunny Racer, 1942............................... $135.00
#476 Cookie Pig, 1966-70 ....$40.00
#476 Mickey Mouse Drummer, 1941-45 & Easter 1946 . $275.00
#476 Rooster Pop-Up Kritter, 1936..................... $250.00
#477 Dr Doodle, 1940-41 .... $275.00
#478 Pudgy Pig, 1962-64 & Easter 1965 ....$40.00
#479 Donald Duck & Nephews, 1941-42 .... $400.00
#479 Peter Pig, 1959-61 & Easter 1962.................$40.00
#480 Leo the Drummer, 1952 & Easter 1953............. $225.00
#480 Teddy Station Wagon, 1942 .... $200.00
#485 Mickey Mouse Choo-Choo, 1949-54, new litho version of
    #432 .... $100.00
#488 Popeye Spinach Eater, 1939-40 .... $625.00
#491 Boom-Boom Popeye.............................. $575.00

Fisher-Price
#465 Mickey Mouse Choo-Choo, 1938, VG, $450.00. (Photo courtesy Morphy Auctions on LiveAuctioneers.com)

Fisher-Price
#530 Mickey Mouse Band, 1934, 12" long, NM+, $1,840.00. (Photo courtesy James D. Julia, Inc.)

Fisher-Price
#544 Donald Duck Cart, 1942, EX, $300.00. (Photo courtesy www.serioustoyz.com)

#494 Pinocchio, 1939-40......................................$600.00
#495 Running Bunny Cart, 1941 ....$200.00
#495 Sleepy Sue Turtle, 1962-63 & Easter 1964..............$40.00
#499 Kitty Bell, 1950-51....................................$100.00
#500 Donald Duck Cart, 1937, unpnt wheels $375.00
#500 Donald Duck Cart, 1951-53 ....$350.00
#500 Pick-Up & Peek Puzzle, 1972-86......................$10.00
#500 Pushy Pig, 1932-35.....................................$650.00
#502 Action Bunny Cart, 1949 ....$200.00
#503 Pick-Up & Peek Wood Puzzle, Occupations, 1972-76..$10.00
#505 Bunny Drummer, 1946, bell on front $175.00
#507 Pushy Doodle, 1933 ....$575.00
#510 Pick-Up & Peek Wood Puzzle, Nursery Rhymes, 1972-81...$10.00
#510 Strutter Donald Duck, 1941 ....$150.00
#512 Bunny Drummer, 1942................................$175.00
#515 Pushy Pat, 1933-35 ....$550.00
#517 Choo-Choo Local, 1936 ....$375.00
#517 Pick-Up & Piece Wood Puzzle, Animal Friends, 1977-84..$10.00
#520 Bunny Bell Cart, 1941 ....$150.00
#520 Pick-Up & Peek Puzzle, Three Little Pigs, 1979-84..$15.00
#525 Cotton Tail Cart, 1940 ....$175.00
#525 Pushy Elephant, 1934-35 ....$425.00
#530 Mickey Mouse Band, 1935-36 ....$775.00
#533 Thumper Bunny, 1942 ....$250.00
#550 Donald Duck Cart, 1938, VG.....................$175.00

Fisher-Price

#549 Toy Lunch Kit, 1962 – 1979, red with barn lithograph, with silo-style plastic bottle, $25.00. (Photo courtesy Carole Bess and L.M. White)

Fisher-Price

#567 Basic Hardboard Puzzle, cat and kittens, 1975, MIB, $10.00. (Photo courtesy Brad Cassity)

#550 Toy Lunch Kit, 1957, red, wht & gr plastic barn shape, no litho $40.00
#552 Basic Hardboard Puzzle, Nature or any other, 1974-75, MIB, ea $10 to $15.00
#563 Basic Hardboard Puzzle, Weather, 1975 ....$10.00
#568 Basic Hardboard Puzzle, bear on log $10.00
#569 Basic Hardboard Puzzle, Airport, 1975.......$10.00
#600 Tailspin Tabby Pop-Up, 1947 ....$200.00
#604 Bunny Bell Cart, 1954-55.............................$50.00
#605 Donald Duck Cart, 1954-56 ....$150.00
#605 Horse & Wagon, 1933, NM $950.00
#605 Woodsey Major Goodgrub Mole & Book, 1981-82, 32 pgs $15.00
#606 Woodsey Bramble Beaver & Book, 1981-82, 32 pgs.$15.00
#607 Woodsey Very Blue Bird & Book, 1981-82, 32 pgs....$15.00
#615 Tow Truck, 1960-61 & Easter 1962 ....$65.00
#616 Chuggy Pop-Up, 1955-56............................$75.00
#616 Patch Pony, 1963-64 & Easter 1965 ....$25.00
#617 Prancy Pony, 1965-70................................$25.00
#621 Suzie Seal, 1965-66, ball on nose $30.00
#623 Suzie Seal, 1964-65, umbrella on nose $30.00
#625 Playful Puppy, 1961-62 & Easter 1963, w/shoe $50.00
#629 Fisher-Price Tractor, 1962-68 ....$30.00
#630 Fire Truck, 1959-62....................................$45.00
#634 Drummer Boy, 1967-69...............................$60.00
#634 Tiny Teddy, 1955-57...................................$50.00
#637 Milk Carrier, 1966-85.................................$15.00
#640 Wiggily Woofer, 1957-58 & Easter 1958....................$75.00
#641 Toot Toot Engine, 1962-63 & Easter 1964, bl litho..$60.00
#642 Bob-Along Bear, 1979-84 ....$5.00
#642 Dinky Engine, 1959, blk litho $60.00
#642 Smokie Engine, 1960-61 & Easter 1962, blk litho....$60.00
#649 Stake Truck, 1960-61 & Easter 1962.............$50.00
#653 Allie Gator, 1960-61 & Easter 1962..............$50.00
#654 Tawny Tiger, 1962 & Easter 1963..................$75.00
#656 Bossy Bell, 1960 & Easter 1961, w/bonnet...............$50.00
#656 Bossy Bell, 1961-63, no bonnet, new litho design $50.00
#657 Crazy Clown Fire Brigade, 1983-84...............$45.00
#658 Lady Bug, 1961-62 & Easter 1963 ....$50.00
#662 Merry Mousewife, 1962-64 & Easter 1965 ....$45.00
#663 Play Family, 1966-70, tan dog, MIP.......................$170.00
#674 Sports Car, 1958-60 ....$75.00
#677 Picnic Basket, 1975-79 ....$20.00
#678 Kriss Kricket, 1955-57 ....$50.00
#679 Little People Garage Squad, 1984-90, MIP..............$15.00
#684 Little Lamb, 1964-65..................................$45.00
#685 Car & Boat, 1968-69, wood & plastic, 5 pcs............$50.00
#686 Car & Camper, 1968-70 ....$50.00
#686 Perky Pot, 1958-59 & Easter 1960 ....$50.00
#694 Suzie Seal, 1979-80...................................$10.00
#695 Pinky Pig, 1956-57, wooden eyes $75.00
#695 Pinky Pig, 1958, litho eyes.........................$75.00
#698 Talky Parrot, 1963 & Easter 1964..................$50.00
#700 Cowboy Chime, 1951-53 ....$125.00
#700 Popeye, 1935..$700.00
#700 Woofy Wowser, 1940 & Easter 1941 ....$125.00
#703 Bunny Engine, 1954-56...............................$50.00
#703 Popeye the Sailor, 1936 ....$825.00

#705 Mini Snowmobile, 1971-73 ....$40.00
#705 Popeye Cowboy, 1937 ....$700.00
#710 Scotty Dog, 1933 ....$375.00
#711 Cry Baby Bear, 1967-69 ....$15.00
#711 Raggedy Ann & Andy, 1941 ....$1,100.00
#711 Teddy Trucker, 1949-51 ....$125.00
#712 Fred Flintstone Xylophone, 1962, Sears only $250.00
#712 Johnny Jumbo, 1933-35 ....$525.00
#712 Teddy Tooter, 1957-58 & Easter 1959 ....$200.00
#714 Mickey Mouse Xylophone, 1963, Sears only $175.00
#715 Donald Duck Delivery, 1936, VG $200.00
#715 Ducky Flip Flap, 1964-65 ....$50.00
#717 Ducky Flip Flap, 1937, NM $350.00
#718 Tow Truck & Car, 1969-70, wood & plastic $45.00
#719 Busy Bunny Cart, 1936-37 ....$275.00
#720 Pinnochio Express, 1939-40 ....$625.00
#721 Peter Bunny Engine, 1949-51 ....$150.00
#722 Racing Bunny Cart, 1937 ....$175.00
#722 Running Bunny, 1938-40 ....$225.00
#723 Bouncing Bunny Cart, 1936 ....$175.00
#724 Ding-Dong Ducky, 1949-50 ....$200.00
#725 Musical Mutt, 1935-36 ....$375.00
#725 Play Family Bath/Utility Room Set, 1972 ....$10.00
#726 Play Family Patio Set, 1970-73 ....$10.00
#728 Buddy Bullfrog, 1959-60, yel body w/red coat $50.00
#728 Pound & Saw Bench, 1966-67 ....$30.00
#730 Racing Rowboat, 1952-53 ....$150.00
#732 Happy Hauler, 1968-70 ....$20.00
#734 Teddy Zilo, 1964, no coat $40.00
#734 Teddy Zilo, 1965-66, w/coat $55.00
#735 Juggling Jumbo, 1958-59 ....$225.00
#737 Galloping Horse & Wagon, 1948-49 ....$175.00
#737 Ziggy Zilo, 1958-59 ....$550.00
#738 Shaggy Zilo, 1960-61 & Easter 1962 ....$75.00
#738 Walt Disney's Circus Racer, 1941 & Easter 1942 ... $400.00
#738 Walt Disney's Dumbo Circus, 1941 ....$400.00
#739 Poodle Zilo, 1962-63 & Easter 1964 ....$50.00
#741 Teddy Zilo, 1967 ....$35.00
#741 Trotting Donald Duck, 1937 ....$575.00
#742 Dashing Dobbin, 1938-40 ....$425.00
#744 Doughboy Donald, 1942 ....$575.00
#745 Elsie's Dairy Truck, 1948-49, w/2 bottles $600.00
#746 Pocket Radio, 1977-78, It's a Small World, wood & plastic $10.00
#747 Chatter Telephone, 1962-67, wooden wheels $25.00
#747 Talk-Back Telephone, 1961 & Easter 1962 ....$75.00
#749 Egg Truck, 1947 ....$225.00
#750 Hot Dog Wagon, 1938 ....$300.00
#750 Space Blazer, 1953-54 ....$175.00
#755 Jumbo Rolo, 1951-52 ....$225.00
#756 Pocket Radio, 1973, 12 Days of Christmas, wood & plastic $25.00
#757 Howdy Bunny, 1939-40 ....$325.00
#757 Humpty Dumpty, 1957 & Easter 1958 ....$250.00
#757 Snappy-Quacky, 1950 ....$200.00
#758 Pocket Radio, 1970-72, Mulberry Bush, wood & plastic $10.00
#758 Pony Chime, 1948-50 ....$175.00

Fisher-Price
#711 Huckleberry Hound, 1961, Sears only, NM+, $200.00. (Photo courtesy Morphy Auctions on LiveAuctioneers.com)

Fisher-Price
#727 Bouncing Bunny Wheelbarrow, 1939, VG, $425.00. (Photo courtesy Morphy Auctions on LiveAuctioneers.com)

Fisher-Price
#733 Mickey Mouse Safety Patrol, 1956 – 1957, 10", VG, $250.00. (Photo courtesy www.serioustoyz.com)

#758 Push-Along Clown, 1980-81 ....$5.00
#759 Pocket Radio, 1969-73, Do-Re-Me, wood & plastic.$10.00
#760 Racing Ponies, 1936.............................$425.00
#761 Play Family Nursery Set, 1973...................$10.00
#762 Pocket Radio, 1972-77, Raindrops, wood & plastic..$10.00
#763 Music Box, 1962, Farmer in the Dell, yel litho $40.00
#763 Pocket Radio, 1978, I Whistle a Happy Tune, wood & plastic $10.00
#764 Music Box, 1960-61 & Easter 1962, Farmer in the Dell, red litho $40.00
#764 Pocket Radio, 1975-76, My Name Is Michael $10.00
#765 Dandy Dobbin, 1941-44 ....$275.00
#765 Talking Donald Duck, 1955-58 ....$125.00
#766 Pocket Radio, 1968-70, Where Has My Little Dog Gone?, wood & plastic $10.00
#766 Pocket Radio, 1977-78, I'd Like To Teach the World To Sing...................................$10.00
#767 Pocket Radio, 1977, Twinkle Twinkle Little Star $25.00
#768 Pocket Radio, 1971-76, Happy Birthday, wood & plastic..$10.00
#772 Pocket Radio, 1974-76, Jack & Jill............$10.00
#775 Gabby Goofies, 1956-59 & Easter 1960 ....$25.00

#775 Pocket Radio, 1967-68, Sing a Song of Six Pence, wood & plastic...$10.00

#775 Teddy Drummer, 1936 .... $325.00

#777 Squeaky the Clown, 1958-59 .... $225.00

#778 Ice-Cream Wagon, 1940 & Easter 1941 .... $300.00

#779 Pocket Radio, 1976, Yankee Doodle, wood & plastic ..$15.00

#780 Jumbo Xylophone, 1937-38 .... $250.00

#780 Snoopy Sniffer, 1955-57 & Easter 1958 .... $50.00

#784 Mother Goose Music Chart, 1955-56 & Easter 1957...$50.00

#785 Blackie Drummer, 1939 .... $525.00

#788 Rock-A-Bye Bunny Cart, 1940-41 .... $200.00

#789 Lift & Load Road Builders, 1978-82.....................$15.00

#793 Jolly Jumper, 1963-64 & Easter 1965 ....$30.00

#794 Big Bill Pelican, 1961-63, w/cb fish $100.00

#795 Mickey Mouse Drummer, 1937............................ $300.00

#795 Musical Duck, 1952-54 & Easter 1955....................$75.00

#798 Chatter Monk, 1957-58 & Easter 1959....................$75.00

#798 Mickey Mouse Xylophone, 1939, w/hat................ $250.00

#798 Mickey Mouse Xylophone, 1942, no hat.............. $350.00

#799 Quacky Family, 1940-42 ....$75.00

#800 Hot Diggety, 1934, w/up $625.00

#808 Pop'n Ring, 1956-58 & Easter 1959 ....$50.00

#810 Timber Toter, 1957 & Easter 1958 ....$75.00

#845 Farm Truck, 1954-55, w/booklet............................. $250.00

#870 Pull-A-Tune Xylophone, 1957-69, w/song book.......$25.00

#875, Looky Push Car, 1962-65 & Easter 1966 ....$45.00

#900 Fisher-Price Circus, 1962, NM $300.00

#900 Struttin' Donald Duck, 1939 & Easter 1940 .... $475.00

#900 This Little Pig, 1956-58 & Easter 1959.....................$25.00

#902 Junior Circus, 1963-70.................................... $100.00

#904 Beginner's Circus, 1965-68 ....$50.00

#905 This Little Pig, 1959-62....................................$25.00

#909 Play Family Rooms, 1972, Sears only $175.00

#910 Change-A-Tune Piano, 1969-72, Pop Goes the Weasel, This Old Man & The Muffin Man $25.00

#915 Play Family Farm, 1968-79, 1st version w/Masonite base ..$25.00

#919 Music Box Movie Camera, 1968-70, plays This Old Man, w/5 picture disks $35.00

#923 Play Family School, 1971-78, 1st version.................$20.00

#926 Concrete Mixer Truck, 1959-60 & Easter 1961 ..... $150.00

#928 Play Family Fire Station, 1980-82 ....$30.00

#929 Play Family Nursery School, 1978-79 ....$30.00

#931 Play Family Children's Hospital, 1976-78................$75.00

#932 Amusement Park, 1963-65 .... $150.00

#932 Ferry Boat, 1979-80 ....$25.00

#934 Play Family Western Town, 1982-84.........................$75.00

#935 Tool Box Work Bench, 1969-71 ....$20.00

#937 Play Family Sesame Street Clubhouse, 1977-79 ....$50.00

#938 Play Family Sesame Street House, 1975-76 ....$50.00

#942 Play Family Lift & Load Depot, 1977-79 ....$40.00

#943 Lift & Load Railroad, 1978-79 ....$40.00

#944 Lift & Load Lumber Yard, 1979-81 ....$40.00

#945 Offshore Cargo Base, 1979-80 ....$50.00

#960 Woodsey's Log House, 1979-81, complete $20.00

#961 Woodsey's Store, 1980-81, complete.......................$25.00

#962 Woodsey's Airport, 1980-81, complete $10.00

#969 Musical Ferris Wheel, 1966-72, 1st version w/4 wooden straight-body figures $50.00

#979 Dump Truckers Playset, 1965-67 ....$50.00

#982 Hot Rod Roadster, 1983-84, riding toy w/4-pc take-apart engine $40.00

#983 Safety School Bus, 1959, w/6 figures, Fisher-Price Club logo $150.00

#985 Play Family Houseboat, 1972-76, complete $25.00

#987 Creative Coaster, 1964-82 ....$40.00

#990 Play Family A-Frame, 1974-76 ....$35.00

#991 Music Box Lacing Shoe, 1964-67.........................$50.00

#991 Play Family Circus Train, 1973-78, w/gondola car....$15.00

#991 Play Family Circus Train, 1979-86, no gondola car ..$10.00

#992 Play Family Car & Camper, 1980-84 ....$25.00

#993 Play Family Castle, 1974-77, 1st version...............$75.00

#994 Play Family Camper, 1973-76..............................$25.00

#996 Play Family Airport, 1972-76, 1st version w/bl airport & clear look-out tower $25.00

#997 Musical Tick-Tock Clock, 1962-63 ....$30.00

#997 Play Family Village, 1973-77 ....$40.00

#998 Music Box Teaching Clock, 1968-83 ....$10.00

#999 Huffy Puffy Train, 1958-62 .... $100.00

#2352 Little People Construction Set, 1985.....................$15.00

#2360 Little People Jetliner, 1986-88.............................$10.00

#2361 Little People Fire Truck, 1989-90.........................$10.00

#2453 Little People Beauty Salon, 1990 ....$15.00

#2454 Little People Drive-In Movie $15.00

#2455 Little People Gas Station, 1990...........................$15.00

#2501 Little People Farm, 1986-89 ....$15.00

#2504 Little People Garage, 1986 ....$25.00

#2524 Little People Cruise Boat, 1989-90 ....$15.00

#2525 Little People Playground, 1986-90 ....$10.00

#2551 Little People Neighborhood, 1988-90....................$20.00

#2552 McDonald's Restaurant, 1990, 1st version $30.00

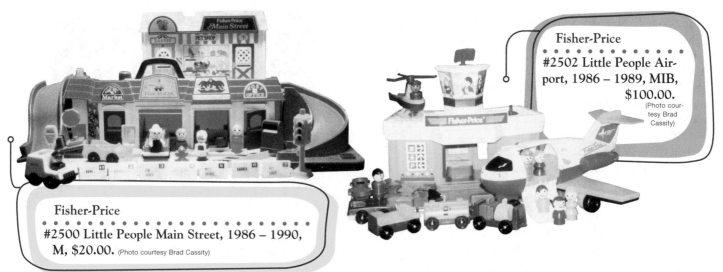

Fisher-Price
#2502 Little People Airport, 1986 – 1989, MIB, $100.00.
(Photo courtesy Brad Cassity)

Fisher-Price
#2500 Little People Main Street, 1986 – 1990, M, $20.00. (Photo courtesy Brad Cassity)

#2552 McDonald's Restaurant, 1991-92, 2nd version, same pcs as 1st version but lg-size figures $25.00
#2580 Little People Little Mart, 1987-89.........................$15.00
#2581 Little People Express Train, 1987-90.....................$10.00
#2582 Little People Floating Marina, 1988-90 ....$15.00

#2712 Pick-Up & Peek Wood Puzzle, any, 1985-88, ea.....$10.00
#3002 Pre-Educational Blocks, 1935, VGIB $315.00
#4500 Husky Helpers Workmen, 1985-86, 6 different, MOC, ea.. $10.00
#4520 Highway Dump Truck, 1985-86 ....$15.00
#4521 Dozer Loader, 1985-86..$15.00
#4523 Gravel Hauler, 1985-86 ....$15.00

• Games • • • • • • • • • • • • • • • • • •

Early games (those from 1850 to 1910) are very often appreciated more for their wonderful lithographed boxes than their 'play-ability,' and you'll find collectors displaying them as they would any fine artwork. Many boxes and boards were designed by commercial artists of the day. The 'boomer' games are still highly sought after for their nostalgic quality.

Some game prices have come down a little since the last edition, with the internet being an influencing factor.

When you buy a game, check to see that all pieces are there. The games listed below are complete unless noted otherwise. For further information we recommend *Baby Boomer Games* by Rick Polizzi and *Board Games of the '50s, '60s, and '70s* by David Dilley.

See also Advertising; Black Americana; Halloween; other relevant categories.

4 Alarm Game, Milton Bradley, 1963, EXIB $20.00
77 Sunset Strip, Lowell, 1960, EXIB.................................$35.00
$10,000 Pyramid, Milton Bradley, 1972, NMIB.................$20.00
20,000 Leagues Under the Sea, Gardner, 1950s, EXIB......$30.00
$64,000 Question, Lowell, 1955, EXIB $15.00
A Cycling Tour, Spears, EXIB $225.00
A-Team, Parker Bros, 1984, EX+IB...................................$10.00
A-Team Grenade Toss, Placo Toys, 1983, NRFB (sealed) .$30.00
Addams Family, Ideal, 1960s, NMIB..................................$75.00
Addams Family (Cartoon Series), Milton Bradley, 1970s, NMIB $25.00
Addams Family Card Game, Milton Bradley, 1965, NMIB ..$20.00
Advance to Boardwalk, Parker Bros, 1985, NMIB $15.00
Air Ship Game, McLoughlin Bros, c 1904, VGIB $800.00
Alfred Hitchcock Presents 'Why' Mystery Game, Milton Bradley, 1958, unused, MIB $40.00
Alice in Wonderland Card Game, McLoughlin Bros, c 1898, EXIB $400.00
Alien, Kenner, 1979, EXIB...$15.00
All in the Family, Milton Bradley, 1972, NM+IB.............$25.00
Alvin & the Chipmunks Acorn Hunt, Hasbro, 1960, EXIB .$20.00
Amazing Chan & the Chan Clan, Whitman, 1973, NMIB..$20.00
Amazing Spider-Man, Milton Bradley, 1966, EXIB...........$25.00

American Boys Game, McLoughlin Bros, 1913, VGIB .. $285.00
Animal Ten Pins, McLoughlin Bros, EXIB $1,200.00
Annette's Secret Passage Game, Parker Bros, 1958, EX+IB..$15.00
Annie Oakley Game, Milton Bradley, 1950s, lg, NMIB....$45.00
Annie Oakley Game, Milton Bradley, 1950s, sm, NMIB ..$35.00
Annie the Movie Game, Parker Bros, 1981, NMIB...........$10.00
Apple's Way, Milton Bradley, 1974, NMIB.......................$18.00
Archie Bunker's Card Game, Milton Bradley, #4239, 1972, NM+IB...$15.00
Archies, Whitman, 1969, NMIB.......................................$25.00
Around the World in 80 Days, Transogram, NMIB...........$25.00
As the World Turns, Parker Bros, 1966, NMIB $25.00
Ask Popeye's Lucky Jeep/2 Games in 1, King Features, c 1929-36.$230.00
Atom Ant Saves the Day, Transogram, 1966, NMIB $50.00
Auto Game, Milton Bradley, 1906, EXIB $135.00
Babe Ruth's Baseball Game, Milton Bradley, 1920s, EX+IB...$500.00
Babes in Toyland, Whitman, 1961, EXIB $20.00
Bamboozle, Milton Bradley, 1962, NMIB $25.00
Barbie Queen of the Prom, Mattel, 1960s, NM+IB..........$75.00
Baretta, Milton Bradley, 1976, NMIB $45.00
Bargain Hunter, Milton Bradley, 1981, NMIB..................$20.00
Barnabas Collins Dark Shadows Game, Milton Bradley, 1969, NMIB $50.00

Barney Google & Spark Plug Game, Milton Bradley, c 1923, EXIB $55.00

Barney Miller, Parker Bros, 1977, NMIB $35.00

Base Ball, JH Singer, 7x7", VGIB................................$425.00

Base Ball Card Game, George Norris, Pat 1903, EXIB... $375.00

Base Ball Game, McLoughlin Bros, c 1897, 8x8", GIB... $600.00

Baseball & Checkers (Two-Game Combination), Milton Bradley, VGIB..$275.00

Baseball Game, All-Fair, 1930, EX+IB.......................$150.00

Baseball Pitching Game, Marx, 1940s, NMIB $225.00

Bash!, Milton Bradley, 1965, NMIB............................$15.00

Bat Masterson, Lowell, 1958, NMIB.............................$45.00

Batman, Milton Bradley, 1966, NMIB...........................$35.00

Batman & Robin, Hasbro, 1965, EXIB $35.00

Batman & Robin Pinball Game, Marx, 1966, NM......... $125.00

Batman Pinball Game, AHI, 1976, NMIB.....................$100.00

Battle Cry, Milton Bradley, 1962, EXIB $30.00

Battle of the Planets, Milton Bradley, 1970s, NMIB.........$30.00

Battlestar Galactica, Parker Bros #58, 1978, NM+IB........$20.00

Beany & Cecil Match It, Mattel, 1960s, EXIB $35.00

Beany & Cecil Ring Toss, Pressman, 1961, EX+IB............$35.00

Beat the Clock, Lowell, 1954, NMIB.............................$35.00

Beat the Clock, Milton Bradley, 1960s, NMIB $15.00

Beatles Flip Your Wig Game, Milton Bradley, 1964, NM+IB.$175.00

Beetle Bailey The Old Army Game, Milton Bradley, 1963, EXIB $25.00

Ben Casey MD, Transogram, 1961, NMIB.....................$20.00

Bermuda Triangle, Milton Bradley, 1976, EX+IB $15.00

Betsy Ross Flag Game, Transogram, 1960s, NM+IB..........$40.00

Beverly Hillbillies 'Set Back' Card Game, Milton Bradley, 1963, NMIB $12.00

Beverly Hillbillies, Standard Toycraft, 1963, NM+IB $45.00

Bewitched, T Cohn Inc, 1965, NMIB.............................$65.00

Bewitched Card Game, Milton Bradley, 1965, EXIB.........$30.00

Bicycle Race, McLoughlin Bros, 1891, GIB....................$350.00

Big Game (Pinball), Marx, 1950s, NM $50.00

Big Maze, Marx, 1955, MIB...$50.00

Billionaire, Parker Bros, 1973, NMIB $12.00

Bionic Crisis, Parker Bros, 1975, NMIB.........................$12.00

Bionic Woman, Parker Bros, 1976, NMIB.......................$12.00

Black Beauty, Transogram, 1957, NMIB $25.00

Black Hole Space Alert Game 'Escape the Doomed Cygnus,' Whitman, 1979, NMIB..$25.00

Blondie, Parker Bros, 1970s, NMIB.............................$12.00

Bo Bang & Hong Kong, Parker Bros, 1890s, EXIB $300.00

Bobbsey Twins, Milton Bradley, 1957, MIB $25.00

Bonanza Michigan Rummy, Parker Bros, 1960s, EXIB $25.00

Boots & Saddles, Chad Valley, 1960s, EX+IB....................$50.00

Boris Karloff's Monster Game, Gems, 1960s, EXIB $125.00

Bozo Ed-U Cards, 1972, EXIB $15.00

Bozo the Clown in Circus Land, Transogram, 1960s, NMIB.$20.00

Brady Bunch, Whitman, 1973, MIB $75.00

Branded, Milton Bradley, 1966, EXIB............................$25.00

Brett Ball/George Brett's Ninth Inning Baseball Game, Raymond O Kentner MD, MIB..$75.00

Buck Rogers & His Cosmic Rocket Wars, Lutz & Scheimkman, 1934, EXIB $450.00

Buck Rogers Game, Milton Bradley, 1970, EXIB..............$15.00

Bugaloos, Milton Bradley, 1971, EXIB $20.00

Bullwinkle Hide 'N Seek Game, Milton Bradley, 1961, NMIB..$50.00

Bullwinkle's Supermarket Game, Whitman, 1970s, EXIB.$25.00

Buy & Sell, Whitman, 1953, EXIB $10.00

Calling Superman, Transogram, 1950s, EXIB $175.00

Candid Camera, Lowell, 1963, NM+IB $30.00

Candyland, Milton Bradley, 1955, EXIB.........................$20.00

Captain America, Milton Bradley, 1966, EXIB...................$30.00

Captain Gallant of the Foreign Legion Adventure Game, Transogram, 1950s, EXIB..$25.00

Captain Kangaroo, Milton Bradley, 1956, NMIB $50.00

Captain Kangaroo TV Lotto, Ideal, 1961, EXIB.................$25.00

Captain Video, Milton Bradley, 1952, EXIB......................$50.00

Captive Princess, McLoughlin Bros, 1890s, G+IB..........$175.00

Car 54 Where Are You?, Allison, 1963, NMIB $75.00

Careers, Parker Bros, 1965, NMIB $20.00

Casey Jones, Saalfield, 1959, EXIB................................$25.00

Cat & Mouse Game, Parker Bros, 1964, EXIB...................$10.00

Champion Game of Base Ball, Proctor Amusement, 1915, NMIB $200.00

Charlie McCarthy's Flying Hats, Whitman, 1930s, EXIB .$30.00

Charlie's Angels (Farrah Fawcett on box), Milton Bradley, 1970s, NMIB $25.00

Charlotte's Web, Hasbro, 1974, NMIB $30.00

Checkered Game of Life, Milton Bradley, VGIB............ $150.00
Cheyenne, Milton Bradley, 1950s, EXIB.............................$30.00
Chicken Lotto, Ideal, 1960s, EXIB......................................$15.00
CHiPS, Ideal, 1981, MIB...$15.00
CHiPS Game, Milton Bradley, 1977, NMIB.........................$10.00
Chiromagica, McLoughlin Bros, early 1910s, EX+IB $300.00
Chug-A-Lug, Dynamic, 1969, NMIB...................................$15.00
Cinderella, Parker Bros, 1964, EXIB $25.00
Cinderella, A Game, Parker Bros, 1875, NMIB...................$75.00
Circination (Or Swinging 'Round the Circle), McLoughlin Bros,
    c 1897, GIB $225.00
Close Encounters of the Third Kind, Parker Bros, 1977, EXIB.$10.00
Clue, Parker Bros, 1970s, NMIB $10.00
Columbo, Milton Bradley, 1973, NMIB..............................$12.00
Combat, Ideal, 1963, NMIB..$50.00
Combat Card Game, Milton Bradley, 1960s, EXIB $12.00
Comical Tivoli Game, JW Spear, VGIB $100.00
Commercial Traveler, McLoughlin Bros, EXIB.............. $325.00
Conflict, Parker Bros, 1960, EXIB......................................$30.00
Count Down Space Game, Transogram, 1960, NMIB.......$25.00
Countdown, Lowe, 1967, NMIB...$35.00
Crazy Clock, Ideal, 1964, NMIB..$30.00
Creature from the Black Lagoon, Hasbro, 1963, EX+IB. $175.00
Crokinole, Selchow & Righter, EXIB $475.00
Crusader Rabbit TV Game, Tryne 1960s, NMIB $125.00
Cycling Tour Game, JW Spear & Co, VGIB $125.00
Dallas, Marcus Industries, 1985, EXIB $20.00
Dangerous World of James Bond 007, Milton Bradley, 1965,
    NMIB $50.00
Daniel Boone Wilderness Trail Card Game, Transogram, 1960s,
    NMIB $45.00
Dark Crystal Game, Milton Bradley, 1980s, NM+IB.........$25.00
Dark Shadows, Whitman, 1968, NMIB $45.00
Dark Towers, Milton Bradley, 1981, NMIB................... $150.00
Dastardly & Muttley, Milton Bradley, 1969, EX+IB..........$25.00
Dating Game, Hasbro, 1967, EXIB $15.00
Dave Garroway's Today Game, Quality Games, 1960, unused,
    MIB..$25.00
Davy Crockett Adventures, Gardner, 1950s, EXIB $50.00
Davy Crockett Radar Action, Ewing, 1950s, EX+IB $50.00
Daytona 500 Race Game, Milton Bradley, 1989, NMIB ...$30.00
Dennis the Menace Baseball Game, MTP, 1960, NMIB ...$45.00
Denny McClain Magnetik Baseball Game, Gotham, 1968,
    NMIB $175.00
Deputy (Starring Henry Fonda...), Bell, 1960s, EXIB........$25.00
Deputy Dawg TV Lotto, Ideal, 1960s, EXIB $20.00
Derby Day, Parker Bros, 1959, NMIB.................................$40.00
Derby Steeple Chase, McLoughlin Bros, 1880s, EXIB.... $175.00
Detectives, Transogram, 1961, NMIB $35.00
Dick Tracy Card Game, Whitman, 1934, EXIB.................$35.00
Dick Tracy Crime Stopper Game, Ideal, 1963, EXIB.........$25.00
Dick Tracy the Master Detective, Selchow & Righter, 1960s,
    EX+IB...$35.00
Dick Van Dyke Board Game, Standard Toykraft, 1960s, EX+IB..$100.00
Dig, Parker Bros, 1930s, EXIB $25.00
Diner's Club Credit Card Game, Ideal, 1961, NMIB........$25.00
Direct Hit, Northwestern Prod, 1950s, EX+IB $165.00
Disney True Life Electric Quiz Game, 1952, VGIB $25.00

Games
Davy Crockett Rescue Race Game, Gabriel, EX
(EX box), $25.00. (Photo courtesy Bill Bruegman)

Games
Donald Duck's Tiddley Winx, 1950s, $100.00
to $135.00. (Photo courtesy David Longest)

Games
Dracula Mystery Game, Hasbro, 1962,
EXIB, $75.00. (Photo courtesy www.serioustoyz.com)

Disneyland Game, Transogram, 1954, EXIB.....................$30.00
District Messenger, McLoughlin Bros, 1880s, VGIB $250.00
Doc Holiday Wild West Game, Transogram, 1960, NMIB.$35.00
Dogfight, McLoughlin Bros, 1962, EXIB............................$40.00
Don't Break the Ice, Schaper, 1960s, NMIB $15.00
Don't Have a Cow Dice Game (Simpsons), Milton Bradley 1990,
    NMIB $15.00
Donnie & Marie Osmond TV Game Show, Mattel, 1977,
    NMIB $30.00
Dr Kildare, Ideal, 1962, NMIB..$30.00

Games
• • • • • • • • • •
The Dukes of Hazzard Card Game, International Games, 1981, unused, MIB, $10.00.
(Photo courtesy www.whatacharacter.com)

Games
• • • • • • • • • •
Fishing Banks Game, EXIB, $500.00. (Photo courtesy Morphy Auctions on LiveAuctioneers.com)

Games
• • • • • • • • • •
Game of Aladdin, Singer, 1890, VG+IB, $4,310.00. (Photo courtesy James D. Julia, Inc.)

Dragnet, Transogram, 1955, NMIB $55.00
Dream House, Milton Bradley, 1968, EXIB $25.00
Dukes of Hazzard, Ideal, 1981, EXIB $10.00
Dynomutt, Milton Bradley, 1970s, NM+IB $20.00
Ed Wynn the Fire Chief, Selchow & Righter, 1930s, EXIB.. $50.00
Eliot Ness and the Untouchables, Transogram, 1960s, EX+IB. $40.00
Emergency, Milton Bradley, 1970s, NMIB $30.00
Emily Post Popularity Game, Selchow & Righter, 1970s, NMIB $20.00
Ensign O'Toole USS Appleby Game, Hasbro, 1968, NMIB. $30.00
Escape from New York, TSR, 1980s, EX+IB $15.00
Escort Game of Guys & Gals, Parker Bros, 1955, unused, MIB.. $30.00
Evel Knievel Stunt World, Ideal, 1975, self-contained suitcase unfolds to Coliseum & Snake River, NMIB $80.00
Excuse Me! A Game of Manners, Parker Bros, NMIB $25.00
Eye Guess, Milton Bradley, 1966, EXIB $15.00
F-Troop, Ideal, 1960s, VGIB $35.00
Fall Guy, Milton Bradley, 1980s, NMIB $30.00
Family Affair, Whitman, 1960s, EX+IB $30.00
Family Feud, Milton Bradley, 1970s, NMIB $15.00
Family Ties, Apple Street, 1986, EXIB $15.00
Fantastic Voyage, Milton Bradley, 1968, NMIB $30.00
Fantasy Island, Ideal, 1978, NMIB $45.00
Farmer Jones Pigs, McLoughlin Bros, VGIB $125.00
FBI, Transogram, 1950s, EX+IB $45.00
Felix the Cat, Milton Bradley, 1960, 1st version, EXIB $35.00
Felix the Cat Dandy Candy Game, Built-Rite, 1950s, EX+IB.. $10.00
Felix the Cat Target, Lido, 1960s, EXIB $25.00
Ferdinand's Chinese Checkers w/the Bee!, Parker Bros, 1939, EXIB $150.00
Fess Parker Trail Blazers Game, Milton Bradley, 1964, NMIB.. $40.00
Fish Pond, Milton Bradley, EX+IB $65.00
Flintstones Brake Ball, Whitman, 1962, EXIB $85.00
Flintstones, Milton Bradley, 1971, NMIB $20.00
Flintstones Stone Age Game Transogram, 1961, NMIB ... $55.00
Flipper Flips, Mattel, 1960s, EX+IB $35.00
Flying Nun Marble Maze Game, Milton Bradley, 1967, NMIB.. $45.00
Fonz Hanging Out at Arnold's Card Game, Milton Bradley, 1976, MIB.. $30.00
Foot Ball, Parker Bros, 8x8", VGIB $500.00
Formula 1 Car Racing Game, Parker Bros, 1968, NMIB ... $55.00
Fox & the Hounds, Parker Bros, 1948, NM $25.00
Frankenstein Mystery Game, Hasbro, 1960s, EXIB $75.00
Fugitive, Ideal, 1964, NMIB $75.00
Fu Manchu's Hidden Hoard, Ideal, 1960s, VGIB $15.00

Gambler, Parker Bros, 1970s, EX+IB $10.00
Game of A Dash for the North Pole, McLoughlin Bros, 1897, VG+IB $2,760.00
Game of Alley Oop, Royal Toy Co, 1930s, VG (rnd tin canister) $75.00
Game of Base-Ball, McLoughlin Bros, c 1886, 9x17", GIB. $1,400.00
Game of Boy Scouts, Milton Bradley, EXIB $300.00
Game of Boy Scouts, Parker Bros, 1920s, EXIB $250.00
Game of Famous Men, Parker Bros, VGIB $50.00
Game of Flags, McLoughlin Bros, VGIB $75.00
Game of Going to the Klondike, McLoughlin Bros, 1890s, EXIB,... $4,600.00
Game of Golf, Singer, VGIB $550.00
Game of International Spy, All-Fair, 1940s, EXIB $50.00
Game of Jaws, Ideal, 1975, MIB (sealed) $80.00
Game of Life, Milton Bradley, 1960s, NM+IB $25.00
Game of Napoleon (Little Corporal), Parker Bros, 1895, EXIB... $450.00
Game of Phoebe Snow, McLoughlin Bros, ca 1909, EXIB.. $550.00
Game of Playing Department Store, McLoughlin Bros, EXIB.. $2,750.00
Game of Red Riding Hood, Parker Bros, 1895, VGIB $150.00
Game of Redoubt, JH Singer, VGIB $350.00
Game of Rival Armies (The Merry Christmas Series), McLoughlin Bros, VGIB... $600.00
Game of Sailor Boy, JH Singer, 1880s-90s, GIB $275.00
Game of Snap, Milton Bradley, 1910s, VG+IB $50.00
Game of the Man in the Moon, McLoughlin Bros, c 1912, EXIB $850.00
Game of Trip Around the World, McLoughlin Bros, 1890s, VGIB $2,000.00

Game of Yuneek, McLoughlin Bros, 1880s, VGIB $200.00

Games People Play, Alpsco, 1967, NMIB $25.00

Games You Like to Play, Parker Bros, 1920s, EX+IB $50.00

Gang Way for Fun, Transogram, 1960s, VGIB $15.00

Garrison's Gorillas, Ideal, 1967, EXIB $50.00

Gee-Wiz The Racing Game Sensation, Wolverine, 1920s, EX+ (VG box) $100.00

Gene Autry's Dude Ranch Game, Built-Rite, 1950s, EXIB .. $25.00

General Hospital, Parker Bros, 1970s, EX+IB $10.00

Gentle Ben Animal Hunt Game, Mattel, 1960s, EX+IB ... $40.00

George of the Jungle, Parker Bros, 1968, NMIB $75.00

Get in That Tub, Hasbro, 1969, unused, NMIB $30.00

Get Smart Card Game, Ideal, 1966, EXIB $20.00

Get Smart, Ideal, 1966, NMIB $35.00

GI Joe Adventure, Hasbro, 1980s, EX+IB $25.00

GI Joe Card Game, Whitman, 1960s, NM+IB $20.00

Gidget, Standard Toycraft, 1965, MIB $75.00

Gilligan's Island, Game Gems/T Cohn, 1965, EXIB $150.00

G-Men Clue Games, Whitman #3930, 1930s, VGIB $75.00

Gnip Gnop, Parker Bros, 1971, NMIB $15.00

Godzilla, Mattel, 1978, EXIB $35.00

Gomer Pyle, Transogram, 1964, EXIB $20.00

Goodbye Mr Chips, Parker Bros, 1969, EXIB $10.00

Gray Ghost, Transogram, 1958, NMIB $90.00

Great Charlie Chan Detective Game, Milton Bradley, 1930s, EXIB $350.00

Great Escape, Ideal, 1967, EX+IB $12.00

Great Grape Ape Game, Milton Bradley, 1975, EX+IB $20.00

Green Acres, Standard Toykraft, 1960s, EXIB $75.00

Green Ghost Game, Transogram, 1965, NMIB $165.00

Green Hornet Quick Switch Game, Milton Bradley, 1960s, EX+IB $100.00

Gremlins, International Games, 1980s, VGIB $5.00

Groucho Marx TV Quiz, Pressman, 1950s, EXIB $45.00

Groucho TV Quiz, Pressman, 1954, EXIB $50.00

Gulliver's Travels, Milton Bradley, 1930s, EXIB $135.00

Gumby & Pokey Playful Trails, 1968, NMIB $25.00

Gunsmoke, Lowell, 1958, NMIB $75.00

Hang on Harvey, Ideal, 1969, EXIB $15.00

Happy Days, Parker Bros, 1976, NMIB $20.00

Hardy Boys Mystery Game, Milton Bradley, 1968, EX+IB . $10.00

Hardy Boys Treasure Game, Parker Bros, 1957, NMIB $35.00

Haunted House Game, Ideal, 1960s, EXIB $125.00

Haunted Mansion Lakeside, 1970s, EX+IB $75.00

Hawaii Five-O, Remco, 1960s, EXIB $25.00

Hawaiian Eye, Transogram, 1960s, EXIB $50.00

Hen That Laid the Golden Egg, Parker Bros, 1900s, EXIB .. $125.00

Hi-Way Henry Cross Country 'The Lizzy' Race, All-Fair, 1920s, EXIB $895.00

Hide 'N Seek, Ideal, 1960s, EXIB $25.00

Hit & Run Baseball Game, Wilder, 1930s, NMIB $175.00

Hogan's Heroes, Transogram, 1960s, VGIB $25.00

Hollywood Squares, Ideal, 1970s, EX+IB $10.00

Honey Bee Game, Milton Bradley, 1913, EX+IB $60.00

Honey West, Ideal, 1960s, EXIB $40.00

Hopalong Cassidy, Milton Bradley, 1950, NMIB $80.00

Hopalong Cassidy Game, Marx, 1950s, EXIB $115.00

Hopalong Cassidy Lasso Game, Transogram, 1950, NMIB . $135.00

Hoppity Hooper Pinball Game, Lidu, 1965, NMIB $85.00

Horseless Carriage Race, McLoughlin Bros, EXIB $2,750.00

Hot Wheels Wipe Out Race Game, Mattel, 1968, NMIB . $40.00

House Party, Whitman, 1968, EX+IB $15.00

Howdy Doody Adventure Game, Milton Bradley, 1950s, VGIB $25.00

Howdy Doody Bean Bag Game, Parker Bros, 1950s, EXIB . $75.00

Howdy Doody Card Game, Russell, 1950s, NMIB $15.00

Howdy Doody's Own Game, Parker Bros, 1949, EXIB $45.00

Howdy Doody's TV Game, Milton Bradley, 1950s, EXIB .. $25.00

Huckleberry Hound Tiddly Winks, Milton Bradley, 1959, EXIB $20.00

Huckleberry Hound Western Game, Milton Bradley, 1959, EXIB $30.00

Hullabaloo, Remco, 1965, EXIB $30.00

Humpty Dumpty Game, Lowell, 1950s, EXIB $30.00

Hungry Ant, Milton Bradley, 1970s, NMIB $15.00

Hurry Waiter!, Ideal, 1969, EXIB $10.00

I Dream of Jeannie, Milton Bradley, 1965, NMIB $60.00

I Spy, Ideal, 1965, EXIB $40.00

I Wanna Be President, JR Mackey, 1983, NMIB $15.00

Incredible Hulk, Milton Bradley, 1970s, NMIB $10.00

Indiana Jones in Raiders of the Lost Ark, Kenner, 1981, NMIB $15.00

Intercollegiate Football, Hustler, 1920s, EXIB................ $200.00

International Automobile Race, Parker Bros, 1903, EXIB..$625.00

Intrigue, Milton Bradley, 1954, NMIB...........................$35.00

Ipcress File Game (The), Milton Bradley, 1966, MIB........$30.00

Ironside, Ideal, 1976, EXIB..$50.00

Jack & Jill, Milton Bradley, early 1900s, VGIB.............. $100.00

Jackie Gleason & Away We Go! TV Fun Game, Transogram, 1956, EXIB $50.00

James Bond Message From M, Ideal, 1966, EXIB............. $150.00

James Bond Secret Agent 007, Milton Bradley, 1964, NMIB...$35.00

Jan Murray's Treasure Hunt, Gardner, 1950s, NMIB $30.00

Jeopardy, Milton Bradley, 1964, NMIB $20.00

Jerome Park Steeple Chase, McLoughlin Bros, EXIB $400.00

Jetsons Fun Pad Game, Milton Bradley, 1963, NMIB.......$80.00

Jetsons Game, Milton Bradley, 1985, NM+IB $12.00

Jetsons Out of This World Game, Transogram, 1963, unused, EXIB $50.00

John Drake Secret Agent, Milton Bradley, 1966, EXIB.....$18.00

Jolly Jungleers, Milton Bradley, VGIB............................ $100.00

Jungle Book, Parker Bros, 1966, NMIB.............................$35.00

Justice League of America, Hasbro, 1967, EXIB $75.00

Kaboom Balloon Busting Game, Ideal, 1965, NMIB.........$30.00

King Kong Game, Ideal, 1970s, EXIB $50.00

King Kong Game, Milton Bradley, 1960s, NMIB $25.00

King Leonardo & His Subjects, Milton Bradley, 1960, EXIB...$20.00

King of the Hill, Schaper, 1960s, EXIB $30.00

KISS on Tour, Aucoin, 1978, EXIB...................................$30.00

Knight Rider, Parker Bros, 1983, NMIB............................$15.00

Kojak Stake Out Detective, Milton Bradley, 1975, EXIB..$15.00

Kooky Carnival, Milton Bradley, 1969, NMIB $40.00

Kukla & Ollie – A Game, Parker Bros, 1962, NMIB.........$30.00

Lame Duck, Parker Bros, 1928, VGIB............................. $125.00

Lancer, Remco, 1968, EX+IB...$50.00

Land of the Giants, Ideal, 1968, NMIB.......................... $100.00

Laramie, Lowell, 1960, VGIB...$25.00

Lassie, Game Gems, 1965, EXIB $25.00

Laugh-In's Squeeze Your Bibby, Hasbro, 1960s, VGIB.......$25.00

Laverne & Shirley, Parker Bros, 1970s, EXIB $10.00

Le Dirigeable Ball Toss Game, France, ca 1895, 29x31x10", VG..$4,500.00

Legend of Jesse James, Milton Bradley, 1965, EXIB...........$35.00

Let's Make a Deal, Milton Bradley, 1960s, EX+IB.............$15.00

Letter Carrier, McLoughlin Bros, VGIB.......................... $275.00

Lie Detector, Mattel, 1961, NMIB $50.00

Little Drummer, J Ottmann Litho Co, EXIB $275.00

Little Orphan Annie Game, Parker Bros, 1981, EXIB.......$15.00

Little Rascals Clubhouse Bingo, Gabriel, 1958, NM (G box) .$30.00

Little Red Riding Hood, McLoughlin Bros, 1900s, EXIB . $200.00

Lone Ranger Target Game, Marx, 1939, EXIB $75.00

Looney Tunes, Milton Bradley, 1968, NMIB $35.00

Lost in Space, Milton Bradley, 1965, NMIB $75.00

Louisa, McLoughlin Bros, EXIB $165.00

Lucy's Tea Party Game, Milton Bradley, 1971, EXIB.........$20.00

M Squad, Bell Toys, 1950s, VGIB $25.00

MAD Magazine, Parker Bros, 1979, NMIB.......................$10.00

MAD's Spy vs Spy, Milton Bradley, 1986, NMIB $25.00

Games

Jonny Quest Game, Transogram, 1964, EXIB, $225.00. (Photo courtesy Morphy Auctions on LiveAuctioneers.com)

Games

Land of the Lost Game, Milton Bradley, 1975, NMIB, $30.00. (Photo courtesy Greg Davis and Bill Morgan)

Games

Liberty Airport and Flying Airplanes, Liberty Playthings, EXIB, $880.00. (Photo courtesy Bertoia Auctions)

Magilla Gorilla, Ideal, 1960s, EX+IB $50.00

Magnetic Fish Pond, McLoughlin Bros, 1890s, VGIB.... $400.00

Magnetic Fish Pond, Milton Bradley, 1948, NMIB $25.00

Major League Baseball Game, Philadelphia Game Mfg, Pat 1912, EXIB $625.00

Man From UNCLE Illya Kuryakin Card Game, Milton Bradley, 1966, NMIB...$20.00

Man From UNCLE Target Game, Marx, 1965, NM....... $250.00

Man From UNCLE the Pinball Game, 1966, EX $100.00

Man From UNCLE Thrush Ray Gun Affair Game, Ideal, 1966, NMIB $75.00

Manhunt, Milton Bradley, 1972, NMIB.........................$15.00

Marlin Perkins' Zoo Parade, Cadaco-Ellis, 1960s, EXIB....$15.00

Marvel Comics Super-Heroes Card Game, Milton Bradley, 1970s, MIB (sealed) $75.00

Mary Hartman Mary Hartman, Reiss Games, 1970s, EXIB ..$15.00

Mary Poppins Carousel Game, Parker Bros, 1964, NMIB .$20.00

Masquerade Party, Bettye B, 1955, EX+IB $40.00

McHale's Navy, Transogram, 1962, NMIB.........................$35.00

Melvin Pervis' G-Men Detective Game, Parker Bros, 1936, EXIB $100.00

Melvin the Moon Man, Remco, 1960s, NMIB.................$75.00

Merry-Go-Round, Chaffee & Selchow, 1890s-1910s, VGIB..$1,500.00

Merry-Go-Round Game, Parker Bros, VG+IB................ $355.00

Miami Vice, Pepper Lane, 1984, EXIB...........................$15.00

Mickey Mantle's Big League Baseball, Gardner, 1958, VGIB..$100.00

Mickey Mouse Circus Game, Marks Bros, 1930s, NMIB. $500.00

Mickey Mouse Kiddy Keno, Jaymar, 1950s-60s, NMIB $20.00

Mickey Mouse Picture Matching Game, Parker Bros, 1953, EX+IB...$25.00

Mickey Mouse Pop Up Game, Whitman, 1970s, MIB $25.00

Mighty Comics Super Heroes, Transogram, 1966, NMIB..$75.00

Mighty Hercules Game, Hasbro, 1960s, NMIB $325.00

Mighty Mouse Rescue Game, Harett-Gilmer, 1960s, NMIB...$55.00

Milton the Monster, Milton Bradley, 1966, EXIB.............$15.00

Mini Golf, Technofix, 1960s, NMIB $150.00

Mission Impossible, Ideal, 1967, EXIB $50.00

Mister Ed, Parker Bros, 1962, EXIB.............................$25.00

Monkees Game, Transogram, 1968, NMIB $115.00

Monopoly, Parker Bros, 1950s, NMIB.............................$65.00

Monster Old Maid Card Game, Milton Bradley, 1964, EXIB...$20.00

Monster Squad, Milton Bradley #4716, 1977, EXIB..........$15.00

Mork & Mindy, Milton Bradley, 1978, NMIB $20.00

Motor Cycle Game, Milton Bradley, early, EX+IB $425.00

Motor Race, Wolverine, 1922, VGIB $50.00

Mr Novak, Transogram, 1963, NMIB...............................$25.00

Munsters Card Game, Milton Bradley, 1964, NMIB $45.00

Munsters Masquerade Game, Hasbro, 1960s, VGIB....... $175.00

Munsters Picnic Game, Hasbro, 1960s, EXIB $250.00

Muppet Show, Parker Bros, 1977, EXIB...........................$20.00

Murder on the Orient Express, Ideal, 1967, EXIB $25.00

Murder She Wrote, Warren, 1985, NMIB $8.00

Mushmouth & Punkin Puss, Ideal, 1964, EXIB $50.00

My Favorite Martian, Transogram, 1963, EXIB $45.00

Mystery Date Game, Milton Bradley, 1965, NMIB $75.00

Mystic Skull The Game of Voodoo, Ideal, 1964, NMIB....$35.00

Name That Tune — A Music Bingo Game, Milton Bradley, 1957, unused, MIB $20.00

Nancy & Sluggo Game, 1944, rare, NMIB $100.00

National Velvet, Transogram, 1950s, NMIB.....................$30.00

Nebbs on the Air, Milton Bradley, 1930s, EXIB $100.00

New Game of Hunting, McLoughlin Bros, EXIB............ $990.00

New Pretty Village, McLoughlin Bros, 1890s, EXIB....... $200.00

Newlywed Game, Hasbro, 1st Edition, 1967, NMIB $20.00

No Time for Sergeants, Ideal, 1964, EXIB $15.00

Nurses, Ideal, 1963, NMIB...$45.00

Office Boy — The Good Old Days, Parker Bros, 1889, EXIB.. $150.00

Oh Magoo, Warren, 1960s, NMIB...................................$25.00

Old Maid & Old Bachelor (Or Beaux & Belles), McLoughlin Bros, 1890s, EXIB...$3,000.00

Operation, Milton Bradley, 1965, NMIB $40.00

Orbit, Parker Bros, 1959, NMIB......................................$25.00

Outer Limits, Milton Bradley, 1964, NMIB $175.00

Overland Trail, Transogram, 1960, NMIB.........................$60.00

Park & Shop, Milton Bradley, 1960, NMIB.......................$45.00

Parlor Football Game, McLoughlin Bros, VGIB.......... $1,200.00

Partidge Family, Milton Bradley, 1971, NMIB...................$25.00

Patty Duke Show, Milton Bradley, 1963, NMIB...............$30.00

Games
● ● ● ● ● ● ● ● ● ●
Paladin Checkers, Ideal, 1960, NMIB, $200.00. (Photo courtesy www.serioustoyz.com)

Games
● ● ● ● ● ● ● ● ● ●
Peter Pan Games, Hunt-Wesson Foods Premium, 1969, unused, MIB, $75.00. (Photo courtesy www.gasolinealleyantiques.com)

Peanuts, The Game of Charlie Brown & His Pals, Selchow & Righter, 1959, EXIB $25.00

Pebbles Flintstone Game, Transogram, 1962, NMIB.........$25.00

Peg Base Ball Game, Parker Bros, VGIB.........................$150.00

Perry Mason Case of the Missing Suspect, Transogram, NMIB... $25.00

Peter Gunn Detective Game, Lowell, 1960, NMIB...........$30.00

Peter Pan, Selchow & Righter, 1920s, EX+IB $100.00

Peter Pan, Transogram, 1953, EXIB $12.00

Peter Potamus Game, Ideal, 1964, NMIB.......................$45.00

Peter Rabbit Game, Milton Bradley, 1910s, EXIB.............$50.00

Petticoat Junction, Standard Toycraft, 1963, NMIB $75.00

Philip Marlow, Transogram, 1960, EXIB.........................$15.00

Ping-Pong, Parker Bros, EXIB $200.00

Pink Panther, Warren, 1977, NMIB...............................$20.00

Pinky Lee & the Runaway Frankfurters, Lisbeth Whiting Co, 1954, NM (G+ box)....................$65.00

Pirate & Traveler, Milton Bradley, 1953, NMIB................$30.00

Pirate's Cove, Gabriel, 1950s, EX+IB.............................$20.00

Pirates of the Caribbean, Parker Bros, 1967, NMIB $35.00

Planet of the Apes, Milton Bradley, 1974, EXIB...............$25.00

Popeye Jet Pilot Target Game, Japan, NMIB $150.00

Popeye Menu Marble Game, Durable Toys & Novelty, c 1935, EX $440.00

Popeye Ring Toss Game, Rosebud Art Co, 1933, NMIB. $285.00

Popeye's Game, Parker Bros, 1948, unused, MIB............$200.00

Price Is Right, Milton Bradley, 1958, 1st ed, EXIB............$25.00

Prince Valiant, Transogram, 1950s, EXIB $25.00

PT 109, Ideal, 1963, VGIB..$45.00

Quick Draw McGraw Private Eye Game, Milton Bradley, 1960, EXIB $10.00

Raggedy Ann & Andy Game, Milton Bradley, 1956, NMIB...$15.00

Raise the Titanic, Hoyle, 1987, EXIB $15.00

Rat Patrol, Transogram, 1966, NMIB.............................$75.00

Rebel, Ideal, 1961, NMIB...$80.00

Red Riding Hood With Big Bad Wolf & 3 Little Pigs/Walt Disney's Own Game, Parker Bros, 1933, NMIB $200.00

Restless Gun, Milton Bradley, 1950s, EXIB $20.00

Rich Uncle — The Stock Market Game, Parker Bros, 1955, EXIB..$15.00

Ricochet Rabbit Game, Ideal, 1965, EXIB........................$50.00

Rifleman, Milton Bradley, 1959, NMIB $50.00

Rin-Tin-Tin (Adventures of), Transogram, 1955, EXIB....$35.00

Risk!, Parker Bros, 1959, NMIB....................................$35.00

Rival Doctors (A Comic Game), McLoughlin Bros, 1890s, EXIB.. $425.00

Road Runner, Milton Bradley, 1968, NMIB $30.00

Road Runner Card Game, 1976, NMIB...........................$10.00

Robin Hood, Parker Bros, 1970s, EXIB...........................$10.00

Rocket Race to Saturn, Lido, 1950s, NM+IB $25.00

Rocky & His Friends, Milton Bradley, 1960s, EXIB $50.00

Round the World with Nellie Bly, McLoughlin Bros, 1890, VG+IB....................$350.00

Ruff & Reddy Spelling Game, Exclusive Playing Card Co, 1958, EXIB $24.00

Run-Pig-Run Game, Schoenhut, EXIB............................$500.00

Sailor Boy, United Games Co, EXIB...............................$200.00

Scooby Doo Where Are You?, Milton Bradley, 1973, NMIB...$25.00

Sealab 2020, Milton Bradley, 1973, NM+IB.....................$15.00

Secret Agent Man, Milton Bradley, 1966, EXIB................$30.00

Shenanigans, Milton Bradley, 1964, EXIB $20.00

Shuffled Symphonies Card Game, England/WD, ca 1938, NMIB . $65.00

Skeezix & the Air Mail, Milton Bradley, 1930s, EXIB $60.00

Skippy, Milton Bradley, 1930s, EXIB $80.00

Skirmish at Harper's Ferry, McLoughlin Bros, 1890s, VG+IB ...$900.00

Sleeping Beauty, see Walt Disney's Sleeping Beauty

Smitty, Milton Bradley, 1930s, EX+IB $250.00

Snake's Alive, Ideal, 1967, NMIB..................................$25.00

Snoopy & the Red Baron, Milton Bradley, 1970, MIB......$40.00

Snoopy Card Game, Ideal, 1965, NMIB..........................$25.00

Snoopy Game, Selchow & Righter, 1960, VGIB..............$15.00

Snoopy Snake Attack, Gabriel, 1980, MIB $25.00

Snow White & the Seven Dwarfs, Cadaco, 1970s, NMIB .$20.00

Snow White & the Seven Dwarfs, Milton Bradley, 1930s, EXIB....................$75.00

Snow White & the Seven Dwarfs, Parker Bros, 1930s, EXIB.. $150.00

Soldiers on Guard, McLoughlin Bros, VGIB $125.00

Space Patrol Magnetic Target Game, American Toy, 1950s, EX .. $50.00

Space: 1999, Milton Bradley, 1975, NMIB $25.00

Sparky Marble Maze, Built-Rite, 1971, NMIB...................$30.00

Spider's Web, McLoughlin Bros, late 1800s, EXIB $80.00

Spider-Man w/the Fantastic Four, Milton Bradley, 1977, NMIB. $35.00

Spot Shot Marble Game, Wolverine, 1930s, NM...............$50.00

Spy Detector, Mattel, 1960, NMIB $75.00

Stagecoach, Milton Bradley, 1958, NMIB $25.00

Star Trek, Milton Bradley, 1979, EXIB..............................$45.00

Star Trek Adventure Game, West End Games, 1985, NMIB...$25.00

Star Trek: The Next Generation, Classics Games, 1990s, NM+IB.$35.00

Star Wars Escape From Death Star, Kenner, 1971, NMIB.$25.00

Stars Wars Monopoly, Parker Bros, 1997, unused, MIB.....$30.00

Starsky & Hutch Detective, Milton Bradley, 1977, NMIB.$25.00

Steeple Chase, Singer, 1890s, VGIB $150.00

Steve Canyon Air Force Game, Lowell, 1950s, NM+IB ...$50.00

Stop Thief, Parker Bros, 1979, NMIB $30.00

Superboy Game, Hasbro, 1960s, NMIB $80.00

Super Heroes Card Game, Milton Bradley, 1978, EXIB....$20.00

Superman's Deadliest Enemy, Hasbro, 1965, EXIB...........$85.00

Superman III, Parker Bros, 1983, MIB............................$25.00

Superstition, Milton Bradley, 1977, NMIB $25.00

Surfside 6, Lowell, 1961, unused, EXIB............................$35.00

Susceptibles (A Parlor Amusement), McLoughlin Bros, 1890s,
     VGIB $500.00

Tales of Wells Fargo, Milton Bradley, 1959, EXIB $45.00

Tennessee Tuxedo, Transogram, 1963, EXIB....................$100.00

That Girl, Remco, 1969, EXIB.......................................$70.00

The Big Squeeze, Ideal, 1968, EXIB $17.00

The Charge (Toralon Series), EO Clark, VGIB.............. $700.00

The Last Straw, Schafer Mfg, 1966, NMIB $15.00

This Is Your Life, Lowell, 1954, EXIB $25.00

Tic-Tac-Dough, Transogram, 1957, EXIB $15.00

Tight Squeeze, Mattel, 1967, NMIB...............................$25.00

Tim Holt Rodeo Dart Games, American Toys, unused, NMIB..$100.00

Time Bomb, Milton Bradley, 1965, NMIB $88.00

Time Tunnel, Ideal, 1966, EXIB $100.00

Tiny Tim Game of Beautiful Things, Parker Bros, 1970, EXIB.$25.00

Tiny Town Bank, Spear's New Edition, EXIB $300.00

To Tell the Truth, Lowell, 1957, EXIB...........................$20.00

Toll Gate, McLoughlin Bros, c 1894, VGIB $800.00

Tom & Jerry, Milton Bradley, 1977, EXIB........................$10.00

Tom & Jerry, Adventure in Blunderland, Transogram, EXIB...$20.00

Tom Sawyer & Huck Finn (Adventures of), Stoll & Edwards,
     VGIB $125.00

Top Cat, Cadaco-Ellis, 1961, NMIB $100.00

Town & Country Traffic, Ranger Steel, 1940s, NMIB.......$85.00

Town Hall, Milton Bradley, 1939, NMIB........................$20.00

Train for Boston, Parker Bros, c 1900, GIB.................. $850.00

Truth or Consequences, Gabriel, 1950s, NMIB.................$35.00

Turn Over, Milton Bradley, EXIB..................................$75.00

Twelve O'Clock High, Ideal, 1965, VGIB $25.00

Twiggy, Milton Bradley, 1967, EXIB..............................$65.00

Twilight Zone, Ideal, 1964, unused, NMIB $180.00

Uncle Remus Shooting Gallery, B&B Novelties, 1917 patent,
     VGIB $690.00

Uncle Sam's Mail, McLoughlin Bros, 1890s, VGIB........ $150.00

Uncle Wiggily, Parker Bros, 1979, NMIB $25.00

Untouchables, Marx, 1950s, NMIB $225.00

Untouchables Target Game, Marx, 1950s, NM $350.00

Vassar Boat Race, Chaffee & Selchow, c 1899, EXIB..$1,500.00

Virginian, Transogram, 1962, EXIB............................. $100.00

Voodoo Doll Game, Schaper, 1967, EXIB.......................$30.00

Voyage to the Bottom of the Sea Card Game, Milton Bradley,
     1964, NMIB $50.00

Wagon Train, Milton Bradley, 1960, EXIB $50.00

Wally Gator Game, Transogram, 1963, NMIB $100.00

Walt Disney's Fantasyland, PB, 1950, MIB $50.00

Walt Disney's Sleeping Beauty, Whitman, 1958, EXIB $35.00

Walt Disney's Treasure Island, Gardner Games, 1950s, EXIB.. $100.00

Wanted Dead or Alive, Lowell, 1959, EXIB $50.00

War at Sea (Or Don't Give Up the Ship), McLoughlin Bros,
     VGIB $2,100.00

Warner's Baseball Game, early, VG+IB........................... $630.00

Wendy the Good Little Witch, Milton Bradley, 1966, VGIB...$25.00

Westpoint — A Game for the Nation, Otooman Litho Co, 1902,
     EX+ (G+ box) $125.00

Which Witch?, Milton Bradley, 1970, EXIB.....................$50.00

Who Framed Roger Rabbit?, Milton Bradley, 1987, NMIB ...$30.00

Wide World Travel Game, Parker Bros, 1957, NMIB........$30.00

Wild Bill Hickok's Cavalry & Indians Game, Built-Rite, NMIB.....$25.00

Wilder's Baseball Game, Wilder, 1936, NMIB................ $200.00

Wonderful Game of Oz, Parker Bros, EXIB.................... $200.00

Wonder Woman, Hasbro, 1967, NMIB............................$30.00

Woody Woodpecker Game, Milton Bradley, 1959, NM+IB.. $30.00

World's Fair Ed-U Cards, 1965, NMIB............................$15.00

Wyatt Earp, Transogram, 1958, EXIB.............................$40.00

Yachting, Singer, 1890, EXIB $150.00

Yacht Race Game, McLoughlin Bros, GIB...................... $140.00

Yale-Harvard Game, Parker Bros, 1890s, EX+IB $2,750.00

Yogi Bear Break a Plate Game, Transogram, 1960s, NMIB....$45.00

Yogi Bear Rummy Ed-U Cards, 1961, MIB (sealed) $15.00

You Don't Say, Milton Bradley, 1963, EXIB.....................$20.00

Zoom the Airplane Card Game, Whitman, 1941, NM (VG box).$65.00

Zorro, Parker Bros, 1966, EXIB $30.00

Gasoline-Powered Toys

Two of the largest companies to manufacture gas-powered models are Cox and Wen-Mac. Since the late 1950s they have been faithfully making detailed models of airplanes as well as some automobiles and boats. Condition of used models will vary greatly because of the nature of the miniature gas engine and damage resulting from the fuel that has been used. Because of this, 'new in box' gas toys command a premium.

Advisor: Richard Trautwein

All-American Hot Rod, cast aluminum, 9", VG $250.00
BB Korn Meteor #3 (Korn Spl), 1970s, 18", VG+ $4,540.00
Bremer #42 Atwood Special, silver-tone metal w/yel flames on nose, burgundy leather seat, Super Champion engine, 18", NM $1,600.00
Bremer Whirlwind #2, gr & wht, 18", 1939, NM $2,900.00
Bremer Whirlwind #300, red, Brown Jr engine, 1939, VG . $1,250.00
Butch Marx Bowes Seal Fast Sprint Car #26, 1952, wht w/bl & red, 18", EX $5,750.00
Butch Marx Caruso #2 One-Off Midget, pre-war, McCoy .19 ignition engine, 16", VG+ $4,025.00
Cameron Racer #4, red w/yel flames, 8", VG, $200 to.... $275.00
Cameron Rodzy Standard Racer, 1950s, 8", MIB............ $500.00
Cox AA Fuel Dragster, bl & red, 1968-70, M................. $125.00
Cox Acro-Cub, 1960s, MIB (sealed), $60 to $85.00
Cox Baja Bug, yel & orange, 1968-73, M...........................$65.00
Cox Chopper, MIB, $70 to $100.00
Cox Commanche, E-Z Flyer series, 1993-95, NMIB..........$35.00
Cox Delta F-15, Wing Series, gray, 1981-86, M.................$30.00
Cox E-Z Flyer Commanche, wht, NMIB $35.00
Cox Golden Bee, .49 engine, M.......................................$30.00
Cox Marine Helicopter, NM $35.00
Cox ME-109 Airplane, 1994, MIB (sealed), $40 to...........$60.00
Cox Mercedes Benz W196 Racer, red, 1963-65, EX $85.00
Cox Navy Hilldiver, 2-tone bl, 1963-66, EX, $65 to $80.00
Cox PT-19 Flight Trainer, yel & bl, EX............................$45.00
Cox Sandblaster, brn & tan, 1968-72, M, $45 to...............$65.00
Cox Shrike Bonneville Special, MIB, $130 to................ $150.00
Cox Sky Rider, gray, EXIB...$85.00

Cox Snowmobile, silver, 1968, M $100.00
Cox Stealth Bomber, blk, 1987-89, EX, $30 to.................$50.00
Cox Super Stunter, 1974-79, EX, $30 to...........................$45.00
Cox Thimble Drome Prop-Rod, yel & red, 12", EXIB.... $200.00
Cox Thimble Drome Racer #92, diecast, 8½", VG......... $150.00
Cox Thimble Drome TD-1 Airplane, NMIB, $95 to $125.00
Cox Thimble Drome TD-3 Airplane, 1950s, NMIB $85.00
Cox UFO Flying Saucer, Wings Series, wht, 1990-91, M..$25.00
Curtiss Jenny Airplane, WWI era, 65" WS, EX, $250 to.. $300.00
Curtiss P-40D Tiger Shark, 13½", MIB, $95 to $135.00
Don Edmunds Elcar Special #18, modeled after Indy 500 racer driven by John Duff in 1926, red & yel, w/driver, 21", VG+ $5,460.00
Don Edmunds Trackmaster #23, ca 1975, Atwood Champion .60 ignition engine, silver w/red & yel trim, VG+ $3,220.00
Dooling Knoxville Champ F Racer #3, red, 19", EX, $1,000 to $1,400.00
Dooling Mercury Racer #59, Hornet engine, 1940s, 18½", $1,800 to..$2,300.00
Dooling Racer #34, orange w/bl & wht 'Autographics of California' decals, 16", EX.. $860.00
Dooling Racer #4, orange articulated front end, McCoy engine, EX rstr $1,500.00
Dooling Racer #5, red, 16", EX.................................. $1,200.00
Dooling Racer #6, bl, Super Cyclone engine, 1941, 18", EX . $2,300.00
Dooling Racer #8, Atwood .60 Champion engine, 1939, 19", EX, $1,500 to.. $1,800.00
Dooling Sostilo Offy F Racer #54, VG, $2,000 to........ $2,450.00
Dooling Streamline (Frog), Super Cyclone .60 engine, 1940, EX+..$1,725.00

Gasoline-Powered Toys
Cox Thimble Drome Champion, single cylinder engine, VG, $350.00. (Photo courtesy RM Auctions on LiveAuctioneers.com)

Gasoline-Powered Toys
Dooling 'F' Type Racer #3, with Dooling 61 and Smith coil, 16", VG, $2,000.00. (Photo courtesy Dirk Soulis Auctions on LiveAuctioneers.com)

Gasoline-Powered Toys
Cox Thimble Drome Racer #15, 10", EX, $400.00. (Photo courtesy Morphy Auctions)

Dooling Tether Racing Boat, red, .61 engine, 1955, 35", EX,
$500 to.. $700.00
Fairchild 22 Model Airplane, 47" WS, NM, $250 to $350.00
Frog Racer w/Hornet Engine, bare silver-tone metal, 16",
VG...$1,450.00
Hiller Comet #5, red, 1942, 19", EX, $1,200 to $1,800.00
Hiller T Racer #19, yel, Hiller .60 engine, 20", EX, $900 to .$1,200.00
Hot Rod Roadster, red, Hornet .60 engine, 15", EX $950.00
Jim Carmellini One-Off Boattail #2, Black Panther 10cc ignition
engine, red & silver w/wood trim, 20", EX $4,885.00
Matthews Fresno California, silver metal streamlined style w/slot-
ted vents at windshield, back & radiator, 18", VG $5,175.00
McCoy Streamline, gray, never drilled engine, 17", NM .. $800.00
Melcraft Racer, ignition engine, 1940s, 16", EX, $600 to . $800.00
Ohlsson & Rice Racer #54, orig #29 engine, unused, NMIB,
$600 to.. $850.00
Papina Spl #5, .60 McCoy ignition engine, ca 1955, VG+ . $3,600.00
Popp Spl #2, Ignition .60 Super Cyclone engine, ca 1940, 20",
VG+...$2,880.00
Railton Champion Racer #12, red & yel, 17", NM $2,700.00
Randy Giovenale Froggie's Cafe Streamline, 1948 McCoy .60
ignition engine, EX $2,070.00
Reuhl Racer #39, .49 McCoy engine, 1940, 17", EX, $1,900
to $2,200.00
Rexner Bowes Seal Fast Special #33, 1939, .60 Atwood Cham-
pion ignition engine, 18½", VG+ $4,715.00
Richter Streamliner #99, twin spark plug Super Cyclone .60 igni-
tion engine, 18", 1940, never run, EX+.................... $4,225.00
Roy Cox Thimble Drome Champion Racer, VGIB, $400 to .$600.00
Synchro Rocket #25 (Syncro Ace), Synchro Ace ingnition
engine, centrifugal clutch, wht w/red, 20", VG+ $1,725.00
Synchro Rocket Special #41, 1939, Synchro Rocket Super
Ace iggnition engine, wht w/red trim, Gilmore Oil Co, 20",
VG+ $2,300.00
Testors Avion Mustang Fighter Airplane, NMIB............. $100.00
Testors Cosmic Wind, Spirit of the '76, M.........................$60.00
Testors OD P-51 Mustang, VG...$30.00

Gasoline-Powered Toys
Dooling Rear Drive Mercury Tether Racer #42, Dennymite engine, full suspension, 18", VG, $1,825.00.
(Photo courtesy Dirk Soulis Auctions on LiveAuctioneers.com)

Gasoline-Powered Toys
McCoy Invader #6 , yellow, McCoy, .49 engine, 17", EX, $1,400.00.

Wen-Mac A-24 Army Attack Bomber, 1962-64, EX.........$45.00
Wen-Mac Albatross, Flying Wing Series, EX....................$40.00
Wen-Mac Boeing P-26 Pursuit Plane, 1960s, unused, MIB .$125.00
Wen-Mac Cutlass, bl, blk & yel, 1958-60, EX $50.00
Wen-Mac Marine Corsair, red, 1960s, EX........................$40.00
Wen-Mac P-63 King Cobra, chrome, 1962-64, EX...........$50.00
Wen-Mac RAF Day Fighter, wht, 1963-64, EX $50.00
Wen-Mac Yellow Jacket Corsair, yel, 1959-64, EX $40.00

GI Joe

GI Joe, the 'Real American Hero' and probably the most famous action figure, has been made in hundreds of variations since Hasbro introduced him in 1964. The first of these jointed figures was 12" tall; this size can be identified by the mark each carried on his back: GI Joe T.M. (trademark), Copyright 1964. They came with four different hair colors: blond, auburn, black, and brown, each with a scar on his right cheek. They were sold in four basic packages: Action Soldier, Action Sailor, Action Marine, and Action Pilot. A black figure was also included in the line, and there were representatives of many nations as well — France, Germany, Japan, Russia, etc. These figures did not have scars and are more valuable. Talking GI Joes were issued in 1967 when the only female (the nurse) was introduced. Besides the figures, uniforms, vehicles, guns, and accessories of many varieties were produced. The Adventure Team series (AT in the listings), made from 1970 to 1976, included Black Adventurer, Air Adventurer, Talking Astronaut, Sea Adventurer, Talking Team Commander, Land Adventurer, and several variations. In 1974 Joe's hard plastic hands were replaced with kung fu grips, so that he could better grasp his weapons. Assorted playsets allowed young imaginations to run wild, and besides the doll-size items, there were wristwatches, foot lockers, toys, walkie-talkies, etc., made for the kids themselves. Due to increased production costs, the large GI Joe was discontinued in 1976.

In 1982, Hasbro brought out the smaller 3¾" GI Joe figures, each with its own descriptive name. Of the first series, some characters were produced with either a swivel or straight arm. Vehicles, weapons, and playsets were available, and some characters could only be had by redeeming flag points from the backs of packages. This small version proved to be the most successful action figure line ever made. Loose items are common; collectors value those still mint in the original packages at two to four times higher.

The 1990s through today has seen the exit and return of the 3¾" figures in various series along with the reintroduction of the 12" figure in a few different collections including the Classic Collection and the 30th Anniversay, among others. Joe is still going strong today.

For more information we recommend *Collectible Male Action Figures* by Paris and Susan Manos; *Encyclopedia to GI Joe* and *The 30th Anniversary Salute to GI Joe*, both by Vincent Santelmo; *Official Collector's Guide to Collecting and Completing Your GI Joe Figures and Accessories, Vol. I*, *Official Guide to Completing 3¾" Series and Hall of Fame: Vol II*, and *Official Guide To GI Joe: '64 – '78*, all by James DeSimone. There is also a section on GI Joe in *Dolls in Uniform*, by Joseph Bourgeois. Note: All items are American issue unless indicated otherwise. (Action Man was made in England by Hasbro circa 1960 into the 1970s.) All listings are for complete figures/sets unless otherwise noted.

See also Games; Lunch Boxes; Puzzles.

12" GI Joe Figures and Figure Sets

GI Joe, 12" Figures
Action Sailor, #7600, MIB, $375.00 to $425.00. (Photo courtesy Cotswold Collectibles)

Action Marine, #7700, EX to NM, $100 to $150.00
Action Marine, #7700, MIB, $375 to $425.00
Action Marine, Medic, #90711, EX to NM, $300 to $400.00
Action Marine, Medic, #90711 MIB, $1,475 to $1,525.00
Action Marine, Talking, #7790, EX to NM, $150 to $200.00
Action Marine, Talking, #7790, MIB, $775 to $825.00
Action Nurse, #8060, EX to NM, $1,800 to $2,100.00
Action Nurse, #8060, MIB, $4,500 to $4,750.00
Action Pilot, #7800, EX to NM, $150 to $175.00
Action Pilot, #7800, MIB, $500 to $600.00
Action Pilot, Talking, #7890, EX to NM $200 to $250.00
Action Pilot, Talking, #7890, MIB, $1,200 to $1,500.00
Action Sailor, #7600, EX to NM, $150 to $250.00
Action Sailor, Talking, #7690, EX to NM, $200 to $325.00
Action Sailor, Talking, #7690, MIB, $1,000 to $1,300.00
Action Soldier, #7500, EX to NM, $100 to $200.00
Action Soldier, #7500, MIB, $400 to $450.00
Action Soldier, black, #7900, EX to NM, $475 to $775.00
Action Soldier, black, #7900, MIB, $2,000 to $2,400.00
Action Soldier, Canadian Mountie, #5904, EX to NM, $800 to $1,600.00
Action Soldier, Canadian Mountie, #5904, MIB, $3,500 to .. $4,000.00
Action Soldier, Forward Observer, #5969, EX to NM, $225 to $350.00
Action Soldier, Forward Observer, #5969, MIB, $700 to. $800.00
Action Soldier, Green Beret, #7536, EX to NM, $300 to ... $500.00
Action Soldier, Green Beret, #7536, MIB, $2,500 to .. $3,000.00
Action Soldier, Talking, #7590, EX to NM, $75 to $125.00
Action Soldier, Talking, #7590, MIB, $775 to $800.00
Adventures of GI Joe, Adventurer, black, #7905, MIP, $2,500 to $3,000.00
Adventures of GI Joe, Adventurer, black, #7905, NM, $400 to $800.00
Adventures of GI Joe, Aquanaut, #7910, EX to NM, $200 to $500.00
Adventures of GI Joe, Aquanaut, #7910, MIB, $2,750 to... $3,250.00
Adventures of GI Joe, Astronaut, Talking, #7915, EX to NM, $100 to $300.00
Adventures of GI Joe, Astronaut, Talking, #7915, MIB, $1,000 to $1,200.00
Adventures of GI Joe, Sharks Surprise Set w/Frogman, #7980, EX to NM, $100 to $275.00
Adventures of GI Joe, Sharks Surprise Set w/Frogman, #7980, MIB, $725 to $775.00
AT, Adventurer, black, #7404, EX to NM, $100 to $175.00
AT, Adventurer, black, #7404, MIB, $350 to $400.00

AT, Adventurer, black, Life-Like Hair, Kung Fu Grip, #7283, EX to NM, $75 to $175.00
AT, Adventurer, black, Life-Like Hair, Kung Fu Grip, #7283, MIB, $225 to $275.00
AT, Air Adventurer, Kung Fu Grip, #7282, EX to NM, $100 to..$175.00
AT, Air Adventurer, Kung Fu Grip, #7282, MIB, $300 to ... $350.00
AT, Air Adventurer, Kung Fu Grip, #7403, EX to NM, $125 to..$325.00
AT, Air Adventurer, Kung Fu Grip, #7403, MIB, $375 to..$425.00
AT, Air Adventurer, Life-Like Hair & Beard, #7282, EX to NM, $75 to $125.00
AT, Air Adventurer, Life-Like Hair & Beard, #7282, MIB, $175 to $225.00
AT, Astronaut, Talking, #7590, MIB, $400 to $450.00
AT, British Commando, #8204, EX to NM, $150 to $250.00
AT, British Commando, #8204, MIB, $1,500 to $1,800.00
AT, Bullet Man, #8026, EX to NM, $50 to $100.00
AT, Bullet Man, #8026, MIB, $150 to $200.00
AT, Commander, black, Talking, #7406, EX to NM, $125 to.. $450.00
AT, Commander, black, Talking, #7406, MIB, $800 to .. $850.00
AT, Commander, black, Talking, Kung Fu Grip, #7291, 1974, EX to NM, $100 to $325.00
AT, Commander, black, Talking, Kung Fu Grip, #7291, 1974, MIB, $675 to $775.00
AT, Commander, Talking, Kung Fu Grip, #7290, EX to NM, $100 to $200.00
AT, Commander, Talking, Kung Fu Grip, #7290, MIB, $450 to $550.00
AT, Commander, Talking, Life-Like Hair & Beard, #7400, EX to NM, $75 .... $125.00
AT, Eagle Eye Commando, black, #7278, EX to NM, $75 to $150.00
AT, Eagle Eye Commando, black, #7278, MIB, $225 to. $275.00
AT, Eagle Eye Land Commander, #7276, EX to NM, $50 to... $100.00
AT, Eagle Eye Land Commander, #7276, MIB, $125 to . $175.00

AT, Eagle Eye Man of Action, #7277, EX to NM, $50 to..$100.00

AT, Eagle Eye Man of Action, #7277, MIB, $150 to $175.00

AT, Intruder Commander, #8050, EX to NM, $50 to........$75.00

AT, Intruder Commander, #8050, MIB, $125 to............. $150.00

AT, Intruder Warrior, #8051, EX to NM, $50 to...............$75.00

AT, Intruder Warrior, #8051, MIB, $150 to $200.00

AT, Land Adventurer, #7270, EX to NM, $25 to.............$50.00

AT, Land Adventurer, #7270, MIB, $150 to $175.00

AT, Land Adventurer, #7401, EX to NM, $50 to............ $100.00

AT, Land Adventurer, #7401, MIB, $150 to $175.00

AT, Land Adventurer, Life-Like Hair & Beard, Kung Fu Grip, #7280, EX to NM, $25 to......................................$50.00

AT, Land Adventurer, Life-Like Hair & Beard, Kung Fu Grip, #7280, MIB, $125 to $175.00

AT, Man of Action, #7274/#7284, EX to NM, $25 to.......$50.00

AT, Man of Action, #7274/#7284, MIB, $150 to $200.00

AT, Man of Action, #7500, EX to NM, $50 to $100.00

AT, Man of Action, #7500, MIB, $200 to........................ $250.00

AT, Man of Action, Life-Like Hair & Beard, Kung Fu Grip, #7284, EX to NM, $50 to.. $100.00

AT, Man of Action, Talking, 7292, EX to NM, $100 to . $200.00

AT, Man of Action, Talking, #7292, MIB, $625 to......... $675.00

AT, Man of Action, Talking, #7590, EX to NM, $50 to. $150.00

AT, Man of Action, Talking, #7590, MIB, $325 to......... $375.00

AT, Man of Action, Talking, Life-Like, Kung Fu Grip, #7292, EX to NM, $100 to... $200.00

AT, Man of Action, Talking, Life-Like, Kung Fu Grip, #7292, MIB, $625 to $675.00

AT, Mike Powers Atomic Man, #8025, EX to NM, $25 to.$50.00

AT, Mike Powers Atomic Man, #8025, MIB, $100 to $150.00

AT, Sea Adventurer, #7271, EX to NM, $50 to $100.00

AT, Sea Adventurer, #7271, MIB, $225 to...................... $275.00

AT, Sea Adventurer, #7281, EX to NM, $75 to $125.00

AT, Sea Adventurer, #7281, MIB, $275 to...................... $325.00

AT, Sea Adventurer, #7402, MIB, $225 to...................... $275.00

AT, Sea Adventurer, #7402, NM......................................$75.00

Australian Jungle Fighter, #8105, EX to NM, $225 to.... $375.00

Australian Jungle Fighter, #8105, MIB, $2,000 to $2,750.00

Australian Jungle Fighter, #8205, EX to NM, $125 to.... $250.00

Australian Jungle Fighter, #8205, MIB, $1,000 to $1,200.00

British Commando, #8104, MIB, $2,225 to $1,800.00

British Commando, #8204, EX to NM, $125 to $250.00

British Commando, #8204, MIB, $1,500 to......................$18.00

French Resistance Fighter, #8103, EX to NM, $175 to... $225.00

French Resistance Fighter, #8103, MIB, $2,000 to $2,500.00

French Resistance Fighter, #8203, EX to NM, $100 to... $200.00

French Resistance Fighter, #8203, MIB, $1,000 to $1,500.00

German Storm Trooper, #8100, EX to NM, $250 to....... $400.00

German Storm Trooper, #8100, MIB, $2,250 to $2,400.00

German Storm Trooper, #8200, EX to NM, $250 to....... $350.00

German Storm Trooper, #8200, MIB, $1,000 to $1,500.00

Japanese Imperial Soldier, #8101, EX to NM, $400 to ... $650.00

Japanese Imperial Soldier, #8101, MIB, $2,500 to $2,800.00

Japanese Imperial Soldier, #8201, EX to NM, $275 to ... $350.00

Japanese Imperial Soldier, #8201, MIB, $1,200 to $1,500.00

Russian Infantry Man, #8102, EX to NM, $250 to $375.00

Russian Infantry Man, #8202, MIB, $1,000 to............. $1,500.00

GI Joe, 12" Figures

Adventure Team, Astronaut, Talking, #7590, EX to NM, $100.00 to $200.00. (Photo courtesy Cotswold Collectibles)

GI Joe, 12" Figures

Adventure Team, Man of Action, Life-Like Hair and Beard, Kung Fu Grip, MIB, $175.00 to $225.00. (Photo courtesy Cotswold Collectibles)

GI Joe, 12" Figures

Adventure Team, Commander, Talking, life-like hair and beard, #7400, MIB, $375.00 to $425.00. (Photo courtesy Cotswold Collectibles)

GI Joe, 12" Figures

Russian Infantry Man, #8202, NM (EX box), $725.00. (Photo courtesy Cotswold Collectibles)

GI Joe, 12" Figures

Russian Infantry Man, #8102, GI Joe Combat Series, complete, MIB, $1,000.00 to $1,500.00.

ACCESSORIES FOR 12" GI JOE

Action Combat Mess Kit, #7509, MIP, $75 to $100.00

Action Marine Basics Set, #7722, EX, $55 to $60.00

Action Marine Beachhead Assault Field Pack Set, #7713, EX, $75 to $100.00

Action Marine Beachhead Flamethrower Set, #7718, NM, $25 to $35.00

Action Marine Communications Field Radio & Telephone, #7703, MIP, $250 to $300.00

Action Marine Communications Poncho, #7702, NM, $45 to . $55.00

Action Marine Demolition Set, #7730, NM, $75 to $85.00

Action Marine Dress Parade Set, #7710, MIP, $425 to .. $475.00

Action Marine Medic Set, #7720, MIP, $100 to $150.00

Action Marine Paratrooper Helmet Set, #7707, MIP, $80 to .. $90.00

Action Marine Tank Commander Set, #7731, MIP, $1,200 to .. $1,500.00

Action Pilot Air Acadamy Cadet Set, #7822, MIP, $900 to .. $1,200.00

Action Pilot Air Force Police Equipment, #7813, NM, $100 to $125.00

Action Sailor Annapolis Cadet Outfit, #7624, MIP, $1,200 to .. $1,500.00

Action Sailor Breeches Buoy, #7625, NM, $400 to $450.00

Action Sailor Deep Sea Diver Set, #7620, EX+, $300 to.. $350.00

Action Sailor Frogman Scuba Tank Set, MIP, $75 to $125.00

Action Sailor MP Uniform Set, #7521, EX+ $500.00

Action Sailor Navy Attack Helmet Set, #7610, MIP, $125 to $175.00

Action Sailor Navy Basics Set, #7628, NM+, $50 to $60.00

Action Sailor Navy Machine Gun Set, #7618, NM $75.00

Action Sailor Shore Patrol Dress Jumper Set, #7613, MIP .. $200.00

Action Sailor Shore Patrol Dress Pant Set, #7614, EX+, $35 to $45.00

Action Soldier Adventure Pack, #8005-83, 12 pcs, MP, $550 to $625.00

Action Soldier Adventure Pack, #8008-83, 14 pcs, MIP, $550 to $625.00

Action Soldier Air Police Equipment, #7813, MIP, $175 to... $225.00

Action Soldier Bivouac Machine Gun Set, #7514, MIP, $120 to $130.00

Action Soldier Bivouac Machine Gun Set, #7514, reissue, MIP, $175 to $200.00

Action Soldier Bivouac Sleeping Bag, #7515, MIP, $100 to $135.00

Action Soldier Combat Construction Set, #7572, EX+ . $350.00

Action Soldier Combat Construction Set, #7572, MIP, $550 to $600.00

Action Soldier Combat Fatigue Pants, #7504, NM, $20 to .. $30.00

Action Soldier Combat Field Jacket, #7505, EX, $50 to .. $60.00

Action Soldier Combat Field Pack Deluxe Set, #7502, MIP .. $300.00

Action Soldier Combat Helmet Set, #7505, MIP, $65 to .. $85.00

Action Soldier Combat Rifle Set, #7510, MIP, $300 to.. $350.00

Action Soldier Green Beret & Small Arms Set, #7533, EX .. $75.00

Action Soldier Heavy Weapons Set, #7538, EX+, $150 to... $200.00

Action Soldier Life Ring (USN), #7627C, MIP $70.00

Action Soldier MP Ike Jacket, #7524, NM+, $50 to $60.00

Action Soldier Ski Patrol Deluxe Set, #7531, EX+, $150 to.. $175.00

Action Soldier Snow Troop Set, #7529, MIP, $150 to.... $200.00

Action Soldier Special Forces Bazooka Set, #7528, NM, $40 to $50.00

Action Soldier West Point Cadet Uniform Set, #7537, EX+, $225 to $275.00

Adventures of GI Joe Adventure Locker, #7940, EX $175.00

Adventures of GI Joe Hidden Missile Discovery Set, #7952, EX, $65 to $75.00

Adventures of GI Joe Mysterious Explosion Set, #7921, MIP, $400 to $450.00

Adventures of GI Joe Perilous Rescue Set, #7923, MIP, $500 to $550.00

AT, Secret Mountain Outpost, #8040, EX, $50 to $75.00

AT, Secret Mountain Outpost, #8040, MIB, $125 to $175.00

AT Black Widow Rendezous Super Deluxe Set, #7414, EX+.. $150.00

AT Danger of the Depths, #7412, NM+ $200.00

AT Dangerous Climb Outfit, #7309E, MOC $70.00

AT Dangerous Climb Set, #7309-2, EX+ $25.00

AT Demolition Set, #7370, MIP, $100 to $150.00

AT Desert Explorer Outfit, #7309, MIP, rom $75 to $85.00

AT Desert Survival Set, #7308-6, NM+ $50.00

AT Diver's Distress, #7328-6, NM $75.00

AT Emergency Rescue Set, #7374, EX+ $50.00

AT Fantastic Freefall Set, #7423, EX+ $150.00

AT Fight For Survival Set, #7308-2, NM+ $50.00

AT Fight For Survival Set, #7431, NM, $525 to $575.00

GI Joe, Accessories for 12"

Signal Flasher, battery-operated, MIB,
$65.00 to $75.00.

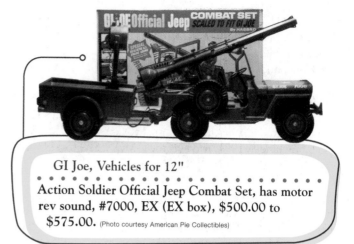

GI Joe, Vehicles for 12"

Action Soldier Official Jeep Combat Set, has motor
rev sound, #7000, EX (EX box), $500.00 to
$575.00. (Photo courtesy American Pie Collectibles)

AT Flying Rescue Set, #7361, MIP, $75 to $100.00
AT Footlocker, #8000, NM+ $100.00
AT Headquarters, #7490, MIB $325.00
AT Hidden Treasure, #7308-1, MIP $50.00
AT Hurricane Spotter Set, #7343, NM $100.00
AT Jungle Ordeal Set, #7309-3, MIP, $65 to $75.00
AT Laser Rescue, #7311, MOC...$65.00
AT Magnetic Flaw Detector Set, #7319-2, NM $25.00
AT Race For Recovery, #8028-1, EX $25.00
AT Radiation Detection Set, #7341, MIP..........................$95.00
AT Rocket Pack Set, #7315, NM..$25.00
AT Secret Agent Set, #7375, NM.......................................$60.00
AT Seismograph, #7319C, MIP..$80.00
AT Signal Flasher Set, #7362, MIP....................................$75.00
AT Special Assignment, #8028-3, EX $35.00
AT Training Center, #7495, MIB $250.00
AT Trouble at Vulture Pass, #59289, MIP, $300 to $350.00
AT Underwater Demolitioin Set, #7310, MIP....................$50.00
AT Volcano Jumper Set, #7344, NM+ $200.00
AT White Tiger Hunt Set, #7436, NM+ $200.00
Australian Jungle Fighter Set, #8305, MIP $225.00
British Commando Set, #8304, MIP $335.00
French Resistance Fighter Set, #8303, NM+ $65.00
German Soldier Equipment Set, #8300, MOC.............. $350.00
German Storm Trooper, #8300, EX+ $150.00
Japanese Imperial Soldier Set, #8301, NM+ $300.00
Russian Infantryman Equipment, #8302, MOC $350.00

VEHICLES FOR 12" GI JOE

Action Pilot Official Space Capsule Set, #8020, MIB, $325
    to $375.00
Action Pilot Spacewalk Mystery, #7981, EXIB, $125 to.. $150.00
Action Sailor Official Sea Sled & Frogman Set, #8050, NMIB,
    $275 to $325.00
Action Soldier Armored Car, #5397, EXIB, $150 to...... $175.00
Action Soldier Jet Fighter Plane, #5396, NMIB, $450 to ...$500.00
Adventures of GI Joe Sharks Surprise Set, w/ or w/o figure, #7980
    or #7980-83, NMIB, ea $300 to $350.00

Adventures of GI Joe Spacewalk Mystery Set, w/ or w/o figure,
    #7981 or #7981-83, EXIB, ea $100 to.......................... $150.00
AT Big Trapper, #7498, NMIB, $100 to.......................... $125.00
AT Capture Copter, #7480, MIB, $300 to $350.00
AT Chopper Cycle, #59114, EXIB, $25 to.........................$35.00
AT Combat Action Jeep, #59751, NMIB, $60 to..............$75.00
AT Fantastic Sea Wolf Submarine, #7460, NMIB, $75 to..$125.00
AT Giant Air-Sea Helicopter, #59189, NMIB, $100 to . $150.00
AT Sandstorm Survival Adventure, #7493, NMIB, $175 to..$225.00
AT Sky Hawk, #7470, EXIB, $50 to...................................$75.00
AT Vehicle Set, #7005, NMIB, $75 to............................. $100.00

3¾" GI JOE FIGURES

Airborne, 1983, MOC, $75 to.. $100.00
Air Commandos, 1991, any character, MOC, ea $25 to ...$35.00
Airtight, 1985, MOC, $55 to $65.00
Alley-Viper, 1989, MOC, $20 to $30.00
Alpine, 1985, MOC, $50 to $60.00
Ambush, 1990, MOC, $12 to $18.00
Astro-Viper, 1988, MOC, $20 to $30.00
Backblast, 1989, MOC, $12 to $18.00
Barbecue, 1985, MOC, $65 to $75.00
Barbecue, 1992, MOC, $8 to $12.00
Baroness, 1984, MOC, $175 to $200.00
BAT, 1986, MOC, $60 to $70.00
BAT, 1991, MOC, $12 to $18.00
Battleforce 2000 Dee Jay, 1989, MOC, $12 to...................$18.00
Bazooka, 1985, MOC, $60 to $70.00
Bazooka, 1993, MOC, $12 to $18.00
Beach-Head, 1986, MOC, $50 to......................................$75.00
Beach-Head, 1993, MOC, $12 to.......................................$18.00
Big Ben, 1991, MOC, $18 to $25.00
Big Boa, 1987, MOC, $15 to $25.00
Blizzard, 1988, MOC, $15 to $25.00
Blow Torch, 1984, MOC, $65 to.......................................$85.00
Breaker, 1982, MOC, $75 to $100.00
Breaker, 1983, MOC, $75 to $100.00
Budo, 1988, MOC, $15 to $25.00
Buzzer, 1985, MOC, $55 to..$65.00
Captain Grid Iron, 1990, MOC, $12 to $18.00
Charbroil, 1988, MOC, $15 to $25.00

Chuckles, 1987, MOC, $20 to $30.00
Cobra, 1982, MOC, $175 to $200.00
Cobra, 1983, MOC, $175 to $200.00
Cobra Commander, 1982, mail-in, MOC, $175 to.........$200.00
Cobra Commander, 1983, MOC, $250 to.....................$275.00
Cobra Commander, 1984, MOC, $35 to........................$45.00
Cobra Commander, 1987, MOC, $25 to........................$35.00
Cobra Commander, 1991, w/eyebrows, MOC, $45 to.......$55.00
Cobra Commander, 1991, w/o eyebrows, MOC, $20 to....$30.00
Cobra Commander, 1993, MOC, $12 to........................$18.00
Cobra-La Team, 1987, set of 3, MOC, $70 to...................$80.00
Cobra Ninja Viper, 1992, MOC, $25 to..........................$35.00
Cobra Officer, 1982, MOC, $175 to...............................$200.00
Cobra Officer, 1983, MOC, $175 to...............................$200.00
Countdown, 1989, Hasbro, MOC, $18 to........................$25.00
Crazy Legs, 1987, MOC, $25 to.....................................$35.00
Crimson Guard, 1985, MOC, $100 to.......................... $125.00
Crimson Guard Commander, 1993, MOC, $12 to.............$15.00
Croc Master, 1987, MOC, $20 to...................................$30.00
Crystal Ball, 1987, MOC, $15 to....................................$25.00
DEF, 1992, any character, MOC, $10 to..........................$15.00
Destro, 1983, MOC, $125 to.. $150.00
Destro, 1992, MOC, $10 to..$15.00
Dial-Tone, 1986, MOC, $40 to.......................................$50.00
Doc, 1983, MOC, $75 to... $100.00
Downtown, 1989, MOC, $15 to......................................$25.00
Dr Mindbender, 1986, MOC, $30 to..............................$40.00
Dr Mindbender, 1993, MOC, $10 to..............................$15.00
Duke, 1983, MOC, $75 to.. $100.00
Duke, 1984, MOC, $100 to..$125.00
Dusty, 1985, MOC, $60 to...$70.00
Eco Warriors, 1991, any character, MOC, ea $10 to.........$15.00
Eels, 1985, MOC, $60 to..$70.00
Eels, 1993, MOC, $10 to..$15.00
Evil Headhunters, 1992, any character, MOC, $10 to.......$15.00
Falcon, 1987, MOC, $45 to..$55.00
Fast Draw, 1987, MOC, $25 to.......................................$35.00
Firefly, 1984, MOC, $175 to...$200.00
Firefly, 1992/1993, MOC, ea $12 to................................$18.00
Flak-Viper, 1993, MOC, $12 to......................................$18.00

Flash, 1982, MOC, $75 to... $100.00
Flash, 1983, MOC, $75 to...$10.00
Flint, 1985, MOC, $65 to..$75.00
Footloose, 1985, MOC, $55 to..$65.00
Frag-Viper, 1989, MOC, $20 to......................................$30.00
Freefall, 1990, MOC, $12 to...$18.00
Fridge (The), 1986, MOC, $25 to....................................$35.00
Gnawgahyde, 1989, MOC, $18 to...................................$25.00
Grunt, 1982, MOC, $75 to.. $100.00
Grunt, 1983, MOC, $75 to.. $100.00
Gung-Ho, 1983, MOC, $100 to...................................... $125.00
Gung-Ho, 1987, MOC, $25 to...$35.00
Hardball, 1988, MOC, $20 to..$25.00
Hawk, 1986, MOC, $45 to...$55.00
Headhunter Stormtrooper, 1993, MOC, $10 to $15.00
HEAT Viper, 1989, MOC, $18 to.....................................$25.00
HEAT Viper, 1993, MOC, $10 to.....................................$15.00
Hit & Run, 1988, MOC, $20 to.......................................$30.00
Hydro-Viper, 1988, MOC, $20 to....................................$30.00
Ice Sabre, 1991, MOC, $12 to..$18.00
Iceberg, 1986, MOC, $35 to...$45.00
Iron Grenadier, 1988, MOC, $20 to................................$30.00
Iron Grenadiers Annihilator, 1989, MOC, $18 to.............$25.00
Iron Grenadiers Metal-Head, 1990, MOC, $12 to $18.00
Iron Grenadiers Underflow, 1990, MOC, $20 to..............$30.00
Jinx, 1987, MOC, $40 to...$50.00
Lady Jaye, 1985, MOC, $80 to.. $100.00
Laser-Viper, 1990, MOC, $20 to.....................................$30.00
Law & Order, 1987, MOC, $40 to....................................$50.00
Leatherneck, 1986, MOC, $40 to....................................$50.00
Lifeline, 1986, MOC, $55 to...$65.00
Lightfoot, 1988, MOC, $20 to...$30.00
Low-Light, 1986, MOC, $70 to..$80.00
Low-Light, 1991, MOC, $15 to..$20.00
Mainframe, 1986, MOC, $45 to.......................................$55.00
Major Bludd, 1982, MOC, $125 to.................................. $150.00
Major Bludd, 1983, MOC, $125 to.................................. $150.00
Major Bludd, 1994, MOC, $12 to....................................$18.00
Mercer, 1991, MOC, $18 to..$25.00
Monkeywrench, 1986, MOC, $30 to................................$40.00
Muskrat, 1988, MOC, $20 to..$30.00
Mutt, 1984, MOC, $75 to... $100.00
Night Creeper, 1990, MOC, $12 to.................................$15.00
Night Creeper Leader, 1993, MOC, $10 to $15.00
Night Force, 1988, any set of 2, MOC, ea $65 to.........$75.00
Night-Viper, 1989, MOC, $20 to.....................................$30.00
Ninja Force Dice or Slice, 1992, MOC, ea $12 to............$18.00
Ninja Force Dojo, Nunchuk, Storm Shadow or TJ'bang, 1992, MOC, ea $22 to $28.00
Outback, 1987, MOC, $45 to..$55.00
Pathfinder, 1990, MOC, $12 to.......................................$18.00
Psyche-Out, 1987, MOC, $15 to.....................................$25.00
Python Patrol, 1989, any figure, MOC, $20 to $30.00
Quick Kick, 1985, MOC, $75 to...................................... $100.00
Rampart, 1990, MOC, $12 to $18.00
Range-Viper, 1990, MOC, $20 to....................................$30.00
Raptor, 1987, MOC, $15 to...$25.00
Recoil, 1989, MOC, $12 to...$18.00

GI Joe, 3¾" Figures
• • • • • • • •
Deep Six, 1989, MOC, $15.00 to $25.00.

Recondo, 1984, MOC, $75 to $100.00
Red Star, 1991, MOC, $18 to...$25.00
Repeater, 1988, MOC, $20 to $30.00
Rip Cord, 1983, MOC, $65 to..$85.00
Ripper, 1985, MOC, $50 to...$60.00
Roadblock, 1984, MOC, $75 to $100.00
Roadblock, 1986, MOC, $40 to $50.00
Road Pig, 1988, MOC, $15 to $25.00
Rock 'N Roll, 1982, MOC, $100 to $125.00
Rock 'N Roll, 1983, MOC, $100 to $125.00
Rock 'N Roll, 1989, MOC, $12 to..$18.00
Rock-Viper, 1990, MOC, $20 to $30.00
Salvo, 1990, MOC, $12 to $18.00
Scarlett, 1982 or 1983, MOC, ea $200 to $225.00
Sci-Fi, 1986, MOC, $40 to..$50.00
Sci-Fi, 1991, MOC, $15 to..$20.00
Scrap-Iron, 1984, MOC, $75 to $100.00
Sgt Slaughter's Renegades, 1987, set of 3, MOC, $60 to ...$70.00
Shipwreck, 1985, MOC, $75 to $100.00
Shockwave, 1988, MOC, $20 to $30.00
Short-Fuze, 1982 or 1983, MOC, $75 to....................... $100.00
Sky Patrol, 1990, any character, MOC, ea $20 to.............$30.00
Slaughter's Maruaders, 1989, any figure, MOC, ea $20 to.$30.00
Snake Eyes, 1982 or 1983, MOC, ea $300 to................. $325.00
Snake Eyes, 1985, MOC, $225 to $250.00
Snake Eyes, 1989, MOC, $40 to...$50.00
Snake Eyes, 1991, MOC, $20 to...$30.00
Sneak Peek, 1987, MOC, $25 to...$35.00
Snow Job, 1983, MOC, $75 to $100.00
Snow Serpent, 1985, MOC, $65 to...$75.00
Snow Serpent, 1991, MOC, $12 to...$18.00
Snow Storm, 1993, MOC, $10 to..$15.00
Sonic Fighters, 1990, any character, MOC, ea $20 to $30.00
Spearhead & Max, 1988, MOC, $20 to $30.00
Spirit, 1984, MOC, $75 to $100.00
Stalker, 1982 or 1983, MOC, ea $100 to $125.00
Stalker, 1989, MOC, $20 to $30.00
Starduster, 1987, MOC, $55 to..$65.00
Steel Brigade, 1987, MOC $35 to..$45.00
Storm Shadow, 1984, MOC, $175 to $200.00
Storm Shadow, 1988, MOC, $70 to $80.00
Stretcher, 1990, MOC, $12 to..$18.00
Super Sonic Fighters, 1991, any character, MOC, $18 to .$25.00
Super Trooper, 1988, MOC, $25 to..$35.00
Talking Battle Commanders, 1991, any character MOC, ea $18
    to...$25.00
Techno-Viper, 1987, MOC, $15 to $25.00
Tele-Viper, 1985, MOC, $50 to...$75.00
Tiger Force, 1988, any character, MOC, $40 to..................$50.00
Tomax & Xamot, 1985, MOC, $150 to $175.00
Topside, 1990, MOC, $12 to...$18.00
Torch, 1985, MOC, $55 to..$65.00
Torpedo, 1983, MOC, $75 to $100.00
Toxo-Viper, 1988, MOC, $20 to $30.00
Toxo-Zombie, 1992, MOC, $10 to...$15.00
Tracker, 1991, MOC, $15 to...$20.00
Tripwire, 1983, MOC, $75 to $100.00
Tripwire, 1985, MOC, $65 to..$75.00

Tunnel Rat, 1987, MOC, $40 to..$50.00
Viper, 1986, MOC, $40 to...$50.00
Viper, 1994, MOC, $15 to...$25.00
Voltar, 1988, MOC, $15 to..$25.00
Wet Suit, 1986, MOC, $55 to..$65.00
Wild Bill, 1992, MOC, $10 to..$15.00
Wild Bill, 1993, MOC, $10 to..$15.00
Zandar, 1986, MOC, $30 to $40.00
Zap, 1982, MOC, $125 to... $150.00
Zap, 1983, MOC, $125 to... $150.00
Zarana, 1985, MOC, $30 to $40.00
Zarana, 1986, w/earrings, MOC, $75 to $100.00

VEHICLES AND ACCESSORIES FOR 3¾" GI JOE

Air Defense, 1985, MIP, $20 to...$30.00
Anti-Aircraft Gun, 1987, MIP, $10 to....................................$20.00
Armadillo Mini Tank, 1985, MIP, $30 to...............................$40.00
Attack Cruiser, 1991, MIP, $20 to...$25.00
Avalanche, 1990, MIP, $25 to..$35.00
Barracuda, 1992, MIP, $15 to..$20.00
Battle Copter, 1991, MIP, $20 to...$30.00
Battle Copter w/Heli-Viper, 1992, MIP, $20 to....................$25.00
Bomb Disposal, 1985, MIP, $20 to...$30.00
CAT, 1985, MIP, $85 to.. $100.00
CLAW, 1984, MIP, $40 to...$60.00
Cobra Adder, 1988, MIP, $20 to..$25.00
Cobra Battle Barge, 1988, MIP, $18 to..................................$22.00
Cobra Glider, 1983, MIP, $125 to $175.00
Cobra Hydro Sled, 1986, MIP, $20 to $30.00
Cobra Rat, 1992, MIP, $20 to...$25.00
Cobra Rifle Range Unit, 1985, MIP, $20 to $30.00
Condor Z25, 1989, $50 to...$60.00
Conquest X-30, MIP, $20 to..$30.00

GI Joe, Vehicles and Accessories for 3¾"
∙∙∙∙∙∙∙∙∙∙∙∙∙∙∙∙∙∙∙∙∙∙∙∙∙∙∙∙∙∙∙∙∙∙∙
Battle Copter with Pilot Interrogator figure, 1991, MIP,
$20.00 to $30.00. (Photo courtesy Morphy Auctions on LiveAuctioneers.com)

GI Joe, Vehicles and Accessories for 3¾"

Cobra Pogo Ballistic Battle Ball, 1987, MIP,
$25.00 to $35.00. (Photo courtesy Morphy Auctions on LiveAuctioneers.
com)

GI Joe, Vehicles and Accessories for 3¾"

SLAM (Strategic Long-Range Artillery Machine),
1987, MIP, $25.00 to $35.00. (Photo courtesy Morphy Auctions on
LiveAuctioneers.com)

GI Joe,
Vehicles and
Accessories for 3¾"

Star Brigade Armor-
Bot, 1990s, MIP,
$15.00 to $18.00.
(Photo courtesy Morphy Auctions
on LiveAuctioneers.com)

Crossfire-Alfa, 1987, MIP, $75 to $100.00
Devilfish, 1986, MIP, $20 to $30.00
Dominator Snow Tank, 1988, MIP, $20 to...................... $30.00
Dreadnok Air Skiff, 1987, MIP, $25 to $35.00
Dreadnok Thunder Machine, 1986, MIP, $30 to $40.00
Earth Borer, 1987, MIP, $10 to $15.00
Eco Warriors Toxo-Lab, 1992, MIP, $25 to $35.00
Falcon, 1983, MIP, $125 to $175.00
FANG II, 1989, MIP, $25 to $35.00
FLAK, 1982, MIP, $75 to $85.00
Flight Pod, 1985, MIP, $30 to $40.00
General, 1990, MIP, $55 to $65.00
GI Joe Headquarters, 1992, MIP, $50 to........................ $75.00
Hammerhead, 1990, MIP, $40 to $60.00
Headquarters Command Center, 1983, MIP, $150 to $200.00
Headquarters Missile-Command Center, 1983, MIP, $200
    to $225.00
Hovercraft Killer WHALE, 1984, MIP, $125 to $150.00
Ice Sabre, 1991, MIP, $12 to... $18.00
Iron Grenadiers DEMON, 1988, MIP, $40 to $50.00
Machine Gun Nest, 1988, MIP, $10 to $15.00
Mamba, 1987, MIP, $25 to $35.00
Mean Dog, 1988, MIP, $45 to $55.00
Mine Sweeper, 1988, MIP, $10 to $15.00
MOBAT, 1982, MIP, $125 to $150.00
Moray, 1985, MIP, $75 to $85.00
Mountain Climber, 1987, MIP, $10 to $15.00
Mobile Command Center, 1987, MIP, $90 to................... $115.00
Night Raven S-3P, 1986, MIP, $70 to $80.00
Outpost Defender, 1986, MIP, $12 to............................. $18.00
Overlord's Dictator, 1990, MIP, $25 to $35.00
Patriot, 1992, MIP, $30 to... $35.00
Python Patrol ASP, 1989, MIP, $25 to $35.00
Raider, 1989, MIP, $55 to $65.00
Rattler, 1984, MIP, $100 to... $125.00
Rocket Sled, 1988, MIP, $10 to $15.00
Rolling Thunder, 1988, MIP, $100 to.............................. $115.00
Rope Crosser, 1987, MIP, $12 to $18.00
Sky Hawk, 1984, MIP, $40 to $50.00
Sky Patrol Hawk, 1990, MIP, $30 to $35.00
Skystorm X-Wing Chopper, 1988, MIP, $25 to................ $35.00
Slugger, 1984, MIP, $50 to $75.00
Snow Cat, 1985, MIP, $65 to $85.00
Storm Eagle Jet, 1992, MIP, $20 to............................... $30.00
Surveillance Port, 1986, MIP, $20 to............................. $30.00
Swamp Skier, 1984, MIP, $140 to $150.00
Tiger Cat, 1988, MIP, $45 to $55.00
Tiger Fish, 1989, MIP, $20 to.. $30.00
Tiger Rat, 1988, MIP, $100 to $125.00
Tomahawk, 1986, MIP, $130 to $150.00
Transportable Tactical Battle Platform, 1985, MIP, $50
    to.. $75.00
USS Flagg, 1985, MIP, $475 to $500.00
VAMP, 1982, MIP, $80 to... $100.00
VAMP Mark II, 1984, MIP, $75 to $95.00
Weapon Transport, 1985, MIP, $20 to............................ $30.00
Whirlwind, 1983, MIP, $40 to $50.00
Wolverine, 1983, MIP, $100 to....................................... $125.00

• Guns •

Toy guns were first produced in the late 1800s. Made of cast iron, they tended to be small and very stylized with little resemblance to real guns. Many were more novelty than toy, and are often referred to as 'animated cap guns.' One had two goats on the barrel that butted heads when the trigger was pulled. Another had a train that moved down the barrel. And, another reflected the politics of the time with a worker in a steel hat kicking a pig-tailed Chinese worker in the rear. Western movies of the 1930s and 1940s had every kid wanting to be a cowboy, and cast iron guns evolved into more realistic designs. By the late 1930s, toy guns were produced under license with names like Roy Rogers, Gene Autry, and The Lone Ranger. During World War II, toy guns were mostly made from wood byproducts. After the war, manufacturers utilized inexpensive diecast metal. Toy guns and holsters reached their zenith during the 1950s and 1960s. These were the golden years of television westerns, and kids were offered a dazzling array of choices.

Space guns made popular by Flash Gordon and Tom Corbett kept pace with the robots coming from Japan. Some of these early lithographed tin guns were fantastic futuristic styles that spat out rays of sparks when you pulled the trigger. But gradually the space race losts its fervor and westerns ran their course, being replaced with detective shows and sitcoms. Guns in disfavor is a recent phenomenon, not relevent before the mid-1980s.

Learn to be realistic when you assess condition; it's critical when evaluating the price of a toy gun. Advisor Bill Hamburg tells us that 'Old toy gun values have stabilized after being negatively impacted for several years by the internet auctions. Prices for relatively common toy guns have remained fairly constant over the last year with values for hard-to-find cap guns steadily increasing. I believe we can be fairly certain that most vintage toy guns from the late 1800s to the early 1960s, in excellent or better condition, will hold their value and continue to increase over the foreseeable future. In recent times, some pretty astounding prices have been paid at auctions for both relatively common and scarcer models, especially if they have their original boxes. We have reached a point where the boxes are worth almost as much as the toy they contained.'

Bill goes on to say that 'All vintage toy guns have become increasingly difficult to find at flea markets, antique shops, and toy shows. The exception being a few small regional shows specializing just in toy guns and related collectibles. eBay continues to be the best marketplace to buy and sell collectible toy guns. This is in spite of eBay's penchant for political correctness such as requiring sellers to insert orange plugs in the barrels of these vintage toy pistols. They also no longer allow the sales of toy caps (only the empty boxes) and restrict shipment of toy guns to within the United States. Failure to observe these requirements will result in the auction being cancelled by the eBay 'police.' Although eBay claims otherwise, these restrictions have nothing to do with federal or local law. It's just their rules. Other auction sites do not have these restrictions.'

Finally, Bill says 'Overall enthusiasm for vintage toy guns remains strong with the circle of collectors growing all the time. And why not? These great artifacts of simpler times are beautiful to behold. The quality of these toys will never be duplicated and the boxes that contain them are truly wonderful works of art. Even general collectors can add depth and interest to their collections by including those nostalgic toys of a time long past.'

Advisor: Bill Hamburg

Air Blaster Gun & Target Set, Wham-O, 1963, EX+IB. $175.00
American Cap Pistol, Kilgore, 1940s, 1st version, flying eagle on
    ivory-colored grips, 9", EX $325.00
American Cap Pistol, Kilgore, 1940s, 1st version, flying eagle on
    ivory-colored grips, 9", NMIB.................................. $500.00
Army .45 Cap Gun, Hubley, 1940, CI, blk w/wht grips, 6½", NM..$125.00
Atomic Buster Myster Gun, Webb Electronics Co, plastic, 11",
    MIB.. $250.00
Atomic Disintegrator Repeating Cap Pistol, Hubley, 1954,
    diecast metal w/plastic grips, 8", EX............................ $250.00
Atomic Gun, Japan, 1960s, tin, friction w/sparking action, red,
    wht & bl on gold, 5", NM+.....................................$35.00
Atomic Space Patrol, Rosko, b/o, tin, MIB......................$75.00
Automatic Repeater Cap Pistol No 50, Wyandotte, steel, 8",
    EX+IB...$60.00
Baby Space Gun, Daiya, litho tin, friction, 6", NM+IB. $150.00
Big Game Rifle, Marx, MIB.. $125.00
Bronco, Kilgore, 1950s, NMIB $100.00
Buck 'n Bronc Cap Guns w/Cowboy Double Holster Set, Russell,
    NMIB $350.00
Colt .45 Cap Pistol, Hubley, 1950s, silver w/removable gold-tone
    cylinder, plain wht grips, VG+..................................... $160.00
Combat Machine Gun #305 w/Automatic Bullet Action, TN,
    1960s, tin, b/o, MIB $150.00

Guns
• •
**Civil War Centennial Sidearm set, Cap Gun
and Holster, unused, complete EXOC (NOS),
$250.00.** (Photo courtesy Morphy Auctions on LiveAuctioneers.com)

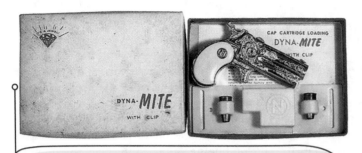

Cork Shooting Submachine Gun, Marx, 1951, MIB...... $175.00

Cowboy King 50-Shot Repeater Pistol, J&E Stevens, 1940s, antique brass-looking finish w/blk grips, 8½", NMIB .. $200.00

Cowboy Repeating Cap Pistol, Hubley, 1950s, wht grips, 11½", unused, NMIB $200.00

Cowboy 6-Shooter Water Pistol, Irwin, MIB..................... $75.00

Crack Shot Dart Pistol, Wyandotte, steel, w/2 darts, 7", NMIB $60.00

De Luxe Holster for Stallion .45, 'Left or Right,' EXIB .. $200.00

Deputy Pistol, Hubley, 10", MIB $150.00

Derringer w/Dagger, Hubley, 1960s, w/red plastic push-out dagger, blk grips, 7", unused, NM+ $75.00

Detective Automatic Repeater Cap Gun, Roth American Inc, 1970s, MOC $60.00

Dixi Cap Pistol, Kenton, 1930s, checked patterns on blk grips, red jewels, 6½", VG.. $100.00

Fanner-50 Smoking Cap Pistol, Mattel, revolving cylinder, 11", VGIB $150.00

Flashy Ray Gun, TN, 1950s, b/o, 18", NMIB................. $200.00

Frontier Smoker, PR Co, 1950s, 9", NMIB $150.00

Jet Jr 'S' Cap Gun, J&E Stevens, 6", MIB $200.00

Junior Rifle (Commando Auto Rifle), Nomura, tin, friction/ sparking shooting action, NMIB............................... $100.00

Little Burp Gurilla Machine Gun, Mattel, NMIB $100.00

Machine Gun (Cap Firing), Mattel, 1960s, plastic & metal, 17", NM $75.00

Mac Machine Gun (No 100), McDowell Mfg Co, 1920s, pump action, EXIB $100.00

Marshall Revolving Cap Pistol, Leslie-Henry, 1950s, w/blk oval on wht grips, 10½", EX+ $150.00

Model 1860 Colt .44 Cap Pistol, Hubley, 1971, silver & gold-tone w/wht grips, 13½", NMIB $200.00

Mountie Repeating Cap Pistol, Hubley, 1950s, w/engraved grips, 7", MIB $50.00

New Flash Gun, Horikawa, litho tin, b/o, barrel lights as it makes a shooting sound, 9½", EXIB............................... $175.00

Padlock Cap Gun, Hubley, 1950s, NM+...........................$75.00

Park's Lugar Water Gun, Park's Plastics, 1950s, w/2 refillable water clips, 7", NM (VG box) $50.00

Pioneer Cap Pistol, Hubley, translucent brn grips, 9½", EX .. $75.00

Pirate Pistol, Hubley, 2 hammers, NM $125.00

Private Eye 50 Shot Repeater Cap Pistol, #2038, Kilgore, 1960s, M (VG+ card) $30.00

Radar Raider (Cap Shooting Tommy Gun), Arliss/Premier Plastics, 18", unused, MIB $100.00

Ranger Cap Pistol, Kilgore, 1940s, w/dk reddish brn grip, 8", unused, EX+ $175.00

Ray Gun, Japan, 1960s, tin, friction w/sparking action, 5", EX...$22.00

Rocket Dart Pistol, Daisy, litho steel, complete w/7" gun, 2 darts & target, NMIB... $475.00

Rocket-2 Sparking Space Gun, Marx, tin & plastic, NMIB . $400.00

Rodeo Cap Gun, Hubley, 1950s, w/longhorn steer heads emb on wht grips, 8", MIB $750.00

Scout Cap Rifle, Hubley, 1960s, 36", unused, M............. $140.00

Sheriff Repeating Cap Pistol, J&E Stevens, 1940s, w/red jewels on blk horse-head grips, 8", NMIB $200.00

Shootin' Shell Colt 6 Shooter Rifle, Mattel, 1960, 31", MIB .. $350.00

Shootin' Shell Fanner .45 Cap Pistol, Mattel, 1959, w/6 shells, M $300.00

Sixfinger, Topper Toys (De Luxe Reading), 1965, plastic finger form shoots 6 different projectiles, MOC $75.00

Sky Robot, Horikawa, plastic, b/o, 9", NMIB $100.00

Space Jet (Space Super Jet Gun), Yoshiya, tin & plastic, friction, 9½", NMIB $150.00

Space Patrol 2019 (Flying Saucer), Yonezawa, tin & plastic, b/o, 8" dia, EXIB $65.00

Spinner Rifle, Marx, NMOC............................. $125.00

Stallion .32 Six Shooter, Nichols, NP, 8", NMIB $125.00

Stallion .38 Repeater Cap Pistol, Nichols, MIB $150.00

Stallion 41-50 Flip-Out Six Shooter, Nichols, NMIB $300.00

Stallion .45 MK11 Cap Pistol, Nichols, 1950s, w/wht & blk interchangeable grips, 6 bullets in clip, MIB $400.00

Stallion .45 Six Shooter Cap Pistol, Nichols, 1950, wht grips w/ single red jewel & emb w/stallion, 12", unused, NMIB . $550.00

Stallion 300 Saddle Gun, NMIB $250.00

Texan .38 Cap Pistol, Hubley, 1950s, w/blk steer head emb on wht grips, 10½", MIB.. $200.00

Texan Double Gun & Holster Set, Halco, MIB.............. $300.00

Texan Gold De Luxe Pistol, Hubley, NMIB.................... $200.00

Texan Jr Double Gun & Holster Set, Hubley, 1950s, brn leather w/star medallions, steer heads emb on wht grips, NM. $150.00

Texan Jr Repeating Cap Pistol, Hubley, EXIB................. $100.00

Tiny Tommy Machine Gun, Hubley, 10", MIB.................$75.00

Tommy-Burp Mattel-O-Matic Cap Gun, Mattel, 1960s, rapid-fire 50 shots, smoking barrel, 24", unused, NM $175.00

X-Ray Gun, Nomura, litho tin, b/o, sits on tripod, 16½", NM+IB...$325.00

CHARACTER

Agent Zero Radio-Rifle, Mattel, 1964, NMIB $75.00

Annie Oakley Cowgirl Outfit, 2 9" guns in wht holsters w/ bl images & trim, red & blk skirt w/wht fringe & trim, NMIB... $675.00

Annie Oakley Golden Smoke Rifle Outfit, Daisy, complete, NMIB $650.00

Annie Oakley Pistol, wht grips, 9", EX $200.00

Bonanza Genuine Leather Holster Set, 2 guns w/blk holsters, EXIB $700.00

Bonanza Guns The Hoss Range Pistol, Marx, plastic, 12", EXOC $150.00

Buck Rogers Atomic Pistol, Daisy, metallic gold, sparks, 1936, 10", VG $200.00

Buck Rogers Atomic Pistol, Daisy #U-235, metallic gold, sparks, 1936, 10", NMIB.. $500.00

Buck Rogers Rocket Pistol, 10", VGIB.............................. $250.00

Buck Rogers XZ-44 Liquid Helium Water Pistol, Daisy, steel, 7", 1936, NM $300.00

Buffalo Bill Repeating Cap Pistol, J&E Stevens, NP w/emb horse heads & red jewels on wht grips, 8", NMIB................. $175.00

Captain Gallant Foreign Legion Holster Set, Halco, w/Hubley 'Army 45' diecast gun, canteen, handcuffs & ID, NMIB............. $350.00

Cheyenne Singin' Saddle Gun, Daisy, 33", NMIB.......... $250.00

Dale Evans Shootin' Iron, Schmidt, crosshatched grips w/red 'jewel' & logo, NMIB $600.00

Dan Dare Planet Guns, Merit Toys, 1950s, complete, NMIB.$150.00

Davy Crockett Cap Pistol, Marx, 1950s, pnt marblized plastic w/ working metal 'flintlock' hammer & trigger, 10½", NM+ .. $75.00

Davy Crockett Cap Pistols, Schmidt, metal w/blk grips, 7½", EX, pr... $250.00

Davy Crockett Double Gun & Holster Set, R&S Toys, tan & brn leather w/jeweled buckle, name & image on pockets, NMIB... $200.00

Davy Crockett Frontier Rifle, Marx, metal, 34", NMIB . $175.00

Davy Crockett Pistol, Lacto, w/bronze-type floral grips, 10½", unused, NM+.. $125.00

Dick Tracy Jr Click Pistol #78, Marx, 1930s, aluminum, EX+.. $65.00

Dick Tracy Police Siren Pistol, Marx, VGIB.................... $125.00

Dick Tracy Power Jet Squad Gun, Mattel, 1962, 29", EX+ ...$75.00

Dick Tracy Sub-Machine Gun, Tops Plastics, 1951, plastic water gun, 12", EXIB...$225.00

Dick Tracy Tommy Gun, Parker Jones Co, 20", EXIB $300.00

Dragnet Detective Special Repeating Revolver Cap Gun, Knickerbocker, EXOC $95.00

Dragnet Double-Barrel Cap Riot Gun, plastic, 33", EXIB ..$250.00

Dragnet (Official) Police Holster Set, gun, holster, badge & handcuffs, EXIB..$200.00

Flash Gordon Arresting Ray Gun, Marx, 1950s, litho tin, 10", VG+...$275.00

Flash Gordon Radio Repeater, Marx, 1930s, litho tin, clicker action, 10" L, EX $300.00

Flash Gordon Signal Pistol, Marx, 7", NMIB.................$800.00

G-Man Automatic, Marx, 4", NMIB $100.00

G-Man Gun, Marx, litho tin w/wood stock, 23" L, EX+ . $250.00

G-Man Gun/Siren Alarm Pistol, Marx, 9", EXIB $175.00

G-Man Machine Gun, Japan, 1950s, 18", MIB...............$125.00

G-Man Sparkling Pop Pistol, Marx, 8", NMIB...............$100.00

G-Man Sparkling Sub-Machine Gun, Marx, plastic, 26", VGIB...$125.00

Gene Autry '44' Western Pistol, Leslie-Henry, 50-shot repeater, revolving barrel, auto release, side loader, NMIB........$350.00

Gene Autry Cap Pistol, Kenton, 1940s, 3rd version, red grips, 8", VG $150.00

Gene Autry Cap Pistol, Leslie-Henry, 1950s, transparent amber horse-head grips, 11", EX $175.00

Gene Autry Double Gun & Holster Set, blk leather w/silver studs & yel jewels, 2 8½" Kenton guns w/wht grips, VG $325.00

Gene Autry Repeating Cap Pistol, wht grips w/name scripted in red, 6", EXIB..$250.00

Get Smart Agent 86 Headquarters Signal Ray Gun, Marx, 1966, plastic, b/o, 7½", MOC $300.00

Gun Smoke Holster Set, Halco, 2 8" Pinto guns, leather holsters, GIB..$125.00

Hopalong Cassidy Cap Pistol, Schmidt, blk grips w/wht cameo bust image, 9½", NM+ $275.00

Hopalong Cassidy Cap Pistol, Wyandotte, 1950s, gold-plated w/ blk grips, 7½", EXIB $400.00

Hopalong Cassidy Cap Pistol, Wyandotte, 1950s, w/blk outlined bust image of Hoppy & signature on wht grips, 8", EX. $200.00

Hopalong Cassidy Double Holster Set, Wyandotte, 1950s, blk leather w/silver studs & red jewels, 8" guns w/wht grips, VG...$500.00

Hopalong Cassidy Single Holster Set, Wyandotte, 1950s, blk leather holster w/silver studs, pistol w/ivory grips, MIB. $725.00

James Bond 007 Harpoon Gun, Lone Star, 1960s, EXIB . $100.00

James Bond 007 Hideaway Pistol, Coibel, 1985, NMIB....$75.00

James Bond 007 Multi-Buster Machine Gun, plastic, complete, 19", EXIB...$250.00

Johnny Ringo Lanyard Pull Action Gun & Holster Set, Marx, 10" gun, blk open holster w/straps to hold gun in place, EXIB...$250.00

Jr-Ranger Cap Pistol, J&E Stevens, 1940s, single shot, NP w/horse heads & cowboys emb on wht grips, 7½", NMIB...........$125.00

Kit Carson Pistol, Kilgore, lever opening, profile bust emb on blk grips, 9½", NMIB...$250.00

Laramie Genuine Leather Holster Set, 2 8½" guns w/blk holsters, EXIB $500.00

Lawman Lever Gun (New Smoke/Bang Rifle), Daisy, 33", EXIB...$225.00

Lone Ranger Carbine Rifle, Leslie-Henry, plastic, shoots caps, 26", NMIB...$350.00

Lone Ranger Double Gun & Holster Set, Esquire, 1947, blk leather, silver trim, red jewels, 2 Pony Boy guns, MIB (NOS).......$300.00

Lone Ranger Hi-Yo Silver Pistol, Kilgore, 1938, NP w/brn plastic grips, 8", EX $200.00

Lone Ranger Official Outfit, double holster set w/nonfiring compo guns, NMIB $350.00

Lone Ranger Single Gun & Holster Set, Esquire, blk leather, silver trim, red jewels, Pony Boy gun, MIB $250.00

Lone Ranger Sparkling Pop Pistol, Marx, 1938, metal, 7½", EXIB $150.00

Lost in Space Helmet & Gun Set, Remco, 1966, NMIB. $500.00

Lost in Space Signal Ray Gun & Helmet, Remco, 11½", EXIB...$625.00

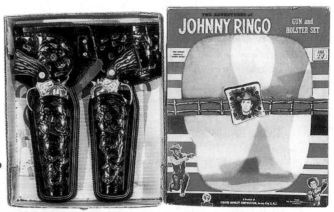

Guns, Character

Johnny Ringo Gun and Holster Set, double gun, unused, NMIB, $1,600.00. (Photo courtesy Morphy Auctions on LiveAuctioneers.com)

Guns, Character

Hopalong Cassidy Holster Set, double gun, Schmidt, EX guns, NM Holster, with box, $1,100.00. (Photo courtesy Morphy Auctions on LiveAuctioneers.com)

Man From UNCLE Illya Kuryakin Gun Set, Ideal, 13" gun, EXIB $350.00

Man From UNCLE Napoleon Solo Gun Set, Ideal, converts to rifle, complete, NMIB $400.00

Maverick (Double) Gun & Holster Set, Leslie Henry, 1958, NM (EX box w/James Garner image) $650.00

Mickey Mouse Explorers Club Outfit, gun & holster, binoculars & hat, NMIB $200.00

Overland Trail/Kelly's Rifle, Hubley, 35", EXIB $300.00

Planet Patrol (Rocket-2) Sparkling Space Gun, tin & plastic, w/ up, NMIB $200.00

Popeye Gun Set, Halco, 1961, dbl gun & holster set on 98¢ die-cut Popeye card, EX $300.00

Popeye Pirate Pistol, Marx, litho tin, NMIB $250.00

Red Ranger Jr Cap Pistol, Wyandotte, w/horse heads & star medallion on wht grips, 7½", NMIB $75.00

Red Ranger Jr Cap Pistol, Wyandotte, 1950s, wht grips emb w/ rope & horseshoe, 9", EX $50.00

Restless Gun & Holster Set, 2 10" guns w/lt tan holsters, VGIB $400.00

Rifleman Flip Special Rifle, Hubley, NMIB $450.00

Rin Tin Tin Cap Pistol, Actoy, copper-colored metal w/wht grips, 9", NM $125.00

Rin Tin Tin 101st Cavalry Outfit, w/single gun & holster, belt & telescope, EXIB $500.00

Roy Rogers Cap Pistol, Kilgore, 1950s, gold-tone finish, w/blk horse-head grips, 8", VG $175.00

Roy Rogers Cap Pistol, Leslie-Henry, 1950s, 2nd version, revolving cylinder, gold-tone w/blk grips, 9", EX+ $200.00

Roy Rogers Cap Pistol, Schmidt, emb 'Roy Rogers' & 'RR,' copper color metal grips w/red jewel, 9", EX $250.00

Roy Rogers Cap Shooting Carbine Rifle, Marx, 25½", NM+IB. $200.00

Roy Rogers Double Gun & Holster Set, Classy, brn & wht leather w/silver pockets, jewels, 10", Schmidt guns, EXIB $600.00

Roy Rogers Forty Niner Pistol & Spurs Set, Lelsie Henry, diecast w/gold finish, blk grips, complete, NMIB $900.00

Roy Rogers Shootin' Iron, Kilgore, simulated pearl grips, 9", MIB $400.00

Roy Rogers Signal Gun, Langson, 5½", NM+IB $125.00

Sergeant Bilko Holster Outfit, Halco, Hubley 'Army 45' gun w/ hat & holster set, EXIB $300.00

Shane Single Gun & Holster Set, marked Alan Ladd, EX+ ... $900.00

Tom Corbett Space Cadet Atomic Pistol Flashlite, Marx, plastic, 7½", NMIB $200.00

Tom Corbett Space Cadet Sparkling Space Gun, Marx, litho tin & plastic, 22½", NMIB (NOS) $400.00

Untouchables Tommy Gun, Marx, plastic, b/o, 24", EXOC. $325.00

Wagon Train Complete Western Outfit, Leslie-Henry, w/'50-Shot Repeater Rifle,' 2 guns & holsters, Derringer spurs, NMIB $700.00

Wagon Train Gun & Holster Set, Halco, 2 10" diecast Fanner 50 guns, NMIB $900.00

Wanted Dead or Alive 'The Mare's Laig' Cap Rifle/Pistol, Marx, 1960, MOC (card reads 'Collector Series,') $80.00

Wanted Dead or Alive Official Mare's Laig Rapid Fire Rifle Pistol, Marx, 19", NMIB $700.00

Wells Fargo Gun & Holster Set, 2 11" 'Wells Fargo' guns, lt tan holsters w/brn accents, EXIB $800.00

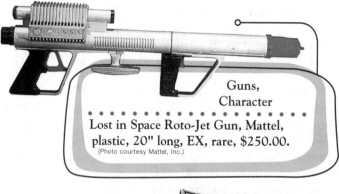

Guns, Character

Lost in Space Roto-Jet Gun, Mattel, plastic, 20" long, EX, rare, $250.00.
(Photo courtesy Mattel, Inc.)

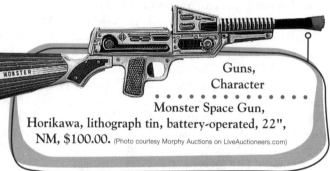

Guns, Character

Monster Space Gun, Horikawa, lithograph tin, battery-operated, 22", NM, $100.00. (Photo courtesy Morphy Auctions on LiveAuctioneers.com)

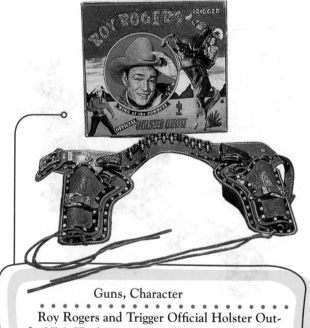

Guns, Character

Roy Rogers and Trigger Official Holster Outfit, NM+IB, $900.00. (Photo courtesy Morphy Auctions on LiveAuctioneers.com)

Wild Bill Hickok & Jingles Official Cowby Outfit, Canadian, 2 9" guns, blk holsters w/wht fringe, NMIB $900.00

Wild Bill Hickok Cap Pistol, Leslie-Henry, 'Marshall Wild Bill Hickok' on grips, 9½", EX, pr $250.00

Wilma Deering's Gun & Holster (Buck Rogers), NM $500.00

Wyatt Earp (Double) Holster, Hubley, guns w/blk grips, tan & blk holsters, NMIB $550.00

Wyatt Earp Gun Belt, Esquire Novelty, 2 guns w/wht grips, double holster, NMIB $650.00

Zorro Cap Pistol, flintlock style, NM $100.00

EARLY CAST-IRON CAP SHOOTERS

The early cap shooters listed are single-shot and action unless noted otherwise.

Best Butter, 2 goats butting heads on barrel, 5" L, very rare, EX+ $7,500.00
Butting Match, Ives, 1885, NM+ $600.00
Chinese Must Go, Ives, 1880, 5", NM $2,200.00
Clown & Mule, Ives, 5", VG...$750.00
Clown Seated on Keg, Ives, 4", VG+ $400.00
Lion, Stevens, octagonal barrel, japanned, cross-hatched grip, emb 'Lion' & Dec 17 1878/Mar 22 1887/June 21/1887, VG..$350.00
Lion, Stevens, rnd barrel, japanned, emb 'Lion' & June 21 1887/June 17 1890, 4½", EX+ $300.00
Locomotive Lightning Express, Kenton, 1910, japanned, variation of AN17, 5", VG+ $175.00
Monkey w/Coconut, japanned finish, 4", VG.................$230.00
Mule, Ives, 5", VG $750.00
Snap Shot Camera, Ives, 1893, 3", NM $950.00
Two Monkeys, J&E Stevens, 4½", G $600.00
Zip, J&E Stevens, 1890, 5", EX+ $150.00

Guns, Early Cast-Iron Cap Shooters
J&ES & Co, 1868, open handle, EX, $500.00. (Photo courtesy Bertoia Auctions on LiveAuctioneers.com)

RELATED ITEMS AND ACCESSORIES

Col Tim McCoy Pin-back w/'Pluck' Cap Pistol & Holster, 3" button attached to holster w/3" gun, 1920s, EX (Poor holster)..$95.00
Greenie Stik-M-Caps, Mattel, 1958, MIP (sealed)............$45.00
Holster & Belt, Dale Evans, unmarked, 1950s, tan leather w/blk trim & silver-tone studs, VG....................................$150.00
Holster Set, Buck Rogers, 1930s, tan w/red images on yel rnd patches & stud & star trim on tan felt-type material, EX+ $250.00
Holster Set, Lone Ranger, Smallman & Sons, blk leather w/ silver-tone studs & jewels, NMIB $300.00
Holster Set, Roy Rogers, brn leather, NM+IB $500.00
Holster Set, Wild Bill Hickok, blk & tan leather w/silver tone studs, diamond detail, VG, pr $200.00
Mechanical Shooting Gallery, Wyandotte, litho tin, w/up, complete w/plastic gun & accessories, 14" L, EXIB.............$125.00
Rifle Rack, Tales of Wells Fargo, wood, holds 2 rifles, 1959, NM..$75.00
Shootin' Shells for Shootin' Shell Guns, Mattel, 1959, MIP $50.00
Shooting Gallery, Wolverine #151-A, litho tin, complete, NMIB...$175.00
Stallion Round Caps, Nichols, 1950, box w/100 caps for use w/ Nichols .45 guns, M $15.00

Guns, Early Cast-Iron Cap Shooters
Punch and Judy, Ives, 1882, 5", $725.00. (Photo courtesy Bertoia Auctions on LiveAuctioneers.com)

• • • • • • • • • • • Halloween • • • • • • • •

Halloween items are very collectible right now with old, new, and folk art items demanding great attention from collectors. Many items are being made 'new' in Germany and being sold as vintage items (pre-WWII), and collectors must beware of these items as they are creative and well designed and aged. The rising amount of important folk artists making Halloween-related items is very exciting as is reflected in the difficulty of these artists to supply the demand. Haunted-House prop items are also being noticed by collectors. There is even the Castle Halloween Museum dedicated to the fun-loving 'kids' who embrace this most popular holiday. For more information about the museum, see the Directory of Advisors and Contributors in the back of the book.

For more information we recommend *Halloween Decorations and Games*; *Salem Witchcraft and Souvenirs*; and *Tastes and Smells of Halloween* by our advisor, Pamela E. Apkarian-Russell, The Halloween Queen™ (See Directory).

See also Halloween Costumes.

Key: J-O-L   jack-o-lantern

Book, 'Games for Halloween,' by Mary E Blain, 1912, hardcover, 60 pgs, w/dust jacket, EX...$50.00

Book, 'Ghosts What Ain't,' EX+...$50.00

Cake Decoration Set, plastic figures on picks, orange & blk, 5 different, 1950s, 2½", NM+..$40.00

Candle Set, 5 orange J-O-L's w/wht candles, Gurley, 1950s, unused, MIP (sealed)..$50.00

Candy Container, blk cat w/carrot body, cucumber arms, hat & tie, EX.. $225.00

Candy Container, cat on rnd container, compo & cb, 2", Germany, EX $200.00

Candy Container, ghost, wht muslin-dressed figure w/cb tube body, wht-pnt compo hands, skull head, 6", VG+....... $325.00

Candy Container, girl nodder pulling pumpkin house w/2 molded wheels, pnt compo, 4", EX $350.00

Candy Container, J-O-L man w/body, pressed cb, orange w/blk top hat, gr vest, blk jacket, orange legs, 9", VG+ $350.00

Candy Container, owl, pulp w/plastic eyes, orange & cream w/gr base, 10", US, VG+... $135.00

Candy Container, witch head w/cat body, compo, 5½", Germany, 1920, EX $700.00

Candy Container, witch figure, pnt compo w/cb hat, straw broom, 6½", G $300.00

Candy Container, witch w/J-O-L head holding broom, bisque & paper, 7", EX $425.00

Candy Pail, Buck Rogers head, molded plastic, wht w/red trim, 10", Renzi, 1979, NM+...$25.00

Candy Pail, Casper the Friendly Ghost, molded wht plastic bust form w/name emb on chest, Renzi, NM $35.00

Coloring Book, Halloween..., Dell #163, 1957, unused, NM...$40.00

Decoration, blk cat on J-O-L, die-cut cb, 12", US, 1930s, EX .$125.00

Decoration, blk cat or J-O-L, blk & orange crepe paper diecuts w/long streamers, 1930s-40s, 54x20", EX+, ea................$45.00

Decoration, cat w/feet attached to lg rnd head, blk-pnt paper material, 6", Germany, G+...$50.00

Decoration, scarecrow w/J-O-L head, die-cut cb w/string tissue paper arms & legs, Beistle, 1950s, 28", EX+ $30.00

Decoration, skull & crossbones, wht-pnt pulp w/blk eyes & nose, EX...$55.00

Decoration, witch w/broom, crepe paper, 4", EX $25.00

Decoration, J-O-L figure playing saxophone, die-cut cb stand-up, blk, orange & wht, 27", EX $250.00

Fan, blk cat, dbl-sided, 13", Germany, 1920s, EX $100.00

Figure, J-O-L man w/sm top hat & bowtie seated, pulp, 8", VG.. $350.00

Figure, owl, pulp, US, 1940s, 7", NM............................... $250.00

Figure, witch standing, holding broom & J-O-L, compo face & hands, cloth dress, apron & blk cape w/hood, 11", 1920s, EX... $2,200.00

Game, Halloween Party, Saalfield #702, unused, NM $75.00

Hand Puppet, goblin type w/striped body, pointy ears & hat, vinyl, 1950s, 10", EX+..$50.00

Horn, cb cone shape w/lithoed witch & screaming cat, 1921, EX..$20.00

Lantern, blk cat's head on fence, pulp, gr insert eyes, toothy scowl, 7½", EX $135.00

Lantern, devil's bust, pulp, orange, paper inserts, wire hdl, 7", EX...$225.00

Lantern, devil's head, red-pnt compo w/blk detail, inserted eyes & teeth, 4", EX.. $750.00

Halloween

Candle Set, three black cats in various poses, Gurley, 3½" each, unused, VG, $35.00. (Photo courtesy Classic Edge Auctions on LiveAuctioneers.com)

Halloween

Candy Container, black cat atop jack-o-lantern, painted composition, 3½", NM, $400.00. (Photo courtesy Morphy Auctions on LiveAuctioneers.com)

Halloween

Decoration, black cat dressed as muskateer, die-cut and embossed cardboard, 20", $140.00. (Photo courtesy Morphy Auctions on LiveAuctioneers.com)

Halloween

Game, Fortune Teller, Whitman, 1930s, complete, EXIB, $75.00. (Photo courtesy Pamela Apkarian-Russell)

Halloween

Lantern, cat head, painted cardboard, inserted eyes, bale handle, 4", $350.00. (Photo courtesy James D. Julia, Inc.)

Halloween

Nodder, ghost figure with jack-o-lantern face, painted composition with wood base, 7", G, $450.00. (Photo courtesy James D. Julia, Inc.)

Halloween

Noisemaker, black witch silhouette, 6½", EX, $100.00. (Photo courtesy Morphy Auctions on LiveAuctioneers.com)

Halloween

Tambourine, lithographed tin, goose and witch, 7" diameter, $165.00. (Photo courtesy Homestead Auctions on LiveAuctioneers.com)

Lantern, hexagonal top & bottom, emb cb w/various Halloween images, wire handle, 11" dia, VG+ $55.00

Lantern, J-O-L, cb, orange scowling face w/cut-out eyes & wide mouth, bail hdl, 5½", EX............................... $170.00

Lantern, J-O-L, tin, cut-out rnd eyes, long triangle nose, and 'toothy' mouth, 9", Toledo OH, 1908, EX $900.00

Lantern, witch's head, pnt compo w/cb hat, inserted eyes & toothy mouth, blk hat, gray hair, orange collar, 5", VG+ $1,750.00

Mechanical Toy, 'goblin' man waddles when wound, compo head w/wooden arms, metal feet, cloth outfit, 7", EX $700.00

Mechanical Toy, blk man in cloth costume on stick, when string is pulled prop turns & devil pops out of head, 14", EX. $275.00

Nodder, cat standing playing cello, pnt compo, spring neck, 10", EX $100.00

Noisemaker, pan knocker, tin, 6", Japan, 1930s, EX $65.00

Noisemaker, pumpkin head, pressed cb w/wooden hdl, 6", Germany, 1930, NM... $150.00

Noisemaker, ratchet, happy face lithoed on cb on wooden ratchet, 5", Germany, G+.....................................$35.00

Noisemaker, ratchet, wood w/carved wood cat straddling top, 8½x7", EX $100.00

Plastic Toy, clown pirate marching w/drum, orange, gr, blk & yel, 7", very rare, EX $250.00

Plastic Toy, witch w/broom & J-O-L on motorcycle, orange & blk w/gr wheels, 7", EX................................... $350.00

Ramp walkers, pumpkin man & woman, plastic, 3" $60.00

Rattle, rnd flat-sided J-O-L w/lithoed face on stick, crepe collar, 13", VG+ $100.00

Rattle, vegetable man (dbl-faced), celluloid, orange w/blk silhouette on belly, 4½", NM $575.00

Tambourine, litho tin, blk cat face, T Cohn, 1940s, EX+. $250.00

• • • • • • • • • Halloween Costumes • • • • • • • • •

During the 1950s, 1960s, and 1970s, Ben Cooper and Collegeville made Halloween costumes representing the popular TV and movie characters of the day. If you can find one in excellent to mint condition and still in its original box, some of the better ones can go for over $100.00. MAD's Alfred E. Neuman (Collegeville, 1959 – 1960) usually carries an asking price of $150.00 to $175.00 and The Green Hornet (Ben Cooper, 1966) upwards of $200.00. Earlier handmade costumes are especially valuable if they are 'Dennison-Made.'

Advisor: Pamela E. Apkarian-Russell, The Halloween Queen™

Admiral Ackbar (Return of the Jedi), 1983, NMIB $25.00

Alf, Collegeville, MIB $35.00

Alfred E Neuman, mask only, Ben Cooper, 1960s, NM.....$50.00

Aquaman, Ben Cooper, 1967, NMIB............................ $125.00

Archie, Collegeville, 1960, MIB $50.00

Barbarino, Collegeville, 1976, MIB.....................................$40.00

Barbie, TV-Comic/Collegeville, 1975, MIB.......................$55.00

Barbie Super Star Bride, Collegeville, 1975, MIP.............$60.00

Baretta, NMIB (box reads 'TV Comic')..............................$75.00

Batgirl, 1977, NMIB $35.00

Batman, Ben Cooper, 1969, NMIB $60.00
Batman (Super Heroes), Ben Cooper, 1973, EXIB $35.00
Beany & Cecil, Ben Cooper, 1950, NMIB......................$50.00
Beatles, any member, Ben Cooper, MIB, ea $450.00
Boss Hogg (Dukes of Hazzard), Ben Cooper, 1982, MIB ...$40.00
Brady Bunch, any character, Collegeville, 1970s, MIB, ea $25
    to $35.00
C-3PO (Star Wars), Ben Cooper, 1977, MIB $45.00
Casper the Friendly Ghost, Collegeville, 1960s, EXIB $50.00
Cookie Monster, Ben Cooper, 1989, MIB.........................$30.00
Daffy Duck, Collegeville, 1960s, EXIB.............................$25.00
Darth Vader, Ben Cooper, 1977, MIP $25.00
Donald Duck, Ben Cooper, orig box, $25 to $50.00
Donny & Marie, Collegeville, 1977, MIB..........................$35.00
Droopy Dog, Collegeville, 1953, EXIB.............................$50.00
Electra Woman, Ben Cooper, 1976, MIB..........................$60.00
Flipper, Collegeville, 1964, MIB......................................$75.00
Fred Flintstone, Famous Faces, Ben Cooper, 1973, unused,
    MIB $65.00
GI Joe, Halco, 1960s, EXIB $65.00
Great Grape Ape, Ben Cooper, 1975, EXIB $50.00
Green Hornet, Ben Cooper, 1966, NMIB......................$200.00
Gumby, Collegeville, EXIB..$65.00
Hardy Boys, Collegeville, 1978, MIB, ea...........................$45.00
He-Man, mask only, Mattel, M $10.00
Hong Kong Phooey, 1974, NMIB...................................$20.00
HR Pufnstuf, Collegeville, 1970s, MIB $75.00
Hush Puppy (Shari Lewis), Halco, 1961, EXIB.................$75.00
Impossibles, Ben Cooper, 1967, NMIB $50.00
Jimmy Osmond, Collegeville, 1977, MIB $20.00
Joker, vinyl, 1989, MIB...$35.00
King Kong, Ben Cooper, 1976, MIB...............................$100.00
KISS, Gene Simmons, Collegeville, 1978, MIB $100.00
Lambchop (Shari Lewis), mask only, Halco, 1962, NM $40.00
Land of the Giants, 1968, EX+ (no box) $50.00
Laugh-In, Ben Cooper, MIP $40.00
Lavern & Shirley, Collegeville, 1977, MIB, ea $30.00
Li'l Abner, Ben Cooper, 1957, NMIB $45.00
Li'l Tiger, 1960s, VGIB...$25.00
Little Audrey, Collegeville, 1959, MIB..............................$50.00
Lone Ranger, 'Western Hero,' Ben Cooper, 1977, NMIB..$25.00
Lost in Space, silver, Ben Cooper, EX (no box)................$60.00
Luke Skywalker (Return of the Jedi), Ben Cooper, EXIB . $125.00
Mandrake the Musician, Collegeville, 1950s, EXIB $85.00
Marie Osmond, 1977, NMIB...$35.00
Maverick, 1959, EX (no box) $50.00
Mickey Mouse, Ben Cooper, 1940s, VGIB........................$45.00
Miss Kitty (Gunsmoke), Halco, EXIB.............................$125.00
Monkees, any member, Blan Charnas, 1967, NMIB....... $200.00
Mork, Ben Cooper, 1978, NM (no box) $35.00
Morticia Addams, Ben Cooper, 1965, VG+IB..................$50.00
Mr Spock (Star Trek), Ben Cooper, MIB..........................$50.00
Raggedy Andy, Ben Cooper, 1965, MIB...........................$30.00
Raggedy Ann, Ben Cooper, 1965, MIB.............................$30.00
Rin-Tin-Tin, 1950s, NMIB..$50.00
Sabrina the Teenage Witch, Ben Cooper, 1971, NMIB $25.00
Samantha (Bewitched), Ben Cooper, 1965-67, VG (no box)..$35.00
Six Million Dollar Man, Ben Cooper, 1965, MIB.............$40.00

Halloween Costumes
· · · · · · · · · · · · · · ·
Bewitched, Ben Cooper, 1965, vinyl, MIB, $45.00. (Photo courtesy Greg Davis and Bill Morgan)

Halloween Costumes
· · · · · · · · · · · · · · ·
Charlie's Angles, Collegeville, 1976, box labeled as Charlie's Angels but mask resembles Sabrina, $50.00 to $75.00. (Photo courtesy Greg Davis and Bill Morgan)

Halloween Costumes
· · · · · · · · · · · · · · ·
CHiPs, officer, Ben Cooper, 1978, MIB, $25.00. (Photo courtesy Greg Davis and Bill Morgan)

Halloween Costumes
· · · · · · · · · · · · · · ·
I Dream of Jeannie, Ben Cooper, 1974, MIB, $50.00.

Space: 1999, Commander Koenig, 1975, EXIB..................$35.00
Spider-Man, Ben Cooper, 1972, NMIB.......................$50.00
Starsky & Hutch, Collegeville, 1976, MIB, ea...................$50.00
Steve Canyon, Halco, 1959, NMIB $50.00
Superman, Ben Cooper, early, EXIB.............................$150.00
SWAT, Ben Cooper, 1975, NMIB $35.00
Tattoo (Fantasy Island), Ben Cooper, 1978, MIB $30.00

Top Cat, Ben Cooper, 1965, NMIB.........................$75.00
Underdog, Collegeville, 1974, MIB $40.00
Winky Dink, Halco, 1950s, EX (no box) $65.00
Witchiepoo, Collegeville, 1971, MIB $50.00
Yoda (Empire Strikes Back), EXIB $35.00
Zorro, Ben Cooper #233, 1950s, deluxe edition, EXIB... $100.00

Hartland Plastics, Inc.

Originally known as the Electro Forming Co., Hartland Plastics Inc. was founded in 1941 by Ed and Iola Walters. They first produced heels for military shoes, birdhouses, and ornamental wall decor. It wasn't until the late 1940s that Hartland produced their first horse and rider. Figures were hand painted with an eye for detail. The Western and Historic Horsemen, Miniature Western Series, Authentic Scale Model Horses, Famous Gunfighter Series, and the Hartland Sports Series of Famous Baseball Stars were symbols of the fine workmanship of the 1940s, 1950s, and 1960s. The plastic used was a virgin acetate. Paint was formulated by Bee Chemical Co., Chicago, Illinois, and Wolverine Finishes Corp., Grand Rapids, Michigan. Hartland figures are best known for their uncanny resemblance to the TV Western stars who portrayed characters like the Lone Ranger, Matt Dillon, and Roy Rogers.

The prices listed are for figures that are complete with original accessories. For more information, we recommend *Hartland Horses and Riders* by Gail Fitch. See also Clubs, Newsletters, and Other Publications in the back of the book.

GUNFIGHTERS

Bat Masterson, NMIB..$500.00
Bret Maverick, NM...$250.00
Bret Maverick, NMIB.......................................$480.00
Chris Colt, NM..$250.00
Jim Hardy, NM...$150.00
Johnny McKay, EX..$550.00
Johnny McKay, NM+ $800.00
Paladin, NM...$400.00
Vint Bonner, NMIB...$850.00

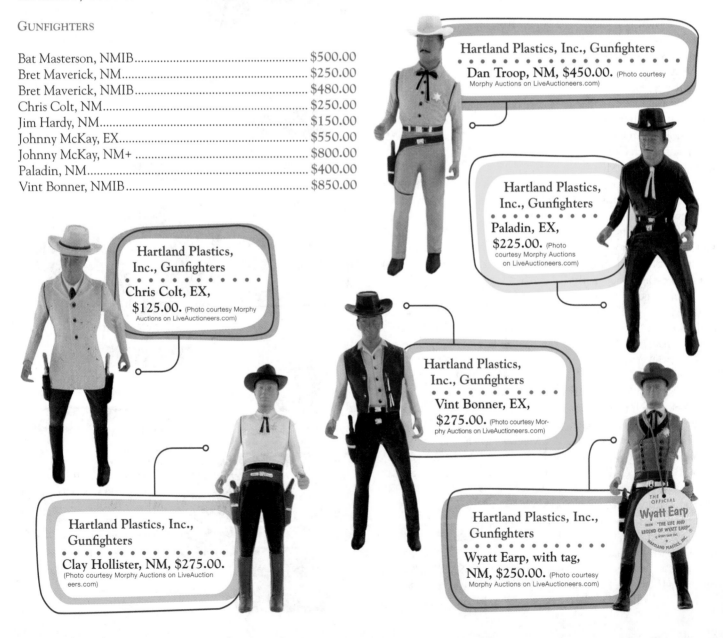

Hartland Plastics, Inc., Gunfighters Dan Troop, NM, $450.00. (Photo courtesy Morphy Auctions on LiveAuctioneers.com)

Hartland Plastics, Inc., Gunfighters Paladin, EX, $225.00. (Photo courtesy Morphy Auctions on LiveAuctioneers.com)

Hartland Plastics, Inc., Gunfighters Chris Colt, EX, $125.00. (Photo courtesy Morphy Auctions on LiveAuctioneers.com)

Hartland Plastics, Inc., Gunfighters Vint Bonner, EX, $275.00. (Photo courtesy Morphy Auctions on LiveAuctioneers.com)

Hartland Plastics, Inc., Gunfighters Clay Hollister, NM, $275.00. (Photo courtesy Morphy Auctions on LiveAuctioneers.com)

Hartland Plastics, Inc., Gunfighters Wyatt Earp, with tag, NM, $250.00. (Photo courtesy Morphy Auctions on LiveAuctioneers.com)

HORSEMEN

Alkine Ike, NM	$150.00
Annie Oakley, NM	$275.00
Bill Longley, EX+IB	$500.00
Brave Eagle, NM	$200.00
Brave Eagle, NMIB	$300.00
Bret Maverick, coffee/dunn horse, NM	$500.00
Bret Maverick, gray horse, rare, NMIB	$600.00
Bret Maverick, miniature series	$75.00
Buffalo Bill, NM	$300.00
Bullet, NM	$100.00
Bullet, w/tag, NM	$150.00
Cactus Pete, NM	$150.00
Champ Cowgirl, very rare, NM	$275.00
Cheyenne, miniature series, NM	$190.00
Chief Thunderbird, rare shield, rearing, NM	$150.00
Commanche Kid, NM	$150.00
Dale Evans, bl, rare, NM	$500.00
Dale Evans, gr, NM	$175.00
Dale Evans, gr, w/tag, NM	$250.00
Davy Crockett, EX+	$375.00
General Custer, NM	$150.00
General Custer, NMIB	$350.00
General George Washington, NMIB	$175.00
General Robert E Lee, EX	$100.00
General Robert E Lee, NMIB	$250.00
Gil Favor, prancing, very rare, M	$1,100.00
Gil Favor, semi-rearing, NM+	$800.00
Hoby Gillman, NM	$200.00
Jim Bowie, NM	$200.00
Jim Hardy, NM	$350.00
Jim Hardy, NMIB	$300.00
Jockey, NM	$150.00

Hartland Plastics, Inc., Horsemen
Bullet, MIB, $250.00.
(Photo courtesy Morphy Auctions on LiveAuctioneers.com)

Hartland Plastics, Inc., Horsemen
Cheyenne, with tag, NM, $250.00. (Photo courtesy Morphy Auctions on LiveAuctioneers.com)

Hartland Plastics, Inc., Horsemen
Chief Thundercloud, with spear, EX, $100.00. (Photo courtesy Morphy Auctions on LiveAuctioneers.com)

Hartland Plastics, Inc., Horsemen
Cochise, NM, $150.00. (Photo courtesy Morphy Auctions on LiveAuctioneers.com)

Hartland Plastics, Inc., Horsemen
Annie Oakley, with tag, EX, $225.00.
(Photo courtesy Morphy Auctions on LiveAuctioneers.com)

Hartland Plastics, Inc., Horsemen
Buffalo Bill, EX, $150.00. (Photo courtesy Morphy Auctions on LiveAuctioneers.com)

Hartland Plastics, Inc., Horsemen
Dale Evans, purple, NM, $250.00. (Photo courtesy Morphy Auctions on LiveAuctioneers.com)

Hartland Plastics, Inc., Horsemen
General Custer, EX, $100.00. (Photo courtesy Morphy Auctions on LiveAuctioneers.com)

Hartland Plastics, Inc., Horsemen

General George Washington, EX, $75.00. (Photo courtesy Morphy Auctions on LiveAuctioneers.com)

Hartland Plastics, Inc., Horsemen

Josh Randall, NM, $650.00. (Photo courtesy Morphy Auctions on LiveAuctioneers.com)

Hartland Plastics, Inc., Horsemen

Lone Ranger, walking (Trigger), with tag, M, $300.00. (Photo courtesy Morphy Auctions on LiveAuctioneers.com)

Hartland Plastics, Inc., Horsemen

Rebel, M, $600.00. (Photo courtesy Morphy Auctions on LiveAuctioneers.com)

Lone Ranger, miniature series, NM	$75.00
Lone Ranger, NM	$300.00
Lone Ranger, rearing, NMIB	$350.00
Matt Dillon, NM	$200.00
Matt Dillon, NM (VG+ box)	$250.00
Paladin, NMIB	$350.00
Rebel, EX	$250.00
Rebel, miniature series, NM	$125.00
Rifleman, EX+	$275.00
Rifleman, miniature series, EX	$75.00

Ronald MacKenzie, NM	$1,200.00
Roy Rogers, semi-rearing, NMIB	$600.00
Roy Rogers, walking, NM	$275.00
Seth Adams, EX	$125.00
Seth Adams, M	$200.00
Sgt Lance O'Rourke, NMIB	$300.00
Sgt Preston, EX	$425.00
Tom Jeffords, EX	$125.00
Tom Jeffords, NM	$175.00
Tom Jeffords, NMIB	$250.00
Tonto, EX	$200.00
Tonto, miniature series, NM	$75.00
Tonto, semi-rearing, rare, NM	$650.00
Wyatt Earp, EX+	$125.00

Sports Figures

Bat Boy, 25th Anniversary, NM	$50.00
Dick Groat, w/bat, NM, minimum value	$1,000.00
Dick Groat, 25th Anniversary, MIB, $30 to	$40.00
Don Drysdale, EX, $275 to	$350.00
Duke Snyder, EX+	$360.00
Ernie Banks, NM, $200 to	$250.00
Ernie Banks, 25th Anniversary, MIB, $30 to	$40.00
Hank Aaron, EX	$250.00
Hank Aaron, M	$350.00
Hank Aaron, 25th Anniveasy, MIB	$35.00
Harmon Killebrew, 25th Anniversary, MIB, $30 to	$45.00
Little Legure, 4", EX, $50 to	$75.00
Luis Aparicio, NM, $250 to	$300.00
Luis Aparicio, 25th Anniversary, MIB	$32.00
Mickey Mantle, NM, $285 to	$320.00
Mickey Mantle, 25th Anniversary, MIB	$50.00
Nellie Fox, EX, $135 to	$165.00
Rocky Colavito, NM, $600 to	$700.00

Hartland Plastics, Inc., Sports Figures

Babe Ruth, NM, $175.00 to $225.00. (Photo courtesy David Longest)

Hartland Plastics, Inc., Sports Figures

Mickey Mantle, VG, $150.00. (Photo courtesy David Longest)

Hartland Plastics, Inc., Sports Figures
Roger Maris, NM, $325.00 to $375.00. (Photo courtesy David Longest)

Hartland Plastics, Inc., Sports Figures
Yogi Berra, with mask, NM, $165.00 to $200.00. (Photo courtesy David Longest)

Stan Musial, NM $235.00	Willie Mays, NM, $255 to $285.00
Ted Williams, VG $145.00	Willie Mays, 25th Anniversary, MIB $50.00
Ted Williams, 25th Anniversary, MIB $50.00	Yogi Berra, no mask, NM, $100 to $150.00
Warren Spahn, limited edition, 2002, MIB $25.00	Yogi Berra, w/mask, 25th Anniversary, M (NM box) $38.00
Washington Redskins, running back, NM, minimum value . $500.00	Yogi Berra, w/mask, 25th Anniversary, MIB $50.00

• Horses • • • • • • • • • • • • • • • • • •

Horse riding being the order of the day, many children of the nineteenth century had their own horses to ride indoors; some were wooden while others were stuffed, and many had glass eyes and real horsehair tails. There were several ways to construct these horses so as to achieve a galloping action. The most common types had rocker bases or were mounted with a spring on each leg.

Horse on Wheels, dappled, glass eyes, w/saddle & trappings, pull string & horse whinnys, 13" L, VG.............................. $225.00

Horse on 4-Wheeled Platform, real horsehide over straw-stuffed frame, horsehair mane & tail, harness, 31", G............. $450.00

Mobo Bronco, pedal horse on wheels, 26", 1940s, VG... $250.00

Rocking Horse, hide covered w/hair mane & tail, wood snout, hooves & base, leather trappings, saddle & blanket, 39x30", G $350.00

Rocking Horse, pnt wood, wht w/gr mottled look, pnt eyes, gr-pnt rocker base, w/trappings, 60" L, EX $525.00

Rocking Horse, pnt wood & canvas w/leather saddle & bridle, wht w/blk circles, red wooden rockers, 27x41½", VG. $500.00

Rocking Horse, pnt wood 2-sided horse w/interior upholstered seat, 31½" L, G $100.00

Shoofly, oilcloth upholstered seat in pnt wood frame w/dbl horse heads on rockers, 35" L, VG $1,300.00

Wheeled Horse on Rocker base, wheels fit in slots on wooden rocker base, fur-covered, w/saddle & reins, German, EX.$175.00

Horses
Gliding Horse, gray-painted carved wood, leather saddle, red-painted glider base, 37x39", G, $875.00. (Photo courtesy James D. Julia, Inc.)

Horses
Rocking Horse, wood, primitive, 46" long, EX, $350.00. (Photo courtesy Morphy Auctions on LiveAuctioneers.com)

• • • • • • • • • • • • • • • ‹ Hot Wheels › • • • • • • • • • • • • • • •

When introduced in 1968, Hot Wheels were an instant success. Sure, the racy style and flashy custom paint jobs were attention-getters, but what the kids loved most was the fact that the cars were fast! Fastest on the market! It's estimated that more than two billion Hot Wheels have been sold to date — every model with a little variation, keeping up with the big cars. The line has included futuristic vehicles, muscle cars, trucks, hot rods, racers, and some military vehicles. A lot of these can still be found for very little, but if you want to buy the older models (collectors call them 'Red Lines' because of their red sidewall tires), it's going to cost you a little more, though many can still be found for under $25.00. By 1977, black-wall tires had become the standard and by 1978, 'Red Lines' were no longer used.

A line of cars with Goodyear tires called Real Riders was made from 1983 until about 1987. (In 1983 the tires had gray hubs with white lettering; in 1984 the hubs were white.) California Customs were made in 1989 and 1990. These had the Real Rider tires, but they were not lettered 'Good Year' (and some had different wheels entirely).

Chopcycles are similar to Sizzlers in that they have rechargable batteries. The first series was issued in 1972 in these models: Mighty Zork, Blown Torch, Speed Steed, and Bruiser Cruiser. Generally speaking, these are valued at $35.00 (loose) to $75.00 (MIB). A second series issued in 1973 was made up of Ghost Rider, Rage Coach, Riptide, Sourkraut, and Triking Viking. This series is considerably harder to find and much more expensive today; expect to pay as much as $600.00 to $1,000.00 for a mint-in-package example.

Though recent re-releases have dampened the collector market somewhat, cars mint and in the original packages are holding their values and are still moving well. Near mint examples (no package) are worth about 50% to 60% less than those mint and still in their original package, excellent condition about 65% to 75% less.

Advisor: Steve Stephenson

'31 Doozie, 1986, maroon w/red-brn fenders, MIP.............$12.00
'32 Ford Delivery, 1989, yel w/orange & magenta tampo, M...$15.00
'56 Flasher Pickup, 1990s, turq, MIP...................................$5.00
'57 T-Bird, 1990, Park 'n Plates, aqua, M $10.00
'65 Mustang Convertible, 1980s, lt bl, MIP $40.00
Air France Delivery Truck, 1990, wht, M (International box) $20.00
Alive '55 Chevy Station Wagon, 1974, lt bl, M $300.00
Alive '55 Chevy Station Wagon, 1976, Super Chromes, dk bl, lt gr & yel in tampo, M...$75.00
Ambulance, 1970, Heavyweights, aqua, bl, gr or red, MIP ..$125.00
American Tipper, 1976, red, M $60.00
American Victory, 1983, lt bl w/dk bl tampo, France, MIP...$70.00
AMX/2, 1971, purple, M $170.00
Assault Crawler, 1987, olive w/gr, tan & brn camp tampo, MIP $25.00
Backwoods Bomb, 1975, lt bl, M..$75.00
Backwoods Bomb, 1977, dk gr, blk-wall tires, M.................$35.00
Backwoods Bomb, 1977, dk gr, M.......................................$50.00
Battle Tank, 1984, tan, MIP $25.00
Beach Patrol, 1983, Real Riders, wht, gray hubs, MIP.......$30.00
Beach Patrol, 1990, fluorescent gr, M................................$15.00
Beatnik Bandit, 1968, aqua, US or Hong Kong, M $65.00
Beatnik Bandit, 1968, bl, US, M..$45.00
Beatnik Bandit, 1968, orange, US, M $70.00
Beatnik Bandit, 1968, rose, US, M....................................$60.00
Big Bertha, 1988, tan, M $10.00
Bronco Four-Wheeler, 1985, red, M..................................$10.00
Bugeye, 1971, gold, US, M $225.00
Bugeye, 1971, gold, US, MIP...$425.00
Buzz Off, 1973, dk bl, M $200.00
Buzz Off, 1973, fluorescent pk, M $400.00
Buzz Off, 1973, red, M $250.00
Cadillac Seville, 1983, metal-flake gold, M $8.00
Captain America Hot Bird, 1979, red, wht & bl, M..........$30.00
Carabo, 1970, hot pk, Hong Kong, M............................ $300.00
Carabo, 1970, lt gr, US, M...$75.00

Carabo, 1974, yel, M... $1,000.00
Carabo, 1977, lt gr, M..$75.00
Cargoyle, 1986, orange, M...$7.00
Cement Mixer, 1970, Heavyweights, purple, MIP......... $225.00
Chevy Monza 2+2, 1975, lt gr, Mexico, M $400.00
Chevy Monza 2+2, 1975, orange, M.............................$75.00
Choppin' Chariot, 1970, Rumblers, MOC....................$175.00
Classic '31 Ford Woody, 1969, aqua, MIP $100.00
Classic '31 Ford Woody, 1969, creamy pk w/blk roof, M.. $400.00
Classic '31 Ford Woody, 1969, orange, M $75.00
Classic '32 Vicky, 1994, metal-flake pk, MIP $900.00
Classic '35 Caddy, 1989, silver w/beige interior, pk fenders, wht-walls, NM $25.00
Classic '36 Ford Coupe, 1969, Antifreeze, MIP $120.00
Classic '57 T-Bird, 1969, bl, MIP................................$100.00
Classic Nomad, 1970, magenta, M................................$150.00
Classic Nomad, 1970, red, MIP (unpunched).................$225.00
Cockeny Cab, 1971, magenta, clear windows, US, M.... $160.00
Cockeny Cab, 1971, magenta, Hong Kong, M $200.00
Cockney Cab, 1971, bl, US, M $140.00
Combat Medic, 1988, gold & chrome, no horizontal lines, from 20th Anniversary set, M $45.00
Continental Mark III, 1969, hot pk, M..........................$180.00

Custom AMX, 1969, bl, M..............................$110.00
Custom Baracuda, 1968, lt bl, Hong Kong, M................$500.00
Custom Baracuda, 1968, lt bl, US, M..........................$500.00
Custom Camaro, 1968, lt bl, US, M.............................$650.00
Custom Camaro, 1968, rose, US, M..............................$900.00
Custom Corvette, 1968, Antifreeze, US, M....................$300.00
Custom Corvette, 1968, bl, Hong Kong, M...................$150.00
Custom Cougar, 1968, bl, pnt tooth, Hong Kong, M $250.00
Custom Cougar, 1968, bl, pnt tooth, US, M..................$500.00
Custom Cougar, 1968, orange, US, MIP.......................$500.00
Custom Eldorado, 1968, bl, US, M...............................$90.00
Custom Eldorado, 1968, olive, Hong Kong, M..............$125.00
Custom Firebird, 1968, red, Hong Kong, M..................$125.00
Custom Firebird, 1968, red, US, M..............................$100.00
Custom Fleetside, 1968, purple, US, M.........................$100.00
Custom Mustang, 1968, Antifreeze, smooth rear window, US, M...$350.00
Custom Mustang, 1968, purple, closed hood scoops, Hong Kong, M $450.00
Custom Mustang, 1968, purple, smooth rear window, US, M . $425.00
Custom Mustang, 1968, red w/red interior, Hong Kong, M .. $200.00
Custom Mustang, 1994, brn, MIP $10.00
Custom T-Bird, 1968, gold, all interiors except wht, US, M . $325.00
Custom T-Bird, 1968, gold, blk roof, Hong Kong, M......$125.00
Custom T-Bird, 1968, gold, blk roof, US, M $150.00
Custom T-Bird, 1968, gold, wht interior, US, M $500.00
Custom Volkswagen, 1968, bl, opening sunroof, Hong Kong, M $100.00
Custom Volkswagen, 1968, bl, US, M...........................$75.00
Custom Volkswagen, 1968, hot pk, US, M $900.00
Demon, 1970, lt gr, M...$150.00
Demon, 1994, metal-flake bl, Toy Fair Limited Edition, M... $150.00
Deora, 1968, Antifreeze, Hong Kong, MIP....................$250.00
Deora, 1968, Antifreeze, US, MIP $500.00
Deora, 1968, purple, Hong Kong, M $100.00
Deora, 1968, purple, US, M.......................................$150.00
Double Header, 1973, dk bl, M...................................$250.00
Double Header, 1973, dk bl, MIP $700.00
Double Header, 1973, lt bl, M....................................$300.00
Double Header, 1973, lt bl, MIP.................................$650.00
Double Vision, 1973, dk bl, M....................................$150.00
Double Vision, 1973, dk gr, M....................................$250.00
Double Vision, 1973, fluorescent lime gr, engine exposed in back, M $300.00
Double Vision, 1973, fluorescent lime gr, engine exposed in back, MIP..$600.00
Double Vision, 1973, lt bl or red, M, ea $250.00
Double Vision, 1973, lt gr, M....................................$250.00
Dump Truck, 1970, Heavyweights, orange, MIP.............$165.00
Dump Truck, 1970, Heavyweights, purple, MIP $175.00
Dump Truck, 1982, yel, MIP $10.00
Dumpin' A, 1983, gray w/chrome motor, M..................$65.00
Dumpin' A, 1983, gray w/gray motor, M......................$15.00
Dune Daddy, 1973, dk bl or red, M $100.00
Dune Daddy, 1973, fluorescent pk, M $375.00
Dune Daddy, 1973, lt gr, M.......................................$150.00
Dune Daddy, 1973, red, M...$100.00
Dune Daddy, 1973, yel or lemon yel, M $150.00

Dune Daddy, 1973, yel or lemon yel, MIP.....................$400.00
El Rey Special, 1974, dk bl, M...................................$400.00
El Rey Special, 1974, dk bl, MIP................................$750.00
El Rey Special, 1974, dk gr, M.....................................$80.00
El Rey Special, 1974, dk gr, MIP................................$150.00
El Rey Special, 1974, gr, M..$75.00
El Rey Special, 1974, gr, MIP.....................................$175.00
El Rey Special, 1974, lt bl, M.....................................$850.00
El Rey Special, 1974, lt bl, MIP................................$1,500.00
Emergency Squad, 1982, red, MIP................................$50.00
Ferrari 512P, 1973, lt bl, M.......................................$475.00
Ferrari 512S, 1972, red, M..$200.00
Fire Chief Cruiser, 1970, red, M...................................$50.00
Fire Chief Cruiser, 1970, red, MIP $125.00
Fire Eater, 1977, red w/yel & blk tampo, blk-wall tires, M..$20.00
Fire Eater, 1977, red w/yel & blk tampo, blk-wall tires, MIP....$50.00
Fire Eater, 1977, red w/yel & blk tampo, M $45.00
Fire Eater, 1977, red w/yel & blk tampo, MIP...............$100.00
Firebird Funny Car, 1989, yel w/orange, blk & bl tampo, MIP ..$5.00
Flame Stopper, 1988, red, MIP...................................$10.00
Ford J-Car, 1968, Antifreeze, US, M...........................$250.00
Ford J-Car, 1968, red, US, M......................................$50.00
Ford J-Car, 1968, wht enamel, Hong Kong, M $95.00
Formula Fever, 1983, yel, MIP....................................$10.00
Formula PACK, 1976, blk, M.......................................$75.00
Formula PACK, 1976, blk, MIP...................................$135.00
Formula PACK, 1978, blk, M.......................................$20.00
Formula 5000, 1976, wht, M $40.00
Formula 5000, 1976, wht, MIP....................................$80.00
Funny Money, 1977, gray, blk-wall tires, MIP.................$50.00
Funny Money, 1977, gray, MIP....................................$50.00

Hot Wheels
• • • • • • • •
Dump Truck, 1970, Heavy-weights, copper, MIP, $140.00
(Photo courtesy Jack Clark and Robert P. Wicker)

Hot Wheels
• • • • • • • •
Ferrari 512S, 1973 Shell promotional, fluorescent pink, MIP, $245.00.
(Photo courtesy Jack Clark and Robert P. Wicker)

Hot Wheels

Funny Money, 1974, plum, M, $85.00. (Photo courtesy Jack Clark and Robert P. Wicker)

Hot Wheels

Grass Hopper, 1974, light green, M, $60.00.
(Photo courtesy Jack Clark and Robert P. Wicker)

Hot Wheels

Hiway Robber, 1973, flourescent pink, EX, $175.00. (Photo courtesy Worldwide Diecast Toy Auctions on LiveAuctioneers.com)

Hot Wheels

Lotus Turbine, 1969, Grand Prix, olive, blue-tinted windows, Hong Kong only, M, $65.00.
(Photo courtesy Jack Clark and Robert P. Wicker)

Grass Hopper, 1971, lt gr, M................................. $100.00

Grass Wheels, 1975, lt gr w/bl & orange 'Grass Hopper' tampo, M $100.00

Gremlin Grinder, 1975, dk gr, Herfy's logo on sides, M.. $350.00

Gremlin Grinder, 1975, dk gr, M............................$65.00
Gremlin Grinder, 1975, gr, M................................$45.00
Gulch Stepper, 1985, yel w/tan roof, mc tampo, MIP........$10.00
Gulch Stepper, 1987, red, MIP...............................$22.00
Gun Slinger, 1975, lt olive, M...............................$40.00
Hairy Hauler, 1971, magenta, M $55.00
Hairy Hauler, 1971, salmon pk, M $165.00
Heavy Chevy, 1970, Spoilers, gr, M $125.00
Heavy Chevy, 1970, Spoilers, orange, M $175.00
Heavy Chevy, 1970, Spoilers, purple w/blk roof, M........$850.00
Heavy Chevy, 1974, lt gr, M...............................$1,200.00
Heavy Chevy, 1974, yel, M...................................$175.00
Hiway Robber, 1973, dk gr, M..............................$250.00
Hiway Robber, 1973, dk gr, MIP...........................$600.00
Hot Bird, 1980, bl w/orange & yel tampo, M...............$75.00
Hot Heap, 1968, orange, Hong Kong, M $80.00
Hot Heap, 1968, orange, Hong Kong, MIP...............$175.00
Hot Heap, 1968, orange, US, M.............................$50.00
Hot Heap, 1968, orange, US, MIP.........................$150.00
Hummer, 1990s, beige camo, M...............................$8.00
Hummer, 1990s, beige camo, MIP...........................$10.00
Ice T, 1971, yel, M $60.00
Ice T, 1971, yel, MIP.......................................$200.00
Indy Eagle, 1969, aqua, M $40.00
Indy Eagle, 1969, olive, M..................................$90.00
Inferno, 1976, yel, M...$60.00
Inside Story, 1979, gray w/red, yel & bl tampo, M............$15.00
Jack Rabbit Special, 1970, wht w/blk interior, clear windshield, US, M..$40.00
Jet Threat, 1971, red, M $150.00
Jet Threat, 1971, yel, M....................................$90.00
Jet Threat, 1976, purple, M $200.00
King 'Kuda, 1970, bl, M...................................$125.00
King 'Kuda, 1970, bl, MIP.................................$350.00
Large Charge, 1975, Super Chromes, blk, orange & yel in tampo, M $45.00
Letter Getter, 1977, wht (redline variation only available in the Truckin' Machines Gift Set), M $550.00
Letter Getter, 1977, wht, blk-wall tires, M................$25.00
Light-My-Firebird, 1970, Spoilers, red, MIP $225.00
Lola GT 70, 1969, Grand Prix, dk gr, Hong Kong, MIP....$80.00
Lola GT 70, 1969, Grand Prix, dk gr, US, MIP $75.00
Lotus Turbine, 1969, Grand Prix, copper, bl-tinted windows, Hong Kong only, MIP $125.00
Lowdown, 1977, gold chrome, blk-wall tires, M $35.00
Lowdown, 1977, gold chrome, red-line tires, M.............$50.00
Mantis, 1970, hot pk, Hong Kong, MIP.....................$300.00
Mantis, 1970, hot pk, US, MIP.............................$200.00
Maserati Mistral, 1969, gr, M..............................$100.00
Maserati Mistral, 1969, gr w/blk roof, M.................$130.00
Maserati Mistral, 1969, red, MIP.........................$300.00
Maserati Mistral, 1969, red w/blk roof, MIP $300.00
Mazda MX-5 Miata, 1992, yel, M.............................$5.00
Mean Machine, 1970, Rumblers, MOC $175.00
Mercedes-Benz C-11, 1972, lt gr, M $125.00
Mercedes-Benz SL, 1991, MIP..............................$10.00
Mighty Mantis, 1970, lime-yel, US, M $125.00
Mighty Maverick, 1970, aqua w/blk interior, US, M......$125.00

Mighty Maverick, 1970, aqua w/blk interior & blk roof, Hong Kong, M $250.00

Mighty Maverick, 1970, orange w/brn interior, Hong Kong, M $250.00

Minitrek 1983, wht, M $95.00

Mod Quad, 1970, magenta, Hong Kong, M $125.00

Mod Quad, 1970, magenta, US, M $125.00

Mongoose (Funny Car), 1970, Mongoose vs Snake, red, M .. $90.00

Mongoose (Funny Car), 1970, Mongoose vs Snake, red, MIP $300.00

Monte Carlo Stocker, 1979, dk bl, M $60.00

Moving Van, 1970, metallic gr w/blk interior & gray trailer, M $75.00

Mustang Stocker, 1976, Super Chromes, red, wht & bl tampo, M $100.00

Mustang Stocker, 1976, Super Chromes, red, wht & bl tampo, MIP $225.00

Mutt Mobile, 1971, aqua, M $65.00

Mutt Mobile, 1971, bl, M $100.00

Mutt Mobile, 1994, metallic magenta, MIP $10.00

Neet Streeter, 1976, lt bl, MIP $100.00

Nitty Gritty Kitty, 1970, Spoilers, bl, MIP $300.00

Odd Job, 1973, lemon yel, M $250.00

Odd Job, 1973, pk, M $450.00

Olds 442, 1971, purple, M $4,000.00

Olds 442, 1971, yel, M $475.00

Omni 024, 1981, gray, unpnt base, MIP $10.00

Open Fire, 1972, bl, M $800.00

Open Fire, 1972, gold, M $450.00

Open Fire, 1972, magenta, M $450.00

Open Fire, 1972, red, M $750.00

P-911, 1988, blk, np tampo, M $10.00

Packin' Pacer, 1980, orange, MIP $10.00

Paddy Wagon (Police 3), 1973, dk bl, M $90.00

Peeping Bomb, 1970, aqua w/chrome headlights, Hong Kong, M $75.00

Peeping Bomb, 1970, aqua w/chrome headlights, US, M .. $50.00

Peeping Bomb, 1970, orange w/chrome headlights, US, M .. $75.00

Peeping Bomb, 1970, orange w/orange headlights, US, M .. $450.00

Peeping Bomb, 1970, yel, US, M $50.00

Peterbilt Dump Truck, 1983, yel, MIP $10.00

Peugeot 205 Rallye, 1989, wht w/#2 tampo MIP $15.00

Pit Crew Car, 1971, wht, M $150.00

Poison Pinto, 1976, lt gr, M $50.00

Porsche Targa Christmas Car, 1996, red w/Santa & passenger, MIP $30.00

Porsche 911, 1976, Super Chromes, M $40.00

Porsche 959, 1991, yel, Getty promo, MIP $10.00

Power Plower Cabover, 1990, blk, tandem axle, M $10.00

Pro Circuit #2, 1993, wht w/'Texaco' logo, gray Pro Circut Indy wheels, NM+ $6.00

Prowler, 1978, Super Chrome, M $40.00

Python, 1968, brn, US, MIP $300.00

Python, 1968, gold, Hong Kong, MIP $200.00

Python, 1968, purple, US, M $85.00

Quik Trik, 1984, metallic magenta, M $5.00

Ranger Rig (Dept of Agriculture/Forest Service), 1975, dk gr, MIP $100.00

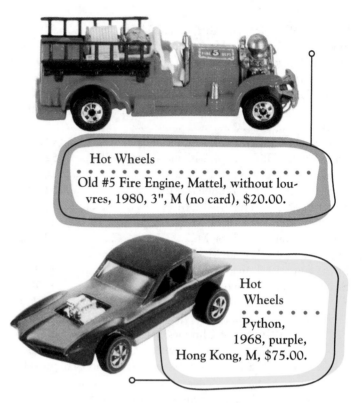

Hot Wheels
• • • • • • • • • • • •
Old #5 Fire Engine, Mattel, without louvres, 1980, 3", M (no card), $20.00.

Hot Wheels
• • • • • • •
Python, 1968, purple, Hong Kong, M, $75.00.

Rapid Transit School Bus, 1984, yel, MIP $7.00

Rear Engine Snake, 1972, Mongoose vs Snake, yel, M .. $250.00

Rear Engine Snake, 1972, Mongoose vs Snake, yel, MIP .. $70.00

Red Baron, 1973, red, MIP $250.00

Renault 5 Turbo, 1991, bl w/yel, orange & wht tampo, MIP .. $8.00

Revolution, Rumblers, 1970, MOC $125.00

Road Torch, 1987, red w/blk, wht & yel #9 tampo, MIP .. $10.00

Rock Buster, 1976, yel, MIP $25.00

Rock Buster, 1977, Super Chrome, M $20.00

Rocket-Bye-Baby, 1971, aqua, M $80.00

Rocket-Bye-Baby, 1971, gold, M $160.00

S'Cool Bus, 1971, Heavyweights, yel, M $375.00

Sand Crab, 1970, magenta, US, MIP $130.00

Sand Crab, 1970, red, Hong Kong, M $125.00

Sand Crab, 1970, red, Hong Kong, MIP $250.00

Sand Crab, 1970, red, US, M $50.00

Sand Crab, 1970, red, US, MIP $125.00

Second Wind, 1977, wht, blk-wall tires, MIP $65.00

Second Wind, 1977, wht, MIP $150.00

Sheriff Patrol, 1990, blk, MIP $10.00

Short Order, 1971, gold w/blk interior, M $80.00

Short Order, 1971, magenta, M $400.00

Show Hoss II, 1977, lemon yel, blk-wall tires, MIP $75.00

Show Hoss II, 1977, yel, blk-wall tires, MIP $75.00

Show Hoss II, 1977, yel, MIP $750.00

Silhouette, 1968, creamy pk, Hong Kong, M $150.00

Silhouette, 1968, creamy pk, US, M $150.00

Silhouette, 1968, pk w/wht interior, M $250.00

Six Shooter, 1971, aqua, M $100.00

Six Shooter, 1971, aqua, MIP $225.00

Six Shooter, 1971, magenta, M $250.00

Snake, 1994, metal-flake gr, MIP $15.00

Snorkle, 1971, Heavyweights, purple, M $250.00

Spider-Man, 1979, blk, M $15.00

Splittin' Image, 1969, aqua or gold, MIP $95.00

Splittin' Image, 1969, bl, MIP $100.00

Splittin' Image, 1969, gr or red, MIP $90.00

Spoiler Sport, 1980, gr w/blk, yel & dk red tampo, 1 lg window, MIP $15.00

State Police Cruiser, 1974, wht, metal base, M $100.00

State Police Cruiser, 1974, wht, metal base, MIP $200.00

Sting Rod, 1988, olive, MIP $20.00

Straight Away, 1970, Rumblers, MIP $100.00

Street Beast, 1991, red w/wht, MIP $25.00

Street Snorter, 1973, dk bl, M $225.00

Street Snorter, 1973, lt bl, M $275.00

Strip Teaser, 1971, gold, M $150.00

Strip Teaser, 1971, magenta, M $300.00

Sugar Caddy, 1971, Spoilers, red, MIP $250.00

Super Van, 1976, Super Chromes, yel & red tampo, blk plastic chassis, M $45.00

Super Van, 1976, Super Chromes, yel & red tampo, blk plastic chassis, MIP $75.00

Super Van, 1976, Super Chromes, yel & red tampo, chrome plastic chassis, M $50.00

Super Van, 1976, Super Chromes, yel & red tampo, chrome plastic chassis, MIP $75.00

Superfine Turbine, 1973, dk bl or red, M $450.00

SWAT Van Scene, 1979, dk bl, M $15.00

Sweet 16, 1973, fluorescent lime gr, M $225.00

Sweet 16, 1973, red, M $250.00

T-Bird Stocker, 1996, red & wht Bill Elliot car, Kellogg's promo, MIP $15.00

T-4-2, 1971, bl, MIP $215.00

T-4-2, 1971, lime yel, MIP $175.00

Tall Rider, 1985, grape, MIP $10.00

Team Trailer, 1971, Heavyweights, red, M $140.00

Thing, 1979, dk bl, M $15.00

Thor Van, 1979, yel, M $12.00

Thunderstreak, 1989, bl, Kraco, MIP $10.00

Top Eliminator, 1974, bl, M $125.00

Top Eliminator, 1974, dk bl, M $90.00

Torino Stocker, 1975, red, M $75.00

Torino Stocker, 1975, red, MIP $150.00

Torino Stocker, 1979, blk w/yel, orange & wht #3 tampo, M ... $25.00

Tough Customer, 1975, olive, MIP $75.00

Tow Truck, 1970, Heavyweights, aqua or bl, MIP $125.00

Tow Truck, 1970, Heavyweights, gr, M $75.00

Tri-Baby, 1970, aqua, Hong Kong, M $100.00

Tri-Baby, 1970, aqua, US, M $125.00

Tri-Baby, 1970, rose, US, M $50.00

Tricar X8, 1988, yel, MIP $10.00

Turbo Heater, 1986, magenta, MIP $15.00

Turbo Streak, Real Riders, 1983, yel, gray hubs, MIP $25.00

Turbo Streak, 1988, wht, M $10.00

Turbo Streak, 1996, dk bl, Union 76 promo, M $6.00

Turbofire, 1969, rose, M $35.00

Turismo, 1981, red, MIP $10.00

Turismo, 1983, yel, MIP $10.00

Twin Mill, 1969, aqua, M $40.00

Twin Mill, 1969, olive, M $100.00

Twin Mill, 1969, yel, M $50.00

Vega Bomb, 1975, lt gr, M, minimum value $900.00

Vega Bomb, 1975, lt gr, MIP, minimum value $1,500.00

Vega Bomb, 1975, orange, MIP $200.00

Volkswagen, 1975, orange w/wht, yel & blk striped tampo on hood, roof & back, unpnt metal base, MIP $1,000.00

Volkswagen Beach Bomb, 1969, bl, M $250.00

Volkswagen Beach Bomb, 1969, red, M $325.00

Waste Wagon, 1971, Heavyweights, bl, MIP $225.00

What-4, 1971, aqua or gr, M $100.00

Whip Creamer, 1970, purple, Hong Kong, M $150.00

Whip Creamer, 1994, dk metal-flake red, MIP $5.00

Xploder, 1973, lt bl or dk bl, M $150.00

MISCELLANEOUS

Action City Playset, 1969, yel, EX+ $50.00

Autorama, 1970, MIB $250.00

Bad to the Bone Watch, 1994, blk, MIB $15.00

Button, Beatnik Bandit, metal, NM $8.00

Button, Cement Mixer, metal, NM+ $5.00

Button, Classic '31 Ford Woody, metal, NM $5.00

Button, Custom Barracuda, metal, NM $5.00

Button, Jet Threat, plastic, M $10.00

Button, Racer Ring, metal, NM+ $8.00

Button, S'Cool Bus, plastic, rare, NM $10.00

Button, Short Order, plastic, M $4.00

Button, Strip Tease, plastic, NM+ $4.00

Case, 12-car, 1969, yel w/red car on front, NM $20.00

Case, 12-car pop-up, 1968, orange w/name on front, cars on back, EX $35.00

Hot Wheels

Street Eater, 1975, yellow, MIP, $400.00. (Photo courtesy Jack Clark and Robert P. Wicker)

Hot Wheels

Volkswagen, 1975, orange, M, $550.00. (Photo courtesy Jack Clark and Robert P. Wicker)

Case, 24-car, 1969, yrl w/wht & bl cars on front, adjustable, EX . $30.00

Case, 24-car, 1975, bl w/wht trays, Porsche 917, Super Van & Emergency Squad on front, NM $40.00

Case, 48-car, 1969, yel, adjustable, M $50.00

Case, 72-car, 1970, blk w/snake & Mongoose on front, EX .$40.00

City Burger Stand, aqua mini truck, MIB $30.00

City Machines, 1982, set of 6, MIB...................................$45.00

Club Kit, issued w/Boss Hoss, Heavy Chevy or King Kuda cars, unused, MIB (sealed) $285.00

Coloring Book, Whitman #1052, 1970, unused, EX..........$28.00

Competition Pak, 1968, MIB (sealed) $25.00

Crossover Pak, 1969, 21" L, MIB (sealed).........................$55.00

Cutoff Canyon Set, 1975, MIB............................... $150.00

Dual-Lane Lap Counter, 1968, MIB....................................$10.00

Dual-Lane Rod Runner Hand-Shift Power Booster, 1970, MIB. $35.00

Flyin' Circus, 1971, EXIB $450.00

Funny Car Gift Pak, 1991, MIB $30.00

Gran Toros Chevy Astro 11, 1970, gray, complete, NM.. $125.00

Gran Toros Match Race Set, 1970, complete, MIB........ $575.00

Hot Curves Race Action Track Set, 1968, MIB (no cars) ..$150.00

Hot Wheels Factory, 1970, MIB.................................. $200.00

Jigsaw Puzzle, Whitman, 1970s, 100 pcs, MIB $25.00

Pop-Up Service Station, 1968, MIB....................................$75.00

Pop-Up Speed Shop, 1968, MIB $75.00

Road King Highway Drive-Ins, 1974, MIB $250.00

Sizzlers Laguna Oval Set, complete, MIB...................... $250.00

Hot Wheels

Bridge 3-Pak, 1970, track accessory, three bridge sections, M, $45.00. (Photo courtesy Jack Clark and Robert P. Wicker)

Hot Wheels

Ontario Trio, 1971, M, $200.00 (plus price of cars that came with set). (Photo courtesy Jack Clark and Robert P. Wicker)

Hot Wheels

Bug Bite Set, 1972, $125.00 (plus price of car that came with set). (Photo courtesy Jack Clark and Robert P. Wicker)

Hot Wheels

Super-Charger Speed Test Set, 1970, M, $225.00 (plus price of car that came with set). (Photo courtesy Jack Clark and Robert P. Wicker)

Hot Wheels

Hazard Hill Race Set, 1970, M, $550.00 (plus price of car that came with set). (Photo courtesy Jack Clark and Robert P. Wicker)

Hot Wheels

Thundershift 500, version 2, 1975, $125.00 (plus price of cars that came with set). (Photo courtesy Jack Clark and Robert P. Wicker)

Speed Stunter Set, 1974, MIB...........................$125.00
Sto & Go Baywatch, MIB $25.00
Sto & Go Fix & Fill Center, MIB $25.00
Strip Action Set, 1969, MIB (sealed) $125.00

Super-Charger Double Action Set, 1969, MIB (no cars). $300.00
Super-Charger Rally 'N Freeway Set, 1968, EXIB $450.00
Talking Service Center, 1969, complete, scarce, NM.....$100.00
Tune-Up Tower, NMIB.................................$125.00

Housewares

Little girls used to love to emulate their mothers and pretend to sew and bake, sweep, do laundry, and iron (gasp!). They imagined what fun it would be when they were big like mommy. Those little gadgets they played with are precious collectibles today, and any child-size houseware item is treasured, especially those from the 1940s and 1950s. If you're interested in learning more we recommend *Toy and Miniature Sewing Machines* by Glenda Thomas; *Encyclopedia of Children's Sewing Collectibles* by Darlene J. Gengelbach; and *Collector's Guide to Housekeeping Toys, 1870 – 1970*, by our advisor Margaret Wright.

CARRIAGES AND STROLLERS

Canoe-Shape w/Parasol, brn wicker type w/4 wooden spoke wheels, bent wood hdl, silk-type parasol, 58x50" L, EX...........$3,000.00
Pressed Steel Buggy, wht rubber wheels, wire hdl, 9" L, Wyandotte, EXIB...................................$350.00

Tin w/Embossed Wicker Design, folding top, 4 spoke wheels, 6", EX $250.00
Wicker Buggy, metal frame, 4 spoke wheels, scrolled metal hdl w/ wooden grip, parasol on wire holder above seat, VG ..$250.00
Wicker Buggy, metal frame, 4 spoke wheels, swinging hood, corduroy interior, med brn, G+...........................$100.00
Wicker Chair Type w/Scrolled Arms, 2 lg wooden spoke wheels & 2 sm wheels, curved hdl, 27", G $250.00
Wicker Sleigh Type w/Scroll Design, 2 lg spoke wheels & 2 sm wheels, curved hdl, 36" L, Ex.......................$500.00
Wood Ellis Style 3-Wheeler w/Canvas Fold-Down Top, 31" L, VG..$100.00
Wood Pram w/Wicker Strapped Sides, 4 lg metal strapped wooden spoke wheels, curved hdl, w/bedding, 34" L, VG..........$100.00
Wood Sleigh Body w/Velvet Upholstered Seat, CI scroll work on runners, turned wood hdl, 31x25", VG.................$225.00
Wood Surry Type w/Red Fringed Top, upholstered seat, wooden spoke wheels, 25" L, VG $850.00

CLEANING AND LAUNDRY

Clothes Drying Rack, wood fold-out type, 12", American, 1915, EX...$35.00
Doll Pin Clothesline & Pin Set, rayon line w/plastic clothespins, Hoflion, 1950s, unused, NMIB $25.00
Doll-E-Do Dish Set, w/dish pan & drainer, Ajax can, box of Vel, Brillo box, etc, Amsco, 1950s, EX+................$85.00
Doll-E Housekeeper Set, 14-pc set w/sweeper, broom, mop, bucket & cleaning products in cabinet, Amsco, 1950s, EX+.......$200.00
Iron, electric, Wolverine #24A or #25A, 1940, NMIB, ea .$75.00
Ironing Board & Iron, Sunny Suzy, litho tin, Wolverine-Spang, 1970s, EX...$50.00
Ironing Set, Little Sweetheart, w/iron, clothesline & 6 clothespins, Wolverine #295, unused, MIB (cut-out doll/clothes).......$75.00
Kidd-E-Kitchen Set, w/dish pan, drainer, towel, dishes, apron, flatware, etc, Amsco, 1950s, complete, NMIB $175.00
Laundry Set, Mickey Mouse, litho tin tub w/scrub board & clothesline stand, NMIB.........................$450.00
Laundry Set, Mickey Mouse, litho tin tub w/scrub board & clothesline stand, VGIB.........................$275.00
Laundry Set, Three Little Pigs, litho tin tub w/scrub board, Ohio Art, 5½", VG $150.00

Housewares, Carriages and Strollers

Wicker Auto Carriage, with black cloth top and side lanterns, spoke wheels, 36" long, attributed to Heywood-Wakefield Co., EX, $2,500.00.
(Photo courtesy Bertoia Auctions on LiveAuctioneers.com)

Housewares, Carriages and Strollers

Wire Buggy, with dolls and fabric insert, 6½", Germany, 1920, VG, $650.00. (Photo courtesy Noel Barrett Antiques & Auctions Ltd. on LiveAuctioneers.com)

Sweeper, Bissell Little Queen, 1957, EX $50.00

Sweeper Set, Golden Girl Carpet Sweeper, w/sweeper, dustpan, apron & broom, 1960s, NMIB.......................................**$65.00**

Washing Machine, Dick Tracy, litho tin, Kalon Redo Corp, EXIB $100.00

Washing Machine, Dolly's Washer, litho tin, crank-op, 9", Chein, EXIB.. $300.00

Washing Machine, Dolly's Washer, litho tin, crank-op, 9", Chein, VG.. $125.00

Washing Machine, Maytag ringer type, 9", Hubley, 1940s, EX+ $650.00

Washing Machine, Mickey & Minnie Mouse, litho tin, 3-legged, lid w/blk knob, electric, 9", VG $175.00

Washing Machine, Three Little Pigs, litho tin, crank-op, 9", Chein, EX $450.00

Wash Tub & Washboard, Mickey Mouse & Minnie graphics, 2x5½" dia tub, 5" washboard, Ohio Art, 1930s, VG+ . $135.00

COOKING AND KITCHENWARE

Automatic Dollee Blender, b/o, EXIB $75.00

Baking Set, Bake-A-Cake Set, Wolverine, MIB............. $100.00

Baking Set, Betty Jane, 9-c clear glass set w/covered casserole, 4 custards, pie plate, etc, Glasbake, 1940s, EXIB $150.00

Baking Set, Busy Baker Pastry Set, Transogram, 1957, complete, MIB... $250.00

Baking Set, Cake Box Set, litho tin, Blue Delph motif, Wolverine #260, 1940s, complete, EXIB $225.00

Baking Set, Cinderella Pastry Set, w/baking utensils & scale, Peerless Playthings, 1950s, complete, EXIB....................$90.00

Baking Set, Junior Chef Cake Mix Set, Argo Industries, 1956, complete & unused, NMIB...................................... $100.00

Baking Set, Sunny Suzy Bake-A-Cake, w/hand beater, wooden board, measuring spoons, bowl, etc, Wolverine, complete, EXIB $100.00

Baking Set, Sunny Suzy, 7-pc set marked Fire-King Oven Glass, Wolverine #260, complete, EXIB $140.00

Betty Crocker Mini-Wave Oven, Kenner, NMIB.............$50.00

Housewares, Cleaning and Laundry

Sweeper, Ohio Art, lithographed tin, Donald Duck and Minnie Mouse, 1930s, $275.00 to $400.00.
(Photo courtesy David Longest)

Housewares, Cleaning and Laundry

Washer-Dryer, Sparkle Bright, pressed steel, pink, 10", Structo, EX+IB, $130.00.

Housewares, Cooking and Kitchenware

Coffee Mill, Juvenile, Arcade, wooden with paper lithograph in construction, 4" square, VG+, $165.00. (Photo courtesy Randy Inman Auctions)

Housewares, Cleaning and Laundry

Washing Machine, Mickey Mouse, lithographed tin, crank-operated, Ohio Art, without wringer, VG, $300.00. (Photo courtesy David Longest)

Housewares, Cooking and Kitchenware

Food Chopper, nickel-plated cast iron, embossed with 'AC' logo, 5", Arcade, NM, $60.00. (Photo courtesy Arneson Auctions Service on LiveAuctioneers.com)

Cabinet, Little Miss Structo Corner Cabinet, PS, pk, 12", EX+IB $100.00

Cabinet, Little Miss Structo Counter-Top, PS, pk, w/top shelves, 11", MIB $85.00

Eggbeater, A&J (label reads Baby Bingo No 68...,) or Betty Taplin, EX, ea $25.00

Granite Ware Set, 18-pc gray set w/pots, pans, colander, ladles, grater, etc, EX $60.00

Kitchen Set, litho tin, 4 canisters, 'Pastry Board,' 'Cookie Sheet,' rolling pin, 3 bowls, 2 plates, Ohio Art, EX $200.00

Pan Set, aluminum, w/coffeepot, tube cake pan, roaster, skillet, 2 saucepans, dbl boiler, 1930s, EX+ $85.00

Pan Set, Revere Ware, 12 pcs, 1950s, EX+ $150.00

Percolator, metal w/emb motif such as Cinderella, Bo Peep, or Three Little Kittens, Mirro, 1950s, EX, ea $20.00

Refrigerator, metal w/2 doors, food lithoed on inside of bottomd oor, wht w/red hdls, 13½", Wolverine, EX (no food)......$50.00

Sink, lithoed tin, footed base, tall back w/lithoed glassware & shelves, red & cream, 10x11x6", Wolverine, 1930s, EX $65.00

Sink 'n Stove Combination (Holiday), tin, pk, b/o, running water, 6½x8" to 11" L, TN/Japan, 1950s, MIB $275.00

Stove, Bird, blk CI, plain base w/emb legs, nickel top plate, stovepipe, 10½", VG $200.00

Stove, Charm, NP CI, backshelf & stovepipe, 5", Grey Iron, G $100.00

Stove, Eagle, NP CI, name on oven door, ornate casting, short legs, stove pipe, 18½" L, VG $230.00

Stove, Globe, Kenton, CI, 18", EX $800.00

Stove, Karr Range Co, bl enamel w/NP feet & trim, CI burners, back shelf, 21½x13x10", EXIB $6,325.00

Stove, Little Chef, wht metal, 13x13x7", Ohio Art, 1950s, EX+ $150.00

Stove, Little Eva, blk CI w/3 removable legs, low front plate emb T Southard, 14" L, early rpnt $925.00

Stove, Little Miss Structo, PS, pk, 11½" L, MIB............. $150.00

Stove, Little Orphan Annie, electric, 9x10x5½", Marx, 1930s, EX+ $125.00

Stove, Marvel, CI, ornate casting, short legs, stove pipe, w/ assorted accessories, 20" L, VG $315.00

Stove, Union, ornate casting w/short legs, 9", F $200.00

Waffle Iron, CI, rectangular, 5½", Arcade, VG $100.00

Waffle Iron, CI, rnd w/CI hdl & top & bottom wooden hdls, 8" L (w/hdl), Arcade, VG+ $125.00

FURNITURE

Armoire, Renaissance Revival, rosewood parquetry veneer, mirrored door, bottom drawer, footed, 13½x10x6", VG ... $275.00

Bed, Renaissance Revival style w/marquetry inlay on bedposts & siderails, w/mattress & bedspread, rosewood, 18" L, G. $100.00

Chair, armless dk wood side chair w/open kidney-shaped bentwood back & wicker crosshatch seat, VG $50.00

Chair, Lolling or Martha Washington style, mahogany w/patterened silk upholstery & decorative braid, 12½", VG. $125.00

Chest, English, bottom has 3 drawers w/wht rnd knobs, top has 2 doors w/rope-patterened trim, footed, 14", VG $150.00

Chest of Drawers, Regency-style mahogany 4-drawer w/rnd brass pulls, bracket feet, no mirror, 13½x12½x6", VG $50.00

Chest of Drawers, 5 drawers w/top double drawers, lg bottom drawer, ball feet, dk pine & maple w/brass knobs, 19", EX $100.00

Cradle, red-pnt wood w/spindle sides, blk striping, arched ends, slat board bottom, 21" L, VG...$90.00

Housewares, Cooking and Kitchenware

Stove, Favorite, 11½", NM, $3,000.00. (Photo courtesy Morphy Auctions on LiveAuctioneers.com)

Housewares, Cooking and Kitchenware

Stove, Spirit Fired, tin, with backplate and stovepipe, three burners, accessories, 10½x9", Germany, VG+, $350.00. (Photo courtesy Noel Barrett Antiques & Auctions Ltd. on LiveAuctioneers.com)

Housewares, Furniture

Patio Furniture, for 8" dolls, Strombecker, 1950, EXIB, $175.00. (Photo courtesy McMasters Harris Auction Co.)

Cradle, wire oval w/pillow bottom on ornate CI 4-legged frame, scrolled hanger w/2 dangling tassels, 60", VG $200.00

Desk, Davenport, more modern style w/3 side drawers, slots & drawers under lid, footed, 10", VG $375.00

Desk, Davenport, 4 drawers on 1 side, 3 drawers & 5 pigeonholes inside lid, wood w/leather writing surface, 13" H, EX . $550.00

Desk, drop front, 9 sm inner drawers & 8 slots, bracket feet, walnut w/brass drawer pulls, 18", VG $150.00

Desk, French style writing desk w/6 drawers & legs, bird's-eye maple, oak & satinwood veneer w/leather inset, 12", EX $850.00

Desk, French Tambour style, glazed cupboard & Rococo ormolu decorative mounts, animal paw feet, hinged top, 16", G .$400.00

Desk/Bookcase Combination, drop-front desk attached to bookcase w/glass door, balsa w/mahogany inlay, 14", VG ... $125.00

Dresser, bl-pnt wood w/red detail, 3 drawers, attached die-cut panel w/vertical oblong mirror, blk knobs, 24½x14", G............. $150.00

Dresser, 3-drawer w/decorative brass pulls, scrollwork-trimmed attached mirror, pine, 12", VG $50.00

Dry Sink, 19th C, 2 front doors open to reveal 2 shelves, wood w/faux grain pnt surface, 12x17x8", VG $1,200.00

Highchair, cord-type wrapping over wooden frame, open back, plain wood seat & footrest, no tray, gr tone, 28", G $140.00

Highchair, wht bentwood w/scroll design on back, knobs on back & arm ends, pillow cushion, no tray, 28x14", VG.........$50.00

Ice Cream Parlor Table & 4 Chairs, wire w/round wooden table top & seats, 17", VG $125.00

Mirror, cheval style w/elaborately turned supports & inlaid frame, rosewood, 13", F......................................$50.00

Rocking Chair, brn wicker w/gr-pnt accents, wht cushion, 26x21", VG $150.00

Rocking Chair, wicker over wooden frame, loosely woven design, wooden turned legs, med brn tone, VG....................... $100.00

Table, center, w/rnd hinged top, pedestal foot, mahogany w/satinwood birch, rosewood & walnut, 10½" dia, VG....... $100.00

Table, dining, w/4 leaves, curved legs, mahogany, 9½x14x25½" L (w/leaves), G $50.00

Table, Eastlake 4-legged pedestal w/oblong lift top that converts to a desk, polished oak, felt writing surface, 12", VG .. $475.00

Table, gate-leg w/round drop-leaf top, primitive, pine, 15x17" L, VG..$60.00

Table, hexagonal hinged top, 3-legged, mahogany w/rosewood, birch & ash inlay, 5", G... $125.00

Table & Chairs, bistro type, twisted CI w/rnd wooden table top & seats, 17" table w/2 20½" chairs, VG..........................$75.00

SEWING

Big Knitting Set, Parker Bros, 1956, complete w/instructions..$30.00

Spears Elite Edition Art Needlework, VG+IB................ $100.00

Jolly Dolly Sewing Cards, #T184, Samuel Gabriel & Co, ca 1940 ....$30.00

Junior Miss Embroidery Set, hatbox style case, Hassenfeld #1586, 1950s, complete, unused, NMIB....................................$75.00

Junior Miss Hat Shop, Advance Games millinery set #868, 1950s, complete, NMIB $100.00

Junior Miss Sewing Kit, Hassenfeld Bros #1535, complete, unused, NMIB $75.00

Housewares, Sewing

Handkerchief Set to Embroider, American Toy Works, #5, 1940s, complete, unused, NMIB, $35.00. (Photo courtesy Darlene J. Gengelbach)

Housewares, Sewing

Needlepoint Set, Transogram, 1959, complete with yarn, needle threader, and needle, MIB, $30.00. (Photo courtesy Darlene J. Gengelbach)

Housewares, Sewing

Singer Sewhandy Sewing Machine, Model #20, 1950s, MIB, $180.00. (Photo courtesy Stout Auctions on LiveAuctioneers.com)

Knitting Nancy, #6001, JW Spears & Sons, 1940, complete w/ instructions, MIB..$30.00

Modes Nouveautes Chapeau Millinery Set, complete in paper-covered wooden box w/hinged lid & clasp, VG+........ $500.00

Sew Ette Sewing Machine, Jaymar, 1950s, complete w/attachments & instructions, MIB $75.00

Sew Young, Sew Fun Pattern Kit, 1999, projects shown on TV program, EXIB..$15.00

Shirley Temple Luncheon Embroidery Set, Gabriel #311, 1960s, complete, unused, NMIB $100.00

Singer Sewing Machine, early table model, complete, EXIB (box reads 'A Singer For The Girls')................................. $200.00

Take Along Sew-Rite Sewing Machine, Hasbro #1543, 1969, complete, unused, NMIB (suitcase type).......................$75.00

Weaving Loom, #860, Concord Toy Co, 1943, complete w/ wooden shuttle, yarn & instructions............................$30.00

TABLE SERVICE

See also Character, TV, and Movie Collectibles; Disney.

Akro Agate Chiquita Dishes (My Carnival Colors), 8-pc set, MIB.. $225.00

Akro Agate Chiquita Toy Dishes, 22-pc gr set, MIB $400.00

Akro Agate Little American Maid Tea Set, 11-pc wht set w/bl decals, MIB.. $100.00

Akro Agate Little American Maid Tea Set, 17-pc Lemonade & Oxblood set, MIB.. $450.00

Akro Agate Little American Maid Tea Set, 21-pc amber Interior Panel Depression glass set, MIB................................... $175.00

Akro Agate Little American Maid Tea Set, 21-pc wht & maroon marble set, MIB.. $550.00

Akro Agate Little American Maid Tea Set, 29-pc bl, orange, yel & gr set, unused, MIB $350.00

Akro Agate Play-Time Dish Set, 19-pc bl, yel & gr set, MIB..$375.00

Akro Agate Play-Time Glass Dishes, 8-pc bl & wht marble set, MIB.. $300.00

Akro Agate Play-Time Glass Dishes, 16-pc gr Interior Panel Stacked Disc w/Darts set, MIB................................... $600.00

Akro Agate Play-Time Glass Dishes, 16-pc transparent gr set, MIB.. $225.00

Akro Agate Play-Time Glass Water Set, gr pitcher w/6 yel glasses, ribbed pattern, MIB $100.00

Akro Agate Play-Time Glass Water Set, pitcher & 6 glasses, bl, yel, gr & wht octagonal set, MIB................................ $150.00

Jeannette Junior Dishes, 14-pc Cherry Blossom Depression glass set, MIB $300.00

Marx Plastic Tea Set #2093, 44-pc mc set w/4 clear goblets & 4 clear sherbets, complete w/napkins & flatware, EXIB....$75.00

Mirro Flatware Set, 26-pc set w/knives, forks, spoons & serving pcs, 1950s, complete, EX+IB.............................$50.00

Housewares, Table Service
● ● ● ● ● ● ● ● ● ● ● ● ● ● ●
Ohio Art Tea Service, Donald Duck, 1930s, $75.00 to $100.00. Ohio Art tea tray, 1930s, $75.00 to $100.00. (Photos courtesy David Longest)

Housewares, Table Service
● ● ● ● ● ● ● ● ● ● ● ● ● ● ● ● ● ●
USA Children's Tea Set, six-piece litho-graphed tin with kitten motif, teapot with lid, two cups, two saucers, MIB, $75.00.
(Photo courtesy Livingston Auctions on LiveAuctioneers.com)

Housewares, Table Service
● ● ● ● ● ● ● ● ● ● ● ● ● ● ●
Ohio Art Tea Service, Busy Squirrel, 1938 – 1940, pieces shown came from a 31-piece set, rare, EX, $250.00. (Photo courtesy Margaret Wright)

Mirro Like Mother's Tea Set, 27-pc aluminum set w/'Three Little Kittens' emb images, 1950s, EXIB.............................. $150.00

Ohio Art Children's Tea Set, 9-pc litho tin set w/'She Loves Me She Loves Me Not' motif, artist sgn 'Elaine,' NMIB... $125.00

Ohio Art Good Morning Breakfast Set, 15-pc litho tin set w/rooster-&-sunshine motif, complete w/toaster, 1960s, EXIB.........$100.00

Ohio Art Sunshine Breakfast Set, litho tin set w/sunflower motif, complete w/toaster & fruit bowl, 1970s, EXIB $85.00

Wolverine Little Sweetheart Salad Set #253, litho tin set w/4 serving bowls, tossing fork & spoon, EXIB $75.00

MISCELLANEOUS

Doll-E-Feeder Set, divided dish, sterilizer, tongs, funnel, juicer, box off Vel, 6 bottles in rack, etc, Amsco, 1950s, EX.. $100.00

Doll-E-Feedette, 12-pc w/Gerber's Oatmeal box, Evenflo cleanser, etc, Amsco, 1950s, complete, NMIB $125.00

Doll-E-Nurser, '22-Piece Feeding Set,' 6 bottles in rack, sterilizer pot, bottle brush, etc, Amsco, 1948, MIB.................... $150.00

Little Yankee Carpenter & Joiner Set, Arcade, 1923, VG (wooden box) $225.00

My Merry Shoe Shining Set, Merry Mfg, 1950s, MIB $35.00

Popcorn Junior Machine, complete, 20", EXIB............... $225.00

Rocking Horse, for dolls, pnt compo, suspended from rods on scrolled CI rockers w/4 wheels, leather saddle, 27x25", EX..........$2,000.00

Sleigh, pnt wood w/upholstered seat, wood runners & push handle, VG... $110.00

Sno-Cone Maker, plastic snowman shape, Hasenfeld Bros, 1960s, 9½", NM $75.00

Suzy Homemaker Sweet Shoppe Soda Fountain, Topper, 1960s, MIB..$50.00

Tiny Tools Set, 4-pc garden set, NP, Arcade, 1941, MOC..$125.00

Toy Carpenter Set, NP, 5-pc, Arcade, 1941, MOC $55.00

Toy Garden Tools, 5-pc, Arcade, 1941, MOC $55.00

Typewriter, Berwin, 1940s, NMIB.............................. $175.00

Typewriter, Marx Junior Dial, litho tin, EX........................ $25.00

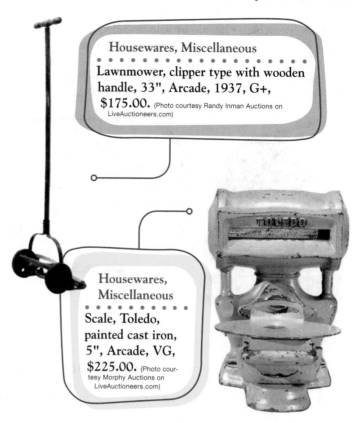

Housewares, Miscellaneous

Lawnmower, clipper type with wooden handle, 33", Arcade, 1937, G+, $175.00. (Photo courtesy Randy Inman Auctions on LiveAuctioneers.com)

Housewares, Miscellaneous

Scale, Toledo, painted cast iron, 5", Arcade, VG, $225.00. (Photo courtesy Morphy Auctions on LiveAuctioneers.com)

Jack-in-the-Boxes

A jack-in-the-box is a children's toy that essentially mimics the game peek-a-boo. The toy appears to be a closed box with a lid and a hand crank on the side. When the crank is turned, it plays a tune, typically 'Pop Goes the Weasel.' At the end of the melody, the lid pops open and out jumps a character of some sort. The first jack-in-the-boxes usually held clowns or jesters. Early jack-in-the-boxes were usually made with painted composition heads and paper lithograph on wood boxes with various motifs. Most vintage jack-in-the-boxes were made in Germany, but the toy has been adopted and produced by many companies in many countries over the years, including the U.S. The following listings are from current auctions.

Black Man, compo head w/pnt features, cloth outfit, paper litho on wood box, 5" (when opened), VG.......................... $125.00

Clown, tin litho & plastic, 1960s, $75 to....................... $125.00

Happy Hooligan, molded compo head w/pnt features, paper litho on wood box, 6½" (when opened), VG....................... $175.00

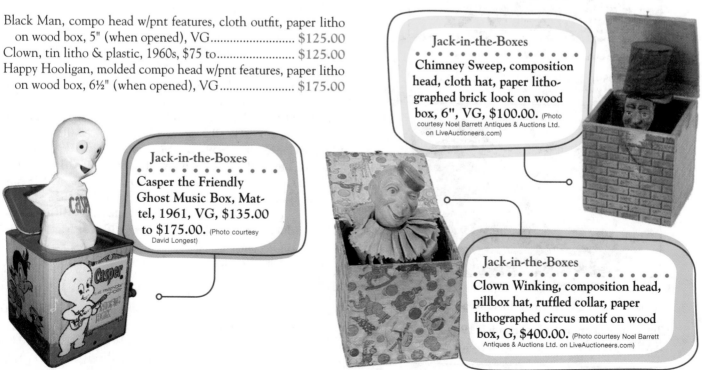

Jack-in-the-Boxes

Chimney Sweep, composition head, cloth hat, paper lithographed brick look on wood box, 6", VG, $100.00. (Photo courtesy Noel Barrett Antiques & Auctions Ltd. on LiveAuctioneers.com)

Jack-in-the-Boxes

Casper the Friendly Ghost Music Box, Mattel, 1961, VG, $135.00 to $175.00. (Photo courtesy David Longest)

Jack-in-the-Boxes

Clown Winking, composition head, pillbox hat, ruffled collar, paper lithographed circus motif on wood box, G, $400.00. (Photo courtesy Noel Barrett Antiques & Auctions Ltd. on LiveAuctioneers.com)

Jester, molded compo head, pnt features, cloth cone hat, wht goat's hair, paper litho on wood box, 7½" (when opened), VG $500.00

Pig, compo head w/pnt features, cloth outfit, paper (kids playing graphics) on wood box, 6¼" (when opened), EX $325.00

Punch & Judy, compo heads w/pnt faces, cloth outfits, mounted on springs, paper litho on wood box, 5" (when opened), VG ..$350.00

Jack-in-the-Boxes
Farm Woman, composition head in bonnet, paper lithograph with chickens on green, wood box, 6", VG, $175.00. (Photo courtesy Noel Barrett Antiques & Auctions Ltd. on LiveAuctioneers.com)

Jack-in-the-Boxes
Flipper in the Music Box, tin lithograph, Mattel, 1960s, VG, $200.00 to $300.00. (Photo courtesy David Longest)

• • • • • • • • • • Japanese and Other Tin Vehicle Replicas • • • • • • • • • •

Listed here are the model vehicles (most of which were made in Japan during the 1950s and 1960s) that were designed to realistically represent the muscle cars, station wagons, convertibles, budget models, and luxury cars that were actually being made at the time. Most are tin and many are friction or battery-operated, some have remote control. In our descriptions, all are tin unless noted otherwise. Values listed are from current auctions.

Japanese and Other Tin Vehicle Replicas
Buick (1959), TN, friction, 12", NMIB, $1,000.00. (Photo courtesy Morphy Auctions on LiveAuctioneers.com)

Japanese and Other Tin Vehicle Replicas
Chevy Impala Sport Sedan, Bandai, 1961, 11", NMIB, $400.00. (Photo courtesy Morphy Auctions on LiveAuctioneers.com)

Alfa Romeo Giuletta Sprint Veloce Coupe (1960s), Bandai, friction, 8", EX $275.00

Austin Healy 100 SIX Convertible (1958), Bandai, friction, 8", EXIB $500.00

BMW Isetta B-588 (1950s), Bandai, friction, 6½", NM+IB .$350.00

Buick Century (1958), friction, 14", VGIB..................$1,800.00

Buick LaSabre Concept Convertible (1950s), Yonezawa, friction, 8", EX+ $525.00

Buick LeSabre 4-Door Hardtop (1961), Nomura, friction, 16", NMIB (box reads 'New Buick')......................$650.00

Buick Riviera Convertible (1964), Haji, friction, 11", EX+IB (box reads Giant Door-Matic Car) $300.00

Buick Sedan (1961), Ichiko, friction, 17", NMIB........$2,750.00

Buick 2-Door (1959), MT, friction, 8", EXIB..................$275.00

Cadillac (1950), Nomura, b/o, 8½", NMIB.....................$175.00

Cadillac Convertible (1950), Nomura/Nikko, b/o, 13", NMIB.$1,750.00

Cadillac Convertible (1959), Bandai, friction, 12", NMIB...$325.00

Cadillac Convertible (1960), Yonezawa, friction, 18", EXIB.$1,300.00

Cadillac Convertible (1961), SSS, b/o, 17", EXIB $750.00

Cadillac Convertible (1963), Bandai, friction, 8", NM+IB ..$150.00

Cadillac Convertible (1965), Yonezawa, friction, 22", NMIB.$900.00

Cadillac Fleetwood (1960), Yonezawa #10798, friction, 18", VGIB $1,475.00

Cadillac Sedan (1954), Marusan, friction, 12", NMIB .$1,900.00

Cadillac Sedan (1961), Bandai, 8", MIB........................$375.00

Cadillac 2-Door (1960s), ATC, friction, 17", NMIB...$1,400.00

Celica Cobra GT, ATC, friction, 14", NMIB..................$225.00

Chevy Bel Air Station Wagon (1960s), ATC, friction, 10", VGIB $300.00

Chevy Camaro (1960s), Bandai, b/o, 13", NM+IB........$175.00

Chevy Camaro SS (1968), Nomura, friction, 11", NMIB...$375.00
Chevy Corvair (1960), Yonezawa, friction, 9", NM+IB . $300.00
Chevy Corvair (1961), Bandai, friction, 8", NM+IB...... $175.00
Chevy Corvair (1961), Ichiko, friction, 9", EX+IB $250.00
Chevy Corvette (1958), Yonezawa, friction, 10",
    EX+IB $400.00
Chevy Corvette Sting Ray (1963), Ichida, b/o, 12", EX. $225.00
Chevy Pickup (1950s), Bandai, friction, 10", EX+IB $350.00
Chevy Sedan (1954), Marusan, friction, 11", EX $750.00
Chevy Sedan (1959), TS, friction, 12", EXIB................ $850.00
Chevy 2-Door (1954), Linemar, friction, 11", EX........... $150.00
Chevy 2-Door (1954), Marusan, b/o, electric lights, 11",
    NMIB $2,750.00
Chrysler Convertible (1952), Yonezawa/Sato, friction, 10",
    NMIB $575.00
Chrysler Imperial Convertible (1959), Bandai, friction, 8",
    NMIB $150.00
Chrysler Imperial Hardtop (1959), Bandai, friction, 8",
    NM+IB $150.00
Chrysler New Yorker (1958), Alps, friction, 14", EX+ . $2,900.00
Chrysler 2-Door Hardtop (1955), Irco, friction, 8½", VG+ .. $250.00
Citreon Convertible DS19, Bandai, friction, 8", EXIB... $600.00
Dodge Sedan, TN, friction, 11", EXIB $1,400.00
Edsel, KKS, friction, 8", EXIB $400.00
Edsel, Nomura, friction, 9", NMIB............................. $475.00
Edsel Station Wagon, Nomura, friction, 10½", EX $200.00
Edsel 4-Door Hardtop, Sato, friction, 7", NMIB............. $150.00
Ferrari (1960s), Bandai, friction, 11", NMIB $450.00
Fiat 600, Bandai, friction, w/sun roof, 7", NMIB $350.00
Ford Capri GT (1970s), Ichiko, friction, 15", NM+IB... $150.00
Ford Fairlane 2-Door Hardtop (1958), Sato, friction, 8",
    NMIB $175.00
Ford Fairlane 500 Skyliner (Convertible), Cragstan, r/c, retract-
    able top, 10½", EX+IB... $300.00
Ford Falcon Station Wagon (1962), Alps, friction, woodgrain
    trim, luggage rack on roof, rear opening door, 9", NM . $150.00
Ford Flower Delivery Station Wagon (1956), Bandai, friction,
    12", VG $250.00
Ford Gyron Concept Car (1950s), Ichida, r/c, 11", NMIB...$300.00
Ford Gyron Concept Car (1960s), friction, 9", NM+IB . $400.00
Ford Mustang Convertible, Bandai/Sears, b/o, w/gear shift, 11",
    EXIB $150.00
Ford Mustang Fastback (1960s), ATC, friction, 11", NMIB.. $75.00
Ford Mustang Fastback (1960s), Taiyo, b/o, blinking lights,
    NMIB $75.00
Ford Mustang GT, Nomura, friction, w/mirrors & antenna, 15½",
    EXIB $450.00
Ford Pickup (1955), Bandai, friction, elephant decal, 12",
    EXIB...$800.00
Ford Ranchero (1957), Bandai, friction, 12", NM $250.00
Ford Skyliner Retractable (1958), Nomura, b/o, 9", NM+IB..$250.00
Ford Station Wagon (Country Sedan), TN, friction, removable
    plastic roof, 10", EXIB.. $350.00
Ford Station Wagon (Custom Ranch), Bandai, friction, 12",
    NMIB $300.00
Ford Station Wagon (1961), Ichimura, friction, 10", NMIB. $125.00
Ford T-Bird, ATC, friction, 13", EXIB $400.00
Ford T-Bird, Bandai, friction, 11", EXIB $175.00

Ford T-Bird, Ichiko, friction, 11", EXIB $300.00
Ford T-Bird (1956), Nomura, b/o, 11", NMIB $400.00
Ford T-Bird (1956), Nomura, friction, w/snap-on clear plastic
    top, 11", NM $225.00
Ford T-Bird Convertible (1964), Ichiko/Sears, friction, retract-
    able roof, 15", NMIB... $300.00
Ford T-Bird Convertible (1962), Haji, friction, 8", NMIB...$200.00
Ford 2-Door Hardtop, ATC, friction, 10", NMIB.......... $500.00
Ford 2-Door Hardtop (1954), Marusan, friction, 10", EX ...$250.00

Japanese and Other Tin Vehicle Replicas

Lincoln Sedan (1950s), Ichiko, friction, 12", NMIB, $3,750.00. (Photo courtesy Morphy Auctions on LiveAuctioneers.com)

Japanese and Other Tin Vehicle Replicas

Lotus Elan (1960s), Bandai, GT Car Series, 8½", MIB, $100.00. (Photo courtesy www.serioustoyz.com)

Ford 2-Door Hardtop (1956), Yonezawa, r/c, 12½", EX... $1,100.00
Jaguar E Type, TT, friction, 11", EXIB $200.00
Jaguar XKE Coupe (1960s), Nomura, friction, 11½", NM ..$350.00
Jaguar XK120 Convertible, Alps, friction, 6½", NMIB .. $300.00
Jaguar XK150 Convertible (1950s), Bandai, friction, 10", NM.$200.00
Jaguar 3.4 Sedan, Bandai, friction, 8", EXIB $250.00
Lincoln Continental Mark III Sedan (1959), Bandai, friction, 12", EXIB.. $5,500.00
Lincoln Sedan (1950s), Ichiko, friction, 12", EX............ $750.00
Lincoln XL-500 Sundeck Convertible Concept Car (1950s), Yonezawa, friction, 7", EX.. $500.00
Mercedes Benz Convertible (1960s), M, friction, 8", NM+IB...$275.00
Mercedes Convertible, Schuco #5503, 9", NMIB........... $450.00
Mercedes 219 Convertible (1950s), Bandai, friction, 8", EX .$1,500.00
Mercedes 220, Bandai, b/o, 10", EXIB............................ $200.00
Mercedes 220S (1960s), Bandai, friction, 10", NM $200.00
Mercedes 230 Taxi (1960s), Bandai, b/o, doors open, 10½", NMIB $150.00
Mercedes 250S Sedan (1960s), Daiya, friction, 14", NM.. $150.00
Mercedes 300 Adenaur Limosuine (1950s), Alps, b/o, 9½", NMIB $1,300.00
Mercedes 300SE (1960s), Ichiko, rider, 24", unused, MIB ...$300.00

Mercedes 300SL Convertible Coupe, Bandai, 1950s, friction, 8", NMIB $175.00
Mercury Montclair Sedan (1958), Yonezawa, friction, 11½", EX.. $200.00
MG Midget, Bandai, friction, 8", EXIB........................... $300.00
MG Midget Convertible (1950s), Yoshiya, friction, 8½", EXIB..$275.00
MGA Convertible (1950s), Terai, friction, 9½", NM..... $150.00
MGA 1600 Convertible (1950s), ATC, friction, 10", NM..$150.00
MGA 1600 Coupe (1950s), Bandai, friction, 8", NM+IB ..$225.00
MGA 1600 MKII Rally Car (1960s), Bandai, friction, 8", VG+ $175.00
Nash Cross Country Station Wagon (1954), Marusan, friction, w/luggage rail on roof, 10", EX+IB............................ $1,850.00
Nissan Gloria GL (1960s), Ichiko, friction, 16", MIB $175.00
Oldsmobile Sedan (1952), Yonezawa, friction, 10½", NMIB...$175.00
Oldsmobile Sedan (1960s), Cragstan, friction, 12", EXIB...$450.00
Oldsmobile Super 88 Pickup, Nakamura, friction, bl-tinted windows, 7", NMIB $200.00
Oldsmobile Toronado, ATC, friction, 16", NMIB $300.00
Oldsmobile Toronado (1967), Bandai, b/o, 11", MIB..... $150.00
Oldsmobile 2-Door (1959), Ichiko, friction, 13", EXIB.. $350.00
Opel Olympia Rekord (1959), Yonezawa, b/o, 11½", EX+IB...$575.00
Plymouth Belvedere, Alps, friction, 8", EXIB $500.00
Plymouth Fury (1956), Alps, b/o, 12", NM.................... $500.00
Plymouth Fury (1965), Bandai, friction, 8", NM $85.00
Plymouth Fury Convertible (1958), Bandai, friction, 8", EX... $100.00
Pontiac (1950s), KS, friction, 14", EX $750.00
Porsche Sportomatic, Takatoku, b/o, 11", NMIB............ $125.00
Rambler Classic (1961), Bandai/Frankonia Import, 1960s, 8", NMIB $115.00

Japanese and Other Tin Vehicle Replicas

Saab, Bandai, friction, 7", NMIB, $400.00. (Photo courtesy Morphy Auctions on LiveAuctioneers.com)

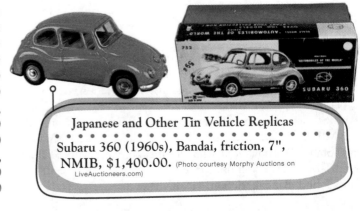

Japanese and Other Tin Vehicle Replicas

Subaru 360 (1960s), Bandai, friction, 7", NMIB, $1,400.00. (Photo courtesy Morphy Auctions on LiveAuctioneers.com)

Rambler Classic Station Wagon, Bandai, friction, 11",
  EXIB $225.00
Rambler Station Wagon w/Shasta Trailer, Bandai, friction, 21"
  overall, NM $1,100.00
Renault (1960), Yonezawa, friction, 7", NMIB............ $1,000.00
Renault Floride, ATC, friction, 9", VGIB..................... $225.00
Rolls-Royce Silver Cloud, Bandai, friction, 12", NMIB . $400.00
Rolls-Royce Silver Cloud (1960s), Yonezawa, friction, 8½",
  NM+IB $150.00

Studebaker Avanti Coupe, Bandai, 1963, friction, 8½", NM..$125.00
Toyota 2000, Ichiko, 16", EXIB.............................. $350.00
Volkswagen Beetle (1960s), Taiyo, b/o, 10", NMIB..........$75.00
Volkswagen Beetle Convertible (1960s), Nomura, b/o, visible
  lighted engine w/working pistons, 10", EX $225.00
Volkswagen Bus, Bandai, b/o, 9½", NM+IB................. $575.00
Volkswagen Sedan (Kingsize), Bandai, b/o, 15", NMIB.. $250.00
Volvo 1800ES, Ichiko, r/c, 9", NMIB......................... $450.00
Volvo 1800S, Ichiko, friction, 9", NMIB $450.00

Japanese and Other Tin Vehicle Replicas
Triumph TR-3 Convertible, friction, Bandai, 8", NMIB, $750.00.
(Photo courtesy Morphy Auctions on LiveAuctioneers.com)

Japanese and Other Tin Vehicle Replicas
Volkswagen Convertible (Lited Piston Action), Showa, battery-operated, 9", NMIB, $400.00.
(Photo courtesy Morphy Auctions on LiveAuctioneers.com)

Keystone

Though this Massachusetts company produced a variety of toys during their years of operation (ca. 1920 – late 1950s), their pressed-steel vehicles are the most collectible, and that's what we've listed here. As a rule they were very large, with some of the riders being around 30" in length.

Air Mail Plane NX-273, ride-on, 27" L, EX................. $1,500.00
Airplane (Rapid Fire Motor), 24" WS, VG $750.00
American Railway Express, #43, 26", G........................ $800.00
Circus Truck, ride-on, 26", G $2,700.00
Coast-to-Coast Bus, #84, 32", EX+ $5,300.00
Coast-to-Coast Bus, #84, 32", G............................. $1,265.00
Dairy Truck, 1930, 26", G..................................... $1,950.00
Delivery Truck, 1920s, doorless cab, 26", VG $675.00
Dump Truck, cabover, 25", G $450.00
Dump Truck, doorless cab, crank-op, 26", G $550.00
Dump Truck, doorless cab, crank-op, 26", VG............. $1,000.00
Fire Chemical Pump Truck, #57, 28", G+.................... $1,375.00
Fire Ladder Truck, #79, 31", rstr $575.00
Fire Water Tower Truck, #56, 30", EX....................... $1,200.00
Fire Water Tower Truck, #56, 30", G........................ $350.00
Hydraulic Dump Truck, 28", G................................ $975.00
Pennsylvania Railroad Coach Bus, gray & maroon, BRT w/olive
  hubs, 31", EX.. $2,000.00

Keystone, Dugan Brothers Bakery Truck, ride-on, 26", G, $2,000.00.
(Photo courtesy Morphy Auctions on LiveAuctioneers.com)

Keystone Fire Ladder Truck, 1939, ride-on, 26", EX, $2,750.00.
(Photo courtesy Morphy Auctions on LiveAuctioneers.com)

Keystone Ambulance, #73, 27", VG, $925.00. (Photo courtesy Randy Inman Auctions on LiveAuctioneers.com)

Keystone Moving Van, #58, 27", VG, $1,375.00. (Photo courtesy Morphy Auctions on LiveAuctioneers.com)

Police Patrol, #51, 27", VG $1,375.00
Sprinkler Tank Truck, #53, 27", VG $1,250.00
Steam Shovel, #46, 21", VG.. $150.00
Train Locomotive #6400, ride-on, 28", VG $400.00
Train Pullman Car No 6800, 25", NM $2,300.00
Train Tender No 6500, 18", EX $725.00
Truck Loader, #44, 18", EX.. $400.00
US Mail Truck, #45, screened van, 26", EX................. $2,500.00
US Mail Truck, #45, screened van, 26", G $800.00
Water Tower Truck, 1920s, 33", VG $850.00
Wrecker, #78, 26", VG $800.00

MISCELLANEOUS

Elevator Garage, pressed wood, 14x23", complete, GIB. $175.00
Traffic Outfit, w/electric traffic light, gas pump, auto, 2 penny-
operated parking meters, VGIB $200.00

Keystone

Sprinkler Tank Truck #53, 1920s, 27", EX, $1,725.00. (Photo courtesy Morphy Auctions on LiveAuctioneers.com)

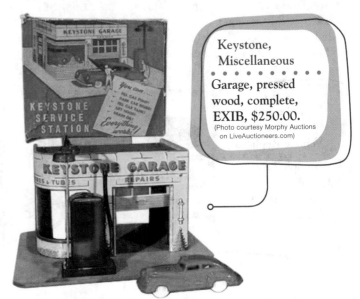

Keystone, Miscellaneous

Garage, pressed wood, complete, EXIB, $250.00. (Photo courtesy Morphy Auctions on LiveAuctioneers.com)

Keystone

Tank Department Truck, 1920s, 24", VG, $2,000.00. (Photo courtesy Morphy Auctions on LiveAuctioneers.com)

Keystone, Miscellaneous

Lumber Yard, #223, EXIB, $550.00. (Photo courtesy Morphy Auctions on LiveAuctioneers.com)

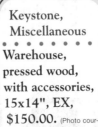

Keystone

US Army Truck, #48, 26", VG, $775.00. (Photo courtesy Morphy Auctions on LiveAuctioneers.com)

Keystone

Water Tower Fire Truck, 1939, ride-on, $9,200.00. (Photo courtesy Morphy Auctions on LiveAuctioneers.com)

Keystone, Miscellaneous

Warehouse, pressed wood, with accessories, 15x14", EX, $150.00. (Photo courtesy Morphy Auctions on LiveAuctioneers.com)

Lehmann

Lehmann toys were made in Germany as early as 1881. Early on they were sometimes animated by means of an inertia-generated flywheel; later, clockwork mechanisms were used. Some of their best-known turn-of-the-century toys were actually very racist and unflattering to certain ethnic groups. But the wonderful antics they perform and the imagination that went into their conception have made them and all the other Lehmann toys favorites with collectors today. Though the company faltered with the onset of WWI, they were quick to recover and during the war years produced some of their best toys, several of which were copied by their competitors. Business declined after WWI. Lehmann died in 1934, but the company continued for awhile under the direction of Lehmann's partner and cousin, Johannes Richter.

Advisor: Scott Smiles

Lehmann
Africa Ostrich Cart, red, G, $400.00.

Lehmann
Baldur (Taxi), EX+, $2,500.00.
(Photo courtesy James D. Julia, Inc.)

Lehmann
Duo, NMIB, $6,250.00. (Photo courtesy James D. Julia, Inc.)

Lehmann
Echo Cycle, EX, $1,500.00. (Photo courtesy James D. Julia, Inc.)

Acrobat, VG	$750.00
Adam the Porter, EX	$850.00
Adam the Porter, EX+IB	$1,950.00
Adam the Porter, NM	$1,150.00
Africa Ostrich Cart, EX+	$800.00
AHA Delivery Truck, EX	$775.00
AHA Delivery Truck, NM+IB	$4,000.00
Ajax, NM+	$1,500.00
Alabama Coon Jigger, EX	$650.00
Alabama Coon Jigger, EX+IB	$1,200.00
ALSO Auto, NM+	$650.00
AM POL, EX	$1,500.00
AM POL, G	$750.00
AM POL, NM	$2,200.00
Anxious Bride, EX	$2,000.00
Anxious Bride, VG	$1,500.00
Autin, EX	$500.00
Autobus #590, EX	$1,500.00
Autobus #590, NM	$2,500.00
Autobus #590, VG	$850.00
Autohutte (Garage) w/Galop Racer & Sedan, NM	$1,500.00
Baker & Sweep, #450, NM+IB	$6,500.00
Baker & Sweep, #450, VG+	$1,825.00
Balky Mule, EX+IB	$725.00
Balky Mule, VG	$300.00
Ballerina (Magic Ball Dancer), G	$2,500.00
Beetle, VG	$150.00
Berolina Automobile, NM	$4,300.00
Boxer, EPL #530, EX	$7,500.00
Bucking Bronco, EXIB	$1,200.00
Bucking Bronco, VG	$675.00
Buster Brown Auto, NM+	$2,200.00
Captain of Kopevnik, NM	$1,550.00
Climbing Miller, EXIB	$700.00
Climbing Monkey (Kletter-Affe), VG+IB	$175.00
Coach w/Driver, VG+	$700.00
Coco, native climbing palm tree, EX+IB	$2,000.00
Coco, native climbing palm tree, VG	$725.00
Crocodile, NM	$375.00
Dancing Sailor (Columbia), EX	$725.00
Dancing Sailor (HMS Dreadnaught), EX+IB	$1,200.00
Dancing Sailor (MARS), EXIB	$900.00
Dare Devil, EX	$500.00
Dare Devil, VG	$300.00
Duo, EX	$1,500.00
Duo, VG	$1,000.00
EHE & Co Truck, EX+	$700.00

EHE & Co Truck, EX+IB	$1,675.00
EPL-I Zeppelin, GIB	$725.00
EPL-I Zeppelin, VG	$325.00
EPL-II Zeppelin, GIB	$500.00
Express Porter, EX	$500.00
Express Porter, G	$200.00
Fala Sedan, bl & wht, rare, VG	$750.00
Flying Bird, EX+IB	$2,000.00
Futurus Peace Chime, VG	$650.00
Galop Zebra Cart, EX+IB	$350.00
Garage w/Single Sedan, VG	$450.00
Going to the Fair, NM+	$3,500.00
Gustaf the Miller, NMIB	$700.00
Gustaf the Miller, VG	$325.00
Halloh Cycle, EX+	$2,100.00
Hop Hop, EXIB	$350.00
IHI Meat Van, NM+	$3,000.00
Ito Auto, EX	$600.00
Kadi, EX	$1,200.00
Kadi, NMIB	$2,200.00
Kamerun Ostrich Cart, EX	$825.00
Lehmann Family (Couple Walking Dog), see Walking Down Broadway	
Li La Hansom Cab, EX+	$1,950.00
Lo Lo Auto, EX+	$525.00
Los Angeles Zeppelin 757, EXIB	$3,600.00
Man Da Rin, EX	$2,500.00
Mars Motorcycle, VG	$950.00

Masuyama, NM	$2,300.00
Masuyama, NMIB	$3,500.00
Masuyama, VG+	$1,200.00
Mensa, EX	$2,000.00
Mensa, NMIB	$6,000.00
Mikado Family, VG	$1,650.00
Miller, EX+IB	$725.00
Minstrel Man, flat tin figure, scarce, NM	$600.00
Miss Blondin (Tightrope Walker), EXIB	$5,000.00
Mixtum, NMIB	$5,500.00
Mixtum, VG	$800.00
Model Airplane Kit, EXIB	$300.00
Motor Car, EX	$575.00
NA-OB, EX	$300.00
Nanu, EX+	$650.00
Naughty Boy, EX	$850.00
Naughty Boy, VG	$600.00
New Century Cycle, EX+	$700.00
Nina (Cat & Mouse), EX	$2,000.00
Nu-Nu, EX+	$1,200.00
Oh My, see Alabama Coon Jigger	
Oho Auto, EX	$575.00
Paak-Paak Quack-Quack Duck Cart, EX	$500.00
Paak-Paak Quack-Quack Duck Cart, NM+IB	$1,000.00
Paddy's Dancing Pig, EX+	$1,250.00
Paddy's Dancing Pig, NMIB	$3,000.00
Panne Touring Car, EX	$700.00
Performing Sea Lion	$350.00
Peter, EX	$1,100.00
Peter, NM	$1,800.00
Playing Mice, EX	$175.00
Primus No 840, NMIB	$650.00
Rooster Cart w/Rabbit Rider, EX	$1,450.00
Royal Mail Van, EXIB	$3,200.00
Shenandoah Zeppilin, EX	$225.00
Snik-Snak, EX+IB	$6,000.00
Stiller (Ad) on EPL No 760 Auto, EX+	$2,500.00
Stubborn Donkey (Clown), EX	$300.00
Stubborn Donkey (Clown), NMIB	$700.00

Lehmann
EPL-II Zeppelin, EXIB, $2,250.00. (Photo courtesy Morphy Auctions on LiveAuctioneers.com)

Lehmann
Paak-Paak Quack-Quack Duck Cart, NM+, $800.00. (Photo courtesy Morphy Auctions on LiveAuctioneers.com)

Lehmann
Zulu Ostrich Cart, yellow, NMIB, $4,800.00. (Photo courtesy James D. Julia, Inc.)

Swinging Doll, EX	$3,000.00	UHU Amphibious Car, EX	$1,300.00
Tap-Tap, EX	$700.00	Velleda, EX	$1,025.00
Tap-Tap, NMIB	$1,000.00	Vineta 656 Streetcar, EX+IB	$2,185.00
Terre Sedan, G	$550.00	Walking Down Broadway, EX	$7,800.00
Terre Sedan, VG	$800.00	Waltzing Doll, NMIB	$950.00
Tit-Bits Automatic Money-Box, EX	$5,600.00	Zig-Zag, EX+	$1,600.00
Tut-Tut, EXIB	$2,400.00	Zig-Zag, G	$650.00
Tut-Tut, VG	$1,000.00	Zirka Dare Devil, EX+IB	$950.00
Tyras Walking Dog, EX	$875.00	Zulu Ostrich Cart, EX+	$825.00

• • • • • • • • • • • • • • • • • Lunch Boxes • • • • • • • • • • • • • • • •

When the lunch box craze began in the mid-1980s, it was only the metal boxes that so quickly soared to sometimes astronomical prices. But today, even the plastic and vinyl ones are collectible. So pick a genre and have fun. There are literally hundreds to choose from, and just as is true in other areas of character-related collectibles, the more desirable lunch boxes are those with easily recognized, well-known subjects — western heroes, TV, Disney and other cartoon characters, and famous entertainers. Bottles are collectible as well.

The listings are ranged from excellent to near mint values. Bottles for metal boxes are listed under each lunch box. Plastic and vinyl listings are complete with bottles.

If you would like to learn more, we recommend *A Pictorial Price Guide to Metal Lunch Boxes and Thermoses* and a companion book, *A Pictorial Guide to Vinyl and Plastic Lunch and Plastic Lunch Boxes* by Larry Aikins, and *Collector's Guide to Lunchboxes* by Carole Bess White & L.M. White.

Advisor: Terri Mardis Ivers, Terri's Toys & Nostalgia

METAL

18 Wheeler, 1970s, $25 to	$50.00
18 Wheeler, 1970s, plastic bottle, $5 to	$10.00
240 Robert, 1970s, $2,500 to	$3,500.00
240 Robert, 1970s, plastic bottle, $350 to	$450.00
A-Team, 1980s, $15 to	$30.00
A-Team, 1980s, plastic bottle, $5 to	$10.00
Action Jackson, 1970s, $550 to	$750.00
Action Jackson, 1970s, metal bottle, $150 to	$175.00
Adam-12, 1970s, $35 to	$55.00
Adam-12, 1970s, plastic bottle, $8 to	$12.00
Addams Family, 1970s, $50 to	$75.00
Addams Family, 1970s, plastic bottle, $25 to	$50.00
America on Parade, 1970s, $15 to	$25.00
America on Parade, 1970s, plastic bottle, $5 to	$10.00
Animal Friends, 1970s, $15 to	$25.00
Annie, 1980s, $15 to	$25.00
Annie, 1980s, plastic bottle, $5 to	$10.00
Annie Oakley & Tag, 1950s, $75 to	$125.00
Annie Oakley & Tag, 1950s, metal bottle, $25 to	$35.00
Apple's Way, 1970s, $25 to	$35.00
Apple's Way, 1970s, plastic bottle, $10 to	$15.00
Archies, 1969, $50 to	$75.00
Archies, 1969, plastic bottle, $15 to	$25.00
Astronauts, 1960, dome, $55 to	$75.00
Astronauts, 1960, metal bottle, $15 to	$25.00
Astronauts, 1969, $25 to	$50.00
Astronauts, 1969, plastic bottle, $15 to	$30.00
Atom Ant, 1960s, $60 to	$80.00
Atom Ant, 1960s, metal bottle, $20 to	$30.00
Auto Race, 1960s, $25 to	$50.00
Auto Race, 1960s, metal bottle, $10 to	$15.00

Lunch Boxes, Metal
Beatles, 1965, $275.00 to $350.00; metal bottle, VG, $125.00 to $175.00. (Photo courtesy Morphy Auctions on LiveAuctioneers.com)

Back in '76, 1970s, $20 to	$40.00
Back in '76, 1970s, plastic bottle, $5 to	$15.00
Batman & Robin, 1960s, $75 to	$100.00
Batman & Robin, 1960s, metal bottle, $40 to	$50.00
Battle Kit, 1960s, $75 to	$125.00
Battle Kit, 1960s, metal bottle, $25 to	$35.00
Battle of the Planets, 1970s, $30 to	$60.00
Battle of the Planets, 1970s, plastic bottle, $10 to	$20.00
Battlestar Galactica, 1970s, $25 to	$50.00
Battlestar Galactica, 1970s, plastic bottle, $5 to	$10.00
Bee Gees, 1970s, $35 to	$65.00
Bee Gees, 1970s, plastic bottle, $10 to	$20.00
Berenstain Bears, 1980s, $40 to	$65.00
Berenstain Bears, 1980s, plastic bottle, $10 to	$20.00
Betsey Clark, 1970s, $25 to	$50.00
Betsey Clark, 1970s, plastic bottle, $5 to	$15.00

Lunch Boxes, Metal
Blondie, 1969, $150.00. (Photo courtesy Carole Bess & L.M. White)

Lunch Boxes, Metal
Cabbage Patch Kids, 1980s, $15.00 to $30.00. (Photo courtesy Carole Bess & L.M. White)

Lunch Boxes, Metal
Care Bear Cousins, 1980s, $10.00 to $25.00; plastic bottle, $5.00 to $8.00. (Photo courtesy Carole Bess & L.M. White)

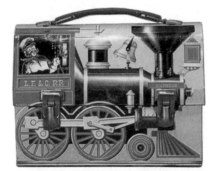

Lunch Boxes, Metal
Casey Jones, 1960, dome top, $100.00 to $200.00. (Photo courtesy Morphy Auctions on LiveAuctioneers.com)

Beverly Hillbillies, 1960s, $75 to $125.00
Beverly Hillbillies, 1960s, metal bottle, $30 to $55.00
Bionic Woman, 1970s, $30 to $60.00
Bionic Woman, 1970s, plastic bottle, $10 to $20.00
Black Hole, 1970s, $30 to $60.00
Black Hole, 1970s, plastic bottle, $10 to $20.00
Bobby Sherman, 1970s, $50 to $75.00
Bobby Sherman, 1970s, metal bottle, $25 to $35.00
Bonanza, 1960s, any of 3 versions, ea $60 to................... $100.00
Bonanza, 1960s, metal bottle, any of 3 versions, ea $25
   to $35.00
Bozo the Clown, 1960s, dome, $75 to $125.00
Bozo the Clown, 1960s, metal bottle, $25 to $45.00
Brady Bunch, 1970s, $100 to $150.00
Brady Bunch, 1970s, metal bottle, $25 to $45.00
Brave Eagle, 1950s, $75 to $125.00
Brave Eagle, 1950s, metal bottle, $20 to $40.00
Buccaneer, 1950s, dome, $75 to $125.00
Buccaneer, 1950s, metal bottle, $45 to $55.00
Buck Rogers, 1970s, $35 to $65.00
Buck Rogers, 1970s, plastic bottle, $10 to $20.00
Bullwinkle & Rocky, 1960s, $200 to $300.00
Bullwinkle & Rocky, 1960s, metal bottle, $100 to $150.00
Cabbage Patch Kids, 1980s, plastic bottle, $5 to $10.00
Campbell's Kids, 1970s, $40 to $60.00
Campbell's Kids, 1970s, metal bottle, $10 to $20.00
Campus Queen, 1960s, $50 to $75.00
Campus Queen, 1960s, metal bottle, $10 to $20.00
Captain Astro, 1960s, $50 to $100.00
Care Bears, 1980s, $10 to $25.00
Care Bears, 1980s, plastic bottle, $5 to $8.00
Carnival, 1950s, $100 to $175.00
Carnival, 1950s, metal bottle, $30 to $60.00
Cartoon Zoo Lunch Chest, 1960s, $100 to $200.00
Cartoon Zoo Lunch Chest, 1960s, metal bottle, $75 to . $125.00
Casey Jones, 1960s, metal bottle, $60 to $100.00
Chan Clan, 1970s, $50 to $100.00
Chan Clan, 1970s, plastic bottle, $10 to $20.00
Charlie's Angels, 1970s, $50 to $100.00
Charlie's Angels, 1970s, plastic bottle, $10 to $20.00
Chavo, 1970s, $40 to $90.00
Chavo, 1970s, plastic bottle, $15 to $25.00
Chitty Chitty Bang Bang, 1960s, $50 to $100.00
Chitty Chitty Bang Bang, 1960s, metal bottle, $20 to $40.00
Chuck Conners, 1960s, Cowboy in Africa, $150 to $200.00
Chuck Conners, 1960s, Cowboy in Africa, metal bottle, $75
   to $100.00
Clash of the Titans, 1980s, $30 to $60.00
Clash of the Titans, 1980s, plastic bottle, $10 to $20.00
Close Encounters of the Third Kind, 1970s, $50 to........ $100.00
Close Encounters of the Third Kind, 1970s, plastic bottle, $10
   to $20.00
Cracker Jack, 1970s, plastic bottle, $5 to $10.00
Cyclist, 1970s, $25 to.. $50.00
Cyclist, 1970s, plastic bottle, $10 to................................. $20.00
Daniel Boone, Aladdin, 1950s, $75 to $150.00
Daniel Boone, Aladdin, 1950s, metal bottle, $30 to......... $60.00
Daniel Boone, Aladdin, 1960s, $50 to $100.00

Daniel Boone, Aladdin, 1960s, metal bottle, $35 to..........$50.00
Daniel Boone, KST, 1960s, Fess Parker, $50 to.............. $100.00
Daniel Boone, KST, 1960s, Fess Parker, metal bottle, $20 to...$40.00
Davy Crockett, 1955, At the Alamo, $100 to $200.00
Davy Crockett, 1955, At the Alamo, metal bottle, $200 to....$400.00
Davy Crockett, 1955, gr rim, $100 to............................ $200.00
Davy Crockett, 1955, gr rim, metal bottle, $25 to.............$50.00
Davy Crockett, 1955, Official (Fess Parker), no bottle, $50 to....$100.00
Davy Crockett/Kit Carson, 1955, no bottle, $100 to...... $200.00
Dick Tracy, 1960s, $50 to.. $100.00
Dick Tracy, 1960s, metal bottle, $20 to......................$40.00
Disney Express, 1970s, $15 to.................................$30.00
Disney Express, 1970s, plastic bottle, $5 to.................$10.00
Disneyland, 1950s-60s, $50 to................................ $100.00
Disneyland, 1950s-60s, metal bottle, $15 to $30.00
Disney on Parade, 1970s, $15 to..............................$30.00
Disney on Parade, 1970s, plastic bottle, $5 to...................$10.00
Disney's Magic Kingdom, 1970s, $15 to.......................$30.00
Disney's Magic Kingdom, 1970s, plastic bottle, $5 to........$10.00
Disney's Wonderful World, 1980s, $10 to $20.00
Disney's Wonderful World, 1980s, plastic bottle, $5 to $10.00
Disney School Bus, 1960s-70s, dome, $25 to $50.00
Disney School Bus, 1960s-70s, metal bottle, $10 to $20.00
Disney World, 1970s, 50th Anniversary, $15 to $30.00
Disney World, 1970s, 50th Anniversary, plastic bottle, $5 to $10.00
Doctor Dolittle, 1960s, $35 to...............................$75.00
Doctor Dolittle, 1960s, metal bottle, $20 to.................$35.00
Double-Deckers, 1970s, $30 to..............................$60.00
Double-Deckers, 1970s, plastic bottle, $15 to..................$25.00
Dr Seuss, 1970s, $50 to.. $100.00
Dr Seuss, 1970s, plastic bottle, $15 to..........................$25.00
Dudley Do-Right, 1960s, $500 to.......................... $800.00
Dudley Do-Right, 1960s, metal bottle, $225 to $325.00
Dukes of Hazzard, 1980s, orig Duke boys, $35 to $50.00
Dukes of Hazzard, 1980s, plastic bottle, $5 to $10.00
Dyno Mutt, 1970s, $35 to.....................................$55.00
Dyno Mutt, 1970s, plastic bottle, $10 to........................$20.00
Early West, 1982-84, ea $30 to..............................$60.00
Emergency!, 1973, $35 to......................................$65.00
Emergency!, 1973, plastic bottle, $10 to $20.00
Emergency!, 1977, dome, $75 to $150.00
Emergency!, 1977, plastic bottle, $20 to $40.00
Empire Strikes Back, 1980s, $15 to $30.00
Empire Strikes Back, 1980s, plastic bottle, $5 to $10.00
ET, 1980s, $15 to $30.00

ET, 1980s, plastic bottle, $5 to $10.00
Evel Knievel, 1970s, $50 to............................... $100.00
Evel Knievel, 1970s, plastic bottle, $15 to $30.00
Fall Guy, 1980s, $20 to......................................$40.00
Fall Guy, 1980s, plastic bottle, $5 to.......................$10.00
Family Affair, 1960s, $50 to............................... $100.00
Family Affair, 1960s, metal bottle, $15 to $30.00
Flintstones, 1960s, $125 to $175.00
Flintstones, 1960s, metal bottle, $30 to $60.00
Flintstones, 1970s, $50 to $100.00
Flintstones, 1970s, plastic bottle, $15 to $20.00
Flintstones & Dino, 1960s, $125 to.......................... $175.00
Flintstones & Dino, 1960s, metal bottle, $30 to...............$60.00
Flipper, 1960s, $75 to...................................... $125.00
Flipper, 1960s, metal bottle, $20 to $40.00
Flying Nun, 1960s, $100 to................................. $150.00
Flying Nun, 1960s, metal bottle, $20 to $40.00
Fraggle Rock, 1980s, $50 to.................................$75.00
Fraggle Rock, 1980s, plastic bottle, $10 to $20.00
Frontier Days, 1950s, $50 to $100.00
Gene Autry Melody Ranch, 1950s, $75 to $150.00
Gene Autry Melody Ranch, 1950s, metal bottle, $25 to...$50.00
Gentle Ben, 1960s, metal bottle, $15 to $30.00
Get Smart, 1960s, $75 to................................... $150.00
Get Smart, 1960s, metal bottle, $25 to $50.00
Ghostland, 1970s, $25 to...................................$50.00
GI Joe, 1960s, $80 to...................................... $130.00
GI Joe, 1960s, metal bottle, $25 to.........................$50.00
GI Joe, 1980s, $25 to......................................$40.00
GI Joe, 1980s, plastic bottle, $10 to $20.00
Gomer Pyle, 1960s, $75 to................................. $125.00
Gomer Pyle, 1960s, metal bottle, $30 to....................$55.00
Goober & the Ghost Chasers, 1970s, $30 to $60.00
Goober & the Ghost Chasers, 1970s, plastic bottle, $15 to..$25.00
Great Wild West, 1950s, $100 to $200.00
Great Wild West, 1950s, metal bottle, $50 to...................$75.00
Green Hornet, 1960s, $100 to............................... $200.00
Green Hornet, 1960s, metal bottle, $40 to $80.00
Gremlins, 1980s, $25 to.....................................$50.00
Gremlins, 1980s, plastic bottle, $10 to.....................$20.00
Grizzly Adams, 1970s, dome, $100 to....................... $150.00
Grizzly Adams, 1970s, plastic bottle, $10 to $20.00
Guns of Will Sonnet, 1960s, $50 to $100.00

Guns of Will Sonnet, 1960s, metal bottle, $25 to $50.00
Gunsmoke, 1959, $100 to.. $200.00
Gunsmoke, 1959, metal bottle, $50 to........................... $100.00
Gunsmoke, 1959, Marshall, $100 to $200.00
Gunsmoke, 1959, Marshall, metal bottle, $50 to........... $100.00
Gunsmoke, 1962, $75 to...$125.00
Gunsmoke, 1962, metal bottle, $25 to.............................$45.00
Gunsmoke, 1972, $60 to...$80.00
Gunsmoke, 1972, plastic bottle, $20 to............................$30.00
Gunsmoke, 1973, $60 to...$80.00
Gunsmoke, 1973, plastic bottle, $15 to............................$25.00
Hair Bear Bunch, 1970s, $50 to $100.00
Hair Bear Bunch, 1970s, metal bottle, $15 to...................$25.00
Hansel & Gretel, 1980s, $25 to...$50.00
Happy Days, 1970s, 2 versions, ea $50 to.........................$75.00
Happy Days, 1970s, 2 versions, plastic bottle, ea $10 to....$20.00
Hardy Boys Mysteries, 1970s, $25 to $50.00
Hardy Boys Mysteries, 1970s, plastic bottle, $5 to $15.00
Harlem Globetrotters, 1950s, dome, $75 to..................... $125.00
Harlem Globetrotters, 1950s, metal bottle, $15 to $25.00
Harlem Globetrotters, 1970s, $30 to.................................$60.00
Harlem Globetrotters, 1970s, metal bottle, $15 to $25.00
Heathcliff, 1980s, $20 to $30.00
Heathcliff, 1980s, plastic bottle, $5 to $10.00
Hector Heathcote, 1960s, $75 to $125.00
Hector Heathcote, 1960s, metal bottle, $20 to.................$40.00
Hee Haw, 1970s, $50 to... $100.00
Hee Haw, 1970s, metal bottle, $15 to $30.00
Highway Signs, 1960s or 1970s, 2 versions, ea $15 to $30.00
Hogan's Heroes, 1960s, dome, $100 to.......................... $200.00
Hogan's Heroes, 1960s, metal bottle, $30 to $75.00
Holly Hobbie, 1970s, any version, $20 to $30.00
Holly Hobbie, 1970s, plastic bottle, $5 to.........................$10.00
Hopalong Cassidy, 1950-53, bl or red w/cloud or sq decal, ea
   $100 to $200.00
Hopalong Cassidy, 1950-53, metal bottle, ea $50 to..........$75.00
Hopalong Cassidy, 1954, $125 to $225.00
Hopalong Cassidy, 1954, metal bottle, $50 to....................$75.00
How the West Was Won, 1970s, $30 to..............................$50.00

How the West Was Won, 1970s, plastic bottle, $10 to......$20.00
HR Pufnstuff, 1970s, $50 to... $100.00
HR Pufnstuff, 1970s, plastic bottle, $20 to.......................$30.00
Huckleberry Hound & Friends, 1960s, $100 to $175.00
Huckleberry Hound & Friends, 1960s, metal bottle, $20 to ..$40.00
Incredible Hulk, 1970s, $60 to $100.00
Incredible Hulk, 1970s, plastic bottle, $10 to $20.00
Indiana Jones, 1980s, $20 to..$40.00
Indiana Jones, 1980s, plastic bottle, $5 to........................$15.00
James Bond 007, 1960s, $150 to $225.00
James Bond 007, 1960s, metal bottle, $25 to $50.00
Jet Patrol, 1950s, $100 to.. $200.00
Jet Patrol, 1950s, metal bottle, $50 to $100.00
Jetsons, 1960s, dome, $500 to.....................................$1,000.00
Jetsons, 1960s, metal bottle, $150 to $250.00
Joe Palooka, oblong box w/2 swing handles, removable lid, 5x7"
   L, EX...$75.00
Johnny Lightning, 1970s, $40 to $75.00
Johnny Lightning, 1970s, plastic bottle, $15 to $30.00
Jr Miss, 1956, $30 to...$65.00
Jr Miss, 1956, metal bottle, $20 to.....................................$30.00
Jr Miss, 1960, $25 to $50.00
Jr Miss, 1960, metal bottle, $15 to.....................................$20.00
Jr Miss, 1962, $25 to...$75.00
Jr Miss, 1962, metal bottle, $15 to.....................................$25.00
Jr Miss, 1966, $25 to...$45.00
Jr Miss, 1966, metal bottle, $15 to.....................................$20.00
Jr Miss, 1970, $20 to...$40.00
Jr Miss, 1970, plastic bottle, $5 to.....................................$15.00
Jr Miss, 1973, $15 to...$30.00
Jr Miss, 1973, plastic bottle, $5 to.....................................$15.00
Julia, 1960s, $50 to.. $100.00
Julia, 1960s, metal bottle, $15 to.......................................$40.00
Jungle Book, 1960s, $45 to..$90.00
Jungle Book, 1960s, metal bottle, $15 to...........................$30.00
Knight Rider, 1980s, $20 to...$40.00
Knight Rider, 1980s, plastic bottle, $5 to..........................$15.00
Korg, 1970s, $35 to...$65.00
Korg, 1970s, plastic, $10 to..$20.00

Lunch Boxes, Metal
Home Town Airport, 1960s, dome top, VG, $200.00 to $300.00; metal bottle, $50.00 to $75.00. (Photo courtesy Morphy Auctions on LiveAuctioneers.com)

Lunch Boxes, Metal
Laugh-In, 1968, $100.00 to $150.00; plastic bottle, $15.00 to $30.00. (Photo courtesy www.serioustoyz.com)

Lunch Boxes, Metal
Pac-Man, 1980s, $20.00 to $35.00. (Photo courtesy Carole Bess & L.M. White)

Lunch Boxes, Metal

Lost in Space, 1967, dome, $750.00 to $1,000.00; metal bottle, VG, $50.00 to $75.00. (Photo courtesy Morphy Auctions on LiveAuctioneers.com)

Krofft Supershow, 1970s, $50 to	$100.00
Krofft Supershow, 1970s, plastic bottle, $15 to	$25.00
Kung Fu, 1970s, $40 to	$80.00
Kung Fu, 1970s, plastic bottle, $5 to	$15.00
Lance Link Secret Chimp, 1970s, $75 to	$125.00
Lance Link Secret Chimp, 1970s, metal bottle, $15 to	$30.00
Land of the Giants, 1960s, $100 to	$160.00
Land of the Giants, 1960s, plastic bottle, $20 to	$40.00
Land of the Lost, 1970s, $75 to	$125.00
Land of the Lost, 1970s, plastic bottle, $15 to	$30.00
Lassie, Magic of, 1970s, $45 to	$75.00
Lassie, Magic of, 1970s, plastic bottle, $15 to	$30.00
Laugh-In, 1971, $75 to	$100.00
Laugh-In, 1971, plastic bottle, $15 to	$30.00
Lawman, 1960s, $75 to	$150.00
Lawman, 1960s, metal bottle, $20 to	$40.00
Legend of the Lone Ranger, 1980s, $45 to	$75.00
Legend of the Lone Ranger, 1980s, plastic bottle, $15 to	$30.00
Little Dutch Miss, 1959, $50 to	$100.00
Little Dutch Miss, 1959, metal bottle, $20 to	$40.00
Little Friends, 1980s, $150 to	$250.00
Little Friends, 1980s, plastic bottle, $75 to	$150.00
Little House on the Prairie, 1970s, $50 to	$100.00
Little House on the Prairie, 1970s, plastic bottle, $20 to	$40.00
Little Orphan Annie, 1980s, $25 to	$50.00
Little Red Riding Hood, 1982, $40 to	$80.00
Lone Ranger, 1950s, $100 to	$200.00
Looney Tunes, 1959, $100 to	$200.00
Looney Tunes, 1959, metal bottle, $25 to	$50.00
Lost in Space, repro, dome, $20 to	$40.00
Ludwig Von Drake in Disneyland, 1960s, $125 to	$175.00
Ludwig Von Drake in Disneyland, 1960s, metal bottle, $20 to	$40.00
Man From UNCLE, 1960s, $100 to	$150.00
Man From UNCLE, 1960s, metal bottle, $20 to	$40.00
Marvel Super Heroes, 1970s, $25 to	$50.00
Mary Poppins, 1960s, $50 to	$100.00
Mary Poppins, 1960s, metal bottle, $15 to	$30.00
Masters of the Universe, 1980s, $30 to	$60.00
Masters of the Universe, 1980s, plastic bottle, $5 to	$10.00
Mickey Mouse & Donald Duck, 1950s, $250 to	$350.00
Mickey Mouse & Donald Duck, 1950s, metal bottle, $75 to	$150.00
Mickey Mouse Club, 1960s, $65 to	$100.00
Mickey Mouse Club, 1960s, metal bottle, $15 to	$30.00
Mickey Mouse Club, 1970s, $30 to	$60.00
Mickey Mouse Club, 1970s, plastic bottle, $5 to	$15.00
Miss America, 1970s, $50 to	$100.00
Miss America, 1970s, plastic bottle, $15 to	$30.00
Monkees, 1990s, $25 to	$50.00
Monroes, 1960s, $75 to	$150.00
Monroes, 1960s, metal bottle, $25 to	$50.00
Mork & Mindy, 1970s, $25 to	$50.00
Mork & Mindy, 1970s, plastic bottle, $5 to	$15.00
Mr Merlin, 1980s, $20 to	$35.00
Mr Merlin, 1980s, plastic bottle, $5 to	$15.00
Munsters, 1960s, $300 to	$400.00
Munsters, 1960s, metal bottle, $50 to	$100.00
Muppet Babies, 1980s, $20 to	$40.00
Muppet Babies, 1980s, plastic bottle, $5 to	$10.00
Muppets, 1970s, any, ea $20 to	$50.00
Muppets, 1970s, plastic bottle, $5 to	$10.00
Nancy Drew Mysteries, 1970s, $30 to	$60.00
Nancy Drew Mysteries, 1970s, plastic, $10 to	$20.00
Orbit, 1950s, $30 to	$60.00
Orbit, 1960s, metal bottle, $10 to	$20.00
Osmonds, 1970s, $50 to	$75.00
Osmonds, 1970s, plastic bottle, $15 to	$25.00
Our Friends, 1980s, $100 to	$200.00
Our Friends, 1980s, metal bottle, $50 to	$75.00
Pac-Man, 1980s, plastic bottle, $5 to	$10.00
Paladin, 1960s, $100 to	$200.00
Paladin, 1960s, metal bottle, $40 to	$80.00
Partridge Family, 1970s, $50 to	$100.00
Partridge Family, 1970s, metal bottle, $20 to	$30.00
Pathfinder, 1959, $100 to	$200.00
Pathfinder, 1959, metal bottle, $40 to	$80.00
Peanuts, 1960, $30 to	$60.00
Peanuts, 1960, metal bottle, $10 to	$20.00
Peanuts, 1973, $25 to	$50.00
Peanuts, 1973, plastic bottle, $5 to	$15.00
Peanuts, 1976, $20 to	$35.00
Peanuts, 1976, plastic bottle, $5 to	$15.00
Peanuts, 1980, $15 to	$30.00
Peanuts, 1980, plastic bottle, $6 to	$12.00

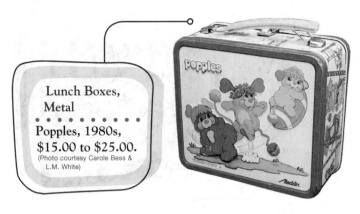

Pebbles & Bamm Bamm, 1970s, $40 to $80.00
Pebbles & Bamm Bamm, 1970s, plastic bottle, $15 to $30.00
Pele, 1970s, $50 to.. $100.00
Pele, 1970s, plastic bottle, $15 to $30.00
Pete's Dragon, 1970s, $50 to.................................... $100.00
Pete's Dragon, 1970s, plastic bottle, $15 to......................$25.00
Peter Pan, 1960s, $50 to... $100.00
Peter Pan, 1960s, plastic bottle, $20 to $40.00
Pigs in Space, 1970s, $35 to..$50.00
Pigs in Space, 1970s, plastic bottle, $5 to........................$15.00
Pink Panther & Sons, 1980s, $20 to $40.00
Pink Panther & Sons, 1980s, plastic bottle, $5 to $15.00
Pinocchio, 1970s, $50 to $100.00
Pinocchio, 1970s, plastic bottle, $15 to $30.00
Pit Stop, 1960s, $50 to... $100.00
Planet of the Apes, 1970s, $50 to $100.00
Planet of the Apes, 1970s, plastic bottle, $15 to...............$20.00
Play Ball, 1960s, $40 to..$80.00
Play Ball, 1960s, metal bottle, $15 to.............................$30.00
Police Patrol, 1970s, $100 to $150.00
Police Patrol, 1970s, plastic bottle, $15 to $25.00
Polly Pal, 1970s, $20 to..$35.00
Polly Pal, 1970s, plastic bottle, $5 to.............................$10.00
Pony Express, 1950s, $100 to..................................... $200.00
Popeye, 1962, $100 to.. $200.00
Popeye, 1962, metal bottle, $50 to $75.00
Popeye, 1964, $75 to.. $150.00
Popeye, 1964, metal bottle, $30 to $60.00
Popeye, 1980, $40 to..$80.00
Popeye, 1980, plastic bottle, $10 to...............................$20.00
Popples, 1980s, plastic bottle, $5 to $10.00
Porky's Lunch Wagon, 1959, $200 to............................. $300.00
Porky's Lunch Wagon, 1959, metal bottle, $50 to $75.00

Raggedy Ann & Andy, 1970s, $30 to................................$60.00
Raggedy Ann & Andy, 1970s, plastic bottle, $10 to..........$20.00
Rambo, 1980s, $20 to $30.00
Rambo, 1980s, plastic bottle, $5 to $10.00
Rat Patrol, 1960s, $75 to $125.00
Rat Patrol, 1960s, metal bottle, $20 to...........................$40.00
Rescuers, $25 to $50.00
Rescuers, 1970s, plastic bottle, $15 to $25.00
Return of the Jedi, 1980s, plastic bottle, $10 to.................$20.00
Rifleman, 1960s, $200 to... $300.00
Rifleman, 1960s, metal bottle, $50 to.............................$80.00
Road Runner, 1970s, $40 to $80.00
Road Runner, 1970s, metal bottle, $15 to........................$30.00
Robin Hood, 1950s, $100 to...................................... $200.00
Robin Hood, 1950s, metal bottle, $25 to.........................$50.00
Robin Hood, 1970s, $50 to.. $100.00
Robin Hood, 1970s, plastic bottle, $15 to........................$30.00
Ronald McDonald, 1980s, $15 to...................................$30.00
Ronald McDonald, 1980s, plastic bottle, $6 to.................$12.00
Rose Petal Place, 1980s, $20 to $40.00
Rose Petal Place, 1980s, plastic bottle, $5 to $15.00
Rough Rider, 1970s, $50 to...$75.00
Rough Rider, 1970s, plastic bottle, $18 to.......................$28.00
Roy Rogers & Dale Evans, 1950s, many variations, ea $250.00
   to... $350.00
Satellite, 1950s, $80 to... $120.00
Satellite, 1950s, metal bottle, $20 to.............................$40.00
Satellite, 1960s, $50 to $75.00
Satellite, 1960s, metal bottle, $15 to.............................$30.00
School Days, 1980s, $350 to....................................... $450.00
School Days, 1980s, plastic bottle, $65 to...................... $125.00
Scooby Doo, 1970s, any, ea $50 to............................. $100.00
Scooby Doo, 1970s, plastic bottle, $22 to........................$38.00
Secret Agent T, 1960s, $50 to $100.00
Secret Agent T, 1960s, metal bottle, $25 to.....................$50.00
Secret of NIMH, 1980s, $15 to $30.00
Secret of NIMH, 1980s, plastic bottle, $5 to $10.00
Secret Wars, 1980s, $50 to $75.00
Secret Wars, 1980s, plastic bottle, $18 to $28.00
Sesame Street, 1970s, $25 to $50.00
Sesame Street, 1970s, plastic bottle, $5 to $10.00
Sesame Street, 1980s, plastic bottle, $5 to $10.00
Sigmund & the Sea Monsters, 1970s, $65 to $125.00
Sigmund & the Sea Monsters, 1970s, plastic bottle, $25 to... $45.00
Six Million Dollar Man, 1970s, any, ea $35 to..................$55.00

Six Million Dollar Man, 1970s, plastic bottle, ea $18 to...$28.00
Skateboarder, 1970s, $35 to..$65.00
Skateboarder, 1970s, plastic bottle, $15 to.......................$25.00
Smokey Bear, 1970s, $225 to..$300.00
Smokey Bear, 1970s, metal bottle, $75 to $150.00
Smurfs, 1980s, $100 to...$150.00
Smurfs, 1980s, plastic bottle, $5 to....................................$15.00
Snoopy, 1969, metal bottle, $15 to.....................................$25.00
Snow White, 1975, $35 to...$70.00
Snow White, 1975, plastic bottle, $10 to.............................$20.00
Snow White, 1977 or 1980, ea $25 to..................................$50.00
Space Shuttle Orbiter Enterprise, 1970s, $45 to.................$85.00
Space Shuttle Oribter Enterprise, 1970s, plastic bottle, $15 to.$25.00
Space: 1999, 1970s, $50 to $75.00
Space: 1999, 1970s, plastic bottle, $15 to $25.00
Spider-Man & The Hulk, 1980s, $40 to................................$70.00
Spider-Man & The Hulk, 1980s, plastic bottle, $10 to $20.00
Sport Goofy, 1980s, $20 to..$40.00
Sport Goofy, 1980s, plastic bottle, $5 to.............................$15.00
Star Trek, 1960s, dome, $750 to $950.00
Star Trek, 1960s, metal bottle, $300 to $400.00
Star Trek: The Motion Picture, 1980, $35 to.....................$60.00
Star Trek: The Motion Picture, 1980, plastic bottle, $15 to...$25.00
Star Wars, 1970s, any, ea $50 to $100.00
Star Wars, 1970s, plastic bottle, any, ea $10 to.................$20.00
Strawberry Shortcake, 1980s, $20 to..................................$40.00
Strawberry Shortcake, 1980s, plastic bottle, $5 to............$10.00
Street Hawk, 1980s, $70 to...$135.00
Street Hawk, 1980s, plastic bottle, $20 to..........................$40.00
Submarine, 1960, $50 to...$100.00
Submarine, 1960, metal bottle, $15 to $30.00
Super Friends, 1970s, $40 to...$80.00
Super Friends, 1970s, plastic bottle, $10 to.......................$20.00
Super Heroes, 1970s, $35 to $70.00
Super Heroes, 1970s, plastic bottle, $10 to $20.00
Super Powers, 1980s, $45 to $85.00
Super Powers, 1980s, plastic bottle, 1980s, $10 to............$20.00
Superman, 1960s, $100 to $175.00
Superman, 1960s, metal bottle, $50 to................................$75.00
Superman, 1970s, $50 to $100.00
Superman, 1970s, plastic bottle, $15 to $25.00
Tarzan, 1960s, $100 to $150.00
Tarzan, 1960s, metal bottle, $20 to $40.00
Three Little Pigs, 1980s, $40 to..$80.00
Thundercats, 1980s, $25 to...$50.00
Thundercats, 1980s, plastic bottle, $5 to............................$10.00
Tom Corbett Space Cadet, 1952, $75 to $125.00
Tom Corbett Space Cadet, 1952, metal bottle, $30 to $55.00
Tom Corbett Space Cadet, 1954, $125 to.........................$275.00
Tom Corbett Space Cadet, 1954, metal bottle, $35 to $65.00
Track King, 1970s, $200 to..$300.00
Track King, 1970s, metal bottle, $75 to $100.00
Transformers, 1980s, $25 to...$50.00
Transformers, 1980s, plastic bottle, $5 to...........................$15.00
Treasure Chest, 1960s, dome, $100 to $200.00
Treasure Chest, 1960s, metal bottle, $25 to $50.00
UFO, 1970s, $50 to...$85.00
UFO, 1970s, plastic bottle, $15 to......................................$30.00

Lunch Boxes, Metal
• • • • • • • •
Sesame Street, 1980s, $20.00 to $40.00. (Photo courtesy Carole Bess & L.M. White)

Lunch Boxes, Metal
• • • • • • • •
Snoopy, 1969, dome, $50.00 to $100.00. (Photo courtesy Carole Bess & L.M. White)

Lunch Boxes, Metal
• • • • • • • • • • • • •
Steve Canyon, 1959, $150.00 to $250.00; metal bottle, $55.00 to $85.00. (Photo courtesy Carole Bess & L.M. White)

Lunch Boxes, Metal
• • • • • • • •
Superman, 1954, $750.00 to $1,000.00. (Photo courtesy Carole Bess & L.M. White)

US Mail/Zippy, 1969, dome, $35 to..................................$65.00
US Mail/Zippy, 1969, plastic bottle, $15 to $30.00
V, 1980s, $75 to..$125.00
V, 1980s, plastic bottle, $20 to...$40.00
Voyage to the Bottom of the Sea, 1960s, $175 to $250.00

Lunch Boxes, Metal

Underdog, 1970s, $350.00 to $750.00; metal bottle, $150.00 to $250.00. (Photo courtesy Carole Bess & L.M. White)

Lunch Boxes, Metal

Yogi Bear, 1970s, $75.00 to $125.00. (Photo courtesy Carole Bess & L.M. White)

Voyage to the Bottom of the Sea, 1960s, metal bottle, $50 to	$75.00
Wagon Train, 1960s, $100 to	$200.00
Wagon Train, 1960s, metal bottle, $25 to	$50.00
Waltons, 1970s, $50 to	$75.00
Waltons, 1970s, plastic bottle, $15 to	$30.00
Welcome Back, Kotter, 1970s, $50 to	$75.00
Welcome Back, Kotter, 1970s, plastic bottle, $10 to	$20.00
Wild Bill Hickok & Jingles, 1950s, $150 to	$200.00
Wild Bill Hickok & Jingles, 1950s, metal bottle, $40 to	$80.00
Wild Wild West, 1960s, $175 to	$250.00
Wild Wild West, 1960s, plastic bottle, $35 to	$65.00
Winnie the Pooh, 1970s, $150 to	$200.00
Winnie the Pooh, 1970s, plastic bottle, $25 to	$50.00
Woody Woodpecker, 1970s, $150 to	$250.00
Woody Woodpecker, 1970s, plastic bottle, $50 to	$75.00
Yankee Doodle, 1970s, $25 to	$50.00
Yellow Submarine, 1968, $500 to	$800.00
Yellow Submarine, 1968, metal bottle, $100 to	$200.00
Yogi Bear, 1970s, plastic bottle, $25 to	$50.00
Yogi Bear & Friends, 1960s, $85 to	$135.00
Yogi Bear & Friends, 1960s, metal bottle, from, $20 to	$40.00
Zorro, 1950s or 1960s, ea $100 to	$200.00
Zorro, 1950s or 1960s, metal bottle, ea $40 to	$75.00

PLASTIC

A-Team, 1980s, $15 to	$20.00
Astrokids, 1980s, $15 to	$25.00

Barbie, 1990s, $10 to	$15.00
Barney & Baby Bop, 1990s, $5 to	$10.00
Batman, 1989, dk bl, $15 to	$25.00
Batman, 1989, lt bl, $30 to	$40.00
Batman Returns, 1991, $15 to	$20.00
Benji, 1970s, $20 to	$30.00
Cabbage Patch Kids, $15 to	$20.00
Care Bears, 1980s, $10 to	$15.00
Casper the Friendly Ghost, 1990s, $8 to	$15.00
CB Bears, 1970s, $15 to	$20.00
Chip 'n Dale, 1980s, $5 to	$10.00
Chuck E Cheese, 1990s, $25 to	$35.00
Crest Toothpaste, 1980s, tubular, $50 to	$75.00
Dick Tracy, 1990s, red, $10 to	$15.00
Disney School Bus, 1990s, $20 to	$30.00
Dr Seuss, 1990s, $20 to	$25.00
Fat Albert, 1970s, $20 to	$30.00
Flintstones (A Day at the Zoo), 1989, Denny's logo, $20 to	$30.00
Garfield, 1980s, $15 to	$20.00
Holly Hobbie, 1989, $20 to	$25.00
Hot Wheels, 1990s, $15 to	$20.00
Incredible Hulk, 1980s, dome, $40 to	$50.00
Jabberjaw, 1970s, $30 to	$40.00
Jem, 1980s, $8 to	$15.00
Jurassic Park, 1990s, w/recalled bottle, $25 to	$30.00
Keebler Cookies, 1980s, $30 to	$50.00
Little Orphan Annie, 1970s, dome, $35 to	$45.00
Looney Tunes, 1970s, $15 to	$25.00
Lucy Luncheonette, 1980s, dome, $20 to	$30.00
Mickey Mouse, boarding school bus, yel, $40 to	$60.00
Mickey Mouse, 1980s, head form, $25 to	$35.00
Mickey Mouse & Donald Duck, 1980s, $10 to	$15.00
Mighty Mouse, 1970s, $25 to	$35.00
Minnie Mouse, 1980s, head form, $30 to	$40.00
Muppet Babies, 1980s, $15 to	$25.00
Muppets, 1990s, $10 to	$18.00
Nestlé Quik, 1980s, $25 to	$30.00
New Kids on the Block, 1990s, $15 to	$25.00
Nosey Bears, 1990s, $10 to	$20.00
Pee Wee Herman, 1980s, $20 to	$30.00
Pepsi, 1980s, $30 to	$40.00
Pink Panther, 1980s, $25 to	$30.00
Popeye, 1979, dome, $30 to	$40.00
Rap It Up, 1990s, $20 to	$25.00

Lunch Boxes, Plastic

Flintstones, dome box, 1981, $40.00. (Photo courtesy Carole Bess & L.M. White)

Lunch Boxes, Vinyl

Alvin and The Chipmunks Lunch Kit, 1963, EX, $200.00 to $300.00. (Photo courtesy Morphy Auctions on LiveAuctioneers.com)

Lunch Boxes, Plastic

Kermit the Frog, 1980s, dome top, $30.00 to $40.00. (Photo courtesy Carole Bess & L.M. White)

Lunch Boxes, Plastic

St. Louis Cardinals (Gatorade), 1990s, $20.00. (Photo courtesy Carole Bess & L.M. White)

Lunch Boxes, Vinyl

Annie, 1980s, $50.00 to $75.00. (Photo courtesy Carole Bess & L.M. White)

Robot Man, 1980s, $20 to	$30.00
Rocky Roughneck, 1970s, $25 to	$35.00
Rover Dangerfield, 1990s, $20 to	$30.00
Shadow, 1990s, $10 to	$20.00
Smurfs, 1980s, dome, $20 to	$30.00
Snoopy & Woodstock, 1970s, dome, $20 to	$30.00
Snoopy as Joe Cool, 1970s, $15 to	$25.00
Star Trek (TNG), 1970s, $10 to	$20.00
Star Wars Ewoks, 1980s, $20 to	$30.00
Sunnie Miss, 1970s, $50 to	$75.00
Superman, 1980s, phone booth scene, $30 to	$40.00
SWAT, 1970s, dome, $30 to	$40.00
The Tick, 1990s, $25 to	$50.00
Tom & Jerry, 1990s, $10 to	$20.00
Train Engine #7, 1990s, $15 to	$25.00
Winnie the Pooh, 1990s, $15 to	$25.00
Yogi Bear, 1990s, $15 to	$25.00
Young Astronauts, 1980s, $20 to	$30.00

Vinyl

Alice in Wonderland, 1970s, $150 to	$200.00
All Dressed Up, 1970s, $50 to	$75.00
Banana Splits, 1969, $425 to	$475.00
Barbarino, 1970s, brunch bag, $225 to	$275.00
Barbie, 1970s, $65 to	$85.00
Barbie & Francie, 1960s, $125 to	$175.00
Barbie & Midge, 1960s, $125 to	$175.00
Barbie & Midge, 1960s, dome, $425 to	$475.00
Barbie Lunch Kit, 1960s, $300 to	$400.00

Batman, 1990s, $15 to	$25.00
Beany and Cecil, $750 to	$850.00
Beatles, 1960s, no bottle, $750 to	$850.00
Bullwinkle, 1960s, $400 to	$500.00
Captain Kangaroo, 1960s, $350 to	$450.00
Casper the Friendly Ghost, 1960s, $365 to	$425.00
Charlie's Angels, 1970s, brunch bag, $150 to	$200.00
Denim, 1970s, $45 to	$65.00
Deputy Dawg, 1960s, $325 to	$375.00
Donny & Marie, 1970s, $80 to	$120.00
Donny & Marie, 1970s, brunch bag, $75 to	$125.00
Donny & Marie, 1970s, long or short hair versions, ea $75 to	$125.00

Lunch Boxes, Vinyl

Dr. Seuss (World of), Cat in the Hat, 1970, $30.00 to $60.00. (Photo courtesy Carole Bess & L.M. White)

Lunch Boxes, Vinyl

Ziggy, 1979, $50.00 to $75.00. (Photo courtesy Carole Bess & L.M. White)

Fire Station Engine Co #1, 1970s, $115 to	$135.00
Holly Hobbie, 1970s, $50 to	$75.00
Jr Deb, 1960s, $100 to	$150.00
Jr Nurse, 1960s, $175 to	$150.00

Li'l Jodie, 1980s, $50 to	$75.00
Lion in the Van, 1970s, $50 to	$75.00
Little Old Schoolhouse, 1970s, $50 to	$75.00
Mardi Gras, 1970s, $50 to	$110.00
Mary Poppins, 1970s, $75 to	$100.00
Monkees, 1960s, $300 to	$350.00
Pac-Man, 1980s, $40 to	$60.00
Pepsi-Cola, 1980s, yel, $50 to	$75.00
Pink Panther, 1980s, $75 to	$100.00
Psychedelic Blue, 1970s, $40 to	$60.00
Ringling Bros & Barnum & Bailey Circus, 1970s, $125 to	$175.00
Ronald McDonald, 1980s, lunch bag, $15 to	$25.00
Smokey Bear, 1960s, $425 to	$475.00
Snoopy, 1970s, brunch bag, $75 to	$125.00
Snoopy at Mailbox, 1969, red, $65 to	$85.00
Sophisticate (The), 1970s, drawstring bag, $50 to	$75.00
Soupy Sales, 1960s, $300 to	$375.00
Speedy Turtle, 1970s, drawstring bag, $15 to	$25.00
Tic-Tac-Toe, 1970s, $50 to	$75.00
Wonder Woman, 1970s, $100 to	$150.00
World of Barbie, 1971, $50 to	$75.00

Marbles

Marbles have been popular with children since the mid-1800s. They have been made in many styles, and from a variety of materials. Glass marbles have been found in archaeological digs in both early Roman and Egyptian settlements. Other marbles were made of china, pottery, steel, and natural stone. Below is a listing of various types along with a brief description of each.

Agates: stone marbles; amber, blue, green, or black with white rings encircling the marble.

Ballot Box: often handmade with pontils. Opaque black or white. Used in lodge elections.

Bloodstone: green chalcedony with red spots, a type of quartz.

China: glazed or unglazed, in a variety of hand-painted designs. Parallel lines or spirals most common.

Clambroth: opaque glass with evenly spaced outer lines of one or more colors.

Clay: commies, one of the most common older types. Painted ones are more desirable.

Comic Strip/Comic: a series of 12 marbles with faces of comic strip characters. Peltier Glass Co., Illinois.

Crockery (or Benningtons): brown, blue, or multicolored. Glazed and fired in a kiln.

End of Day: single pontil glass marbles; the colored part often appears as a multicolored blob or mushroom cloud.

Fluorescent: glows under an ultraviolet blacklight.

Goldstone: sparkling gold colored marble, made of aventurine.

Indian Swirls: usually black glass with colored bands on the surface. Often irregular.

Latticinio Core Swirls: double pontil marble with a net-like core.

Lutz Type: glass with colored or clear bands alternating with gold bands of copper flecks. Comes in several styles.

Micas: clear or colored glass with silver mica flecks. Red is rare and very desirable.

Machine Mades: after WWI, machine-made marbles were manufactured in the U.S. by companies like Akro Agate, Peltier Glass, Christensen Agate, Marble King, and many others.

Onionskin: marble with a thin onion-like layer of colorful decoration just below the surface.

Peppermint Swirls: glass with alternating red, white, and blue bands.

Ribbon Core Swirls: center core is shaped like a ribbon.

Solid Core Swirls: solid core in a tube-like fashion.

Steelies: hollow steel spheres marked with a cross where the steel was bent together to form a marble.

Sulfides: generally made of clear glass with figures inside. Rarer types have colored figures or colored glass.

Tiger Eye: stone marble of golden quartz with inclusions of asbestos; dark brown with gold highlights.

Prices listed are for marbles in near-mint condition. Polished or damaged marbles have a greatly reduced value. For a more thorough study of the subject, we recommend *Everett Grist's Big Book of Marbles*. Also refer to MCSA's *Marble Identification and Price Guide*, re-written by Robert Block (Schiffer Publishing). See Clubs, Newsletters, and Other Publications for club information.

Advisor: Lloyd Huffer

Speech bubble: I YAM WAT I YAM, I YAM A MARBLE SHOOTER, ARF!

Akro Agate, 3-color corkscrew, ⅝" $15.00
Akro Agate, bl slag, ⅝" $2.00
Akro Agate, carnelian oxbloo, ⅝" $45.00
Akro Agate, corkscrew, limeade, ¾" $40.00
Akro Agate, corkscrew, snake, ⅝" $10.00
Akro Agate, corkscrew, wht base, ⅝" $2.00
Banded Opaque, gr w/red bands, wht & bl streaks, ¾" ... $185.00
Banded Opaque, wht opaque w/red & bl swirls, 1¾" ... $2,200.00
China, glazed, decorated, geometrics, spirals, ¾" $20.00
Christensen Agate, flame, bl w/red flames, ⅝" $85.00
Christensen Agate, Guinea, clear base, mc spots & streaks, 11⁄16" $375.00
Christensen Agate, swirl, blk & orange, ⅝" $35.00
Clambroth, bl base w/evenly spaced wht lines, ⅞" $750.00
Clambroth, wht w/pk, gr & bl lines, ⅝" $200.00
Clay, very common, pnt, ⅝" $0.10
Clown Onionskin, wht core, 4 stretched colored bands, 13⁄16" ...$435.00
Comic, Peltier Picture Marble, Andy Gump, 11⁄16" $75.00
Comic, Peltier Picture Marble, Herbie, 11⁄16" $65.00
Comic, Peltier Picture Marble, Kayo, 11⁄16" $375.00
Comic, Peltier Picture Marble, Moon Mullins, 11⁄16" $265.00
Comic, Peltier Picture Marble, Orphan Annie, 11⁄16" $110.00
Divided Core Swirl, red, wht & bl ribbons, ¾" $20.00
Joseph's Coat, clear base, streaks & flecks of 7 colors, 19⁄16" ..$950.00
Lined Crockery, clay, wht w/gr & bl swirls, ¾" $35.00
Lutz, bl banded, 2" $540.00
Lutz, bl opaque, gold & wht lines, ¾" $350.00
Lutz, blk opaque, gold & red lines, ¾" $275.00

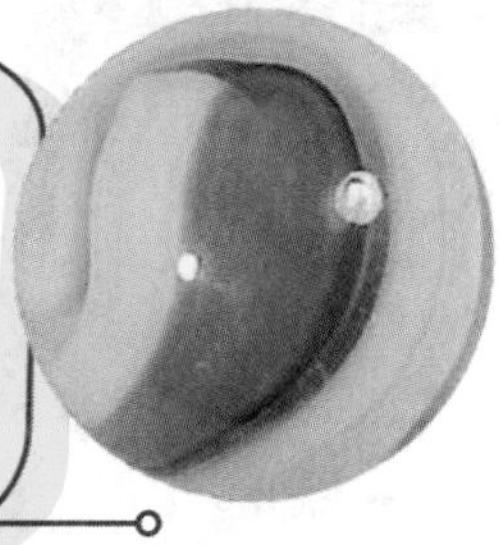

Lutz, clear core, gold, yel & wht bands, ⅝" $85.00
Lutz, red ribbon core, gold swirl w/wht edges, 1¾" $1,500.00
Lutz, ribbon core, red & gr edged w/gold bands, ¾" $225.00
Marble King, Bumblebee, blk & yel patch & ribbon, ⅝" $1.00
Marble King, cloth tournament bag $35.00
Marble King, Cub Scout, bl & yel patch & ribbon, 1" $25.00
Mica, bl glass w/silver mica flecks, ¾" $35.00
Mica, clear base w/silver mica flecks, 1" $100.00
Millefiori, flower pattern, single pontil, 1½" $575.00
Onionskin, bl, wht & orange panels, 25⁄16" $400.00
Onionskin, pk, 113⁄16" $335.00
Onionskin, speckled, 4 color w/silver mica, 13⁄16" $600.00
Onionskin, yel & red w/silver mica, 27⁄16" $660.00
Peltier Glass, Rebel, red, blk & wht, NLR, ⅝" $65.00
Peltier Glass, Superman, bl, red & yel, NLR, 11⁄16" $150.00
Peppermint Swirl, red, wht & bl, 11⁄16" $75.00
Peppermint Swirl, red, wht & bl w/silver mica in bl, ⅝" $375.00
Pottery, Stoneware, w/bl slip decoration, 1¼" $110.00
Solid Opaque, melon balls, pastel colors, ⅞" $100.00
Sulfide, Bear, wearing dress, nice detail, 1¾" $1,000.00
Sulfide, Bird, prairie chicken, 1¾" $175.00
Sulfide, Boy in top hat & dress clothes, gr glass, 1¾" ...$4,000.00
Sulfide, Boy on hobbyhorse, blowing horn, 19⁄16" $650.00
Sulfide, Buffalo, molded figure, lacks detail, 1¾" $125.00
Sulfide, Cherub Head w/wings, well centered, 1⅝" $875.00
Sulfide, Crucifix, lg, well centered, 23⁄16" $400.00
Sulfide, Dog, RCA 'Nipper,' 1¾" $275.00
Sulfide, Elephant, w/long trunk, 1¼" $140.00
Sulfide, Girl sitting in chair, bubble around figure, 19⁄16" .. $275.00
Sulfide, Hawk, gr glass, 1" $840.00
Sulfide, Indian head penny, rare, 1⅛" $350.00
Sulfide, Jenny Lind, well centered, 15⁄16" $350.00
Sulfide, Lamb, common figure, 1¾" $125.00
Sulfide, Man, politician, standing on a stump, 1¼" $450.00
Sulfide, Moses in the Bulrushes, baby in basket, 1¾" $450.00
Sulfide, Number One, nicely detailed, 1¾" $400.00
Sulfide, Parrot, uncommon figure, 1⅝" $330.00
Sulfide, Peacock, 3-color pnt figure, 1¾" $8,000.00

Swirl, Latticino, wht thread form net-like core, ⅝" $15.00
Swirl, Latticinio, yel threads form net-like core, 2⅛" $275.00
Swirl, red solid core, 4 color outer bands, 2⅝" $910.00
Swirl, wht solid core, bl, pk, gr lines, yel outer bands, 2¹³⁄₁₆".. $360.00

Transition, Leighton, 1" $1,000.00
Vitro Agate, Chinese checkers, orig box, ⅝" game marbles (60 total) $70.00
Vitro Agate, Parrot, mc, 1" $40.00

• • • • • • • • • • • • • • • • • • • Marx • • • • • • • • • • • • • • • • • • •

Louis Marx founded this company in New York in the 1920s. He was a genius not only at designing toys but also marketing them. His business grew until it became one of the largest toy companies ever to exist, eventually expanding to include several factories in the United States as well as other countries. Marx sold his company in the early 1970s, and died in 1982. Although toys of every description were produced, collectors today admire his mechanical toys above all others. For more information on Marx battery-operated toys, refer to *Battery-Operated Toys* by Don Hultzman.

Advisors: Tom Lastrapes, battery-operated; Scott Smiles, windups

See also Advertising; Banks; Character, TV, and Movie Collectibles; Disney; Dollhouse Furniture; Games; Guns; Plastic Figures; Playsets; and other categories. For toys made by Linemar (Marx's subsidiary in Japan), see Battery-Operated Toys and Windup, Friction, and Other Mechanical Toys.

BATTERY-OPERATED

Alley the Roaring Stalking Alligator, 18", NMIB........... $225.00
Barking Terrier Dog, plush, w/collar, 8", EXIB................ $100.00
Baseball Pitching Game, EXIB $100.00
Bengali Tiger, r/c, 13", 1960s, MIB.................................. $225.00
Big Loo, 1965, 38", EX+IB $1,800.00
Big Parade (Drill Team), plastic, 1963, unused, MIB...... $225.00
Brewster the Rooster, plush, 10", EXIB $75.00
Buttons the Puppy w/a Brain, plush & tin, 12", EX $75.00
Chief Big Mouth Ball Blowing Target Game, unused, NMIB . $200.00
Colonel Hap Hazzard, litho tin, 12", NMIB.................... $850.00
Electric Robot & Son, plastic, lighted eyes, 17½" w/5" son, EX+IB $150.00
Farm Tractor (Forward & Reverse), plastic, w/driver & 3 trailers, 7" tractor, 1960s, NM (VG+ box) $100.00
Fred Flintstone on Dino, plush, 1961, NM $325.00
Fred Flintstone on Dino, plush, 1961, NMIB $475.00
Great Garloo, 1960, 24", EX+IB $450.00
Hootin' Hollow Haunted House, 11", EX $450.00
Hootin' Hollow Haunted House, 11", NMIB.............. $1,250.00

Marx, Battery-Operated

Mickey Mouse Little Big Wheel, in original box, Mickey riding tricycle, 10" long, EX, $75.00.

Marx, Battery-Operated

Mighty Kong, in original box, 11", EX, $500.00. (Photo courtesy Randy Inman Auctions)

Marx, Battery-Operated

Hootin' Hollow Haunted House, 11", EXIB, $850.00. (Photo courtesy Bertoia Auctions on LiveAuctioneers.com)

Locomotive, r/c, 6", EXIB... $75.00
Mr Mercury, r/c, plastic, 13", EXIB................................... $500.00
Mr Mercury, r/c, tin, gold version, 13", NMIB............. $1,000.00
Nutty Mad Car, 9½", EX.. $150.00
Nutty Mad Indian, EX $100.00
Nutty Mad Indian, MIB $225.00
Ride-Er Convertible, 32", NRFB (sealed) $550.00
Scootin'-Tootin' Hot Rod, 13", GIB $175.00
Walking Tiger, r/c, plush, 12", EXIB................................. $225.00
Whistling Spooky Kooky Tree, 14", EX+IB $1,075.00
Whistling Spooky Kooky Tree, 14", VG $500.00
Yeti the Abominable Snowman, r/c, 11", NMIB $675.00

VEHICLES

A&P Super Market Delivery Truck Van, tin, red & silver, 19½", Nm.. $575.00

ACE Hauler & Van Trailer, tin, 21", NMIB $450.00

American Trucking Co (The Van), litho tin, friction, 5" L, EX+ (F box).. $825.00

Armored Trucking Co Truck, litho tin, opening rear door, 9½", EXIB $2,450.00

Army Transport Truck (marked RA) w/Mobile Field Cannon, tin w/canvas cover, gr, 13", NMIB......................... $325.00

Automatic (Minit Car Wash), 6x9" garage w/7" car, litho tin, w/ up, 1950s, NMIB $450.00

Cadillac, tin, w/up, orange & blk, w/driver, 12", VG...... $800.00

Carpenter's Truck, PS, red w/bl stake bed, w/tool kits, 13½", NMIB $825.00

Caterpillar Heavy Duty Tractor w/Road Grader, tin, w/up, 10", EXIB $125.00

Cities Service Tow Truck, tin, gr & wht, 21", NM $225.00

City Coal Co Truck, tin, w/up, 13", VG....................... $350.00

Deluxe Auto Transport, PS, 22½", no ramps or cars o/w EX. $225.00

Deluxe Auto Transport PS, w/2 plastic cars, 24", unused, NMIB $400.00

Deluxe Delivery Service, PS w/litho tin wheels, grille & hood trim, 14½", EX $600.00

Dick Tracy Police Station w/Riot Car, PS, friction, 9x6" station w/7" car, EX+ $175.00

Dick Tracy Siren Squad Car, litho tin, w/up, w/electric flasing light, 11", EX+IB $350.00

Dick Tracy Siren Squad Car, litho tin, w/up, w/electric flashing light, 11", VG $150.00

Drive-Ur-Self Car, tin, w/up, 13½", VG+ $200.00

Dump Truck, PS, friction, red, wht & bl, covered wheels, 12", 1950s, NMIB $230.00

Electric Coupe, litho tin, w/up, electric lights, red & cream w/ BRT, 15", EX $475.00

Emergency Squad No 2, PS w/plastic ladders, b/o, 14", VG... $75.00

Fire (VFD) Ladder Truck, litho tin, w/up, 14", EX $550.00

Fire Aerial Ladder Truck, tin, friction, red w/yel ladder, figures lithoed in windows, 14", NMIB $125.00

Fire Dept Car, PS, w/up, electric lights, red w/BRT, 15", VG..$475.00

Fire Dept Chief Car No 1, litho tin, 'Friction Drive' on hood, red w/figures lithoed in windows, 6½", EX............................$75.00

Fire Truck w/Automatic Flashing Light & Siren, plastic, w/up, b/o lights, 'NYCFD' decals, 13", MIB $75.00

Fix-All Jeep, plastic, complete w/tools & instructions, 7", 1953, NM (VG box) $100.00

G-Man Pursuit Car, litho tin, w/up, bl, red & blk, BRT, 14", EX... $625.00

G-Man Pursuit Car, PS, w/up, red & bl, 14", 1930s, EXIB..$3,150.00

Giant Reversing (Construction) Tractor Truck, litho tin, w/up, blk rubber treads, 14", VG $325.00

Grocery Truck, PS, red w/bl stake bed, 13½", NMIB...... $825.00

Hess Fire Hose Truck, 11", 1970, NM $575.00

Hess Tanker, plastic, B-Mack cab, 13", 1964, NM+IB.... $625.00

Hi Way Express, litho tin, rear door opens, 16", EX+..... $275.00

Highboy Climbing Tractor, tin, w/up, copper color w/blk rubber treads, mc lithoed driver, 8", NM+IB $100.00

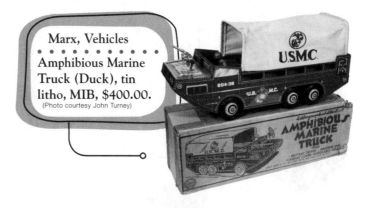

Hook & Ladder Fire Truck, PS, wht, 28", EXIB.............. $525.00

Hydraulic Dump Truck, #1017, 22", MIB (sealed).......... $500.00

Ice Truck, PS, red w/yel stake bed, w/ice tongs, NMIB... $825.00

Industrial Tractor Set, metal, w/up, 7" L tractor w/treads & 2 5" L hauling cars, lithoed driver, rare, EXIB.................. $725.00

LaSalle Convertible Coupe, PS w/litho tin wheels, red w/wht top, 10½", ca 1939, VG................................... $275.00

LeSabre Convertible, plastic, friction, gr, w/driver, 10", EX+..$225.00

Lightning Express Locomotive 3000, PS, rider, 24", VG+..$100.00

Lumar Contractors Dump Truck, PS w/litho tin wheels, hand-op dump bed, 17", EX................................... $100.00

Lumar Dump Truck w/Front Loader, tin, red, wht & bl, 15", EX $125.00

Lumar Wrecker Service Truck, 16", NM....................... $650.00

Marvel Car, extended bumpers for bump-&-go action, 16" L, VG+... $425.00

Marx Tractor #5, tin, w/up, gr & yel w/blk rubber treads, wht plastic driver, NMIB... $125.00

Merchant's Transfer Truck, tin, w/up, Mac style w/stake bed, mc, 10½", EX+ $575.00

Midget Racer #11, plastic, w/up, BRT w/chrome hubs, 6", NMIB $350.00

Milk Truck, PS, stake bed, wht, w/3 glass bottles & orig card, 13½", NMIB $825.00

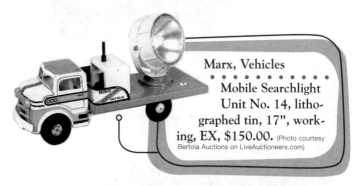

Marx, Vehicles
Pathe News Car, pressed steel, 10", VG, $600.00. (Photo courtesy Morphy Auctions on LiveAuctioneers.com)

Marx, Vehicles
Powerhouse Dump Truck, pressed steel, MIB, $300.00. (Photo courtesy John Turney)

Marx, Vehicles
Powerhouse Turnpike Wrecker Service, pressed steel, 24", NMIB, $375.00. (Photo courtesy Morphy Auctions on LiveAuctioneers.com)

Marx, Vehicles
Railway Express Agency Truck, pressed steel, 19", VG, $425.00. (Photo courtesy Morphy Auctions on LiveAuctioneers.com)

Marx, Vehicles
Stake Truck, pressed steel, red and yellow, 14", NMIB, $275.00. (Photo courtesy Morphy Auctions on LiveAuctioneers.com)

Marx, Vehicles
U.S. Army Transport, pressed steel, canvas cover, 18", EX, $150.00. (Photo courtesy Morphy Auctions on LiveAuctioneers.com)

North American Van Lines, litho tin, 13½", VG $125.00
Polar Ice Co Stake Truck, PS, red & yel, 14", EX+......... $250.00
Power Snap Climbing Caterpillar, tin, silver color w/blk rubber treads on red wheels, lithoed driver, 8", EX+IB........... $250.00
Racer #12, litho tin, w/up, red, yel, blk & wht w/blk & wht striped wheels, 17", EX.. $275.00
Reversible Coupe, tin, w/up, red, 16", 1930s, EXIB..... $1,600.00
Rider-er Fire Truck, PS, #3322-S, 31", MIB (sealed) $975.00
Royal Bus Line Bus, litho tin, w/up, red, orange, gr & bl, 10", G $175.00
Royal Van Co Box Truck, tin, w/up, Mack style, 2-tone orange & gr, 9", VG+ $275.00
Sanitation Truck, PS, 13", unused, NM+IB $800.00
Siren Fire Chief Car, PS, w/up, electric lights, BRT, 15", EX ..$675.00
Speed Racer #27, tin, w/up, orange & yel w/wht plastic driver, 'Grand National 500..' & '...Champ 1948,' 12", NMIB ..$300.00
Stake Truck, PS, #675, red, wht & blk, 12", VGIB (Box held 12 trucks)... $225.00
Toyland Farms Milk/Cheese Delivery Truck, tin, red, wht & bl, wooden bottles w/box, 10½", EX $1,000.00
Tractor, tin, w/up, mc lithoed tractor & driver, blk rubber front tires w/blk tin back tires, 5½", NMIB $100.00
Tractor & Implements (Farm Machinery), PS, w/3 implements & front scoop, VGIB.. $250.00
Trailer Truck, PS, red tractor w/yel & red stake trailer, wheels covered, 14", NMIB $325.00
US Army 5th Divison Truck, tin, gr w/yel trim, tan canvas top, w/5 plastic soldiers, 16", NM+IB $275.00
US Mail Truck, litho tin, w/up, rear door opens, 9", G... $275.00
US Mail Truck, PS, red, wht & bl tractor-trailer, 24", #3632, VGIB $575.00
White's Semi, PS, #3631, 24", VGIB $1,265.00
Willy's Jeep, PS, 11", EX (partial box) $225.00

WINDUPS

American Trucking Co #65, 5½", EXIB.......................... $725.00
Amos 'N' Andy Fresh Air Taxi, 8", EX $450.00
Amos 'N' Andy Fresh Air Taxi, 8", EX+IB...................... $900.00
Balky Mule, 9", NMIB.. $200.00
Beat It! The Komikal Kop, 7", VG................................. $450.00
Big Parade, 24" L, VG.. $375.00
Blondie's Jalopy, 16" L, EX... $3,000.00
BO Plenty, 9", EX $100.00
BO Plenty, 9", NMIB.. $225.00
Buck Rogers Rocket Police Patrol, 12", EX..................... $600.00
Buck Rogers Rocket Police Patrol, 12", NMIB $1,675.00

Busy Bridge, 24" L, EX......................................$350.00
Busy Driver, 9½", NM...................................$1,100.00
Busy Miner, 16", EXIB......................................$300.00
Charleston Trio, 9", EX+..................................$850.00
Charleston Trio, 9", NMIB.............................$1,800.00
Charlie McCarthy Benzine Mobile, 7", NMIB...............$875.00
Charlie McCarthy Benzine Mobile, 7", VG................$250.00
Charlie McCarthy the Drummer Boy ('Strike Up the Band'/'Here
    Comes Drummer Boy'), 9", G.......................$525.00
Charlie McCarthy Walker, 8", EX.......................$225.00
Chompy the Beetle, 5½", EXIB.........................$250.00
Cirko the Clown Cyclist, 9", EXIB..................$4,300.00
Climbing Fireman, 22", VG.............................$200.00
Coast Defense, 9" dia, EX+IB........................$1,000.00
Coast Defense, 9" dia, VG.............................$400.00
College Jalopey, 6", VG...............................$275.00
Coo-Coo Car, 8", EX....................................$275.00
Coo-Coo Car, 8", G.....................................$125.00
Dagwood's Solo Flight (Aeroplane), 8", VG............$550.00
Dagwood the Driver, 8", EX+IB......................$1,500.00
Dapper Dan, 10", EXIB...............................$1,275.00
Dare Devil Flyer, 13", G..............................$350.00
Dare Devil Flyer, 13", NMIB.........................$1,650.00
Dick Tracy Police Station, w/car, 9" L, EXIB..........$500.00
Dick Tracy's Bonnie Braids, 11", EXIB................$150.00
Dippy Dumper, celluloid figure in tin vehicle, 9" L, VG..$450.00
Disney Dipsy Car (Mickey Mouse), 6", NMIB...........$725.00
Disney Parade Roadster, 11", NM....................$500.00
Disney Parade Roadster, 11", NMIB..................$750.00
Disneyland Express, 13½", EXIB (box reads Mechanical Wind-
    Up Train)...$100.00
Donald (Duck) the Driver, 7", EX+IB..................$600.00
Donald Duck Duet, 10", EX.............................$450.00
Donald Duck Duet, 10", VGIB..........................$775.00
Donald Duck on Tractor, plastic, friction, 4" L, EX.........$75.00
Donald Duck Racing Kart, friction, plastic, 6", EXIB.....$325.00
Donald Duck the Drummer, plastic w/tin drum, 10", EX.$200.00
Donald Duck the Skier, plastic w/tin skis & poles, 10", EX..$300.00
Dopey Walker, 8", EXIB................................$550.00
Dopey Walker, 8", VG..................................$225.00
Dottie Driver, celluloid nodder figure, 8" L, EXIB.........$100.00
Doughboy Tank, 9", VG+IB.............................$250.00
Drummer Boy (Let the Drummer Boy Play...), 9", EX....$550.00
Drummer Boy (Let the Drummer Boy Play...), 9", G......$300.00
Dumbo the Acrobat Elephant, 4", EXIB................$375.00
Ferdinand & Matador, 9" L, VG.......................$225.00
Ferdinand & Matador, 9" L, VGIB.....................$600.00
Ferdinand the Bull, 4", NMIB.........................$325.00
Figaro, 5", NMIB.......................................$350.00
Flash Gordon Rocket Fighter, 12", 1939, EX..........$400.00
Flintstones Cars, any character, NM+IB................$350.00
Flintstones Flivver, friction, NM......................$275.00
Flintstones Pals on Dino, any character, MIB.........$525.00
Flintstones Rollover Tank, 4", EX.....................$225.00
Flintstones Tricycle, any character, 4", NMIB........$300.00
Frankenstein (Walker), 1963, 5½", NMIB...............$575.00
Funny Face (Harold Lloyd), 11", EXIB.................$475.00
Funny Flivver, 7½", EX................................$200.00

George the Drummer Boy, 9", NMIB.......................$175.00
Gobbling Goose, 8", EX+IB...............................$75.00
Goofy (Twirling Tail), 8", NMIB........................$250.00
Gorilla, 7½", MIB......................................$225.00
Harold Lloyd, see Funny Face
Hey! Hey! Chicken Snatcher, 9", G......................$650.00
Hey! Hey! Chicken Snatcher, 9", NM...................$1,500.00
Hi-Yo Silver the Lone Ranger, 8", EXIB.................$450.00
Honeymoon Cottage, 7x7", NM...........................$100.00
Honeymoon Express, 9" dia, EX+IB......................$300.00
Honeymoon Special, 6" dia, EX..........................$100.00
Hopalong Cassidy, rocker base, 10", EXIB..............$475.00
Hoppo the Monkey, 8½", VG+............................$125.00
Huckleberry Hound Car, any character, friction, 4", NMIB..$225.00
Jazzbo Jim, 9", EXIB...................................$975.00

Jazzbo Jim, 9", VG.. $375.00

Jetson Express/Jetson Choo Choo Train, 12", NM+ $350.00

Jetsons Hopping Elroy, 4", EXIB.............................. $275.00

Joe Penner & His Duck, 8", EX................................ $375.00

Jolly Joe Jeep, 6", VG (partial box) $275.00

Joy-Rider, 8" L, EX... $350.00

Joy-Rider, 8" L, EX+IB.. $525.00

Jumpin' Jeep, 6", NM+IB...................................... $250.00

Knockout Champs, 7x7", EX+IB.............................. $750.00

Limping Lizzy, 7", EX $300.00

Limping Lizzy, 7", VGIB.. $375.00

Little Orphan Annie & Sandy, Annie skipping rope & Sandy w/
   suitcase in mouth, EX, pr $450.00

Looping Plane, 7½" WS, EXIB................................. $300.00

Lucky Stunt Flyer, 7" L, EX+.................................. $350.00

Main Street, 24" L, EX+IB $425.00

Mammy's Boy, 10½", EX+IB.................................. $1,500.00

Merchants Transfer Wagon, 13", EXIB $2,300.00

Merry Makers, conductor, w/marquee, 8x9", EX (partial
   box) $1,300.00

Merry Makers, violinist, no marquee, 8x9", VG+........... $750.00

Mickey (Mouse) the Driver, 6" L, EXIB...................... $285.00

Mickey (Mouse) the Musician (I Play the Xylophone), 10",
   VGIB $225.00

Mickey Mouse Dipsy Car, 5½", G............................ $150.00

Mickey Mouse Express, 9" dia, NM+IB...................... $1,100.00

Mickey Mouse Express, 9" dia, VG........................... $300.00

Mickey Mouse Express, 9" dia, VGIB........................ $500.00

Mickey Mouse Meteor Train, 5-pc, 43" overall, EX........ $450.00

Mickey Mouse (Whirling Tail), 7½", EX+IB $200.00

Midget Climbing Fighting Tank, 5" L, NMIB................ $125.00

Milton Berle Car, 6", EX+IB.................................. $425.00

Monkey Tumbling w/2 Chairs, 5", EX........................ $300.00

Moon Creature, 5½", 1968, VG+IB $200.00

Moon Mullins & Kayo Handcar, 6", EX...................... $375.00

Moon Mullins & Kayo Handcar, 6", G........................ $175.00

Moon Mullins & Kayo Handcar, 6", VG...................... $275.00

Mortimer Snerd's Home Town Band, 9", VG $500.00

Mortimer Snerd Tricky Auto, 7", EX $425.00

Mortimer Snerd Tricky Auto, 7", NMIB...................... $575.00

Mortimer Snerd Walker, 9", EX $250.00

Mortimer Snerd Walker, 9", EX+IB $350.00

Motorcycle Cop & Car Single Track Speedway, VGIB .. $575.00

Mountaineer #721 (Sparkling Mountain Climber), 41" overall
   length, NMIB.. $150.00

Mysterious Pluto, see Pluto (Mysterious)

Mystery Space Ship, gyro-powered, plastic, 1960s, NMIB ..$125.00

Pinocchio the Acrobat, 17", VGIB $325.00

Pinocchio Walker, 9", EXIB $625.00

Pinocchio Walker, 9", VG $300.00

Planet Patrol X-1 Space Tank, 10" L, EX $225.00

Planet Patrol X-1 Space Tank, 10" L, EXIB $350.00

Pluto, yel plastic, metal tail spins, 5½", 1950s, NM $50.00

Pluto (Roll-Over), 8", VG+ $150.00

Pluto (Wise Pluto), 8", VGIB.................................. $285.00

Police (PD) Motorcycle, 3-wheeled w/integral driver, 3½" L..$250.00

Police Siren Motorcycle, 8½", NMIB.......................... $375.00

Police Squad Motorcycle #3 w/Sidecar, integral driver, 8½",
   NMIB $625.00

Popeye & Olive Oyl Dancing on Roof (Jiggers), 9½", NM. $1,450.00

Marx, Windups
Pinched!, 10x10", EX+IB, $1,000.00. (Photo courtesy Bertoia Auctions on LiveAuctioneers.com)

Marx, Windups
Popeye Express (Parrot on Trunk), 8", EX, $575.00; Popeye Walker with two parrot cages, 8", EX, $375.00. (Photo courtesy James D. Julia, Inc.)

Marx, Windups
Pluto (Mysterious), 10", EX+IB, $250.00. (Photo courtesy Bertoia Auctions on LiveAuctioneers.com)

Marx, Windups
Red the Iceman, 8½", NMIB, $4,000.00. (Photo courtesy Morphy Auctions on LiveAuctioneers.com)

Popeye & Olive Oyl Dancing on Roof (Jiggers), 9½", VG .. $650.00
Popeye Champ, 7", EX+IB $3,000.00
Popeye Dancing on Roof (Jigger), 10", VG $500.00
Popeye Express (Blow Me Down Airport), 9" dia, EX+IB . $2,500.00
Popeye Express (Pushing Baggage Cart), 8½" $800.00
Popeye Express (Two Planes on Tower), 18½", EX+ $650.00
Popeye Handcar, 6" L, VG $300.00
Popeye Pilot/Eccentric Airplane, 8" WS, EX $850.00
Popeye Pilot/Eccentric Airplane, 8" WS, EX+IB $1,300.00
Popeye Pilot/Eccentric Airplane, 8" WS, VG $500.00
Range Rider (Cowboy), 10", VGIB $300.00
Range Rider (Lone Ranger), 11", EX+IB $450.00
Red the Iceman, 8½", EX+IB $3,500.00
Ring-A-Ling Circus, 7½" dia, EX $1,450.00
Rocket Fighter, 12", EX $350.00
Rocket Fighter, 12", NMIB $1,150.00
Rollover Plane, 6" WS, NMIB $425.00
Roll-Over Pluto, see Pluto (Roll-Over)
Rookie Cop, 8½", EX+IB $325.00
Roy Rogers Stage Coach Wagon, 14½" L, NM+IB $350.00
Sandy (Orphan Annie) & Sandy's Dog House, 8" 3-wheeled
    Sandy w/cb 'Dog House' box, EX/VG box $250.00
Scenic Express Train Set, Mickey Mouse & Donald Duck hand
    car on track w/tin base, 13x21", VGIB $230.00
Sheriff Sam & His Whoopee Car, 6", NMIB $175.00
Sky Bird Flyer, 9x24", EX+IB $475.00
Sky Hawk w/Popeye & Olive Oyl, 9", VG $325.00
Somstepa Coon Jigger, blk man dancing on box $475.00
Son of Garloo (Walking), 1960s, 6", EXIB $300.00
Sparkling Climbing Fighting Tank, camo w/blk rubber treads,
    9½", EXIB $200.00
Sparkling Doughboy Tank, 10", EXIB $250.00
Speed Boy 4 (Motorcycle Delivery Cart), 9½", EX $400.00
Superman Rollover Plane, 1940s, 6" L, VGIB $1,825.00
Tidy Tim, 9", EX $300.00
Tom Corbett Space Cadet # 2 Sparkling Space Ship, 12", VG. $550.00
Toylands Horse-Drawn Dairy Wagon, 10", EX $225.00
Tricky Taxi on Busy Street, 4½" car w/6x10" base, EXIB. $325.00
Turnover Tank, 4", EXIB $125.00
Twinkle Toes Ballet Dancer, 6", EXIB $225.00
Uncle Wiggily Crazy Car, 8", EX+IB $950.00
US Army Tank No 3, 8" L, EX $125.00
Walking Pinocchio, see Pinocchio Walker
Walking Porter (Carrying Luggage), 8", EXIB $650.00
Walking Porter (Carrying Luggage), 8", VG $350.00
Walking Porter (Pushing Cart w/Trunk), 8", EXIB $600.00
Walking Porter (Pushing Cart w/Truck), 8", VG $375.00

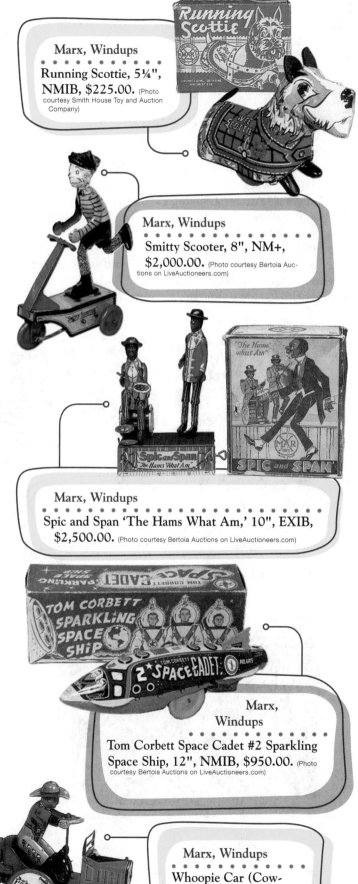

Marx, Windups

Running Scottie, 5¼", NMIB, $225.00. (Photo courtesy Smith House Toy and Auction Company)

Marx, Windups

Smitty Scooter, 8", NM+, $2,000.00. (Photo courtesy Bertoia Auctions on LiveAuctioneers.com)

Marx, Windups

Spic and Span 'The Hams What Am,' 10", EXIB, $2,500.00. (Photo courtesy Bertoia Auctions on LiveAuctioneers.com)

Marx, Windups

Tom Corbett Space Cadet #2 Sparkling Space Ship, 12", NMIB, $950.00. (Photo courtesy Bertoia Auctions on LiveAuctioneers.com)

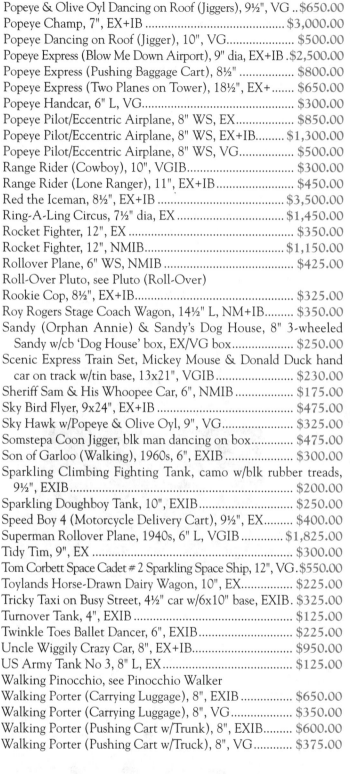

Marx, Windups

Rocket Racer, lithographed tin, 16", EX, $750.00. (Photo courtesy Bertoia Auctions on LiveAuctioneers.com)

Marx, Windups

Whoopie Car (Cowboy), EX, $425.00. (Photo courtesy Scott Smiles)

Whee-Whiz Auto Racer, complete, EXIB....................... $850.00

Whirling Tail Mickey Mouse, see Mickey Mouse (Whirling Tail)

Whoopie Car (College Student), 8", EX......................... $350.00

Whoopie Car (Cowboy), 8", VG................................... $300.00

MISCELLANEOUS

Automatic (Minit) Car Wash, litho tin, 6x9" garage w/7" car, w/ up, NMIB $450.00

Brightlite Filling Station, litho tin, 9" L, EXIB............... $550.00

Bus (Universal) Terminal, litho tin, w/2 Wyandotte vehicles scaled for station, EXIB... $600.00

City (Universal) Airport, litho tin, 12" L, EX $225.00

City (Universal) Airport, litho tin, 12" L, EXIB............. $325.00

Cross Country Flyer, litho tin, building marked 'Air Mail Hangar,' w/biplane, 17½" H building (w/tower), VG......... $300.00

Farm Set, litho tin, tractor, horse-drawn flat-bed wagon & implements in 'barn' box, NMIB $200.00

Fire Dept Headquarters, litho tin, complete, EXIB......... $450.00

Freight (Universal) Station, litho tin, NMIB $475.00

Gas Station Service Island, litho tin, gas pump, oil rack, air pump & IN/Out signs on curved base, 6x9½" L, EX ... $500.00

Glendale Depot (Electro Lighted Railroad Station w/Automatatic Gate), PS & litho tin, 13½", VG+IB................. $550.00

Hangar & Top Wing Plane, litho tin, 6x7" hangar & plane w/6" WS, plane is nonpowered, EX+ to NM $125.00

Midtown Service Station, complete & unused, MIB...... $400.00

Roadside Rest Service Station (Electric Lighted Filling Station), litho tin, 2 gas pumps w/electric light globes, complete, 10x13", EXIB... $625.00

Roadside Rest Service Station, litho tin, 2 gas pumps w/electric light globes, complete, 10x13", EX $350.00

Sunny Side Service Station, complete, 10x14" w/6" auto, EXIB (box reads 'Electric Lighted Filling Station')............... $700.00

Tractor Sales & Service Farm Machinery Set, 1950s, unused, NMIB $350.00

TV & Radio Station, tin & plastic, NMIB $225.00

Union Station, litho tin, 6½x12", EX $150.00

Marx, Miscellaneous

Grand Central Station, lithographed tin with celluloid windows, electric light, 11x17", EX, $375.00. (Photo courtesy Morphy Auctions on LiveAuctioneers.com)

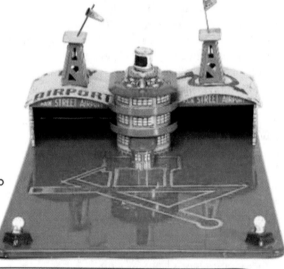

Marx, Miscellaneous

Main Street Airport, lithographed tin with circular tower and two hangars, electric lights, 17" long, EX, $300.00. (Photo courtesy Bertoia Auctions on LiveAuctioneers.com)

Marx, Miscellaneous

Home Town Police Station, lithographed tin, 5" long, complete, NM (VG box), $275.00. (Photo courtesy Morphy Auctions on LiveAuctioneers.com)

Marx, Miscellaneous

Telescope, 14" long, VGIB, $100.00. (Photo courtesy Randy Inman Auctions)

• Matchbox •

The Matchbox series of English and American-made autos, trucks, taxis, Pepsi-Cola trucks, steamrollers, Greyhound buses, etc., was very extensive. By the late 1970s, the company was cranking out more than five million cars every week, and while those days may be over, Matchbox still produces about 75 million vehicles on a yearly basis.

Introduced in 1953, the Matchbox Miniatures series has always been the mainstay of the company. There were 75 models in all but with enough variations to make collecting them a real challenge. Larger, more detailed models were introduced in 1957; this series, called Major Pack, was replaced a few years later by a similar line called King Size. To compete with Hot Wheels, Matchbox converted most models over to a line called Superfast that sported thinner, low-friction axles and wheels. (These are much more readily available than the original 'regular wheels,' the last of which were made in 1969.) At about the same time, the King Size series became known as Speed Kings; in 1977 the line was reintroduced under the name Super Kings.

In the early 1970s, Lesney started to put dates on the baseplates of their toy cars. The name 'Lesney' was coined from the first names of the company's founders, Leslie and Rodney Smith. The last Matchbox toys that carried the Lesney mark were made in 1982. Today many models can be bought for less than $10.00, though a few are priced much much higher.

In 1988, to celebrate the company's 40th anniversary, Matchbox issued a limited set of five models that were replicas of the originals except for a few minor variations. These five were repackaged in 1991 and sold under the name Matchbox Originals. In 1993 a second series expanded the line of reproductions.

Another line that's become very popular is Models of Yesteryear. These are slightly larger replicas of antique and vintage vehicles.

The Matchbox brand has changed hands several times, first to David Yeh and Universal Toy Company in 1982, then to Tyco Toys in 1992, and finally to Mattel, which purchased Tyco, and along with it, Matchbox, Dinky, and several other Tyco subsidiaries, such as Fisher-Price, Milton-Bradley, and View-Master. Mattel still owns Matchbox today.

To learn more, we recommend *Matchbox Toys, 1947 to 2007*, by Dana Johnson.

To determine values of examples in conditions other than given in our listings, based on MIP prices, deduct a minimum of 10% if the original container is missing, 30% if the condition is excellent, and as much as 70% for a toy graded only very good.

Key:
KS — King Size, Speed Kings, and Super Kings
MP — Major Packs
RW — regular wheels

SF — Superfast
YY — Models of Yesteryear

AA & RAC Matchbox Garages Breakdown Service Wreck Truck, RW, #13, 1955, MIP..............................$70.00
AA & RAC Matchbox Garages Breakdown Service Wreck Truck, RW, #13, 1961, MIP..........................$100.00
AEC Ergomatic 8-Wheel Tipper, RW, #51, 1969, MIP......$30.00
AEC Y-Type Lorry (1916), YY, #Y-6, 1958, MIP $100.00
Airport Coach, SF, #65, 1979, various tampos, MIP..........$10.00
Alvis Stalwart BP Exploration, RW, #61, 1966, MIP.........$35.00
Ambulance/Emergency Medical Service, SF, #41, MIP.....$18.00
Armored Jeep, SF, #38, 1977, MIP $8.00
Army Ambulance, RW, #63, Ford 3-Ton truck, 1959, MIP ...$50.00
Army Ferret Scout Car, RW, #61, 1959, MIP.....................$35.00
Army Half Track Mark III, RW, #49, 1958, MIP $60.00
Army Saracen Personnel Carrier, RW, #54, 1958, MIP $50.00
Aston Martin Racer, RW, #19, 1961, MIP $10.00
Auburn 851 Boattail Speedster (1933), YY, #Y-19, 1980, MIP ..$30.00
Austin A55 Cambridge Sedan, RW, #29, 1961, MIP.........$85.00
Austin Mk 2 Radio Truck, RW, #68, 1959, olive, MIP $60.00
Aveling Bradford Diesel Road Roller, RW, #1, 1953, dk gr, MIP..$125.00
Aveling Barford Tractor Shovel, RW, #43, 1962, yel w/yel base & driver, red shovel, MIP.................................$60.00
Baja Buggy, SF, #13, 1971, flower tampo, MIP $15.00
Bazooka Custom Street Rod, RW, #K-44, 1973, MIP $15.00
Beach Buggy RW, #30, 1970, MIP...................................$15.00
Beach Hopper, SF, #47, 1973, MIP..................................$10.00
Bedford Coach, RW, #21, 1956, 'London to Glasgow' decal, MIP $85.00

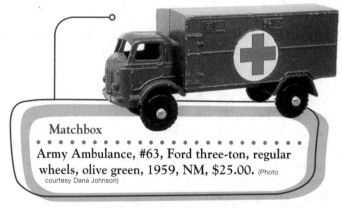

Matchbox
• •
Army Ambulance, #63, Ford three-ton, regular wheels, olive green, 1959, NM, $25.00. (Photo courtesy Dana Johnson)

Matchbox
• •
Army Flammable CD-34-94 Articulated Tanker, BK, #MM1, MIP, $95.00. (Photo courtesy Worldwide Diecast Toy Auctions on LiveAuctioneers.com)

Bedford Dunlop 12CWT Van, RW, #25, 1956, MIP....... $100.00

Bedford Ice Cream Truck, MP, #M-2, 1957, 'Wall's Ice Cream' decals, MIP...$65.00

Bedford Lomas Ambulance, RW, #14, 1962, MIP.............$50.00

Bedford Low Loader, RW, #27, 1958, MIP $135.00

Bedford Milk Delivery Van, RW, #29, 1956, MIP.............$75.00

Bedford Milk Delivery Van, RW, #29, 1956, NM $40.00

Bedford Petrol Tanker, RW, #25, 1964, MIP $30.00

Bedford Ton Tipper, RW, #3, 1961, blk wheels, MIP $65.00

Bedford Ton Tipper, RW, #3, 1961, gray wheels, MIP..... $100.00

Bedford Tractor & York Trailer, MP, #M-2, 1961, 'Lep International Transport' decals, MIP $100.00

Bently (4.5 Litre), YY, #Y-5, 1962, MIP.........................$25.00

Berkley Cavalier Travel Trailer, RW, #23, 1956, pale bl, MIP ...$75.00

Bertone Runabout, KS, #K-31, 1972, MIP........................$15.00

Big Banger, SF, #26, 1973, MIP $20.00

Big Foot 4x4, SF, #22, 1982, MIP $15.00

Blaze Buster, SF, #22, 1976, MIP $8.00

Blaze Trailer Fire Chief's Car, KS, #K-40, 1973, MIPo $15.00

BMW 3.0 CSL, SF, #45, 1975, MIP $12.00

Boss Mustang, RW, #44, 1972, MIP................................$18.00

Bridge Transporter, KS, #K-44, 1981, MIP.......................$15.00

Cabin Cruiser & Trailer, RW, #9, 1966, bright bl deck, MIP....$30.00

Cadillac Sixty Special, RW, #27, 1960, MIP.....................$75.00

Cambuster Custom Street Rod, KS, #K-43, 1973, MIP.....$15.00

Car Transport, SF, #11, 1978, MIP $10.00

Car Transporter, MP, #M-8, 1964, 'Farnborough Measham'/'Car Auction Collection' decals, MIP $135.00

Case Bulldozer, #16, 1969, MIP......................................$35.00

CAT Bulldozer, SF, #64, 1981, MIP...............................$8.00

Caterpillar Crawler Bulldozer, RW, #18, 1964, MIP $45.00

Caterpillar DB Bulldozer, RW, #18, 1956, MIP.................$75.00

Caterpillar Earth Mover, MP, #M-1, 1957, EXIB...............$60.00

Caterpillar Earth Scraper, MP, #M-12, 1957, MIP.............$75.00

Caterpillar Tractor, RW, #8, 1959, MIP.............................$85.00

Caterpillar Tractor, RW, #8, 1961, MIP.............................$60.00

Cement Mixer, RW, #3, 1953, MIP $125.00

Cement Truck, KS, #K-26, 1980, red, 'McAlpine' decal, MIP .$20.00

Cement Truck, KS, #K-26, 1980, yel, MIP $12.00

Cement Truck, SF, #19, 1977, MIP $5.00

Chevy ('57), SF, #4, 1981, MIP $6.00

Chevy Corvette, SF, #62, MIP...$10.00

Chevy Impala Taxi Cab, RW, #20, 1965, MIP $35.00

Chevy Pro Stocker, RW, #34, 1981, MIP $20.00

Citroen DS19, RW. #66, 1959, MIP.................................$55.00

Citroen Station Wagon, SF, #66, 1980, MIP $8.00

Claas Combine Harvester, RW, #65, 1967, MIP $30.00

Cleansing Service Refuse Truck, RW, #15, 1963, MIP $40.00

Commer Ice Cream Canteen, RW, #47, 1963, w/figure, MIP ..$70.00

Commer Milk Delivery Truck, RW, #21, 1961, MIP..........$65.00

Commer Pickup Truck, RW, #50, 1958, gray plastic wheels, MIP $150.00

Corvette Caper Cart, KS, #K-55, 1975, bronze & dk bl, MIP .$15.00

Corvette Caper Cart, KS, #K-55, 1975, lt bl, MIP $20.00

Crossley (1918) Ambulance Truck, YY, #Y-13, 1973, 'RAF' decal, MIP $75.00

DAF Girder Truck, RW, #58, 1968, MIP..........................$25.00

DAF Tipper Container Truck, RW, #47, 1968, MIP $25.00

Daimler (1911), YY, #Y-13, 1966, MIP $60.00

Daimler (1922), YY, #Y-13, 1966, MIP $40.00

Daimler Ambulance, RW, #14, 1956, MIP....................... $100.00

Daimler Bus, RW, #74, 1966, cream, Esso Extra Petrol decals, MIP...$30.00

Datsun 260Z, Rally Car, KS, #K-52, 1975, MIP.................$15.00

Datsun 260Z, SF, #75, 1979, MIP $10.00

Dennis Fire Escape, RW, #9, 1955, MIP $65.00

Dennis Refuse Truck, RW, #15, 1963, MIP $35.00

Denver LaFrance Fire Pumper Truck, RW, #29, 1966, MIP ..$30.00

De Tomasa Pantera, SF, #8, 1975, MIP $8.00

Diddle Trolley Bus (1931), YY, #Y-10, 1988, MIP $35.00

Diesel Road Roller, RW, #1, 1953, MIP $125.00

Dodge Ambulance, KS, #K-38, 1980, MIP $15.00

Dodge Articulated Horse Box, KS, #K-18, 1966, MIP $80.00

Dodge Cattle Truck, RW, #37, 1966, MIP.........................$35.00

Dodge Challenger, SF, #1, 1976, bl or red, MIP.................$20.00

Dodge Challenger, SF, #1, 1982, yel, MIP........................$10.00

Dodge Charger Funny Car Dragster, RW, #70, 1972, MIP.$18.00

Dodge Charger Mark III, SF, #52, 1970, MIP $20.00

Dodge Crane Truck, RW, #63, 1968, red hook, MIP..........$20.00

Dodge Dragster, KS, #K-22, 1969, dk bl, MIP..................$75.00

Dodge Monaco Fire Chief, KS, #K-67, 1978, yel, 'Hackensack' decal, MIP, $15 to..$20.00

Dodge Stake Truck, RW, #4, 1967, MIP..........................$30.00

Dodge Tractor w/Twin Tippers, KS, #K-16, 1966, MIP .. $150.00

Dodge Wreck Truck, RW, #13, 1965, 'BP' decal, MIP $30.00

Dragon Wheels, RW, #43, 1972, MIP $20.00

Drott Excavator, RW, #58, 1962, MIP..............................$65.00

Dumper, RW, #2, 1953, MIP.. $100.00

Dumper, RW, #2, 1957, MIP...$85.00

Dumper, RW, #2, 1961, 'Laing' decal, MIP $28.00

Dumper, RW, #2, 1961, 'Muir-Hill' decal, MIP $35.00

Dunlop Van, RW, #25, 1956, NM $35.00

Matchbox
• • • • • • • • •
Cement Mixer, regular wheels, #3, 1953, $60.00 to $85.00. (Photo courtesy Dana Johnson)

Matchbox
• • • • • • • • •
Chevy Pro Stocker, regular wheels, #34, 'Lightning' tampo, 1981, unpainted base, $6.00 to $8.00. (Photo courtesy Dana Johnson)

Easy Rider Motorcycle, KS, #K-47, 1973, lt brn or orange driver, MIP $15.00

Easy Rider Motorcycle, KS, #K-47, 1973, wht driver, MIP.$40.00

Eight-Wheel Crane Truck, RW, #30, 1965, MIP $25.00

Eight-Wheel Tipper Truck, RW, #17, 1963, 'Hoveringham' decal, MIP $45.00

Eight-Wheel Tipper Truck, RW, #51, 1969, 'Douglas' or 'Pointer' decals, MIP $25.00

Euclid Quarry Truck, RW, #6, 1954, orange, MIP.............$90.00

Euclid Quarry Truck, RW, #6, 1959, yel, MIP $80.00

Euclid Quarry Truck, RW, #6, 1964, yel, MIP $30.00

Ferrari F1 Racing Car, RW, #73, 1962, MIP......................$75.00

Fiat 1500, RW, #56, 1965, MIP $20.00

Field Car, RW, #18, 1969, MIP...$25.00

Fire Chief Car, RW, #64, 1976, MIP.................................$15.00

Fire Pumper, SF, #29, 1970, MIP $40.00

Flying Bug, SF, #11, 1973, MIP $25.00

Foden Concrete Truck, RW, #21, 1968, MIP $20.00

Ford Angila, RW, #7, 1961, blk wheels, MIP $100.00

Ford Angila, RW, #7, 1961, gray wheels, MIP $150.00

Ford Capri, SF, #54, 1971, MIP $10.00

Ford Corsair & Boat, RW, #45, 1965, MIP........................$40.00

Ford Cortina, RW, #25, 1968, MIP....................................$15.00

Ford Escort RS2000, SF, #9, 1978, MIP $10.00

Ford Fairlane Fire Chief Car, RW, #59, 1963, MIP $75.00

Ford Fairlane Station Wagon, RW, #31, 1960, MIP........ $100.00

Ford Galaxie Police Car, RW, #55, 1966, MIP $65.00

Ford Group Six, #RW, 45, 1970, MIP.................................$20.00

Ford GT, SF, #41, 1970, MIP $25.00

Ford Heavy Wreck Truck, RW, #71, 1968, 'Esso' decals, MIP..$40.00

Ford Model A Breakdown Truck (1930), YY, #Y-7, 1984, MIP..$25.00

Ford Model T Tanker (1912), YY, #Y-3, MIP.....................$50.00

Ford Mustang Cobra, KS, #K-60, 1978, red or metallic red, MIP $25.00

Ford Mustang Cobra, KS, #K-60, 1978, wht, MIP.............$15.00

Ford Mustang Fastback, RW, #8, 1966, MIP $40.00

Ford Mustang Fastback, SF, #8, 1970, MIP $100.00

Ford Mustang GT-350, SF, #23, 1981, MIP.......................$20.00

Ford Pickup, RW, #6, 1969, w/camper, MIP......................$25.00

Ford Pickup, SF, #6, 1970, w/camper, MIP.......................$20.00

Ford Pickup Truck (1930), YY, #Y-35, 1990, MIP $20.00

Ford Prefect, RW, #30, 1956, M..$40.00

Ford Prefect, RW, #30, 1956, MIP....................................$80.00

Ford Refuse Truck, RW, #7, 1966, MIP $30.00

Ford Refuse Truck, SF, #7, 1970, MIP $10.00

Ford Thames Estate Car, RW, #70, 1959, MIP..................$65.00

Ford Thames Trader Compressor Truck, RW, #28, 1959, yel, MIP $80.00

Ford Thames Trader Wreck Truck, RW, #13, 1961, MIP . $100.00

Ford Tractor RW, #39, 1967, MIP......................................$28.00

Ford Tractor, SF, #39, 1970, MIP......................................$22.00

Ford Tractor w/Dyson Low Loader & Case Tractor, KS, #K-11, 1966, MIP $75.00

Ford Zephyr 6 MKIII, RW, #33, 1963, MIP.......................$40.00

Ford Zodiac MK IV, RW, #53, 1968, MIP...........................$25.00

Fordson Tractor, RW, #72, 1959, MIP $75.00

Formula 5000 Racer, SF, #36, 1977, MIP $10.00

Freeman Inter-City Commuter Coach, SF, #22, 1970, MIP...$10.00

GMC Tipper Truck, RW, #26, 1968, MIP $18.00

GMC Tipper Truck, SF, #26, 1970, MIP $25.00

GMC Van (1937), YY, #Y-12, 1988, various ads, MIP $20.00

Grand Prix Mercedes, YY, #Y-10, 1958, wht, MIP......... $150.00

Gran Fury Fire Chief Car, KS, #K-78, 1990, orange or wht, MIP $8.00

Gran Fury Fire Chief Car, KS, #K-78, 1990, red, IAAFC, MIP .$15.00

Gran Fury Police Car, KS, #K-78, 1979, blk & wht w/'City Police' decal or plain wht, MIP...................................$10.00

Gran Fury Police Car, KS, #K-78, 1979, blk w/bl interior, MIP $30.00

Gran Fury Taxi, KS, #K-79, 1979, MIP..............................$15.00

Greyhound Bus, RW, #66, 1967, MIP $35.00

Greyhound Bus, SF, #66, 1971, MIP $25.00

Grit Spreading Truck, RW, #70, 1966, MIP $25.00

Gruesome Twosome, SF, #4, 1971, MIP.............................$15.00

Guildsman 1, RW, #40, 1971, MIP....................................$15.00

Hairy Hustler, SF, #7, MIP $12.00

Hay Trailer, RW, #40, 1967, MIP......................................$18.00

Helicopter Transporter, KS, #K-92, 1982, MIP..................$20.00

Hillman Minx, RW, #43, 1958, MIP..................................$65.00

Honda Motorcycle w/Trailer, RW, #38, 1967, MIP...........$40.00

Horse Box, RW, #17, 1969, MIP.......................................$20.00

Horse Box, SF, #17, 1971, AEC Ergomatic truck cab, MIP...$15.00

Horse Box, SF, #40, 1978, MIP...$12.00

Horse-Drawn Double-Decker Bus, YY, #Y-12, 1959, 'Lipton's Tea' advertising, NMIB $40.00

Hot Fire Engine, KS, #K-53, 1975, MIP.............................$15.00

Hot Rocker, SF, #67, 1973, MIP..$10.00

Hot Rod Draguar, RW, #36, 1970, MIP.............................$25.00

Hovercraft, SF, #2, 1976, MIP...$10.00

Hydraulic Shovel, KS, #K-1, 1960, MIP.............................$80.00

Interstate Double Freighter, MP, #M-9, 1962, EX (EX box) .$80.00

Matchbox

Ford 1933 Coupe, Super-fast, #13, bright orange-red with flame graphics, 2005, $3.00 to $4.00. (Photo courtesy Dana Johnson)

Matchbox

Horse Box (Ascot Stables), #K-18, 1966, articulated, with three horses, Dodge, 6½", 1966, NM, $50.00.

Matchbox

Hummer Bus (Blue's Clues), 2004, white, $2.00 to $3.00. (Photo courtesy Dana Johnson)

Matchbox

Jaguar Racer, regular wheels, #41, MIP, $65.00. (Photo courtesy Worldwide Diecast Toy Auctions on LiveAuctioneers.com)

Matchbox

Jaguar XK8 Convertible, #24, green with butterscotch interior, no markings, $1.00 to $2.00. (Photo courtesy Dana Johnson)

Matchbox

Laing Dump Truck, #2, 1961, NM, $10.00.

Matchbox

Land Rover Ninety (Safari Park), #35, 1993 'Off-Road' five-pack, $1.00 to $2.00. (Photo courtesy Dana Johnson)

Interstate Double Freighter, MP, #M-9, 1962, MIP......... $100.00
Iron Fairy Crane, RW, #42, 1969, MIP.............................$20.00
Iso Grifo, SF, #14, 1970, MIP......................................$22.00
Jaguar XKE, RW, #32, 1957, blk wheels, MIP $50.00
Jaguar XKE, RW, #32, 1962, gray wheels, MIP $100.00
Jaguar XK140 Coupe, RW, #32, 1962, MIP.......................$65.00
Jaguar SS100 (1936), YY, #Y-1, 1977, MIP......................$15.00
Jaguar 3.4 Litre Saloon, RW, #65, 1962, MIP....................$65.00
Javelin AMX, SF, #9, 1972, MIP $8.00
JCB Excavator, KS, #K-41, 1981, MIP $20.00
Jeep CJ6, SF, #53, 1978, MIP $10.00
Jeep Hot Rod, SF, #2, 1972, MIP....................................$15.00
John Deere Tipping Trailer, RW, #51, 1964, MIP $20.00
John Deere-Lanz Tractor, RW, #50, 1964, blk or gray wheels,
  MIP..$35.00
Jumbo Crane, RW, #11, 1965, MIP $40.00
Kennel Truck, RW, #50, 1970, MIP.................................$45.00
Lagonda Drophead Coupe (1938), YY, #Y-11, 1973, gold & red,
  MIP..$450.00
Lamborghini Countach, SF, #27, 1973, MIP......................$15.00
Lamborghini Marzai, SF, #20, 1970, MIP.........................$22.00
Land Rover, RW, #12, 1957, left-side steering, MIP $30.00
Land Rover, RW, #12, 1960, right-side steering, MIP........$70.00
Land Rover Fire Truck, RW, #57, 1966, 'Kent Fire Brigade'
  decals, MIP...$40.00
Lemans Bently (1929), YY, #Y-5, 1958, MIP $175.00
Leyland Petrol Tanker, 1968, 'BP' decals, MIP $25.00
Leyland Royal Tiger Bus, RW, #40, 1961, blk plastic wheels,
  MIP $35.00
Leyland Royal Tiger Coach, RW, #40, 1961, silver plastic wheels,
  MIP...$50.00
Leyland Royal Tiger Coach, RW, #40, 1961, silver wheels,
  MIP...$65.00
Leyland Tanker, SF, #32, 1970, MIP................................$20.00
Leyland Tipper Truck, KS, #K-37, 1979, MIP...................$15.00
Leyland Van (4-Ton), YY, #Y-7, 1957, cream roof, blk plastic
  wheels, 3 lines of text, MIP...........................$1,500.00
Leyland Van (4-Ton), YY, #Y-7, 1957, wht or cream roof, metal
  wheels, 3 lines of text, MIP.............................. $100.00
Lincoln Continental, SF, #28, 1979, MIP $18.00
Lincoln Continental, SF, #31, 1970, MIP.........................$35.00
Lincoln Continental Mark V, RW, #28, 1979, MIP.............$8.00
Lomas Ambulance, RW, #14, 1962, MIP $40.00
London Bus, RW, #5, 1965, Longlife decals, MIP $28.00
London E Class Tram Car (1907), YY, #Y-3, 1956, Dewars,
  MIP $500.00
Lotus Europa, SF, #5, 1979, MIP $12.00
Lotus Racing Car, RW, #19, 1966, MIP...........................$35.00
Lyons Maid Ice Cream Mobile Shop, RW, #47, 1963, MIP... $125.00
Mack Dump Truck, RW, #28, 1968, MIP $35.00
Mack Dump Truck, SF, #28, 1970, MIP $20.00
Maserati Bora, KS, #K-56, 1975, metallic gold, MIP.........$50.00
Maserati Bora, KS, #K-56, 1975, metallic gray, MIP..........$15.00
Maserati Bora, KS, #K-56, 1975, red, MIP $20.00
Maserati Bora, SF, #32, 1973, MIP $15.00
Massey-Ferguson Combine Harvester, MP, #M-5, 1960, MIP . $175.00
Matra Rancho, KS, #K-90, 1982, MIP $15.00
McCormick International Tractor B-250, RW, #4, 1960, MIP .$70.00

Mercedes 230SL, SF, #27, 1970, MIP $22.00
Mercedes 300SE, RW, #46, 1970, MIP $20.00
Mercedes Ambulance, KS, #K-63, 1977, MIP $15.00
Mercedes Ambulance, RW, #3, MIP $30.00
Mercedes Ambulance, SF, #3, 1970, MIP...........................$22.00
Mercedes-Benz 36/220 (1928), YY, #Y-10, 1963, wht, MIP ..$140.00
Mercury Cougar, SF, #62, 1970, MIP...................................$28.00
Mercury Cougar Dragster, KS, #K-21, 1968, MIP............$50.00
Mercedes Lorry, RW, #1, 1968, MIP....................................$20.00
Mercedes Lorry, SF, #1, 1970, MIP.....................................$20.00
Mercedes Trailer, RW, #2, 1968, MIP.................................$15.00
Mercedes Trailer, SF, #2, 1970, MIP...................................$18.00
Mercedes Truck Stuttgarter (1913), 1988, MIP $20.00
Mercedes Unimog, RW, #49, 1967, MIP...............................$20.00
Mercedes 220SE, RW, #53, 1963, MIP $50.00
Mercer Raceabout (1913), YY, #Y-7, 1961, lilac w/blk tires,
    MIP $50.00
Mercer Raceabout (1913), YY, #Y-7, 1961, lilac w/gray tires,
    MIP $125.00
Mercury Station Wagon, RW, #73, 1968, MIP...................$30.00
Merryweather Marquis Fire Engine, RW, #9, 1959, MIP ...$43.00
MG 1100 Sedan, RW, #64, 1966, w/driver and dog, MIP ..$45.00
MGA Sports Car, RW, #19, 1958, MIP..............................$130.00
Mod Rod, SF, #1, 1971, wildcat head decal, MIP $18.00
Mod Tractor, SF, #25, 1972, MIP...$8.00
Model A Ford Van (1930), YY, #Y-22, 1982, MIP...............$15.00
Monteverdi Hai, SF, #3, 1973, MIP.....................................$15.00
Morris J2 Pickup, RW, #60, 1958, 'Builders Supply Company'
    decal, MIP $65.00
M3 Personnel Carrier, RW, #49, 1958, gray wheels & treads w/
    silver rollers, NMIP $35.00
Opal Diplomat, RW, #36, 1966, MIP...................................$25.00
Orange Peel, RW, #74, 1981, MIP..$55.00
Peterbilt Wreck Truck, KS, #K-20, 1979, dk gr, MIP.........$15.00
Peterbilt Wreck Truck, KS, #K-20, 1979, lt gr, MIP $20.00
Peterbilt Wreck Truck, KS, #K-20, 1979, wht, MIP $50.00
Petrol Tanker, KS, #K-16, 1974, gr, 'Texaco' decal, MIP ...$75.00
Petrol Tanker, KS, #K-16, 1974, red, 'Texaco' decal, MIP.$25.00
Petrol Tanker, RW, #25, 'BP' decals, MIP............................$35.00
Peugeot (1907), YY, #Y-5, 1969, MIP $25.00
Pickford's Removal Van, RW, #46, 1960, MIP $100.00
Pipe Truck, RW, #10, 1966, MIP $30.00
Pipe Truck, RW, #10, 1970, MIP $20.00
Piston Popper, SF, #10, 1974, MIP $12.00
Piston Popper, SF, #60, 1982, MIP $5.00
Plymouth Grand Fury, SF, #10, 1979, Police tampos, MIP .$10.00
Plymouth Police Car, RW, #10, 1979, MIP $15.00
Plymouth Trail Duster Rescue Vehicle, KS, #K-65, 1978, red,
    MIP $15.00
Pontiac Convertible, RW, #39, 1962, yel w/blk wheels, MIP ...$60.00
Pontiac Firebird, SF, #4, 1975, MIP.......................................$8.00
Pontiac Grand Prix, SF, #22, 1970, MIP.............................$50.00
Pony Trailer, RW, #43, 1968, dk gr base, red wheels, MIP .$40.00
Porsche 911 Turbo, SF, #3, 1979, MIP $6.00
Prime Mover, RW, #15, 1956, rear tow hook missing o/w
    NM+...$575.00
Prince Henry Vauxhall (1914), YY, #Y-2, MIP.................$25.00
Quarry Truck, RW, #6, 1954, metal wheels, MIP $90.00

Matchbox
Leyland Site Office Truck, Superfast, 1970, NM, $12.00. (Photo courtesy Dana Johnson)

Matchbox
Mack Model AC Truck (1920), Models of Yesteryear, #Y-30, 1985, 'Acorn Storage Co.' advertising, MIP, $25.00. (Photo courtesy Dana Johnson)

Matchbox
Maserati Racer 4CL T/1948 #52, 1958, yellow, $60.00 to $80.00. (Photo courtesy Dana Johnson)

Matchbox
Plymouth Estate Station Wagon, #344, EX+, $40.00. (Photo courtesy Worldwide Diecast Toy Auctions on LiveAuctioneers.com)

Matchbox
Rolls-Royce Silver Cloud, regular wheels, #44, MIP, $45.00. (Photo courtesy Worldwide Diecast Toy Auctions on LiveAuctioneers.com)

Racing Mini, RW, #29, 1971, MIP $20.00
Ranger Wild Life Truck, SF, #57, 1973, MIP.....................$15.00
Ready Mix Concrete Truck, RW, #26, 1961, blk wheels, MIP.$35.00
Ready Mix Concrete Truck, RW, #26, 1961, gray wheels, MIP...$80.00
Refrigerator Truck, RW, #44, 1967, red wheels, MIP $25.00
Refrigerator Truck, SF, #44, 1970, MIP............................$18.00
Renault 5TL, SF, #21, 1979, MIP.....................................$10.00
Renault Type AG (1910), YY, #Y-25, 1983, MIP $25.00
Road Dragster, SF, #19, 1971, MIP....................................$8.00
Road Tanker, RW, #11, 1955, MIP $100.00
Rolls-Royce (1912), YY, #Y-7, 1968, silver w/gray roof, MIP ..$200.00
Rolls-Royce (1912), YY, #Y-7, 1968, silver w/red roof, MIP .$40.00
Rolls-Royce Convertible Coupe, SF, #69, 1970, MIP........$20.00
Rolls-Royce Fire Engine (1920), YY, #Y-6, 1977, MIP $25.00
Rolls-Royce Phantom, RW, #44, 1964, blk plastic wheels, MIP...$50.00
Rolls-Royce Silver Cloud, RW, #44, 1958, NM.................$40.00
Rolls Royce Silver Ghost (1906), YY, #Y-10, 1969, MIP ..$25.00
Rolls-Royce Silver Shadow, RW, #24, 1967, MIP $40.00
Rolls-Royce Silver Shadow, SF, #24, 1970, MIP................$18.00
Routemaster London (Double-Decker) Bus, RW, #5, 1965, 'Visco-Static' decals, MIP...$30.00
Ruston Bucyrus Power Shovel, MP, #M-4, 1959, MIP.... $350.00
Saab Sonnet, SF, #65, MIP $12.00
S&S Cadilaac Ambulance, RW, #54, 1965, MIP...............$65.00
Safari Land Rover, SF, #12, 1970, gold, MIP.....................$22.00
Santa Fe Locomotive, YY, #Y-13, 1959, MIP....................$60.00
Scaffold Truck, RW, #11, 1969, MIP $25.00
Scaffold Truck, RW, #11, 1970, MIP................................$15.00

Scammell Mountaineer Snowplow, RW, #16, 1964, blk plastic wheels, MIP..$55.00
Scoop Coopa, SF, #37, 1973, MIP....................................$10.00
Seafire, SF, #5, 1976, MIP...$6.00
Seasprite Rescue Helicopter, SF, #75, 1977, MIP..............$10.00
Sentinel Steam Wagon, YY, #Y-4, 1956, blk wheels, MIP ...$225.00
Sentinel Steam Wagon, YY, #Y-4, 1956, unpnt metal wheels, MIP...$60.00
Serta Coach, RW, #12, 1970, MIP.....................................$20.00
Site Dumper, SF, #26, 1976, MIP $35.00
Site Engineer Vehicle, SF, #20, 1977, MIP........................$15.00
Slingshot Dragster, RW, #64, 1971, MIP...........................$15.00
Snorkel Fire Engine, SF, #13, 1977, MIP $10.00
Snow-Trac Tractor, RW, #36, 1964, MIP...........................$35.00
Spyker (1904), YY, #Y-16, 1961, lt gr w/blk tires, MIP .$2,000.00
Spyker (1904), YY, #Y-16, 1961, maroon w/blk tires, MIP..$1,200.00
Spyker (1904), YY, #Y-16, 1961, yel w/blk tires, MIP........$35.00
Spyker (1904), YY, #Y-16, 1961, yel w/gray tires, MIP ... $100.00
Stake Truck, SF, #4, 1970, MIP $18.00
Studebaker Lark Station Wagon, RW, #42, 1965, MIP......$40.00
Stutz Bearcat (1931), YY, #Y-14, 1974, lime or cream, MIP ..$20.00
Stutz Bearcat (1931), YY, #Y-15, 1974, bl w/chrome wheels, MIP $25.00
Sugar Container Truck, RW, #10, 1961, Tate & Lyle, MIP.$85.00
Swamp Rats Patrol Boat, SF, #30, 1977, MIP....................$10.00
Tanzara, SF, #53, 1973, MIP $8.00
Taylor Jumbo Crane, RW, #11, 1965, MIP $25.00
T-Bird Convertible ('57), SF, #42, 1981 or 1982, MIP $8.00
Ten-Ton Pressure Refuler Truck, RW, #73, 1959, gray plastic wheels, MIP...$100.00
Tractor Shovel, RW, #69, 1965, MIP.................................$35.00
Tractor Transporter, KS, #K-20, 1968, MIP $125.00
Tractor Transporter, KS, #K-21, 1974, MIP $50.00
Trailer Caravan, RW, #23, 1965, MIP $35.00
TV Service Van, RW, #62, 1963, 'Rentaset' decals, MIP . $125.00
Tyre Fryer, SF, #42, 1973, MIP..$10.00
Vantastic, SF, #34, 1976, MIP $10.00
Vauxhall Cresta, RW, #22, 1956, MIP...............................$75.00
Vauxhall Cresta, RW, #22, 1958, MIP............................ $150.00
Vauxhall Victor, RW, #45, 1958, MIP................................$75.00
Vauxhall Victor Estate Car, RW, #38, 1963, MIP $65.00
Volks-Dragon, RW, #31, 1971, MIP $18.00
Volkswagen Beetle (Dragon Wheels), SF, #43, 1973, MIP.$15.00
Volkswagen Beetle (Hi Ho Silver), SF, #15, 1981, MIP $10.00
Volkswagen Beetle (Hot Chocolate), SF, #46, 1982, MIP.$10.00

Matchbox

Rolls-Royce Silver Shadow Convertible Coupe, Superfast, #69, 1969, metallic blue, orange-brown interior, tan tonneau, black base, $20.00 to $30.00. (Photo courtesy Dana Johnson)

Matchbox

Scammell Breakdown Lorry, #64, 1959, NM, $50.00.

Matchbox

Volkswagen 1500 Saloon (1968), Superfast, #15, 1970, ivory, $20.00 to $25.00. (Photo courtesy Dana Johnson)

Matchbox
Volvo XC90, #55, 2005, metallic silver, $1.00 to $2.00. (Photo courtesy Dana Johnson)

Matchbox
Wynn's Race Car #16, Superfast, #34, pink, MIP, $85.00. (Photo courtesy Worldwide Diecast Toys on LiveAuctioneers.com)

Volkswagen Camper, RW, #23, 1970, MIP..........................$35.00
Volkswagen Camper, RW, #34, 1968, silver, MIP $50.00
Volkswagen Carvette Camper, RW, #34, 1962, lt gr, M.....$90.00
Volkswagen Caravette Camper, RW, #34, 1962, lt gr, MIP ..$125.00
Volkswagen Golf, RW, #7, 1976, MIP $15.00
Volkswagen Golf, SF, #7, 1977, MIP $10.00
Volkswagen 1200 Sedan, RW, #25, 1960, MIP...................$75.00
Volkswagen 1600TL, RW, #67, 1967, red, no roof rack, MIP ..$25.00
Volkswagen 1600TL, SF, #67, 1970, MIP...........................$30.00
Volvo Ambulance, KS, #K-96, 1984, MIP...........................$15.00
Walker Electric Van, YY, #Y-29, 1985, any ad, MIP..........$20.00
Weatherhill Hydraulic Excavator, RW, #24, 1959, blk wheels, MIP..$39.00

Wells Fargo Truck, SF, #69, 1979, MIP $15.00
Wheel Tipper Truck, KS, #K-1, 1964, MIP........................$50.00
Whitlock Dinkum Dumoer, MP, #M-10, 1962, MIP..........$75.00
Wildcat Dragster, SF, #8, 1971, MIP $10.00
4.5 Litre Supercharged Bently, YY, #Y-2, 1984, purple, MIP..$20.00

• • • • • • • • • • • • • • • • • Model Kits • • • • • • • • • • • • • • • •

Though model kits were popular with kids of the '50s who enjoyed the challenge of assembling a classic car or two or a Musketeer figure now and then, when the monster series hit in the early 1960s, sales shot through the ceiling. Made popular by all the monster movies of that decade, ghouls like Vampirella, Frankenstein, and the Wolfman were eagerly assembled by kids everywhere. They could (if their parents didn't object too strongly) even construct an actual working guillotine. Aurora had other successful series of figure kits, too, based on characters from comic strips and TV shows, as well as a line of sports stars.

But the vast majority of model kits were vehicles. They varied in complexity, some requiring much more dexterity on the part of the model builder than others, and they came in several scales, from 1/8 (which might be as large as 20" to 24") down to 1/43 (generally about 3" to 4"), but the most popular scale was 1/25 (usually between 6" to 8"). Some of the largest producers of vehicle kits were AMT, MPC, and IMC. Though production obviously waned during the late 1970s and early 1980s, with the intensity of today's collector market, companies like Ertl (who is now producing 1/25 scale vehicles using some of the old AMT dies) are proving that model kits still sell very well.

As a rule of thumb, assembled kits (built-ups) are priced at about 25% to 50% of the price range for a boxed kit, but this is not always true on the higher-priced kits. One mint in the box with the factory seal intact will often sell for up to 15% more than if the seal were broken, though depending on the kit, a sealed perfect box may add as much as $100.00. Condition of the box is crucial. Last but not least, one must factor in internet sales, which could cause some values to go down considerably. Unless noted, condition is for 'unbuilt' kits, and boxes are excellent or better.

For more information, we recommend *Classic Model Kits* by Rick Pollizi, and *Collectible Figure Kits of the '50s, '60s, and '70s* by Gordy Dutt.

See also Plasticville.

Addar, Evel Knievel, 1974, #152, MIB $50.00
Addar, Jaws, 1975, MIB..$100.00
Addar, Planet of the Apes, Caesar or Gen Aldo, 1974, MIB, ea... $50.00
Addar, Planet of the Apes, Cornelius, 1974, MIB $50.00
Addar, Planet of the Apes, Dr Zaius, 1974, MIB $40.00
Addar, Planet of the Apes, Dr Zira, 1974, MIB $40.00
Addar, Planet of the Apes, Gen Ursus 1973-74, MIB........$45.00
Addar, Planet of the Apes, Jail Wagon, 1975, NMIB........$45.00
Addar, Planet of the Apes, Stallion & Soldier, 1974, MIB ..$100.00
Addar, Planet of the Apes, Tree House, 1975, NMIB........$45.00
Addar, Super Scenes, Jaws in a Bottle, 1975, MIB.............$75.00
Addar, Super Scenes, Spirit in a Bottle, 1975, MIB...........$50.00

Model Kits
Airfix, Stegosaurus, $25.00. (Photo courtesy www.gasolinealleyantiques.com)

Airfix, Bigfoot, 1978, MIB..................................$75.00

Airfix, Boy Scout, 1965, MIB.............................$30.00

Airfix, Flying Saucer, 1981, MIB.........................$35.00

Airfix, James Bond & Odd Job, 1966, MIB...............$200.00

Airfix, James Bond's Aston Martin, 1965, MIB...........$250.00

Airfix, Julius Caesar, 1973, MIB.........................$40.00

Airfix, Napoleon, 1978, MIB.............................$25.00

Airfix, Royal Sovereign, #F901S, 1950s, EXIB..........$15.00

Airfix, 2001: A Space Odyssey, Orion, 1970, #701, MIB. $100.00

AMT, Farrah's Foxy Vet, 1977, MIB......................$65.00

AMT, Flintstones Rock Crusher, 1974, MIB...............$75.00

AMT, Flintstones Sports Car, 1974, MIB..................$75.00

AMT, Ford Pinto, 1974, MIB (sealed) $55.00

AMT, Girl From UNCLE, 1974, MIB.....................$350.00

AMT, KISS Custom Chevy Van, 1977, MIB...............$100.00

AMT, Laurel & Hardy '27 Touring Car, 1976, MIB.........$65.00

AMT, Man From UNCLE Car, MIB........................$225.00

AMT, My Mother the Car, 1965, MIB.....................$45.00

AMT, Sonny & Cher Mustang, 1960s, MIB................$325.00

AMT, Star Trek, Klingon Cruiser, #S952-802, 1968, MIB....$225.00

AMT, Star Trek, Spock, 1973, NMIB (sm box)............$150.00

AMT, Star Trek, USS Enterprise Command Bridge, 1975, MIB $75.00

AMT/Ertl, A-Team Van, 1983, MIB......................$30.00

AMT/Ertl, Back to the Future Delorian, 1991, MIB (sealed) ..$35.00

AMT/Ertl, Batman (movie), Batman Cocoon, 1989, MIB....$20.00

AMT/Ertl, Batman (movie), Batwing, 1990, MIB (sealed) ..$30.00

AMT/Ertl, Monkeemobile, 1990, MIB (sealed) $100.00

AMT/Ertl, Robocop 2, Robo 1 Police Car, 1990, MIB......$25.00

AMT/Ertl, Star Trek, USS Enterprise, Chrome Set, Special Edition #6005, MIB...$35.00

AMT/Ertl, Star Trek (TV), Kirk, 1994, MIB (sealed) $25.00

AMT/Ertl Star Trek: TNG, USS Enterprise, 1988, MIB...$30.00

Anubis, Jonny Quest, Robot Spy, 1992, MIB...............$60.00

Anubis, Jonny Quest, Turu the Terrible, 1992, MIB..........$60.00

Aurora, Addams Family Haunted House, 1964, MIB.....$850.00

Aurora, Anzio Beach, 1968, MIB.........................$80.00

Aurora, Archie's Car, 1969, MIB.........................$100.00

Aurora, Banana Splits Banana Buggy, 1969, MIB..........$525.00

Aurora, Batboat, 1968, MIB.............................$475.00

Aurora, Batcycle, 1967, MIB.............................$425.00

Aurora, Batman, Comic Scenes, 1974, MIB (sealed) $125.00

Aurora, Batmobile, 1966, MIB...........................$450.00

Aurora, Big Frankie, see Aurora, Frankenstein (Big Frankie)

Aurora, Bloodthirsty Pirates, Blackbeard, 1965, MIB.....$225.00

Aurora, Bride of Frankenstein, 1965, MIB.................$300.00

Aurora, Captain America, 1966, MIB.....................$325.00

Aurora, Captain Kid, 1965, MIB.........................$125.00

Aurora, Castle Creatures, Vampire, 1966, MIB.............$225.00

Aurora, Creature from the Black Lagoon, 1963, MIB $450.00

Aurora, Creature from the Black Lagoon, glow-in-the-dark, 1969, MIB...$200.00

Aurora, Cro-Magnon Man or Woman, see Aurora, Prehistoric Scenes

Aurora, Dick Tracy in Action, 1968, MIB $350.00

Aurora, Dr Jekyll as Mr Hyde, 1964, MIB.................$375.00

Aurora, Dr Jekyll as Mr Hyde, glow-in-the-dark, 1969, MIB ..$200.00

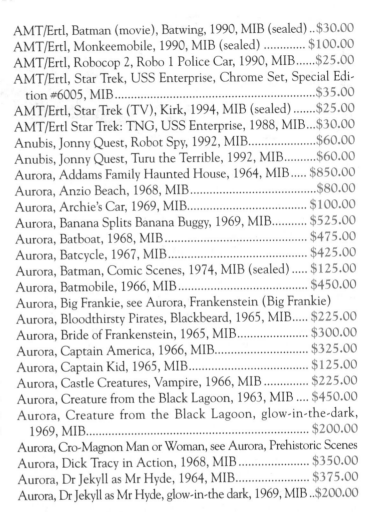

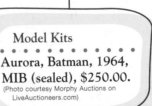

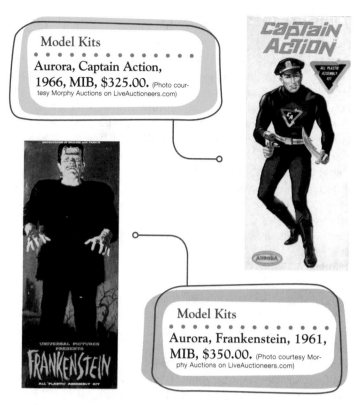

Model Kits
• • • • • • • • •
Aurora, Captain Action, 1966, MIB, $325.00. (Photo courtesy Morphy Auctions on LiveAuctioneers.com)

Model Kits
• • • • • • • • •
Aurora, Incredible Hulk, 1966, MIB, $325.00. (Photo courtesy Morphy Auctions on LiveAuctioneers.com)

Model Kits
• • • • • • • • •
Aurora, Frankenstein, 1961, MIB, $350.00. (Photo courtesy Morphy Auctions on LiveAuctioneers.com)

Model Kits
• • • • • • • • •
Aurora, Invaders, UFO, 1968, MIB, $100.00. (Photo courtesy Morphy Auctions on LiveAuctioneers.com)

Model Kits
• • • • • • • • •
Aurora, Lone Ranger, 1967, MIB, $200.00. (Photo courtesy Morphy Auctions on LiveAuctioneers.com)

Aurora, Dracula, 1967, MIB............................... $300.00
Aurora, Dracula, Monsters of the Movies, 1975, MIB.... $350.00
Aurora, Fantastic Voyage, Voyager, 1969, MIB.............. $500.00
Aurora, Flying Sub, 1968, MIB $235.00
Aurora, Flying Sub, 1975, MIB $100.00
Aurora, Forgotten Prisoner, 1966, MIB.......................... $425.00
Aurora, Forgotten Prisoner, Frightening Lightning, 1969,
    MIB $475.00
Aurora, Forgotten Prisoner, Frightening Lightning, glow-in-the-
    dark, 1969, MIB.. $200.00
Aurora, Frankenstein (Big Frankie), #470, 1964, 19", EX...$275.00
Aurora, Frankenstein (Big Frankie), #470, 1964, 19", MIB..$1,200.00
Aurora, Frankenstein, glow-in-the-dark, 1971, MIB $150.00
Aurora, Frankenstein, Monster Scenes, 1971, MIB........ $125.00
Aurora, Frankenstein, Monsters of the Movies, 1975 MIB..$325.00
Aurora, George Washington, 1965, MIB (sealed) $100.00
Aurora, Ghidrah, Monsters of the Movies, 1975, MIB... $325.00
Aurora, Gladiator w/Trident, Famous Fighters, 1959, MIB... $175.00
Aurora, Godzilla, 1964, MIB.. $550.00
Aurora, Godzilla, glow-in-the-dark, 1964, MIB.............. $350.00
Aurora, Godzilla, glow-in-the-dark, 1972, MIB............. $225.00
Aurora, Godzilla's Go-Cart, 1966, assembled, NM...... $1,000.00
Aurora, Godzilla's Go-Cart, 1966, MIB $3,500.00
Aurora, Gold Knight of Nice, 1957, MIB $325.00
Aurora, Gold Knight of Nice, 1965, MIB $275.00
Aurora, Green Beret, 1966, MIB.................................... $175.00
Aurora, Green Hornet Black Beauty, 1966, MIB........... $525.00
Aurora, Gruesome Goodies, Monster Scenes, 1971, MIB....$100.00
Aurora, Hunchback of Notre Dame, Anthony Quinn, 1964,
    MIB... $300.00
Aurora, Hunchback of Notre Dame, glow-in-the-dark, 1969,
    MIB... $150.00
Aurora, Incredible Hulk, Comic Scenes, 1974, MIB...... $100.00

Aurora, Invaders, UFO, 1975, MIB..................................$75.00
Aurora, James Bond 007, 1966, MIB.............................. $350.00
Aurora, Jesse James, 1966, MIB.................................... $200.00
Aurora, John F Kennedy, 1965, MIB.............................. $150.00
Aurora, King Kong, 1964, MIB...................................... $475.00
Aurora, King Kong, glow-in-the-dark, 1969, MIB.......... $300.00
Aurora, King Kong, glow-in-the-dark, 1972, MIB.......... $200.00
Aurora, Knights in Shining Armour, Sir Galahad, 1973, MIB...$35.00
Aurora, Knights in Shining Armour, Sir Kay, 1973, MIB .$35.00
Aurora, Land of the Giants, Diorama, 1968, MIB.......... $450.00
Aurora, Land of the Giants, Space Ship, 1968, MIB...... $425.00
Aurora, Lone Ranger, Comic Scenes, 1974, MIB (sealed) .$75.00
Aurora, Lost in Space, Robot, 1968, MIB....................... $875.00
Aurora, Man From UNCLE, Illy Kuryakin, 1966, MIB.. $275.00
Aurora, Man From UNCLE, Napoleon Solo, 1966, MIB. $275.00
Aurora, Mummy, 1963, MIB $375.00

Aurora, Mummy, Frightening Lightning, 1969, MIB...... $425.00

Aurora, Mummy, glow-in-the-dark, 1969, MIB............. $200.00

Aurora, Mummy's Chariot, 1965, MIB $575.00

Aurora, Munster's Living Room, 1964, MIB................$1,500.00

Aurora, Odd Job, Gold Finger, 1966, MIB..................... $475.00

Aurora, Pendulum, Monster Scenes, 1971, MIB............ $100.00

Aurora, Phantom of the Opera, Frightening Lightning, 1969, MIB... $375.00

Aurora, Phantom of the Opera, glow-in-the-dark, 1969, MIB..$175.00

Aurora, Phantom of the Opera, glow-in-the-dark, 1972, MIB..$100.00

Aurora, Phantom of the Opera, 1963, MIB $325.00

Aurora, Prehistoric Scenes, Cave Bear, MIB $50.00

Aurora, Prehistoric Scenes, Cro-Magnon Man, 1971, MIB..$50.00

Aurora, Prehistoric Scenes, Cro-Magnon Woman, 1971, MIB $50.00

Aurora, Prehistoric Scenes, Neanderthal Man, 1971, MIB ..$75.00

Aurora, Prehistoric Scenes, Tar Pit, 1972, MIB............. $150.00

Aurora, Robin, Comic Scenes, 1974, MIB..................... $100.00

Aurora, Robin, 1966, MIB... $175.00

Aurora, Robin the Boy Wonder, Comic Scenes, 1974, MIB ..$125.00

Aurora, Rodan, Monsters of the Movies, 1975, rare, MIB ..$425.00

Aurora, Spider-Man, 1966, MIB $300.00

Aurora, Spider-Man, Comic Scenes, 1974, MIB $125.00

Aurora, Steve Canyon, Famous Fighters, 1958, MIB...... $200.00

Aurora, Superboy, Comic Scenes, 1974, MIB................. $100.00

Aurora, Superboy, 1964, MIB....................................... $250.00

Aurora, Superman, 1963, MIB $400.00

Aurora, Superman, 1975, M (EX sealed box) $165.00

Aurora, Tarzan, 1967, MIB... $200.00

Aurora, Tarzan, Comic Scenes, 1974, MIB..................... $100.00

Aurora, Tonto, 1967, MIB... $250.00

Aurora, Tonto, Comic Scenes, 1974, MIB......................$75.00

Aurora, Viking, Famous Fighters, 1959, MIB................. $250.00

Aurora, Voyage to the Bottom of the Sea, Seaview, 1966, MIB $325.00

Aurora, Voyage to the Bottom of the Sea, Seaview, 1975, MIB $200.00

Aurora, Whoozis, Alfalfa, 1966, MIB...........................$85.00

Aurora, Whoozis, Kitty, 1966, MIB..............................$75.00

Aurora, Whoozis, Snuffy, 1966, MIB............................$75.00

Aurora, Witch, 1965, MIB $325.00

Aurora, Witch, glow-in-the-dark, 1969, MIB $200.00

Aurora, Wolfman, Frightening Lightning, 1969, MIB.... $425.00

Aurora, Wolfman, glow-in-the-dark, 1969, MIB $175.00

Aurora, Wolfman, glow-in-the-dark, 1972, MIB $75.00

Aurora, Wolfman, Monsters of the Movies, 1975, MIB . $250.00

Aurora, Wolfman, 1962, MIB.. $300.00

Aurora, Wolfman, #425, Toys R Us reissue, MIB (sealed).$30.00

Aurora, Wolfman's Wagon, 1965, MIB $450.00

Aurora, Wonder Woman, 1965, MIB............................. $550.00

Bandai, Armoured Car (Bogey Wheeled Puma), #K-108, 1970s, MIB $100.00

Bandai, Godzilla, 1984, MIB $50.00

Bandai, Jeep, #PA1, 1970s, MIB....................................$35.00

Bandai, Pzkw-IV Heuschrecke (German Army Tank IV Grasshopper), #4254H, 1970s, MIB $40.00

Billiken, Batman, type A, 1989, MIB.......................... $125.00

Billiken, Batman, type B, 1989, MIB $150.00

Billiken, Bride of Frankenstein, 1984, MIB $225.00

Billiken, Colossal Beast, 1986, MIP $45.00

Billiken, Creature from the Black Lagoon, 1991, MIB ... $150.00

Billiken, Cyclops, 1984, MIB $225.00

Billiken, Dracula, 1989, MIB....................................... $175.00

Billiken, Frankenstein, 1988, MIB $150.00

Billiken, Joker, 1989, MIB... $150.00

Billiken, Mummy, 1990, MIB $175.00

Billiken, Phantom of the Opera, 1980s, MIB.................. $300.00

Billiken, Predator, 1991, MIB.......................................$80.00

Billiken, She-Creature, 1989, MIB...............................$75.00

Billiken, The Thing, 1984, MIP $325.00

Billiken, Ultraman, 1987, MIB.....................................$65.00

Dark Horse, King Kong, 1992, vinyl, MIB.....................$75.00

Dark Horse, Mummy, 1995, MIB $150.00

Dark Horse, Predator II, 1994, MIB $175.00

Model Kits

Hawk, Francis the Foul, Weird-ohs, 1963, MIB, $100.00.

Eldon, Pink Panther, 1970s, MIB $75.00

Gabriel/Hubley, Duesenberg Straight 8 Model SJ, 1975, metal, MIB $75.00

Gabriel/Hubley, Model A Roadster, 1975, metal, MIB......$75.00

Gabriel/Hubley, 1912 Model T Delivery Truck, 1977, MIB...$60.00

Hawk, Beach Bunny Catchin' Rays, 1964, MIP $125.00

Hawk, Bobcat Roadster, 1962, MIB $50.00

Hawk, Cobra II, 1950s, MIB.. $100.00

Hawk, Davy the Way-Out Cyclist, 1963, MIP............. $100.00

Hawk, Digger & Dragster, 1963, MIB $125.00

Hawk, Drag Hag, 1963, MIP $100.00

Hawk, Endsville Eddie, 1963, MIP................................ $100.00

Hawk, Frantic Banana, 1965, MIB $150.00

Hawk, Freddie Flame Out, 1963, MIP............................ $110.00

Hawk, Hidad Silly Surfer, 1964, MIP $125.00

Hawk, Hot Dogger Hangin' Ten, 1964, MIP.................. $100.00

Hawk, Huey's Hut Rod, 1963, MIP $75.00

Hawk, Killer McBash, 1963, MIB $175.00

Hawk, Leaky Boat Louie, 1963, MIB $125.00

Hawk, Sling Rave Curvette, 1964, MIB............................$85.00

Hawk, Steel Pluckers, 1965, MIB $110.00

Hawk, Thunderbird, Indian Totem Poles, 1966, MIB $50.00

Hawk, Totally Fab, 1965, MIP.. $125.00

Hawk, Wade A Minute, 1963, MIP $135.00

Hawk, Woodie on a Surfari, 1964, MIB $125.00

Horizon, Bride of Frankenstein, 1990s, MIB....................$70.00

Horizon, Creature from the Black Lagoon, 1990s, MIB.. $100.00

Horizon, Dracula, 1990s, MIP $75.00

Horizon, Dr Doom, Marvel Universe, 1991, MIB..............$65.00

Horizon, Frankenstein, 1990s, MIB..................................$75.00

Horizon, Incredible Hulk, Marvel Universe, 1990, MIB ...$50.00

Horizon, Invisible Man, 1990s, MIB.................................$65.00

Horizon, Mole People, Mole Man #2, 1988, MIB..............$65.00

Horizon, Mummy, 1990s, MIB..$65.00

Horizon, Punisher, Marvel Universe, 1988, MIB...............$50.00

Horizon, Robocop, ED-209, MIB $75.00

Horizon, Robocop, Robocop #30, 1992, MIB $75.00

Horizon, Spider-Man, Marvel Universe, 1988, MIB...........$50.00

Horizon, The Thing, Marvel Universe, 1991, MIB $50.00

Horizon, Wolfman, 1990s, MIB...$60.00

Imai, Captain Blue, 1982, MIB $15.00

Imai, Missile Tank BB-1 (Motorized), #524, 1960s, MIB.. $400.00

Imai, Orguss, Cable, 1994, MIB $40.00

Imai, Orguss, Incredible Hulk, 1990, MIB $45.00

Imai, Orguss, Spider-Man (new pose), 1994, MIB.............$30.00

ITC, USS Oregon Battleship (Motorized), #H-3680, 1950s, VGIB $75.00

Lindberg, Big Wheeler, 1965, MIB....................................$125.00

Lindberg, Creeping Crusher, 1965, MIB $50.00

Lindberg, Fat Max, 1971, MIB $75.00

Lindberg, Flintstone's Flintmobile, 1994, MIB $25.00

Lindberg, Flying Saucer, 1952, MIB $200.00

Lindberg, Giant American Bullfrog, 1973, MIB $40.00

Lindberg, Green Ghoul, 1965, MIB $50.00

Lindberg, Jurassic Park, Velociraptor, MIB.......................$20.00

Lindberg, Krimson Terror, 1965, MIB $50.00

Lindberg, Road Hog, 1965, MIB $75.00

Lindberg, Satan's Crate, 1964, MIB $150.00

Lindberg, Sick Cycle, 1971, MIB $75.00

Lindberg, Zopp, 1964, MIB $100.00

Monogram, Bad Machine, 1970s, MIB $60.00

Monogram, Bathtub Buggy, 1960s, MIB (sealed)............ $100.00

Monogram, Battlestar Galactica, Colonial Viper, 1979, MIB....$55.00

Monogram, Battlestar Galactica, Cylon Base Star, 1979, MIB...$50.00

Monogram, Battlestar Galactica, Cylon Raider, 1979, MIB ..$55.00

Monogram, Buck Rogers, Marauder, 1970, MIB $75.00

Monogram, Devil Chopper, 1971, unused, MIB (sealed).. $110.00

Monogram, Dracula, 1983, MIB..$45.00

Monogram, Elvira Macabre Mobile, 1988, MIB $35.00

Monogram, Flip Out, 1965, MIB $200.00

Monogram, Frankenstein, 1983, MIB $35.00

Monogram, Godzilla, 1978, MIB..................................... $100.00

Monogram, Indianapolis Racer (Kurtis Kraft Roadster), 1965, unused, MIB $55.00

Monogram, Model Missile Paket, #MP6, 1950s, MIP........$35.00

Monogram, Predicta, 1964, MIB..$60.00

Monogram, Sand Crab, 1969, MIB $50.00

Monogram, Smug Bug, 1971, unused, MIB (sealed) $75.00

Monogram, Snoopy as Joe Cool, 1971, MIB................... $100.00

Monogram, Snoopy w/Motorcyle, 1971, MIB................. $100.00

Monogram, Speed Shift, 1965, MIB $200.00

Monogram, Superman, 1978, MIB.....................................$50.00

Model Kits

Monogram, Jaguar XK-E GT Sports Coupe, 1964, MIB, $25.00. (Photo courtesy Morphy Auctions on LiveAuctioneers.com)

Model Kits

MPC, Beverly Hillbillies Truck, 1968, MIB, $200.00. (Photo courtesy Morphy Auctions on LiveAuctioneers.com)

Model Kits

MPC, Hot Curl, The Surfer's Idol, 1960s, MIB, $50.00.

Model Kits

MPC, Pirates of the Caribbean, Dead Men Tell No Tales, 1972, MIB, $100.00.

Model Kits

Revell, Bonanza, #1931, 1966, MIB, $150.00. (Photo courtesy Morphy Auctions on LiveAuctioneers.com)

Monogram, Three Stooges, any character, 1999, MIB.......$25.00
Monogram, TV Orbiter, 1959, MIB $150.00
Monogram, Voyage to the Bottom of the Sea, Flying Sub, 1979, MIB..$50.00
Monogram, Wolfman, 1983, MIB $50.00
MPC, Alien, 1979, MIB (sealed) $100.00
MPC, Barnabas, Dark Shadows, 1968, MIB...................$425.00
MPC, Barnabas Vampire Van, Dark Shadows, 1969, MIB...$275.00
MPC, Batman, Super Powers, 1984, MIB $65.00
MPC, Bionic Woman, Bionic Repair, 1976, MIB.............$80.00
MPC, Black Hole, Cygnus, 1979, MIB $175.00
MPC, Black Hole, Maximillian, 1979, MIB $100.00
MPC, Black Hole, Vincent, 1979, MIB $100.00
MPC, Curl's Gurl, 1960s, MIB $75.00
MPC, Darth Vader, glow-in-the-dark lightsaber, 1979, MIB $50.00
MPC, Dukes of Hazzard, Cooter's Tow Truck, 1981, MIB .$30.00
MPC, Dukes of Hazzard, Daisy's Jeep CJ, 1980, MIB.........$40.00
MPC, Dukes of Hazzard, General Lee, #661, 1979, MIB...$45.00
MPC, Dukes of Hazzard, Sheriff Rosco's Police Car, 1982, MIB $30.00
MPC, Empire Strikes Back, AT-AT, 1980, MIB.................$50.00
MPC, Empire Strikes Back, Luke Skywalker's Snowspeeder, 1980, MIB...$45.00
MPC, Empire Strikes Back, Star Destroyer, 1980, MIB.....$70.00
MPC, Fonzie & Motorcycle, 1976, MIB $50.00
MPC, Hardcastle & McCormick, GMC Truck, MIB $40.00
MPC, Hogan's Heroes Jeep, 1968, MIB $125.00
MPC, Incredible Hulk, 1978, MIB (sealed) $50.00
MPC, Incredible Hulk Van, 1977, MIB $25.00
MPC, Knight Rider, KITT 2000, 1982, MIB $25.00
MPC, Mannix Roadster, 1968, MIB...............................$50.00
MPC, Monkeemobile, 1967, MIB $225.00
MPC, Pirates of the Caribbean, Ghost of the Treasure Guard, 1974..$75.00
MPC, Raiders of the Lost Ark Chase Scene, 1982, MIB...$50.00
MPC, Return of the Jedi, C-3PO, 1983, MIB...................$50.00
MPC, Return of the Jedi, R2-D2, MIB............................$40.00
MPC, Road Runner & the Beep-Beep T, 1972, MIB.........$75.00
MPC, Six Million Dollar Man, Jaws of Doom, 1975, MIB .$50.00
MPC, Space: 1999, Alien Creature & Vehicle, 1976, MIB ..$60.00
MPC, Space: 1999, Eagle I Transporter, 1976, MIB........ $130.00
MPC, Space: 1999, Hawk Spaceship, 1977, MIB $55.00
MPC, Star Wars, AT-AT, 1981, MIB................................$35.00
MPC, Star Wars, Boba Fett's Slave I, 1982, MIB...............$35.00
MPC, Star Wars, Darth Vader TIE Fighter, 1978, MIB.....$40.00
MPC, Star Wars, R2-D2, 1979, MIB................................$35.00
MPC, Strange Changing Mummy, 1974, MIB...................$40.00
MPC, Strange Changing Time Machine, 1974, MIB $50.00
MPC, Strange Changing Vampire, 1974, MIB $50.00
MPC, Stroker McGurk & Surf Rod, 1960s, MIB............ $135.00
MPC, Super Powers, Superman, 1984, MIB $50.00
MPC, Sweathogs 'Dream Machine,' 1976, MIB $35.00
MPC, TJ Hooker, Police Car, 1982, MIB........................$25.00
MPC, Walt Disney's Haunted Mansion, Escape from the Crypt, 1974, MIB.. $100.00
Polar Lights, Jetson Spaceship, #6810, 2001, NRFB..........$50.00
Pyro, Gladiator Show Cycle, 1970, MIB...........................$65.00
Pyro, Indian Warrior, 1960s, MIB $75.00

Pyro, Prehistoric Monsters Gift Set, 1950s, MIB $125.00
Pyro, Rawhide, Gil Favor, 1956, MIB $75.00
Pyro, Restless Gun, Deputy, 1959, MIB $60.00
Pyro, Surf's Up!, 1970, MIB $40.00
Renwal, Duesenberg ('66), 1960s, unused, MIB $40.00
Renwal, General Patton II Medium Tank, Series M, 1960s, MIB
    (Sealed) $40.00
Renwal, Visible Man, 1959, 1st issue, unused, M (NM box) . $80.00
Renwal, Visible V8 Engine, 1960s, MIB (sealed) $200.00
Renwal, Visible V8 Transparent Operating Auto Engine, 1950s,
    unused, MIB $235.00
Renwal, Visible Woman, 1960, 1st issue, unused, M (NM
    box) $165.00
Revell, Alien Invader, w/lights, 1979, MIB (sealed)..........$50.00
Revell, Amazing Moon Mixer, 1970, MIB $35.00
Revell, Apollo Astronaut on Moon, 1970, MIB $125.00
Revell, Apollo II, Columbia/Eagle, 1969, MIB (sealed) . $100.00
Revell, Apollo II Tranquility Base, 1975, MIB $100.00
Revell, Ariane 4 Rocket, 1985, MIB $35.00
Revell, Baja Humbug, 1971, MIB......................................$85.00
Revell, Beatles, any member, 1965, MIB, ea $250.00
Revell, Big Daddy Roth, Beatnik Bandit, MIB $225.00
Revell, Charlie's Angels Mobile Unit Van, 1977, MIB $75.00
Revell, CHiPs, any kit, 1980s, MIB, ea $35.00
Revell, Code Red, Fire Chief's Car, 1981, MIB $25.00
Revell, Disney's Love Bug Rides Again, 1974, MIB........ $100.00
Revell, Disney's Robin Hood Set #1, 1974, MIB $100.00
Revell, Dr Seuss Horton the Elephant, 1960, MIB......... $400.00
Revell, Dr Seuss Zoo, Kit #1, 1959, MIB........................ $400.00
Revell, Dr Seuss Zoo, 1960, Kit #2, MIB........................ $525.00
Revell, Dune, Ornithopter, 1985, MIB (sealed) $60.00
Revell, Dune, 1985, Sand Worm, MIB (sealed)................$75.00
Revell, Ed 'Big Daddy' Roth, Fink-Eliminator, 1965, MIB... $200.00
Revell, Ed 'Big Daddy' Roth, Mr Grasser, 1964, MIB $100.00
Revell, Ed 'Big Daddy' Roth, Road Agent, 1960, MIB $80.00
Revell, Ed 'Big Daddy' Roth, Tweedy Pie, 1963, MIB........$80.00
Revell, Flash Gordon & the Martian, 1965, MIB........... $150.00
Revell, GI Joe, Attack Vehicle, 1982, MIB........................$25.00
Revell, GI Joe, Rapid Fire Motorcycle, 1982, MIB............$25.00
Revell, Hardy Boys Van, 1977, MIB..................................$35.00
Revell, Love Bug, 1970s, MIB $50.00
Revell, Magnum PI, any kit, 1980s, MIB, ea.....................$50.00
Revell, McHale's Navy PT-73, 1965, MIB $75.00
Revell, Moon Ship, 1957, MIB $225.00
Revell, Moonraker Space Shuttle, 1979, MIB $25.00
Revell, Moonraker Space Shuttle, 1979, MIB (sealed) $35.00
Revell, Penny Pincher VW Bug, 1980, MIB......................$35.00
Revell, Peter Pan Pirate Ship, 1960, MIB....................... $100.00
Revell, Red October Submarine, 1990, MIB $65.00
Revell, Rif Raf & Hid Spitfire, 1971, MIB.........................$50.00
Revell, Robotech, Commando, 1984, MIB (sealed) $50.00
Revell, Robotech, Condar, 1984, MIB (sealed) $35.00
Revell, Robotech Defenders Thoren, 1984, MIB
    (sealed) $35.00
Revell, Space Explorer Solaris, 1969, MIB.................... $125.00
Revell, Terrier Missile, 1958, MIB.................................. $200.00
Revell, US Army Nike Hercules, 1958, MIB....................$60.00
Screamin', Contemplating Conquest, 1995, MIB (sealed) .$50.00

Model Kits

Revell, Dr. Seuss, Cat in the Hat, Beginner's Hobby Kit, MIB, $125.00. (Photo courtesy Morphy Auctions on LiveAuctioneers.com)

Model Kits

Revell, Drag Nut, Ed 'Big Daddy' Roth, 1963, MIB, $150.00.

Model Kits

Revell, Flipper, 1965, MIB, $150.00. (Photo courtesy Morphy Auctions on LiveAuctioneers.com)

Model Kits

Revell, Jaguar XK-E Roadster, 1963, MIB, $25.00. (Photo courtesy Morphy Auctions on LiveAuctioneers.com)

Screamin', Friday the 13th's Jason, MIB $125.00
Screamin', Star Wars, Stormtrooper, 1993, MIB............... $45.00
Screamin', Werewolf, MIB $100.00
Strombecker, Disneyland Stagecoach, 1950s, MIB......... $200.00
Strombecker, Walt Disney's Spaceship, 1958, MIB $300.00
Toy Biz, Ghost Rider, 1996, MIB.......................................$30.00
Toy Biz, Hulk, 1996, MIB...$25.00
Toy Biz, Spider-Man, w/ or w/o wall, 1996, MIB, ea $25.00
Toy Biz, Storm, 1996, MIB $20.00
Toy Biz, Thing, 1996, MIB $20.00
Toy Biz, Wolverine, 1996, MIB $25.00
Tsukuda, Ghostbusters, Stay Puft Man (sm), 1984, MIB...$40.00
Tsukuda, Creature from the Black Lagoon, MIB............. $150.00
Tsukuda, Frankenstein, 1985, MIB................................. $100.00
Tsukuda, Ghostbusters Terror Dog, MIB $125.00
Tsukuda, Metaluna Mutant, MIB $100.00
Tsukuda, Mummy, MIB.. $100.00
Tsukuda, Wolfman, MIB.. $100.00

• • • • • • • • • • • • Movie Posters and Lobby Cards • • • • • • • • • • • •

This field is a natural extension of the interest in character collectibles, and one where there is a great deal of activity. Listed here are posters relating to the great monster classics, Disney, westerns, adventure movies, and cartoons.

Advisor: Rick Toler

Aladdin, 1-sheet, Disney, rolled, regular style, 40x27", NM+ ..$35.00
Aladdin, 2-sheet, Disney, rolled, advance, 40x27", NM+ .$50.00
Alien, 1-sheet, title above Alien egg-like image on blk w/gr &
   yel blaze of light, 1979, 41x27", NM $150.00
Back to the Future, 1-sheet, Michael J Fox, folded, 1985, 41x27",
   NM+ $125.00
Back to the Future, 1-sheet, Michael J Fox, rolled, 1985, 41x27",
   NM+ $350.00
Batman, 1-sheet, image of Batman symbol, rolled, 1989, 40x27",
   NM $25.00
Border Legion, 1-sheet, 1940, Roy Rogers & Gabby Hayes,
   41x27", EX+ $250.00
Border Vigilantes, 1-sheet, 1941, William Boyd (Hopalong
   Cassidy) & Andy Clyde, 41x17", NM $250.00
Boy & the Pirates, 3-sheet, 1960, EX $25.00
Bride of Frankenstein, lobby card, R53, EX+, $150 to.... $400.00
Charlotte's Web, 1-sheet, Hanna-Barbera, 1973, NM.......$50.00
Cinderella, 1-sheet, 1950, 41x27", NM+ $500.00
Close Encounters of the Third Kind, 1-sheet, Steven Spielberg
   movie, 41x27", NM+ $100.00
Dumbo, lobby card, Walt Disney, 1941, 11x14", VG+, $250 to.$750.00
Empire Strikes Back, ½-sheet, Lucasfilms Ltd, 1980, 22x28", style
   A, NM $150.00
Empire Strikes Back, ½-sheet, Lucasfilms Ltd, 1980, 22x28", style
   B, NM... $125.00
Empire Strikes Back, 1-sheet, style B, 1980, Darth Vader overshad-
   owing cast members on lt bl bkgrd, folded, 41x27", M $150.00
Empire Strikes Back, 1-sheet, style B, 1980, Darth Vader overshad-
   owing cast members on lt bl bkgrd, rolled, 41x27", M......$300.00
Gulliver's Travels, lobby card, 1957 reissue, EX+, $20 to ..$50.00
Heart of the Golden West, 1-sheet, Roy Rogers, Gabby Hayes &
   Smiley Burnette, 1942, NM $200.00

In Search of the Castaways (Walt Disney's), lobby card, 1962, NM+, $5 to.................................$10.00

James & the Giant Peach, 1-sheet, dbl-sided, 1996, NM+, $6 to.................................$30.00

Jaws, lobby card, set of 8, various scenes, EX+, $200 to.. $300.00

Mad Max, 1-sheet, Mel Gibson w/gun drawn, American Int'l, 1980, 41x27", folded, NM.................................$200.00

Mighty Joe Young, window card, style A, 1949, cowboys trying to lasso Mighty Joe Young, 14x22", VG+ $725.00

New Adventures of Batman & Robin in 'Robin Meets the Wizard' Chapter 8, lobby card, Columbia, 1949, 11x14", EX.....$200.00

One Million Years BC, window card, Raquel Welch stands before prehistoric scene on yel bkgrd, 22x14", EX $125.00

Peter Pan, insert, Disney, 1953, 36x14", NM.................$475.00

Peter Pan, 3-sheet, 1969 reissue, 81x41", NM $125.00

Return of the Jedi, 1-sheet, style B, 1983, Darth Vader looms lg in background w/descending cast members, 41x27", EX+ . $275.00

Riders of the Deadline, 1-sheet, 'William Boyd as Hopalong Cassidy,' 1-sheet, United Artist, 1943, 41x27", NM (G sleeve).................................$300.00

Robin Hood of Texas, 1-sheet, Gene Autry, 1947, 41x27", EX.$375.00

Rodan the Flying Monster, 1-sheet, Japanese sci-fi w/Rodan attacking crowd on wht bkgrd, 41x27", VG+.............. $600.00

Movie Posters and Lobby Cards

Jetsons, one-sheet, Universal, 1990, NM+, $50.00. (Photo courtesy Stephen Bennett Auctions on LiveAuctioneers.com)

Movie Posters and Lobby Cards

Jitterbugs, window card, Laurel and Hardy, 20th Century Fox, 1943, 14x20", EX, $150.00. (Photo courtesy Stephen Bennett on LiveAuctioneers.com)

Movie Posters and Lobby Cards

Pinocchio, lobby card, Walt Disney, 1940, Coachman, Foulfellow, and Gideon gathered around table, 11x4", EX, $58.00. (Photo courtesy Morphy Auctions on LiveAuctioneers.com)

Movie Posters and Lobby Cards

Peter Pan, one-sheet, Disney, reissue, 1982, $50.00. (Photo courtesy Stephen Bennett Auctions on LiveAuctioneers.com)

Movie Posters and Lobby Cards

Spider-Man, two-sheet, advance recalled poster, 2002, 27x40", rolled, M, $350.00. (Photo courtesy Rick Toler)

Roll on Texas Moon, 6-sheet, Roy Rogers, Dale Evans, Gabby Hayes & Sons of the Pioneers, 81x81", NM+ $750.00

Snow White & the Seven Dwarfs, lobby card, Disney, 1951, VG+ $125.00

Star Wars, 1-sheet, style D, Princess Leia shooting gun while holding onto Luke surrounded by space scenes, 41x27", EX $325.00

Star Wars, 3-sheet, Princess Leia and Luke Skywalker in glowing wht against lg Darth Vader, 41x81", EX+ $750.00

Tarzan & the Ape Man, ½-sheet, Johnny Weissmuller, Maureen O'Sullivan, 1954 reissue, 22x28", EX+ $175.00

Tarzan's Magic Fountain, 3-sheet, Lex Barker, Brenda Joyce, 1949, 81x41", EX $375.00

Tom Mix the Miracle Rider in Chapter 5 'Double Barrelled Doom,' 1-sheet, Mascot Serials, 1935, 41x27", NM.... $450.00

Walt Disney's Davy Crockett, lobby cards, 1955, set of 8, 11x14", EX $400.00

Winnie the Pooh & Tigger Too, ½-sheet, 1974, 22x28", EX+..$50.00

Yellow Submarine, lobby cards, set of 8, limited ed lithos of orig US release cards, ea 11x14" $48.00

• • • • • • • • • • • • • • • Musical Toys • • • • • • • • • • • • • •

Whether meant to soothe, entertain, or inspire, musical toys were part of our growing-up years. Some were as simple as a windup music box, others as elaborate as a lacquered French baby grand piano.

See also Character, TV, and Movie Collectibles; Disney; Rock 'n Roll; Western Heroes and Frontiersmen.

Church Organ, litho tin, hand crank, 10", Chein, EXIB. $150.00

Drum, children on parade, litho tin w/decorative wood bands, zigzag string, 9" dia, 1920s, EX+ $500.00

Drum, circus graphics, litho tin w/paper heads, spring tension body, wooden sticks, 11" dia, Chein, EX+ $100.00

Drum, Noah's Ark graphics, litho tin, Ohio Art, NM $150.00

Drum, The Queen of Hearts, tin w/paper heads, 8" dia, EX+ .$225.00

Drum, Uncle Wiggily's Parade scene, litho tin w/paper top, wooden bands, drumsticks, 1920s, EX $500.00

Electric Player Piano, Chein, NM $300.00

Farmer in the Dell Music Maker, litho tin, crank-op, Mattel, 1950s, EX $125.00

Golden Banjo, Emenee, 1960s, NMIB $125.00

Harmonica, detachable horn, Strauss, 1925, EXIB $150.00

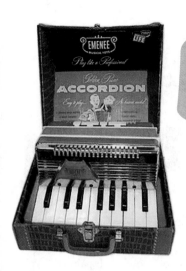

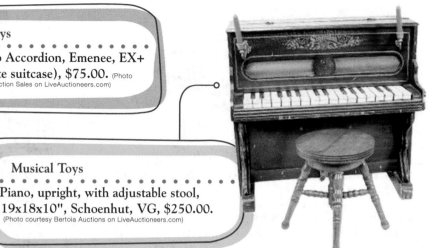

Musical Toys

Golden Piano Accordion, Emenee, EX+
(in leatherette suitcase), $75.00. (Photo
courtesy Bodnar's Auction Sales on LiveAuctioneers.com)

Musical Toys

Piano, upright, with adjustable stool,
19x18x10", Schoenhut, VG, $250.00.
(Photo courtesy Bertoia Auctions on LiveAuctioneers.com)

Kiddyphone Record Player, litho tin, w/up, 7½" dia,
   VG $300.00
Piano, grand style w/internal xylophone, 16", Bliss, EX . $115.00
Piano, Little Bo Peep, wood, 10" H, Marks Bros, VG..... $275.00
Piano, pnt wood w/decal trim, wooden stool, 24x23", Schoenhut,
   EX $550.00

Piano, baby grand, dk stain, 15 wht keys w/simulated blk keys,
   16x10x15", Schoenhut, G+ $100.00
Play-Away Piano, songbook w/16 tunes to play, 10x9", Marx,
   EXIB $100.00
Showboat Band Set #50, plastic, Spec-Toy-Culars Inc, 1952,
   EXIB $35.00

Noah's Ark

The story of Noah building his ark is well known, but few know the story behind the making of the thousands of toy arks that were produced and designed in the nineteenth and early twentieth centuries. The tradition of ark making is embedded deeply in the region of Erzgebirge, the former kingdom of Saxony, in Germany. Entire families took part in the process of constructing these toys from beginning to end in order to put food on the table each week. During this time, children of Victorian households as well as western pioneers strictly observed the Sabbath and were required and expected to play biblical games, and Noah's family members were chief characters in these make-believe games. The toys were favorite gifts to give on Christmas. When the Berlin wall came down in 1990, workers had to change to 'free market' rules and many ark-building families did not outlast the transition, but some survive to this day. There is outstanding detail and workmanship on not only the arks but also the carefully stenciled, brightly decorated animals that came with them. Most arks with accessories were made of wood and produced by Bliss or in Germany. Some of the earliest arks date back to the 1700s; many of these have found respected places in museums and private collections and carry price ranges in the thousands of dollars.

Barge, 7½", pnt & straw decorated wood, sliding panel, 13 pnt
   animals & 2 figures, G+ $400.00
Barge, 14", pnt wood, wht w/reddish brn roof & bottom, 2 church-
   type pointed windows on sides, 8 prs of animals, VG $100.00
Barge, 15", varnished & pnt wood, scalloped roof line, 2 cut-out port-
   holes ea side, 4 spoke wheels, 27 unpnt animals, VG $200.00
Barge, 22", paper litho on wood, The Wonder of Noah's Ark, 1
   figure, Bliss (?), VG $275.00
Barge, 22", pnt wood, log appearance w/brn wavy roof design, pane
   windows/door on side, 69 prs of animals/2 figures, VG . $1,200.00
Barge, 23", pnt wood, 3 pane windows w/shutters, roofed entry at
   1 end, 41 prs of animals plus insects, 2 figures, VG ..$2,000.00
Barge, 27", pnt wood, gray w/4 birds on red roof, floral band, pnt
   pane windows, 200+ animals, Erzgebirge style, VG+.$32,000.00
Flat Bottom, 7", pnt wood, wht w/lavender/red zigzag-striped
   roof, pane windows, 12 carved & pnt animals, EX...... $350.00
Flat Bottom, 12", pnt wood, bird nesting on roof w/wavy design,
   arched pane windows, 19 prs of animals & 2 figures, VG.$225.00
Flat Bottom, 12", pnt wood, red, gr, blk & tan, 4 windows ea side,
   7 wht rubber animals, 'Converse' over end doors, EX.......$75.00

Noah's Ark

Barge, 29", painted wood, 'log' sides with
green gabled roof, fold-down ramp, with
40 Elastolin animals, VG, $650.00. (Photo
courtesy Bertoia Auctions on LiveAuctioneers.com)

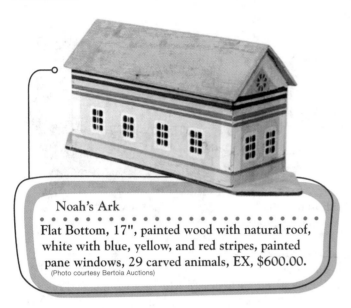

Noah's Ark

Flat Bottom, 17", painted wood with natural roof, white with blue, yellow, and red stripes, painted pane windows, 29 carved animals, EX, $600.00.
(Photo courtesy Bertoia Auctions)

Noah's Ark

Flat Bottom, 18", lithograph on wood with painted roof, animals, and swagging garland, lithoed at windows, 32 animals and one figure, VG, $650.00.
(Photo courtesy Bertoia Auctions)

Flat Bottom, 13", paper litho on wood, 8 animals & 1 figure, VG $475.00

Flat Bottom, 13½", pnt/natural wood, brn wavy stripes on roof, gr stripes on sides, pane windows, unpnt animals, VG+.. $300.00

Flat Bottom, 14", paper litho on wood, stained roof & bottom, pane windows, 70 animals & 8 figures, EX $400.00

Flat Bottom, 17", paper litho on wood, shingle-look roof, animals lithoed in 2 lg windows, 37 animals & 2 figures, G $550.00

Flat Bottom, 18", pnt wood, bird on roof, pnt bands under roof line, pane windows, 43 prs of animals & 2 figures, VG $1,000.00

Flat Bottom, 21", pnt & litho on wood, brn & wht log cabin/lath roof, lithoed windows, VG $275.00

Flat Bottom, 24", litho on wood, log-look, wheeled fold-up, 12 molded animals, G $100.00

Flat Bottom, 25", pnt wood w/paper frieze, roof w/2 ribs ea side, 9 pnt compo animals & 1 Noah figure, G+ $450.00

Flat Bottom, 27", pnt wood, 2 levels, very sm spoke wheels, 12 pr of carved animals, VG.. $1,050.00

Sleigh Base, 5½" H, litho on wood, ends turned up, 7 flat lithoed animals, Bliss, VG $250.00

• Nodders • • • • • • • • • • • • • • • •

Most of the nodders listed are papier-maché or ceramic and made in Japan in the 1960s and 1970s. Some are earlier bisque and ceramic figures made in Germany around the 1930s. They reflect accurate likenesses of the characters they portray and have become popular collectibles. Many of the newer ones were sold as souvenirs from Disney, Universal Studios, and Six Flags amusement parks, as well as roadside concessions. Values are for nodders in near mint condition. To calculate prices for examples in excellent or very good condition reduce these prices by 25% to 40%.

See also Character, TV, and Movie Collectibles; other specific categories.

Advisors: Matt and Lisa Adams

Nodders

Andy and Barney, Mayberry, ceramic, 7", 1992, mail-order only from Time Warner, EX, each $75.00 to $100.00. (Photo courtesy June Moon)

Beetle Bailey, $150 to $250.00

Bugs Bunny, $175 to $350.00

Charlie Brown, 1970s, $45 to... $75.00

Charlie Brown as Baseball Player, ceramic..........................$75.00

Chinaman, compo, Japan, 1960s...$65.00

Chinese Boy & Girl, 5½", pr $65.00

Colonel Sanders, 2 different, ea $150 to $250.00

Dagwood, compo, 'Kiss Me' on gr base, 1950s, $150 to .. $250.00

Danny Kaye & Girl Kissing, pr $150 to $200.00

Dobie Gillis, $300 to.. $400.00

Donald Duck, Irwin/WDP, $100 to $125.00

Donald Duck, rnd gr base, 1970s, $75 to......................... $100.00

Donald Duck, 'Walt Disney World,' sq wht base, $75 to . $125.00

Donny Osmond, wht jumpsuit w/microphone, $100 to.. $150.00

Dr Ben Casey, $150 to $250.00

Dr Kildare, compo, rnd wht base, 1960s, $150 to $250.00

Nodders
Just Kids, Nicodemus, Mush, and Fatso, bisque, German, EX, each $175.00. (Photo courtesy Morphy Auctions on LiveAuctioneers.com)

Dumbo, rnd red base, $100 to............................. $150.00
Elmer Fudd, $200 to... $350.00
Foghorn Leghorn, $200 to................................. $350.00
Goofy, arms at side, $100 to............................. $125.00
Goofy, arms folded, $100 to............................. $125.00
Hobo, compo, Japan, 1960s............................... $60.00
Linus, sq blk base, $100 to............................... $150.00
Linus as Baseball Catcher, ceramic, Japan........... $75.00
Little Audrey, $150 to...................................... $200.00
Lt Fuzz (Beetle Bailey), $150 to........................ $250.00
Lucy, no base, sm, 1970s, $75 to....................... $100.00
Lucy as Baseball Player, ceramic, $75 to............. $100.00
Mammy (Dogpatch USA), $75 to........................ $125.00
Mary Poppins, wood, Disneyland, 1960s, $150 to.......... $200.00
Maynard G Krebs Holding Bongos (Dobie Gillis), $300 to . $400.00
Mickey Mouse, red & yel outfit, rnd gr base, $100 to..... $125.00
Mickey Mouse, red, wht & bl outfit, Disney World, $75 to .. $125.00
Mickey Mouse, red, wht & bl outfit, Disneyland, sq wht base,
    $100 to... $150.00
Mr Peanut, moves at waist, $150 to $200.00
Mutt & Jeff, bisque, Germany, 1920s, 3" & 2", VG+, pr . $150.00
NY World's Fair Boy & Girl Kissing, $100 to $125.00
Oodles the Duck (Bozo the Clown), $200 to.......... $250.00
Peppermint Patti as Baseball Player, ceramic, Japan, $45 to .. $75.00
Phantom of the Opera, gr face, rare, $150 to $400.00

Pig Pen, Lego, 1960s, $100 to............................ $150.00
Pluto, rnd gr base, 1970s, NM, $100 to............... $125.00
Porky Pig, $200 to.. $350.00
Raggedy Andy, bank, 'A Penny Earned,' $75 to $100.00
Raggedy Ann, bank, 'A Penny Saved,' $75 to $100.00
Roy Rogers, compo, sq gr base, Japan, 1960s, $150 to $250.00
Schroeder, sq blk base, Lego, $100 to............... $150.00
Sgt Snorkel (Beetle Bailey), $150 to................. $250.00
Smokey the Bear, rnd base, $150 to $200.00
Smokey the Bear, sq base, $150 to.................... $200.00
Snoopy as Baseball Player, ceramic, Japan, $45 to $75.00
Snoopy as Flying Ace, 1970s, $60 to.................. $75.00
Snoopy as Joe Cool, no base, sm, 1970s, $60 to $75.00
Snoopy as Santa, 1970s, $60 to........................ $75.00
Space Boy, blk spacesuit & helmet................... $75.00
Speedy Gonzales, $200 to............................... $350.00
Three Little Pigs, red rnd base, ea $150 to.......... $200.00
Three Stooges, bisque, set of 3, MIB, $150 to....... $200.00
Topo Gigio, w/fruit or w/o fruit, ea $60 to............ $75.00
Topo Gigio, 9", Rossini/Japan, 1960s, $60 to $75.00
Tweety Bird, $200 to....................................... $350.00
Wile E Coyote, $200 to $350.00
Winnie the Pooh, rnd gr base, 1970s, $100 to $150.00
Wolfman, $200 to $400.00
Woodstock, no base, sm, 1970s, $45 to................ $75.00
Woodstock, 1970s, $45 to................................ $75.00
Woodstock as Baseball Player, ceramic, Japan, $45 to....... $75.00
Yosemite Sam, $200 to.................................... $350.00

Nodders
Zero, Beetle Bailey, $150.00 to $250.00.

Optical Toys

Compared to the bulky viewers of years ago, contrary to the usual course of advancement, optical toys of more recent years have tended to become more simplified in concept.

See also Character, TV, and Movie Collectibles; Disney; View-Master and Tru-Vue; Western Heroes and Frontiersmen.

Automatic Space Viewer, Stephens, 1950s, EX $175.00
Bingoscope, Ideal Home Cinema, b/o, w/Mickey Mouse 9.5mm
    films, 10½", VGIB $115.00
Cinderella Pixie Viewer, Stori-Views, 1950s, complete,
    NMIB $20.00
Cini Vue, 1939 Golden Gate International/100 Movie Views &
    Pathegrams, complete, EXIB........................... $55.00

Comicscope Viewer, Remington Moris, 1900s, comic strip viewer
    w/3 comic strips, EX $50.00
Easy Show Motorized Movie Projector, Kenner, 1960s, b/o,
    MIB $110.00
Flashy Flickers Magic Picture Gun, Marx, 1960s, NMIB... $77.00
Give-A-Show Projector, Kenner, 1971-73, features various cartoon characters, MIB... $75.00

Kaleidoscope, Du-All Products, 1940s, leatherette camera shape w/interior glass stems, VG+ $250.00

Kaleidoscope Wonder Wheel, Steven Mfg, 1975, NM......$20.00

Kiddie Kamera, Allied, 1934, features various comic characters, EXIB $75.00

Komic Kamera, Allied, 1934, features various comic characters, EXIB $75.00

Magic Lantern, Bing, tin, w/orig glass sliders & instructions, 6½", EX (in cb box)...$80.00

Magic Lantern, Carette, ca 1885, blk metal & brass w/brass filigree trim, w/boxed set of 'Primus' slides, 9½", VG $225.00

Magic Lantern, Carette, ca 1900, metal & brass upright box w/ wooden base, wick oil illuminate, w/slided, 10", VG .. $175.00

Magic Lantern, Ernst Plank, ca 1890, 'Climax,' metal & brass w/wooden base, orante slide mount, circular slides, 4", G $200.00

Magic Lantern, Ernst Plank, footed box type, 9", VG $225.00

Magic Lantern, Hersteller, ca 1890, wood box w/metal lens & chimney, w/slides, 'Jung Amerika Gesetzel: Geschutzt,' VGIB...$400.00

Magic Lantern, Jean Schoenner, ca 1880, metal & brass upright w/figural lens mount, w/circular slides, 12", G............. $110.00

Magic Lantern, Jean Schoenner, ca 1895, blk & red metal & brass, wooden base, w/various slides, 11½", VG $225.00

Magic Lantern, JS, tin w/CI feet, kerosene lamp w/glass chimney, lens & slides, 9", EXIB $150.00

Magic Lantern, Max Dannborn, ca 1885, red-pnt metal & brass w/wooden base, blk-pnt ornate slide stand, w/slides, 14", VG $110.00

Magic Lantern, Plank, pnt tin w/wooden base, glass chimney, 22 glass slides of storybook scenes, 13" overall, EXIB....... $220.00

Mickey Mouse Movie Jector, VGIB $225.00

Mickey Mouse Safe-Toy Cinema, Pathescope/England, b/o crank projector w/2 films, 9", EXIB...................................... $150.00

Movie Viewer Theater, Fisher-Price, 1977-86, #463, MIB .$25.00

Optical Illusions Science Kit, Remco, 1961, NM (orig can)....$25.00

See-Action Football, Kenner, 1973, NMIB $25.00

Starmaster Astronomy Set, Reed, 1950s, complete, EX+IB... $45.00

Stereo Viewer, wood viewer w/adjustable mirror, over 100 various views of mostly European subjects, EX (in divided box) $500.00

• • • • • • • • • • • • • • • • • Paper Dolls • • • • • • • • • • • • • • • • •

Turn-of-the-century paper dolls are seldom found today and when they are, they're very expensive. Advertising companies used them to promote their products, and some were printed on the pages of leading ladies' magazines. By the late 1920s, most paper dolls were being made in book form — the doll on the cover, the clothes on the inside pages. Because they were so inexpensive, paper dolls survived the Depression and went on to peak in the 1940s. Although the advent of television caused sales to decline, paper doll companies were able to hang on by making paper dolls representing Hollywood celebrities and TV stars. These are some of the most collectible today. Even celebrity dolls from more recent years like the Brady Bunch or the Waltons are popular. Remember, condition is very important; if they've been cut out, even when they're still in fine condition and have all their original accessories, they're worth only about half as much as an uncut book or box set. Our values are for mint and uncut dolls unless noted otherwise.

For more information, refer to *Price Guide to Lowe and Whitman Paper Dolls*, *Price Guide to Saalfield and Merrill Paper Dolls*, and *20th Century Paper Dolls*, all by Mary Young, our advisor for this category.

Airline Stewardess, Lowe #4913, 1957................................$45.00
Alice in Wonderland Dolls, Milton Bradley #4109...........$35.00
Angel Face, Gabriel #293...$20.00
Animated Goldilocks with the Three Bears, Milton Bradley #4101..$35.00
Annie Oakley, Whitman #2056, 1955 ....$75.00
Baby Beans & Pets, Whitman #1950, 1978 ....$12.00
Baby Sparkle Plenty, Saalfield #2500, 1948, $50 to...........$75.00
Ballerina Dolls, Gabriel #D115, 1956 ....$35.00
Bedknobs & Broomsticks, Whitman #1999, 1971, $35 to.$55.00
Betsy McCall, Whitman #1969, 1971.................................$25.00
Betty Bo-Peep/Billy Boy Blue, Lowe #1043, 1942 ....$75.00
Betty Grable, Whitman #962, 1946, $200 to $300.00
Betty Grable, Whitman #989, 1941, $200 to.................. $300.00
Big & Little Sister, Whitman #4411, 1962 ....$25.00
Blondie, Saalfield #4434, 1968 ....$65.00
Bob Hope & Dorothy Lamour, Whitman #976, 1942 .... $300.00
Brenda Lee, Lowe #2785, 1961, $50 to $75.00
Bronco Bess, Milton Bradley #4043, 1950 ....$35.00
Career Girls, Lowe #958, 1950..$35.00
Career Girls, Lowe #1045, 1942 ....$75.00
Carol Lynley, Whitman #2089, 1960 ....$70.00
Cheerleaders, Lowe #2741, 1962.......................................$25.00
Chitty Chitty Bang Bang, Whitman #1982, 1968 ....$45.00
Cinderella, Golden #1545, 1989 ....$10.00
Clothes Crazy, Lowe #1046, 1945 ....$35.00
Connie Darling & Her Dolly, Saalfield #6092, 1964, $20 to .$30.00
Coronation Paper Dolls & Coloring Book, Saalfield #4312-29, 1953 ....$75.00
Cuddles & Rags, Lowe #1283, 1950...................................$50.00
Cute Quintuplets, Western #1818-5, 1964, $15 to............$30.00
Cyd Charisse, Whitman #2084, 1956 .... $150.00
Daisy & Donald, Whitman, #1990-21, 1978, $10 to.........$20.00
Daisy Dolly, Goldsmith #2005, 1930.................................$30.00
Deanna Durbin, Merrill #3480, 1940 .... $175.00
Debbie Reynolds, Whitman #1178, 1953, $125 to $175.00

Dolls of Many Lands, Whitman #3046, 1931, MIB...........$85.00
Dolls of Other Lands, Whitman #2074, 1963 ....$25.00
Dolly Rosycheeks With Her Pretty Dresses & Hats, JW Spears $150.00
Doris Day Doll, Whitman #1977, 1957, $100 to $150.00
Dorothy Provine, Whitman #1964, 1962...........................$70.00
Dottie Dress-Up, Dot & Peg Productions, 1950 ....$35.00
Dy-Dee Baby Doll, Whitman #969, 1938 .... $125.00
Family Affair Dolls (5), Whitman #4767, 1968.................$40.00
Farmer Fred, Lowe #523, 1943 ....$25.00
Fashion Previews, Lowe #1246, 1949 ....$60.00
'Five Paper Dolls' (Dionne Quints), Whitman #998, 1935... $125.00
Flatsy, Whitman #1994, 1970, $20 to $35.00
Flatsy, Whitman #4756, 1969, $15 to $25.00
Flying Nun, Artcraft/Screen Gems Inc #4417, 1968, $40 to ...$60.00
Fonzie, Toy Factory #105, 1976.......................................$25.00
Funny Bunnies Cut-Out Book, McLoughlin Bros #553, 1938 ..$100.00
Gene Autry's Melody Ranch, Whitman #990, 1950 ...... $150.00

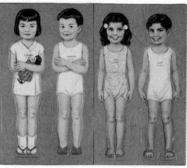

Paper Dolls

Dolls of Far-Off Lands, Platt & Munk #228B, 1965, $20.00. (Photo courtesy Mary Young)

Paper Dolls

Lennon Sisters, Whitman #1979, 1958, cut, EX, $40.00; uncut, $75.00 to $100.00.

Paper Dolls

Gidget, Avalon/ Standard Toy-kraft #601, 1965, $50.00. (Photo courtesy Mary Young)

Paper Dolls

Magic Mary Ann, Milton Bradley #4010-2, 1972, $25.00. (Photo courtesy Mary Young)

Gene Tiereny, Whitman #992, 1947	$225.00
Gigi Perreau, Saalfield #2605, 1951	$75.00
Glamour Girl, Whitman #973, 1942	$50.00
Goldilocks & the Three Bears, Lowe #2561, 1955	$35.00
Goldilocks & the Three Bears, Peck-Gandré, 1988, $5 to	$10.00
Good Neighbor, Saalfield #2487, 1944	$40.00
Gretchen, Whitman #4613, 1966	$15.00
Gulliver's Travels, Saalfield #1261, 1939	$125.00
Hayley Mills Summer Magic Cutouts, Whitman #1966, 1963, $50 to	$75.00
Hedy Lamar, Saalfield #2600, 1951	$150.00
Heidi, Whitman #1952, 1966	$35.00
Here Comes the Bride, Saalfield #1320, 1967, $40 to	$50.00
High School Dolls, Merrill #1551, 1948, $75 to	$100.00
Ivy With Magic Fabric Fashions, Janex #2001, 1971	$15.00
Jane Russell, Saalfield #4328, 1955	$95.00
Janet Leigh, Lowe #2405, 1957, $75 to	$100.00
Jet Airline Stewardess, Jaymar #913	$40.00
Josie & the Pussycats, Whitman #1982, 1971, EX	$30.00
Julie Andrews, Saalfield #4424, 1958	$125.00
June Allyson, Whitman #970, 1950	$175.00
Kewpie Dolls, Saalfield-Artcraft #6088, 1963, $50 to	$80.00
Lacy Daisy, Kits Inc #1050, 1949	$25.00
Let's Play Paper Dolls, McLoughlin Bros #551, 1938	$60.00
Liddle Kiddles, Whitman #1981, 1967	$75.00
Linda Darnell, Saalfield #1584, 1953	$100.00
Little Audrey, Gabriel #250 (no date)	$50.00
Little Miss Christmas & Holly-Belle, Merrill #2968, 1965, $65 to	$85.00
Little Miss Muffet, Lowe #2787, 1969, $15 to	$25.00
Little Orphan Annie, Saalfield #299, 1943	$100.00
Little Women, Artcraft #5127, $30 to	$40.00
Lucille Ball/Desi Arnaz w/Little Ricky, Whitman #2116, 1953	$150.00
Magic Mindy, Whitman #1991, 1970	$15.00
Malibu Francie, Whitman #1955, 1973	$30.00
Mary Ann Goes to Mexico, Reuben H Lilja #912	$20.00
Mary Poppins, Whitman #1977, 1973, $30 to	$45.00
Me & Mimi, Lowe #L144, 1942	$40.00
Mother & Daughter, Lowe #1860, 1963	$18.00
Mother Goose Village Cut Outs, Harter #H-164, 1935	$30.00
Mouseketeers, Whitman #1974, 1963	$85.00
Movie Starlets, Whitman #960, 1946	$150.00
Munsters, Whitman #1959, 1966	$125.00
My Best Friend, Whitman #1978-23, 1980	$10.00
My Doll Jack/Jill, Gabriel #D78/#D79, ea	$40.00
National Velvet, Whitman #1948, 1962	$65.00
Ozzie & Harriet, Saalfield #4319, 1954	$125.00
Patti Page, Lowe #2488, 1958, $75 to	$100.00
Patty Duke, Whitman #4775, 1965	$45.00
Patty Duke Fashion Dolls, Milton Bradley #4441, 1963	$50.00
Pebbles Flintstone, Whitman #1997, 1963, $40 to	$50.00

Peter Rabbit, Saalfield #963, 1934, stand-ups $40.00
Petticoat Junction, Whitman #1954, 1964 .... $100.00
Pixie Doll & Pup, Lowe #2764, 1968, $25 to.................$35.00
Raggedy Ann & Andy, Whitman #1979, 1966.................$30.00
Raggedy Ann & Andy, Whitman #1987-32, 1980 ....$15.00
Riders of the West, Saalfield #2716, 1950.....................$35.00
Rock Hudson, Whitman #2087, 1957, $65 to $75.00
Round About Dolls on Parade, McLoughlin Bros #2992, 1941 .... $80.00
Sally, Sue & Sherry, Lowe #2785, 1969 ....$10.00
Sandy, Western #1805D, 1964, $8 to $12.00
School Days, Gabriel, #D118 ....$50.00
Sheree North, Saalfield #4420, 1957 .... $100.00
Shirley Temple, Whitman #1986, 1976 ....$20.00
Skooter, Whitman/Mattel #1985, 1965, $50 to $75.00
Sleeping Beauty, Whitman #4723, 1958, $75 to............ $100.00
Sonja Henie, Merrill #3418, 1941...............................$250.00
Square Dance, Lowe #2707, 1957 ....$20.00

Strawberry Shortcake Playhouse, Random House, 1980 ...$15.00
Suzie Sweet, Grinnell #N2009, 1940 ....$40.00
Sweet-Treat Kiddles, Whitman #1993, 1969 ....$55.00
Tammy & Her Family, Whitman #1997, 1964...................$75.00
Teen Queens, Lowe #2710, 1957...............................$20.00
Tender Love 'N Kisses, Whitman #1944-1, 1978...............$15.00
This Is the House That Jack Built, Harter #H-169, 1935..$85.00
Tiny Chatty Twins, Whitman #1985, 1963.....................$45.00
Tom the Aviator, Lowe #1074, 1941 ....$75.00
Tropical Barbie, Golden #1523-1, 1986, $12 to.................$15.00
Tuesday Weld, Saalfield #5112, 1960, $60 to....................$75.00
TV Tap Stars, Lowe #990, 1952 ....$35.00
Velva Doll (Jill), Kingston #D21, 1932........................$30.00
Vera Miles, Whitman #2086, 1957 .... $150.00
Virginia Weidler, Whitman #1016, 1942, $60 to..............$80.00
Wedding Belles, Dot & Peg Productions, 1945.................$50.00
Wedding Dolls, Whitman #1953, 1958, $65 to $85.00
White House Party Dresses, Merrill #1550, 1961, $35 to.. $55.00
Wide Awake & Fast Asleep Doll, Samuel Gabriel & Sons #D114...$100.00
Winnie the Pooh & Friends, Whitman #1977-24, 1980, $15 to..$25.00
Wishnik, Whitman #1954, 1965, $30 to..........................$40.00

Paper Dolls
Mickey & Minnie Steppin' Out, Whitman/Walt Disney #1986-41, 1977, $20.00 to $35.00.
(Photo courtesy Carol Nichols)

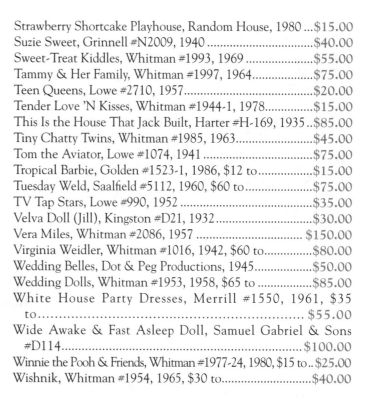

Paper Dolls
Mini Moppets, Saalfield #1320, 1969, $12.00 to $20.00. (Photo courtesy Carol Nichols)

Paper Dolls
Pals and Pets, Saalfield #2612, 1952, $35.00.
(Photo courtesy Mary Young)

Paper Dolls
The Nurses, Whitman #1975, 1963, unused, MIP, $65.00. (Photo courtesy www.gasolinealley antiques.com)

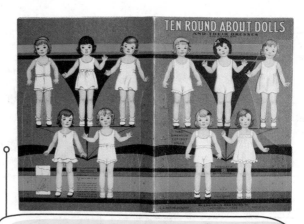

Paper Dolls
Ten Round About Dolls and Their Dresses, McLoughlin Brothers, #555, 1936, $60.00.
(Photo courtesy Mary Young)

Paper-Lithographed Toys

Following the development of color lithography, early toy makers soon recognized the possibility of using this technology in their own field. By the 1800s, both here and abroad, toys ranging from soldiers to involved dioramas of entire villages were being produced of wood with colorful and well detailed paper lithographed surfaces. Some of the best known manufactures were Crandell, Bliss, Reed, and McLoughlin Brothers. This style of toy remained popular until well after the turn of the century.

Advisors: Mark and Lynda Suozzi

See also Black Americana; Dollhouses; Games; Puzzles; Schoenhut.

Block Set, ABC Blocks, alphabet & pictures on oblong blocks in 10x11" wooden box, EX.................................. $850.00
Block Set, Cob House Blocks (Three Little Kittens), McLoughlin Bros, ca 1875, EXIB................................. $950.00
Block Set, Comic Cubes, McLoughlin Bros, 6-pc, forms 10 figures, VG+IB $550.00
Block Set, Cubes Alphabetiques, cubes depicting Victorian era children & nursery rhyme scenes, 8½x10" box, VGIB. $350.00
Block Set, Lyman's Grama Blocks, ea block has verse corresponding to ea letter w/animals & kids, VG (8x8" box)....... $350.00
Block Set, Mammoth Alphabet Picture Blocks, 12-pc, VGIB..$500.00
Block Set, Mother Goose, McLoughlin Bros, 1890s, EXIB. $1,000.00

Paper-Lithographed Toys
• • • • • • • • • • • • • • • • • •
Boat, Terror battleship,
Bliss, 22" long, VG,
$550.00. (Photo courtesy Bertoia Auctions on LiveAuctioneers.com)

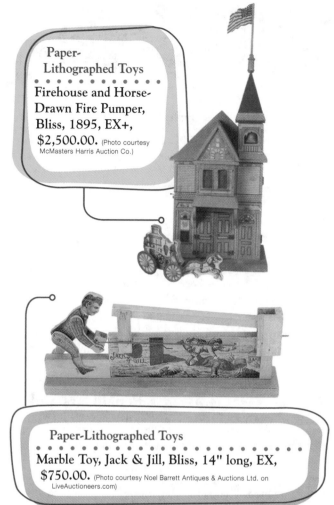

Paper-Lithographed Toys
• • • • • • • • • • • • • • • • • •
Firehouse and Horse-Drawn Fire Pumper,
Bliss, 1895, EX+,
$2,500.00. (Photo courtesy McMasters Harris Auction Co.)

Paper-Lithographed Toys
• • • • • • • • • • • • • • • • • •
Cinderella Coach, Reed, roof opens to access six ABC blocks with story images, 26" long, VG+,
$4,000.00. (Photo courtesy Noel Barrett Antiques & Auctions Ltd. on LiveAuctioneers.com)

Paper-Lithographed Toys
• • • • • • • • • • • • • • • • • •
Marble Toy, Jack & Jill, Bliss, 14" long, EX,
$750.00. (Photo courtesy Noel Barrett Antiques & Auctions Ltd. on LiveAuctioneers.com)

Block Set, Tower of Babel, Stirn & Lyon, EX (w/11½x13½" wooden box)... $950.00
Boat, America fishing boat, Reed, 29" L, VG $650.00
Boat, Conqueror battleship, Bliss, 21" L, VG $1,200.00
Boat, Fairy paddlewheeler on 4 wheels, 12" L, EX.......... $600.00
Boat, Iowa battleship, Bliss, 28½", VG........................... $875.00
Boat, New York battleship, Bliss, 35", G $1,450.00
Boat, Philadelphia battle cruiser, Reed, 31" L, G......... $1,750.00
Boat, Providence side-wheeler, Reed, 20", VG.............. $950.00
Boat, River Queen side-wheeler, Reed, 24" L, G $1,150.00
Boat, Thetis yacht, 12", VG+... $625.00
Boat, Twilight paddlewheeler, Reed, 20" L, EX............ $1,050.00
Boat, Volunteer fishing vessel, Reed, ca 1883, 32" L, G . $675.00
Building Blocks & Museum Set, circus scenes/Arabian palace, 11x18" box, EXIB.. $800.00
Captain Kidd's Castle, complete, 16½x11", G $850.00
Civil War Fort, foldable box forms fort w/2 cannons, American flag pole & 6 die-cut soldiers at attention, VG............ $650.00
Game, Animal Ten Pins, McLoughlin Bros, 9" ea, EXIB. $675.00
Game, Animal Ten Pins, Parker Bros, ca 1900, 9" to 11", VG..$450.00
Game, Performing Acrobats, 1 doing handstand atop shoulders of another flips when target is hit, 20", EX $300.00
Game, target w/bird & flower motif, hit target & hinged door drops to reveal nest, 15x8", EX $225.00
Mother Goose Cart, Bliss, goose on lg wheel pulling 2-wheeled cart w/Mother Goose driving, 14", L, VG $550.00

Paper-Lithographed Toys
• • • • • • • • • • • • • • • • • •
Train, Golden Gate Special, Bliss, 1889, 37",
EX, $1,750.00. (Photo courtesy Bertoia Auctions)

Mother Goose Tower, EIH, 1880s, complete, VG+ (w/wooden box) $325.00
Nesting Blocks, set of 5, bright graphics & alphabet, from 2" to 4", VG $100.00
Nesting Blocks, Surprise, McLoughlin Bros, scenes w/animals dressed as people, 61" (stacked), VG+........................ $450.00

Noah's Ark, Bliss, The Wonder, 16 pr & 5 single animals on wheeled platforms, 22", VG+...................................... $325.00

Pansy Tally Ho Coach, Bliss, 29" L, VG $1,900.00

Tiny Town Zoo, JW Spears & Son, complete, VGIB...... $275.00

Toboggan Slide, sleigh runners marked 'Puritan,' 36" overall, VG $725.00

Train, New York Central Railroad, Bliss, locomotive w/baggage car & coach, 26½" L overall, VG................................. $600.00

Train, Nickel Plate Railroad, Bliss, locomotive, tend #295 & 2 coaches, 26" overall, EX... $825.00

Trolley, 'Bowery Central Park,' horse-drawn, 25", VG ... $650.00

Turcos (Turkish) Soldiers, 2 mounted & 5 parade soldiers on sq wooden bases, 4½", G (w/hinged box)......................... $525.00

Wild Animal Picture Cubes, McLoughlin Bros, complete, VGIB...$425.00

· · · · · · · · · · · · Pedal Cars and Other Wheeled Vehicles · · · · · · · · · · · ·

Just like Daddy, all little boys (and girls as well) are thrilled and happy to drive a brand new shiny car. Today both generations search through flea markets and auto swap meets for cars, boats, fire engines, tractors, and trains that run not on gas but pedal power. Some of the largest manufacturers of wheeled goods were AMF (American Machine and Foundry Company), Murray, and Garton. Values depend to a very large extent on condition, and those that have been restored may sell for $1,000.00 or more, depending on the year and model. The following listings are in original condition unless noted otherwise.

Advisor: Nate Stoller

Airplane, American National, 1920s, wood fuselage w/steel nose cone, wings, seat & tail, CI steering wheel, 53", G ..$1,950.00

Boycraft Chrysler Airflow (1935), Steelcraft, working headlights w/glass inserts, 45", VG+ $2,750.00

Chrysler, Murray, 1941, 40", VG $700.00

Chrysler, Steelcraft, full fenders, simulated wht-wall pneumatic tires, 40", VG.. $1,600.00

Comet, Murray, 1950s, G.. $300.00

Dodge, American National, working headlights, 34", VG.$1,100.00

Durant Fire Chief Car, Steelcraft, 1920s, bell on hood, lights w/ glass lenses, NP trim, 48", G $2,050.00

Essex, American National, 1930s, celluloid windshield, crank-op horn, 35", G..$2,300.00

Fire Chief Car, Gendron, 47", prof rstr....................... $2,000.00

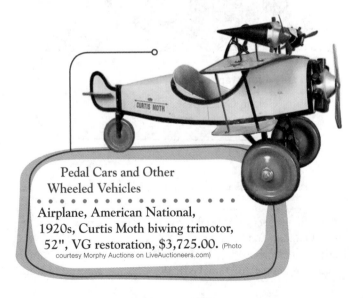

Pedal Cars and Other Wheeled Vehicles

Buick Coupe, Toledo, 1920s, simulated soft top, celluloid windshield, 29", VG, $8,050.00. (Photo courtesy Morphy Auctions on LiveAuctioneers.com)

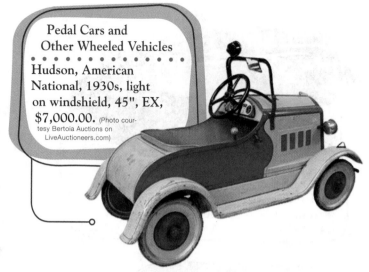

Pedal Cars and Other Wheeled Vehicles

Hudson, American National, 1930s, light on windshield, 45", EX, $7,000.00. (Photo courtesy Bertoia Auctions on LiveAuctioneers.com)

Pedal Cars and Other Wheeled Vehicles

Buick Phaeton Touring Car, Gendron, 1925, cloth top, disk wheels, VG+, $12,000.00. (Photo courtesy Bertoia Auctions on LiveAuctioneers.com)

Pedal Cars and Other Wheeled Vehicles

Hupmobile, Steelcraft, 1932, 45", EX, $8,500.00. (Photo courtesy Bertoia Auctions on LiveAuctioneers.com)

Pedal Cars and Other Wheeled Vehicles

Chrysler (1941), Steelcraft, 37", restored, $4,125.00. (Photo courtesy Randy Inman Auctions)

Pedal Cars and Other Wheeled Vehicles

Lincoln, Steelcraft, 1920s, 38", full restoration, $1,300.00. (Photo courtesy Morphy Auctions on LiveAuctioneers.com)

Fire Fighter Unit No 508, bell on hood, rpl ladders, 44", EX ..$150.00
Fire W/F City Batallion No 1, Murray, 1950s, bell on hood, 35", VG $125.00
Ford, Steelcraft, 1937, perforated wheels, 34", G............ $650.00
Hummer, Pioneer, 1914, 33", VG................................$1,800.00
Kiddilac, Murray, 1950s, rstr..$550.00

LaSalle, American National, 45", EX........................$7,000.00
Lincoln Zephyr, Steelcraft, ca 1937, 40", VG $1,900.00
Oakland, American National, 41", VG $2,250.00

Pedal Cars and Other Wheeled Vehicles

Mercedes, Tri-Ang, 60", professionally restored, $16,000.00. (Photo courtesy Bertoia Auctions on LiveAuctioneers.com)

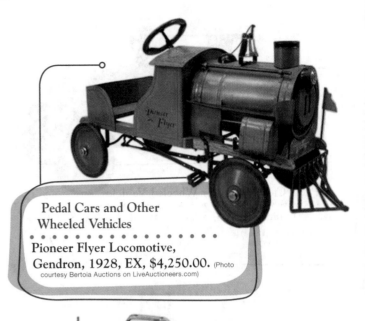

Pedal Cars and Other Wheeled Vehicles

Pioneer Flyer Locomotive, Gendron, 1928, EX, $4,250.00. (Photo courtesy Bertoia Auctions on LiveAuctioneers.com)

Pedal Cars and Other Wheeled Vehicles

Packard, American National, with roof, side spare and running boards, black rubber tires, 28", EX, $16,500.00. (Photo courtesy Morphy Auctions)

Pedal Cars and Other Wheeled Vehicles

Radio Cruiser, Toledo, electric lights and spotlight, bell on hood, 50", EX, $7,500.00. (Photo courtesy Bertoia Auctions on LiveAuctioneers.com)

Pedal Cars and Other Wheeled Vehicles

Packard, Gendron, 1920s, 50", VG+, $7,000.00. (Photo courtesy Bertoia Auctions on LiveAuctioneers.com)

Pedal Cars and Other Wheeled Vehicles

Ranch Wagon, Garton, chain drive, electric lights, antenna, 45", restored, $250.00. (Photo courtesy Randy Inman Auctions)

Pierce-Arrow, Steelcraft, 1935, flared rear fenders, disk wheels, 42", G $1,200.00
Pontiac, Garton, perforated wheels, 40", EX................... $900.00
Pontiac Station Wagon, Murray, 1949, 47", G $600.00

Roadster, Gendron, ca 1929, spoke wheels, 42", EX $1,600.00
Skippy, Gendron, 1930s, 36", VG $1,100.00
Skippy, La Salle, Gendron, perforated wheels, 45", VG+...$1,900.00
Stutz Roadster, Gendron, 1920s, fold-down top, side spare, NP trim, 29", VG.. $5,750.00

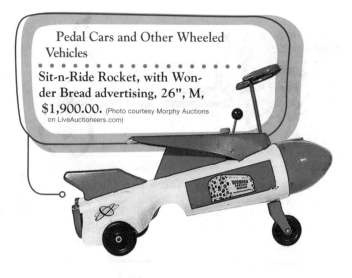

Pedal Cars and Other Wheeled Vehicles

Sit-n-Ride Rocket, with Wonder Bread advertising, 26", M, $1,900.00. (Photo courtesy Morphy Auctions on LiveAuctioneers.com)

Pedal Cars and Other Wheeled Vehicles

Woody Station Wagon, Garton, 1940s, 46", VG, $2,875.00. (Photo courtesy Morphy Auctions on LiveAuctioneers.com)

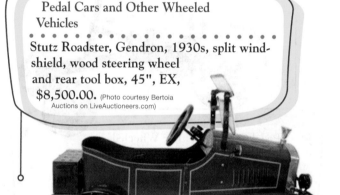

Pedal Cars and Other Wheeled Vehicles

Stutz Roadster, Gendron, 1930s, split windshield, wood steering wheel and rear tool box, 45", EX, $8,500.00. (Photo courtesy Bertoia Auctions on LiveAuctioneers.com)

WAGONS

Aero-Flite, 1930s, streamlined style working headlights, 47", EX $950.00

Alliance, Paris Mfg, 1920s, wood body coaster w/name stenciled on sides, disk wheels, 45", VG $400.00

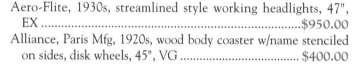

Pedal Cars and Other Wheeled Vehicles, Wagons

Greyhound De Luxe, 40", VG+, $275.00. (Photo courtesy Morphy Auctions on LiveAuctioneers.com)

Pedal Cars and Other Wheeled Vehicles

Super Sport, Murray, 1953, EX+, $2,250.00. (Photo courtesy Morphy Auctions on LiveAuctioneers.com)

Pedal Cars and Other Wheeled Vehicles, Wagons

Multi-Use Scoot Wagon, MTD, 1960s, unused, NM+IB, $400.00. (Photo courtesy Morphy Auctions on LiveAuctioneers.com)

Stutz Sedan, Steelcraft, 1930s, front & back seats, side spare, wht-wall tires, 61", EX $6,325.00

Tee Bird, Murray, 31", rstr.................................$125.00

Willys Knight, Steelcraft, 32", overpnt, G $650.00

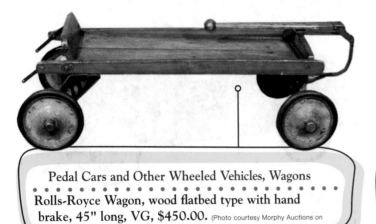

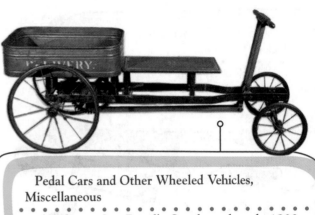

Auto Wagon, Pat 1917, wicker seat in wood wagon frame w/ steering wheel, gearing allows forward & reverse motion, 45", VG $6,000.00
Hercules De Luxe, wood w/stake sides, dual rear wheels, 52", VG $150.00
Lindy Flyer, 1933 World's Fair decal, working lights, VG ...$900.00
Wolverine Speedster, 34", VG............................... $200.00
Wood Wagon, 2 lg/2 sm spoke wheels, 39", EX $300.00

MISCELLANEOUS

Bell Car, name stenciled on paddle-form seat, 27" L, VG... $225.00
Benteco Speedster Scooter, Metalcraft, 1920s, 3-wheeled, stick hdl, yel, 37x32", unused, NM $300.00
Boycraft Handcar, 32½" L, G............................. $225.00
Chief Scooting Star Scooter, 1930s, streamlined fenders, 40x33", VG... $400.00
Flying Scot Irish Mail, 40" L, unused, M......................... $175.00
Henley Roll About Scooter, wood w/4 metal spoke wheels, 30", EX $350.00
Irish Mail, Gendron, 1920s, steel frame w/wooden seat, 2 sm/2 lg spoke wheels, 37", G $460.00
Irish Mail, Jenny-Boy, 1930s, iron frame w/wooden seat, 1 sm/2 lg spoke wheels, 32", EX.............................. $315.00
Pioneer Flyer Locomotive, Gendron, 1928, EX $4,250.00
Scooter, w/seat & straight wooden hand grip, 20" L, VG . $125.00
Scooter, 2-wheeled, w/pump pedal, front & back kickstands over spoke wheels, 39", G $350.00
Skippy Scooter, 1920s, streamline fenders, w/foot brake, 44x32", EX.. $400.00
Super Sport, Murray, 1953, EX+.................................$2,250.00

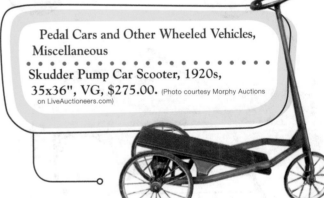

• • • • • • • • • • • • • Penny Toys • • • • • • • • • • • • •

Penny toys were around as early as the late 1800s and as late as the 1920s. Many were made in Germany, but some were made in France as well. With few exceptions, they ranged in size from 5" on down; some had moving parts, and a few had clockwork mechanisms. Although many were unmarked, you'll sometimes find them signed 'Kellermann,' 'Meier,' 'Fischer,' or 'Distler,' or carrying an embossed company logo such as the 'dog and cart' emblem. They were made of lithographed tin with exquisite detailing — imagine an entire carousel less than 2½" tall. Because of a recent surge in collector interest, many have been crossing the auction block of some of the country's largest galleries. The values listed are prices realized from some of these auctions.

Airship w/Observer in Gondola, when properly strung ship goes up & down when prop turns, 3", VG.......... $375.00

Armored Car, Distler, WWI style, 3" L, EX $100.00

Auto 948, Meier, seat curved around driver, long bonnet, spoke wheels, 3⅝", VG.......... $425.00

Baby Girl in Carriage Holding Doll, Meier, 3¾", EX+ ... $550.00

Baby in Carriage, Fischer, 3¼" L, EX+ $400.00

Barrel Maker on Platform, Fischer, 4", EX $325.00

Barrel Truck, Distler, 1914, open bench seat w/driver, stacked barrels lithoed on stake bed, 3⅝", EX $475.00

Battleship w/Cannon, Germany, spring-loaded cannon & containment chamber, 3½", EX.......... $375.00

Beer Truck, Distler, open cab, 3½", EX $450.00

Billiards Player, Kellermann, 4" L, EX.......... $325.00

Biplane, Meier, 3", EX $500.00

Birdcage w/Canary, Germany, bl, red & yel, 2¾" W, EX+...$125.00

Boat Swing w/2 Kids, Meier, 3¼", EX.......... $200.00

Boy Feeding Dog on Platform, Meier, 4" L, VG.......... $200.00

Boy in Rocking Chair, Meier, 2¾", EX.......... $250.00

Boy Kneeling in Stake Wagon, Fischer, 2¾", EX $725.00

Boy on Horse on 4-Wheeled Platform, Germany, dappled gray horse, spoke wheels, 3" L, VG.......... $325.00

Boy on Irish Mail, Kellermann, 3", VG.......... $300.00

Boy on Rocking Horse, Meier $110.00

Boy Seated on Sled w/Wheels, Meier, 3", EX $300.00

Boy w/Butterfly Net After Butterfly on Large Toadstool on Platform, Fischer, 4", EX+ $475.00

Boy w/Butterfly Net Puts Butterfly in Box, Fischer, 3", EX...$425.00

Penny Toys

Auto with Driver, Meier, open with fold-down top, center steering, 3¾", EX, $800.00. (Photo courtesy Bertoia Auctions on LiveAuctioneers.com)

Penny Toys

Boat with Sailor, Meier, 4½", EX, $500.00. (Photo courtesy Bertoia Auctions on LiveAuctioneers.com)

Penny Toys

Airplane and Hangar, Distler, pilot in open cockpit, 5" long hangar, EX, $425.00. (Photo courtesy Lloyd Ralston Gallery on LiveAuctioneers.com)

Penny Toys

Child in Chair with Attached Table, Germany, 2½", EX, $300.00. (Photo courtesy Lloyd Ralston Gallery on LiveAuctioneers.com)

Penny Toys

Auto with Driver and Lady Passenger, Germany, 3½", VG, $450.00. (Photo courtesy Morphy Auctions on LiveAuctioneers.com)

Bugler on Galloping Horse on 4-Wheeled Platform, Meier, 2½", EX $550.00

Camel w/Backpack on 4-Wheeled Platform, Meier, 2½", EX.$550.00

Camel w/Rider on 4-Wheeled Platform, 3½", EX........ $2,200.00

Candy Truck, bed w/sliding lid to hold candy, 3½", EX.. $550.00

Cargo Truck, Distler, open w/driver, tarp over back, 3¾", EX .$325.00

Carousel w/Bicycle Riders, Meier, 2¼", EX $650.00

Castle Bank, slot in hinged roof, emb w/knight rider & princess, 3" L, VG $225.00

Cat & Dog Fight on 4-Wheeled Platform, 3½", VG...... $275.00

Cat Confronting Dog in Doghouse on Platform, Meier, 4", EX..$165.00

Chicken & Egg, Fischer, chicken pecks at lg egg to reveal chick on oblong platform, 3¼" L, EX+ $475.00

Chicken & Egg, Fischer, chicken pecks at lg egg to reveal chick on oblong platform, 3¼" L, VG $250.00

Church Bank, slot in hinged roof, w/key, 3¼", VG......... $175.00

Cito Cycle, 3-wheeled w/driver in open cab, 3¾", VG... $550.00

Cito Trike Car, Kellermann, w/rider, 3½", EX............. $1,650.00

Clock Candy Container, wall type w/pendulum & movable hands, 4½", EX $200.00

Clown Prodding Mule on Platform, Meier, 4", EX.......... $250.00

Clowns (2) Tossing Ball on Footed Platform, Meier, 3¾", VG..$400.00

Coffee Mill, Germany, top crank hdl, sm opening front drawer, 2⅜", VG...$75.00

Cow on 4-Wheeled Platform, Distler, 2½", G................. $150.00

Cow on 4-Wheeled Platform, Meier, 3¼", EX................. $550.00

Crane (Winch), crank-op w/box on hook, oblong base, 5¾" L, EX... $225.00

Cross Country Skier, Meier, 3½", VG+........................... $400.00

Dachshund on 4-Wheeled Platform, Distler, 4", VG+ ... $225.00

Delivery Van #245, Fischer, 3½", EX.............................. $165.00

Diabolo Player, Meier, oblong base, 2¾x3" L, EX $1,900.00

Dog & Stork w/Babies in Nest on Platform, Meier, dog dressed & standing upright, 4" L, VG+ $825.00

Dog (Spaniel) on 4-Wheeled Platform, Meier, 2⅞", EX.......$550.00

Dog w/Cat in Basket on Platform, 4", VG $275.00

Dog w/Coiled Tail on 4-Wheeled Platform, Distler, 2½", EX ..$300.00

Double-Decker Bus, Distler, 4½", EX $275.00

Electric Omnibus, Meier, many passengers on upper deck, 3¼", VG+..$600.00

Elephant on 4-Wheeled Platform, Meier, 2¾", VG+...... $520.00

Elephant Pulling 2-Wheeled Cart, Fischer, 5" L, EX $110.00

Elephant Trumpeting on 4-Wheeled Platform, Distler, 3½", EX..$550.00

Penny Toys

Chinaman with Parasol on Four-Wheeled Cart, Distler, 3", NM, $550.00. (Photo courtesy Bertoia Auctions on LiveAuctioneers.com)

Penny Toys

Covered Wagon Truck (JD), Distler, 1914, 3½", EX, $375.00. (Photo courtesy Bertoia Auctions on LiveAuctioneers.com)

Penny Toys

Flying Hollander, Meier, 3¼", VG, $350.00. (Photo courtesy Bertoia Auctions on LiveAuctioneers.com)

Penny Toys

Fire Ladder Truck, Germany, with figures, 4¼", $400.00. (Photo courtesy Bertoia Auctions on LiveAuctioneers.com)

Penny Toys

Geese Pecking, Meier, 2x2¼", EX+, $300.00. (Photo courtesy Bertoia Auctions on LiveAuctioneers.com)

Penny Toys

Girl Feeding Chicken on Platform, Meier, 4", EX+, $475.00. (Photo courtesy Bertoia Auctions on LiveAuctioneers.com)

Penny Toys

Grand Hotel Coach, Meier, passengers in windows, 3" long, EX, $400.00. (Photo courtesy Bertoia Auctions on LiveAuctioneers.com)

Penny Toys

Goose on Four-Wheeled Platform, Fischer, with nodding neck, 2x3½", EX, $600.00. (Photo courtesy Lloyd Ralston Gallery on LiveAuctioneers.com)

Penny Toys

Horse-Drawn Caisson, Germany, 5½", EX, $275.00. (Photo courtesy Lloyd Ralston Gallery on LiveAuctioneers.com)

Equestrian Riders (3) on Base, Meier, 3¾" L, EX+ $1,700.00
Equestrian Riders (3) on Base, Meier, 3¾" L, G.............. $250.00
Express Parcels Delivery Truck, Distler, 4", EX $110.00
Flying Machine, Meier, w/4 side props, standing pilot, 3¼", VG.. $785.00
Frog Jumps at Butterfly on Box on Platform, Fischer, 3", EX...$375.00
Garage w/Touring Car, 4" L garage, EX $135.00
Gas Station w/Reversing Car, lever-op, 3¼", EX $65.00
General Double-Decker Bus, Fischer, 3½", EX $110.00
Gingerbread House Bank, Germany, lady at door greeting kids, 2½" L, EX+ $150.00
Girl at School Desk Candy Container, Meier, 2¾", EX.. $475.00
Girl in Swing, Distler, 2¾", EX.. $250.00
Girl w/Doll in Rocking Chair Candy Container, Meier, 3", EX...$650.00
Gnome Feeding Bird on 4-Wheeled Platform, Meier, 3¼", EX.. $225.00
Gnome on Easter Egg Chasing Rabbit on 4-Wheeled Platform, Meier, 3½", VG+ $750.00
Gnomes Sawing on 4-Wheeled Platform, 3½", VG+ $225.00
Goat Pulling Lady in 2-Wheeled Cart, 4" L, VG............ $275.00
Goat w/Candy Box on Platform, Fischer, 3", EX............. $325.00
Goat Walking on 4-Wheeled Cart, Meier, 3", VG+....... $500.00
Henhouse w/Chickens Feeding From Trough, 2½", EX .. $350.00
Horse-Drawn Ambulance, Meier, 2 horses & 1 w/rider, 4½", EX... $650.00

Penny Toys

Mattoni's Delivery Cart, box lid opens, 5" long, EX+, $900.00. (Photo courtesy Bertoia Auctions on LiveAuctioneers. com)

Horse-Drawn Cab, w/flag reading 'For Hire,' lady passenger lithoed in window, single horse, 4", EX $475.00
Horse-Drawn Carriage w/Driver, 5", EX......................... $225.00
Horse-Drawn Coach, Fischer, enclosed passenger cab w/driver in open seat, single horse, 5½", EX+ $500.00
Horse-Drawn Coach, Meier, passengers lithoed in windows, 4¾", VG+.. $325.00
Horse-Drawn Delivery Wagon, Germany, w/driver & single box on flatbed wagon, 2 horses $250.00

Horse-Drawn Gig, w/driver, single horse, 5", EX $360.00

Horse-Drawn Hansom Cab, w/driver at rear on high seat, single horse, 3½", EX $250.00

Horse-Drawn Open Carriage, Meier, w/driver, 2 horses, 4½", EX.. $390.00

Horse-Drawn Postal Coach, Meier, 'Post' & French horn emb on sides of coach, no driver, single horse, 5¼", EX $550.00

Horse-Drawn Wagon, Fischer, cab over driver on bench seat, open bed, single horse, 5", EX................................. $250.00

Horse-Drawn Wagon (Candy Container), Germany, 2 horses & driver, 4½" L, EX $275.00

Horseless Carriage, Fischer, enclosed passenger compartment w/ driver in open seat, 2¾", EX+ $550.00

Horseless Carriage, Meier, 3¼", VG $325.00

House w/Trip Hammer, Meier, 2" H, EX $385.00

Interurban Bus, Fischer, 5⅞", EX $450.00

Jockey on Horse on 4-Wheeled Platform, 2¾", EX........ $190.00

Jockey on Horse-Drawn Sulky, 4", EX............................ $440.00

Jockey on Rocking Horse, Meier, 3½", EX.....................$300.00

Lady Pushing Child in Rolling Chair, Meier, 3¼", EX.... $450.00

Lady Pushing Child in Sleigh-Type Chair, 3", EX+ $750.00

Leopard on 4-Wheeled Platform, Distler, 4", VG+......... $475.00

Limousine, Distler, doorless driver's compartment w/driver, images of passengers in windows, luggage on top, 4¼", EX $475.00

Limousine, Meier, luggage rack on roof, doorless front seat w/ driver, passengers cut-out in windows, 4½", EX........... $400.00

Lion on 4-Wheeled Platform, Distler, spring tail, 3", VG+ $250.00

Locomotive & Tender, Distler, red & blk, 5½", EX $165.00

Lorry w/Covered Back, Meier, bench seat w/driver, tent-shaped covered back, 4⅝", EX.. $325.00

Los Angeles Zeppelin, marked 'Made in Germany,' 4" L, VG+ $350.00

Man Dancing Atop Box, Distler, 3¾", VG+ $355.00

Man Lying on Sled, 4½", EX.. $275.00

Mobile Gas Station w/Passenger Car & Jet Racer, 1½" wide, EX $85.00

Monkey & Rooster Facing Each Other on Platform, Meier, 3¾", Fair+ $110.00

Monkey on Great Dane, Meier (?), rocker base, 4½", F.. $400.00

Monkey on Irish Mail, Meier, 3¼", EX......................... $1,300.00

Monkey on Rocking Dog on 4-Wheeled Platform, Meier, 3", EX $900.00

Motorcycle, see also Triumph Motorcycle w/Civilian Rider

Motorcycle w/Civilian Rider, Kellermann, 3-wheeled version, 3¾", EX $500.00

Motorcycle w/Civilian Rider, Kellermann, 4", EX.......... $465.00

Motorcycle w/Sidecar, Kellermann, w/driver & passenger, 4" L, VG $1,750.00

Motorcycle w/Uniformed Rider, Kellermann, 2¾", EX... $550.00

Movie Projector Showing Man's Face, trapezoidal base, 4¼" L, EX $550.00

Mule-Drawn Hay Wagon, Fischer, w/driver, 6", EX+ $200.00

Ocean Liner, Fischer, 2 stacks, 4¾", EX $300.00

Ocean Liner, Meier, 4½", EX.. $600.00

Omnibus, Germany, roof over open cab, rear stairs lead to railed top deck, 4½", VG.. $300.00

Optical, paper litho scroll pertaining to the British royal family is viewed through lens, scroll turns, 2x2", EX $1,000.00

Parrots (2) Facing Each Other w/Candy Box in between on Platform, 4" L, VG+ $275.00

Pig Pulling Clown in 2-Wheeled Cart, 3¾", EX $875.00

Pool Player, see Billiards Player

Porter Pushing 2-Wheeled Cart w/Trunk, Fischer, 3¼", EX.. $400.00

Punch & Judy Show, Meier, 2¼", EX $875.00

Puppet Show Bank, slot in hinged roof, w/key, 2¾", EX. $550.00

Rabbit (Dressed) Standing Upright Rocking on Platform, Fischer, 2½", EX.. $300.00

Rabbit & Lamb in Stake Wagon, Fischer, 2½", EX......... $550.00

Rabbit Candy Container, upright w/basket on back on grassy base, 3¼", EX.. $300.00

Rabbit on 4-Wheeled Platform, IJF/France, 3", EX $400.00

Rabbit on 4-Wheeled Platform, Meier, 2¾", VG+ $150.00

Rabbits (2) Riding on Back of Larger Rabbit on Base, Meier, 3¼", EX $650.00

Racer #4, Meier, 3½", EX.. $1,750.00

Racer #11, Distler, 4¼", VG $1,425.00

Racer #948, Fischer, 3½", VG+ $600.00

Racer w/Bobbing Head Driver, Fischer, inertia driver, F+ ...$110.00

Racing Skull w/2 Rowers, Germany, gr, 6½" L, EX $800.00

Reindeer on 4-Wheeled Platform, Meier, 2¾", EX $650.00

Rocking Horse, box resting on rockers holds candy, 3½", EX .. $335.00

Roosters (2) Pecking at Box on Platform, Meier, 4", EX.. $400.00
Roosters (2) Pecking at Box on Platform, Meier, 4", VG.. $250.00
Sailboat, Fischer, red, wht & bl w/gold trimmed masts & ladders, flywheel on deck, 4½", VG... $300.00
Saloon Car, Distler, doorless driver's compartment w/driver, lady passenger lithoed in rear window, 3", G...................... $390.00
Sheep in Pen w/Tree, 3", VG+ $275.00
Soldier Marching on 4-Wheeled Platform, 3¾", VG+ ... $225.00
Soldiers Engaging, Germany, 2 soldiers w/rifles on oblong base lunge at each other w/rifles, 4" L, NM $500.00
Squirrel on 4-Wheeled Platform, Meier, 3", VG+ $200.00
St Bernard on 4-Wheeled Base, Meier, 3" L, EX+ $525.00
Stake Truck, Meier (?), open cab w/driver, gr w/red bed, wht & gold hood, bl seat & trim, wht spoke wheels, 2¼", EX. $175.00
Steam Engine, crank-op, 4", EX $135.00
Steam Engine Whistle, 2½", EX.. $140.00
Streetcar 129, Germany, 4½", VG..................................... $375.00
Swordsmen Fighting, Kellermann, squeeze action, 2¼", EX.$330.00
Tap Dancer on Roof, Distler, 4", EX................................ $600.00
Taxi, Distler, open front seat w/driver, simulated top down in back, no passenger, 3", EX.................................... $350.00
Telefon (Telephone) 946, old wall crank-type, 4½", EX. $300.00
Tiny Town Train, GR Schwarz, penny toy train w/paper litho floor layout & cb building, EX+IB (9x13" box) $700.00
Tonneau (Auto), Germany, open w/front & back seats, w/driver, spoke wheels, 4½", EX.................................... $425.00
Toonerville Trolley (Cracker Jack), 1¾", EX $350.00
Touring Car, Meier, 3¼", EX.. $465.00
Touring Car (Open), Kellerman, long flat auto w/2 compatments & driver, yel w/gray wheels, 3" L, VG...........................$85.00
Toy Town Garage, Parker Bros, w/3 3" vehicles, 6" garage, VGIB..$1,000.00
Toy Town Railroad, Parker Bros, w/train set, 2 horse-drawn coaches & auto w/2 figures, 4 standing figures, etc, NMIB........$6,500.00
Train on Round Tracks, locomotive, coach & tender, 8" train overall, EXIB $475.00
Transfer Truck, Meier, w/driver, 3¼" L, EX+ $250.00
Triumph Motorcycle w/Civilian Rider, Meier, 2¾", EX.. $715.00
Truck, early model w/roof over open seat, bed w/horizontal slats, MSW, 5¼", VG+ $110.00

Penny Toys

Three-Wheeled Motorized Cart with Driver, Kellerman, with steering rod, 3¾", EX, $875.00. (Photo courtesy Bertoia Auctions on LiveAuctioneers.com)

Penny Toys

Touring Car with Kangaroo Driver, Distler, 1914, 3½", NM, $1,400.00. (Photo courtesy Bertoia Auctions on LiveAuctioneers.com)

Truck w/Lamb, Meier, open w/driver, 3¼", EX................ $250.00
Vis-a-Vis, Meier, 3", VG.. $250.00
Wheel of Fortune Candy Container, Meier, oblong base, 2¾", EX $550.00
Wild Boar on 4-Wheeled Platform, 2½", VG $100.00
Windmill Candy Container, spinning blades, 3", EX $165.00
Zeppelin, Meier, 4 props on top, 2 gondolas w/passengers, 4½", EX $625.00

• • • • • • • • • • • • • • • • • • PEZ Dispensers • • • • • • • • • • • •

PEZ was originally designed as a breath mint for smokers, but by the 1950s kids were the target market, and the candies were packaged in the dispensers that we all know and love today. There are several hundred variations to collect, with more arriving on the store shelves every day, most retailing for about $2.00 each. Early PEZ dispensers came without 'feet' on the base of the stem. Feet are little plastic protrusions that were added in 1987 to PEZ dispensers to help them stand. Since then almost every dispenser has come with feet. Some dispensers have variations in color and design that can influence their values. Don't buy any that are damaged, incomplete, or that have been tampered with in any way; those are nearly worthless. For more information refer to *A Pictorial Guide to Plastic Candy Dispensers Featuring PEZ* by David Welch, and *Collector's Guide to PEZ* by Shawn Peterson.

In the listings below, (A), (B), and (C) refer to different versions of dispensers, (A) being an earlier version with a noticeable difference in the design or look.

Advisor: Richard Belyski

Aardvark, w/ft $5.00
Angel, no ft $65.00
Arlene, w/ft, pk, $3 to...$5.00

Asterix Line, Asterix, Obelix, Roman or Getafix, ea $5.00
Baloo, w/ft...$30.00
Bambi, no ft $50.00

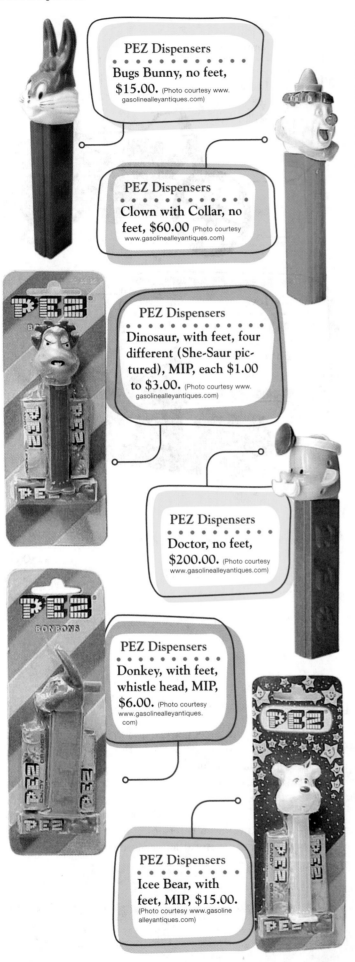

PEZ Dispensers
. . . .
Bugs Bunny, no feet, $15.00. (Photo courtesy www.gasolinealleyantiques.com)

PEZ Dispensers
. . . .
Clown with Collar, no feet, $60.00 (Photo courtesy www.gasolinealleyantiques.com)

PEZ Dispensers
. . . .
Dinosaur, with feet, four different (She-Saur pictured), MIP, each $1.00 to $3.00. (Photo courtesy www.gasolinealleyantiques.com)

PEZ Dispensers
. . . .
Doctor, no feet, $200.00. (Photo courtesy www.gasolinealleyantiques.com)

PEZ Dispensers
. . . .
Donkey, with feet, whistle head, MIP, $6.00. (Photo courtesy www.gasolinealleyantiques.com)

PEZ Dispensers
. . . .
Icee Bear, with feet, MIP, $15.00. (Photo courtesy www.gasolinealleyantiques.com)

Barney Bear, no ft $40.00
Barney Bear, w/ft $30.00
Baseball Glove, no ft.. $150.00
Batgirl, no ft, soft head $160.00
Batman, no ft $15.00
Batman, no ft, w/cape $125.00
Batman, w/ft, bl or blk, ea $3 to $5.00
Betsy Ross, no ft $150.00
Bouncer Beagle, w/ft $5.00
Boy, w/ft, brn hair $3.00
Bozo, no ft, die-cut $150.00
Bubble Man, w/ft $3.00
Bubble Man, w/ft, neon hat $3.00
Bugs Bunny, w/ft, $1 to $3.00
Bullwinkle, no ft $200.00
Candy Shooter, red & wht, w/candy & gun license, unused...$125.00
Captain America, no ft $90.00
Captain Hook, no ft $75.00
Casper, no ft $175.00
Charlie Brown, w/ft, $1 to $3.00
Charlie Brown, w/ft & tongue $30.00
Chicago Cubs 2000, Charlie Brown in pkg w/commemorative
   card $30.00
Chick, w/ft, $1 to $3.00
Chick in Egg, no ft $15.00
Chick in Egg, no ft, w/hair $125.00
Chip, w/ft $55.00
Clown, w/ft, whistle head $6.00
Cockatoo, no ft, bl face, red beak $50.00
Cool Cat, w/ft $55.00
Cow (A or B), no ft, bl, ea, $80 to $90.00
Creature from the Black Lagoon, no ft................................ $300.00
Crocodile, no ft $95.00
Crystal Hearts, eBay, limited edition................................... $10.00
Daffy Duck, no ft.. $15.00
Daffy Duck, w/ft, $1 to $3.00
Dalmatian Pup, w/ft $50.00
Daniel Boone, no ft $175.00
Dino, w/ft, purple, $1 to $3.00
Donald Duck, no ft, die-cut $150.00
Donald Duck, no ft, $10 to $15.00
Donald Duck's Nephew, no ft $30.00
Donald Duck's Nephew, w/ft, gr, bl or red hat, ea $10.00
Droopy Dog (A), no ft, plastic swivel ears $25.00
Droopy Dog (B), w/ft, pnt ears, MIP $6.00
Duck Tales, any character, w/ft, ea $6.00
Dumbo, w/ft, bl head $35.00
Eerie Spectres, Air Spirit, Diabolic or Zombie (no ft), ea ...$185.00
Elephant, no ft, orange & bl, flat hat $85.00
Elvis Presley, dispenser set in collector's tin $20.00
Fat-Ears Rabbit, no ft, pk head $20.00
Fat-Ears Rabbit, no ft, yel head $15.00
Fireman, no ft... $80.00
Fishman, no ft, gr $185.00
Foghorn Leghorn, w/ft $65.00
Football Player $175.00
Fozzie Bear, w/ft, $1 to $3.00
Frankenstein, no ft $275.00

Fred Flintstone, w/ft, $1 to $3.00
Frog, w/ft, whistle head $35.00
Garfield, w/ft, orange w/gr hat, $1 to $3.00
Garfield, w/ft, teeth, $1 to $3.00
Garfield, w/ft, visor, $1 to $3.00
Gargamel, w/ft $5.00
Ghosts (Glowing), Happy Henry, Naughty Neil, or Slimy Sid,
 ea $2.00
Ghosts (Non-Glowing), Happy Henry, Naughty Neil, or Slimy
 Sid, ea $2.00
Girl, w/ft, yel hair $3.00
Gonzo, w/ft, $1 to $3.00
Goofy, no ft, ea $15.00
Gorilla, no ft, blk head $80.00
Green Hornet, 1960s, $200 to $250.00
Gyro Gearloose, w/ft $6.00
Henery Hawk, no ft $65.00
Hulk, no ft, dk gr $45.00
Hulk, no ft, lt gr, remake $3.00
Indian, w/ft, whistle head $15.00
Indian Brave, no ft, reddish $130.00
Indian Chief, no ft, yel headdress $115.00
Indian Maiden, no ft $150.00
Inspector Clouseau, w/ft $5.00
Jerry Mouse, w/ft, plastic face $15.00
Jerry Mouse, w/ft, pnt face $6.00
Joker (Batman), no ft, soft head $175.00
Jungle Mission, interactive dispenser $2.00
Kermit the Frog, w/ft, red $2.00
Knight, no ft $250.00
Koala, w/ft, whistle head $10.00
Krazy Animals, Blinky Bill, Lion, Hippo, Elephant or Gator, ea,
 $4 to $6.00
Lamb, no ft $15.00
Lamb, w/ft $2.00
Lamb, w/ft, whistle head $20.00
Lazy Garfield, w/ft $2.00
Li'l Bad Wolf, w/ft $25.00
Lion's Club Lion, minimum value $1,500.00
Lucy w/Crown, no ft $100.00
Lucy, w/ft $2.00
Make-A-Face, works like Mr Potato Head $2,000.00
Mary Poppins, no ft $500.00
Merlin Mouse, w/ft $15.00
Merry Melody Makers, rhino, donkey, panda, parrot, clown, tiger
 or penguin, w/ft, MOC, ea $6.00
Mexican, no ft $200.00
Mickey Mouse, no ft, removable nose or cast nose, ea $10 to .. $15.00
Mickey Mouse, w/ft $2.00
Mimic Monkey (monkey w/ball cap), no ft, several colors, ea .. $50.00
Miss Piggy, w/ft $2.00
Miss Piggy, w/ft, eyelashes $15.00
Monkey Sailor, no ft, w/wht cap $50.00
Mowgli, no ft $30.00
Mr Ugly, no ft $45.00
Muscle Mouse (gray Jerry), w/ft, plastic nose $15.00
NASCAR Helmets, various numbers $2.00
Nermal, w/ft, gray $3.00

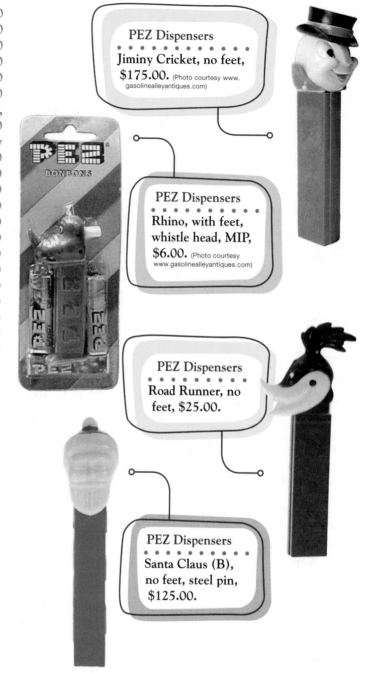

PEZ Dispensers
Jiminy Cricket, no feet,
$175.00. (Photo courtesy www.
gasolinealleyantiques.com)

PEZ Dispensers
Rhino, with feet,
whistle head, MIP,
$6.00. (Photo courtesy
www.gasolinealleyantiques.com)

PEZ Dispensers
Road Runner, no
feet, $25.00.

PEZ Dispensers
Santa Claus (B),
no feet, steel pin,
$125.00.

Nintendo, Diddy Dong, Koopa Trooper, Mario or Yoshi, ea $4
 to $6.00
Nurse, no ft $175.00
Octopus, no ft, blk $85.00
Odie, w/ft $2.00
Olive Oyl, no ft $200.00
Orange County Chopper, dispenser set in collector's tin ... $15.00
Panda, no ft, die-cut eyes $20.00
Panda, w/ft, remake $2.00
Panda, w/ft, whistle head $6.00
Papa Smurf, w/ft, red $6.00
Parrot, w/ft, whistle head $6.00
Pebbles Flintstone, w/ft $2.00
Penguin, w/ft, whistle head $6.00
Penguin (Batman), no ft, soft head $175.00

Peter Pez (A), no ft..$55.00
Peter Pez (B & C), w/ft....................................$2.00
Pilgrim, no ft..$125.00
Pink Panther, w/ft...$5.00
Pinocchio, no ft..$150.00
Pirate, no ft...$65.00
Pluto, no ft..$15.00
Pluto, w/ft...$2.00
Pokemon (non-US), Kottins, Meowith, Mew, Pikachu, or Psy-
    duck, ea..$5.00
Policeman, no ft...$50.00
Popeye (B), no ft..$90.00
Popeye (C), no ft, w/removable pipe..........$110.00
Practical Pig (B), no ft.....................................$30.00
Psychedelic Eye, no ft......................................$250.00
Psychedelic Eye, remake, blk or pk, MOC, ea..........$10.00
Psychedelic Flower, no ft, minimum value.............$250.00
Pumpkin (A), no ft...$15.00
Pumpkin (B), w/ft...$2.00
Raven, no ft, yel beak.......................................$70.00
Ringmaster, no ft..$300.00
Ringmaster, w/ft..$350.00
Road Runner, w/ft...$15.00
Rooster, w/ft, whistle head...............................$35.00
Rooster, w/ft, wht or yel head, ea.....................$30.00
Rudolph, no ft...$50.00
Santa Claus, w/ft, $1 to....................................$3.00
Santa Claus (A), no ft, steel pin.......................$130.00
Santa Claus (C), no ft, $5 to.............................$15.00
Santa Claus (C), w/ft, $1 to..............................$2.00
Scrooge McDuck (A), no ft...............................$20.00
Scrooge McDuck (B), w/ft.................................$6.00
Sheik, no ft..$55.00
Skull (A), no ft, $10 to......................................$15.00
Skull (B), w/ft..$2.00
Smurf, w/ft...$5.00
Smurfette, w/ft...$5.00
Snoopy, w/ft..$2.00
Snow White, no ft...$200.00
Snowman (A), no ft...$15.00
Snowman (B), w/ft...$2.00
Space Trooper Robot, no ft, full body...............$325.00
Spaceman, no ft...$125.00
Speedy Gonzales (A), w/ft.................................$15.00
Speedy Gonzales (B)...$2.00
Spider-Man, no ft, $10 to...................................$15.00
Spider-Man, w/ft...$2.00
Spike, w/ft...$6.00
Star Wars, Boba Fett, Ewok, Luke Skywalker or Princess Leia, ea .$2.00
Star Wars, C3PO, Chewbacca, Darth Vader or Stormtrooper,
    ea...$2.00
Sylvester (A), w/ft, cream or wht whiskers, ea.....................$5.00
Sylvester (B), w/ft, $1 to....................................$3.00
Teenage Mutant Ninja Turtles, 8 different, w/ft, ea............$2.00
Thor, no ft..$300.00
Thumper, w/ft, no copyright..............................$50.00
Tiger, w/ft, whistle head....................................$6.00
Tinkerbell, no ft...$225.00

Tom, no ft..$35.00
Tom, w/ft, plastic face......................................$15.00
Tom, w/ft, pnt face..$6.00
Truck, many variations, ea................................$2.00
Tweety Bird, no ft..$15.00
Tweety Bird, w/ft, $1 to.....................................$3.00
Tyke, w/ft...$15.00
Uncle Sam, EX...$110.00
Uncle Sam, no ft...$175.00
Valentine Heart..$2.00
Vitamin Flinthart, EX..$15.00
Wal-Mart Smiley Pez, ea $1 to..........................$2.00
Whistle, w/ft, $1 to..$3.00
Wile E Coyote, w/ft..$40.00
Wimpy, EX...$18.00
Winnie the Pooh (A), w/ft.................................$75.00
Winnie the Pooh (B), Eeyore, Piglet, Pooh or Tigger, ea $2.00
Witch, 3-pc, no ft..$15.00
Wolfman, no ft...$275.00
Wonder Woman, no ft, soft head........................$175.00
Wonder Woman, w/ft..$2.00
Woodstock, w/ft..$2.00
Woodstock, w/ft, pnt feathers............................$15.00
Yappy Dog, no ft, orange or gr, ea....................$75.00
Yosemite Sam, w/ft...$2.00
Zorro...$65.00

Miscellaneous

Bank, truck #1, metal..$200.00
Bank, truck #2, metal..$40.00
Body Parts, fit over stem of dispenser & make it look like a per-
    son, many variations, ea..............................$1.00
Bracelet, pk...$5.00

PEZ Dispensers, Miscellaneous
• • • • • • • • • •
Money Clip, metal with color insert showing PEZ clown holding dispenser, unused, M, $15.00.
(Photo courtesy www.gasolinealley antiques.com)

PEZ Dispensers, Miscellaneous
• • • • • • • • • •
Yo-yo, tin version, 2¼" diameter, Made in Germany, 1950s, EX, $375.00. (Photo courtesy www.gasolinealleyantiques.com)

Bubble Wand $3.00
Clicker, US Zone Germany, 1955, litho tin, 3½", NM... $150.00
Clicker, 1960s, metal, 2", EX $45.00
Coin Plate $15.00
Coloring Book, Safety #2, non-English $15.00
Costume, lithoed frontal image of headless PEZ motorcyclist on cb, cut-out hole for head, folds over shoulders, EX $25.00
Giant PEZ Dispenser, various, 12", ea $15 to....................$25.00
Instruction Pamphlet, came in 1960s PEZ package, 2¾x1¾" (when folded), M $35.00
Mini PEZ Sets, various sets, Japan, ea set $15 to $35.00
PEZ Pinz, metal collector pins, various designs, ea $10 to.$75.00
Power Pez, rnd mechanical dispenser $2.00
Puzzle, Ceaco, 550 pcs, MIB $30.00

Puzzle, Springbok/Hallmark, 500 pcs....................$15.00
Refrigerator Magnet Set $10.00
Snow Dome, Bride & Groom, 4½", M $20.00
Snow Dome, ringmaster & elephant, M $20.00
Tin, Pez Specials, stars & lines on checked bkgrd, gold colors, 2½x4½", rare, EX...................... $225.00
Toy Car, Johnny Lightning Psychedelic Eye racer $20.00
Toy Car, Johnny Lightning Racing Dreams PEZ racer.......$10.00
Watch, pk face w/yel band or yel face w/bl band, ea...........$5.00
Watch, Psychedelic Hand.................................$10.00
Yo-yo, plastic, 2¼" dia, Made in Germany, any variation, M, ea.. $12.00
Yo-yo, 1950s, litho metal w/peppermint pkg, rare, NM.. $300.00

• • • • • • • • • • • • • • • • • Pin-Back Buttons • • • • • • • • • • • • • • •

Pin-back buttons, produced from the late 1890s up to the early 1920s, were made with a celluloid covering. After that time, a large number of buttons were lithographed on tin; these are referred to as tin 'lithos.'

Character and toy-related buttons represent a popular collecting field. There are countless categories to base a collection on. Buttons were given out at stores and theaters, offered as premiums, attached to dolls, or received with club memberships.

In the late 1940s and into the 1950s, some cereal companies packed one in each box of their product. Quaker Puffed Oats offered a series of movie star pin-backs, but probably the best known are Kellogg's PEP pins. There were 86 in all, so theoretically if you wanted the whole series as Kellogg's hoped you would, you'd have to buy at least that many boxes of their cereal. PEP pins came in five sets, the first in 1945, three more in 1946, and the last in 1947. They were printed with full-color lithographs of comic characters licensed by King Features and Famous Artists — Maggie and Jiggs, the Winkles, and Dagwood and Blondie, for instance. Superman, the only D.C. Comics character, was included in each set. Most PEP pins range in value from $10.00 to $15.00 in NM/M condition, but some sell for much more.

Nearly all pin-backs are collectible. Be sure that you buy only buttons with well-centered designs, well-aligned colors, no fading or yellowing, no spots or stains, and no cracks, splits, or dents. In the listings that follow, sizes are approximate.

Advisors: Michael and Polly McQuillen

Bat Kids Fan Club, bl head image on gold-tone, 2½" dia, 1960s, M $20.00
Buck Jones for US Marshall, lettering surrounds portrait on wht, 1½", 1930s, scarce, EX...$60.00

Pin-Back Buttons
Dale Evans, 1" diameter, 1950s, plain back (no Post Cereal advertising), NM, $25.00.
(Photo courtesy www.gasolinealley antiques.com)

Pin-Back Buttons
Batman and Robin, duo bursting through orange background, 6" diameter, 1982, M, $35.00.
(Photo courtesy www.gasolinealley antiques.com)

Pin-Back Buttons
Brave Eagle, Green Duck, 1", 1950s, M, $25.00. (Photo courtesy www. gasolinealleyantiques.com)

Pin-Back Buttons
Jerry Lewis as 'The Nutty Professor,' 2¾x1¾", 1950s, M, $30.00. (Photo courtesy www.gasoline alleyantiques.com)

Pin-Back Buttons

Smokey the Bear, Join Smokey's Campaign Prevent Forest Fires!, head image, brown and yellow, 1950s, 1½", M, $24.00. (Photo courtesy www.gasolinealleyantiques.com)

Pin-Back Buttons

Laurel & Hardy, ⅞", 1930s movie theater premium, NM, $20.00. (Photo courtesy www.gasolinealleyantiques.com)

Pin-Back Buttons

Lone Ranger (The), Lone Ranger and Silver in orange cloud of dust with blue sky, yellow ribbon, boots adornment, 1¼" diameter button, $70.00. (Photo courtesy www.serioustoyz.com)

Pin-Back Buttons

Pet-Koko (Member) Circus Club, 1¼" diameter, 1930s, Pet Milk premium, NM, $15.00. (Photo courtesy www.gasolinealleyantiques.com)

Pin-Back Buttons

Kids Ken L Klub, Official Member, 3" diameter, $15.00. (Photo courtesy www.gasolinealleyantiques.com)

Pin-Back Buttons

Pat Brady, 1" diameter, 1950s, plain back (no Post Cereal advertising), NM, $25.00. (Photo courtesy www.gasolinealleyantiques.com)

Daisy Air Rifle/World-Wide Safety League/Shoot Safe Buddy, red, wht & bl bull's-eye design, ⅞" dia, 1930s-40s, EX...$18.00

Davy Crockett, artist's image of Davy w/gun & powder horn against trees & bl sky, 1¾", 1950s, M...........................$50.00

Disneyland, color portrait of Donald Duck on wht w/yel border, WDP, 3½", M..$8.00

Green Hornet Club/WCMU/FM, blk lettering around head image in mask on gr, 2" dia, Bastian Bros, EX $55.00

Grumpy, full image of Snow White's Grumpy w/a disgruntled look & actions on wht, 3", WDP, NM..........................$12.00

Hopalong Cassidy Daily in the Chicago Tribune, blk & wht half-figure w/yel glow on red bkgrd, 1½", M.....................$35.00

Howdy Doody Safety Club CBC, wht lettering on red band around blk & wht head image on wht, 1¼" dia, M $200.00

I Rode It! Magic Mountain's Colossus The Greatest Roller Coaster in the World, blk & orange on wht, 3" dia, Fast Seal, 1978, NM $20.00

John Payne/Restless Gun, lettering around blk & wht half-image on lt gr bkgrd, 3", 1950s, M (VG package w/header) $30.00

Little Orphan Annie/Member Funny Frostys Club, bl lettering around bust portrait on wht, 1¼", 1930s, EX.............. $200.00

Mickey Mouse Undies/1928-30 WE Disney, image of Mickey 'hawking' underware, blk & red on wht, rnd, NM $28.00

Monkees, name in red guitar shape on yel, 2¼" dia, 1967, NM+ $48.00

Official Green Hornet Agent, mc, 4" dia, Greenway Prod, 1966, MIP (w/header card) $50.00

Oliver & Company, dog & cat looking lovingly at each other on bl & wht checked ground, 3" dia, Disney, 1988, NM.....$10.00

Orphan Annie/Some Swell Sweater, blk lettering around yel profile image of Annie on white, 1¼", 1920s, EX...........$75.00

Rex Allen, blk & wht portrait photo & name on red, 1¼" dia, 1940s, M $25.00

Roy Rogers & Trigger, blk & wht image on yel, 1¾" dia, 1953, NM $35.00

Roy Rogers, blk & wht portrait on deep yel w/red, wht & bl ribbon, 1¼", 1940s, EX+..$50.00

Pin-Back Buttons

Robin, 1" diameter, NPP Inc/Creative House, 1966, M, $15.00. (Photo courtesy www.gasolinealleyantiques.com)

Pin-Back Buttons

Supermen of America, 1961, $75.00. (Photo courtesy www.gasolinealleyantiques.com)

Pin-Back Buttons
- - - - - - - - - -
Trigger, 1" diameter, 1950s, plain back (no Post Cereal advertising), NM, $25.00. (Photo courtesy www.gasolinealleyantiques. com)

Pin-Back Buttons, Kellogg's PEP Pins
- - - - - - - - - -
Beezie, VG, $10.00. (Photo courtesy www.gasolinealleyantiques.com)

Pin-Back Buttons
- - - - - - - - - -
Universal Studios, 3" diameter, 1970s, NM, $20.00. (Photo courtesy www. gasolinealleyantiques.com)

Pin-Back Buttons, Kellogg's PEP Pins
- - - - - - - - - -
Chester Gump, EX, $15.00. (Photo courtesy www.gaso linealleyantiques.com)

Roy Rogers, color portrait w/red name on yel, 3/4" dia, Post Grape Nuts/Canadian issue, 1953, very scarce, EX $45.00
Roy Rogers King of the Cowboys, color portrait, name & phrase on wht, 1¾" dia, Post Grape Nuts, 1953, EX.................$30.00
Santa Claus Gave This To Me At..., blk lettering around frontal image of Santa in open auto on gr, 1¼" dia, VG $45.00
Yogi Bear for President & Huck Vice Pres, 2 head images w/blk & red lettering on yel, round, 1960s, NM+ $15.00

KELLOGG'S PEP PINS

Pin-Back Buttons, Kellogg's PEP Pins
- - - - - - - - - -
Emmy, VG, $10.00. (Photo courtesy www.gasolinealleyantiques.com)

Andy Gump, EX	$10.00
Barney Google, VG	$10.00
BO Plenty, NM	$30.00
Chief Brandon, VG	$10.00
Cindy, EX	$15.00
Corky, EX	$10.00
Dagwood, NM	$30.00
Dick Tracy, G	$12.00
Dick Tracy, NM	$30.00
Don Winslow, EX	$20.00
Fat Stuff, NM	$15.00
Felix the Cat, NM	$40.00
Fire Chief, VG	$10.00
Flash Gordon, NM	$25.00
Flat Top, NM	$23.00
Fritz, VG	$12.00
Goofy, NM	$10.00
Gravel Gertie, NM	$15.00
Harold Teen, NM	$15.00
Herby, VG	$12.00
Inspector, NM	$12.00
Jiggs, NM	$25.00
Judy, NM	$10.00
Junior Tracy, VG	$12.00
Kayo, NM	$12.00
Lillums, EX	$8.00

Pin-Back Buttons, Kellogg's PEP Pins
- - - - - - - - - -
Lord Plushbottom, EX, $11.00. (Photo courtesy www. gasolinealleyantiques.com)

Pin-Back Buttons, Kellogg's PEP Pins
- - - - - - - - - -
Pop Jenks, NM, $15.00. (Photo courtesy www.gasolinealleyantiques.com)

Pin-Back Buttons, Kellogg's PEP Pins
- - - - - - - - - -
Sandy, NM, $12.00. (Photo courtesy www.gasolinealleyantiques.com)

Pin-Back Buttons, Kellogg's PEP Pins Shadow, VG, $10.00. (Photo courtesy www.gasolinealleyantiques.com)

Pin-Back Buttons, Kellogg's PEP Pins Vitamin Flinthart, EX, $15.00. (Photo courtesy www.gasolinealleyantiques.com)

Pin-Back Buttons, Kellogg's PEP Pins Superman, NM, $25.00. (Photo courtesy www.gasolinealleyantiques.com)

Pin-Back Buttons, Kellogg's PEP Pins Wimpy, EX, $18.00. (Photo courtesy www.gasolinealleyantiques.com)

Little King, NM $15.00	Punjab, VG $15.00
Little Moose, NM $15.00	Rip Winkle, NM $20.00
Maggie, NM $25.00	Skeezix, NM $15.00
Mama De Stross, NM $30.00	Smilin' Jack, EX $12.00
Mama Katzenjammer, NM.............................$25.00	Smokey Stover, VG $20.00
Mamie, NM.............................$15.00	Spud, VG $12.00
Min Gump, VG $12.00	Superman, EX $20.00
Moon Mullins, EX $10.00	Tess Trueheart, VG $14.00
Mr. Barley, VG $12.00	Toots, NM $15.00
Nina, VG $10.00	Uncle Bim, EX $11.00
Olive Oyl, NM $18.00	Uncle Walt, NM $20.00
Orphan Annie, NM.............................$25.00	Uncle Walt, VG.............................$10.00
Pat Patton, NM $15.00	Uncle Willie, NM $12.00
Perry Winkle, NM $15.00	Winkle Twins, NM $25.00
Phantom, NM.............................$45.00	Winnie Winkle, NM $15.00
Popeye, NM $30.00	Winnie Winkle, EX $12.00

• • • • • • • • • Plastic Figures • • • • • • • • •

Plastic figures were made by many toy companies. They were first boxed with playsets, but in the early 1950s, some became available individually. Marx was the first company to offer single figures (at 10¢ each), and even some cereal companies included one in boxes of their products. (Kellogg's offered a series of 16 54mm Historic Warriors, and Nabisco had a line of ten dinosaurs in marbleized, primary colors.) Virtually every type of man and beast has been modeled in plastic; today some have become very collectible and expensive. There are lots of factors you'll need to be aware of to be a wise buyer. For instance, Marx made cowboys during the mid-1960s in a flat finish, and these are much harder to find and more valuable than the later figures with a waxy finish. Marvel Super Heroes in the fluorescent hues are worth about half as much as the earlier, light gray issue. Beware that internet sales may cause values to change greatly.

Because of limited space, it isn't possible to evaluate more than a representative few of these plastic figures in a general price guide, so if you would like to learn more about them, we recommend *Playset Magazine*, published by our advisors, Rusty and Kathy Kern.

See also Clubs, Newsletters, and Other Publications for information concerning *Prehistoric Times*, a magazine for dinosaur figure collectors, published by Mike Fredericks, and *Playset Magazine*.

Note: All listings below are figures by Marx unless noted otherwise.

See also Playsets.

Advisors: Rusty and Kathy Kern

Size Conversion:

20mm — ¾"	45mm — 1¾"	50mm — 2"
54mm — 2⅛"	60mm — 2½"	70mm — 2¾"

ACTION AND ADVENTURE

Apollo Astronaut, 6", w/American Flag, wht, NM.............$4.00
Apollo Astronaut Explorers, 54mm, set of 8 in 7 poses, orange, NM, $20 to $25.00
Arctic — Dew Line, scientists, any, bl, NM, ea.............$4.00
Ben Hur, 54mm, set of 16, cream, Ben Hur/Empress/Emperor marked MGM on base, rare, NM..............................$200.00
Ben Hur, 54mm, set of 16, gray, M............................$50.00
Ben Hur, 54mm, set of 16, tan, NM............................$60.00
Ben Hur characters, set of 3 (Ben Hur, Emperor, Empress), purple, M $150.00
Captain Video, 50mm, any, various colors, Lido, 1950s, M, ea $25.00
Deep Sea Diver, 3", Ideal...$35.00
Fox Hunt, 60mm, fox running, NM..............................$10.00
Fox Hunt, 60mm, hound sniffing, NM...........................$10.00
GIs, 54mm, gr, set of 16, M..$65.00
Indians, 54mm, red/br, khaki or tan, set of 16, M.............$65.00
Man From UNCLE, 6", Alexander Waverly, Illya Kuryakin or Napoleon Solo, turq or tan, NM, ea $12 to...................$20.00
Man From UNCLE, 6", Illya Kuryakin or Napoleon Solo, lt gray, turq or tan, NM (watch for Mexican copies in stiff plastic gray), ea...$25.00
Man From UNCLE, 6", Thrush Agents, tan, ea $20.00
Man From UNCLE, 6", Thrush Agents, turq, ea..............$15.00

Plastic Figures, Action and Adventure
• • • • • • • • • • • • • • • •
Arctic — Dew Line, Eskimo, towing seal with rope intact (no splits), $25.00. (Photo courtesy Rusty and Kathy Kern)

Plastic Figures, Action and Adventure
• • • • • • • • • • • • • • • • •
Ben Hur, set of three (Ben Hur, Emperor, Empress), cream, M, $175.00. (Photo courtesy Rusty and Kathy Kern)

Royal Canadian Police, Dulcop, NM.................................$5.00
Spaceman, 3", various poses & colors, Premier, ea............$5.00
Spaceman, 45mm, metallic bl or yel, NM, ea $5.00
Space Patrol, 45mm, any, tan & orange, NM, ea.............$18.00
Space People, set of 11, Archer, MIB............................$345.00
Sports, 60mm, bowler, boxer, figure skater, golfer or runner, wht, NM, ea $2.50 to $3.00
Sports, 60mm, hockey player, lt bl, NM.........................$12.00
Super Heroes, Captain America, 7", gr, 1967, NM............$22.00
Super Heroes, Dare Devil, 7", red, NM.........................$20.00
Super Heroes, Incredible Hulk, 5½", orange, 1967, NM ...$20.00
Super Heroes, Iron Man, 7", red, 1967, NM $22.00
Super Heroes, Thor, 7½", gr, 1967, NM.........................$30.00
Untouchables, 54mm, NM, ea $15.00

ANIMALS

Arctic Animals, any, cream, ea......................................$4.00
Ben Hur, lion or tiger, orange, ea.................................$20.00
Champion Dogs, 84mm, any, NM, ea $6.50
Circus Animals, elephant w/howdah, NM.........................$10.00
Circus Animals, giraffe, tan, NM $10.00
Circus Animals, gorilla, NM $3.00
Farm Stock, 54mm, 2nd issue, any, NM, ea......................$2.00
Farm Stock, 60mm, any, NM, ea $2 to $5.00
Ice-Age Mammals, any, NM, $10 to $20.00
Prehistoric Dinosaurs, any color, NM, ea $8 to.................$12.00
Prehistoric Dinosaurs, pot belly 1st issue, T-Rex, NM.......$20.00
Ranch & Rodeo, 54mm, Indian pony running, various colors, EX $3.50
Ranch & Rodeo, 60mm, bucking bronco, reddish brn, NM.$5.00
Ranch & Rodeo, 60mm, longhorn steer haulting, reddish brn, NM $8.00

CAMPUS CUTIES AND AMERICAN BEAUTIES

American Beauties, any figure besides reclining nude, M, ea $20.00
American Beauties, reclining nude, never sold to public, M....$75.00
Campus Cuties, any figure, 1st series, M, ea $8 to.............$20.00
Campus Cuties, any figure, 2nd series, M, ea $8 to...........$40.00

COMIC, DISNEY, AND NURSERY CHARACTERS

Disneykin Play Sets, 19 figures in 3 complete sets in 1 box, Snow White, Pinocchio & assorted, 1961, NRFB.................$220.00
Disneykings, any character, MIB, ea $15 to $20.00
Disneykins, any character, MIB, ea $10 to........................$15.00
Fairykins, any, MIB (individual window boxes), ea $20.00
Fairykins, book-shaped box set of 21 different plastic figures, 1962 issue, M (VG box)..$300.00
Fairykins, various characters, MIB, ea $20.00
Nursery Rhymes, 60mm to 70mm, any, NM, ea $5 to.......$10.00
Oz-Kins, set of 10, Aurora/MGM, 1967, unused, NMOC ..$100.00
Rolykins, any, NM, ea $10 to $15.00
Rolykins, 6 different figures on 1 card, M (G card)............$100.00
Tinykins, any character, NM, ea $15 to $20.00
Tinykins, any character, NMIB, ea $25 to $30.00

Famous People and Civilians

Civilians & Workmen, cameraman, 60mm, NM..............$15.00
Civilians & Workmen, racetrack pit crew, 54mm, cream, NM $100.00
Civilians & Workmen, railroad station people, 45mm, cream, set of 5, NM $20.00
International VIPs, Queen Elizabeth, 60mm, wht, NM $30.00
International VIPs, Royal Family, any except Queen Elizabeth II, 60mm, wht, NM..............................$20.00
Louis Marx on base w/name, giveaway, cigar held down.. $100.00
Politicians, Adlai Stevenson, NM..............................$50.00
Religious Leaders, Cardinal Spellman, NM $20.00
US Presidents, Eisenhower, 60mm, NM $20.00
US Presidents, Lincoln, 60mm, NM $6.50
US Presidents, Nixon, 60mm, NM $12.50
US Presidents, Washington, 60mm, NM $8.00

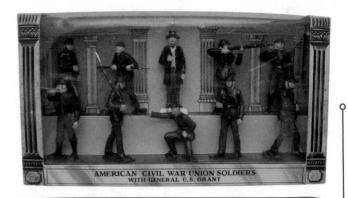

AMERICAN CIVIL WAR UNION SOLDIERS
WITH GENERAL U.S. GRANT

Plastic Figures, Military and Warriors
• •
Warriors of the World, Union, two-tier set, $150.00. Display carton, $350.00. (Photo courtesy Rusty and Kathy Kern)

Plastic Figures, Famous People and Civilians
• • • • • • • • • • • • • • • •
Louis Marx on base w/name, giveaway, cigar held out, $25.00. (Photo courtesy Rusty and Kathy Kern)

LOUIS MARX

Warriors of the World, Confederate, 2-tier set................ $150.00
Warriors of the World, German, 2-tier set $200.00
Warriors of the World, Knights, 6", any, silver, ea $8.00
Warriors of the World, US Combat Soldiers, set of 6, NMIB.. $125.00
Warriors of the World, Vikings, 6", any, NM, ea $18.00

Nutty Mads

All Heart Hogan, pk w/cream swirl, NM $20.00
Bullpen Boo Boo, dk gr, NM $30.00
Dippy the Sea Diver, cobalt, 1st issue, EX.........................$10.00
End Zone Football Player, dk gr, 1st issue, NM, $15 to......$20.00
Lost Teepee, fluorescent red, NM, $15 to..........................$20.00
Manny the Reckless Mariner, lime gr, NM $20.00
Manny the Reckless Mariner, lt gr, 1st issue, NM............$35.00
Rocko the Champ, lime gr, 1st issue, NM, $15 to..............$20.00
Rocko the Champ, pk, NM $16.50
Roddy the Hotrod, chartreuse gr, 1st issue, NM, $15 to $20.00
Suburban Sidney, maroon, 1st issue, NM...........................$35.00
The Thinker, dk gr, NM $35.00
Waldo the Weight Lifter, pk, 1st issue, NM $25.00

Military and Warriors

American Heroes, Gen Arnold, 60mm, wht......................$20.00
American Heroes, Gen Bradley, 60mm, wht.....................$20.00
American Heroes, Gen Eisenhower, 60mm, wht $20.00
American Heroes, Gen Grant, 60mm, wht, NM $30.00
American Heroes, Gen Gruenther, 60mm, wht, NM........$15.00
American Heroes, Gen Jackson, 60mm, wht, NM $40.00
American Heroes, Gen Lee, 60mm, wht, NM...................$40.00
American Heroes, Gen Lemay, 60mm, wht, NM $15.00
American Heroes, Gen MacArthur, 60mm, wht, NM.......$20.00
American Heroes, Gen Pershing, 60mm, wht, NM...........$40.00
American Heroes, Gen Pickett, 60mm, wht $50.00
American Heroes, Gen Ridgeway, 60mm, wht, NM..........$25.00
American Heroes, Gen Sheridan, 60mm, wht, NM $40.00
American Heroes, Gen Spaatz, 60mm, wht, NM $20.00
American Heroes, Gen Taylor, 60mm, wht, NM..............$40.00
American Heroes, Gen Washington, 60mm, wht, NM $40.00
Civil War, Confederate soldiers, any, Andy Guard, ea $3 to $4.00
Civil War, Union officers or soldiers, any, Andy Guard, ea $6 to $8.00
Warriors of the World, British, 2-tier set.......................$180.00
Warriors of the World, Cadets, set of 6, NMIB..............$125.00

Western and Frontier Heroes

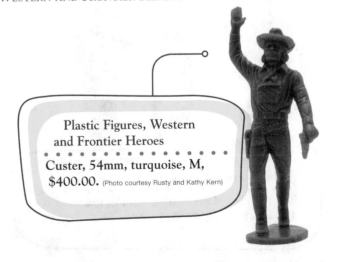

Plastic Figures, Western and Frontier Heroes
• • • • • • • • • • • • • • • • •
Custer, 54mm, turquoise, M, $400.00. (Photo courtesy Rusty and Kathy Kern)

Plastic Figures, Western and Frontier Heroes

Gunsmoke, Marshall Dillon, M, minimum value, $700.00. (Photo courtesy Rusty and Kathy Kern)

Plastic Figures, Western and Frontier Heroes

Wyatt Earp, gray, rare, NM, $25.00. (Photo courtesy Rusty and Kathy Kern)

Buffalo Bill, Atlantic #1202, MIP (sealed) $50.00
Buffalo Bill, 60mm, beige, EX..$5.00
Cavalry, 60mm, metallic bl SP, mounted, ea.....................$12.00
Cavalry, 60mm, metallic bl SP, standing or kneeling firing, ea..$20.00

Cavalry, metallic bl, set of 12 ....$140.00
Cavalry, 60mm, powder bl, set of 12............................$200.00
Cowboy, 45mm, mounted w/rope, NM $36.00
Cowboy, 54mm, set of 9, NM....................................$35.00
Cowboy, 6", any, Crescent, NM, ea...............................$10.00
Dale Evans, 60mm, cream, NM....................................$12.00
Davy Crockett, 50mm, cream, NM..............................$25.00
Gunsmoke, Chester, NM..$375.00
Gunsmoke, cowboys, bl, NM, ea $75 to......................$100.00
Gunsmoke, cowboys, tan, NM, ea................................$3.00
Gunsmoke, Doc, NM...$375.00
Gunsmoke, driver seated, bl, NM..............................$100.00
Gunsmoke, Miss Kitty, cream, earrings intact, NM $375.00
High Chaparral, ½", 42-pc set, Airfix, unused, MIB.........$25.00
Indians, 54mm, set of 15, w/totem pole, NM..................$45.00
Johnny Ringo, portrayed by Don Durant (from playset), cream, soft plastic, NM..$1,800.00
Lone Ranger & Tonto, 54mm, NM................................$65.00
Pioneer, 60mm, clubbing, NM $5.00
Ranch Hand, 60mm, kneeling, NM $125.00
Ranch Kids, Roy Rogers Ranch Set, full set of 14, rare .. $125.00
Rough Rider, 60mm, mounted, NM..............................$18.00
Roy Rogers, 54mm, set of 4, cream SP $45.00
Roy Rogers, 60mm, hands on hips, NM..........................$15.00
Roy Rogers on Trigger, 5", Ideal, M.............................$150.00
Tonto, 60mm, cream, NM.......................................$110.00
Trappers & Miners, 54mm, gray SP, set of 16.................$300.00
Wagon Driver, 6", cream, NM....................................$5.00
Zorro, 54mm, w/Horse, Tornado, NM...........................$60.00
7th Cavalry, 6", shot w/arrow intact, set of 6 ....$100.00

Plastic Toys

During the 1940s and into the 1960s, plastic was often the material of choice for consumer goods ranging from dinnerware and kitchenware items to jewelry and even high-heeled shoes. Toy companies used brightly colored plastic to produce cars, dolls, pull toys, banks, games, and thousands of other types of products. Of the more imaginative toys, those that have survived in good collectible condition are beginning to attract a considerable amount of interest, especially items made by major companies.

Atomic Cannon Truck, Ideal, 1960s, 43", complete, unused, NMIB $225.00
Benny Rabbit on Scooter w/Sidecar, Canada, 1940s-50s, 5" L, NM $40.00
Car Wash, Ideal, #3031, NMIB.................................... $125.00
Cement Mixer Truck, Renwal, 1948, mixer revolves, red w/yel & bl trim, door opens to reveal bl driver, 7", NM........... $180.00
Drawbridge Set #155, Renwal, crank-op bridge, 2 cars & 2 boats, unused, NM+IB... $175.00
Easy Does It Searchlight Truck Assembly Kit, Thomas, complete & unused, MIB $175.00
Fire Chief Car, Saunders Tool & Die, red convertible w/yel siren, clear windshield, friction, 9", VG.............................$15.00
Fix-It Car of Tomorrow, Ideal #XP-600, working horn & headlights, EXIP.. $125.00
Friction Explorer With Siren, #609, 6", Hong Kong, 1960s, NMIB $30.00

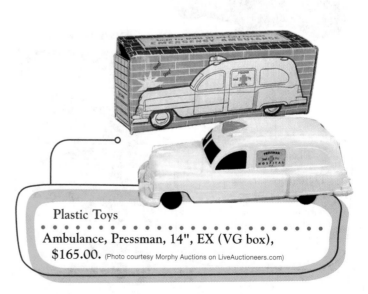

Plastic Toys

Ambulance, Pressman, 14", EX (VG box), $165.00. (Photo courtesy Morphy Auctions on LiveAuctioneers.com)

Gilmark's Service & Hi-Way Fleet, 10-pc, EXIB $75.00

Hardy County Fair, unused, MIB $100.00

Hardy Farm, complete, EXIB $75.00

Hot Dog Wagon, Ideal, 7", NM+IB $85.00

Hot Rod #3, Saunders Tool & Die, #400, 1950, open w/driver, exposed engine, friction, 7", NM $80.00

Hot Rod #8 (1930s), Lincoln Line, 1950s, friction motor, BRT, 5", NM $65.00

Ice Cream Trike, Renwal, 1950s, w/metal bell, red, wht, bl & yel, 4½", EX $35.00

Ice Cream Trike, Renwal, 1950s, w/metal bell, red, wht, bl & yel, 4½", NM $48.00

Jet Bomber Escort Squadron, Payton Prod, 7-pc set w/6 fighter jets & 1 bomber, unused, MIB $125.00

Jetgo Freedom Plane, Nosco, EXIB (box mk United Nations Peace Toy) $150.00

Kiddie Toy (4) Assortment, Hubley, 4 vehicles including taxi, fire pumper truck, fire hose truck & sedan, EX+IB $500.00

Li'l Beep Bus, Arrow, 1960s, beeps when squeezed, w/pull string, 11", EX $20.00

Modern Toys Auto & Planes Set, Kilgore, ca 1937, w/sedan, coupe, truck & 2 planes, 5" to 12", EXIB $350.00

Mystery Space Ship, Marx, 1960s, gyro-powered, w/astronaut & alien figures, lg flying saucer & 2 rockets, NMIB $125.00

Police Motorcycle, Hubley Kiddy Toys, 1950s, removable driver, 5", M $33.00

Race Car #5 w/Motor, Rite Spot Plastic Prod, w/up, 10", NMIB $100.00

Rocket Tank, red, gr & yel, 6", EXIB $30.00

Satellite Launcher, EXIB $275.00

Service & Hi-Way Fleet, Gilmark, 10-pc vehicle set in various colors, EXIB $75.00

Speed King Racer #8, Renwal, #107, 1950s, friction motor, red, bl & yel, NMIB $90.00

Speedway Racer #7, Renwal, #173, 1953, w/driver, 9½", NM . $40.00

Sportorama Sports Car, Payton, 1950s, Healy, LeSabre, Jaguar or Allard, 8½", MIP, ea $20.00

Steer-O Car, Product Miniature Co Inc, convertible w/wht-wall tires, chrome-look hubs, 12", EXIB $250.00
Super-X Gasoline Truck, Renwal, 1950, tank holds water, doors open to reveal driver, bl & yel w/wht tires, 7", NM $140.00
Trailer Fleet, Banner, 3½" truck cab w/3 different 4½" trailers, NMIB $425.00
US Army Set (21-pc), Pyro, NMIB $220.00
Witch on Rocket, 1950s-60s, 4", NM+ $175.00

Zoo Fire Truck Pull Toy, Irwin, truck's eyes roll & bell rings, driver bobs head & 2 animal riders spin, 13", NMIB .. $100.00

Plasticville

From the 1940s through the 1960s, Bachmann Brothers produced plastic accessories for train layouts such as buildings, fences, trees, and animals. Buildings often included several smaller pieces — for instance, ladders, railings, windsocks, etc. — everything you could ever need to play out just about any scenario. Beware of reissues.

Advisor: Gary Mosholder, Gary's Trains

Airport Administration Building, #AD-4, EXIB $55.00	Church, #113, Littletown, EXIB $20.00
Bank, #1801, EXIB $28.00	Church, #1600, EXIB $16.00
Barbeque, EX..$3.00	Church, #1818, EXIB (sm box)..$12.00
Barn, #BN-1, wht w/red roof, chrome silo top, EXIB.........$18.00	Colonial Mansion, #1703, Littletown, EX $29.00
Barn, #BN-1, wht w/red roof, EXIB.........................$15.00	Covered Bridge, #1920, MIB..$25.00
Barnyard Animals, EX, ea....................................$1.00	Diner, #DE-7, yel roof & trim, EXIB.............................$15.00
Bridge (Trestle), #BR-2, EXIB................................$18.00	Figure Set, #953, Lionel, VGIB......................................$65.00
Bridge & Pond, #BL-2, EXIB................................$6.00	Fire House, #FH-4, w/hollow siren, EXIB $25.00
Cape Cod House, #HP-9, dk gray roof, red trim, EXIB......$10.00	Fire House, #FH-4, w/lg base siren, EXIB........................$16.00

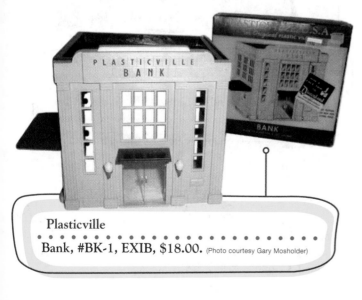

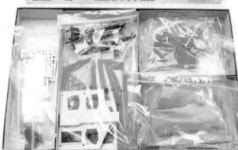

Plasticville

Colonial House (Two-Story), #LH-4, EXIB, $18.00.
(Photo courtesy Gary Mosholder)

Plasticville

Countryside Farm Set, #5606-498, O- and S-gauge, complete, VGIB, $180.00. (Photo courtesy Stout Auctions on LiveAuctioneers.com)

Plasticville

Corner Store, #1626, gray with white roof, VGIB, $65.00. (Photo courtesy Gary Mosholder)

Plasticville

Homes for Town and Country, #HU-5, complete, EX+IB, $50.00. (Photo courtesy Stout Auctions on LiveAuctioneers.com)

Fire House, #FH-4, w/sm base siren, EXIB	$15.00
Five & Ten Cent Store, #CS-5, EXIB	$15.00
Frosty Store, #FB-1, yel w/chrome bar, EXIB	$18.00
Gas Station, #1800, w/auto, EXIB	$18.00
Hardware-Pharmacy, #DH-1, EXIB	$18.00
Hospital, #HS-6, w/furniture, EXIB	$35.00
Hospital, #HS-6, w/o furniture, EXIB	$22.00
House & Yard Set, #HY-6, VGIB	$18.00
House Under Construction, #1624, lt gray, complete, VGIB	$60.00
Loading Platform, #1817, MIB	$16.00
Log Cabin, #LC-2, w/chimney & rustic fence, EXIB	$18.00
Log Cabin, #LC-2, w/rustic fence & tree, VGIB	$18.00
Motel, #1621, EXIB	$15.00
Pine Trees, #2410, set of 8, VGIB (HO box)	$18.00
Plasticville Hall, #PH-1, EXIB	$35.00
Platform Fence & Gate Unit, #3F, VGIB	$20.00
Playground, #1406, EXIB	$30.00
Police Dept, #PD-3, dk gray, EXIB	$25.00
Police Dept, #PD-3, lt gray, EXIB	$20.00
Ranch House, #RH-1, EXIB	$15.00
Ranch House, #1603, wht sides, lt bl roof, EXIB	$16.00
Ranch House, EX	$10.00
School, #SC-4, EX	$10.00
School, #SC-4, VGIB	$15.00
Split-Level, #1908, EXIB	$22.00

Street Signs, EX	$1.00
Suburban Station, #RS-8, GIB	$10.00
Switch Tower, #1814, EXIB	$12.00
Telephone Booth, EX	$15.00
Union Station, #1901, EXIB	$25.00
Watchman's Chanty, #1407, EXIB	$12.00

• • • • • • • • • • • • • • • • • • •   Playsets   • • • • • • • • • • • • • •

Originally issued as early as 1948 in the form of farms and service stations, the Marx playset quickly became a Baby Boomer sensation offered in many variations containing tiny buildings and forts with soft plastic figures and accessories such as tanks and wagons. Fort Apache, Revolutionary War, and Battle of the Blue & Gray were generic playset titles while Roy Rogers Western Town, Zorro, Walt Disney's Davy Crockett at the Alamo and even The Flintstones, based on then-popular TV shows, are among the licensed property titles. Johnny Ringo, a short-lived TV series, has the distinction of being the most valuable set since it was only sold for half a year.

In general, illustrated cartons contain the more valuable sets, while photo boxes of the late 1960s and 1970s are by far less valuable and contain parts in less desirable waxy plastics. Miniature (HO scale) sets containing 1" tall painted figures from Marx Hong Kong do often have photo covers and are in high demand.

Near-mint boxes double the value of a complete set; sets still stapled sealed earn stratospheric values at auction. A $350.00 Fort Apache earns thousands for the privilege of opening it and getting 1960 factory air. Boxes with tears, stains, or holes, missing parts, or damaged figures greatly decrease values since key items ('Velardi' sign and character figure from Marx Johnny Ringo set) elevate sets above the average. Damaged parts like a split trail in a wagon hitch devalue the total piece. A mint yellow wagon will sell for $300.00; with split traces, it's $150.00. Likewise, the hard plastic caisson in Civil War sets: intact it fetches $125.00; but with the tiny hitches broken, it's worth less than half that. A Matt Dillon character figure from the Gunsmoke set gets $700.00 to $1,200.00, depending on who's bidding; but with scuffed hat brim or dimpled torso he drops to $350.00 or less.

The listings below are for complete examples unless noted otherwise. See the Clubs, Newsletters, and Other Publications section for information on how to order *Prehistoric Times*, by Mike Fredericks, and *Playset Magazine*, published by our advisors, Rusty and Kathy Kern.

Adventures of Robin Hood, Marx #4722, EXIB $400.00

Adventures of Robin Hood, Marx #4722, NMIB $800.00

Alamo, Marx #3534, NMIB $2,000.00

Alamo, Marx/Sears #3543, John Wayne set, 1960s, NMIB ..$1,100.00

Alaska, Marx #3707-8, NMIB, w/knife & accessories $800.00

Alaska, Marx #3707-8, used, M $900.00

Allstate Service Station (4-level), Marx #3499, EX+IB. $400.00

American Airlines Astro Jet Port, Marx #4821-2, NMIB...$435.00

American Airlines International Jetport, Marx #4811, Series 2000, w/friction cars, NMIB...................... $650.00

Anzio Beach, Aurora, HO scale, VGIB $50.00

Arctic Explorer, Marx #3702, EXIB $1,100.00

Army Combat Set, Marx #4158, EXIB $150.00

Army Combat Training Center, Marx #2654, VGIB........$25.00

Army Combat Training Center, Marx #4152, unused, NMIB (sealed) $275.00

Bar-M Ranch, Marx #3956, EXIB $75.00

Battlefield, Marx #4756, Series 5000, NMIB $3,900.00

Battleground, Marx #4139, EXIB $125.00

Battleground, Marx #4150, EX $500.00

Battleground, Marx #4749-50, Series 1000, basic set, NMIB..$400.00

Battleground, Marx #4751, EX.. $450.00

Battleground, Marx #4752, EX.. $500.00

Battleground, Marx #4756, photobox set, EXIB $100.00

Battleground Convoy, Marx #3745-6, NMIB $2,000.00
Battle of Iwo Jima, Marx #4154, EXIB $1,200.00
Battle of Iwo Jima, Marx #4147, NMIB, $750 to $800.00
Battle of Iwo Jima, Marx #6057, giant set, NMIB........ $1,500.00
Battle of Little Big Horn, Marx #4679MO, w/Custer, MIB .$900.00
Battle of the Alamo (Heritage), Marx #59091, EX+IB .. $300.00
Battle of the Blue & Gray, Marx #2646, rare half set, M. $1,500.00
Battle of the Blue & Gray, Marx #4658, Series 2000, EXIB.$450.00
Battle of the Blue & Gray, Marx #4744, NMIB.............. $750.00
Battle of the Blue & Gray, Marx #4760, Series 2000, EXIB.$900.00
Beach Head Landing Set, Marx #4939, NMIB $75.00
Ben Hur, Marx #2648, MOC.. $900.00
Ben Hur, Marx #4696, EXIB.. $750.00
Ben Hur, Marx #4696, MIB.. $1,200.00
Ben Hur, Marx #4701, Series 5000, 8 chariots, G........ $1,400.00
Ben Hur, Marx #4701, Series 5000, 8 chariots, M $1,900.00
Ben Hur, Marx #4702, Series 2000, 4 chariots, NMIB.. $1,200.00
Beyond Tomorrow Lunar Station, Multiple Toys, EXIB. $125.00
Big Inch Pipeline, Marx #6008, EXIB............................. $650.00
Big Top Circus, Marx #4310, EXIB $350.00
Big Top Circus, Marx #4310, NMIB $475.00
Blue & Gray Battle Set (Giant), Marx, MIB.............. $1,500.00

Boot Camp (Carry-All), Marx #4645, EX+IB $75.00
Boy's Camp, Marx #4103, EXIB $900.00
Cape Canaveral, Marx #4524, Series 2000, NMIB......... $225.00
Cape Canaveral Missile Base, Marx #4524, NMIB......... $375.00
Cape Canaveral Missile Base, Marx #4528, EXIB $150.00
Cape Canaveral Missile Base, Marx #5935, NMIB......... $675.00
Cape Kennedy (Carry-All), Marx #4625, tin box, NMIB.$75.00
Captain Gallant, Marx #4729, NMIB......................... $1,600.00
Captain Space Solar Academy, Marx #7026, EXIB........ $400.00
Captain Space Solar Port, Marx #7018, EXIB $400.00
Castle, Elastolin #9756, EXIB $300.00
Castle & Moat Set, Marx/Sears #4734, EXIB $500.00
Cattle Drive, Marx #3983, NMIB $375.00
Charge of the Light Brigade, HO set w/Arabs $600.00
Civil War Centennial (Happi-Time), Marx/Sears #5927,
    MIB $2,000.00
Combat! (Official Play Set), Cohn, NMIB..................... $125.00
Commanche Pass, Marx #3416, NMIB........................... $150.00
Construction Camp, Marx #4442, EX+IB $200.00
Construction Camp, Marx #4444, w/tin friction vehicles...$650.00
Cowboy & Indian Camp, Marx #3950, NMIB $800.00
Custer's Last Stand, HO set, MIB.................................. $600.00
Custer's Last Stand, Marx #4670, NMIB.................... $3,000.00
Custer's Last Stand, Marx #4779, Series 500, NMIB $750.00
D-Day Army, Marx #6027, medium set, NMIB $800.00
Daktari, Marx #3717, EXIB $700.00
Daktari, Marx #3718, EXIB $800.00
Daktari, Marx #3720, NMIB $900.00
Daniel Boone Frontier, Marx #1393, NMIB $275.00
Daniel Boone Wilderness Scout, Marx #0631, NMIB.... $250.00
Daniel Boone Wilderness Scout, Marx #0670, NMIB.... $250.00
Daniel Boone Wilderness Scout, Marx #2640, EXIB...... $175.00
Davy Crockett at the Alamo, Marx #3442, NMIB......... $375.00
Davy Crockett at the Alamo, Marx #3530, NMIB......... $300.00
Davy Crockett at the Alamo, Marx #3530, EXIB........... $150.00
Davy Crockett at the Alamo, Marx #3544, Walt Disney,
    EXIB $850.00

Playsets
Boy's Camp, Marx, #4103, unused, MIB (sealed),
$1,200.00. (Photo courtesy Morphy Auctions on LiveAuctioneers.com)

Playsets
Cape Canaveral Missile Base, Marx, #2656,
unused, MIB (sealed), $400.00. (Photo courtesy Morphy
Auctions on LiveAuctioneers.com)

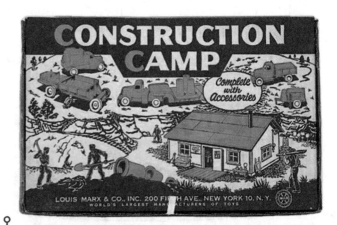

Playsets
Construction Camp, Marx, #4439, unused, MIB
(NOS), $325.00. (Photo courtesy Morphy Auctions on LiveAuctioneers.com)

Desert Fox, Marx #4177, NMIB.................................. $325.00
Desert Fox, Marx #4178, NMIB.................................. $500.00
Desert Patrol, Marx #4174, MIB $350.00
Desert Patrol, Marx #4174, VGIB................................$75.00
Farm, Marx #3948, Series 2000, NMIB.................... $275.00
Farm, Marx #5942, EXIB...$75.00
Farm, Marx #6006, NMIB... $225.00
Farm, Marx #6050, EXIB $100.00
Farm, Platform #5990, EX $650.00
Farm (Happi-Time), Marx #3480, NMIB $100.00
Farm (Happi-Time), Marx #3943, NMIB $175.00
Farm (Lazy Day), Marx #3942, NMIB...................... $175.00
Farm (Lazy Day), Marx #3945, EX+IB $100.00
Farm (Modern), Marx #3931, NMIB $175.00
Farm (Modern), Marx #3932, EXIB $100.00
Fighting Knights (Carry-All), Marx #4635, EX+IB....... $100.00
Fire House, Marx #4819, VG+IB $100.00
Fireball XL5 Space City, Multiple Prod, VGIB....... $650.00
Flintstones, Marx #4672, EXIB................................ $300.00
Fort Apache, Marx #3616, NMIB.............................. $125.00
Fort Apache, Marx #3647, NMIB.............................. $300.00
Fort Apache, Marx #3680, open, complete, EX............. $500.00
Fort Apache, Marx #3680, unused, MIB (sealed) $3,025.00
Fort Apache, Marx #3681, EXIB................................$75.00
Fort Apache, Marx #3682A, EX+IB $50.00
Fort Apache, Marx #4202, NMIB................................$50.00
Fort Apache, Marx #6059, NMIB............................ $1,300.00
Fort Apache, Marx #6063, EXIB............................... $150.00
Fort Apache, Marx #6068, EX+IB $50.00
Fort Apache Stockade, Marx #3612, NMIB $200.00
Fort Apache Stockade, Marx #3660, Series 2000, NMIB...$250.00
Fort Boone, Multiple, NMIB.................................... $175.00
Fort Dearborn, Marx #3510, NMIB $200.00
Fort Dearborn, Marx #3514, EXIB $30.00
Fort Dearborn, Marx #3688, NMIB $225.00
Fort Laramie (Giant), Ideal, NMIB........................... $175.00
Fort Liberty, Hong Kong, 1970s, MIB $50.00

Fort Mohawk, Marx #3751-2, EXIB.......................... $650.00
Fort Pitt, Marx #3741, Series 750, NMIB $650.00
Fort Pitt, Marx #3742, Series 1000, NMIB $350.00
Freight Trucking Terminal, Marx #5220, EX+IB $50.00
Freight Trucking Terminal, Marx #5422, NMIB............. $100.00
Galaxy Command, Marx #4206, NMIB.........................$75.00
Gallant Men, Marx #4634, EX+IB............................ $2,600.00
Gallant Men Army, Marx #4632, EX+IB.................... $100.00
Gunsmoke (Dodge City), Marx #4268, Series 2000, EXIB. $5,000.00
History in the Pacific, Marx #4164, NMIB $300.00
Holiday Turnpike, Marx #5230, NMIB.........................$25.00
Home Farm Set, Blue Box #6042, EX+IB......................$50.00
IGY Arctic Satellite Base, Marx #4800, Series 1000, EX+IB... $850.00
Indian Warfare, Marx #4778, Series 2000, EXIB $850.00
International Airport, Marx #4814, EXIB $50.00
International Airport, Marx #4814, NM+IB $100.00
Johnny Apollo Launch Center, Marx #4630, EXIB........ $100.00
Johnny Ringo Western Frontier, Marx #4784, Series 2000,
    NM+IB $3,000.00
Johnny Tremain Revolutionary War, Marx #3401-2, VGIB. $1,500.00
Jungle, Marx #3705, Series 500, NMIB.......................... $350.00

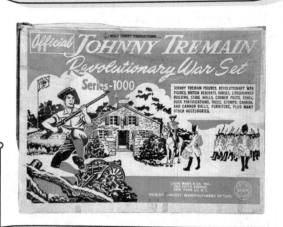

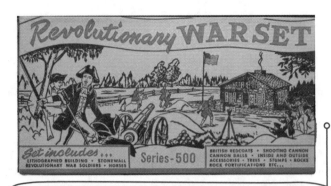

Playsets
• •
Jungle Jim Play Set, Marx #3706, Series 1000, unused, sealed, MIB, $1,500.00. (Photo courtesy Morphy Auctions on LiveAuctioneers.com)

Playsets
• •
Revolutionary War, Marx #3404, Series 500, with Indians, EX+IB, $825.00. (Photo courtesy Morphy Auctions on LiveAuctioneers.com)

Jungle, Marx #3716, NMIB $300.00
Jungle Jim Play Set, Marx, #3705-6, Series 1000, unused, MIB (sealed) $2,000.00
Jungle Jim, Marx #3705-6, EXIB $1,200.00
Keystone Fire Department, Keystone, 1940, EX+IB $100.00
King Arthur's Castle, Marx #4800, NMIB $225.00
Knights & Vikings, Marx #4733, EX+IB $100.00
Knights & Vikings, Marx #4733, NM+IB $200.00
Knights & Vikings, Marx #4743, EX+IB $100.00
Knights & Vikings, Marx #4773, NMIB $100.00
Lazy Day Farm Set, see Farm Set (Lazy Day)
Legend of the Lone Ranger, MPC, later issue, MIB (sealed).. $25.00
Little Red Schoolhouse, Marx #3381-2, EX+IB $750.00
Lone Ranger Ranch, Marx #3969, Series 500, NMIB $300.00
Lone Ranger Rodeo, Marx #3696, NMIB $150.00
McDonaldland, Remco, 1976, unused, MIB $50.00
Medieval Castle, Marx #4707, EXIB $50.00
Medieval Castle, Marx #4708/Sears, Series 2000, EX+IB..$200.00
Medieval Castle, Marx #4733, EXIB $250.00
Medieval Castle, Marx/Sears #4734, NMIB $300.00
Medieval Castle Fort, Marx #4709-10, NMIB $175.00
Midtown Service Station, Marx #5953, EXIB $600.00
Midtown Shopping Center, Marx #2644, NMIB $700.00
Military Academy, Marx #4718, EX+IB $400.00
Mobile Army Battlefront, MPC #3501, EXIB $75.00
Modern Farm Set, see Farm Set (Modern)
Modern Service Center, see Service Center (Modern)
Mountain Assault, Atlantic #202, unused, MIB $175.00
Navarone Mountain Battleground, Marx #3412, MIB ... $225.00
New Car Sales Service Center, Marx #3465, NMIB....... $325.00
Noah's Ark, Marx, miniature, EX+IB $45.00
One Million BC, Marx #59842, EXIB $350.00
Operation Moon Base, Marx #4653-1, MIB $600.00
Operation Moon Base, Marx #4653-4, EXIB $500.00
Parking Garage (4-level), Marx #3502, EX+IB..................$75.00
Pet Shop, Marx #4209, NMIB $250.00
Pet Shop, Marx #4209-10, EXIB $400.00
Pirate's Canoe, Multiple Toys, 1950s, MIP......................$50.00

Prehistoric, Marx #3398, NMIB $125.00
Prehistoric Dinosaur, Marx #4208, NMIB $125.00
Prehistoric Times, Marx #2650, NMIB $150.00
Prehistoric Times, Marx #3389, NMIB $125.00
Prehistoric Times, Marx #3390, NMIB $250.00
Prehistoric Times, Marx #3391, NMIB $50.00
Prince Valiant Castle, Marx #4705, EXIB $350.00
Prince Valiant Castle, Marx #4706, EXIB $175.00
Project Apollo Cape Kennedy, Marx #4523, EX+IB $50.00
Project Apollo Moon Landing, Marx #4646, NMIB $100.00
Project Mercury Cape Canaveral, Marx #4524, EXIB.... $250.00
Raytheon Missile Test Center, Marx #603-A, EXIB....... $100.00
Ready Gang Action-Town Set, Marx, 1970s, unused, NMIB...$75.00
Real Life Western Wagon, Marx #4998, NMIB.................$50.00
Red River Gang, Marx #4104, NMIB $100.00
Revolutionary War, Marx #3401, EXIB $400.00
Rex Mars Planet Patrol, Marx #7040, EX+IB $150.00
Rex Mars Space Dome, Marx #7016, EXIB $175.00
Rifleman Ranch, Marx #3997-8, NMIB..................... $500.00
Rin Tin Tin Fort Apache, Marx #3686R, Series 5000, EX+IB $300.00
Robin Hood Castle, Marx #4717, NMIB..................... $400.00
Robin Hood Castle, Marx #4718, EXIB $200.00
Robin Hood Castle, Marx #4723, EXIB $150.00
Roman Warship (Motorized), Remco, cb fort, big Caesar w/32 Romans, unused, NMIB $500.00
Roman Warship (Motorized), Remco, no fort, big Caesar w/32 Romans, unused, NMIB $300.00
Roy Rogers Double R Bar Ranch, Marx #3982, EXIB $150.00
Roy Rogers Double R Bar Ranch, Marx #3982, NMIB .. $350.00
Roy Rogers Mineral City, Marx #4227, NMIB $500.00
Roy Rogers Ranch, Marx #3980, EXIB $200.00
Roy Rogers Rodeo, Marx #3689-90, NMIB $100.00
Roy Rogers Rodeo Ranch, Marx #3979, NMIB $175.00
Roy Rogers Rodeo Ranch, Marx #3985, NMIB $275.00
Roy Rogers Rodeo Ranch, Marx #3986R, EXIB $300.00
Roy Rogers Rodeo Ranch, Marx #3992, NMIB $300.00
Roy Rogers Rodeo Ranch, Marx #3996, MIB $575.00
Roy Rogers Rodeo Ranch (Happi-Time), Marx #3990, EXIB. $100.00

Roy Rogers Western Town, Marx #4216, NMIB $475.00
Roy Rogers Western Town, Marx #4227, 54mm set $550.00
Roy Rogers Western Town, Marx #4259, Series 5000, EXIB..$125.00
Sands of Iwo Jima (296-pc), Marx Miniature, EXIB....... $300.00
Sears 4-Level Garage, w/gas truck $650.00
Sears Store, Marx #5490, EXIB $1,250.00
See & Play Disney Castle, Marx Miniature #48-24388,
     EXIB $475.00
Service Station, Marx #5459, NMIB $75.00
Service Station (Modern), Marx #6044, EXIB $75.00
Service Station (Steel), T Cohn, 1960s, unused, NMIB . $125.00
Shopping Center, Marx #3755-6, NMIB $300.00
Silver City Frontier Town, Marx #4219-20, NMIB $300.00
Silver City Western Town, Marx #4220, NMIB $525.00
Silver City Western Town, Marx #4256, EXIB............... $300.00
Skyscraper, Marx #5449-50, EXIB............................... $400.00
Skyscraper, Marx #5450, NMIB $850.00
Sons of Liberty (Sears Heritage), Marx #59147C, NMIB...$325.00
Strategic Air Command, Marx #6013, EXIB $1,600.00
Super Circus, Marx #4319, EXIB $150.00
Super Circus, Marx #4320, EXIB $200.00
Tactical Air Command, Marx #4106, NMIB.....................$75.00
Tales of Wells Fargo, Marx #4262, NMIB $375.00
Tales of Wells Fargo, Marx #4263, NMIB $300.00
Tales of Wells Fargo Train Set, Marx #54752, NMIB $450.00
Tank Battle, Marx/Sears #6056, NMIB $600.00
Television Playhouse, Marx #4350 or #4352, NMIB, ea. $400.00
Tiny Town Zoo, Spear Works/England, die-cut paper litho ani-
     mals & buildings, EXIB.. $200.00
Tom Corbett Space Academy, Marx #7010, EXIB.......... $600.00
Tom Corbett Space Academy, Marx #7012, NMIB........ $825.00
Torpedoes Away Sea Battle, Kentline, 1940s, EX+IB........$75.00
Undersea Attack, Atlantic #206, EXIB $100.00
Untouchables, Marx #4676, EXIB............................. $2,500.00
US Armed Forces, Marx #4151, EXIB $100.00
US Armed Forces Training Center, Marx #4144, NMIB. $175.00
US Armed Forces Training Center, Marx #4149-50, EXIB... $100.00
US Armed Forces Training Center, Marx #4158, EXIB . $200.00
US Armed Forces Training Center, Marx #4158, NMIB. $375.00
US Army Mobile Set, Marx #3655, NMIB..................... $150.00
US Army Training Center, Marx #3146, EXIB..................$50.00
US Army Training Center, Marx #4123, NMIB............. $200.00
Vikings & Knights, Marx #6053, NMIB $200.00
Viking Ship, Eldon, 1960s, 18" L, unused, MIP (sealed) . $125.00
Voice Control Kennedy Airport, Remco, 1960s, unused, NRFB...$250.00
Voyage to the Bottom of the Sea Submarine Explorer Set,
     Remco, 1967, NMIB.. $400.00
Wagon Train, Marx #4788, Series 2000, NMIB........... $1,100.00
Wagon Train, Marx #4888, Series 5000, NMIB........... $3,500.00
Ward's Service Center, Marx #3488, NMIB $400.00
Western Frontier Town, Ideal #3298, EXIB................... $150.00
Western Mining Town, Marx #4266, NMIB................... $400.00
Western Ranch Set, Marx #3980, NMIB....................... $100.00
Western Town, Marx #4229, EXIB............................... $250.00
Wild West, Multiple, NMIB.. $175.00
Wyatt Earp Dodge City Western Town, Marx #4228, Series
     1000, NMIB $800.00
Yogi Bear at Jellystone National Park, Marx #4363-4, EXIB. $350.00

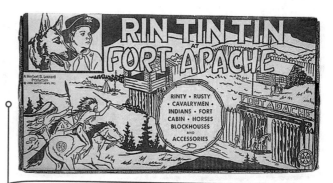

Playsets

Rin Tin Tin Fort Apache, Marx #3628, unused, sealed, MIB, $500.00. (Photo courtesy Morphy Auctions on LiveAuctioneers.com)

Playsets

Service Center (Modern), Marx, unused, M (EX sealed box), $400.00. (Photo courtesy Morphy Auctions on LiveAuctioneers.com)

Playsets

Super Circus, Marx, #4320, unused, MIB (sealed), $600.00. (Photo courtesy Morphy Auctions on LiveAuctioneers.com)

Zoo Set, 1960s, EXIB... $400.00
Zorro, Marx #3554, Series 1000, unused, MIB (sealed)... $1,800.00
Zorro, Marx #3753, Series 1000, NMIB.......................... $800.00
Zorro, Marx #3754, Series 1000, EXIB........................... $650.00
Zorro, Marx #3754, Series 1000, unused, MIB (sealed)... $1,500.00

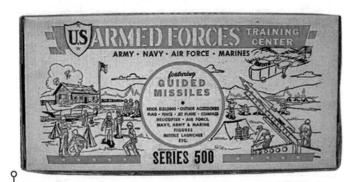

Playsets

US Armed Forces Training Center, Marx #4149-50, Series 500, unused, MIB (sealed), $550.00.
(Photo courtesy Morphy Auctions on LiveAuctioneers.com)

Playsets

Westgate Auto Center, Marx, unused, MIB (NOS), $300.00. (Photo courtesy Morphy Auctions on LiveAuctioneers.com)

Playsets

Wagon Train, Marx #4805, Series 2000, NMIB, $2,000.00.

Playsets

Yogi Bear at Jellystone National Park, Marx #4363-4, unused, MIB (sealed), $1,200.00.
(Photo courtesy Morphy Auctions on LiveAuctioneers.com)

Premiums

Those from the 'pre-boomer' and 'boomer' eras remember waiting in anticipation for that silver bullet ring, secret membership kit, decoder pen, coloring book, or whatever other wonderful item they'd seen advertised in their favorite comic book or heard about on the Tom Mix show. Tom wasn't the only one to have these exciting premiums. Just about any top character-oriented show from the 1930s through the 1940s made similar offers, and even through the 1950s some were still being distributed. Often they could be had free for a cereal boxtop or an Ovaltine inner seal, and if any money was involved, it was usually only a dime. Not especially durable and often made in somewhat limited amounts, few have survived to the present. Today some of these are bringing fantastic prices, but the market at present is very volatile.

Note: Those trademark/logo characters created to specifically represent a cereal product or company (for example Cap'n Crunch) are listed in the Advertising category.

Condition is very important in assessing value; items in pristine condition bring premium prices.

Advisor: Bill Campbell

See also Advertising; Character, TV, and Movie Collectibles; Pin-Back Buttons.

Ace Williams, badge, ...Holsum Observer, brass-tone metal w/bl lettering, 1930s, EX..$45.00

Amos & Andy, map, Eagles View of Weber City, Pepsodent, 1935, NM+ (w/mailer)..$95.00

Andy Pafko, ring, baseball scorekeeper, EX $215.00

Annie, book, Radio Orphan Annie's Book About Dogs, Ovaltine, 1936, VG $65.00

Annie, cup, plastic, Beetleware, EX $215.00

Annie, decoder, 1935, EX................................$35.00
Annie, decoder, 1936, EX................................$40.00
Annie, decoder, 1937 or 1938, EX, ea................$50.00
Annie, decoder, 1939, EX................................$55.00
Annie, decoder, 1940, EX................................$75.00
Annie, game, Treasure Island, Ovaltine, 1933, framed, 12x17",
    complete, EX $75.00
Annie, Little Orphan Annie Circus/The All-Star Action Show,
    Ovaltine, 1930s, NM (w/envelope)...............$275.00
Annie, manual & badge, Secret Society, EX (orig mailer) .$75.00
Annie, map of Simmons Corner, NM $125.00
Annie, mask, die-cut paper, Ovaltine, 1933, EX+ $40.00
Annie, mug, Shake-Up, 1931, ivory w/orange top, EX......$50.00
Annie, mug, Shake-Up, 1935, beige w/orange top, EX $75.00
Annie, mug, Shake-Up, 1938, aqua w/orange top, EX ... $175.00
Annie, mug, Shake-Up, 1939, brn w/orange top, EX $150.00
Annie, mug, Shake-Up, 1940, gr w/red top, EX.............. $150.00
Annie, mug, 50th Anniversary, ceramic, EX $25.00
Annie, Orphan Annie Circus, Ovaltine, 1930s, NM+ (w/
    mailer) $600.00
Annie, ring, face, EX $65.00
Annie, ring, face, NM+ $100.00
Annie, ring, intitial, EX................................. $125.00
Annie, ring, Mystic Eye, w/instructions, EX $200.00
Annie, ring, Secret Guard Magnifying, 1940s, EX....... $2,500.00
Annie, ring, secret message, EX $250.00
Annie, ring, Secret Society, silver finish w/emb crossed keys on
    starburst, Ovaltine, 1930s, EX........................$75.00
Annie, ring, silver star, EX................................ $350.00
Annie, sheet music, Little Orphan Annie's Song, Ovaltine,
    1931, M $65.00
Annie, stationery, 5 sheets w/images of gang, NM (w/orig
    mailer) $15.00
Annie, watch, Miracle Compass, NM+ $60.00
Babe Ruth, ring, Baseball Club, EX................... $165.00
Batman, ring, Nestlé, M $90.00
Bobby Benson, cereal bowl, red glass w/blk graphics in center
    (name/Howdy Pard/H-O Ranger/cowboy on horse), 6½",
    NM+..$75.00
Buck Rogers, badge, Solar Scouts Chief Explorer, burgundy,
    EX.. $360.00
Buck Rogers, badge/whistle, Space Commander, NM $325.00
Buck Rogers, book, City of Floating Globes, Big Little Books,
    Cocomalt, EX+.. $175.00
Buck Rogers, coloring book, 25th Century, Kellogg's, 1933,
    EX...$65.00
Buck Rogers, Cut-Out Adventure Book, Cocomalt, 1933,
    unused, VG.. $375.00
Buck Rogers, Flying Saucer, heavy cb disk w/steel rim, 1939, 6¼",
    dia, NM $100.00
Buck Rogers, manual, Solar Scouts, Cream of Wheat, 1936, EX
    (w/orig mailer).. $300.00
Buck Rogers, Penny Card, American Amoco Gas, 3x3", any
    number, ea $275.00
Buck Rogers, pocket knife, Cream of Wheat/Camillus Cutlery,
    1935, 3", EX.. $975.00
Buck Rogers, pop gun, XZ-31, Cocomalt, 1934, EX $350.00
Buck Rogers, ring, birthstone, EX $565.00

Buck Rogers, ring, birthstone/initial, Cocomalt & Popcicle pre-
    mium, 1934, EX+ $150.00
Buck Rogers, ring, Saturn, NM+ $600.00
Buck Rogers, Satellite Pioneers Confidential Bulletin, EX+.$75.00
Buck Rogers, Solar System Map, Cocomalt, 1930s, matted &
    framed, 21x40" overall, EX $1,050.00
Buck Rogers, Space Ranger Kit, Sylvania TV, 1952, unused,
    NM+ (in sealed envelope)............................ $150.00
Buck Rogers, tab pin, Member of ...Rocket Rangers, red, wht &
    bl litho tin, very scarce, EX+ $225.00
Buck Rogers, tab pin, Satellite Pioneers, red, wht & blk litho tin,
    unbent tab/unused, NM $125.00
Bulldog Drummond, bomber airplane, cb punchout, w/4 cut-out
    battleships, Horton's Ice Cream, 1930s, 9½", EX $150.00
Bullwinkle, Electric Quiz Fun Game, General Mills, 1961,
    EX... $50.00
Buster Brown, bandana, Buster & Tige & pals' images around
    Smilin' Ed McConnell, MC, 1940s, 23x20", VG...........$50.00
Capt America, badge, Sentinels of Liberty, metal shield w/eagle
    on top, EX+ $700.00
Capt Frank Hawks, manual, Sky Patrol Pilot's..., NM $75.00
Capt Marvel, key ring, Capt Marvel Club, EX...................$75.00
Capt Marvel, Magic Flute, MOC $100.00
Capt Marvel, Magic Whistle, EX $50.00
Capt Marvel, patch, Capt Marvel Club, rectangular, red, wht &
    bl, EX.. $225.00

Capt Midnight, badge, Mysto-Magic Weather Forecasting Wings, w/litmus paper, Skelly Oil, 1939, EX $50.00
Capt Midnight, badge, pilot's wings, 24k gold-finished brass, 1943, EX $225.00
Capt Midnight, badge, Secret Squadron Decoder, brass-plated tin, 2¼", EX $125.00
Capt Midnight, cup, red plastic w/decal, EX......................$35.00
Capt Midnight, decoder, 1941, Code-O-Graph, EX $100.00

Capt Midnight, decoder, 1945, EX.................................. $125.00
Capt Midnight, decoder, 1946, EX.................................. $100.00
Capt Midnight, decoder, 1948, EX....................................$70.00
Capt Midnight, decoder, 1949, EX+ $110.00
Capt Midnight, decoder, 1949, Key-O-Matic, w/key, EX.. $225.00
Capt Midnight, decoder, 1955, EX.................................. $175.00
Capt Midnight, decoder, 1955, w/membership card & manual, EX $300.00
Capt Midnight, decoder, 1957, badge w/tailfin, EX $200.00
Capt Midnight, manual, 1942, NM+ $100.00
Capt Midnight, manual, 1945, EX....................................$75.00
Capt Midnight, manual, 1947, EX....................................$75.00
Capt Midnight, manual, 1948, NM $100.00
Capt Midnight, manual, 1955-56, w/code book, EX....... $200.00
Capt Midnight, manual, 1957, EX (w/mailer) $100.00
Capt Midnight, manual, 1957, G....................................$75.00
Capt Midnight, manual, 1957, w/letter, EX (w/mailer).. $150.00
Capt Midnight, membership kit, 1957, complete, EX $575.00
Capt Midnight, patch, Secret Squadron, stick-on type, 1956, MIP..$75.00
Capt Midnight, plane detector tube, 1942, no accessories, o/w NM $250.00
Capt Midnight, whistle, 1947, EX....................................$75.00
Davy Crockett, ring, TV screen flicker action, Karo Syrup, 1955, NM $125.00
Detectives Black & Blue, badge, metal, Iodent Toothpaste, 1930s, NM+.. $120.00
Dick Tracy, badge, Inspector General/Secret Service Patrol, emb star w/eagle & leaf swag, Quaker, 1938, 2½", NM....$1,035.00
Dick Tracy, badge, metal wreath w/emb star & Captain on ribbon banner, EX $500.00
Don Winslow, badge, Lt Commander/Squadron of Peace, silvered brass, Kellogg's, 1939, VG+...................................... $175.00
Hop Harrigan, wings badge, All American Flying Club, brass, EX $95.00

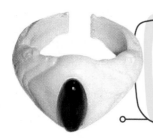

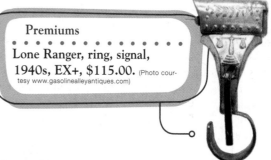

Premiums
Lone Ranger, ring, signal, 1940s, EX+, $115.00. (Photo courtesy www.gasolinealleyantiques.com)

Premiums
Red Ryder, badge, Victory Patrol, glow-in-the-dark fiberboard, rare WWII era, NM+, $500.00. (Photo courtesy www.gasoline alleyantiques.com)

Howdy Doody/Poll Parrot, ring, plastic w/raised image of Howdy's head, Poll Parrot incised on sides, open band, EX+...... $150.00

Jack Armstrong, badge, JA/Lieutenant/Listening Squad, 1940s, EX+.. $100.00

Jack Armstrong, Stamp Set, Wheaties, 1935, M (w/mailer).$50.00

Jimmy Allen, membership club kit, NM (w/mailer)....... $275.00

Little Orphan Annie, see Annie

Lone Ranger, coloring book, Lone Ranger Health & Safety Club, 5x7", Merita Bread, 1955, unused, NM $50.00

Lone Ranger, Flashlight Pistol, b/o, plastic, secret compartment in hdl, w/instructions, 6", General Mills, 1949, NMIB.. $275.00

Lone Ranger, pedometer, w/ankle strap, EX......................$25.00

Lone Ranger, ring, atomic bomb, EX $215.00

Lone Ranger, ring, flashlight, w/instructions, EX............ $150.00

Lone Ranger, ring, gold ore/meteorite, EX $2,000.00

Lone Ranger, ring, Six Shooter, 1947, EX $150.00

Lone Ranger, Western Tattoos, Fritos, 1959, unused, EX+ .$45.00

Mandrake the Magician, pin, profile bust image in top hat, enamel on brass, Tastee Bread, 1934, 1", scarce, EX ... $125.00

Maverick, spinner coin, silver-dollar size w/emb images of the Maverick brothers, Kaiser Aluminum, NM+ $20.00

Melvin Pervis, manual, Secret Operator's, Post Toasties, 1937, NM+ (w/mailer).. $100.00

Melvin Pervis, ring, Jr G-Men Corps, EX $85.00

Mickey Mouse, book, Merry Christmas from Mickey Mouse, 1939 store premium, VG... $200.00

Mickey Mouse, Globetrotters, w/map & 12 pictures from MM Globetrotter weekly publications, EX (VG mailer) $100.00

Mighty Mouse, Merry Pack punchouts, Post Cereal/CBS-TV Ent, 1956, unused, EX...$75.00

Orphan Annie, see Annie

Our Gang, comic book, March of Comics Featuring MGM Our Gang, Poll Parrot, 1947, EX+ $50.00

Our Gang, Fun Kit, 12 die-cut pgs featuring the gang & different activies, Morton Salt, 1930s, NM................................ $175.00

Phantom, Pilot Patrol, membership kit, complete, Langendorf Bread, 1930s, extremely rare, NM+ $2,000.00

Phantom, ring, skull, brass w/red eyes, 1950s, EX $800.00

Philip H Lord's Gang Busters, badge, brass w/enameled detail, 1930s, EX... $100.00

Radio Orphan Annie, see Annie

Red Ryder, postcard, Victory Patrol application, unused, M . $100.00

Rin Tin Tin, dexterity (B-B) puzzle, rnd w/image of Rinny, Nabisco cereal premium, 1950s, EX+ $18.00

Roy Rogers, Double-R-Bar Ranch, cut-out on paper, Post Cereal, 1955, unused, M $150.00

Roy Rogers, harmonica, Cowboy Band, chrome top w/etched name & head image, offered as premium only, 4", NM+..$75.00

Premiums
Roy Rogers, Hobby-Art Plaque Set, paint-by-numbers, molded plastic plaque, Collector's Brand/Nestlé Quik, unused, NMIB, $200.00. (Photo courtesy Morphy Auctions on LiveAuctioneers.com)

Premiums
Sergeant Preston, pedometer, 1952, EX, $25.00. (Photo courtesy www.gasolinealley antiques.com)

Premiums
Tom Mix, badge, Straight Shooter, EX, $75.00. (Photo courtesy www. gasolinealleyantiques.com)

Roy Rogers, lantern, litho tin, 8" (w/hdl up), EX $50.00

Roy Rogers, paint-by-numbers set, RRE Set C/Post Sugar Crisp, 1954, unused, MIB $75.00

Roy Rogers, ring, microscope, EX $125.00

Roy Rogers, ring, saddle, silver, EX $350.00

Scoop Ward, badge & brochure, How to Become a Member of Scoop Ward's Press Club, NM+ $125.00

Sergeant Preston, Ore Detector, NM (w/orig mailer box) ..$200.00

Sergeant Preston, 10-in-1 Trail Kit, complete, 1958, EX...$75.00

Shadow, ring, bust, EX $150.00

Shadow, ring, Magic, plastic, Carey Salt, 1941, EX $450.00

Sky King, Detecto-Microscope, 1950s, NM (EX mailer) . $225.00

Sky King, Detecto-Writer, aluminum or brass, EX, ea $125.00

Sky King, ring, Aztec, EX $800.00

Sky King, ring, MagniGlo Writing, EX $115.00

Sky King, ring, radar, EX $125.00

Sky King, ring, Telebinger, EX................................. $255.00

Sky King, Stamping Kit, Your Personal Name & Address..., litho tin, 1953, complete, EX $50.00

Smokey the Bear, badge, Jr Forest Ranger, 1960s, 2", NM.$25.00

Smokey the Bear, Jr Forest Ranger Kit, USDA, 1956-57, complete, EX+ (w/mailer)..$65.00

Snow White & the Seven Dwarfs, game board, Tek Toothbrush, WDE, 1930s, EX...$60.00

Space Patrol, badge, red, wht & bl under plastic, EX $350.00

Space Patrol, binoculars, Ralston, 1953, NM $150.00

Space Patrol, decoder belt buckle, brass & aluminum, Ralston, 1950s, EX... $175.00

Space Patrol, ring, Hydrogen Ray Gun, Wheat Chex, 1950s, EX $250.00

Space Patrol, Space-O-Phone, plastic, Ralston Purina Wheat or Rice Chex, complete w/instruction sheet & mailer, NM ..$85.00

Straight Arrow, ring, face, EX......................................$70.00

Straight Arrow, ring, Nugget Cave w/photo, EX $275.00

Straight Arrow, War Drum, complete, scarce, MIB........ $450.00

Superman, airplane, Kellogg's PEP, EX........................... $200.00

Superman, ring, Crusader, EX.. $235.00

Superman, ring, S logo, gold finish, Nestlé, 1978, EX+ $25.00

Superman, Stereo Pix, Kellogg's 1954, 8", NM, ea $10 to .$15.00

Terry & the Pirates, ring, gold detector, EX $125.00

Tom Corbett, patch (from membership kit), bl, gold & red stitched fabric, Kellogg's, 1951, NM+...........................$50.00

Tom Corbett, ring, face, EX.. $125.00

Tom Corbett, ring, rocket, w/expansion band, unused, M ..$475.00

Tom Mix, badge, Deputy Sheriff of Dobie County whistler, w/ papers, EX...$75.00

Tom Mix, badge, Straight Shooter, MOC (w/catalog & mailer) $150.00

Tom Mix, belt buckle, brass w/emb portrait image & name on checkerboard bkgrd, EX $100.00

Tom Mix, belt buckle, brass w/rope design encircling diagonal red, wht & bl Straight Shooters emblem, EX $75.00

Tom Mix, booklet, 'Tom Mix Escapes the Poison Death,' #14, Chicle Co, 1934, 2¾x2½", EX.................................$35.00

Tom Mix, comic book, 'Ralston Straight Shooters #3,' EX..$50.00

Tom Mix, compass, brass w/western symbols & rope border, EX... $85.00

Tom Mix, compass, Ralston Straight Shooters, ca 1936, EX+ .$35.00

Tom Mix, Golden Bullet Telescope, 1949, NM $35.00

Tom Mix, ID bracelet, 1947, NM+ $50.00

Tom Mix, periscope, Straight Shooters, cb w/tin cap ends, Ralston, 1939, EX...$50.00

Tom Mix, Postal Telegraph Signal Set/International System, 1927, MIB (mailer) $175.00

Tom Mix, postcard promoting premiums to Ralston dealers, reads 'Check your stock...build Ralston displays!,' 1940s, NM.$50.00

Tom Mix, puzzle, 125-pc jigsaw, Rexall, 1920s, complete, NM (w/envelope) $150.00

Tom Mix, ring, Look Around, EX $125.00

Tom Mix, ring, Straight Shooter, EX $100.00

Tom Mix, ring, target, Marlin Guns, 1937 (also issued in the 1950s), EX+ $125.00

Tom Mix, Telegraph Set, Ralston Straight Shooters, EX+..$150.00

Wild Bill Hickok, Colt 6-Shooter Pistol, Sugar Pops, 1958, 10", MIB... $300.00

Wild Bill Hickok, Treasure Map & Secret Treasure Guide, Kellogg's Sugar Pops, 1950s, M (w/mailer).........................$125.00

Wonder Woman, ring, Nestlé, 1977, EX......................... $110.00

Woody Woodpecker, ring, Club Stamp, EX.................... $150.00

Zorro, ring, silver plastic w/logo on black top, EX $60.00

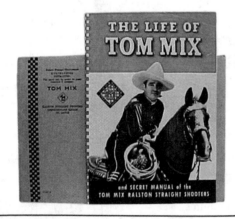

Premiums
Tom Mix, book, 'The Life of Tom Mix and Secret Manual of the Tom Mix Ralston Straight Shooters,' M (with mailer), $125.00. (Photo courtesy www.gasolinealley antiques.com)

Premiums
Tom Mix, gold ore watch fob, 1940, NM, $75.00. (Photo courtesy www. gasolinealleyantiques.com)

Pressed Steel

Many companies were involved in the manufacture of pressed-steel automotive toys which were often faithfully modeled after actual vehicles in production at the time they were made. Because they were so sturdy, some from as early as the 1920s have survived to the present, and those that are still in good condition are bringing very respectable prices at toy auctions around the country. Some of the better-known manufacturers are listed in other sections or their own categories. The following listings and values are from recent auctions.

See also Aeronautical; Buddy L; Keystone; Marx; Pedal Cars and Other Wheeled Vehicles; Structo; Tonka; Wyandotte.

AUTOMOBILES

Amazing Car No 600, Nylint, 1930s, w/up, rubber bumpers, 14", VG $150.00

Brougham, Kingsbury, w/up, electric headlights, open front seat w/coverd passenger compartment, bl & gray, WRT, 13", VG+ $825.00

Chrysler Airflow, Cor-Cor, 1930s, w/up, electric lights, red w/NP trim, BRT, 17", VG $850.00

Chrysler Airflow, Kingsbury, w/up, electric lights, bl w/NP trim, WRT w/spoke wheels, 14", EX.................................. $925.00

Coupe, Dayton, friction, long nosed, simulated cloth top up, MDW w/rear spare, red, blk & rust, 18", EX $420.00

Coupe, Kingsbury, w/up musical version, electric lights, 2-tone purple, WRT, 13", EX.................................... $2,520.00

Coupe, Kingsbury, w/up, w/rumble seat, 2-tone gr w/orange trim, WRT, rear spare, 13", G $350.00

Graham Sedan, Cor-Cor, 1930s, red, NP grille, BRT, 21", G..$725.00

Jaguar Convertible Coupe, Doepke, lt bl, BRT, 18", VG. $400.00

Lincoln Sedan, Turner, 1930s, BRT, 27", G $3,450.00

Lincoln Zephyr Pulling Travel Trailer, Kingsbury, 1930s, w/up, gr, 23", EX.. $400.00

Mercury Sedan, Doepke, 1950s, yel w/blk top, BRT, 14", EX .$400.00

MG Roadster, Doepke, open, dk gr w/tan seat, rear spare, BRT, 15" L, EX+ $425.00

Monterey Auto, Mason & Parker, friction w/chain-driven spoke wheels, high bench seat w/driver, blk, yel & red, 9", VG .$550.00

Oldsmobile Tourer, Acme, w/up, early sleigh-type w/center steering, blk, red scroll trim, WRT, gold spoke wheels, 11", G........$500.00

Packard Coupe, Turner, 1920s, friction, simulated cloth top up, rear-mounted trunk, red, BRT, 26", VG $1,850.00

Packard Roadster, Turner, 1920s, side spare, NP trim, 18", rstr ..$575.00

Pierce-Arrow, Girard, 1930s, w/up, electric lights, blk wooden disk wheels, 13½", VG $250.00

Roadster, Kingsbury, w/up, electric lights, open w/rumble seat, tan, red & gr, WRT, 13", VG $500.00

Roadster, Kingsbury, w/up, open w/driver, gr, WRT w/red hubs, extended wire front bumper, 11", EX........................... $400.00

Roadster, Schieble, extra-long nose, flat roof w/no windshield support, MSW w/rear spare, blk, 17", VG $150.00

Sedan, Schieble, 1920s, MSW, 17½", G $325.00

Touring Car, Converse, w/up, open w/canvas top, red w/gr trim, wooden lights, MSW, 15", G $1,200.00

Touring Car, Dayton, friction, open w/2-seat front, rear bench seat, red w/gold trim, MSW, 11", EX $325.00

Touring Car, Kingsbury, w/up, open 1-seater, BRT w/spoke wheels, emb carpet & seat, lady driver, 9", G+............ $450.00

Touring Car, Kingsbury, w/up, open 2-seater, BRT w/spoke wheels, male driver on right side, 10", G.................... $350.00

Towncar, Kingsbury, w/up, electric lights, 2-tone gr w/orange trim, WRT, 13", EX+... $5,500.00

Pressed Steel, Automobiles

Convertible Coupe, Kingsbury, 1920s, windup, electric lights, red and tan, green hubs, rumble seat, white rubber tires, 12", VG, $1,500.00. (Photo courtesy Morphy Auctions on LiveAuctioneers.com)

Pressed Steel, Automobiles

Graham Sedan, Cor-Cor, 1930s, 21", EX, $2,185.00. (Photo courtesy Morphy Auctions on LiveAuctioneers.com)

Pressed Steel, Automobiles

Lincoln Sedan, Turner, 1930s, 27", EX+, $9,000.00. (Photo courtesy Morphy Auctions on LiveAuctioneers.com)

Towncar, Kingsbury, w/up, electric lights, 2-tone gr w/orange trim, WRT, 13", G... $1,200.00

Yellow Cab Co Taxi, Neff Moon, orange & brn, MDW, 12", VG $250.00

Pressed Steel, Automobiles
**Packard Roadster, Turner, 1920s, friction, 26",
EX, $2,875.00.** (Photo courtesy Morphy Auctions on LiveAuctioneers.com)

Pressed Steel, Buses and Trolleys
**Pay as You Enter Trolley, Dayton, friction, 23",
EX, $600.00.** (Photo courtesy Bertoia Auctions on LiveAuctioneers.com)

Pressed Steel, Automobiles
**Touring Car, Mason and Parker, high bench seat,
six-sided radiator, red with gold trim, gold painted
metal spoke wheels, marked April 27 1909, 11",
VG, $130.00.** (Photo courtesy Bertoia Auctions)

BUSES AND TROLLEYS

City Hall Park/Union Depot Trolley, Converse, w/up, yel-orange,
15½", EX.. $475.00
Greyhound Bus, Kingsbury, 1930s, 18", EX+ $600.00
Inter-City Bus, Steelcraft, 1930s, 24", EX $800.00
Inter-City Bus, Steelcraft, 1930s, 24", G $375.00
Overland Stage Lines, cream & red w/2 wht-wall side spares, 32",
MIB.. $1,500.00
Pay As You Enter Trolley, Converse, cow catchers at both ends,
21", G $175.00

Pickwick Stages System Double-Decker, newer model, blk, red &
yel, chrome grille, BRT, MIB $650.00
Rapid Transit Trolley, Schieble, flywheel action, bl w/red roof,
21", no roof rod, Fair $275.00
Trolley, Hill Climber, Pat 1897, 4 lg CI spoke wheels, brn w/red
striping, 14½", VG $225.00
Trolley #784, Kingsbury, w/up, orange, 14", EX $350.00

CONSTRUCTION

Adams Motor Grader, orange, BRT, 26", VG $250.00
Barber-Greene Bucket Loader, Doepke, track version, metal
treads, 19", EX.. $325.00
Barber-Greene Bucket Loader, Doepke, vehicle version w/steer-
ing wheel, BRT, 24", EX.. $300.00
Barber-Greene Conveyor Belt, Doepke, tractor-type vehicle, gr
w/BRT, VG $200.00
Barber-Greene Grain Elevator, Doepke, chain treads, 18" H,
VG $200.00
Big Boy Coal Loader/Chute, Kelmet, 1920s, wooden base, 23",
VG $800.00
Big Boy Coal Pocket Chain Bucket, #508, EX................. $700.00
Big Boy Steam Shovel, Kelmet, 1920s, 20", EX............. $400.00
Big Boy Steam Shovel, Kelmet, 1920s, 20", VG............. $250.00
Caterpillar Bulldozer, Doepke, yel & blk, 15", EX $375.00
Cement Mixer, Doepke, yel, 4-wheeled, VG $200.00
Construction Co Truck, Sturditoy, doorless cab, open dump bed,
disk wheels, 27½", VG..$800.00
Crane, Doepke, orange & blk, BRT, 28", VG $300.00
Crane Truck, Kelmet, open White cab w/bench seat, 27",
VG+ $5,175.00
Emmets No 50 Ready Mixed Concrete Truck, 19", VG.. $1,250.00

Pressed Steel, Buses and Trolleys
**New York – San Francisco Bus, Steelcraft,
1940s, 21", EX, $1,725.00.** (Photo courtesy Morphy
Auctions on LiveAuctioneers.com)

Pressed Steel,
Construction
**Road Roller Trumatic,
1920s, VG, $275.00.**
(Photo courtesy Morphy Auctions on
LiveAuctioneers.com)

Pressed Steel, Construction
Steam Shovel Truck, Kelmet/Big Boy, #507, restored, $3,600.00. (Photo courtesy Leslie Hindman Auctioneers)

Euclid, Doepke, 27", NM.. $325.00
Helliner Earth Mover, Doepke, BRT, 28", EX+ $300.00
Jaeger Mixer, Doepke, 15", VG $225.00
Lumar Rocker Dump, 18", VG+ $125.00
Road Grader, Doepke, 26", NMIB............................. $325.00
Steam Roller, Steelcraft, 1920s-30s, 16", EX.................. $500.00
Steam Roller, Steelcraft, 1920s-30s, 16", G+ $175.00
Steam Shovel, Bowman, 1920s, 18", EX $300.00
Steam Shovel, Sturditoy, 1920s, 20", EX $315.00
Steam Shovel Truck, Steelcraft 'Little Jim,' 1930s, enclosed
    White cab, no visor or lights, BRT w/spoke wheels, 28",
    EX.. $1,950.00
Steam Shovel Truck, Steelcraft, 1930s, enclosed White cab, no
    visor, b/o lights, BRT, disk wheels, 28", EX.............. $1,035.00
Steam Shovel Truck, Steelcraft, 1930s, enclosed White cab w/
    visor, b/o lights, folding boom, MDW w/emb spokes, 28",
    VG $725.00
Tournahopper, Ny-Lint #1500, MIB (sealed).................. $800.00
Turnpike 28-Wheeled Hydraulic Dump Truck, SSS, 1960, fric-
    tion, 20", EX.. $50.00
Wooldridge Bottom Dump, Doepke, 1950s, 25", VG $125.00
Wooldridge Loader, Doepke, 24", EX........................ $150.00

FIREFIGHTING

Aerial Ladder Truck, Doepke, 1950s, open cab, red w/aluminum
    ladders, BRT, 34", EX $200.00
Aerial Ladder Truck, Kelmet, 1920s, open White cab, crank-op
    rotating platform, wooden ladders, 37", VG............ $1,000.00
Aerial Ladder Truck, Kingsbury, 1930s, open cab w/upholstered
    seat, crank-op ladders, non-motor version, 35", EX . $2,185.00
American LaFrance Chemical Truck, Sturditoy, 1920s, 26", EX . $3,750.00
American LaFrance Pumper Truck, Sturditoy, 1920s, open cab,
    BRT, 26", EX $2,875.00
American LaFrance Water Tower Truck No 9, Sturditoy, red,
    BRT w/red hubs, 31", G+ $900.00
Big Boy Ladder Truck, Kelmet, 1920s, White open cab, 27",
    EX... $625.00
Chemical Truck, see also Giant Chemical Truck
Chemical Truck, Grendron, 1920s, open cab w/front crank, 2
    ladders on racks, hose reel, red, BRT, 29", rstr.......... $1,150.00

Chemical Truck, Schieble, 1913, open high bench seat w/
    driver, chemical drum on open bed, red w/gold trim, MSW,
    12", EX.. $1,400.00
Chemical Truck, Toledo, 1920s, Mack open cab, crank-op, BRT,
    29", G $975.00
City Fire Dept Ladder Truck, Steelcraft, 1920s, Mack open cab,
    26", EX.. $1,250.00
City Fire Dept Ladder Truck, Steelcraft, 1930s, Mack open cab,
    arched ladder rack, 24", G.............................. $500.00
Fire Chief Car, Hoge, w/up, b/o lights, NP rear spare, 14",
    VG... $350.00

Pressed Steel, Firefighting
Chemical Truck, Toledo, 1920s, 29", EX+, $4,000.00. (Photo courtesy Bertoia Auctions on LiveAuctioneers.com)

Pressed Steel, Firefighting
Ladder Truck, Converse, with driver, NM, $2,875.00. (Photo courtesy Morphy Auctions on LiveAuctioneers.com)

Pressed Steel, Firefighting
Ladder Truck, Dayton, 1910, friction, 19½", VG, $500.00. (Photo courtesy Bertoia Auctions on LiveAuctioneers.com)

Fire Chief Coupe, Kingsbury, w/up, b/o lights, red, WRT, 12", VG $475.00

Fire Chief Siren Car, Girard, w/up, b/o lights, 14", VG+. $300.00

Fire Station & Ladder Cart, Kingsbury, w/up, 13" cart w/front & rear figures, 20" station, EX $2,875.00

Giant Chemical Truck, American National, 1920s, Mack open cab, front crank, 29", EX $1,950.00

Hook & Ladder Truck, Hill Climber, 6 MSW, front & rear drivers, red w/gold trim, some wooden features, 19", some rpnt $400.00

Hook & Ladder Truck, Kingsbury #255, crank-op, NP ladders, WRT, 31", VG $1,375.00

Ladder Truck, see also Big Boy Ladder Truck

Ladder Truck, Kelmet, open seat, MDW, wooden ladders, 34", G $900.00

Ladder Truck, Kingsbury, open seat, side lever for extension ladder, WRT w/red hubs, 34", F $700.00

Ladder Truck, Kingsbury, w/up, b/o lights, open seat, red, 2 ladders, WRT, 14", VG $325.00

Ladder Truck, Kingsbury, w/up, open frame w/CI driver on bench seat, wht w/red wooden ladders, 18", VG $425.00

Ladder Truck, Kingsbury, w/up, open horseless frame w/drivers front & back, bl w/yel ladders & spoke wheels, 13", VG $600.00

Ladder Truck, Republic, open frame, red w/gr running boards & grille, gold trim, 3 ladders, driver, 17", EX $300.00

Ladder Truck, Schieble, 1920s, flywheel, crank-op extension ladder, wht w/yel perforated hubs, bell on hood, 21", EX.. $500.00

Ladder Truck, Steelcraft, 1920s, Mack open cab, 'City Fire Dept' decals, red, MDW, 27", G $575.00

Little Jim Pumper Truck, Schieble/JC Penney, red, blk MDW w/ orange trim, 21", VG $500.00

Oh-Boy! Fire Patrol Truck, Kiddies Metal Toys, 1920s, enclosed cab, railed bed, 12", VG+ $1,400.00

Oh-Boy! Pumper Truck, Kiddies Metal Toys, open seat, copper-finish boiler, MDW, 12", VG $1,100.00

Pumper Truck, Kingsbury, w/up, open motor cart, 4 spoke wheels w/rubber tires, wood steam domes, CI driver, 10", VG. $225.00

Pumper Truck, Schieble, 1913, friction, open, spoke wheels, red w/gold trim, w/driver, 12", VG $375.00

Pumper Truck, Turner, 1930s, open Lincoln cab, red w/brass-pnt boiler, 2 ladders on racks, MDW, 29", EX $1,150.00

Rossmoyne Aerial Ladder Truck, Doepke, open cab, aluminum ladders, 33", MIB $1,265.00

Rossmoyne Searchlight Truck, Doepke, wht, BRT, 19", EX..$2,900.00

Suburban Fire Pumper, Nylint #81W, 1965-70, hooks up to garden hose for real water use, 12½", NMIB $200.00

Water Tower Truck, Sturditoy, 1920s, open cab, 33", EX. $2,575.00

RACE CARS

Auto Racer, Wilkins, 1913, w/up, silver, red MSW, right-sided driver, 10", VG $400.00

Golden Racer, Gunthermann, w/up, metallic gold, BRT, no driver, 20½", rpnt $225.00

Lionel Racer, electric track racer w/driver, WRT, spoke wheels, rear spare, brass trim, 8", VG $525.00

Pressed Steel, Firefighting

Little Jim Aerial Ladder Truck, Steelcraft/ JC Penney, 28", EX, $650.00. (Photo courtesy www.serioustoyz.com)

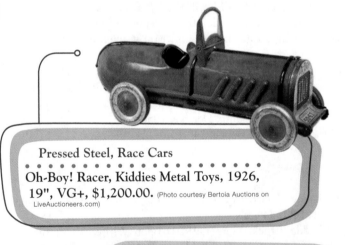

Pressed Steel, Race Cars

Oh-Boy! Racer, Kiddies Metal Toys, 1926, 19", VG+, $1,200.00. (Photo courtesy Bertoia Auctions on LiveAuctioneers.com)

Pressed Steel, Firefighting

Water Tower Truck, No. 9, Sturditoy, American La France, red, black rubber tires with red hubs, 31", G+, $900.00. (Photo courtesy Bertoia Auctions)

Pressed Steel, Race Cars

Two-Seater Racer, Wilkins, 1912, windup, 10", VG, $400.00. (Photo courtesy Bertoia Auctions on LiveAuctioneers.com)

Racer #5, Republic, friction, boattail rear, red w/gold trim, MDW, w/driver, 11", VG $275.00

Two-Seater Racer, Republic, 1920s, w/up, gray w/bl running boards, red fuel tank, hand crank on front, 2 figures, 11", G $500.00

TRUCKS AND VANS

Ambulance, Clark Hill Climber, 1908, enclosed wagon type w/ wooden floor, open seat w/driver at center steering, 11", G.$350.00

American Airlines Baggage Train, Doepke, 4-wheeled open car w/open box trailer & flatbed, 27" overall, EX.............. $350.00

American Dump Truck, Gendron 1929, doorless cab, blk w/ orange dump bed, BRT w/orange hubs, 26", G......... $1,350.00

American Emergency Unit No 6000, Nylint, 1963, red & wht, 11", NMIB.. $375.00

American Railway Express Van, Sturditoy, roof extends over open seat, screened sides, blk & gr w/red hubs, BRT, 26", EX+ $2,000.00

Armored Car, Dayton, 1911, friction, 2 guns protrude from roof, red w/gold trim, MSW, 10½", VG................................ $225.00

Army Truck, see also Little Jim Army Truck

Army Truck & Searchlight, Lumar, 19" truck & 12½" search-light, EX $200.00

Army Truck, Cor-Cor, 1930s, enclosed cab w/flat roof, army gr, 23", missing canvas cover & supports, VG $225.00

Army Truck, Steelcraft, 1920s, Mack 'C'-style cab, cloth cover, tan w/red hubs, 26", VG.. $725.00

Army Truck, Steelcraft, 1930s, Mack enclosed cab, cloth cover, tan w/red hubs, 24", EX.. $250.00

Army Truck, Toledo, 1920s, open Mack cab w/front crank, can-vas topper stamped 'US Army,' disk wheels, 27", VG . $675.00

Army Truck, Turner, army gr w/tan canvas Conestoga-type cover, 18", VG $325.00

Big Boy Army Truck, Kelmet, 1920s, White open-seat cab, blk & red undercarriage, tan canvas canopy, WRT, 25½", VG $1,100.00

Big Boy Tank Truck, Kelmet, 1920s, White doorless cab, WRT w/spoke wheels, blk & red, 27", EX $1,600.00

Big Boy Tank Truck, Kelmet, 1920s, White doorless cab, WRT w/spoke wheels, blk & red, 27", G $725.00

Bloomingdale's Delivery Truck, Steelcraft, 'C'-style roof extends over open seat, electric lights, med gr, BRT, 23", G $550.00

Blue Streak Express Truck, Toledo, crank-op, blk open cab w/bench seat, 3-panel screened van, BRT w/red hubs, 27", G.... $3,900.00

Boy Craft Dump Truck, Steelcraft, 1930s, enclosed Mack cab, lever-op dump bed, red & gr, 25", VG $300.00

Boy Craft Dump Truck, Steelcraft, 1930s, enclosed Mack cab, lever-op dump bed, wht & bl, 25", NM $1,000.00

Brighton Place Dairy Co Truck, Steelcraft, 1930s, box truck, open side doors, electric lights, blk & cream, 18", EX $2,585.00

Cannon Truck, Dayton, swivel cannon on open bed, spoke wheels, olive gr w/red fenders, driver, 11", VG............ $200.00

Circus Truck, see also Giant Circus Truck

Circus Truck, Gendron, 1920s, van roof extends over open cab, 'Sampson' & 3 images of caged animals on 3 panels, 27", VG..$925.00

City Dairy Co Truck, Steelcraft, open cab, bl & gr, 24", prof rstr..$250.00

City Delivery Box Truck, Steelcraft, BRT, disk wheels, 2-tone tan, 18½", VG $550.00

City Ice Co Truck, Steelcraft, 1930s, enclosed Mack cab, wht w/ gr rails & hubs, 24", EX rstr.................................... $500.00

City Ice Co Truck, Steelcraft, 1930s, open Mack cab, canvas cover, gr w/red hubs, 23", VG $400.00

Coal & Ice Truck, friction, gr w/red running boards/front fenders, stenciled sides, MSW, 13", VG $1,100.00

Coal Truck, Steelcraft, 1920s, open GMC cab, hopper bed, red & blk w/yel hubs, BRT, 26", EX rstr........................... $500.00

Coal Truck, Sturditoy, doorless cab, hopper w/chute & sliding door, blk w/red chassis & hubs, 26", VG................... $1,250.00

Coal Truck, Toledo, 1920s, doorless 'Bull Dog' Mack cab, hopper w/sliding door shoot, red & blk, BRT, 26", VG $1,950.00

Cream-Crest Milk Products Delivery Truck, Steelcraft, ca 1935, box truck w/open doorway on sides, red & cream, 18", EX $725.00

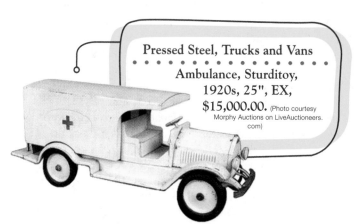

Pressed Steel, Trucks and Vans

Ambulance, Sturditoy, 1920s, 25", EX, $15,000.00. (Photo courtesy Morphy Auctions on LiveAuctioneers. com)

Pressed Steel, Trucks and Vans

Artillery Truck, Dayton, fric-tion, 12", $2,240.00. (Photo courtesy Bertoia Auctions on LiveAuc tioneers.com)

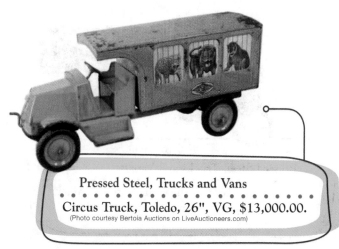

Pressed Steel, Trucks and Vans

Circus Truck, Toledo, 26", VG, $13,000.00. (Photo courtesy Bertoia Auctions on LiveAuctioneers.com)

Crean's Clean Coal Truck, American National, 1920s, 'C'-style Mack cab w/celluloid windshield, hopper w/chute, 26", EX $9,775.00

Delivery Box Truck, Metalcraft, blk w/gr box van, NP grille, NPDW, 11", G... $110.00

Delivery Panel Truck, Republic, friction, doorless, yel w/gr trim, MDW, w/drier, G.. $900.00

Delivery Truck, Kingsbury, w/up, early open seat vehicle w/center steering, WRT w/spoke wheels, pnt driver, 15", EX $400.00

Delivery Truck, Kingsbury, w/up, very early open wagon type w/ driver at center wheel, rubber tires w/MSW, 15", EX.. $400.00

Delivery Truck, Metalcraft, 1930s, 'Plee-Zing Quality Products' on gr box van, blk cab, MDW, 11", VG $300.00

Dray, see Motorized Dray

Dump Truck, see also American, Boy Craft Giant, Little Jim, Oh-Boy!, Sampson, Son-ny, and Sturditoy Construction Co Dump Truck

Dump Truck, American National, 1920s, open Mack cab, crank-op dump bed, blk & red, BRT, 28", G........................ $675.00

Dump Truck, Burdette-Murray, 1920s, doorless White cab w/ crank-op dump bed, blk/gray w/red chassis & spokes, 26", EX... $1,250.00

Dump Truck, Dayton, doorless 'C'-style cab, gr w/gold trim, MDW, w/driver, 13", VG $225.00

Dump Truck, Kelmet, 1920s, open White cab, lever-op dump bed, blk & red, WRT, 26", VG $625.00

Dump Truck, Republic, 1920s, doorless cab w/lever-op dump bed, pnt-tin driver, orange w/red trim, BRT, 20", EX $450.00

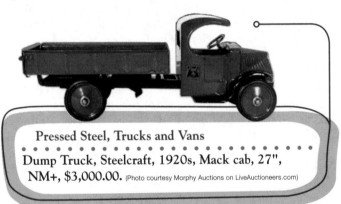

Pressed Steel, Trucks and Vans
Dump Truck, Steelcraft, 1920s, Mack cab, 27", NM+, $3,000.00. (Photo courtesy Morphy Auctions on LiveAuctioneers.com)

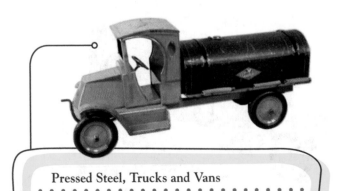

Pressed Steel, Trucks and Vans
Giant Tanker Truck, American National, Mack cab, crank-operated, 26", EX, $10,650.00.
(Photo courtesy Bertoia Auctions on LiveAuctioneers.com)

Dump Truck, Steelcraft, 1920s, GMC open cab, crank-op dump bed, BRT w/disk wheels, 26", EX $750.00

Dump Truck, Steelcraft, 1920s, Mack 'C'-style cab, lever-op dump bed, lt yel & gr, no tailgate, 25", EX $2,050.00

Dump Truck, Steelcraft, 1920s, Mack 'C'-style cab, red w/blk chassis & fenders, cowl lights & rear duals, 27", G $850.00

Dump Truck, Steelcraft, 1930s, Mack enclosed cab w/'C'-style windows, lever-op dump bed, orange & gr, 26", EX $225.00

Dump Truck, Steelcraft, 1930s, enclosed cab w/flat top, crank-op dump bed w/slanted back, electric lights, 20", EX....... $175.00

Dump Truck, Steelcraft, 1930s, enclosed cab w/visor, lever-op dump bed, bl & off wht, disk wheels, 24", EX $250.00

Dump Truck, Sturditoy, crank-op gondola dump bed swivels from side to side, blk, gr & red, BRT, 25", EX rstr............... $975.00

Dump Truck, Toledo, 1920s, Mack doorless cab w/celluloid windshield, lt gr & orange, 28", G $975.00

Dump Truck, Turner, 1930s, Lincoln cab w/lever-op dump bed, red w/yel roof, MDW, 30", G $400.00

Electronic Cannon Truck, Ny-Lint #2400, w/3 plastic rockets, 22", VGIB.. $175.00

Emergency Van, Neff Moon, bl & blk w/'Emergency' stenciled on sides, railed rear platform, gr MDW, 12½", VG...... $900.00

Express Truck, Cecaso, 1930s, open cab w/wooden bench seat, gr overpnt, MDW, 25", G.................................. $250.00

Express Truck, Steelcraft, 1920s, open GMC cab, open bed, bl, gr, gray & red, 26", VG $450.00

Express Truck, Toledo, 1920s, Mack open cab, front crank, rear open bed, orange & gray, 28", VG $1,050.00

Fro-joy Ice Cream Truck, Steelcrat, 1930s, box van w/open door-way on ea side, red & cream, BRT, 22", VG................ $325.00

Giant Circus Truck, American National, 1920s, van roof extends over Mack cab, 3 animal images, blk/wht/red, 27", EX rstr $1,075.00

Giant Coal Truck, American National, 1920s, doorless Mack cab w/front crank, hopper bed, blk & red, BRT, EX rstr $1,375.00

Giant Delivery Van, American National, 1920s, roof on screened van extends over open Mack cab, blk & tan, 27", G.$1,500.00

Giant Delivery Van, American National, 1920s, roof on screened van extends over open Mack cab, gr & orange, 27", EX.........$6,325.00

Giant Dump Truck, American National, 1920s, doorless Mack cab w/front crank, blk & red, BRT, 28", VG $3,500.00

Giant Express Truck, American National, 1920s, open Mack cab w/front crank, open bed, red, BRT, 28", VG................ $900.00

Giant Stake Truck, American National, 1920s, doorless Mack cab, bright bl & red, BRT, 27", EX rstr $1,150.00

Giant Tanker Truck, American National, Mack doorless cab, crank-op, orange & bl, BRT, 26", G $3,500.00

Gilmore Red Lion Tank Truck, Mack cab, 27", rstr..... $2,000.00

Gun Truck, Hill Climber, friction, armored car look w/2 guns atop roof, sm dbl porthole window, MSW, 11", VG+ . $300.00

Hendler's Ice Cream Truck, Steelcraft, visor over windshield, open side doors on box van, yel w/Kewpie doll ad, 22", G $350.00

Hood's Ice Cream Truck, Steelcraft, ca 1935, box van w/open doorways on ea side, enclosed cab, red, BRT, 21", VG . $575.00

Huckster, Kingsbury, w/up, gr, WRT w/red hubs, 15", VG .$2,900.00

Huckster, Sturditoy, ca 1925, roof w/stake sides extends over open bench seat, blk & gray w/red hubs, BRT, 27", rstr.......... $975.00

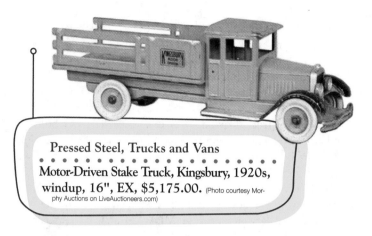

Pressed Steel, Trucks and Vans
• •
Motor-Driven Stake Truck, Kingsbury, 1920s, windup, 16", EX, $5,175.00. (Photo courtesy Morphy Auctions on LiveAuctioneers.com)

Pressed Steel, Trucks and Vans
• •
Oh-Boy! American Express Truck, Kiddies Metal Toys, 1920s, 22", VG+, $1,900.00. (Photo courtesy Bertoia Auctions on LiveAuctioneers.com)

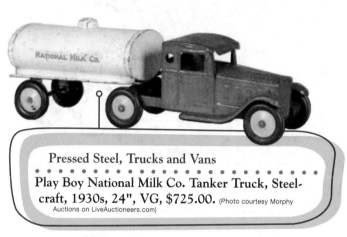

Pressed Steel, Trucks and Vans
• •
Play Boy National Milk Co. Tanker Truck, Steelcraft, 1930s, 24", VG, $725.00. (Photo courtesy Morphy Auctions on LiveAuctioneers.com)

Ice Truck, American National, open cab w/bench seat, railed bed labeled 'Pure Ice,' BRT, rstr $775.00

Ice Truck, Cor-Cor, 1920s, blk w/orange bed, orange hubs, 23½", EX $550.00

Jungle Wagon, Nylint #9000, 1966-72, 2-tone gr, w/all 6 orig animals, NMIB $500.00

Little Jim Army Truck, Steelcraft/JC Penney, 1930s, open Mack cab, canvas top, tan w/red hubs, 23", VG+ $250.00

Little Jim Dump Truck, Steelcraft/JC Penney, 1930s, Mack enclosed cab, red w/tan bed, BRT w/red hubs, 24", G. $225.00

Little Jim Stake Truck, Steelcraft/JC Penney, 1930s, blk & orange, WRT w/blk hubs, 24½", VG $850.00

Lumar Van Lines Semi, red PS cab w/bl, yel & red litho tin trailer, 14", EX $350.00

Lumber Truck, All American Toy Co, yel cab w/horn on hood, red bed w/load of lumber, 10-wheeled, 20", VG $400.00

Machinery Hauling Truck, Metalcraft, red enclosed cab w/gr open back, orig Goodrich rubber tires, 14", G+ $100.00

Mandel Bro's Delivery Van, Steelcraft, roof extends over open seat, lt bl, 22", G $525.00

Morey-La Rue Laundry Truck, Steelcraft, electric headlamps, yel w/red lettering, chrome grille, BRT, 19", G+ $700.00

Motor-Driven Stake Truck, Kingsbury, 1920s, w/up, WRT, 16", G $1,600.00

Motorized Dray, Kingsbury, w/up, open seat w/driver at center steering wheel, rubber tires on spoke wheels, bl, 11", VG $400.00

Moving Van, Steelcraft, 1920s, van roof extends over open GMC cab, blk, tan & red, disk wheels, 24", EX $2,585.00

Moving Van, Steelcraft, 1920s, van roof extends over open Mack cab, red, gr & blk, MDW, 24", G $800.00

National Milk Co Tanker Truck, see Play Boy National Milk Co Tanker Truck

Oh-Boy! Delivery Stake Truck, Kiddie Metal Toys, 1920s, enclosed cab, MDW, 19", rpnt $350.00

Oh-Boy! Dump Truck, Kiddies Metal Toys, 1920s, open seat, blk & gray, MDW w/orange hubs, 18½", G+IB $500.00

Oh-Boy! Ice Truck, Kiddies Metal Toys, open seat, railed bed, gr, MDW w/red hubs, 19", VG $350.00

Oh-Boy! Moving Van, Kiddies Metal Toys, 1920s, roof extends over open seat, MDW, 22", VG $950.00

Oh-Boy! Wrecking Truck, open cab, MDW, red & blk, 19", VGIB $550.00

Panel Truck, Kingsbury, electric headlights, bl w/orange hubs, WRT, 13", Fair+ $1,150.00

Parcel Delivery Truck, Kingsbury, w/up, doorless, orange, 9½", VG $225.00

Parcel Post Truck, Dayton, friction, open w/high bench seat, long opening hood, red w/gold trim, 12", G $165.00

Pickup Truck, Schieble Hill Climber, 1927, friction, bl w/red roof, rubber tires w/yel MDW, 18", G+ $350.00

Play Boy Tractor-Trailer, Steelcraft, 1930s, enclosed cab w/box trailer, electric lights, yel w/bl hubs, 24", VG $700.00

Play Boy Trucking Co Delivery Truck, Steelcraft, 1930s, box van, 22", EX $400.00

Play Boy Trucking Co Delivery Truck, Steelcraft, 1930s, box van, 22", VG $275.00

Play Boy Trucking Co Ride-On Truck, Steelcraft, Mack cab, b/o lights, steering wheel on cab top, seat in bed, 19", G.. $900.00

Play Boy Trucking Co Wrecker, Steelcraft, 1930s, electric lights, olive gr w/blk boom, BRT w/red hubs, 22", VG $500.00

Police Department Van, Sturditoy, 25", rstr $1,900.00

Police Patrol, Steelcraft, 1920s, van roof extends over open Mack cab, red, BRT, 26", EX $6,900.00

Pure Oil Tank Truck, Metalcraft, streamline model, bl w/wht lettering, NP grille, BRT, 15", NM $2,500.00

Railway Express Truck, Steelcraft, 1920s, screened van roof extends over open Mack cab, red, gr & blk, 25", G . $1,150.00

Railway Express Van, Steelcraft, 1920s, screened van roof extends over open Mack cab, red, gr & blk, 25", EX $6,900.00

Richfield Tanker Truck, American National, 1920s, Mack doorless cab, front crank, blk w/gold trim, 26", EX $3,000.00

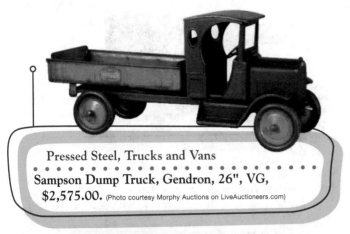

Pressed Steel, Trucks and Vans
Sampson Dump Truck, Gendron, 26", VG, $2,575.00. (Photo courtesy Morphy Auctions on LiveAuctioneers.com)

Pressed Steel, Trucks and Vans
Son-ny Moving Van, Dayton, 1920s, 26", EX, $1,100.00. (Photo courtesy Morphy Auctions on LiveAuctioneers.com)

Pressed Steel, Trucks and Vans
Stake Delivery Truck, Dayton, with driver, 15", VG, $300.00. (Photo courtesy Bertoia Auctions)

Pressed Steel, Trucks and Vans
Tank Truck, Sturditoy, 1920s, doorless cab, steerable wheels, black rubber tires, red, 35", VG, $8,000.00. (Photo courtesy Morphy Auctions on LiveAuctioneers.com)

Richfield Tanker Truck, American National, 1920s, Mack doorless cab, front crank, blk w/gold trim, 26", VG......... $1,725.00
Sampson Dump Truck, Gendron, 1920s, doorless cab, front crank, disk wheels, blk & red, 26", G $1,150.00
Sampson Stake Truck, Gendron, blk & orange, MDW, crank-op, 25½", G.. $925.00
Sand & Gravel Truck, Dayton, yel & red, MDW, 17", VG .$650.00
Sand & Gravel Truck, Metalcraft, red w/yel dump bed, orig Goodrich rubber tires, 10½", G+ $150.00
Sheffield Farms Sealtest Milk Stake Truck, Steelcraft, red, disk wheels, w/2 milk cans, 23", VG+ $1,650.00
Son-ny Artillery Truck, Dayton, 1920s, open cab, rotating rear-mounted artillery gun, army gr, MDW, 24", VG.......... $575.00
Son-ny Artillery Truck, Dayton, 1920s, open cab, rotating rear-mounted gun, army gr, BRT, 24", EX $975.00
Son-ny Dump Truck, Dayton, 1920s, Mack 'C'-style cab, lever-op dump bed, blk & red, MDW, 26", EX $750.00
Son-ny Dump Truck, Dayton, 1920s, Mack 'C'-stlye cab, lever-op dump bed, blk & red, MDW, 26", G $250.00
Son-ny Moving Van, Dayton, 1920s, van roof extends over open cab, blk & gr w/red hubs, 26", VG $800.00
Son-ny Parcel Post Truck, Dayton, 1920s, screened van roof extends over open cb, blk & gr w/red hubs, 26", VG .. $900.00
Son-ny Police Patrol, Dayton, 1920s, screened van roof extends over open cab, blk & bl w/orange hubs, 28", VG $850.00
Son-ny Railway Express, Dayton, 1920s, van roof extends over open cab, blk & gr w/red hubs, 26", EX $850.00
Son-ny US Army Truck, Dayton, 1920s, open cab, cloth cover, army gr, w/2 cannons, 26", EX $850.00
Speedwagon, Republic, 1920s, friction, 'C'-style cab w/open bed, gr w/red fenders & grille, gold MSW, 11", VG $250.00
Speedwagon, Republic, 1920s, friction, doorless cab, orange w/gr running boards/front fenders, gold trim, MDW, 12", VG+ $375.00
St Louis Dairy Co Delivery Truck, Steelcraft, open side doors, blk & wht, BRT w/red hubs, 18", G+ $450.00
Stake Truck, see also Motorized Stake Truck
Stake Truck, American National, Mack cab, doorless, bl & red, BRT, 26", EX $10,350.00
Stake Truck, Steelcraft, blk & orange w/orange MDW, 21", VG .$500.00
Stake Truck, Turner, C-style cab, yel w/red roof & front fenders, no back fenders, BET, 17", G $200.00
Sturditoy Construction Co Dump Truck, 1920s, doorless cab, crank-op bed, blk & gr w/red chassis & hubs, 27", VG .$850.00
Sturditoy Construction Co Dump Truck, 1920s, doorless cab, crank-op bed, lt gr w/red chassis & hubs, BRT, 27", EX........... $1,600.00
Sturditoy Oil Company Tanker Truck, doorless cab, blk, red & gr, BRT, 26½", VG.. $6,325.00
Supplee-Wills-Jones 'A' Milk/Walker Gordon Certified Milk Truck, cream & gr, BRT, 18", EX $3,500.00
Tank Truck, see also Big Boy Tank Truck
Tank Truck, Steelcraft, 1920s, Mack 'C'-style cab, red w/blk trim, BRT, 27", EX $4,300.00
Tank Truck, Toledo, 1920s, Mack doorless cab w/front crank, blk & red, 26", EX $2,725.00
Tractor-Trailer, Steelcraft, 1920s, GMC open cab pulling open 2-wheeled trailer, blk & gray w/red hubs, 29", VG... $1,250.00
USA Defense Truck, Kingsbury, w/up, olive gr w/tan canvas cover, 14", EX $200.00

Pressed Steel, Trucks and Vans
• •
Tractor-Trailer, Steelcraft, 1920s, GMC, 29", EX, $1,725.00. (Photo courtesy Morphy Auctions on LiveAuctioneers.com)

Pressed Steel, Trucks and Vans
• •
White Army Truck, Kelmet #513, black with red undercarriage, 'Army Truck' stamped on canvas cover, white rubber tires, red hubs, restored, $1,200.00. (Photo courtesy Leslie Hindman Auctioneers)

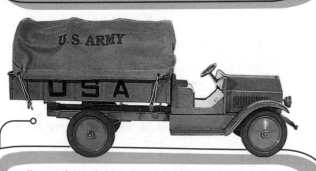

Pressed Steel, Trucks and Vans
• •
US Army Truck, Sturditoy, 1920s, open cab, green with 'US Army' on canvas top, USA in black on bedsides, black rubber tires, green hubs, 27", EX, $3,735.00. (Photo courtesy Morphy Auctions on LiveAuctioneers.com)

US Mail Truck, Steelcraft, 1930s, 'C'-style van roof extends over open Mack cab, red & gr, 22", VG $625.00
Utility Service Truck, Lumar, w/accessories, 20", NM $300.00
Wrecker, Garland, 1950s, ride-on toy w/built-in seat on wrecker trailer, wooden handle, 24", EX $400.00
Wrecker, Schieble, inertia drive, bl w/red top, yel hubs, WRT, 19", EX $875.00
Wrecker, Sturditoy, doorless cab, crank-op, red, BRT, 29", VG $2,800.00

• • • • • • • • • • • • • •   **Promotional Vehicles**   • • • • • • • • • • • • • •

Miniature Model T Fords were made by Tootsietoy during the 1920s, and a few of these were handed out by Ford dealers to promote the new models. In 1932 Tootsietoy was contacted by Graham-Paige to produce a model of their car. These 4" Grahams were sold in boxes as sales promotions by car dealerships, and some were sold through the toy company's catalog. But it wasn't until after WWII that distribution of 1/25 scale promotional models and kits became commonplace. Early models were of cast metal, but during the 1950s, manufacturers turned to plastic. Not only was the material less costly to use, but it could be molded in the color desired, thereby saving the time and expense previously involved in painting the metal. Though the early plastic cars were prone to warp easily, by the early '60s they had become more durable. Some were friction powered, and others battery-operated. Advertising extolling some of the model's features was often embossed on the underside. Among the toy manufacturers involved in making promotionals were National Products, Product Miniature, AMT, MPC, and Jo-Han. Interest in '50s and '60s models is intense, and the muscle cars from the '60s and early '70s are especially collectible. The more popularity the life-size models attain, the more popular the promotional is with collectors.

Check the model for damage, warping, and amateur alterations. The original box can increase the value by as much as 100%. Jo-Han has reissued some of their 1950s and 1960s Mopar and Cadillac models as well as Chrysler's Turbine Car.

Nothing controls values of promos more than color. Thus, the difference can be substantial.

Buick Electra (1962), AMT, wht, VG $40.00
Buick Riviera (1963), silver, wht-line tires w/chrome-like hubs, NM $60.00
Buick Roadmaster Convertible (1958), 2-tone yel, wht-wall tires, 8½", VG $50.00
Cadillac de Ville 2-Door Hardtop (1964), Jo-Han, silver w/blk top, M $110.00
Cadillac Eldorado 2-Door Hardtop (1973), Jo-Han, NM (NM box) $77.00

Cadillac Fleetwood 'Sixty Special' 4-Door Hardtop (1958), Jo-Han, wht w/pk interior, MIB $365.00
Cadillac Fleetwood 4-Door Hardtop (1959), Jo-Han, blk, wht-wall tires, M $120.00
Chevy Corvette (1976), Classic White, 7½", M (EX box) . $75.00
Chevy Corvette (1978 Anniversary Edition), MPC, 2-tone, MIB $53.00
Chevy Corvette (1992 Special Edition 1 Millionth Corvette), AMT, M (M in box) $53.00

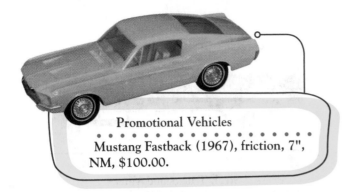

Promotional Vehicles
• • • • • • • • • • • • • • • • • • •
**Mustang Fastback (1967), friction, 7",
NM, $100.00.**

Promotional Vehicles
• •
Buick Invicta (1960), AMT, VG, $60.00. (Photo
courtesy Lloyd Ralston Gallery on LiveAuctioneers.com)

Promotional Vehicles
• •
**Chevy Apache 32 Fleetside Pickup (1959), EX,
$30.00.** (Photo courtesy BS Slosberg, Inc. Auctioneers on LiveAuctioneers.com)

Promotional Vehicles
• •
Chevy Malibu (1964), AMT, G, $50.00. (Photo
courtesy Lloyd Ralston Gallery on LiveAuctioneers.com)

Ford Crestline Sedan (91953), AMT, EX $50.00
Ford Fairlane GT (1966), 390 engine, dk red, EX+ $100.00
Ford Fairlane 2-Door, brn & tan, blk-walls w/tan hubs, friction,
   8", AMT, VG $50.00
Ford Galaxie Convertible w/Top Up (1962), lt bl w/wht top,
   EX $200.00
Ford Galaxie 500XL 2-Door Hardtop (1964), AMT, deep red,
   M $90.00

Ford Galaxie 500XL 2-Door Hardtop (1965), AMT, bl,
   NMIB $68.00
Ford Mustang Coupe (1965), aqua, VG+ $50.00
Ford Mustang Fastback (1967), yel, NM $100.00
Ford Thunderbird Convertible (1955), mint gr, VG+ $150.00
Ford Thunderbird Convertible (1962), lt bl, EX+ $250.00
Ford Thunderbird 2-Door Hardtop (1963), AMT, NM $55.00
Ford Thunderbird 2-Door Hardtop (1964), AMT, NM $55.00
Ford 4-Door Sedan (1950), maroon, NM $125.00
Hudson, 13", EX $550.00
Lincoln Continental Mark III 2-Door Hardtop (1958), AMT,
   missing hood ornament o/w M $125.00
Mercury Park Lane (1959), bl w/wht top, wht-wall tires, friction,
   AMT, 8½", VG $50.00
Mercury Park Lane (1966), burgundy w/silver-tone hubs on wht-
   line tires, 8½", VG $50.00
Oldsmobile Cutlass (1964), cream w/dk gr interior), M . $130.00
Oldsmobile Starfire Convertible (1963), Jo-Han, metallic fleck
   pnt, M $95.00
Oldsmobile Starfire 2-Door Hardtop (1963), Jo-Han, red, M .. $95.00
Oldsmobile Toronado (1970), metallic Gold Nugget w/blk inte-
   rior, M (EX+ box) $85.00
Oldsmobile 442 2-Door Hardtop (1970), Jo-Han, metallic
   orange, M $100.00
Oldsmobile 442 2-Door Hardtop (1971), Jo-Han, metallic deep
   lime gr, NMIB $200.00

Promotional Vehicles
• •
**Chrysler Two-Door Hardtop, Jo-Han #M0166,
NMIB, $130.00.** (Photo courtesy Lloyd Ralston Gallery on LiveAuctioneers.com)

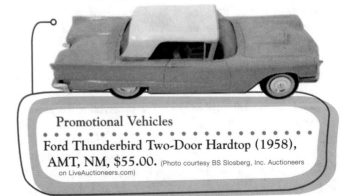

Promotional Vehicles
• •
**Ford Thunderbird Two-Door Hardtop (1958),
AMT, NM, $55.00.** (Photo courtesy BS Slosberg, Inc. Auctioneers
on LiveAuctioneers.com)

Plymouth (1958), aqua gr w/blk top, 8", Jo-Han, G+ $30.00
Pontiac Bonneville 2-Door Hardtop (1958), AMT, M... $200.00
Pontiac Cheiftain Sedan (1951), AMT, NM.................. $150.00
Pontiac V-8 2-Door Hardtop (1955), Jo-Han, 2-tone gr, M..$75.00

Rambler Cross Country Station Wagon (1959), Jo-Han, cream, NMIB $60.00
Tempest (1961), Shelltone Ivory, wht-wall tires w/chrome-like hubs, MIB... $115.00

Pull and Push Toys

Pull and push toys from the 1800s often were hide- and cloth-covered animals with glass or shoe-button eyes on wheels or wheeled platforms. Many were also made of tin or wood. The cast-iron bell toys of that era can be found in the Cast Iron category under Bell Toys.

See also Character, TV, and Movie Collectibles; Disney; Fisher-Price.

Alderney Milk Wagon, horse on 4-wheeled platform, wooden wagon, w/figure in suit & tie, 21", Schoenhut, VG..$3,000.00
Bear on 4-Wheeled Open Tin Platform, brn plush, 18" L, F...$100.00
Borden's Milk Wagon, Rich Toys, wood w/pnt detail, complete w/wooden bottle carrier & bottles, 18", VG................ $575.00
Camel on 4-Wheeled Platform, pnt tin, yel camel w/gr base, 4 MSW, 9" L, A Bergmann, 1880s, G..........................$1,035.00
Cat on 2 Spoke Wheels, wood & tin cat w/articulated limbs supported on 2 CI spoke wheels w/long wooden pull handle, EX $250.00
Central Transportation Trolley, pnt tin w/stenciling, red w/gr roof, MSW, 1 horse, 16", Fallows, VG $2,585.00
Chariot, pnt tin, wht horse w/red saddle, emb chariot w/2 sm spoke wheels, 7", Fallows, 1880s, G $250.00
City Delivery Wagon, pnt tin, 2 dapple horses pulling yel & red wagon w/4 MSW, 20" L, Converse, ca 1912, VG........ $525.00
City Passenger Trolley, pnt tin, horse-drawn, 14½", Hull & Stafford, EX $850.00
Clown on Wooden 4-Wheeled Platform, cloth dressed w/ bisque head, turns head & waves staff when pulled, 11½", VG+ $715.00
Coaster Boy #140, 1941, VG... $500.00
Covered Wagon, Gibbs, 2 paper-litho-on-wood horses w/articulated legs, tin wagon w/cloth cover, 18", VG+ $100.00
Cow on 4-Wheeled Platform, hide-covered w/applied glass eyes, wooden platform w/4 sm MSW, emits 'moo' sound, 9" L, VG...............$100.00
Dog (Large) & Small Boy Walking on 4-Wheeled Platform, pnt tin, 6", Fallows, 1880s, G $300.00
Elephant on 4-Wheeled Platform, CI, brn elephant, gr platform w/red spoke wheels, 4", Kenton, VG $450.00

Pull and Push Toys
Buffalo Bill Chasing Two Buffalo on Four-Wheeled Platform, painted tin, articulated action, 9", Fallows, 1880s, EX, $2,800.00. (Photo courtesy Bertoia Auctions on LiveAuctioneers.com)

Pull and Push Toys
Butcher Wagon, painted tin, 11½", some restoration, $1,775.00. (Photo courtesy Bertoia Auctions on LiveAuctioneers.com)

Pull and Push Toys

City Hall and 51st Horse-Drawn Trolley, painted tin, 12½", Fallows, 1883, VG, $1,500.00. (Photo courtesy Bertoia Auctions on LiveAuctioneers.com)

Pull and Push Toys

Duck, painted cast iron, when pulled bill opens and legs move, 9½", Hubley, 1930s, NM, $2,800.00. (Photo courtesy Morphy Auctions on LiveAuctioneers.com)

Pull and Push Toys

Fine Bread/Cakes Wagon, wood, 20" overall, Schoenhut, VG, $5,000.00. (Photo courtesy Bertoia Auctions on LiveAuctioneers.com)

Pull and Push Toys

German Girl in Horse Cart Pull Toy, wicker cart, tin wheels, animated cloth covered horse, bisque head doll plays music, 15" long, VG, $1,100.00. (Photo courtesy Noel Barrett Antiques & Auctions Ltd.)

Pull and Push Toys

Horse and Colt on Four-Wheeled Platform, painted tin, 7" long, Merriam, 1860s, EX, $2,800.00. (Photo courtesy Bertoia Auctions on LiveAuctioneers.com)

Elephant on 4-Wheeled Platform, pnt tin, friction, w/pull rope, 8x9", Converse, VG $225.00

Express Wagon, pnt tin, wht horse, red wagon w/'Express' on sides, 4 MSW, 17" L, Hull & Stafford, 1870s, VG ... $1,050.00

Fairmount Farms 'A' Milk Dairy Wagon, horse on 4-wheeled platform, w/figure & cans, 25", Schoenhut, EX+ ...$10,350.00

Frogs (2) on Seesaw on 3-Wheeled Platform, CI frogs on wire bar, yel tin platform w/spoke wheels, pull string, 7" L, EX.... $650.00

Goat (Large) & Small Girl Walking on 4-Wheeled Platform, pnt tin, 7" L, Fallows, 1880s, G $275.00

Grand Central Trolley, pnt tin, 2 wht horses pull red trolley w/4 spoke wheels, 14" L, VG $450.00

Grasshopper, pnt CI w/aluminum legs, 2 sm front wheels, 11" L, Hubley, NM.............................. $800.00

Hoop Toy w/Horse, pnt tin, 6¼" dia, A Bergmann, rpnt . $325.00

Horse Cart, tin, 2-wheeled cart w/uniformed driver, 2 horses, 9½", EX.............................. $600.00

Horse-Drawn Delivery Wagon, pnt tin, yel horse pulling 4-wheeled cart w/roof & open sides, Fallows, 1880s, 12" L, G $600.00

Horse-Drawn Stake Cart, horse on 4-wheeled platform pulling 2-wheeled cart, felt-covered horse, pnt wood cart, 15", EX.$250.00

Horse-Drawn Trolley, pnt tin, red w/gr top & yel bottom, 2 blk horses, 19", Fallows, G $1,265.00

Horse-Drawn 2-Wheeled Cart, pnt tin, blk horse, bl cart w/cut-out sides, MSW, 13" L, Hull & Stafford, 1880s, VG+....... $2,250.00

Horse-Drawn 2-Wheeled Cart, pnt tin, wht horse w/red saddle, red cart scalloped front end, 12" L, George Brown, rpnt.............................. $250.00

Horse on 4-Wheeled Platform, brn & wht hide-covered w/ leather harness & saddle, carved wood face w/glass eyes, 26" L, VG.............................. $350.00

Horse on 4-Wheeled Platform, dapple gray & wht pnt wood w/cotton mane, shoe-button eyes, leather trappings, 15" L, VG...$500.00

Horse on 4-Wheeled Platform, felt-covered body w/glass eyes, orig harness & saddle, wooden base w/MSW, 15x13" L, VG...$100.00

Horse on 4-Wheeled Platform, mohair-covered w/horse hair mane & tail, w/full trappings, 20", VG........................ $400.00

Horse on 4-Wheeled Platform, tan hide-covered wood w/dk human mane & tail, glass eyes, leather trappings, 13" L, VG...$250.00

Horse Trotting on 4-Wheeled Platform, pnt tin, blk w/red-saddle, gold harness, gr base w/MSW, 9" L, George Brown, VG.. $450.00

Horse Trotting on 4-Wheeled Platform, pnt tin, brn w/red sad-dle, gold harness, 4½", A Bergmann (?), VG............... $150.00

Horse Trotting on 4-Wheeled Platform, pnt tin, wht w/red-pnt saddle, gr platform w/blk MSW, 4¼", Fallows, 1880s, VG. $300.00

Horse Trotting on 4-Wheeled Platform, pnt tin, wht w/red saddle, spoke wheels, 6½" L, Hull & Stafford, 1870s, VG........ $450.00

Horse w/Figure Standing at Side on 4-Wheeled Platform, pnt tin, wht horse & figure, 5" L, A Bergmann (?), VG $775.00

Jumbo Elephant w/Movable Trunk on 4-Wheeled Platform, gray w/red saddle, gr platform w/blk MSW, 7" L, Fallows, 1880s, G $325.00

Lamb on 4-Wheeled Platform, blk & wht w/emb neck bell, gr platform w/blk MSW, 4½" L, Fallows, ca 1870, EX..... $300.00

Lamb on 4-Wheeled Platform, wht wool body on wooden base w/4 MSW, 7½x6" L, EX $100.00

Lion w/Tamer on 4-Wheeled Platform, pnt tin, yel lion w/bl tamer, 4" L, A Bergmann, 1870s, VG $950.00

Milk Wagon, horse on 4-wheeled platform pulling open box wagon w/5 milk cans, wood w/pnt detail, 22", EX....... $200.00

Motorcycle w/Sidecar, Rich Toys, wood & metal w/articulated driver, pull string, 9", EX $500.00

Ox Cart, pnt tin w/stenciling on 2-wheeled cart, cream & blk, 9½", George Brown, VG $2,645.00

Peacock on 3 Wheels, pnt compo w/red & wht plumage, tin spoke wheels, wooden handle, 43" L (w/handle) $75.00

Perpetual Motion #910, very rare, NMIP........................ $575.00

Ram Pulling 2-Wheeled Cart, pnt tin, wht ram w/bl & yel cart, spoke wheels, 10" L, A Bergmann, 1870s, VG $400.00

Reindeer, tin, on 2 front wheels w/clicker, 8", VG $250.00

Rocking Horse w/Jockey Rider, pnt tin, 7" L, Fallows, EX+ $3,000.00

Rocking Horse w/Jockey Rider, pnt tin, 7" L, Fallows, rpnt .$325.00

Sheep & Dog on 4-Wheeled Platform, pnt tin, gr emb platform w/4 blk MSW, 9" L, Stevens & Brown, 1870, VG $775.00

Sheep on 4-Wheeled Platform, wooly w/glass eyes, wooden plat-form w/CI wheels, Germany, 10", EX $850.00

Sheep on 4-Wheeled Platform w/Bell, pnt tin, wht & gray lamb w/ gold neck bell, lg bell on platform, 8" L, Fallows, EX... $1,500.00

Sheffield Farms Co Milk Wagon, Gibbs, wood w/pnt detail, orig metal bottle carrier w/7 bottles, 20", VG..................... $675.00

Train, locomotive (no engineer's cabin) on 4-wheeled platform & yel coach, pnt tin, 8" L, Fallows (?), 1890s, G........ $350.00

Train, Panama locomotive, Mexican Central RR & Excursion to Coney Island open cars, wood, 42" overall, EX $550.00

Train (Conn Valley RR), locomotive, tender & 2 coaches, 29" L, Fallows, 1880s, EX... $2,520.00

Train (Rocket), locomotive & tender, pnt tin, primary colors, 8", Fallows, EX $275.00

Train (Skip), locomotive w/tender & 2 coaches, pnt tin, spoke wheels, 20" overall, G $115.00

Train Locomotive, pnt tin w/tall wooden stack, wood base, pri-mary colors, 9½", Hull & Stafford, F........................ $1,000.00

Train Locomotive, tin, w/up, 18", Ives, 1876, VG $7,500.00

Train Locomotive (Boss), pnt tin, red w/blk boiler, spoke wheels & cow catcher, 9" L, EX.. $450.00

Train Locomotive (Gladiator), pnt tin w/wooden smoke stack, yel, red & blk, spoke wheels & cow catcher, 13", VG........ $2,750.00

Pull and Push Toys

Trucking Hay Wagon, painted and stenciled wood, 25", EX, $450.00. (Photo courtesy Morphy Auctions on LiveAuctioneers.com)

Train Locomotive (Samson), pnt tin, red, yel & blk, 9½", Hull & Stafford, 1890s, EX..$4,750.00
Train Locomotive (Transit), pnt tin, orange & blk, 4 spoke wheels, w/up, 7" L, Ives, VG $2,000.00
Train Locomotive (Union), pnt tin, 8¼", Ives, F............ $100.00
Train Locomotive & Coach, pnt tin, w/up, 16" L, Hull & Stafford, late 1800s, G to VG $1,300.00
Two-Headed Cart, 2 articulated heads bob as 2-wheeled paper-litho-on-cb cart is pulled or pushed, 30" to handle, VG..$450.00
US Mail Wagon, Converse, litho tin w/wooden wagon floor, roof extends over open seat, 3 horses, VG+........................$750.00

Puppets

Puppet theaters have been a long-lasting form of entertainment for kids and adults alike. What child has not had a puppet or two of their own that they have brought to life? Here we have listed non-character-related hand puppets, marionettes, and push-button puppets. You will find the character puppets listed in related categories.

See also Advertising; Black Americana; Character, TV, and Movie Collectibles; Disney; Western Heroes and Frontiersmen.

HAND PUPPETS

Chinese Girl, Scripture Press, 1968, cloth body w/vinyl face, blk-pnt hair, NM+ $50.00
Chipmunk, Hazelle #100A, 1960s, brn cloth body w/brn vinyl head, MIB..$45.00
Clown (Ringling Bros Barnum & Bailey Circus), cloth body w/ vinyl head, EX $75.00
Dog, Hazelle, 1960s, blk & wht checked cloth body w/blk & wht vinyl head, blk-pnt eyes, brows & nose, MIP $45.00
Dog, 1950s, cloth body w/wht polka-dots, vinyl head w/sm red hat cocked to side & bowtie, wht/blk ears, NM $50.00

Elephant (Ringling Bros Barnum & Bailey Circus), cloth body w/logo, brn vinyl head, EX...$75.00
Elf, Zany, 1950s, silky cloth body w/vinyl head, mouth open, lg plastic eyes, molded pointy hat, EX $50.00

Puppets, Hand

Lion, Mattel, 1960s, talker, EX+, $125.00. (Photo courtesy www.gasolinealley antiques.com)

Puppets, Hand

Red the Clown, Hazelle, 1960s, MIP, $55.00. (Photo courtesy www.gasolinealleyantiques.com)

Puppets, Marionettes

Ballet Dancer, Pelham, MIB, $100.00. (Photo courtesy www.gasoline alleyantiques.com)

Puppets, Marionettes

Fritz the Soldier, M, $95.00. (Photo courtesy www. gasolinealleyantiques.com)

Leopard, Hazelle, 1960s, blk, wht & brn spotted cloth body w/ vinyl head, mouth w/fangs, MIP $45.00

Policeman, Hazelle, plain bl cloth body w/vinyl head & hat, glancing eyed, 9", EX $45.00

Prince Phillip, Gund, 1950s, cloth body w/vinyl head, NM .$75.00

Ralph, Hazelle, 1960s, wht cloth body w/bl polka-dots, vinyl head w/yel hair, pnt-on brn-dotted 'whiskers,' MIP $65.00

Wise Owl, Hazelle, 1960s, wht cloth body w/vinyl head, MIP.. $45.00

MARIONETTES

Bobby (Policeman), Pelham, working mouth, dk bl uniform, about 14", MIB $175.00

Cat, Pelham, wood, beaded legs & tail, blk & wht, red ribbon neck bow, 5½" L, NM+ $100.00

Clown, Hazelle, wht cloth body w/red, bl & yel polka-dots, vinyl head w/yel hair, red vinyl hat & shoes, 12½", VG.........$75.00

Clown, Hazelle, wht face/hands/shoes, blk brows/eyes, red cheeks/ lips, red costume w/wht dots, red hat/collar, 15", EX........$75.00

Clown, Hazelle's Hobby Kit #101, wht face & hands, blk shoes, colorful outfit, 15", NMIB...$125.00

Girl w/Yo-Yo, Pelham, ball-shaped head w/dk hair, yo-yo in hand, NMIB $100.00

Hillbilly, Hazelle #881, 1949-50, nonmovable mouth w/pipe, 13½", NMIB $150.00

Lady, Hazelle, nonmovable mouth, blond hair, print house dress w/long sleeves, wht shoes, 14", NM $85.00

Lady, Hazelle, nonmovable mouth, dk hair, long print skirt w/wht blouse, red ribbon neck bow & sash, wht shoes, 14", NM $85.00

Lady, Hazelle, working mouth, blond hair, bl skirt w/red & wht checked blouse, wht apron, blk-pnt shoes, 14", NM+ .$100.00

Lady in Long Gown, Pelham, yel blond hair, satiny gown, NM $75.00

Minstrel, Pelham, wood, dk brn skin w/red lips, lt bl pants, wht striped jacket, w/banjo, NRFB $175.00

Prince Charming, Hazelle #916, working mouth, NMIB. $175.00

Sailor, Hazelle, working mouth, US Navy uniform, 14", NM+ $100.00

Skeleton, Pelham, boney structure w/lg red-rimmed bug-eyes, very scarce, NM.. $275.00

Small Fry Club Girl, Peter Puppet Playthings, working mouth, NM+ $125.00

Witch, Hazelle, nonmovable mouth, blk w/red belt, buggy eyes outlined in blk w/blk facial markings, wht hair, EX+ .. $125.00

Witch, Hazelle, working mouth, blk outfit, holding broom, 15", NM+.. $150.00

PUSH-BUTTON

Baseball Batter, China, pnt wood, various styles, about 5", M, $15 to...$20.00

Baseball Pitcher, China, pnt wood, 5", M $18.00

Bronco Bill, Kohner, #125, 1940s, pnt wood, 6", EX $20.00

Candy the Cat, Kohner, 1960s, M..................................$75.00

Dancer Dog, Kohner, 1960s, NM $65.00

Football Player, pnt wood, 5¼", M $15.00

Gabriel the Giraffe, Kohner, 1960s, EX+ $65.00

Go Bots, Tonka/Toy Store Ltd, 1986, M $35.00

Happy the Wonder Dog, Kohner, 1940s, pnt wood w/leather ears, 6", EX+IB $28.00

Puppets, Marionettes
School Master, talker, M (poor box), $120.00. (Photo courtesy www.gasolinealleyantiques.com)

Puppets, Marionettes
Snake Charmer, Pelham, MIB, $175.00. (Photo courtesy www.gasoline alleyantiques.com)

Puppets, Push-Button
Cowboy on Horse, Wak-ouwa, 1949, EX+, $150.00. (Photo courtesy www.gasolinealleyantiques.com)

Puppets, Push-Button
Elephant, Kohner, 1950s, NM+, $150.00. (Photo courtesy www.gasolinealleyantiques.com)

Hit & Miss, Kohner, 1940s, pnt wood, wht & blk boxers, sq base, NMIB (red box) $225.00
Hit & Miss, Kohner, 1960s, 2 boxers, pnt plastic, silver foil label on rnd base, NM $75.00
Huba Huba, dog on sq base, wood w/leather ears, EX $75.00
I'm Robot, Kohner, 1960s, EX $35.00
Lion, TM, 1970s, sq base, NM+ $30.00
Skateboarder, China, pnt wood bead type on rnd base, M .. $20.00
Terry the Tiger, Kohner, 1960s, M $65.00
Tiger, TM, 1970s, orange on sq blk base, EX $40.00

Puzzles

Jigsaw puzzles have been around almost as long as games. The first examples were handcrafted from wood, and they are extremely difficult to find. Most of the early examples featured moral subjects and offered insight into the social atmosphere of their time. By the 1900s jigsaw puzzles had become a major form of home entertainment. Cube puzzles or blocks were often made by the same companies as board games. Early examples display lithography of the finest quality. While all subjects are collectible, some (such as Santa blocks) often command prices higher than games of the same period.

Because TV and personality-related puzzles have become so popular, they're now regarded as a field all their own apart from character collectibles in general, and these are listed here as well, under the subtitle 'Character.'

Note: All early jigsaw puzzles are complete and in excellent condition unless indicated otherwise.

See also Advertising; Black Americana; Paper-Lithographed Toys.

Advisor: Bob Armstrong

Arriving at Grandfather's for Christmas (colonial scene), JLG Ferris (artist), 1930s, plywood, 208 pcs, 9x14", orig box . $60.00
Automobile Scroll Puzzle, McLoughlin Bros, orig box ... $400.00
Autumn Along the Seine, Joseph Sterns, 1930s, plywood, 300 pcs, orig box $40.00
Auvers-Sur Oise (cathedral), Jumbo International/Van Gogh (artist), 1980-90, plastic, 210 pcs, 7x7", orig box $15.00
Battle of Lake Erie (War of 1812), JLG Ferris, 1930s, plywood, 204 pcs, 16x11", orig box $50.00
Beautiful Garden of Dreams (idyllic/women), Madmar Quality Co/Interlox, 1930s, plywood, 250 pcs, 10x13", orig box . $65.00
Blooms & Blossoms (house & garden), 1930s, pressed board, 505 pcs, 18x26", rpl box $150.00
Buffeting the Billows (clipper ships), Milton Bradley/Premier, 1930s, plywood, 158 pcs, 9x12", orig box $50.00

Cattle in Pasture (farming), Julien Dupre (artist), 1930s, plywood, 188 pcs, 10x14", rpl box $45.00
Cenotaph (early 20th century London street scene), Chad Valley, 1930s, 200 pcs, 10x14", orig box $40.00
Children & Swan, Red Seal Jig, 1930s, plywood, 545 pcs, 16x20", orig box $200.00
Colonial Picture (Washington & colonists), Percy Morgan (?), 1910-20, wood, 380 pcs, 11x15", rpl box $120.00
Cottage of Mary Arden, Parker Bros/Pastime, 1920-30, plywood, 71 pcs, 8x6", orig box $35.00
Dairy Pride (cow in pasture), Pulver Novelty Co/Idle-Hour, 1930s, plywood, 301 pcs, 12x18", orig box $60.00
Deer in Mountain Valley, Edward Leggart Clark (maker), 1930s, plywood, 850 pcs, 16x22", orig box $250.00
Deer in Mountain Valley, Edward Leggett Clark (maker), 1930s, plywood, 850 pcs, 16x22", orig box $250.00
Derby Day (19th century scene w/many figures), Tuck/Zag-Zaw/BP Smith (artist), 1930s, plywood, 211 pcs, 7x15", orig box $70.00
Fire Department Puzzle Box, Milton Bradley, paper litho, set of 3, 10x16", VGIB $350.00
George Washington's Ancestral Home (garden), Lloyd Clift/Miloy, 1930s, plywood, 607 pcs, 16x20", orig box $175.00
Gleaners (farming scene), Jean-Francois Millet (artist), cb, 325 pcs, 12x16", orig box $10.00
Happy Family (home scene w/peasants), E Zampighi (artist), 1930s, 12x16", rpl box $100.00
Horse, wood, brn w/blk ears & hooves, sq base, 3", M (P box) $65.00
Household Calvary (horse/humor), Thomson (artist), 1909, 200 pcs, 12x18", orig box $225.00

Hunting (fall scene w/dog & hunter), 1930s, plywood, 162 pcs, 8x10", rpl box $35.00

In Northern Climes (fjord scene), Gruittefiem (artist?), 1930s, plywood, 204 pcs, 10x12", orig box........................$40.00

In the Park (WWI/horse & rider), Vallentine Sandberg (artist), 1909, wood, 63 pcs, 5x7", orig box................$15.00

Invocation (Eastern women), Phyllis McLellan (maker), 1930s, plywood, 280 pcs, 10x12", orig box........................$75.00

Jewel Case (woman), Parker Bros/Pastime, 1926, plywood, 257 pcs, 10x13", orig box $110.00

Juawles Pius (Picasso abstract), James Browning, 1960s, plywood, 1000 pcs, 24x30", orig box $375.00

King's Cavalier, Joseph Staus/Regal/Doheny (artist), 1940-50, plywood, 1000 pcs, 22x28", orig box $200.00

Lagoon at Night (Venice), Saybold (artist), 1930s, 500 pcs, orig box $110.00

Mallards (ducks in marsh), Joseph Straus/C Blinks (artist), 1930s, plywood, 300 pcs, 12x16", orig box $35.00

Modern Travel Series Picture Puzzles, Milton Bradley, orig box...$165.00

Moses in the Bullrushes, Parker Bros/Pastime/Relyea (artist), 1920s, plywood, 354 pcs, 12x16½", rpl box $150.00

Mountain Train, Parker Bros/Kohler's Puzzles, 1930s, plywood, 412 pcs, 16x19", orig boxes.......................$150.00

My Garden Is a Glory, Joseph Straus, plywood, 325 pcs, 15½" dia, orig box...$50.00

News of Peace (Civil War/town), Clyde O Deland (artist), 1910s, wood, 321 pcs, 12x16", orig box $140.00

Old Fort Antigua, Lowell, 1920-30, plywood, 116 pcs, 9x8", EXIB $35.00

Old Homestead a Picture Puzzle, jigsaw, outdoor scene w/buildings & people, 14½x17", orig box........................$125.00

Old Mill (stream), Macy's, 1930s, plywood, 200 pcs, 9x12", orig box..$70.00

Over Field & Fence (fox hunt scene), Jewel Puzzle Co, 1930s, plywood, 134 pcs, 8x10", orig box.........................$30.00

Peaceful Hours (romantic colonial courtship), Parker Bros/Pastime, 1933, plywood, 225 pcs, 10x15½", orig box $110.00

Peep at the Circus Puzzle, A (Dissected), McLoughlin Bros, 1887, 12x10", VGIB...$175.00

People's Advocate (Lincoln addressing court), Griswald Fang (artist ?), 1920s, wood, 540 pcs, 16x21", rpl box $150.00

Philadelphia Centennial Expo Puzzle Set, paper on wood, 5 scroll-cut puzzles of various buildings, G (12x22" wood box)....$165.00

Proposal (courtship scene), Parker Bros/Pastime, 1930s, 317 pcs, 1930s, 9x17", orig box...$125.00

Rounding the Capes (clipper ship), Joseph Straus, 1930s, plywood, 300 pcs, 12x16", orig box $40.00

Scene in Brussels (Flemish town & river), 1930s, plywood, 240 pcs, 9x12", rpl box...$85.00

Silvery Afternoon (Dutch harbor scene), Mairaux (artist?)/Ed Smith Mfg, 1930s, plywood, 150 pcs, 10x13", orig box..$30.00

Sir Galahad (knight beside horse), Parker Bros/Pastime, 1910s, plywood, 162 pcs, 7x14½", orig box...................$65.00

Springtime (woman), Parker Bros/Pastime, 1917, plywood, 81 pcs, orig box..$35.00

Steady (setters at point), Olive Novelty, 1909, plywood, 121 pcs, 6x8", orig box...$50.00

Summer on the Riviera (sailing scene), Parker Bros/Pastime, G Roger (artist), 1930s, plywood, 1000 pcs, 24x35", rpl box. $450.00

Sunset in Japan, Parker Bros/Pastime/Armitoka (artist), 1930s, plywood, 205 pcs, 9x12", orig box.................... $100.00

Surprised (bears raiding tent), Saalfield, 1940s, cb, 500 pcs, orig box $12.00

Taj Mahal, Chad Valley, 1930s, plywood, 535 pcs, 20x15", VGIB...$110.00

Tranquil Mountain Waters, Fairchild Corp/Fairco E, 1930-40, cb, 350 pcs, 13x19", orig box $80.00

Tranquility (scenery w/12 figures), 1930s, plywood, 210 pcs, 9x12", orig box...$40.00

Trouble on the Trail, Tuco/Deluxe, 1940s, cb, 357 pcs, 15x19½", orig box...$16.00

Untitled (bears raiding canoe camp), 1930s, plywood, 75 pcs, 6x9", rpl box $12.00

Untitled (cowboy surprising bear family), McCallist (artist), cb, 54 pcs, 10x13", rpl box....................................$8.00

Untitled (ships at sea), Joseph Straus, 1930s, plywood, 750 pcs, 18x23½", rpl box $85.00

Untitled (singing in church), 1909, wood, 134 pcs, 10x12", rpl box $55.00

Untitled (starting at the walk), 1909, wood, 200 pcs, 11x20½", rpl box $75.00

Untitled (winter fashions), English, 1910s, 393 pcs, 11x17", rpl box $100.00

Unwelcome Visitor, AVN Jones (maker)/Delta, 1930s, plywood, 375 pcs, 14x18", rpl box $60.00

Venetian Sunset, Webers Novelty Shop/Ribowsky (artist?), 510 pcs, 16x20", orig box $100.00

Washington & His Birthplace (1732-1932), Adelaide Hiebal (artist), 1930s, plywood, 716 pcs, 17x21", rpl box.......$200.00

Water Gates Haarlem (European town scene), 1928, plywood, 500 pcs, 14x2½", orig box $210.00

Where 'Seconds' Mean 'Minutes' (river action), Philip R Goodwin (artist), 1910s, plywood, 11½x16", rpl box $35.00

White Squadron, McLoughlin Bros, ca 1892, interlocking, 9½x9½", EX+IB...$412.00

Winter Morning in the Country (sleigh scene), Louise Scribner/Currier & Ives, 1950s, 127 pcs, 8½x12", orig box $25.00

Winter on the Spreewald (winter countryside), 1910, plywood, 631 pcs, 24x18", orig box $300.00

York Coach (coaching scene), Victor Venner (English artist), 1909, wood, 14x24", orig box........................$250.00

CHARACTER

Angela Cartwright – America's Little Darling on TV – The Danny Thomas Show, fr-tray, Saalfield #7030, 1962 ....$40.00

Archie, jigsaw, Jaymar, 1960s, malt shop scene, 60 pcs, NMIB... $75.00

Banana Splits, fr-tray, Whitman, boxed set of 4, NM $100.00

Batman & Robin, fr-tray, Watkins-Strathmore #4908-29, 1966, VG+...$65.00

Beatles, jigsaw, Jaymar, 1968, 'Beatles in Pepperland,' medium sz, 100 pcs, sealed, MIB..................................... $140.00

Ben Casey, jigsaw, Milton Bradley, #43, 'The Ordeal is Over,' EXIB...$45.00

Beverly Hillbillies, jigsaw, Jaymar, 1963, shoes, Granny, Elly May & Jeb on staircase, EXIB.....................................$50.00

Buffalo Bill Jr, fr-tray, Built-Rite #1229, 1956 ....$40.00

Captain Kangaroo, fr-tray, Whitman #4446, 1960............$38.00

Captain Kangaroo, jigsaw, Fairchild #4430, 1970s, EXIB..$18.00

Cheyenne Puzzle Set, jigsaw, Milton Bradley #4705-2, set of 3, NMIB $50.00

Dennis the Menace, fr-tray, Whitman, 1960, painting a chair, NM $45.00

Ding Dong School, fr-tray, Whitman, 1953, boat, blk & wht photo of Miss Francis upper right corner, VG+ $20.00

Ding Dong School, fr-tray, Whitman, 1955, jungle animals, VG+...$20.00

Felix the Cat, Bilt-Rite #1229, 1959, fishing scene, NM...$65.00

Flintstones, fr-tray, Warren, 1974, Splat, Dino slips in soapy puddle as Fred tries to give him a bath, NM+ $35.00

Flintstones, fr-tray, Whitman #4434, 1960s $35.00

Goldfinger/James Bond 007, jigsaw, Milton Bradley, 1965, confrontation w/Odd Job by car, 600 pcs, NMIB $50.00

Green Hornet, fr-tray, Whitman, 1966, boxed set of 4, NMIB.. $125.00

Gulliver's Travels, jigsaw, Saalfield, 1930s, set of 3, EXIB . $125.00

Gunsmoke, jigsaw, Whitman #4609, 1969, NMIB $25.00

Hopalong Cassidy, 4 Television Puzzles, inlaid (fr-tray), Milton Bradley, 1950, MIB.. $150.00

Howdy Doody, fr-tray, Whitman #4428, 1953, VG+.........$40.00

Huckleberry Hound Puzzles (4), jigsaw, Milton Bradley/Hanna-Barbera, 1960, boxed set of 4, 14x10½" ea, EXIB...........$40.00

Puzzles, Character
Banana Splits, frame-tray, Whitman #4534, 1969, North Pole, NM, $50.00. (Photo courtesy www.gasolinealleyantiques.com)

Puzzles, Character
Batman, frame-tray, Whitman #4518, 1966, EX+, $25.00. (Photo courtesy www.gasolinealleyantiques.com)

Puzzles, Character
Buck Rogers in the 25th Century, frame-tray, Craft Industries of Chicago, 1945, set of three, G+IB, $85.00. (Photo courtesy Lloyd Ralston Gallery on LiveAuctioneers.com)

Puzzles, Character
• • • • • • • • • • • • • • •
Fantastic Four, frame-tray, Whitman #4559, 1968, $30.00. (Photo courtesy www.gasolinealleyantiques.com)

Puzzles, Character
• • • • • • • • • • • • • • •
Pussy Cat Puzzle Box, set of three litho puzzles in box, 15½x13", $330.00. (Photo courtesy Noel Barrett Antiques & Auctions Ltd.)

Puzzles, Character
• • • • • • • • • • • • • • •
Mickey Mouse Club, Whitman #4428, County Fair, 1950s, NM+, $45.00. (Photo courtesy www.gasolinealley antiques.com)

Puzzles, Character
• • • • • • • • • • • • • • •
Peter Pan Picture Puzzles, Whitman, set of six, EX+IB, $125.00. (Photo courtesy www.gasolinealley antiques.com)

Puzzles, Character
• • • • • • • • • • • • • • •
Sleeping Beauty, frame-tray, Whitman, 1958, $35.00. (Photo courtesy www.gasolinealley antiques.com)

Katzenjammer Kids, jigsaw, Featured Funnies, 1930s, 14x10", EXIB $80.00

Lamb Chop, fr-tray, Golden #8206, 1993, 8x11" $6.00

Lone Ranger & Tonto, jigsaw, American Publishing, 1974, M (M sealed canister) $22.00

Lone Ranger Picture Puzzles, Whitman #3902, set of 2, NMIB $125.00

Marvel Superheroes, jigsaw, Milton Bradley, 1967, 100 pcs, EXIB $50.00

Masters of the Universe, jigsaw, Monstrous Meeting, 1984, 100 pcs, EXIB $8.00

My Little Pony, jigsaw, Milton Bradley #4576-10, 1989, EXIB $8.00

Pinocchio Picture Puzzles, Whitman, 1939, set of 2, 10x8½", NMIB $50.00

Rescuers, jigsaw, Golden, 200 pcs, NMIB $6.00

Rin Tin Tin, fr-tray, Whitman #4128, 1950s, EX+ $45.00

Rocky the Flying Squirrel, fr-tray, Whitman, 1960, Bullwinkle balancing Rocky & aliens Gidney & Cloyd on feet, NM $50.00

Rootie (Kazootie) Wins the Soap Box Race..., fr-tray, Fairchild Corp, 1940s, 10x14" $30.00

Roy Rogers, fr-tray, Artcraft Series 1004, photo image of Marx Double Bar ranch playset w/figures, horses & dogs $35.00

Roy Rogers, fr-tray, Whitman #4427, VG+ $40.00

Santa Claus Puzzle Box, jigsaw, Milton Bradley, 1890s-1900, 3 complete 9x13" puzzles, NM (VG+ box) $325.00

Sgt Preston, jigsaw, Milton Bradley #4828, NMIB $35.00

Smurfs, jigsaw, Milton Bradley, 1983, toboggan scene, EX+IB $8.50

Smurfs, jigsaw, Peyo, 1988, camping scene, EXIB $8.00

Snow White, picture cubes, paper on wood, 20 cubes, complete picture measures 7½x6", VG+IB (wood box) $125.00

Superman, fr-tray, Whitman, 1966, various scenes, EX+, ea.. $30.00

Superman Picture Puzzle, jigsaw, Saalfield, 1940, 'Superman Over the City,' unused, NM (NM box) $500.00

Superman Picture Puzzle, jigsaw, Saalfield, 1940, 'Superman Springs into Action,' NM (G+ box) $400.00

Puzzles,
Character
• • • • • • • •
Top Cat, frame-
tray, Whitman,
#4457, 1961,
NM+, $50.00.
(Photo courtesy www.gasoline
alleyantiques.com)

Puzzles,
Character
• • • • • • • •
Wacky Races,
Whitman, 1969,
One Way, $35.00.
(Photo courtesy www.gasoline
alleyantiques.com)

Superman the Man of Tomorrow, jigsaw, Saalfield, 1940, 300 pcs, EX+IB.. $200.00
Tales of Wells Fargo, fr-tray, Whitman #4427, 1958..........$40.00
Wagon Train, fr-tray, Whitman, 1958, Seth Adams & Flint McCulloch w/guns drawn behind corral fence, EX+ $35.00

Wizard of Oz, fr-tray, Jaymar, 1960s, NM+........................$25.00
Wizard of Oz, jigsaw, Jaymar, 1970s, Departure from Oz, 19x19", EXIB $55.00
Wyatt Earp, fr-tray, Whitman #4427, 1958, NM $45.00
Zorro, fr-tray, Whitman, 1957, Zorro standing by tree, 15x11½", NM $40.00

• **Radios, Novelty** •

Many novelty radios are made to resemble a commercial product box or can, and with the crossover interest into the advertising field, some of the more collectible, even though of recent vintage, are often seen carrying very respectible price tags. Likenesses of famous personalities such as Elvis or characters like Charlie Tuna house transistors in cases made of plastic that scarcely hint at their actual function. Others represent items ranging from baseball caps to Cadillacs. To learn more about this subject, we recommend *Collector's Guide to Novelty Radios, Book I* and *Book II* by Marty Bunis and Robert F. Breed.

Alf, rectangular w/image on front, NMIP $75.00
Ball Form, gr plastic, National Panasonic Model R705, 6 transistors, b/o, 1970s, M $50.00
Batman, Batman figure applied to red oval on bl building, plastic, 6½x5½", Vanity Fair, 1978, NM $175.00

Bert & Ernie, half-figures on figure-8 base w/Sesame Street label, AM, 7", NM $25.00
Bert & Ernie, vaudeville act on stage, AM, 7", NM+........$25.00
Big Bird, head form w/red & wht bow tie, w/strap & belt clip, Radio Shack, 1990, MIB..$90.00
Big Bird, in nest w/Sesame Street sign emb on side, yel strap, AM, 8", NM $25.00
Big Bird, seated on oval base leaning on vintage 'wooden' radio, name on base, AM-FM, 8x7", NM $30.00
Bugs Bunny, w/carrot on round grassy mound, AM, Janex/Sears, 1970s, NM...$30.00
Bullwinkle, 1969, 12", NM... $150.00
Cap'n Crunch, Isis, model #39, NM...................................$40.00
Casper the Friendly Ghost, Harvey Cartoons, Sutton, 1972, M $50.00
Champion Spark Plugs, plastic, Japan, 1950-60s, NM.... $225.00
Charlie Brown, Snoopy & Woodstock, flat decaled plastic figures w/strap, AM, Determined, 1970s, NM $35.00
Charlie McCarthy, Bakelite case w/figure of Charlie seated w/legs crossed & holding mike on front, Majestic, 6x7x5", EX..$650.00
Charlie the Tuna, figural, MIB $30.00
Cheeseburger, w/strap, 5" dia, NM+..................................$20.00
Donnie & Marie, red, 1977, NM.......................................$30.00
Elvis, doll figure singing into microphone on blk base w/name & birth/death dates, UNIC, M...$50.00
Ernie the Keebler Elf, NM+... $50.00
Fonz Jukebox, AM, VG $30.00

Radios, Novelty
• • • • • • • •
B.A. Baracus (Mr. T), Baracus flexing muscles, AM, MIB, $50.00. (Photo courtesy www.gasolinealleyantiques.com)

Radios,
Novelty
• • • • • • • •
Batman, Hong Kong, 1973, NM, $65.00.
(Photo courtesy www.gasolinealley antiques.com)

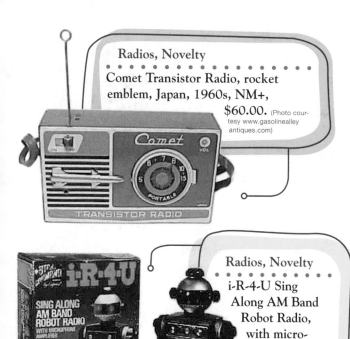

Radios, Novelty

Comet Transistor Radio, rocket emblem, Japan, 1960s, NM+, $60.00. (Photo courtesy www.gasolinealleyantiques.com)

Radios, Novelty

Oscar the Grouch, Concept 2000, 1976, NMIB, $50.00. (Photo courtesy www.gasolinealleyantiques.com)

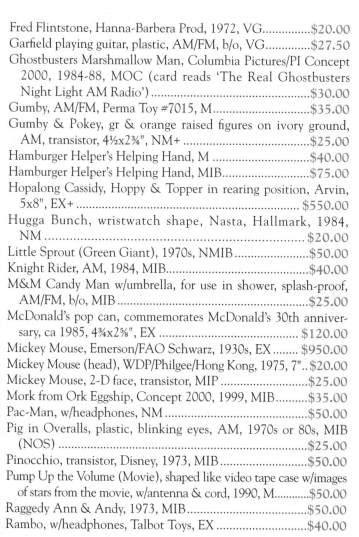

Radios, Novelty

i-R-4-U Sing Along AM Band Robot Radio, with microphone, MIB, $150.00. (Photo courtesy www.gasolinealleyantiques.com)

Radios, Novelty

Planters Cocktail Peanuts Can, NM, $85.00. (Photo courtesy www.gasolinealleyantiques.com)

Radios, Novelty

Punchy, Hawaiian Punch figure, AM/FM, NM+, $50.00. (Photo courtesy www.gasolinealleyantiques.com)

Radios, Novelty

Rocket Radio, Miniman #MG306 (Pioneer), crystal, MIB, $150.00. (Photo courtesy www.gasolinealleyantiques.com)

Fred Flintstone, Hanna-Barbera Prod, 1972, VG..............$20.00
Garfield playing guitar, plastic, AM/FM, b/o, VG..............$27.50
Ghostbusters Marshmallow Man, Columbia Pictures/PI Concept 2000, 1984-88, MOC (card reads 'The Real Ghostbusters Night Light AM Radio')..$30.00
Gumby, AM/FM, Perma Toy #7015, M...........................$35.00
Gumby & Pokey, gr & orange raised figures on ivory ground, AM, transistor, 4½x2¾", NM+ $25.00
Hamburger Helper's Helping Hand, M $40.00
Hamburger Helper's Helping Hand, MIB.........................$75.00
Hopalong Cassidy, Hoppy & Topper in rearing position, Arvin, 5x8", EX+ $550.00
Hugga Bunch, wristwatch shape, Nasta, Hallmark, 1984, NM $20.00
Little Sprout (Green Giant), 1970s, NMIB.......................$50.00
Knight Rider, AM, 1984, MIB......................................$40.00
M&M Candy Man w/umbrella, for use in shower, splash-proof, AM/FM, b/o, MIB $25.00
McDonald's pop can, commemorates McDonald's 30th anniversary, ca 1985, 4¾x2⅝", EX $120.00
Mickey Mouse, Emerson/FAO Schwarz, 1930s, EX........ $950.00
Mickey Mouse (head), WDP/Philgee/Hong Kong, 1975, 7"..$20.00
Mickey Mouse, 2-D face, transistor, MIP $25.00
Mork from Ork Eggship, Concept 2000, 1999, MIB..........$35.00
Pac-Man, w/headphones, NM $50.00
Pig in Overalls, plastic, blinking eyes, AM, 1970s or 80s, MIB (NOS) $25.00
Pinocchio, transistor, Disney, 1973, MIB.........................$50.00
Pump Up the Volume (Movie), shaped like video tape case w/images of stars from the movie, w/antenna & cord, 1990, M...........$50.00
Raggedy Ann & Andy, 1973, MIB.................................$50.00
Rambo, w/headphones, Talbot Toys, EX $40.00

Rocket Radio, crystal, Miniman #MG304, MIB............ $150.00
Rocket Radio, crystal, Miniman #MG305, MIB............ $150.00
Sesame Street, characters in gr stage box draped w/yel swag, oblong dial on front, vinyl w/plastic, electric, 1970s, EX $30.00
Snoopy Doghouse, plastic, Determined, 1970s, 6x4", NMIB. $55.00
Snoopy, seated, 2-D, wht w/blk outline detail, AM, w/earplugs, 1970s, NMIB $50.00

Radios, Novelty
. . . .
Smurf, head form, with strap, 1982, EX, $35.00. (Photo courtesy www. gasolinealleyantiques.com)

Radios, Novelty
. . . .
Snow White and the Seven Dwarfs, Emerson, 1930s, 8x11", EX, $785.00. (Photo courtesy Morphy Auctions on LiveAuctioneers.com)

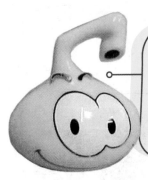

Radios, Novelty
. . . .
Snork, Allstar Seaworthy, yellow plastic, from the Hanna-Barbera cartoon series, Wallace Berrie, 1984, NM, $40.00. (Photo courtesy www.gasoline alleyantiques.com)

Space Embassador, flying saucer shape, transistor, M.........$75.00
Stand By Me (Movie) Locomotive, AM, NMIB $80.00
Tony the Tiger, standing, 2-D, Kellogg's, 1980, MIB $50.00
Transformers Wrist Radio, AM, MIB...............................$25.00
Vending machine, Jack Russell (Japan) Co Ltd, transistors, 1960s.. $120.00
Yogi Bear, head form, NBC, NM+.....................................$25.00

Ramp Walkers

Ramp walkers date back to at least 1873 when Ives produced two versions of a cast-iron elephant walker. Wood and composition ramp walkers were made in Czechoslovakia and the U.S.A. from the 1930s through the 1950s. The most common were made by John Wilson of Pennsylvania and were sold worldwide. These became known as 'Wilson Walkies.' Most are two-legged and stand approximately 4½" tall. While some of the Wilson Walkies were made of a composite material with wood legs (for instance, Donald, Wimpy, Popeye, and Olive Oyl), most are made with cardboard thread-cone bodies with wood legs and head. The walkers made in Czechoslovakia are similar but they are generally made of wood.

Plastic ramp walkers were primarily manufactured by the Louis Marx Co. and were made from the early 1950s through the mid-1960s. The majority were produced in Hong Kong, but some were made in the United States and sold under the Marx logo or by the Charmore Co., which was a subsidiary of the Marx Co. Some walkers are still being produced today as fast-food premiums.

The three common sizes are small, about 1½x2"; medium, about 2¾x3"; and large, about 4x5". Most of the small walkers are unpainted while the medium or large sizes were either spray painted or painted by hand. Several of the walking toys were sold with wooden, plastic, or colorful lithographed tin ramps.

Unless another manufacturer is noted within the descriptions, all of the following Disney ramp walkers were made by the Marx company.

Advisor: Randy Welch

ADVERTISING

Captain Flint, Long John Silver's, 1989, w/plastic coin weight...$15.00
Choo-Choo Cherry, Funny Face Drink Mix, w/plastic coin weight..$60.00
Flash Turtle, Long John Silver's, 1989, w/plastic coin weight...$15.00
Goofy Grape, Funny Face Drink Mix, w/plastic coin weight . $60.00
Quinn Penguin, Long John Silver's, 1989, w/plastic coin weight...$15.00
Root'n Toot'n Raspberry, Funny Face Drink Mix, w/plastic coin weight...$60.00
Sylvia Dinosaur, Long John Silver's, 1989, lavender & pk, w/ plastic coin weight..$15.00

CZECHOSLOVAKIAN

Chicago World's Fair (1933), wooden, G...................... $100.00
Dog...$30.00

Ramp Walkers, Czechoslovakian
. . . .
Man with Beard, $40.00; Penguin, $40.00; Monkey, $45.00; Cow, $35.00; Dutch Girl, $60.00. (Photo courtesy Randy Welch)

Ramp Walkers,
Czechoslovakian
• • • • • • • • • • • • • • •
Bird, large, store display,
$200.00; Bird, small,
$35.00. (Photo courtesy Randy Welch)

Ramp Walkers,
Czechoslovakian
• • • • • • • • • • • • •
Sailor, $40.00. (Photo courtesy
www.gasolinealleyantiques.com)

Ramp Walkers,
Disney
• • • • • • • • • • • • •
Mad Hatter with
March Hare, $50.00.
(Photo courtesy www.gasolinealley
antiques.com)

Ramp Walkers,
Disney
• • • • • • • • • • • • •
Mickey Mouse and Min-
nie Mouse, with basket
of food, $40.00. (Photo
courtesy Randy Welch)

Man w/Carved Wood Hat $45.00
Pig $40.00
Policeman $60.00

DISNEY

Big Bad Wolf & Mason Pig...$50.00
Donald Duck Pulling Nephews in Wagon.........................$35.00

Ramp Walkers, Disney
• •
Big Bad Wolf & Three Little Pigs, $150.00.
(Photo courtesy Randy Welch)

Donald Duck Pushing Wheelbarrow, plastic w/metal legs, sm.$25.00
Donald's Trio, France, Huey, Louie & Dewey dressed as Indian
    Chief, cowboy & 1 carrying flowers $150.00
Fiddler & Fifer Pigs $50.00
Figaro the Cat w/Ball $30.00
Goofy, riding hippo $45.00
Jiminy Cricket, w/cello $30.00
Mickey Mouse & Donald Duck Riding Alligator $40.00
Mickey Mouse & Minnie Mouse, plastic w/metal legs, sm.$40.00
Mickey Mouse & Pluto Hunting $40.00
Minnie Mouse Pushing Baby Stroller...............................$35.00
Pluto, plastic w/metal legs, sm $35.00

HANNA-BARBERA, KING FEATURES & OTHER CHARACTERS BY MARX

Astro $150.00
Astro & George Jetson $75.00
Bonnie Braids' Nursemaid $50.00
Chilly Willy, penguin on sled $25.00

Ramp Walkers,
Disney
• • • • • • • • • • • • •
Donald Duck and Goofy
Riding Go-Cart, $40.00.
(Photo courtesy www.gasolinealleyantiques.
com)

Ramp Walkers,
Hanna-Barbera
• • • • • • • • • • • • •
Astro & Rosey,
$75.00. (Photo courtesy
Randy Welch)

Ramp Walkers, Hanna-Barbera

Fred and Wilma Flintstone on Dino, $60.00. (Photo courtesy Randy Welch)

Ramp Walkers, Hanna-Barbera

Top Cat & Benny, $65.00. (Photo courtesy Randy Welch)

Ramp Walkers, King Features

Popeye Pushing Spinach Can Wheelbarrow, $30.00; Popeye & Wimpy, heads on springs, MIB, $85.00; Popeye, Irwin, celluloid, large, $60.00. (Photo courtesy Randy Welch)

Fred Flintstone & Barney Rubble $40.00
Hap & Hop Soldiers $25.00
Little King & Guard $60.00
Santa, w/gold sack...$45.00
Santa, w/wht sack $40.00
Santa, w/yel sack $40.00
Santa & Mrs Claus, faces on both sides $50.00
Santa & Snowman, faces on both sides...............................$50.00
Spark Plug $200.00
Yogi Bear & Huckleberry Hound...$50.00

MARX ANIMALS WITH RIDERS SERIES

Ankylosaurus w/Clown...$40.00
Bison w/Native..$40.00

Brontosaurus w/Monkey $40.00
Hippo w/Native $40.00
Lion w/Clown $40.00
Stegosaurus w/Black Caveman $40.00
Triceratops w/Native...$40.00
Zebra w/Native..$40.00

PLASTIC

Baby Walk-A-Way, lg $40.00
Bear $20.00
Boy & Girl Dancing...$45.00
Bull...$20.00
Bunny on Back of Dog..$50.00
Bunny Pushing Cart...$60.00
Camel w/2 Humps, head bobs $20.00
Chinese Men w/Duck in Basket $30.00
Chipmunks Carrying Acorns...$35.00
Chipmunks Marching Band w/Drum & Horn $35.00
Cow, w/metal legs, sm $20.00
Cowboy on Horse, w/metal legs, sm $30.00
Dachshund $20.00
Dairy Cow $20.00
Dog, Pluto look-alike w/metal legs, sm................................$20.00
Double Walking Doll, boy behind girl, lg.............................$60.00
Duck...$20.00
Dutch Boy & Girl $40.00
Elephant, w/metal legs, sm..$30.00
Farmer Pushing Wheelbarrow $30.00
Frontiersman w/Dog...$95.00
Goat $20.00
Horse, circus style $20.00
Horse, lg $30.00
Horse, yel w/rubber ears & string tail, lg $30.00
Horse w/English Rider, lg..$50.00
Indian Woman Pulling Baby on Travois $95.00
Mama Duck w/3 Ducklings..$35.00

Ramp Walkers, Plastic

Chicks Carrying Easter Egg, $35.00. (Photo courtesy Randy Welch)

Ramp Walkers, Plastic

Elephant, $20.00. (Photo courtesy www.gasoline alleyantiques.com)

Ramp Walkers, Plastic

Firemen, $35.00.
(Photo courtesy Randy Welch)

Ramp Walkers, Plastic

Kangaroo with Joey in Pouch, $30.00. (Photo courtesy www.gasolinealleyantiques.com)

Ramp Walkers, Plastic

Pumpkin Head Man and Woman, faces both sides, $100.00. (Photo courtesy Randy Welch)

Tin Man Robot Pushing Cart $150.00
Walking Baby, in Canadian Mountie uniform, lg $50.00
Walking Baby, w/moving eyes & cloth dress, lg $40.00
Wiz Walker Milking Cow, Charmore, lg $40.00

WILSON

Clown.. $30.00
Elephant.. $30.00
Eskimo $100.00
Indian Chief.. $70.00
Little Red Riding Hood $40.00
Mammy $40.00
Nurse $30.00
Penguin $25.00
Pig $40.00
Popeye $200.00
Rabbit.. $75.00
Sailor $30.00
Santa Claus $90.00
Soldier $30.00

Ramp Walkers, Wilson

Donald Duck, $175.00; Pinnochio, $200.00. (Photo courtesy Randy Welch)

Ramp Walkers, Wilson

Olive Oyl, $175.00; Wimpy, $175.00. (Photo courtesy Randy Welch)

Marty's Market Lady Pushing Shopping Cart $65.00
Mexican Cowboy on Horse, w/metal legs, sm $30.00
Milking Cow, lg.. $40.00
Mother Goose $45.00
Nursemaid Pushing Baby Stroller $20.00
Pig $20.00
Pigs, 2 carrying 1 in basket $40.00
Reindeer.. $45.00
Slugger the Walking Bat Boy, w/ramp & box $250.00
Teeny Toddler, walking baby girl, Dolls Inc, lg $40.00

Records

Most of the records listed here are related to TV shows, cartoons, and movies, and are specifically geared toward children. The more successful, the more collectible the record. Condition is critical as well, and unless the record is excellent or better, its value is lowered very dramatically. The presence of the original sleeve or cover is crucial to establishing collectibility.

33⅓ RPM

Addams Family (Original Music), RCA Victor #LPM-3421, EX (EX sleeve) $75.00
Adventures of Batman & Robin, Leo/MGM, 1966, EX (EX sleeve)... $30.00

Alice in Wonderland Starring Magilla Gorilla, Columbia, 1977, M (EX sleeve)... $60.00
At Home with the Munsters, Golden #LP139, 1960s, EX (EX sleeve)... $50.00

Records, 33⅓ RPM

The Jetsons/First Family on the Moon, HBR, #HLP 2037, 1965, EX (VG sleeve), $65.00. (Photo courtesy www.gasolinealley antiques.com)

Records, 33⅓ RPM

Superman, Power #8156, NM (EX+ sleeve), $20.00. (Photo courtesy www.gasoline alleyantiques.com)

Records, 33⅓ RPM

John Denver & The Muppets, A Christmas Together, RCA #AFL3451, 1979, VG (EX+ sleeve), $6.00.

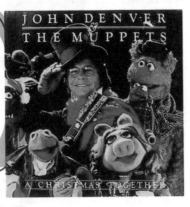

Records, 33⅓ RPM

War of the Worlds, Orson Wells broadcast, LPA #2355, Audio Rarities, NM (NM sleeve), $40.00. (Photo courtesy www.gasolinealley antiques.com)

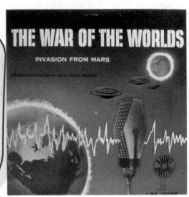

Records, 33⅓ RPM

Rocky & His Friends, Golden #LP64, 1961, EX (EX sleeve), $75.00. (Photo courtesy www. gasolinealley antiques.com)

Records, 33⅓ RPM

You're a Good Man, Charlie Brown, MGM, #A1E90C, EX (VG+ sleeve), $18.00. (Photo courtesy www.gasolinealleyantiques. com)

Babes in Toyland, Disneyland #ST3910, 1961, w/10-pg storybook $15.00

Batman/The Catwoman's Revenge, Power Records 2306, 1975, 7", M (sealed sleeve) $55.00

Car 54 Where Are You?, Golden Records, 1963, EX (EX sleeve) $35.00

Charlie Brown's All-Stars, #2602, 1978, NM (EX+ sleeve)... $30.00

Cinderella, Disneyland #ST3908, 1962, w/10-pg storybook, VG+ (EX sleeve) $15.00

Don Adams, Get Smart, United Artist, 1960s, very scarce, EX (NM sleeve) $75.00

Dr Seuss Presents Yertle the Turtle, RCA/Stereo, 1960s, EX (EX sleeve).. $15.00

Fonzie Favorites, Precision Records #TVLP177602R, 1976, Canadian issue only, EX+ (EX+ sleeve) $35.00

Gizmo & the Gremlins/Story #2, Warner, 1984, w/16-pg story book, M (NM sleeve)....................................... $18.00

Huckleberry Hound & the Great Kellogg's TV Show, Colpix, 1960, EX (EX sleeve) $35.00

Lady & the Tramp, Decca, 1955, EX (EX sleeve) $40.00

Let's All Sing with the Chipmunks, Liberty #LRP3132, 1959, VG+ (VG sleeve).. $8.00

Mary Poppins, RCA Victor #CSO111, 1964, orig soundtrack, VG+ (EX jacket).. $10.00

Merry Merry Merry Christmas from Captain Kangaroo, NM (NM sleeve) $75.00

Mickey Mouse Club, 1975, VG+ (G sleeve)................... $10.00

Mister Ed, 1962, soundtrack, EX (EX sleeve) $40.00

Nancy — Listen Laugh & Learn, Kid Stuff #KSS5020, 1982, NM (EX+ sleeve).. $45.00

Peter Pan, Disneyland #ST3910, 1962, w/10-pg storybook, EX (EX sleeve) $15.00

Popeye & Friends, Merry Records, 1980s, NM+ (EX sleeve) $20.00

Precious Pup & Granny Sweet in Hot Rod Granny, HBR #HLP2039, 1965, VG (G sleeve) $25.00

Reluctant Dragon Starring Touché Turtle & Dum-Dum, 1965, EX (EX sleeve) $100.00

Roger Ramjet & the American Eagles, RCA, 1966, EX (EX
    sleeve)..$40.00

Saggy Baggy Elephant, Little Golden Book & Record #201,
    NM+..$18.00

Snoopy & His Friends the Royal Guardsmen, Laurie #SLP2042,
    Canadian, EX (EX+ sleeve)........................$20.00

Songs From Annette/Walt Disney Serials, Disneyland #MM24,
    NM (EX sleeve)..$65.00

Songs of the Pogo, AA Records #AR2, 1956, 12", EX+ (EX
    sleeve)..$150.00

Tammy's Sing Along Party, Little World Records/Ideal, 1965, EX
    (VG sleeve)..$35.00

Thumbelina/Little Golden Book & Record, Disneyland #206,
    1976, NM (NM sleeve)..............................$18.00

Treasure Island Starring Sinbad Jr, HBR #HLP2039, 1965, VG
    (VG sleeve)..$25.00

Twelve Days of Christmas with the Chipmunks, Pickwick
    Records, 1980, VG (w/sleeve) $8.00

Wonder Woman, Peter Pan, 1977, EX (EX sleeve) $25.00

45 RPM

A Hap-Hap-Happy Christmas from Yogi Bear, Golden #R50, EX
    (EX sleeve) $40.00

Banana Splits/Doin' the Banana Splits & I Enjoy Being a Boy,
    Kellogg's premium, 1969, EX (EX sleeve)........$45.00

Bimbo & Punchy the Clown, Cricket #C754, VG (VG
    sleeve) $10.00

Bozo Under the Sea, Capitol #EAXF3031, w/38-pg illustrated
    story, EX (EX sleeve)................................$35.00

Campaign Songs of Magilla Gorilla & Yogi Bear, Golden #768,
    1964, VG+ (EX sleeve)..............................$35.00

Casper the Friendly Ghost/Little Audrey Says, Little Golden,
    1960s, EX (EX sleeve)................................$30.00

Chipmunk Fun with Chip 'N Dale, Disneyland #LG-704, EX
    (EX sleeve)..$20.00

Felix the Cat, Cricket Records, 1958, EX (EX sleeve) $20.00

Flintstones Goldie Rocks & the Three Bearosauruses, HBR
    #7021, scarce, EX+ (EX+ sleeve)................$50.00

Flipper the King of the Sea, MGM, 1960s, EX (EX sleeve) ..$20.00

Frosty the Snowman, Golden #69, EX (VG sleeve) $10.00

Here Come the Dukes of Hazzard, Kid Stuff #KSR954, 1983,
    w/16-pg storybook, unused, scarce, M (NM+ sleeve).....$40.00

HR Pufnstuf, Capitol, Kellogg's mail-in premiums, 1969, EX (EX
    sleeve)..$65.00

Huck, Yogi & Quick Draw Safety Song #674, 1961, M (NM+ in
    sleeve)..$35.00

Huckleberry Hound Tells the Stories of Uncle Remus, HBR
    #7030, scarce, EX+ (EX+ sleeve)................$50.00

Johnny Appleseed, RCA Victor #EYA6, 1949, Dennis Day, EX
    (VG+ sleeve)..$25.00

King Leonardo & His Short Subjects, Golden, 1961, EX (EX
    sleeve)..$20.00

Laurel & Hardy Chiller Diller Thriller, Peter Pan, 1962, EX (EX
    sleeve)..$15.00

Lone Ranger Theme/Hi-Yo Silver Hi-Yo, Golden #FF521, 1958,
    EX (EX sleeve) $45.00

Maverick, Golden #498, 1958, NM (NM sleeve)..............$45.00

Mickey Mouse Club Pledge, Golden #D223, 1962, EX (NM
    sleeve)..$32.00

Popeye on Parade/Strike Me Pink, Cricket, 1950s, NM+ (EX
    jacket)..$35.00

Quick Draw's A-Comin' (And Baba Looey Too) to Clean Up
    Your Town, Golden #646, 1961, VG+ (EX sleeve)........$35.00

Roy Rogers Had a Ranch, Golden, 1950s, EX (EX sleeve).$45.00

Ruff & Reddy & Professor Gizmo, Golden #558, EX+ (EX+
    sleeve)..$38.00

Sleeping Beauty Once Upon a Dream, Golden #480, EX (EX
    sleeve)..$30.00

Smokey Bear, Peter Pan, NM (EX sleeve) $20.00

Songs from Robin Hood Starring Top Cat, HBR #7038, EX+
    (EX+ sleeve)..$55.00

Songs of the Jetsons/Push Button Blues & Rama Rama Zoom,
    Golden #755, EX (EX sleeve)....................$50.00

Three Little Pigs Sing Polly Wolly Doodle & Alouette, Disney-
    land #LG710, 1962, NM (NM sleeve) $15.00

Tom & Jerry & the Fire Engine, MGM #SK19, M (EX+ sleeve).$40.00

Tom Terrific!, 1959, 3 on 1, rare, NM (NM sleeve)........$100.00

Tweety's Puddy Tat Twouble, Capitol #CBXF-31-2, 2-record set
    w/20-pg story book, EX (EX+ sleeve) $75.00

Wagon Train, Golden, 1950s, EX (EX sleeve) $25.00

War of the Worlds, 1978, EX (EX sleeve) $10.00

Woody Woodpecker & His Friends Andy Panda & Chilly Willy,
    Golden #EP620, M (EX+ sleeve)................$35.00

Yogi Bears Friends, Golden #EP654, 1961, NM (EX+ sleeve)..$50.00

78 RPM PICTURE AND NON-PICTURE

Absent Minded Professor, Golden #648, EX (EX sleeve) ..$25.00

Adventures of Mighty Mouse, Rocking Horse, 1957, EX (w/
    sleeve)..$15.00

Alice in Wonderland Musical Story, Peter Pan #565, EX (EX sleeve $15.00

Animal Supermarket/It's Fun to Go Shopping, CRG #9004, EX+ (EX sleeve) $10.00

Annie Oakley Sings Ten Gallon Hat & I Gotta Crow, Golden, 1950s, EX+ (EX sleeve)....................$10.00

Big Rock Candy Mountain, CRD #509, Tom Glazer, VG+ (EX sleeve)..$8.00

Bongo Fun & Fancy Free, Columbia Records #MJ-41, 1940s, 3 record set, G (G jacket) $35.00

Bozo Under the Sea, Capitol, 1950, w/20-pg booklet, EX (EX sleeve)...$50.00

Bugs Bunny & the Grow-Small Juice, Capitol, 1950s, NM.$75.00

Bugs Bunny & the Tortoise, Capitol, 1949, EX (EX sleeve) ..$30.00

Bugs Bunny Railroad Engineer & Yosemite Sam Hold-Up Man, Golden #R249, EX (EX sleeve) $38.00

Casper the Friendly Ghost & Little Audrey Says, Golden, 1959, EX (EX sleeve) $15.00

Cinderella Work Song (As Sung in the Movie), Golden #RD10, M (NM sleeve)...$35.00

Cowabonga & Big Chief (Howdy Doody), Little Golden Record #R221, NM (NM sleeve) $50.00

Davy Crockett Be Sure You're Right (Davy's Motto), Golden #D213, EX (EX sleeve) $30.00

Dennis the Menace, Golden #534, 1959, EX+ (EX sleeve) $32.00

Disneyland & When You Wish Upon a Star, Golden #D194, EX (EX sleeve) $30.00

Donald Duck Presents Quack Quack Quack, Golden #D251, NM (NM sleeve)...$25.00

Elmer Elephant Capitol, Playtime, 1954, NM (EX sleeve)...$18.00

Flintstones Dino the Dino, Golden #739, 1963, EX..........$35.00

Flipper the Fabulous Dolphin, Golden #1105, EX+ (EX+ sleeve) $35.00

Foodini Goes a Huntin', Caravan, 1949, EX (EX sleeve)..$35.00

Froggy the Gremlin, Capitol, 1947, VG (VG sleeve)........$40.00

Gabby Hayes 1001 Western Nights, RCA #Y420, EX (EX sleeve)..$35.00

Goofy the Toreador, Golden #D151:25, EX (EX+ sleeve).$35.00

Hey Diddle Diddle, Peter Pan, 1948, EX (EX sleeve)........$30.00

Howdy Doody's Laughing Circus, RCA Victor, 1950, EX (EX sleeve)...$25.00

Huckleberry Hound Presents Pixie & Dixie/Iddy Biddy Buddy, Golden #610, 1960, EX (VG sleeve)..............................$30.00

It's Howdy Doody Time, RCA Victor, 1951, EX (EX sleeve) ..$75.00

Little Lulu & Her Magic Tricks, Golden, 1954, EX (EX sleeve) $25.00

Lone Ranger — He Saves the Booneville Gold, Decca, 1952, No 6 in series, EX (EX sleeve) $75.00

March from Peter & the Wolf/Jing-A-Ling, Golden #R65A, EX (EX sleeve)..$25.00

Mickey & the Beanstalk, Capitol, 1948, complete w/booklet, EX (EX sleeve)..$30.00

Mouseketunes, Disneyland Records, 1955, EX (EX sleeve) ..$30.00

Mr Jinks & Boo Boo Bear, Golden #591, 1959, NM (NM sleeve) $35.00

Mr Mickey Mouse/Mickey's New Car, Golden #RD7:25, VG (EX sleeve)...$25.00

Old Yeller Title Song, Golden #D390, NM (NM sleeve)..$25.00

Peter Pan The Second Star to the Right/March of the Lost Boys, Golden #RD36, 1952, EX (EX+ sleeve) $30.00

Pinocchio, RCA Victor #349, 1940, VG (VG sleeve) $65.00

Pinocchio When You Wish Upon a Star, Golden #675, EX (NM sleeve)..$25.00

Popeye the Sailor Man & Blow Me Down, Golden #R60, VG (VG sleeve) $20.00

Raggedy Ann & the Magic Book, Decca #K55, 1952, very scarce, EX (NM sleeve) $100.00

Raggedy Ann's Sunny Songs, RCA, 1933, 3-record set, EX (EX sleeve)..$150.00

Rescue in Space with Tom Corbett Space Cadet, RCA Victor Y#450, 1952, NM (EX sleeve) $100.00

Rootie Kazootie & Polka Dottie Polka, Golden #R98, 1952, EX+ (EX sleeve) $50.00

Ruff & Reddy, Golden, 1959, EX+ (EX sleeve) $15.00

Sleeping Beauty I Wonder, Golden #489, EX+ (EX+ sleeve)... $30.00

Songs of the Flintstones, Golden, 1961, EX (w/sleeve) $25.00

Three Little Pigs, Capitol #DXB3013, 1949, Don Winslow, EX (EX album) $75.00

Top Cat Theme Song, Golden #689, 1962, EX (EX sleeve). $35.00

Tweetie Pie, Capitol, EX (EX sleeve) $25.00

Wagon Train & Square Dance, Golden #R495, NM (EX sleeve) $40.00

Walt Disney's Song of Fantasyland, Golden #D300, EX+ (EX+ sleeve) $35.00

Wild Bill Hickok, Peter Pan #480, unused, M (M sleeve). $25.00

Willie the Whale, Columbia, 1946, 3 records, EX (w/ sleeve) $30.00

Wizard of Oz, Golden #R50, EX (EX sleeve) $35.00

Woody Woodpecker Song/Woodpecker Dance, Golden #R58, EX (EX sleeve) $25.00

Yankee Doodle Mickey, Disneyland, 1980, EX (EX sleeve).. $12.00

Yogi Bear Introduces Loopy de Loop/Let's Have a Song Yogi Bear!, Golden #592, 1961, M (NM sleeve) $35.00

KIDDIE PICTURE DISKS

Listed here is a representative sampling of kiddie picture disks that were produced through the 1940s. Most are 6" to 7" in diameter and are made of cardboard with plastic-laminated grooves. They are very colorful and seldom seen with original sleeves. Value ranges are for items in very good to near-mint condition. Ultimately, the value of any collectible is what a buyer is willing to pay, and prices tend to fluctuate. Our values are for records only (no sleeves except where noted). Unlike other records, the value of a picture disk is not diminished if there is no original sleeve.

Alice in Wonderland, Toy Toon Records, 1952 .... $15.00

Bible Storytime, Standard Publishing, 78 rpm, 1948, 7" $10.00

A Birthday Song to You, Voco #35215, 5" sq. $20.00

Cinderella Toy Toon Records, 1952 .... $15.00

Disneyland Main Street Electrical Parade, 1973, 7" $60.00

Flash Gordon 'City of the Sea Caves' Part 1, Record Guild of America/King Features, 1948, EX $50.00

Gilbert & Sullivan Series, Picture Tone Record Co, 1948, 78 rpm, rare, 6½", EX $40.00

Greetings & Here's Good Wishes for a 14 Carrot Christmas, features Bugs Bunny dressed as Santa, Capitol, 1948, 8" $125.00

Records, Kiddie Picture Disks

The Bunny Easter Party, Voco #EB-1, 1948, EX, $15.00.
(Photo courtesy Peter Muldavin)

Jack and the Beanstalk, Toy Toon Records, 1952 .... $15.00

Kitty Cat, Voco, ca 1948, 7", EX $8.00

Kitty Cat, Vovo 'Pic Disc,' ca 1948, 6" (rare size), EX $15.00

Lionel Train Sound Effects, 1951 .... $60.00

Little White Duck, Red Raven Movie Records $15.00

Red River Valley, Record Guild of America #2002P, 1949, EX (EX rare sleeve) $25.00

Red Ryder, Record Guild of America, 1948 .... $45.00

Round & Round the Village, Voco Pic Disc, 1948, 78 rpm, 6" (rare size), EX $15.00

Round & Round the Village, Voco Pic Disc, 1948, 78 rpm, 7", EX $6.00

Rover the Strongman, Voco, 1948, EX $25.00

Shepherd Boy, Bible Storytime, 1948 .... $10.00

Songs from Mother Goose, Toy Toon Records, 1952 .... $15.00

Swing Your Partner, Picture Play Records #PR11A/Record Guild of America, 1948 .... $100.00

Ten Little Indians, Voco, 1948, 7" $8.00

Ten Little Indians, Voco, 1948, 16" $25.00

Terry & the Pirates, Record Guild of America, F501, 1949, 6½" $45.00

The Fox, Talking Book Corp, 1917, 78 rpm, very rare ... $100.00

The Fox, Talking Book Corp, 1917, 78 rpm, very rare, EX. $85.00

Three Little Bears with Uncle Henry, Kidisks, KD-77A, 1948, rare $75.00

Trial of 'Bumble' the Bee Part 1, Vogue #R-745, 1947, 10", EX $60.00

Winnie the Pooh & Christopher Robin Songs, RCA Victor, 1933, very rare $500.00

- **Robots and Space Toys** -

Space is a genre that anyone who grew up in the '50s and '60s can relate to, but whether you're from that generation or not, chances are the fantastic robots, space vehicles, and rocket launchers from that era are fascinating to you as well. Some emitted beams of colored light and eerie sounds and suggested technology the secrets of which were still locked away in the future. To a collector, the stranger, the better. Some were made of lithographed tin, but even plastic toys (Atom Robot, for example) are high on want lists of many serious buyers. Condition is extremely important, both in general appearance and internal workings. Mint-in-box examples may be worth twice as much as one mint-no-box, since the package art was often just as awesome as the toy itself.

Because of the high prices these toys now command, many have been reproduced. Beware!

The following listings came from recent auctions.

See also Guns; Marx.

Acrobat Robot, Yonezawa, 1960s, b/o, plastic, 9½", EX+IB.$185.00

Action Planet Robot, see Planet Robot (Action)

Answer Game Machine (Robot), Amico, 1960s, b/o, tin, 14½", EX+IB $475.00

Apollo 11 American Eagle Lunar Module, DSK, 1960s, b/o, tin & plastic, 9½", EXIB $200.00

Astro Scout (Robot), Yonezawa, 1960s, friction, tin, 9", NMIB $13,550.00

Astroman, Dux, 1960s, r/c, plastic, 14", NMIB............ $1,575.00

Astroman, Nomura, 1960, w/up, tin & plastic, 10", EX+IB..$9,600.00

Astronaut, Cragstan, b/o, litho tin w/glass dome, holds gun, 13", VG $625.00

Astronaut, Daiya/AHI, 1960s, w/up, tin & plastic, 6½", EX+IB... $300.00

Astronaut, Nomura, b/o, tin & vinyl, 13", EXIB $750.00

Astronaut X-70, Hong Kong, w/up, plastic, 6½", NM+IB ..$200.00

Atomic Boat X-90, EX/Japan, w/up, tin, 14" L, EX $800.00

Atomic Robot Man (lead arm version), Japan, 1940s, w/up, tin, 5", VG+IB $1,175.00

Atomic Robot Man (tin-arm version), Japan, 1950s, w/up, tin, 5", EX+IB $950.00

Atomic Rocket, Masudaya, 1950s, friction, tin, 7" L, NM .$1,075.00

Atomic Rocket, Masudaya, 1950s, friction, tin, 7" L, NMIB.$1,750.00

Attacking Martian, Horikawa, b/o, tin, 11", NM+IB $275.00

Batman Robot, Atom/Japan, 1960s, tin w/vinyl head & arms, 13", EXIB...$13,800.00

Blink-A-Gear Robot, Taiyo, 1960s, b/o, tin & plastic, 14½", NMIB $1,350.00

Brain Robot Controlled Car, Jay V Zimmerman, 1955, b/o, plastic & vinyl, 12½", VG... $115.00

Buck Rogers Rocket Police Patrol, Marx, w/up, tin, 11½", EX..$1,100.00

Buck Rogers Rocket Police Patrol, Marx, w/up, tin, 11½", F..$250.00

Bump 'n Go Space Explorer, Yoshiya, crank-op, tin, vehicle w/ astronaut driver, 6", NMIB.............................. $400.00

Busy Cart Robot, Horikawa, 1960s, b/o, tin & plastic, 11½", EXIB $1,125.00

Buzzer Robot, Yonezawa, 1950s, b/o, tin, 10½", EXIB..$3,550.00

Capsule 6, Masudaya, b/o, tin, 10", NM+IB.................. $900.00

Change Man, Marumiya, 1960, r/c, tin, vinyl & plastic, 13½", NMIB $7,450.00

Chief Robotman, Yoshiya, 1960s, b/o, tin, 12", NMIB .$1,075.00

Chief Robotman, Yoshiya, 1960s, b/o, tin, 12", VG+ $550.00

Chief Smokey Robot, Yoshiya, 1960s, b/o, tin, 12", EX+IB..$4,225.00

Chime Trooper Astronaut, Aoshin, 1950s, w/up, tin, 9", NMIB $17,500.00

Colonel Hap Hazard (Robot), Marx, 1960s, b/o, tin & plastic, 12", EX+IB $750.00

Conehead Space Robot, Yonezawa, 1960s, w/up, tin, 8½", EXIB...$7,675.00

Cragstan Astronaut, Yonezawa, 1960s, friction, tin, 9½", EXIB $675.00

Cragstan Astronaut (no antenna), Daiya, 1960s, b/o, tin, 14", EXIB $1,100.00

Cragstan Astronaut (with antenna), Daiya, 1960s, b/o, tin, 12", EX+IB $950.00

Cragstan Great Astronaut, Alps, 1960s, b/o, tin, 14½", EXIB $1,450.00

Cragstan Mr Atomic, Yonezawa, 1962, b/o, tin, 9", EX...$4,050.00

Cragstan Mr Atomic, Yonezawa, 1962, b/o, tin, 9", EXIB...$5,075.00

Cragstan Ranger Robot, NGS, 1960s, b/o, tin & plastic, 12½", EXIB $2,000.00

Cragstan Robot, Yonezawa, 1960s, b/o, tin, 11", NMIB..$1,400.00

Cragstan's Mr Robot, b/o, tin w/plastic dome, 11", nonworking o/w NM $315.00

Crystal Robot, Hong Kong, plastic, fixed legs, movable arms, 7", EX $850.00

Diamond Planet Robot, Yonezawa, 1960s, w/up, tin, 10", very rare, NMIB $50,850.00

Dino Change Robot, Horikawa, 1960s, b/o, tin & plastic, 11", NMIB $1,000.00

Directional Robot, Yonezawa, 1950s, b/o, tin, 10½", NMIB.$1,100.00

Doctor Moon, Daiya, w/up, tin & plastic, 7", EXIB........ $700.00

Domed Easel-Back Robot, Linemar, 1950s, r/c, 6", EX+ .. $2,300.00

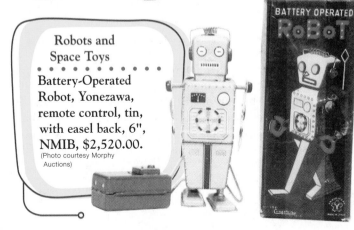

Robots and Space Toys
• • • • • • • • • • • • • •
Astronaut on Tricycle, Japan, windup, celluloid figure on tin trike, 5", EX, $2,250.00. (Photo courtesy Smith House Toy and Auction Company)

Robots and Space Toys
• • • • • • • • • • • • • •
Battery-Operated Robot, Yonezawa, remote control, tin, with easel back, 6", NMIB, $2,520.00. (Photo courtesy Morphy Auctions)

Robots and Space Toys
• • • • • • • • • • • • • •
Change Man, Marumiya, remote control, tin, vinyl, and plastic, 13½", NM, $5,930.00. (Photo courtesy Smith House Toy and Auction Company)

Door Robot, see Revolving Flashing Robot

Earth Man, Nomura, 1950s, r/c, tin, 10", EXIB $1,185.00

Easel-Back Robot, see Domed Easel-Back Robot

Explorer, Masudaya, friction, tin, 7½", NMIB.................$445.00

Explorer (Robot) X-27, Yonezawa, 1960s, friction, tin, 10",
NMIB $12,975.00

Exploration Train, Sankei, b/o, tin, complete, 21½" overall,
NMIB $1,050.00

Fire Bird No 3 (Space Patrol Fire Bird w/Blinking Light), b/o,
tin, 14" L, VG+IB $1,130.00

Firebird Space Car, Alps/Cragstan, 1950s, b/o, tin w/clear plastic
double domes w/2 drivers, bump-&-go, NM...............$390.00

Fire Rocket X-0077, Yonezawa, 1960s, friction, tin, 15" L,
NMIB..$850.00

Flashy Jim, see R7 (Flashy Jim)

Flying Man Robot (Driving Robot), Yoneya, w/up, tin, 11",
EXIB $265.00

Flying Saucer, B&S/West Germany, friction, tin, 4" dia,
NMIB $100.00

Flying Space Saucer, Aoshin, 1950s, b/o, tin, 6½" dia,
EXIB $12,975.00

Friendship 7 Space Rocket, Yonezawa, friction, tin, 13½",
NMIB...$1,575.00

Gatchaman Ken Superhero, Japan, w/up, tin w/vinyl head, 9",
EXIB $315.00

Gear Robot, Horikawa, plastic, w/up, 8", NMIB.............$150.00

Gemini Space Capsule, Horikawa, friction, tin, 6½", EXIB..$485.00

Gettsuko Kamen Robot, Bullmark, w/up, tin, 9", EX+IB..$550.00

Giant Sonic (Train) Robot, Masudaya, 1950s, b/o, tin, 15",
EX..$3,800.00

Golden Robot, see Robot (Golden Robot)

Grandizer Superhero, Poppy/Japan, w/up, tin w/vinyl head, 9",
EXIB $200.00

Hi-Bouncer Moon Explorer (Robot), Marx, 1960s, r/c, tin &
vinyl, 12", EX+IB $2,475.00

High Speed Sparkling Rocket, see Moon ZX-8 (The)

Hook Robot, Marubishi, friction, tin, 7", EXIB (repro box)..$4,350.00

Hook Robot, Waco, 1950s, friction, tin, skirted bottom, 8", EXIB
(box reads Robot)...$13,550.00

ICBM Launching Station, crank-op friction motor, tin, 18½" L,
NMIB $750.00

Interplanetary Explorer, Naito Shoten, 1950s, w/up, tin, 8",
EX..$1,450.00

Interplanetary Explorer, Naito Shoten, 1950s, w/up, tin, 8",
NMIB..$6,325.00

Jumping Rocket, Yoneya, 1960s, w/up, tin, 6", NMIB....$550.00

Jupiter Robot, Yoshiya, r/c, tin & plastic, NM+IB.........$650.00

Jupiter Trailer, Momoya, friction, tin, 13" truck & trailer w/8"
Jupiter rocket, EXIB $2,600.00

King Flying Saucer X-081, Yoshiya, b/o, tin & plastic, 7" dia,
NMIB $100.00

Krome Dome Robot, Yonezawa, 1970s, b/o, tin & plastic, grows
from 10" to 12", NM+IB $1,075.00

Lantern Robot, see Robot (Lantern)

Lavender Robot, see Non-Stop Robot (Lavender Robot)

Magic Color Moon Express, TPS, b/o, tin & plastic, 14½",
NMIB $400.00

Man from Mars, Irwin, w/up, plastic, 11½", NM+ $250.00

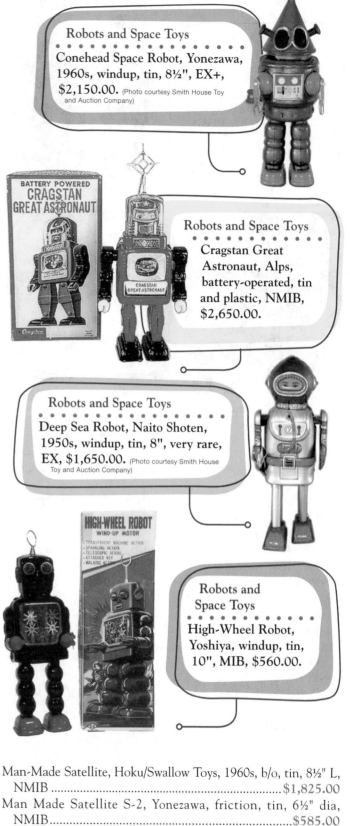

Robots and Space Toys
Conehead Space Robot, Yonezawa, 1960s, windup, tin, 8½", EX+, $2,150.00. (Photo courtesy Smith House Toy and Auction Company)

Robots and Space Toys
Cragstan Great Astronaut, Alps, battery-operated, tin and plastic, NMIB, $2,650.00.

Robots and Space Toys
Deep Sea Robot, Naito Shoten, 1950s, windup, tin, 8", very rare, EX, $1,650.00. (Photo courtesy Smith House Toy and Auction Company)

Robots and Space Toys
High-Wheel Robot, Yoshiya, windup, tin, 10", MIB, $560.00.

Man-Made Satellite, Hoku/Swallow Toys, 1960s, b/o, tin, 8½" L,
NMIB $1,825.00

Man Made Satellite S-2, Yonezawa, friction, tin, 6½" dia,
NMIB..$585.00

Martian Supersensitive Radar Patrol Jeep, Daiya, 1950s, b/o, tin,
10" L, EX+IB $1,025.00

Marvelous Mike Electromatic Robot Tractor #1000, Saunders,
MIB (sealed)...$575.00

Mechanized Robot (early blk version), Nomura, 1950s, b/o, tin,
13", NMIB...$1,450.00

Robots and Space Toys
• • • • • • • • • • • • •
Interplanetary Explorer, Naito Shoten, 1950s, windup, tin, 8", VGIB, $2,200.00. (Photo courtesy Smith House Toy and Auction Company)

Robots and Space Toys
• • • • • • • • • • • • •
Moon Astronaut, Daiya, 1950s, windup, tin, 9", VG+, $2,250.00.
(Photo courtesy Smith House Toy and Auction Company)

Robots and Space Toys
• • • • • • • • • • • • •
Lost in Space Robot, Hong Kong/20ᵗʰ Century Filpin, 1977, battery-operated, plastic, 10", MIB, $400.00. (Photo courtesy Smith House Toy and Auction Company)

Mechanized Robot (later blk version), Nomura, 1950s, b/o, tin, 13", EX+IB $950.00

Mechanized Robot (silver version), Nomura, 1950s, b/o, tin, 13", EXIB $10,375.00

Mechanized Robot (1990s reproduction), Osaka, b/o, tin, NMIB $375.00

Mego Man, Yoneya, w/up, tin, 7", EX+ $250.00

Mego Man, Yoneya, w/up, tin, 7", NMIB $500.00

Mercury X-1 Space Saucer, Yonezawa, b/o, tin & plastic, 8", NM+IB $150.00

Mighty Robot (Athlete Robot), Yonezawa, 1960s, w/up, tin & plastic, 10", EXIB $2,875.00

Mighty Robot, Noguchi, w/up, tin, 5½", NM+IB $125.00

Mighty Robot, Yoshiya, 1960s, b/o, 12", EXIB $3,650.00

Mighty Robot 8 (Magic Color), Masudaya, 1950s, w/up, tin, 12", NMIB $14,950.00

Missile Robot, Alps, 1960s, b/o, tin & plastic, 17", EX+IB . $4,050.00

Missile Rocket MR-45, Masudaya, r/c, plastic, 17½", VGIB ... $325.00

Missile Rocket, see also USAF Missile Rocket

Mobile Space TV Unit w/Trailer, Nomura, 1950s, b/o, tin, 10½" L, EXIB $2,650.00

Moon Astronaut, Daiya, 1950s, w/up, tin, 9", EX+IB .. $4,300.00

Moon Explorer, Alps, 1950s, b/o, tin & plastic, 17½", NMIB . $2,125.00

Moon Explorer, Yoshiya, w/up, tin, EX+ $475.00

Moon Explorer M-27, Yonezawa, r/c, tin, 8" L, NMIB .. $2,000.00

Moon Man 001, OK/Hong Kong, #3379, b/o, plastic, 6", NMIB $150.00

Moon Express XY, Nomura, 1950s, friction, tin, 5½" L, EXIB $1,130.00

Moon Patrol (Moon Car Space Division No 3), Nomura, 1950s, b/o, tin, 13" L, EX+IB $2,250.00

Moon Patrol Vehicle, Yonezawa, 1960s, b/o, tin, 9" L, VGIB $4,600.00

Moon Robot (Ribbon Head Robby), Yonezawa, 1950s, w/up, tin, 10½", EX+IB $3,000.00

Moon Rocket 3, Masudaya, 1950s, friciton, tin, 6½", NM+IB .. $1,200.00

Moon Space Ship (Moon Car), Nomura, 1950s, b/o, tin, 13" L, NMIB $1,900.00

Moon ZX-8 (The High Speed Sparkling Rocket), Marusan, 1950s, w/up, tin, 8½", NMIB $3,920.00

Mr Atomic, see Cragstan Mr Atomic

Mr Machine, Ideal, 1960s, w/up, plastic, 18", EX+ $140.00

Mr Mercury (bl version w/helmet light), Marx, 1960s, r/c, tin & plastic, 13", EXIB $1,050.00

Mr Mercury (bl version w/no helmet light), Marx, 1960s, r/c, tin & plastic, 13", EXIB $450.00

Mr Mercury (gold version w/no helmet light), Marx, 1960s, r/c, tin & plastic, 13", EX+IB $850.00

Mr Robot, Asahi, 1960s, w/up, tin & plastic, bell on chest, 7", EX $250.00

Mr Robot, Asahi, 1960s, w/up, tin & plastic, bell on chest, 7", NMIB $775.00

Mr Robot, Yonezawa, 1960s, b/o, tin w/plastic dome, 11", NM $450.00

Mr Robot, Yonezawa, 1960s, b/o, tin w/plastic dome, 11", NMIB $725.00

Mr Robot the Mechanical Brain, Alps, 1950s, w/up, b/o lights, tin, 9", EXIB $1,675.00

Musical Drummer Robot, Nomura, 1950s, b/o, tin, 8", EXIB .. $5,350.00

Mystery Space Ship (Flying Saucer), Marx, 1960s, gyro-powered, plastic, w/astronaut & alien figures, 2 rockets, NMIB . $125.00

NASA Moon Explorer M-27 (Moon Explorer), Yonezawa, 1970s, r/c, tin, 8", NMIB $675.00

NASA Space Capsule, SH, 1960s, b/o, tin & plastic, 9", NM $100.00

NASA Super Moon Patroler, Junior Toy, 1970s, b/o, tin & plastic, 9" L, NMIB $475.00

Non-Stop Robot (Lavender Robot), Masudaya, 1950s, b/o, tin, 15", EX $3,150.00

Non-Stop Robot (Lavender Robot), Masudaya, 1950s, b/o, tin, 15", NMIB $5,800.00

NP 5357 Robot (Liliput), KT, prewar, w/up, tin, orange, 6", EX $2,575.00

Piston Action Robot (Pug Robby), Nomura, b/o, tin, later version w/1 bent antenna, 8½", EX+IB $650.00

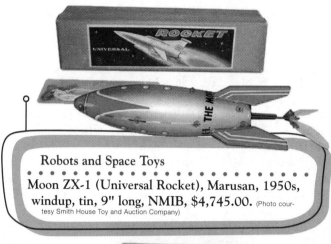

Moon ZX-1 (Universal Rocket), Marusan, 1950s, windup, tin, 9" long, NMIB, $4,745.00. (Photo courtesy Smith House Toy and Auction Company)

Radar Robot (Blinking Lite), Nomura, 1950s, battery-operated, 9", NMIB, $1,500.00. (Photo courtesy Smith House Toy and Auction Company)

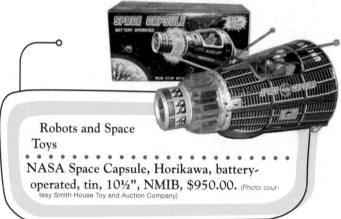

NASA Space Capsule, Horikawa, battery-operated, tin, 10½", NMIB, $950.00. (Photo courtesy Smith House Toy and Auction Company)

Piston Action Robot (Pug Robby), Nomura, r/c, tin, early version w/straight antenna, 8½", EX.............................. $1,675.00
Planet Robot (Action), Yoshiya, 1950s, r/c, tin, 9", NMIB..$650.00
Planet Robot (Action), Yoshiya, 1960s, w/up, tin, 9", EXIB...$475.00
Pom Pom Tank, Suzuki & Edwards, b/o, tin, 12½" L, NMIB..$385.00
Porthole Astronaut, see Spaceman
Prop Flying Robot Car, ATC, 1950s, friction, tin, 8" L, EXIB.$1,185.00
Prop Flying Robot Car, ATC, 1950s, friction, tin, 8" L, NMIB $2,350.00
R-10 (VW Convertible), Nomura, 1960s, b/o, tin, 13" L, EXIB $3,000.00
Radar Robot, Horikawa, b/o, tin & plastic, 13", NM+IB. $150.00
Radicon Robot, Masudaya, 1950s, b/o, tin, 20", NMIB.$17,500.00
Ranger Robot, see also Cragstan Ranger Robot
Ranger Robot, Daiya, 1965, b/o, tin & plastic, 8", EX+ . $1,635.00
Ratchet Robot, Nomura, w/up, tin, 8", NMIB............... $650.00
Revolving Flashing Robot (Door Robot), Alps, r/c, tin, 9", VG+IB $1,750.00
Rex Mars Planet Patrol Space Tank, Marx, 1950s, w/up, tin, 10", NM+IB... $400.00
Ribbon Head Robby, see Moon Robot (Ribbon Head Robby)
Road Construction Roller (Robby Road Roller), Daiya, b/o, tin, 9", EX+IB $2,850.00
Robby Robot, Yonezawa, 1950s, w/up, tin, 8", EX $700.00
Robby Robot, Yonezawa, 1950s, w/up, tin, 8", NMIB..$3,550.00
Robby Space Patrol, Nomura, 1950s, b/o, tin, 13", EXIB...$5,100.00
Robert the Robot, Ideal, 1950s, r/c, plastic, 14", NMIB . $200.00
Robot (Door Robot), Alps, 1950s, b/o, tin, EXIB........$4,900.00

Robot (Electric Remote Control), Linemar, 1950s, r/c, tin, 7½", EX+IB $530.00
Robot (Golden Robot), Linemar, 1950s, r/c, tin, 6½", EXIB.$1,850.00
Robot (Lantern Robot), Linemar, 1950s, r/c, tin, 8", EX+ .$1,635.00
Robot (Lantern Robot), Linemar, 1950s, r/c, tin, 8", EX+IB...$3,100.00
Robot (R-35), Linemar, r/c, tin, 'Robot' lettered on chest, 8", EXIB $400.00
Robot Bulldozer, Yoshiya, r/c, tin w/rubber treads, 6½" L, EX+IB $900.00
Robot Lilliput, KT/CK, 1939, tin, w/up, 6", EXIB....... $6,475.00
Robot Shooting Game, Masudaya, 1950s, tin, b/o, 15", EXIB $16,375.00
Robot Space Trooper, Yoshiya, friction, tin, 6½", NM.... $600.00
Robot Space Trooper, Yoshiya, r/c, tin, 6½", VG $300.00
Robot Space Trooper, Yoshiya, friction, tin, 6½", NMIB . $800.00
Robot ST1 (w/Cart), Strenco, 1950s, tin, w/up, 7", NMIB.$1,150.00
Robot Torpedo, Marusan, 1950s, friction, tin, 12" L, EXIB...$800.00
Robot Torpedo, Marusan, 1950s, w/up, tin, 12" L, NMIB...$1,450.00
Robot 7, Japan, w/up, tin, 4", EX.................................. $150.00
Robotank Z, Nomura, 1970s, b/o, tin, 10", NM+IB........ $550.00
Robot War Boat, Aoshin, crank-op, prop & siren, tin, 12½", rare, EXIB $7,900.00
Roby Robot, Yonezawa, w/up, tin, 8", EX+IB $850.00
Rocket Jeep, Masudaya, friction, tin, 6", EX+IB............. $280.00
Rocket Fighter #5, Marx, w/up, tin, 12", VG................. $350.00
Rocket Man, Alps, 1960s, b/o, tin & plastic, 16", NMIB...$2,350.00
Rocket Racer (Super Sonic Speedster), Masudaya, friction, tin, 6½", NMIB $175.00
Rocket Ranger, Marusan, friction, tin, 6", EX+IB $650.00
Rocket (Sparkling Rocket), Masudaya, 1950s, friction, tin, 12½", NMIB $2,235.00
Rosko Astronaut, Nomura, 1960s, b/o, tin & vinyl, 13", EX+IB $1,800.00
Rosko Astronaut, Nomura, 1960s, b/o, tin & vinyl, 13", VGIB $950.00
R7 (Flashy Jim), Japan, r/c, tin, 8", EXIB..................... $2,175.00
Scouting Rocket X-20, Nomura, friction, tin, 10" L, NM..$1,450.00
Sky Rocket, Guntherman, w/up, tin, 7" rocket propels along 7" L metal track, EX+IB $1,750.00
Silver Ray Secret Weapon Space Scout, Horikawa, 1960s, b/o, tin, 9", EXIB $1,525.00
Smoking Space Man, Yonezawa, 1960s, b/o, tin, 12", VG+..$775.00

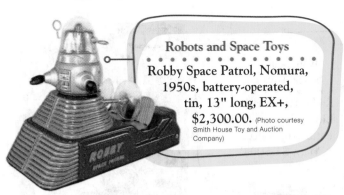

Robots and Space Toys

Robby Space Patrol, Nomura, 1950s, battery-operated, tin, 13" long, EX+, $2,300.00. (Photo courtesy Smith House Toy and Auction Company)

Robots and Space Toys

Robotank-Z, battery-operated, tin, 10", NM+IB, $550.00. (Photo courtesy Morphy Auctions on LiveAuctioneers.com)

Robots and Space Toys

Robot Boat No. 7/Speed Boat, Marusan, windup, tin, 14", EX+IB, $1,900.00. (Photo courtesy Smith House Toy and Auction Company)

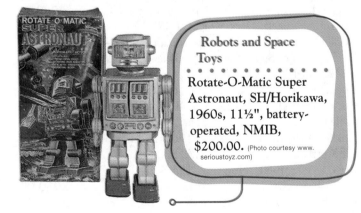

Robots and Space Toys

Rotate-O-Matic Super Astronaut, SH/Horikawa, 1960s, 11½", battery-operated, NMIB, $200.00. (Photo courtesy www.serioustoyz.com)

Smoking Space Man, Yonezawa, 1960s, b/o, tin, 12", EXIB..$1,525.00

Sonicon Rocket (version 1), Masudaya, 1960s, b/o, tin, 14" L, NMIB $2,300.00

Sonicon Rocket (version 2), Masudaya, 1960s, b/o, tin, 14" L, EX+IB...$1,500.00

SP-1 Space Car, Usagiya, friction, tin, scarce, VG+ $315.00

Space Bus, Usagiya/Miura, friction, tin, 15", G+ $450.00

Space Capsule, see Gemini Space Capsule and NASA Space Capsule

Space Capsule 5, Masudaya, 1960s, b/o, tin, 10½" L, EX. $225.00

Space Capsule 5, Masudaya, 1960s, b/o, tin, 10½", NMIB...$800.00

Space Commando, Nomura, 1950s, w/up, tin, 7½", EX.. $625.00

Space Commando, Nomura, 1950s, w/up, tin, 7½", NMIB $1,800.00

Space Conqueror (bl version), Daiya, 1960s, b/o, tin, 12", EX...$775.00

Space Conqueror (bl version), Daiya, 1960s, b/o, tin, 12", GIB...$925.00

Space Conqueror (gr version), Daiya, 1960s, b/o, tin, 12", rare, EXIB...$6,250.00

Space Controlled Tractor, PMC/Hong Kong, b/o, plastic, bull-dozer w/robot driver, 12", EX+IB $550.00

Space Dog, Yoshiya, 1950s, b/o, tin, 7½", EX+IB $2,525.00

Space Dog, Yoshiya, 1950s, friction, tin, 7½", NMIB $575.00

Space Dog, Yoshiya, 1950s, w/up, tin, 7½", EX+IB $525.00

Space Explorer, Yonezawa, 1950s, b/o, tin, 12", NMIB.$3,200.00

Space Explorer, Yonezawa, 1950s, w/up, tin, 9", EXIB.$2,350.00

Space Explorer Ship X-7, MT, 1950s, b/o, tin, 8" dia, NM...$125.00

Space Explorer Z-26, Yoshiya, friction, tin, 5½", VG $200.00

Space FD Robot, SY, 1950s, w/up, tin, 7", EXIB..........$1,800.00

Space Fighter, Horizawa, b/o, tin & plastic, 9", NM+IB. $150.00

Space Jet (Space Patrol), ATC, b/o, tin & plastic, 9" L, EX+IB...$525.00

Spaceman, Nomura/Sonsco, 1950s, r/c, tin, 10", EX+IB.$8,530.00

Spaceman (Porthole Astronaut), Linemar, 1950s, r/c, tin, 8", EXIB $1,575.00

Spaceman (27), Masudaya, 1950s, b/o, 9", EX................. $625.00

Space Patrol, Masudaya, friction, tin, NASA logo on fin & astro-naut's arm, 7" L, EXIB $300.00

Space Patrol Car, Nomura, b/o, tin, 9½", EX+IB.........$1,200.00

Space Patrol Car w/Radio Operator, ATC, friction, celluloid fig-ure in tin space vehicle, 8½", NMIB........................... $315.00

Space Patrol R-10 (VW Beetle), Nomura, b/o, tin, 13" L, NM+IB...$6,000.00

Space Patrol R-3 Car, Asahi, friction, tin, 8", EX........... $575.00

Space Patrol Robot, Horikawa, b/o, tin, 11", NMIB....... $150.00

Space Patrol Super Cycle, Bandai, 1950s, friction, tin, 12" L, NMIB $20,900.00

Space Patrol X-15 (Non-Stop Space Patrol), Masudaya, 1960s, b/o, tin, 8" dia, EX+IB... $475.00

Space Patrol X-27, w/up, tin, 5½", NM+IB.................... $275.00

Space Patrol 7 (Snoopy), Masudaya, b/o, tin & plastic, 11", NMIB $475.00

Space Robot Car, Yonezawa, 1950s, b/o, tin, 9½" L, EX+ ..$2,600.00

Space Robot Car X-9, Masudaya, 1950s, b/o, tin, 7½", EXIB ..$3,200.00

Space Robot Trooper, Yoshiya, r/c, tin, VG $550.00

Space Robot X-70 (Tulip Head), Nomura, 1960s, b/o, tin & plas-tic, 12", NMIB...$2,375.00

Space Rocket, Yoneya, tin, friction, 6", EXIB................ $500.00

Space Saucer X-15, Yoshiya, 1960s, friction, tin, 5½", EX ..$550.00

Space Scout, Yonezawa, 1950s, friction, tin, 10½", EXIB. $6,475.00

Space Ship (Flying Saucer), IY Metal Toys/Cragstan, 1950s, b/o, tin, EX+ $125.00

Space Ship X-2, Masudaya, 1950s, friction, tin, 7½" L, EXIB $375.00

Space Ship X-5, Masudaya, 1950s, friction, tin, 12" L, NM+IB $2,250.00

Space Ship 1, Masudaya, b/o, tin, 12" dia, NMIB $3,220.00

Space Station, Horikawa, 1960s, b/o, tin, 11" dia, EXIB. $1,900.00

Space Station, Horikawa, 1960s, b/o, tin, 11" dia, NMIB .. $2,825.00

Space Surveilant X-7, Masudaya, b/o, tin, 8½" L, VG+IB .. $130.00

Space Traveller w/Moving Head, ATC, friction, celluloid figure in tin space vehicle, 8½", NMIB $315.00

Space Tricycle, Suzuki, w/up, tin & plastic, 4", NM+IB. $775.00

Space Trooper, Haji, 1950s, w/up, tin, 7", EXIB $5,875.00

Space Whale Ship, Yoshiya, 1950s, w/up, tin, 9" L, NM+IB $1,825.00

Sparkling Rocket X-6, Masudaya, 1950s, friction, tin, 5" L, NMIB $575.00

Sparkling Space Dog, Japan, friction, tin w/plastic eyes, 7" L, NMIB $575.00

Sparkling Space Ranger X-36, SI, 1950s, friction, tin, 6½", NMIB $500.00

Sparkling Space Tank, see Rex Mars Planet Patrol Space Tank

Sparky the Robot, Yoshiya, 1960s, w/up, tin, 9", EXIB. $2,825.00

Super Moon Patroler, see NASA Super Moon Patroler

Super Robot, Hiro, w/up, tin & plastic, 6", NM+IB $125.00

Super Space Capsule, Horikawa, b/o, tin & plastic, 9", VG+IB $85.00

Super Space Commander, Horikawa, b/o, plastic, 9½", NM+IB $85.00

Super Space Giant (Robot), Horikawa, 1960s, b/o, tin, 16", EXIB $475.00

Swinging Baby Robot, Yone, w/up, tin, 11", NMIB $300.00

Talking Robot, Yonezawa, 1960s, friction, b/o voice, tin, 11", EXIB $850.00

Television Spaceman, Alps, 1960s, b/o, tin, 14½", NMIB .. $675.00

Tetsujin-28 No 2, Nomura, 1960s, b/o, tin & plastic, 13", EXIB $1,275.00

Tetsujin-28 No 3, Nomura, 1960s, w/up, tin, NMIB ... $1,800.00

Thunder Robot, Asakusa, 1960s, b/o, tin & plastic, 11½", NMIB $3,200.00

Tractor (Robot Driven) w/Visible Lighted Piston Movement, Nomura, b/o, tin, 10", VGIB $400.00

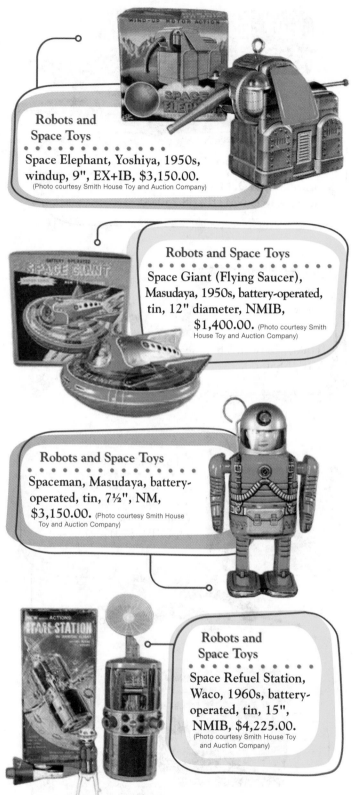

Robots and Space Toys

Space Elephant, Yoshiya, 1950s, windup, 9", EX+IB, $3,150.00. (Photo courtesy Smith House Toy and Auction Company)

Robots and Space Toys

Space Giant (Flying Saucer), Masudaya, 1950s, battery-operated, tin, 12" diameter, NMIB, $1,400.00. (Photo courtesy Smith House Toy and Auction Company)

Robots and Space Toys

Spaceman, Masudaya, battery-operated, tin, 7½", NM, $3,150.00. (Photo courtesy Smith House Toy and Auction Company)

Robots and Space Toys

Space Refuel Station, Waco, 1960s, battery-operated, tin, 15", NMIB, $4,225.00. (Photo courtesy Smith House Toy and Auction Company)

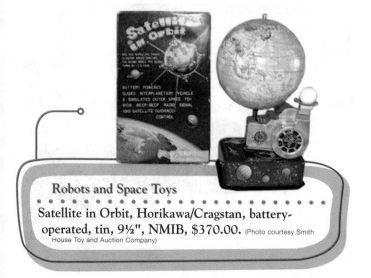

Robots and Space Toys

Satellite in Orbit, Horikawa/Cragstan, battery-operated, tin, 9½", NMIB, $370.00. (Photo courtesy Smith House Toy and Auction Company)

Tremendous Mike, Aoshin, 1960, w/up, tin, 10½", EXIB.. $25,425.00

Tulip Head Robot, see Space Robot X-70 (Tulip Head)

Twikly Whikly Rocket Ride, Alps, b/o, tin, 13", EXIB... $575.00

Ultraman Robot, Bullmark, w/up, tin w/vinyl head, 9", EXIB. $575.00

Ultra Seven Superhero, Bullmark, w/up, tin w/vinyl head, 9½", EXIB $250.00

Universe Car, China, 1970s, b/o, tin & plastic, 10", NM.. $50.00

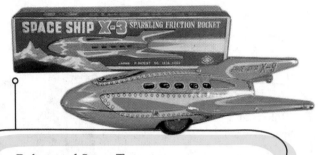

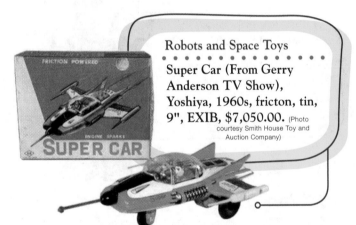

USAF Missile Rocket, Japan, 1950s, friction, in, 14" L, NM+
IB $325.00
Venus Robot, Yoshiya, r/c, tin & plastic, 5½", EXIB....... $135.00
Walking Robot, Hong Kong, b/o, plastic, 8½", EX+IB... $375.00
Walking Space Man, Yoneya, w/up, tin, 7½", EXIB........ $600.00
Walking Space Robot, Hong Kong, b/o, plastic, 9", scarce,
NMIB $200.00
Wander Superhero Robot, Jada/Japan, 1960s, tin w/plastic &
plastic head & arms, 12", VGIB............................... $1,150.00
Winky Robot, Yonezawa, w/up, tin & plastic, 10", EX.. $1,375.00
Winky Robot, Yonezawa, w/up, tin & plastic, 10", EXIB . $2,175.00
Zoomer the Robot, Nomura, 1950s, b/o, tin, 9½", NMIB.. $1,100.00
Zot the Friendly Flashing Robot, Hong Kong, b/o, plastic, 10",
EXIB $250.00

MISCELLANEOUS

Apollo Staging Rockets, Parks Plastics, 1960s, unused, MIB
(sealed) $65.00
Astronaut Space Helmet w/RCA Built-in Speaker, plays set of
45 rpm records, 1960s, complete, NMIB $150.00
Bank, Apollo Moon Bank, resin moon shape w/name on base,
6½", Royal Design of Florida, EX $100.00
Bank, Plan-It Bank, diecast metal w/mc planets in bl ring around
lg silver sun, Astro Mfg, 1950s, 9", VG $50.00
Bank, Guided Missile, Astro Mfg, 12", MIB $110.00
Bank, Satellite, Duro Mold & Mfg, diecast, 10½", MIB . $110.00
Bank, Strato, Duro Mold & Mfg, diecast, 8½" L, unused,
NM+IB $160.00
Bank, Strato, shoots coins from rocket across into moon, Duro
Mfg, 1950s, 8", EX.. $65.00
Bank, Turbo Jet, HWN, 1960s, tin, 7½" L, VG $300.00
Captain Video Rocket Launcher, Lido, plastic, NM+IB. $440.00
Explorer & Vanguard Tracking Station, Structoys, b/o, tin, 7½"
W, EXIB... $435.00
Game, Count Down Space Game, Transogram, 1960,
NMIB.. $150.00
Game, Race to the Moon, All-Fair, 1930s, complete, VGIB. $1,575.00
Gumball Machine, rocket shape w/clear plastic center, solid
color cone top w/astronaut decal, EX $75.00

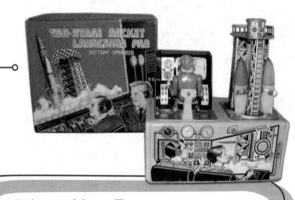

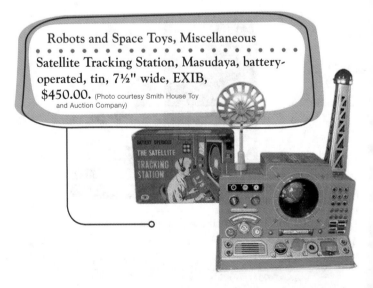

Kite, paper w/wood supports, various space graphics, 28x22", Alox Mfg, 1950s, unused, EX+ $20.00

Lunchbox, bl tin box w/red, wht & bl space scenes, double red swing hdls, 4x7½x5", Decoware, 1950, VG+ $100.00

NASA Control Center, Masudaya, b/o, tin & plastic, 7½", VGIB $200.00

Pencil Sharpener, spaceship, 2½", 1960s, MIP (sealed) $10.00

Rocket Patrol Magnetic Target Game, American Toy Prod, 1950s, complete, EX........................$50.00

Space Faces, Pressman, 1950s, unused, NMIB $175.00

Space Globe, tin, 10", NM........................$450.00

Space Model QX-2 Electronic Walkie Talkies, Remco, plastic, works w/magnetic power, EX+IB $50.00

Space Scope, paper kalidescope w/3 snap-on heads, MIB $85.00

Space Toy Sparkler, Arnold, tin, 5", NM $100.00

Space War Beany, felt w/metal spinning props atop spinning coil, 1950s, EX+ $125.00

Spinner Toy, rnd litho cb w/space graphics, push lever & astronaut spins & stops on a planet, 2½" dia, Japan, M $25.00

• • • • • • • • • • • • • • • • • • • Rock 'n Roll • • • • • • • • • • • • • • • • • • •

From the 1950s on, rock 'n roll music has been an enjoyable part of many of our lives, and the performers themselves have often been venerated as icons. Today some of the all-time great artists such as Elvis, the Beatles, KISS, and the Monkees have fans that not only continue to appreciate their music but actively search for their ticket stubs, concert posters, photographs, and autographs. More easily found, though, are the items that sold through retail stores at the height of their careers — dolls, games, toys, books, magazines, etc. In recent years, some of the larger auction galleries have sold personal items such as guitars, jewelry, costumes, automobiles, contracts, and other one-of-a-kind items that realized astronomical prices. If you're an Elvis or Beatles fan, we recommend *Elvis Collectibles* and *Best of Elvis Collectibles* by Rosalind Cranor; *The Beatles, A Reference and Value Guide,* by Barbara Crawford, Hollis Lamon, and Michael Stern; and *Rock-n-Roll Treasures* by Joe Hilton and Greg Moore.

See also Coloring, Activity, and Paint Books; Lunch Boxes; Paper Dolls; Pin-Back Buttons.

Advisor: Bob Gottuso (Bojo)

Andy Gibb, Wireless FM Microphone, LJN, 1978, MIB ...$50.00

Beatles, bank, Ringo half-figure, papier mache, orange shirt w/ red tie, red & bl striped sweater, 8", 1968, EX $60.00

Beatles, brooch, group photo set in plastic, MOC $60.00

Beatles, bubble bath container, Paul or Ringo, Colgate-Palmolive, 1960s, NM+, ea $120.00

Beatles, bulletin board, Yellow Submarine, 24x24", Unicorn Creations, MIP $700.00

Beatles, charms, set of 4 mc plastic ovals w/head images, 'Beetles' on back, 1½", 1960s, M $50.00

Beatles, Colouring Set, Kitfix, 1964, complete, MIB...$2,000.00

Beatles, dolls, Paul or Ringo, plastic w/lifelike hair, w/instruments, about 4½", Remco, 1964, EX, ea........................$75.00

Beatles, dolls, John or George, plastic w/lifelike hair, w/instruments, about 4½", Remco, 1964, EX, ea........................ $150.00

Beatles, dolls, soft or hard bodies, set of 4, Remco, NM . $400.00

Beatles, guitar, Four Pop, head images of group & name, NM.$500.00

Beatles, pin, rnd John Lennon photo on guitar shape, 4¼", 1960s, NM........................$40.00

Beatles, scrapbook, 'The Beatles Scrap Book,' 4 head images, Whitman/Nems, 1964, EX........................$90.00

Beatles, spatter toy, 16", rare, MIP $250.00

Beatles, squirt gun, Yellow Submarine shape, plastic, 1960s .$90.00

Beatles, watercolor set, 'Yellow Submarine,' Craftmaster, complete, MIB........................ $150.00

Bee Gees, record case for 45 rpm records, photo image on wht, Vanity Fair, 1979, EX+........................$50.00

Bobby Sherman, ring, 'Love & Peace,' 1971, M $25.00

Boy George, doll, 11½", LJN, 1984, rare, MIB...............$150.00

Boy George, puffy stickers, set of 6, 1984, M $15.00

Bruce Springsteen, bandana, gray w/'Bruce' & 'The Boss' graphics, unused, M........................$20.00

Chubby Checker, Twister set, complete w/45 rpm 'practice' record, Empire Plastic Corp, 1960s, EXIB $75.00

David Cassidy, Dress-Up Set, 1972, MIP $30.00

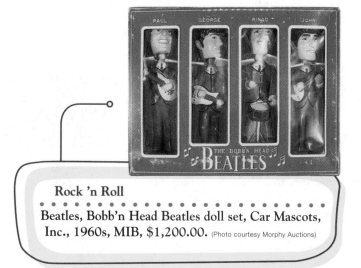

Rock 'n Roll
Beatles, Bobb'n Head Beatles doll set, Car Mascots, Inc., 1960s, MIB, $1,200.00. (Photo courtesy Morphy Auctions)

Rock 'n Roll
Beatles, overnight case, red vinyl, Air Flite, 1964, 13x5½", EX, $670.00. (Photo courtesy www.serioustoyz.com)

Rock 'n Roll

Beatles, wall plaques, set of four 3-D painted ceramic head shapes of the 'Fab Four,' 5x3½", Kelsboro Ware, 1964, NM, $2,400.00. (Photo courtesy www.serioustoyz.com)

Rock 'n Roll

KISS, dolls, Mego, 1978, four different, EX, each $100.00 to $150.00. (Photo courtesy Tom Harris Auctions on LiveAuctioneers.com)

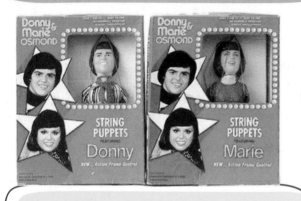

Rock 'n Roll

Donny & Marie, String Puppets, Madison #2321 and #2322, NMIB, each $100.00. (Photo courtesy www.gasolinealleyantiques.com)

David Cassidy, guitar, plastic, 31", Carnival Toys, 1973, MIP .. $400.00
David Cassidy, slide-tile puzzle, 1970s, M $35.00
Dick Clark, autograph doll, cloth body w/vinyl head, 26", 1960s, EX $75.00
Donny & Marie, Poster Pen Set, Craft House, 1971, unused, MIP $20.00
Elvis, autograph book, EP Enterprises, 1950s, unused, NM .. $400.00
Elvis, guitar, Lapin, 1984, MOC (sealed) $75.00
Herman's Hermits, doll, Peter Noone, Show Biz Babies, NMIB. $250.00
KISS, Colorforms, 1979, complete, MIB $75.00
KISS, necklace, ½x1" 'Kiss' logo on chain, 1977, MIB $45.00
KISS, Your Face Makeup, Remco, 1978, MIB (sealed) ... $200.00
Led Zeppelin, blimp, inflatable vinyl, distributed to music stores for record promo, M $100.00

The Mamas & The Papas, Show Biz Babies, Hasbro, MOC, ea. $200.00
Marie Osmond, Hair Care Set, Gordy, 1976, MOC $25.00
Monkees, charm bracelet, gold-tone chain w/4 rnd picture charms, Raybert Prod, 1967, MOC $60.00
Monkees, finger puppets, 1970, EX, ea $35.00
Monkees, flasher rings, various, Vari-Vue, 1967, NM, ea .. $18.00
Monkees, Flip Movies, Topps, 1967, NM (in wrapper) $25.00
Monkees, hand puppet, talker, Mattel, 1966, NM $100.00
Monkees, Show Biz Babies, vinyl, set of 4, 4", NMOC .. $500.00
Monkees, Talking Hand Puppet, Mattel, 1966, NMIB... $200.00
New Kids on the Block, Colorforms Deluxe Playset, 1991, MIB.. $15.00
New Kids on the Block, dolls, In Concert, 5 different, 12", Hasbro, MIB, ea $20.00
New Kids on the Block, dolls, Show Time Kids Rag Dolls, 5 different, 19", Hasbro, 1990, MIB, ea $25.00
New Kids on the Block, Fashion Plates, Hasbro, 1990, unused, MIB $35.00
Pat Boone, pendant, metal heart shape w/etched bust image, record, pr of shoes & signature, NM $25.00
Rick Nelson, Picture Patch, 1950s, MOC $20.00
Rolling Stones, doll, Keith Richards, vinyl w/synthetic hair, Eegee, 1964, NM $100.00
Rolling Stones, doll, Mick Jagger, vinyl w/synthetic hair, 5", Play Pal, 1963, NM $100.00
Rolling Stones, sticker album, Stanley, 1983, NM+ $20.00
Shawn Cassidy, record case, cb, Vanity Fair, 1978, EX $35.00
Van Halen, binoculars, plastic w/'VH' logo, EX $20.00
Village People, guitar, 36", Carnival Toys, 1976, MIP $150.00
ZZ Top, mirror, 6x6", 1980s, M $10.00

• • • • • • • • • • • • • • • Roly Polys • • • • • • • • • • • • • • •

Popular toys with children around the turn of the century, roly polys were designed with a weighted base that caused the toy to automatically right itself after being kicked or knocked over. Their popularity faded to some extent, but they continued to be produced until WWI and beyond. Most were made of papier-maché/composition, although later on, some were made of celluloid and tin. Schoenhut made some in a variety of sizes — up to almost a foot in height. They represented clowns, animals, and children, as well as some well-known storybook characters.

The following listings are composition unless noted otherwise.

See also Black Americana; Chein; Character, TV, and Movie Collectibles; Disney.

Baby, 9½", nodding head, toothy smile, blk hair, wht top w/red bottom, Schoenhut, G $450.00

Chinaman, 9½", bl clothing & hat, wht shirt w/gr tie, hands on belly, NM.. $200.00

Clown, 6", red suit w/yel & bl trim, bald head w/red topknot & bl side hair, hands on belly, VG $60.00

Clown, 7", wht face w/minimal red & blk detail, yel w/wht fluted collar, sm hat cocked, Schoenhut, EX $110.00

Clown, 10", chimes, orange hair, yel jacket, pk vest, bl bottom, blk bowtie, VG+.. $400,00

Clown, 11", chimes, plaid suit, brn hat, spring w/gauze attached to nose, VG $100.00

Clown, 11", orange striped jacket, bl bottom, blk top hat cocked, blk bow tie, VG+.. $275.00

Clown, 11", red hair & jacket, gr bottom, sm blk top hat cocked, arched eyebrows, Germany, VG+ $300.00

Clown, 14", gr formal attire & skull cap, hands on belly holding rolled-up paper, VG.. $275.00

Clown, 14", half bl & half red w/3 decals on chest, 2-layered pleated collar, hands on belly, red/bl cheeks, EX......... $450.00

Clown, 14", orange & cream w/blk & bl line trim, decals of news hawk, etc, Schoenhut, EX................................... $700.00

Clown, 14", swivel head, blk & red on tan, cloth collar, bl & red on wht head, Schoenhut, EX $500.00

Clown, 15", chimes, yel jacket & vest w/orange & gr plaid stripes, bl bottom, bowtie & trim, VG......................... $275.00

Clown, 15", 2-pc w/separate head, red-pnt collar w/points, bl jacket w/yel vest, gr bottom, VG $350.00

Clown, 16", concerned look, gr cheeks, orange & yel w/gr collar & bottom, 2 buttons, Germany, VG.......................... $325.00

Donald Duck, 4", celluloid, jtd figure seated atop ball w/bell inside, NM+ $100.00

Drummer Boy, 4½", holding drumsticks, long hair, bl uniform, wht hat, VG $100.00

Dutch Girl, 9½", nodding head, toothy smile, Schoenhut, VG..$600.00

Foxy Grandpa, 9½", Schoenhut, G $475.00

Foxy Grandpa, 11", Schoenhut, ca 1915, EX............... $600.00

Happy Hooligan, 4", hands in pockets, exaggerated face w/arched eyebrows & lg eyes, gr & red, EX $200.00

Indian Baby, 4", pnt marking on face, yel outfit w/red trim, wht hood, Schoenhut, G...$85.00

Keystone Cop, 5", hands on belly, bl single-breasted jacket & hat, detailed face w/mustache, EX $125.00

Keystone Cop, 10", musical, hands on belly, bl single-breasted jacket, lg buttons, mustache, VG.............................. $165.00

Mother Goose, 8½", holding goose, bl & wht w/red trim, Schoenhut, EX $165.00

Revolutionary Era Figure, 15", red & wht outfit, cloth ruffled collar, Schoenut, VG $650.00

Santa, 9", red, wht & gr, Schoenhut, EX...................... $550.00

Santa, 11", red, wht & gr, Schoenhut, EX...................... $600.00

Uncle Sam, 3", red, wht & bl, VG $225.00

Roly Polys
Clown, 6", Germany, G, $100.00. (Photo courtesy Conestoga Auction Co. on LiveAuctioneers.com)

Roly Polys
Donald Duck, 6", celluloid, push down on head and Donald squeaks, EX, $300.00. (Photo courtesy Bertoia Auctions on LiveAuctioneers.com)

Roly Polys
Felix the Cat, 7½", closed-mouth grin, black and white, original label on belly, NM, $1,500.00. (Photo courtesy Morphy Auctions on LiveAuctioneers.com)

Roly Polys
Grotesque Baby, 10", nodding head, Schoenhut, VG, $275.00. (Photo courtesy Bertoia Auctions on LiveAuctioneers.com)

Roly Polys
Man, 8", Germany, VG, $250.00. (Photo courtesy Morphy Auctions on LiveAuctioneers.com)

Roly Polys
Sailor, Schoenhut, EX+, $550.00. (Photo courtesy Bertoia Auctions on LiveAuctioneers.com)

Sand Toys and Pails

By 1900, companies were developing all sorts of sand toys, free-standing models. The Sand Toy Company of Pittsburgh patented and made 'Sandy Andy' from 1909 onward. The company was later bought by the Wolverine Supply & Manufacturing Co. and continued to produce variations of the toy until the 1970s.

Today if you mention sand toys, people think of pails, spades, sifters, and molds.

We have a rich heritage of lithographed tin pails by manufacturers such as J. Chein & Co., T. Cohn Inc., Morton Converse, Kirchoff Patent Co., Marx Toy Co., and Ohio Art Co., plus the small jobbing companies who neglected to sign their wares. Sand pails have really come into their own and are now recognized for their beautiful graphics and designs. The following listings are lithographed or painted tin. For more information we recommend *Pails by Comparison, Sand Pails and Other Sand Toys, A Study and Price Guide*, by Carole and Richard Smyth.

Beach Set, 5 molds w/screen & scoop, litho tin, Wolverine, VG+IB.. $275.00

Bowler Andy Mill, 20",Wolverine #57A, NMIB............ $400.00

Captain Sandy Andy, 13½", Wolverine #63C, MIB....... $375.00

Coal Loader, 11", Wolverine, MIB................................. $400.00

Crane, 17½", Wolverine #020, MIB.............................. $375.00

Dandy Sandy Andy, 11", Wolverine, G $75.00

Mr Sandman the Robot, tin & wood, take-apart robot for sand play, w/orig shovel, 11½", Wolverine, ca 1945, EX+ ... $600.00

Mr Sandman the Robot, tin w/wooden arms & shovel hdl, body is bucket, sifter top, 11½", Wolverine, 1940s, NM...... $850.00

Pail, Asbury Park, royal bl, bail hdl, 6", G $300.00

Pail, Asbury Park on red, wht & bl patriotic graphics, bail hdl w/ wood grip, 5½", VG+ $1,100.00

Pail, beach scene w/kids, orange band top & bottom, elephant graphics on shovel bowl w/wooden hdl, 6", G+ $220.00

Pail, beach scene w/kids, w/zeppelin & airplane overhead, red, bl & yel, 6", USA, 1930s, EX... $390.00

Pail, beach scene w/kids in goat cart, bail hdl, 6", marked Germany & emb w/horse & MO2O, 1910s, EX $165.00

Pail, beach scene w/kids in water gathering shells, catching fish, digging clams, bail hdl, wood grip, 6", T Bros,............. $140.00

Pail, beach scene w/kids playing on lg ball & playing under lg umbrella, lt bl interior, bail hdl, 5", VG+ $275.00

Pail,, beach scene w/sailor & his girl, fancy floral & vine border, bail hdl, 6", VG+ $330.00

Pail, beach scene w/Victorian kids on path, girl picking flowers & child on donkey, 6", Germany, 1910s, EX+............. $600.00

Pail, circus scene on yel w/lt bl interior, rimmed foot, 7", G+ ..$75.00

Pail, clown heads in metallic gold circles on wht, red trim, bail hdl w/wood grip, shovel, 6½", Converse, VG.............. $550.00

Pail, Disney, Donald Duck appears to be in a dither on beach, red footed base & shovel, 5½", Ohio Art, EX............. $495.00

Pail, Disney, Donald Duck as captain of the ship looking in spyglass backwards, bl shovel, 4½", Ohio Art, EX............ $385.00

Pail, Disney, Donald Duck in beach scene w/nephews, red shovel, 4¼", Ohio Art, 1939, EX $275.00

Pail, Disney, Donald Duck's nephews on merry-go-round & other amusement themes, 5¼", Chein, EX........................... $110.00

Pail, Disney, lg head images of Mickey, Pluto, etc on red middle w/yel, bl & wht, 4", EX $35.00

Pail, Disney, Mickey, Donald & Pluto in rowboat, lt bl sky & wht clouds, w/lt bl shovel, 6", Ohio Art, VG $200.00

Pail, Disney, Mickey & friends in rowboat w/Mickey pointing, wht clouds in bl-gray sky, 3", Ohio Art, NM............$1,100.00

Pail, Disney, Mickey & Minnie standing in front of fenced cottage w/Pluto, 11", Ohio Art/WDE, 1938, VG............. $200.00

Pail, Disney, Mickey Mouse, Donald Duck & Goofy on golf outing, 6", Ohio Art, 1938, EX+...................................... $425.00

Pail, Disney, Mickey Mouse & Donald Duck on yel w/bl & red stars, bl hdl, Happynak #706, EX................................. $250.00

Pail, Disney, Mickey Mouse Band, characters parading in city, w/ shovel, 6", Ohio Art, VG... $325.00

Sand Toys and Pails

Dutch Mill, 12", Max #26 (McDowell), 1930s, 12", NMIB, $200.00. (Photo courtesy Bertoia Auctions on LiveAuctioneers.com)

Sand Toys and Pails

Pail, Atlantic City, red, white, and blue patriotic graphics, bail handle with wooden grip, 6½", VG+, $825.00. (Photo courtesy Noel Barrett Antiques & Auctions Ltd. on LiveAuctioneers. com)

Sand Toys and Pails

Pail, Disney, Atlantic City, Pluto pulling Donald Duck in wagon, 8", Ohio Art, VG, $1,100.00. (Photo courtesy Morphy Auctions on LiveAuctioneers.com)

Pail, Disney, Mickey's Band, w/shovel marked 'Mickey Mouse' & graphics, 10", Ohio Art, EX+ $770.00
Pail, Disney, Snow White & the Seven Dwarfs, w/shovel, 6", Ohio Art, EX (inside worn) $140.00
Pail, Disney, Snow White & the Seven Dwarfs in forest scene, w/shovel, 8", Ohio Art, EX+ $285.00
Pail, Disney, Three Little Pigs lettered at bottom, pigs in front of houses, bl footed base, 5½", EX $385.00
Pail, Disney, Three Little Pigs lettered at bottom, pigs on lt gr bkgrd, 3½", WDE, EX $360.00
Pail, Disney, Treasure Island, Mickey & friends on beach seeking treasure, 4½", NM $1,200.00
Pail, Disney, Who's Afraid.../Three Little Pigs lettered top/bottom, brick wall/gr & yel shovel, 4½", VG $385.00
Pail, eagle on rock/kids at the beach doing various activities, 6", AMSCO, 1920s, EX $450.00
Pail, For a Good Child, red, wht & bl patriotic graphics on wht, bail hdl w/wood grip, 6", VG $715.00
Pail, From Wildwood Beach, metallic gold, bail hdl, 3¼", G ..$300.00
Pail, Funny Face, 3¼", Ohio Art, EX $200.00
Pail, Jumbo at the Seaside, blk graphics on brick red, blk interior, can shape w/bail hdl, 3x4½" dia, VG+ $425.00
Pail, kids playing cowboys & Indians in yel desert scene w/wht mountains & bl sky, 5", Chein, NM $110.00
Pail, Mary Had a Little Lamb, emb images, 6", Germany, 1910s, EX $165.00
Pail, Sea Side in red, wht & bl w/crossed flags & eagle on metallic gold, bail hdl w/wood grip, 6½", T Bros, VG $550.00
Pail, straight sides, Jumbo Sea Side on orange, bail hdl, 3x4½" dia, VG+ $465.00
Pail, Young America, beach scene w/kids, fancy floral & vine border, bail hdl, 7", G+ $525.00
Sand Lift, 11", Ohio Art, VGIB $100.00
Sand Loader, 11", Wolverine, MIB $400.00
Sand Shifter/Watering Can, Donald Duck/donkey graphics, Ohio Art/WDE, 1938, VG+ $150.00

Sand Sifter, tin w/Disney characters & Krazy Kat lithoed on sides, Chein, 1930s, VG $200.00
Sandy Andy Cable Car #53, 10x24", Wolverine, EXIB.. $325.00
Sandy Andy Merry Miller #77, 12", Wolverine, NMIB.. $800.00
Sandy Andy Merry Miller #77, 12", Wolverine, VG...........$100.00
Sandy Andy Sand Loader, Wolverine #50, EX $30.00
Sandy Andy #75, Wolverine, 14", EX+ (VG box) $120.00
Shovel, Mickey, Minnie & Donald Duck in snowball fight on wide fluted tin shovel pan, wooden hdl, 27", Ohio Art, VG ...$385.00
Tub, Three Little Pigs singing & dancing as they work, yel sky, no hdl, 3", EX $250.00
Watering Can, Disney, cylindrical w/blk & wht images on bl, red rim, yel & red spout, side hdl, 3", EX......................... $385.00
Watering Can, Disney, Donald Duck camping graphics, 6½", Ohio Art, c 1938, EX $300.00
Watering Can, Disney, Mickey Mouse watering flowers by fence, yel sky & spout, high loop hdl, 8", VG $385.00
Watering Can, flying gulls/2 mallards in flight over water, 6½" (w/hdl up), Germany 1910s, EX $200.00
Watering Can, kids playing war in military garb, various flag imagery, 8", French, VG+ $470.00

• Schoenhut •

Albert Schoenhut & Co. was located in Philadelphia, Pennsylvania. From as early as 1872 they produced toys of many types including dolls, pianos and other musical instruments, games, and a good assortment of roly polys (which they called Rolly Dollys). From 1902 to 1903 they were granted patents that were the basis for toy animals and performers that Schoenhut designated the 'Humpty Dumpty Circus.' It was made up of circus animals, ringmasters, acrobats, lion tamers, and the like, and the concept proved to be so successful that it continued in production until the company closed in 1935. During the nearly 35 years they were made, the figures were continually altered either in size or by construction methods, and these variations can greatly affect their values today. Besides the figures themselves, many accessories were produced to go along with the circus theme — tents, cages, tubs, ladders, and wagons, just to mention a few. Teddy Roosevelt's 1909 African safari adventures inspired the company to design a line that included not only Teddy and the animals he was apt to encounter in Africa, but native tribesmen as well. A third line in the 1920s featured comic characters of the day, all with the same type of jointed wood construction, many dressed in cotton and felt clothing, among them Felix the Cat, Maggie and Jiggs, Barney Google and Spark Plug, and Happy Hooligan. (See Character, TV, and Movie Collectibles.)

Several factors come into play when evaluating Schoenhut figures. Foremost is condition. Since most found on the market today show signs of heavy wear, anything above a very good rating commands a premium price. Missing parts and retouched paint sharply reduce a figure's value, though a well-done restoration is usually acceptable. The earlier examples had glass eyes; by 1920 eyes were painted. In the early 1920s the company began to make their animals in a reduced size. While some of the earlier figures had bisque heads or carved wooden heads, by the '20s, pressed wood heads were the norm. Full-size examples with glass eyes and bisque or carved heads are generally more desirable and more valuable, though rarity must be considered as well.

During the 1950s, some of the figures and animals were produced by the Delvan Company, who had purchased the manufacturing rights.

For more information we recommend *Schoenhut Toy Price Guide* by Keith Kaonis (our advisor) and Andrew Yaffee.

Advisors: Keith and Donna Kaonis

See also Character, TV, and Movie Collectibles; Pull and Push Toys; Roly Polys.

HUMPTY DUMPTY CIRCUS ANIMALS

Humpty Dumpty Circus animals with glass eyes, circa 1903 – 1914, are more desirable and can demand much higher prices than the later painted-eye versions. As a general rule, a glass-eye version is 30% to 40% more than a painted-eye version. (There are exceptions.) The following list suggests values for both glass-eye and painted-eye versions and reflects a low painted-eye price to a high glass-eye price.

There are other variations and nuances of certain figures: Bulldog — white with black spots or brindle (brown); open-and closed-mouth zebras and giraffes; and ball necks and hemispherical necks on some animals such as the pig, leopard, and tiger, to name a few. These points can affect the price and should be judged individually.

Schoenhut, Humpty Dumpty Circus Animals
• • • • • • • • • • • • •
Buffalo, carved mane, painted/glass eyes, $200.00 to $1,200.00. (Photo courtesy Bertoia Auctions on LiveAuctioneers.com)

Schoenhut, Humpty Dumpty Circus Animals
• • • • • • • • • • • • •
Gazelle, painted/glass eyes, rare, $500.00 to $3,000.00. (Photo courtesy Bertoia Auctions on LiveAuctioneers.com)

Schoenhut, Humpty Dumpty Circus Animals
• • • • • • • • • • • • •
Giraffe, painted/glass eyes, $200.00 to $900.00. (Photo courtesy Bertoia Auctions on LiveAuctioneers.com)

Alligator, PE/GE, $250 to $750.00
Arabian Camel, 1 hump, PE/GE, $250 to $750.00
Bactrain Camel, 2 humps, PE/GE, $200 to $1,200.00
Brown Bear, PE/GE, $200 to.. $800.00
Bulldog, PE/GE, $400 to.. $1,500.00
Burro, farm set, PE/GE, no harness/no belly hole for chariot,
    $300 to... $800.00
Burro, made to go w/chariot & clown, w/leather track, PE/GE,
    $200 to... $800.00
Cat, PE/GE, rare, $500 to $3,000.00
Cow, PE/GE, $300 to... $1,200.00
Deer, PE/GE, $300 to... $1,500.00
Donkey, PE/GE, $75 to... $300.00
Elephant, PE/GE, $75 to... $300.00
Goose, PE only, $200 to.. $750.00
Gorilla, PE only, $1,500 to $4,000.00
Horse, dappled pnt, platform saddle, PE/GL, $250 to..... $700.00

Schoenhut, Humpty Dumpty Circus Animals

Polar Bear, painted/glass eyes, $200.00 to $2,000.00.
(Photo courtesy Noel Barrett Antiques & Auctions Ltd. on LiveAuctioneers.com)

Schoenhut, Humpty Dumpty Circus Animals

Sea Lion, painted/glass eyes, $400.00 to $1,500.00. (Photo courtesy Noel Barrett Antiques & Auctions Ltd. on LiveAuctioneers.com)

Schoenhut, Humpty Dumpty Circus Personnel

Black Dude, one-part head, purple coat, $250.00 to $750.00. (Photo courtesy Noel Barrett Antiques & Auctions Ltd. on LiveAuctioneers.com)

Schoenhut, Humpty Dumpty Circus Personnel

Chinese Acrobat, two-part head, rare, $400.00 to $1,600.00. (Photo courtesy Noel Barrett Antiques & Auctions Ltd. on LiveAuctioneers.com)

Hyena, PE/GE, very rare, $1,000 to	$6,000.00
Kangaroo, PE/GE, very rare, $1,000 to	$6,000.00
Lion, carved mane, PE/GE, $200 to	$1,400.00
Monkey, 1-part head, PE only, $200 to	$600.00
Monkey, 2-part head, wht face, $300 to	$1,000.00
Ostrich, PE/GE, $200 to	$900.00
Pig, 5 versions, PE/GE, $200 to	$800.00
Poodle, PE/GE, $100 to	$300.00
Rabbit, PE/GE, very rare, $500 to	$3,500.00
Rhino, PE/GE, $250 to	$800.00
Sheep (Lamb), w/bell, PE/GE, $200 to	$800.00
Tiger, PE/GE, $250 to	$1,200.00
Wolf, PE/GE, very rare, $500 to	$5,000.00
Zebra, PE/GE, rare, $500 to	$3,000.00

Schoenhut, Humpty Dumpty Circus Personnel

Lady Rider, one-part head, $250.00 to $550.00. (Photo courtesy Noel Barrett Antiques & Auctions Ltd. on LiveAuctioneers.com)

HUMPTY DUMPTY CIRCUS CLOWNS AND OTHER PERSONNEL

Clowns with two-part heads (a cast face applied to a wooden head) were made from 1903 to 1916 and are most desirable — condition is always important. There have been nine distinct styles in 14 different costumes recorded. Only eight costume styles apply to the two-part headed clowns. The later clowns, circa 1920, had one-part heads whose features were pressed, and the costumes were no longer tied at the wrists and ankles.

Note: Use the low end of the value range for items in only fair condition. Those in good to very good condition (having very minor scratches and wear, good original finish, no splits or chips, no excessive paint wear or cracked eyes and, of course, complete) may be evaluated by the high end.

Black Dude, 2-part head, blk coat, $400 to	$1,000.00
Clown, reduced size, $75 to	$125.00
Hobo, reduced size, $200 to	$400.00
Hobo, 1-part head, $200 to	$400.00

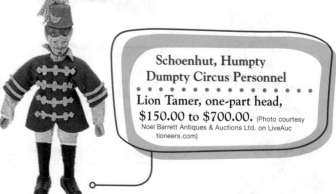

Schoenhut, Humpty Dumpty Circus Personnel

Lion Tamer, one-part head, $150.00 to $700.00. (Photo courtesy Noel Barrett Antiques & Auctions Ltd. on LiveAuctioneers.com)

Hobo, 2-part head, curved-up toes, blk coat, $500 to	$1,200.00
Lady & Gent Acrobats, bisque heads, ea $300 to	$800.00
Lady Acrobat, 1-part head, $150 to	$400.00
Lady Rider, 2-part head, very rare, $500 to	$1,000.00
Lion Tamer, 2-part head, early, very rare, $700 to	$1,600.00
Ringmaster, bisque, $300 to	$800.00
Ringmaster, 2-part head, blk coat, very rare, $800 to	$1,800.00
Ringmaster, 2-part head, red coat, very rare, $700 to	$1,600.00

Schoenhut, Humpty Dumpty Circus Sets
Toy Train to Build, 11" long, VG+IB, $300.00.
(Photo courtesy Noel Barrett Antiques & Auctions Ltd.)

HUMPTY DUMPTY CIRCUS SETS AND ACCESSORIES

There are many accessories: wagons, tents, ladders, chairs, pedestals, tightropes, weights, and various other items.

Cage Wagon, 16", dk gr w/gold detail, scarce, G+ $3,750.00
Cage Wagon w/2 Horses on Single Platform, red w/stenciled marquee, dapple horses, 10" L, G+ $1,700.00
Circus Tent, bl sq base w/red ring, 18x24", VG $300.00
Circus Tent, w/side banner depicting the circus midway measuring 18x49", 26x42" oval tent w/red & wht striped top, VG $2,875.00
Clown in Chariot, GE burro, clown w/2-part head, VG . $5,000.00
Wagon, wood w/papier-maché side panels, flatbed w/chained post, w/2 figures, 17", VG $16,500.00

Schuco

A German company noted for both mechanical toys as well as the teddy bears and stuffed animals we've listed here, Schuco was founded in 1912 as the Spielzeugfirma Schreyer & Co. and changed their name to Schuco in 1921. They manufactured stuffed toys through the 1950s. Items were either marked Germany or US Zone, Germany.

See also Aeronautical; Battery-Operated Toys; Character, TV, and Movie Collectibles; Diecast; Disney; Windup, Friction, and Other Mechanical Toys.

Schuco
Bear, 5½", green mohair (unusual color), glass eyes, NM, $400.00. (Photo courtesy Morphy Auctions)

Schuco
Bear on Roller Skates, 8", blond, 1946, VG, $225.00.
(Photo courtesy Skinner Auctioneers and Appraisers of Antiques and Fine Art on LiveAuctioneers.com)

Bear Tumbler, 9", furry head w/jtd felt body, w/wire tumbling support, VG $660.00
Bingo-Bello Dog, 14", orig clothes, NM $150.00
Black Scottie, 3", Noah's Ark, 1950s, MIB $225.00
Blackbird, 3", Noah's Ark, 1950s, MIB $200.00
Dalmatian, 2½", Noah's Ark, 1950s, rare, M $375.00
Elephant, 2½", Noah's Ark, 1950s, NM $125.00
Monkey, 8", brn & wht shaggy mohair, glass eyes, posable fingers & toes, EX $650.00
Monkey Acrobat, 5", brn, flocked tin face, felt ears, hands & feet, jtd, w/up action, VG $100.00
Monkey on Roller Skates, 7½", dressed in overalls & red & shirt, G $375.00
Mouse, 6", mc dress w/gr shoes, EX+ $200.00
Orangutan, 3", Noah's Ark, 1950s, rare, MIB $300.00
Owl, 3", Noah's Ark, 1950s, M $75.00
Penguin, 3", Noah's Ark, 1950s, EX $150.00
Perfume Bear, 3½", gold, 1920s, no bottle o/w VG $150.00

Schuco
Yes/No Bear, 8", beige mohair, green felt overalls, 1950, VG, $230.00. (Photo courtesy Morphy Auctions)

Bear, 2½", blk, shoe-button eyes, felt pads, VG $200.00
Bear, 2½", cream, tan nose & mouth, metal eyes, 1920s, VG .$150.00
Bear, 2½", pale gold, metal eyes, paper label, 1950s, NM.. $225.00
Bear, 3½", cinnamon, orig ribbon, 1950s, M $250.00
Bear, 4", lt gold, 1940s-50s, EX $125.00
Bear, 12", yel, metal eyes, 1920s, VG $350.00

Perfume Bellboy Monkey, 5", EX.................................. $650.00
Perfume Monkey, 5", cinnamon, G $250.00
Two-Faced Bear, 3½", brn, blk shoe-button eyes, 1950s, EX . $250.00
Yes/No Bear, 5", caramel, glass eyes, 1950s, NM............. $450.00
Yes/No Bear, 12", caramel, glass eyes, G......................... $275.00
Yes/No Bear, 13", caramel, pre-WWI, G $275.00
Yes/No Bear, 17", caramel, amber glass eyes, VG......... $1,000.00
Yes/No Bear, 19", caramel, amber glass eyes, 1920s-30s, EX.. $440.00
Yes/No Bellboy Bear w/Cello, 15", VG $1,150.00
Yes/No Bellboy Monkey, 8" (seated), VG $175.00
Yes/No Bellboy Monkey, 9", 1920s-30s, EX $350.00
Yes/No Bellboy Monkey, 14", 1920s-30s, G $125.00
Yes/No Bulldog, 7", cream & brn, glass eyes, 1930s, NM ...$1,200.00
Yes/No Cat, 5", M.. $650.00
Yes/No Donkey, 5", 1950s, NM $475.00
Yes/No Elephant, 5", 1948, EX $400.00
Yes/No Panda, 3½", 1950s, NM................................. $1,000.00
Yes/No Tricky Bear, 8", 1950, NM............................... $950.00
Yes/No Tricky Bear, 13", 1948, M............................. $1,200.00

Schuco
**Yes/No Panda, 8",
1950s, EX, $475.00.**
(Photo courtesy Noel Barrett Antiques &
Auctions Ltd. on LiveAuctioneers.com)

Yes/No Tricky Monkey, 10", orig tag, 1940s-50s, EX $350.00
Yes/No Tricky Monkey, 14", NM................................. $450.00
Yes/No Tricky Orangutan, 8", EX................................ $375.00
Yes/No Tricky Orangutan, 14", NM $950.00

• Skittles •

Skittles is an early European nine-pin bowling game in which the pins are called skittles. Skittles were made of various materials in many different shapes, sizes, and weights that varied from region to region. The vintage sets, especially if complete and in very good condition, can command some very high values. Unless otherwise noted, the listings refer to complete sets of nine.

Black Musical Troupe, pnt compo, 8½", EX................. $2,800.00
Brownie Nine=Pins, McLoughlin Bros, dated 1892, EXIB. $2,000.00
Camel holder w/6 Nubians on 4-wheeled wooden platform,
    14x14", EX.. $3,000.00
Chickens, 1 rooster w/8 hens, pnt compo, 6½" & 7½", EX+.$1,000.00
Circus Clown w/Horses & Trainer, lg open clown body holds 8
    horses & trainer, pnt compo, 17" L, EX................... $5,040.00
Circus Elephants, 8 upright elephants & trainer, pnt compo w/
    wooden bases, 7½", EX..................................... $3,360.00
English Bobbies, standing w/arms at sides, pnt compo w/wooden
    bases, 10", EX $1,230.00
French Soldiers, standing in short stride, pnt compo, 10½",
    EX+ $2,350.00
German Sailors, pnt compo, in navy bl uniforms w/arms at sides,
    ea w/mustache, 11", EX..................................... $2,800.00
Indian Set, Indian chief lying on his side on 4-wheeled platform
    w/9 smaller Indians, papier-maché, 9x23", EX $4,000.00
Indians & Chief, wearing Seminole-type headdress, pnt compo,
    9" & 9½", EX+... $3,080.00
Louis Bleriot Monoplane, w/pilot & 8 passengers, pnt wood
    plane w/paper wings, 8½" pnt compo figures, EX+ ... $9,520.00
Men of Various Occupations, butcher, carpenter, cobbler, gar-
    dener, blacksmith, etc, pnt compo, 11", EX+ $3,360.00
People of Different Nations, figures in various cultural attire, pnt
    compo, 10", EX... $2,240.00
Rabbits, papier-maché, 6 bunnys in mama rabbit holder on
    5-wheeled wood platform, 10x12", rstr/rpnt............. $1,200.00
Rooster Set, lg rooster holder on 4 metal wheels w/5 smaller rooster
    skittles & 3 wooden balls, pnt papier-maché, EX......... $2,100.00
Snowman & Boys w/Snowballs, mc pnt compo, boys wearing
    suits & ties w/snowballs looking upward, 7½", EX ... $1,790.00

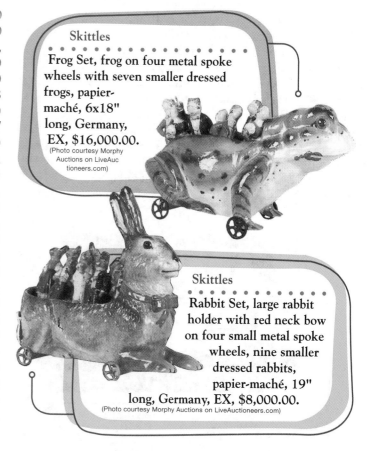

Skittles
**Frog Set, frog on four metal spoke
wheels with seven smaller dressed
frogs, papier-
maché, 6x18"
long, Germany,
EX, $16,000.00.**
(Photo courtesy Morphy
Auctions on LiveAuc
tioneers.com)

Skittles
**Rabbit Set, large rabbit
holder with red neck bow
on four small metal spoke
wheels, nine smaller
dressed rabbits,
papier-maché, 19"
long, Germany, EX, $8,000.00.**
(Photo courtesy Morphy Auctions on LiveAuctioneers.com)

Steiff Animal Set, 9 animals sitting upright on wooden bases, ea
    8", EX...$16,000.00
Teddy Roosevelt, mc pnt compo, 8", EX..................... $1,680.00

Slot Cars

Slot cars first became popular in the early 1960s. Electric raceways set up in retail storefront windows were commonplace. Huge commercial tracks with eight and ten lanes were located in hobby stores and raceways throughout the United States. Large corporations such as Aurora, Revell, Monogram, and Cox, many of which were already manufacturing toys and hobby items, jumped on the bandwagon to produce slot cars and race sets. By the end of the early 1970s, people were losing interest in slot racing, and its popularity diminished. Today the same Baby Boomers that raced slot cars in earlier days are revitalizing the sport. The popularity of the internet has stabilized the pricing of collectible slots. It can confirm prices of common items, while escalating the prices of the 'rare' items to new levels. As the internet grows in popularity, the accessibility of information on slots also grows. This should make the once hard-to-find slot cars more readily available for all to enjoy. Slot cars were generally well used, so finding vintage cars and race sets in like-new or mint condition is difficult. Slot replicating the 'muscle' cars from the '60s and '70s are extremely sought after, and clubs and organizations devoted to these collectibles are becoming more and more commonplace. Large toy companies such as Tomy and Tyco still produce some slots today, but not in the quality, quantity, or variety of years past.

Aurora produced several types of slots: Screachers (5700 and 5800 number series, valued at $5.00 to $20.00); the AC-powered Vibrators (1500 number series, valued at $20.00 to $150.00); DC-powered Thunderjets (1300 and 1400 number series, valued at $20.00 to $150.00); and the last-made AFX SP1000 (1900 number series, valued at $15.00 to $75.00).

Advisor: Gary Pollastro

COMPLETE SETS

AMT, Cobra Racing Set, NMIB	$185.00
Arnold, Minimobil, 1960s, unused, NMIB	$30.00
Atlas, Racing Set #1000, HO scale, GIB	$100.00
Aurora, Ford Street Van, #1943, lt bl & brn, NM	$15.00
Aurora, Home Raceway by Sears, #79N9513C, VG	$225.00
Aurora, Model Motoring Real Racing Set #1980, 1970, NMIB	$400.00
Aurora AFX, Big Ryder, HO scale, EXIB	$70.00
Aurora AFX, Blazer, #1917, bl & wht, VG	$12.00
Aurora AFX, Chevy Nomad, #1760, chrome, EX	$25.00
Aurora AFX, Chevy Nomad, #1760, orange, EX	$20.00
Aurora AFX, Devil's Ditch Set, EX	$40.00
Aurora AFX, Dodge Rescue Van, #1937, red, gr & wht, EX	$15.00
Aurora AFX, Furious Fueler Dragster, #1774, wht & yel, EX	$15.00
Aurora AFX, Peterbilt Shell Rig, #1155, yel, red & wht, EX	$25.00
Aurora AFX, Porsche 917-10, #1747, wht, red & bl, EX	$12.00
Aurora AFX, Shadow Cam Racer, blk, EX	$20.00
Aurora AFX, Speed Banner #11, red, wht & bl, NM	$15.00
Aurora AFX, Ultra 5, EXIB	$75.00

Aurora Cigarbox, Ford Lola GT, red w/wht stripe, G+	$10.00
Aurora G-Plus, Ferrari F1, #1734, red & wht, EX	$25.00
Aurora G-Plus, Indy Valvoline, blk, VG	$12.00
Cox, Baja Raceway, Super Scale, NMIB	$150.00
Cox, Ontario 8 #3070 w/Eagle & McLaren, GIB	$75.00
Eldon, Dodge Charger Road Race Set, NMIB	$75.00
Eldon, Gold Cup Road Race, 1962, 1/32 scale, EXIB	$150.00
Eldon, Raceway Set #24, 1/24 scale, VG	$75.00
Gilbert, Miniature Race Set #19041, VGIB	$95.00
Hong Kong, Speed King Deluxe Road Race Set #6441, EX+IB	$125.00
Ideal, Alcan Highway Torture Track, 1968, MIB	$50.00
Ideal, Dukes of Hazzard Racing Set, MIB	$85.00
Ideal, Mini-Motorific Set, #4939-5, EX	$85.00
Ideal, Motorific Alcan Highway Torture Track, 1966, missing vehicles o/w complete, NMIB	$60.00
Ideal, Motorific GTO Torture Track, lg, EXIB	$100.00
Ideal, Motorific-Racerific Survival Run XL, 1969, unused, MIB	$75.00
Marklin, Sprint, West Germany, 1960s, unused, M (EX box)	$225.00

Meccano Triang, Scalextric, 1960s, unused, NMIB........ $110.00
Remco, Mighty Mike Action Track, NMIB......................$50.00
Strombecker, Plymouth Barracuda, 1/32 scale set.......... $150.00
Strombecker, Thunderbolt Monza, Montgomery Ward,
   VGIB $150.00
Strombecker, 4 Lane Mark IV Race Set, VGIB $250.00
Tyco, '57 Chevy, red & orange w/yel stripes, EX...............$20.00
Tyco, The A-Team, 1980s, unused, MIB..........................$25.00
Tyco, Autoworld Carrera, wht & red w/bl stripe, G $10.00
Tyco, Blazer, red & blk, VG...$10.00
Tyco, Chaparral 2G #66, #8504, VG.............................$14.00
Tyco, Firebird Turbo #12, blk & gold, EX......................$10.00
Tyco, Lighted Porsche #2, silver w/red nose, EX.............$20.00
Tyco, Pinto Funny Car Goodyear, red & yel, EX $20.00
Tyco, Racing Bandits, EX $30.00

SLOT CARS ONLY

Aurora AFX, AMC Javelin Trans-Am, #6, 1972, EX........$10.00
Aurora AFX, Autoworld Porsche #5, wht w/bl stripes, EX.$12.00
Aurora AFX, BMW 3201 Turbo, #1980, yel & orange, EX.$20.00
Aurora AFX, Camaro Z-28, #1901, red, wht & bl, EX $20.00
Aurora AFX, Chevy Nomad, #1760, orange, EX...............$20.00
Aurora AFX, Dodge Challenger, #1773, lime & bl, NM...$35.00
Aurora AFX, Dodge Fever Dragster, wht & yel, EX $15.00
Aurora AFX, Ferrari 612, #1751, yel & blk, EX...............$10.00
Aurora AFX, Ford Thunderbird Stock Car, NMIB............$25.00
Aurora AFX Magna Traction, Dodge 'Police' Van, blk & wht,
   unused, MIP $37.00
Aurora AFX Magna Traction, Dodge 'Rescue Vehicle,' Van,
   orange w/wht roof, gold lettering, unused, MIP.............$45.00
Aurora AFX Magna Traction, Ford Street Van, 2-tone brn,
   unused, MIP $35.00
Aurora AFX, Mario Andretti NGK Indy Car, blk, M........$35.00
Aurora AFX, Monza GT, #1948, wht & gr, EX.................$15.00
Aurora AFX, Pontiac Firebird #9, wht, bl & blk, EX $25.00
Aurora AFX, Porsche Carrera #3, 1933, wht, red & blk, NM ..$12.00
Aurora AFX, Porsche 917 Flamethrower, 1972, EX+ $24.00
Aurora AFX, Rallye Ford Escort, #1737, gr & bl, EX $15.00
Aurora AFX, Speed Beamer, red, wht & bl stripe, VG......$10.00
Aurora Cigarbox, Cobra GT, #6113, chromed w/dbl blk stripe, M
   (EX+ box)..$45.00
Aurora Cigarbox, Dino Ferrari, red, EX $20.00
Aurora Cigarbox, Ford GT, wht w/blk stripe, NM+ $20.00
Aurora Cigarbox, Ford J, #6104, yel & bl w/bl stripe, M (EX+
   box) $25.00
Aurora Cigarbox, Mako Shark, #6103, bl, M (EX+ box) ..$25.00
Aurora, Ford Baja Bronco, #1909, red, EX $15.00
Aurora G-Plus, Corvette, #1011, red, orange & wht, EX ..$15.00
Aurora G-Plus, Indy Valvoline, blk, VG..........................$12.00
Aurora G-Plus, Rallye Ford Escort, #1737, gr & bl, EX.....$15.00
Aurora, McLaren Elva #1397, 1968, NM........................$20.00
Aurora, Model Motoring, Thunderbird, #1544, bl w/wht top, NMIB.$182.00
Aurora, Snowmobile, #1485-400, yel w/bl figure, MIB......$55.00
Aurora Thunderjet, Chaparral 2F #7, #1410, lime & bl, EX ...$25.00
Aurora Thunderjet, Cobra, #1375, yel w/blk stripe, VG+.$30.00
Aurora Thunderjet, Cougar, #1389, wht, EX....................$40.00
Aurora Thunderjet, Dune Buggy, wht w/red striped roof, EX ..$30.00

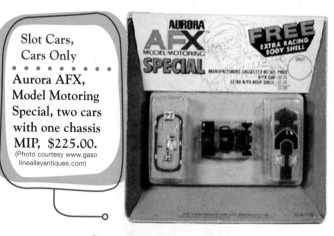

Aurora Thunderjet, Ford Car, #1382, wht & bl, VG.........$25.00
Aurora Thunderjet, Ford GT 40, #1374, red w/blk stripe, EX.$25.00
Aurora Thunderjet, Mangusta Mongoose, #1400, yel, EX.$45.00
Aurora Thunderjet, Mustang Fastback #7 Racer, wht w/red
   stripe, blk interior, EX $65.00
Aurora Vibrators, Ford Galaxie (Sunliner) Convertible (1962),
   red w/blk tonneau, tan interior, EX $85.00
Aurora Vibrators, Mercedes, #1542, yel, EX $50.00
Aurora Vibrators, Thunderbird, bl w/tan roof, silver trim, EX.$120.00
Aurora, Willy's Gasser, #1401, 1969, NMIP $65.00
BZ, Batmobile, 1966, blk, 8", NMIB $335.00
Eldon, Corvette Stingray, bl, VG $65.00
Eldon, Dodge Charger (1968) #9, bl w/2 yel stripes front to back,
   blk top, EX+ $85.00
Eldon, Porsche RSK #2, red, electric lights, EX.................$65.00
Ideal, Jaguar XK-E, #1, Motorific Custom Cars, 1968, gr w/racing
   stripes, chromed side exhausts, MIB $40.00
Ideal Mini Motorific, Custom Hot Rod, w/CU 25 motor, unused,
   MIP...$50.00
Marchon (Tyco Compatible), Donald Duck Firebird, 1980s, yel
   & bl, Donald driver, NM+ $25.00
Marchon (Tyco Compatible), Mickey Mouse Firebird, 1980s,
   red, Mickey driver, NM..$20.00
Marklin Sprint, BMW Formula 2 Race Car #6, wht w/gray-bl,
   EX+IB $150.00
Strombecker, Pontiac Bonneville, EX...............................$40.00

TCR, Maintenance Van, red & whtm, EX.......................$15.00

Tyco, '40 Ford Coupe, #88534, blk w/flames, EX...............$20.00

Tyco, '83 Corvette Challenger #33, silver & yel, EX.........$25.00

Tyco, Bandit Pickup, blk & red, EX $12.00

Tyco, Camel GT Datsun 280-ZX, 1982, EX......................$8.00

Tyco, Caterpillar #96, blk & yel, EX $20.00

Tyco, Corvette Hardtop #3, wht w/orange stripe front to back, dk
windows, NM $20.00

Tyco, Corvette #12, wht & red w/bl stripes, EX..............$12.00

Tyco, Firebird, #6914, cream & red, VG......................$12.00

Tyco, Funny Mustang, orange w/yel flame, EX.................$25.00

Tyco, Jam Car, yel & blk, EX................................$10.00

Tyco, Lamborghini, red, VG.................................$12.00

Tyco, Military Police #45, wht & bl, EX $30.00

Tyco, Open-Wheeled Indy Car #27, 1962, gr, EX+ $65.00

Tyco, Pinto Funny Cargotcha, dk red w/gold stripe, VG ...$20.00

Tyco, Richard Petty STP Dodge Stock Car #43, EX............$45.00

Tyco, Rokar 240-Z, #7, blk, EX..............................$10.00

Tyco, Superbird, #8533, red, wht & bl, VG+.................$15.00

Tyco, Super Pinto Funny Car, 1972, wht w/bl & red stripes, yel
parachute pack on rear, EX+................................$35.00

Tyco TCR, Mark Martin's Valvoline #6 Stock Car, red, wht &
bl, 1992-93, MIP $21.00

Tyco, Turbo Hopper #27, red, EX $12.00

Tyco, Vette (Corvette), 1980s, red w/blk & wht detail, working
headlights, EX $11.00

Tyco, Volvo 850 #3, wht & bl, EX...........................$20.00

Tyco, 7-Eleven Ford Thunderbird, 1970s, red, wht & bl,
NM $6.00

MISCELLANEOUS

AMT Service Parts Kit, #2000, VG $65.00

Aurora AFX Billboard Retaining Walls, set of 8, EXIB.....$15.00

Aurora AFX Pit Kit, G $15.00

Aurora AFX Terminal Track, plug-in or wire-type, EX,
ea $5.00

Aurora AFX 45 OHM Hand Controller w/Brakes, EXIB..$15.00

Aurora Model Motoring Hill Track, 9", EX $8.00

Aurora Model Motoring Service Manual for Thunderjet 500,
1963, 32 pgs, image of Stirling Moss, VG...................$25.00

Aurora Model Motoring Thumb-Style Controller, EX........$6.00

Aurora Model Motoring Y Turn-Off Track w/Switch, EX .$20.00

Aurora Model Motoring 4-Way Stop Track, 9", EX $15.00

Aurora Thunderjet Country Bridge Roadway, EXIB.........$20.00

Eldon Power Track, MOC $10.00

Gilbert Automatic Fly Over Chicane Kit, #19342, MIB...$40.00

Gilbert Automatic Lap Counter, #19339, MIB................$35.00

Gilbert Autorama Grand Stand #19340, MIB.................$25.00

Monogram Lane Change Track, MIB..........................$20.00

Monogram Tapered Chicane Track, MIB.....................$20.00

Strombecker Scale Lap Counter, 1/32 scale, MIB...........$25.00

Tyco HO Scale 1973-74 Handbook, EX.......................$10.00

Tyoc Trigger Controller, orange, EX.........................$8.00

• • • • • • • • • • • • • • • • • • Smith-Miller • • • • • • • • • • • • • • • •

Smith-Miller (Los Angeles, California) made toy trucks from 1944 until 1955. During that time they used four basic cab designs, and most of their trucks sold for about $15.00 each. Over the past several years, these toys have become very popular, especially the Mack trucks which today sell at premium prices. The company made a few other types of toys, such as the train toy box and the 'Long, Long Trailer.'

See also Advertising.

Arden Milk Truck, GMC, red & wht, 8 wooden milk cans, 14",
EX $450.00

Army Materials Truck, L-Mack, 20", VG+IB $650.00

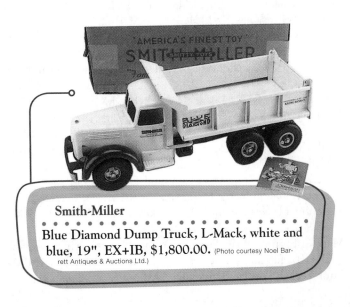

Smith-Miller
• •
**Blue Diamond Dump Truck, L-Mack, white and
blue, 19", EX+IB, $1,800.00.** (Photo courtesy Noel Bar-
rett Antiques & Auctions Ltd.)

Auto Pulling House Trailer, #535, bl & wht, 40" overall, EXIB..$2,050.00

Bank of America Truck, GMC, 14", EX......................$135.00

Barrel Truck, GMC, aluminum high-sided trailer w/open top &
chains, 2 wooden barrels, 14", EX $250.00

Bekins Van Lines Co Semi, B-Mack, wht, 29", EX+ ...$1,300.00

Bekins Van Lines Co Semi, L-Mack, wht, 28", EX......$1,100.00

Bell Telephone System Truck, L-Mack, canvas top arched over
bed, 2-tone gr, 19", EX $550.00

Blue Diamond Dump Truck, B-Mack, wht, 19", EX+.....$825.00

Drive-O-Dump Truck, GMC, remote driving action, 6-wheeled
w/rear duals, 12", VG+.....................................$275.00

Dump Truck, GMC, w/wheel-crank on side of dump bed,
6-wheeled w/rear duals, 11", NM+ $300.00

Emergency Towing Service Truck, GMC, red & wht, 14", EX..$650.00

Fire Aerial Ladder Truck, B-Mack, 'SMFD,' complete w/3 plastic
figures & hang tag, 36" overall, NMIB $1,425.00

Fire Aerial Ladder Truck, open cab, 'LAFD,' 25", EX.....$750.00

Fire Ladder Truck, 'St Louis FD No 7,' 24", NM...........$625.00

Heinz Stake Truck, GMC cab, decals on stake bed, 14", VG .$150.00

Hennis Semi, B-Mack, red w/aluminum enclosed trailer, 29",
EX $1,100.00

Smith-Miller

MIC Road Star Fruehauf Semi, L-Mack, red with aluminum trailer, 29", NMIB, $1,300.00.
(Photo courtesy Noel Barrett Antiques & Auctions Ltd.)

Hollywood Film Ad Truck w/Searchlight on Trailer, GMC, b/o light, 26" overall, EX $750.00

International Paper Co Semi, L-Mack, red & wht, open-top trailer w/curved ends on sides, open back, 28", VG+ .. $700.00

Kraft Delivery Truck, GMC, yel, 14", EX+ $440.00

Lumber Truck, GMC, flatbed trailer w/bundle of lumber, 13", NM $325.00

Lumber Truck, GMC, flatbed trailer w/bundle of lumber, 23", VG+IB $400.00

Lumber Truck, L-Mack, tandem trailers, orig load of wood, 36" overall, EX+ $500.00

Lyon Van Lines, Semi, GMC, trailer w/drop sides, 21", EX . $400.00

Lyon Van Lines Semi, GMC, trailer w/straight sides, 21", VG+ . $350.00

Lyon Van Lines Van Truck, L-Mack, single axle van, 20", EX ... $950.00

Machinery Hauler, GMC, Fruehauf low-boy trailer w/very scarce orig loading ramps, 26", EX+ $900.00

Machinery Hauler, GMC, Fruehauf low-boy trailer, no loading ramps, 26", EXIB $500.00

Materials Truck, GMC, wood bed w/wire rails on ea side, 14", EX $225.00

Materials Truck, L-Mack, wood flatbed w/3 metal posts ea side, no load, 20", VG $450.00

Materials Truck, L-Mack, wood flatbed w/3 metal posts ea side, orig load, 20", EXIB $925.00

MIC Aerial Fire Ladder Truck, open cab, aluminum ladders, 26", EX+IB $750.00

MIC Dump Truck, side lever dump action, yel, 17½", EX....$975.00

MIC Lift-O-Matic Stake Truck, L-Mack, rear gate lifts up & down, wooden barrels, 17", EX+ $550.00

MIC Lift-O-Matic Stake Truck, L-Mack, rear gate lifts up & down, wooden barrels, 17", EX+IB $775.00

MIC Lumber Truck, lever action, yel cab w/gr frame, full load of chained lumber, 19", EX $1,000.00

MIC Official Tow Car, wht, 17", NMIB $1,000.00

Mobilgas Tanker Truck, GMC, retractable hoses & nozzles, 27" L, EX+ $375.00

PIE Semi, B-Mack, 29", EXIB $1,000.00

PIE Semi, L-Mack, 29", EX $450.00

PIE Semi, L-Mack, 29", NMIB $1,200.00

Rexall Delivery Truck, GMC, orange, 14", VG $250.00

Searchlight Truck, B-Mack, 18", VG $1,050.00

Searchlight Truck, L Mack, electric spotlight, 18½", VG . $650.00

Semi w/Stake Trailer, GMC, U-shaped wooden bed w/aluminum stake sides, 23", VG+ $225.00

Silver Streak Semi, GMC, wooden bed w/polished aluminum sides, 23", VG $275.00

Sparkeeta UP Truck, GMC, gr, divided bed, 14", G $825.00

Stake Truck, GMC, 14", EX $225.00

Trans-Continental Freighter Semi, GMC, open aluminum & wood trailer w/open curved back, 23", EXIB $650.00

Union Ice Co Truck, GMC, bl & wht, 14", VG $350.00

US Treasury Truck, GMC, 14", EX+ $650.00

Van Truck w/Tandem Trailer, L-Mack, red, 'Smith-Miller' logo on sides, EX+ $1,400.00

Soldiers and Accessories

Dimestore soldiers were made from the 1920s until sometime in the 1960s. Some of the better-known companies who made these small-scale figures and vehicles were Barclay, Manoil, and American Metal Toys, formerly known as Jones (hollow cast lead); Grey Iron (cast iron); and Auburn Rubber. They are 3" to 3½" high and were sold in Woolworth's, Kresge's, and other five-and-dime stores for a nickel or a dime, hence the name dimestore. Marx made tin soldiers for use in target gun games and these sell for about $10.00 to $25.00. Condition is most important as these soldiers saw lots of action. They are often found with much of the paint worn off and with some serious 'battle wounds' such as missing arms or rifle tips. Such figures have little value to collectors. Nearly 2,000 different figures and vehicles were made by the major manufacturers, plus a number of others by minor makers such as Tommy Toy and All-Nu.

Another very popular line of toy soldiers has been made by Britains of England since 1893. They are smaller and usually more detailed than dimestores, and variants number in the thousands. We recommend *Collecting American Made Toy Soldiers* by Richard O'Brien for more information about dimestore soldiers, and *Collecting Foreign-Made Toy Soldiers* also by Richard O'Brien, for Britains and others not made in America.

You'll notice that in addition to the soldiers, many of our descriptions and values are for vehicles and planes made and sold by the same manufacturers. Note: Percentages in the description lines refer to the amount of original paint remaining, a most important evaluation factor.

The following listings were provided by our advisors, Stan and Sally Alekna. To contact them, see the Dictory of Contributors and Advisors.

See also Dinky; Plastic Figures.

Key:
AA — antianircraft
AC — aircraft
AMT — American Metal Toys
CH — cast helmet
EV — early version
GK — Greyklip
LS — long stride
M — military

PF — pod foot
PH — pot helmet
PW — postwar
SS — short stride
TH — tin helmet
USD — Uncle Sam's Defenders
V — vehicles

AMT, M, AA gun, silver, scarce, NM $50.00
AMT, M, AA gunner, gray, scarce, 98% $170.00
AMT, M, AA gunner, khaki, scarce, 97%......................$120.00
AMT, M, ammo carrier, khaki, very scarce, 96%............$375.00
AMT, M, anti-tank gunner kneeling, khaki, scarce, 97%....$125.00
AMT, M, flag bearer, khaki, very scarce, 97%.................$275.00
AMT, M, grenade thrower, very scrace, 97% $170.00
AMT, M, howitzer, rubber tires, 7", scarce, 99%..............$95.00
AMT, M, machine (dbl) gunner prone, khaki, scarce, 96% ...$133.00
AMT, M, machine gunner firing on stump, gray, scarce, 98% .$135.00
AMT, M, soldier kneeling at searchlight, khaki, scarce, 98% .$105.00
AMT, M, soldier kneeling firing long rifle, khaki, scarce, 98%..$165.00
AMT, M, soldier prone w/rifle, scarce, 95% $180.00
AMT, M, soldier standing firing rifle, khaki, scarce, 99% . $140.00
AMT, M, wire cutter, khaki, very scarce, 93%-95% $400.00
AMT, V, tank, 98%..$55.00
Auburn, M, bugler, khaki, 95% $20.00
Auburn, M, doctor, wht, scarce, 93%-95% $44.00
Auburn, M, infantry officer, M $35.00
Auburn, M, infantry private, wht, NM $25.00
Auburn, M, nurse in brn, M $175.00
Auburn, M, observer w/binoculars, khaki, 97%.................$25.00
Auburn, M, officer, M...$35.00
Auburn, M, Red Cross doctor, scarce, 96%......................$46.00
Auburn, M, soldier charging w/tommy gun, 97% $26.00
Auburn, M, soldier marching at port arms, khaki, EV, NM ..$45.00
Auburn, M, tommy gunner charging, 98% $27.00
Auburn, M, US infantry officer, 98%..............................$19.00
Auburn, M, White Guard officer, 99%............................$40.00
Auburn, V, Marmon-Harrington tank, 3¼", 98% $37.00
Auburn, V, US Army open bed truck, 4½", 97% $42.00
Barclay, AC, dirigible, 1930s, very scarce, 95% $225.00
Barclay, M, AA gun crew, bl barrel, 97% $41.00
Barclay, M, AA gunner, gr, 96%.....................................$21.00
Barclay, M, AA gunner, khaki, 98%................................$22.00

Barclay, M, ammo carrier, silver boxes, 98% $27.00
Barclay, M, machine gunner lying down, khaki, 99%.........$22.00
Barclay, M, machine gunner prone, CH, 97% $28.00
Barclay, M, machine gunner prone, gr pot helmet, 97%....$27.00
Barclay, M, marine, SS, 94% $32.00
Barclay, M, marine, 98%...$28.00
Barclay, M, marine marching, bl cap,LS, 99% $43.00
Barclay, M, marine officer, LS, wht cap, scarce, 99%.........$55.00
Barclay, M, naval officer, LS, bl uniform, very scarce, 98%.$425.00
Barclay, M, naval officer, LS, wht uniform, 99%................$27.00
Barclay, M, naval officer, LS, 95%...................................$29.00
Barclay, M, nurse, blk hair, scarce, 99% $46.00
Barclay, M, nurse w/bag, blond hair, bl cross on cap, 98%.$33.00
Barclay, M, officer, gr PH, 98%..$31.00
Barclay, M, officer, khaki, 96% $16.00
Barclay, M, officer, khaki, on gray horse, 96%...................$50.00
Barclay, M, officer, PF, bl w/wht helmet, very scarce, 98% ..$175.00
Barclay, M, officer in helmet on horse, scarce, NM $125.00
Barclay, M, officer w/gas mask & pistol, CH, 98%.............$31.00
Barclay, M, officer w/sword, gr pot helmet, M...................$31.00
Barclay, M, officer w/sword, LS, TH, 99%.........................$34.00
Barclay, M, radio operator, separate antenna, 94% $55.00
Barclay, M, sailor, bl, PF, 98%..$26.00
Barclay, M, sailor, wht, PF, 96%.......................................$24.00
Barclay, M, sentry in overcoat, TH, 95% $30.00
Barclay, M, shell loader, 99%...$28.00
Barclay, M, soldier on motorcycle, 98% $70.00
Barclay, M, solder, parachutist, 97%.................................$36.00
Barclay, M, soldier, pigeon dispatcher, M $40.00
Barclay, M, soldier prone firing rifle, TH, 98%..................$32.00
Barclay, M, soldier running looking up, gr, PF, M $23.00
Barclay, M, soldier running looking up, khaki, PF, NM $21.00
Barclay, M, soldier running w/rifle, gr, CH, 98%...............$41.00
Barclay, M, soldier standing at searchlight, M $58.00
Barclay, M, soldier standing firing, 99% $23.00

Soldiers and Accessories
Barclay, Aircraft, spaceship with arrow on top, 1930s, very scarce, M, $575.00. (Photo courtesy Stan and Sally Alekna)

Soldiers and Accessories
Barclay, Military, Italian soldier with rifle, in stride, NM, $300.00. (Photo courtesy Bertoia Auctions)

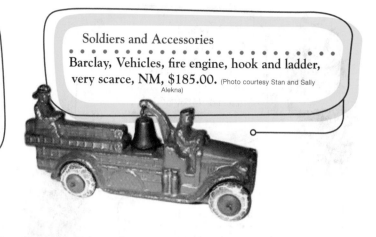

Barclay, M, soldier w/flame thrower, gr, PF, NM $25.00
Barclay, M, soldier w/flame thrower, khaki, PF, 98%..........$20.00
Barclay, M, soldier w/french horn, 96% $27.00
Barclay, M, soldier w/gas mask & rifle charging, tin helmet.$34.00
Barclay, M, soldier w/pistol crawling, khaki, 98%..............$38.00
Barclay, M, soldier w/sentry dog, scarce, 99% $97.00
Barclay, M, soldier wounded head & arm, gr, 95% $46.00
Barclay, M, soldier wounded on crutches, gr, 99% $48.00
Barclay, M, soldier wounded sitting, arm in sling, 98% $33.00
Barclay, M, soldiers on raft, scarce, 95% $94.00
Barclay, M, soldiers at range finder, 97%...........................$41.00
Barclay, M, tommy gunner, gr PH, M $31.00
Barclay, V, ambulance, sm bl cross, WRT, 3½", 98% $74.00
Barclay, V, armoured truck, khaki, WRT, 98%...................$27.00
Barclay, V, cannon (coastal defense), rarest Barclay cannon, NM $185.00
Barclay, V, cannon truck, movable cannon, scarce, M.... $180.00
Barclay, V, circus wagon, no horses, very scarce, 98%..... $325.00
Barclay, V, coupe, blk metal wheels, 2¼", 95% $43.00
Barclay, V, dump truck, SC, plain, movable bed, bl/red, 99% ..$17.00
Barclay, V, fuel truck, SC, plain, gr, 99%...........................$17.00
Barclay, V, futuristic bus, bl w/wht tires, 3½", 97% $64.00
Barclay, V, machine gun car (two-man), scarce, 99% $75.00
Barclay, V, milk wagon, 1 horse, very scarce, 90% $225.00
Barclay, V, moving truck, SC, 'Hertz,' gr/silver, ca 1960s, M..$20.00
Barclay, V, Renault tank, wht tired, 1937, 4", 98%............$59.00
Barclay, V, Sedan, orange w/wht tires, 1935 3½", 96% $83.00
Barclay, V, streamlined coupe, orange, 3¼", 97%.............$55.00
Barclay, V, streamlined sedan, 1936, red w/wht tires, 3⅛", scarce, 97%..$90.00
Barclay, V, taxi, w/'Taxi' stenciled on hood, 99% $62.00
Barclay, V, taxi, w/o 'Taxi' stenciled on hood, 98% $59.00
Barclay, V, US Army truck, 96% $41.00
Barclay, V, US M2 tank, khaki, wht tires, 2½", 99% $35.00
Barclay, V, wrecker, orig wire hook, ca 1931, 3½", 96%....$80.00
Barclay, V, zephyr train, 1-piece, 1930s, the rarest Barclay train, 99%.. $475.00
Grey Iron, GK, drummer charging, EX $7.00
Grey Iron, GK, officer charging, EX.....................................$7.00
Grey Iron, GK, soldier marching w/rifle, EX $4.00
Grey Iron, M, ammo carrier, scarce, 98%........................ $125.00
Grey Iron, M, cadet, EV, 94%...$31.00
Grey Iron, M, cadet marching, 97%....................................$36.00
Grey Iron, M, cadet officer marching, 96%.........................$36.00

Grey Iron, M, cavalryman on brn horse, 97%....................$46.00
Grey Iron, M, US doughboy bomber, crawling, NM..........$37.00
Grey Iron, M, US doughboy charging, PW, 95%...............$21.00
Grey Iron, M, US doughboy combat trooper, PW, 97% $56.00
Grey Iron, M, US doughboy kneeling, firing rifle, 96% $31.00
Grey Iron, M, US doughboy officer, 97%............................$27.00
Grey Iron, M, US doughboy officer w/field glasses, 95%....$40.00
Grey Iron, M, US doughboy sentry in overcoat, 99%........$39.00
Grey Iron, M, US doughboy signaling, 99% $45.00
Grey Iron, M, US infantry charging, EV, 97%...................$23.00
Grey Iron, M, US infantry officer, EV, 97%.......................$25.00
Grey Iron, M, US infantry port arms, EV, 98%.................$23.00
Grey Iron, M, US infantry rt shoulder arms, EV, 98%.......$23.00
Grey Iron, M, US machine gunner, EV, scarce, 98%.........$34.00
Grey Iron, M, US Marine, dk bl tunic, EV, 97%.................32.00
Grey Iron, M, US Marine, lt bl tunic, EV, 99% $34.00
Grey Iron, M, US Naval officer, bl, EV, 99% $29.00
Grey Iron, M, wounded soldier on stretcher, 99% $51.00
Jones, Annapolis cadet port arms, bl, M $35.00
Jones, Kings Royal Rifle Corps, 99%..................................$32.00
Jones, Marines of 1809, #5436, set of 7, very scarce, MIB...$250.00
Jones, Midshipmen of 1928, #544, set of 8, very scarce, MIB..$250.00
Jones, Pilot of the 17th Pursuit Squadron, 1937, 99%.......$25.00
Jones, Scot Highlander of 1814, 98%.................................$29.00
Jones, US infantry, #5413, set of 8, very scarce, MIB $250.00
Jones, US infantry, 1940 (?), 96% $30.00
Jones, US marine, 1809, no pigtail, scarce, 96%...............$35.00
Jones, Waynes Legion soldier on guard w/bayonet, M $34.00
Lincoln Log, M, foot soldier of 1812, scarce, M.................$30.00
Lincoln Log, M, foot soldier of 1918 charging, 99%..........$25.00
Lincoln Log, M, foot soldier of 1918 marching, 99%.........$25.00
Lincoln Log, M, officer of 1918 mounted, 95% $36.00
Manoil, M, AA gunner, 98%..$54.00
Manoil, M, AA gunner w/range finder, NM $38.00
Manoil, M, AA machine gunner, 98%.................................$32.00
Manoil, M, aviator w/bomb, 98%..$43.00
Manoil, M, banjo player, very scarce, M $165.00
Manoil, M, bazooka soldier kneeling, 97%.........................$41.00
Manoil, M, bicycle dispatch rider, 96%..............................$51.00
Manoil, M, bomb thrower, 3 grenades in pouch, 98%.......$37.00
Manoil, M, boxer, scarce, 97% $129.00
Manoil, M, bugler, 2nd version, NM...................................$36.00
Manoil, M, gray, 94%..$30.00
Manoil, M, cadet marching, dk bl, very scarce, 95% $175.00

Soldiers and Accessories

Manoil, Military, soldier at map table with phone, no buttons, 94%, $62.00. (Photo courtesy Mohawk Arms, Inc. on LiveAuctioneers.com)

Soldiers and Accessories

Manoil, Military, sailor in blue uniform, second version, very scarce, 96%, $225.00. (Photo courtesy Stan and Sally Alekna)

Manoil, M, cadet marching, lt bl, M $32.00
Manoil, M, cannon loader, 99% $35.00
Manoil, M, observer w/periscope, scarce, 99% $58.00
Manoil, M, parade soldier, stocky version, 98% $29.00
Manoil, M, parade soldier, thin version, 99% $48.00
Manoil, M, parade soldier, 5th version, 99% $29.00
Manoil, M, parade soldier, 97% $54.00
Manoil, M, radio operator prone, scarce, 96% $69.00
Manoil, M, sailor, wht uniform, 2nd version, M $36.00
Manoil, M, shell loader, 97% $30.00
Manoil, M, signalman, hollow base, 93-95% $67.00
Manoil, M, sniper firing carbine at angle, 98% $45.00
Manoil, M, sniper kneeling, 97% $53.00
Manoil, M, sniper prone, camouflaged, 96% $40.00
Manoil, M, soldier firing rifle in air, 95% $51.00
Manoil, M, soldier in gas mask w/rifle, 95% $32.00

Manoil, M, solider kneeling, firing, 99% $35.00
Manoil, M, soldier marching w/rifle & pack, 97% $37.00
Manoil, M, soldier marching w/right shoulder arms, 98% .$29.00
Manoil, M, soldier on guard duty, scarce, 98% $133.00
Manoil, M, solider sitting w/o rifle, 98% $41.00
Manoil, M, solider standing firing rifle, 99% $36.00
Manoil, M, soldier w/bazooka, 95% $39.00
Manoil, M, soldier w/camera, thick arm, scarce, M $112.00
Manoil, M, solder w/gas mask & flare pistol, 98% $39.00
Manoil, M, solider w/rifle, charging, scarce, 95% $64.00
Manoil, M, soldier wounded, 94% $20.00
Manoil, M, stretcher bearer, gr cross on pouch, NM $15.00
Manoil, M, stretcher bearer, no medical kit, 98% $35.00
Manoil, M, tommy gunner charging, 96% $48.00
Manoil, V, fire engine, red & silver, 96% $43.00
Manoil, V, 'Gasoline' truck, 98% $38.00
Manoil, V, oil tanker, red, 95% $42.00
Manoil, V, oil tanker, yel & silver, scarce, 98% $52.00
Manoil, V, submarine, silver, 98% $58.00
Manoil, V, tank, silver, 98% $34.00
Manoil, V, tractor w/plain front, NM $30.00
Manoil, V, tractor w/tow loop in front, M $32.00
Manoil, V, water wagon (no number), 98% $36.00
Manoil, V, water wagon #72, 97% $35.00
Marx, M, Air Force mechanic w/prop, scarce, VG+ $28.00
Marx, M, French infantry, tin $13.00
Marx, M, howitzer, tin, NM $14.00
Marx, M, infantry colonel reading orders, EX $13.00
Marx, M, infantry private at attention, tin, M $10.00
Marx, M, infantry private kneeling, firing rifle, EX+ $11.00
Marx, M, infantry private marching, EX $9.00
Marx, M, infantry sergeant, EX+ $13.00
Marx, M, nurse in cape, tin, very scarce, EX+ $125.00
Marx, M, paratropper w/tommy gun, scarce, EX $32.00
Marx, M, tank commander, scarce, VG $32.00
Marx, M, US Cavalry, EX+ $12.00

• • • • • • • • • • • • • • • • Star Trek • • • • • • • • • • • • • • • •

   The Star Trek concept was introduced to the public in the mid-1960s via a TV series which continued for many years in syndication. The impact it had on American culture has spanned two generations of loyal fans through its animated TV cartoon series (1977), six major motion pictures, Fox network's 1987 TV show, 'Star Trek, The Next Generation,' and two other television series, 'Deep Space 9,' and 'Voyager.' As a result of its success, vast amounts of merchandise (both licensed and unlicensed) has been marketed in a wide variety of items including jewelry, clothing, calendars, collector plates, comics, costumes, games, greeting and gum cards, party goods, magazines, model kits, posters, puzzles, records and tapes, school supplies, and toys. Packaging is very important; an item mint and in its original box is generally worth 75% to 100% more than one rated excellent.

   See also Character and Promotional Drinking Glasses; Comic Books; Halloween Costumes; Lunch Boxes; Model Kits.

Key: STNG — Star Trek Next Generation   DS9 — Deep Space 9   V— Voyager

FIGURES

Galoob, ST V, 7", any character, 1989, MIP, ea $20 to $25.00
Galoob, STNG, Antican, Ferengi, Q, or Selay, M, ea $30.00
Galoob, STNG, Commander William Riker, MOC $15.00
Galoob, STNG, Data, bl face, M.....................................$25.00
Galoob, STNG, Data, brn face, M $18.00
Galoob, STNG, Data, flesh face, M $10.00

Galoob, STNG, Data, flesh face, MOC $22.00
Galoob, STNG, Data, spotted face, MOC.........................$15.00
Galoob, STNG, LaForge, Lt Worf, Picard or Riker, M,
    ea.. $8.00
Galoob, STNG, Lieutenant Worf, MOC $15.00
Galoob, STNG, Tasha Yar, M $10.00

Star Trek, Figures
• • • • • • • • • • •
Mego, 3¾", Decker, M (EX creased card), $30.00. (Photo courtesy www.gasolinealleyantiques.com)

Star Trek, Figures
• • • • • • • • • • •
Mego, 8", The Keeper, MOC, $180.00. (Photo courtesy Lloyd Ralston Gallery on LiveAuctioneers.com)

Mego, 3¾", Acturian, Betelgeusian, Klingon, Megarite, Rigellian or Zatanite, Series 2, M, ea $80.00

Mego, 3¾", Capt Kirk, Dr McCoy, Mr Spock or Mr Scott, Series 1, M, ea $15.00

Mego, 3¾", Illia, Series 1, M (VG creased card) $27.00

Mego, 8", Andorian, 1970s, M $350.00

Mego, 8", Capt Kirk, 1970s, M...$30.00

Mego, 8", Cheron, 1970s, M...$90.00

Mego, 8", Cheron, 1970s, MOC...................................... $175.00

Mego, 8", Dr McCoy, 1970s, MOC...................................$85.00

Mego, 8", Gorn, 1970s, MOC.. $175.00

Mego, 8", Klingon, 1970s, M $30.00

Mego, 8", Lt Uhura, 1970s, MOC.................................... $135.00

Mego, 8", Mr Scott, 1970s, M..$40.00

Mego, 8", Mr Spock, 1970s, MOC $60.00

Mego, 8", Mugato, 1970s, M.. $300.00

Mego, 8", Neptunian, 1970s, MOC $230.00

Mego, 8", Romulan, 1970s, M.. $800.00

Mego, 8", Talos, 1970s, MOC... $525.00

Mego, 12½", Arcturian, 1979, M.......................................$65.00

Mego, 12½", Capt Kirk, 1979, MIP $80.00

Mego, 12½", Decker, 1979, M $60.00

Mego, 12½", Ilia, 1979, MIP..$80.00

Mego, 12½", Klingon, 1979, M..$60.00

Mego, 12½", Mr Spock, 1979, MIP...................................$80.00

Playmates, DS9, Chief Miles O'Brien, Commander Sisko, Major Kira Nerys, Morn, Odo or Quark, 1994, MIP, ea...........$12.00

Playmates, DS9, Dr Julian Bashir, 1994, M......................$12.00

Playmates, DS9, Lt Jadzia Dax, 1994, MIP.......................$18.00

Playmates, First Contact, 5", The Borg, Dr Beverly Crusher, Capt Picard or Lily, 1996, M, ea $10.00

Playmates, First Contact, 5", The Borg, MOC..................$14.00

Playmates, First Contact, 5", Data, Deanna Troi, La Farge, Cpat Piccard, Riker, Worf or Cochrane, 1996, M, ea...............$8.00

Playmates, First Contact, 9", Capt Picard in 21st C outfit or Cochrane, 1996, M, ea...$20.00

Playmates, First Contact, 9", Data, Capt Picard or Riker, 1996, M $15.00

Playmates, Insurrection, any character, 1998, 9", MIP, ea $10 to..$15.00

Playmates, Insurrection, any character, 1998, 12", M, ea $8.00

Playmates, STNG, 1st Series, Borg, Capt Picard, Commander Riker, Lt Commander Data or Lt Worf, 1992, MOC, ea...$22.00

Playmates, STNG, 1st Series, Deanna Troi or Romulan, 1992, MOC, ea...$35.00

Playmates, STNG, 1st Series, Ferengi, Gowron or Lt Commander La Forge, M, ea..$15.00

Playmates, STNG, 2nd Series, any character, 1993, M, ea $5 to $10.00

Playmates, STNG, 3rd Series, any character except Esoqq or Data in red Redemption outfit, 1994, MOC, ea $16 to..$22.00

Playmates, STNG, 3rd Series, Data in red Redemption outfit, 1994, MOC $325.00

Playmates, STNG, 3rd Series, Esoqq, 1994, M $40.00

Playmates, STNG, 4th Series or 5th Series, any character, 1995, MOC, ea $12 to..$22.00

Playmates, V, Capt Janeway or Lt B'Elanna Torres, 5", MOC, ea $30.00

Playmates, V, Chakotay, Kazon, Lt Carey, Meelix, Seska, Tom Paris, Torres as Klingon, Tuvok or Vidian, 5", M, ea.....................$10.00

Playmates, V, Chakotay the Maquis, Doctor or Harry Kim, 5", M, ea $10.00

PLAYSETS AND ACCESSORIES

Command Communications Console, Mego, 1976, MIB, $125 to $150.00

Communications Set, Mego, 1974, MIB.......................... $150.00

Engineering, Generations Movie, Playmates, MIB...........$35.00

Mission to Gamma VI, Mego, 1975, rare, MIB.............. $400.00

Telescreen Console, Mego, 1975, MIB............................ $125.00

Transporter Room, Mego, 1975, MIB............................. $125.00

USS Enterprise Bridge, Mego, 1975, MIB....................... $130.00

USS Enterprise Bridge, STNG, Playmates, 1991, MIB $50.00

VEHICLES

Borg Ship (sphere), Playmates, MIB $60.00

Klingon Bird of Prey, STNG, Playmates, 1995, MIB.........$80.00

Klingon Cruiser, Mego, 1980, 8" L, MIB..........................$70.00

Klingon Warship, Star Trek II, Corgi #149, MOC $30.00

Romulan Warbird, Playmates, MIB..................................$50.00

Star Trek, Vehicles

Ferengi Fighter, Star Trek the Next Generation, NM (EX box), $50.00. (Photo courtesy www.gasolinealleyantiques.com)

USS Enterprise, Star Trek II, Corgi, 1982, MOC, $25 to..$30.00
USS Enterprise B, Motion Picture, Playmates, M.............$65.00
USS Enterprise E, Motion Picture, Playmates, NMIB.... $135.00

MISCELLANEOUS

Action Toy Book, Motion Picture, 1976, unpunched, EX.$30.00
Bank, Spock, plastic, Play Pal, 1975, 12", MIB.................$60.00
Belt Buckle, marked 200th Anniversary USS Enterprise on back, 3½", M $15.00

Book, Star Trek Pop-Up, Motion Picture, 1977, EX..........$25.00
Book, Where No One Has Gone Before, a History in Pictures, Dillard, M (sealed) $25.00
Bop Bag, Spock, 1975, MIB...$80.00
Classic Science Tricorder, Playmates, MIB $65.00
Colorforms Adventure Set, MIB (sealed) $35.00
Coloring Book, Adventure, Wanderer Books, 1986, unused, NM+ $8.00
Comic Book, Gold Key #1, 1967, M $215.00
Decanter, Mr Spock bust, ceramic, M $40.00
Flashlight Gun, plastic, 1968, NM $50.00
Gum Cards, complete set of 88 w/22 sitckers & display box, Topps, 1976, M cards/VG display box $150.00
Kite, Spock, Hi-Flyer, 1975, unused, MIP.......................$35.00
Metal Detector, Jetco, 1976, EX $150.00
Mix 'n Mold Casting Set, Kirk, Spock, or McCoy, MIB, ea..$65.00
Model Kit, Romulan Scoutship, resin, Amaquest, MIB.....$50.00
Patch, America 1977 Convention, M $40.00
Patch, command insignia, w/instructions for uniform, M..$25.00
Patch, Motion Picture, Kirk or Spock, M $35.00
Phaser Battle, Mego, 1976, NMIB.................................. $200.00
Phaser Ray Gun, clicking flashlight effect, 1976, MOC....$75.00
Phaser Water Gun, Motion Picture, 1976, MOC $55.00
Puzzle Book, Wanderer Books, 1986, unused, NM+ $8.00
Starfleet Phaser, Motion Picture, Playmates, MIB $150.00
Tricorder, Mego, 1976, tape recorder, EXIB $125.00
Utility Belt, Remco, 1975, M $55.00
Wastebasket, Motion Picture, M......................................$35.00

Star Wars

Star Wars exploded onto the movie scene on May 25, 1977, and has engrained itself into popular culture, media, and merchandising every day since. Kenner brought it home for Christmas in 1977 with the invention of the Early Bird Kit, a masterminded marketing ploy in which 'empty' boxes were sold with coupons inside, promising the redeemer a set of four miniature action figures early the next year. To this day Star Wars is closely regarded with dreams and promises fulfilled.

Prior to the Kenner invention of Star Wars action figures, there were no 3¾" scale toys. Boys' dolls were of what we now call the 12" variety, although Kenner got around to creating Star Wars heroes and villains in that scale as well.

Star Wars collectors have broken up the toy timeline into eras. From 1977 to 1986 was the Vintage era, comprised of merchandise released during the original three films, plus two cartoon series — Droids and Ewoks. From 1993 to 1999 was the Power of the Force 2 era, in which merchandising was revitalized after a long stretch of seven dark years. The years 1999 to 2005 provided the Prequel era with the release of the final three films, and today we are collecting in the Saga years. The next generation has already been reserved as the Legacy times. After all, why wait when it can only get better?

Hasbro, formerly Kenner, has released over 1,000 unique action figures to date in more than 20 different packaging styles, and to track the tens of thousands of toys available would require a book in itself. The listings provided here all come from the Vintage era, a selection where values are high, the selection is manageable, and the demand never waivers. All values are for items in mint condition.

For more information, we recommend *Star Wars Super Collector's Wish Book* (Collector Books) by our advisor, Geoffrey T. Carlton, which exhaustively lists over 55,000 Star Wars items.

See also Character and Promotional Drinking Glasses; Halloween Costumes; Lunch Boxes; Model Kits.

Advisor: Geoffrey T. Carlton

Key:
ESB — Empire Strikes Back   POTF — Power of the Force   ROTJ — Return of the Jedi   SW — Star Wars

12" DOLLS

Ben Kenobi $495.00
Boba Fett.. $1,100.00

C-3PO $295.00
Chewbacca $200.00

Star Wars, Action Figures, General
- - - - - - -
Artoo-Detoo (R2-D2), SW-12, MOC, $425.00. (Photo courtesy Geoffrey T. Carlton)

Darth Vader	$550.00
Han Solo	$650.00
IG-88	$1,500.00
Jawa	$310.00
Luke Skywalker	$425.00
Princess Leia Organa	$260.00
R2-D2	$295.00
Stormtrooper	$425.00

ACTION FIGURES, GENERAL

4-LOM, ESB	$300.00
4-LOM, ROTJ	$60.00
8D8, ROTJ	$45.00
A-Wing Pilot, POTF	$100.00
Admiral Ackbar, ROTJ	$45.00
Amanaman, POTF	$260.00
Anakin Skywalker, POTF	$2250.00
Artoo-Detoo (R2-D2), ESB	$140.00
Artoo-Detoo (R2-D2), SW	$280.00
Artoo-Detoo (R2-D2) w/Pop-Up Lightsaber, POTF	$175.00
Artoo-Detoo (R2-D2) w/Sensorscope, ESB	$120.00
Artoo-Detoo (R2-D2) w/Sensorscope, ROTJ	$65.00
AT-AT Commander, ESB	$90.00
AT-AT Commander, ROTJ	$60.00
AT-AT Driver, ESB	$115.00
AT-AT Driver, ROTJ	$70.00
AT-ST Driver, ROTJ	$40.00
AT-ST Driver, POTF	$85.00
B-Wing Pilot, POTF	$45.00
B-Wing Pilot, ROTJ	$45.00
Barada, POTF	$120.00
Ben (Obi-Wan) Kenobi, ESB, gray hair	$125.00
Ben (Obi-Wan) Kenobi, ESB, wht hair	$125.00
Ben (Obi-Wan) Kenobi, POTF	$200.00
Ben (Obi-Wan) Kenobi, ROTJ, gray hair	$60.00
Ben (Obi-Wan) Kenobi, ROTJ, wht hair	$60.00
Ben (Obi-Wan) Kenobi, SW, gray hair	$190.00
Ben (Obi-Wan) Kenobi, SW, wht hair	$165.00
Ben (Obi-Wan) Kenobi, SW-12, dbl telescoping saber	$10,900.00
Ben (Obi-Wan) Kenobi, SW-12, gray hair	$710.00

Ben (Obi-Wan) Kenobi, SW-12, wht hair	$750.00
Bespin Security Guard, ESB, black	$65.00
Bespin Security Guard, ESB, wht	$60.00
Bespin Security Guard, ROTJ, black	$55.00
Bespin Security Guard, ROTJ, wht	$55.00
Bib Fortuna, ROTJ	$45.00
Biker Scout, POTF	$110.00
Biker Scout, ROTJ	$85.00
Boba Fett, ESB	$500.00
Boba Fett, mail-away package	$275.00
Boba Fett, ROTJ, desert scene	$400.00
Boba Fett, ROTJ, fireball	$425.00
Boba Fett, SW	$1650.00
Bossk, ESB	$140.00
Bossk, ROTJ	$100.00
Chewbacca, ESB	$215.00
Chewbacca, POTF	$150.00
Chewbacca, ROTJ	$125.00
Chewbacca, ROTJ, Endor photo	$55.00
Chewbacca, SW	$250.00
Chewbacca, SW-12	$375.00
Chief Chirpa, ROTJ	$45.00
Cloud Car Pilot, ESB	$130.00
Cloud Car Pilot, ROTJ	$60.00
Darth Vader, ESB	$125.00
Darth Vader, POTF	$160.00
Darth Vader, ROTJ, lightsaber drawn	$65.00
Darth Vader ROTJ, pointing	$55.00
Darth Vader, SW	$300.00
Darth Vader, SW-12	$850.00
Darth Vader, SW-12, dbl telescoping saber	$8,600.00
Darth Vader, SW-12, wht card behind bubble	$710.00
Death Squad Commander, ESB	$125.00
Death Squad Commander, SW	$160.00
Death Squad Commander, SW-12	$330.00
Death Star Droid, ESB	$160.00
Death Star Droid, ROTJ	$75.00
Death Star Droid, SW	$230.00
Dengar, ESB	$95.00
Dengar, ROTJ	$45.00
Emperor, POTF	$85.00
Emperor, ROTJ	$65.00
Emperor's Royal Guard, ROTJ	$55.00
EV-9D9, POTF	$245.00
FX-7, ESB	$85.00
FX-7, ROTJ	$75.00
Gamorrean Guard, ROTJ	$45.00
General Madine, ROTJ	$40.00
Greedo, ESB	$155.00
Greedo, ROTJ	$80.00
Greedo, SW	$215.00
Greedo, SW w/o offer	$360.00
Hammerhead, ESB	$120.00
Hammerhead, ROTJ	$75.00
Hammerhead, SW	$270.00
Han Solo, ESB, Bespin	$145.00
Han Solo, ESB, Hoth Battle Gear	$95.00
Han Solo, ESB, lg head	$245.00

Han Solo, ESB, sm head $300.00
Han Solo, POTF, in Carbonite Chamber $275.00
Han Solo, POTF, trench coat $500.00
Han Solo, ROTJ, Bespin $75.00
Han Solo, ROTJ, Death Star scene $165.00
Han Solo, ROTJ, Hoth Battle Gear $75.00
Han Solo, ROTJ, Mos Eisley scene $185.00
Han Solo, ROTJ, trench coat $50.00
Han Solo, SW, lg head $650.00
Han Solo, SW, sm head $540.00
Han Solo, SW-12, lg head $1,000.00
Han Solo, SW-12, sm head $750.00
IG-88, ESB $190.00
IG-88, ROTJ $80.00
Imperial Commander, ESB $85.00
Imperial Commander, ROTJ $50.00
Imperial Dignitary, POTF $155.00
Imperial Gunner, POTF $165.00
Imperial Stormtrooper, ESB, in Hoth Weather Gear $145.00
Imperial Stormtrooper, ROTJ, in Hoth Weather Gear $60.00
Imperial TIE Fighter Pilot, ESB $130.00
Imperial TIE Fighter Pilot, ROTJ $90.00
Jawa, ESB $125.00
Jawa, POTF $140.00
Jawa, ROTJ $50.00
Jawa, SW $200.00
Jawa, SW-12, cloth cape $230.00
Jawa, SW-12, plastic cape $3500.00
Klaatu, ROTJ, palace outfit $50.00
Klaatu, ROTJ, skiff outfit $50.00
Lando Calrissian, ESB $80.00
Lando Calrissian, POTF, general pilot $145.00
Lando Calrissian, ROTJ $45.00
Lando Calrissian, ROTJ, skiff outfit $45.00
Leia Organa, ESB, Bespin Gown, front view, crew neck.. $185.00
Leia Organa, ESB, Bespin Gown, front view, turtleneck . $190.00
Leia Organa, ESB, Bespin Gown, profile, crew neck $200.00
Leia Organa, ESB, Bespin Gown, profile, turtleneck $195.00
Leia Organa, ROTJ, Bespin Gown, crew neck (Princess Leia Organa).$125.00
Leia Organa, ROTJ, Bespin Gown, turtleneck (Princess Leia Organa).$145.00
Lobot, ESB $65.00
Lobot, ROTJ $45.00
Logray, ROTJ $60.00
Luke Skywalker, ESB, Bespin Fatigues, looking, blond hair.. $140.00
Luke Skywalker, ESB, Bespin Fatigues, looking, brn hair.. $200.00
Luke Skywalker, ESB, Bespin Fatigues, walking, blond hair.. $245.00
Luke Skywalker, ESB, Bespin Fatigues, walking, brn hair ...$245.00
Luke Skywalker, ESB, blond hair $250.00
Luke Skywalker, ESB, brn hair $285.00
Luke Skywalker, ESB, Hoth Battle Gear $125.00
Luke Skywalker, ESB, X-Wing Pilot $150.00
Luke Skywalker, POTF, Battle Poncho $170.00
Luke Skywalker, POTF, Jedi $270.00
Luke Skywalker, POTF, Stormtrooper Disguise $425.00
Luke Skywalker, POTF, X-Wing Pilot $165.00
Luke Skywalker, ROTJ, Bespin Fatigues, brn hair $95.00
Luke Skywalker, ROTJ, blond hair, Falcon Gunwell $180.00
Luke Skywalker, ROTJ, blond hair, Tatooine $240.00

Luke Skywalker, ROTJ, brn hair $290.00
Luke Skywalker, ROTJ, Hoth Battle Gear $80.00
Luke Skywalker, ROTJ, Jedi, bl lightsaber $175.00
Luke Skywalker, ROTJ, Jedi, gr lightsaber $95.00
Luke Skywalker, ROTJ, X-Wing Pilot $65.00
Luke Skywalker, SW $235.00
Luke Skywalker, SW-12 .... $850.00
Luke Skywalker, SW-12, dbl telescoping saber $4,800.00
Luke Skywalker, SW, X-Wing Pilot $250.00
Lumat, POTF $75.00
Lumat, ROTJ $60.00
Nien Nunb, ROTJ $70.00
Nikto, ROTJ $40.00
Paploo, POTF $80.00
Paploo, ROTJ $55.00
Power Droid, ESB $130.00
Power Droid, ROTJ $50.00
Power Droid, SW $200.00
Princess Leia Organa, ESB $295.00
Princess Leia Organa, ROTJ $390.00
Princess Leia Organa, ROTJ, Boushh Disguise $60.00
Princess Leia Organa, SW $260.00
Princess Leia Organa, SW-12 .... $675.00
Princess Leia Combat Poncho, POTF $115.00
Princess Leia Combat Poncho, ROTJ $50.00
Princess Leia, ESB, Hoth $160.00
Princess Leia, ROTJ, Hoth $95.00
Pruneface, ROTJ $40.00
R5-D4, ESB $120.00
R5-D4 (Arfive-Defour), ROTJ $60.00
R5-D4, SW $235.00
Rancor Keeper, ROTJ $40.00
Rebel Commander, ESB $140.00
Rebel Commander, ROTJ $50.00
Rebel Commando, ROTJ $50.00
Rebel Soldier, ESB $75.00
Rebel Soldier, ROTJ $40.00
Ree-Yees, ROTJ $40.00
Romba, POTF $100.00
Sandpeople, ESB $120.00
Sandpeople, SW $170.00
Sandpeople, SW-12 .... $390.00
Sandpeople (Tusken Raider), ROTJ $80.00
See-Threepio (C-3PO), ESB $200.00
See-Threepio (C-3PO), ESB, w/removable limbs $100.00
See-Threepio (C-3PO), POTF, w/removable limbs $120.00
See-Threepio (C-3PO), ROTJ, w/removable limbs $75.00
See-Threepio (C-3PO), SW $230.00
See-Threepio (C-3PO), SW-12 .... $350.00
Snaggletooth, ESB $160.00
Snaggletooth, ROTJ $65.00
Snaggletooth, SW $200.00
Squidhead, ROTJ $45.00
Star Destroyer Commander, ESB $125.00
Star Destroyer Commander, ROTJ $80.00
Stormtrooper, ESB $125.00
Stormtrooper, POTF $260.00
Stormtrooper, ROTJ $65.00

Stormtrooper, SW $225.00
Stormtrooper, SW-12 .... $425.00
Teebo, POTF $200.00
Teebo, ROTJ $50.00
Too-Onebee (2-1B), ESB $95.00
Too-Onebee (2-1B), ROTJ $50.00
Ugnaught, ESB $80.00
Ugnaught, ROTJ $45.00
Walrus Man, ESB $135.00
Walrus Man, ROTJ $65.00
Walrus Man, SW $280.00
Warok, POTF $125.00
Weequay, ROTJ $40.00
Wicket Warrick, POTF $200.00
Wicket Warrick, ROTJ $50.00
Yak Face, POTF $1,995.00
Yoda, ESB, brn snake $350.00
Yoda, ESB, orange snake $275.00
Yoda, POTF $585.00
Yoda, ROTJ $175.00
Zuckuss, ESB $125.00
Zuckuss, ROTJ $60.00

Action Figures, Droids

A-Wing Pilot $250.00
Boba Fett $1775.00
C-3PO $200.00
Jann Tosh $65.00
Jord Dusat $75.00
Kea Moll $80.00
Kez-Iban $75.00
R2-D2 .... $150.00
Sise Fromm $275.00
Thall Joben $80.00
Tig Fromm $165.00
Uncle Gundy $80.00

Action Figures, Ewoks

Dulok Scout $65.00
Dulok Shaman $65.00
King Gorneesh $65.00
Logray $65.00
Urgah Lady Gorneesh $65.00
Wicket $100.00

Action Figure Accessories

Ewok Assault Catapult $40.00
Ewok Combat Glider $40.00
Radar Laser Cannon $15.00
Tri-Pod Laser Cannon $15.00
Vehicle Maintenance Energizer $15.00

Action Figure Collector Cases

C-3PO, ROTJ $35.00

Chewbacca Bandolier, ROTJ $20.00
Darth Vader, ESB $40.00
Darth Vader, ROTJ $255.00
Laser Rifle, ROTJ $40.00
Vinyl Case, ESB logo, SW scenes $100.00
Vinyl Case, ESB logo, Yoda $60.00
Vinyl Case, ESB, Yoda, Wampa $80.00
Vinyl Case, ROTJ $135.00
Vinyl Case, SW $45.00

Action Figure Creatures

Hoth Wampa $105.00
Tauntaun, open belly $80.00
Tauntaun, solid belly $75.00
Rancor Monster $85.00

Star Wars, Action Figure Creatures

Patrol Dewback, MIB, $120.00. (Photo courtesy Geoffrey T. Carlton)

Action Figure Playsets

Cloud City, exclusive to Sears $420.00
Cantina Adventure Set, exclusive to Sears $700.00
Creature Cantina $250.00
Dagobah, pkg has Jedi training backpack sticker $135.00

Star Wars, Action Figure Playsets

Droid Factory, MIB, $125.00. (Photo courtesy Geoffrey T. Carlton)

Dagobah, pkg shows Luke & Yoda w/training backpack. $120.00
Dagobah, pkg shows Vader & Luke battling $150.00
Darth Vader's Star Destroyer $145.00
Death Star Space Station $500.00
Ewok Village $300.00
Hoth Ice Planet $225.00
Imperial Attack Base $125.00
Jabba the Hutt $65.00
Jabba the Hutt, exclusive to Sears $75.00
Jabba the Hutt Dungeon, w/8D8, exclusive to Sears $125.00
Jabba the Hutt Dungeon, w/Amanaman $300.00
Land of the Jawas $160.00
Rebel Command Center $245.00
Turret & Probot $145.00

ACTION FIGURE VEHICLES

A-Wing Fighter $450.00
AST-5 Armored Sentinel Transport $25.00
AT-AT All Terrain Attack Transport $450.00
AT-ST Scout Walker $85.00
ATL Interceptor $175.00
B-Wing Fighter $250.00
CAP-2 Captivator $35.00

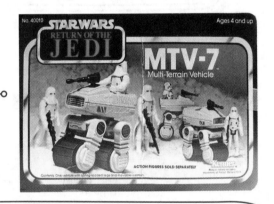

Star Wars, Action Figure Vehicles
• •
MTV-7 Multi-Terrain Vehicle, MIB, $35.00.
(Photo courtesy Geoffrey T. Carlton)

Star Wars, Action Figure Vehicles
• • • • • • • • •
X-Wing Fighter, MIB, $175.00.
(Photo courtesy Geoffrey T. Carlton)

Darth Vader TIE Fighter $175.00
Desert Sail Skiff $55.00
Endor Forest Ranger $75.00
Ewok Battle Wagon $325.00
Imperial Cruiser $125.00
Imperial Shuttle $450.00
Imperial Sniper $125.00
Imperial Troop Transport $150.00
INT-4 Interceptor $30.00
ISP-6 Imperial Shuttle Pod $25.00
Landspeeder $75.00
Landspeeder, Sonic radio controlled $620.00
Millennium Falcon $250.00
MLC-3 Mobile Laser Cannon $35.00
One-Man Sand Skimmer POTF $85.00
PDT-8 Personnel Deployment Transport $30.00
Rebel Armored Snowspeeder, bl bkgrnd $225.00
Rebel Armored Snowspeeder, pk bkgrnd $130.00
Rebel Transport, bl bkgrnd $190.00
Rebel Transport, yel bkgrnd $175.00
Sandcrawler, radio controlled $665.00
Security Scout $95.00
Side Gunner $100.00
Slave I $200.00
Speeder Bike $35.00
Tatooine Skiff $485.00
TIE Fighter, w/Battle Damage $145.00
TIE Fighter $195.00
TIE Interceptor $195.00
Twin-Pod Cloud Car $135.00
X-Wing Fighter, Dagobah box $495.00
X-Wing Fighter, w/Battle Damage $275.00
Y-Wing Fighter $175.00

DIECAST TOYS

Darth Vader TIE Fighter $55.00
Imperial Cruiser $185.00
Land Speeder $85.00
Millennium Falcon $150.00
Slave I $125.00
Snowspeeder $125.00
TIE Bomber $750.00
TIE Fighter $65.00
Twin-Pod Cloud Car $95.00
X-Wing Fighter $75.00
Y-Wing Fighter $200.00

MICRO COLLECTION

Bespin Control Room $35.00
Bespin Freeze Chamber $75.00
Bespin Gantry $35.00
Bespin World $195.00
Death Star Compactor $75.00
Death Star Escape $75.00
Death Star World $175.00
Hoth Generator Attack $35.00

Hoth Ion Cannon...................................$65.00	Imperial TIE Fighter..............................$85.00
Hoth Turret Defense.............................$35.00	Millennium Falcon, exclusive to Sears...........$410.00
Hoth Wampa Cave................................$45.00	Snowspeeder, exclusive to JC Penney...........$200.00
Hoth World.......................................$120.00	X-Wing Fighter...................................$85.00

• Steiff •

Margaret Steiff made the first of her felt toys in 1880, stuffing them with lamb's wool. Later followed toys of velvet, plush, and wool, and in addition to the lamb's wool stuffing, she used felt scraps, excelsior, and kapok. In 1897 and 1898 her trademark was a paper label printed with an elephant; from 1900 to 1905 her toys carried a circular tag with an elephant logo that was different from the one she had previously used. The most famous 'button in ear' trademark was registered on December 20, 1904. The years 1904 and 1905 saw the use of the button with an elephant (extremely rare) and the blank button (which is also rare). The button with Steiff and the underscored or trailing 'F' was used until 1948, and the raised script button is from the 1950s.

Steiff teddy bears, perhaps the favorite of collectors everywhere, are characterized by their long thin arms with curved wrists and paws that extend below their hips. Buyer beware: The Steiff company is now making many replicas of their old bears. For more information about Steiff's buttons, chest tags, and stock tags, as well as the inspirational life of Margaret Steiff and the fascinating history of Steiff toys, we recommend *Button in Ear Book* and *The Steiff Book of Teddy Bears*, both by Jurgen and Marianne Cieslik; *Teddy Bears and Steiff Animals, 2nd* and *3rd Series* by Margaret Fox Mandel; *4th Teddy Bear and Friends Price Guide* by Linda Mullins; *Collectible German Animals Value Guide* by Dee Hockenberry; and *Steiff Sortiment, 1947 – 1995*, by Gunther Pefiffer. (This book is in German; however, the reader can discern the size of the item, year of production, and price estimation).

See also Character, TV, and Movie Collectibles; Disney.

Affen Monkey Seated, 9½", late 1800s, dk brn felt w/furry head, blk bead eyes, holds orange ball, NM $4,025.00

Bear, 3½", 1950s, brn, blk glass eyes, stitched nose & mouth, fully jtd, EX $175.00

Bear, 3½", 1950s, honey blond mohair, blk bead eyes, no pads, jtd, no ID, VG.......................$100.00

Bear, 3½", 1950s, wht, blk glass eyes, fully jtd, ear button, paper tag, EX $350.00

Bear, 4", 1905, blond mohair, shoe-button eyes, no pads, jtd, ear button, EX+.......................$750.00

Bear, 5", beige, glass eyes, ear button, red neck bow, VG. $375.00

Bear, 5½", 1930, blond mohair, glass eyes, no pads, dressed in outfit, EX $350.00

Bear, 8", 1905, blond mohair, shoe-button eyes, no ID, VG .$675.00

Bear, 12", early, lt brn, shoe-button eyes, blk nose & mouth, lt tan pads, VG.......................$1,320.00

Bear, 12", pre-WWI, lt beige, shoe-button eyes, blk-stitched nose, mouth & claws, felt pads, G $975.00

Bear, 12½", 1950s, yel mohair, glass eyes, pads, jtd, ear button, EX $550.00

Bear, 13", 1905, brn, shoe-button eyes, blk-stitched nose, mouth & claws, felt pads, blank ear button, VG.................$1,900.00

Bear, 13", 1915, blond mohair, shoe-button eyes, long snout, pads, jtd, underscored button, VG.......................$350.00

Bear, 14", pre-WWI, apricot, shoe-button eyes, blk-stitched nose, mouth & claws, felt pads, G+ $2,500.00

Bear, 15", early, lt beige, shoe-button eyes, blk-stitched nose, mouth & claws, felt pads, long floppy arms & legs, Fair $2,250.00

Bear, 15", 1950s, beige, glass eyes, shaved snout w/brn nose & mouth, lt tan pads, VG+.......................$300.00

Bear, 16", 1930s (?), wht, glass eyes, lt brn nose, mouth & paws, EX+.......................$4,600.00

Bear, 16", 1930s (?), wht, shoe-button eyes, blk nose, mouth & paws, lt tan pads, G $840.00

Steiff
• • • • • • • • • • • •
Bear, 16", first bear produced by Steiff, cinnamon, head attached by metal rod, VG, $15,500.00. (Photo courtesy Bertoia Auctions)

Steiff
• • • • • • • • • • • •
Bear, 17", pre-WWI, white, shoe-button eyes, stitched nose, mouth, and claws, original metal button, EX, $6,500.00. (Photo courtesy Bertoia Auctions on LiveAuctioneers.com)

Bear, 17", 100th Anniversary certificate, gold mohair, plastic eyes, pads, jtd, ear button, EXIB $225.00

Bear, 17½", ca 1910, lt beige, shoe-button eyes, blk-stitched nose, mouth & claws, felt pads, EX.......................$5,000.00

Bear, 19", med beige, brn-stitched nose, mouth & claws, felt pads, VG.......................$250.00

Bear, 20", wht mohair, glass eyes, red, wht & bl neck ribbon w/ stop watch, EX.......................$750.00

Steiff

Bear, 20", 1907, gold, black shoe-button eyes, stitched nose, mouth, and claws, felt pads, VG, $4,300.00. (Photo courtesy Morphy Auctions on LiveAuctioneers.com)

Steiff

Bear, 29½", pre-WWI, gold, shoe-button eyes, stitched nose, mouth, and claws, original button, EX, $11,500.00. (Photo courtesy Bertoia Auctions on LiveAuctioneers.com)

Steiff

Doll, Coachman, 21", felt, glass eyes, brown overcoat with pleated shoulder cape, black boots, original button, VG, $6,325.00. (Photo courtesy James D. Julia, Inc.)

Steiff

Doll, Coachman's Assistant, 16", felt, side-glancing eyes, black top hat, tan overcoat and spats, red vest, original button, VG+, $6,900.00. (Photo courtesy James D. Julia, Inc.)

Bear, 27", pre-1900, beige, center seam, shoe-button eyes, stiched nose, long floppy arms & legs, blank button, VG..... $8,500.00

Bear, 30", 1940s-50s, blond mohair, glass eyes, pads, jtd, script ear button, VG $1,950.00

Bear on 4-Wheeled Cart, 9" L, gold, blk shoe-button eyes, metal cart w/wooden wheels, VG $1,950.00

Bear on Wheels, 18", brn plush, glass eyes, CI spoke wheels, G+ $400.00

Cow on Wheels, 12", brn & wht, neck bell, w/growler, CI wheels, VG $600.00

Dalmatian, 12x25" L, 1950s, lying down w/front legs outstretched, open mouth w/pk tongue, red leather collar, VG $425.00

Dinosaur (Brosus), 12½", 1960s, beige & yel mohair, googly-eyed, no ID, EX $225.00

Dinosaur (T-Rex Tysus), 8", 1960s, yel & tan mohair, googly-eyed, jtd arms, no ID, EX $200.00

Dolls, Officer & His Wife, 22" and 17", early, felt, period clothing, he w/shoe-button eyes, she w/glass eyes, orig buttons, G+, pr..$4,025.00

Donkey on Wheels, 16" L, 1910s, gray, wooden eyes, red felt blanket under brn leather saddle, ear button, G.......... $700.00

Elephant, 14", 1950s, beige mohair w/airbrushed details, glass eyes, red felt blanket, EX.............................. $125.00

Elephant Ride-On, 19x22", lt gray w/shoe-button eyes, felt tusks, felt & metal removable seat, metal frame/4 wheels, EX.. $575.00

Eric the Bat, larger version, EX $300.00

Felix the Cat on Irish Mail, 9½" H, 1920s (?), w/orig script button, NM...$10,350.00

Fox, 14", red w/wht underbelly & tail tip, jtd head, EX.. $325.00

Fox Standing Upright, 32", jtd forelegs, EX.................... $500.00

German Shepherd, 14x27" L, 1950s, lying down w/fron legs outstretched, open mouth w/pk tongue, blk stitched nose, EX $475.00

Giraffe, 58", glass eyes, head swivels, ear button, VG+ .. $400.00

Horse on Wheels, 30x30", wht & tan pinto markings, metal disk wheels w/rubber tires, EX.............................. $100.00

Kangaroo, 19", 1950s, baby in pouch, glass eyes, jtd neck & arms, stitched nose & mouth, EX........................... $100.00

Rabbit Sitting Upright, 5", 1940s, mc fur, glass eyes, red nose & mouth, ear button w/paper, VG $475.00

Rabbit Standing Upright, 10", 1940s, mc, blk button eyes, head swivels, floppy ears, working squeaker, ear button, VG . $225.00

Santa Bear, 14", 1960s, standing upright in red & wht Santa suit holding toy bag, gold button, yel stock tag, EX $125.00

Somersault Bear, 12", 1909, beige, mechanical somersault action, orig tag & button, EX+ $4,750.00

Stork, 24", 1950s, felt, brn glass eyes, VG...................... $500.00

Steiff

Monkey, 60 PB, 1903, 32", string jointed, VG+, $6,600.00. (Photo courtesy James D. Julia, Inc.)

Woodland Rabbit, 9" L, 1920s, rosy beige w/darker spots, blk shoe-button eyes, Fair.. $225.00

Zotty Bear, 25", 1966, beige, plastic eyes, brn-stitched nose & mouth, felt pads, metal ear tag, orig red bow tie, VG.....$80.00

• Strauss •

Imaginative, high-quality, tin windup toys were made by Ferdinand Strauss (New York, later New Jersey) from the onset of World War I until the 1940s. For about 15 years prior to his becoming a toymaker, he was a distributor of toys he imported from Germany. Though hard to find in good working order, his toys are highly prized by today's collectors, and when found in even very good to excellent condition, many are in the $500.00 and up range.

Advisor: Scott Smiles

Air Devil, w/pilot, EX $550.00
Alabama Coon Jigger, EXIB $725.00
Alabama Coon Jigger, VG $275.00
Auto Jump Cart, EX $350.00
Boob McNutt, EXIB $750.00
Boob McNutt, G $250.00
Bus De Luxe, EX $625.00
Bus De Luxe, VG $425.00
Chek A Cab, EX $650.00
Circus Cage Truck, EX $875.00
Climbing Fireman, EXIB $350.00
Continental Flyer Bus, EX $950.00
Dandy Jim, EXIB $1,000.00
Dandy Jim, VG $700.00
Dizzy Lizzy, NMIB $500.00
Emergency Tow Car #54, VG $1,200.00
Flivver, VG $150.00
Flying Airship, VGIB $400.00
Ham & Sam, EX $750.00
Ham & Sam, EX+IB $1,000.00
Ham & Sam, G $450.00
Ham & Sam, VGIB $700.00
Imperial Bus Lines #214, EX $250.00
Inter-State Bus, EX $600.00
Inter-State Bus, G+ $375.00
Jackee the Hornpipe Dancer, VGIB $650.00
Jazzbo Jim (Banjo Player), EX $500.00
Jazzbo Jim (Jigger), NMIB $650.00
Jazzbo Jim (Jigger), VG $350.00
Jenny the Balking Mule, VG $350.00
Jitney Bus #66, EX $450.00
Knock-Out Prize Fighters, EXIB $625.00
Krazy Kar, EX $500.00
Leaping Lena, EX $450.00

Little Jacko Mechanical Bank, EX $2,000.00
Locomotive #46, EX $100.00
Long Haulage Truck, EX $500.00
Lumber Tractor-Trailer, G $375.00
Lux-A-Cab, VG $375.00
Mail Plane #43, EX+ $375.00
Mail Plane #43, VG $300.00
Miami Sea Sled #38, VG $200.00
Oil Tank Truck #219, EX $350.00
Parcel Post Truck, NM $900.00
Play Golf, EXIB $325.00
Race Car, gr w/yel & blk details, EX $350.00
Santee Claus, G $500.00
Speed-Boat #28, EX $300.00
Speed-Boat #28, EXIB $600.00
Spirit of St Louis, VG $350.00
Standard Oil Truck #73, VG $400.00
Thrifty Tom's Jigger Bank, EX $1,900.00
Timber Truck, VG $400.00
Tip Top Dump Truck, EX $700.00
Tip Top Porter, EXIB $350.00
Tippy Canoe, EX $300.00
Tombo, see Alabama Coon Jigger
Trackless Trolley/Twin Trolleys, VG $300.00
Travelchiks Boxcar, EX $425.00
Trik Auto (Zeppelin), EX $800.00
Trik Auto (Open Auto), red & yel version, EX $425.00
Water Sprinkler Truck #72, EX $450.00
What's Up?, NMIB $800.00
Wildfire, EXIB $350.00
Yel-O-Taxi No 59, VG $450.00
Zeppelin, GZ 2017 Graf…, GIB $375.00
Zeppelin SR-47 (New York), EXIB $1,500.00

Strauss
Big Show Circus Cage Truck, EX, $825.00.
(Photo courtesy Bertoia Auctions on LiveAuctioneers.com)

Strauss
Santee Claus, VG, $650.00.
(Photo courtesy Bertoia Auctions on LiveAuctioneers.com)

• • • • • • • • • • • • • • • Structo • • • • • • • • • • • • • • •

Pressed steel vehicles were made by Structo (Illinois) as early as 1920. They continued in business well into the 1960s, producing several army toys, trucks of all types, and firefighting and construction equipment.

Airlines Doodle Bug, open Jeep-type vehicle, yel, 25½", VG $150.00

Army Engineers Set #915, 6-pc, 7" to 24" trucks, NMIB. $475.00

Army Truck, 1930s, enclosed cab, rpl canvas cover, 18", VG $300.00

Auto-Builder Set #10, complete, EXIB $2,300.00

Auto Dump Car, w/up, open cab, tilting bed, MSW, 18", VG $400.00

Barrel Delivery Truck, 1950s, red snub-nose cab, bl open-top trailer w/doorway-type openings on sides, 2 barrels, 13", NMIB $325.00

Bearcat Build-A-Car, open boattail coupe w/rear spare, 15½", VG $250.00

Cattle Tractor-Trailer, 1950s, wht snub-nose cab w/red stake van trailer, 20", EXIB $275.00

Cement Mixer Truck, 1950s, copper & cream, 21½", NMIB .$100.00

Delivery Van, roof over open seat, screened van sides, open back, gr w/orange hubs, 16", EX $450.00

Dump Truck, open cab, dump bed w/slanted back, 17½", EX.$475.00

Dump Truck, 1938, crank-op dump bed, all gray, 21", EXIB (NOS) $300.00

Express Line Truck, 1940s, 10-wheeled, 24", EX rstr $500.00

Fire Aerial Ladder Truck, marked SFD, 32½", VG+ $150.00

Fire Dept Engine w/Water Tank, long nose, red w/blk front fenders, 2 yel side ladders, 23", VG+ $475.00

Fire Hook & Ladder Truck, #260, marked SFD, EXIB.... $275.00

Fire Hook & Ladder Truck, open cab, side ladders, red w/yel hubs, 18", VG $175.00

Fire Hook & Ladder Truck, open cab, side ladders, red, wht balloon tires w/red hubs, 18", EX+ $500.00

Fire Ladder Truck, open bench seat, 2 ladders on racks, MDW, 18", EX $450.00

Fire Pumper Truck, #262, marked SFD, 1956, 22½", unused, NM (P box) $350.00

Fire Pumper Truck, 1926, marked CFD, live-water pump, side ladders, red w/red hubs, 22", EX $650.00

Fire Rescue Truck, #453, motor sound, 14", unused, NMIB..$75.00

Hi-Way Trasport, bl & yel BRT, 25", G $200.00

Lumber Truck, #714, chrome snub-nose cab, flatbed w/wooden logs, EX $150.00

Moving Van, roof over open cab, orange, 15½", G $400.00

Overland Freight Lines Tractor-Trailer, 1950s, snub-nose cab w/ open U-shaped stake trailer, 22", NMIB $350.00

Pile Driver, 1920s, 13x10", EX $500.00

Police Patrol Car, #409, roof extends over open bench seat, bl w/ red hubs, 16½", VG $275.00

Roadster, ca 1920, simulated top down, rear spare, MDW, w/up, 15", VG $575.00

Rocker Dump, 1950s, bright gr w/gray motor, rubber treads, 20", NMIB $375.00

Stake Truck, 1920s, blk & orange, 22", EX $425.00

Steam Shovel Truck, 1930s, electric headlights, red & lt gr w/pnt wht-walls, 27", EXIB $975.00

Structo Trans Continental Express Moving Van, 1950s, chrome snub-nose cab w/bl van trailer, VG $150.00

Tank (Whippet), 1920s, w/up, metal treats, 11½", GIB . $250.00

Tank (WWI), crank-op, gun turret on top, metal tread, 12", VG+ $600.00

US Army Truck, open seat w/canvas cover, 17", EXIB... $550.00

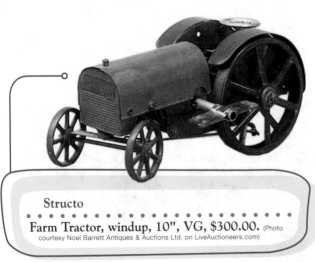

Structo
Ambulance, 18", VG+, $1,500.00. (Photo courtesy Bertoia Auctions on LiveAuctioneers.com)

Structo
Farm Tractor, windup, 10", VG, $300.00. (Photo courtesy Noel Barrett Antiques & Auctions Ltd. on LiveAuctioneers.com)

Structo
Popeye Evening Ledger Delivery Truck, 1931, 23", VG, $1,600.00. (Photo courtesy Bertoia Auctions on LiveAuctioneers.com)

Teddy Bears

The history of teddy bears goes back to about 1902 – 1903. Because most teddies were cherished childhood toys and were usually very well loved, many that survived are well worn, so an early bear in mint condition can be very valuable. Today's collectors often find it difficult to determine exactly what company produced many of these early bears. There are many excellent books available that contain a wealth of information on those early makers: *A Collector's History of the Teddy Bear* by Patricia Schoonmaker; *Teddy Bears Past and Present, Vols. I* and *II*; and *American Teddy Bear Encyclopedia* by Linda Mullins; *Teddy Bears — A Complete Guide to History, Collecting, and Care,* by Sue Pearson and Dottie Ayers; *Teddy Bear Encyclopedia* and *Ultimate Teddy Bear Book* by Pauline Cockrill; and *Big Bear Book* by Dee Hockenberry. The reader can easily see that a wealth of information exists and that it is impossible in a short column such as this to give any kind of a definitive background. If you intend to be a knowledgeable teddy bear collector, it is essential that you spend time in study. Many of these books will be available at your local library or through dealers who specialize in bears.

The following listings are from recent auctions.

See also Schuco; Steiff.

9", brn burlap, felt outfit, bead eyes, stitched nose/mouth, high collar, jtd sleeves/arms, does somersaults, VG $900.00

10", silver-beige, glass eyes, blk stitching, dressed in coat, Germany, 1920s, G $525.00

10½", Merry Thought, beige mohair, amber eyes, blk-stitched nose, mouth & claws, felt pads, Iron Stone/England, VG.........$100.00

10½", tan mohair, blk shoe-button eyes, blk stitched nose, mouth & claws, felt pads, jtd, w/sweater & neck bow, VG..... $275.00

11", brn mohair head w/red, wht & bl felt body, brn feet, glass eyes, wire-hinged arms, wht scalloped collar, VG $175.00

11", lt beige mohiar, glass eyes, brn stitched nose, mouth & claws, lt felt pads, Germany 1920s, G $550.00

12", caramel, swivel head, amber eyes, blk stitched nose & paws, felt pads, VG... $250.00

13", golden beige mohair, blk shoe-button eyes, blk stitching, lt felt pads, 'Ideal' face, EX $1,850.00

14", lt brn mohair, shoe-button eyes, blk stitched nose, mouth & claws, lt felt pads, Germany, G $1,300.00

15", gold, shoe-button eyes, stiched nose & claws, rnd head & ears, jtd football-type body, American, 1915, VG....... $250.00

16", lt golden beige mohair, glass eyes, blk stitched nose & mouth, lt beige pads, fully jtd w/swivel head, VG $600.00

16", red, wht & bl 1-pc head & torso w/jtd arms, brn glass eyes, 1930s, VG.. $450.00

16½", apricot mohair, brn glass eyes, blk-stitched nose & mouth, felt pads, G $200.00

18", apricot mohair, hump back, blk-stitched nose, mouth & claws, felt pads, jtd, VG $800.00

18", wht mohair, hump back, bl glass eyes, brn-stitched nose, mouth & claws, felt pads, long arms, jtd, VG.............. $500.00

19½", beige mohair w/darker end tips, velveteen muzzle w/blk-stitched nose, mouth, claws, felt pads, jtd, G $90.00

20", honey-colored short fur, blk shoe-button eyes, felt pads, English (?), VG $450.00

20", lt gold mohair, blk shoe-button eyes, stitched nose, mouth & claws, felt pads, ca 1915, VG................................. $425.00

21", beige mohair, hump back, pointed snout, suede pads, VG.. $375.00

22", short brn mohair, swivel head, stitched nose, felt pads, growler, G $250.00

24", gold, brn glass eyes, jtd, felt pads, straw-stuffed, American, VG+... $425.00

25", panda, blk & wht w/red tongue, blk eyes, short stubby arms, long legs, 1940s-50s, G..$50.00

25", short honey-colored mohair, blk shoe-button eyes, long football-shaped body, 1920s, VG+............................. $100.00

26", Super Bear, brn, brn plastic eyes, long wht snout w/blk felt nose, beige ears & paws, Commonwealth Toy Co, VG. $125.00

27½", lt beige mohair, swivel head, glass eyes, stitched nose & mouth, felt paws, jtd, VG...................................... $125.00

34", golden plush, dk brn leather pads, blk plastic eyes, fully jtd w/swivel head, later version, VG $60.00

Teddy Bears

13", beige mohair, black shoe-button eyes, stitched nose, mouth, and claws, felt pads, long arms, VG, $500.00. (Photo courtesy James D. Julia, Inc.)

Teddy Bears

24", panda, black and white long shaggy hair, glass eyes, turned down snout, brown velvet pads, VG, $350.00. (Photo courtesy James D. Julia, Inc.)

Tin Vehicles

There is such a huge variety of tin vehicles, that to do them justice, we decided to list some of them in their own category. You will find old painted tin limousines with their intricate details to the newer lithographed tin models. Many are friction, battery-operated, or windups, with a few being just the plain ol' push-pull type. Most of the listings are from recent auctions, and they are bringing very good prices.

See also Aeronautical; Battery-Operated Toys; Boats; Japanese (and Other) Tin Vehicle Replicas; Lehmann; Marx; Strauss; Windup, Friction, and Other Mechanical Toys.

AUTOMOBILES

Batmobile, Alps, 1966, 2-speed friction motor, blk w/bl windshield & Batman driver, 8½", EX+ $375.00

Buick (1959), Yamazaki/Cragstan, r/c, 12", NMIB (box reads 'Remote Driving-Dashboard Control Car') $515.00

Cadillac Coupe DeVille (1955), K, 1950s, b/o, 7½", NM..$75.00

Chevrolet Sedan, KA, friction, plastic lights on front fenders, 13", unused, NMIB...................... $285.00

Citroen B2 'Cloverleaf' Roadster, w/up, open, working steering, forward/reverse gears, 13", VG+ $2,100.00

Citroen B2 Torpedo, w/up, open, working steering, upholstered, MDW w/rear spare, glassene windshield, 15", VG $925.00

Citroen B14 Coupe, w/up, opening door, working steering, MDW w/rear spare, 16", G........................... $700.00

Citroen B14 Sedan, w/up, opening door & trunk, folding front seat, rear spare, working steering, MDW, 16", G+....... $750.00

Citroen Cabriolet, w/up, opening door, working steering, MDW w/rear spare, 16", G $750.00

Citroen C4 Coupe, France, b/o, 2-tone gr w/blk fenders & running boards, NP grille, rear spare, gray tin wheels, 12", G........$800.00

Citroen C4 Petite Sedan, w/up, opening door & trunk, working steering, fold-down front seats, MDW w/rear spare, 12", VG+ $1,000.00

Citroen C6 Victoria Coupe, France, flywheel base, orange w/red top, blk fenders & running boards, gray wheels, 8", VG..$500.00

Citroen Roadster, JEP, crank-op, electric lights, 2-tone gr, blk running boards, gray MDW, blk hubs, rear spare, 16", VG . $975.00

Citroen Roadster, w/up, open, opening door, working steering, folded cloth top, BRT w/rear spare, 16", G.................. $750.00

Convertible Coupe, Distler, w/up, BRT, chrome hubs, 10", NMIB $525.00

Convertible Coupe, Distler, w/up, key on trunk, red, wht-wall tires, 10", EXIB.. $450.00

Convertible Coupe, Stock's #316/Germany, w/up, top up, cream & maroon w/blk fenders, maroon & gray MDW, 8", VGIB ..$1,300.00

Coupe, Gunthermann, w/up, sleek Deco style w/long nose & slanted back, BRT, no driver, 10", EX......................... $250.00

Coupe, JEP, w/up, blk streamline style w/NP grille, 9½", overpnt...$200.00

Cunningham Convertible w/Pig Driver, Marusan, friction, 9", EX $250.00

Delage Phaeton, JEP, w/up, opening, working steering, forward/reverse gears, MDW, 13", G+............................ $650.00

DeLauney Belleville Torpedo, JEP, w/up, red & blk, NP grille, simulated top down, tin wheels, 11", VG $950.00

Ferrari 206 GT Dino (1960s), Yanoman, friction, 11", G+..$150.00

Garage w/Sedan & Open Roadster, Bing, w/up, 8½" L garage, VG... $650.00

Garage w/Two Autos, Bing, w/up, 4x6x9" garage, 6" open auto w/high bench seat, enclosed auto w/doorless front seat, VG .$500.00

GBN Touring Car, Bing, 9", open, red w/yel seats, wht simulated tires w/orange spokes, lithoed driver, G........................ $750.00

Hessmobile, Germany, w/up, dbl front seats w/right-sided driver & passenger, silver w/red trim, MSW, 6", EX $775.00

Hudson, Japan, friction, driver & passengers lithoed in windows, 5", NMIB (plain brn box) $85.00

Jaguar XK 120 Coupe (1950s), Distler, b/o, cut-out windows, BRT w/steerable front wheels, 8½", NM..................... $125.00

KBN Limousine, Germany, w/up, roof slants forward, driver on right side, bl & blk w/orange interior, MSW, 13", VG . $900.00

Limousine, Bing, w/up, cut-out windows, MDW, blk & bl, opening rear doors, 6", VG+ $275.00

Limousine, Carette, w/up, blk & dk burgundy w/red & orange trim, orange emb tuffted seat, red spoke wheel, 12", VG...... $2,250.00

Limousine, Carette, w/up, red w/gray top, gold trim, gold railed top, red spoke wheels, right-sided driver, 12", VG ...$2,500.00

Limousine, Carette, w/up, roof extends over open driver's seat, red & blk, WRT w/spokes, ride-side driver, 14", VG ..$850.00

Limousine, Gt Britain, 2-tone gr w/tan running boards, blk & gr lithoed tires, right-side driver, 13½", VG.................... $350.00

Limousine, Hess, w/up, roof slopes downward over open driver's compartment, bl & blk, right-side driver, MSW, 9", VG..$600.00

Limousine, Karl Bubb, lever-action, glass windows, opening windshield, brn & blk, red trim, MPW, right-side driver, 14", VG $1,600.00

Limousine, Karl Bubb, roof extends over open driver's compartment, red & blk, MSW, right-side driver, 11", VG+ .$2,000.00

Limousine, Karl Bubb, w/up, wht & 2-tone gr, blk undercarriage, opening windshield, NP headlamps, w/driver, 14", EX..$2,500.00

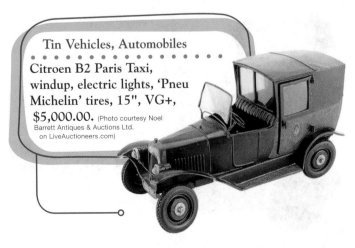

Tin Vehicles, Automobiles

Citroen B2 Paris Taxi, windup, electric lights, 'Pneu Michelin' tires, 15", VG+, $5,000.00. (Photo courtesy Noel Barrett Antiques & Auctions Ltd. on LiveAuctioneers.com)

Limousine, Karl Bubb, 1919, w/up, enclosed, opening doors, side break, 2-tone gray w/NP lamps, WRT w/spokes, 14", VG $2,500.00

Los Ye-Yes Car, Rico, b/o, convertible w/4 vinyl musicians (resembling the Beatles), 20", EX+IB $500.00

Mercedes Cabriolet (1953), Distler, 1950s, w/up, 3 forward gears & 1 reverse, 9½", EX $240.00

Mercury Montclair Sedan (1957), Usagiya, 1950s, friction, 2-tone bl, 8½", NM $285.00

MG Midget Convertible (1950s), Bandai, friction, BRT w/lithoed spoke wheels, rear spare, 7", NMIB $125.00

MG Miget Roadster Convertible (1955), Shioji, friction, 6", NMIB $125.00

Mystery Limo, Gunthermann, 1930s, w/up, long nose, curved back, red w/wht grille & outline trim, lithoed wheels, 15", VG $225.00

Nissan Skyline (1970s), Ichiko, friction, makes engine noise, plastic tires, 16", NM+IB $125.00

Old-Time Car, Taiwan, b/o, some plastic, bump-'n-go w/engine noise & blinking light, 10", NMIB $75.00

Packard (1936), TN, w/up, 8½", EX $900.00

Phaeton, Carette, 1906, w/up, open driver's seat, rear folding canvas top, yel, red trim & spoke wheels, driver, 12", VG $2,800.00

Phaeton, Germany, w/up, open auto w/driver, red w/blk interior, MDW, 6", VG+ $325.00

Pontiac Sedan, Japan, 1950s, friction, tan w/family & dog lithoed in windows, 'Pontiac' lettered on sides, 10½", M.. $840.00

Renault Coupe Series III, JEP, w/up, electric lights, dk gr body w/ lt gr roof, open rumble seat, tin wheels, 11½", VG...... $900.00

Renault Torpedo, JEP, w/up, open, working steering, forward/ reverse gears, MDW, blk w/red interior, 13", G+ $900.00

Roadster, Carette, ca 1906, w/up, open, wht w/red 'upholstered' seat, NP lamps, tan rubber tires w/yel spokes, 11", EX+ $10,000.00

Rolls-Royce Tourer, JEP, 1930s, open, front/back windshields, b/o lights, lady ornament, wht/red, right driver, 20", EX .$3,600.00

Saloon, Karl Bubb, 1910, w/up, glass windows, side hand brake, opening doors, brn & blk, NP lamps, BRT w/spokes, 13", EX...$2,100.00

Sedan (2-Door), Mettoy, 1948, w/up, red w/yel line trim, NP grille & bumper, MDW, 9", EX $250.00

Sport Tourer, G-ndka/Germany, w/up, open auto w/pointed hood, MSW, lady driver, 5½", EX $725.00

Super Buick (Convertible), MT, friction, red w/chrome-plated trim, lithoed interior, BRT w/chrome hubs, 11", EXIB.. $515.00

Super Electric Car, JNF, w/up, b/o headlights, variable forward speed is controlled by lever, 7", EX+ $100.00

Tonneau, Fischer, w/up, open, 2 rear side benches, bl & blk w/ heavy gold trim, simulated spokes, 3 figures, 8", EX. $2,250.00

Tonneau #50, Carette, w/up, open sides, luggage on roof, red & gray w/blk fenders, WRT w/red spokes, 4 figures, 8", VG $2,800.00

Touring Car, Bing, w/up, open, wht w/red trim & emb 'tuffted' front & rear seats, gold spoke wheels, 9", VG $2,250.00

Touring Car, Bing, w/up, simulated cloth top, blk, MSW, driver, 6", EX+ $475.00

Touring Car, Germany, w/up, open w/driver on high bench seat, MSW, 6", VG $275.00

Touring Car, JEP, w/up, gr, gold, red & blk w/brn interior, simulated top down, NP grille, tin wheels, 11", VG $700.00

Town Car, England, 1920s, w/up, open driver's seat w/roof over passenger compartment, bl & wht, 9", VG.................. $300.00

Vis A Vis (Horseless Carriage), Germany, w/up, simulated cloth top down, WRT w/spoke wheels, 7", no figures, Poor pnt.....$4,800.00

BUSES AND TROLLEYS

Airporter Bus, Linemar, 1960s, r/c, working headlights, NMIB $125.00

Broadway (16)/Lexington Avenue Trolley, Morton & Converse, passengers lithoed in windows, 12", G........................ $750.00

Chad Valley Bus, 1930s, w/up, bl & cream w/blk undercarriage & fenders, gray MDW w/bl hubs, 12", EX $300.00

Children Bus, Marusan, friction, 14½", EX+ $2,500.00

Converse, City Hall Park 175, 16", pnt tin, VG............ $390.00.

Cross Country Bus, Girard, w/up, yel, gr, red & blk, red disk wheels, 13", VG.. $450.00

Double-Decker Bus, Bing, w/up, roof over open driver's seat, side bench on upper deck, MSW, gr, maroon & orange, 10", VG........ $1,550.00

Excursion Bus, Hayashi, prewar, w/up, 2-tone orange w/turq lithoed wheels, cut-out windows, 7", NMIB.................. $2,100.00

Express Bus, Wolverine, w/up, red, wht & lt bl w/figures lithoed in windows, 14", EX+IB $100.00

General Parcels Express, Burnett/England, w/up, 7", EX+..$4,000.00

Greyhound Lines, Marusan, friction, shades of gr w/6 figured in seated, 12", VG $325.00

Greyhound Scenicruiser, Tatsuya, b/o, 14½", NM+IB.... $150.00

Happy Speed Car, Hadson, friction, 10½", VG.............. $175.00

Lady & the Tramp Bus, Modern Toys/WDP, 1966, 14", VGIB...$400.00

Long Distance Bus, Girard, w/up, yel w/gr railed top, red wheels & side spares, 13" L, VG $500.00

Municipal Tramway Double-Decker Trolley, Bing, ca 1910, roofed upper deck w/benches, w/roof wire, red & blk, 5x7" L, G+ $1,300.00

Oh-Boy! Bus 105, die-cut curtains in windows, red, wht, bl & blk, 19", VG $725.00

See America First All State Express Bus, MT, 1950s, silver w/red, wht & bl trim, 8½", EX $150.00

Shore Line Cannon Ball Express, Upton, 1925, windows w/die-cut curtains, red, yel & blk, disk wheels, 10", VG $250.00

Volkswagen Animal Bus, Ichiko, friction, animals lithoed in windows & on sides, 10", NM+IB $125.00

CONSTRUCTION

Bulldozer, Linemar, 1960s, b/o, yel w/blk rubber treads, animated driver, bump-&-go action, 7½", MIB $100.00

Dump Car, Mitshashi, friction, lever-op dump bed, 9", EX.$150.00

Magnetic Crane Truck (Electromagne), Excelo, friction, w/truck & crane trailer carrying 3 sections of pipe, 13", NMIB.. $535.00

PCT Power Construction Truck, Alps, b/o, runs in forward & reverse, boom raises & lowers, clam opens & closes, 13", NMIB $200.00

Pipe Hauler Truck, Yamaichi, friction, tractor & trailer w/5 sections of pipe, 14", NMIB $200.00

EMERGENCY AND SERVICE VEHICLES

American Yellow Cab, Bing, w/up, blk & orange, MDW, rear reads 'Lenox 530,' w/driver, 7", G $475.00

Emergency Service Truck, Nomura, b/o, driver w/'AAA' uniform, working headlights, winch on back, 9½", EXIB $300.00

Fire Aerial Ladder Truck (Electro-Toy Fire Engine), Mizuno, b/o, working headlights & ladder light, 9", NMIB $150.00

Fire Aerial Ladder Truck (MFD), Kokyu, friction, lever-op pop-up ladder w/bell, 14½", NMIB $125.00

Fire Car, Marusan, friction, 1950s, fire truck w/ladder extendable atop roof, 5", NM+IB $150.00

Fire Chief Car, Courtland, friction, red & wht w/figures lithoed in windows, 7" L, NM+IB $125.00

Fire Engine, Yonezawa, friction, aerial ladder truck marked FD on cab doors, extensive litho detail, BRT, 10", EXIB.. $100.00

Fire Engine w/Automatic Extension Ladders, Cragstan, w/driver & 4 rear standing firemen, sparking dome light, 14", VGIB.$125.00

Fire Ladder Truck, Germany, w/up, open seat w/bell on curved wire, wire ladder supports, red & blk w/gray MSW, 6", VG........ $150.00

Fire Patrol Auto, SP/France, driver & patrol lithoed in windows, red w/blk roof, 'Dunlop' MDW, 6½", EX $125.00

Fire Truck, Germany, w/up, rotating extension ladder & crank-op water pump w/2 hoses, red w/gold trim, driver, 16", VG..$1,100.00

G-Men Car (Electro-Toy), Mizuno, b/o, 1950s Buick w/working roof light & headlights, machine gun on hood, 8", NM..$300.00

G-Men Car (Sparking), friction, G-Men lithoed on windows, gun on hood, 6½", EXIB $230.00

Louisiana State Police Car, Bandai, 1965, friction, red & wht, 8", EX $100.00

Mercedes Benz 190 SL Police Car (1950s), Seidel/Germany, b/o, gr & wht w/darkened windows, bl roof light, BRT, 11", NM. $175.00

Old Fashioned Fire Engine, Masudaya, b/o, puffs smoke, bell rings, working lights, front & rear figures, 12" L, EXIB..$85.00

Police Car, Lupor, friction, red, blk & wht, figures lithoed in windows, 7", EX+IB $150.00

Police Car (Mystery Action), Komoda, b/o, 1950s blk & wht Buick w/cops lithoed in windows, roof light & siren, 8", NMIB.. $100.00

Police Car, Niedermeir, 1950, friction, 13", EX+IB........ $175.00

Secret Agents Car (007), b/o Chevy sedan w/working siren & flashing light, 14", NMIB $315.00

Taxi, Germany, w/up, early blk & wht auto, MSW, rear spare, w/driver, 8", VG $500.00

Taxi, Electro-Toy/Japan, Mizuno, b/o, 1950 Buick w/roof light, working headlights, 8", NM+IB $325.00

MILITARY

Air Defense Pom Pom Guns, Linemar, friction, b/o guns w/gun operator, 14", NMIB... $125.00

Ambulance, Hausser, w/up, electric lights, opening side & rear doors, gray, wht & blk w/red cross emblems, MDW, 11", VG $1,200.00

Tin Vehicles, Emergency
Fire Ladder Truck, Gunthermann, windup, crank-operated extension ladder, ratchet lever-operated water pump, with firemen figures, 14", EX, $1,800.00.

Tin Vehicles, Military
Armored Car, TN, prewar, windup, gun turrets on top, six-wheeled, tan with blue trim, 9", EX, $750.00.

Artillery Truck, Lionel, w/up, electric lights, open camo body & hubs, MDW, cannon on turret, 6 compo figures, 11", EX.........$1,200.00

Jeep, Minic #2, 1950s, w/up, army gr w/wht star & 2068315-5 on hood, w/spare wheel & plastic jerrycan, NMIB..........$115.00

King Jeep, Yonezawa, friction, hood opens to reveal motor, 7½" L, NM+IB.................$75.00

M-4 US Army Combat Tank, Tano Kogyo Co, 1950s, b/o, bump-&-go action, NMIB................$140.00

M38 (Turn-O-Matic) Military Jeep (1960s), Nomura, b/o, w/2 figures, EXIB................$100.00

Radar Jeep, Nomura, b/o, w/driver & rear radar operators, NMIB................$150.00

Rocket Ranger, Marusan, friction, advances w/siren, gun turret turns & fires at plane on wire, 2 figures, 6", NMIB......$975.00

Touring Car, JEP, w/up, open, front/back windshields, electric lights, BRT w/hubs, yel & red, driver/officer, 20", VG.$4,600.00

Truck, w/up, open bed, allover mc vertical rock-like camouflage detail including wheels, w/driver, 13½", EX $100.00

USAF Radio Jeep (1960s), Momoya, friction, w/3 figures, NMIB.................$85.00

MOTORCYCLES

Arrow Motorcycle, Mitsuhashi, w/up, lithoed spoke wheels, no driver, 6", NMIB.................$1,350.00

Boy on Motorcycle, Kico/Germany, w/up, tall lanky rider w/ orange jacket & hat, thin MSW, 8½", G $3,500.00

Civilian Family on Motorcycle w/Sidecar, Tippco, w/up, couple on cycle w/child in sidecar, 'Dunlop Cord' tires, 9", NM ..$6,900.00

Civilian Motorcycle A 560, Arnold, w/up, integral rider, 7½", NMIB $1,450.00

Delivery Motorcycle, Yoshiya, crank-op friction, 3-wheeled cart w/integral driver, lithoed wheels, 6", NM+IB.............$400.00

G-Men Motorcycle, Hadson, friction, integral driver in wht helmet, 10", NMIB.................$2,200.00

Highway Patrol, Alps, friction, b/o lights, integral driver, 12", EXIB $4,300.00

Highway Patrol, Japan, friction, very detailed litho, w/integral driver, 5½", EX $125.00

Highway Patrol, Masudaya, b/o, driver w/articulated arms & legs, working headlight, NMIB.................$800.00

Indian Motorcycle, Marusan, friction, saddlebags across back fender, integral driver #12, 7", EX+ $1,050.00

Indian Motorcycle, Made in Japan, w/up, integral civilian driver, EX $950.00

Indian Motorcycle (1955), IY Metal Toys, friction, integral civilian driver, 9", unused, NM+IB.................$4,025.00

Mac 700 Motorcycle, Arnold/Germany, w/up, articulated rider, 8", NMIB $900.00

Mirakomet Motorcycle #2, Schuco, w/up, integral driver, 5", NM+IB $375.00

Motorcycle 370 w/Sidecar, Kellerman, w/up, w/driver & passenger, passengers appears to fall out on turns, 5½" L, EX $1,100.00

Motodrill Motorcycle #1, Schuco #1006, w/up, integral driver, 5", NMIB Mirakomet is Schuco #1012.................$375.00

PD Police Motorcycle, Ohta, w/up, integral driver, 7", NM..$500.00

Police Dept (Mystery Police Cycle), Yoshiya, crank-op friction, integral driver, 3 lithoed wheels, 6", NMIB.................$600.00

Police Motorcycle w/Sidecar, Germany, w/up, w/driver & passenger, blk & wht cycle w/red & blk figures, 4" L, EX $300.00

Police Patrol (Patrol Auto-Tricycle), Nomura, b/o, driver whistle in mouth, 10", NMIB.................$425.00

Racing Motoryrcle #4, Technofix, w/up, integral rider, 7", NMIB.................$450.00

Racing Motorcycle #25, Huki/Germany, w/up, w/rider, 3½" L, EX $650.00

Servicycle, Nylint, ca 1948, 3-wheeled w/clear windshield, lithoed integral driver, BRT w/chrome hubs, 7" L, NMIB .$400.00

Sunbeam Motorcycle w/Side Car, Marusan, b/o, blk w/red tank, working lights, no driver, 9", NM+IB.................$1,300.00

Venus Auto Cycle, Nomura, friction, 1960 on license plate, piston action, BRT w/lithoed spokes, rubber grips, 9", NM+IB..$400.00

RACE CARS

Atom Racer #153, Yonezawa, friction, 16", NM..........$3,550.00

Atom Racer #153, Yonezawa, friction, 16", VG $1,450.00

Ball-A-Fire Ford Stock Car, Mitake Toy, 1960s, friction, 13½", NM $110.00

Boattail Racer #5, red pnt, blk tin wheels w/yel hubs, yel #5 on hood, yel seat, 10" L, EX+.................$100.00

Captain Campbell's Blue Bird Racer, Gunthermann, w/up, 1920s, English/American flags on tail, w/driver, NMIB.................$5,750.00

Champions Racer #98, Yonezawa/ETC, friction, BRT, 18", G ..$350.00

Golden Arrow, Racer, Kingsbury, w/up, gun-metal gray, WRT w/ spoke wheels, w/driver, 19½", VG.............................. $325.00

HKN Racing Motorcycle #11, Huki, friction, integral driver, BRT w/2 side wheels, 4", NM $100.00

Indianapolis 500 Racer, Sears, b/o, 15", VGIB................ $400.00

Jaguar Official Pace Car (1950s XK 140 Coupe), Bandai, friction, '500 Mile Race 1956' on trunk, 6", NMIB................... $150.00

JEP Racer #6, JEP/France, BRT w/disk wheels, 18", VG .. $725.00

Jet Racer Y53, Yonezawa, friction, BRT, advances w/siren & spark, w/driver, 12", EX... $325.00

Jumping Racer, Marusan, friction, Jaguar & Tiger racers w/BRT, w/drivers, cb ramp, 4½" ea, NMIB.............................. $350.00

King Jet Racer #8, Tanaguchi, friction, plastic canopy, 12", VG+ $700.00

Mechanical Racer, Chime Toy Prod/Canada, w/up, wooden wheels, flat-sided driver, 12½", EXIB........................ $225.00

Mustang Race Car #12 Convertible, Yonezawa, b/o, lt bl w/yel & blk flag on doors, w/driver, 13", EX+ $275.00

Open Wheel Racer #7, Occupied Japan, 1940s, friction, hand-pnt, integral driver, 5", EX+.....................................$95.00

Race Master #8, Lupor, w/up, 11½", NMIB..................... $150.00

Racer #7, Mettoy, 1930s, w/up, right-sided driver, no size given, EX $275.00

Rocket Racer No 8, Yonezawa, friction, BRT w/orange walls, 11½", VG... $750.00

Speedway Streamlined Blackbird Racer, Lindstrom #1212, w/up, 6", VGIB.. $250.00

TRUCKS AND VANS

American Circus (Circus Trailer), Yoshi/AHI, friction, rear gate opens & animals slide out, 11", NMIB $200.00

Animal Circus Truck, Ohta, w/up, cat pops out of door on roof, 10", EXIB... $125.00

Auto Transporter (Double-Wide), Linemar, 1961, friction, w/6 1961 friction Chevys (holds up to 10), 16", EX $75.00

Auto Transports, Martin #254, 1920s, w/up, open maroon tractor w/ driver towing 4 open trailers w/MSW, 25" L, EX+IB .. $3,250.00

Bakery/Fruit Cake/Bread Delivery Truck (Commercial Van Truck), Tatsuya, friction, 8", EXIB........................... $150.00

Chad Valley Co Ltd Delivery Van, w/up, rear opening door, 10", EX $700.00

Courtland Ice Cream Delivery Truck, w/up, red, wht & bl w/yel bed interior, lithoed driver in window, 8½", EX $55.00

Courtland Roller Truck, w/up, lg roller w/images of zoo animals on red & wht 'candy-cane' background, 9", VG+ $110.00

Delivery Truck, Germany, flywheel in truck bed, open bench seat w/driver, MSW, 10", VG $325.00

Disneyland Van Trailer, Linemar, friction, lt bl w/Disney scene on sides of trailer, 12", VGIB $1,375.00

Dodge Standard Oil Co Gasoline Tanker Truck (Gasoline Car), Mitsuhashi #M-957, friction, 8½", NMIB $200.00

Donald Duck Gasoline Tanker Truck, Linemar, friction, 13", EX $725.00

Dump Truck, Bing (?), w/up, roof over open cab w/right-side driver, horizontally slated bed, MSW, 11", VG $350.00

Esso Gasoline (Tanker) Truck, Asakusa, friction, 18", NMIB..$350.00

Fast Freight/Continental Express Transport Van, Yamaichi, friction, yel & bl, 14", NMIB $200.00

General Parcels Express, Burnette/England, w/up, roof extends over open seat, w/driver, 7", EX+............................... $4,000.00

Glide-A-Ride (NY World's Fair 1964), Lowell Toy Mfg, friction, Greyhound logo, 9", NMIB.................................... $225.00

Menagerie Truck, Y, 1950s, friction, w/2 lions & tamers on a moving seesaw & ball, 10", MIB............................. $150.00

Merry-Go-Round Truck, Nomura, b/o, 10½", NM $300.00

Mickey's Mousekemovers Moving Van, Linemar, 1950s, 12½", VG+.. $265.00

Moving Van/Ware House Truck, NonPariel, w/up, van roof extends over open seat, spoke wheels, w/7" US Gas pump, 6", VG+ $350.00

NAR Television Truck, Linemar, b/o, 11½", NM+IB..$1,150.00

REA Air Express Panel Truck (Corvair), Tatsuya, friction, gr w/ gray top, 8", NM+IB... $150.00

Road Sweeper, Gely/Germany, w/up, red w/NP trim, sweeper brush on front end, MDW, lithoed driver, 5½", EX..... $525.00

Shell Tanker Truck (Mighty Gasoline Truck), Harusame, friction, 10-wheeled, 11", NMIB..................................... $125.00

SIE Cragstan Line Trailer Truck, SSS, friction, GMC cab, 15", NM+IB $150.00

Stake Truck, IY Metal Toys, friction, 16", NMIB............ $400.00

US Mail 15360 Truck, Banner, 1940s, dk gr, 12", EX+... $125.00

Work Truck, Germany, w/up, roof over open seat w/driver on right side, MSW, gr & blk, 7½", VG.......................... $110.00

World Circus Truck, Linemar, friction, w/revolving clown & animals, 9½", EX $200.00

Tonka

Since the mid-'40s, the Tonka Company (Minnesota) has produced an extensive variety of high-quality painted metal trucks, heavy equipment, tractors, and vans.

Allied Van Lines Moving Van, #39, 24", VGIB.............. $325.00
Animal Circus Semi, 1960s, 26", VG............................. $175.00
Army Bulldozer GR-2-243, rubber treads, 1960s, 12", VG ..$100.00
Army Troop Carrier GR-2-243, 1960s, 14", EXIB $125.00
Camper Pickup, #530, 1960s, NMIB.............................. $325.00
Cargo King, aluminum trailer, 1950s, 24", VG $125.00
Fire Aerial Ladder Truck #5, 32", VG $200.00
Fire Ladder Engine #5, w/hose, 17", EX $140.00
Fire Snorkel Pumper Truck, #2950, 17", unused, EX+IB . $100.00
Fire Suburban Pumper Truck, 1950s, red, 17", NMIB..... $400.00
Fire Suburban Pumper Truck, 1960s, wht, 18", VG $125.00
Golf Club Tractor, 12", G $50.00
Grain Hauler, #550, 1952, 23", VG............................... $150.00
Hydraulic Dump Truck, #520, 1963, NMIB.................... $330.00
Lumber Truck, #850-6, 1950s, 17", VG......................... $325.00
Minute Maid Box Truck, wht w/decals, 14", 1950s, VG. $285.00
Parcel Delivery, #750, 1950s, 12", EX+ $440.00
Pickup Truck & Trailer, 1960s, 22" overall, G $75.00
Pickup Truck (De Salle), #880-6, gold w/50th Anniversary decal on doors, 13", EXIB $225.00
Pickup, 1956, red, rstr.. $110.00
Road Grader Diesel No 600, NM $200.00

Serv-I-Car, 1960s, 9", EX+ $100.00
Sportman Pickup, #5, 1959-60, 13", VGIB..................... $350.00
Stake Truck, red w/gr stake sides, 16", 1950s, VG.......... $230.00
State Hi-Way Dept Dump Truck w/Snow Plow, straight plow, 1950s, 15", VG $200.00
State Hi-Way Dept Dump Truck w/Snow Plow, V-shaped plow, 1960s, 18", G $175.00
State Hi-Way Dept Dump Truck w/Two Snow Plows, #975, 13", VG $400.00
State Hi-Way Dept Flatbed Truck w/Steam Shovel, 1950s, 25", VG $125.00
State Hi-Way Dept Pickup 975, EX+ $125.00
State Hi-Way Dept Steam Shovel, rubber treads, NM ... $175.00
State Hi-Way Dept Truck w/Dragline on Low-Boy Trailer, cream, 32", VG $150.00
Steel Carrier, orange snub-nose cab w/gr open U-shaped trailer, EX $75.00
Tonka Airlines Baggage Train, 1960s, 6-pc w/plastic luggage, EX $175.00
Tonka Farms Livestock Truck, 1960s, 17", VG $150.00
Tonka Service Van, 1960s, 13", VG................................ $125.00
Tonka Tanker and Bulk Storage Tanks Set, 28" truck w/2 11" H tanks, VG $400.00
Tonka Toy Transport Semi, snub-nose cab (GMC?), EX. $180.00
Winnebago Motor Home, metal & plastic, 23", GIB $100.00
Wrecker, straight bed, wht w/red crane, 1960s, EX......... $175.00
Wrecker, wht w/Official MM Service Truck decals, EX+. $175.00

Tonka

Fire Suburban Pumper Truck No. 46, unused, MIB (NOS), $900.00. (Photo courtesy Morphy Auctions on LiveAuctioneers.com)

Tonka

Green Giant Semi, #589, 23", EX, $400.00.
(Photo courtesy Morphy Auctions on LiveAuctioneers.com)

Tootsietoys

The first diecast Tootsietoys were made by the Samuel Dowst Company in 1906 when they reproduced the Model T Ford in miniature. Dowst merged with Cosmo Manufacturing in 1926 to form the Dowst Manufacturing Company and continued to turn out replicas of the full-scale vehicles in actual use at the time. After another merger in 1961, the company became known as the Strombecker Corporation. Over the years, many types of wheels and hubs were utilized, varying in both style and material. The last all-metal car was made in 1969; recent Tootsietoy mix plastic components with the metal and have soft plastic wheels. Early prewar mint-in-box toys are scarce and now command high prices on today's market.

Values listed here are current auction prices.

Tootsietoys

Baby Ford and Outfit, #501, complete, EX+IB, $350.00. (Photo courtesy Noel Barrett Antiques & Auctions Ltd. on LiveAuctioneers.com)

Tootsietoys

Roamer Set, Lincoln Zephyr with #1044 Roamer Trailer, EXIB, $1,400.00. (Photo courtesy Bertoia Auctions on LiveAuctioneers.com)

Tootsietoys

Tootsietoy Special, #194, NMIB, $450.00. (Photo courtesy Noel Barrett Antiques & Auctions Ltd. on LiveAuctioneers.com)

Aerial Defense Set #05051, 7 airplanes w/4"-5" WS, VGIB . $375.00

Aero-Dawn, #4660, 1934, red, NM $70.00

Airplane Set, #5698, 5 planes from 3" to 4" WS, VGIB . $225.00

Airplane Set, #7500, 6 military planes, NMIB $700.00

Airport Set, #1689, 1960s, lg plane w/4 vehicles 3 tow trailers, MIP (sealed) $25.00

Auto Transport, #198, EXIB $425.00

Biplane, #4650, 1926, NM $115.00

Buick Touring Sedan, #4641, 1925, VG $200.00

Car & Ramp Set #5798, 6 vehicles & ramp, NMIB $275.00

Carrier, #1036, NM $35.00

Combination Set, #9130A, w/fire ladder truck, US mail truck, stake truck & auto, 3" ea, NMIB $1,840.00

Contractor Set, #0191, 1933-41, NMIB $600.00

Convoy Set, 13 boats, EX+IB $425.00

Deluxe Set, #4700, 4 6" vehicles, VGIB $275.00

DeSoto Air Flow, #0118, 1935-39, NM $50.00

Express Railroad Set, #193, EXIB $200.00

Farm Set, #6800, 1958, complete, MIB $475.00

Fire Department Set, #521, 9" aerial ladder truck, 7" pumper truck, 4" fire chief's car & 4" ambulance, G-NM (VG box) $325.00

Fire Department Set, #5211, complete w/4 vehicles & accessories, EXIB $325.00

Fire Hook & Ladder Truck, #4652, 1927, 3½", EX $30.00

Fire Water Tower Truck, #4653, 1927, 3½", EX+ $60.00

Ford Model A Sedan (1929), #6665, orange, EX $50.00

Ford Station Wagon w/Midget Race Car & Trailer, 1960s, 10½", MOC $160.00

Freight Train Set, #290, 5-pc w/Cracker Jack boxcar, EX+IB . $150.00

Freight Train Set, #5550, locomotive & 4 freight cars, 4½" to 5", EX+IB $175.00

Freight Train Set, #5600, 10-piece, EXIB $225.00

Highway Set, #4700, 1949, complete, MIB $450.00

Insurance Patrol Car, #104, 1932-34, NM $35.00

Interchangeable Truck, w/tank, stake & dump trailers, 3x4", NMIB $800.00

Jumbo Coupe, #1017, 1942-46, EX $40.00

KO Ice Truck, KO seated at rear, 3" L, EX+ $275.00

Mack Anti-Aircraft Gun, #4643, 1931, NM $65.00

Mack B-Line (1955) Cement Mixer Truck, 1950s, 6", M (VG+ card) $75.00

Motorcycle w/Driver & Sidecar, lid on car, 3" L, G $200.00

Navy Set #5750, 6 navy ships from 4" to 6", VGIB $225.00

Playtime Toys Miniature Set, #7005, 1933, 10-pc, rare, EXIB $1,000.00

Playtime Toys Set, #5075, 7-pc, EX+IB $1,500.00

Road Construction Assortment (Set), 4 vehicles w/6 road signs, EX+IB $275.00

Roadgrader, #679, 6" L, EXIB $65.00

Rol-ezy Toys Set #5149, 9 vehicles from 3" to 4" & 1 airplane, NMIB $450.00

Seaplane, #4660, NM $100.00

Smitty on Motorcycle w/Passenger in Sidecar, 3" L, EX+ $450.00

Streamline Train, 3-pc w/US Mail, Union Pacific & Tootsietoy Flyer Cars, 11½" L, EX+IB $650.00

Taxicab Set, #5350, 5-pc, EX+IB $1,500.00

Tootsietoy Dairy Tandem Tanker Truck, 3 tanks, 13½" L overall, EX+IB $325.00

Tootsietoy Funnies Set, 6 vehicles w/comic character drivers, VGIB $2,500.00

Tootsietoy Limited, #5850, 2 locomotives, 2 Broadway cars & 1 Pullman, 5" to 6", EX+IB $650.00

Tootsietoy Line Mack Tanker, #669, NM $100.00

Touring Car, #232, 1940-41, NM $50.00

Tow Truck, #2485, 1960s, NM $45.00

US Army Airplane, #119, 1936, NM $75.00

USN Los Angeles Zeppelin, 1937, 5", MIB $1,400.00

Utility Truck, #869, EXIB $75.00

Waco Dive Bomber, #718, 1937, NM $125.00

Wings, biplane, 3¾" WS, NMIB $500.00

Trains

Some of the earliest trains (from ca. 1860) were made of tin or cast iron, smaller versions of the full-scale steam-powered trains that traversed America from the east to the west. Most were made to simply be pushed or pulled along, though some had clockwork motors. Electric trains were produced as early as the late nineteenth century. Three of the largest manufacturers were Lionel, Ives, and American Flyer.

Lionel trains have been made since 1900. Until 1915 they produced only standard gauge models (measuring 2½" between the rails). The smaller O gauge (1¼") they introduced at that time proved to be highly successful, and the company grew until by 1955 it had become the largest producer of trains in the world. Until discontinued in 1940, standard gauge trains were produced on a limited scale, but O and 027 gauge models dominated the market. Production dwindled and nearly stopped in the mid-1960s, but the company was purchased by General Mills in 1969, and they continue to produce a very limited number of trains today.

The Ives company had been a major producer of toys since 1896. They were the first to initiate manufacture of the O gauge train and at first used only clockwork motors to propel them. Their first electric trains (in both O and 1 gauge) were made in 1910, but because electricity was not yet a common commodity in many areas, clockwork production continued for several years. By 1920, 1 gauge was phased out in favor of standard gauge. The company continued to prosper until the late 1920s when it floundered and was bought jointly by American Flyer and Lionel. American Flyer soon turned their interest over to Lionel, who continued to make Ives trains until 1933.

The American Flyer company had produced trains for several years, but it wasn't until it was bought by AC Gilbert in 1937 that it became successful enough to be considered a competitor of Lionel. They're best noted for their conversion from the standard (wide gauge) three-rail system to the two-rail S gauge (⅞") and the high-quality locomotives and passenger and freight cars they produced in the 1950s. Interest in toy trains waned during the space-age decade of the 1960s. As a result, sales declined, and in 1966 the company was purchased by Lionel. Today both American Flyer and Lionel trains are being made from the original dies by Lionel Trains Inc., privately owned.

All listings below come from current auctions.

For more information we recommend *Collecting Toy Trains* by Richard O'Brien.

Advisor: Gary Mosholder

See also Buddy L (for that company's Outdoor Railroad); Cast Iron, Trains; Paper-Lithographed Toys; Pull and Push Toys.

AMERICAN FLYER

Accessory, Central Station, tin, faux red & gr brick, wht trim, gr roof, 2 red chimneys, electric lights, O-gauge, NMIB . $500.00
Accessory, figure set, #578, complete, VG $200.00
Accessory, Flyerville Station, #163, EXIB...................... $475.00
Accessory, Freight Station, #91 or #95, EX, ea $200.00
Accessory, Switch Tower, #108, EX+ $925.00
Accessory, Talking Station #799, S-gauge, complete, VGIB. $400.00

Accessory, Terminal Station, #97, VG $200.00
Accessory, Union Station #110, prewar, VG $3,600.00
Accessory, water tower, prewar, G $50.00
Accessory, water tower, #596, EX $100.00
Baggage Car, 50, FY & PRR, VG $200.00
Baggage Car, 1108, Penn Line, prewar, G $675.00
Boxcar, 24016, MKT/The Katy, yel w/red top, G........... $325.00
Boxcar, 25061, TNY/Explosives Carrier Service, VG..... $200.00
Caboose, 4021, red, VGIB $225.00
Caboose, 24636, yel, EX $625.00
Cattle Car, 976, Missouri Pacific, VG $30.00
Cattle Car, 4005, gr, VG.. $350.00

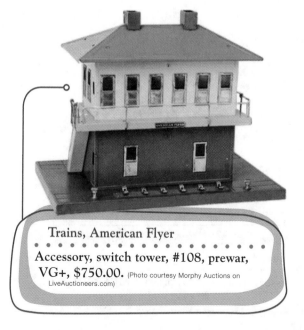

Trains, American Flyer
Accessory, switch tower, #108, prewar, VG+, $750.00. (Photo courtesy Morphy Auctions on LiveAuctioneers.com)

Trains, American Flyer
Caboose, 24632, M, $475.00. (Photo courtesy Stout Auctions on LiveAuctioneers.com)

Flatcar w/2 'American Flyer' trailers, 24536, Monon, EX...$1,300.00

Flatcar, 24558, Canadian Pacific, w/Christmas trees, NMIB.$575.00

Hopper, 4006, red, prewar, VG+IB.................................$500.00

Hopper, 24333, Domino Sugars, yel, G+.......................$250.00

Hopper, Western Maryland 24219, S-gauge, NM.............$80.00

Loco, 499, New Haven EP-5, EX $375.00

Loco, 4637, Shasta, prewar, G $675.00

Loco, 4644, 0-4-0 electric, G......................................$120.00

Loco, 4654, New Haven, G...$100.00

Loco & Tender, 302A, EX..$175.00

Loco & Tender, 343, VG $350.00

Loco & Tender, 3199, G $140.00

Loco & Tender, 4322 2-4-0 locomotive, 433 tender, prewar, VG $425.00

Loco & Tender, 4693, VG+..$600.00

Loco & Tender, 4694 Golden State Tender, VG $400.00

Lumber Loader, 751, VGIB $175.00

Passenger Car, Golden State Wide Lines Coach, VG+ ..$500.00

Passenger Car, 652, Pikes Peak, red, VG $75.00

Passenger Car, 978, Grand Canyon, maroon, G+ $375.00

Tank Car, 910, Gilbert Chemicals, EXIB $325.00

Tank Car, 24320, Deep Rock, VG $275.00

AMERICAN FLYER SETS

Freight, loco & tender 00283/ballast car 924/boxcar 923/gondola 804/gondola 916, S-gauge, VG $150.00

Freight, Reliable, #30705, w/loco & 3 cars, EXIB........$1,500.00

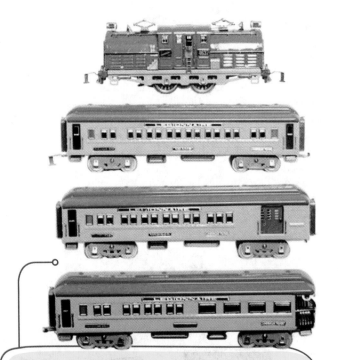

Trains, American Flyer Sets

Passenger, Legionnaire, 4637 locomotive, 4380 Madison car, 4381 Pullman, 4382 Hancock observation car, prewar, VG+, $1,400.00. (Photo courtesy Stout Auctions on LiveAuctioneers.com)

Freight, Union Pacific diesel switcher 372/ballast car 924/boxcars 802 & 803/gondola 805/hopper 921/caboose 806, EX.. $250.00

Passenger, Burlington Zephyr, loco 9900 & 4 cars, silver & blk, VG $225.00

Passenger, Chicago Passenger, loco, tender & 2 coaches, prewar, G...$2,100.00

Passenger, Explorer, electric loco 0-4-0/1211, Great Northern baggage car, 2 Oriental Limited coaches, GIB.............$200.00

Passenger, Golden State, loco 3115 & 3 cars, VGIB $575.00

Passenger, Hamiltonian, loco 4678, baggage car 4341, Pullman 4341 & observation ca 4342, NMIB......................$5,600.00

Passenger, loco 4-4-4/3020, baggage car 3000 & 2 Pullmans 3001, gr, F $350.00

Passenger, Pocahontas, 4-pc, standard gauge, EX.........$3,335.00

Passenger, Potomac loco 3116/baggage car 3180/Pullman 3181/ observation car 3182, O-gauge, EX............................$225.00

Passenger, President's Special, Commander loco 4689/club car 4391/ diner 4393/observation car 4390/Pullman 4391, VG....$2,300.00

Passenger, Santa Fe A&B locos 470 & 473/coaches 960, 962 (2) & 963, plastic, S-gauge, EX..$325.00

Passenger, Viking, w/up loco 0-4-0/13, tender 120, baggage car 1108, coach 1120, VG+IB $350.00

LIONEL

Accessory, bascule bridge, #313, EXIB $275.00

Accessory, crossing signal, #79, prewar, VG...................$325.00

Accessory, dispatching board, #334, complete, EXIB $200.00

Accessory, engine transfer table, Lionel #350 Ton, complete, EXIB $230.00

Accessory, Highway Crossing Gate, #262, postwar, NMIB.$250.00

Accessory, Lionelville, #136, VGIB $350.00

Accessory, lumber loader, #164, O-gauge, electric, complete w/ lumber, prewar, VGIB $175.00

Accessory, signal, #69, prewar, VGIB............................$100.00

Accessory, signal, #79, prewar, EX+IB..........................$500.00

Accessory, signal, #97, prewar, EX+IB..........................$150.00

Accessory, signal tower, #438, prewar, EX+ $1,000.00

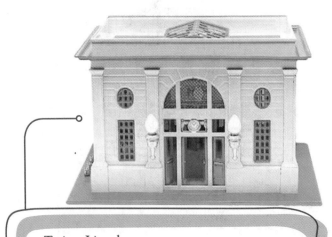

Trains, Lionel

Accessory, station, 115, prewar, MIB, $950.00.
(Photo courtesy Stout Auctions on LiveAuctioneers.com)

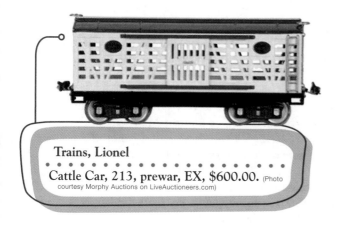

Trains, Lionel

Cattle Car, 213, prewar, EX, $600.00. (Photo courtesy Morphy Auctions on LiveAuctioneers.com)

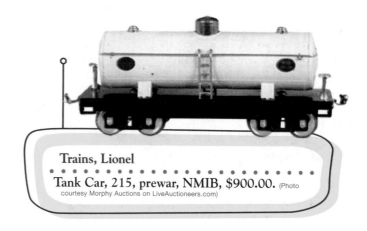

Trains, Lionel

Tank Car, 215, prewar, NMIB, $900.00. (Photo courtesy Morphy Auctions on LiveAuctioneers.com)

Accessory, station, #124, tin, brn faux brick, cream trim, gr roof w/2 chimneys, electric lights, prewar, VG $250.00

Accessory, station, #127, prewar, EXIB $350.00

Accessory, water tank, #93, prewar, NMIB $525.00

Baggage Car, 332, VG $200.00

Baggage Car, 2615, prewar, GIB $300.00

Baggage Car, 2530, Railway Express Agency, aluminum, VG .$400.00

Baggage Car, 19011, NM $250.00

Boxcar, 2814, prewar, EX+IB $800.00

Boxcar, 3484, Pennsylvania RR, EXIB $225.00

Boxcar, 3666, Minuteman, VG+ $425.00

Boxcar, 6044, Airfix, rare purple color, EX $525.00

Boxcar, 6463825, Alaska Railroad, VG $150.00

Boxcar, 6464-475, Boston & Maine, postwar, EX+IB $100.00

Caboose, 2420, DL&W, work caboose w/searchlight, VG.$75.00

Caboose, 2817, postwar, EX $100.00

Caboose, 6447, Pennsylvania, NM+ $500.00

Caboose, 6824, USMC, work caboose, EX $325.00

Cattle Car, 13, prewar, VG $850.00

Cattle Car, 513, GIB $300.00

Flatcar, 3409, w/satellite launcher, VG $300.00

Flatcar, 6816, w/Allis Chalmers dozer, VG $425.00

Hopper, 716, Baltimore & Ohio, prewar, VG+ $450.00

Hopper, 716, B&O 532000/Baltimore & Ohio, EXIB .$1,150.00

Hopper, 716, B&O 532000/Baltimore & Ohio, G+ $525.00

Hopper, 00216, NM+IB $400.00

Hopper, 6456-75, Lehigh Valley, VG+IB $150.00

Lionelville Rapid Transit Trolley, #60, postwar, VG $90.00

Loco, 8, maroon, electric, prewar, G $150.00

Loco, 33, EX $115.00

Loco, 38, New York Central Lines, prewar, EX+ $650.00

Loco, 42, prewar, VG $4,300.00

Loco, 54, 0-4-4-0 electric, brass w/red catchers, VG.... $2,000.00

Loco, 634, Santa Fe, diesel, VG $150.00

Loco, 2329, Virginian, G $300.00

Loco, 8859, Conrail, NMIB $100.00

Loco & Tender, 51-gauge steam loco, 8-wheeled tender, prewar, G $575.00

Loco & Tender, 385E loco, 384T tender, prewar, VG $325.00

Loco & Tender, 685 loco, 6026W tender, NMIB (2 boxes).$400.00

Passenger Car, 400, Baltimore & Ohio, G $200.00

Passenger Car, 2442, Pullman, G $50.00

Passenger Car, 2523, Presidential, aluminum, VG $150.00

Passenger Car, 2559, RDC Budd, Baltimore & Ohio, VG ..$250.00

Switcher, 42, Picatinny Arsenal, VGIB $400.00

Switcher, 56, M St L Mine Transport, G+ $200.00

Switcher, 59, Minuteman, G+ $325.00

Switcher & Tender, 1615 & 3335, ea EXIB $150.00

Tank Car, 715, Sunoco, VG $450.00

Tank Car, 2555, Sunoco, EX+IB $325.00

Tank Car, 8126, Shell, prewar, VG+IB (#45 on box)..... $450.00

Transformer Car, 6461, NMIB $150.00

Trolley, Electric Rapid Transit No 3, standard-gauge, EX ..$12,650.00

Trolley Car, City Hall Park, open sides, F $1,400.00

Trolley Car, Electric Rapid Transit 1, rstr $800.00

Trolley Car, Electric Rapid Transit 100, F $2,250.00

LIONEL SETS

Freight, #141W, 2-6-2 loco 224E w/4 cars, caboose & whistle controller, prewar, EX (VG box) $250.00

Freight, #228W, Virginian FM Trainmaster 2331 w/4 cars, caboose & transforrmer, VG to NM (VG boxes).....$1,150.00

Freight, #256E, loco 256 w/3 cars, O-gauge, preware, EX+ (no boxes) $2,500.00

Freight, #293, electric loco 252 w/3 cars & caboose, O-gauge, prewar, EX+ (EX+ boxes) $325.00

Freight, #11268, Chesapeake & Ohio loco 2365 w/4 cars & caboose, VG to EX (VG boxes).................................. $875.00

Freight, #11288, Minneapolis 229 & St Louis Alco AB units w/4 cars & caboose, tracks & instructions, unused, EX to M (VG+ boxes) $975.00

Freight, #11730, Union Pacific switcher 645 w/4 cars, caboose, track & transformers, unused, NMIB....................... $375.00

Freight, Cascade Range Logging Train, #30021, NMIB . $125.00

Freight, Chesapeake & Ohio, #31904, NMIB $200.00

Freight, Girl's Set, #15875, G+ to EX+ cars (VG+ boxes).$2,450.00

Freight, Girl's Set, #31700 (Celebration Series), NMIB. $450.00

Freight, Great Plains Express, #1866, EXIB $200.00

Freight, Pennsylvania Flyer, #30018, MIB (sealed) $150.00

Freight, Santa Fe Work Train, #1632SSS, MIB (sealed) . $150.00

Freight, Union Pacific, #11736, O gauge, MIB (sealed) . $100.00

Passenger, #255, loco 152 w/3 cars, O gauge, prewar, EX+IB..$550.00

Passenger, #260, loco 152 w/3 cars, O gauge, prewar, EX+IB..$500.00

Passenber, #294, loco 252 w/3 cars, O gauge, prewar, NM (EX boxes) $550.00

Passenger, #1088, 2-4-2 loco 1664 w/tender, 3 cars & transformer, VG to EX (VG boxes) $500.00

Passenger, #1088W, loco 1664 & tender w/3 cars, O gauge, prewar, EX (worn box) $400.00

Passenger, Blue Comet, 4-6-4 steam engine 8801 w/5 cars, plastic, paperwork marked 1976, EX (EX boxes) $250.00

Passenger, Polar Express, #31960, O gauge, complete, EX+IB ... $200.00

Passenger, Steamline, #1551, loc 1816 w/2 cars, O gauge, prewar, EX+ (VG box) $2,250.00

MISCELLANEOUS

Bing, boxcar, Swift's Premium Hams, O gauge, 6½", VG .. $125.00

Bing, loco 0-4-0 Pennsylvania Lines, electric, EX $425.00

Bing, loco, 0-4-4-0 electric #3238, 1 gauge, VG $1,800.00

Bing, loco 4-4-0 & tender, w/up, O gauge, G+ $250.00

Bing, loco 4-4-0 Sydney & tender, 1 gauge, EX $3,500.00

Bing, Postal-Telegraph coach, 1 gauge, 18", G $475.00

Bing, set, electric loco 0-4-4-0, baggage car 1250, coach 1207, maroon & brn, F $650.00

Bing, set, freight #5136, w/up, loco 0-4-0, tender 1012 w/7 cars, O-gauge, VGIB $550.00

Bing, set, Mercury, w/up, loco 4-4-0/5320, 2 LMS dining cars, EX+IB $2,500.00

Bing, set, New York Central Lines, 5-pc train w/1-pc oval track, EX+IB $400.00

Bing, set, passenger, electric, 4-4-0 loco, tender 1012, baggage car 1250, 2 coaches 1207, G to VG $1,000.00

Bing, set, passenger, loco 0-4-0 & tender, baggage car 501, observation car 529, coach 617, G loco/VG+IB cars $500.00

Bing, set, passenger, w/up, loco 4-4-0, PRR tender, baggage car 5285, 2 Pullmans 5208, O gauge, EX $1,500.00

Ives, gate house w/dbl gates & base for track, litho tin, 22", VG $300.00

Ives, loco, w/up, 'Smoker' stenciled on sides of boiler, blk, red & yel w/brass looking bell on wire, 11½", VG $1,150.00

Ives, loco NY Central 3243R, 4-4-4 electric, orange, 16", rpnt .. $8.00

Ives, loco 0-4-0 3242 NYC & PR, maroon w/blk frame, wide gauge, G $350.00

Ives, loco 0-4-0/20 & tender 25, O gauge, G+ $250.00

Ives, loco 0-4-0/3241, buffet car 184 & observation car 186, VG .$375.00

Ives, loco 4-4-0 & tender 25, O gauge, VG $275.00

Ives, loco 4-4-4, O gauge, VG $200.00

Ives, set, loco 4-4-4/3243R, buffet car 180, observation car 182, parlor car 181, orange, wide-gauge, VGIB $1,000.00

Ives, set, Olympian, electric loco 3245R w/orange frame, club car 241, observation car 243, parlor car 242, VG $1,000.00

Ives, set, #704, 3243 loco, 187-3 buffet car, 188-3 parlor car, 189-3 observation car, prewar, VGIB $900.00

Ives, station, Union Station, litho tin w/glass canopy that mounts to base of station, 22" L, G $950.00

Karl Bub, set, passenger, w/up, loco, tender, diner, & 2 coaches, O gauge, G to EXIB $2,250.00

Knapp, passenger set, loco, tender & 3 coaches, VG $400.00

Marklin, bridge, trestle w/2 attachable approaches w/pnt shrubbery accents, 48" overall, VG $200.00

Marklin, bridge, 2-pc trestle span construction, emb 'stone' base, 42" overall, EX $3,250.00

Marklin, loco & tender, Pacific 4-6-2, G+ $1,600.00

Marklin, loco & tender, pnt, tin, 15", VG $700.00

Marklin, loco & tender, Union Pacific 4-6-2/5021, 1 gauge, some rpr $3,250.00

Marklin, loco & tender, w/up, 4-4-0/1030 & NYC & HR tender, O gauge, VG $700.00

Marklin, loco 4-6-2 & NYC & HR tender (8-wheeled), O gauge NMIB $1,000.00

Marklin, set, American passenger, w/up, loco 0-4-0 NY Central Lines, tender, baggage car, 2 coaches, 1 gauge, G+ $600.00

Marklin, set, freight, electric, loco 0-4-0 #1031, NYC & HR tender, Coke car, stake car & tank car, 1 gauge, VG $1,000.00

Marklin, set, freight, w/up, loco 0-4-0, tender, boxcar, dump car, stock car & caboose, 1 gauge, VG+ $1,300.00

Marklin, station, Stuttgart, HO scale, 14x33", NM..... $2,875.00

Marklin, station, Stuttgart, HO scale, 14x33", VG+ .. $1,675.00

Marklin, switcher, #13728/8, 20-volt, litho tin building, 9", EX+IB $375.00

Marx, accessory, Bell Ringing Crossing Signal, #414, 7½", 1950s, NMIB $20.00

Marx, set, Allstate New York Central, plastic, Sears exclusive, 1959, complete, NMIB $88.00

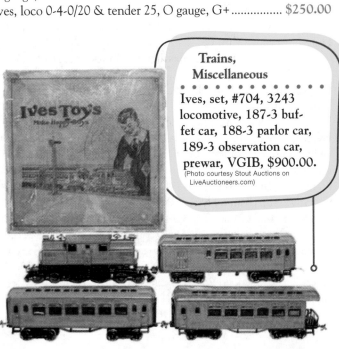

Trains, Miscellaneous

Ives, set, #704, 3243 locomotive, 187-3 buffet car, 188-3 parlor car, 189-3 observation car, prewar, VGIB, $900.00. (Photo courtesy Stout Auctions on LiveAuctioneers.com)

Trains, Miscellaneous

Marklin, roundhouse, painted tin, O gauge, EX, $600.00. (Photo courtesy Morphy Auctions on LiveAuctioneers.com)

Marx, set, Diesel Type Electric w/B&O A&B locos, tender, gondola, PA Merchandise car, transformer & track, EXIB...$85.00

Marx, set, Mickey Mouse Meteor Train, tin, w/up, 5-pc, VG .$500.00

Marx, set, Tales of Wells Fargo, 54752, 1959, VG+IB.... $775.00

Marx, set, Union Pacific loco w/Omaha, Squaw Bonnet & LA coaches, tin, electric, VG.................................... $115.00

Marx, set, Union Pacific M10005 Streamliner Train, litho tin, electric, 5-pc, HO scale, NM $220.00

Schoenhut, Railroad Station/Telegraph Office, pnt wood & emb paper, 17" W, EX $225.00

Steelcraft, set, Twentieth Century Limited loco w/boxcar, Erie coal car, tank car & Chesapeake & Ohio wrecking car, Fair $650.00

TCA, Bicentennial Passenger set, loco 1776 w/3 coaches, NMIB $115.00

Voltamp, caboose, B&O 2110, F $1,000.00

Voltamp, loco, Suburban 2210, rstr $1,600.00

Voltamp, loco 0-4-0 #220, electric, EX $2,250.00

Voltamp, loco 2100 & Pennsylvania tender 2102, VG+.. $3,500.00

Voltamp, trolley, United Electric, electric light, 11½", rstr..$1,300.00

• **Transformers** •

Produced by Hasbro, Transformers were introduced in the United States in 1984. Originally there were 28 figures — 18 Autobots, robots that transformed into cars, and ten Decepticons, evil robots capable of becoming such things as jets or handguns. Eventually the line was expanded to more than 200 different models. The first Transformers were remakes of earlier Japanese robots that had been produced by Takara in the 1970s and early 1980s from such series as *Microman* and *Diaclone*. These Transformers figures can be differentiated from their earlier counterparts through color differences and, in the case of the *Diaclone* series, the absence of the small driver or pilot figures.

The stories of the Transformers and their epic adventures were told through several different comic books and animated series as well as a highly successful movie in 1986. Their popularity was reflected internationally and eventually made its way back to Japan. There the American Transformer animated series was translated into Japanese and soon inspired several parallel series of the toys which were again produced by Takara. Transformers were sold until 1990 when the line ended in the U.S., although the toys continued to be sold in Japan and Europe.

In 1993, Hasbro reintroduced the line with *Transformers: Generation 2*. Transformers once again had their own comic book, and the old animated series was brought back in revamped format. In 1996, Hasbro reinvented the series by introducing the series *Transformers Beast Wars* that featured toys that changed from robot to animal. Transformers returned to its roots with the *Robots In Disguise, Armada*, and *Energon* series, again featuring robots that transformed into vehicles. Sustained interest in the Transformers has spawned international fan clubs, conventions such as the BotCon, an original series produced at Cartoon Network (*Transformers Animated)*, and two highly successful feature films produced by Paramount Pictures, *Transformers* (2007) and *Transformers: Revenge of the Fallen* (2009).

All of the Transformers' success has resulted in a massive amount of merchandise. Everything from Transformers backpacks, to costumes to Transformers edition vehicles from GM have been produced. As of yet there is no complete catalog of all Transformers Hasbro licensed products. The following listings focus on the core group of Transformers action figures produced by Hasbro, with a complete list of all Transformers action figures released between 1984 and 1990. After that year only representative items are listed, as well as ones of significant value.

Because Transformers came in a number of sizes, you'll find a wide range of pricing. Values listed here are for Transformers that are mint figures in mint or nearly mint original boxes. One that has been used is worth much less — about 25% to 75%, depending on whether it has all its parts (weapons, instruction book, tech specs, etc.), and what its condition is — whether decals are well applied or if it is worn. Generally, a loose Transformer complete and in near-mint condition is worth only about half as much as one mint in the box. A Transformer still sealed in its box or package is worth 25% more than the list price.

Advisor: Dahveed Kolodny-Nagy

SERIES 1, 1984

Autobot Car, Bluestreak (Datsun), bl $350.00

Autobot Car, Bluestreak (Datsun), silver...................... $300.00

Autobot Car, Camshaft (car), silver, mail-in $40.00

Autobot Car, Downshaft (car), wht, mail-in $40.00

Autobot Car, Hound (jeep).. $250.00

Autobot Car, Mirage (Indy car) $235.00

Autobot Car, Overdrive (car), red, mail-in....................$40.00

Autobot Car, Powerdasher #1 (jet), mail-in $20.00

Autobot Car, Powerdasher #2 (car), mail-in....................$20.00

Autobot Car, Powerdasher #3 (drill), mail-in....................$40.00

Autobot Car, Rachet (ambulance)................................ $150.00

Autobot Car, Sunstreak (Countach), yel...................... $300.00

Autobot Car, Trailbreaker (camper)............................ $150.00

Autobot Car, Wheeljack (Mazzerati)............................. $275.00

Autobot Commander, Optimus Primus w/Roller (semi).. $175.00

Cassette, Frenzy & Lazerbreak....................................$50.00

Cassette, Ravage & Rumble $50.00

Collector's Case $30.00

Collector's Case, red 3-D version $50.00

Collector's Showcase $15.00

Decepticon Jet, Skywrap, blk.. $150.00

Decepticon Jet, Starcream, gray $200.00

Decepticon Jet, Thundercracker, bl................................ $150.00

Decepticon Leader, Megatron, Walther P-38................. $175.00

Minicar, Brawn (jeep)..$65.00

Minicar, Bumblebee (VW Bug), red or yel.................... $100.00

Transformers, Series 1

Autobot Car, Jazz (Porsche), $275.00; Autobot Car, Prowl (police car), $300.00; Autobot Car, Sideswipe, $275.00. (Photo courtesy Morphy Auctions on LiveAuctioneers.com)

Minicar, Cliffjumper (race car), gr, red or yel.....................$75.00
Minicar, Gears (truck) $65.00
Minicar, Huffer (semi), orange cab.................................$55.00
Minicar, Windcharger (Firebird)....................................$60.00
Watch, Time Warrior, w/Autobot insignia, mail-in........ $100.00

SERIES 2, 1985

Autobot, Red Alert (fire chief) $150.00
Autobot Air Guardian, Jetfire (F-14 jet)....................... $325.00
Autobot Car, Grapple (crane)..................................... $150.00
Autobot Car, Hoist (tow truck).................................... $150.00
Autobot Car, Inferno (fire engine) $150.00
Autobot Car, Skids (Le Car) $225.00
Autobot Car, Smokescreen (Datsun), red, wht & bl $200.00
Autobot Car, Tracks (Corvette) $200.00
Autobot Commander, Blaster (radio/tapeplayer)............ $125.00
Autobot Scientist, Perceptor (microscope)................... $100.00
Constructicon, Bonecrusher (1)....................................$60.00
Constructicon, Hook (4) $50.00
Constructicon, Long Haul (5)......................................$50.00
Constructicon, Mixmaster (6).......................................$50.00
Constructicon, Scavenger (2) $50.00
Constructicon, Scrapper (3)...$50.00
Decepticon, Dirge $110.00
Decepticon, Ramjet $110.00
Decepticon, Shockwave $170.00
Decepticon, Thrust, maroon....................................... $120.00
Deluxe Insecticon, Chop Chop.......................................$70.00
Deluxe Insecticon, Ransack..$65.00
Deluxe Vehicle, Roadbuster $175.00
Deluxe Vehicle, Whirl (helicopter) $150.00
Dinobot, Grimlock (Tynnosaurus) $200.00
Dinobot, Slag (Triceratops) $125.00
Dinobot, Sludge (Brontosaurus)................................... $150.00
Dinobot, Snarl (Stegosaurus) $150.00
Insecticon, Bombshell..$50.00
Insecticon, Kickback..$50.00
Insecticon, Sharpnel..$50.00

Transformers, Series 2

City Commander, Ultra Magnus, $125.00. (Photo courtesy Morphy Auctions on LiveAuctioneers.com)

Insecticon, Venom..$50.00
Jumpstarter, Topspin $45.00
Jumpstarter, Twin Twist (drill tank) $50.00
Minicar, Beachcomber (dune buggy) $30.00
Minicar, Brawn (jeep)..$65.00
Minicar, Bumblebee (VW Bug), w/ or w/o minispy $100.00
Minicar, Cliffjumper (race car), red or yel, ea.................$45.00
Minicar, Cliffjumper (race car), w/minispy $100.00
Minicar, Cosmos (spaceship)..$30.00
Minicar, Gears (truck), bl..$60.00
Minicar, Gears (truck), w/minispy..................................$75.00
Minicar, Huffer (semi)..$50.00
Minicar, Huffer (semi), w/minispy..................................$50.00
Minicar, Powerglide (plane) $35.00
Minicar, Seaspray (hovercraft) $30.00
Minicar, Warpath (tank) $50.00
Minicar, Windcharger (Firebird) $50.00
Minicar, Windcharger (Firebird), w/minispy $75.00
Motorized Autobit Defense Base, Omega Supreme $300.00
Triple Charger, Astrotrain (shuttle/train) $100.00
Triple Charger, Blitzwing (tank/plane)........................... $100.00

SERIES 3, 1986

Aerialbot, Air Raid (1)..$50.00
Aerialbot, Fireflight (3) $50.00
Aerialbot, Silverbot (5)... $100.00
Aerialbot, Skydive (2)..$60.00
Autobot Car, Blurr (futuristic car) $100.00
Autobot Car, Hot Rod (race car) $200.00
Autobot Car, Kup (pickup truck) $100.00
Autobot City Commander, Ultra Magnus (car carrier).. $135.00
Battlecharger, Runabout (Trans Am)...............................$30.00
Battlecharger, Runamuck (Corvette)...............................$35.00
Combaticon, Blast Off (3) $60.00
Combaticon, Brawl (1)..$50.00
Combaticon, Onslaught (5) $75.00
Combaticon, Swindle (3) $50.00
Combaticon, Vortex (4) $60.00
Decepticon City Commander, Galvatron $150.00
Heroes, Rodimus Prime (futuristic RV)......................... $150.00

Heroes, Wreck-Car (futuristic motorcycle)..................... $100.00
Jet, Cyclous Space Jet $125.00
Jet, Scrouge (hovercraft) $125.00
Minicar, Hubcap (race car).. $35.00
Minicar, Outback (jeep).. $50.00
Minicar, Pipes (semi).. $50.00
Minicar, Swerve (truck)... $40.00
Minicar, Tailgate (Firebird)... $40.00
Minicar, Wheelie (futuristic car)...................................... $35.00
Predacon, Gnaw (futuristic shark) $100.00
Predacon, Rampage (2)... $85.00
Predacon, Razorclaw (1)... $85.00
Predacon, Tantrum (4)... $85.00
Predocon, Divebomb (3).. $85.00
Stunticon, Breakdown (2).. $50.00
Stunticon, Dead End (1).. $50.00
Stunticon, Drag Strip (4)... $50.00
Stunticon, Motormaster (semi).. $75.00
Stunticon, Wildrider (Ferrari).. $50.00
Triple Charger, Broadside (aircraft carrier/plane)............. $75.00
Triple Charger, Octane (tanker truck/jumbo jet)............. $100.00
Triple Charger, Sandstorm (dune buggy/helicopter)....... $100.00
Triple Charger, Springer (armored car/copter)............... $125.00

Series 4, 1987

Clone, Fastlane & Cloudraker (dragster & spaceship) $65.00
Clone, Pounce & Wingspan (puma & eagle) $45.00
Double Spy, Punch-Counterpunch (Fiero) $75.00
Duocon, Battlestap (jeep/copter) $40.00
Duocon, Flywheels (jet/tank) $30.00
Headmaster Autobot, Brainstorm w/Arcana (jet) $100.00
Headmaster Autobot, Chromedome w/Stylor (futuristic car)... $10.00
Headmaster Autobot, Hardhead w/Duros (tank)............ $100.00
Headmaster Autobot, Highbrow w/Gort (copter) $100.00
Headmaster Decepticon, Mindwipe w/Vorath (bat)....... $100.00
Headmaster Decepticon, Skullrunner w/Grax (alligator) . $100.00
Headmaster Decepticon, Weirdwolf w/Monzo (wolf)..... $100.00
Headmaster Horrorcon, Apeface w/Spasma (jet/ape)..... $100.00
Headmaster Horrorcon, Snapdragon w/Krunk (jet/dinosaur).$100.00
Monsterbot, Doublecross (2-headed dragon) $75.00
Monsterbot, Grotusque (tiger) $75.00
Monsterbot, Repugnus (insect) $75.00

Targetmaster Autobot, Blurr w/Haywire (futuristic car &
   gun) $250.00
Targetmaster Autobot, Crosshairs w/Pinpointer (truck &
   gun) $100.00
Targetmaster Autobot, Hot Rod & Firebolt (race car & gun) . $400.00
Targetmaster Autobot, Kup & Recoil (pickup truck & gun) ..$150.00
Targetmaster Autobot, Pointblank w/Peacemaker (race car w/
   gun) $100.00
Targetmaster Autobot, Sureshot w/Spoilsport (off-road buggy &
   gun) $75.00
Targetmaster Decepticon, Misfire w/Aimless (spaceship &
   gun) $135.00
Targetmaster Decepticon, Scrouge w/Fracas (hovercraft &
   gun) $375.00
Targetmaster Decepticon, Slugslinger w/Caliburts (twin jet &
   gun) $100.00
Technobot, Afterburner... $45.00
Technobot, Afterburner, w/decoy...................................... $55.00
Technobot, Lightspeed... $45.00
Technobot, Lightspeed, w/decoy...................................... $50.00
Technobot, Nosecone... $40.00
Technobot, Nosecone, w/decoy.. $45.00
Terrocon, Blot.. $40.00
Terrocon, Blot (moster), w/decoy..................................... $50.00
Terrocon, Cutthroat (Vulture), w/decoy $50.00
Terrocon, Cutthroat (3)... $40.00
Terrocon, Ripperspapper.. $40.00
Terrocon, Rippersapper, w/decoy..................................... $50.00
Terrocon, Sinnertwin... $40.00
Terrocon, Sinnertwin, w/decoy... $50.00
Throttlebot, Chase (Ferrari)... $35.00
Throttlebot, Chase (Ferrari), w/decoy............................... $40.00
Throttlebot, Freeway (Corvette).. $35.00
Throttlebot, Freeway (Corvette), w/decoy.......................... $40.00
Throttlebot, Goldbug (VW bug).. $50.00
Throttlebot, Rollbar (jeep)... $20.00
Throttlebot, Rollbar (jeep), w/decoy................................. $35.00
Throttlebot, Searchlight (race car) $30.00
Throttlebot, Shearchlight (race car), w/decoy.................... $35.00
Throttlebot, Wideload (dump truck) $30.00
Throttlebot, Wideload (dump truck), w/decoy $35.00

Series 5, 1988

Firecon, Cindersaur (dinosaur).. $35.00
Firecon, Flamefeather (monster bird).................................. $35.00
Firecon, Sparkstalker (monster) $45.00
Headmaster Autobot, Hosehead w/Lug (fire engine)......... $85.00
Headmaster Autobot, Nightbeat w/Muzzle (race car) $85.00
Headmaster Autobot, Siren w/Quig (fire chief car)........... $85.00
Headmaster Decepticon, Fangry w/Brisko (winged wolf) ..$85.00
Headmaster Decepticon, Horri-Bull w/Kreb (bull)............ $85.00
Headmaster Decepticon, Squeezeplay w/Lokos (crab)....... $85.00
Powermaster Autobot, Getaway w/Rev (Mr2)................... $75.00
Powermaster Autobot, Joyride w/Hotwire (off-road buggy) .$75.00
Powermaster Autobot, Slapdash w/Lube (Indy car).......... $75.00
Powermaster Autobot Leader, Optimus Prime w/HiQ (semi) . $200.00
Pretender, Bomb-burst (spaceship), w/shell $65.00

Pretender, Cloudburst (jet), w/shell $65.00
Pretender, Finback (sea skimmer), w/shell.....................$65.00
Pretender, Groundbreaker (race car), w/shell $150.00
Pretender, Iguanus (motorcycle), w/shell........................$65.00
Pretender, Landmine (race car), w/shell...........................$65.00
Pretender, Skullgrin (tank), w/shell $65.00
Pretender, Sky High (jet), w/shell.....................................$75.00
Pretender, Submarauder (submarine), w/shell..................$75.00
Pretender, Waverider (submarine), w/shell.......................$65.00
Pretender Beast, Carnivac (wolf), w/shell.........................$65.00
Pretender Beast, Catilla (sabertooth tiger), w/shell $65.00
Pretender Beast, Chainclaw (bear), w/shell $65.00
Pretender Beast, Snarler (boar), w/shell............................$65.00
Pretender Vehicle, Gunrunner (jet) w/vehicle shell, red...$65.00
Pretender Vehicle, Roadgrabber (jet) w/vehicle shell, purple ..$85.00
Seacon, Nautilator..$60.00
Seacon, Overbite...$60.00
Seacon, Seawing $50.00
Seacon, Skalor..$60.00
Seacon, Tenakil...$60.00
Sparkbot, Fizzle (off-road buggy) $30.00
Sparkbot, Guzzle (tank)..$30.00
Sparkbot, Sizzle (funny car)...$35.00
Targetmaster Autobot, Landfill w/Flintlock & Silencer (dump
　truck & 2 guns) $65.00
Targetmaster Autobot, Quickmix w/Boomer & Ricochet (cement
　mixer & 2 guns) $65.00
Targetmaster Autobot, Scoop w/Tracer & Holepunch (front-end
　loader & 2 guns) $65.00
Targetmaster Decepitcon, Needlenose w/Sunbeam & Zigzag (jet
　& 2 guns) $100.00
Targetmaster Decepticon, Spinster & Singe & Hairsplitter (heli-
　copter & 2 guns)..$85.00
Tiggerbot, Backstreet (race car)..$30.00
Tiggerbot, Override (motorcycle).......................................$30.00
Triggercon, Crankcase (jeep)..$30.00
Triggercon, Rucus (dune buggy) $35.00
Triggercon, Windsweeper (B-1 bomber) $35.00

SERIES 6, 1989

Mega Pretender, Crossblades (copter w/shell)................. $115.00
Mega Pretender, Thunderwing (jet w/shell) $165.00
Mega Pretender, Vroom (dragster w/shell)...................... $150.00
Micromaster Base, Skyhopper w/Micromaster (copter & F-15)..$55.00
Micromaster Base, Skystalker (Space Shuttle Base & Micromas-
　ter Porsche) $55.00
Micromaster Patrol, Battle Patrol Series, 4 different, ea....$30.00
Micromaster Patrol, Off-Road Series, 4 different, ea $30.00
Micromaster Patrol, Sports Car Patrol Series, 4 different, ea .$30.00
Micromaster Station, Greasepit, pickup w/gas station.......$30.00
Micromaster Station, Ironworks (semi w/construction site) ..$30.00
Micromaster Transport, Flattop (aircraft carrier)...............$30.00
Micromaster Transport, Overload (car carrier)..................$30.00
Micromaster Transport, Roughstuff (military transport)....$30.00
Pretender, Bludgeon (tank), w/shell.................................. $150.00
Pretender, Doubleheader (twin jet), w/shell $85.00
Pretender, Longtooth (hovercraft), w/shell........................$85.00

Pretender, Pincher (scorpion), w/shell $85.00
Pretender, Stranglehold (rhino), w/shell...........................$75.00
Pretender Monster, Wildfly...$65.00
Ultra Pretender, Roadblock (tank w/figure & vehicle)......$85.00
Ultra Pretender, Skyhammer (race car w/figure & vehicle)..$65.00

SERIES 7, 1990

Action Masters, Devastator $30.00
Action Masters, Grimlock...$30.00
Action Masters, Gutcruncher..$50.00
Action Masters, Inferno..$30.00
Action Masters, Over-Run..$40.00
Action Masters, Prowl..$60.00
Action Masters, Rad...$15.00
Action Masters, Shockwave..$30.00
Action Masters, Skyfall...$30.00
Action Masters, Soundwave..$30.00
Action Masters, Wheeljack..$70.00
Micromaster Patrol, Air Patrol: Thread Bolt, Eagle Eye, Sky
　High & Blaze Master...$30.00
Micromaster Patrol, Hot Rod Patrol: Big Daddy Trip-Up, Greaser
　& Hubs $40.00
Micromaster Patrol, Military Patrol: Bombshock, Tracer, Drop-
　shot 7 Growl...$45.00
Micromaster Patrol, Race Track Patrol: Barricade, Roller Force,
　Ground Hog Motorhead $15.00

GENERATION 2, SERIES 1, 1992 –1993

Autobot Car, Inferno (fire truck) $30.00
Autobot Car, Jazz (Porsche) $35.00
Autobot Leader, Optimus Prime w/Roller (semi w/electronic
　sound effect box) $150.00
Autobot Minicar, Bumble (VW bug), metallic..................$30.00
Autobot Minicar, Hubcap, metallic $25.00
Autobot Minicar, Seaspray (hovercraft), metallic $20.00
Autobot Obliterator (Europe only), Spark..........................$45.00
Color Change Transformer, Deluge $25.00
Color Change Transformer, Gobots.....................................$25.00
Constructicon, Bonecrusher (1), orange $12.00
Constructicon, Bonecrusher (1), yel....................................$10.00
Constructicon, Hook (4)orange $30.00

Constructicon, Hook (4) yel $30.00
Constructicon, Mixmaster (6) orange $15.00
Constructicon, Mixmaster (6) yel $30.00
Constructicon, Long Haul (5), orange $12.00
Constructicon, Long Haul (5), yel $10.00
Constructicon, Scavenger (2), orange $30.00
Constructicon, Scavenger (2), yel $30.00
Constructicon, Scrapper (3), orange $12.00
Constructicon, Scrapper (3), yel $10.00
Decepticon Jet, Starscream (jet w/electronic light & sound effect
    box), gray...$30.00
Decepticon Leader, Megatron (tank w/electronic sound effect
    treads) $45.00
Decepticon Obliterator (Europe only), Colossus $75.00
Dinobot, Grimlock (Tyrannosaurus), bl.........................$25.00
Dinobot, Grimlock (Tyrannosaurus), turq $140.00
Dinobot, Snarl (Stegosaurus), gray or bl, ea...................$50.00
Small Autobot Car, Skram $15.00
Small Autobot Car, Turbofire $15.00
Small Decepticon Jet, Afterburner $15.00
Small Decpeticon Jet, Eagle Eye $15.00
Small Decepticon Jet, Terredive......................................$15.00
Small Decepticon Jet, Windrazor $15.00

Generation 2, Series 2, 1994 – 1995

Aerialbot, Fireflight (3) $10.00
Aerialbot, Silverbot (5) $25.00
Aerialbot, Skydive (1) $15.00
Combaticon, Blast Off (3) $10.00
Combaticon, Brawl (1) $10.00
Combaticon, Onslaught (5) $25.00
Heroes, Autobot Hero Optimus Prime.............................$40.00
Heroes, Decepticon Hero Megatron.................................$35.00
Laser Rod Transformer, Electro.......................................$25.00
Laser Rod Transformer, Jolt $25.00
Rotor Force: Leadfoot, Manta Ray, or Ransack, ea $15.00
Stunticon, Breakdown (2), BotCon '94 Exclusive.......... $300.00
Watches: Superion, Ultra Magnus, or Scorpia, ea $25.00

Beast Wars, 1996 – 2001

Maximal, Airrazor $30.00
Maximal, Blackarachina..$85.00
Maximal, Cheeter $18.00
Maximal, Depth Charge $50.00
Maximal, Optimus Primal (gorilla) $110.00
Maximal, Polar Claw $15.00
Maximal, Rattrap $100.00
Predacon, Dinobot... $110.00
Predacon, Inferno $35.00
Predacon, Megatron (Dragon), Transmetal II $30.00
Predacon, Megatron (T-Rex)... $110.00
Predacon, Scorponok, dk purple/bl $85.00
Predacon, Shokaract, BotCon 2000 exclusive $70.00
Predacon, Terroraur $90.00
Predacon, Tripedacus $60.00
Predacon, Waspinator... $110.00

Transformers,
Beast Wars
• • • • • • • • • •
Maximal, Windra-
zor, 1999, MOC,
$120.00. (Photo courtesy
Dahveed Kolodny-Nagy)

Robots in Disguise, 2001 – 2002

Autobot, Optimus Prime $50.00
Autobot, Prowl $25.00
Autobot, Side Burn...$25.00
Decepticon, Scourge $70.00
Predacon, Sky Byte $30.00

Armada, 2002 – 2004

Autobot, Ironhide...$30.00
Autobot, Jetfire $25.00
Autobot, Optimus Prime $50.00
Autobot, Sentinel Maximus $55.00
Decepticon, Megatron $50.00
Decepticon, Tidal Wave $30.00

Energon, 2004 –2005

Autobot, Hot Shot...$15.00
Autobot, Ironhide..$30.00
Autobot, Jetfire $25.00
Autobot, Optimus Prime $50.00
Decepticon, Demolisher $30.00
Decepticon, Megatron $50.00

Cybertron, 2005 – 2006

Autobot, Ironhide..$30.00
Autobot, Landmine $25.00
Autobot, Optimus Prime $50.00
Autobot, Wing Saber $15.00
Decepticon, Megatron $50.00
Decepticon, Starscream $30.00

Transformers Movie, 2007

Autobot, Deluxe, Final Battle Jazz $15.00
Autobot, Leader, Optimus Prime.....................................$80.00
Autobot, Voyager, Optimus Prime $40.00
Decepticon, Leader, Megatron $70.00
Evolution of a Hero, Bumblebee, Target Exclusive Set......$75.00

TRANSFORMERS ANIMATED, 2008 – 2009

Autobot, Deluxe, Bumblebee $15.00
Autobot, Deluxe, Ratchet $20.00
Autobot, Voyager, Grimlock $45.00
Autobot, Voyager, Optimus Prime $25.00
Decepticon, Voyager, Megatron $20.00

TRANSFORMERS MOVIE 2: REVENGE OF THE FALLEN, 2009

Autobot, Leader, Jetfire $60.00
Autobot, Leader, Optimus Prime $60.00
Decepticon, Deluxe, The Fallen...........................$35.00
Decepticon, Devastator Giftset $140.00

GENERATION 1 REISSUES, 2002 – 2009

Autobot, Hot Rod...$60.00
Autobot, Jazz $35.00
Autobot, Prowl $35.00
Decepticon Leader, Megatron, Walther P-38 ....$150.00
Powermaster Autobot Leader, GodGinrai w/ Godbomber..$140.00
Ratchet, MIB (sealed) $50.00
Red Alert, MIB (sealed) $90.00
Rodimus Prime, MIB (sealed)..............................$60.00
Sixshot, MIB (sealed) $60.00
Skids, MIB (sealed)..$35.00
Skywrap, MIB (sealed) $120.00
Tracks, MIB (sealed) $35.00

• • • • • • • • • • • • • • • • View-Master and Tru-Vue • • • • • • • • • • • • • • • •

View-Master, the invention of William Gruber, was introduced to the public at the 1939 – 1940 New York World's Fair and the Golden Gate Exposition in California. Since then, View-Master reels, packets, and viewers have been produced by five different companies — the original Sawyers Company, G.A.F (1966), View-Master International (1981), Ideal Toys, and Tyco Toys (the present owners). Because none of the non-cartoon single reels and three-reel packets have been made since 1980, these have become collectors' items. Also highly sought after are the three-reel sets featuring popular TV and cartoon characters. The market is divided between those who simply collect View-Master as a field all its own and collectors of character-related memorabilia who will often pay much higher prices for reels about Barbie, Batman, The Addams Family, etc. Our values tend to follow the more conservative approach.

The first single reels were dark blue with a gold sticker and came in attractive gold-colored envelopes. They appeared to have handwritten letters. These were followed by tan reels with a blue circular stamp. Because these were produced for the most part after 1945 and paper supplies were short during WWII, they came in a variety of front and back color combinations, tan with blue, tan with white, and some were marbleized. Since print runs were low during the war, these early singles are much more desirable than the printed white ones that were produced by the millions from 1946 until 1957. Three-reel packets, many containing storybooks, were introduced in 1955, and single reels were phased out. Nearly all viewers are very common and have little value except for the very early ones, such as the Model A and Model B. Blue and brown versions of the Model B are especially rare. Another desirable viewer, unique in that it is the only focusing model ever made, is the Model D. For more information we recommend *View-Master Single Reels, Volume I*, by Roger Nazeley.

Note: Unless noted otherwise, the following values are for complete, mint in package (MIP) reels with cover and book.

Adam & the Ants, BD199.................................$20.00
Annie Oakley, B470 ....$22.00
Apple's Way, B558...$15.00
Aristocats, B365..$8.00
Barbie & the Rockers, 4071...............................$12.00
Barbie's Around the World Trip, B500....................$28.00
Battle of the Planets, BD185 ....$16.00
Beverly Hillbillies, B570..................................$22.00
Black Beauty, D135..$12.00

Brave Eagle, B466 ....$26.00
Bullwinkle, B515..$22.00
Captain Kangaroo, 755-abc $18.00
Care Bears, BD264 ....$8.00
Chip 'n Dale Rescue Rangers, 3075 ....$8.00
Cinderella, B318..$10.00
City Beneath the Sea, B496 ....$28.00
Danger Mouse, BD214.....................................$20.00
Daniel Boone, B479..$25.00

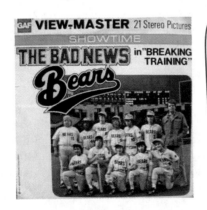

Davy Crockett, 935-abc.................................$70.00
Disneyland (Fantasyland), A178...................$22.00
Dr Who, BD216...$70.00
Dracula, B324 ....$18.00
Dumbo, J60 ....$10.00
Eight Is Enough, K76 ....$15.00
Emergency, B597...$10.00
Family Matters, 4118 ....$10.00
Fat Albert & the Cosby Kids, B554................$8.00
Ferdy, BD269...$8.00
Fonz, BJ103 ....$10.00
Fraggle Rock, 4053..$8.00
Full House, 4119 ....$5.00
Godzilla, J23 ....$18.00
Green Hornet, B488......................................$65.00
Grimm's Fairy Tales.....................................$10.00
Hair Bear Bunch, B552 ....$10.00
Heidi, B425 ....$12.00
Here's Lucy, B588...$45.00
Howard the Duck, 4073................................$12.00
Inspector Gadget, DB232 ....$15.00
Isis, T100 ....$10.00
James Bond (Moonraker), K68......................$18.00
Jimbo & the Jet Set, BD261 ....$10.00
King Kong, B392...$10.00
Knight Rider, 4054..$8.00
Lassie & Timmy, B472 ....$12.00
Lassie Rides the Log Flume, B489 ....$14.00
Little Mermaid, 3078.....................................$5.00
Lost in Space, B482 ....$55.00
Man From UNCLE, B484.............................$22.00
Mannix, BB450...$30.00
Mork & Mindy, K67 ....$10.00
Munsters, B481 ....$100.00
Muppets Go Hawaiian, L25............................$6.00
Nanny & the Professor, B573 ....$30.00
One of the Dinosaurs Is Missing, B377 ....$10.00
Pete's Dragon, H38 ....$10.00
Pinocchio, B311..$10.00
Planet of the Apes, B507 or BB507, ea $40.00
Pluto, B529 ....$12.00
Popeye's Fun, B527 ....$10.00
Poseidon Adventure, B301 ....$28.00
Power Rangers, 36870.....................................$5.00
Red Riding Hood, FT1 ....$4.00
Rescuers, BH026..$8.00
Rin-Tin-Tin, B467 ....$20.00
Rookies, BB452...$18.00
Rugrats, 36343 ....$5.00
Run Joe Run, B594 ....$18.00
Sebastian, D101 ....$35.00

View-Master
• • • • • • • •
Flintstones (Cartoon Favorites), B514, $15.00. (Photo courtesy www.gasolinealley antiques.com)

View-Master
• • • • • • • •
Space Mouse, B509, $22.00. (Photo courtesy www.gasoline alleyantiques.com)

Secret Valley, BD208 ....$10.00
Sesame Street Goes on Vacation, 4077............$6.00
Shazam, B550...$8.00
Silverhawks, 1058..$6.00
Six Million Dollar Man, B556.......................$18.00
Smith Family, B490.......................................$25.00
Smokey Bear, B404..$18.00
Snow White, B300..$8.00
Snowman, BD262..$10.00
Space: 1999, BB451 ....$20.00
Star Trek the Motion Picture, K57................$10.00
Superman, 1064..$6.00
SWAT, BB453..$10.00
Tarzan of the Apes, 976-abc $20.00
Teenage Mutant Ninja Turtles (Movie), 4114.......$8.00
Thor, H39 ....$6.00
Thunderbirds, B453.......................................$45.00
Tom Corbett Space Cadet, 970-abc $28.00
Tom Sawyer, B340 ....$10.00
Treasure Island, B432....................................$25.00
Tweety & Sylvester, BD1161..........................$10.00
Voyage to the Bottom of the Sea, B483.........$10.00
Wind in the Willows, 4084 ....$12.00
Winnetou, BB731..$22.00
Woody Woodpecker, B522.............................$18.00
X-Men (Captive Hearts), 1085 ....$15.00

• • • • • • • • • • • **Western Heroes and Frontiersmen** • • • • • • • • • • • •

No friend was ever more true, no brother more faithful, no acquaintance more real to us than our favorite cowboys of radio, TV, and the silver screen. They were upright, strictly moral, extremely polite, and tireless in their pursuit of law and order in the American West. How unfortunate that such role models are practically extinct nowadays.

For more information and some wonderful pictures, we recommend *Character Toys and Collectibles, First* and *Second Series,* by David Longest and *Guide to Cowboy Character Collectibles* by Ted Hake. Other publications include *The Lone Ranger* by Lee Felbinger and *The W.F. Cody Buffalo Bill Collector's Guide* by James W. Wojtowicz.

Advisors: Donna and Ron Donnelly

See also Advertising Signs, Ads, and Displays; Books; Character and Promotional Drinking Glasses; Character Clocks and Watches; Coloring, Activity, and Paint Books; Guns; Lunch Boxes; Premiums; Puzzles; Windup, Friction, and Other Mechanical Toys.

Annie Oakley, belt, blk & wht leather emb w/'Annie Oakley' & 'Tag' names, silver-tone buckle, 1950s, NMOC $60.00

Annie Oakley, musical figurine, ceramic, figure on rnd base w/ name, gold trim, 9", Schmid, 1960s or 1970s, NM+ $40.00

Annie Oakley, Sparkle Picture Craft w/Sequins & Beads, Gabriel, 1955, unused, MIB.............$50.00

Bat Masterson, outfit w/shirt, pants & tie, Gene Barry labels, Kaynee, MIB.............$160.00

Cisco Kid, marionette, compo head, hands & boots, cloth outfit & straw hat, 15", unmarked, 1950s, NM $150.00

Cisco Kid, play watch, 'Roundup Time,' Japan, 1950s, NMOC.$35.00

Cisco Kid, Star-cal Decals, 'Cisco Kid...Duncan Renaldo,' Meyercord Co, MIP (sealed) $15.00

Cisco Kid, stick horse, vinyl head w/fur-like mane & name, 32" L wooden stick, 1950s, VG $35.00

Dale Evans, washcloth mitten, terry cloth w/color image of Dale & inscribed name & Queen of the West, EX $25.00

Daniel Boone, coonskin cap, Fess Parker as Daniel Boone, Arligton/American Tradition Co, 1964, EX $50.00

Daniel Boone, figure, pnt plastic w/soft vinyl head, fur cap & powder horn, 5½", American Tradition Co, 1964, NM .$50.00

Daniel Boone, magic slate, 'Fess Parker Super Slate,' Saalfield, 1964, unused, M $75.00

Davy Crockett, Auto Magic Picture Gun, 1950s, complete, EX+IB.............$175.00

Davy Crockett, doll, hard plastic walker in cloth costume, hat & musket, red wig, 8", Madame Alexander, 1955, EXIB. $120.00

Davy Crockett, figure set, Davy Crockett & His Horse, plastic, 4" figure w/5" horse, Ideal, 1950s, EXIB $100.00

Davy Crockett, Frontierland Pencil Case, brn vinyl holster w/ gun-shaped pencil case, 8", 1950s, VG $50.00

Davy Crockett, guitar, 'Walt Disney's Official Davy Crockett Guitar,' wood, Peter Puppet Playthings, 1950s, VG (EX case) $100.00

Davy Crockett, pencil case, 'Walt Disney's Official...' 'Fronterland...,' slide-out box, 5x8", Hassenfeld, 1950s, EX........$50.00

Davy Crockett, pin, diecast metal rectangle w/scalloped border, crossed swords emb on front, NMOC.............$65.00

Davy Crockett, play horse, Pied Piper Toys, MIB.............$125.00

Davy Crockett, Sharpshooter Pin, Davy's muzzle loader w/name on plaque hanging from gun barrel, 4" L, NMOC.........$28.00

Davy Crockett, tent, brn & wht Davy graphics on tan canvas Empire Mfg/WDP, 1950s, complete, NM $135.00

Davy Crockett, tie clip, sq copper-tone metal w/emb image of musket & powder horn w/name, 1950s, M.............$18.00

Davy Crockett, towel, wht terry w/litho bust image of Davy/Fess Parker, Cannon/WDP, 1950s, 37x20", NM+ $40.00

Davy Crockett, tray, litho tin w/image of Davy fighting Indian, WDP, 1955, 13x17", VG.............$75.00

Gabby Hayes, Champion Shooting Target, Haccker/Ind, 1950s, NMIB $225.00

Gabby Hayes, doll, stuffed cloth w/fur beard & felt hat, name on belt, 13", 1960s, M $40.00

Gabby Hayes, Fishing Outfit, steel 2-part rod & reel, VG (in litho tin cylindrical container) $175.00

Gabby Hayes, hand puppet, cloth body w/rubber head, JVZ, 1949, EX.............$175.00

Gene Autry, badge, Gene Autry Deputy Sherrif, 12-point star, embossed bronze, Daniel Smilo & Sons, MOC.........$125.00

Gene Autry, doll (Terry Lee), compo, cloth outfit & felt hat, 16", NM+.............$500.00

Gene Autry, figure, ceramic, lg-headed Gene in full western dress standing on base, 8", Wilfred Ent, 1940s, EX $575.00

Gene Autry, figure, pnt compo w/name emb on sides of chaps, w/ lasso, wood base, 12", EX $275.00

Western

Annie Oakley, Cowgirl Outfit, 9" guns, NMIB, $690.00. (Photo courtesy Morphy Auctions on LiveAuctioneers.com)

Western

Dale Evans, lamp, figural plaster base of Dale on rearing Buttercup, printed shade, 8", EX, $150.00. (Photo courtesy Morphy Auctions on LiveAuctioneers.com)

Gene Autry, Medal of Honor, 'Champ Crackshot Cowboy,' embossed bronze, David Smilo & Sons, MOC............ $125.00

Gene Autry, Official Ranch Outfit, G+IB...........................$75.00

Gene Autry, rug, tan chenille w/signature name & Champ above & below image of horse's head, 37x25", EX+ $75.00

Gene Autry, wallet, leather w/zipper closure, image of Gene & Champion, Aristocrat, 1950s, VGIB.............................$75.00

Gene Autry, writing tablet, cover shows Gene seated w/leg over knee playing guitar, 8x10", 1940s, unused, NM $45.00

Gun Smoke, writing tablet, cover shows Miss Kittie hugging horse head, unused, NM+ $45.00

Gunsmoke, cowboy hat, brn felt w/Gunsmoke & Marshal Matt Dillon emblem on front, vinyl trim, tie string, 1950s, EX .$65.00

Gunsmoke, slippers, blk vinyl w/yel & red image of Matt, Chester & Doc, Columbia, 1959, unused, NM+IB $200.00

Gunsmoke, vest, blk leatherette w/yel screen-printed image of Matt Dillon & 'Gunsmike,' w/star badge, unused, MIB .$45.00

Hoot Gibson Wornova Play Clothes............................. $225.00

Hopalong Cassidy, badge, Sheriff, 6-pointed star w/circular image of Hoppy & 'Copyright 1950,' 4", unused, NMOC..... $125.00

Hopalong Cassidy, bank, 'Hoppy Savings Club,' plastic bust figure w/removable hat, copper color, 4", 1950s, EX $50.00

Hopalong Cassidy, coin, front w/emb image of Hoppy, back marked 'Good Luck From Hoppy,' 1¼" dia, VG.............$15.00

Hopalong Cassidy, Coloring Outfit, Transogram, 1950s, slight use, NM+IB...$85.00

Hopalong Cassidy, doll, rubber head, cloth outfit, w/gun & holster, 21", 1950s, NM...................................... $300.00

Hopalong Cassidy, drinking straws, cut-out photo of Hoppy on back of box, 1950s, unused, NM.....................................$75.00

Hopalong Cassidy, Figure & Paint Set, Laurel Ann, complete, used, EXIB $250.00

Hopalong Cassidy, figure set, Hoppy on Topper, plastic, 6", Ideal, 1950s, NMIB $285.00

Hopalong Cassidy, hand puppet, cloth body w/vinyl head, 1950s, scarce, NM.. $200.00

Hopalong Cassidy, Junior Chow Set, knife, fork & spoon w/emb name & image on hdls, Imperial, 1950, NMIB $83.00

Hopalong Cassidy, lamp, rotating cylinder picturing Hoppy & Topper chasing stagecoach, plastic, 10", Econolite, NM+ $500.00

Hopalong Cassidy, Lasso Game, Transogram, 1950, complete, NMIB $175.00

Hopalong Cassidy, night light, figural glass gun in holster w/ image of Hoppy, Aladdin, 1950s, NM $350.00

Hopalong Cassidy, night-light set, decaled milk glass wall-mount guns & holsters w/free-standing footed cylinder, 9", EX ..$750.00

Hopalong Cassidy, pants, blk cloth chaps-like w/2 images of Hoppy & Topper, covered wagons & steer heads, 1950s, VG...$50.00

Hopalong Cassidy, pencil case, vinyl w/zipper opening, blk/wht image of Toppy w/name & 'Pencil Case,' 5x8", EX+......$95.00

Hopalong Cassidy, play watch, colorful half-image of Hoppy on round face, laminated paper strap, MT, 1956, NMOC...$30.00

Hopalong Cassidy, playhouse, 4 lithoed panels, William Boyd/ Charcook, 1950, EX+.. $650.00

Hopalong Cassidy, potato chip can, close-up image of Hoppy & Topper on cream, slip lid, 11", 1950s, EX $175.00

Hopalong Cassidy, rocking chair, image on tan vinyl back w/back seat, chrome tubing-like frame w/flat rockers, 24", EX . $225.00

Hopalong Cassidy, scrapbook, tan vinyl hard cover w/emb image of Hoppy on Topper, string-bound pgs, 1950s, unused, NM.$125.00

Hopalong Cassidy, shoe caddy, red vinyl w/8 shoe pockets showing various yel & blk scenes, 1950s, EX...................... $125.00

Hopalong Cassidy, spurs, silver-tone & brass w/blk leather straps, NM $200.00

Hopalong Cassidy, Stagecoach Toss beanbag target, litho tin & masonite, 24x18", Transogram, 1950s, EX.....................$75.00

Hopalong Cassidy, stationery folio, w/paper & envelopes, complete, VG+...$50.00

Hopalong Cassidy, sweater, tan w/color images showing Hoppy & name, child-size, 1950s, EX.. $100.00

Hopalong Cassidy, TV set, plastic w/pull-out knob, filmstrips revolve inside TV, 5x5", Automatic Toy, EXIB.......... $250.00

Hopalong Cassidy, wallet, brn leather w/cloth litho head images of Hoppy & Topper, zippered closure, 4x5", 1950s, EX ..$50.00

Hopalong Cassidy, Western Frontier Set, Milton Bradley, 1950s, complete, NMIB... $300.00

Hopalong Cassidy, Woodburning Set, American Toy, 1950s, unused, EXIB... $100.00

Hopalong Cassidy, wrist cuffs, 'Hoppy' on blk w/silver stud trim, EX+.. $200.00

Johnny Ringo, hand puppet, Laura (girlfriend), cloth body w/ vinyl head, felt hands, 10", Tops in Toys, 1959-60, EX+.$40.00

Kit Carson, 3-Powered Binocular, 1950s, EXIB $125.00

Lone Ranger, binoculars, plastic, Harrison, EX+IB......... $135.00

Lone Ranger, costume, Western Hero, w/mask, child's size, Ben Cooper, 1977, NMIB..................$25.00

Lone Ranger, De Luxe Movie Views, Acme Plastics, NM+IB. $150.00

Lone Ranger, Hi-Yo Silver the Lone Ranger Target Game, Marx, EXIB.........................$65.00

Lone Ranger, horseshoe set, rubber, Gardner, NMIB.........$85.00

Lone Ranger, lantern, 'Lone Ranger Chuck Wagon Lantern,' real metal & glass working hurricane-type, Dietz, 1950s, VG..$35.00

Lone Ranger, Movie Style Viewer, viewer w/2 films, Acme Plastics, 1955, NMIP (sealed) $150.00

Lone Ranger, neck scarf & concho slide, purple silk-type material w/images of Lone Ranger & Silver, 1940s-50s, EX...$50.00

Lone Ranger, Official Outfit, leather holster w/compo gun, blk mask & red scarf, Feinburg-Henry, 1938, EXIB...........$200.00

Lone Ranger, Official Outfit, fringed pants & shirt w/images & name, Seneca Mfg. Co, NMIB.....................$125.00

Lone Ranger, Official Outfit, w/chaps, shirt, vest, hat, wrist cuffs, neckerchief & lasso, Henry, 1940s, NMIB $475.00

Lone Ranger, Pop-Up Rub-Ons, Hasbro, 1968, MIB (sealed) ..$50.00

Lone Ranger, record player, molded plastic image of the Lone Ranger on Silver on front panel, Mercury, 1950s, VG+..$85.00

Lone Ranger, record player, wood case, 10x12", Decca/Lone Ranger Inc, EX $350.00

Lone Ranger, ring-toss, die-cut cb, complete, Rosebud Art, MIB $250.00

Lone Ranger, school bag, canvas w/plastic hdl, image of Lone Ranger on side pocket, 1950s, EX.................$100.00

Lone Ranger, soap figure, 4½", Kerk Guild, unused, EXIB. $65.00

Lone Ranger, soap figure set, Lone Ranger, Tonto & Silver, 4", Kerk, 1939, VG $50.00

Lone Ranger, target game, Hi-Yo Silver..., Marx, EXIB.....$65.00

Maverick, belt, tooled leather w/names & images, Maverick emb on brass-tone cast-metal rectangular buckle, EX+ $65.00

Maverick, Eras-O-Picture Book, Hasbro, 1958, complete, EX....$40.00

Maverick, paint-by-number set, Hasbro, 1958, complete, EXIB.....................$75.00

Red Ryder, gloves, Playmates, brn, red & bl cloth, tag w/premium offers, Wells Lamont Corp & SS, 1950s, NM $30.00

Rin Tin Tin, canteen, 'Official Rin Tin Tin 101st Cavalry' on front, Nabisco premium, 1957, EX $20.00

Rin Tin Tin, figure, Rinny, pnt plaster w/blk & bronze-tone finish, rhinestone eyes, 1939, 11x8x4", EX.................$75.00

Rin Tin Tin, outfit, Fighting Blue Devil 101st Cavalry shirt, leather belt, pouch w/bullets & holster, NMIB $175.00

Roy Rogers, archery set, Ben Pearson, scarce, unused, MOC..$175.00

Roy Rogers, bank, metal boot form w/copper finish, 5½", Almar Metal Arts Co, 1950s, EX.....................$75.00

Roy Rogers, Camera w/Telescopic Sight, Herbert George Co, NMIB $225.00

Roy Rogers, Crayon Set, w/Roy Rogers Pictures & Stencils, Standard Toycraft, 1950s, complete & unused, MIB... $400.00

Roy Rogers, Fix-It Chuck Wagon & Jeep Set, 24", Ideal, 1950s, complete, NMIB.....................$350.00

Roy Rogers, flashlight, 'Signal Siren,' tin, 7", Usalite, unused, MIB.....................$150.00

Roy Rogers, game, Lucky Horseshoe, Ohio Art, 1950s, complete, EX.....................$50.00

Roy Rogers, gloves, 2-tone brn suede w/name in wht, studded horseshoe & image of Roy on Trigger on cuffs w/ fringe, VG.....................$75.00

Roy Rogers, guitar, Rich Toys/Ranger Rhythm Toys, 30", EXIB.....................$150.00

Roy Rogers, guitar, 'Roy Rogers & Trigger,' w/Dale's portrait & RR 'the Plus Brand,' rope-like border, 29", unmarked, VG+ ...$80.00

Roy Rogers, hand puppet, cloth w/vinyl head & hat, 1950s, EX.....................$75.00

Roy Rogers, hat, taupe felt w/Roy Rogers band, wht whipstitching around hat rim, NM+.....................$100.00

Roy Rogers, paint-by-number paint set, RRE Set C/Post Sugar Crisp, 1954, used, EXIB.....................$40.00

Roy Rogers, Pony Contest entry form, 12x9", Hudson's Bay Co, 1950s, used, NM.....................$50.00

Roy Rogers, postcard, image of Roy on rearing Trigger, acknowledges contest entry, Quaker Oats, 1948, NM $50.00

Roy Rogers, pull toy, horse-drawn covered wagon, paper litho on wood, removable cloth cover, 20", NN Hill, EX $250.00

Western

Lone Ranger and Tonto, push-button puppet set, both on horses, Kohner, 1965, NMIB, $400.00.

(Photo courtesy Morphy Auctions on LiveAuctioneers.com)

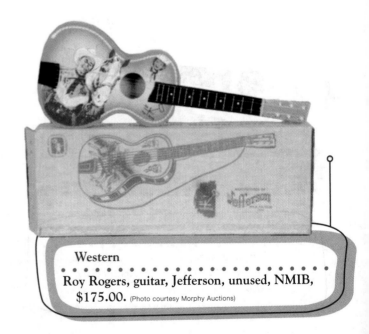

Western

Roy Rogers, guitar, Jefferson, unused, NMIB, $175.00. (Photo courtesy Morphy Auctions)

Western

Tom Mix, rocking horse, lithographed details, 25x40", VG, $100.00. (Photo courtesy Morphy Auctions)

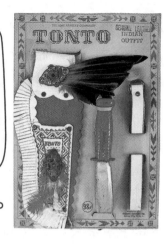

Western

Tonto, Genuine Leather Indian Outfit, Esquire, 1950s, unused, MOC, $35.00. (Photo courtesy www.serioustoyz.com)

Roy Rogers, rodeo program, Chicago Stadium, 1946, 20-pg w/ back showing Tom Mix, Buck Jones, etc, EX $75.00
Roy Rogers, scarf, red & gold silk-like material w/vignette graphics, 25x25", King of Cowboys, 1950s, EX $75.00
Roy Rogers, school bag, brn textured vinyl w/brn leather strap, badge above graphics on front pocket flap, 1950s, G+ . $100.00
Roy Rogers, Signal Siren Flashlight, Usalite, NMIB $175.00
Roy Rogers, telescope, plastic, H George, 9", MIB $200.00
Roy Rogers, Trick Lasso, Classy, 1950s, EXIP $75.00
Roy Rogers, woodburning set, Burn-Rite, complete, EXIB .$175.00
Tales of Wells Fargo, paint-by-number set, 1959, complete, unused, NMIB $65.00
The Texan (Rory Calhoun), hand puppet, full body in wht shirt w/blk vest & pants, holster, Tops in Toys, 1960s, NM.. $175.00
Tom Mix, cowboy boots, tan & gr leather w/wht detail, child's size, 1930s, MIB (box numbered 4427) $260.00
Tom Mix, gloves, heavy tan suede w/fringe, blk diamond shaped logo on cuffs, 1930s, unused condition, M $150.00
Tom Mix, School Tablet, salesman's sample w/4 different photo covers attached, M $450.00
Tom Mix, Shooting Gallery, Parker Bros, c 1930, complete, EXIB $230.00
Tonto, doll, stuffed body w/compo head, cloth outfit, guns & holster, headband w/feather, EX $500.00
Tonto, hand puppet, printed body & name on gr vinyl w/vinyl head, 1966, NM+ $125.00
Tonto, soap figure, 4", Kerk Guild, 1939, EXIB (unopened)..$50.00
Virginian, Movie Viewer, Chemtoy, 1966, MIB.................$40.00
Wild Bill Hickok, wallet, fastens w/western buckle, NM+ .$75.00

Wyatt Earp, badge, Junior Sheriff, 6-point tin star, 20th Century Toys, 1958, MOC (sealed) $25.00
Wyatt Earp, Crayon by Number & Stencil Set, Transogram, 1958, some use, G (VG box) $50.00
Zorro, accessory set w/mask, whip, lariat & ring, Shimmel/WDP, M (w/24" L card picturing Guy Williams)..................$150.00
Zorro, bolo tie, metal medallion w/plastic insert featuring Zorro portrait in red logo, NM......................................$50.00
Zorro, bookends, ceramic, figural w/red 'Z' on wht base, glossy w/ red cold pnt, Enesco, 1960s, NM $225.00
Zorro, hand puppet, Don Diego, cloth body w/vinyl head, Gund, 1950s, NM......................................$85.00
Zorro, hand puppet, tag reads 'Zorro' but looks like Don Diego, Canadian issue, Reliable, 1950s, EX+......................... $100.00
Zorro, hand puppet, vinyl head w/cloth body, felt hat, Gund/ WDP, 1950s, EX+......................................$75.00
Zorro, key chain/flashlight, c WDP, 1950s, EX+ $75.00
Zorro, magic slate, Watkins/Strathmore/WDP, 1950s-60s, EX .$75.00
Zorro, magic slate, Whitman, 1965, unused, NM..............$50.00
Zorro, Official 'Secret Slight' Scarf Mask 49¢, Disney, 1959, NRFC $75.00
Zorro, oil-paint-by-number-set, Hassenfeld Bros, 1960s, complete, VGIB......................................$65.00
Zorro, ring, blk plastic w/Zorro lettered in gold tone on blk stone, M $75.00
Zorro, target board, litho tin w/cb stand-up back, 15x23", T Cohn/WDP, 1950s-60s, EX......................................$75.00
Zorro, Target Shoot, Lido/WDP, MIB $225.00
Zorro, tote bag, red vinyl, EX $275.00

• • • • • • • • • • • • Windup, Friction, and Other Mechanical Toys • • • • • • • • • •

Windup toys represent a fun and exciting field of collecting — our fascination with them stems from their simplistic but exciting actions and brightly colored lithography, and especially the comic character or personality-related examples greatly in demand by collectors today. Though most were made through the years of the 1930s to the 1950s, they carry their own weight against much earlier toys and are considered very worthwhile investments. Various types of mechanisms were used — some are key wound while others depend on lever action to tighten the mainspring and release the action of the toy. Tin and celluloid were used in their production, and although it is sometimes possible to repair a tin windup, experts advise against investing in a celluloid toy whose mechanism is not working, since the material is usually too fragile to withstand the repair.

Many of the boxes that these toys came in are almost as attractive as the toys themselves and can add considerably to their value.
Advisor: Scott Smiles
See also Aeronautical; Boats; Chein; Japanese (and Other) Tin Vehicle Replicas; Lehmann; Marx; Robots and Space Toys; Strauss.

Acrobats (2) Performing on Seesaw, Guntherman, w/up, litho tin, 8" L, VG...$2,000.00

Acrobat Monkeys, Wyandotte, w/up, litho tin, 10" dia, VG...$225.00

Acrocycle, Alps, w/up, litho tin, clown rider on motorcycle, 6" L, NMIB $650.00

Airport, Ohio Art, w/up, litho tin, 2 airplanes spiral down center rod atop rnd 2-tiered building, 9", EXIB...................... $275.00

American Circus, Japan, w/up, litho tin, monkey circus act, 6" H, NM $350.00

Artie the Clown in Crazy Car, Unique Art, w/up, litho tin, 7", EX $500.00

Astro Boy & Girl Fire Truck, Japan, friction, litho tin truck w/ vinyl figures, 12", VG...$1,300.00

Astro Boy Train, Japan, friction, tin 'bullet' type train w/lithoed Astro Boy, Astro Girl & passengers, 28", VG...........$1,150.00

Babes in Toyland Marching Soldier, Linemar, w/up, litho tin, 6", EXIB $300.00

Baby Swinging, KK, w/up, celluloid figure swings on wire apparatus, 7", NMIB $125.00

Balloon & Toy Vendor, Distler, 1930s, w/up, litho tin, w/Mickey Mouse & other toys on string, 6½", VG+ $400.00

Barney Google Riding Spark Plug, Nifty, w/up, litho tin, 7", G $550.00

Bar-X Cowboy (Cowboy on Horse w/Lasso), Alps, w/up, litho tin, 5", NMIB $250.00

Bashful Groom, Germany, w/up, litho tin, EX................ $800.00

Batman, Biliken, 1989, w/up tin figure w/cloth cape, walks & swings arms, MIB.. $100.00

Bavarian Dancing Couple, Schuco, w/up, boy lifts girl into the air, celluloid w/felt outfits, 5", G $175.00

Bear, Ives, w/up, fur-covered w/wooden feet & claws, rears up, moves head back & forth, opens & closes mouth, 10", EXIB $880.00

Bear Playing Drum, w/up, brn fur-covered bear w/Santa hat & muzzled mouth standing upright w/drums & cymbals, 15", EX $350.00

Bear Riding Tricycle w/2 Cubs, Rico/Spain, w/up, litho tin, cub in front basket & cub on rear springboard, 9" L, EX $1,750.00

Bear Walker, w/up, brn fur w/glass eyes, wooden paws, moves muzzled head, opens & closes mouth while walking, 10" L, EX $250.00

Bears Playing Ball, TPS, w/up, tin, bears standing facing each other on tin base bounce ball back & forth, 19" L, NMIB........$275.00

Beatrix in Horse-Drawn Cart, ca 1910, w/up, litho tin, lady driver w/whip in 2-wheeled card, 8" L, EX+............. $1,450.00

Beatrix in 3-Wheeled Auto, Germany, ca 1904, w/up, litho tin, 4" L, EX $550.00

Beetle, Gunthermann, w/up, pnt tin, lifelike, 7½" L, EX+IB..$500.00

Betty's (Boop) Acrobat, Kuramochi & Co/Fleischer Studios, 1930s, w/up, 6" celluloid figure on wire apparatus, EXIB.............$800.00

Big Bad Wolf, Linemar, 1960s, w/up, tin hopping figure, 4½", NM $200.00

Big Chief Mechanical Motorcycle, Mettoy, w/up, litho tin, 7½", NM+IB...$3,600.00

Billiard Table, Ranger Steel, w/up, tin, 2 figures in suits at either end of pool table, 14" L, NMIB...................... $450.00

Bird Singing, Kohler, w/up, tin & plastic, colorful bird sings, flaps wings & moves head, 8" L, NMIB $75.00

Black Boy Riding 2-Wheeled Donkey Cart, Gunthermann, w/up, pnt tin, gray-flocked donkey, boy w/whip in hand, 8" L, EX $600.00

Boat Ride, Unique Art, w/up, litho tin, 3 boats w/passengers on rods swing from tower, 9", EX $200.00

Boat w/Oarsman, Ives, 1869, cloth-dressed metal & wood figure w/2 oars in boat, 12½" L, VG+ $2,500.00

Bonzo on 3-Wheeled Scooter, Germany, 1920s, w/up, tin, 8", EX $1,400.00

Bo Bo the Juggling Clown, TPS, w/up, litho tin, clown w/spring-loaded arms bounces ball from side to side, 5", EXIB .. $425.00

Boy at Chalkboard Easel, Tipp, w/up, litho tin, standing on tall beveled platform, 7½", EX.....................................$1,550.00

Boy Driving Early Tiller Being Chased by Dog, Germany, w/up, litho tin, 7½", VG+.....................................$1,300.00

Boy Drummer (Lovely Boy Drummer), Y, w/up, tin figure w/celluloid head, 8½", NM+IB...................................... $550.00

Boy on Bicycle w/Dog Running Along Side, Gunthermann, w/up, pnt tin, spoke wheels w/wht rubber tires, 6" L, VG...$2,000.00

Boy on Irish Mail, SE/Germany, w/up, litho tin, 4 spoke wheels, 5" L, EX $650.00

Boy on Tricycle (Teddy's Cycle), Occupied Japan, w/up, celluloid figure on tin trike w/bell, 5" H, NM+IB $200.00

Boy on Tricycle (Wonder Cyclist), Unique Art, w/up, litho tin, spoke wheels, 8" L, VG $275.00

Boy on Velocipede, w/up, cloth-dressed figure w/molded & pnt cb head rides tricycle, 11" L, EX $1,450.00

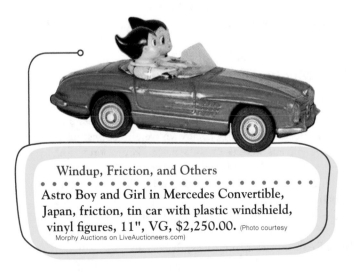

Windup, Friction, and Others

Astro Boy and Girl in Mercedes Convertible, Japan, friction, tin car with plastic windshield, vinyl figures, 11", VG, $2,250.00. (Photo courtesy Morphy Auctions on LiveAuctioneers.com)

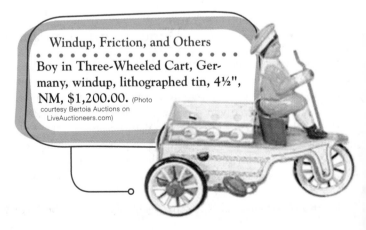

Windup, Friction, and Others

Boy in Three-Wheeled Cart, Germany, windup, lithographed tin, 4½", NM, $1,200.00. (Photo courtesy Bertoia Auctions on LiveAuctioneers.com)

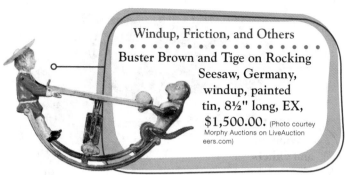

Boy on 3-Wheeled Cart, Germany w/up, litho tin, boy in early lt bl playsuit w/hat on wht cart w/spoke wheels, 4½", EX . $800.00

Boy Riding Turtle, w/up, litho tin, 5", VG $225.00

Boy Twirling Ball & American Flag, Germany, w/up, pnt tin, 8½", VG.. $325.00

Bozo (Playing Drum), Alps, w/up, litho tin, 8", NMIB... $350.00

Brutus (Popeye), Linemar, w/up, litho tin, head bobs while body hops, EX+IB $1,150.00

Bubble Blowing Bear, Alps, w/up,litho tin, plush & plastic, 8", EX+... $350.00

Bucking Car, Japan, w/up, tin car w/celluloid clown that bobs up & down, 8" L, EX+IB $450.00

Buster Brown & Tige on Seesaw on Turning Base, Mueller & Kadeder, w/up, pnt tin, 10" L, EX $2,500.00

Buster Brown & Tige Ringing Bell by Lamppost, Germany, w/up, pnt tin, 8", EX $4,000.00

Buster Brown & Tige Ringing Bell by Lamppost, Germany, w/up, pnt tin, 8", G $1,200.00

Busy Betty, Lindstrom, w/up, litho tin, 8", VG $150.00

Busy Lizzy Sweeper, Fischer, w/up, litho tin, lady in long dress an apron w/sweeper, 7", VG... $400.00

Buttercup (Crawling baby), Germany, 1920s, w/up, tin, 8", EXIB $800.00

Can-Can Dancer, lever action, litho tin flat-sided articulated figure, 8", VG $175.00

Candy Cart, Ohta, friction, litho tin, monkey vendor pedals 3-wheeled 'Candy' cart & bell rings, 5½" H, EX+....... $175.00

Carnival, Wyandotte, w/up, litho tin & PS w/cb front pcs, 12x16", EX.. $550.00

Casper the Friendly Ghost, Linemar, w/up, litho tin figure w/bobing head, 4½", VG $175.00

Cat, Decamps, w/up, fur-covered w/glass eyes, several motions, 13" L, VG+ $125.00

Cat Guarding Mouse in Cage, Germany, w/up, pnt tin, cat on 2 wheels & cage on single wheel, 10" L, VG................. $475.00

Cat Guarding Mouse in Cage, Germany, w/up, pnt tin, cat on 2 wheels & cage on single wheel, 10" L, EX................... $750.00

Cat Knitting, TN, w/up, wht plush, 6", EX $100.00

Cat Pushing 2 Mice in Caged Cart, Gunthermann, w/up, litho tin, cat in red jacket stands behind 2-wheeled cart, 7" L, EX. $2,250.00

Cat Standing Upright, Germany, w/up, pnt tin, wearing red glasses & pnt clothing, 6", VG.................................... $375.00

Cat Standing Upright w/Fan on 3-Wheeled Round Platform, Gunthermann, w/up, pnt tin, 7¼", VG $750.00

Catapult Aeroplane, Henry Katz, w/up, litho tin, spring-activated plane on wire flies around hangar, 9" L.............. $450.00

Charlie Chaplin Dancer, KW/DRGM/WK/Germany, 1920s, lever-op, litho tin flat-sided figure w/jtd knees holding cane, 6", EX... $2,050.00

Charlie Chaplin Squeeze Toy, Distler, plunger-activated, tin figure holding cat plays the cymbals, 7", VG................. $375.00

Charlie Chaplin Squeeze Toy, Germany, squeeze lever & tin figure makes facial expressions, 8", EX $450.00

Charlie Chaplin Walker, Germany, w/up, litho tin w/CI shoes, dk bl & blk, jtd arms, 9", EX...................................... $725.00

Charlie Chaplin Walker, Schuco, w/up, felt-covered outfit & cane, 6½", NMIB.. $850.00

Chef on Roller Skates, TPS, w/up, litho tin blk figure w/articulated arms, 6", G... $300.00

Cinderella Railcar, Wells of London, w/up, complete, EX+IB.$1,200.00

Circus Act w/Acrobat in Wheel & Motorcyclist on Ramp, Arnold, w/up, acrobat revolves as cyclist provides power, 11", VG+... $550.00

Circus Bugler, TPS, w/up, tin long-legged clown figure in cloth outfit, 9", MIB $425.00

Circus Clown, Cragstan, clown climbs along string, cloth suit w/ litho tin head & limbs, celluloid feet, 9", EXIB.......... $150.00

Circus Cyclist (Clown), TPS, w/up, litho tin w/cloth outfit, w/ bell, 6½", NMIB $600.00

Clown Balancing Ball on Nose, Germany, w/up, pnt tin w/cloth costume, 9½", EX $800.00

Clown Crouching on 3-Wheeled Cycle, Doll, w/up, pnt tin, arms extend to reach front wheel, 10½" L, EX.................. $650.00

Clown Driving Goat Cart, Germany, w/up, pnt tin, disk wheels, 9" L, EX $825.00

Clown Driving Open Runabout, Gunthermann, ca 1905, w/up, litho & pnt tin, 6½" L, VG $2,000.00

Clown Guiding 2 Clowns on Pigs, Germany, pnt tin, clown guide on 2-wheeled platform & pigs on 2 wheels, 10" L, G .. $3,250.00

Clown Holding Cane on Skis w/Cat at Rear, Germany, pnt tin, 7½", VG.. $1,000.00

Clown Jalopy Cycle, TPS, 1960s, friction, litho tin, handlebars & front end break away when bumped, 9", NMIB...... $400.00

Clown Juggler, Alps, cloth dressed figure, compo hands, clockwork, orig tin pocket watch, w/colorful orig box, EX .. $350.00

Clown Juggler w/Monkey, TPS, w/up, 1950s, litho tin, clown balancing monkey seated in chair, 9", NMIB............. $450.00

Clown Juggler w/Monkey, TPS, w/up, 1950s, litho tin, clown balancing monkey seated in chair, 9", VGIB.............. $375.00

Clown Musicians, West Germany, w/up, litho tin, seated facing each other playing drums & cymbals on oblong base, 9", EX..... $450.00

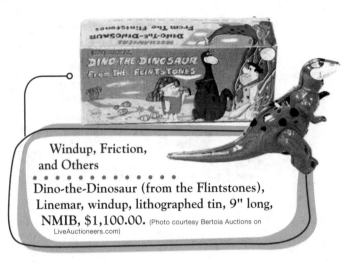

Clown on Balking Donkey, Germany, w/up, litho tin, donkey w/ articulated legs, 6", EX $125.00

Clown on Horse (Circus), SY, w/up, celluloid horse & clown rider w/lg front litho tin wheel, 7" H, NMIB $175.00

Clown on Rocking Mule, Gama/US Zone Germany, w/up, rocker base, 6½" H, EX $225.00

Clown on Unicycle (Circus Clown), att to TPS, w/up, litho tin, pedals & advances, 5½", NMIB $600.00

Clown Performing w/Flying Boats & Banjo Player, Gunthermann, w/up, pnt tin, juggling 4 flying boats w/feet, 15", EX .. $5,000.00

Clown Playing Guitar, Germany, w/up, litho tin, clown in long plaid coat on diagonally striped rnd musical base, 9", EX $200.00

Clown Pulled by 2 Dogs on 4-Wheeled Open Frame, Tippco, 1920s, litho tin, 8" L, VG $800.00

Clown Riding Donkey Cart, Doll, w/up, pnt tin, 10" L, EX. $650.00

Clown Roller Skater, TPS, w/up, litho tin w/cloth pants, 6", EX .$200.00

Clown Walker, German/US Zone, w/up, litho tin, plaid jacket w/wht collar & lg mc buttons, red/wht striped pants, 6", EX $125.00

Clown Walker, pnt tin, clockwork, head w/flocked hat goes side to side as arms swing, 8½", VG $600.00

Clown Walker w/Tambourine, Japan, w/up, celluloid, 8", EX..$400.00

Coney Island Coaster, Goso/Germany, ca 1949, w/up, litho tin roller coaster w/2 4" cars, VGIB.................................. $575.00

Couple Dancing, Ives (?), pull wound string to activate spinning motion, pnt tin, 3½", G.. $300.00

Couple Walking w/Dog, w/up, pnt tin, Victorian style, 6½", EX... $5,500.00

Cowboy on Rocking Horse, Cragstan, w/up, litho tin, wht horse w/red rocker, 7" L, EXIB... $250.00

Cowboy w/Guns Drawn, Japan, friction, litho tin, advances w/ sparks & shooting sound, 5½", NM $1,200.00

Cowboy w/Lasso on Rearing Horse, Alps, w/up, celluloid w/wire lasso, 7" H, NM+IB... $100.00

Crazy Car, Kuramochi, prewar, w/up, litho tin, man driving, red & gr w/yel trim, 3" L, EX... $150.00

Creeping Baby, Ives, w/up, cloth-dressed pnt compo, wood & metal baby realistically crawls, 11" L, EX+IB........... $1,300.00

Cubby the Reading Bear, Alps, w/up, plush w/cloth overalls, 7", EXIB $125.00

Cycling Quacky, Alps, w/up, litho tin duck on tricycle, 6", NMIB $150.00

Dagwood's Solo Flight, Marx, King Features Syndicate, 1935. $675.00

Dandy Jim w/Clown Violinist Atop Roof, Unique Art, w/up, litho tin, 10½", EX $725.00

Daredevil Motor Cop, Unique Art, w/up, litho tin, 'Police' lettered on tank, 8½", NMIB $1,350.00

Derby Horse Roundabout, German, Wilhelm Krauss, embossed litho tin, spiral rod mechanism, 6 horses, 12½", VG. $1,650.00

Disney Dipsy Car, see Donald Duck Dipsy Car

Disney Dipsy Car, see Mickey Mouse Dipsy Car

Donald Duck Carousel, Borfeldt, prewar, w/up, celluloid Donald under parasol w/beads, wheeled base, 7½", EXIB $3,500.00

Dog Cart w/Girl Driver, OK, w/up, celluloid girl & dog w/tin 2-wheeled cart, 10" L, VG+ $300.00

Doin' the Howdy Doody, Unique Art, w/up, litho tin, 5½x6½", EX..$800.00

Doin' the Howdy Doody, Unique Art, w/up, litho tin, 5½x6½", EXIB $1,150.00

Donald Duck, France, w/up, pnt compo figure w/hands (wings) up, 7", EXIB $400.00

Donald Duck & Elmer the Elephant Dancing, w/up, w/up, celluloid integral figures w/Donald as girl in pk skirt, 5", EX+.... $3,750.00

Donald Duck & Nephews Hunting, Linemar, w/up, litho tin, Donald & 3 nephews w/guns on a string, 11" L, EX.... $400.00

Donald Duck Carousel, Borgfeldt, prewar, w/up, celluloid Donald under parasol w/beads, wheeled base, 7½", EXIB $3,450.00

Donald Duck Carousel, Borgfeldt, prewar, w/up, celluloid Donald under parasol w/beads & characters, wheeled base, 9", EX. $1,500.00

Donald Duck Carousel, Occupied Japan, w/up, celluloid Donald under parasol w/beads, wheeled base, 7½", EX $350.00

Donald Duck Cart w/Minnie Mouse Driver, Japan, prewar, w/up, celluloid figures, tin 2-wheeled cart, 6" L, EX........... $2,000.00

Donald Duck Climbing Fireman, Linemar, litho tin, 14", EX. $350.00

Donald Duck Crawler, Borgfeldt, prewar, w/up, celluloid, long bill, winking eyes, 9" L, VG $600.00

Donald Duck Crawler, Occupied Japan, w/up, celluloid, short bill, open eyes, 7" L, NM... $350.00

Donald Duck Dipsy Car (Disney Dipsy Car), Linemar, w/up, litho tin w/plastic Donald driver, 6" L, EX+IB $500.00

Donald Duck Dipsy Car (Disney Dipsy Car), Linemar, w/up, litho tin w/plastic Donald driver, 6" L, VGIB $325.00

Donald Duck Drummer, Linemar, w/up, litho tin, 6", VG+.$300.00

Donald Duck Nodder, w/up, celluloid winking Donald figure w/hands on hips on rnd tin base, head nods when wound, 6", EX.....$400.00

Donald Duck on Pluto Rocker, Japan, prewar, celluloid Donald & Pluto figures on wooden rocker base, 8" L, VG $850.00

Donald Duck on Skis, Linemar, w/up, litho tin, 6", VG. $450.00

Donald Duck on Trapeze, Japan, 1930s, w/up, 5" celluloid Donald figure on 8½" wire apparatus, EXIB........................ $600.00

Donald Duck on Tricycle, Paradise Novelty, 1930s, celluloid Donald w/cloth pants on tin trike, 5½x4", EX $450.00

Donald Duck Racer, Linemar, w/up, celluloid Donald driver in silver metal racer w/BRT, 6", EX+ $225.00

Donald Duck Rail Car, Lionel, w/up, tin w/compo Donald & Pluto figures, PS doghouse, 9x12" L, VGIB................. $375.00

Donald Duck, Schuco, 1930s, tin w/cloth jacket & hat, jtd arms & legs make quacking sound, w/ID tag, 6", EXIB..... $2,000.00

Donald Duck w/Huey & Voice, Linemar, friction, litho tin, 7½", EX+IB.. $475.00

Donald Duck Waddler, Japan, prewar, w/up, articulated celluloid figure, winking expression, 5½", EXIB $450.00

Donald Duck Waddler, Japan, prewar, w/up, articulated celluloid figure, winking expression, 5½", VG........................... $300.00

Donald Duck Waddler, Linemar, w/up, plush w/tin beak & feet, 5", VGIB.. $300.00

Donald Duck Walker, Lewis & Scott/Borgfeldt, w/up, compo, 12", NMIB.. $950.00

Donald Duck Walker, Schuco, 1930s, w/up, tin w/cloth jacket & hat, articulated arms & legs, makes quacking sound, 6", EXIB...$2,100.00

Drum Major, Wolverine #27, w/up, litho tin, 14", NMIB. $450.00

Dopey (Snow White) Walker, Great Britian, w/up, litho tin, 5", NMIB $500.00

Drummer, Japan, w/up, celluloid figure standing playing tin drum in helmet w/tassle on top, 10", EX............................... $575.00

Drummer Boy, Y, w/up, celluloid moving head on litho tin body, tin drum, 8½" H, NM.. $275.00

Drummer Marching, Rossignol (marked CR), inertia drive, tin figure bangs drum on 2 spoke wheels/clangs cymbal, 3½", G....... $425.00

Drunkard, Martin, w/up, tin w/cloth outfit, 8", VG........ $475.00

Duck & 2 Ducklings, Germany, w/up, pnt tin, 2 yel duckling out front on 2 wheels w/mama on wheels behind, 9" L, VGIB.......... $275.00

Duck the Mailman w/2 Goose Cages, TPS, w/up, litho tin, 4", EX+.. $275.00

Ducky Darlings, Wyandotte, w/up, litho tin, mama duck pulling 2 ducklings, EXIB.. $100.00

Dumbo (Disney) Merry-Go-Round, Linemar #48-15392, w/up, musical, 6", EXIB... $1,150.00

Elephant, Decamps, w/up, hide-covered w/glass eyes, realistic walking motion w/flapping ears & moving trunk, 13", VG+ ..$650.00

Elephant, Masudaya, w/up, celluloid, head moves & ears swing, w/molded back blanket, 8" L, NM+IB...................... $150.00

Elephant w/Native Rider & 2-Wheeled Music Box, Eberl, w/up, litho tin, artiulated elephant's head, 8" L, EX+........ $2,200.00

Felix the Cat in Race Car, Nifty/Borgfeldt, pnt wood, articulated axle allows Felix to jump up & down, 12" L, VG........ $325.00

Felix the Cat on 3-Wheeled Scooter, Nifty, w/up, litho tin, marked 'Felix' on tail, 8", L, EX+............................... $750.00

Felix the Cat on 3-Wheeled Scooter, Nifty, w/up, litho tin, marked 'Felix' on tail, 8" L, VG................................. $500.00

Felix the Cat Sparkler, Nifty/Borgfeldt, litho tin, blk & wht cat face, 5½", EXIB... $675.00

Felix the Cat Walker, Germany, w/up, pnt tin, balances on long tail, flat-sided legs, 6½", VG.................................... $450.00

Ferdinand the Bull, Linemar, w/up, litho tin, tail spins & head moves, 6" L, VG.. $175.00

Ferry Boat, Yonezawa, w/up, tin, boat shuttles w/up bus back & forth between lighthouses, 27" L, NMIB.................... $200.00

Finnegan In Again Out Again, Unique Art, w/up, litho tin, 13½" L, EXIB.. $300.00

Firehouse Toy, Eberl, w/up, tin, truck comes out of firehouse to blazing building on rnd track on sq base, 9" sq, G....... $325.00

Flying Circus, Unique Art, windup, litho tin, 12", EXIB. $900.00

Fox the Magician, Nomura, w/up, plush fox w/litho tin trick case, rabbit appears & disappears, 6½", EX+IB............ $175.00

Foxy Grandpa on Knees w/Boy on Back, Gunthermann, w/up, pnt tin, 8", G $1,550.00

Frankenstein Mechanical Monster, Linemar, w/up, plastic, 6", MIB... $500.00

Fred Flintstone on Dino, Linemar, 1960s, w/up, litho tin w/vinyl head, 8" L, EX.. $125.00

Frog Banjo Player, w/up, pnt tin, gr frog in pnt top hat & red coat, yel bow tie, 6¼", EX $450.00

Fruit Vendor, Martin, w/up, litho tin, 4x7½" L, EX $1,200.00

Gay 90s Cyclist, TPS, w/up, litho tin w/cloth outfit, 7", NM+IB...$350.00

Gem-Toys Acrobat, see Pluto Acrobat

General Butler Walker, Ives, 1880s, w/up, CI & wood w/cloth outfit, 10", EX..$1,900.00

German Swing Roundabout, pnt tin, clockwork w/plunk-plank music, 6 seats w/riders, orig flag, 14", EX $1,320.00

Giant Ride, Ohio Art, w/up, litho tin Ferris wheel, 16½", EX+IB $225.00

GI Joe & His Jouncing Jeep, Unique Art, w/up, litho tin, 7½", EX+IB.. $300.00

GI Joe & His Jouncing Jeep, Unique Art, w/up, litho tin, 7½", EX $175.00

Girl Chasing Duck on 4-Wheeled Platform, friction, pnt PS, 10½" L, VG $225.00

Girl Pushing Baby in Pram, Germany, w/up, litho tin, 7" L, EX .$1,200.00

Good Time Charlie, Alps, w/up, clown w/cloth outfit & paper hat blows on party whistle, 13", NMIB........................ $200.00

Goofy Cyclist, Linemar, w/up, litho tin, Goofy on tricycle w/bell, 7½", EX+IB.. $1,250.00

Goofy Riding Unicycle, w/up, litho tin, 5", EX $500.00

Goofy Whirling Tail, Linemar, w/up, litho tin, 5", EX ... $325.00

Goose-Drawn Barrel Cart, Germany, w/up, litho tin, butcher seated atop 2-wheeled barrel cart pulled by goose, 10" L, EX... $1,200.00

Grandpa's New Car, ETC/Yonezawa, w/up, litho tin, 6" H, NMIB $175.00

Gus & Jaq Handcar (Cinderella Mouse Characters), England, w/up, compo figures w/tin arms, 8" L, EX $275.00

Gymnast, pat by William Hubbell in 1875, w/up, cloth-dressed figure on wooden platform w/tall wooden housing, 8", EX $1,800.00

Happy Bunny, Yonezawa, friction, litho tin, bunny in open car, 1957 on license plate, 6" H, EX+IB............................ $150.00

Happy Clown, Distler, w/up, tin, neck elongates as eyes open & close, 6", NMIB... $425.00

Happy Easter Hand Car, Wyandotte, 1940s, w/up, litho tin, bunny steering 4-wheeled car w/basket, 6½", VG $250.00

Happy Penguin, Marusan, w/up, litho tin, 6", NMIB $150.00

Happy Pig (Boo-Tong), Kuramochi, w/up, celluloid pig standing driving chick cart, 7" L, EXIB................................... $1,250.00

Harold Lloyd Sparkler, Germany, litho tin head, 5", EX.. $650.00

Harold Lloyd Waddler, Germany, 1920s, w/up, litho tin, 7", EX... $1,350.00

Henry & Porter on Elephant, Borgfeldt, prewar, w/up, celluloid, Henry on elephant's trunk & Porter on back, 8" L, EX. $850.00

Henry Eating Candy, Linemar, 1950s, w/up, litho tin, 5½", EX $400.00

Horse Chair, Clark (?), friction, stained & pnt tin, 2 horses frame seat w/4 MSW, 10" L, F+.............................. $1,200.00

Howdy Doody, see also Doin' the Howdy Doody

Howdy Doody Acrobat, Arnold, lever action, cloth clothed Howdy on litho tin apparatus, 16", NMIB $175.00

Howdy Doody Cart, Nylint, w/up, litho tin, 9", VG....... $300.00

Howdy Doody Clock-A-Doodle, Bandai, w/up, litho tin, 9½", VG $600.00

Huckleberry Hound Hopper, Linemar, 1962, w/up, litho tin hopping figure, 4", EX+ $175.00

Humphrey Mobile, Wyandotte, w/up, tin, 9", EX+IB..... $500.00

Indian Rowing in Canoe, Arnold, w/up, tin, 8", NM $775.00

Indian w/Bow & Arrow, Germany, w/up, tin, rocks back & forth, 7½", G.. $300.00

Jazzbo Jim, Unique Art, w/up, litho tin, 10", NMIB....... $775.00

Jazzbo Jim, Unique Art, w/up, litho tin, 10", VGIB........ $475.00

Jazzi Jim, Distler, w/up, litho tin, blk man in top hat & plaid pants plays accordion & dances on sm sq base, 8", EX+IB... $1,750.00

JFK in Rocking Chair, Kamar, w/up, vinyl figure in cloth suit reading newspaper in wooden rocker, 11½", NM+IB.. $450.00

Jiggler, Schoenhut, 12" wood figure w/compo head & cloth outfit on curved wire apparatus on 20½" wood hand-press, EX $1,300.00

Jiggs Jazzcar, Nifty, w/up, litho tin, 6½", NM $1,750.00

Johnny the Clown, Lindstrom, w/up, litho tin, 8", EX ... $150.00

Kiddie Kampers, Wolverine, 1930s, w/up, litho tin, 14" L, EXIB... $400.00

Kiddie Cyclist, Unique Art, w/up, tin, 8" L, EX $200.00

Kiddy Television, Masudaya, w/up, tin w/chrome trim, 5", EX..$275.00

Krazy Kar, Unique Art, w/up, litho tin, clown driving pk car w/kids playing lithoed on sides, bl wheels, 7", NMIB .. $1,900.00

Lady w/Whirlygig on 2-Wheeled Platform, Germany, w/up, pnt tin, 6", VG... $700.00

Lasso Range Rider, Y, 1950s, w/up, tin, cowboy w/lasso on rocking horse, 7" H, NM (G box)................................. $125.00

Lester the Jester, Alps, w/up, celluloid & tin clown figure in cloth costume twirls cane, 9½", NMIB $250.00

Li'l Abner & His Dogpatch Band, Unique Art, w/up, litho tin, 6½", EXIB... $625.00

Li'l Abner & His Dogpatch Band, Unique Art, w/up, litho tin, 6½", VG+ $400.00

Lincoln Tunnel, Unique Art, w/up, litho tin, 24" L, EX.. $300.00

Lion, Decamps, w/up, hide-covered w/glass eyes, various motions, 15½", VG.. $700.00

Loop the Loop, Wolverine, #30, 1930s, w/up, litho tin, 19", NMIB $725.00

Lucky Monkey Cycle, Sato, w/up, litho tin, umbrella spins & bell rings, 6", NM $325.00

Magic Car No 2, Masudaya, friction, litho tin, 6", EX+IB ..$175.00

Maggie & Jiggs, Nifty, w/up, litho tin, figures facing off on 2-wheeled platforms connected by wire spring, 7", EX $1,000.00

Maggie & Jiggs Squeeze Toy, Nifty, Maggie chases Jiggs w/rolling pin when apparatus is squeezed, 8", VG $675.00

Mammy Walker, Lindstrom, w/up, litho tin, 8", VG $225.00

Man at Grindstone, w/up, pnt tin, man works treadle while he holds knife to grindstone, 6" H, VG+........................ $125.00

Man Holding Whirligig, Paya/Spain, w/up, litho tin, 8", EX ..$325.00

Man in Tux Swinging Girl, w/up, tin & celluloid w/cloth outfits, 5½", EX $375.00

Man on Rearing Horse, Germany, w/up, pnt tin, horse has articulated legs, EX... $200.00

Man on the Flying Trapeze, Wyandotte, w/up, litho tin, 9", VG+IB $125.00

Mary & Her Lamb, Germany, w/up, pnt tin, both on wheels, 7½", VG... $800.00

Merry Cockyolly See-Saw, Yoneya, w/up, litho tin, NMIB.$300.00

Merry-Go-Round, Doll, w/up, pnt tin, 4 horses w/riders, flag atop scalloped canopy, wht w/bl trim, 14½" H, rstr $425.00

Merry-Go-Round, Germany, w/up, pnt tin, 3 horses/riders, 'plink-plunk' music, flag atop, perforated top/base, 17", VG+ $650.00

Merry-Go-Round, Wolverine #31A, w/up, litho tin, 12", NMIB $500.00

Merry-Go-Round, Wyandotte #2010, 1930s, w/up, litho tin, 5", EXIB $600.00

Merry-Go-Round (Musical Merry-Go-Round), Japan, w/up, litho tin w/celluloid balls, 4 cars & riders, 9½", NM+IB...... $325.00

Mickey (Mouse) the Magician, Linemar, w/up, litho tin, 6", VG $1,725.00

Mickey & Minnie Mouse Playland, Borgfeldt/WDE, prewar, w/up, celluloid figures on wire apparatus w/awning, 11x9", NMIB.. $3,800.00

Mickey & Minnie Mouse (Swinging Exhibition Fights), Japan, prewar, w/up, celluloid figures on wire apparatus, 12", G $225.00

Mickey & Minnie Mouse (Swinging Exhibition Fights), Japan, prewar, w/up, celluloid figures on wire apparatus, 12", VGIB.. $450.00

Mickey & Minnie Mouse Acrobats, Japan, w/up, celluloid figures facing each other on wire apparatus, 13", GIB $500.00

Mickey & Minnie Mouse on Seesaw, Japan, lead weight allows pendulum action, celluloid figures, tin base, 6", EX $550.00

Mickey Mouse Carousel, Occupied Japan, w/up, celluloid figure under beaded parasol on tin 4-wheeled platform, 7", VG.$325.00

Mickey Mouse Circus Train, Lionel, w/up, tin, complete w/circular track, tent & all accessories, NMIB..................... $7,000.00

Mickey Mouse Circus Train, Lionel, w/up, tin, complete w/circular track, tent & all accessories, VGIB $2,000.00

Mickey Mouse Circus Train, Lionel, w/up, tin, engine & tender w/Mickey figure & 3 cars, no tracks, 23" overall, G+.. $600.00

Mickey Mouse Cowboy on 4-Wheeled Horse (Bucking Bronco), Japan, prewar, w/up, celluloid & wood, 8½" L, VG..... $725.00

Mickey Mouse Hand Car, Lionel, w/up, tin car w/compo Mickey & Minnie figures, 8" L, NMIB $900.00

Mickey Mouse Hand Car, Lionel, w/up, tin car w/compo Mickey & Minnie figures, 8" L, VGIB.................................. $675.00

Mickey Mouse Hand Car, Wells, w/up, tin car w/compo Mickey & Donald figures, Goofy images on sides of car, 8" L, VGIB.. $575.00

Mickey Mouse Head Sparkler, Nifty, plunger-activated, litho tin, 5½", EX.. $400.00

Mickey Mouse Hurdy Gurdy, Germany, 1930s, w/up, litho tin, Minnie tap dances atop wheeled organ pushed by Mickey, 6", EX $5,750.00

Mickey Mouse Nodder, Japan, prewar, swinging pendulum rubber band mechanism, celluloid figure w/instrument, 7", EXIB $800.00

Mickey Mouse Nodder, Japan, prewar, swinging pendulum rubber band mechanism, celluloid figure w/instrument, 7", VG.. $400.00

Mickey Mouse on Bell Trike (Walt Disney's Mechanical Tricycle), Linemar, w/up, celluloid & litho tin, 4", EXIB . $325.00

Mickey Mouse on Rocking Horse, Borgfeldt, prewar, w/up, celluloid Mickey & horse on wooden rockers, 8" H, VG..... $475.00

Mickey Mouse on Rocking Pluto, Linemar, w/up, litho tin, Pluto w/rocker base, 7" L, EX+ $875.00

Mickey Mouse on Trapeze, Borgfeldt, prewar, w/up, 4" celluloid figure on 6½" H wire apparatus, EXIB......................... $575.00

Mickey Mouse Pulled by Pluto, Japan, w/up, celluloid, Mickey on 2 wheels pulled by Pluto on 3-wheeled mechanism, 9", VG $700.00

Mickey Mouse Race Car #5, w/up, tin w/rubber tires, Mickey driving, 4", VG+ $350.00

Mickey Mouse Roller Skater, Linemar, w/up, 6½", VGIB. $750.00

Mickey Mouse the Unicyclist, Linemar, w/up, litho tin w/cloth pants, 6", EX+IB.. $1,225.00

Mickey Mouse Xylophone, Linemar, w/up, litho tin, 6", EX. $350.00

Minnie Mouse Driving Pluto Cart, Japan, prewar, w/up, celluloid figures w/tin casrt, 9" L, VG.................................. $625.00

Minnie Mouse Knitting in Rocking Chair, Linemar, w/up, litho tin, 7", EX $350.00

Minnie Mouse Knitting in Rocking Chair, Linemar, w/up, litho tin, 7", EXIB $450.00

Minnie Mouse Knitting in Rocking Chair, Linemar, w/up, litho tin, 7", NMIB $650.00

Minnie Mouse on Tricycle w/Bell, Japan, prewar, celluloid figure on tin trike, chrome bell, 5½" H, G.......................... $200.00

Monkey Batter, Sanei, w/up, litho tin, 'Our Team' on shirt, 7½", EX+IB $275.00

Monkey Drummer, Yoneya, w/up, litho tin, tail spins & hat raises & lowers on monkey in band uniform, 7", NMIB....... $100.00

Windup, Friction, and Others
• • • • • • • • • • •
Mickey Mouse Cowboy on Rocking Pluto, Japan, windup, celluloid figures, wooden rocker base, 8", NMIB, $5,000.00. (Photo courtesy Morphy Auctions on LiveAuctioneers.com)

Windup, Friction, and Others
• • • • • • • • • • •
Mickey (Mouse) the Magician, Linemar, windup, lithographed tin, 6", NMIB, $4,750.00.
(Photo courtesy Morphy Auctions on LiveAuctioneers.com)

Monkey Jockey on Wheeled Horse, w/up, litho tin, 7¼" L, EX ..$275.00

Monkey on Motorcycle (Monkey Cycle), Haji, friction, tin & vinyl, monkey in lithoed police uniform, 5", NMIB ... $125.00

Monkey Rider, Kanto, w/up, litho tin, civilian driver on motorcycle w/monkey rider getting on & off back, 6", NMIB............$500.00

Monkeys (2) on Skooter, Germany, pnt tin, lg monkey on front 3-wheeled skooter w/sm monkey on 1 wheel behind, 12" L, VG.....................$2,000.00

Motorcycle w/Rider (Trick Cyclist), Technofix, w/up, litho tin, 7" L, EX $225.00

Mouse Dancing w/Baby Mouse, Schuco, w/up, felt-covered, 4", NM $100.00

Mysterious Ball Toy, Martin, w/up, litho tin, figure concealed in ball able to traverse spiral band, 14½", EX $1,500.00

Native Figure Dancing on Platform, Hubley, crank-op, CI figure in grass skirt on CI footed platform, 17x14", EX $1,100.00

Observation Tank, M, friction, litho tin, soldier in tank w/binoculars spins as her watches plane circle, 5" L, NMIB $100.00

Octopus Ride, B&S/West Germany, w/up, 4 litho tin cars w/riders twirl around on rnd base, 7" dia, NM+IB...............$200.00

Old Woman, Gunthermann, w/up, pnt tin, wearing scarf & glasses, w/closed umbrella & wicker basket, 7", VG....$725.00

Olive Oyl Ballet Dancer, Linemar, friction, litho tin, 5½", EX+ IB $900.00

Olive Oyl Roadster, Linemar, friction, litho tin, 8" L, EX. $925.00

Oliver Hardy Sparkler, Isla, 1920s, articulated limbs, litho tin, 9", very rare, VG $1,100.00

Pan-Gee the Funny Dancer, CE Carter, w/up, litho tin, 10", EX $425.00

Pao-Pao Peacock, Germany, w/up, tin, 9" L, nonworking o/w VG $275.00

Peacock Walking, Eberle/Germany, w/up, litho tin, 10" L, EX+ $475.00

Percy Penguin, Nomura, friction, tin, advances & flaps wings moves beak, 5", VG+ $125.00

Peter Rabbit Chick Mobile, Lionel, #1103, 1935, w/up, tin w/ celluloid rabbit, 9", VG.................$175.00

Piano Player w/Twirling Umbrella, Japan, w/up, celluloid & tin, 7", EX.................$350.00

Pig Drinking Mug of Beer, Schuco, w/up, tin figure w/cloth outfit, ceramic beer mug, 4½", VG+ $275.00

Pig Pulling Butcher on 2-Wheeled Barrel Cart (Paddy's Pride), Germany, w/up, litho tin, 8" L, EX $1,000.00

Pig Pulling Butcher on 2-Wheeled Barrel Cart (Paddy's Pride), Germany, w/up, litho tin, 8" L, EX+IB $1,800.00

Piggy Cook, Yonezawa, w/up, vinyl figure in chef's garb holding tin skillet, 5", NMIB.................$175.00

Pinocchio, France, w/up, pnt compo figure holding books & an apple, 8", EXIB.................$300.00

Pinocchio Walker, Linemar, w/up, litho tin, 6", EX........$250.00

Pluto, see also Running Pluto, Stretching Pluto, or Wise Pluto

Pluto Acrobat, Linemar, plastic figure on wire apparatus w/'Disneyland' flag, 13" H (to top of flag), VGIB........$175.00

Pluto Acrobat, Linemar/Gym Toy, larger celluloid Pluto figure on 9" wire apparatus, VGIB $275.00

Pluto Drum Major, Linemar, w/up, litho tin, horn in mouth & baton in hand, 6½", VG.................$225.00

Pluto Drum Major, Linemar, w/up, litho tin, horn in mouth & baton on hands, 6", EX $325.00

Pluto Drum Major, Linemar, w/up, litho tin, horn in mouth & baton in hands, 6", EXIB.................$425.00

Pluto Slinky, Linemar, w/up, litho tin, 8", VG.................$200.00

Polar Bear, w/up, wht fur covered w/glass eyes, wooden paws, moves head back & forth, opens mouth & walks, 10" L, EX.......$300.00

Pop Eye Pete, TPS, w/up, litho tin figure moves side to side & eyes pop in & out, 5", NMIB $400.00

Popeye, see also Tumbling Popeye

Popeye & Mean Man Fighting, Linemar, w/up, ea celluloid figure stands on 2-wheeled litho tin platform, 6" L, VG $850.00

Popeye & Olive Oyl Playing Ball, Linemar, w/up, tin, 19" L, EX+IB.................$750.00

Popeye Acrobat, Linemar, w/up, tin, 13", NMIB.........$1,750.00

Popeye Air-O-Plane, Linemar, w/up, tin, 6" L, EX+ $2,500.00

Popeye in Rowboat, Hoge Mfg, w/up, pnt PS boat w/litho tin Popeye figure, 14" L, VG.................$1,200.00

Popeye in Rowboat, Hoge Mfg, w/up, pnt PS boat w/litho tin Popeye figure, 14" L, EX+ $2,000.00

Popeye on Tricycle w/Bell, Linemar, w/up, litho tin w/cloth pants, 5x7", EX.................$325.00

Popeye Rollover Tank, Linemar, w/up, litho tin, 4" L, EX ...$250.00

Popeye Skater, Linemar, w/up, litho tin w/cloth pants, holding up spinach can on plate, 6", VG $500.00

Windup, Friction, and Others

Olive Oyl, Linemar, windup, lithographed tin with plastic nose, head bobs while body hops, 5", EXIB, $1,550.00. (Photo courtesy Morphy Auctions on LiveAuctioneers.com)

Windup, Friction, and Others

Popeye Spinning Olive Oyl, Linemar, windup, lithographed tin, VG, $1,800.00. (Photo courtesy Morphy Auctions on LiveAuctioneers.com)

Popeye Standing, celluloid, 1929, head moves up & down, King Features Syndicate, MIB $900.00

Popeye Transit Co Truck, friction, 12", Linemar, NM $550.00

Powerful Katrinka Holding Jimmy, Nifty, w/up, litho tin, 6", EX $1,900.00

Powerful Katrinka Pushing Jimmy in Wheelbarrow, Nifty, w/up, litho tin, 6", EX $1,800.00

Professor Von Drake Walker, Linemar, w/up, litho tin, 6", EX. $350.00

Quick Draw McGraw Go-Mobile, Linemar, 1960s, friction, tin, 6", NMIB (box reads Huckleberry Go-Mobile) $350.00

Red Ranger Ride 'Em Cowboy, Wyandotte, w/up, litho tin, 7x7", EXIB $225.00

Riding on the Boardwalk — Atlantic City, Germany, w/up, litho tin, 7", EX+ $3,500.00

Rocking Horse w/Rider, Germany, w/up, pnt tin, 7" L, VG. $850.00

Rodeo Joe Crazy Car, Unique Art, 1950s, w/up, tin, 9", NM .. $200.00

Roundabout, Germany, w/up, pnt tin, 6 flying chairs & riders, 15½" H, rstr $350.00

Roundabout, Germany, w/up, tin, 5 seats w/figures facing counter clockwise, 12" dia, G+ $2,200.00

Roundabout, Muller & Kadeder, w/up, pnt tin, flying canoes w/ riders, 17" H, G $2,100.00

Roundabout, Muller & Kaderer, w/up, litho tin, 3 lady riders in chairs twirl about on base w/outdoor scenes, 9", EX.... $850.00

Roundabout, USA, w/up, litho tin, 3 flying seats & riders, 10½", EX $750.00

Running Pluto, Linemar, friction, litho tin, 5" L, EXIB . $400.00

Sambo the Minstrel Man, Alps, w/up, tin & celluloid, monkey in gold top hat seated on stump playing guitar, 7", NM+IB.. $175.00

Sandy Andy Full Back, Wolverine #25, Pat 1919, lever-action, tin w/celluloid football, 8", NMIB $900.00

Santa Claus Hand Car, Lionel #1105, w/up, Mickey Mouse doll in Santa's toy sack, 8" L, EX.. $400.00

Seesaw Toy, Gibbs, couple on seesaw spirals down pole that can be turned upside down for continuous action, 14½", VG..... $350.00

Seesaw w/Elephant & Zebra, Hishimo, w/up, litho tin, seesaw rocks as elephant & zebra play the drum, 7" L, NM.... $450.00

Sewing Machine w/Girl, Marusan, w/up, celluloid figure seated at litho tin sewing machine, 5" H, EXIB $175.00

Shooting Cowboy, Technofix, 1940s, w/up, tin, eyes shift as his waist twists, MIB $200.00

Skeeter Bug, Lindstrom, 1940s, w/up, litho tin, 2 figures in car, 10" L, EXIB... $375.00

Skiing Duck, Linemar, w/up, litho tin, 4", NMIB $250.00

Sky Ride Roller Coaster, Motion Toys, #121, 1950s, w/up, tin w/ plastic cars, unused, MIB.. $150.00

Speed King Scooter, Wyandotte, 1940s, w/up, litho tin, boy on scooter w/box, 6½" L, EXIB $600.00

Spirit of Saint Louis w/Pilot, Schuco, friction, litho tin, 4", EX..$625.00

Sports Land, Japan, prewar, litho tin amusement ride, celluloid balls hanging from lg parasol, 5½x6" sq, VG $1,575.00

Stretching Pluto, WDP, w/up, litho tin w/'Slinky'-type body on wheels, 8" L, EX+IB $600.00

Strongman, Gely, spring activated, litho tin flat-sided articulated figure swings hammer & object runs up pole, 7", VG+.. $450.00

Sunny Andy Fun Fair, Wolverine, 1928, BB's & gravity powers 4 playground rides, tin, NM+.. $300.00

Windup, Friction, and Others

Red Ranger Ride 'Em Cowboy, Wyandotte, 1930s, windup, EX, $150.00. (Photo courtesy www.serioustoyz.com)

Windup, Friction, and Others

School Master, Kellerman, windup, 6" square, VG+, $1,950.00. (Photo courtesy James D. Julia, Inc.)

Windup, Friction, and Others

Sky Rangers, Unique Art, windup, lithographed tin, 8", EXIB, $350.00. (Photo courtesy Morphy Auctions on LiveAuctioneers.com)

Windup, Friction, and Others

Sunny Andy Kiddie Kampers No. 66A, Wolverine, 1920s, 14", EXIB, $675.00. (Photo courtesy Morphy Auctions on LiveAuctioneers.com)

Windup, Friction, and Others

Swinging Sam the Jazz Man, DRGM/Germany, 1890, lithographed tin, squeeze handle in back and arms extend, exposes teeth, eyes move, NM, $650.00. (Photo courtesy www.serioustoyz.com)

Windup, Friction, and Others

Walt Disney Character Carousel, Linemar, windup, celluloid characters move around on tin carousel, 6½", NMIB, $3,000.00. (Photo courtesy Morphy Auctions on LiveAuctioneers.com)

Windup, Friction, and Others

Waltzing Couple, Gunthermann, clockwork, painted tin, classic toy, 8", G, $600.00. (Photo courtesy Noel Barrett Antiques & Auctions Ltd.)

Windup, Friction, and Others

Wimpy (Popeye), Linemar, windup, lithographed tin, head bobs while body hops, 5", EXIB, $1,200.00. (Photo courtesy Morphy Auctions on LiveAuctioneers.com)

Superman Turnover Tank M-25, Linemar, 1950s, w/up, litho tin, 4" L, VGIB $725.00

Swan in Castle Moat, Fleischman, w/up, pnt tin, center tower w/arched walls on each side, 8¾" dia, VG $325.00

Teddy Bear on Tricycle w/Umbrella, Sato/Alps, friction, litho tin w/celluloid beaded umbrella, 6", NM $325.00

Teddy's Cycle, see Boy on Tricycle

Three Little Pigs, Schuco, w/up, tin figures w/cloth outfits, ea playing instruments, 4½", VG $1,000.00

Tiger, Decamps, w/up, hide-covered w/glass eyes, realistic motions, 15" L, VG $925.00

Toonerville Trolley, Nifty, 1920s, w/up, litho tin, 7", EX+ ...$875.00

Toonerville Trolley, Nifty, 1920s, w/up, litho tin, 7", VG....$650.00

Topo Gigio Motorcycle, Gorgo/Argentina, friction, tin, 8" L, EXIB $200.00

Topsy Turvy Tom, Distler, w/up, litho tin, clown in colorful car w/wide roll-over bar, disk wheels, 10" L, EX $800.00

Touchdown Pete, Linemar, w/up, litho tin, football player bends up & downat waist in running motion, 5½", EX $325.00

Trans World Flyer, #100, Biller, 1950s, Germany, w/up, NMIB.. $330.00

Traveller, Alps, Germany, w/up, plush monkey in cloth outfit w/camera, 6", EXIB $175.00

Trick Cyclist, see Motorcycle w/Rider

Tumbling Popeye, Linemar, w/up, litho tin, 4½", NMIB.. $1,250.00

Turkey Walking, B&S/Germany, w/up, litho tin, tail feathers spread as her walks, 4", NMIB $250.00

Ul-Ul Cycle, Germany, w/up, tin, driver on 3-wheeled cycle, 6½" L, EX.. $2,000.00

Uncle Wiggily Crazy Car, Distler, w/up, litho tin, 9½", 1920s, EX $3,100.00

US Navy Couple Dancing, Japan, w/up, celluloid, 8", EX ..$300.00

Victory Locomotive, Ives, w/up, pnt & stenciled tin, 9½" L, EX.. $2,750.00

Walking Donald Duck, see Donald Duck Walker

The Whip, Germany, litho tin, 9x1x3", EX (VG box) . $2,800.00

Whirligig w/Elephant, KT, celluloid elephant stands on wheeled base under turning beaded umbrella, musical, 9", NMIB..$275.00

Whirligig w/Airplanes, Japan, w/up, 6 celluloid planes w/riders on beaded lines twirl around tin base, 14", EX $800.00

Whoopee Plane, Nonpareil Toy & Novelty Co, w/up, litho tin, 9" L, EX+ (partial box) $350.00

Windup, Friction, and Others

Woman Feeding Chickens, German, windup, tin, 7", old restoration, $850.00. (Photo courtesy James D. Julia, Inc.)

Wild West Bucking Bronco, Lehmann, 1906, w/up........ $750.00
Wimpy (Popeye's Pal), Japan, w/up, celluloid figure vibrates & shakes, 7", VG $250.00
Wise Pluto, Marx, w/up, tin, 1939, Walt Dinsey, w/orig box. $425.00

Xylophone Player, Masudaya, w/up, tin & celluloid, articulated man in tux w/tails plays xylophone, 6", NMIB............ $200.00
Yogi Bear Go-Mobile, Linemar, 1960s, friction, tin, 6" L, NMIB (box reads Huckleberry Go-Mobile)............................ $325.00

Windup, Friction, and Others

Yogi Bear (Hopping), Linemar, windup, lithographed tin, 4", EXIB, $350.00. (Photo courtesy Morphy Auctions on LiveAuctioneers.com)

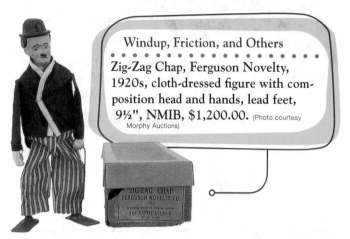

Windup, Friction, and Others

Zig-Zag Chap, Ferguson Novelty, 1920s, cloth-dressed figure with composition head and hands, lead feet, 9½", NMIB, $1,200.00. (Photo courtesy Morphy Auctions)

Wyandotte

Wyandotte produced toys mostly of heavy gauge steel with a few being tin or plastic. The following listings are of vehicles and related toys from the 1920s to the 1960s. All are steel unless noted otherwise.

See also Aeronautical; Boats; Character, TV, and Movie Collectibles; Guns; Windup, Friction, and Other Mechanical Toys.

Airflow Coupe, 1930s, 5½", friction, G+ $100.00
Allied Van Lines, 1950s, 24", 14-wheeled, Chiefton Lines on door, aluminum trailer w/advertising, VG $75.00
Ambulance, 1930s, 6", streamline styling w/'Ambulance' imprinted on top, EX+ $375.00
Ambulance, 1950s, 9", plastic w/friction motor, wht w/red lettering & cross symbol, VG $25.00
Army Supply Corps No 42 Truck, 1940s, 18", 4-wheeled, w/cloth cover, EX+ $125.00
Auto-Transport, 1950s, 9", 6-wheeled, #455, EX+ $75.00
Auto-Transport, 1950s, 23", 8-wheeled, sq-nose cab, EXIB. $150.00
Automatic Loading Dump Truck, 1950s, 15", 4-wheeled, front loader, NM+ $225.00
Automobile Society Tow Truck, 1950s, 10", 4-wheeled, blk & yel checked band, VG... $150.00
Car-A-Van Automobile Transport, 1950s, 22", 8-wheeled, EX... $125.00
Cargo Lines Motor Transport Fleet Semi, 1950s, 26", 6-wheeled, EX... $150.00
Circus Cage Tandem Truck, 20" overall, EX.................... $875.00
Circus Cage Truck, 10½", VG $400.00
Cloverdale Farms Delivery Van, 11", wht w/red hubs, VG .$140.00
Club Coupe, 1930s, 9", electric lights, red w/NP grille, WRT, EX $225.00
Construction Endloader & Dump Trailer, 1950s, 21", 4-wheeled, EX+...$50.00
Cord Coupe, 1936, 13", friction, red w/cream top, NP bumpers, BRT, VG.. $300.00
Cord Coupe & Streamlined Trailer, 23½" overall, lt bl w/cream top, VG.. $450.00
Delivery Truck, 1930s, 6", 4-wheeled, slanted bed sides, EX . $175.00

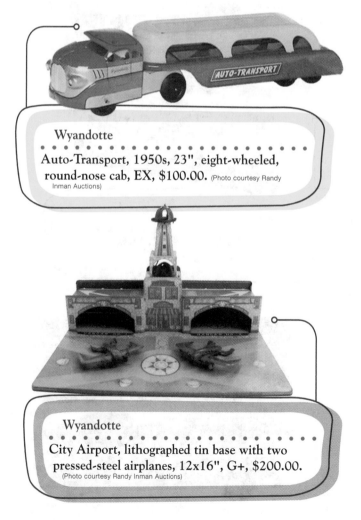

Wyandotte

Auto-Transport, 1950s, 23", eight-wheeled, round-nose cab, EX, $100.00. (Photo courtesy Randy Inman Auctions)

Wyandotte

City Airport, lithographed tin base with two pressed-steel airplanes, 12x16", G+, $200.00. (Photo courtesy Randy Inman Auctions)

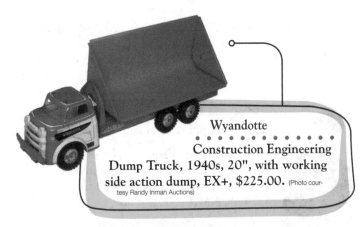

Wyandotte
Construction Engineering
Dump Truck, 1940s, 20", with working side action dump, EX+, $225.00. (Photo courtesy Randy Inman Auctions)

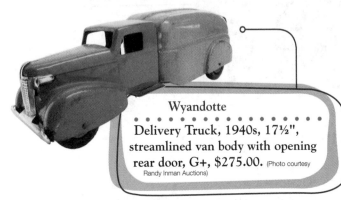

Wyandotte
Delivery Truck, 1940s, 17½", streamlined van body with opening rear door, G+, $275.00. (Photo courtesy Randy Inman Auctions)

Wyandotte
Dump Truck, 1950s, 11", #352, MIB, $100.00. (Photo courtesy Jeff Bub)

Wyandotte
Pumper Fire Engine, 12", EXIB, $175.00. (Photo courtesy Morphy Auctions on LiveAuctioneers.com)

Dot Towing Service, rider, wht & bl w/red, VG $150.00

Dump Truck, 1930s, 7", 4-wheeled, WRT, slanted bed sides, VG $60.00

Dump Truck, 1930s, 12", 4-wheeled, MDW, slanted bed sides, EX+ $200.00

Dump Truck, 1950s, 11", 4-wheeled, high dump bed w/tailgate, front wheels covered, blk & yel check, EX $126.00

Dump Truck, 1950s, 13", 4-wheeled, sq nose, straight-sided bed w/tailgate, all wheels covered, EX $150.00

Dump Truck, 1950s, 17", 6-wheeled, rnd-nose cab w/covered wheels, oblong bed w/side dump, NM $175.00

Dump Truck, 1960s, 22", 4-wheeled, long-nosed sq cab, straight-sided bed w/tailgate, EX $75.00

Dump Truck, 1960s, 22", 6-wheeled, hydraulic, long-nosed sq cab, straight-sided bed w/tailgate, VG $65.00

Emergency Auto Service Tow Truck, 1950s, 15", 4-wheeled, plastic cab, boom w/2 wheels, NM.................................... $200.00

Express Co Stake Truck, 1940s, 22", 6-wheeled, U-shaped stake trailer, EX $85.00

Express Semi, 1940s, 20", 6-wheeled, U-shaped stake bed, VG.. $360.00

Express Service Delivery Truck, 1950s, 10", 4-wheeled, snub-nose cab w/covered wheels, EXIB $300.00

Fire Dept #5 Truck, 1950s, 10", 4-wheeled, EX............... $100.00

Fire Engine Co No 1, 1950s, 24", 6-wheeled, NM.......... $250.00

Fire Engine Co No 4, 1950s, 12", 4-wheeled, cab slants forward, red w/yel trim, EX.. $100.00

Fire Hook & ladder No 10, 23", crank-op ladder, VG+.. $350.00

Flatbed Truck, 1950s, 13", 4-wheeled, all wheels covered, EX.$75.00

Giant Construction Co Dump Truck, 1950s, 19", 6-wheeled, VG+.. $125.00

Green Valley Stock Ranch Stake Truck, 1950s, 17", 6-wheeled, NM $150.00

Igloo Ice Co Truck, 1950s, 10", 4-wheeled, EX+ $150.00

Log Truck, 1950s, 10", 4-wheeled, yel & blk checks, EX+ ..$125.00

Log Truck, 1950s, 26", 14-wheeled, open framed trailer w/logs, VG..$75.00

Lowboy Machinery Re-Hauler, 1940s, 22", 6-wheeled, 4 cab wheels covered, open trailer wheels, G+ $75.00

Moto-Fix Towcar, 1950s, 15", 4-wheeled, VG $125.00

Motor Freight Lines Semi, 1950s, 23", 14-wheeled, U-shaped trailer w/open back, EX+... $225.00

National Bank, litho tin, 3", G+ $30.00

Nation-Wide Air Rail Service Delivery Van, 1950s, 11", 4-wheeled, plastic cab, VG $100.00

North American Van Lines Semi, 14", 6-wheeled, long-nose cab w/covered wheels, red, yel & blk, NM........................ $175.00

Racer, 1930s, 9½", streamlined Deco styling, friction, red w/NP grille, EX.. $140.00

Racer, 1930s, 10", electric lights, boattail w/wheel covers, red w/ WRT, EX $365.00

Reads Stake Truck, 13", 4-wheeled, 'Run Right to Reads' stenciled on ad panels on stake bed, VG+ $200.00

Sand Truck, #443, 1950s, 13", 4-wheeled, whole truck slants forward, front loader, VG $100.00

Sedan, 1930s, 15", streamlined, NP headlights, grille & bumpers, red, WRT, EX $365.00

Sinclair Tank Truck, 1930s, 18", gr w/NP grille & headlights, VG $450.00

Stake Truck, 1950s, 16", 4-wheeled, cab wheels covered, VG. $100.00

Super Service Garage, 9x9", litho tin, EX $250.00

Tank Truck, 1930s, 9", 4-wheeled, chrome grille & bumper, covered wheels, NM+ $375.00

Tow Truck, 1950s, 14", 4-wheeled, rnd-nose cab w/covered wheels, NM $250.00

Toy Town Delivery Wagon, doors open, 21", EX $300.00

Wrecker & Service Truck, 1950s, 6", 4-wheeled, all wheels covered, VG $110.00

Wyandotte Construction Co Stake Truck, 1950s, 23", 14-wheeled, NM+ $375.00

Wyandotte Van Lines, 1950s, 15", plastic cab, EX+ $200.00

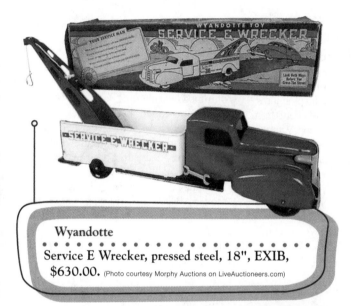

Wyandotte
Service E Wrecker, pressed steel, 18", EXIB, $630.00. (Photo courtesy Morphy Auctions on LiveAuctioneers.com)

Wyandotte
Woody Convertible, 1940s, 12½", retractable top, opening trunk, VG, $250.00. (Photo courtesy Randy Inman Auctions)

Wyandotte
Shady Glen Stock Ranch Cattle Truck, 1950s, 17", six-wheeled, EX, $150.00. (Photo courtesy Randy Inman Auctions)

Wyandotte
Wyndot (sic) Package Delivery Truck, 1950s, 12", four-wheeled, G, $100.00. (Photo courtesy Richard Opfer Auctioneering, Inc.)

• • • • • • • • • • • • • • Directory of Advisors and Contributors • • • • • • • • • • • • • •

In this section we have listed dealers, authors, specialists, and collectors who have contributed photographs, served as our advisors, or in any other way assisted us in preparing this guide. (See also Clubs, Newsletters, and Other Publications, as some of our advisors who represent a club or a publication are listed in that section.) This is a complimentary service; none of these people are under any obligation to answer questions. Some may have the time to respond to you; others may not. If you write to them, please include a SASE (self-addressed, stamped envelope). Your phone number and/or your e-mail address may expedite a response as well.

Matt and Lisa Adams
Tatonka Toys
904-772-6911
beatles@bellsouth.net
www.stores.ebay.com/tatonkatoys
Bubble bath containers (including foreign issues), nodders, character collectibles, character bobbin' head nodders,
   Dr. Dolittle, Beatles, and movie posters

Stan and Sally Alekna
732 Aspen Lane
Lebanon, PA 17042-9073
717-228-2361
fax: 717-228-2362
Soldiers: Barclay, Manoil, Grey Iron,
   other Dimestore soldiers and accessories, also Syroco figures

Pamela E. Apkarian-Russell
The Halloween Queen™
1595 Boggs Run Rd.
Benwood (Wheeling), WV 26031-1050
304-233-1031
castlehalloween@comcast.net
www.castlehalloween.com
Author and curator of Castle Halloween
   Museum. Halloween memorabilia —
   costumes, fortune telling, folk art, candy
   containers, toys, games, Harry Potter,
   Nightmare Before Christmas, papier
   mache jack-o-lanterns, and much more

Bob Armstrong
15 Monadnock Rd.
Worcester, MA 01609
508-799-0644
raahna@oldpuzzles.com
www.oldpuzzles.com
Puzzles: wood jigsaw-type, from before
   1950

Richard Belyski
P.O. Box 14956
Surfside Beach, SC 29587
843-457-3413
richie@pezcollectorsnews.com
www.pezcollectorsnews.com
Pez candy dispensers

Felicia Browell
123 Hooks Lane
Cannonsburg, PA 15317
felicia.browell@gmail.com

Breyer horses and other animals; author
   of Breyer Animal Collector's Guide, order
   direct

Bill Campbell
3501 Foxbriar Ln.
Cibolo, TX 78108
830-626-1077
captainmarvel1940@satx.rr.com
eBay store: go to www.google.com, Search
   for Bill and Anne's Wonderful Toys
Character clocks and watches, radio premiums
   and decoders, P-38 airplane-related items from
   World War II, Captain Marvel, Hoppy items,
   Lone Ranger books with jackets, selected old
   comic books, toys, and cap guns, Buck Rogers, Doc Savage, Universal Monsters, Tarzan,
   space-related items, Superman, Shadow

Geoffrey T. Carlton
403 Matlock Meadow Drive
Arlington, TX 76002-3353
Collector@StarWarsGuide.net
www.starwarsguide.net
Author of Star Wars Super Collector's
   Wish Book (Collector Books)

Joel J. Cohen
Cohen Books and Collectibles
P.O. Box 810310
Boca Raton, FL 33481-0403
561-487-7888
fax: 561-487-3117
disney@disneycohen.com
www.disneycohen.com
Disney books, animation cels, ephemera,
   toys, figurines, and more

Cotswold Collectibles
P.O. Box 716
Freeland, WA 98249
877-404-5637 (toll free)
fax: 360-331-5344
www.elitebrigade.com
GI Joe, diecast, Star Wars

Dawn Diaz
20460 Samual Dr.
Saugus, CA 91350-3812
661-263-TOYS (8697)
jamdiaz99@earthlink.net
Liddle Kiddles and other small dolls
   from the late 1960s and early 1970s

Ron and Donna Donnelly

Saturday Heroes
15847 Edwardian Dr.
Northport, AL 35475
Early Disney, Gone With the Wind, Western
   heroes, premiums, and other related collectibles

Marcia Fanta
Marcia's Fantasy
4275 33rd St. SE
Tappen, ND 58487-9411
701-327-4441
tofantas@bektel.com
www.fantastiquedollsandcollectibles.com
www.stores.ebay.com/MarciasFantasy
Ad dolls, Barbie and other Mattel dolls, premiums, baby dolls, artist designer dolls, character memorabilia, Strawberry Shortcake,
   Madame Alexander, Raggedy Ann & Andy,
   modern dolls, doll clothing, related items

Mike Fredericks
145 Bayline Circle
Folsom, CA 95630-8077
916-985-7986
Plastic figures and playsets, GI Joe, Star
   Trek, and dinosaurs

Gasoline Alley Antiques
Keith Schneider, Proprietor
Liz Cormier, Manager
6501 20th NE
Seattle, WA 98115
206-524-1606
fax: 206-524-6343
www.gasolinealleyantiques.com
Model kits, diecast scale models, character
   collectibles, sports memorabilia, nostalgia

Bob Gottuso (Bojo)
P.O. Box 1403
Cranberry Township, PA 16066-0403
phone/fax: 724-776-0621
bojo@zbzoom.net
www.bojoonline.com
Buying and selling old and new Beatles
   memorabilia; one piece or collection;
   also dolls, rock 'n roll personalities

Bill Hamburg
Happy Memories Collectibles
6023 Lubao Ave.
Woodland Hills, CA 91367
818-346-0215
webcollect@aol.com
Guns, especially cap guns

George Hardy
Charlottesville, VA 22901
804-295-4863
fax: 804-295-4898
georgeh@comet.net
Building blocks and construction toys,
  especially Anchor Stone Building
  Blocks by Richter

Lloyd Huffer
Antique Marbles
11 Meander Ridge
Damascus, PA 18415
570-224-4012
olmarblz@ptd.net
Marbles

Dan Iannotti
212 W. Hickory Grove Rd.
Bloomfield Hills, MI 48302-1127
248-335-5042
modernbanks@prodigy.net
Modern mechanical banks: Reynolds,
  Sandman Designs, James Capron,
  Book of Knowledge, Richards, Wilton;
  sales lists available

Terri Mardis Ivers
Terri's Toys & Nostalgia
114 Whitworth Ave.
Ponca City, OK 74601-3438
580-762-8697
toyladyt@gmail.com
Lunch boxes, Halloween, character
  collectibles, and Hartland figures

Harriet Joyce
415 Soft Shadow Lane
DeBary, FL 32713
386-668-8006
Cracker Jack and Checkers prizes, and
  Flossie Fisher items

Keith and Donna Kaonis
c/o Antique Doll Collector Magazine
P.O. Box 239
Northport, NY 11768
kkaonis@gmail.com
Schoenhut

Rusty & Kathy Kern
729 Crown Ridge Dr.
Colorado Springs, CO 80904
719-634-7430
playsetmagazine@aol.com
www.playsetmagazine.com
Plastic figures (Marx), playsets, publish-
  ers of *Playset Magazine*

Dahveed Kolodny-Nagy
Toy Hell
P.O. Box 381208
Hollywood, CA 90038
toyhell@yahoo.com

www.toyhell.com
Specializing in Transformers, Robotech,
  Shogun Warriors, Gadaikins, and any other
  robot; want to buy these MIP — also selling

Tom Lastrapes
6050 86th Ave.
Pinellas Park, FL 33782
727-230-0801
tomlas1@fastmail.fm
Battery-operated toys

Michael and Polly McQuillen
McQuillen's Collectibles
P.O. Box 50022
Indianapolis, IN 46250-0022
317-845-1721
michael@politicalparade.com
www.politicalparade.com
Political toys, pin-back buttons

Gary Mosholder
Gary's Trains
186 Pine Springs Camp Road
Boswell, PA 15531
814-629-9277
gtrains@floodcity.net
Trains: Lionel, American Flyer; and Plasticville

Judith A. Mosholder
186 Pine Springs Camp Road
Boswell, PA 15531
814-629-9277
jlytwins@floodcity.net
Dollhouse furniture: Renwal, Ideal, Marx, etc.

Peter Muldavin
173 W 78th St., Apt. 5-F
New York, NY 10024
212-362-9606
kiddie78s@aol.com
www.Kiddierekordking.com
Records: 78 rpm children's records and
  picture disks; buys, sells, and trades
  records as well as makes cassette
  recordings for a small fee

Gary Pollastro
5160 Mercer Way
Mercer Island, WA, 89040-5128
206-232-3199
Slot cars and model racing from the
  '60s – '70s, especially complete sets in
  original boxes

Judy Posner
P.O. Box 2194
Englewood, FL 34295
judyposner@yahoo.com
www.judyposner.com
Character-related pottery, china, ceramics,
  salt and pepper shakers, cookie jars, tea sets,
  and children's china with special interest in
  Black Americana and Disneyana

John Rammacher
Son's a Poppin' Ranch
1610 Park Ave.
Orange City, FL 32763-8869
386-775-2891
sonsapoppin@embarqmail.com
www.sonsapoppin.com
Ertl banks, farm toys, trucks, and construction toys

Cindy Sabulis
P.O. Box 642
Shelton, CT 06484
toys4two@snet.net
www.toysofanothertime.com
Author of *Collector's Guide to Dolls of the
  1960s and 1970s* (Collector Books); co-
  author of *Collector's Guide to Tammy,
  the Ideal Teen* (Collector Books); spe-
  cializes in dolls from the 1960s – 1970s,
  including Liddle Kiddles, Barbie,
  Tammy, Tressy, etc.

Scott T. Smiles
157 Yacht Club Way, Apt. 112
Hypoluxo, FL 33462-6048
561-582-6016
stsmiles@bellsouth.net
Windups, friction and battery-operated
  toys, fast food displays, Lehmann,
  Chein; Antique Toy Information Service: Send SASE, good photos (35mm
  preferred), and $9.95 per toy

Steve Stephenson
11117 NE 164th Pl.
Bothell, WA 98011-4003
425-488-6265
fax: 425-488-2841
Hot Wheels

Nate Stoller
960 Reynolds Ave.
Ripon, CA 95366
209-599-5933
multimotor@aol.com
www.maytagclub.com
Pedal cars, also specializing in Maytag
  collectibles

Stout Auctions
Greg Stout
529 State Road 28 East
Williamsport, IN 47993
765-764-6901
fax: 765-764-1516
info@stoutauctions.com
www.stoutauctions.com
Trains of all types; holds cataloged auctions,
  seeking quality collections for consignment

Mark and Lynda Suozzi
Mark & Lyn's Antiques
P.O. Box 102

Ashfield, MA 01330
phone/fax: 413-628-3241 (9am to 5pm)
info@marklynantiques.com
www.marklynantiques.com
Antiques & Americana, iron penny
  banks, mechanical tin toys, penny
  arcade machines, country store advertising, folk art trade signs, campaign
  political items, early baseball souvenirs,
  historical & exposition material, photographs of young America, and paper-
  lithographed toys. Buy and sell; lists
  available upon request. Mail order and
  shows only.

Rick Toler
Rick's Hollywood
2301 Cornerstone Ave.
Claremore, OK 74017
918-341-RICK (7425)
rokmod@aol.com
eBay ID: rockmodataol
Movie posters, Elvis, music items, trains,
  planes, boats, and more

Richard Trautwein
437 Dawson St.
Sault Ste. Marie, MI 49783
906-635-0356
rtraut@up.com
Character collectibles, especially tin-
  plate toys and cars, battery-operated

toys and toy trains, boats, bicycles &
  tricycles, gasoline-powered toys

Marci Van Ausdall
4532 Fertile Valley Road
Newport, WA 99156
509-292-1311
betsymcallfanclub@hotmail.com
Betsy McCall

Randy Welch
Raven'tiques
27965 Peach Orchard Rd.
Easton, MD 21601-8203
410-822-5441
Ramp walkers, mechanical sparklers,
  and other plunger-type toys

www.whatacharacter.com
Hugh Klein, hugh@whatacharacter.com
or Ken Ossman, bazuin32@aol.com
Comic & cartoon character, television series

Larry White
108 Central St.
Rowley, MA 01969-1317
978-948-8187
larrydw@erols.com
Cracker Jack; author of *Cracker Jack
  Toys* and *Cracker Jack, The Unauthorized Guide to Advertising Collectibles*

Bob Wilson
Phoenix Toy Soldier Co.
8912 E. Pinnacle Peak Rd.
PMB 552
Scottsdale, AZ 85255-3659
480-699-5005
877-269-6074 (toll free)
Plastic figures and playsets, especially
  Marx, but also figures from about 100
  other old manufacturers; buying parts
  of playsets as well

Margaret Wright
10974 Bland Ridge Dr.
Petersburg, VA 23805
Housewares/housekeeping toys, author
  of *Collector's Guide to Housekeeping
  Toys, from Metal to Plastic, 1870 – 1970*
  (Collector Books)

Mary Young
Box 9244
Dayton, OH 45409
937-751-9141
bus2003@att.net
Paper dolls; author of books

• • • • • • • • • • • • • • Clubs, Newsletters, and Other Publications • • • • • • • • • • • • • •

There are hundreds of clubs, newsletters, and magazines available to toy collectors today. Listed here are some devoted to specific areas of interest. You can obtain a copy of many newsletters simply by requesting a sample.

We will list other organizations and publications upon request. Please send your information to Amy Sullivan, Collector Books, P.O. Box 3009, Paducah, Kentucky 42002-3009; or e-mail amysullivan@collectorbooks.com.

A.C. Gilbert Heritage Society
9 Bristol Knoll Road
Newark, DE 19711
www.acghs.org

Antique Advertising Association of America
Past Times newsletter
P.O. Box 76
Petersburg, IL 62675
twgeneral@comcast.net
www.pastimes.org

Antique Doll Collector
P.O. Box 239
Northport, NY 11768
888-800-2588 or 631-261-4100
antiquedoll@gmail.com
www.antiquedollcollector.com

Antique Trader
700 East State Street
Iola, WI 54990-001
715-445-2214
fax: 715-445-4087
sandra.sparks@fwpubs.com
www.antiquetrader.com

Association of Game & Puzzle Collectors
(AGPC)
PMB 321
197M Boston Post Road W.
Marlborough, MA 01752
membership@agpc.org
agpcinfo@gmail.com
www.agpc.org

Beatlefan
P.O. Box 33515
Decatur, GA 30033
770-492-0444
fax: 404-321-3109
goodypress@mindspring.com
www.beatlefan.com

Betsy's Fan Club (Betsy McCall)
Marci Van Ausdall
P.O. Box 946
Quincy, CA 95971-0946
916-283-2770
dreams@psln.com

Beyond the Rainbow
P.O. Box 31672
St. Louis, MO 63131
314-217-2727
fax: 314-909-6617

www.jgdb.com/mfaq4.htm
Wizard of Oz dolls, toys, and collectibles

Big Little Times
Big Little Book Collectors Club of America
Larry Lowery
P.O. Box 1242
Danville, CA 94526
925-837-2086
larry@biglittlebooks.com
www.biglittlebooks.com

Bojo (Bob Gottuso)
P.O. Box 1403
Cranberry Township, PA 16066-0403
724-776-0621 (9 am to 8 pm EST, phone or fax)
bojo@zbzoom.net
www.bojoonline.com
Beatles and rock 'n roll memorabilia

Brian's Toys, Inc.
W730 Hwy 35
Fountain City, WI 54629
608-687-7572
fax: 608-687-7573
sales@brianstoys.com
www.brianstoys.com
Star Wars, GI Joe, Transformers. Masters of the Universe, Indiana Jones, Lord of the Rings, and more

Buckeye Marble Collectors' Club
(BMCC)
Brian Estepp
10380 Taylor Rd. SW
Reynoldsburg, OH 43068
614-975-1203
bemarbles@aol.com
www.buckeyemarble.com

Candy Container Collectors of America
The Candy Gram newsletter
Jim Olean, Membership Chairperson
115 Mac Beth Dr.
Lower Burrell, PA 15068-2628
lostincandyland2004@yahoo.com
or
Jeff Bradfield
90 Main St.
Dayton, VA 22821
www.candycontainer.org

The Coca-Cola Collectors Club
PMB 609
4780 Ashford-Dunwoody Rd., Suite A

Atlanta, Georgia 30338
joinccclub@yahoo.com
www.cocacolaclub.org

Cracker Jack® Collectors Association
The Prize Insider Newsletter
Linda Farris (membership chairperson)
4908 N. Holborn Dr.
Muncie, IN 47304
lindajfarris@comcast.net
www.crackerjackcollectors.com

Doll Castle News
P.O. Box 247
Washington, NJ 07882
800-572-6607
info@dollcastlemagazine.com
www.dollcastlemagazine.com

The Fisher-Price Collector's Club
The Gabby Goose newsletter
Jacquie Hamblin
38 Main St.
Oneonta, NY 13820-2519
jacham@dmcom.net
www.fpclub.org

Hopalong Cassidy Fan Club International
Laura Bates
6310 Friendship Dr.
New Concord, OH 43762-9708
LBates1205@cs.com
www.hopalong.com

Gene Autry
Autry National Center of the Midwest
4700 Western Heritage Way
Los Angeles, CA 90027-1462
323-667-2000
fax: 323-660-5721
www.autrynationalcenter.org

International Association of Marble Collectors
Ernie Kirk
4006 North 10th
Tacoma, WA 98406
zaboo222@comcast.net
www.iamc.us

Liddle Kiddle Konvention
Paris Langford
415 Dodge Ave.
Jefferson, LA 70121
504-733-0667
bbean415@aol.com

Specializing in all small vinyl dolls of the '60s and '70s; Author of *Liddle Kiddles Identification and Value Guide* (now out of print). Please include SASE when requesting information; Contact for information concerning Liddle Kiddle Konvention

Lone Ranger Fan Club
Silver Bullet newsletter
P.O. Box 1742
Rosenberg, TX 77471
lonerangerfanclub@sbcglobal.net
www.lonerangerfanclub.com

Marl & B — Simply the Best in Fashion Dolls
Marl Davidson
10301 Braden Run
Bradenton, FL 34202
941-751-6275
fax: 941-751-5463
marlbe@aol.com
www.marlbe.com

McDonald's Collector Club
P.O. Box 148
Fremont, OH 43420
www.mcdclub.com

National Fantasy Fan Club (NFFC)
   (Disneyana)
P.O. Box 19212
Irvine, CA 92623-9212
714-731-4705
info@nffc.org
www.nffc.org
Includes newsletters, free ads, chapters, conventions, etc.

Peanut Pals (Mr. Peanut, Planters collectibles)
Ruth Augustine
6052 Canter Glen Ave.
Las Vegas, NV 89122
info@peanutpals.org
www.peanutpals.org

Pepsi-Cola Collectors Club
Pepsi-Cola Collectors Club Express
www.pepsicolacollectorsclub.com

Pez Collector's News
Richard Belyski
P.O. Box 14956
Surfside Beach, SC 29587
info@pezcollectorsnews.com
www.pezcollectorsnews.com

PGCA (Promotional Glass Collectors
   Association)
Marilyn Johnston, Treasurer
528 Oakley
Central Point, OR 97502
www.pgcaglassclub.com

Playset Magazine
Rusty & Kathy Kern
729 Crown Ridge Drive
Colorado Springs, CO 80904
719-634-7430
playsetmagazine@aol.com
www.playsetmagazine.com

Prehistoric Times
Mike Fredericks
145 Bayline Circle
Folsom, CA 95630-8077
916-985-7986 (before 5pm PST)
pretimes@comcast.net
www.prehistorictimes.com

The Replica (Ertl, toy tractors)
Craig Purcell, Editor
P.O. Box 111
Hwys 136 & 20
Dyersville, IA 52040
319-875-2000
www.toytractorshow.com/the_replica.htm
Marketing tool that previews upcoming diecast releases and articles of interest to collectors; included are Wm Britain pewter figures, Ertl diecast automotive replicas, and John Deere kits (preschool)
Free online newsletter

Robert Tonner Dolls
Tonner Doll Company, Inc.
459 Hurley Avenue
Kingston, NY 12443
845-339-9537
fax: 845-339-1259
www.tonnerdirect.com

Schoenhut Collectors Club
Joe Wells
72 Barre Dr.
Lancaster, PA 17601-3206
734-662-6676
fax: 717-569-9697
jwellsjr47@aol.com
www.schoenhutcollectorsclub.org

Star Wars online guide
Geoffrey T. Carlton
info@starWarsGuide.net
www.StarWarsGuide.net
Author of *Star Wars Super Collector's Wish Book* (Collector Books)
Star Wars online newsletter

Still Bank Collectors Club of America
   (SBCCA)
SBCCA Membership Chairman
440 Homestead Ave.
Metairie, LA 70005
contact@stillbankclub.com
www.stillbankclub.com

Toy Collector Club (SpecCast toys)
1235 16th Ave. Ct. SW
Dyersville, IA 52040
563-875-9263 or 800-452-3303
fax: 563-875-8056
www.speccast.com
www.toycollectorclub.com

Toy Car Colletors Association
Toynutz.com (online catalog for toy cars)
Dana Johnson Enterprises
P.O. Box 1824
Bend, OR 97709-1824
541-318-7176 (24 hour message line)
toynutz@earthlink.net
www.toynutz.com

Toy Scouts, Inc.
137 Casterton Ave.
Akron, OH 44303
330-836-0668
fax: 330-869-8668
info@toyscouts.com
www.toyscouts.com

Toy Soldier Collectors of America
   (TSCA)
Charlie Duval
P.O. Box 179
New Ellenton, SC 29809-0179
803-652-7932
toysoldiercollectorsamerica@yahoo.com
www.toysoldiercollectors.homestead.com

Train Collectors Association/National
   Toy Museum
300 Paradise Lane or
P.O. Box 248
Strasburg, PA 17579-0248
717-687-8623 (business office)
717-687-8976 (toy museum)
fax: 717-687-0742
tca-office@traincollectors.org
info@nttmuseum.org
www.traincollectors.org

Trick or Treat Trader
Pamela E. Apkarian-Russell
   (The Halloween Queen™)
Castle Halloween Museum
1595 Boggs Run Road
Benwood, WV 26031-1050
304-233-1031
castlehalloween@comcast.net
www.castlehalloween.com

United Federation of Doll Clubs, Inc.
10900 N. Pomona Ave.
Kansas City, MO 64153
816-891-7040
fax: 816-891-8360
info@ufdc.org
www.ufdc.org

Auction Houses

We would like to thank the following auction houses for letting us use their catalogs, online sources, and photographs in this guide. They have been an invaluable source for all 12 editions.

Americana Auctions
c/o Glen Rairigh
12633 Sandborn
Sunfield, MI 48890
Specializing in Skookum dolls

Bertoia Auctions
2141 DeMarco Dr.
Vineland, NJ 08360
856-692-1881
fax: 856-692-8697
toys@bertoiaauctions.com
www.bertoiaauctions.com
Toys, dolls, advertising, and related
 items

Gasoline Alley Antiques
6501 20th Ave. NE
Seattle, WA 98115
206-524-1606
fax: 206-524-6343
www.gasolinealleyantiques.com

Henry-Peirce Auctioneers
Double Tree Hotel
75 West Algonquin Rd.
Arlington Heights, IL 60005
847-364-7600
hpacutions@comcast.net
www.henrypeirceauctions.com
Specializing in still banks, mechanical
 banks, cast iron toys, and ephemera.

High Noon Western Americana
9929 Venice Blvd.
Los Angeles, CA 90034-5111
310-202-9010
fax: 310-202-9011
info@highnoon.com
www.highnoon.com
Cowboy and western collectibles

Jackson's International Auctioneers &
 Appraisers of Fine Art and Antiques
2229 Lincoln St.
Cedar Falls, IA 50613
319-277-2256
fax: 319-277-1252
www.jacksonsauction.com

James D. Julia, Inc.
P.O. Box 830
Rt. 201, Skowhagen Rd.
Fairfield, ME 04937
207-453-7125
fax: 207-453-2502
jjulia@juliaauctions.com
www.juliaauctions.com

LiveAuctioneers LLC
2nd Floor
220 12th Avenue
New York, NY 10001
info@liveauctioneers.com
www.liveauctioneers.com

McMasters Harris Auction Co.
P.O. Box 341096
5855 John Glenn Hwy
Columbus, OH 43234-1096
740-297-1054
800-842-3526
fax: 614-396-6285
info@mcmastersharris.com
www.mcmastersharris.com

Morphy Auctions
2000 N. Reading Rd.
Denver, PA 17517
717-335-3435
fax: 717-336-7115
morphy@morphyauctions.com
www.morphyauctions.com

Noel Barrett Antiques & Auctions, Ltd.
P.O. Box 300
Carversville, PA 18913
215-297-5109
fax: 215-297-0457
toys@noelbarrett.com
www.noelbarrett.com

Randy Inman Auctions Inc.
P.O. Box 726
Waterville, ME 04903
www.liveauctioneers.com/auctioneers/
 inmanauctions

Serious Toyz
Box 189
Croton-on-Hudson, NY 10520
866-OLD-TOYZ (866-653-8699)
914-271-8699
fax: 914-827-9366
tom@serioustoyz.com
www.serioustoyz.com

Smith House Toy & Auction Company
P.O. Box 129
Telford, PA 18969
215-721-1389
fax: 215-721-1503
smithhousetoys@comcast.net
www.smithhousetoys.com

Stout Auctions
529 State Road 28 East
Williamsport, IN 47993-1034
765-764-6901
fax: 765-764-1516
info@stoutauctions.com
www.stoutauctions.com

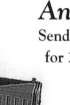

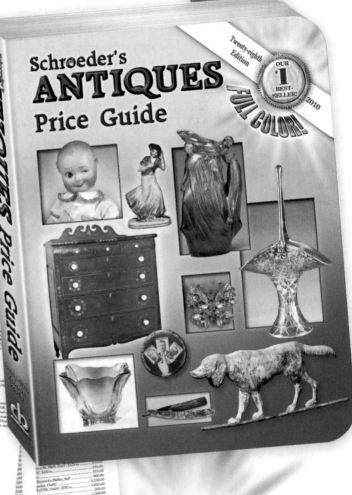